These maps of the World, United States and Europe indicate locations of the regional maps found on pages 27-160. The colored outlines show the scale of each map (per the accompanying legend) and the extent of each map's coverage. Page numbers of the same color are found in the center of each outline. Large scale map insets are noted by outline, name and page number. Small scale maps are indicated by name and page number only. A map of the world appears on pages 22-23.

HAMMOND

CENTENNIAL WORLD ATLAS

HAMMOND

CENTE

WORLD

NNIAL
ATLAS

HAMMOND INCORPORATED, MAPLEWOOD, NEW JERSEY

MAPMAKERS AND PUBLISHERS FOR THE 21ST CENTURY

Contents

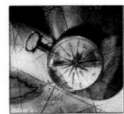

INTERPRETING MAPS

Designed to enhance your knowledge and enjoyment of maps, these pages explain such cartographic principles as scale, projection and symbology. This section also includes a brief explanation of the boundary and name policies followed in this atlas.

6   Map Projections
7   Using This Atlas

GLOBAL RELATIONSHIPS

This section highlights key social, economic and geographic factors, unveiling the complex relationships between people and their environments. Coverage includes: demographic trends, population distribution and growth; assessing the consequences of pollution; acid rain, deforestation, ozone depletion and global warming; also revealing comparisons of GDP per capita and literacy and life expectancy around the globe.

8-9   Population
10-11   Standards of Living
12-13   Climate
14-15   Environmental Concerns

WORLD REFERENCE GUIDE

This colorful section presents the national flag and important geographic data about each independent country, including area, population, capital, type of government, date of independence, U.N. admission, life expectancy, GDP and monetary unit.

16-21   World Flags & Reference Guide

MAPS OF THE WORLD

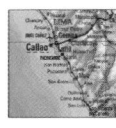

This collection of regional maps is completely generated from a computer database structured by latitude and longitude. The realistic topography is achieved by combining the political map data with digital hypsometric and bathymetric relief data. The maps are arranged by continent, with a stunning satellite image and political map introducing each section. Continent thematic maps are also included in each section, which provide special geographical comparisons. Over 70 inset maps highlight metropolitan and other areas of special interest. Numbers following each entry indicate map scale (M=million, K=thousand).

22-23   World - Political Map 1:70M
24-25   World - Physical Map 1:70M

Europe and Northern Asia

27   Europe 1:18M
28   Geographical Comparisons: Temperature, Climate, Vegetation
29   Geographical Comparisons: Rainfall, Population, Land Use, Minerals
30   Metropolitan London, Metropolitan Paris 1:500K
31   United Kingdom, Ireland 1:3M
32-33   Southern England and Wales 1:1M
34-35   Northeastern Ireland, Northern England and Wales 1:1M
36   Central Scotland 1:1M
37   Scandinavia and Finland 1:6M
     Iceland 1:6M
38-39   Baltic Region 1:3M
40-41   North Central Europe 1:3M
     Berlin 1:1M
42-43   West Central Europe 1:3M
44-45   Spain, Portugal 1:3M
     Barcelona, Madrid, Lisbon 1:1M
     Azores, Canary Islands, Madeira 1:6M
46-47   Southern Italy, Albania, Greece 1:3M
     Athens, Malta 1:1M
48-49   Hungary, Northern Balkan States 1:3M
     Vienna, Budapest 1:1M
50-51   Netherlands, Northwestern Germany 1:1M
52-53   Belgium, Northern France, Western Germany 1:1M
54-55   Southern Germany, Czech Republic, Upper Austria 1:1M
56-57   Central Alps Region 1:1M
58-59   Northern Italy 1:1M
     Monaco 1:58K
60-61   Northeastern Europe 1:6M
     St. Petersburg, Moscow 1:1M
62-63   Southeastern Europe 1:6M
64-65   Russia and Neighboring Countries 1:18M

Asia

67   Asia 1:42M
68   Geographical Comparisons: Temperature, Climate, Vegetation
69   Geographical Comparisons: Rainfall, Population, Land Use, Minerals
70-71   Eastern Asia 1:12M
     Hong Kong 1:1M
72   Northeastern China 1:6M
     Beijing-Tianjin, Shanghai 1:3M
73   Korea 1:3M
     Seoul 1:1M
74-75   Central and Southern Japan 1:3M
     Ryukyu Islands 1:6M
76   Northern Japan 1:3M
77   Tokyo-Yokohama, Osaka-Nagoya 1:1M
78   Indochina 1:6M
79   Southeastern China, Taiwan, Philippines 1:9M
80-81   Indonesia, Malaysia 1:9M
82-83   Southern Asia 1:9M
84-85   Ganges Plain 1:3M
86   Punjab Plain 1:3M
87   Central Asia 1:9M
88-89   Southwestern Asia 1:9M
90   Northern Middle East 1:6M
91   Eastern Mediterranean Region 1:3M
     Central Israel 1:1M

Africa

93   Africa 1:30M
     Cape Verde 1:6M
94   Geographical Comparisons: Temperature, Climate, Vegetation
95   Geographical Comparisons: Rainfall, Population, Land Use, Minerals
96-97   Northern Africa 1:15M
98-99   Northern West Africa 1:6M
100   Northern Morocco, Algeria, Tunisia 1:3M
101   Northeastern Africa 1:6M
102-103   Southern West Africa 1:6M
104   East Africa 1:6M
105   Southern Africa 1:15M
106-107   South Africa 1:6M
     Cape Town, Johannesburg, Mauritius and Réunion 1:3M
     Madagascar 1:6M

Australia, New Zealand and Pacific

109	Australia, New Zealand 1:16.6M
110	Geographical Comparisons: Temperature, Climate, Vegetation
111	Geographical Comparisons: Rainfall, Population, Land Use, Minerals
112-113	Western and Central Australia 1:6M Perth, Adelaide 1:1M
114	Northeastern Australia 1:6M Brisbane, Sydney 1:1M
115	Southeastern Australia 1:6M Melbourne 1:1M
116-117	Central Pacific Ocean 1:27M New Zealand 1:9M

North America

119	North America 1:30M
120	Geographical Comparisons: Temperature, Climate, Vegetation
121	Geographical Comparisons: Rainfall, Population, Land Use, Minerals
122-123	Canada 1:12M
124-125	United States 1:12M Hawaii 1:3M Oahu 1:1M
128-129	Southwestern United States 1:6M
130-131	Southeastern Canada, Northeastern United States 1:6M Montreal, Toronto-Buffalo 1:1M
132-133	Southeastern United States 1:6M
134	Alaska 1:9M
135	Seattle-Tacoma, Sacramento-San Francisco-San Jose, Detroit, Chicago-Milwaukee 1:1M
136	Los Angeles-San Diego 1:1M Metropolitan Los Angeles 1:500K
137	Phoenix, Salt Lake City, Denver, Oklahoma City, Kansas City, St. Louis, San Antonio, New Orleans 1:1M
138-139	New York-Philadelphia-Washington 1:1M Metropolitan New York 1:500K
140-141	Middle America 1:9M Puerto Rico, Lesser Antilles 1:6M
142-143	Northern and Central Mexico 1:6M Distrito Federal-Veracruz 1:3M Distrito Federal 1:1M
144-145	Southern Mexico, Central America, Western Caribbean 1:6M

South America and Polar Regions

147	South America 1:24M
148	Geographical Comparisons: Temperature, Climate, Vegetation
149	Geographical Comparisons: Rainfall, Population, Land Use, Minerals
150-151	Northern South America 1:13M
152-153	Colombia, Venezuela, Ecuador 1:6M
154	Northeastern Brazil 1:6M
155	Southeastern Brazil 1:6M Rio de Janeiro-São Paulo 1:3M
156	Peru 1:6M Galápagos Islands 1:6M
157	Southern South America 1:13M
158-159	Southern Chile and Argentina 1:6M Santiago-Valparaíso, Buenos Aires 1:3M
160	Arctic Regions 1:30M Antarctica 1:50M

STATISTICS, TIME ZONES AND INDEX

The section on World Statistics includes the planets of the solar system, dimensions of the earth, oceans and major seas, major mountain peaks, longest rivers, largest lakes and major islands. The computer-generated Time Zones of the World is completely new and reflects the world's most recent time zone changes. A Master Index lists 60,000 places and other features appearing in this atlas, complete with page numbers and easy-to-use alpha-numeric references.

162-163	World Statistics
164-165	Time Zones of the World
166	Index Abbreviations
167-223	Index of the World (60,000 entries)
224	Acknowledgements

Centennial World Atlas

ENTIRE CONTENTS
© COPYRIGHT 1999 BY
HAMMOND INCORPORATED

PHOTO CREDITS: Neal & Molly Jansen: Cover and title page; Chris Lomas: Compass-p.4.; NASA - National Aeronautics and Space Administration Earth from Space images: Greece-Peloponnisos Peninsula-p.26; Pakistan-Indus River Delta-p.66; Egypt-Sinai Peninsula-p.92; Australia-Lake Eyre-p.108; United States-Grand Canyon-p.118; Argentina/Chile-Andes Mountains-p.146.

LIBRARY OF CONGRESS
CATALOGING-IN-PUBLICATION DATA

Hammond Incorporated.
  Hammond centennial world atlas.
    p. cm.
  Includes index.
  ISBN 0-8437-1150-7 (hc: alk. paper).
  ISBN 0-8437-1151-5 (sc: alk. paper).
  1. Atlases. I. Title. II. Title: Centennial world atlas.
  G1021. H2668   1998 <G&M>

  912--DC21   98-12386
                                   CIP
                                   MAPS

Map Projections

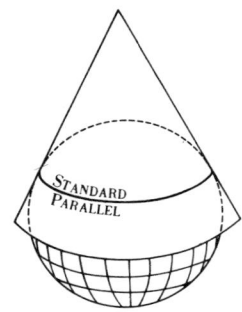

FIGURE 3
Conic Projection
The original idea of a conic projection is to cap the globe with a cone, and then project onto the cone from the planet's center the lines of latitude and longitude (the parallels and meridians). To produce a working map, the cone is simply cut open and laid flat. The conic projection used here is a modification of this idea. A cone can be made tangent to any standard parallel you choose. One popular version of a conic projection, the Lambert Conformal Conic, uses two standard parallels near the top and bottom of the map to further reduce errors of scale.

FIGURE 4
Hammond Optimal Conformal Projection
Like all conformal maps, the Optimal projection preserves angles exactly and minimizes distortion in shapes. This projection is more successful than any previous projection at spreading curvature across the entire map, producing the most distortion-free map possible.

S imply stated, the map-maker's challenge is to project the earth's curved surface onto a flat plane. To achieve this elusive goal, cartographers have developed map projections — equations which govern this conversion of geographic data.

This section explores some of the most widely used projections. It also introduces a new projection, the Hammond Optimal Conformal.

GENERAL PRINCIPLES AND TERMS
The earth rotates around its axis once a day. Its end points are the North and South poles; the line circling the earth midway between the poles is the equator. The arc from the equator to either pole is divided into 90 degrees of latitude. The equator represents 0° latitude. Circles of equal latitude, called parallels, are traditionally shown at every fifth or tenth degree.

The equator is divided into 360 degrees. Lines circling the globe from pole to pole through the degree points on the equator are called meridians, or great circles. All meridians are equal in length, but by international agreement the meridian passing through the Greenwich Observatory near London has been chosen as the prime meridian or 0° longitude. The distance in degrees from the prime meridian to any point east or west is its longitude.

While meridians are all equal in length, parallels become shorter as they approach the poles. Whereas one degree of latitude represents approximately 69 miles (112 km.) anywhere on the globe, a degree of longitude varies from 69 miles (112 km.) at the equator to zero at the poles. Each degree of latitude and longitude is divided into 60 minutes. One minute of latitude equals one nautical mile (1.15 land miles or 1.85 km.).

HOW TO FLATTEN A SPHERE: THE
ART OF CONTROLLING DISTORTION
There is only one way to represent a sphere with absolute precision: on a globe. All attempts to project our planet's surface onto a plane unevenly stretch or tear the sphere as it flattens, inevitably distorting shapes, distances, area (sizes appear larger or smaller than actual size), angles or direction.

Since representing a sphere on a flat plane always creates distortion, only the parallels or the meridians (or some other set of lines) can maintain the same length as on a globe of corresponding scale. All other lines must be either too long or too short. Accordingly, the scale on a flat map cannot be true everywhere; there will always be different scales in different parts of a map. On world maps or very large areas, variations in scale may be extreme. Most maps seek to preserve either true area relationships (equal area projections) or true angles and shapes (conformal projections); some attempt to achieve overall balance.

PROJECTIONS:
SELECTED EXAMPLES
Mercator (Fig. 1): This projection is especially useful because all compass directions appear as straight lines, making it a valuable navigational tool. Moreover, every small region conforms to its shape on a globe — hence the name conformal. But because its meridians are evenly-spaced vertical lines which never converge (unlike the globe), the horizontal parallels must be drawn farther and farther apart at higher latitudes to maintain a correct relationship.

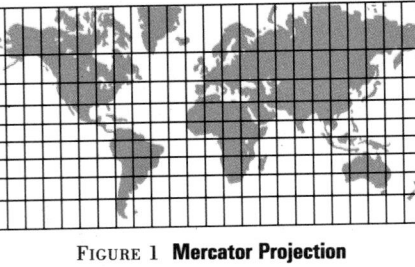

FIGURE 1 **Mercator Projection**

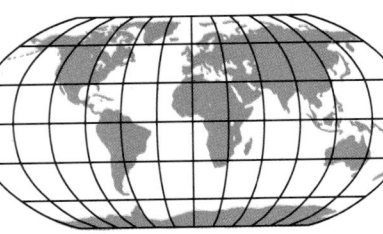

FIGURE 2 **Robinson Projection**

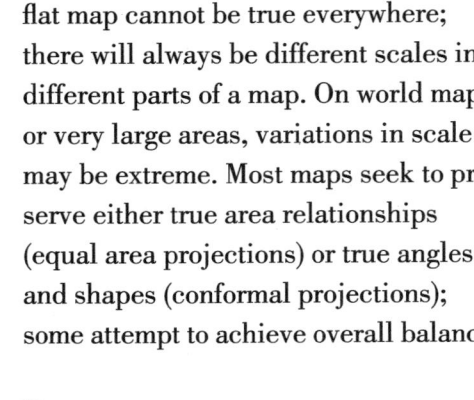

Only the equator is true to scale, and the size of areas in the higher latitudes is dramatically distorted.

Robinson (Fig. 2): To create the World-Physical and World-Political maps on pages 22-25, the Robinson projection was used. It combines elements of both conformal and equal area projections to show the whole earth with relatively true shapes and reasonably equal areas.

Conic (Fig. 3): This projection has been used frequently for air navigation charts and to create most of the national and regional maps in this atlas. (See text in margin at right).

HAMMOND OPTIMAL CONFORMAL
As its name implies, this new conformal projection (Fig. 4) presents the optimal view of an area by reducing shifts in scale over an entire region to the minimum degree possible. While conformal maps generally preserve all small shapes, large shapes can become very distorted because of varying scales, causing considerable inaccuracy in distance measurements. The concept underlying the Optimal Conformal is that for any region on the globe, there is an ideal projection for which scale variation can be made as small as possible. Consequently, unlike other projections, the Optimal Conformal does not use one standard formula to construct a map. Each map is a unique projection — the optimal projection for that particular area.

After a cartographer defines the subject area, a sophisticated computer program evaluates the size and shape of the region, and projects the most distortion-free conformal map possible.

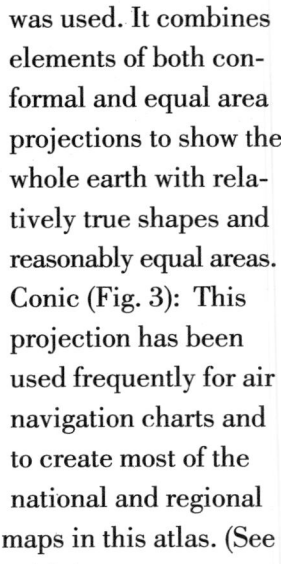

Using This Atlas

SYMBOLS USED ON MAPS OF THE WORLD

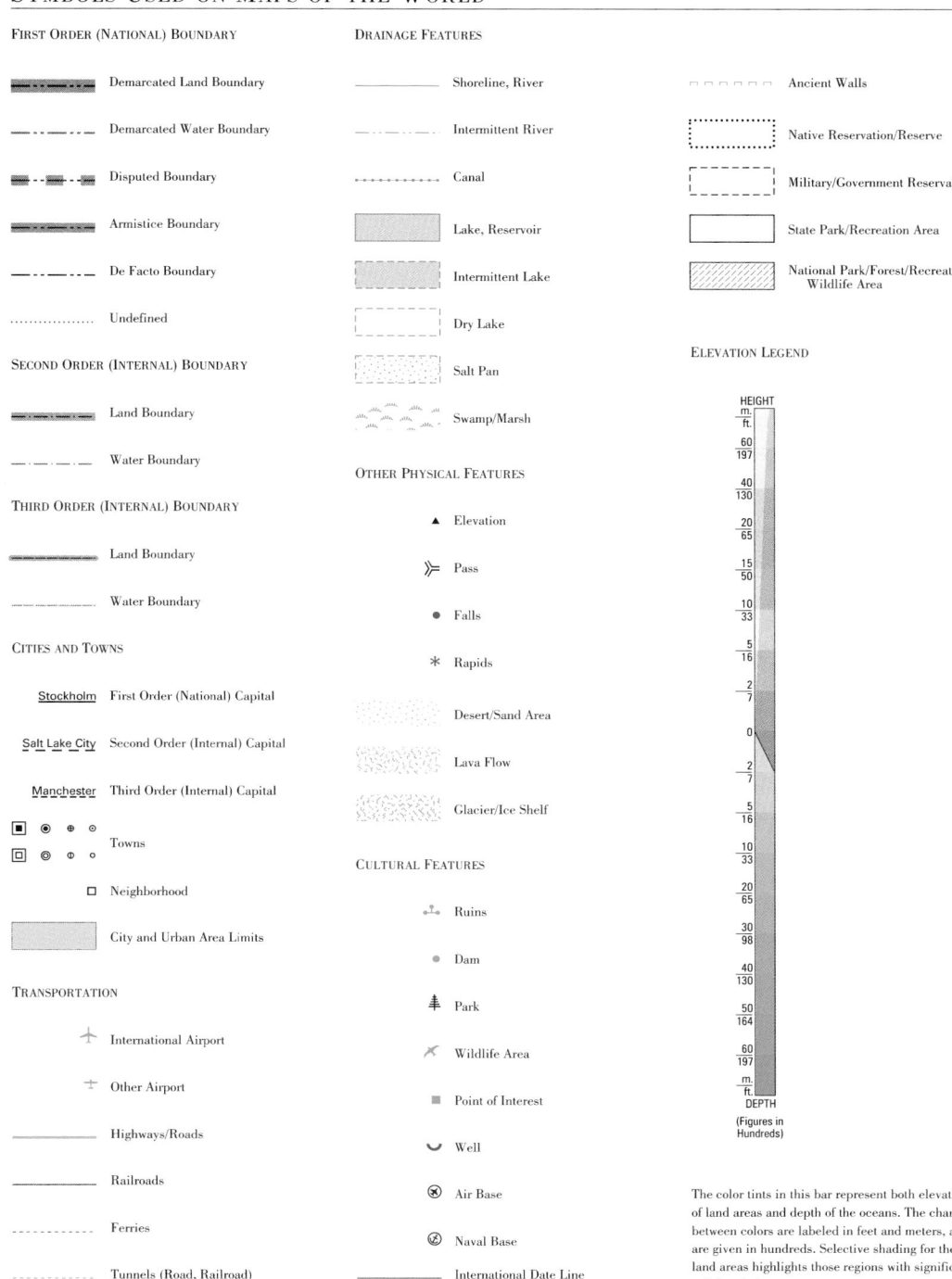

FIRST ORDER (NATIONAL) BOUNDARY

Demarcated Land Boundary

Demarcated Water Boundary

Disputed Boundary

Armistice Boundary

De Facto Boundary

Undefined

SECOND ORDER (INTERNAL) BOUNDARY

Land Boundary

Water Boundary

THIRD ORDER (INTERNAL) BOUNDARY

Land Boundary

Water Boundary

CITIES AND TOWNS

Stockholm   First Order (National) Capital

Salt Lake City   Second Order (Internal) Capital

Manchester   Third Order (Internal) Capital

Towns

Neighborhood

City and Urban Area Limits

TRANSPORTATION

International Airport

Other Airport

Highways/Roads

Railroads

Ferries

Tunnels (Road, Railroad)

DRAINAGE FEATURES

Shoreline, River

Intermittent River

Canal

Lake, Reservoir

Intermittent Lake

Dry Lake

Salt Pan

Swamp/Marsh

OTHER PHYSICAL FEATURES

▲ Elevation

⤝ Pass

● Falls

✳ Rapids

Desert/Sand Area

Lava Flow

Glacier/Ice Shelf

CULTURAL FEATURES

Ruins

Dam

Park

Wildlife Area

Point of Interest

Well

Air Base

Naval Base

International Date Line

Ancient Walls

Native Reservation/Reserve

Military/Government Reservation

State Park/Recreation Area

National Park/Forest/Recreation/Wildlife Area

ELEVATION LEGEND

HEIGHT
m.
ft.
60
197
40
130
20
65
15
50
10
33
5
16
2
7
0
2
7
5
16
10
33
20
65
30
98
40
130
50
164
60
197
m.
ft.
DEPTH
(Figures in Hundreds)

The color tints in this bar represent both elevation of land areas and depth of the oceans. The changes between colors are labeled in feet and meters, and are given in hundreds. Selective shading for the land areas highlights those regions with significant relief variations.

PRINCIPAL MAP ABBREVIATIONS

ABOR. RSV.	ABORIGINAL RESERVE	FT.	FORT	NCA	NATIONAL	PLAT.	PLATEAU
ADMIN.	ADMINISTRATION	G.	GULF		CONSERVATION AREA	PN	PARK NATIONAL
AFB	AIR FORCE BASE	GOVT.	GOVERNMENT	NHP	NATIONAL	PROM.	PROMONTORY
AMM. DEP.	AMMUNITION DEPOT	GD.	GRAND		HISTORICAL PARK	PRSV.	PRESERVE
ARCH.	ARCHIPELAGO	GT.	GREAT	NHS	NATIONAL	PT.	POINT
AUT.	AUTONOMOUS	HAR.	HARBOR		HISTORIC SITE	R.	RIVER
B.	BAY	HIST.	HISTORIC(AL)	NL	NATIONAL LAKESHORE	REC.	RECREATION(AL)
BFLD.	BATTLEFIELD	HTS.	HEIGHTS	NM	NATIONAL MONUMENT	REF.	REFUGE
BK.	BROOK	I., IS.	ISLAND(S)	NMEM	NATIONAL MEMORIAL	REG.	REGION
BR.	BRANCH	IND. RES.	INDIAN RESERVATION	NMILP	NATIONAL	REP.	REPUBLIC
C.	CAPE	INT'L	INTERNATIONAL		MILITARY PARK	RES.	RESERVOIR,
CAN.	CANAL	IR	INDIAN RESERVATION	NO.	NORTHERN		RESERVATION
CAP.	CAPITAL	ISTH.	ISTHMUS	NP	NATIONAL PARK	SA.	SIERRA
C.G.	COAST GUARD	JCT.	JUNCTION	NPP	NATIONAL PARK	SD.	SOUND
CHAN.	CHANNEL	L.	LAKE		AND PRESERVE	SO.	SOUTHERN
CO.	COUNTY	LAG.	LAGOON	NPRSV	NATIONAL PRESERVE	SP	STATE PARK
CONSV.	CONSERVATION	MEM.	MEMORIAL	NRA	NATIONAL	SPR., SPRGS.	SPRING, SPRINGS
CORD.	CORDILLERA	MIL.	MILITARY		RECREATION AREA	ST.	STATE
CR.	CREEK	MON.	MONUMENT	NRIV	NATIONAL RIVER	STA.	STATION
CTR.	CENTER	MT.	MOUNT	NRSV	NATIONAL RESERVE	STM.	STREAM
DEP.	DEPOT	MTN.	MOUNTAIN	NS	NATIONAL SEASHORE	STR.	STRAIT
DEPR.	DEPRESSION	MTS.	MOUNTAINS	NWR	NATIONAL	TERR.	TERRITORY
DES.	DESERT	NAT.	NATURAL		WILDLIFE REFUGE	TUN.	TUNNEL
DIST.	DISTRICT	NAT'L	NATIONAL	OBL.	OBLAST	TWP.	TOWNSHIP
DMZ	DEMILITARIZED ZONE	NAV.	NAVAL	OCC.	OCCUPIED	UNDOF	UNITED NATIONS
EST.	ESTUARY	NB	NATIONAL	OKR.	OKRUG		DISENGAGEMENT
FED.	FEDERAL		BATTLEFIELD	PASSG.	PASSAGE		OBSERVER FORCE
FK.	FORK	NBP	NATIONAL	PEN.	PENINSULA	VAL.	VALLEY
FOR.	FOREST		BATTLEFIELD PARK	PK.	PEAK	VILL.	VILLAGE

*T*he Centennial World Atlas has been thoughtfully designed to be easy and enjoyable to use. Only a short time is needeed to familiarize yourself with its organization.

MAP SYMBOLS, COLORS AND LABELS

The cartographer selects the natural and cultural features most valuable to the map user. Map legibility requires that small features be represented by symbols that are actually larger than true scale size. Due to the larger symbol sizes and the resulting loss of map space, it is necessary to omit less important features in congested areas.

Most map features are represented by the use of conventional symbols, lines, and patterns printed in appropriate colors. The chart to the left shows the standard symbols used in this atlas. Water features are shown in blue. Lines of various weights, styles, and colors represent the many different linear features in this atlas. Individual point features are represented by a pictorial and/or generic symbol.

Notes may also be added to explain features that cannot be depicted clearly.

MAP SCALES

A map's scale is the relationship of any length on the map to an identical length on the earth's surface. A scale of 1:3M means that one inch on the map represents 3,000,000 inches (47 miles, 76 km.) on the earth's surface. Thus, a 1:1M scale is larger than 1:3M, just as 1/1 is larger than 1/3.

The most densely populated areas are shown at a scale of 1:1M, while selected metropolitan areas are covered at either 1:500,000 or 1:1M. Other populous areas are presented at 1:3M and 1:6M, allowing you to accurately compare areas and distances of similar regions. Remaining regions, including the continent maps, are presented at 1:9M and smaller scales.

BOUNDARY POLICIES

This atlas observes the boundary policies of the U.S. Department of State. Disputed, armistice and de facto boundaries are handled with a special symbol treatment. The portrayal of independent nations follows their recognition by the United Nations and/or United States government.

Map Type Styles
Cartographers use a variety of type styles to differentiate between map features. The following styles are used in this Atlas.

Major Political Areas
LUXEMBOURG

Internal Political Divisions
SAXONY-ANHALT

Regions
Polabská Nížina

Cities and Towns
Norfolk Sumter Smyrna

Neighborhoods
BIGGIN HILL

Points of Interest
MISSION SAN BUENAVENTURA

Water Features
L. Elsinore

Capes, Points, Peaks, Passes
Pt. La Jolla   Pacifico Mtn.

Islands, Peninsulas
Cape Breton I.

Mountains, Uplands
Serra do Norte

Deserts, Plains, Valleys
San Fernando Valley

A Word About Names
Our source for all foreign names is the decision lists of the U.S. Board of Geographic Names and/or official foreign government maps and official gazetteers. This atlas also uses accepted conventional names for certain major foreign place names. The U.S. Board of Geographic Names defines a conventional name as "a name approved for use in addition to, or in lieu of, an approved local official name or names."

In order to make the maps more readily understandable to English-speaking readers, many foreign physical features are translated into more recognizable English forms.

The rendering of city, town and village names for the United States follows the forms and spelling of the U.S. Postal Service.

In 6,000 B.C., earth's entire population stood between 5 and 20 million people. It took almost 8,000 years to reach the one billion mark, yet just 100 years more to reach two billion in 1930. Sixty years later, that figure has nearly tripled, to about 5.8 billion people today. This massive expansion has been fueled not by an increasing birth rate, but by a gradual extension of life expectancy and a huge reduction in infant mortality.◉ By 2025, the United Nations projects that our global population could exceed 8.3 billion. Ninety percent of this growth will be concentrated in the poorest countries. The most dramatic increases will take place in sub-Saharan Africa, where fertility rates have remained high.◉ Population shifts are often driven by economic forces. In the late 15th and early 16th centuries, Europe's conquest of the sea spurred trade, exploration and settlements across the globe. The temperate zones of the Americas were especially well-suited to their crops and flocks. Between the 16th and mid-19th centuries, millions of black Africans were brought to the Americas by the Atlantic slave trade, victims of the New World's voracious need for labor.◉ In the industrialized nations of Europe, Japan, Canada and the United States, the trend is towards zero growth. Birth rates have also fallen in India and China, yet 17 percent of the world's people live in India, and 20 percent — 1 of every 5 people — live in China. Aggressive educational programs are helping to change traditional beliefs, which held childbirth as a woman's duty, and viewed large families as proof of wealth, fortification against hardship and security for aging parents. Government-sponsored birth control programs are also showing positive results.◉ Not all of the factors which could limit population growth are so well planned. In the end, the environmental pressures created by rapidly expanding population may deplete the very resources necessary for survival.

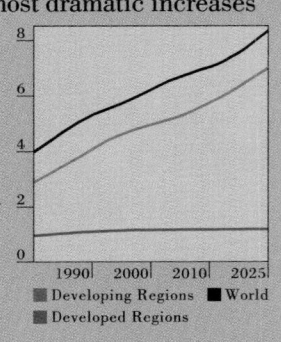

World population in billions

Developing Regions ■ World ■
Developed Regions ■

CROWDED PLACES

THOUSANDS OF PERSONS PER SQUARE MILE (SQ. KM.)

Macau
81(31)
95(36)

Monaco
32(17)
34(18)

Hong Kong
16(6)
20(8)

Singapore
14(5)
18(7)

Gibraltar
9(4)
10(5)

Gaza Strip
7(3)
18(7)

1997 ■ 2020 (estimate) ■

Source: U.S. Bureau of the Census, International Database

Population

WORLD'S LARGEST URBAN AREAS

MILLIONS OF INHABITANTS

TOKYO, Japan 26.5

NEW YORK, U.S. 18.0

SÃO PAULO, Brazil 16.9

OSAKA, Japan 16.9

SEOUL, Korea, 15.8

MEXICO, Mexico 15.5

SHANGHAI, China 14.7

MUMBAI, India 14.5

LOS ANGELES, U.S. 14.5

MOSCOW, Russia 13.1

BEIJING, China 12.0

CALCUTTA, India 11.4

LONDON, U.K. 11.1

RIO DE JANEIRO, Brazil 11.0

JAKARTA, Indonesia 11.0

URBAN & RURAL POPULATION COMPONENTS

SELECTED COUNTRIES

URBAN ▨ RURAL ▨

Uruguay 87% / 13%

Australia 85% / 15%

Japan 77% / 23%

United States 74% / 26%

Russia 73% / 27%

Hungary 62% / 38%

Iran 54% / 46%

Egypt 44% / 56%

Philippines 37% / 63%

Portugal 30% / 70%

China 26% / 74%

Maldives 20% / 80%

Bangladesh 15% / 85%

Nepal 6% / 94%

AGE DISTRIBUTION

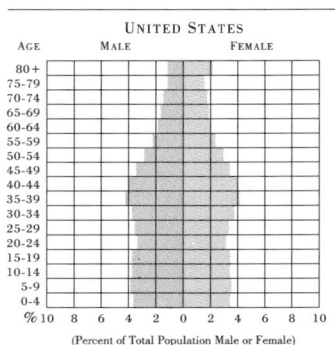

UNITED STATES

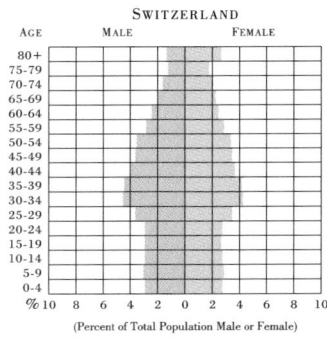

SWITZERLAND

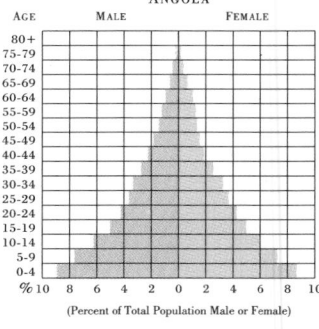

ANGOLA

SOURCE: U.S. BUREAU OF THE CENSUS, INTERNATIONAL DATABASE

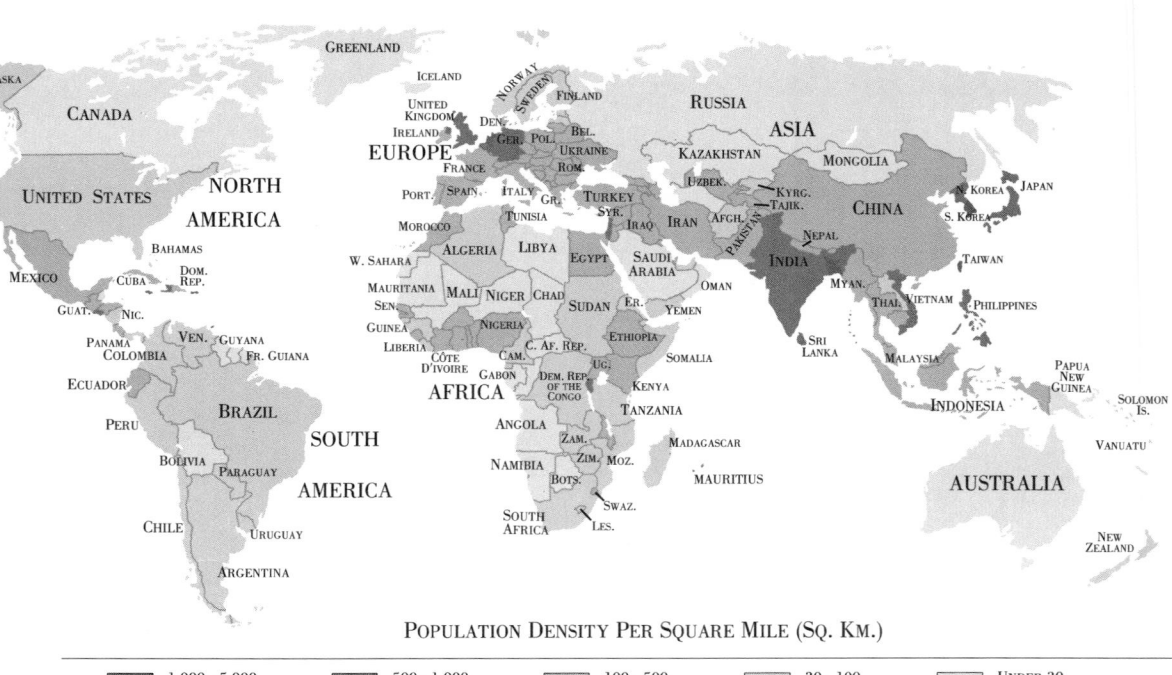

POPULATION DENSITY PER SQUARE MILE (SQ. KM.)

| ■ 1,000 - 5,000 (390 - 2,000) | ■ 500 - 1,000 (195 - 390) | ■ 100 - 500 (39 - 195) | ■ 30 - 100 (12 - 39) | ■ UNDER 30 (UNDER 12) |

Source: U.S. Bureau of the Census, International Database

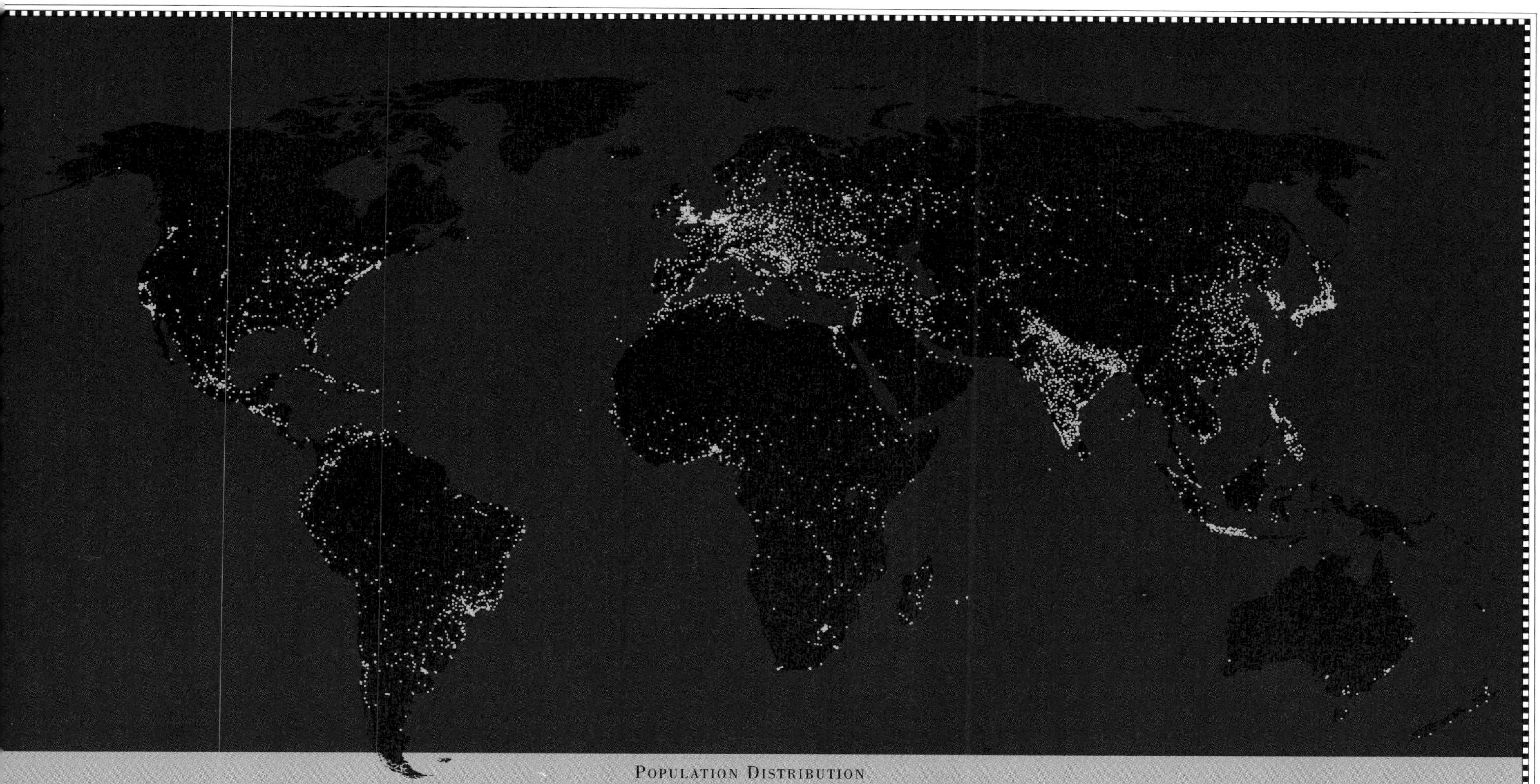

POPULATION DISTRIBUTION

This map provides a dramatic perspective by illuminating populated areas with one point of light for each city over 50,000 residents. Over 675 million people live in cities with populations in excess of 500,000. According to the latest census data, there are 10,000 people per square mile (3,860 per sq km) in London. In New York, there are 11,000 (4,250). Hong Kong has over 16,000 people per square mile (6,200 per sq km), and the Tokyo-Yokohama agglomeration includes over 25,000 (9,650). During the last decade, the movement to the cities has accelerated dramatically, particularly in developing nations. In Lagos, Nigeria, where there are over 24,000 people per square mile (9,290 per sq km), most live in shantytowns. In São Paulo, Brazil, 2,000 buses arrive each day, bringing field hands, farm workers and their families in search of a better life. By the year 2000, the United Nations predicts that 17 of the world's 20 largest urban agglomerations will be in the third world. Tokyo-Yokohama, Mexico and São Paulo will top the list.

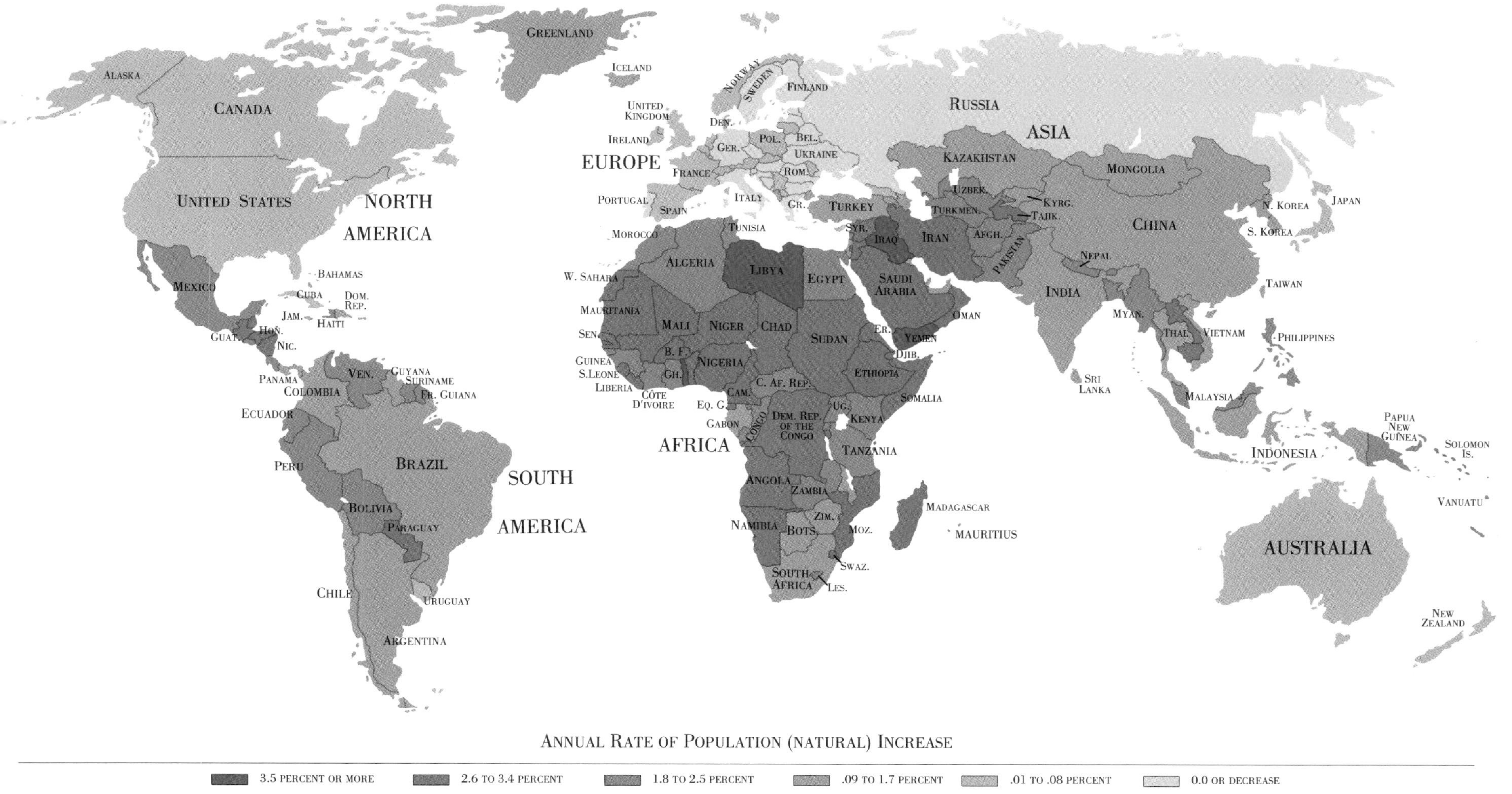

ANNUAL RATE OF POPULATION (NATURAL) INCREASE

3.5 PERCENT OR MORE	2.6 TO 3.4 PERCENT	1.8 TO 2.5 PERCENT	.09 TO 1.7 PERCENT	.01 TO .08 PERCENT	0.0 OR DECREASE

Source: U.S. Bureau of the Census, International Database

The living standards of less than two dozen highly industrialized nations stand in vivid contrast to conditions in the rest of the world. Though the developed countries represent only about a quarter of the earth's population, they create 80 percent of its wealth. The rest of the world must subsist on one-fifth of the total goods. ✸ Political instability, inadequate education and health care, and the lack or misuse of natural resources all contribute to this disparity. Most people in the developing world still live off the land, leaving them prey to natural disasters and market prices which no longer keep pace with rising costs. Drought, desertification, swelling populations and aggressive development further challenge traditional lifestyles. In third world nations from Mexico to Nigeria, the exodus from rural communities has resulted in intensely overcrowded cities where housing, jobs and clean water are inadequate. ✸ Despite these challenges, advances in education and health care have wrought stunning improvements in average life expectancy. In the developing world, it has risen from 46 years in 1960 to 62 years in 1993. Between 1962 and 1997, life expectancy in China jumped from 39 to 70 years. Antibiotics and immunizations have significantly reduced infant mortality levels in many third world countries. In North America, Western Europe and Japan, the average life expectancy is 71 years for men and 77 years for women. Elsewhere, in Afghanistan and sub-Saharan Africa, average life expectancy still hovers around 40. ✸ Literacy is the cornerstone of a healthy industrial nation. Yet by the year 2000, more than a billion people may be unable to read or write. Most of them will live in the 5 most populous Asian countries: China, India, Indonesia, Pakistan and Bangladesh. Ambitious literacy programs now underway in countries from Iraq to Chile and Mexico have reported significant reductions in their illiteracy rates. With each success comes new hope — for an individual, a family and a nation.

In the United States, the average person earns about $27,500 — the highest per capita Gross Domestic Product in the world. In Rwanda, the same person would earn about $400 in a year.

American workers typically get only 2 or 3 weeks of annual paid vacation, while western Europeans enjoy 4 to 6 weeks off.

Standards of

GREENLAND

ALASKA

CANADA

UNITED STATES

EUROPE
The healthy, high-tech economies of many western European nations stand in sharp relief to the obsolete factories, high unemployment and ethnic rivalries of Eastern Europe.

ICELAND NORWAY SWEDEN FINLAND
UNITED KINGDOM DEN. E.
IRELAND N. L.
B. GER. POLAND BEL.
CZ. UKRAINE
FRANCE S. A. HUN. ROM. M.
ITALY C. BUL.
PORTUGAL SPAIN GR. TURKE
C. L.S.
TUNISIA ISR.
MOROCCO ALGERIA LIBYA EGYPT
WESTERN SAHARA
MAURITANIA MALI NIGER CHAD SUDAN
SEN. G.
G.B. B. F. NIGERIA
GUINEA
S. LEONE GH. C. AF. REP.
LIBERIA CÔTE CAM.
D'IVOIRE EQ. G. UG.
GABON CONGO DEM. REP. KE
OF THE
CONGO
TANZA

UNITED STATES
The United States and other developed countries have committed greater resources to both public and private education. This has helped their populations develop the skills that are necessary in more complex, technical and competitive societies.

MEXICO
BAHAMAS
CUBA
DOM. REP.
BEL. JAM. HAITI
HON.
GUAT. NIC.
EL SAL.
C.R. VENEZUELA GUYANA
PANAMA SURINAME
COLOMBIA FR. GUIANA
ECUADOR

PERU

BRAZIL

AFRICA
Disastrous droughts, discriminatory government policies and ancient tribal rivalries, particularly in South Africa and the Sudan, have resulted in political instability and economic hardship.

ANGOLA ZAMBIA
ZIM.
NAMIBIA MOZ
BOTS.
SOUTH SWAZ
AFRICA LES.

LATIN AMERICA
The gulf between rich and poor continues to widen, despite efforts to reform oppressive governments, increase literacy and relieve overburdened cities.

BOLIVIA
PARAGUAY

CHILE
URUGUAY
ARGENTINA

SOUTH AMERICA
Political unrest, rising inflation and slow economic growth continue to thwart efforts to bring unity and prosperity to the nations of South America.

WORKER COMPARISONS OF SELECTED COUNTRIES

COUNTRY	AVG. ACTUAL HOURS WORKED PER WEEK	YEARS OF FORMAL SCHOOLING	PERCENT WOMEN OF LABOR FORCE
AUSTRALIA	39	13.6	38
AUSTRIA	34	14.6	39
BELGIUM	33	14.4	33
CANADA	38	17.6	40
FRANCE	39	14.6	41
GERMANY	38	14.6	39
GREECE	41	13.2	27
HUNGARY	37	12.0	44
IRELAND	41	13.1	29
ISRAEL	42	NA	34
JAPAN	38	13.5	40
LUXEMBOURG	41	NA	32
NETHERLANDS	40	15.5	31
NEW ZEALAND	42	15.4	36
NORWAY	37	15.5	41
ROMANIA	38	10.8	45
SOUTH AFRICA	46	12.0	36
SOUTH KOREA	49	13.7	34
SPAIN	37	14.7	25
UNITED KINGDOM	43	14.9	39
UNITED STATES	42	16.0	41

NA=DATA NOT AVAILABLE   SOURCE: UNITED NATIONS

GROSS DOMESTIC PRODUCT GROWTH RATES

BEST GROWTH RATES		WORST GROWTH RATES	
LESOTHO	13.5	AZERBAIJAN	-17
CHINA	10.3	TAJIKISTAN	-12.4
EQUATORIAL GUINEA	10	GEORGIA	-11
ERITREA	10	BELARUS	-10
MALAWI	9.9	TURKMENISTAN	-10
MALAYSIA	9.5	KAZAKHSTAN	-8.9
VIETNAM	9.5	CONGO, DEM. REP. OF THE	-7.4
SOUTH KOREA	9	MEXICO	-6.9
SINGAPORE	8.9	MOROCCO	-6.5
THAILAND	8.6	KYRGYZSTAN	-6
CHILE	8.5	NORTH KOREA	-5
LAOS	8	ARGENTINA	-4.4
SOLOMON ISLANDS	8	RUSSIA	-4
INDONESIA	7.5	SIERRA LEONE	-4
ISRAEL	7.1	UKRAINE	-4
UGANDA	7.1	DJIBOUTI	-3
IRELAND	7	MOLDOVA	-3
MYANMAR	6.8	PAPUA NEW GUINEA	-3
PERU	6.8	RWANDA	-2.7
TURKEY	6.8	MOZAMBIQUE	-2.5

Source: CIA World Factbook

Living

EASTERN EUROPE AND RUSSIA
In the former Soviet republics, population growth is slowing because of rising mortality due to a breakdown in health care services, heavy smoking, and heavy consumption of alcohol. Russia's life expectancy has dropped so dramatically that its population is shrinking at the fastest rate ever recorded for an industrial society.

CHINA
The limited relaxation of Communist dogma has encouraged growing industrialization and exports, creating new wealth in parts of China.

EAST ASIA
The economies of this region (excluding China) have experienced annual per capita growth of 7.6 percent between 1960 and 1993 with relatively low inequality in incomes. This rare combination has been known to achieve dramatic reductions in poverty.

MIDDLE EAST
Water has emerged as a significant factor in Middle East politics. Projected water shortages could lead to economic hardship and regional conflicts.

AUSTRALIA
An influx of Japanese tourists and investors is generating new capital and development, escalating coastal real estate prices and regional tensions.

GROSS DOMESTIC PRODUCT PER CAPITA IN DOLLARS (PER YEAR)

10,000 AND MORE	2,500-4,999	700-999	DATA NOT AVAILABLE
5,000-9,999	1,000-2,499	UNDER 700	

Source: CIA World Factbook

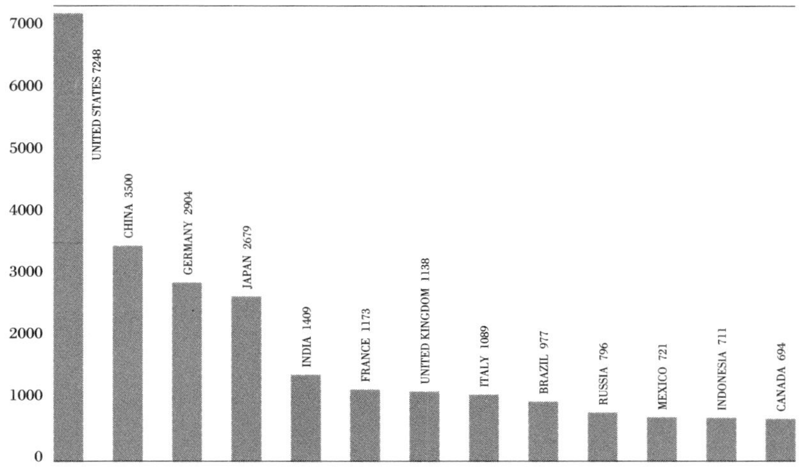

TOTAL GROSS DOMESTIC PRODUCT
BILLIONS OF DOLLARS

- UNITED STATES 7248
- CHINA 3500
- GERMANY 2904
- JAPAN 2679
- INDIA 1409
- FRANCE 1173
- UNITED KINGDOM 1138
- ITALY 1089
- BRAZIL 977
- RUSSIA 796
- MEXICO 721
- INDONESIA 711
- CANADA 694

Source: CIA World Factbook

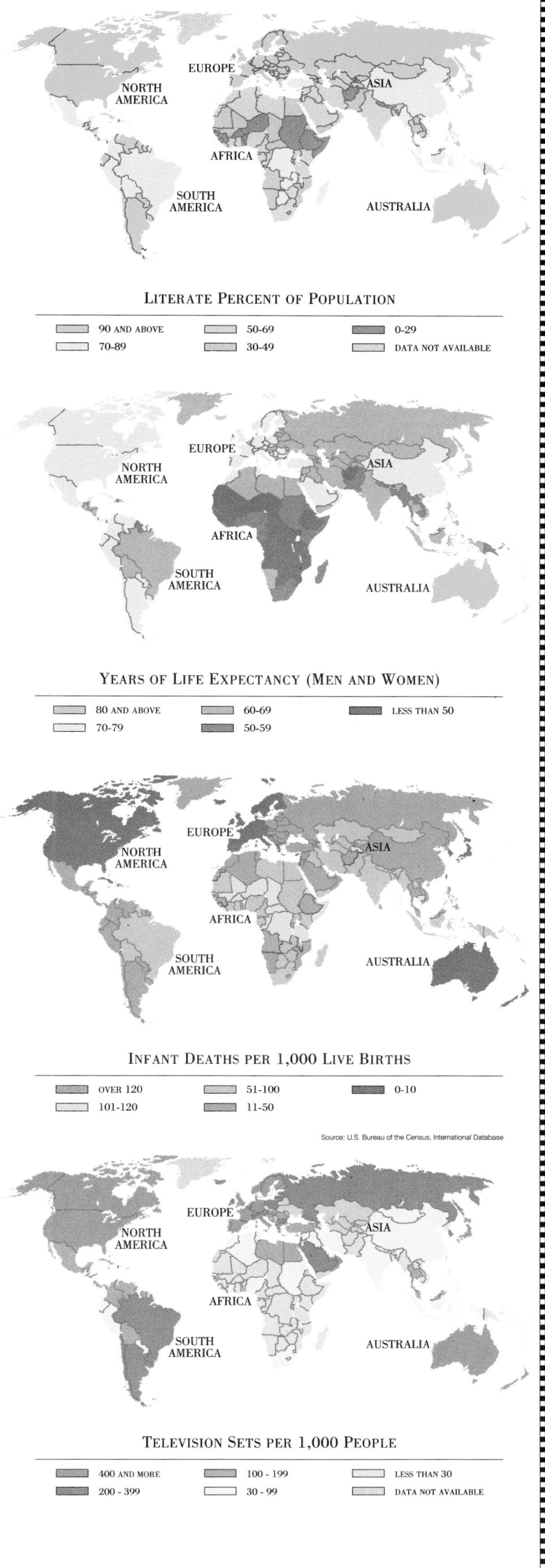

LITERATE PERCENT OF POPULATION

90 AND ABOVE	50-69	0-29
70-89	30-49	DATA NOT AVAILABLE

YEARS OF LIFE EXPECTANCY (MEN AND WOMEN)

80 AND ABOVE	60-69	LESS THAN 50
70-79	50-59	

INFANT DEATHS PER 1,000 LIVE BIRTHS

OVER 120	51-100	0-10
101-120	11-50	

Source: U.S. Bureau of the Census, International Database

TELEVISION SETS PER 1,000 PEOPLE

400 AND MORE	100 - 199	LESS THAN 30
200 - 399	30 - 99	DATA NOT AVAILABLE

T he earth is a living organism. It breathes ceaselessly, as the forces of convection circulate air in an endless stream around the globe. Warm air rises at the equator and flows north or south, while cold air moves down from the poles towards the equator. In this way, global air currents direct the weather. ❂ All weather occurs in the troposphere, the atmospheric level closest to the earth's surface. Chemical exchanges between air and sea help stabilize the oxygen and carbon dioxide content of both. Wind also whips up and carries along invisible droplets of salty water. Water condenses around the salt crystals to produce mists, clouds and rain. ❂ Climate, the average weather in an area as measured over many years, is determined by two key variables: temperature and precipitation. Humidity, sunshine, air pressure and wind play supporting roles. Since temperature depends upon the strength of the sun's rays, the earth's 14 climatic zones (see map) are related to latitude — though winds and elevation can modify these zones. ❂ Climates differ for many reasons, from variations in latitude, elevation and topography to changes in land and water temperatures. Every place on earth has its own climate and ecosystem which, in turn, influences the food, clothing, homes and culture of the local population. ❂ How do climates change? Climatologists point to several causes, from shifts in solar energy to volcanic ash in the atmos-

Antarctica, the earth's coldest place, is also one of its driest. Its vast inland plateau is really a desert of ice and snow.

phere, which can severely reduce the amount of sunlight reaching the earth's surface — sometimes for years. ❂ Almost 3 billion pounds (1.36 million kg.) of chemicals are released into the air in the United States each year. The sky then transports the pollutants hundreds of miles. During the journey, the atmosphere functions as a complex chemical reactor where fossil fuel emissions interact with sunlight, water vapor and hundreds of man-made compounds. ❂ Our atmosphere, which rises 30 miles (48 km.) above the planet's surface and covers 260 billion cubic miles (1.08 trillion cubic km.), may seem too vast to pollute. But the ability of the atmosphere to warm and cool the earth, to shield us from ultraviolet rays and to enable life to flourish is diminishing. The changes we have wrought are altering our atmosphere, our climate and our lives.

Climate

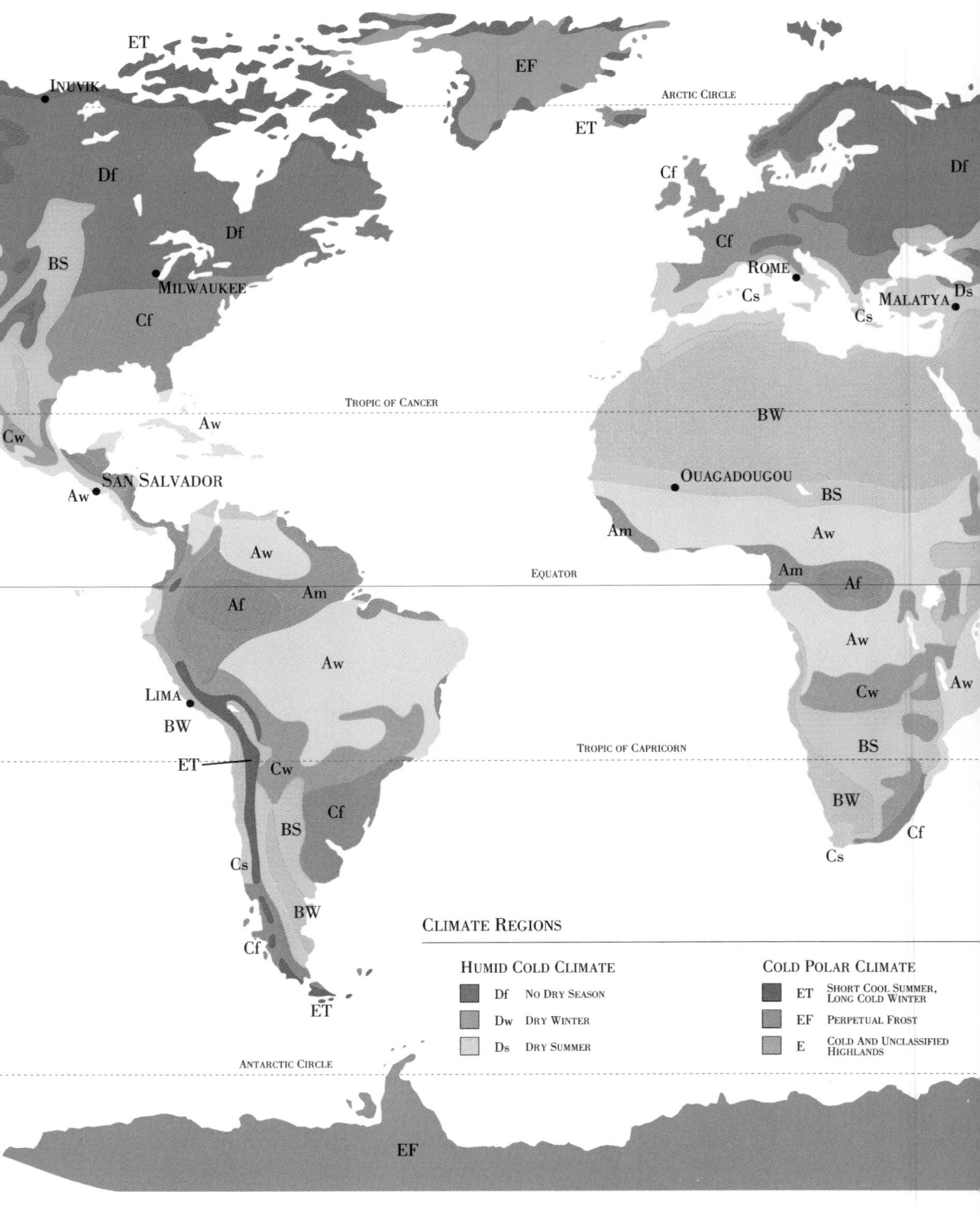

CLIMATE REGIONS

HUMID COLD CLIMATE

■	Df	No Dry Season
■	Dw	Dry Winter
□	Ds	Dry Summer

COLD POLAR CLIMATE

■	ET	Short Cool Summer, Long Cold Winter
■	EF	Perpetual Frost
□	E	Cold And Unclassified Highlands

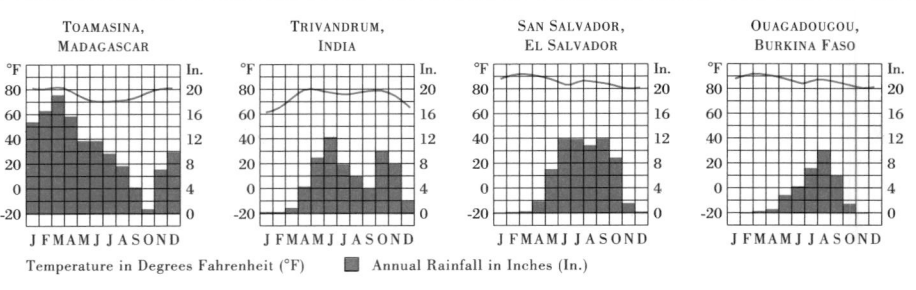

Temperature in Degrees Fahrenheit (°F)   ■ Annual Rainfall in Inches (In.)

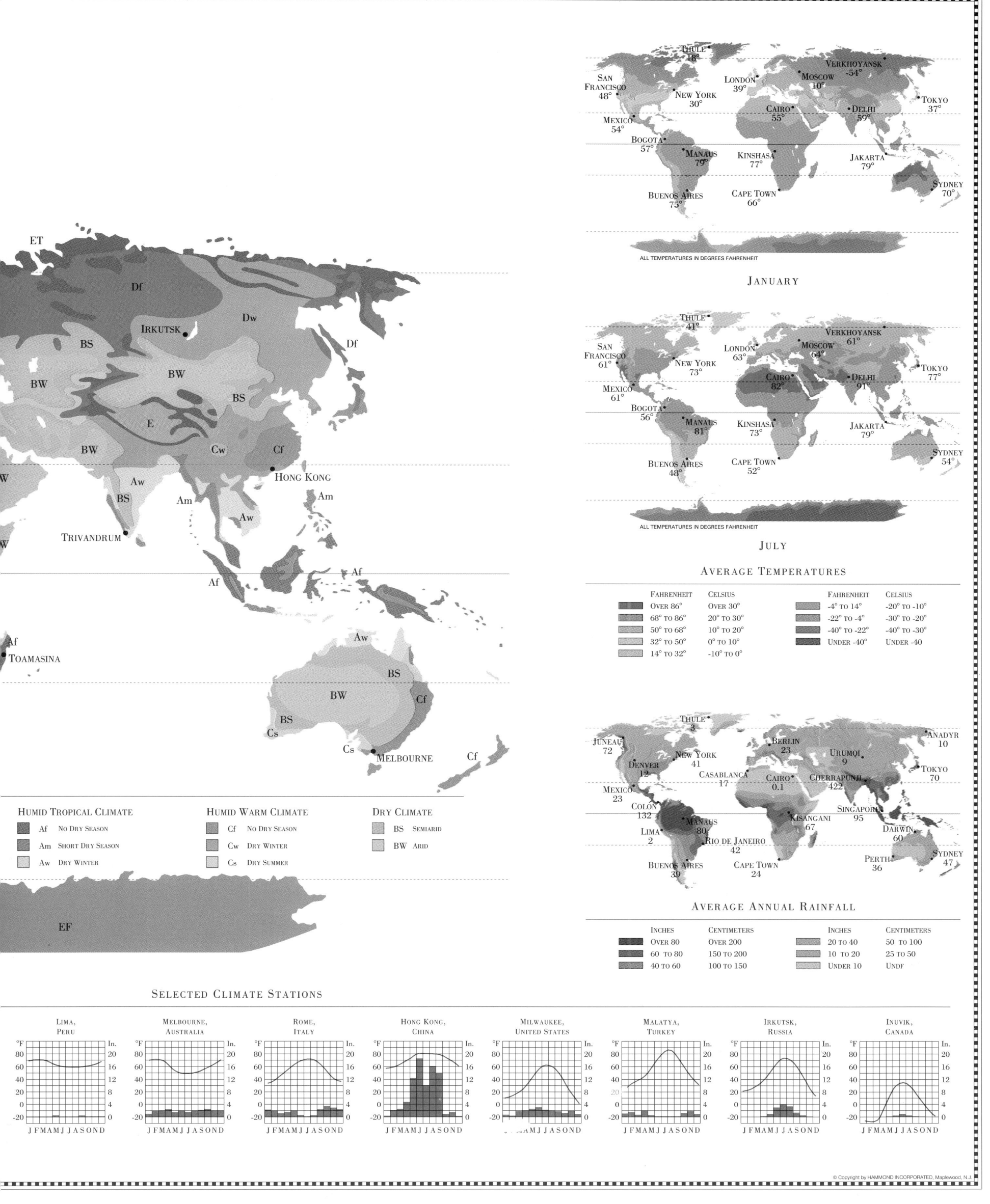

The earth's human population, already 5.8 billion, is growing at a rate of 80 million people a year. This rapid rise is straining the global environment, devouring forests, fresh water and oil reserves while polluting the very resources necessary for survival. ✹ Each year, the burning of fossil fuels releases more than 23 billion tons (21 billion metric tons) of carbon dioxide into the air. Man-made chlorofluorocarbons are eating away at the layer of ozone which shields earth from harmful ultraviolet radiation. Highly acidic rains created by fossil fuel emissions are destroying lakes, forests and historic monuments from North America to Africa. ✹ "Greenhouse gases" such as carbon dioxide, sulphur and nitrogen oxides trap heat within our atmosphere and warm the planet by absorbing earth's infrared radiation. Tropical rainforests, with their capacity to consume carbon dioxide, generate fresh oxygen and regulate rainfall, might offer an antidote. Yet from South America to Indonesia, they are being levelled for lumber and land at the rate of 44.5 million acres (18 million hectares) per year. ✹ Some experts predict that "global warming" could raise the earth's temperature significantly in the next century, leading to unpredictable changes in climate. Soaring temperatures could bring severe recurring droughts, dust storms, forest fires and wildlife extinction. Melting glaciers and rising seas would flood coastal areas, drown wetlands, contaminate estuaries and pollute drinking water. ✹ While industrialized nations can afford to invest in environmental preservation, third world countries, home to most of the world's population and rainforests, must focus their limited resources on immediate economic survival. Feeding a nation takes precedence over saving a forest, even if the long-term cost could be incalculable. ✹ The United Nations Conference on Environment and Development, held at Rio de Janeiro, set in motion initiatives which may help to repair our environment. It seems the solution requires nothing less than a unified global effort to transform the way we live, with nature conservation, population control and clean, efficient energy use as our goals.

In Mumbai (Bombay) India, as well as other cities around the world, smog is making it difficult to breathe.

Is a global warming trend under way? Containing the four warmest years in history, the 1990's are already the warmest decade ever recorded . Record droughts, floods and forest fires have become increasingly common throughout the world.

Environmental

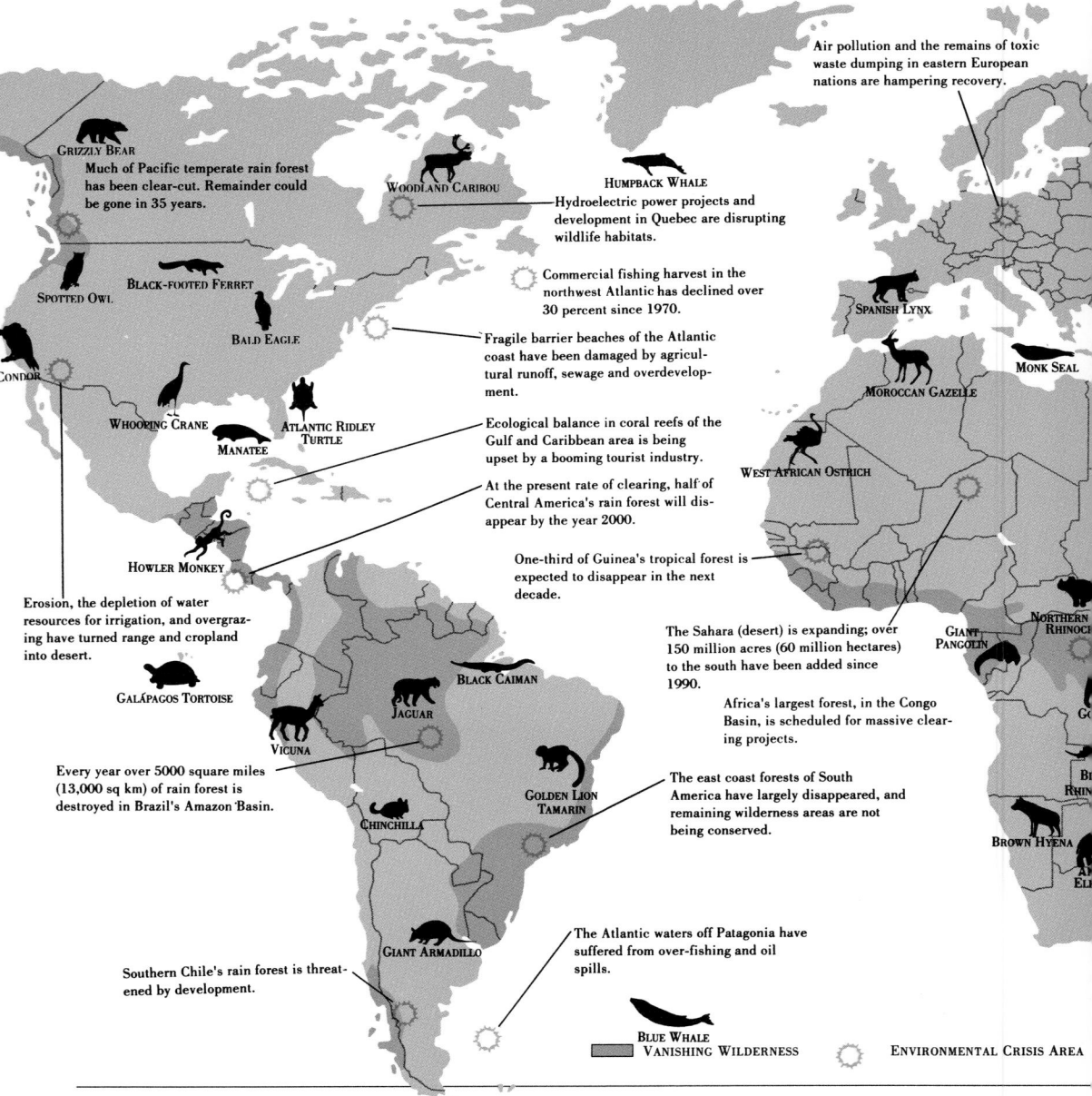

Air pollution and the remains of toxic waste dumping in eastern European nations are hampering recovery.

GRIZZLY BEAR
Much of Pacific temperate rain forest has been clear-cut. Remainder could be gone in 35 years.

WOODLAND CARIBOU

HUMPBACK WHALE
Hydroelectric power projects and development in Quebec are disrupting wildlife habitats.

SPOTTED OWL

BLACK-FOOTED FERRET

BALD EAGLE

CONDOR

WHOOPING CRANE

MANATEE

ATLANTIC RIDLEY TURTLE

Commercial fishing harvest in the northwest Atlantic has declined over 30 percent since 1970.

Fragile barrier beaches of the Atlantic coast have been damaged by agricultural runoff, sewage and overdevelopment.

Ecological balance in coral reefs of the Gulf and Caribbean area is being upset by a booming tourist industry.

At the present rate of clearing, half of Central America's rain forest will disappear by the year 2000.

HOWLER MONKEY

Erosion, the depletion of water resources for irrigation, and overgrazing have turned range and cropland into desert.

GALÁPAGOS TORTOISE

BLACK CAIMAN

JAGUAR

VICUNA

Every year over 5000 square miles (13,000 sq km) of rain forest is destroyed in Brazil's Amazon Basin.

CHINCHILLA

GOLDEN LION TAMARIN

GIANT ARMADILLO

Southern Chile's rain forest is threatened by development.

SPANISH LYNX

MONK SEAL

MOROCCAN GAZELLE

WEST AFRICAN OSTRICH

One-third of Guinea's tropical forest is expected to disappear in the next decade.

The Sahara (desert) is expanding; over 150 million acres (60 million hectares) to the south have been added since 1990.

Africa's largest forest, in the Congo Basin, is scheduled for massive clearing projects.

The east coast forests of South America have largely disappeared, and remaining wilderness areas are not being conserved.

The Atlantic waters off Patagonia have suffered from over-fishing and oil spills.

GIANT PANGOLIN

NORTHERN RHINOC

BROWN HYENA

BLUE WHALE
VANISHING WILDERNESS   ENVIRONMENTAL CRISIS AREA

Air Pollution
Billions of tons of industrial emissions and toxic pollutants — including carbon dioxide, sulphur, nitrogen oxide, lead, mercury and cadmium — are released into the air each year, depleting our ozone layer, killing our forests and lakes with acid rain and threatening our health: in some parts of the world, lung cancer has become a leading cause of death.

Water Pollution
Only 3 percent of the earth's water is fresh. Unfortunately, pollution from cities, farms and factories has made much of it unfit to drink. In the developing world, most sewage flows untreated into lakes and rivers; health officials estimate that 5 million people die each year from diseases caused by unclean water. Regional struggles to secure adequate water are becoming more intense.

Ozone Depletion
The layer of ozone in the stratosphere shields earth from harmful ultraviolet radiation. But man-made gases are destroying this vital barrier, increasing the risk of skin cancer and eye disease — with equally harmful effects for all plant and animal species. A hole in the ozone layer over Antarctica is now the size of the continental United States.

Concerns

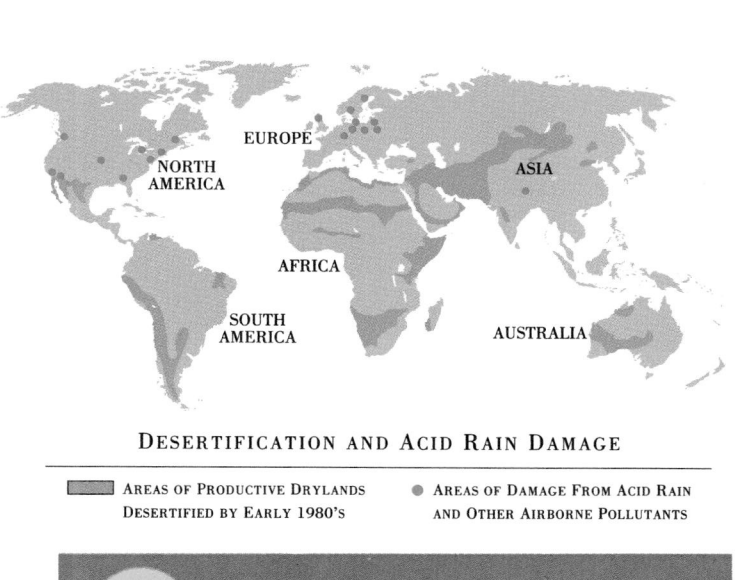

DESERTIFICATION AND ACID RAIN DAMAGE

AREAS OF PRODUCTIVE DRYLANDS DESERTIFIED BY EARLY 1980'S

AREAS OF DAMAGE FROM ACID RAIN AND OTHER AIRBORNE POLLUTANTS

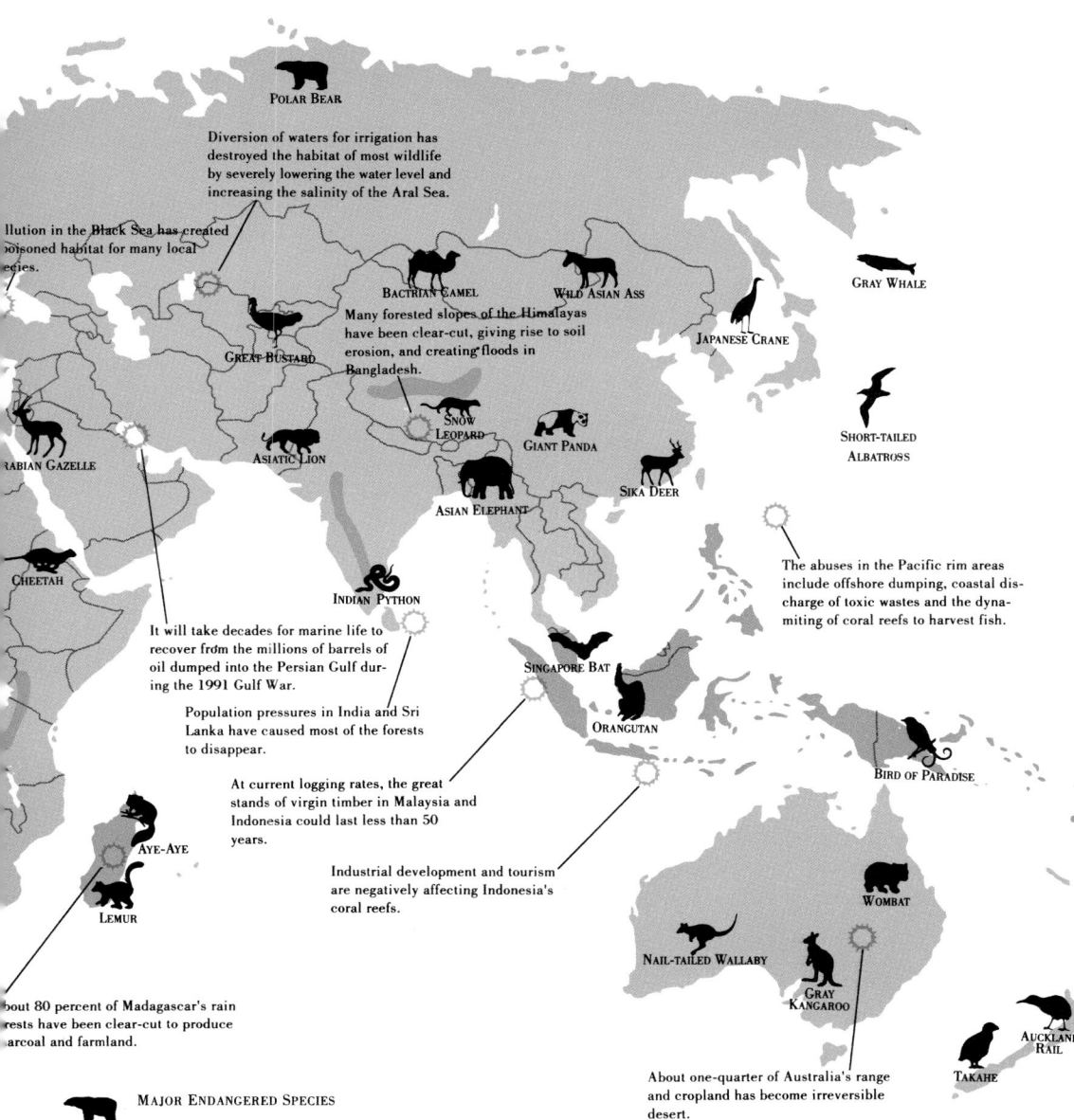

Diversion of waters for irrigation has destroyed the habitat of most wildlife by severely lowering the water level and increasing the salinity of the Aral Sea.

Pollution in the Black Sea has created poisoned habitat for many local species.

Many forested slopes of the Himalayas have been clear-cut, giving rise to soil erosion, and creating floods in Bangladesh.

It will take decades for marine life to recover from the millions of barrels of oil dumped into the Persian Gulf during the 1991 Gulf War.

The abuses in the Pacific rim areas include offshore dumping, coastal discharge of toxic wastes and the dynamiting of coral reefs to harvest fish.

Population pressures in India and Sri Lanka have caused most of the forests to disappear.

At current logging rates, the great stands of virgin timber in Malaysia and Indonesia could last less than 50 years.

Industrial development and tourism are negatively affecting Indonesia's coral reefs.

About 80 percent of Madagascar's rain forests have been clear-cut to produce charcoal and farmland.

About one-quarter of Australia's range and cropland has become irreversible desert.

POLAR BEAR, GRAY WHALE, BACTRIAN CAMEL, WILD ASIAN ASS, JAPANESE CRANE, GREAT BUSTARD, SNOW LEOPARD, GIANT PANDA, SHORT-TAILED ALBATROSS, ARABIAN GAZELLE, ASIATIC LION, ASIAN ELEPHANT, SIKA DEER, CHEETAH, INDIAN PYTHON, SINGAPORE BAT, AYE-AYE, ORANGUTAN, BIRD OF PARADISE, LEMUR, WOMBAT, NAIL-TAILED WALLABY, GRAY KANGAROO, TAKAHE, AUCKLAND RAIL

MAJOR ENDANGERED SPECIES

GREENHOUSE EFFECT

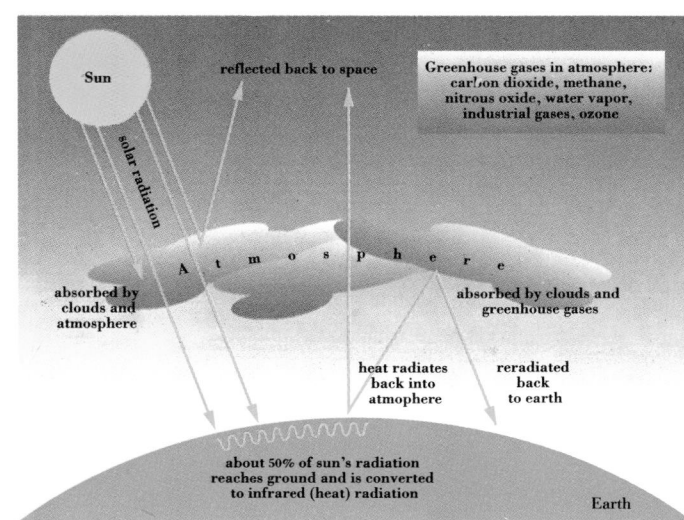

Sun

solar radiation

reflected back to space

Greenhouse gases in atmosphere: carbon dioxide, methane, nitrous oxide, water vapor, industrial gases, ozone

Atmosphere

absorbed by clouds and atmosphere

absorbed by clouds and greenhouse gases

heat radiates back into atmophere

reradiated back to earth

about 50% of sun's radiation reaches ground and is converted to infrared (heat) radiation

Earth

GREENHOUSE EMISSIONS

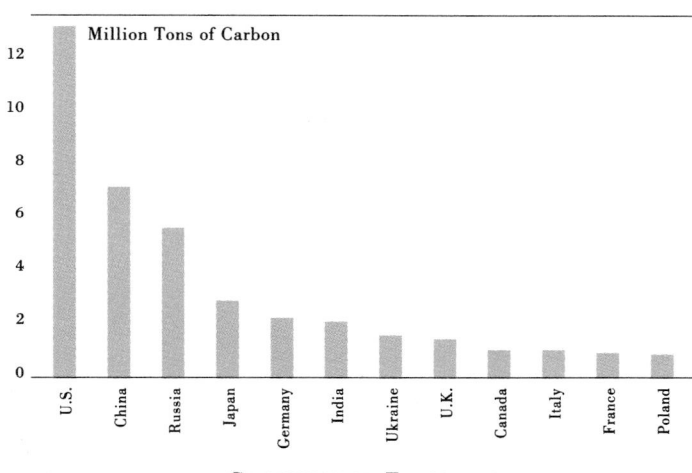

Million Tons of Carbon

U.S., China, Russia, Japan, Germany, India, Ukraine, U.K., Canada, Italy, France, Poland

CARBON DIOXIDE EQUIVALENTS

Source: Handbook of International Economic Statistics

MAIN TANKER ROUTES AND MAJOR OIL SPILLS

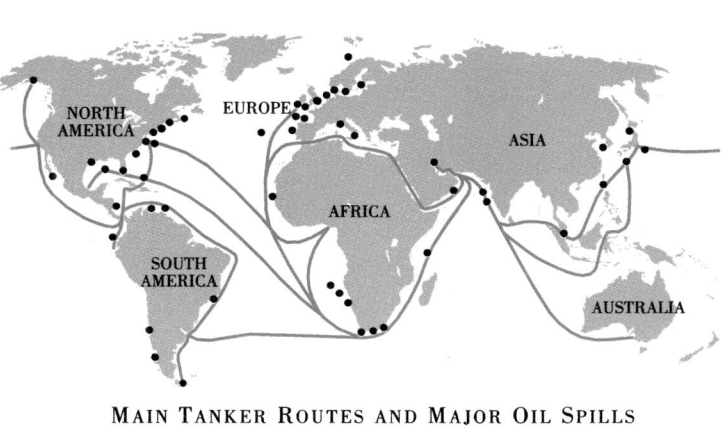

NORTH AMERICA, EUROPE, ASIA, AFRICA, SOUTH AMERICA, AUSTRALIA

ROUTES OF VERY LARGE CRUDE OIL CARRIERS

MAJOR OIL SPILLS

Acid Rain

Acid rain is created when fossil fuel emissions interact with sunlight and water vapor. The resulting clouds of nitric and sulfuric acids are carried thousands of miles. Acid rain has killed all life in thousands of lakes, and over 15 million acres (6 million hectares) of virgin forest in Europe and North America — and even some third world countries — are dead or dying.

Deforestation

Each year, 60 million acres (25 million hectares) of tropical rainforests are being felled by loggers — an area larger than Uruguay or Syria. Trees are vital to the prevention of both soil erosion and silting of rivers. They also remove heat-trapping carbon dioxide from the atmosphere.

Extinction

Biologists estimate that over 50,000 plant and animal species inhabiting the world's rain forests are disappearing each year due to pollution, unchecked hunting and the destruction of natural habitats. The loss of plant and animal species means fewer potential sources of new foods and medicines.

World Flags and Reference Guide

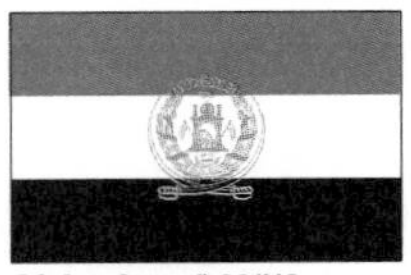

Afghanistan* 89/H2
Capital: Kabul
Area: 250,000 sq. mi.
647,500 sq. km.
Population: 23,738,085; growth rate: 4.48%
Government : transitional government
Independence: August 19, 1919
U.N. Admission: November 19, 1946
Life expectancy: 46 yrs
GDP : $18.1 billion; per capita: $800
Currency: afghani

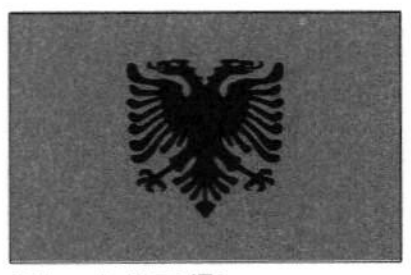

Albania* 75/F2
Capital: Tiranë
Area: 11,100 sq. mi.
28,749 sq. km.
Population: 3,293,252; growth rate: 1.36%
Government : emerging democracy
Independence: November 28, 1912
U.N. Admission: December 14, 1955
Life expectancy: 68 yrs
GDP : $4.4 billion; per capita: $1,290
Currency: lek

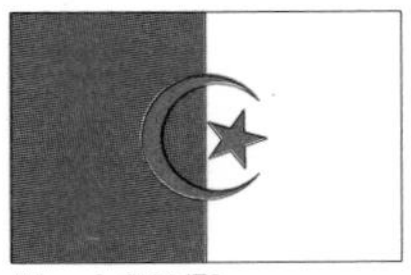

Algeria* 96/F2
Capital: Algiers
Area: 919,591 sq. mi.
2,381,740 sq. km.
Population: 29,830,370; growth rate: 2.18%
Government : republic
Independence: July 5, 1962
U.N. Admission: October 8, 1962
Life expectancy: 69 yrs
GDP : $115.9 billion; per capita: $4,000
Currency: Algerian dinar

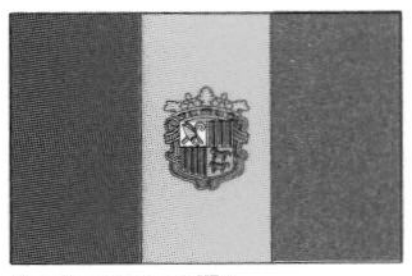

Andorra* 73/F1
Capital: Andorra la Vella
Area: 174 sq. mi.
450 sq. km.
Population: 74,839; growth rate: 2.66%
Government : parliamentary democracy
Independence: 1278
U.N. Admission: July 28, 1993
Life expectancy: 91 yrs
GDP : $1.2 billion; per capita: $18,000
Currency: French franc

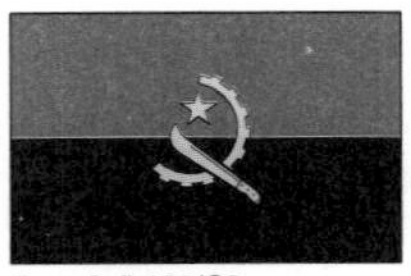

Angola* 105/C3
Capital: Luanda
Area: 481,351 sq. mi.
1,246,700 sq. km.
Population: 10,623,994; growth rate: 3.06%
Government : transitional government
Independence: November 11, 1975
U.N. Admission: December 1, 1976
Life expectancy: 47 yrs
GDP : $8.3 billion; per capita: $800
Currency: new kwanza

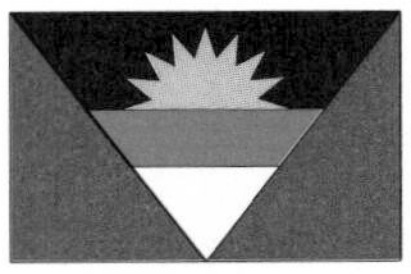

Antigua & Barbuda* 141N8
Capital: St. John's
Area: 170 sq. mi.
440 sq. km.
Population: 66,175; growth rate: .44%
Government : parliamentary democracy
Independence: November 1, 1981
U.N. Admission: November 11, 1981
Life expectancy: 71 yrs
GDP : $446 million; per capita: $6,800
Currency: EC dollar

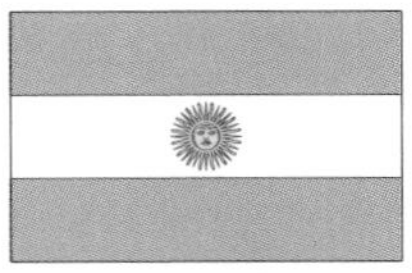

Argentina* 157/C4
Capital: Buenos Aires
Area: 1,068,296 sq. mi.
2,766,890 sq. km.
Population: 35,797,536; growth rate: 1.3%
Government : republic
Independence: July 9, 1816
U.N. Admission: October 24, 1945
Life expectancy: 74 yrs
GDP : $296.9 billion; per capita: $8,600
Currency: nuevo peso argentino

Armenia* 63/H5
Capital: Yerevan
Area: 11,506 sq. mi.
29,800 sq. km.
Population: 3,465,611; growth rate: .09%
Government : republic
Independence: September 23, 1991
U.N. Admission: March 2, 1992
Life expectancy: 69 yrs
GDP : $9.7 billion; per capita: $2,800
Currency: dram

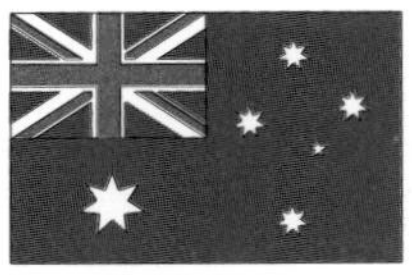

Australia* 109
Capital: Canberra
Area: 2,967,893 sq. mi.
7,686,850 sq. km.
Population: 18,438,824; growth rate: .96%
Government : federal parliamentary state
Independence: January 1, 1901
U.N. Admission: November 1, 1945
Life expectancy: 80 yrs
GDP : $430.5 billion; per capita: $23,600
Currency: Australian dollar

Austria* 43/L3
Capital: Vienna
Area: 32,375 sq. mi.
83,851 sq. km.
Population: 8,054,078; growth rate: .36%
Government : federal republic
Independence: 1156
U.N. Admission: December 14, 1955
Life expectancy: 77 yrs
GDP : $157.6 billion; per capita: $19,700
Currency: Austrian schilling

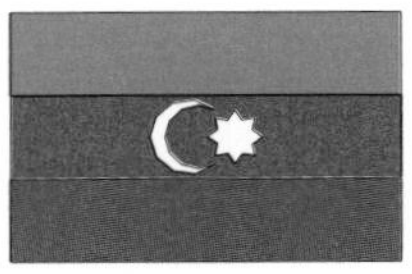

Azerbaijan* 63/H4
Capital: Baku
Area: 33,436 sq. mi.
86,600 sq. km.
Population: 7,735,918; growth rate: .75%
Government : republic
Independence: August 30, 1991
U.N. Admission: March 9, 1992
Life expectancy: 65 yrs
GDP : $11.9 billion; per capita: $1,550
Currency: manat

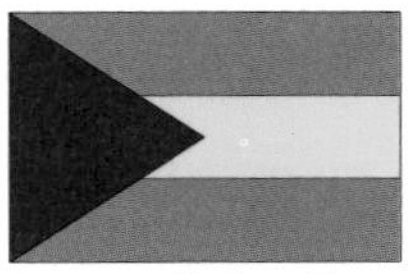

Bahamas, The* 141/F2
Capital: Nassau
Area: 5,382 sq. mi.
13,939 sq. km.
Population: 262,034; growth rate: 1.41%
Government : commonwealth
Independence: July 10, 1973
U.N. Admission: September 18,1973
Life expectancy: 74 yrs
GDP : $4.8 billion; per capita: $18,700
Currency: Bahamian dollar

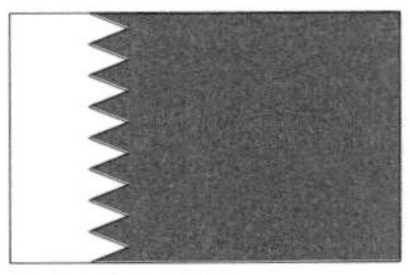

Bahrain* 88/F3
Capital: Manama
Area: 240 sq. mi.
622 sq. km.
Population: 603,318; growth rate: 2.18%
Government : traditional monarchy
Independence: August 15, 1971
U.N. Admission: September 21, 1971
Life expectancy: 75 yrs
GDP : $7.7 billion; per capita: $13,000
Currency: Bahraini danar

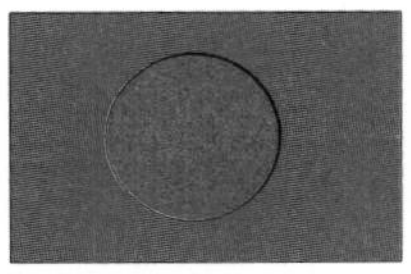

Bangladesh* 82/E3
Capital: Dhaka
Area: 55,598 sq. mi.
144,000 sq. km.
Population: 125,340,261; growth rate: 1.82%
Government : republic
Independence: December 16, 1971
U.N. Admission: September 17, 1974
Life expectancy: 56 yrs
GDP : $155.1 billion; per capita: $1,260
Currency: taka

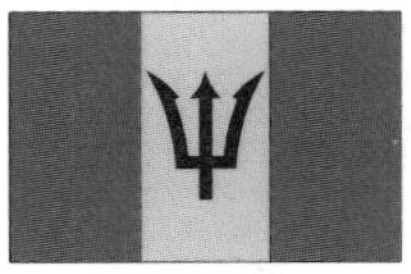

Barbados* 141/P9
Capital: Bridgetown
Area: 166 sq. mi.
430 sq. km.
Population: 257,731; growth rate: .28%
Government : parliamentary democracy
Independence: November 30, 1966
U.N. Admission: December 9, 1966
Life expectancy: 75 yrs
GDP : $2.65 billion; per capita: $10,300
Currency: Barbadian dollar

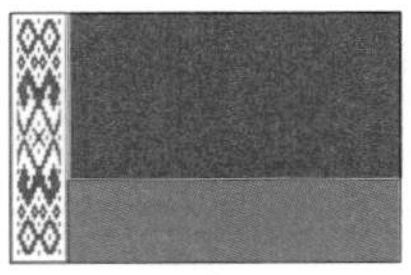

Belarus* 27/G3
Capital: Minsk
Area: 80,154 sq. mi.
207,600 sq. km.
Population: 10,439,916; growth rate: .26%
Government : republic
Independence: August 25, 1991
U.N. Admission: October 24, 1945
Life expectancy: 69 yrs
GDP : $51.9 billion; per capita: $5,000
Currency: Belarusian ruble

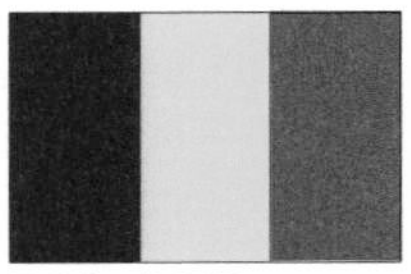

Belgium* 40/C3
Capital: Brussels
Area: 11,780 sq. mi.
30,510 sq. km.
Population: 10,203,683; growth rate: .32%
Government : constitutional monarchy
Independence: October 4, 1830
U.N. Admission: December 27, 1945
Life expectancy: 77 yrs
GDP : $204.8 billion; per capita: $20,300
Currency: Belgian franc

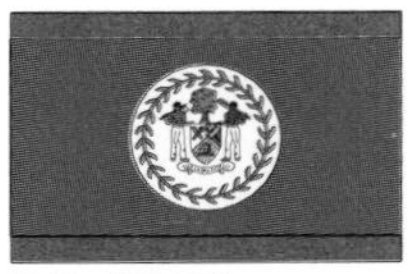

Belize* 144/D2
Capital: Belmopan
Area: 8,865 sq. mi.
22,960 sq. km.
Population: 224,663; growth rate: 2.42%
Government : parliamentary democracy
Independence: September 21, 1981
U.N. Admission: September 25, 1981
Life expectancy: 69 yrs
GDP : $649 million; per capita: $2,960
Currency: Belizean dollar

Benin* 103/F4
Capital: Porto-Novo
Area: 43,483 sq. mi.
112,620 sq. km.
Population: 5,902,178; growth rate: 3.31%
Government : republic
Independence: August 1, 1960
U.N. Admission: September 20, 1960
Life expectancy: 53 yrs
GDP : $8.2 billion; per capita: $1,440
Currency: CFA franc

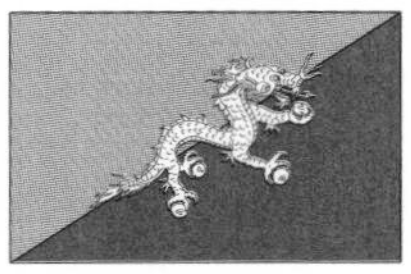

Bhutan* 82/E2
Capital: Thimphu
Area: 18,147 sq. mi.
47,000 sq. km.
Population: 1,865,191; growth rate: 2.3%
Government : monarchy
Independence: August 8, 1949
U.N. Admission: September 21, 1971
Life expectancy: 52 yrs
GDP : $1.3 billion; per capita: $730
Currency: ngultrum

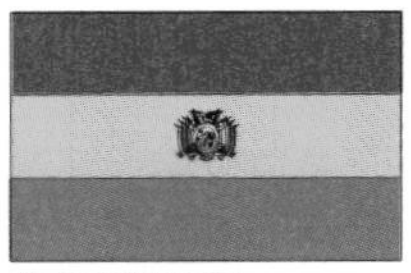

Bolivia* 150/F7
Capital: La Paz; Sucre
Area: 424,163 sq. mi.
1,098,582 sq. km.
Population: 7,669,868; growth rate: 2.04%
Government : republic
Independence: August 6, 1825
U.N. Admission: November 14, 1945
Life expectancy: 60 yrs
GDP : $21.5 billion; per capita: $3,000
Currency: boliviano

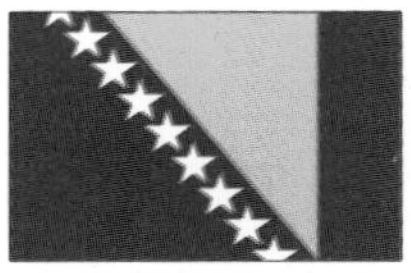

Bosnia & Herzegovina* 48/C3
Capital: Sarajevo
Area: 19,781 sq. mi.
51,233 sq. km.
Population: 2,607,734; growth rate: -.83%
Government : emerging democracy
Independence: April 1992
U.N. Admission: May 22, 1992
Life expectancy: 60 yrs
GDP : $1.9 billion; per capita: $600
Currency: dinar

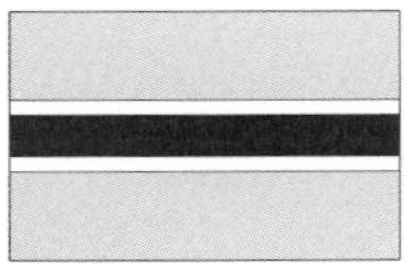

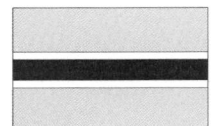

Botswana* 105/D5
Capital: Gaborone
Area: 231,803 sq. mi.
600,370 sq. km.
Population: 1,500,765; growth rate: 1.48%
Government : parliamentary republic
Independence: September 30, 1966
U.N. Admission: October 17, 1966
Life expectancy: 45 yrs
GDP : $4.6 billion; per capita: $3,100
Currency: pula

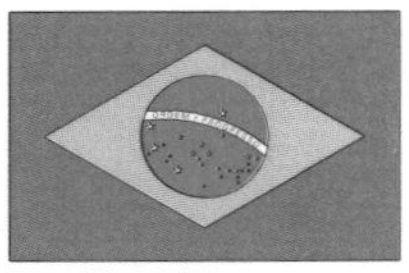

Brazil* 150/F5
Capital: Brasília
Area: 3,286,470 sq. mi.
8,511,965 sq. km.
Population: 164,511,366; growth rate: 1.1%
Government : federal republic
Independence: September 7, 1822
U.N. Admission: October 24, 1945
Life expectancy: 61 yrs
GDP : $1.022 trllion; per capita: $6,300
Currency: real

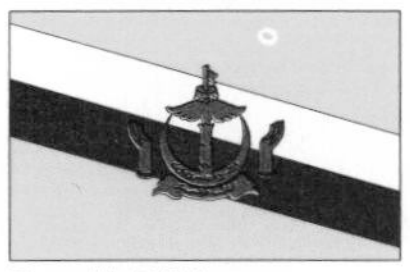

Brunei* 80/D2
Capital: Bandar Seri Begawan
Area: 2,228 sq. mi.
5,770 sq. km.
Population: 307,616; growth rate: 2.5%
Government : constitutional sultanate
Independence: January 1, 1984
U.N. Admission: September 21, 1984
Life expectancy: 72 yrs
GDP : $4.6 billion; per capita: $15,800
Currency: Bruneian dollar

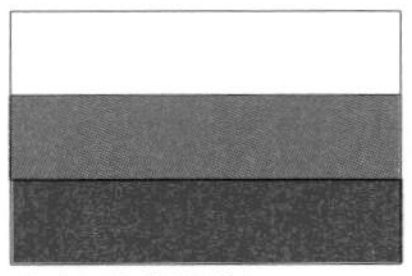

Bulgaria* 62/C4
Capital: Sofia
Area: 42,823 sq. mi.
110,912 sq. km.
Population: 8,652,745; growth rate: .47%
Government : emerging democracy
Independence: September 22, 1908
U.N. Admission: December 14, 1955
Life expectancy: 71 yrs
GDP : $39.9 billion; per capita: $4,630
Currency: lev

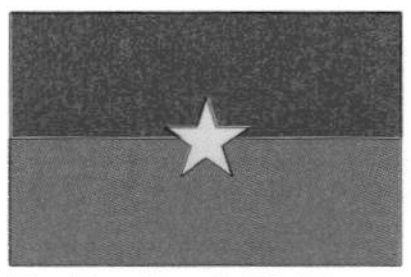

Burkina Faso* 141/E3
Capital: Ouagadougou
Area: 105,869 sq. mi.
274,200 sq. km.
Population: 10,891,159; growth rate: 2.45%
Government : parliamentary
Independence: August 5, 1960
U.N. Admission: September 20, 1960
Life expectancy: 42 yrs
GDP : $8 billion; per capita: $740
Currency: CFA franc

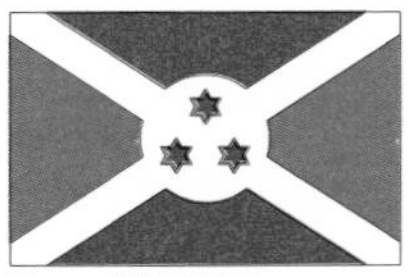

Burundi* 104/A3
Capital: Bujumbura
Area: 10,745 sq. mi.
27,830 sq. km.
Population: 6,052,614; growth rate: 2.11%
Government : republic
Independence: July 1, 1962
U.N. Admission: September 18, 1962
Life expectancy: 49 yrs
GDP : $4 billion; per capita: $600
Currency: Burundi franc

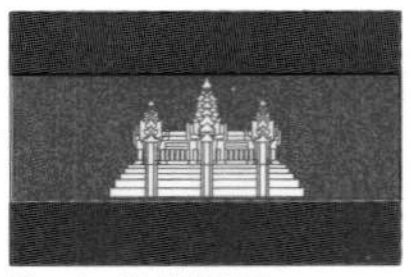

Cambodia* 83/H5
Capital: Phnom Penh
Area: 69,900 sq. mi.
181,040 sq. km.
Population: 11,163,861; growth rate: 2.72%
Government : constitutional monarchy
Independence: November 9, 1949
U.N. Admission: December 14, 1955
Life expectancy: 50 yrs
GDP : $7.7 billion; per capita: $710
Currency: new riel

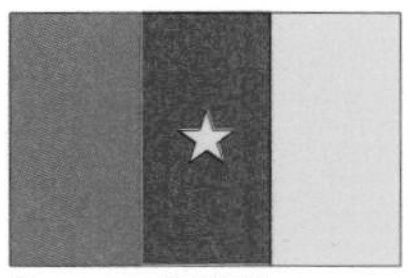

Cameroon* 96/H7
Capital: Yaoundé
Area: 183,568 sq. mi.
475,441 sq. km.
Population: 14,677,510; growth rate: 2.86%
Government : unitary republic
Independence: January 1, 1960
U.N. Admission: September 20, 1960
Life expectancy: 52 yrs
GDP : $17.5 billion; per capita: $1,230
Currency: CFA franc

* United Nations member (Yugoslavia suspended)
Note – Page and letter-number references in blue type follow the country names. For example: **Bulgaria** 62/C4 refers to page 62, index grid square C4.

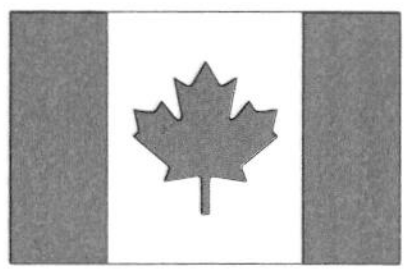

Canada* 166
Capital: Ottawa
Area: 3,851,787 sq. mi.
9,976,139 sq. km.
Population: 29,123,194; growth rate: 1.13%
Government : parliamentary democracy
Independence: July 1, 1867
U.N. Admission: November 9, 1945
Life expectancy: 79 yrs
GDP : $721 billion; per capita: $25,000
Currency: Canadian dollar

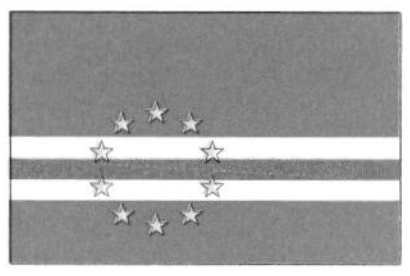

Cape Verde* 93/J9
Capital: Praia
Area: 1,556 sq. mi.
4,030 sq. km.
Population: 393,843; growth rate: 1.54%
Government : republic
Independence: July 5, 1975
U.N. Admission: September 16, 1975
Life expectancy: 70 yrs
GDP : $472 million; per capita: $1,000
Currency: Cape Verdean escudo

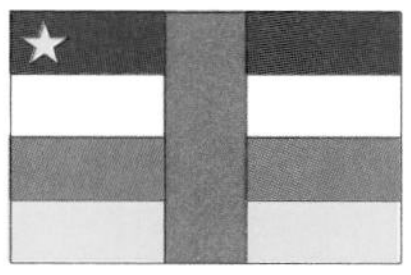

Central African Republic* 97/J6
Capital: Bangui
Area: 240,533 sq. mi.
622,980 sq. km.
Population: 3,342,051; growth rate: 2.01%
Government : republic
Independence: August 13, 1960
U.N. Admission: September 20, 1960
Life expectancy: 45 yrs
GDP : $2.5 billion; per capita: $800
Currency: CFA franc

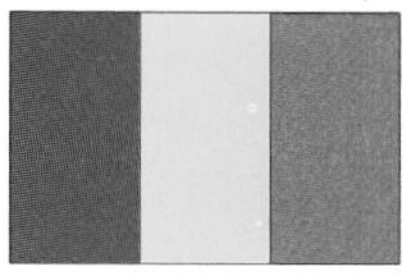

Chad* 97/J4
Capital: N'Djamena
Area: 495,752 sq. mi.
1,283,998 sq. km.
Population: 7,166,023; growth rate: 2.67
Government : republic
Independence: August 11, 1960
U.N. Admission: September 20, 1960
Life expectancy: 48 yrs
GDP : $3.3 billion; per capita: $600
Currency: CFA franc

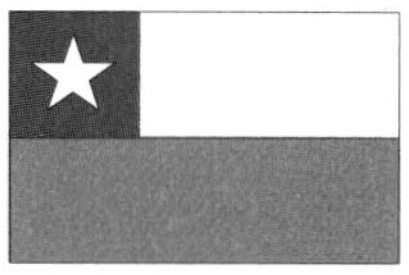

Chile* 147/B6
Capital: Santiago
Area: 292,258 sq. mi.
756,950 sq. km.
Population: 14,508,168; growth rate: 1.18%
Government : republic
Independence: September 18, 1810
U.N. Admission: October 24, 1945
Life expectancy: 75 yrs
GDP : $120.6 billion; per capita: $8,400
Currency: Chilean peso

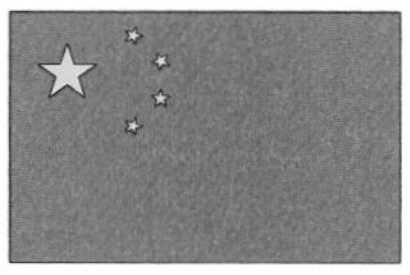

China* 70/G4
Capital: Beijing
Area: 3,705,386 sq. mi.
9,596,960 sq. km.
Population: 1,221,591,778; growth rate: .93%
Government : Communist state
Independence: October 1, 1949
U.N. Admission: October 24, 1945
Life expectancy: 70 yrs
GDP : $3.39 trillion; per capita: $2,800
Currency: yuan

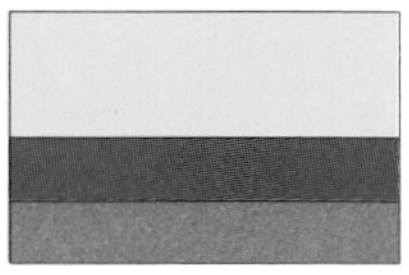

Colombia* 150/D3
Capital: Bogotá
Area: 439,733 sq. mi.
1,138,910 sq. km.
Population: 37,418,290; growth rate: 1.61%
Government : republic
Independence: July 20, 1810
U.N. Admission: November 5, 1945
Life expectancy: 73 yrs
GDP : $201.4 billion; per capita: $5,400
Currency: Colombian peso

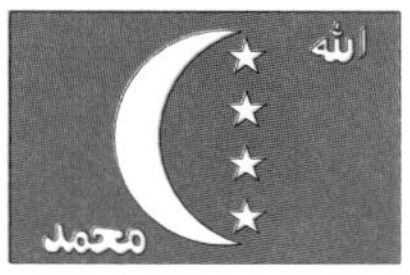

Comoros* 107/G5
Capital: Moroni
Area: 838 sq. mi.
2,170 sq. km.
Population: 589,797; growth rate: 3.09%
Government : independent republic
Independence: July 6, 1975
U.N. Admission: November 12, 1975
Life expectancy: 60 yrs
GDP : $370 million; per capita: $650
Currency: Comoran franc

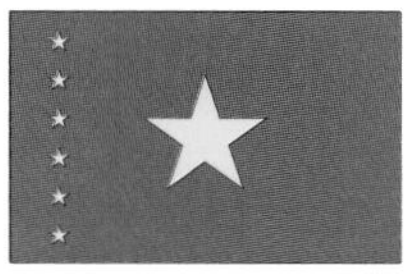

Congo, Dem. Rep. of the* 93/E5
Capital: Kinshasa
Area: 905,563 sq. mi.
2,345,410 sq. km.
Population: 47,440,362; growth rate: 2.34%
Government : republic
Independence: June 30, 1960
U.N. Admission: September 20, 1960
Life expectancy: 47 yrs
GDP : $16.5 billion; per capita: $400
Currency: zaire

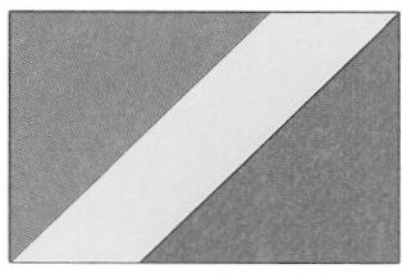

Congo, Rep. of the* 93/D4
Capital: Brazzaville
Area: 132,046 sq. mi.
342,000 sq. km.
Population: 2,583,198; growth rate: 2.15%
Government : republic
Independence: August 15, 1960
U.N. Admission: September 20, 1960
Life expectancy: 46 yrs
GDP : $4.9 billion; per capita: $1,960
Currency: CFA franc

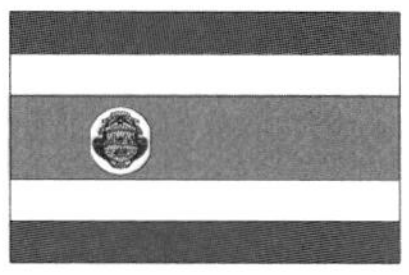

Costa Rica* 145/F4
Capital: San José
Area: 19,730 sq. mi.
51,100 sq. km.
Population: 3,534,174; growth rate: 2%
Government : democratic republic
Independence: September 15, 1821
U.N. Admission: November 2, 1945
Life expectancy: 76 yrs
GDP : $19 billion; per capita: $5,500
Currency: Costa Rican colon

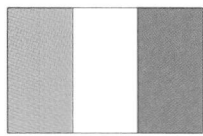

Côte d'Ivoire* 102/D5
Capital: Yamoussoukro
Area: 124,502 sq. mi.
322,460 sq. km.
Population: 14,986,218; growth rate: 2.35%
Government : republic
Independence: August 7, 1960
U.N. Admission: September 20, 1960
Life expectancy: 45 yrs
GDP : $23.9 billion; per capita: $1,620
Currency: CFA franc

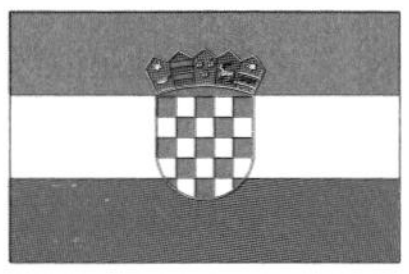

Croatia* 48/B3
Capital: Zagreb
Area: 22,050 sq. mi.
56,538 sq. km.
Population: 5,026,995; growth rate: .33%
Government : parliamentary democracy
Independence: June 25, 1991
U.N. Admission: May 22, 1992
Life expectancy: 73 yrs
GDP : $21.4 billion; per capita: $4,300
Currency: Croatian kuna

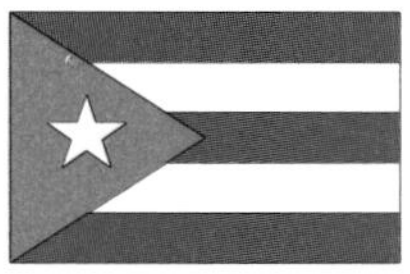

Cuba* 145/F1
Capital: Havana
Area: 42,803 sq. mi.
110,860 sq. km.
Population: 10,999,041; growth rate: .42%
Government : Communist state
Independence: May 20, 1902
U.N. Admission: October 24, 1945
Life expectancy: 75 yrs
GDP : $16.2 billion; per capita: $1,480
Currency: Cuban peso

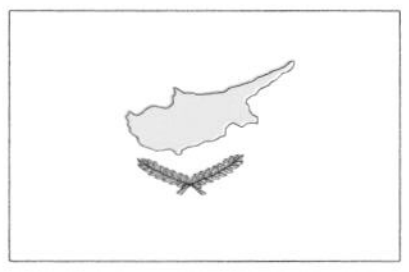

Cyprus* 91/C2
Capital: Nicosia
Area: 3,571 sq. mi.
9,250 sq. km.
Population: 752,808; growth rate: 1.08%
Government : republic
Independence: August 16, 1960
U.N. Admission: September 20, 1960
Life expectancy: 77 yrs
GDP : $8.8 billion; per capita: $11,800
Currency: Cypriot pound

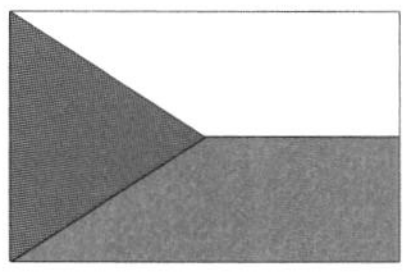

Czech Republic* 41/H4
Capital: Prague
Area: 30,387 sq. mi.
78,703 sq. km.
Population: 10,318,958; growth rate: -.02%
Government : parliamentary democracy
Independence: January 1, 1993
U.N. Admission: January 19, 1993
Life expectancy: 74 yrs
GDP : $114.3 billion; per capita: $11,100
Currency: koruna

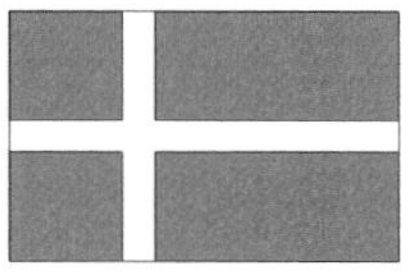

Denmark* 38/C4
Capital: Copenhagen
Area: 16,629 sq. mi.
43,069 sq. km.
Population: 5,268,775; growth rate: .35%
Government : constitutional monarchy
Independence: 1849
U.N. Admission: October 24, 1945
Life expectancy: 77 yrs
GDP : $118.2 billion; per capita: $22,700
Currency: Danish krone

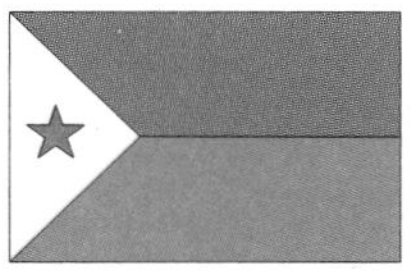

Djibouti* 97/P5
Capital: Djibouti
Area: 8,494 sq. mi.
22,000 sq. km.
Population: 434,116; growth rate: 1.51%
Government : republic
Independence: June 27, 1977
U.N. Admission: September 20, 1977
Life expectancy: 51 yrs
GDP : $500 million; per capita: $1,200
Currency: Djiboutian franc

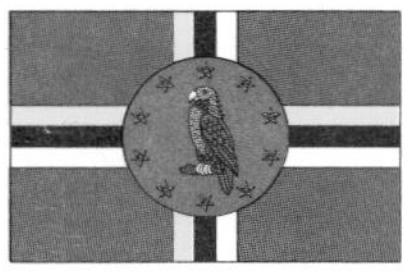

Dominica* 141/N9
Capital: Roseau
Area: 290 sq. mi.
751 sq. km.
Population: 83,226; growth rate: -1.26%
Government : parliamentary democracy
Independence: November 3, 1978
U.N. Admission: December 18, 1978
Life expectancy: 78 yrs
GDP : $208 million; per capita: $2,500
Currency: EC dollar

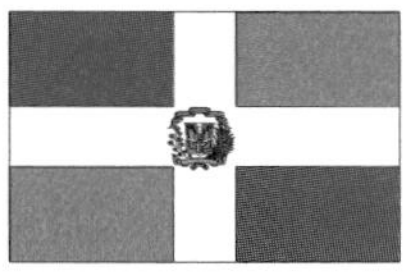

Dominican Republic* 141/H4
Capital: Santo Domingo
Area: 18,815 sq. mi.
48,730 sq. km.
Population: 8,228,151; growth rate: 1.68%
Government : republic
Independence: February 27, 1844
U.N. Admission: October 24, 1945
Life expectancy: 69 yrs
GDP : $29.8 billion; per capita: $3,670
Currency: Dominican peso

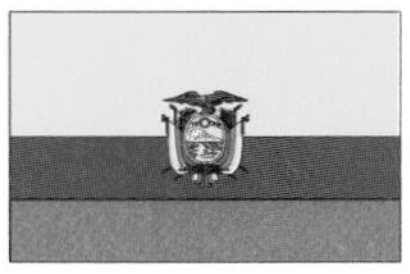

Ecuador* 150/C4
Capital: Quito
Area: 109,483 sq. mi.
283,561 sq. km.
Population: 11,690,535; growth rate: 1.93%
Government : republic
Independence: May 24, 1822
U.N. Admission: December 21, 1945
Life expectancy: 71 yrs
GDP : $47 billion; per capita: $4,100
Currency: sucre

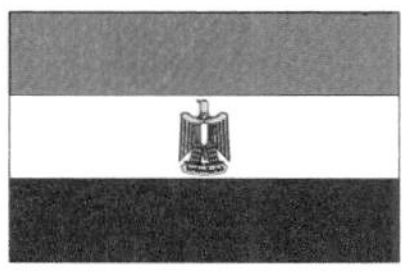

Egypt* 97/L2
Capital: Cairo
Area: 386,659 sq. mi.
1,001,447 sq. km.
Population: 64,791,891; growth rate: 1.89%
Government : republic
Independence: February 28, 1922
U.N. Admission: October 24, 1945
Life expectancy: 62 yrs
GDP : $183.9 billion; per capita: $2,900
Currency: Egyptian pound

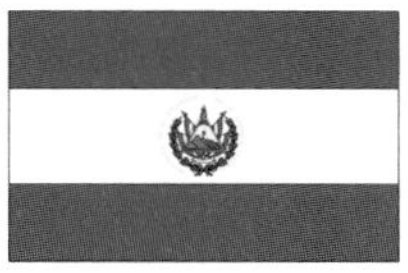

El Salvador* 144/D3
Capital: San Salvador
Area: 8,124 sq. mi.
21,040 sq. km.
Population: 5,661,827; growth rate: 1.6%
Government : republic
Independence: September 15, 1821
U.N. Admission: October 24, 1945
Life expectancy: 69 yrs
GDP : $12.2 billion; per capita: $2,080
Currency: Salvadoran colon

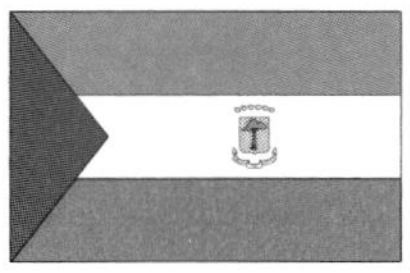

Equatorial Guinea* 96/G7
Capital: Malabo
Area: 10,831 sq. mi.
28,052 sq. km.
Population: 442,516; growth rate: 2.57%
Government : republic in transition
Independence: October 12, 1968
U.N. Admission: November 12, 1968
Life expectancy: 53 yrs
GDP : $328 million; per capita: $800
Currency: CFA franc

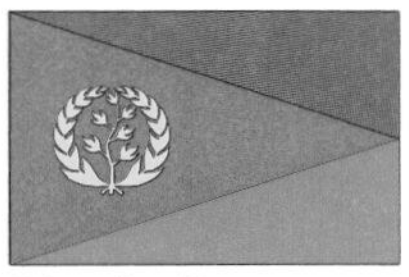

Eritrea* 97/N5
Capital: Asmara
Area: 46,842 sq. mi.
121,320 sq. km.
Population: 3,589,687; growth rate: 6.35%
Government : transitional government
Independence: May 27, 1993
U.N. Admission: May 28, 1993
Life expectancy: 51 yrs
GDP : $2 billion; per capita: $570
Currency: nakfa

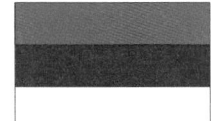

Estonia* 39/L2
Capital: Tallinn
Area: 17,413 sq. mi.
45,100 sq. km.
Population: 1,444,721; growth rate: -.89%
Government : republic
Independence: September 6, 1991
U.N. Admission: September 17, 1991
Life expectancy: 68 yrs
GDP : $8.1 billion; per capita: $5,560
Currency: Estonian kroon

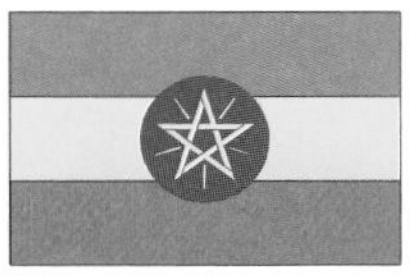

Ethiopia* 97/N5
Capital: Addis Ababa
Area: 435,184 sq. mi.
1,127,127 sq. km.
Population: 58,732,577; growth rate: 2.67%
Government : federal republic
Independence: c. 2nd cent. A.D.
U.N. Admission: November 13, 1945
Life expectancy: 47 yrs
GDP : $24.8 billion; per capita: $430
Currency: birr

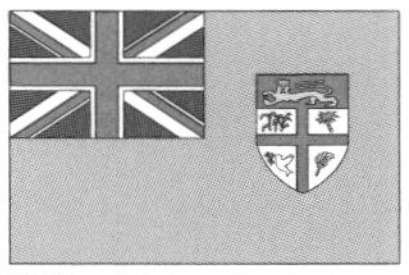

Fiji* 116/G6
Capital: Suva
Area: 7,055 sq. mi.
18,272 sq. km.
Population: 792,441; growth rate: 1.28%
Government : republic
Independence: October 10, 1970
U.N. Admission: October 13, 1970
Life expectancy: 66 yrs
GDP : $5.1 billion; per capita: $6,500
Currency: Fijian dollar

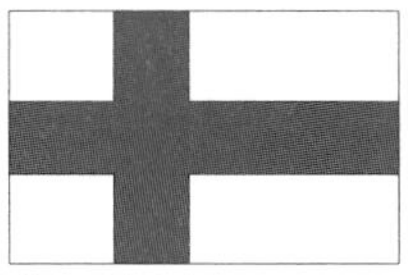

Finland* 37/H2
Capital: Helsinki
Area: 130,128 sq. mi.
337,032 sq. km.
Population: 5,109,148; growth rate: .06%
Government : republic
Independence: December 16, 1917
U.N. Admission: December 14, 1955
Life expectancy: 76 yrs
GDP : $97.1 billion; per capita: $19,000
Currency: markka

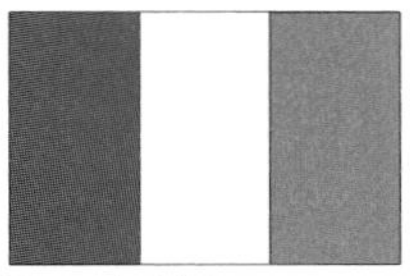

France* 42/D3
Capital: Paris
Area: 211,208 sq. mi.
547,030 sq. km.
Population: 58,470,421; growth rate: .29%
Government : republic
Independence: 486
U.N. Admission: October 24, 1945
Life expectancy: 79 yrs
GDP : $1.22 trillion; per capita: $20,900
Currency: French franc

Gabon* 96/H7
Capital: Libreville
Area: 103,347 sq. mi.
267,670 sq. km.
Population: 1,190,159; growth rate: 1.47%
Government : republic
Independence: August 17, 1960
U.N. Admission: September 20, 1960
Life expectancy: 56 yrs
GDP : $6.3 billion; per capita: $5,400
Currency: CFA franc

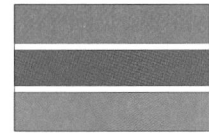

Gambia, The* 102/B3
Capital: Banjul
Area: 4,363 sq. mi.
11,300 sq. km.
Population: 1,248,085; growth rate: 3.48%
Government : republic
Independence: February 18, 1965
U.N. Admission: September 21, 1965
Life expectancy: 53 yrs
GDP : $1.1 billion; per capita: $1,100
Currency: dalasi

Georgia* 63/G4
Capital: T'bilisi
Area: 26,911 sq. mi.
69,700 sq. km.
Population: 5,174,642; growth rate: -.72%
Government : republic
Independence: April 9, 1991
U.N. Admission: July 31, 1992
Life expectancy: 68 yrs
GDP : $7.1 billion; per capita: $1,350
Currency: lari

Germany* 40/E3
Capital: Berlin
Area: 137,803 sq. mi.
356,910 sq. km.
Population: 84,068,216; growth rate: .6%
Government : federal republic
Independence: January 18, 1871
U.N. Admission: September 18, 1973
Life expectancy: 76 yrs
GDP : $1.7 trillion; per capita: $23,100
Currency: deutsche mark

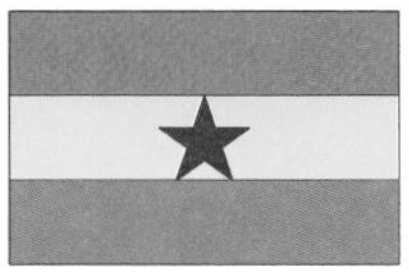

Ghana* 103/E4
Capital: Accra
Area: 92,100 sq. mi.
238,540 sq. km.
Population: 18,100,703; growth rate: 2.21%
Government : constitutional democracy
Independence: March 6, 1957
U.N. Admission: March 8, 1957
Life expectancy: 56 yrs
GDP : $27 billion; per capita: $1,530
Currency: new cedi

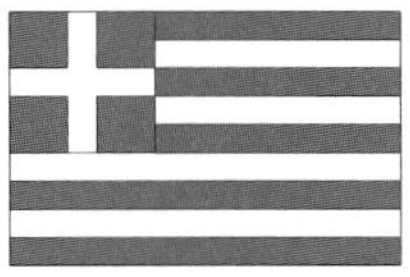

Greece* 47/G3
Capital: Athens
Area: 50,942 sq. mi.
131,940 sq. km.
Population: 10,583,126; growth rate: .42%
Government : parliamentary republic
Independence: 1829
U.N. Admission: October 25, 1945
Life expectancy: 78 yrs
GDP : $106.9 billion; per capita: $10,000
Currency: drachma

Sources: The Flag Research Center; U.S. Bureau of the Census, International Data Base; CIA World Factbook

World Flags and Reference Guide

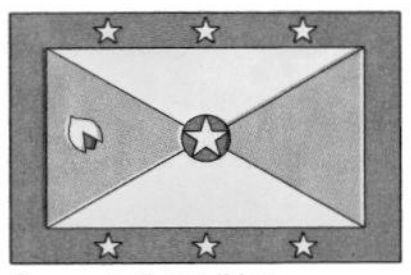

Grenada* 141/N10
Capital: St. George's
Area: 131 sq. mi.
340 sq. km.
Population: 95,537; growth rate: .66%
Government : parliamentary democracy
Independence: February 7, 1974
U.N. Admission: September 17, 1974
Life expectancy: 71 yrs
GDP : $300 million; per capita: $3,160
Currency: EC dollar

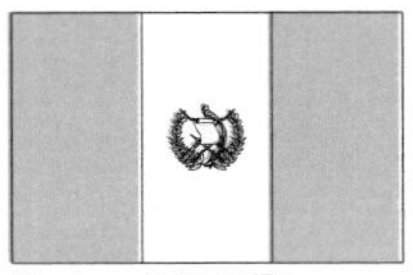

Guatemala* 144/D3
Capital: Guatemala
Area: 42,042 sq. mi.
108,889 sq. km.
Population: 11,558,407; growth rate: 2.44%
Government : republic
Independence: September 15, 1821
U.N. Admission: November 21, 1945
Life expectancy: 66 yrs
GDP : $39 billion; per capita: $3,460
Currency: quetzel

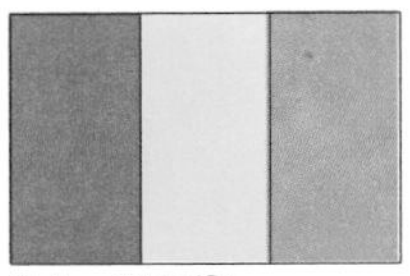

Guinea* 102/C4
Capital: Conakry
Area: 94,927 sq. mi.
245,860 sq. km.
Population: 7,405,375; growth rate: 1.1%
Government : republic
Independence: October 2, 1958
U.N. Admission: December 12, 1958
Life expectancy: 46 yrs
GDP : $7.1 billion; per capita: $950
Currency: Guinean franc

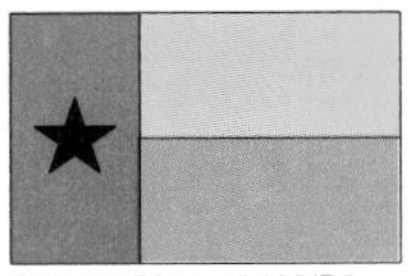

Guinea-Bissau* 102/B3
Capital: Bissau
Area: 13,946 sq. mi.
36,120 sq. km.
Population: 1,178,584; growth rate: 2.33%
Government : republic
Independence: September 10, 1974
U.N. Admission: September 17, 1974
Life expectancy: 49 yrs
GDP : $1.1 billion; per capita: $950
Currency: Guinea-Bissauan peso

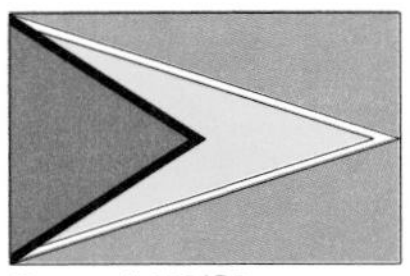

Guyana* 153/G3
Capital: Georgetown
Area: 83,000 sq. mi.
214,970 sq. km.
Population: 706,116; growth rate: -.78%
Government : republic
Independence: May 26, 1966
U.N. Admission: September 20, 1966
Life expectancy: 59 yrs
GDP : $1.8 billion; per capita: $2,490
Currency: Guyanese dollar

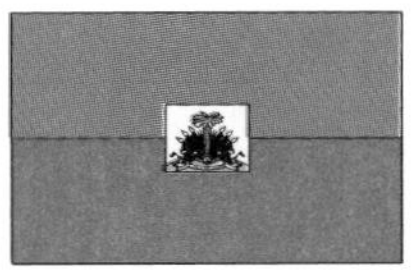

Haiti* 145/H2
Capital: Port-au-Prince
Area: 10,714 sq. mi.
27,750 sq. km.
Population: 6,611,407; growth rate: 1.39%
Government : republic
Independence: January 1, 1804
U.N. Admission: October 24, 1945
Life expectancy: 50 yrs
GDP : $68 billion; per capita: $1,000
Currency: gourde

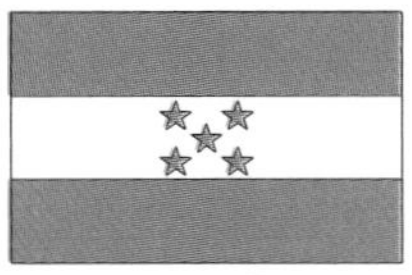

Honduras* 144/E3
Capital: Tegucigalpa
Area: 43,277 sq. mi.
112,087 sq. km.
Population: 5,751,384; growth rate: 2.55%
Government : republic
Independence: September 15, 1821
U.N. Admission: December 17, 1945
Life expectancy: 69 yrs
GDP : $11.5 billion; per capita: $2,000
Currency: lempira

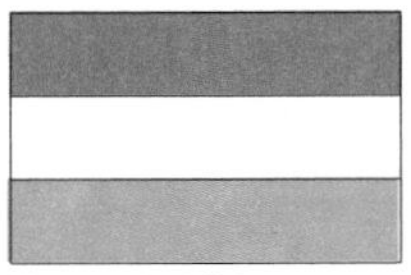

Hungary* 48/D2
Capital: Budapest
Area: 35,919 sq. mi.
93,030 sq. km.
Population: 9,935,774; growth rate: .66%
Government : republic
Independence: 1001
U.N. Admission: December 14, 1955
Life expectancy: 69 yrs
GDP : $74.7 billion; per capita: $7,500
Currency: forint

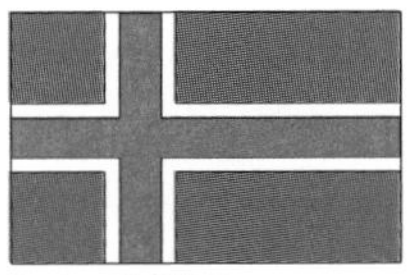

Iceland* 37/N7
Capital: Reykjavík
Area: 39,768 sq. mi.
103,000 sq. km.
Population: 272,550; growth rate: .84%
Government : constitutional republic
Independence: June 17, 1944
U.N. Admission: November 19, 1946
Life expectancy: 80 yrs
GDP : $5.3 billion; per capita: $19,800
Currency: krona

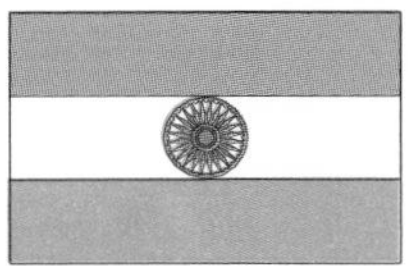

India* 67/G7
Capital: New Delhi
Area: 1,269,339 sq. mi.
3,287,588 sq. km.
Population: 967,612,804; growth rate: 1.72%
Government : federal republic
Independence: August 15, 1947
U.N. Admission: October 30, 1945
Life expectancy: 62 yrs
GDP : $1.538 trillion; per capita: $1,600
Currency: Indian rupee

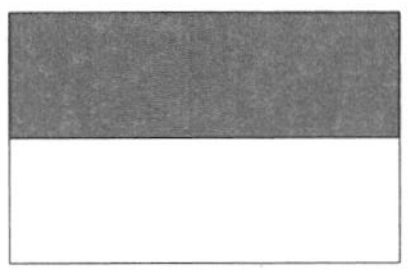

Indonesia* 81/E4
Capital: Jakarta
Area: 741,096 sq. mi.
1,919,440 sq. km.
Population: 209,774,138; growth rate: 1.51%
Government : republic
Independence: August 17, 1945
U.N. Admission: September 28, 1950
Life expectancy: 62 yrs
GDP : $779.7 billion; per capita: $3,770
Currency: Indonesian rupiah

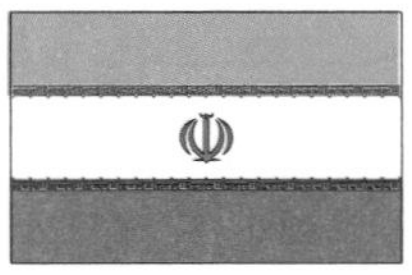

Iran* 67/E6
Capital: Tehran
Area: 636,293 sq. mi.
1,648,000 sq. km.
Population: 67,540,002; growth rate: 2.12%
Government : theocratic republic
Independence: April 1, 1979
U.N. Admission: October 24, 1945
Life expectancy: 68 yrs
GDP : $343.5 billion; per capita: $5,200
Currency: Iranian rial

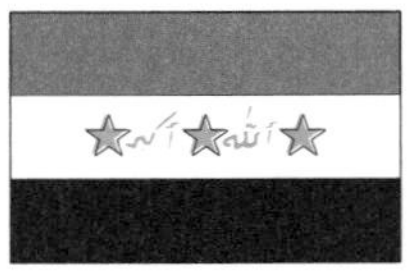

Iraq* 88/D2
Capital: Baghdad
Area: 168,753 sq. mi.
437,072 sq. km.
Population: 22,219,289; growth rate: 3.62%
Government : republic
Independence: October 3, 1932
U.N. Admission: December 21, 1945
Life expectancy: 67 yrs
GDP : $42 billion; per capita: $2,000
Currency: Iraqi dinar

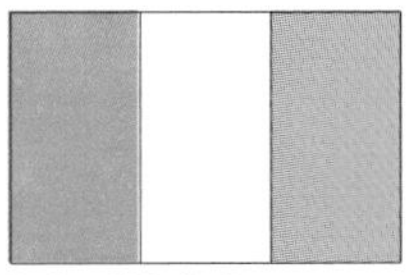

Ireland* 31/P10
Capital: Dublin
Area: 27,136 sq. mi.
70,282 sq. km.
Population: 3,555,500; growth rate: -.42%
Government : republic
Independence: December 6, 1921
U.N. Admission: December 14, 1955
Life expectancy: 76 yrs
GDP : $59.9 billion; per capita: $16,800
Currency: Irish pound

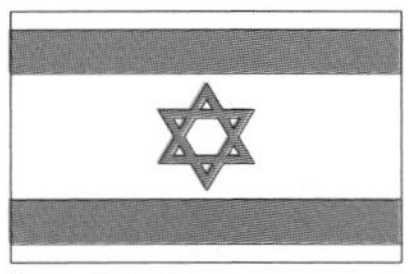

Israel* 91/C3
Capital: Jerusalem
Area: 8,019 sq. mi.
20,770 sq. km.
Population: 5,534,672; growth rate: 2.01%
Government : republic
Independence: May 14, 1948
U.N. Admission: May 11, 1949
Life expectancy: 78 yrs
GDP : $585.7 billion; per capita: $16,400
Currency: new Israeli shekel

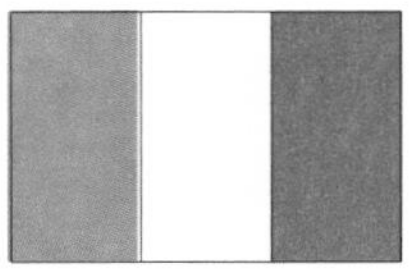

Italy* 27/F4
Capital: Rome
Area: 116,305 sq. mi.
301,230 sq. km.
Population: 57,534,088; growth rate: .13%
Government : republic
Independence: March 12, 1861
U.N. Admission: December 14, 1955
Life expectancy: 78 yrs
GDP : $1.12 trillion; per capita: $19,600
Currency: Italian lira

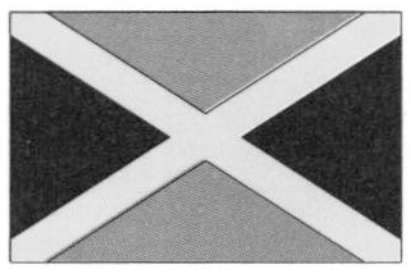

Jamaica* 145/G2
Capital: Kingston
Area: 4,243 sq. mi.
10,990 sq. km.
Population: 2,615,582; growth rate: .75%
Government : parliamentary democracy
Independence: August 6, 1962
U.N. Admission: September 18, 1962
Life expectancy: 75 yrs
GDP : $8.4 billion; per capita: $3,260
Currency: Jamaican dollar

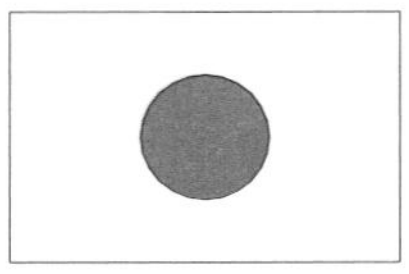

Japan* 71/Q4
Capital: Tōkyō
Area: 145,882 sq. mi.
377,835 sq. km.
Population: 125,716,637; growth rate: .23%
Government : constitutional monarchy
Independence: 660 B.C.
U.N. Admission: December 18, 1956
Life expectancy: 80 yrs
GDP : $2.85 trillion; per capita: $22,700
Currency: yen

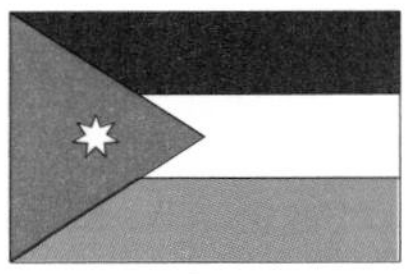

Jordan* 88/C2
Capital: Amman
Area: 34,445 sq. mi.
89,213 sq. km.
Population: 4,324,638; growth rate: .26%
Government : constitutional monarchy
Independence: May 25, 1946
U.N. Admission: December 14, 1955
Life expectancy: 73 yrs
GDP : $20.9 billion; per capita: $5,000
Currency: Jordanian dinar

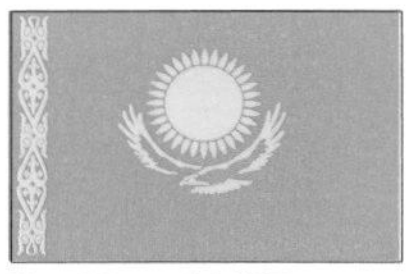

Kazakhstan* 64/G5
Capital: Astana
Area: 1,049,150 sq. mi.
2,717,300 sq. km.
Population: 16,898,572; growth rate: -.6%
Government : republic
Independence: December 16, 1991
U.N. Admission: March 2, 1992
Life expectancy: 64 yrs
GDP : $48.6 billion; per capita: $2,880
Currency: Kazakstani tenge

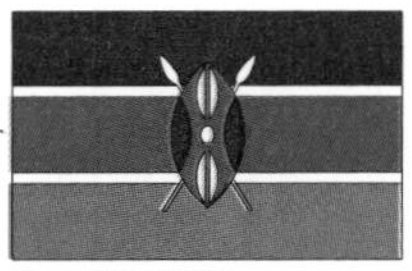

Kenya* 104/C2
Capital: Nairobi
Area: 224,960 sq. mi.
582,646 sq. km.
Population: 28,803,085; growth rate: 2.13%
Government : republic
Independence: December 12, 1963
U.N. Admission: December 16, 1963
Life expectancy: 54 yrs
GDP : $39.2 billion; per capita: $1,400
Currency: Kenyan shilling

Kiribati 116/H5
Capital: Tarawa
Area: 277 sq. mi.
717 sq. km.
Population: 82,449; growth rate: 1.85%
Government : republic
Independence: July 12, 1979
U.N. Admission: non-member
Life expectancy: 62 yrs
GDP : $62 million; per capita: $800
Currency: Australian dollar

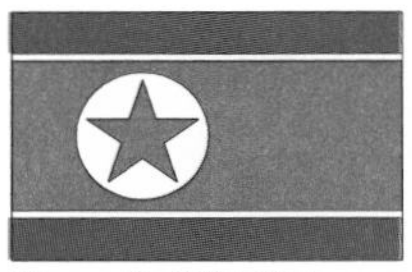

Korea, North* 73/D2
Capital: P'yŏngyang
Area: 46,540 sq. mi.
120,539 sq. km.
Population: 24,317,004; growth rate: 1.68%
Government : Communist state
Independence: September 9, 1948
U.N. Admission: September 17, 1991
Life expectancy: 71 yrs
GDP : $20.9 billion; per capita: $900
Currency: North Korean won

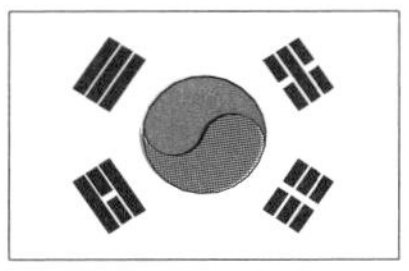

Korea, South* 73/D4
Capital: Seoul
Area: 38,023 sq. mi.
98,480 sq. km.
Population: 45,948,811; growth rate: 1.02%
Government : republic
Independence: August 15, 1948
U.N. Admission: September 17, 1991
Life expectancy: 74 yrs
GDP : $647.2 billion; per capita: $14,200
Currency: South Korean won

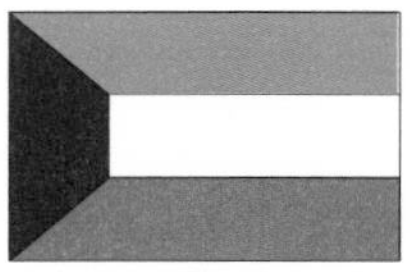

Kuwait* 88/E3
Capital: Kuwait
Area: 6,880 sq. mi.
17,820 sq. km.
Population: 2,076,805; growth rate: 5.96%
Government : constitutional monarchy
Independence: June 19, 1961
U.N. Admission: May 14, 1963
Life expectancy: 76 yrs
GDP : $32.5 billion; per capita: $16,700
Currency: Kuwaiti dinar

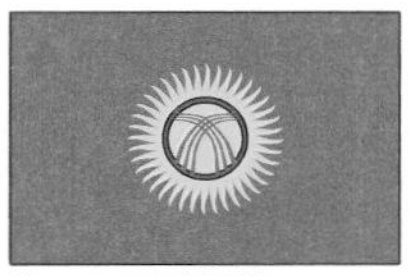

Kyrgyzstan* 87/F4
Capital: Bishkek
Area: 76,641 sq. mi.
198,500 sq. km.
Population: 4,540,185; growth rate: .4%
Government : republic
Independence: August 31, 1991
U.N. Admission: March 2, 1992
Life expectancy: 64 yrs
GDP : $5.8 billion; per capita: $1,290
Currency: Kyrgyzstani som

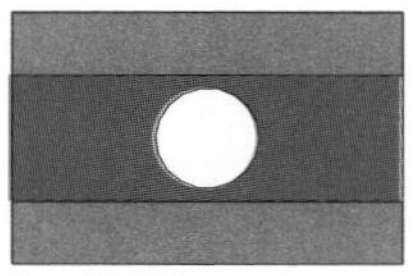

Laos* 78/C2
Capital: Vientiane
Area: 91,428 sq. mi.
236,800 sq. km.
Population: 5,116,959; growth rate: 2.78%
Government : Communist state
Independence: July 19, 1949
U.N. Admission: December 14, 1955
Life expectancy: 53 yrs
GDP : $5.7 billion; per capita: $1,150
Currency: new kip

Latvia* 39/L3
Capital: Riga
Area: 24,749 sq. mi.
64,100 sq. km.
Population: 2,437,649; growth rate: -1.16%
Government : republic
Independence: September 6, 1991
U.N. Admission: September 17, 1991
Life expectancy: 67 yrs
GDP : $9.4 billion; per capita: $3,800
Currency: Latvian let

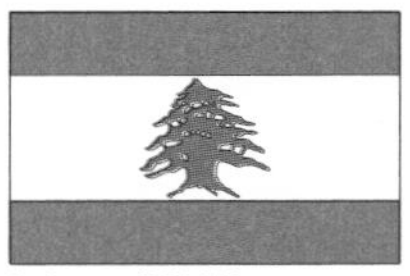

Lebanon* 91/D3
Capital: Beirut
Area: 4,015 sq. mi.
10,399 sq. km.
Population: 3,858,736; growth rate: 1.62%
Government : republic
Independence: November 22, 1943
U.N. Admission: October 24, 1945
Life expectancy: 70 yrs
GDP : $13 billion; per capita: $3,400
Currency: Lebanese pound

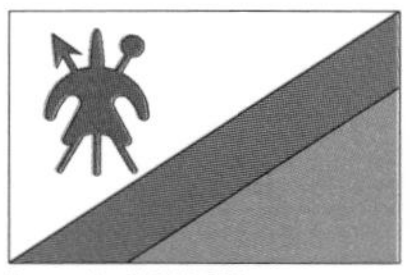

Lesotho* 106/E6
Capital: Maseru
Area: 11,718 sq. mi.
30,350 sq. km.
Population: 2,007,814; growth rate: 1.83%
Government : constitutional monarchy
Independence: October 4, 1966
U.N. Admission: October 17, 1966
Life expectancy: 52 yrs
GDP : $27 billion; per capita: $1,860
Currency: loti

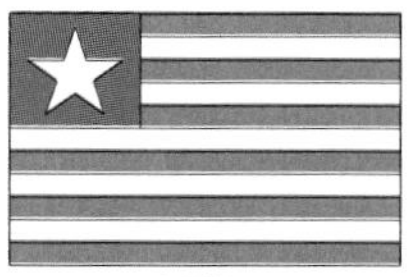

Liberia* 102/C5
Capital: Monrovia
Area: 43,000 sq. mi.
111,370 sq. km.
Population: 2,602,068; growth rate: 6.92%
Government : republic
Independence: July 26, 1847
U.N. Admission: November 2, 1945
Life expectancy: 59 yrs
GDP : $2.4 billion; per capita: $1,100
Currency: Liberian dollar

Libya* 97/J2
Capital: Tripoli
Area: 679,358 sq. mi.
1,759,537 sq. km.
Population: 5,648,359; growth rate: 3.64%
Government : military dictatorship
Independence: December 24, 1951
U.N. Admission: December 14, 1955
Life expectancy: 65 yrs
GDP : $34.5 billion; per capita: $6,570
Currency: Libyan dinar

Liechtenstein* 57/F3
Capital: Vaduz
Area: 62 sq. mi.
160 sq. km.
Population: 31,461; growth rate: 1.09%
Government : constitutional monarchy
Independence: January 23, 1719
U.N. Admission: September 18, 1990
Life expectancy: 79 yrs
GDP : $713 million; per capita: $23,000
Currency: Swiss franc

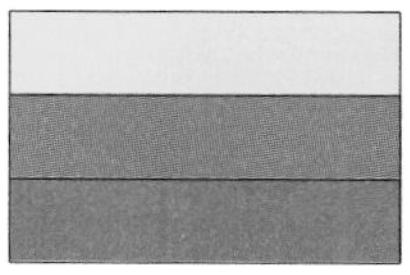

Lithuania* 39/K4
Capital: Vilnius
Area: 25,174 sq. mi.
65,200 sq. km.
Population: 3,635,932; growth rate: -.21%
Government : democratic republic
Independence: September 6, 1991
U.N. Admission: September 17, 1991
Life expectancy: 68 yrs
GDP : $14.1 billion; per capita: $3,870
Currency: Lithuanian litas

Luxembourg* 53/E4
Capital: Luxembourg
Area: 999 sq. mi.
2,587 sq. km.
Population: 422,474; growth rate: 1.58%
Government : constitutional monarchy
Independence: 1839
U.N. Admission: October 24, 1945
Life expectancy: 79 yrs
GDP : $10 billion; per capita: $24,500
Currency: Luxembourg franc

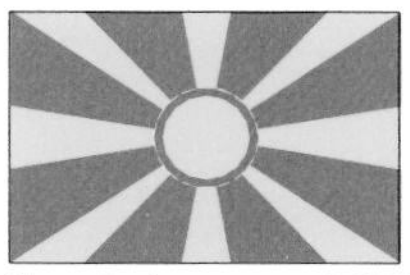

Macedonia (F.Y.R.O.M.)* 47/G2
Capital: Skopje
Area: 9,781 sq. mi.
25,333 sq. km.
Population: 2,113,866; growth rate: .47%
Government : emerging democracy
Independence: September 17, 1991
U.N. Admission: April 8, 1993
Life expectancy: 72 yrs
GDP : $2 billion; per capita: $960
Currency: Macedonian denar

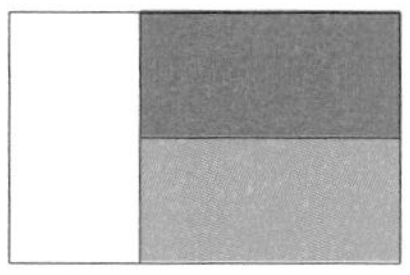

Madagascar* 107/H8
Capital: Antananarivo
Area: 226,657 sq. mi.
587,041 sq. km.
Population: 14,061,627; growth rate: 2.82%
Government : republic
Independence: June 26, 1960
U.N. Admission: September 20, 1960
Life expectancy: 53 yrs
GDP : $12.1 billion; per capita: $880
Currency: Malagasy franc

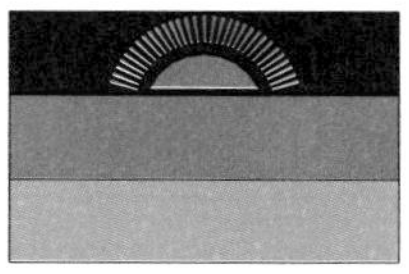

Malawi* 105/F3
Capital: Lilongwe
Area: 45,745 sq. mi.
118,480 sq. km.
Population: 9,609,081; growth rate: 1.57%
Government : multiparty democracy
Independence: July 6, 1964
U.N. Admission: December 1, 1964
Life expectancy: 35 yrs
GDP : $7.5 billion; per capita: $800
Currency: Malawian kwacha

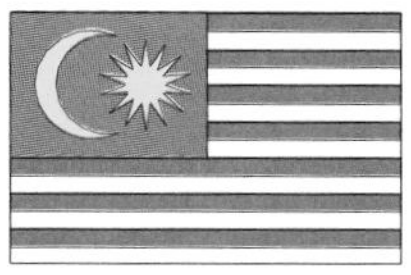

Malaysia* 80/C2
Capital: Kuala Lumpur
Area: 127,316 sq. mi.
329,750 sq. km.
Population: 20,376,235; growth rate: 2.15%
Government : constitutional monarchy
Independence: August 31, 1957
U.N. Admission: September 17, 1957
Life expectancy: 70 yrs
GDP : $214.7 billion; per capita: $10,750
Currency: ringgit

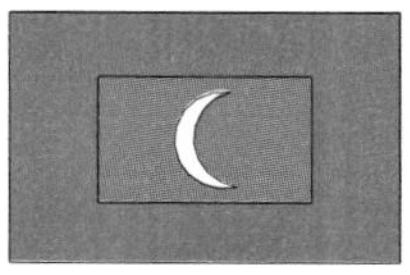

Maldives* 67/F9
Capital: Male
Area: 116 sq. mi.
300 sq. km.
Population: 280,391; growth rate: 3.47%
Government : republic
Independence: July 26, 1965
U.N. Admission: September 21, 1965
Life expectancy: 67 yrs
GDP : $423 million; per capita: $1,620
Currency: rufiyaa

Mali* 96/E4
Capital: Bamako
Area: 478,764 sq. mi.
1,240,000 sq. km.
Population: 9,945,383; growth rate: 3.01%
Government : republic
Independence: September 22, 1960
U.N. Admission: September 28, 1960
Life expectancy: 47 yrs
GDP : $5.8 billion; per capita: $600
Currency: CFA franc

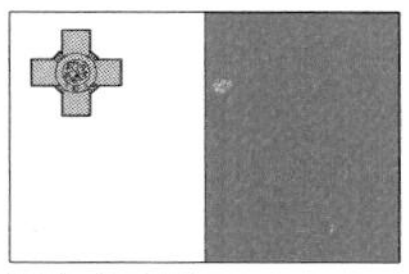

Malta* 46/L7
Capital: Valletta
Area: 124 sq. mi.
320 sq. km.
Population: 379,365; growth rate: 1%
Government : parliamentary democracy
Independence: September 21, 1964
U.N. Admission: December 1, 1964
Life expectancy: 79 yrs
GDP : $4.7 billion; per capita: $12,600
Currency: Maltese lira

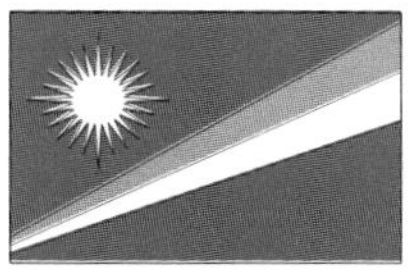

Marshall Islands* 116/G3
Capital: Majuro
Area: 70 sq. mi.
181 sq. km.
Population: 60,652; growth rate: 3.85%
Government : constitutional government
Independence: October 21, 1986
U.N. Admission: September 17, 1991
Life expectancy: 64 yrs
GDP : $94 million; per capita: $1,680
Currency: United States dollar

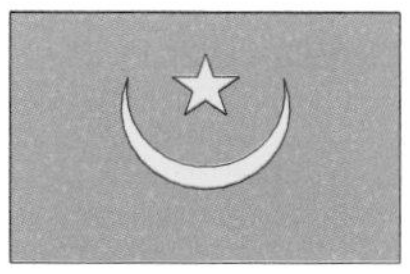

Mauritania* 96/C4
Capital: Nouakchott
Area: 397,953 sq. mi.
1,030,700 sq. km.
Population: 2,411,317; growth rate: 3.17%
Government : republic
Independence: November 28, 1960
U.N. Admission: October 7, 1961
Life expectancy: 49 yrs
GDP : $12.8 billion; per capita: $1,200
Currency: ouguiya

Mauritius* 107/T15
Capital: Port Louis
Area: 718 sq. mi.
1,860 sq. km.
Population: 1,154,272; growth rate: 1.21%
Government : parliamentary democracy
Independence: March 12, 1968
U.N. Admission: April 24, 1968
Life expectancy: 71 yrs
GDP : $11.7 billion; per capita: $10,350
Currency: Mauritian rupee

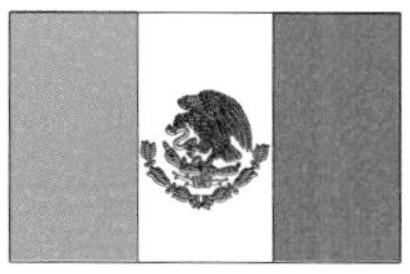

Mexico* 142
Capital: Mexico
Area: 761,601 sq. mi.
1,972,546 sq. km.
Population: 97,563,374; growth rate: 1.84%
Government : federal republic
Independence: September 16, 1810
U.N. Admission: November 7, 1945
Life expectancy: 74 yrs
GDP : $777.3 billion; per capita: $8,100
Currency: new Mexican peso

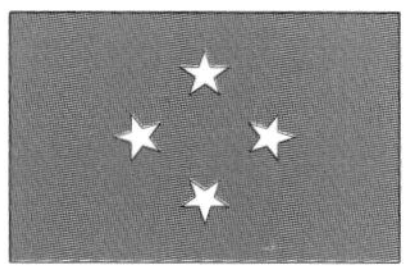

Micronesia* 116/D4
Capital: Palikir
Area: 271 sq. mi.
702 sq. km.
Population: 122,950; growth rate: 3.33%
Government : constitutional government
Independence: November 3, 1986
U.N. Admission: September 17, 1991
Life expectancy: 68 yrs
GDP : $205 million; per capita: $1,700
Currency: Untied States dollar

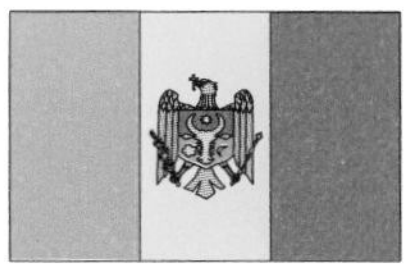

Moldova* 49/H2
Capital: Chişinău
Area: 13,012 sq. mi.
33,700 sq. km.
Population: 4,475,232; growth rate: .33%
Government : republic
Independence: August 27, 1991
U.N. Admission: March 2, 1992
Life expectancy: 65 yrs
GDP : $10.8 billion; per capita: $2,400
Currency: Moldovan leu

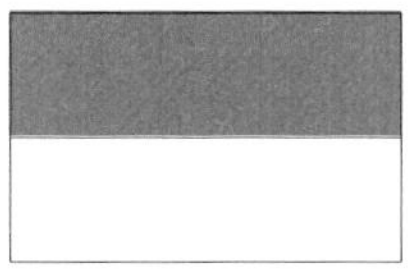

Monaco* 58/J8
Capital: Monaco
Area: 0.7 sq. mi.
1.9 sq. km.
Population: 31,892; growth rate: .49%
Government : constitutional monarchy
Independence: 1419
U.N. Admission: May 28, 1993
Life expectancy: 78 yrs
GDP : $800 million; per capita: $25,000
Currency: French franc

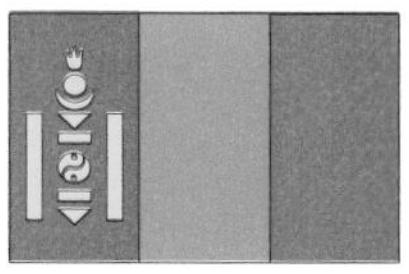

Mongolia* 70/G2
Capital: Ulaanbaatar
Area: 606,163 sq. mi.
1,569,962 sq. km.
Population: 2,538,211; growth rate: 1.62%
Government : republic
Independence: March 13, 1921
U.N. Admission: October 27, 1961
Life expectancy: 61 yrs
GDP : $5.1 billion; per capita: $2,060
Currency: tughrik

Morocco* 98/D2
Capital: Rabat
Area: 172,414 sq. mi.
446,550 sq. km.
Population: 30,391,423; growth rate: 2.02%
Government : constitutional monarchy
Independence: March 2, 1956
U.N. Admission: November 12, 1956
Life expectancy: 70 yrs
GDP : $897.6 billion; per capita: $3,260
Currency: Moroccan dirham

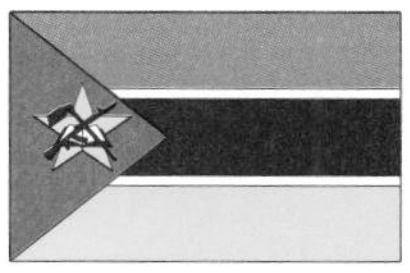

Mozambique* 105/G4
Capital: Maputo
Area: 309,494 sq. mi.
801,590 sq. km.
Population: 18,165,476; growth rate: 2.6%
Government : republic
Independence: June 25, 1975
U.N. Admission: September 16, 1975
Life expectancy: 45 yrs
GDP : $12.2 billion; per capita: $670
Currency: metical

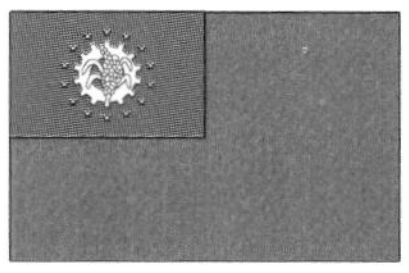

Myanmar (Burma)* 83/G3
Capital: Yangon (Rangoon)
Area: 261,969 sq. mi.
678,500 sq. km.
Population: 46,821,943; growth rate: 1.81%
Government : military regime
Independence: January 4, 1948
U.N. Admission: April 19, 1948
Life expectancy: 57 yrs
GDP : $51.5 billion; per capita: $1,120
Currency: kyat

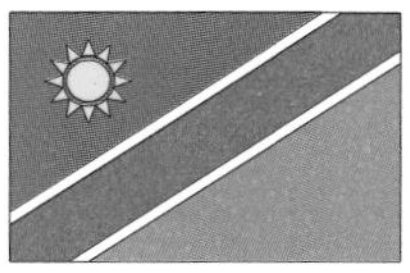

Namibia* 105/C5
Capital: Windhoek
Area: 318,694 sq. mi.
825,418 sq. km.
Population: 1,727,183; growth rate: 2.94%
Government : republic
Independence: March 21, 1990
U.N. Admission: April 23, 1990
Life expectancy: 65 yrs
GDP : $6.2 billion; per capita: $3,700
Currency: Namibian dollar

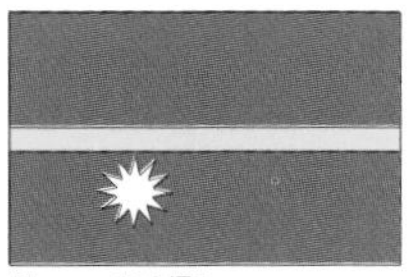

Nauru 116/F5
Capital: Yaren (district)
Area: 8 sq. mi.
21 sq. km.
Population: 10,390; growth rate: N/A
Government : republic
Independence: January 31, 1968
U.N. Admission: non-member
Life expectancy: 67 yrs
GDP : $100 million; per capita: $10,000
Currency: Australian dollar

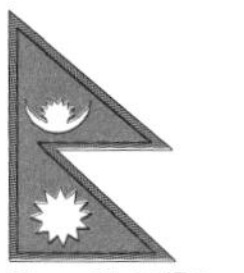

Nepal* 84/D1
Capital: Kāthmāndu
Area: 54,363 sq. mi.
140,800 sq. km.
Population: 22,641,061; growth rate: 2.45%
Government : parliamentary democracy
Independence: 1768
U.N. Admission: December 14, 1955
Life expectancy: 54 yrs
GDP : $26.5 billion; per capita: $1,200
Currency: Nepalese rupee

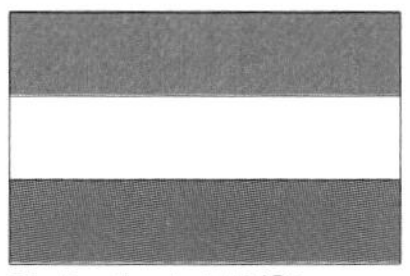

Netherlands* 40/C3
Capital: The Hague; Amsterdam
Area: 14,413 sq. mi.
37,330 sq. km.
Population: 15,653,091; growth rate: .53%
Government : constitutional monarchy
Independence:1579
U.N. Admission: December 10, 1945
Life expectancy: 78 yrs
GDP : $317.8 billion; per capita: $20,500
Currency: Netherlands guilder

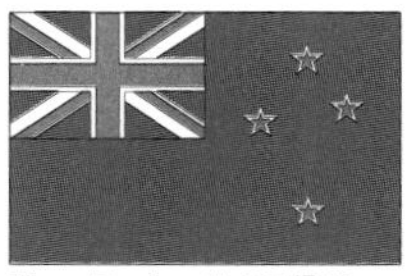

New Zealand* 117/R10
Capital: Wellington
Area: 103,736 sq. mi.
268,676 sq. km.
Population: 3,587,275; growth rate: 1.08%
Government : parliamentary democracy
Independence: September 26, 1907
U.N. Admission: October 24, 1945
Life expectancy: 77 yrs
GDP : $65.6 billion; per capita: $18,500
Currency: New Zealand dollar

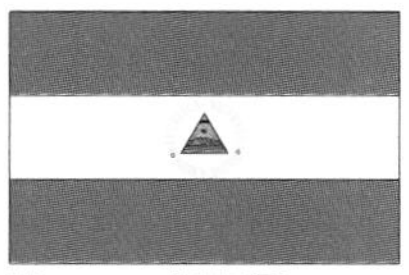

Nicaragua* 145/E3
Capital: Managua
Area: 49,998 sq. mi.
129,494 sq. km.
Population: 4,386,399; growth rate: 2.6%
Government : republic
Independence: September 15, 1821
U.N. Admission: October 24, 1945
Life expectancy: 66 yrs
GDP : $7.7 billion; per capita: $1,800
Currency: gold cordoba

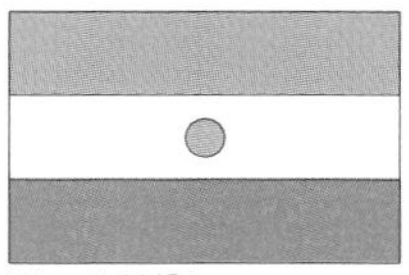

Niger* 96/G4
Capital: Niamey
Area: 489,189 sq. mi.
1,267,000 sq. km.
Population: 9,388,859; growth rate: 2.98%
Government : republic
Independence: August 3, 1960
U.N. Admission: September 20, 1960
Life expectancy: 41 yrs
GDP : $5.9 billion; per capita: $640
Currency: CFA franc

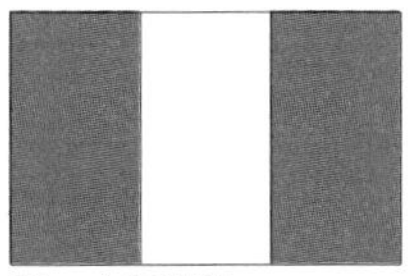

Nigeria* 96/G6
Capital: Abuja
Area: 356,668 sq. mi.
923,770 sq. km.
Population: 107,129,469; growth rate: 3.05%
Government : military government
Independence: October 1, 1960
U.N. Admission: October 7, 1960
Life expectancy: 55 yrs
GDP : $143.5 billion; per capita: $1,380
Currency: naira

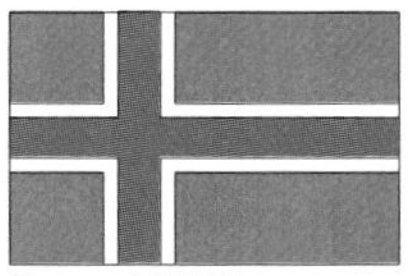

Norway* 37/C3
Capital: Oslo
Area: 125,181 sq. mi.
324,220 sq. km.
Population: 4,404,456; growth rate: .46%
Government : constitutional monarchy
Independence: October 26, 1905
U.N. Admission: November 27, 1945
Life expectancy: 78 yrs
GDP : $114.1 billion; per capita: $26,200
Currency: Norwegian krone

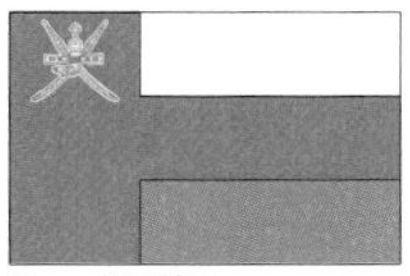

Oman* 89/G4
Capital: Muscat
Area: 82,031 sq. mi.
212,460 sq. km.
Population: 2,264,590; growth rate: 3.49%
Government : monarchy
Independence: 1650
U.N. Admission: October 7, 1971
Life expectancy: 71 yrs
GDP : $20.8 billion; per capita: $9,500
Currency: Omani rial

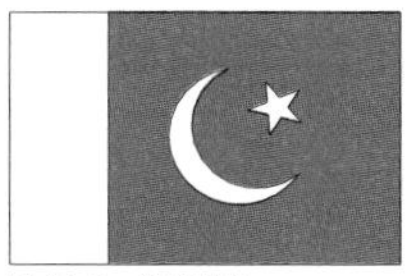

Pakistan* 89/H3
Capital: Islamabad
Area: 310,403 sq. mi.
803,944 sq. km.
Population: 132,185,299; growth rate: 2.22%
Government : federal republic
Independence: August 14, 1947
U.N. Admission: September 30, 1947
Life expectancy: 59 yrs
GDP : $296.5 billion; per capita: $2,300
Currency: Pakistani rupee

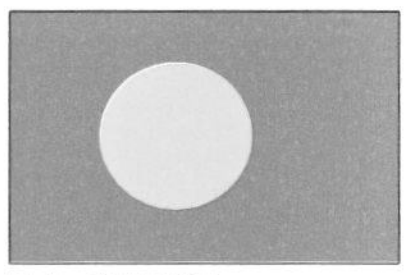

Palau* 116/C4
Capital: Koror
Area: 177 sq. mi.
458 sq. km.
Population: 17,240; growth rate: 1.66%
Government : constitutional government
Independence: October 1, 1994
U.N. Admission: December 15, 1994
Life expectancy: 71 yrs
GDP : $81.8 million; per capita: $5,000
Currency: United States dollar

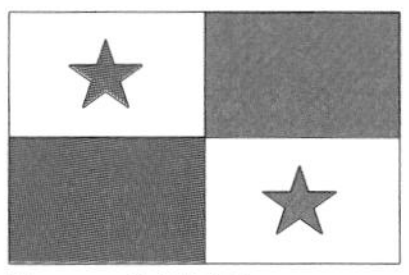

Panama* 145/F4
Capital: Panamá
Area: 30,193 sq. mi.
78,200 sq. km.
Population: 2,693,417; growth rate: 1.58%
Government : constitutional republic
Independence: November 3, 1903
U.N. Admission: November 13, 1945
Life expectancy: 74 yrs
GDP : $14 billion; per capita: $5,300
Currency: balboa

World Flags and Reference Guide

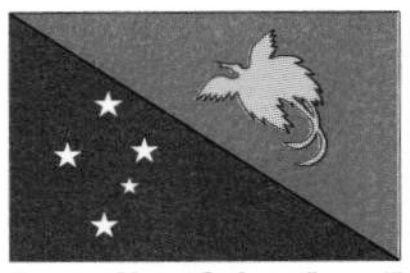

Papua New Guinea* 116/D5
Capital: Port Moresby
Area: 178,259 sq. mi.
461,690 sq. km.
Population: 4,496,221; growth rate: 2.28%
Government : parliamentary democracy
Independence: September 16, 1975
U.N. Admission: October 10, 1975
Life expectancy: 58 yrs
GDP : $10.7 billion; per capita: $2,400
Currency: kina

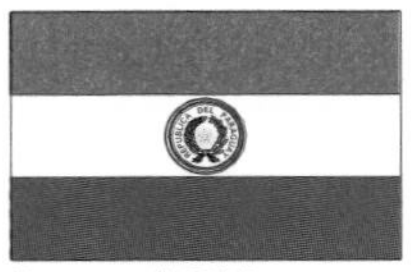

Paraguay* 42/E1
Capital: Asunción
Area: 157,047 sq. mi.
406,752 sq. km.
Population: 5,651,634; growth rate: 2.62%
Government: republic
Independence: May 14, 1811
U.N. Admission: October 24, 1945
Life expectancy: 74 yrs
GDP : $17.7 billion; per capita: $3,200
Currency: guarani

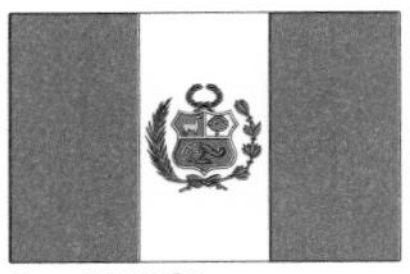

Peru* 156/C3
Capital: Lima
Area: 496,223 sq. mi.
1,285,220 sq. km.
Population: 24,949,512; growth rate: 1.7%
Government: republic
Independence: July 28, 1821
U.N. Admission: October 31, 1945
Life expectancy: 70 yrs
GDP : $92 billion; per capita: $3,800
Currency: nuevo sol

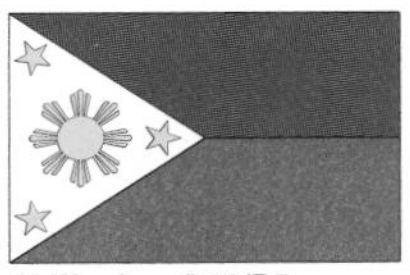

Philippines* 79/D5
Capital: Manila
Area: 115,830 sq. mi.
300,000 sq. km.
Population: 76,103,564; growth rate: 2.13%
Government: republic
Independence: July 4, 1946
U.N. Admission: October 24, 1945
Life expectancy: 66 yrs
GDP : $194.2 billion; per capita: $2,600
Currency: Philippine peso

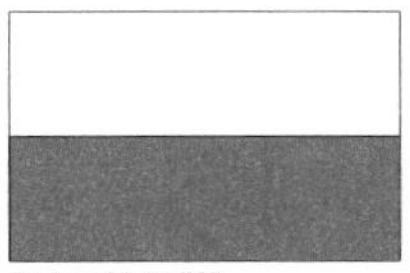

Poland* 41/K2
Capital: Warsaw
Area: 120,725 sq. mi.
312,678 sq. km.
Population: 38,700,291; growth rate: .16%
Government: democratic state
Independence: November 11, 1918
U.N. Admission: October 24, 1945
Life expectancy: 72 yrs
GDP : $246.3 billion; per capita: $6,400
Currency: zloty

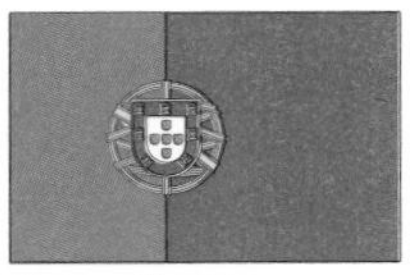

Portugal* 44/A3
Capital: Lisbon
Area: 35,552 sq. mi.
92,080 sq. km.
Population: 9,867,654; growth rate: .04%
Government : parliamentary democracy
Independence: October 5, 1910
U.N. Admission: December 14, 1955
Life expectancy: 76 yrs
GDP : $122.1 billion; per capita: $12,400
Currency: Portuguese escudo

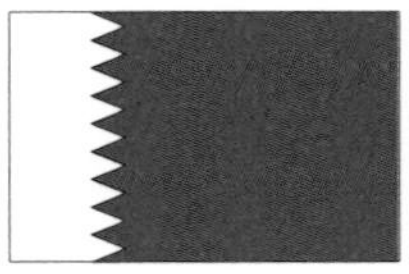

Qatar* 88/F3
Capital: Doha
Area: 4,247 sq. mi.
11,000 sq. km.
Population: 665,485; growth rate: 4.04%
Government : traditional monarchy
Independence: September 3, 1971
U.N. Admission: September 21, 1971
Life expectancy: 73 yrs
GDP : $11.7 billion; per capita: $21,300
Currency: Qatari riyal

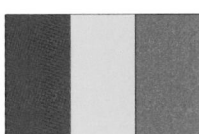

Romania* 49/F3
Capital: Bucharest
Area: 91,699 sq. mi.
237,500 sq. km.
Population: 21,399,114; growth rate: -1.19%
Government : republic
Independence:1881
U.N. Admission: December 14, 1955
Life expectancy: 70 yrs
GDP : $113.2 billion; per capita: $5,200
Currency: leu

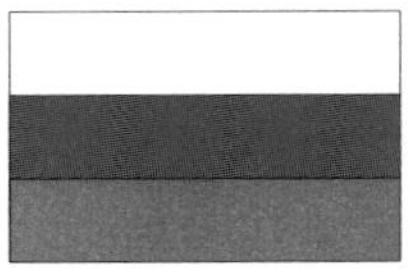

Russia* 64/H3
Capital: Moscow
Area: 6,592,735 sq. mi.
17,075,200 sq. km.
Population: 147,987,101; growth rate: .19%
Government : federation
Independence: August 24, 1991
U.N. Admission: October 24, 1945
Life expectancy: 64 yrs
GDP : $767 billion; per capita: $5,200
Currency: ruble

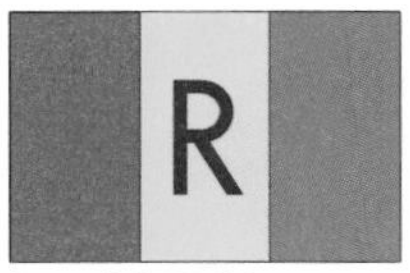

Rwanda* 104/A3
Capital: Kigali
Area: 10,169 sq. mi.
26,337 sq. km.
Population: 7,737,537; growth rate: 8.24%
Government : republic
Independence: July 1, 1962
U.N. Admission: September 18, 1962
Life expectancy: 39 yrs
GDP : $3.8 billion; per capita: $400
Currency: Rwandan franc

Saint Kitts & Nevis* 141/N8
Capital: Basseterre
Area: 104 sq. mi.
269 sq. km.
Population: 41,803; growth rate: 1.1%
Government : constitutional monarchy
Independence: September 19, 1983
U.N. Admission: September 23, 1983
Life expectancy: 67 yrs
GDP : $235 million; per capita: $5,700
Currency: EC dollar

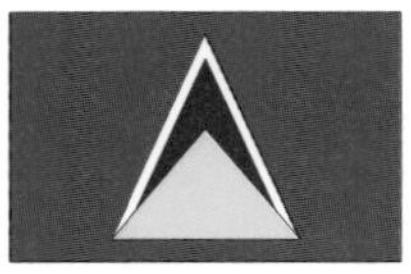

Saint Lucia* 141/N9
Capital: Castries
Area: 239 sq. mi.
620 sq. km.
Population: 159,639; growth rate: 1.14%
Government : parliamentary democracy
Independence: February 22, 1979
U.N. Admission: September 18, 1979
Life expectancy: 71 yrs
GDP : $695 million; per capita: $4,400
Currency: EC dollar

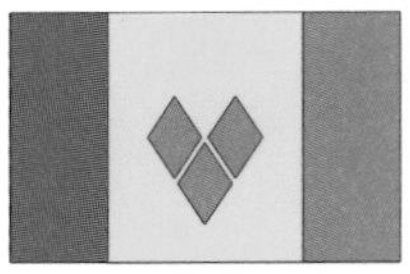

St. Vincent & the Grenadines* 141/N9
Capital: Kingstown
Area: 131 sq. mi.
340 sq. km.
Population: 119,092; growth rate: 1.62%
Government : parliamentary democracy
Independence: October 27, 1979
U.N. Admission: September 16, 1980
Life expectancy: 73 yrs
GDP : $259 million; per capita: $2,190
Currency: EC dollar

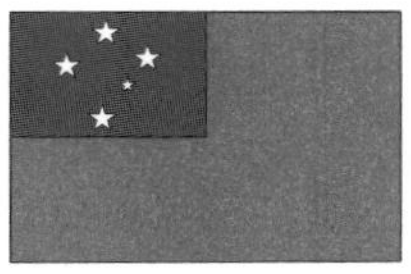

Samoa* 117/H6
Capital: Apia
Area: 1,104 sq. mi.
2,860 sq. km.
Population: 219,509; growth rate: 2.34%
Government : parliamentary democracy
Independence: January 1, 1962
U.N. Admission: December 15, 1976
Life expectancy: 69 yrs
GDP : $415 million; per capita: $1,900
Currency: tala

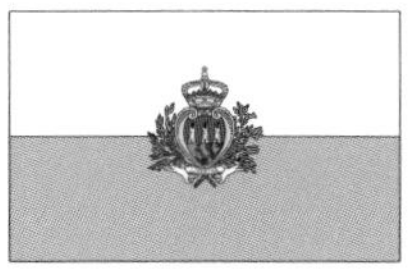

San Marino* 59/F5
Capital: San Marino
Area: 23.4 sq. mi.
60.6 sq. km.
Population: 24,714; growth rate: .76%
Government : republic
Independence: 301 A.D.
U.N. Admission: March 2, 1992
Life expectancy: 81 yrs
GDP : $408 million; per capita: $16,900
Currency: Italian lira

São Tomé & Príncipe* 96/F7
Capital: São Tomé
Area: 371 sq. mi.
960 sq. km.
Population: 147,865; growth rate: 2.54%
Government : republic
Independence: July 12, 1975
U.N. Admission: September 16, 1975
Life expectancy: 64 yrs
GDP : $149 million; per capita: $1,000
Currency: dobra

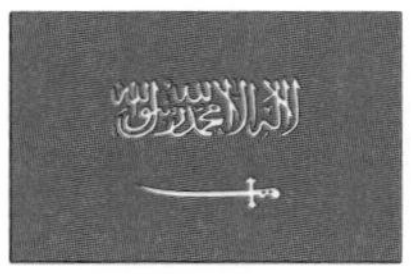

Saudi Arabia* 88/D4
Capital: Riyadh
Area: 756,981 sq. mi.
1,960,582 sq. km.
Population: 20,087,965; growth rate: 3.42%
Government : monarchy
Independence: September 23, 1932
U.N. Admission: October 24, 1945
Life expectancy: 70 yrs
GDP : $205.6 billion; per capita: $10,600
Currency: Saudi riyal

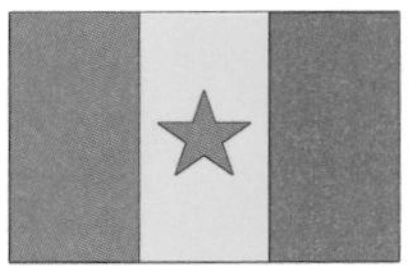

Senegal* 102/B3
Capital: Dakar
Area: 75,749 sq. mi.
196,190 sq. km.
Population: 9,403,546; growth rate: 3.35%
Government : multiparty democracy
Independence: April 4, 1960
U.N. Admission: September 28, 1960
Life expectancy: 57 yrs
GDP : $15.6 billion; per capita: $1,700
Currency: CFA franc

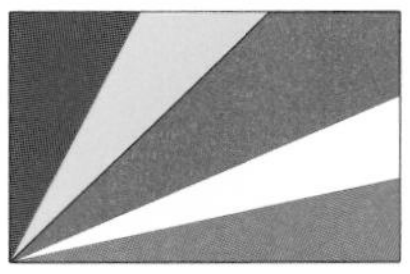

Seychelles* 23/M6
Capital: Victoria
Area: 176 sq. mi.
455 sq. km.
Population: 78,142; growth rate: .7%
Government : republic
Independence: June 29, 1976
U.N. Admission: September 1, 1976
Life expectancy: 70 yrs
GDP : $450 million; per capita: $6,000
Currency: Seychelles rupee

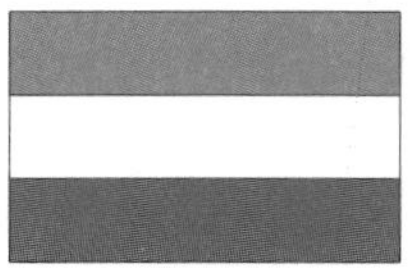

Sierra Leone* 102/B4
Capital: Freetown
Area: 27,699 sq. mi.
71,740 sq. km.
Population: 4,891,546; growth rate: 3.54%
Government : constitutional democracy
Independence: April 27, 1961
U.N. Admission: September 27, 1961
Life expectancy: 48 yrs
GDP : $4.7 billion; per capita: $980
Currency: leone

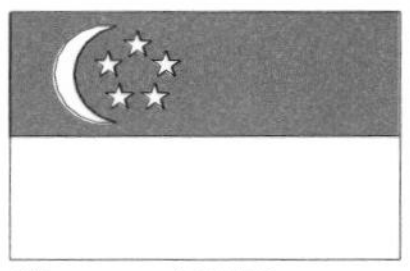

Singapore* 80/B3
Capital: Singapore
Area: 244 sq. mi.
632.6 sq. km.
Population: 3,461,929; growth rate: 1.67%
Government : republic
Independence: August 6, 1965
U.N. Admission: September 21, 1965
Life expectancy: 78 yrs
GDP : $72.2 billion; per capita: $21,200
Currency: Singapore dollar

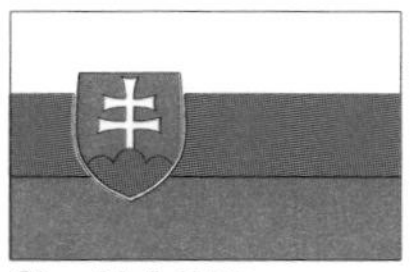

Slovakia* 41/K4
Capital: Bratislava
Area: 18,859 sq. mi.
48,845 sq. km.
Population: 5,393,016; growth rate: .35%
Government : parliamentary democracy
Independence: January 1, 1993
U.N. Admission: January 19, 1993
Life expectancy: 73 yrs
GDP : $42.8 billion; per capita: $8,000
Currency: koruna

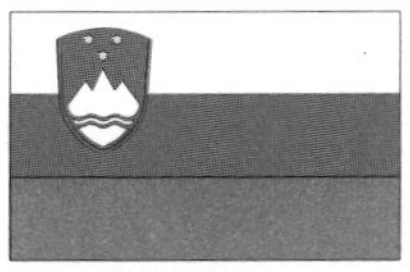

Slovenia* 48/B3
Capital: Ljubljana
Area: 7,836 sq. mi.
20,296 sq. km.
Population: 1,945,998; growth rate: -.29%
Government : emerging democracy
Independence: June 25, 1991
U.N. Admission: May 22, 1992
Life expectancy: 75 yrs
GDP : $24 billion; per capita: $12,300
Currency: tolar

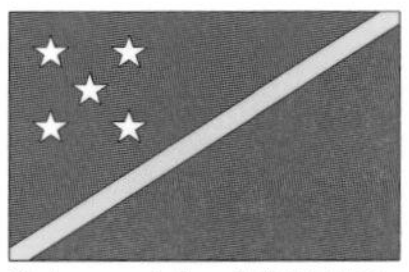

Solomon Islands* 116/E6
Capital: Honiara
Area: 10,985 sq. mi.
28,450 sq. km.
Population: 462,855; growth rate: 3.3%
Government : parliamentary democracy
Independence: July 7, 1978
U.N. Admission: September 19, 1978
Life expectancy: 71 yrs
GDP : $1.2 billion; per capita: $3,000
Currency: Solomon Islands dollar

Somalia* 97/Q6
Capital: Mogadishu
Area: 246,200 sq. mi.
637,658 sq. km.
Population: 9,940,232; growth rate: 3.03%
Government : none
Independence: July 1, 1960
U.N. Admission: September 20, 1960
Life expectancy: 46 yrs
GDP : $3.6 billion; per capita: $500
Currency: Somali shilling

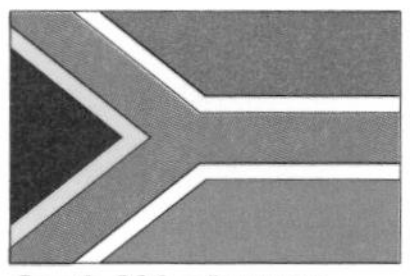

South Africa* 105/D6
Capital: Cape Town; Pretoria
Area: 471,008 sq. mi.
1,219,912 sq. km.
Population: 42,327,458; growth rate: 1.51%
Government : republic
Independence: May 31, 1910
U.N. Admission: November 7, 1945
Life expectancy: 56 yrs
GDP : $227 billion; per capita: $5,400
Currency: rand

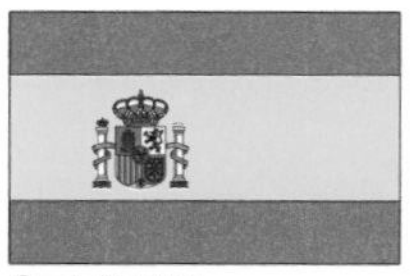

Spain* 44/C2
Capital: Madrid
Area: 194,884 sq. mi.
504,750 sq. km.
Population: 39,244,195; growth rate: 1.6%
Government : parliamentary monarchy
Independence: 1492
U.N. Admission: December 14, 1955
Life expectancy: 78 yrs
GDP : $593 billion; per capita: $15,300
Currency: peseta

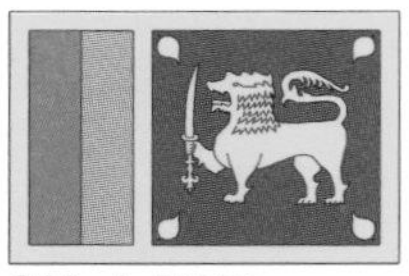

Sri Lanka* 82/D6
Capital: Colombo
Area: 25,332 sq. mi.
65,610 sq. km.
Population: 18,762,075; growth rate: 1.11%
Government : republic
Independence: February 4, 1948
U.N. Admission: December 14, 1955
Life expectancy: 73 yrs
GDP : $69.7 billion; per capita: $3,760
Currency: Sri Lankan rupee

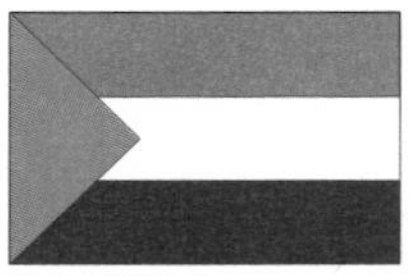

Sudan* 97/L5
Capital: Khartoum
Area: 967,494 sq. mi.
2,505,809 sq. km.
Population: 32,594,128; growth rate: 3.06%
Government : transitional
Independence: January 1, 1956
U.N. Admission: November 12, 1956
Life expectancy: 56 yrs
GDP : $26.6 billion; per capita: $860
Currency: Sudanese pound

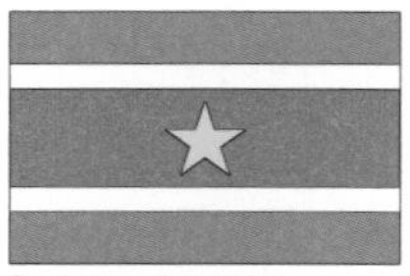

Suriname* 153/G3
Capital: Paramaribo
Area: 63,039 sq. mi.
163,270 sq. km.
Population: 443,446; growth rate: .83%
Government : republic
Independence: November 25, 1975
U.N. Admission: December 4, 1975
Life expectancy: 70 yrs
GDP : $1.4 billion; per capita: $3,150
Currency: Surinamese guilder

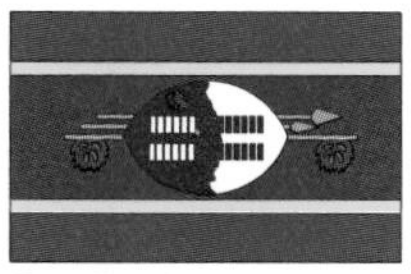

Swaziland* 107/E2
Capital: Mbabane; Lobamba
Area: 6,703 sq. mi.
17,360 sq. km.
Population: 1,031,600; growth rate: 3.24%
Government : monarchy
Independence: September 6, 1968
U.N. Admission: September 24, 1968
Life expectancy: 58 yrs
GDP : $3.8 billion; per capita: $3,800
Currency: lilangeni

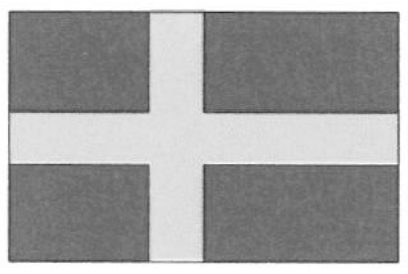

Sweden* 37/E3
Capital: Stockholm
Area: 173,731 sq. mi.
449,964 sq. km.
Population: 8,946,193; growth rate: .45%
Government : constitiutional monarchy
Independence: June 6, 1523
U.N. Admission: November 19, 1946
Life expectancy: 78 yrs
GDP : $184.3 billion; per capita: $20,800
Currency: Swedish krona

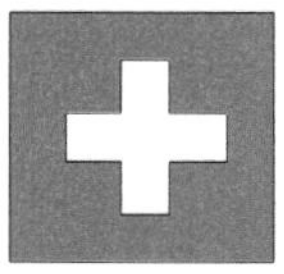

Switzerland 59/D4
Capital: Bern
Area: 15,943 sq. mi.
41,292 sq. km.
Population: 7,248,984; growth rate: .57%
Government : federal republic
Independence: August 1, 1291
U.N. Admission: observer status
Life expectancy: 78 yrs
GDP : $161.3 billion; per capita: $22,600
Currency: Swiss franc

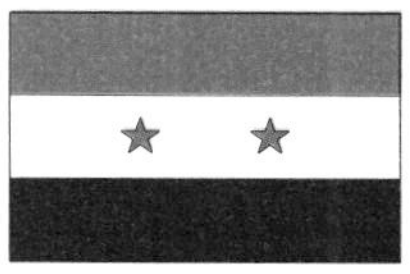

Syria* 90/D3
Capital: Damascus
Area: 71,498 sq. mi.
185,180 sq. km.
Population: 16,137,899; growth rate: 3.3%
Government : military regime
Independence: April 17, 1946
U.N. Admission: October 24, 1945
Life expectancy: 67 yrs
GDP : $98.3 billion; per capita: $6,300
Currency: Syrian pound

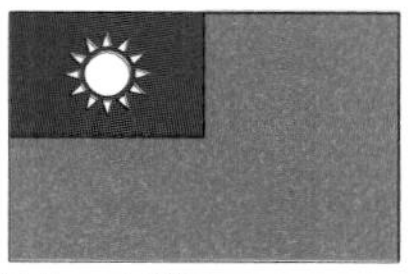

Taiwan 79/D3
Capital: T'aipei
Area: 13,892 sq. mi.
35,980 sq. km.
Population: 21,655,515; growth rate: .95%
Government : multiparty democracy
Independence: 1949 (Nationalist govt.)
U.N. Admission: non-member
Life expectancy: 77 yrs
GDP : $315 billion; per capita: $14,700
Currency: New Taiwan dollar

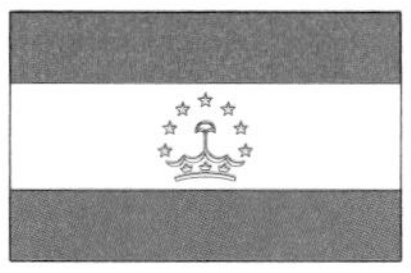

Tajikistan* 87/E5
Capital: Dushanbe
Area: 55,251 sq. mi.
143,100 sq. km.
Population: 6,013,855; growth rate: 1.73%
Government : republic
Independence: September 9, 1991
U.N. Admission: March 2, 1992
Life expectancy: 65 yrs
GDP : $5.4 billion; per capita: $920
Currency: Tajikistani ruble

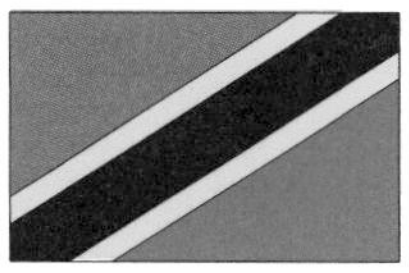

Tanzania* 104/B4
Capital: Dar es Salaam
Area: 364,699 sq. mi.
945,090 sq. km.
Population: 29,460,753; growth rate: 1.6%
Government : republic
Independence: April 26, 1964
U.N. Admission: December 14, 1961
Life expectancy: 42 yrs
GDP : $18.9 billion; per capita: $650
Currency: Tanzanian shilling

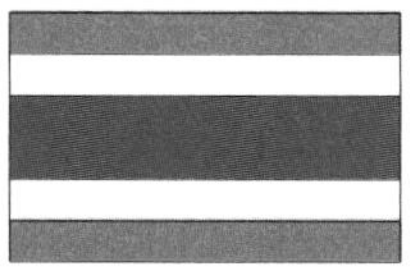

Thailand* 78/C3
Capital: Bangkok
Area: 198,455 sq. mi.
513,998 sq. km.
Population: 59,450,818; growth rate: 1%
Government : constitiutional monarchy
Independence: 1238 (traditional date)
U.N. Admission: December 16, 1946
Life expectancy: 69 yrs
GDP : $455.7 billion; per capita: $7,700
Currency: baht

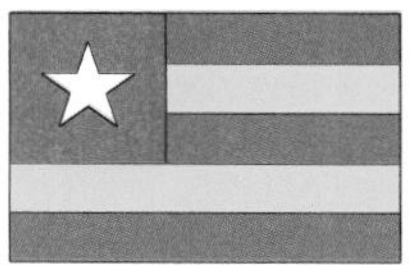

Togo* 103/F4
Capital: Lomé
Area: 21,927 sq. mi.
56,790 sq. km.
Population: 4,735,610; growth rate: 3.54%
Government : transitional government
Independence: April 27, 1960
U.N. Admission: September 20, 1960
Life expectancy: 58 yrs
GDP : $4.45 billion; per capita: $970
Currency: CFA franc

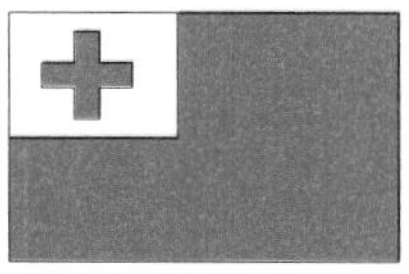

Tonga 117/H7
Capital: Nuku'alofa
Area: 289 sq. mi.
748 sq. km.
Population: 107,335; growth rate: .81%
Government : constitutional monarchy
Independence: June 4, 1970
U.N. Admission: non-member
Life expectancy: 69 yrs
GDP : $228 million; per capita: $2,140
Currency: pa'anga

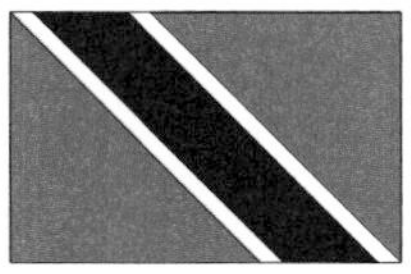

Trinidad & Tobago* 141/N10
Capital: Port-of-Spain
Area: 1,980 sq. mi.
5,128 sq. km.
Population: 1,273,141; growth rate: -1.18%
Government : parliamentary democracy
Independence: August 31, 1962
U.N. Admission: September 18, 1962
Life expectancy: 70 yrs
GDP : $17.1 billion; per capita: $13,500
Currency: Trinidad and Tobago dollar

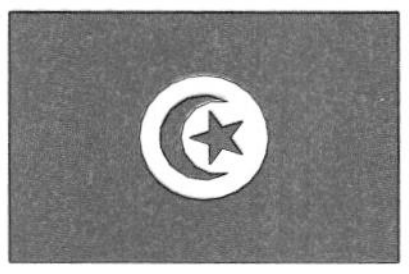

Tunisia* 99/H2
Capital: Tunis
Area: 63,170 sq. mi.
163,610 sq. km.
Population: 9,183,097; growth rate: 1.78%
Government : republic
Independence: March 20, 1956
U.N. Admission: November 12, 1956
Life expectancy: 73 yrs
GDP : $43.3 billion; per capita: $4,800
Currency: Tunisian dollar

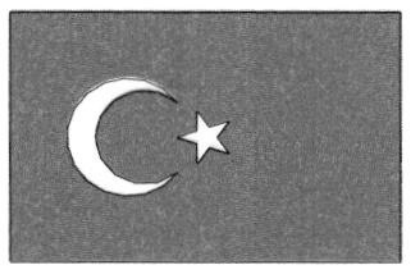

Turkey* 90/C2
Capital: Ankara
Area: 301,382 sq. mi.
780,580 sq. km.
Population: 63,528,225; growth rate: 1.64%
Government: parliamentary democracy
Independence: October 29, 1923
U.N. Admission: December 24, 1945
Life expectancy: 72 yrs
GDP : $379.1 billion; per capita: $6,100
Currency: Turkish lira

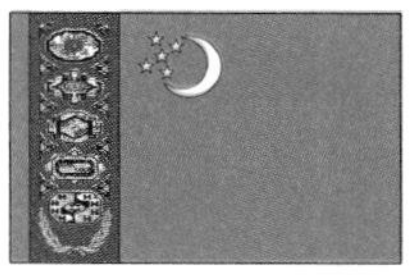

Turkmenistan* 87/C5
Capital: Ashgabat
Area: 188,455 sq. mi.
488,100 sq. km.
Population: 4,225,351; growth rate: 1.82%
Government : republic
Independence: October 27, 1971
U.N. Admission: March 2, 1992
Life expectancy: 62 yrs
GDP : $11.8 billion; per capita: $2,840
Currency: Turkmen manat

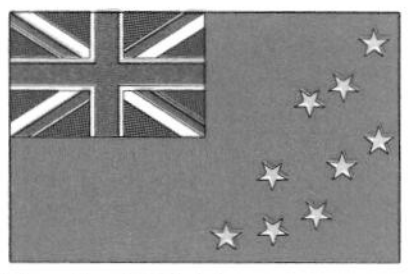

Tuvalu 116/G5
Capital: Funafuti
Area: 10 sq. mi.
26 sq. km.
Population: 10,297; growth rate: 1.45%
Government : democracy
Independence: October 1, 1978
U.N. Admission: non-member
Life expectancy: 64 yrs
GDP : $57.8 million; per capita: $800
Currency: Tuvaluan or Australian dollar

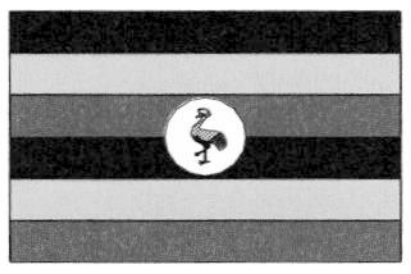

Uganda* 104/B2
Capital: Kampala
Area: 91,135 sq. mi.
236,040 sq. km.
Population: 20,604,874; growth rate: 2.14%
Government : republic
Independence: October 9, 1962
U.N. Admission: October 25, 1962
Life expectancy: 40 yrs
GDP : $16.8 billion; per capita: $900
Currency: Ugandan shilling

Ukraine* 62/D2
Capital: Kiev
Area: 233,089 sq. mi.
603,700 sq. km.
Population: 50,684,635; growth rate: -.31%
Government : republic
Independence: December 1, 1991
U.N. Admission: October 24, 1945
Life expectancy: 67 yrs
GDP : $161.1 billion; per capita: $3,170
Currency: hryvnia

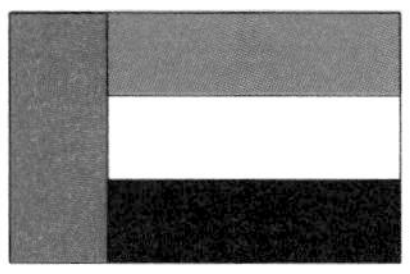

United Arab Emirates* 88/F4
Capital: Abu Dhabi
Area: 29,182 sq. mi.
75,581 sq. km.
Population: 2,262,309; growth rate: 1.79%
Government : federation
Independence: December 2, 1971
U.N. Admission: December 9, 1971
Life expectancy: 75 yrs
GDP : $72.9 billion; per capita: $23,800
Currency: Emirian dirham

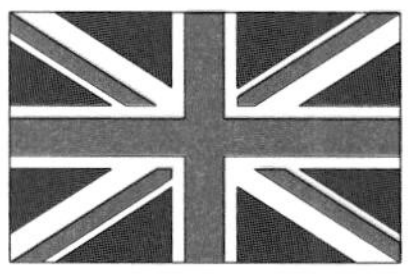

United Kingdom* 31/R9
Capital: London
Area: 94,525 sq. mi.
244,820 sq. km.
Population: 58,610,182; growth rate: .19%
Government : constitutional monarchy
Independence: January 1, 1801
U.N. Admission: October 24, 1945
Life expectancy: 77 yrs
GDP : $1.19 trillion; per capita: $20,400
Currency: British pound

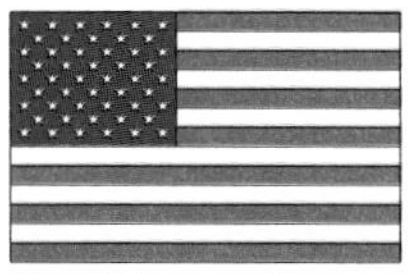

United States* 124
Capital: Washington, D.C.
Area: 3,618,765 sq. mi.
9,372,610 sq. km.
Population: 267,954,767; growth rate: .89%
Government : federal republic
Independence: July 4, 1776
U.N. Admission: October 24, 1945
Life expectancy: 76 yrs
GDP : $7.61 trillion; per capita: $28,600
Currency: United States dollar

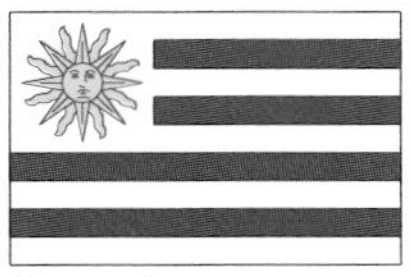

Uruguay* 157/E3
Capital: Montevideo
Area: 68,039 sq. mi.
176,220 sq. km.
Population: 3,261,707; growth rate: .7%
Government : republic
Independence: August 25, 1828
U.N. Admission: December 18, 1945
Life expectancy: 75 yrs
GDP : $26 billion; per capita: $8,000
Currency: Uruguayan pesos

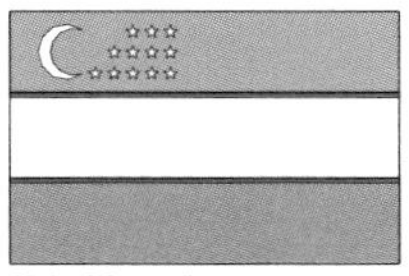

Uzbekistan* 87/D4
Capital: Tashkent
Area: 172,741 sq. mi.
447,400 sq. km.
Population: 23,860,452; growth rate: 1.87%
Government : republic
Independence: August 31, 1991
U.N. Admission: March 2, 1992
Life expectancy: 65 yrs
GDP : $57 billion; per capita: $2,430
Currency: som

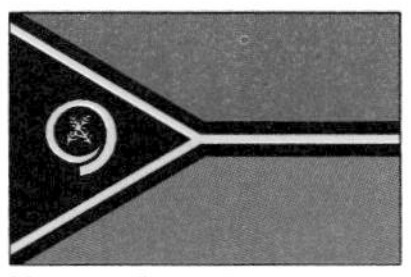

Vanuatu* 116/F6
Capital: Port-Vila
Area: 5,699 sq. mi.
14,760 sq. km.
Population: 181,358; growth rate: 2.12%
Government : republic
Independence: July 30, 1980
U.N. Admission: September 15, 1981
Life expectancy: 61 yrs
GDP : $219 million; per capita: $1,230
Currency: vatu

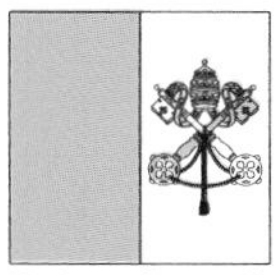

Vatican City 46/C2
Capital: —
Area: 0.17 sq. mi.
0.44 sq. km.
Population: 830; growth rate: 1.15%
Gov. : monarchial-sacredotal state
Independence: February 11, 1929
U.N. Admission: observer status
Life expectancy: N/A
GDP : N/A
Currency: Vatican lira

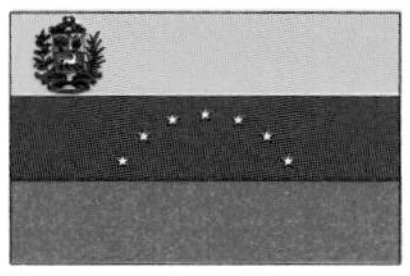

Venezuela* 153/E3
Capital: Caracas
Area: 352,143 sq. mi.
912,050 sq. km.
Population: 22,396,407; growth rate: 1.83%
Government : republic
Independence: July 5, 1811
U.N. Admission: November 15, 1945
Life expectancy: 72 yrs
GDP : $197 billion; per capita: $9,000
Currency: bolivar

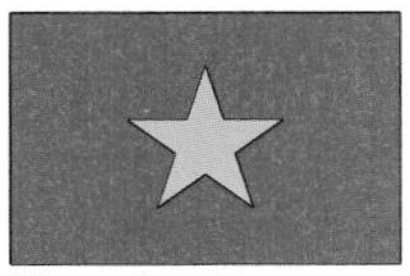

Vietnam* 78/D2
Capital: Hanoi
Area: 127,243 sq. mi.
329,560 sq. km.
Population: 75,123,880; growth rate: 1.51%
Government : Communist state
Independence: September 2, 1945
U.N. Admission: September 20, 1977
Life expectancy: 67 yrs
GDP : $108.7 billion; per capita: $1,470
Currency: new dong

Yemen* 88/E5
Capital: Sanaa
Area: 203,849 sq. mi.
527,970 sq. km.
Population: 13,972,477; growth rate: 3.57%
Government : republic
Independence: May 22, 1990
U.N. Admission: September 30, 1947
Life expectancy: 60 yrs
GDP : $39.1 billion; per capita: $2,900
Currency: Yemeni rial

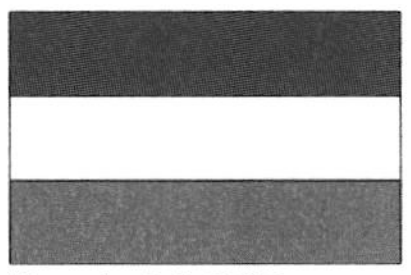

Yugoslavia* 48/D3
Capital: Belgrade
Area: 39,517 sq. mi.
102,350 sq. km.
Population: 10,655,317; growth rate: .39%
Government : republic
Independence: April 11, 1992
U.N. Admission: October 24, 1945
Life expectancy: 74 yrs
GDP : $21 billion; per capita: $1,900
Currency: Yugoslav new dinar

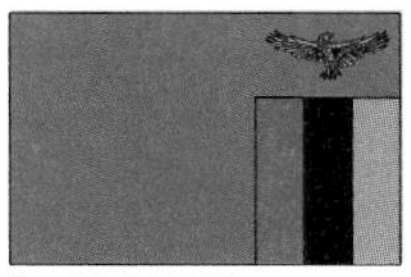

Zambia* 105/E3
Capital: Lusaka
Area: 290,583 sq. mi.
752,610 sq. km.
Population: 9,349,975; growth rate: 2.02%
Government : republic
Independence: October 24, 1964
U.N. Admission: December 1, 1964
Life expectancy: 36 yrs
GDP : $9.7 billion; per capita: $1,060
Currency: Zambian kwacha

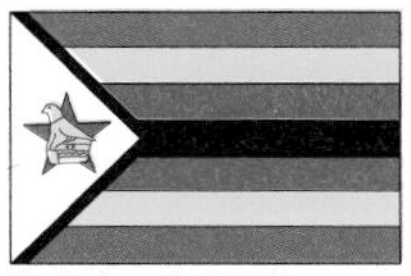

Zimbabwe* 105/E4
Capital: Harare
Area: 150,803 sq. mi.
390,580 sq. km.
Population: 11,423,175; growth rate: 1.26%
Government : parliamentary democracy
Independence: April 18, 1980
U.N. Admission: August 25, 1980
Life expectancy: 41 yrs
GDP : $26.4 billion; per capita: $2,340
Currency: Zimbabwean dollar

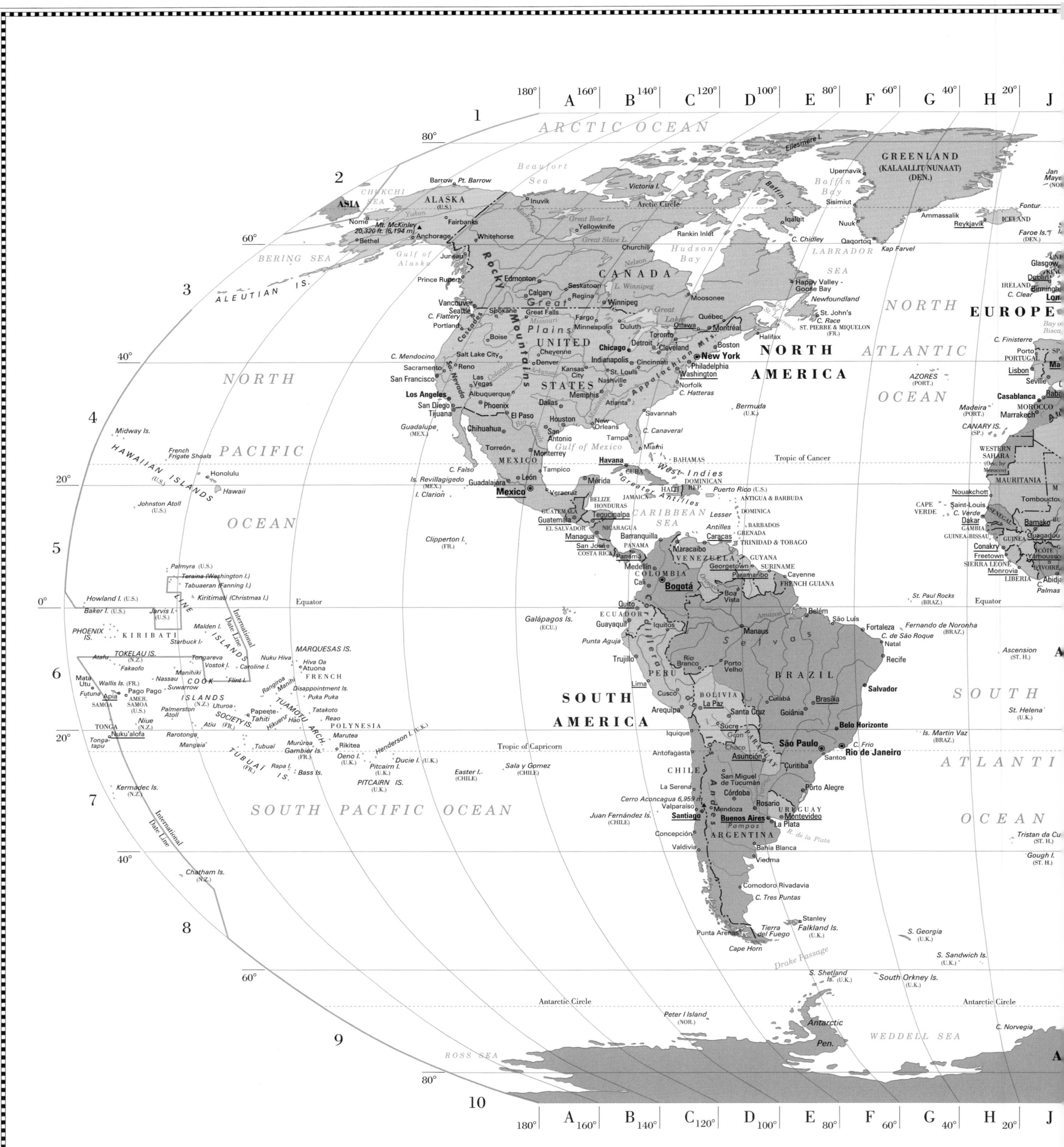

World

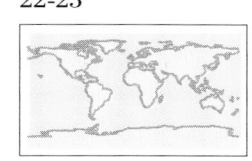

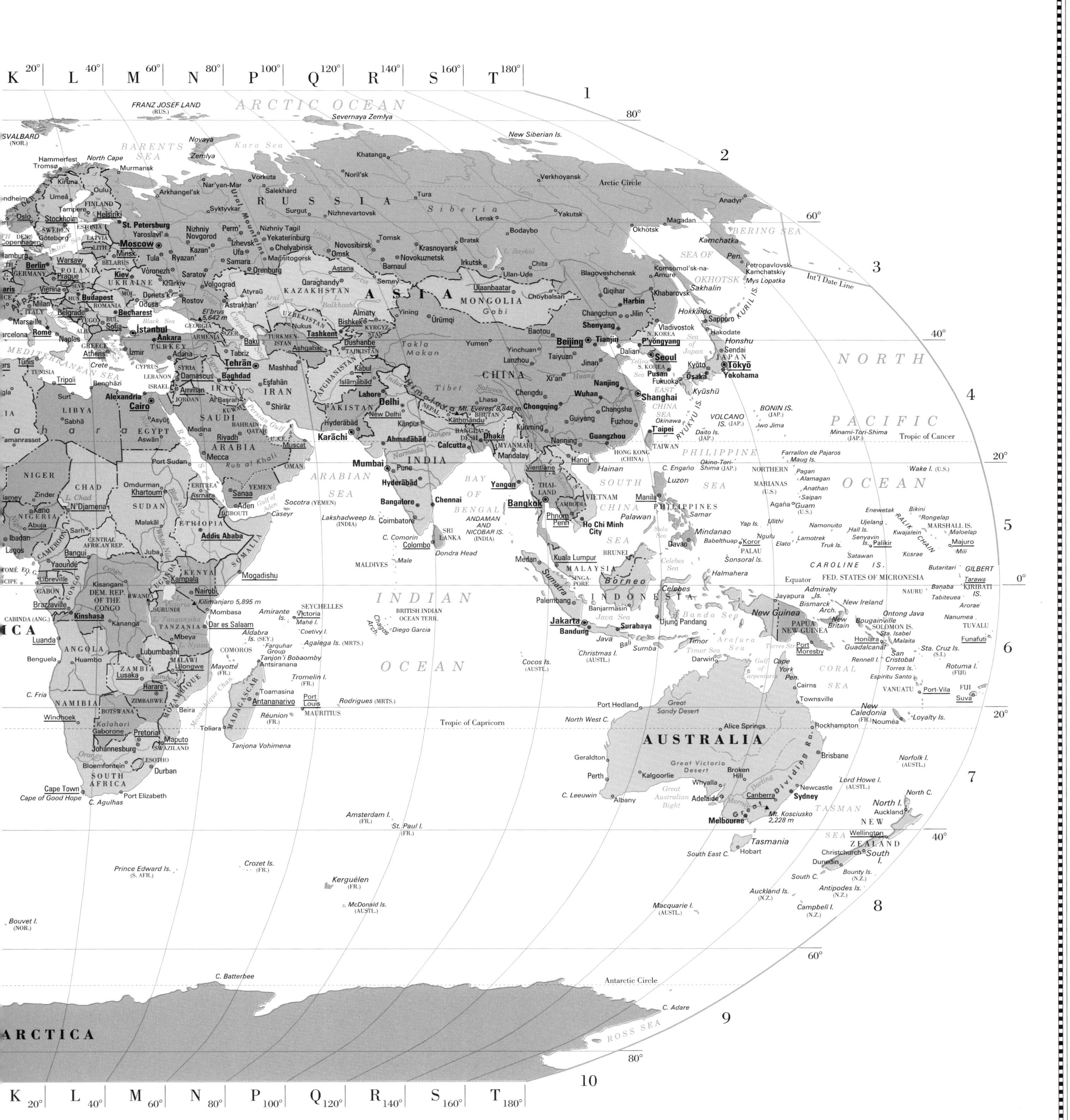

POPULATION OF CITIES AND TOWNS
- ⊛ OVER 5,000,000
- ⊙ 500,000 - 1,999,999
- ◉ 2,000,000 - 4,999,999
- ○ UNDER 500,000

SCALE 1:70,000,000   ROBINSON PROJECTION   STANDARD PARALLELS 38°N AND 38°S

MILES 0 .... 1000 .... 2000 .... 3000 4000
KILOMETERS 0 .... 1000 .... 2000 .... 3000 4000

World - Physical

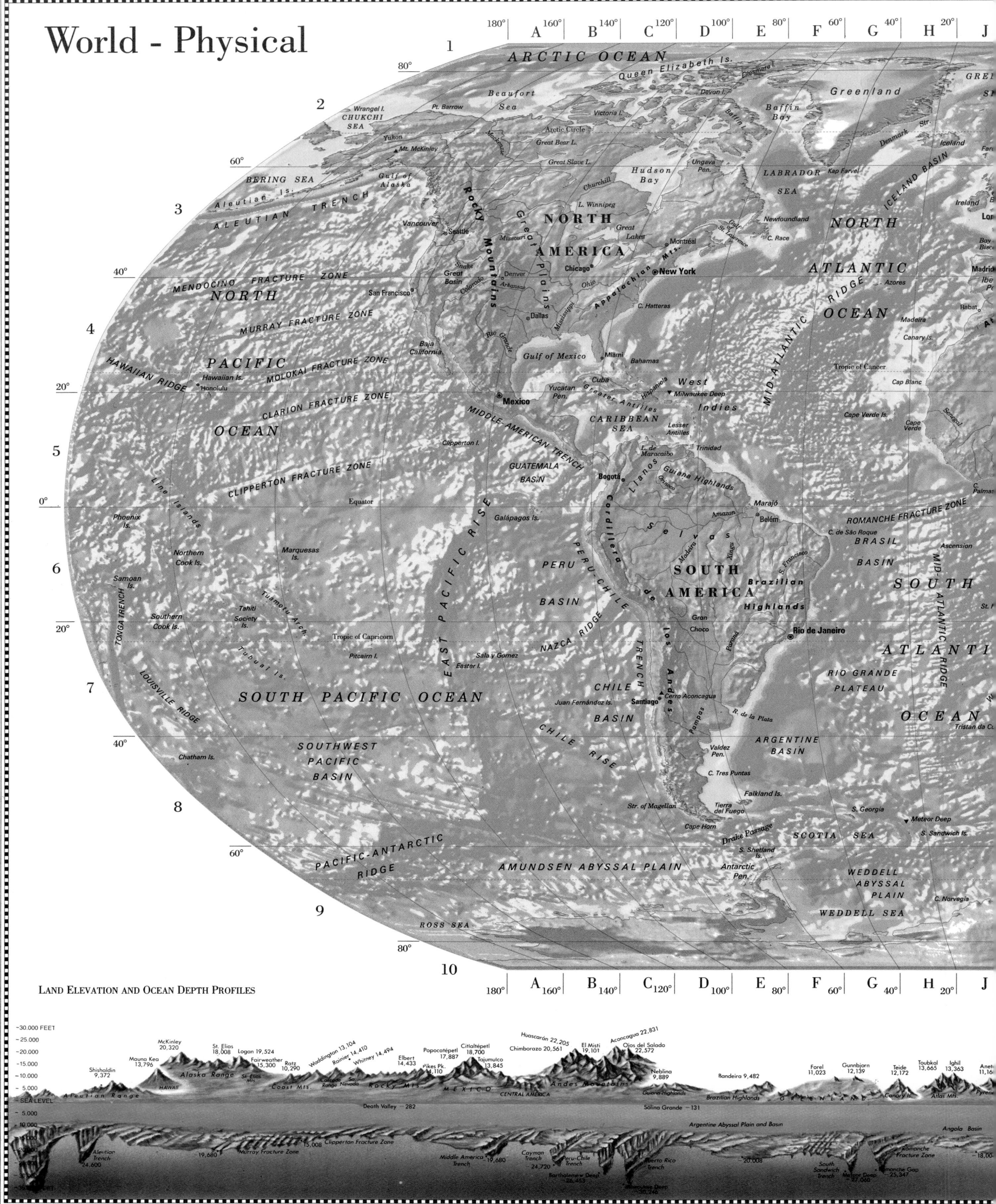

ARCTIC OCEAN
Queen Elizabeth Is.
Ellesmere I.
Greenland
GRE
SM
Beaufort Sea
Devon I.
Baffin Bay
Pt. Barrow
Wrangel I.
CHUKCHI SEA
Victoria I.
Baffin I.
Denmark Str.
Iceland
Yukon
Arctic Circle
Great Bear L.
Str.
Mt. McKinley
Mackenzie
Great Slave L.
Hudson Bay
LABRADOR
Kap Farvel
ICELAND BASIN
BERING SEA
Churchill
Ungava Pen.
SEA
Ireland
Bi.
Aleutian Is.
ALEUTIAN TRENCH
L. Winnipeg
Great Lakes
Montréal
NORTH
NORTH
Lor
Gulf of Alaska
NORTH AMERICA
St. Lawrence
Newfoundland
C. Race
Vancouver
Seattle
Great Plains
Missouri
Chicago
Ohio
Appalachian Mts.
ATLANTIC
Madr
Ibe
Rocky Mountains
Denver
Arkansas
MENDOCINO FRACTURE ZONE
NORTH
Great Basin
Colorado
OCEAN
Azores
San Francisco
Dallas
Mississippi
C. Hatteras
A
MURRAY FRACTURE ZONE
Rio Grande
Madeira
Rabat
PACIFIC
Baja California
Gulf of Mexico
Miami
Bahamas
Canary Is.
Tropic of Cancer
HAWAIIAN RIDGE
Hawaiian Is.
MOLOKAI FRACTURE ZONE
Cuba
Greater Antilles
Hispaniola
West
Cap Blanc
Honolulu
Yucatan Pen.
Milwaukee Deep
Indies
OCEAN
CLARION FRACTURE ZONE
Mexico
CARIBBEAN SEA
Lesser Antilles
Cape Verde Is.
Cape Verde
Clipperton I.
MIDDLE AMERICAN TRENCH
GUATEMALA BASIN
L. de Maracaibo
Trinidad
Senega
CLIPPERTON FRACTURE ZONE
Bogotá
Llanos
Guiana Highlands
C. Palmas
Equator
Galápagos Is.
Cordillera
Orinoco
Amazon
Marajó
Belém
ROMANCHE FRACTURE ZONE
Phoenix Is.
Selvas
Madeira
Xingu
C. de São Roque
BRASIL
Ascension
Northern Cook Is.
Marquesas
PERU
de los
SOUTH AMERICA
São Francisco
BASIN
MID-ATLANTIC RIDGE
SOUTH
Samoan Is.
BASIN
Brazilian Highlands
TONGA TRENCH
Tahiti
Society Is.
Tuamotu Arch.
PERU-CHILE
NAZCA RIDGE
Gran Choco
ATLANTIC
Southern Cook Is.
Tropic of Capricorn
Andes
Paraná
Rio de Janeiro
Pitcairn I.
Sala y Gomez
RIO GRANDE PLATEAU
Easter I.
TRENCH
CHILE
R. de la Plata
OCEAN
LOUISVILLE RIDGE
SOUTH PACIFIC OCEAN
Juan Fernández Is.
Cerro Aconcagua
Tubuai Is.
BASIN
Santiago
Pampas
EAST PACIFIC RISE
ARGENTINE BASIN
Tristan da Cu
Chatham Is.
SOUTHWEST PACIFIC BASIN
Valdez Pen.
CHILE RISE
C. Tres Puntas
Falkland Is.
Str. of Magellan
Tierra del Fuego
S. Georgia
Meteor Deep
PACIFIC-ANTARCTIC RIDGE
Cape Horn
Drake Passage
SCOTIA SEA
S. Sandwich Is.
S. Shetland Is.
AMUNDSEN ABYSSAL PLAIN
Antarctic Pen.
WEDDELL ABYSSAL PLAIN
ROSS SEA
WEDDELL SEA
C. Norvegia

LAND ELEVATION AND OCEAN DEPTH PROFILES

30,000 FEET
25,000
20,000
15,000
10,000
5,000
SEA LEVEL
5,000
10,000

McKinley 20,320
St. Elias 18,008
Logan 19,524
Huascarán 22,205
Aconcagua 22,831
Mauna Kea 13,796
Fairweather 15,300
Ratz 10,290
Waddington 13,104
Rainier 14,410
Popocatépetl 17,887
Citlaltépetl 18,700
Chimborazo 20,561
El Misti 19,101
Ojos del Salado 22,572
Forel 11,023
Gunnbjørn 12,139
Teide 12,172
Toubkal 13,665
Ighil 13,363
Anet 11,16
Shishaldin 9,372
Elbert 14,433
Whitney 14,494
Tajumulco 13,845
Neblina 9,889
Bandeira 9,482
Aleutian Range
Alaska Range
St. Elias Range
Coast Mts.
Range
Nevada
Rocky Mts.
MEXICO
CENTRAL AMERICA
Andes Mountains
Guiana Highlands
Brazilian Highlands
GREENLAND
Canary Is.
Atlas Mts.
Pyrenee
HAWAII
Pikes Pk. 14,110
Death Valley -282
Salina Grande -131
Argentine Abyssal Plain and Basin
Angola Basin
Aleutian Trench 24,600
19,680
Murray Fracture Zone
15,008
Clipperton Fracture Zone
Middle America Trench 19,680
Cayman Trench 24,720
Peru-Chile Trench
Puerto Rico Trench
20,008
South Sandwich Trench
Meteor Deep 27,000
Romanche Gap 25,347
Romanche Fracture Zone
18,0
Bartholomew Deep 26,453
Sandwich Deep
FEET

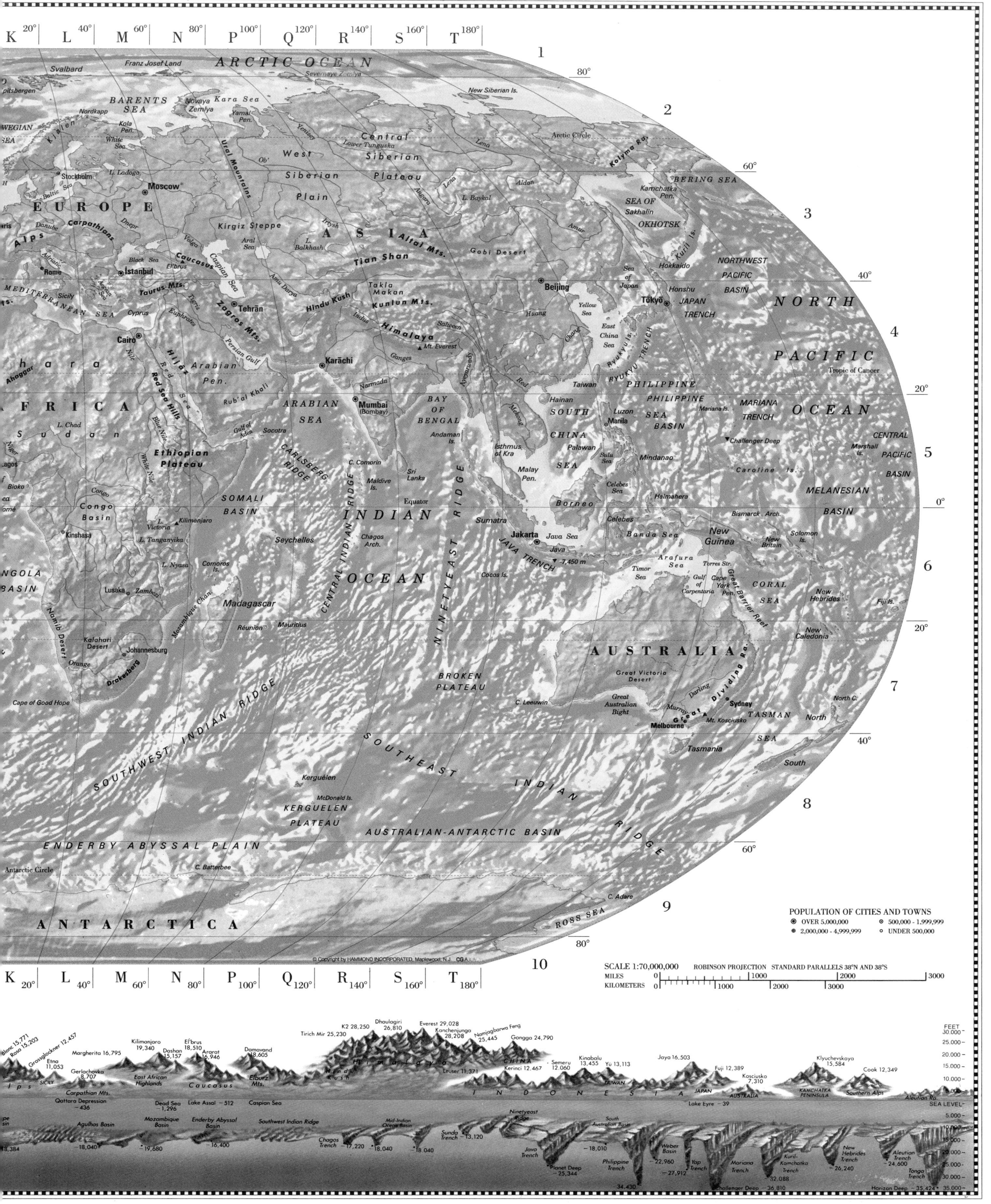

ARCTIC OCEAN

Svalbard
Franz Josef Land
Severnaya Zemlya
New Siberian Is.
80°

Spitsbergen
BARENTS
SEA
Nordkapp
Novaya
Zemlya
Kara Sea
Yamal
Pen.

2
60°

WEGIAN
SEA
Kola
Pen.
White
Sea
L. Ladoga
Yenisey
Lower Tunguska
Central
Siberian
Plateau
Arctic Circle
Kolyma Ra.
BERING SEA

Stockholm
Moscow
West
Siberian
Plain
Ob'
Lena
L. Baykal
Aldan
Kamchatka
Pen.
SEA OF
Sakhalin
OKHOTSK
3

Baltic Sea
EUROPE
Dnepr
Kirgiz Steppe
Irtysh
A S I A
Altai Mts.
Angara
Amur
Kuril Is.
Hokkaido
NORTHWEST
PACIFIC
BASIN
40°

Paris
Danube
Carpathians
Volga
Aral
Sea
L.
Balkhash
Tian Shan
Gobi Desert
Beijing
Sea
of
Japan
Honshu
Tōkyō
JAPAN
TRENCH
NORTH

Alps
Black Sea
Caucasus
Caspian Sea
Elbrus
Amu Darya
Hindu Kush
Takla
Makan
Kunlun Mts.
Huang
Yellow
Sea
Chang
East
China
Sea
RYUKYU TRENCH
4

Rome
Istanbul
Taurus Mts.
Zagros Mts.
Tehrān
Tigris
Indus
Himalaya
▲ Mt. Everest
Salween
Kwangtung
Ryukyu Is.
PACIFIC

MEDITERRANEAN SEA
Sicily
Cyprus
Euphrates
Persian Gulf
Ganges
Mt. Everest
Red
Tropic of Cancer
20°

Cairo
Nile
Hills
Arabian
Pen.
Narmada
Hainan
Taiwan
PHILIPPINE
SEA
BASIN
MARIANA
TRENCH

Sahara
Ahaggar
Red Sea
Mumbai
(Bombay)
BAY
OF
BENGAL
Mekong
SOUTH
CHINA
Luzon
Manila
Mariana Is.
▼ Challenger Deep
Marshall
Is.
OCEAN
CENTRAL
PACIFIC
5

AFRICA
Sudan
L. Chad
Blue Nile
Gulf
of Aden
Socotra
ARABIAN
SEA
CARLSBERG
RIDGE
C. Comorin
Maldive
Is.
Sri Lanka
Andaman
Is.
Isthmus
of Kra
SEA
Palawan
Sulu
Sea
Mindanao
Caroline Is.
MELANESIAN
BASIN

White Nile
Niger
Lagos
Ethiopian
Plateau
SOMALI
BASIN
Seychelles
INDIAN
Equator
Malay
Pen.
Celebes
Sea
Halmahera
0°

Bioko
São Tomé
Congo
Congo
Basin
L.
Victoria
Kilimanjaro
L. Tanganyika
Chagos
Arch.
Sumatra
Jakarta
Java Sea
Celebes
Borneo
Banda Sea
New
Guinea
New
Britain
Solomon
Is.
BASIN

NGOLA
BASIN
Kinshasa
L. Nyasa
Comoros
Is.
CENTRAL INDIAN RIDGE
NINETYEAST RIDGE
OCEAN
JAVA TRENCH
Java −7,450 m
Cocos Is.
Timor
Sea
Arafura
Sea
Bismarck Arch.
New
Hebrides
6

Lusaka
Zambezi
Madagascar
Réunion
Mauritius
Torres Str.
Gulf
of
Carpentaria
Cape
York
Pen.
CORAL
SEA
Fiji Is.
20°

Namib Desert
Orange
Kalahari
Desert
Johannesburg
BROKEN
PLATEAU
AUSTRALIA
Great
Dividing Ra.
New
Caledonia

Cape of Good Hope
Drakensberg
C. Leeuwin
Great Victoria
Desert
Great
Australian
Bight
Darling
Sydney
North C.
7

SOUTHWEST INDIAN RIDGE
SOUTHEAST
INDIAN
Murray
Great
Melbourne
▲ Mt. Kosciusko
TASMAN
North
40°

Kerguélen
McDonald Is.
KERGUELEN
PLATEAU
RIDGE
Tasmania
SEA
South

ENDERBY ABYSSAL PLAIN
AUSTRALIAN-ANTARCTIC BASIN
8
60°

Antarctic Circle
C. Batterbee
C. Adare
9

ANTARCTICA
ROSS SEA
80°
10

POPULATION OF CITIES AND TOWNS
◉ OVER 5,000,000   ⊙ 500,000 - 1,999,999
◉ 2,000,000 - 4,999,999   ○ UNDER 500,000

SCALE 1:70,000,000   ROBINSON PROJECTION   STANDARD PARALLELS 38°N AND 38°S
MILES 0 [___] 1000 [___] 2000 [___] 3000
KILOMETERS 0 [___] 1000 [___] 2000 [___] 3000

Blanc 15,771
Rosa 15,203
Grossglockner 12,457
Etna 11,053
Gerlachovka 8,707
Margherita 16,795
Kilimanjaro 19,340
Dashan 15,157
El'brus 18,510
Ararat 16,946
Damavand 18,605
Tirich Mir 25,230
K2 28,250
Dhaulagiri 26,810
Everest 29,028
Kanchenjunga 28,208
Namjagbarwa Feng 25,445
Gongga 24,790
Leuser 11,371
Kerinci 12,467
Semeru 12,060
Kinabalu 13,455
Yu 13,113
Jaya 16,503
Fuji 12,389
Kosciusko 7,310
Klyuchevskaya 15,584
Cook 12,349
FEET
30,000
25,000
20,000
15,000
10,000

Alps
SICILY
Carpathian Mts.
East African
Highlands
Caucasus
Elburz
Mts.
CHINA
INDONESIA
TAIWAN
JAPAN
AUSTRALIA
KAMCHATKA
PENINSULA
Southern Alps
Aleutian Ra.
SEA LEVEL
5,000

Qattara Depression −436
Dead Sea −1,296
Lake Assal −512
Caspian Sea
Lake Eyre −39
10,000

Agulhas Basin
−18,040
Mozambique
Basin
−19,680
Enderby Abyssal
Basin
−16,400
Southwest Indian Ridge
Mid-Indian
Ocean Basin
Ninetyeast
Ridge
Chagos
Trench
−7,220
−18,040
−18,040
Sunda
Trench
−13,120
South
Australian Basin
15,000

8,384
Java
Trench
Planet Deep
−25,344
Philippine
Trench
−32,088
Weber
Basin
−22,960
Yap
Trench
−27,912
Moriana
Trench
Kuril-
Kamchatka
Trench
−26,240
New
Hebrides
Trench
−24,600
Aleutian
Trench
Tonga
Trench
20,000
25,000
30,000
35,000

Challenger Deep −36,810
Horizon Deep −35,424
34,430

Europe

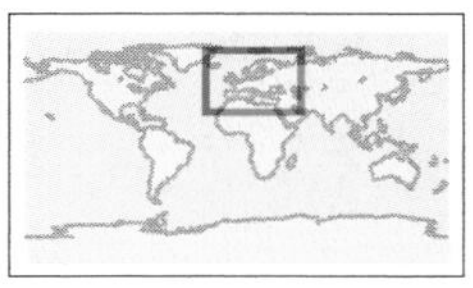

The terrain in this high-oblique, northwest-looking image, is indicative of the rugged, mountainous landscape characterizing most of Greece. Two major landform regions are captured in this image: the northwest to southeast-trending Mountains of Pindus in central Greece (north of the Gulf of Corinth), and the Peloponnisos Peninsula (south of the Gulf of Corinth). The Pindus, a massive continuation of the Dinaric Alps of Albania and the former Yugoslavia, make the land inhospitable and travel difficult. This rugged terrain caused the Greeks to become a seafaring people.

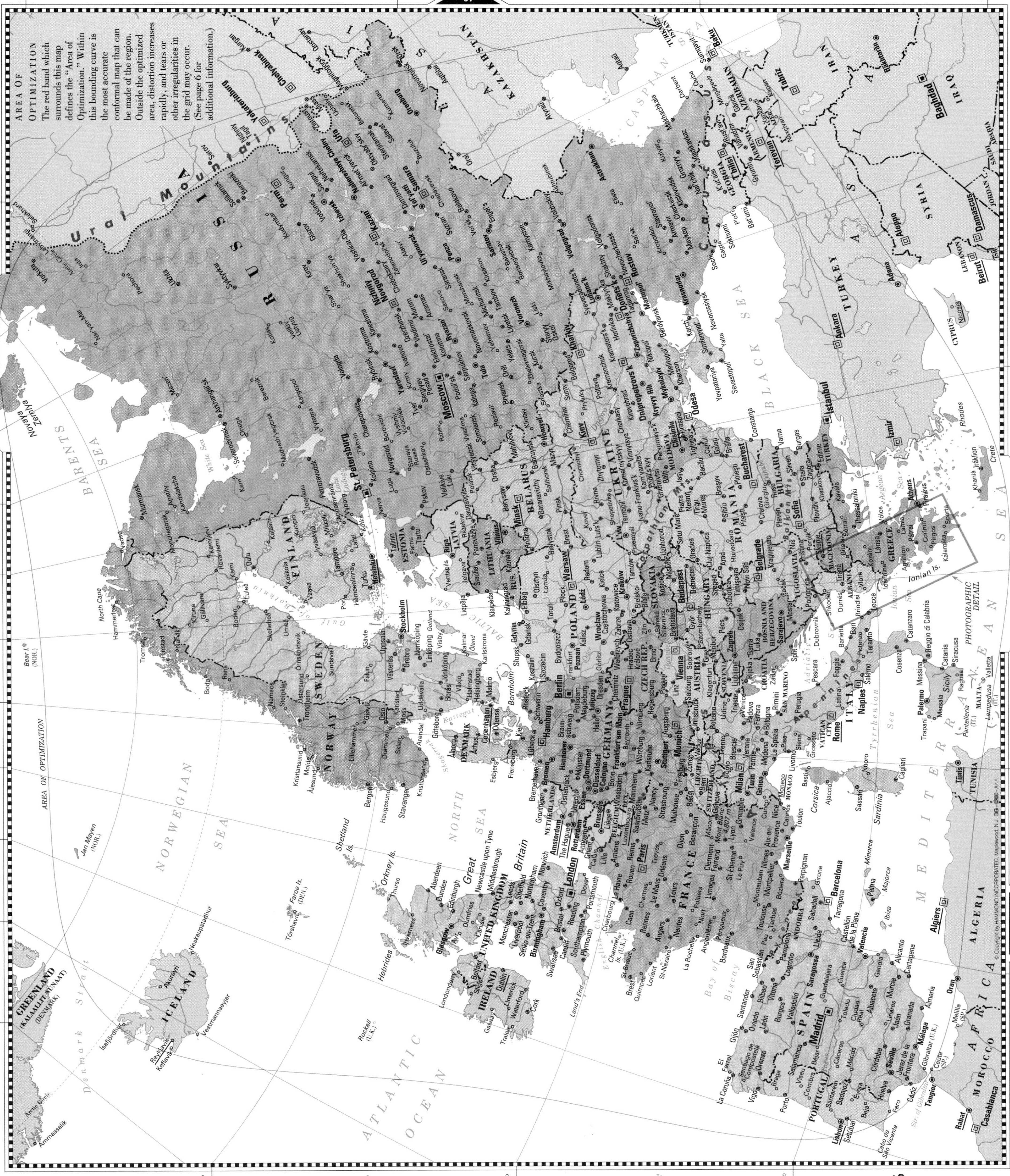

AREA OF OPTIMIZATION The red band which surrounds this map defines the "Area of Optimization." Within this bounding curve is the most accurate conformal map that can be made of the region. Outside the optimized area, distortion increases rapidly, and tears or other irregularities in the grid may occur. (See page 6 for additional information.)

POPULATION OF CITIES AND TOWNS

- ▣ OVER 3,000,000
- ▣ 1,000,000 - 2,999,999
- ● 500,000 - 999,999
- ● 100,000 - 499,999
- ○ UNDER 100,000

SCALE 1:18,000,000   OPTIMAL CONFORMAL PROJECTION

MILES 0 — 300 — 600 — 900

KILOMETERS 0 — 300 — 600 — 900

● Reykjavik 30°

Oslo 25° Helsinki 23° Moscow 12° Samara 2°

London 30° Berlin 30° Kiev 19°

Paris 39°

Madrid 41° Rome 45° Belgrade 30°

Athens 48°

● Athens 48°
Average January temperature
degrees Fahrenheit at
selected stations

AVERAGE JANUARY TEMPERATURE

● Reykjavik 48°

Oslo 63° Helsinki 61° Moscow 66° Samara 64°

London 63° Berlin 64° Kiev 68°

Paris 66°

Madrid 75° Rome 77° Belgrade 73°

Athens 81°

● Athens 81°
Average July temperature
degrees Fahrenheit at
selected stations

AVERAGE JULY TEMPERATURE

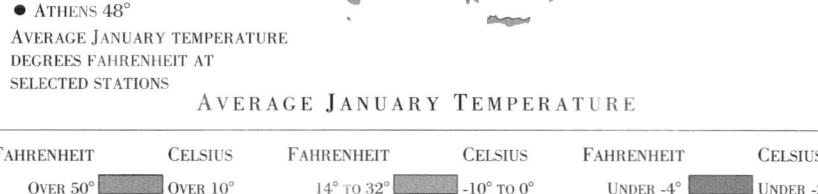

Fahrenheit	Celsius	Fahrenheit	Celsius	Fahrenheit	Celsius
Over 50°	Over 10°	14° to 32°	-10° to 0°	Under -4°	Under -20°
32° to 50°	0° to 10°	-4° to 14°	-20° to -10°		

Fahrenheit	Celsius	Fahrenheit	Celsius
Over 68°	Over 20°	32° to 50°	0° to 10°
50° to 68°	10° to 20°	Under 32°	Under 0°

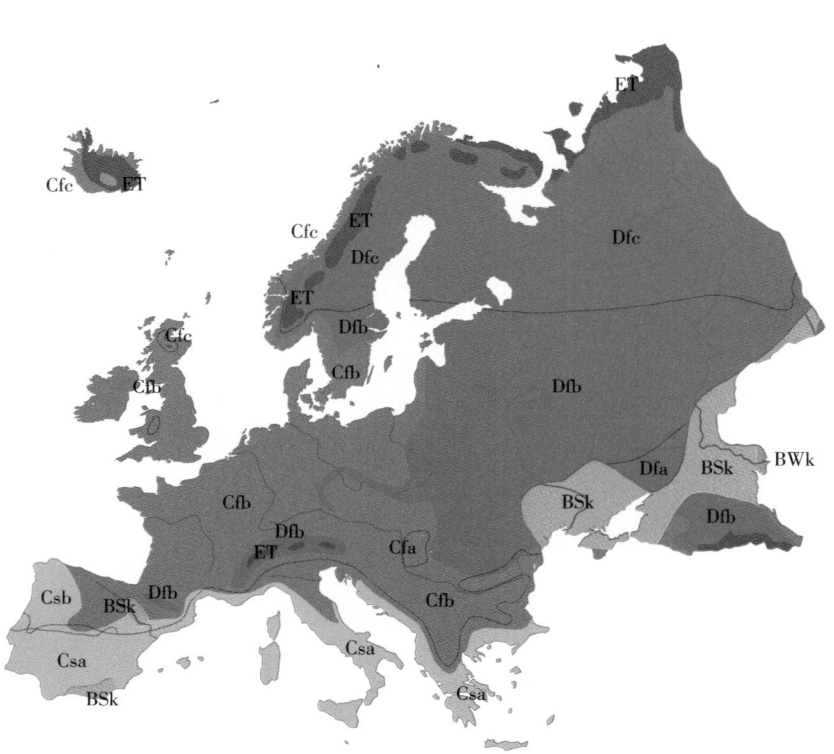

ET

Cfc ET

Cfc ET Dfc

Cfc Dfc

ET Dfb

Cfc Cfb

Cfb Dfb

Cfb Dfa BSk BWk

BSk

Dfb Dfb

Cfb Dfb Cfa

ET

Csb BSk

Csa Dfb Csa

BSk Csa

CLIMATE

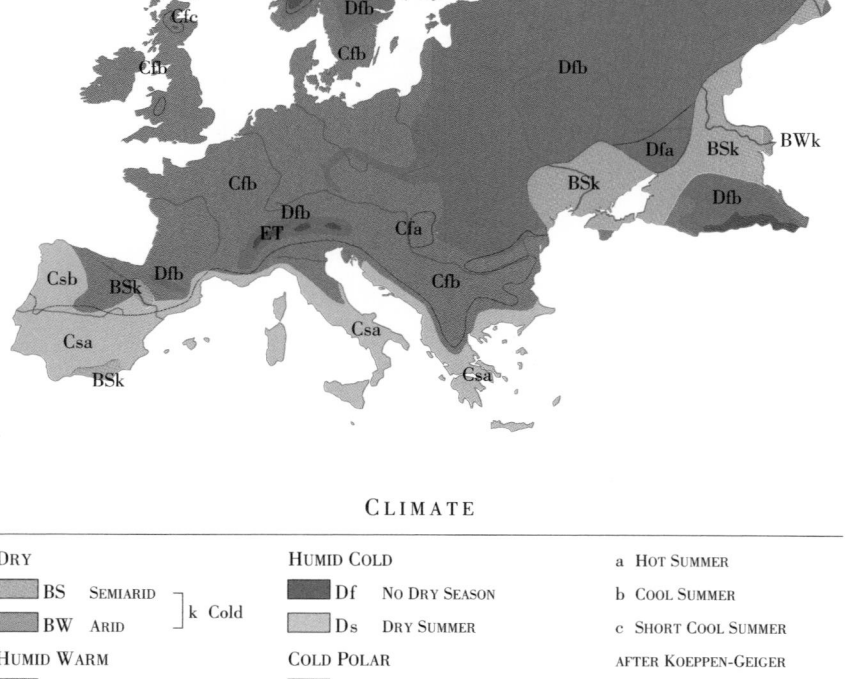

Dry

| | BS | Semiarid | } k Cold |
| | BW | Arid | |

Humid Warm

| | Cf | No Dry Season |
| | Cs | Dry Summer |

Humid Cold

| | Df | No Dry Season |
| | Ds | Dry Summer |

Cold Polar

| | ET | Short Cool Summer, Long Cold Winter |
| | EF | Perpetual Frost |

a Hot Summer
b Cool Summer
c Short Cool Summer

After Koeppen-Geiger

VEGETATION

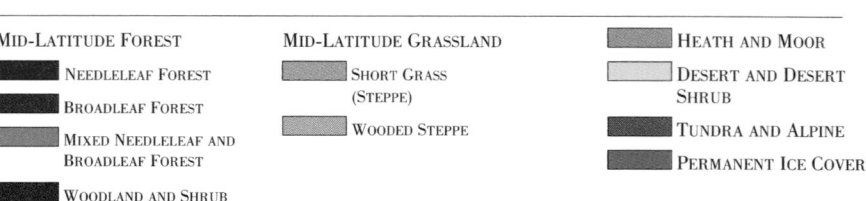

Mid-Latitude Forest

	Needleleaf Forest
	Broadleaf Forest
	Mixed Needleleaf and Broadleaf Forest
	Woodland and Shrub (Mediterranean)

Mid-Latitude Grassland

| | Short Grass (Steppe) |
| | Wooded Steppe |

	Heath and Moor
	Desert and Desert Shrub
	Tundra and Alpine
	Permanent Ice Cover

Europe - Geographical Comparisons

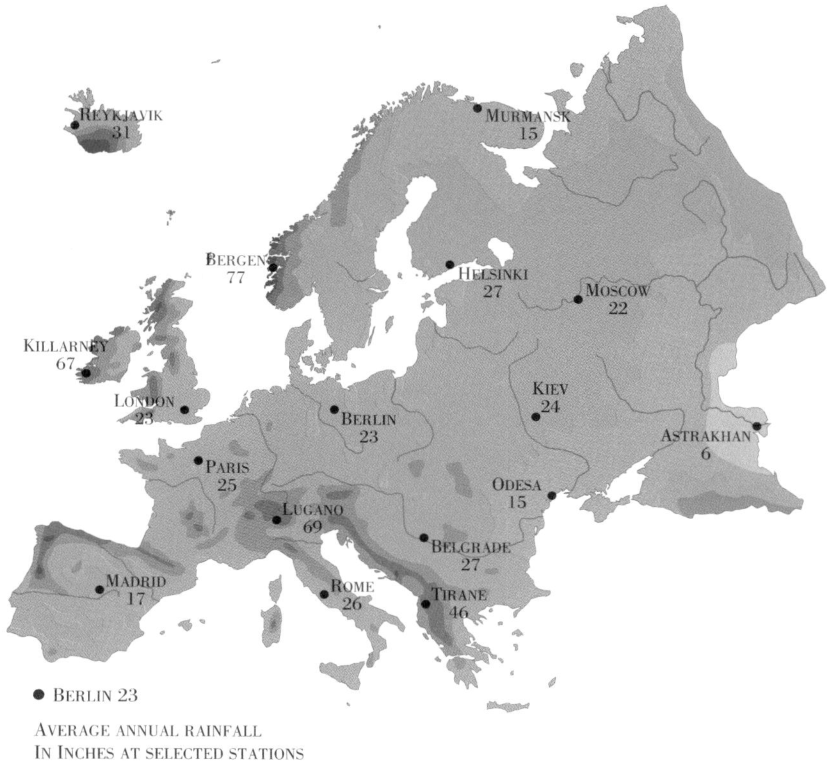

AVERAGE ANNUAL RAINFALL

REYKJAVIK 31

MURMANSK 15

BERGEN 77

HELSINKI 27

MOSCOW 22

KILLARNEY 67

KIEV 24

LONDON 23

BERLIN 23

ASTRAKHAN 6

PARIS 25

LUGANO 69

ODESA 15

BELGRADE 27

MADRID 17

ROME 26

TIRANE 46

● BERLIN 23

AVERAGE ANNUAL RAINFALL
IN INCHES AT SELECTED STATIONS

AVERAGE ANNUAL RAINFALL

INCHES	CM	INCHES	CM	INCHES	CM
OVER 80	OVER 200	40 TO 60	100 TO 150	10 TO 20	25 TO 50
60 TO 80	150 TO 200	20 TO 40	50 TO 100	UNDER 10	UNDER 25

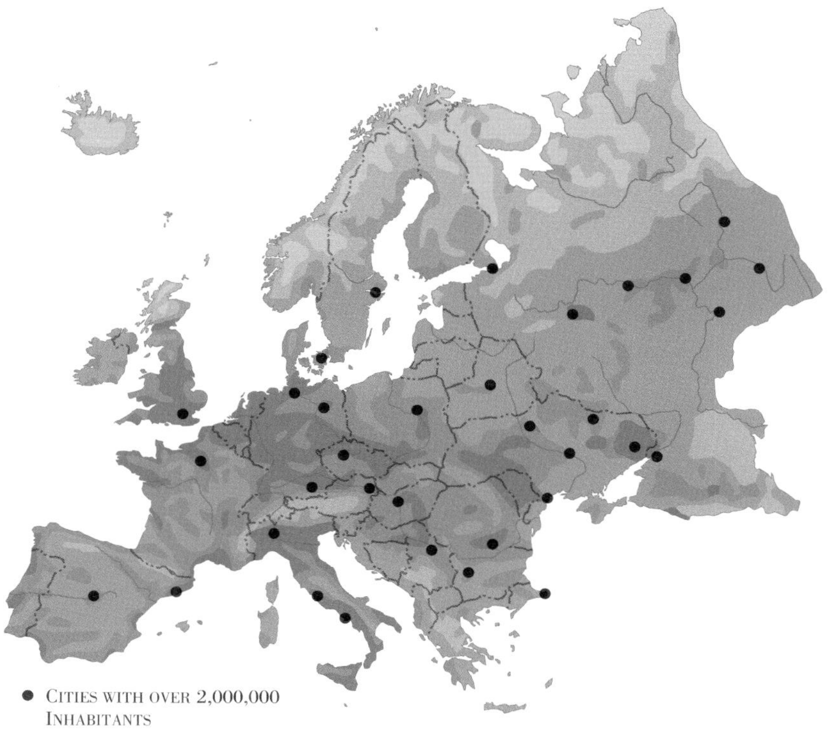

POPULATION DISTRIBUTION

● CITIES WITH OVER 2,000,000
INHABITANTS

POPULATION DISTRIBUTION

DENSITY PER		SQ. MI.	SQ. KM.	SQ. MI.	SQ. KM.
SQ. MI.	SQ. KM.	130 TO 260	50 TO 100	3 TO 25	1 TO 10
OVER 260	OVER 100	25 TO 130	10 TO 50	UNDER 3	UNDER 1

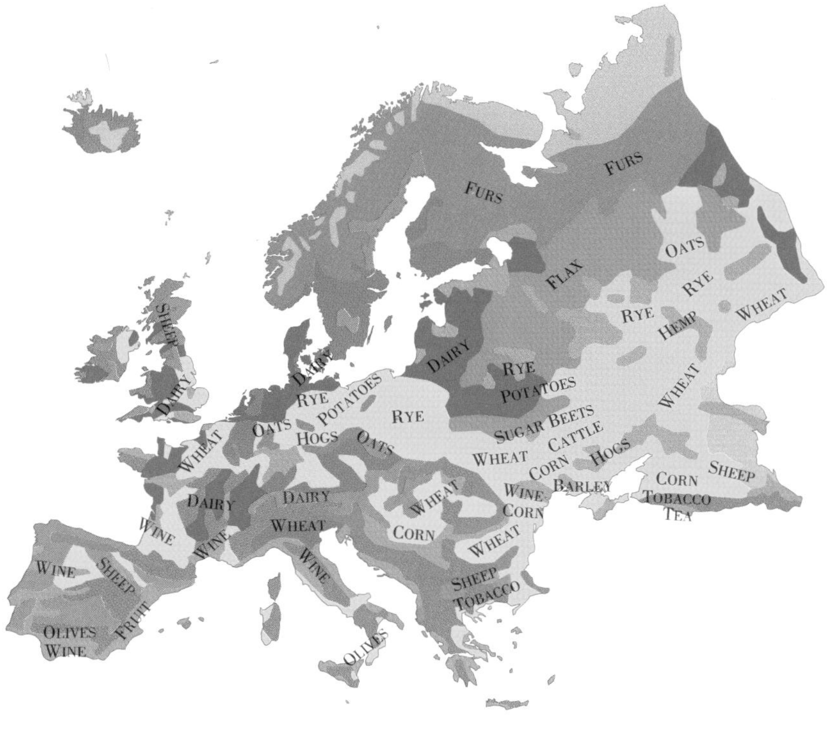

LAND USE

FURS

FURS

FURS

OATS

FLAX

RYE

RYE

WHEAT

DAIRY

HEMP

RYE

POTATOES

WHEAT

DAIRY

RYE

POTATOES

RYE

WHEAT

OATS

HOGS

SUGAR BEETS

CATTLE

WHEAT

CORN

HOGS

SHEEP

DAIRY

DAIRY

WHEAT

WINE

CORN

BARLEY

CORN

TOBACCO

TEA

WINE

WINE

CORN

WHEAT

WINE

SHEEP

WHEAT

OLIVES

FRUIT

SHEEP

WINE

TOBACCO

OLIVES

LAND USE

CEREALS, LIVESTOCK	FRUIT AND TRUCK FARMING	GENERAL FARMING, LIVESTOCK	
DAIRY, LIVESTOCK	PASTURE LIVESTOCK		
LIVESTOCK HERDING	DAIRY, CEREALS	FORESTS	
SPECIAL CROPS		NONPRODUCTIVE	

MINERAL RESOURCES

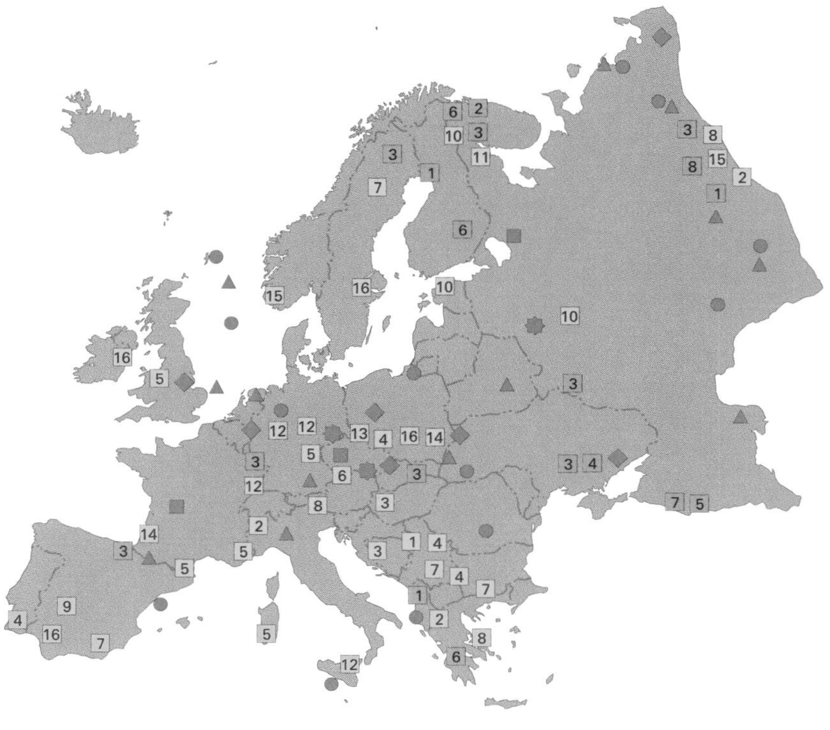

MINERAL RESOURCES

ENERGY & FUELS

◆ COAL
⬡ LIGNITE
▲ NATURAL GAS
● PETROLEUM
■ URANIUM

IRON & FERROALLOYS

1 CHROMIUM
2 COBALT
3 IRON ORE
4 MANGANESE
5 MOLYBDENUM
6 NICKEL
7 TUNGSTEN
8 VANADIUM

OTHER MAJOR RESOURCES

1 ANTIMONY
2 ASBESTOS
3 BAUXITE
4 COPPER
5 FLORSPAR
6 GRAPHITE
7 LEAD
8 MAGNESITE
9 MERCURY
10 PHOSPHATES
11 PLATINUM
12 POTASH
13 SILVER
14 SULFER
15 TITANIUM
16 ZINC

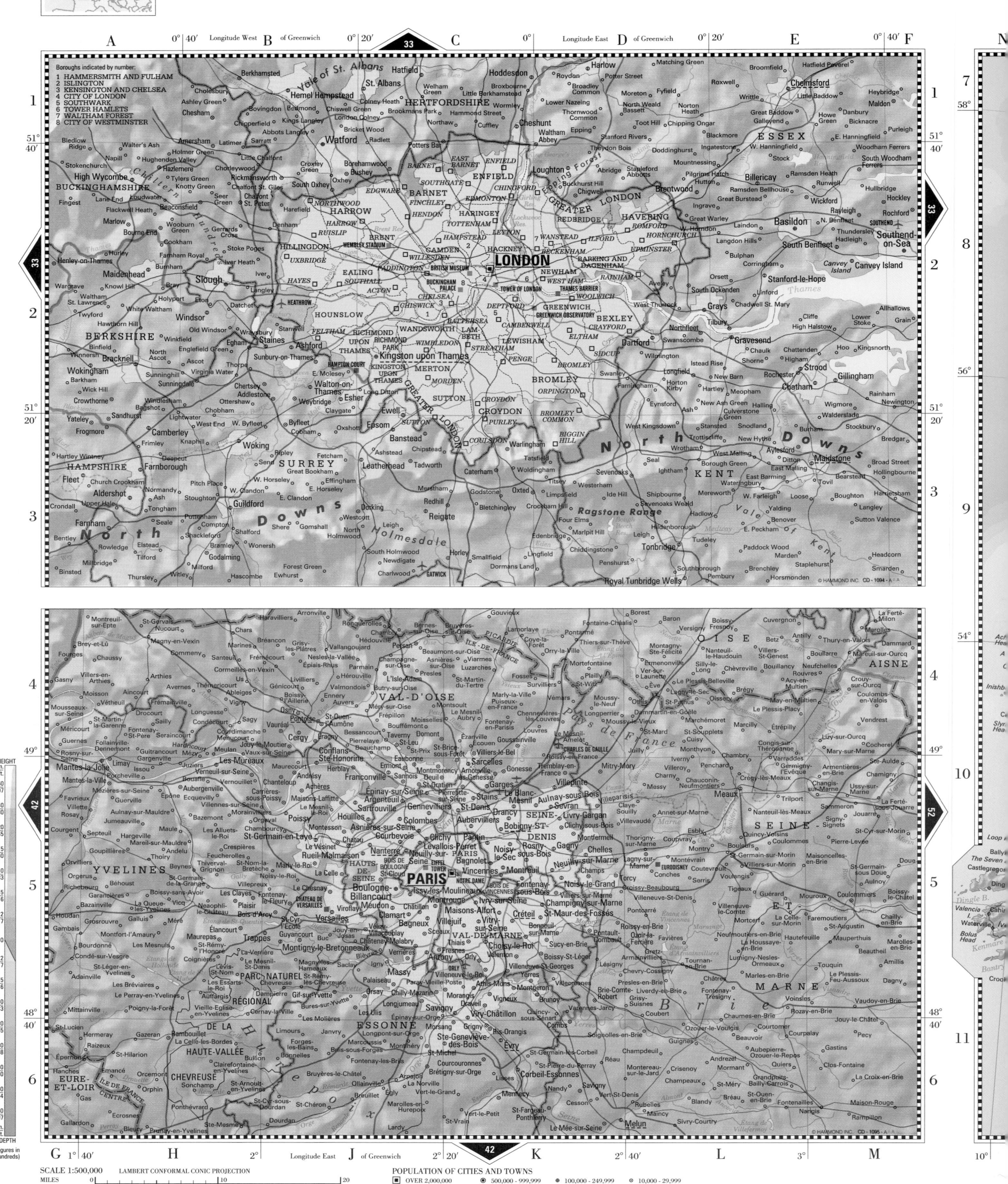

SCALE 1:500,000   LAMBERT CONFORMAL CONIC PROJECTION

MILES

KILOMETERS

POPULATION OF CITIES AND TOWNS

□ OVER 2,000,000   ● 500,000 - 999,999   ● 100,000 - 249,999   ○ 10,000 - 29,999
□ 1,000,000 - 1,999,999   □ 250,000 - 499,999   ● 30,000 - 99,999   ○ UNDER 10,000

HEIGHT
m.   ft.
60 197
40 130
20   65
15   50
10   33
5   16
2   7
0   0
2   7
5   16
10   33
20   65
30   98
40 130
50 164
60 197
m.   ft.
DEPTH
(Figures in
Hundreds)

Boroughs indicated by number:
1. HAMMERSMITH AND FULHAM
2. ISLINGTON
3. KENSINGTON AND CHELSEA
4. CITY OF LONDON
5. SOUTHWARK
6. TOWER HAMLETS
7. WALTHAM FOREST
8. CITY OF WESTMINSTER

United Kingdom, Ireland

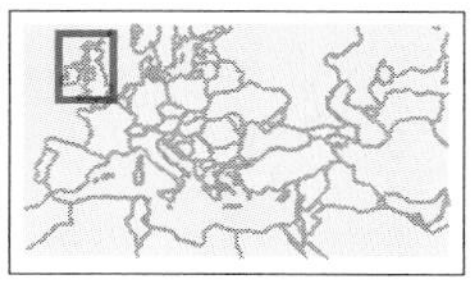

Inset (top right): Shetland Is. / Orkney Is.

Same scale as main map

Shetland Is. (U.K.)

Herma Ness, Yell, Unst, Point of Fethaland, Hillswick, Esha Ness, Mid Yell, Whalsay, Walls, Mainland, Aith, Scalloway, Bressay, Lerwick, Foula, Hoswick, Fitful Head, Sumburgh Head

ATLANTIC OCEAN

NORTH SEA

Fair Isle

Papa Westray, Westray, N. Ronaldsay, Hollandstoun, Start Pt., Pierowall, Rousay, Eday, Sanday, Stronsay, Brough Head, Mainland, Finstown, Kirkwall, Downby, Stromness, **Orkney Is.**, Saint Mary's, Saint Margaret's Hope, S. Ronaldsay, OLD MAN OF HOY, Hoy, Lyness, Duncansby Head

Map continued at left

© HAMMOND INC. CD-1096

SCOTLAND

Main map

ATLANTIC OCEAN

Outer Hebrides — St. Kilda, Lewis, Butt of Lewis, Port of Ness, North Tolsta, Carloway, Stornoway, Tarbert, Harris, North Uist, Benbecula, South Uist, Barra, Barra Head

Inner Hebrides — I. of Skye, The Storr 719 m, Portree, Rhum, Eigg, Muck, Coll, Tiree, Iona, I. of Mull, Ben More 966 m, Colonsay, Islay, Jura, Rhinns Pt., Mull of Oa

The Minch, Little Minch, Sea of the Hebrides

SCOTLAND — North West Highlands, Cape Wrath, Tongue, Thurso, Dunnet Head, Duncansby Head, John O'Groats, Scourie, Ben Hope 927 m, Kinbrace, Wick, Ullapool, Inchnadamph, Ben More Assynt 998 m, Berriedale, Dornoch Firth, Tain, Dingwall, Inverness, Nairn, Forres, Elgin, Buckie, Banff, Fraserburgh, Kinnairds Head, Peterhead, Huntly, Turriff, Maud, Cruden Bay, Grantown, Aviemore, Ben Macdui 1,309 m, Aberdeen, Girdle Ness, Grampian Mts., Braemar, Ballater, Aboyne, Banchory, Stonehaven, Montrose, Forfar, Arbroath, Perth, Dundee, Saint Andrews, Crieff, Callander, Stirling, Kinross, Cupar, Fife Ness, Dunfermline, Kirkcaldy, Firth of Forth, EDINBURGH, GLASGOW, Paisley, Hamilton, Motherwell, Airdrie, Greenock, Ayr, Kilmarnock, Prestwick, Troon, Irvine, Kintyre, Mull of Kintyre, Campbeltown, Goat Fell 874 m, I. of Arran, I. of Bute, Southern Uplands, Merrick 843 m, Dumfries, Lockerbie, Moffat, Broad Law 840 m, Hawick, Cheviot Hills, The Cheviot 817 m, Peebles, Galashiels, Selkirk, Kelso, Berwick-upon-Tweed

NORTHERN IRELAND — Londonderry, Coleraine, Ballymena, Larne, Antrim, Lurgan, BELFAST, Lisburn, Armagh, Newry, Omagh, Enniskillen, Strabane, Dungannon, Downpatrick, Slieve Donard 852 m

Isle of Man — Ramsey, Douglas, Peel, Point of Ayre, Spanish Head

IRELAND — Donegal Bay, Sligo, Galway, DUBLIN, Dún Laoghaire, Bray, Wicklow, Lugnaquillia 926 m, Wexford, Waterford, Cork, Limerick, Tralee, Killarney, MUNSTER, LEINSTER, CONNACHT, Mt. Leinster 796 m, Mizen Head, Hook Head

WALES — Cambrian Mts., Snowdonia, Isle of Anglesey, Caernarfon, Aberystwyth, Cardigan Bay, Cardigan, Llandudno, Wrexham, Newtown, Welshpool, Brecon Beacons, Merthyr Tydfil, CARDIFF, Newport, Swansea, St. George's Channel, Bristol Channel

ENGLAND — Carlisle, Cumbrian Mts., LAKE DISTRICT NP, Cross Fell 893 m, Pennine Chain, Newcastle upon Tyne, Sunderland, Durham, Middlesbrough, Hartlepool, Scarborough, Lancaster, Barrow-in-Furness, Whitby, YORK, NORTH YORK MOORS NP, Harrogate, LEEDS, Bradford, Blackpool, Preston, Blackburn, MANCHESTER, LIVERPOOL, Stockport, Sheffield, Kingston upon Hull, Grimsby, Cleethorpes, Scunthorpe, Doncaster, Rotherham, Chesterfield, Lincoln, Stoke-on-Trent, Derby, NOTTINGHAM, Crewe, Chester, Shrewsbury, Wolverhampton, West Bromwich, BIRMINGHAM, Coventry, Leicester, Peterborough, PEAK DISTRICT NP, Norwich, Great Yarmouth, Lowestoft, THE BROADS NP, King's Lynn, The Wash, Worcester, Hereford, Gloucester, Cheltenham, Stratford-upon-Avon, Northampton, Bedford, Cambridge, Bury Saint Edmunds, Ipswich, Colchester, Oxford, Milton Keynes, Luton, Stevenage, Harlow, Chelmsford, Southend, Bristol, Bath, Swindon, Reading, LONDON, Gravesend, Maidstone, Canterbury, Dover, Folkestone, Ashford, Royal Tunbridge Wells, Hastings, Brighton, Eastbourne, Beachy Head, Worthing, Crawley, Guildford, Basingstoke, Winchester, Southampton, Portsmouth, Isle of Wight, Bournemouth, Poole, Dorchester, Weymouth, Bill of Portland, Salisbury Plain, SOUTH DOWNS, NORTH DOWNS, Chilterns, Cotswolds, MENDIP HILLS, EXMOOR NP, DARTMOOR NP, Taunton, Exeter, Plymouth, Torquay, Paignton, Newton Abbot, Bodmin, Truro, Penzance, Land's End, Isles of Scilly, Lizard Pt., Lyme Bay

Irish Sea, **Celtic Sea**, **NORTH SEA**, **Great Britain**, **UNITED KINGDOM**, **ENGLISH CHANNEL**

FRANCE — Boulogne-sur-Mer, Cap Gris-Nez, Saint-Martin

© Copyright by HAMMOND INCORPORATED, Maplewood, N.J. CD-1004

Scale

SCALE 1:3,000,000 — LAMBERT CONFORMAL CONIC PROJECTION

MILES 0 50 100 150
KILOMETERS 0 50 100 150

Longitude West of Greenwich / Longitude East of Greenwich

HEIGHT / DEPTH (Figures in Hundreds)

Southern England and Wales

E 1° 35 F 0°

Scolt Head
Wells-next-the-Sea Sheringham
Hunstanton Weybourne Overstrand
Heacham Docking Cromer
Snettisham Walsingham Mundesley
Dersingham Holt North Walsham
THE BROADS NP Stalham
Sutton Bridge King's Lynn Reepham Cawston Coltishall Hoveton Norfolk
Castle Acre North Elmham Taverham NORWICH Wroxham Broads
East Dereham Costessey Caister-on-Sea
Swaffham Watton NORFOLK Norwich Sprowston
LEICESTERSHIRE Downham Market Wymondham Brundall Great Yarmouth
Feltwell Mundford Reedham Beltom
The Southery Loddon
Fens Manea Littleport Breckland Brandon Thetford Bungay Beccles Lowestoft
Bedford Ely Lakenheath Harleston Kessingland
Level Isle of Stretham East Diss Reydon
Ely Mildenhall Anglia Halesworth Southwold
Huntingdon Soham Ixworth Stanton Eye Leiston-cum-Sizewell
Saint Ives Isleham Great Barton Framlingham Saxmundham
CAMBRIDGESHIRE Newmarket Bury Saint Elmswell Debenham
Bar Hill Moulton Edmunds SUFFOLK Aldeburgh
Cambridge Fulbourn Stowmarket Needham Market Orford
CAMBRIDGE Great Shelford Kesgrave Woodbridge Orford Ness
Linton Haverhill Sudbury Claydon Hollesley
Saffron Walden Sible Hedingham Capel Saint Mary Ipswich
Great Halstead Nayland Holbrook Shotley
Cornard East Bergholt Mistley Harwich Felixstowe
HERTFORD- Bocking Earls Colne Manningtree Parkeston Hoek Van Holland
SHIRE STANSTED Braintree West Bergholt Horsey I. Zeebrugge
Great Dunmow Coggeshall Colchester Wivenhoe
Bishop's Stortford Kelvedon Thorpe-le-Soken The Naze Oostende
Hertford ESSEX Tiptree Brightlingsea Walton-on-the-Naze
Ware Witham West Mersea Frinton
Harlow Clacton-on-Sea Jaywick
Chelmsford Maldon
Hoddesdon Writtle Danbury Mayland NORTH
Epping Chipping Ongar Southminster
South Woodham Burnham SEA
Waltham Abbey Pilgrims Hatch Ferrers Foulness Pt.
Brentwood Wickford Rayleigh Rochford Foulness I.
Basildon Benfleet SOUTHEND
Havencore Pt.
Stanford-le- Canvey Southend
Hope Island Shoeburyness
Grain Warden Pt. Vlissingen
Tilbury Sheerness Isle of
Grays Queenborough Sheppey Margate Foreness Pt.
Northfleet Gravesend Leysdown North Foreland
Dartford Rochester Shell Ness Herne Saint Peter's Broadstairs
Hartley Chatham Milton Whitstable Bay Swalecliffe Isle of Thanet Ramsgate
Ash Gillingham Faversham Broughton Street Minster Pegwell
Snodland Sittingbourne Bay
Eynsford Aylesford Sturry Sandwich
Maidstone CANTERBURY CATHEDRAL Wingham
KENT Canterbury Eastry Deal
Vale of Kent Challock Wye Aylesham
Headcorn Brabourne Saint Margaret's
Staplehurst Lees at Cliffe South Foreland
NORTH SEA
Tonbridge Paddock Wood Pembury Capel le Ferne Dover Zeebrugge
Royal Tunbridge Wells Tenterden Romney Hythe Folkestone Oostende
Wadhurst Marsh Dymchurch
Ticehurst Channel Tunnel Calais
Robertsbridge Rye New Romney Calais
Heathfield Lydd FERRYFIELD Sangatte
Battle Winchelsea Dungeness Cap Blanc Nez
Herstmonceux Hastings Rye Bay
HASTINGS BATTLESITE FRANCE
(1066) Bexhill Cap Gris-Nez Wimereux
Hailsham Langney Pt. Boulogne-sur-Mer Saint-Martin
Pevensey Le Portel
Eastbourne Équihen Outreau Saint
Saint-Étienne Léonard
Beachy Hardelot-Plage
Head Neufchâtel-Hardelot
PICARDIE
Le Touquet-Paris-Plage

SCALE 1:1,000,000 LAMBERT CONFORMAL CONIC PROJECTION

POPULATION OF CITIES AND TOWNS

- OVER 2,000,000
- 1,000,000 - 1,999,999
- 500,000 - 999,999
- 250,000 - 499,999
- 100,000 - 249,999
- 30,000 - 99,999
- 10,000 - 29,999
- UNDER 10,000

SCALE 1:1,000,000   LAMBERT CONFORMAL CONIC PROJECTION

MILES 0 10 20 30 40 50

KILOMETERS 0 10 20 30 40 50

Longitude West of Greenwich   Longitude East of Greenwich

© Copyright by HAMMOND INCORPORATED, Maplewood, N.J.

Central Scotland

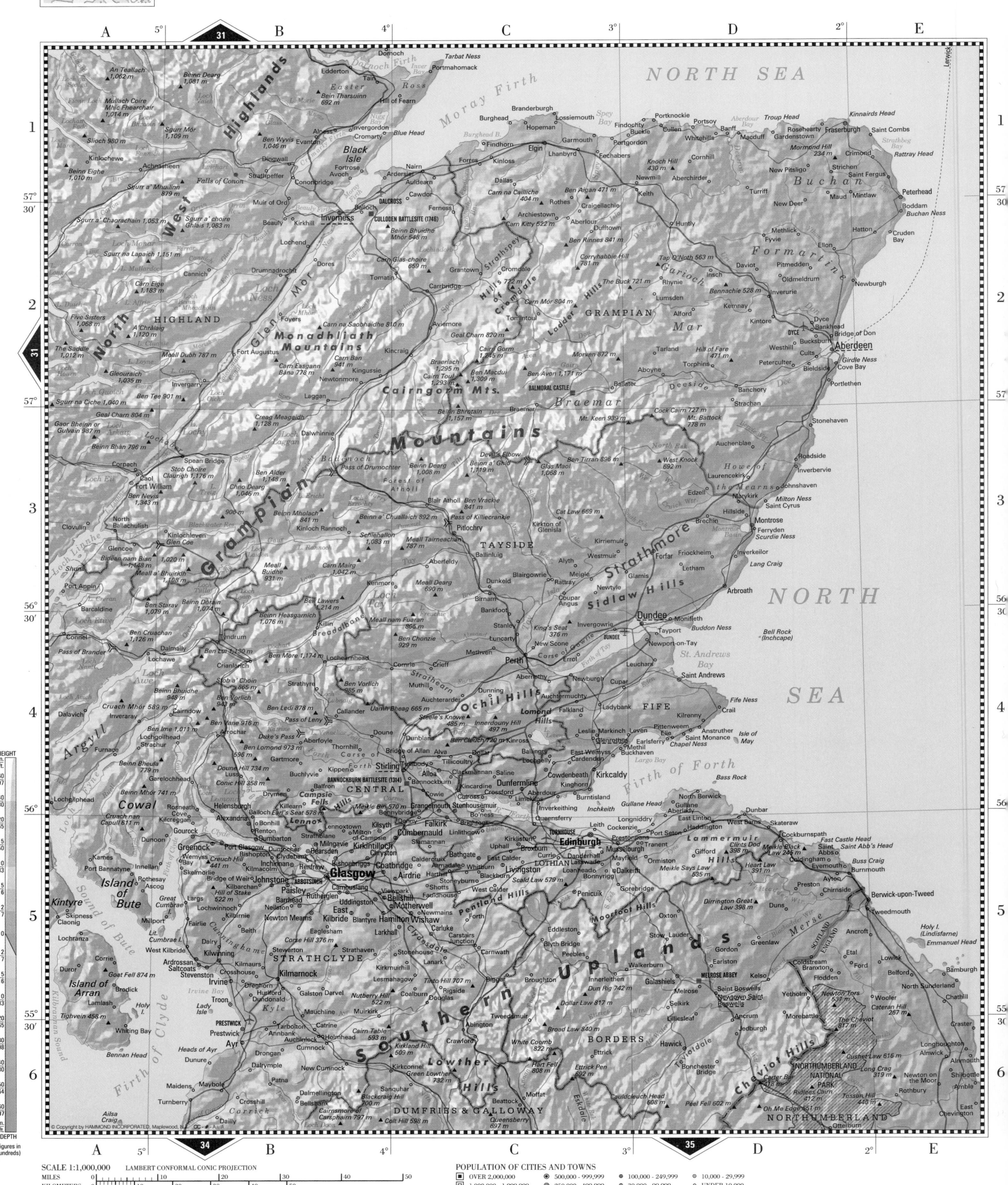

SCALE 1:1,000,000   LAMBERT CONFORMAL CONIC PROJECTION

MILES 0   10   20   30   40   50

KILOMETERS 0   10   20   30

POPULATION OF CITIES AND TOWNS

▪ OVER 2,000,000   ● 500,000 - 999,999   ● 100,000 - 249,999   ○ 10,000 - 29,999
▫ 1,000,000 - 1,999,999   ● 250,000 - 499,999   ● 30,000 - 99,999   ○ UNDER 10,000

Scandinavia and Finland, Iceland

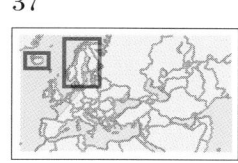

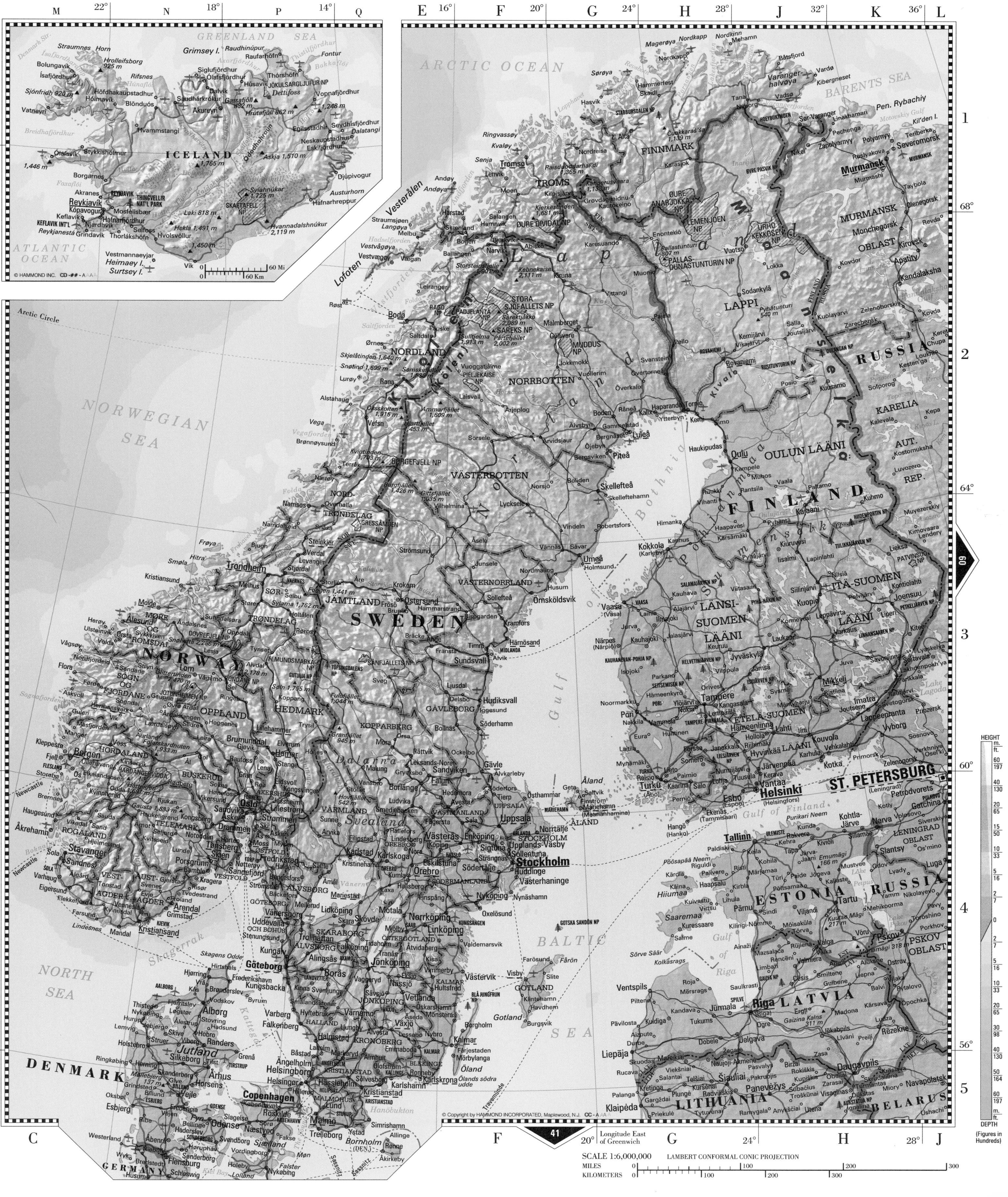

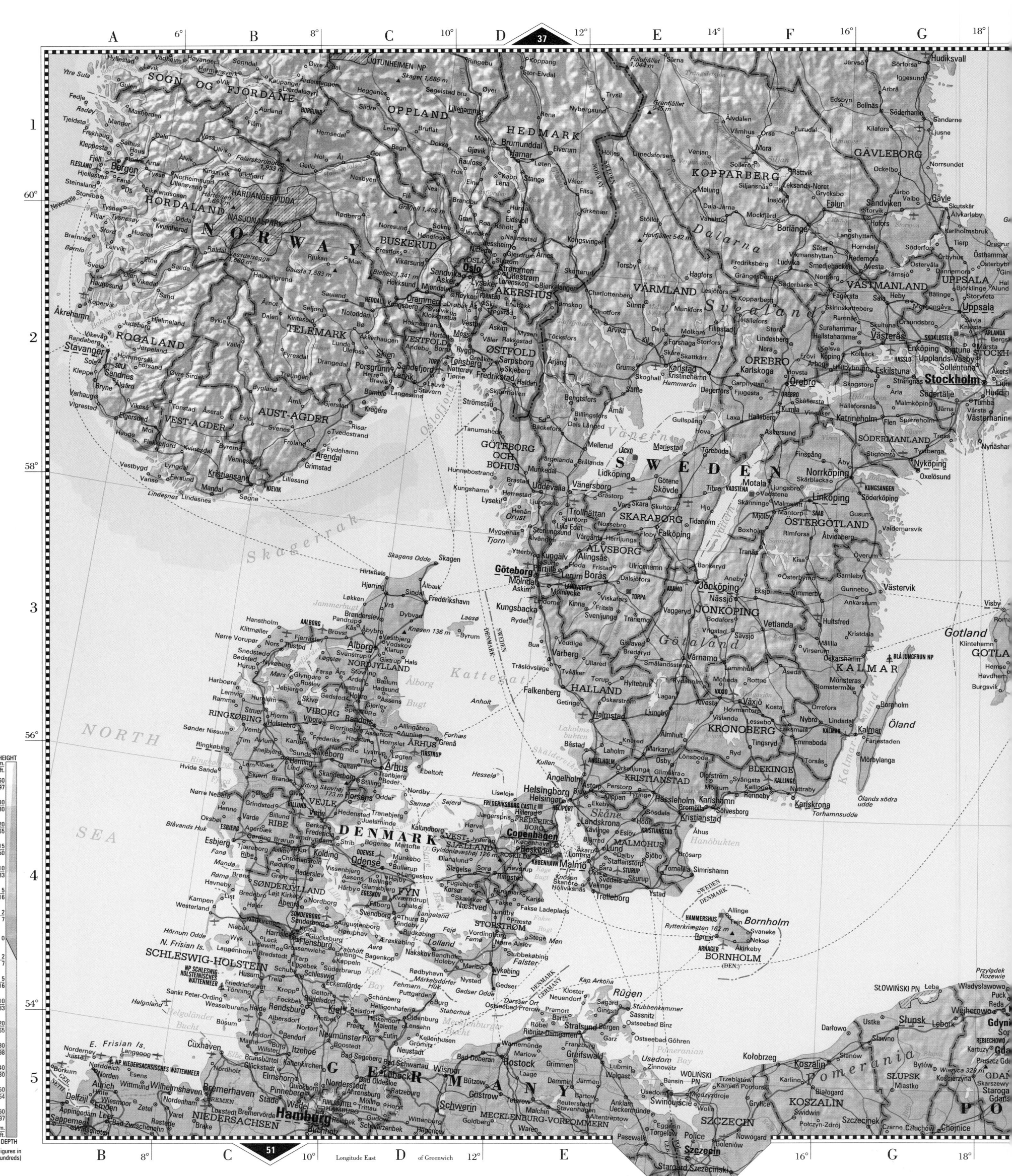

Baltic Region

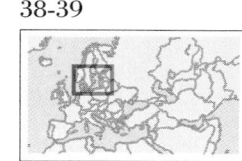

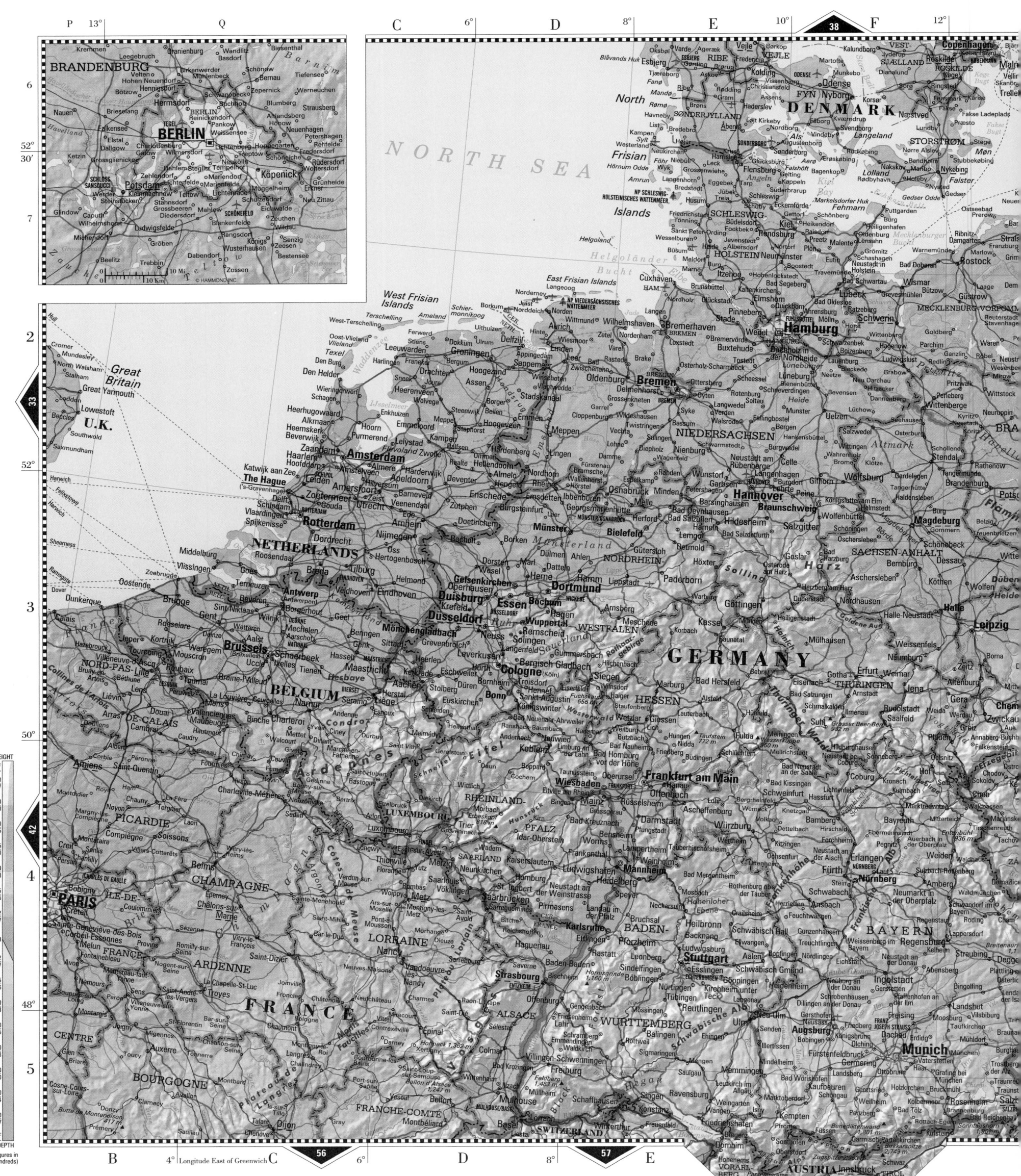

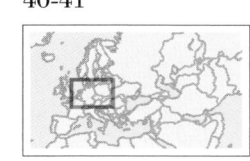

POPULATION OF CITIES AND TOWNS

| ■ OVER 2,000,000 | ● 500,000-999,999 | ● 100,000-249,999 | ○ 10,000-29,999 |
| □ 1,000,000-1,999,999 | ● 250,000-499,999 | ○ 30,000-99,999 | ○ UNDER 10,000 |

SCALE 1:3,000,000   LAMBERT CONFORMAL CONIC PROJECTION

MILES 0   50   100   150

KILOMETERS 0   50   100   150

West Central Europe

POPULATION OF CITIES AND TOWNS

| ■ OVER 2,000,000 | ● 500,000 - 999,999 | ● 100,000 - 249,999 | ○ 10,000 - 29,999 |
| □ 1,000,000 - 1,999,999 | ● 250,000 - 499,999 | ○ 30,000 - 99,999 | ○ UNDER 10,000 |

SCALE 1:3,000,000 LAMBERT CONFORMAL CONIC PROJECTION

MILES 0   50   100   150

KILOMETERS 0   50   100   150

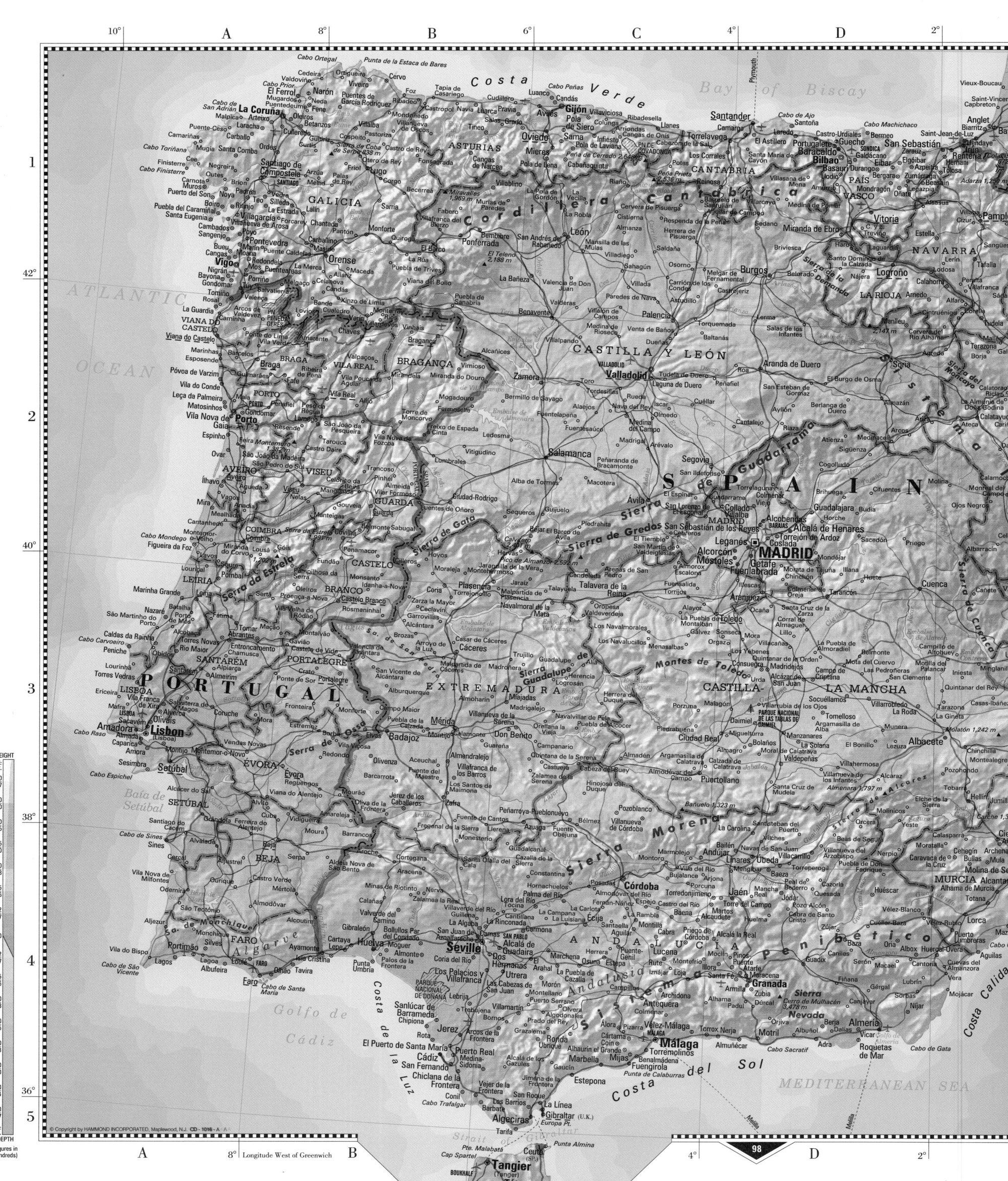

Spain, Portugal

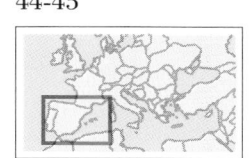

SCALE 1:3,000,000 LAMBERT CONFORMAL CONIC PROJECTION

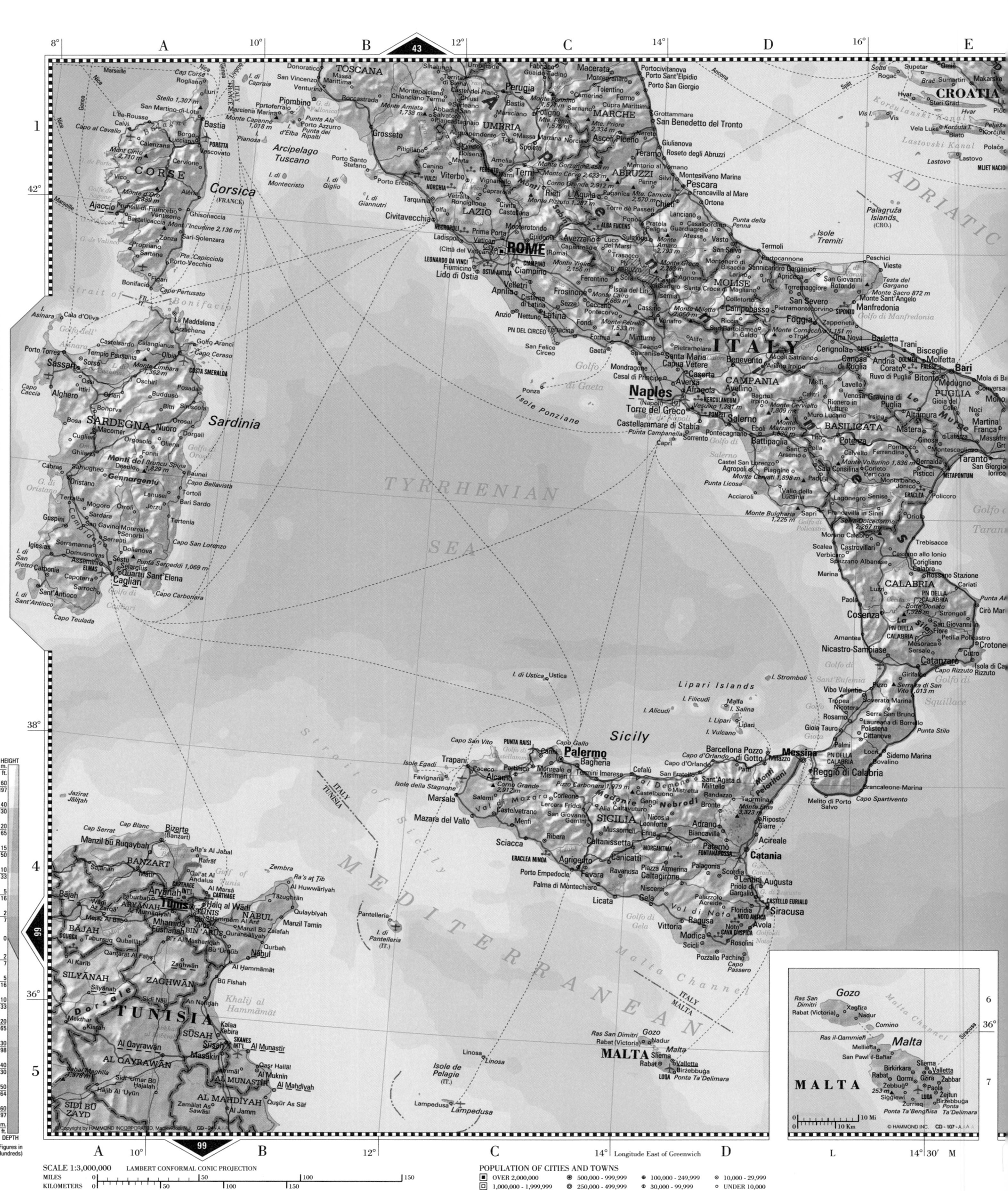

SCALE 1:3,000,000   LAMBERT CONFORMAL CONIC PROJECTION
MILES 0 ⊢ 50 ⊢ 100 ⊢ 150
KILOMETERS 0 ⊢ 50 ⊢ 100 ⊢ 150

POPULATION OF CITIES AND TOWNS
■ OVER 2,000,000   ● 500,000 - 999,999   ● 100,000 - 249,999   ◉ 10,000 - 29,999
▣ 1,000,000 - 1,999,999 ● 250,000 - 499,999   ● 30,000 - 99,999   ○ UNDER 10,000

MALTA

© HAMMOND INC.   CD-107-A

Southern Italy, Albania, Greece

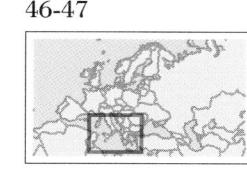

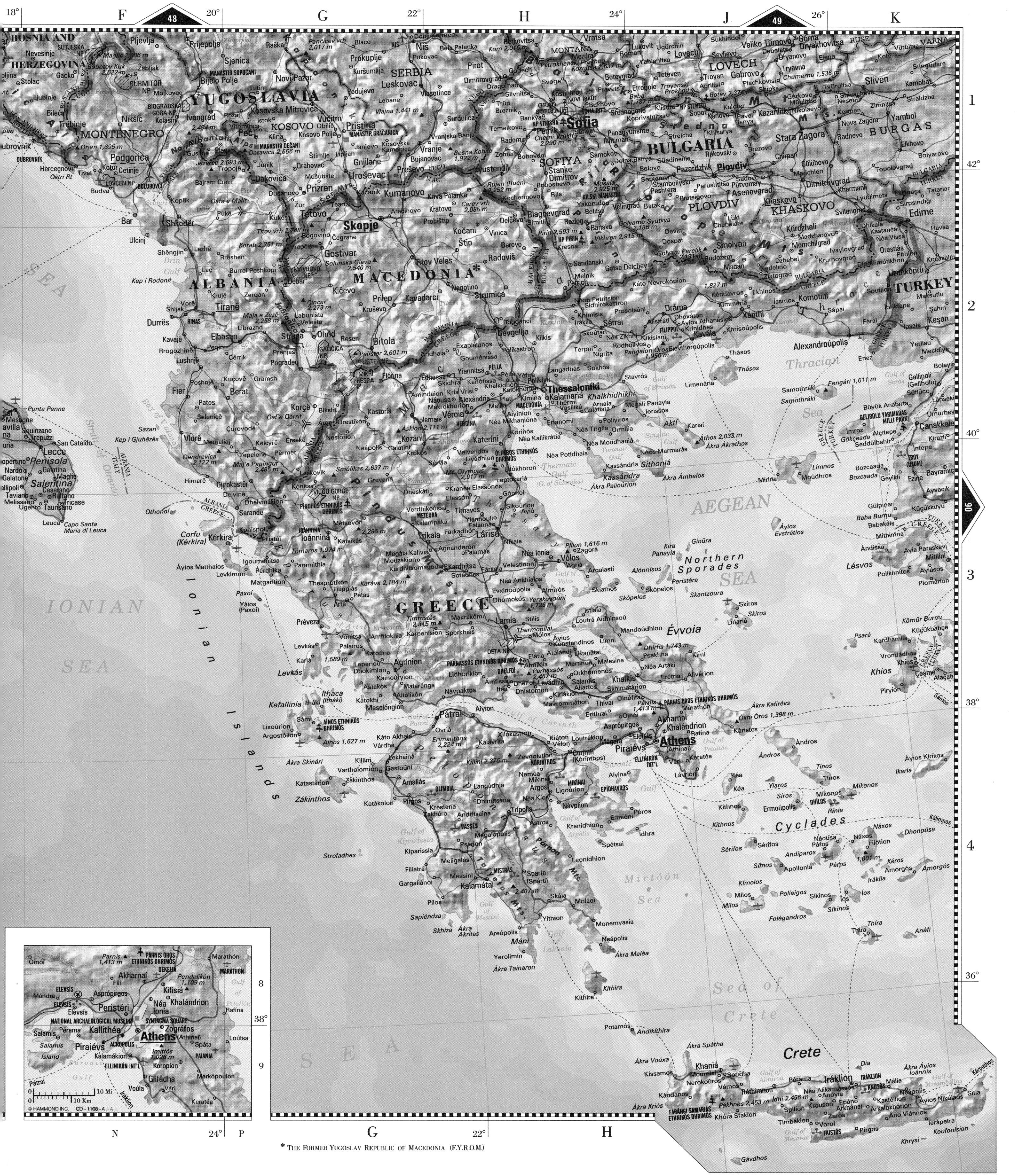

* THE FORMER YUGOSLAV REPUBLIC OF MACEDONIA (F.Y.R.O.M.)

SCALE 1:3,000,000   LAMBERT CONFORMAL CONIC PROJECTION

MILES

KILOMETERS

POPULATION OF CITIES AND TOWNS

■ OVER 2,000,000   ● 500,000 - 999,999   ⊕ 100,000 - 249,999   ○ 10,000 - 29,999
□ 1,000,000 - 1,999,999   ◉ 250,000 - 499,999   ⊙ 30,000 - 99,999   ∘ UNDER 10,000

* THE FORMER YUGOSLAV REPUBLIC OF MACEDONIA (F.Y.R.O.M.)

Hungary, Northern Balkan States

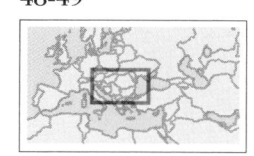

Netherlands, Northwestern Germany

NORTH SEA

West Frisian Islands

Waddenzee

GRONINGEN

FRIESLAND

DRENTHE

IJsselmeer

NOORD-HOLLAND

OVERIJSSEL

FLEVOLAND

Amsterdam

Haarlem

UTRECHT

GELDERLAND

The Hague ('s-Gravenhage)

Rotterdam

Utrecht

Arnhem

Nijmegen

ZUID-HOLLAND

Dordrecht

ZEELAND

Middelburg

NOORD-BRABANT

Breda

Tilburg

's Hertogenbosch

Eindhoven

LIMBURG

Venlo

ANTWERPEN

Antwerp (Antwerpen)

OOST-VLAANDEREN

Ghent (Gent)

BELGIUM

LIMBURG

Duisburg

Mönchengladbach

Düsseldorf

GERMANY

NETHERLANDS

Texel

Den Helder

Alkmaar

Zaanstad

Leiden

Delft

Gouda

Zwolle

Apeldoorn

Deventer

Enschede

Almelo

Hengelo

Groningen

Leeuwarden

Assen

Emmeloord

Lelystad

Amersfoort

Zutphen

Terschelling

Vlieland

Ameland

Schiermonnikoog

Borkum

HEIGHT
m. ft.
60 197
40 130
20 65
15 50
10 33
2 7
0
2 7
5 16
10 33
20 65
30 98
40 130
50 164
60 197
m. ft.
DEPTH
(Figures in Hundreds)

POPULATION OF CITIES AND TOWNS

- ■ OVER 2,000,000
- □ 1,000,000 - 1,999,999
- ⦾ 500,000 - 999,999
- ⦿ 250,000 - 499,999
- ⦿ 100,000 - 249,999
- ⊙ 30,000 - 99,999
- ⊙ 10,000 - 29,999
- ○ UNDER 10,000

SCALE 1:1,000,000   LAMBERT CONFORMAL CONIC PROJECTION

MILES 0 ... 10 ... 20 ... 30 ... 40 ... 50

KILOMETERS 0 ... 10 ... 20 ... 30 ... 40 ... 50

Belgium, Northern France, Western Germany

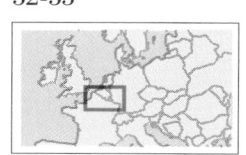

POPULATION OF CITIES AND TOWNS

- ■ OVER 2,000,000
- ▣ 1,000,000 - 1,999,999
- ◉ 500,000 - 999,999
- ◍ 250,000 - 499,999
- ◕ 100,000 - 249,999
- ◐ 30,000 - 99,999
- ○ 10,000 - 24,999
- ○ UNDER 10,000

SCALE 1:1,000,000   LAMBERT CONFORMAL CONIC PROJECTION

MILES   0   10   20   30   40   50

KILOMETERS   0   10   20   30   40   50

© Copyright by HAMMOND INCORPORATED, Maplewood, N.J.   CD-12-A-A

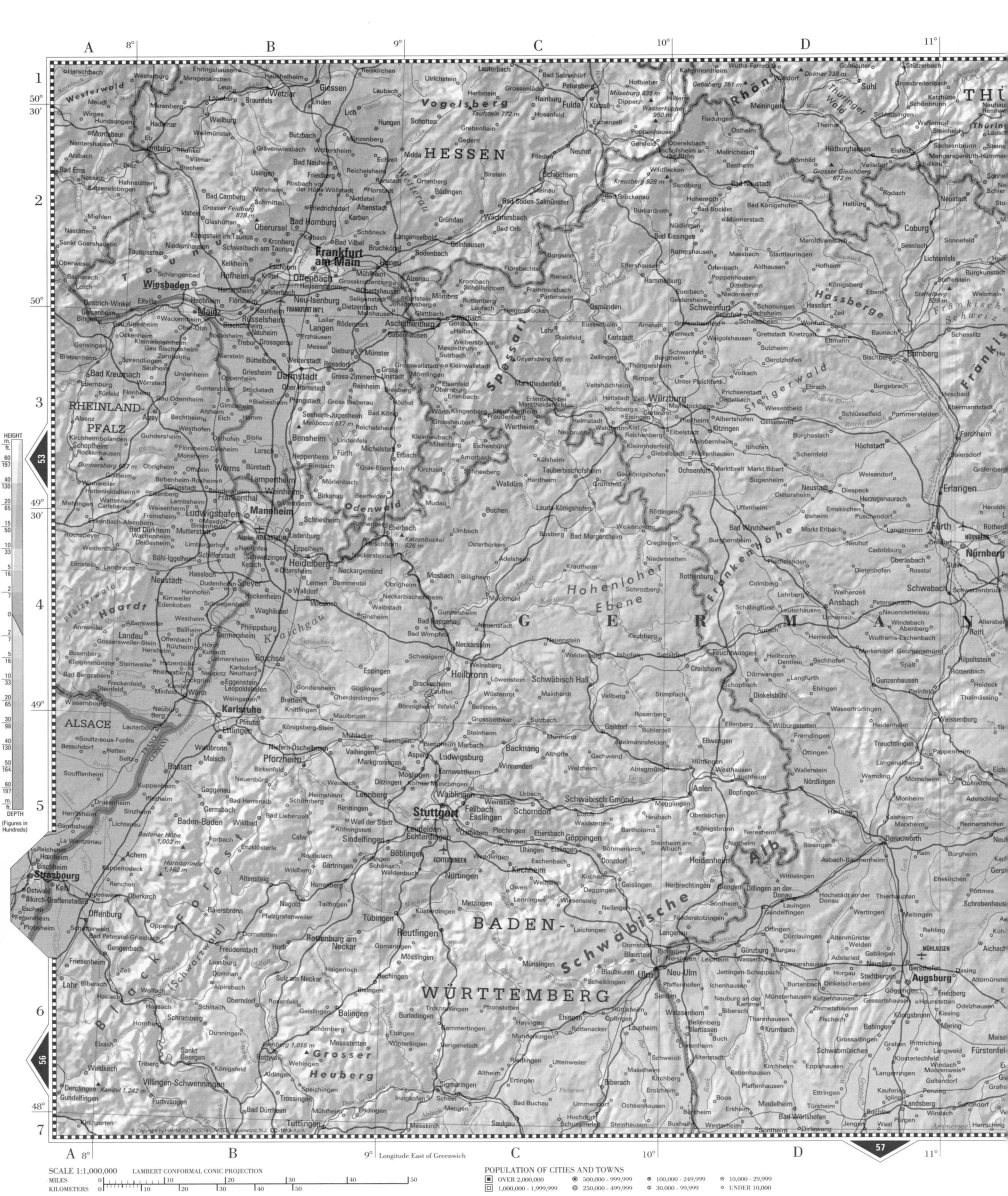

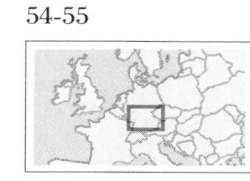

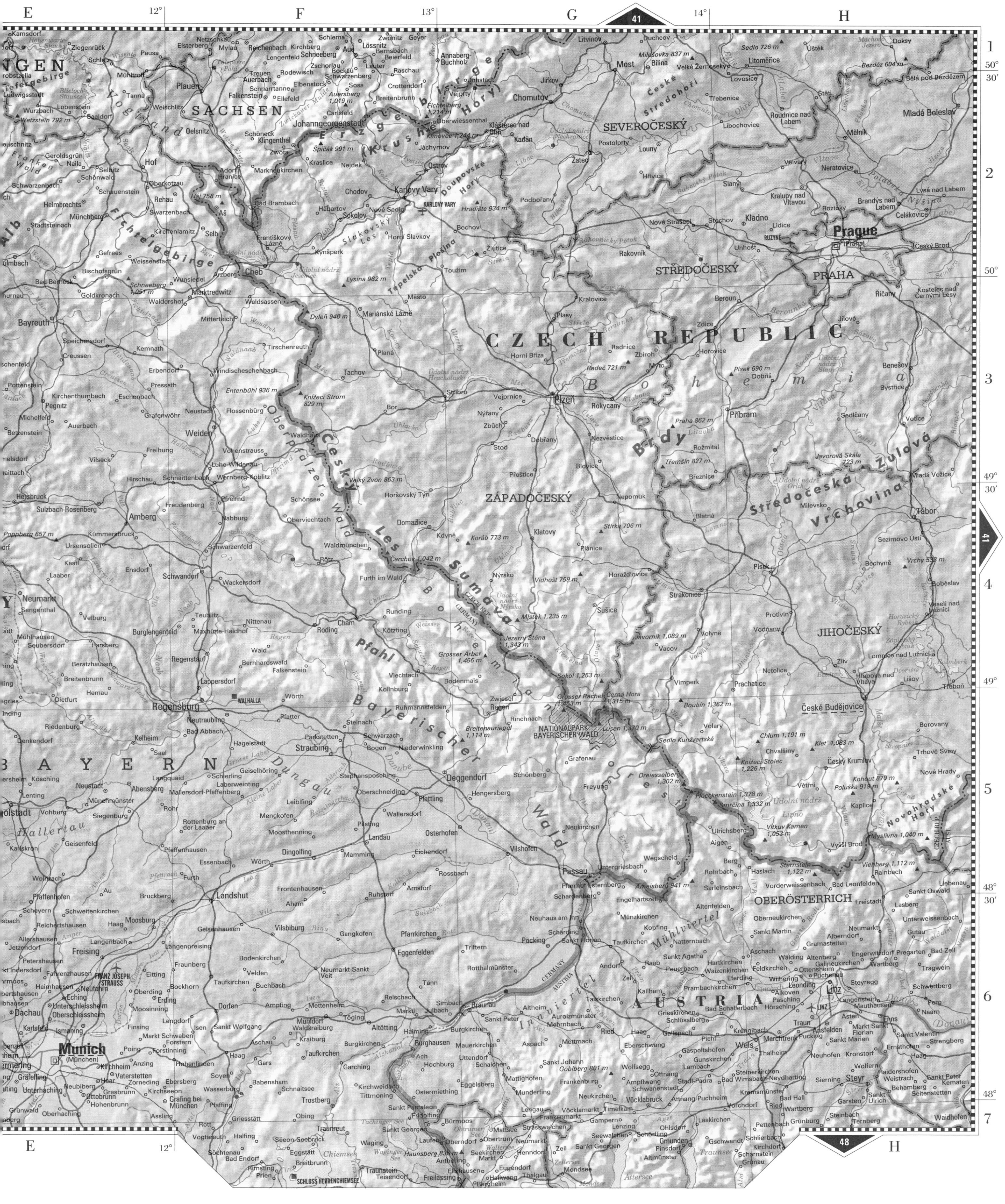

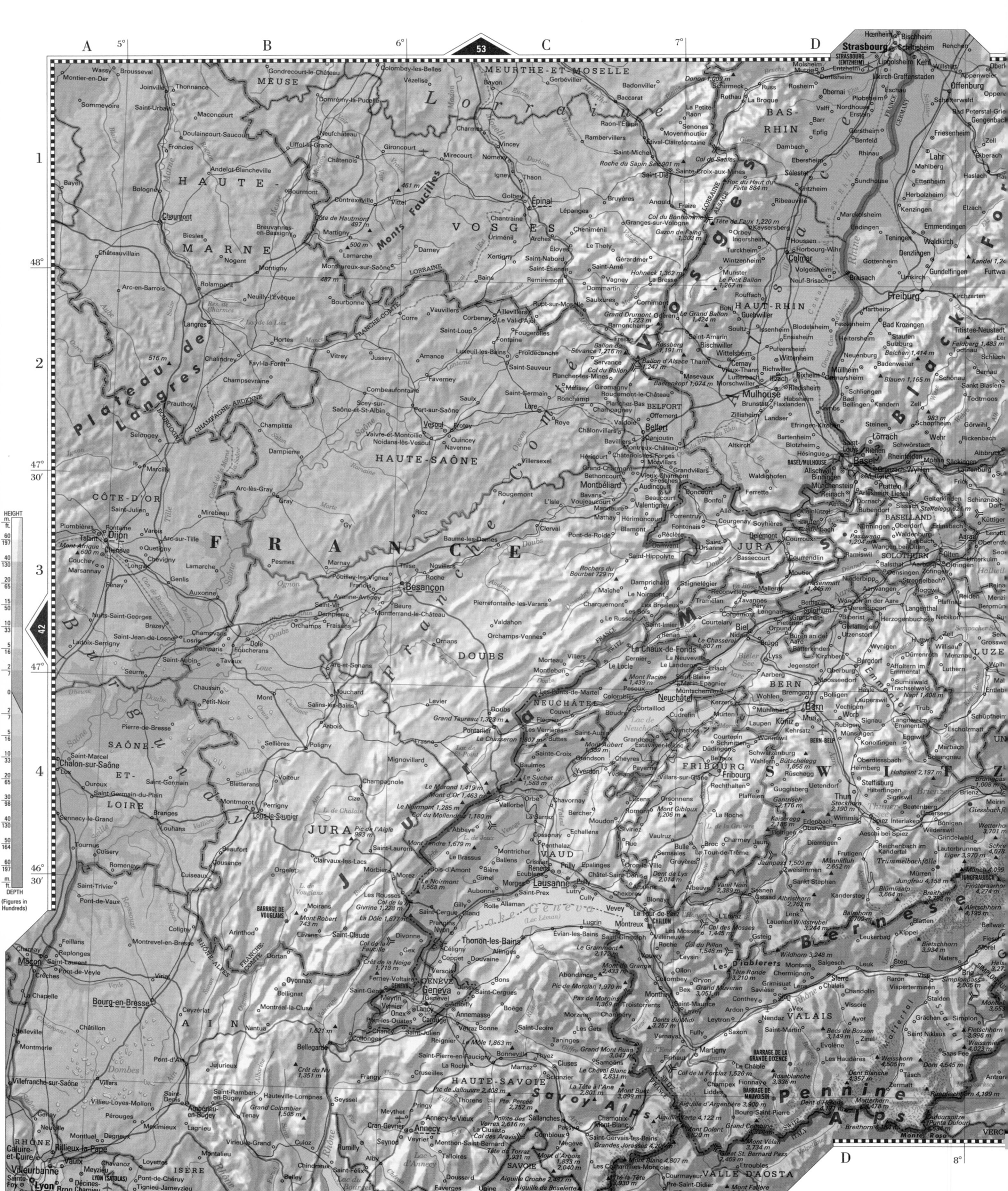

Central Alps Region

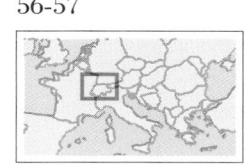

POPULATION OF CITIES AND TOWNS

| ■ OVER 2,000,000 | ● 500,000 - 999,999 | ⊕ 100,000 - 249,999 | ○ 10,000 - 29,999 |
| □ 1,000,000 - 1,999,999 | ● 250,000 - 499,999 | ⊙ 30,000 - 99,999 | ∘ UNDER 10,000 |

SCALE 1:1,000,000   LAMBERT CONFORMAL CONIC PROJECTION

MILES 0 10 20 30 40 50

KILOMETERS 0 10 20 30 40 50

Longitude East of Greenwich

© Copyright by HAMMOND INCORPORATED, Maplewood, N.J.   CC-1018-A

SLOVENIA

CROATIA

Golfo di Venezia

ADRIATIC

SEA

Mouths of the Po

TRENTO

BELLUNO

VICENZA

PORDENONE

UDINE

GORIZIA

TREVISO

VENEZIA

VERONA

PADOVA

ROVIGO

Polesine

Po

FERRARA

BOLOGNA

RAVENNA

Romagna

Emiliano

FORLÌ

Montefeltro

SAN MARINO

PESARO E URBINO

PISTOIA

FIRENZE

Florence

Firenze

AREZZO

Chianti

Casentino

Monti Palomagno

Umbro-Marchigiano

ANCONA

PESARO

PERUGIA

SIENA

MACERATA

Alpi di S. Benedetto

Trieste

TRIESTE

Istria

Pula

Rt Kamenjak

POPULATION OF CITIES AND TOWNS

| ■ | OVER 2,000,000 | ◉ | 500,000 - 999,999 | ⊕ | 100,000 - 249,999 | ⊙ | 10,000 - 29,999 |
| □ | 1,000,000 - 1,999,999 | ◉ | 250,000 - 499,999 | ⊙ | 30,000 - 99,999 | ○ | UNDER 10,000 |

SCALE 1:1,000,000   LAMBERT CONFORMAL CONIC PROJECTION

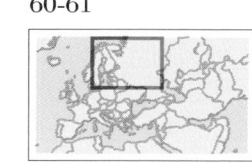

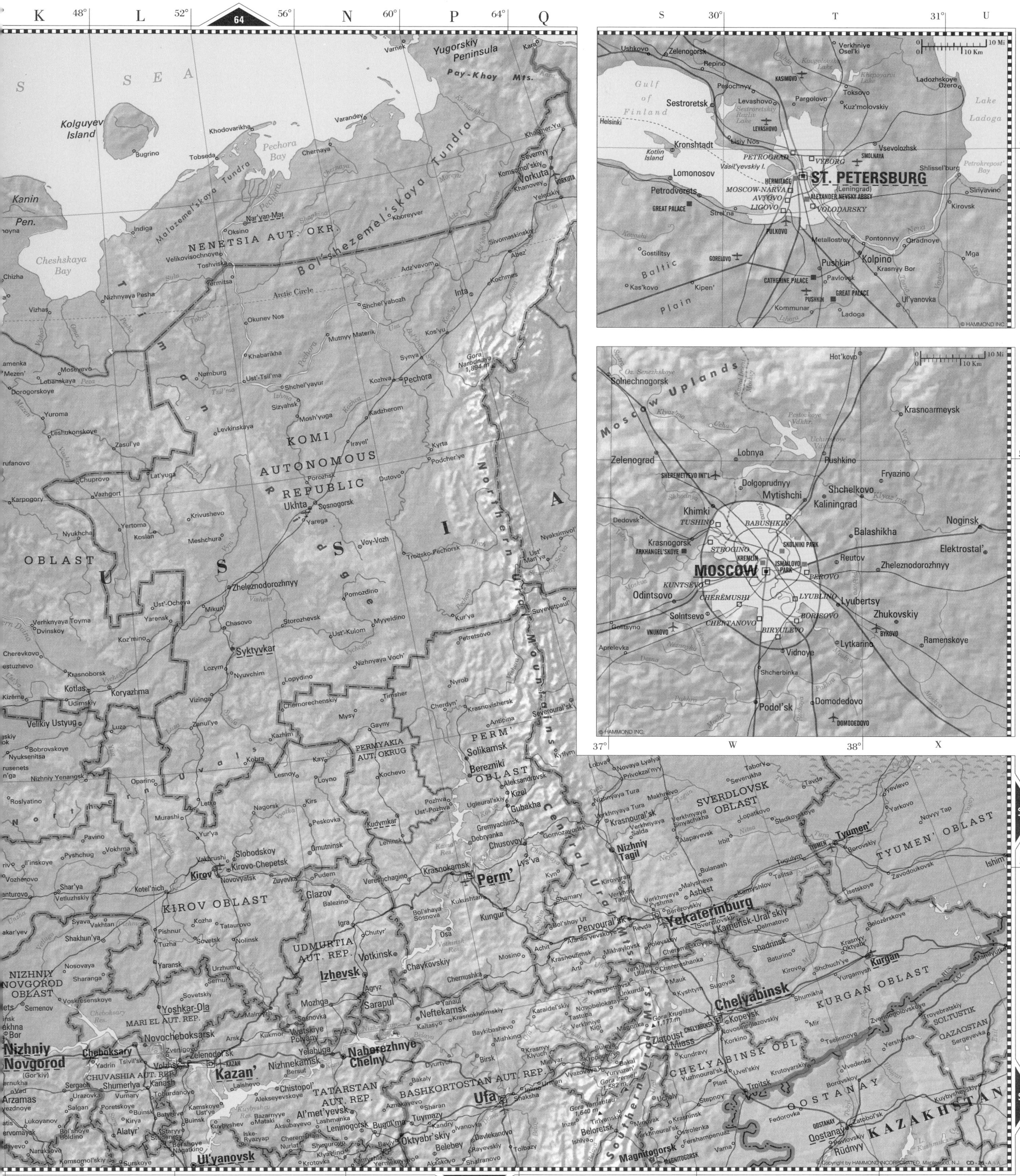

POPULATION OF CITIES AND TOWNS
- ■ OVER 2,000,000
- ◉ 500,000 - 999,999
- ● 100,000 - 249,999
- ○ 10,000 - 29,999
- □ 1,000,000 - 1,999,999
- ◉ 250,000 - 499,999
- ● 30,000 - 99,999
- ○ UNDER 10,000

SCALE 1:6,000,000   LAMBERT CONFORMAL CONIC PROJECTION

MILES 0   100   200   300
KILOMETERS 0   100   200   300

© Copyright by HAMMOND INCORPORATED, Maplewood, N.J.   CD-28-A-A-A

Southeastern Europe

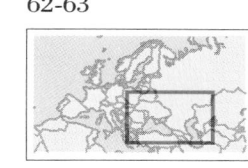

Russia and Neighboring Countries

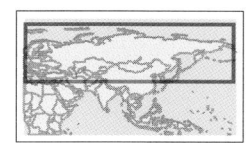

RUSSIA
(Administrative divisions are named only when they differ from their respective capitals.)

1. ADYGEA AUT. REP.
2. KARACHAY-CHERKESSIA AUT. REP.
3. KABARDINO-BALKARIA AUT. REP.
4. NORTH OSSETIA AUT. REP.
5. INGUSHETIA AUT. REP.
6. CHECHNYA AUT. REP.
7. DAGESTAN AUT. REP.
8. MORDOVIA AUT. REP.
9. CHUVASHIA AUT. REP.
10. MARI EL AUT. REP.
11. TATARSTAN AUT. REP.
12. BASHKORTOSTAN AUT. REP.
13. UDMURTIA AUT. REP.
14. PERMYAKIA AUT. OKRUG
15. KHAKASSIA AUT. REP.
16. UST'-ORDA AUT. OKRUG
17. AGA AUT. OKRUG

POPULATION OF CITIES AND TOWNS

- ■ OVER 2,000,000
- ▣ 1,000,000 - 1,999,999
- ● 500,000 - 999,999
- ◉ 100,000 - 499,999
- ⊙ 50,000 - 99,999
- ○ UNDER 50,000

SCALE 1:18,000,000   LAMBERT CONFORMAL CONIC PROJECTION

MILES   0   300   600   900
KILOMETERS   0   300   600   900

Occupied by Russia since 1945, claimed by Japan.

© Copyright by HAMMOND INCORPORATED, Maplewood, N.J.   CC-29-A A

Asia

The delta of the Indus River, the longest river in southwest Asia, is the highlight of this southeast-looking, low-oblique image. Fed by snowmelt and glacial meltwater from the mountains of the Tibet Plateau, the Indus River flows nearly 1800 miles (2897 km.) before emptying into the Arabian Sea. After leaving the Tibet Plateau, the river flows onto the Punjab Plains of western Pakistan and through a vast alluvial lowland where it receives its major tributary, the Panjnad (five streams). In this severely arid landscape the rivers form precarious strips of fertile land.

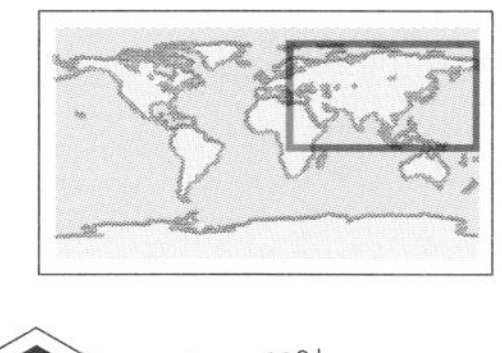

AREA OF OPTIMIZATION

The red band which surrounds this map defines the "Area of Optimization." Within this bounding curve is the most accurate conformal map that can be made of the region. Outside the optimized area, distortion increases rapidly, and tears or other irregularities in the grid may occur. (See page 6 for additional information.)

POPULATION OF CITIES AND TOWNS
- ■ OVER 3,000,000
- ◉ 500,000 - 999,999
- ○ UNDER 100,000
- ▣ 1,000,000 - 2,999,999
- ◉ 100,000 - 499,999

SCALE 1:42,000,000   OPTIMAL CONFORMAL PROJECTION

MILES 0 — 700 — 1400 — 2100
KILOMETERS 0 — 700 — 1400 — 2100

Longitude East F of Greenwich

© Copyright by HAMMOND INCORPORATED, Maplewood, N.J.   CG - 1030 - A

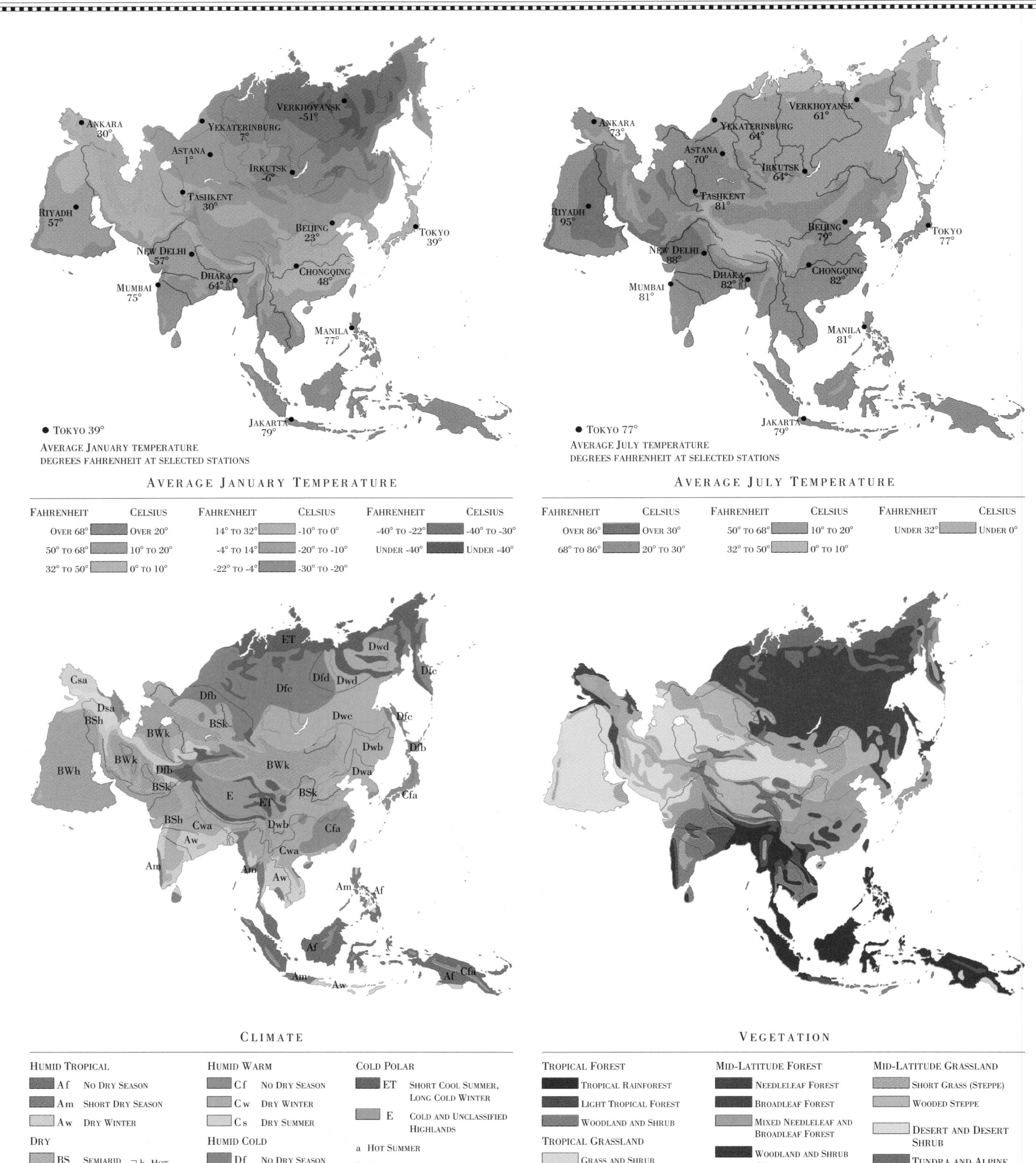

AVERAGE JANUARY TEMPERATURE

ANKARA 30°
RIYADH 57°
VERKHOYANSK -51°
YEKATERINBURG 7°
ASTANA 1°
IRKUTSK -6°
TASHKENT 30°
BEIJING 23°
TOKYO 39°
NEW DELHI 57°
DHAKA 64°
CHONGQING 48°
MUMBAI 75°
MANILA 77°
JAKARTA 79°

● TOKYO 39°
AVERAGE JANUARY TEMPERATURE
DEGREES FAHRENHEIT AT SELECTED STATIONS

FAHRENHEIT	CELSIUS	FAHRENHEIT	CELSIUS	FAHRENHEIT	CELSIUS
OVER 68°	OVER 20°	14° TO 32°	-10° TO 0°	-40° TO -22°	-40° TO -30°
50° TO 68°	10° TO 20°	-4° TO 14°	-20° TO -10°	UNDER -40°	UNDER -40°
32° TO 50°	0° TO 10°	-22° TO -4°	-30° TO -20°		

AVERAGE JULY TEMPERATURE

ANKARA 73°
RIYADH 95°
VERKHOYANSK 61°
YEKATERINBURG 64°
ASTANA 70°
IRKUTSK 64°
TASHKENT 81°
BEIJING 79°
TOKYO 77°
NEW DELHI 88°
DHAKA 82°
CHONGQING 82°
MUMBAI 81°
MANILA 81°
JAKARTA 79°

● TOKYO 77°
AVERAGE JULY TEMPERATURE
DEGREES FAHRENHEIT AT SELECTED STATIONS

FAHRENHEIT	CELSIUS	FAHRENHEIT	CELSIUS	FAHRENHEIT	CELSIUS
OVER 86°	OVER 30°	50° TO 68°	10° TO 20°	UNDER 32°	UNDER 0°
68° TO 86°	20° TO 30°	32° TO 50°	0° TO 10°		

CLIMATE

Csa, Dsa, BSh, BWk, Dfb, BSk, BWh, BWk, Dfb, BSk, BSh, Cwa, Aw, Am, E, ET, Dwb, Am, Aw, Af, Am, Aw, Af, ET, Dfb, Dfc, Dfd, Dwd, Dwd, Dfc, Dwe, Dfc, Dwb, Dfb, Dwa, BWk, BSk, Cfa, Cwa, Cfa, Af, Cfa

HUMID TROPICAL
Af NO DRY SEASON
Am SHORT DRY SEASON
Aw DRY WINTER

DRY
BS SEMIARID ⌉ h HOT
BW ARID ⌋ k COLD

AFTER KOEPPEN-GEIGER

HUMID WARM
Cf NO DRY SEASON
Cw DRY WINTER
Cs DRY SUMMER

HUMID COLD
Df NO DRY SEASON
Dw DRY WINTER
Ds DRY SUMMER

COLD POLAR
ET SHORT COOL SUMMER, LONG COLD WINTER
E COLD AND UNCLASSIFIED HIGHLANDS

a HOT SUMMER
b COOL SUMMER
c SHORT COOL SUMMER
d VERY COLD WINTER

VEGETATION

TROPICAL FOREST
TROPICAL RAINFOREST
LIGHT TROPICAL FOREST
WOODLAND AND SHRUB

TROPICAL GRASSLAND
GRASS AND SHRUB (SAVANNA)
WOODED SAVANNA

MID-LATITUDE FOREST
NEEDLELEAF FOREST
BROADLEAF FOREST
MIXED NEEDLELEAF AND BROADLEAF FOREST
WOODLAND AND SHRUB (MEDITERRANEAN)

MID-LATITUDE GRASSLAND
SHORT GRASS (STEPPE)
WOODED STEPPE
DESERT AND DESERT SHRUB
TUNDRA AND ALPINE
UNCLASSIFIED HIGHLANDS

Asia - Geographical Comparisons

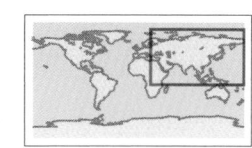

AVERAGE ANNUAL RAINFALL

Cities labeled on map:
- ANKARA 13
- VERKHOYANSK 6
- ASTANA 12
- TEHRAN 9
- TASHKENT 17
- ULAANBAATR 7
- RIYADH 4
- BEIJING 25
- TOKYO 61
- NEW DELHI 28
- CHONGQING 43
- MUMBAI 82
- CHERRAPUNJI 449
- MANILA 82
- PADANG 151

● TOKYO 61
AVERAGE ANNUAL RAINFALL
IN INCHES AT SELECTED STATIONS

INCHES	CM	INCHES	CM	INCHES	CM
OVER 80	OVER 200	40 TO 60	100 TO 150	10 TO 20	25 TO 50
60 TO 80	150 TO 200	20 TO 40	50 TO 100	UNDER 10	UNDER 25

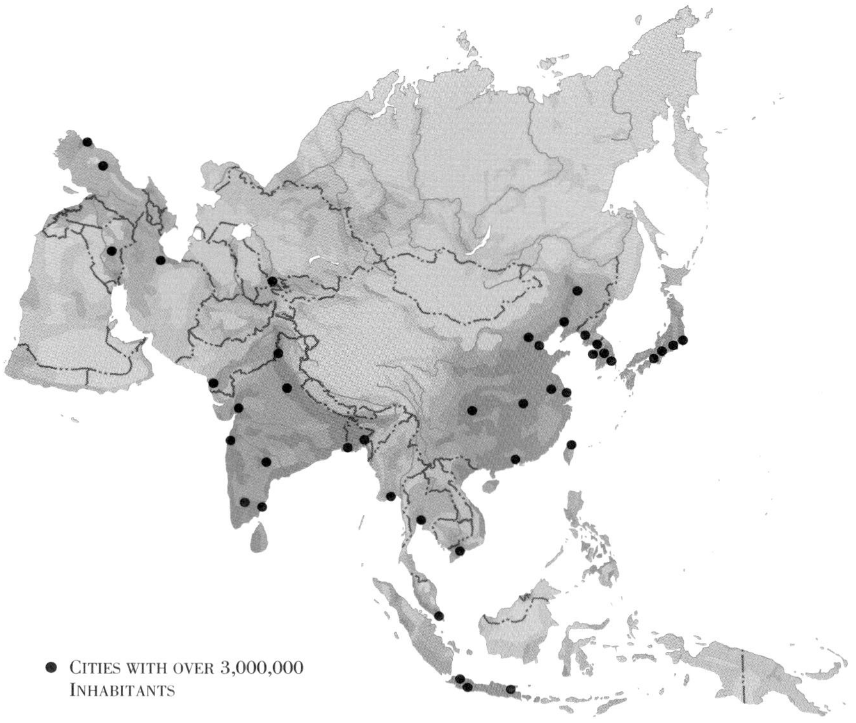

POPULATION DISTRIBUTION

● CITIES WITH OVER 3,000,000 INHABITANTS

DENSITY PER		SQ. MI.	SQ. KM.	SQ. MI.	SQ. KM.
SQ. MI.	SQ. KM.	130 TO 260	50 TO 100	3 TO 25	1 TO 10
OVER 260	OVER 100	25 TO 130	10 TO 50	UNDER 3	UNDER 1

LAND USE

Labels on map: TOBACCO, OLIVES, WHEAT, SHEEP, FRUIT, DATES, SHEEP, FURS, CATTLE, OATS, POTATOES OATS WHEAT, WHEAT, OATS, FURS, SHEEP, COTTON, SHEEP, POTATOES SOYBEANS, WHEAT, SHEEP, RICE, WHEAT SOYBEANS CORN, RICE TEA FRUIT TEA, DATES, CATTLE, WHEAT, COTTON RICE TEA, COTTON, RICE, HOGS, PEANUTS, RICE JUTE, RICE, CASSAVA CORN RICE, SUGARCANE, RICE TEA, FRUIT SUGARCANE, ABACA, RUBBER, RUBBER, RUBBER, COCONUTS, SPICES, RICE COFFEE, SPICES, COCONUTS, COCONUTS, COCOA

CEREALS, LIVESTOCK	DIVERSIFIED TROPICAL & SUBTROPICAL CROPS
CASH CROPS, MIXED FARMING	LIVESTOCK RANCHING & HERDING
DAIRY, LIVESTOCK	SPECIAL CROPS
	FORESTS
	NONPRODUCTIVE

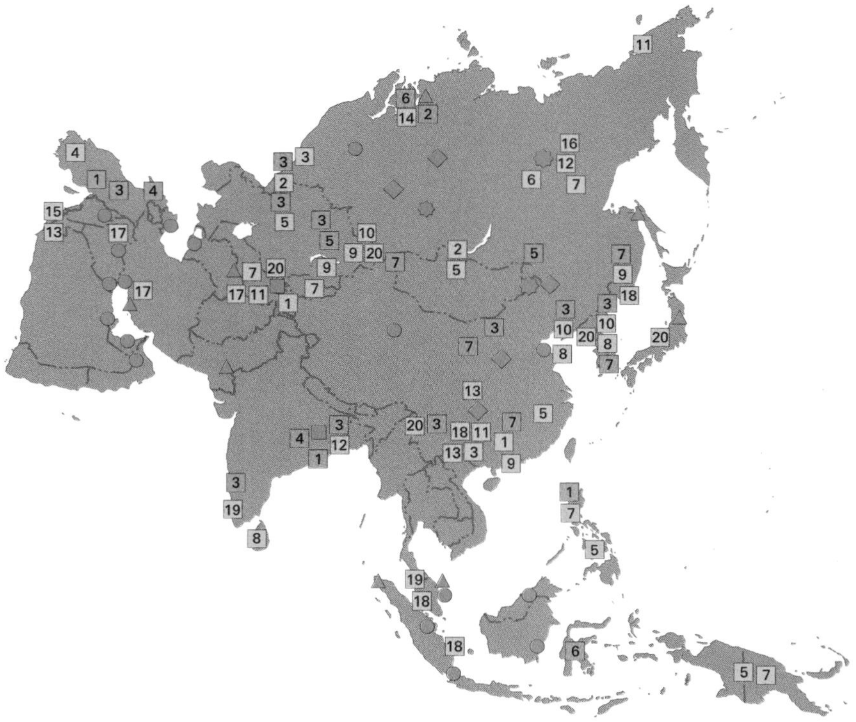

MINERAL RESOURCES

ENERGY & FUELS
- ◆ COAL
- ⬡ LIGNITE
- ▲ NATURAL GAS
- ● PETROLEUM
- ▪ URANIUM

IRON & FERROALLOYS
- 1 CHROMIUM
- 2 COBALT
- 3 IRON ORE
- 4 MANGANESE
- 5 MOLYBDENUM
- 6 NICKEL
- 7 TUNGSTEN

OTHER MAJOR RESOURCES
- 1 ANTIMONY
- 2 ASBESTOS
- 3 BAUXITE
- 4 BORAX
- 5 COPPER
- 6 DIAMONDS
- 7 GOLD
- 8 GRAPHITE
- 9 LEAD
- 10 MAGNESITE
- 11 MERCURY
- 12 MICA
- 13 PHOSPHATES
- 14 PLATINUM
- 15 POTASH
- 16 SILVER
- 17 SULFER
- 18 TIN
- 19 TITANIUM
- 20 ZINC

Eastern Asia

POPULATION OF CITIES AND TOWNS
- ■ OVER 2,000,000
- □ 1,000,000 - 1,999,999
- ● 500,000 - 999,999
- ◉ 100,000 - 499,999
- ◎ 50,000 - 99,999
- ○ UNDER 50,000

SCALE 1:12,000,000   LAMBERT CONFORMAL CONIC PROJECTION

MILES
0   200   400   600

KILOMETERS
0   200   400   600

© HAMMOND INC.

Northeastern China

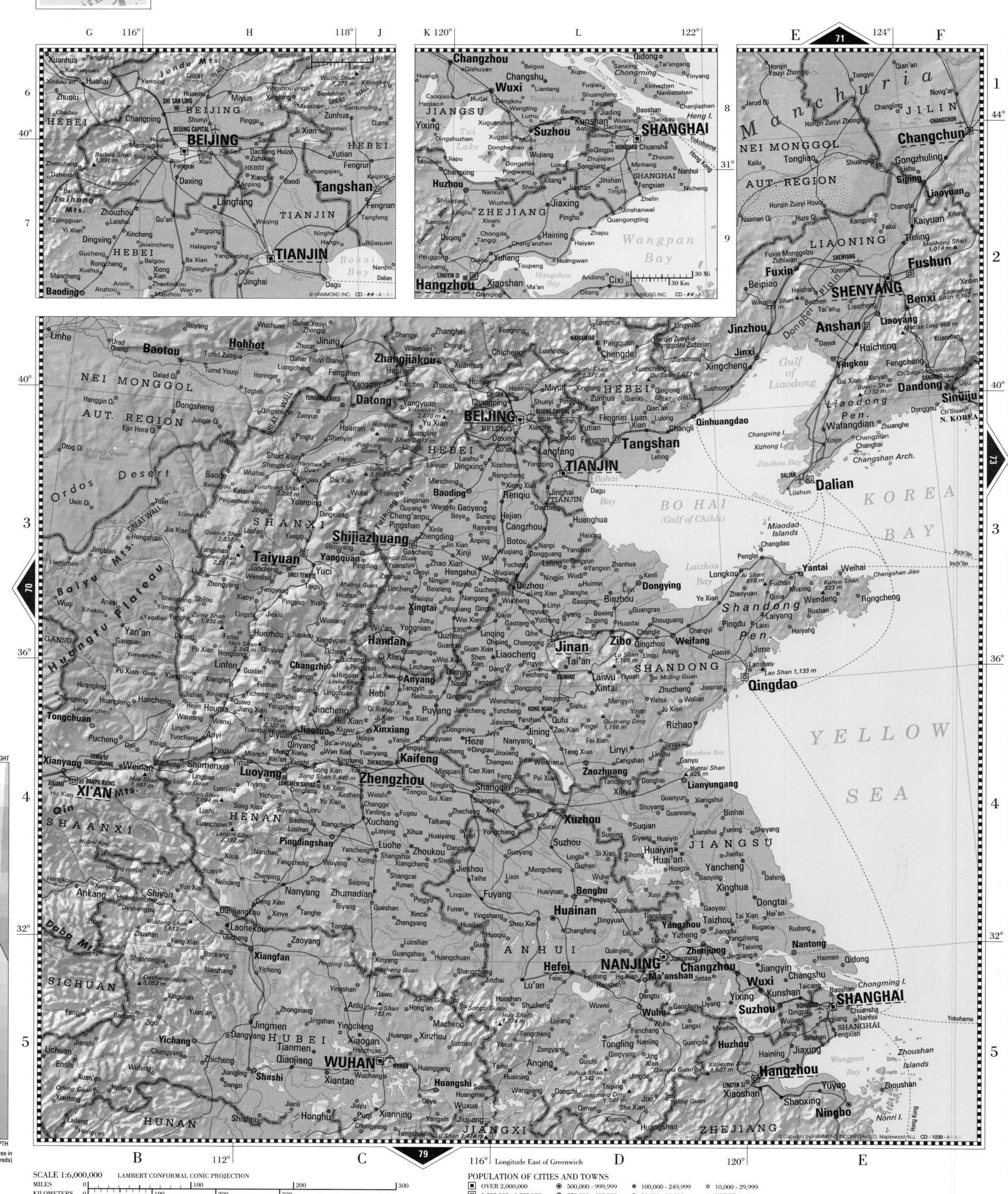

SCALE 1:6,000,000 LAMBERT CONFORMAL CONIC PROJECTION

Longitude East of Greenwich

MILES

KILOMETERS

POPULATION OF CITIES AND TOWNS

- ▣ OVER 2,000,000
- ▣ 1,000,000-1,999,999
- ● 500,000-999,999
- ● 250,000-499,999
- ● 100,000-249,999
- ● 30,000-99,999
- ○ 10,000-29,999
- ○ UNDER 10,000

HEIGHT
m. ft.
60 197
40 130
15 50
10 33
2 7
0
2 7
10 33
20 65
30 98
40 130
50 164
60 197
m. ft.
DEPTH
(Figures in Hundreds)

© Copyright by HAMMOND INCORPORATED, Maplewood, N.J. CD-1039-A·A·A

Korea

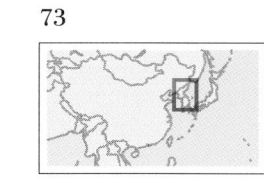

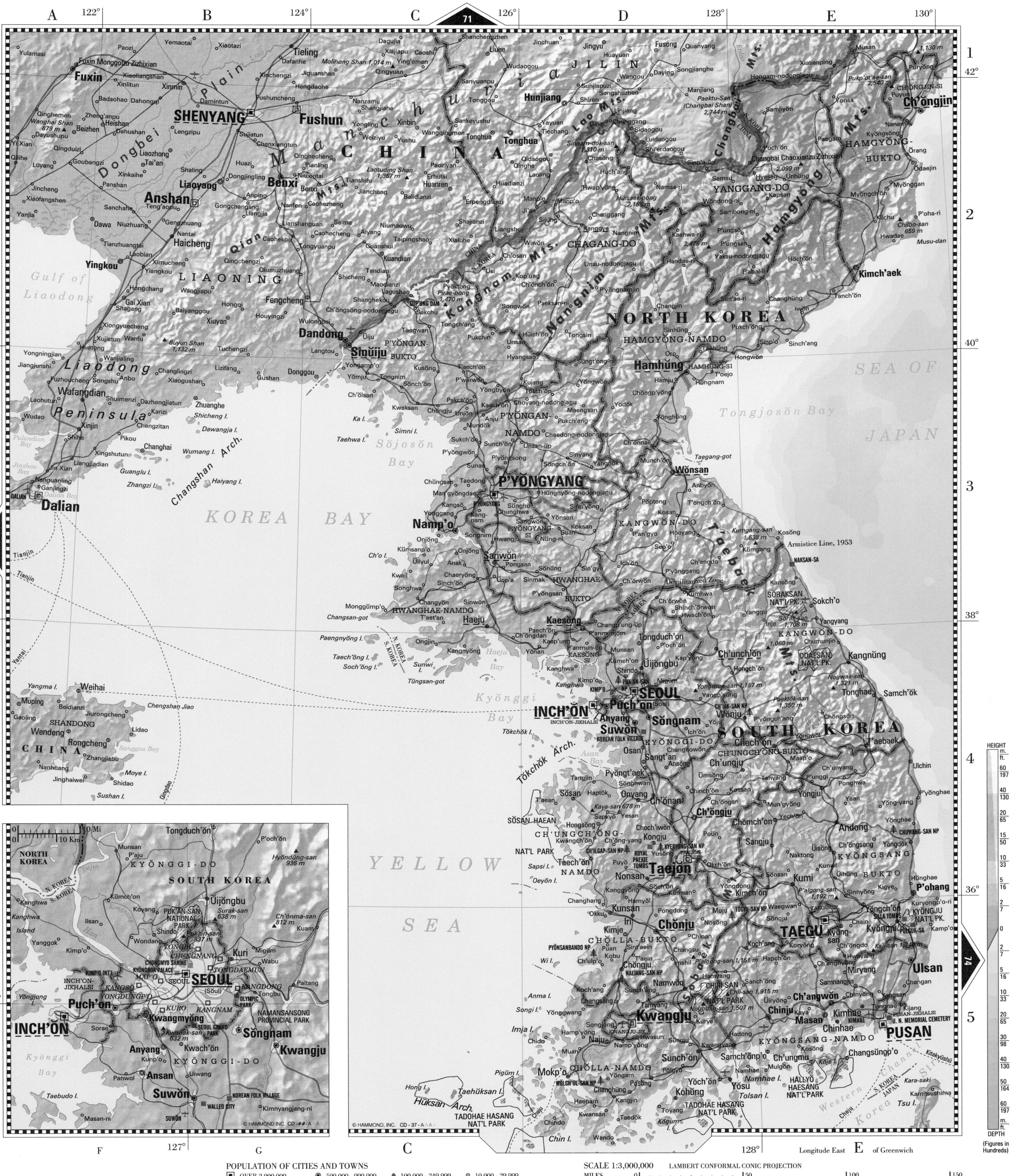

Central and Southern Japan

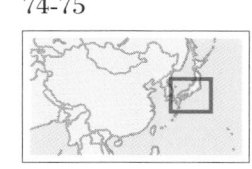

E | 138° | F | 140° | **76** | MIYAGI | 142° | H | 144° | J

Ishinomaki
Awa-shima · Higashine · Yamato · Onagawa
Hajiki-zaki · Sagae · YAMAGATA · Matsushima
Murakami · Asahi-dake · Tendō · **Sendai** · Shiogama
1,870 m · Yamagata · Iwanuma · *Sendai*
Aikawa · Ryōtsu · Nakajō · BANDAI-ASAHI · Nagai · Takahata · SENDAI · *Bay*
NIIGATA · Yonezawa · Watari
Itaya · Kakuda
Suzu-misaki · **Niigata** · Niitsu · Shibata · Kitakata · Sōma
Suzu · Niitsu · Gosen · **Fukushima** · Haramachi
Tsubame · Shirone · **Yamato** · Nihonmatsu · Namie
Kamo · BANDAI-ASAH · Miharu
Nagaoka · Sanjō · Mitsuke · Aizu · Bandai-san 1,819 m · NP · Motomiya · Ōtakine-yama
Kashiwazaki · Tochio · FUKUSHIMA · **Kōriyama** · 1,193 m
Toyama · CHŪBU · Tajima · Sukagawa · Towada
Bay · Ojiya · Tōkamachi · Nasu-dake 1,917 m · Yabuki
Itoigawa · TŌHOKU · Shirakawa · **Iwaki**
Jōetsu · Shirane-san 2,578 m · Kuroiso · Shioya-saki
Arai · NIIGATA · NIKKO NAT'L · Yaita · Ishikawa · Kita-Ibaraki
KAWA · Nyūzen · Myōkō-san 2,446 m · Mikuni-tōge · PARK Nikkō · Ōtawara · Takahagi
Uozu · JOSHIN-ETSU · Nakano · Nantai-san 2,484 m · Imaichi · TOCHIGI · Hitachi
Himi · Namerikawa · **Nagano** · KOGEN · Numata · Kanuma · Moka · Kasama · Hitachi-ōta
minato · **Toyama** · Tate-yama · Asama-yama 2,544 m · Ishibashi · Utsunomiya · Katsuta
Oyabe · TOYAMA 3,015 m · GUMMA · Ueda · Kiryū · Tochigi · Ōyama · **Mito** · Nakaminato
TOYAMA · Yatsuo · Hotaka · **Maebashi** · Shimodate · Ōmiya
Yarike-take 3,180 m · Matsumoto · Saku · Takasaki · Ōta · Sano · Yūki · IBARAKI · Ishioka
Toyoshina · Hotaka-dake 3,190 m · JAPANESE · Isesaki · Fujioka · Iwai · Yatabe · Tsuchiura
Takayama · Nonkura-dake 3,026 m · ALPS NAT'L · Chichibu · Kumagaya · SAITAMA · Sakai Ishige · Mitsukaidō
· PARK · Okaya · Kōnosu · Kuki · Misukaidō · Kashima
GIFU · Suwa · MATSUMOTO · Kawagoe · Kasukabe · Ryūgasaki
Ontake-san 3,063 m · Ina · MINAMI · Kōbushi-gatake 2,475 m · Sayama · **Kawagoe** · Koshigaya · Sawara
NAGANO · Komagane · ALPS · Enzan · NAT'L · Tokorozawa · **Urawa** · Ryūgasaki · Chōshi
Shirahe-san 3,192 m · NAT'L · CHICHIBU-TAMA · Tachikawa · PARK · **Kawaguchi** · Narita · Inubō-zaki
Seki · Nakatsugawa · PARK · NAT'L PARK · Hachiōji · **TŌKYŌ** · NARITA INT'L · Asahi
inomiya · Tajimi · Iida · Nirasaki · **Kōfu** · Ōme · Chōfu · **Chiba**
Kakamigahara · Akaishi-dake 3,120 m · Tsuru · Otsuki · **TOKYO** · CHIBA
Inuyama · Mizunami · Enzan · Fujiyoshida · Hadano · Sagamihara · **Kawasaki**
NAGOYA · AICHI · SHIZUOKA · YAMANASHI · Chigasaki · **YOKOHAMA** · Kisarazu
Seto · Fuji-san 3,776 m · **Fujisawa** · KANA- · Kimitsu
Toyota · Okazaki · Minobu · Fujiyama · HAKONE · **Yokosuka** · Futtsu
Nishio · Tenryū · Fujieda · Numazu · IZU · GAWA · Kyonan · Kamogawa
Gamagōri · Toyokawa · Yaizu · **Mishima** · Susono · Odawara · Tomiyama
Toyohashi · Iwata · Fukuroi · Atami · Katsuura
HŪBU · Kosai · Shimizu NAT'L PARK · Amagi-san 1,407 m · Tateyama
Hamamatsu · **Hamakita** · Suruga · Shimoda · Nojima-zaki
Irago-misaki · Omae-zaki · *Bay* · IMA NAT'L PARK · FUJI-HAKONE- · Irō-zaki · Ōshima
Daiō-zaki · Toba · ZU NAT'L · CHŪBU · Nii I. · *Honshū*
· PARK · KANTŌ · **TŌKYŌ**
Kōzu I.

J A P A N · Miyake I. · MIYAKEJIMA

Mikura I.

Izu

FUJI-HAKONE-
IZU NAT'L
PARK
(JAPAN)

Islands

Hachijō I.
Hachijō · **HACHIJŌJIMA**

Aoga I.

Beyoneisu-Retsugan

Inset (bottom right):

Koshiki · Sendai · Kokubu · Miyakonojo
Is. · Kushikino · Ijuin · KAGOSHIMA · Nichinan
Kagoshima · Kanoya · Kushima
Kaseda · Tarumizu · Koyama
Makurazaki · KIRISHIMA-YAKU NP · **Kyūshū**
Sata-misaki
Nishino'omote
Tanega
Kamiyaku · Nakatane
Yaku · Kamiyaku · 1,935 m
Shanghai · KIRISHIMA
YAKU NP
Kuchino

Tokara Islands

KAGOSHIMA

Suwanose

EAST
CHINA
SEA · Amami-Ō-Shima
· Naze · Kikai
Setouchi

Tokuno · Amami
Islands · Tokunoshima

Ryukyu · Okinoerabu
Islands · (Nansei-Shotō) · Yoron
· Okinawa Is. · Iheya · Hedo-misaki
· Ie · Yonaha-dake
· Motobu · 498 m
· Nago · Okinawa
· Kumé · Ginowan · Gushikawa
· **Naha** · Urasoe · Kitadaitō
· Itoman · Minamidaitō
· Kyan-zaki

Keelung · Senkaku-Shotō · OKINAWA

PACIFIC
OCEAN

Sakishima Islands · Hirara
Yonaguni · Tamara · Miyako
Ishigaki · **Ishigaki** · Miyako Is. · Okidaitō
Iriomote
Yaeyama Is.

© Copyright by HAMMOND INCORPORATED, Maplewood, N.J. · CD-1035-A-A-A · © HAMMOND INC. CC-1116-A

SCALE 1:3,000,000   LAMBERT CONFORMAL CONIC PROJECTION
MILES 0   50   100   150
KILOMETERS 0   50   100   150

E · 138° · F · G · 124° · H · 126° · J · 128° · K · 130° · L

Northern Japan

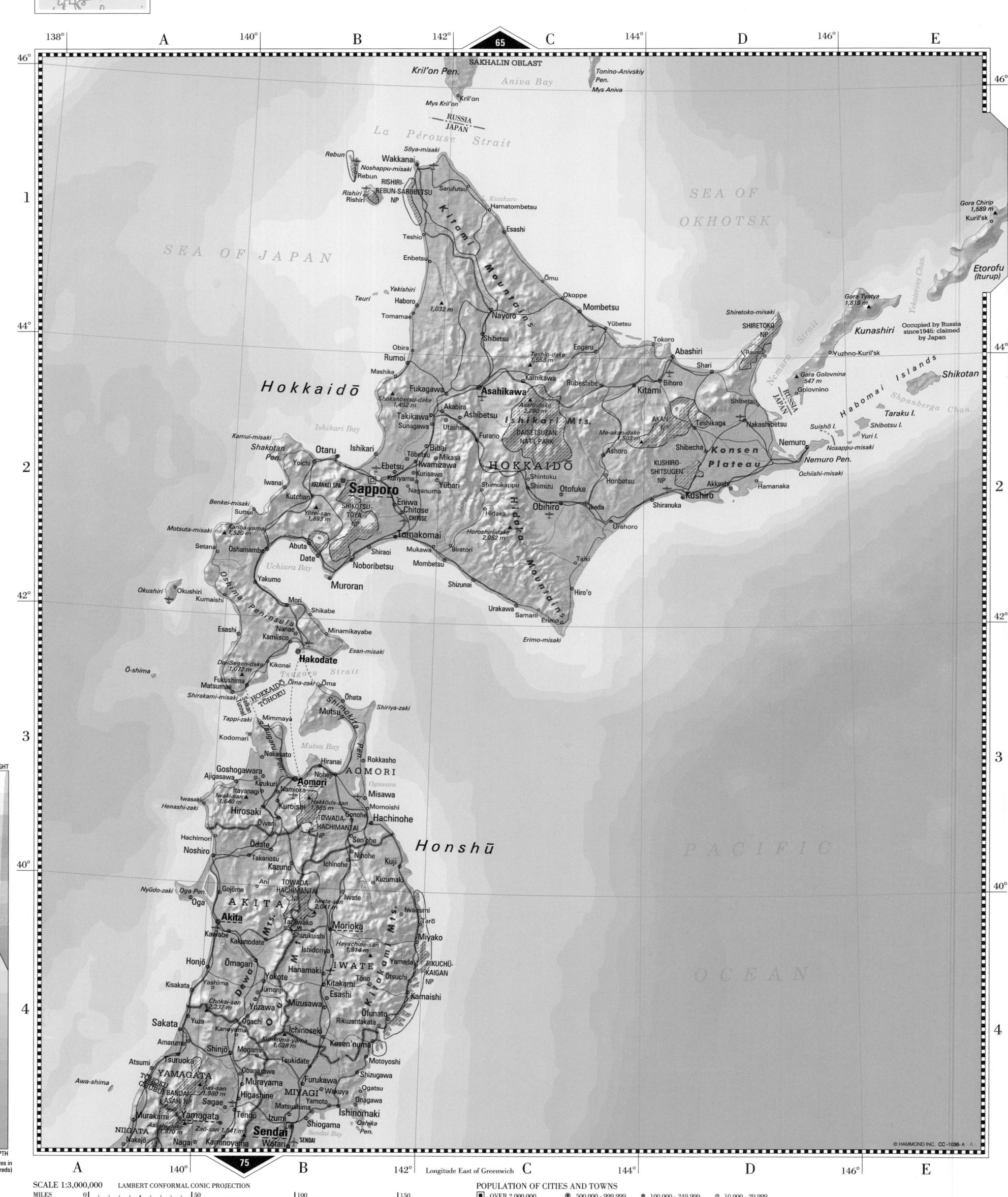

SAKHALIN OBLAST

Kril'on Pen.

Aniva Bay

Tonino-Anivskiy Pen.

Mys Aniva

Mys Kril'on

Kril'on

SEA OF OKHOTSK

Gora Chirip 1,589 m

Kuril'sk

La Pérouse Strait

RUSSIA
JAPAN

Sōya-misaki

Rebun

Etorofu (Iturup)

Wakkanai

Noshappu-misaki

Rebun

Sarufutsu

RISHIRI-REBUN-SAROBETSU NP

Kutcharo

Hamatombetsu

SEA OF JAPAN

Rishiri

Rishiri

Teshio

Esashi

Ōmu

Gora Tyatya 1,819 m

Enbetsu

Okoppe

Mombetsu

Shiretoko-misaki

Yakishiri

Haboro

1,032 m

Nayoro

Yūbetsu

SHIRETOKO NP

Kunashiri

Occupied by Russia since 1945; claimed by Japan

Teuri

Tomamae

Shibetsu

Engaru

Tokoro

Abashiri

Rausu

Yuzhno-Kuril'sk

Obira

Rumoi

Teshio-dake 1,553 m

Kamikawa

Shari

Habomai Islands

Hokkaidō

Mashike

Fukagawa

Shokanbetsu-dake 1,492 m

Akabira

Asahikawa

Rubeshibe

Kitami

Bihoro

Gora Golovnina 547 m

Golovnino

Shikotan

Kamui-misaki

Takikawa

Ashibetsu

Asahi-dake 2,290 m

Ishikari Mts.

Shibetsu

Nakashibetsu

Shpanberga Chan.

Taraku I.

Shakotan Pen.

Otaru

Ishikari

Sunagawa

Utashinai

Furano

DAISETSUZAN NAT'L PARK

Shintoku

Teshikaga

AKAN NP

Suishō I.

Yuri I.

Shibotsu I.

Yoichi

Bibai

Tōbetsu

Mikasa

HOKKAIDŌ

Me-akan-dake 503 m

Shibecha

KUSHIRO-SHITSUGEN NP

Konsen Plateau

Nosappu-misaki

Benkei-misaki

JŌZANKEI SPA

Ebetsu

Kurisawa

Yūbari

Shimukappu

Ashoro

Honbetsu

Nemuro

Kamui-misaki

Sapporo

Kutchan

Naganuma

Shimizu

Otofuke

Kushiro

Nemuro Pen.

Iwanai

Yōtei-san 1,893 m

SHIKOTSU-TOYA NP

Eniwa

Chitose

Shikumappu

Hidaka

Horoshiri-dake 2,052 m

Ikeda

Akkeshi

Hamanaka

Ochiishi-misaki

Suttsu

CHITOSE

Obihiro

Shiranuka

Motsuta-misaki

Kariba-yama 1,520 m

Abuta

Date

Tomakomai

Mukawa

Biratori

Urahoro

Setana

Oshamambe

Shiraoi

Taiki

Yakumo

Noboribetsu

Mombetsu

Shizunai

Hidaka Mountains

Hiro'o

Uchiura Bay

Muroran

Shikabe

Urakawa

Samani

Erimo

Okushiri

Okushiri

Mori

Kumaishi

Nanae

Minamikayabe

Erimo-misaki

Esashi

Kamiisco

Esan-misaki

Dai-Segen-dake 1,072 m

Kikonai

Hakodate

Ō-shima

Fukushima

HOKKAIDŌ
TŌHOKU

Ōma-zaki

Ōma

Matsumae

Tsugaru Strait

Shirakami-misaki

Shiriya-zaki

Ōhata

Tappi-zaki

Mimmaya

Mutsu

Shimokita Pen.

Kodomari

Mutsu Bay

Rokkasho

Nakasato

Hiranai

Tsugaru Pen.

AOMORI

Goshogawara

Noheji

Ogawara

Ajigasawa

Iwaki-san 1,640 m

Itayanagi

Kizukuri

Aomori

Mamioka

Misawa

Iwasaki

Kuroishi

Hakkōda-san 1,585 m

Momoishi

Henashi-zaki

Hirosaki

TOWADA-HACHIMANTAI NP

Gonohe

Hachinohe

Ōwani

Honshū

Hachimori

Ōdate

San'he

Ninohe

Kuji

Noshiro

Takanosu

Kazuno

Ichinohe

Iwate-san 2,041 m

Ani

TOWADA-HACHIMANTAI NP

Kuzumaki

Nyūdo-zaki

Oga Pen.

Gojōme

Iwaizumi

Tarō

Oga

AKITA

Tazawako

Shizukuishi

Morioka

Miyako

Yamada

RIKUCHŪ-KAIGAN NP

Akita

Kakunodate

Ishidoriya

Hayachine-san 1,914 m

Ōtsuchi

Kawabe

Dewa Mts.

Ōmagari

IWATE

Kamaishi

Honjō

Yokote

Hanamaki

Kitakami Mts.

Kisakata

Yashima

Jumonji

Kitakami

Tōno

Ōfunato

Chōkai-san 2,237 m

Yuzawa

Mizusawa

Esashi

Rikuzentakata

Sakata

Yuza

Kaneyama

Kurikoma-yama 1,628 m

Ichinoseki

Kesen'numa

Amarume

Shinjō

Mogami

IWATE

Motoyoshi

Awa-shima

YAMAGATA

Atsumi

Tsuruoka

Obanazawa

Furukawa

Shizugawa

Onagawa

Murakami

CHŌKAI BANDAI-ASAHI NP

Gas-san 1,980 m

Murayama

Higashine

MIYAGI

Yamoto

Wakuya

Ishinomaki

NIIGATA

Sagae

Matsushima

Nakajō

Asahi-san 1,870 m

Yamagata

Tendō

Izumi

Oshika Pen.

Nagai

Zaō-san 1,841 m

Kaminoyama

Sendai

Shiogama

SENDAI

Watari

Sendai Bay

© HAMMOND INC.   CC-1036-A

SCALE 1:3,000,000   LAMBERT CONFORMAL CONIC PROJECTION

MILES   0 ___ 50 ___ 100 ___ 150

KILOMETERS   0 ___ 50 ___ 100 ___ 150

Longitude East of Greenwich

HEIGHT
m.   ft.
60   197
40   130
15   50
10   33
5   16
2   7
0
2   7
5   16
10   33
20   65
30   98
50   164
60   197
m.   ft.
DEPTH
(Figures in Hundreds)

POPULATION OF CITIES AND TOWNS

■ OVER 2,000,000	● 500,000 - 999,999	● 100,000 - 249,999	○ 10,000 - 29,999
▣ 1,000,000 - 1,999,999	● 250,000 - 499,999	● 30,000 - 99,999	○ UNDER 10,000

Tōkyō-Yokohama, Ōsaka-Nagoya

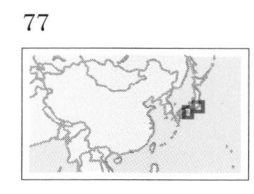

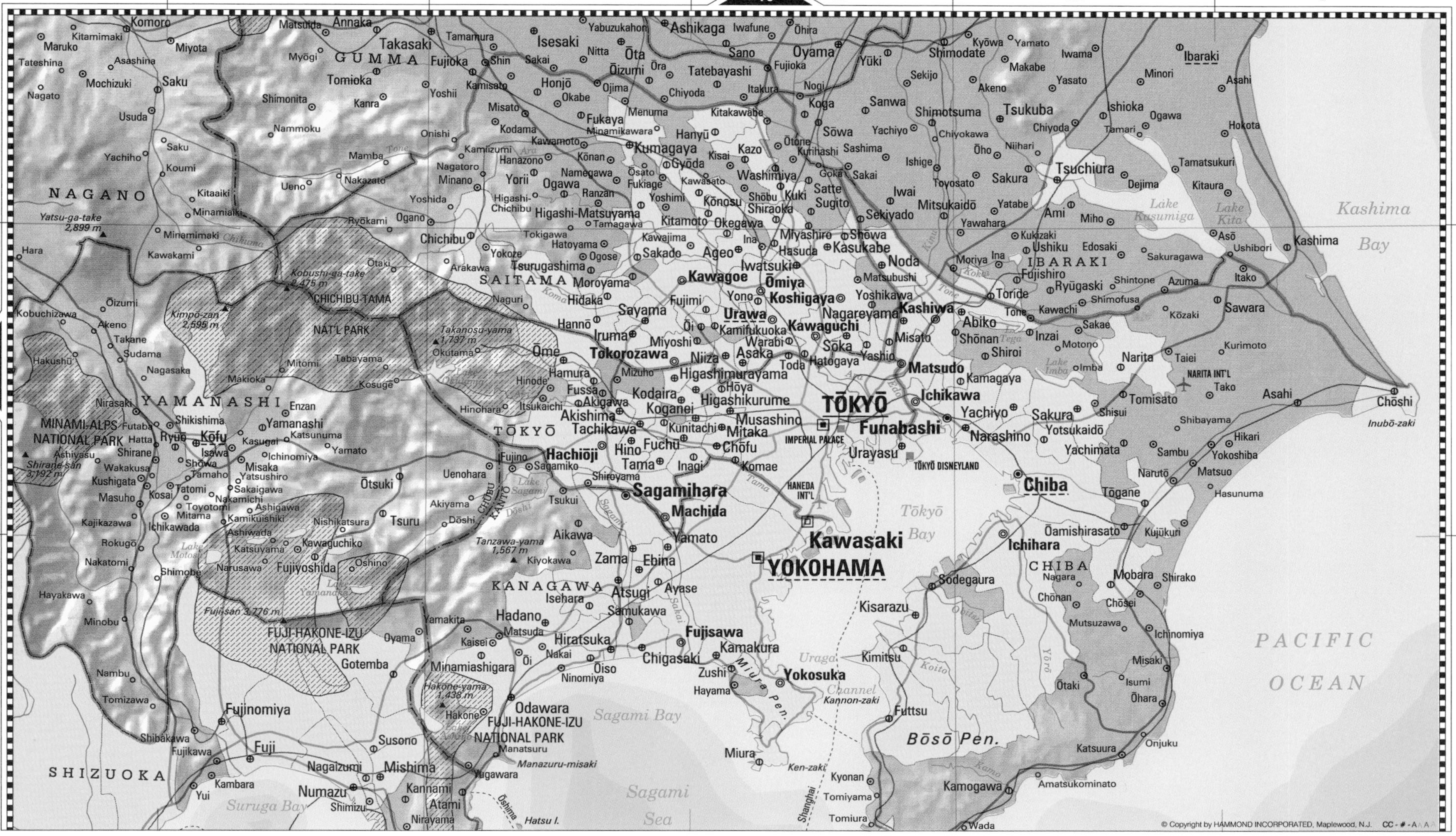

POPULATION OF CITIES AND TOWNS
■ OVER 2,000,000 ⊙ 500,000 - 999,999 ⊙ 100,000 - 249,999 ∘ 10,000 - 29,999
▣ 1,000,000 - 1,999,999 ⊙ 250,000 - 499,999 ⊙ 30,000 - 99,999 ∘ UNDER 10,000

SCALE 1:1,000,000 LAMBERT CONFORMAL CONIC PROJECTION
MILES 0 10 20 30 40 50
KILOMETERS 0 10 20 30 40 50

© Copyright by HAMMOND INCORPORATED, Maplewood, N.J.

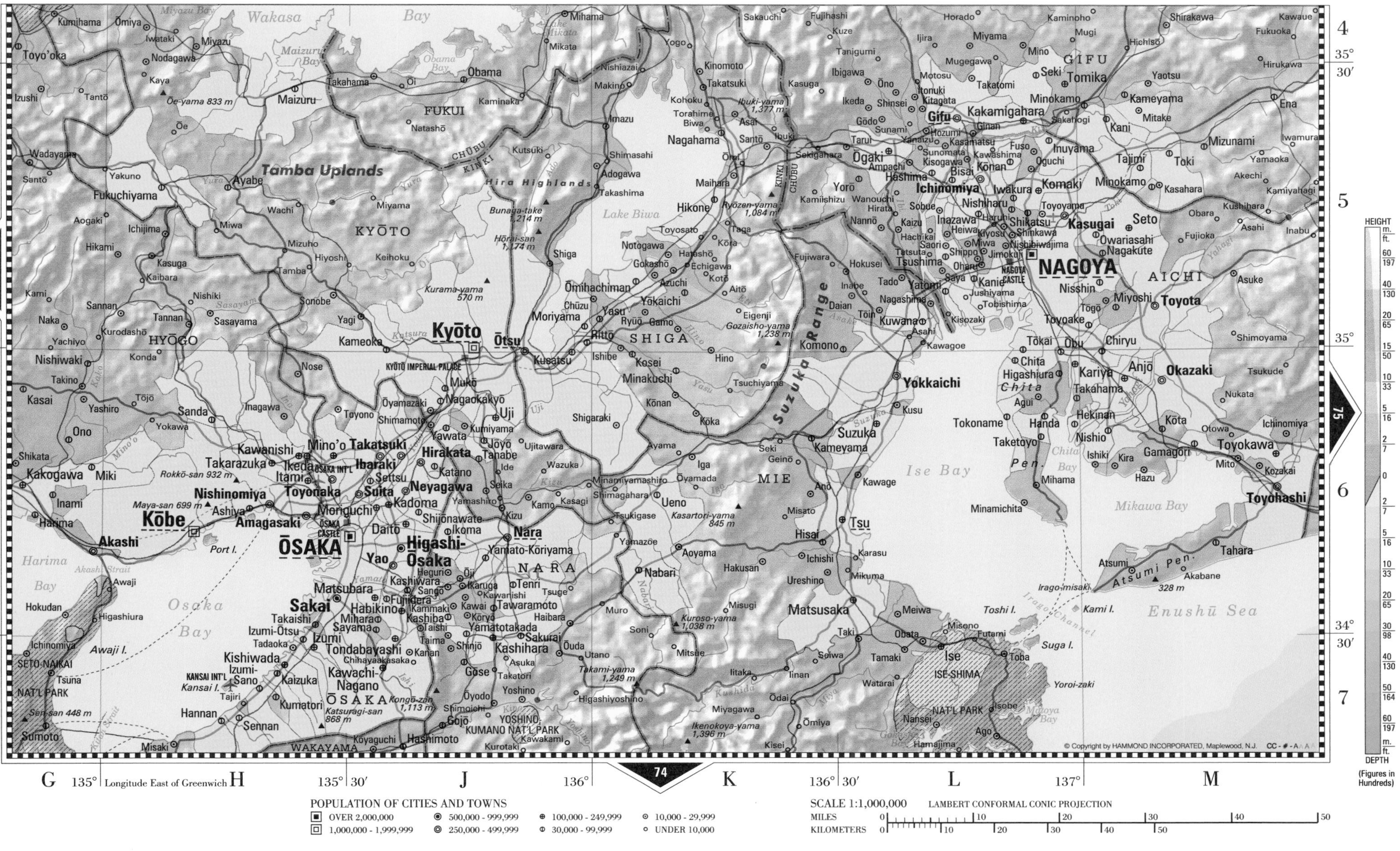

HEIGHT
m. ft.
40 130
20 65
15 50
10 33
7 23
5 16
2 7
0 0
DEPTH
5 16
10 33
30 98
60 197
(Figures in Hundreds)

Indochina

Longitude East of Greenwich

SCALE 1:6,000,000   LAMBERT CONFORMAL CONIC PROJECTION

MILES
KILOMETERS

HEIGHT
m.   ft.
60   197
40   130
20   65
15   50
10   33
5   16
0
—   —
7   2
5   16
10   33
20   65
30   98
40   130
50   164
60   197
m.   ft.
DEPTH
(Figures in
Hundreds)

Southeastern China, Taiwan, Philippines

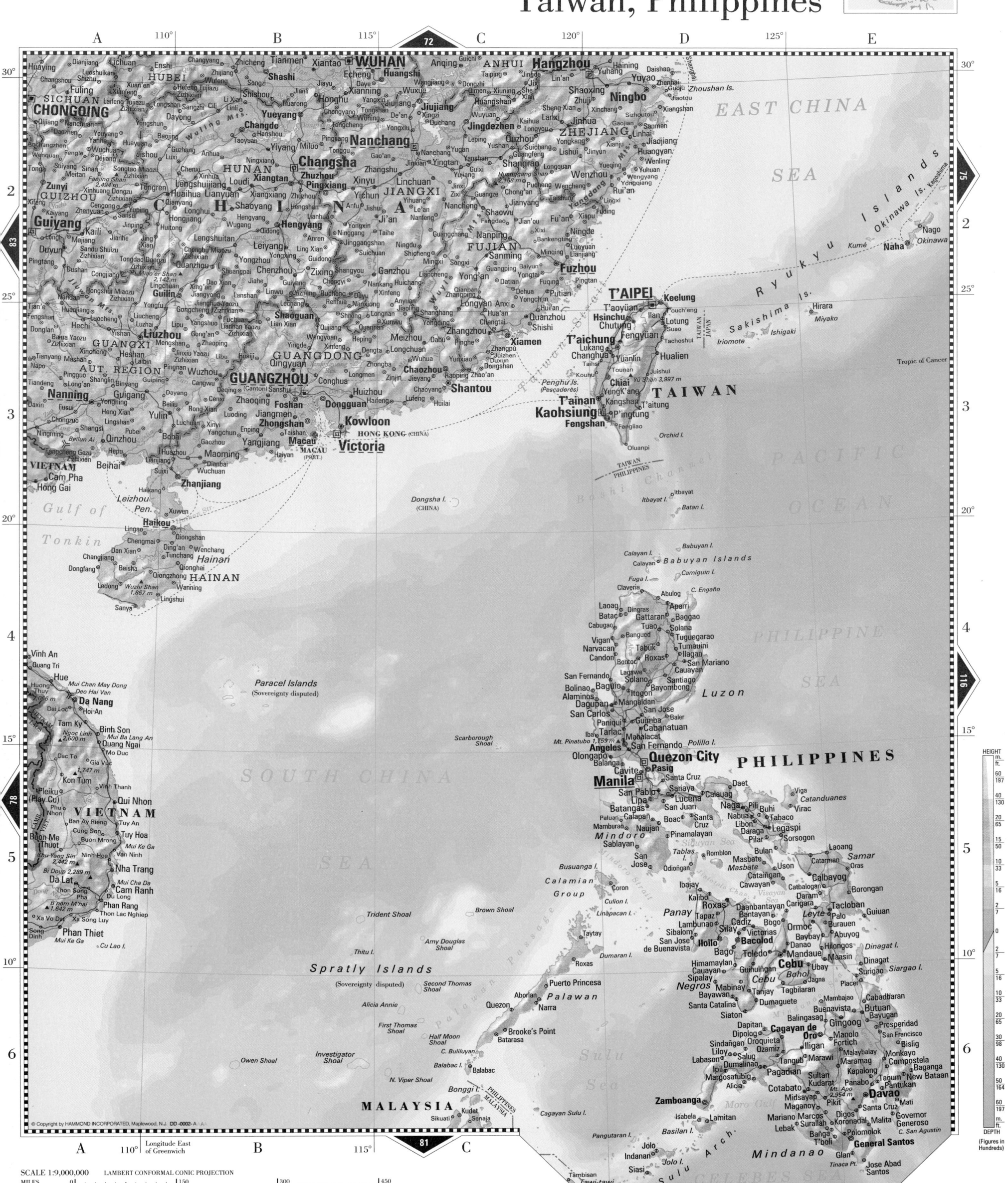

SCALE 1:9,000,000   LAMBERT CONFORMAL CONIC PROJECTION

MILES   0   150   300   450

KILOMETERS   0   150   300   450

POPULATION OF CITIES AND TOWNS

■ OVER 2,000,000   ● 500,000 - 999,999   ● 100,000 - 249,999   ○ 10,000 - 29,999

▣ 1,000,000 - 1,999,999   ● 250,000 - 499,999   ● 30,000 - 99,999   ○ UNDER 10,000

Longitude East of Greenwich

Indonesia, Malaysia

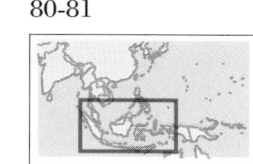

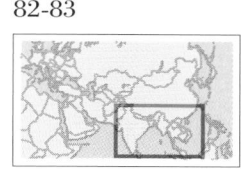

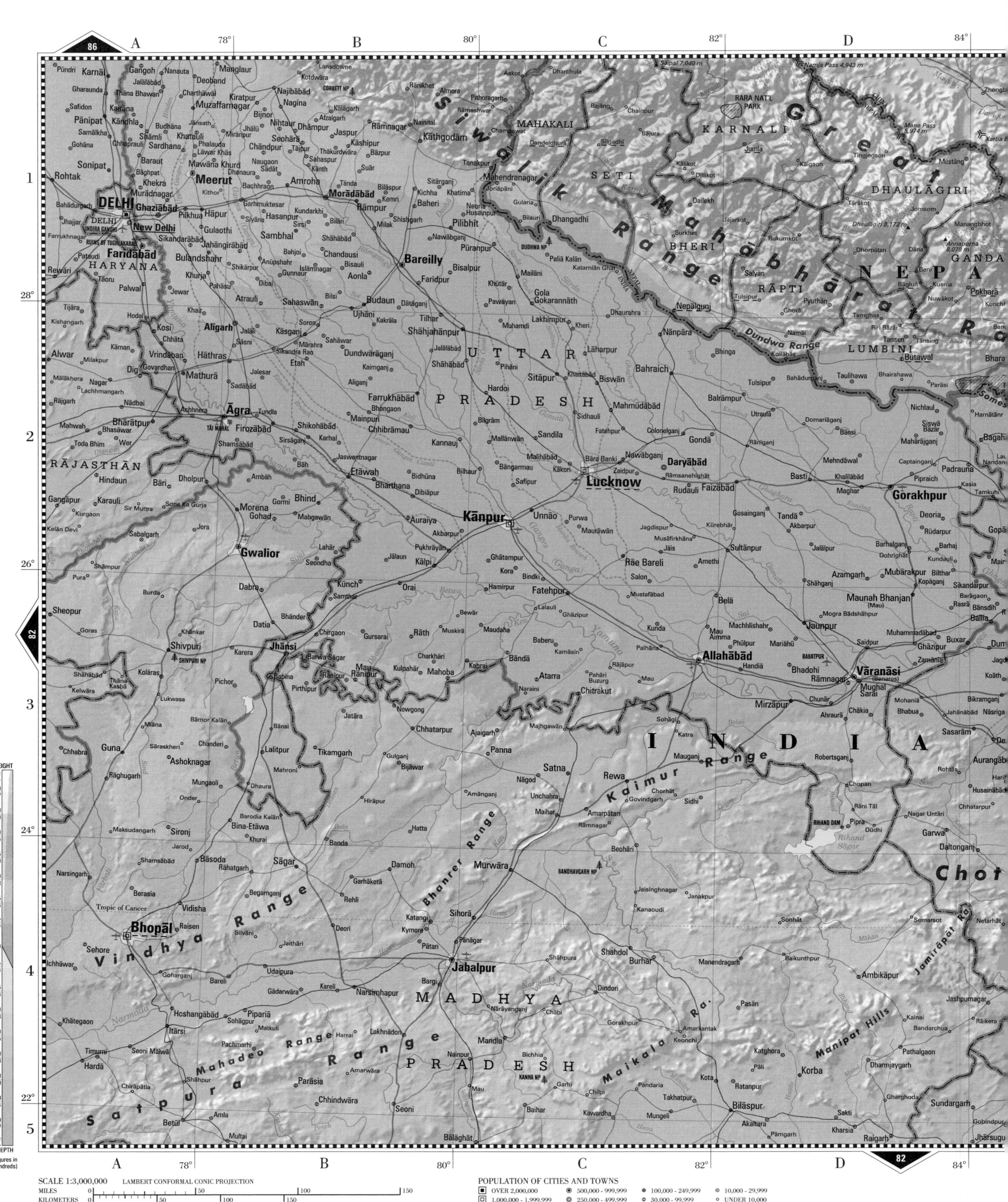

A · 78° · B · 80° · C · 82° · D · 84°

1

28°

2

26°

82

3

24°

22°

4

5

HEIGHT
m.
ft.
60 / 197
40 / 130
20 / 65
15 / 50
10 / 33
5 / 16
2 / 7
0
2 / 7
5 / 16
10 / 33
20 / 65
30 / 98
40 / 130
50 / 164
60 / 197
m.
ft.
DEPTH
(Figures in
Hundreds)

SCALE 1:3,000,000   LAMBERT CONFORMAL CONIC PROJECTION

MILES   0   50   100   150

KILOMETERS   0   50   100   150

POPULATION OF CITIES AND TOWNS

■ OVER 2,000,000   ◉ 500,000 - 999,999   ● 100,000 - 249,999   ◦ 10,000 - 29,999

▣ 1,000,000 - 1,999,999   ◉ 250,000 - 499,999   ● 30,000 - 99,999   ◦ UNDER 10,000

Ganges Plain

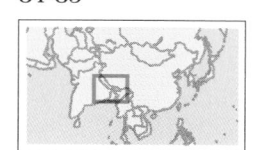

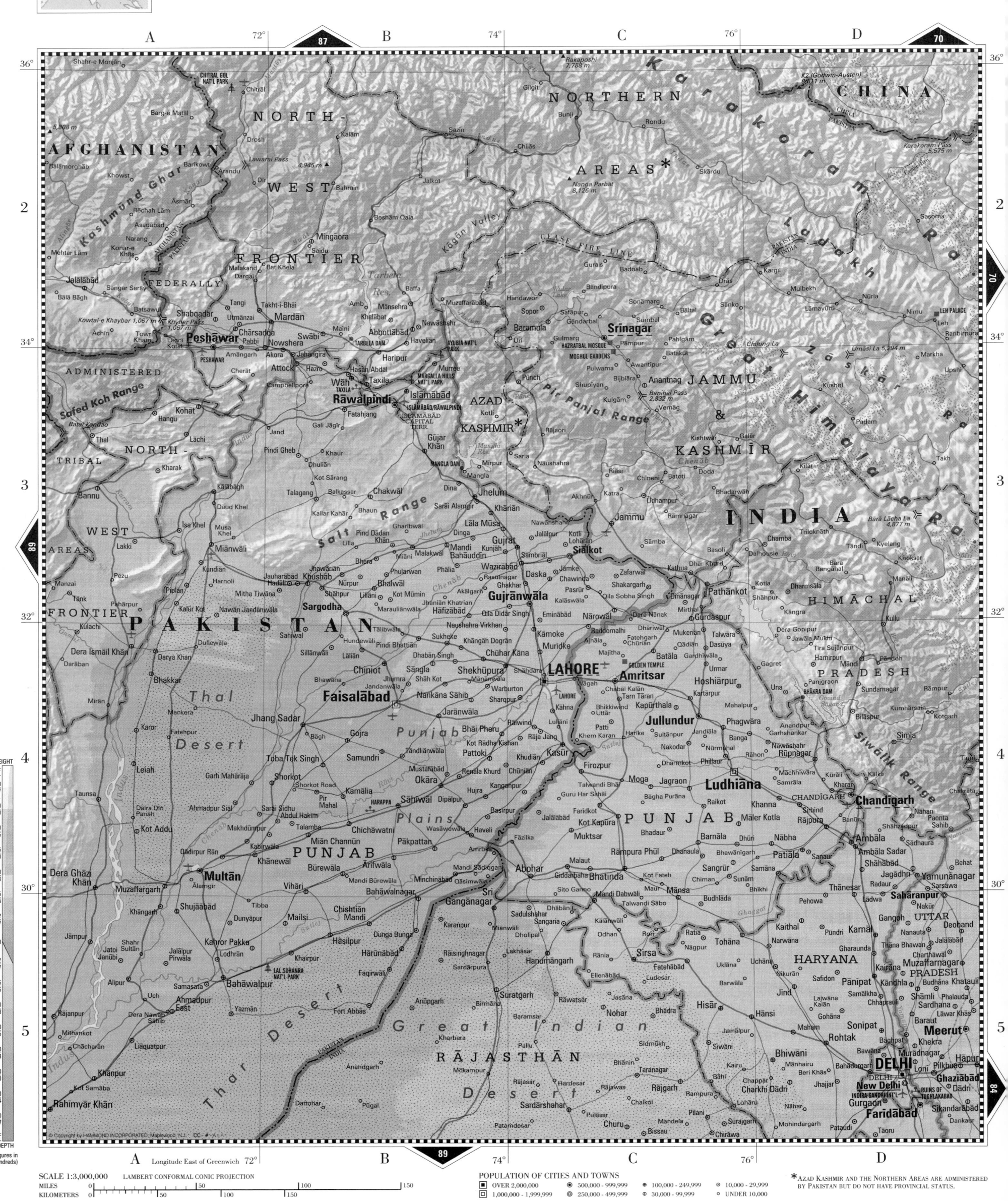

SCALE 1:3,000,000   LAMBERT CONFORMAL CONIC PROJECTION

MILES 0 — 50 — 100 — 150

KILOMETERS 0 — 50 — 100 — 150

POPULATION OF CITIES AND TOWNS

■ OVER 2,000,000
□ 1,000,000 - 1,999,999
◉ 500,000 - 999,999
⊙ 250,000 - 499,999
⊙ 100,000 - 249,999
⊙ 30,000 - 99,999
○ 10,000 - 29,999
○ UNDER 10,000

*Azad Kashmir and the Northern Areas are administered by Pakistan but do not have provincial status.

HEIGHT
m.   ft.
        60 197
        40 130
        20 65
        15 50
        5 16
        2 7
        0
        2 7
        5 16
        20 65
        30 98
        40 130
        50 164
        60 197
        m.   ft.
DEPTH
(Figures in Hundreds)

Central Asia

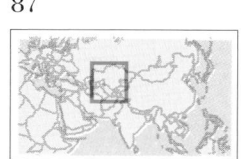

POPULATION OF CITIES AND TOWNS

■ OVER 2,000,000
□ 1,000,000 - 1,999,999
● 500,000 - 999,999
◉ 250,000 - 499,999
◉ 100,000 - 249,999
● 30,000 - 99,999
• 10,000 - 29,999
○ UNDER 10,000

SCALE 1:9,000,000   LAMBERT CONFORMAL CONIC PROJECTION

MILES   0   150   300   450
KILOMETERS   0   150   300   450

Longitude East of Greenwich

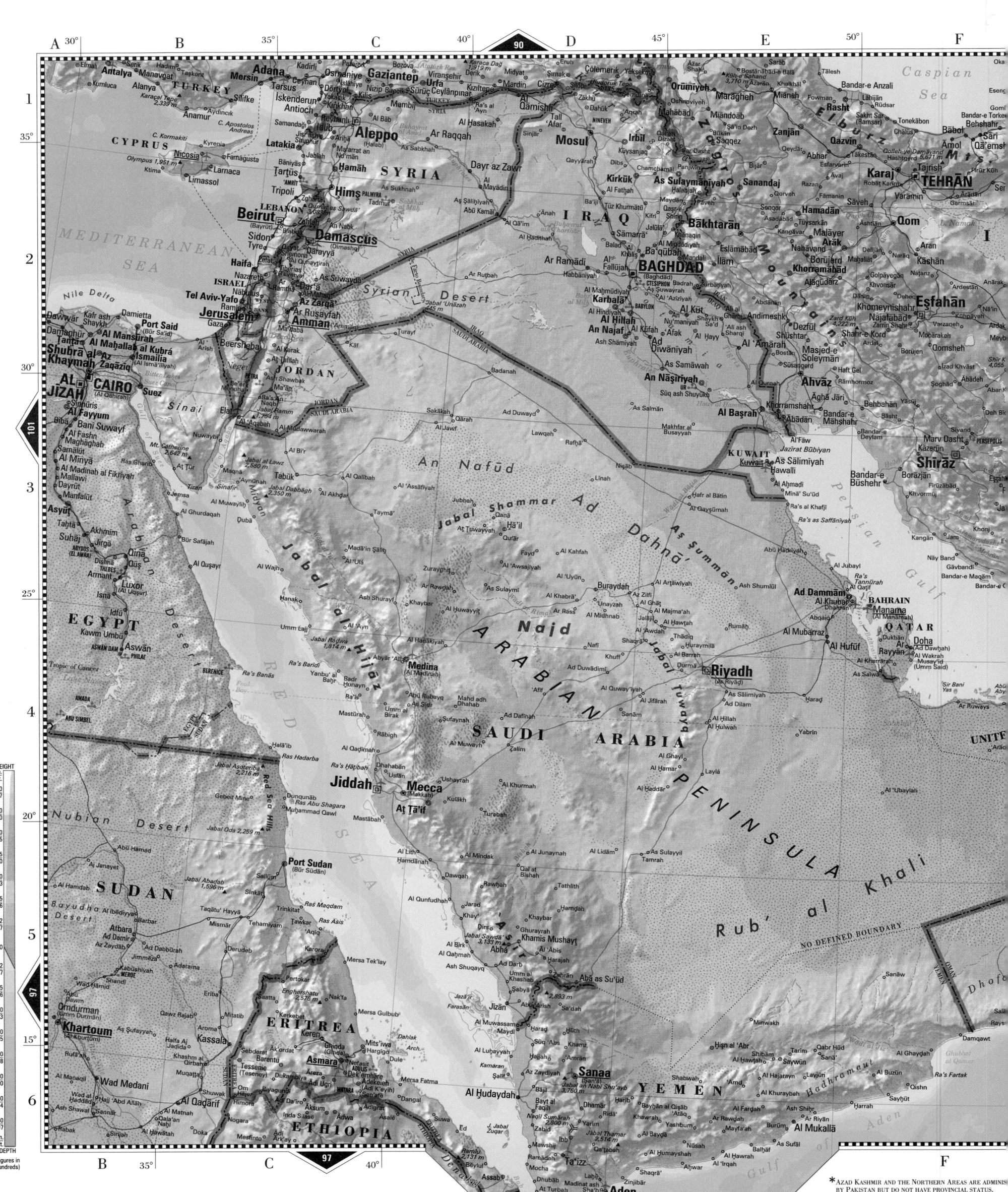

POPULATION OF CITIES AND TOWNS

■ OVER 2,000,000	● 500,000 - 999,999	● 100,000 - 249,999	○ 10,000 - 29,999
◻ 1,000,000 - 1,999,999	● 250,000 - 499,999	● 30,000 - 99,999	○ UNDER 10,000

SCALE 1:9,000,000 LAMBERT CONFORMAL CONIC PROJECTION

MILES 0   150   300   450
KILOMETERS 0   150   300   450

Longitude East of Greenwich

© Copyright by HAMMOND INCORPORATED, Maplewood, N.J.

Northern Middle East

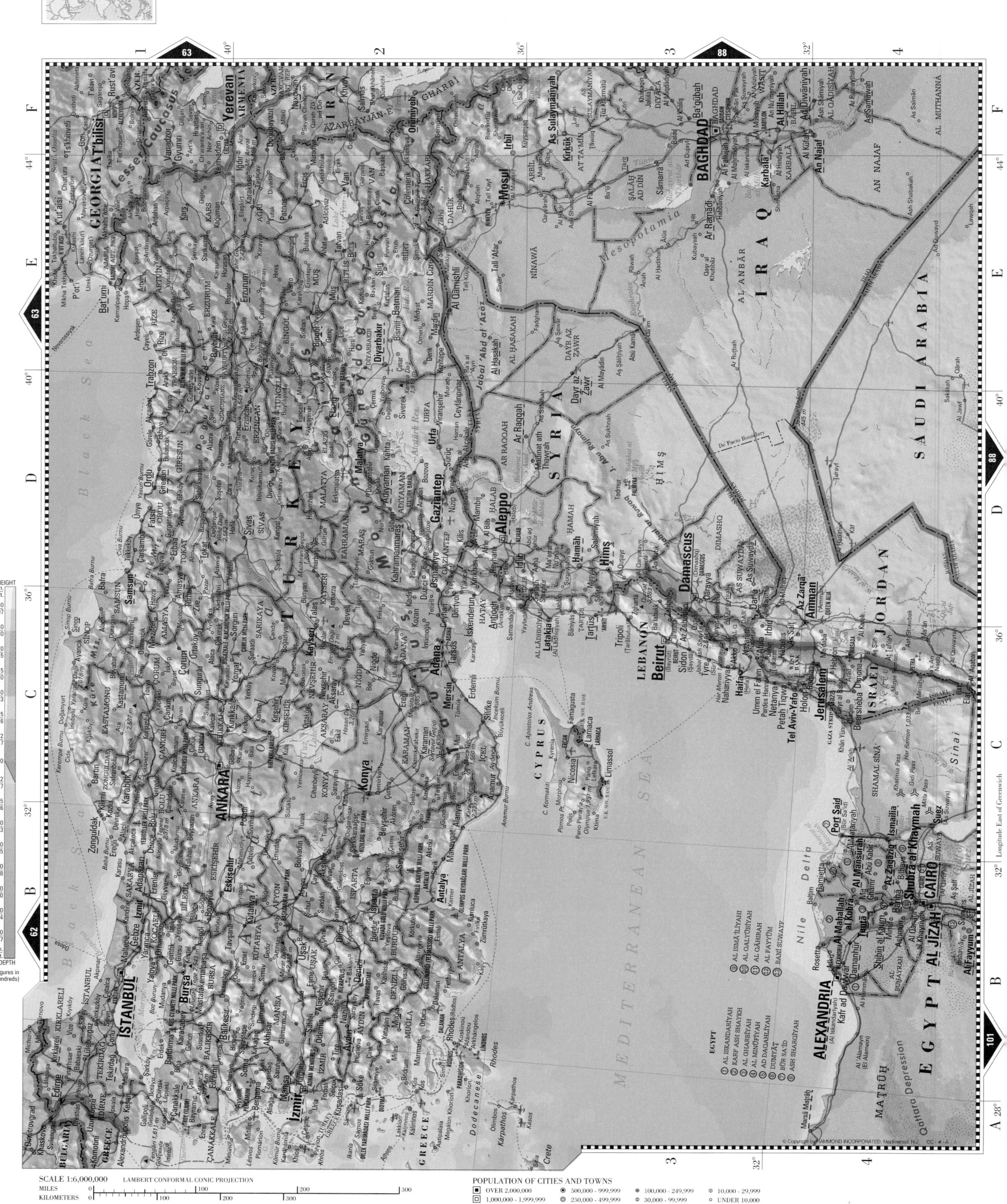

SCALE 1:6,000,000   LAMBERT CONFORMAL CONIC PROJECTION

MILES 0 ___ 100 ___ 200 ___ 300

KILOMETERS 0 ___ 100 ___ 200 ___ 300

POPULATION OF CITIES AND TOWNS

- ■ OVER 2,000,000
- □ 1,000,000 - 1,999,999
- ● 500,000 - 999,999
- ⊙ 250,000 - 499,999
- ⊕ 100,000 - 249,999
- ⊙ 30,000 - 99,999
- ○ 10,000 - 29,999
- ○ UNDER 10,000

Eastern Mediterranean Region

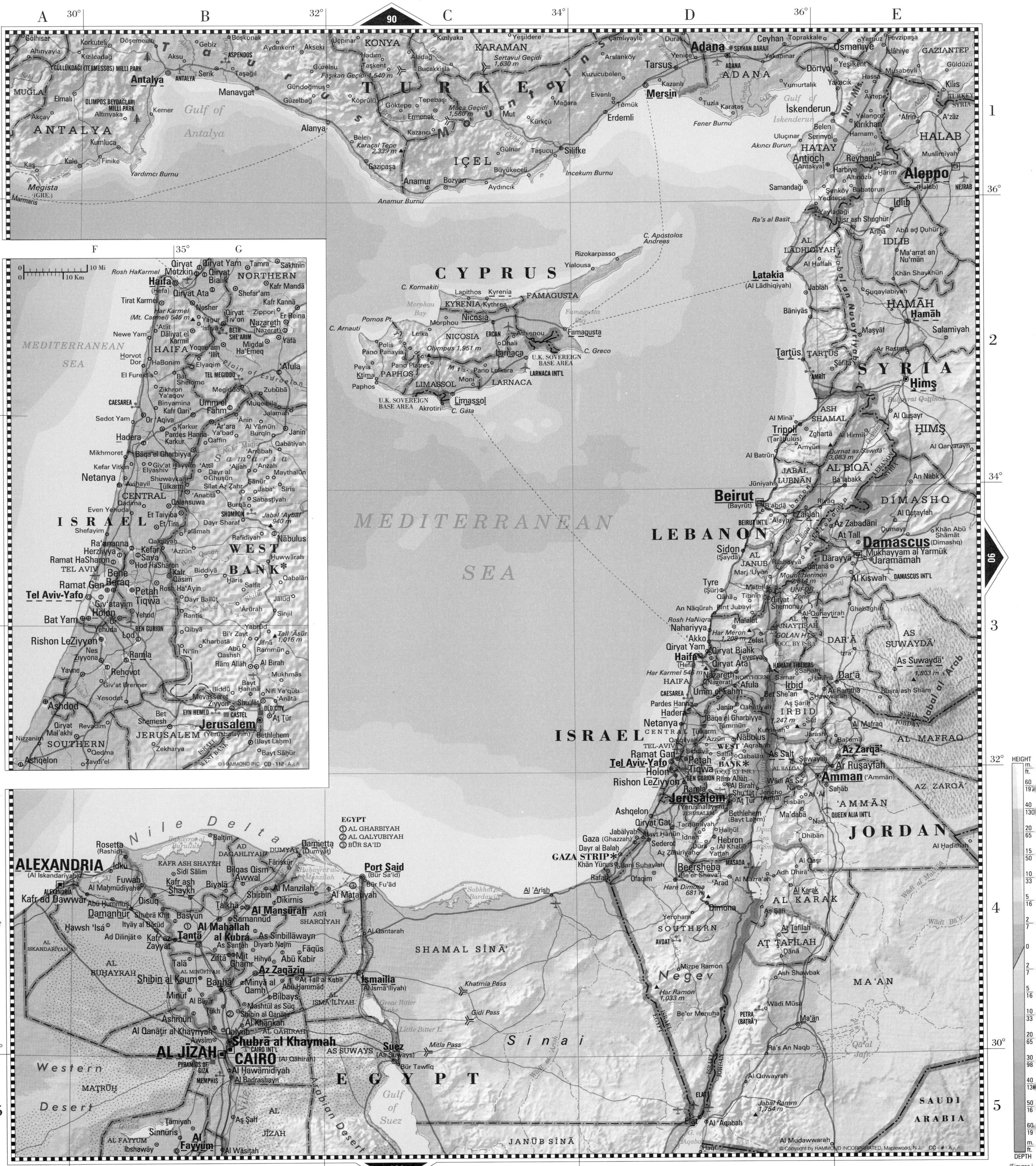

Africa

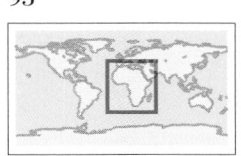

Several physiographic features are captured in this southeast-looking, high-oblique image. The Nile River Delta, the large, dark area at the bottom of the image, extends from the capital city of Cairo at the apex of the delta to the Suez Canal. The entire region is classified as desert (less than 10 inches [25 cm.] of rainfall per year). Desert-like areas are visible southwest of the delta and in the northwestern Sinai. Major rock outcrops (darker areas) are seen encircling the Red Sea. The two bodies of water flanking the southern end of the Sinai Peninsula are the Gulf of Suez and the Gulf of Aqaba.

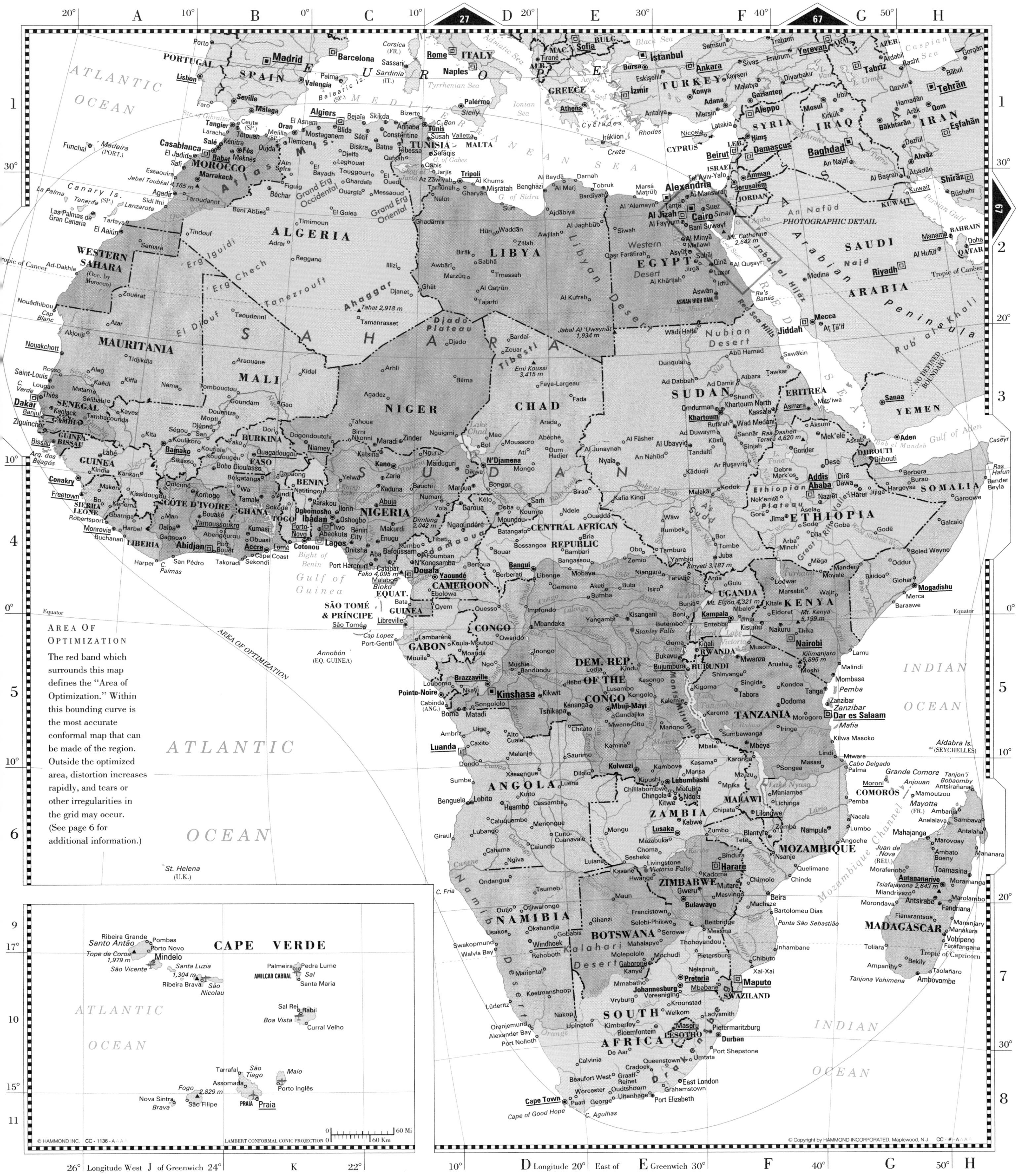

AREA OF OPTIMIZATION

The red band which surrounds this map defines the "Area of Optimization." Within this bounding curve is the most accurate conformal map that can be made of the region. Outside the optimized area, distortion increases rapidly, and tears or other irregularities in the grid may occur. (See page 6 for additional information.)

PHOTOGRAPHIC DETAIL

POPULATION OF CITIES AND TOWNS

■ OVER 3,000,000	● 500,000 - 999,999	○ UNDER 100,000
▣ 1,000,000 - 2,999,999	○ 100,000 - 499,999	

SCALE 1:30,000,000   OPTIMAL CONFORMAL PROJECTION

LAMBERT CONFORMAL CONIC PROJECTION

© HAMMOND INC.   CC - 1136 - A - A

© Copyright by HAMMOND INCORPORATED, Maplewood, N.J.   CC - # - A - A

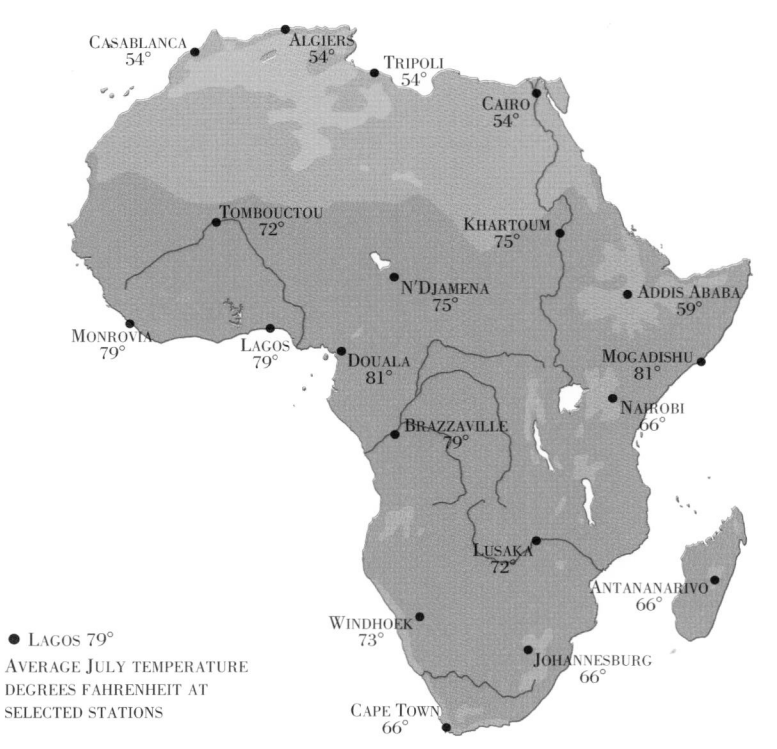

CASABLANCA 54°
ALGIERS 54°
TRIPOLI 54°
CAIRO 54°
TOMBOUCTOU 72°
KHARTOUM 75°
N'DJAMENA 75°
ADDIS ABABA 59°
MONROVIA 79°
LAGOS 79°
DOUALA 81°
MOGADISHU 81°
BRAZZAVILLE 79°
NAIROBI 66°
LUSAKA 72°
ANTANANARIVO 66°
WINDHOEK 73°
JOHANNESBURG 66°
CAPE TOWN 66°

● LAGOS 79°
AVERAGE JULY TEMPERATURE
DEGREES FAHRENHEIT AT
SELECTED STATIONS

AVERAGE JANUARY TEMPERATURE

FAHRENHEIT	CELSIUS		FAHRENHEIT	CELSIUS
OVER 68°	OVER 20°		32° TO 50°	0° TO 10°
50° TO 68°	10° TO 20°		UNDER 32°	UNDER 0°

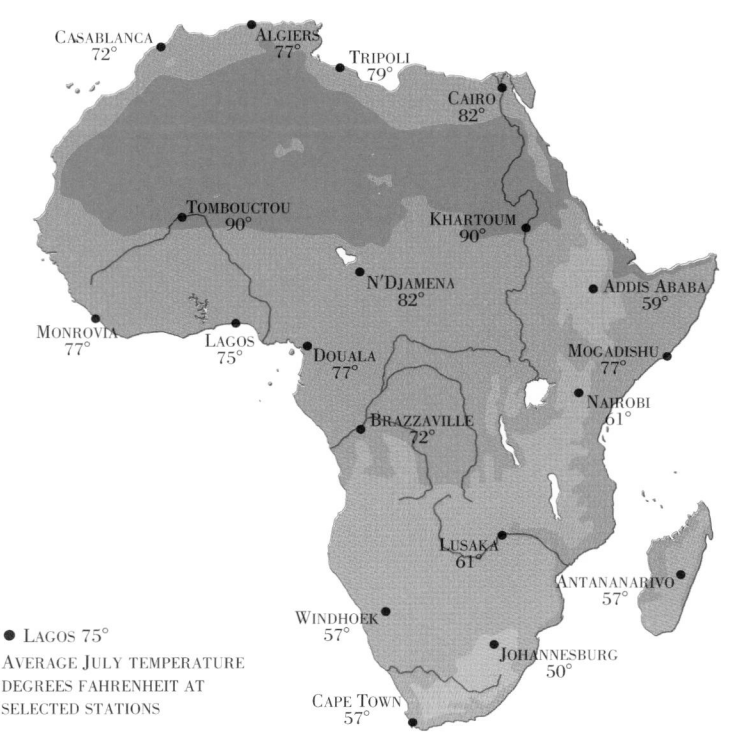

CASABLANCA 72°
ALGIERS 77°
TRIPOLI 79°
CAIRO 82°
TOMBOUCTOU 90°
KHARTOUM 90°
N'DJAMENA 82°
ADDIS ABABA 59°
MONROVIA 77°
LAGOS 75°
DOUALA 77°
MOGADISHU 77°
BRAZZAVILLE 72°
NAIROBI 61°
LUSAKA 61°
ANTANANARIVO 57°
WINDHOEK 57°
JOHANNESBURG 50°
CAPE TOWN 57°

● LAGOS 75°
AVERAGE JULY TEMPERATURE
DEGREES FAHRENHEIT AT
SELECTED STATIONS

AVERAGE JULY TEMPERATURE

FAHRENHEIT	CELSIUS		FAHRENHEIT	CELSIUS
OVER 86°	OVER 30°		50° TO 68°	10° TO 20°
68° TO 86°	20° TO 30°		UNDER 50°	UNDER 10°

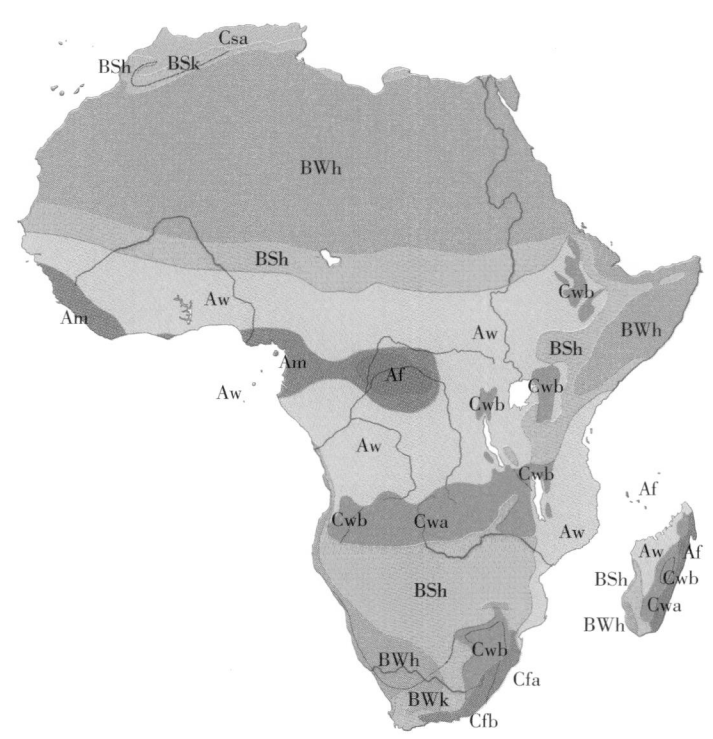

Csa
BSh
BSk
BWh
BSh
Aw
Am
Aw
Am
Af
Aw
Cwb
BSh
BWh
Cwb
Cwb
Cwb
Af
Aw
Cwb
Cwa
Aw
Af
BSh
Cwb
Cwa
BWh
Cwb
Cfa
BWk
Cfb

CLIMATE

HUMID TROPICAL
- Af NO DRY SEASON
- Am SHORT DRY SEASON
- Aw DRY WINTER

DRY
- BS SEMIARID
- BW ARID
- h HOT
- k COLD

HUMID WARM
- Cf NO DRY SEASON
- Cw DRY WINTER
- Cs DRY SUMMER
- a HOT SUMMER
- b COOL SUMMER

AFTER KOEPPEN-GEIGER

VEGETATION

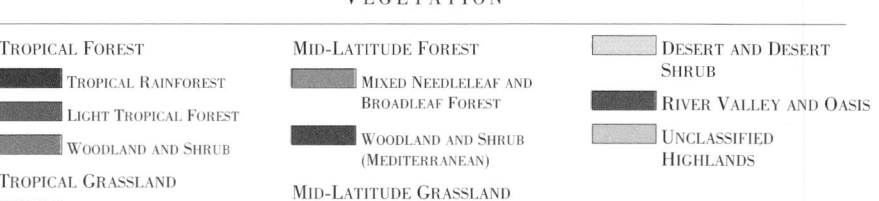

TROPICAL FOREST
- TROPICAL RAINFOREST
- LIGHT TROPICAL FOREST
- WOODLAND AND SHRUB

TROPICAL GRASSLAND
- GRASS AND SHRUB (SAVANNA)
- WOODED SAVANNA

MID-LATITUDE FOREST
- MIXED NEEDLELEAF AND BROADLEAF FOREST
- WOODLAND AND SHRUB (MEDITERRANEAN)

MID-LATITUDE GRASSLAND
- SHORT GRASS (STEPPE)

- DESERT AND DESERT SHRUB
- RIVER VALLEY AND OASIS
- UNCLASSIFIED HIGHLANDS

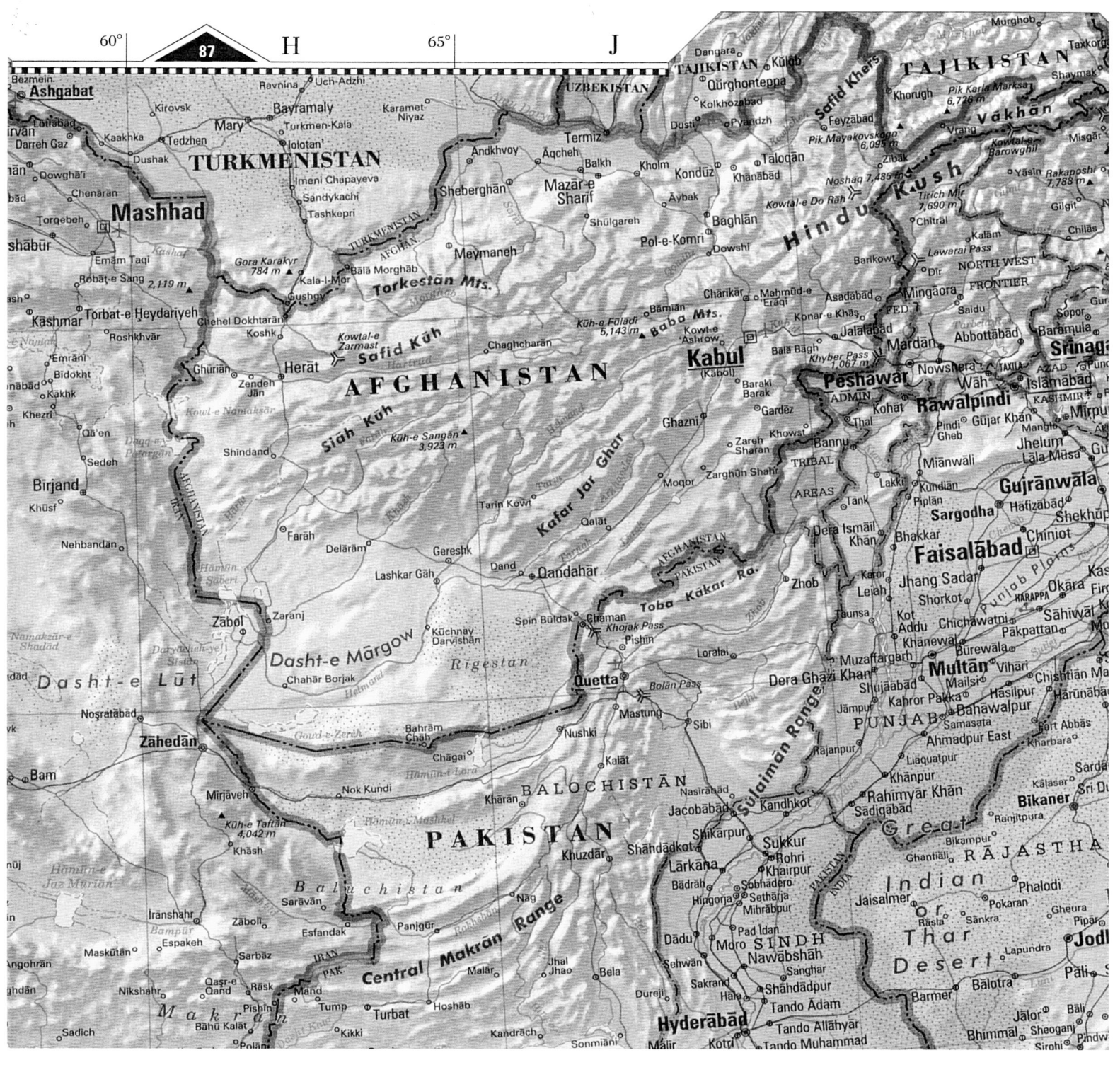

Africa - Geographical Comparisons

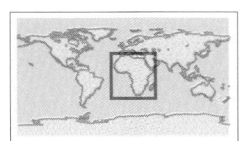

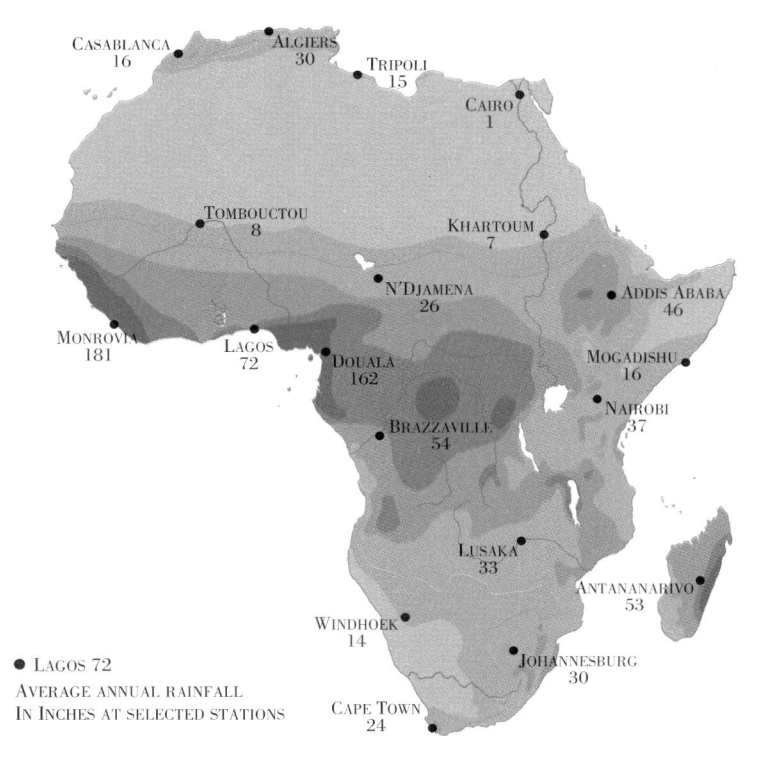

CASABLANCA 16
ALGIERS 30
TRIPOLI 15
CAIRO 1
TOMBOUCTOU 8
KHARTOUM 7
N'DJAMENA 26
ADDIS ABABA 46
MONROVIA 181
LAGOS 72
DOUALA 162
MOGADISHU 16
BRAZZAVILLE 54
NAIROBI 37
LUSAKA 33
ANTANANARIVO 53
WINDHOEK 14
JOHANNESBURG 30
CAPE TOWN 24

● LAGOS 72
AVERAGE ANNUAL RAINFALL
IN INCHES AT SELECTED STATIONS

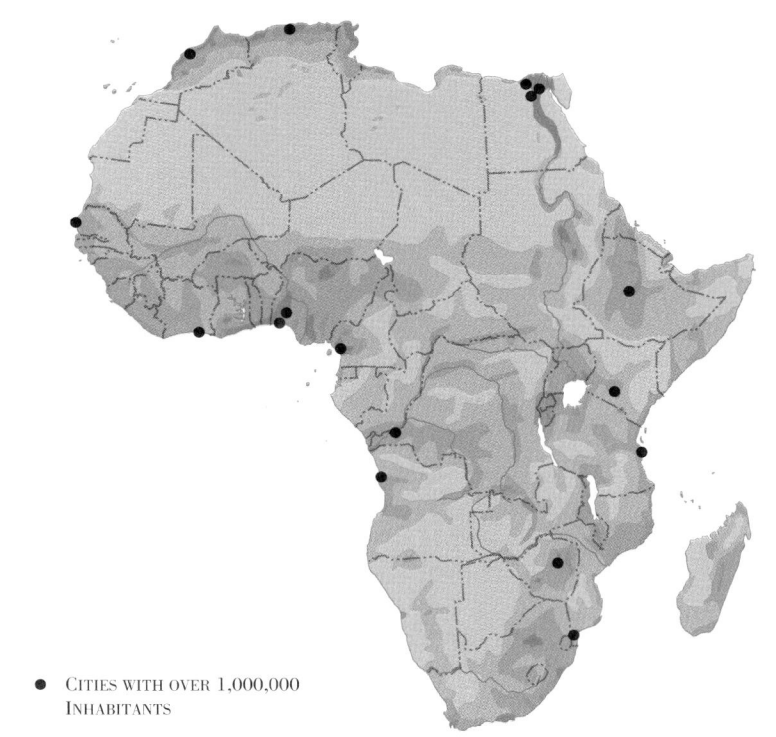

● CITIES WITH OVER 1,000,000
INHABITANTS

AVERAGE ANNUAL RAINFALL

INCHES	CM	INCHES	CM	INCHES	CM
OVER 80	OVER 200	40 TO 60	100 TO 150	10 TO 20	25 TO 50
60 TO 80	150 TO 200	20 TO 40	50 TO 100	UNDER 10	UNDER 25

POPULATION DISTRIBUTION

DENSITY PER		SQ. MI.	SQ. KM.	SQ. MI.	SQ. KM.
SQ. MI.	SQ. KM.	130 TO 260	50 TO 100	3 TO 25	1 TO 10
OVER 260	OVER 100	25 TO 130	10 TO 50	UNDER 3	UNDER 1

FRUIT WINE
SHEEP
CORN
COTTON
DATES
PEANUTS
CATTLE
CATTLE
COTTON
CATTLE
HOGS
COFFEE
PEANUTS
SHEEP
COFFEE
COCOA
COCOA
PALM OIL
BANANAS
COCOA
COFFEE
CATTLE
SISAL
PALM OIL
COFFEE
CORN
TOBACCO
CORN
SHEEP
CORN
CATTLE
SHEEP
SHEEP

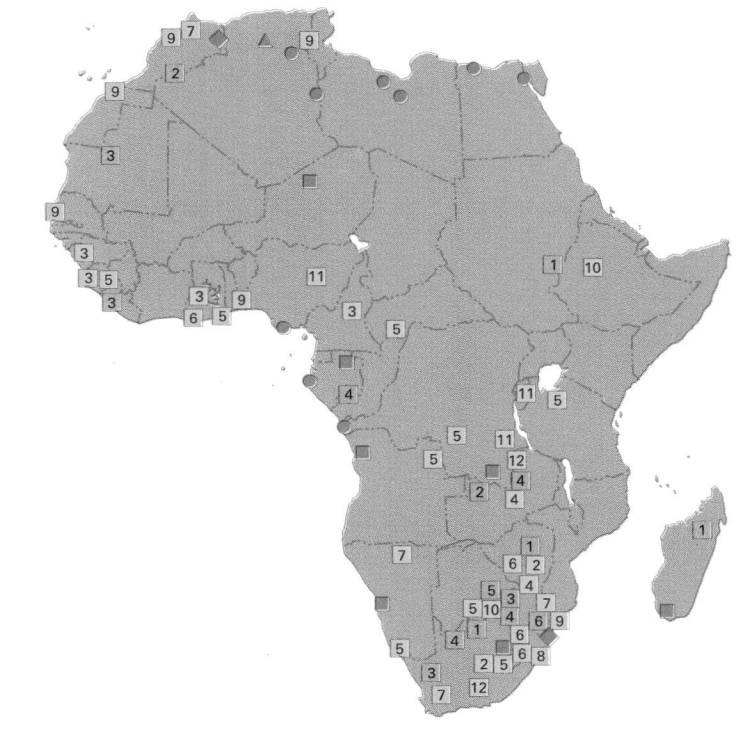

LAND USE

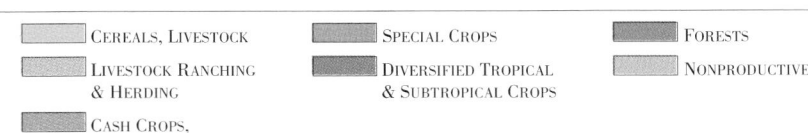

CEREALS, LIVESTOCK
SPECIAL CROPS
FORESTS
LIVESTOCK RANCHING & HERDING
DIVERSIFIED TROPICAL & SUBTROPICAL CROPS
NONPRODUCTIVE
CASH CROPS, MIXED FARMING

MINERAL RESOURCES

ENERGY & FUELS
◆ COAL
▲ NATURAL GAS
● PETROLEUM
▪ URANIUM

IRON & FERROALLOYS
1 CHROMIUM
2 COBALT
3 IRON ORE
4 MANGANESE
5 NICKEL
6 VANADIUM

OTHER MAJOR RESOURCES
1 ANTIMONY
2 ASBESTOS
3 BAUXITE
4 COPPER
5 DIAMONDS
6 GOLD
7 LEAD
8 MICA
9 PHOSPHATES
10 PLATINUM
11 TIN
12 ZINC

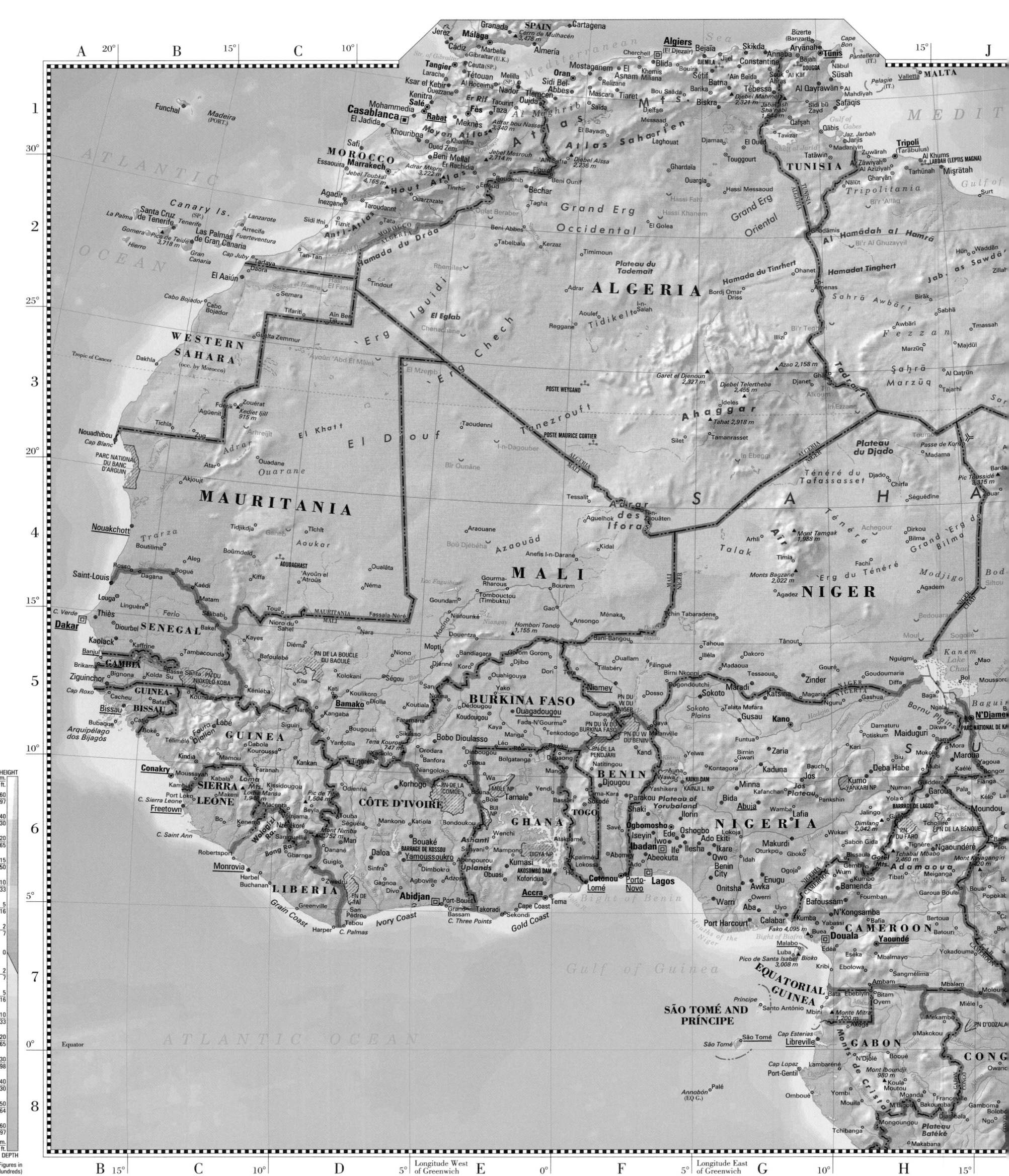

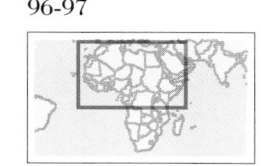

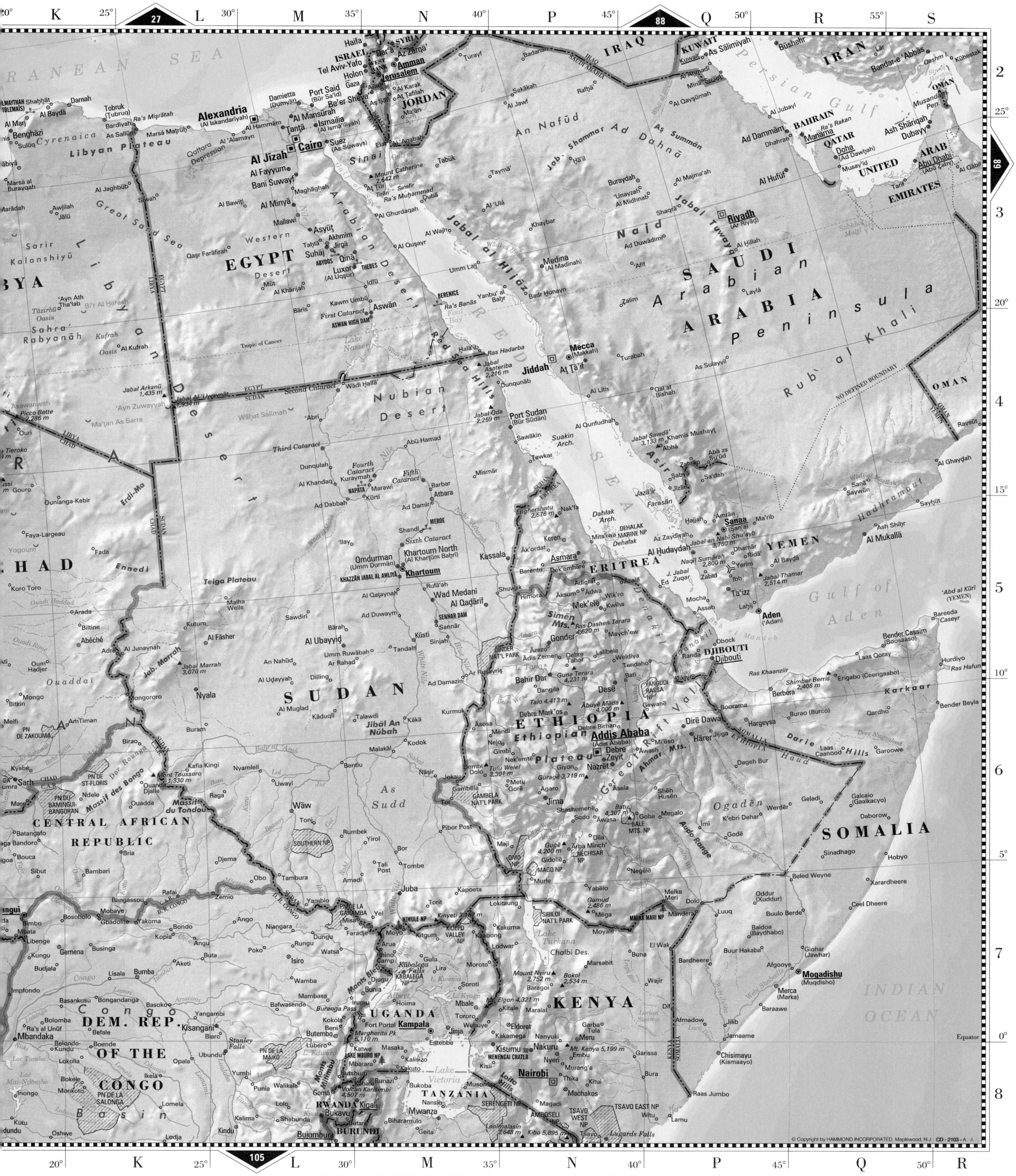

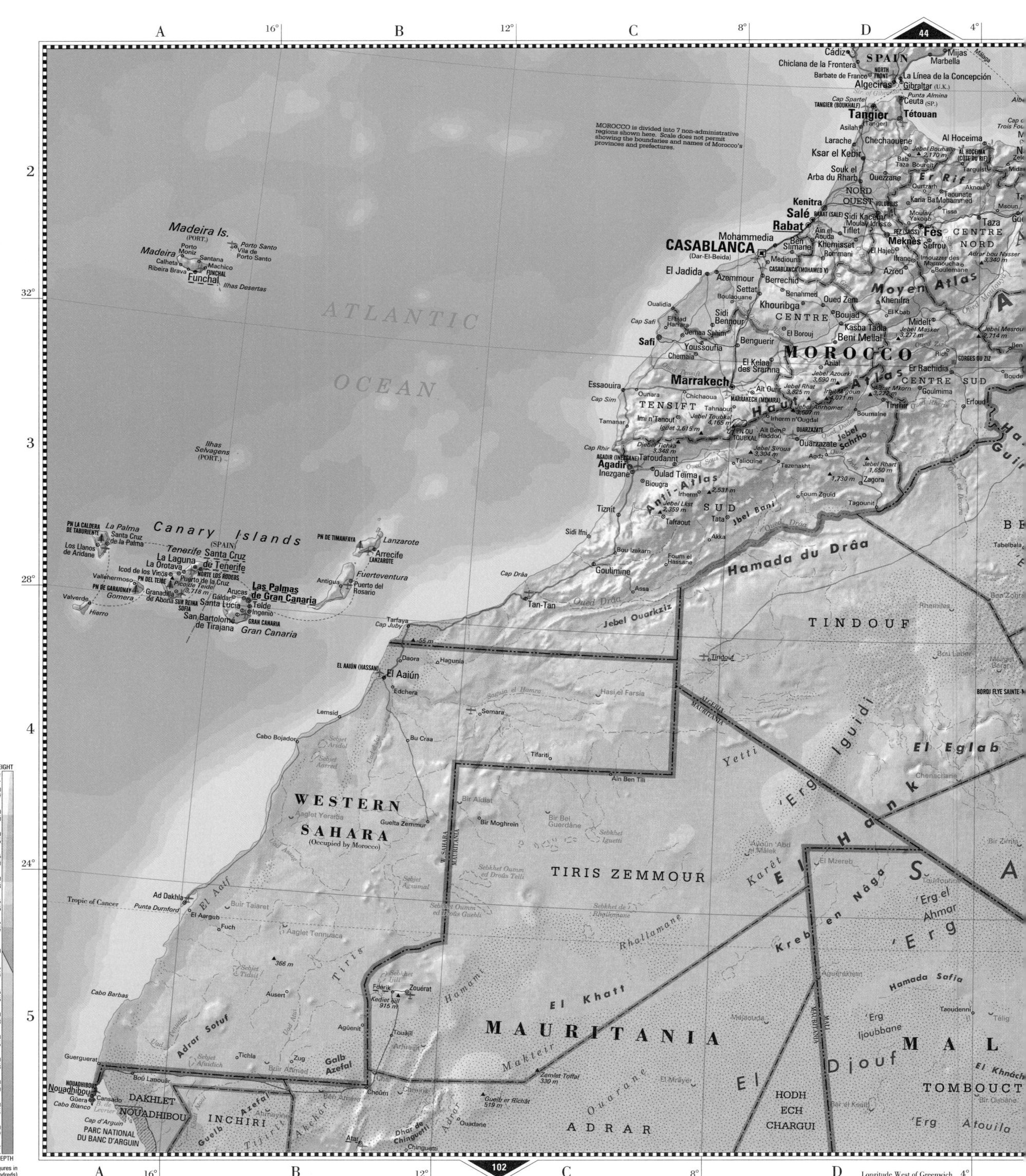

ATLANTIC OCEAN

SPAIN

Cádiz
Chiclana de la Frontera
Barbate de Franco
Algeciras
Gibraltar (U.K.)
Punta Almina
Ceuta (SP.)
Mijas
Marbella
Málaga
La Línea de la Concepción

NORTH FRONT

Cap Spartel
TANGIER (BOUKHALF)
Asilah
Tangier (Tánger)
Tétouan

Larache
Chechaouene
Ksar el Kebir
Al Hoceima
AL HOCEIMA (COTE DU RIF)
Jebel Bouhalla
2,170 m
Bab
Taza Bourel
Er Rif

Souk el
Arba du Rharb
Ouezzane
Ourtzarh
Taounate
Akroum

Kenitra
Salé
Rabat
RABAT (SALE)
Sidi Kacem
Mouley Idriss
Tiflet
Ain el
Aouda
Ben
Slimane
Khemisset
Rommani
Karia Ba Mohammed
Mouley Yakoub
Tissa
Taza
Fes

NORD OUEST

VOLUBILIS
Meknès
Sefrou
NORD CENTRE
Ifrane
Adrar bou Nasser
3,340 m

CASABLANCA
(Dar-El-Beida)
Mohammedia
CASABLANCA (MOHAMED V)
Medíouna
Berrechid
Azrou
Imouzzer des
Marmoucha
Boulemane

El Jadida
Azemmour
Settat
Oued Zem
Boujad
Khenifra
Moyen Atlas

Oualidia
Boulaouane
Benahmed
Khouribga
El Kbab
Midelt
Jebel Masker
3,277 m
Jebel Mesroui
2,714 m

Cap Safi
El Hadd
Harrara
Sidi
Bennour
Jemaa Sahim
El Borouj
Kasba Tadla
Beni Mellal
Rich

Safi
Youssoufia
Benguerir
Azilal
Jebel Azourki
3,690 m
El Kelaa
des Srarhna
MOROCCO
Er Rachidia
GORGES DU ZIZ

Chemaia
Essaouira
Marrakech
Chichaoua
MARRAKECH (MENARA)
Jebel Rhat
3,825 m
Irhil M'goun
4,071 m
Adrar Mkorn
3,228 m
Goulmima
CENTRE SUD

Cap Sim
TENSIFT
Tahnaout
Ounara
Haut Atlas
Jebel Anrhomer
3,607 m
Irherm n'Ougdal
Tinrhir
Erfoud

Tamanar
Imi n'Tanout
Iguit 3,615 m
Jebel Toubkal
4,165 m
PN OU
TOUBKAL
Aït Ben
Haddou
OUARZAZATE
Ouarzazate
Jebel Siroua
3,304 m
Jebel
Sarhro
Agd.
Boumalne
Oued Ziz

Cap Rhir
AGADIR (INEZGANE)
Taroudannt
Djebel Tichka
3,348 m
Anti Atlas
Taliouine
Tazenakht
Jebel Rhart
1,650 m
Zagora

Agadir
Inezgane
Biougra
Oulad Teima
Irherm
Jebel Siroua
2,531 m
Foum Zguid
Tagounit

Tiznit
Jebel Lkst
2,359 m
SUD
Jebel Bani
Taffraout
Tata

Sidi Ifni
Bou Izakarn
Akka
Foum el
Hassane
Hamada du Drâa

TINDOUF

Goulimine
Assa
Tan-Tan
Jebel Ouarkziz
Tindouf

PN LA CALDERA
DE TABURIENTE
La Palma
Santa Cruz
de la Palma

Los Llanos
de Aridane
Tenerife
Santa Cruz
de Tenerife

Canary Islands
(SPAIN)

PN DE TIMANFAYA
Lanzarote
Arrecife
LANZAROTE

La Laguna
La Orotava
Vallehermoso
NORTE LOS RODEOS
Icod de los Vinos
Puerto de la Cruz
PN DEL TEIDE
Pico del Teide
3,718 m
Granadilla
de Abona
Gomera
SUR REINA
SOFIA
Arucas
Las Palmas
de Gran Canaria
Telde
Fuerteventura
Puerto del
Rosario
Antigua

Valverde
Hierro
PN DE GARAJONAY
San Bartolomé
de Tirajana
Santa Lucía
Ingenio
GRAN CANARIA
Gran Canaria

Tarfaya
Cap Juby

55 m

Daora
Hagunia
El Mzereb

EL AAIÚN (HASSANI)
El Aaiún
Edchera
Saguia el Hamra
Hasi el Farsia

Lemsid
Semara

Cabo Bojador
Bu Craa
Tifariti

Sebjet
Aridal
Sebjet
Aarred
Aïn Ben Tili

WESTERN
SAHARA
Aaglet Yeraiba
Guelta Zemmur
Bir Aidiat
Bir Bel
Guerdâne
Sebkhet
Iguetti

SAHARA
(Occupied by Morocco)
Bir Moghrein

TIRIS ZEMMOUR

Sebjet
Agsamal
Sebkhet Oumm
ed Drous Telli

Tropic of Cancer
Ad Dakhla
Punta Durnford
El Aargub
Fuch
El Aatf
Buir Taiaret
Sebjet
Tidsit
Sebkhet Oumm
ed Drous Guebli

Aaglet Tennuaca
366 m
Foderik
Zouérat
Kediet Ijill
915 m

Cabo Barbas
Auseri
Aguent
Touâjîl

MAURITANIA

Cabo Blanco
NOUADHIBOU
Nouadhibou
DAKHLET
NOUADHIBOU
Bóu Lanouâr
Boú Nagra
Zug
INCHIRI
Tichla
Galb
Azefal
Choûm
El Khatt
Zemlet Toffal
330 m
El M'rayer
El Djouf
Taoudenni
TOMBOUCT

Cap d'Arguin
PARC NATIONAL
DU BANC D'ARGUIN
Guerguerat
Guelb
Azefal
Tijirît Akchâr
Adrar
Ben Amira
Guelb er Richât
519 m
Ouarâne
ADRAR
Ouadane
Chinguetti
HODH
ECH
CHARGUI
Bir Oublane
'Erg Atouila

MOROCCO is divided into 7 non-administrative
regions shown here. Scale does not permit
showing the boundaries and names of Morocco's
provinces and prefectures.

Madeira Is.
(PORT.)

Porto
Moniz
Santana
Machico
Porto Santo
Vila de
Porto Santo

Madeira
Calheta
Ribeira Brava
FUNCHAL
Funchal
Ilhas Desertas

Ilhas
Selvagens
(PORT.)

ALGERIA
MAURITANIA

TINDOUF

El Eglab

'Erg Iguidi

Yetti

BORDJ FLYE SAINTE-N

El Hank

Karêt

Kreb en Nâga

El Mzereb

Hamada Safia

'Erg el
Ahmar

'Erg

Aguerraktem

MALI
MAURITANIA

'Erg
Ijoubbane

El Khnâch

M A L

TOMBOUCT

HEIGHT
m.   ft.
60   197
40   130
20   65
15   50
10   33
5   16
2   7
0
2   7
5   16
10   33
20   65
30   98
40   130
50   164
60   197
m.   ft.
DEPTH
(Figures in
Hundreds)

A   16°   B   12°   C   8°   D   4°

Longitude West of Greenwich

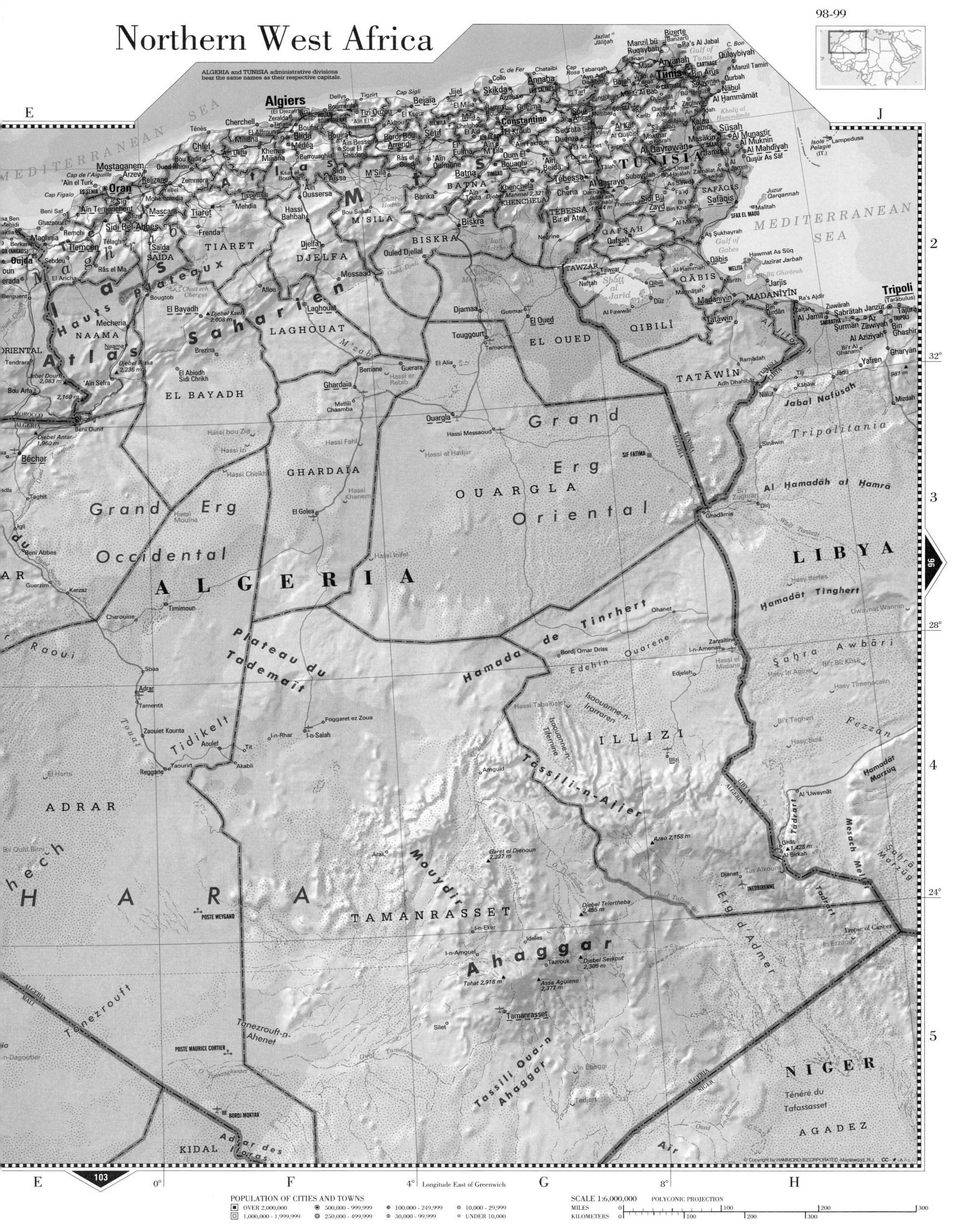

Northern West Africa

ALGERIA and TUNISIA administrative divisions
bear the same names as their respective capitals.

POPULATION OF CITIES AND TOWNS
- ■ OVER 2,000,000
- ◉ 500,000 - 999,999
- ● 100,000 - 249,999
- ◌ 10,000 - 29,999
- □ 1,000,000 - 1,999,999
- ◉ 250,000 - 499,999
- ● 30,000 - 99,999
- ○ UNDER 10,000

SCALE 1:6,000,000   POLYCONIC PROJECTION

MILES 0 ___ 100 ___ 200 ___ 300

KILOMETERS 0 ___ 100 ___ 200 ___ 300

Longitude East of Greenwich

© Copyright by HAMMOND INCORPORATED, Maplewood, N.J.

Northern Morocco, Algeria, Tunisia

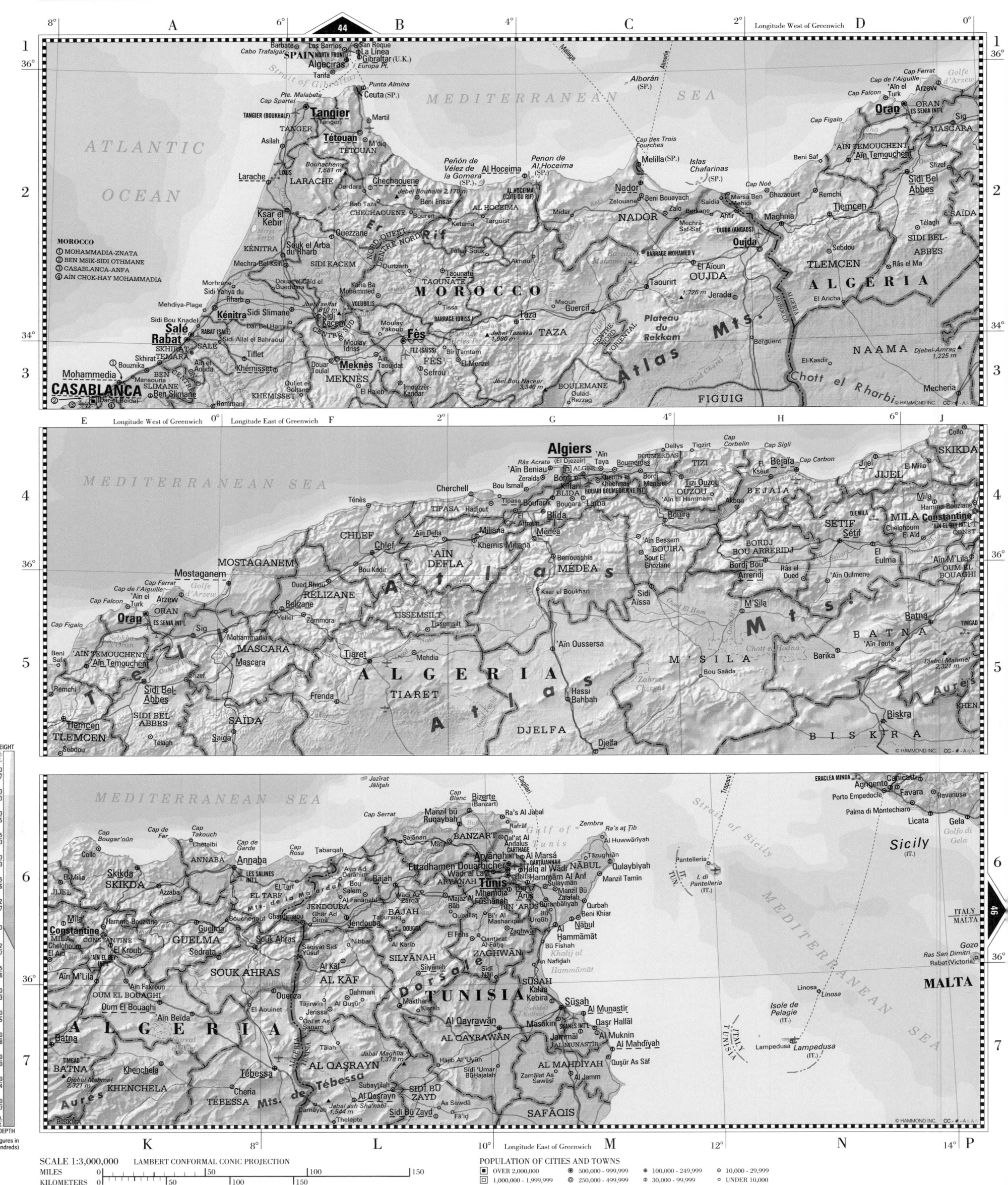

MOROCCO
① MOHAMMADIA-ZNATA
② BEN MSIK-SIDI OTHMANE
③ CASABLANCA-ANFA
④ AÏN CHOK-HAY MOHAMMADIA

SCALE 1:3,000,000   LAMBERT CONFORMAL CONIC PROJECTION

MILES 0 |||||||| 50 |||||||| 100 |||||||| 150

KILOMETERS 0 |||| 50 |||| 100 |||| 150

POPULATION OF CITIES AND TOWNS
■ OVER 2,000,000   ● 500,000 - 999,999   ◉ 100,000 - 249,999   ○ 10,000 - 29,999
□ 1,000,000 - 1,999,999   ⊙ 250,000 - 499,999   ⊙ 30,000 - 99,999   ∘ UNDER 10,000

HEIGHT
m.
ft.
60 197
20 65
15 50
5 16
2 7
0
DEPTH
m.
ft.
(Figures in Hundreds)

Northeastern Africa

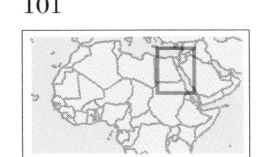

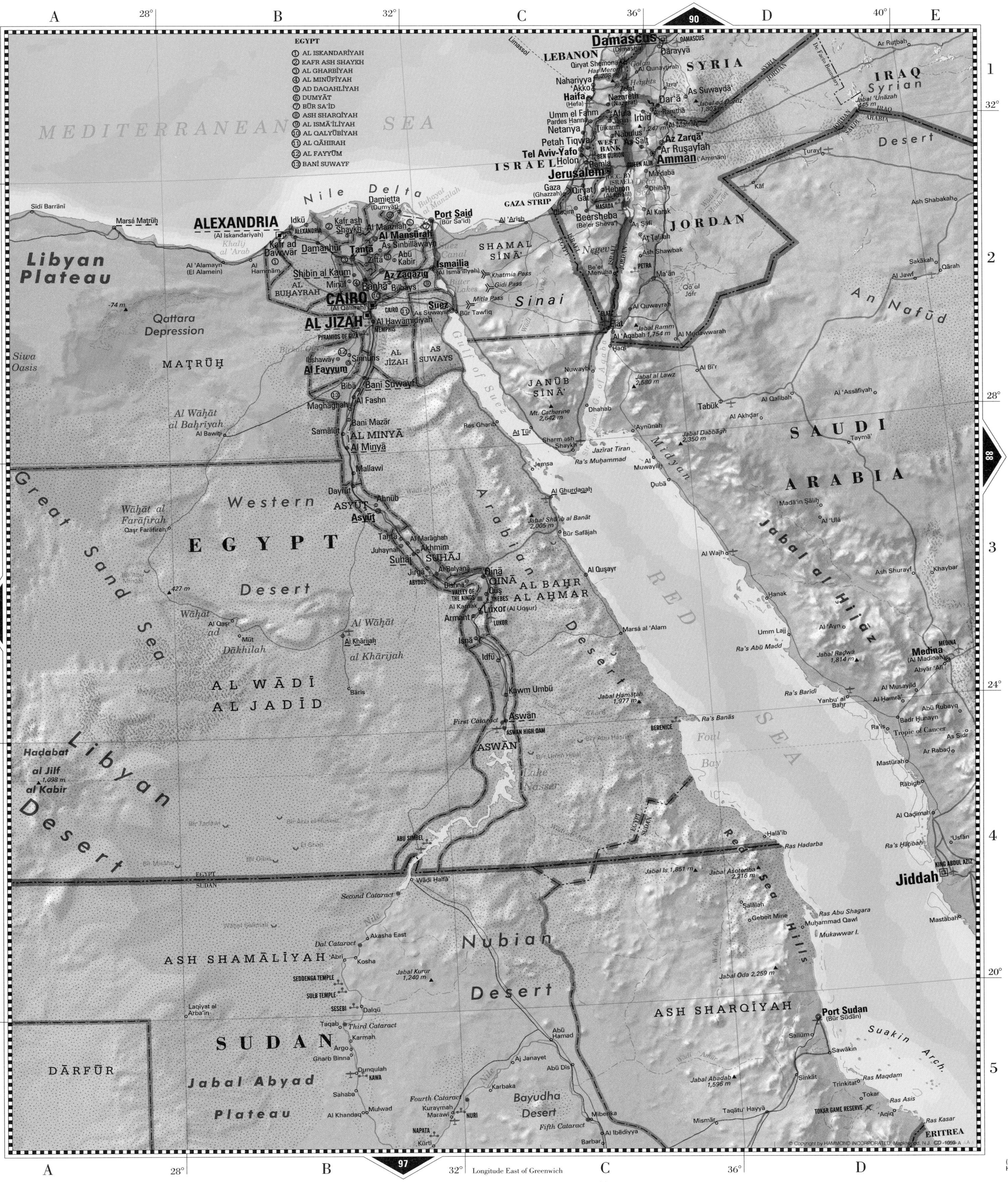

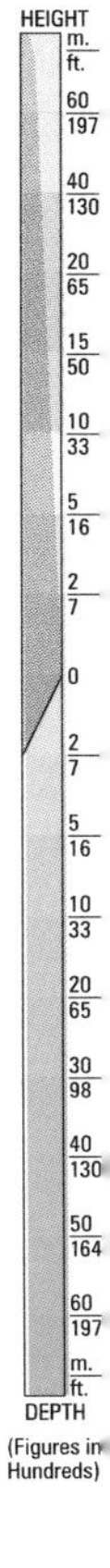

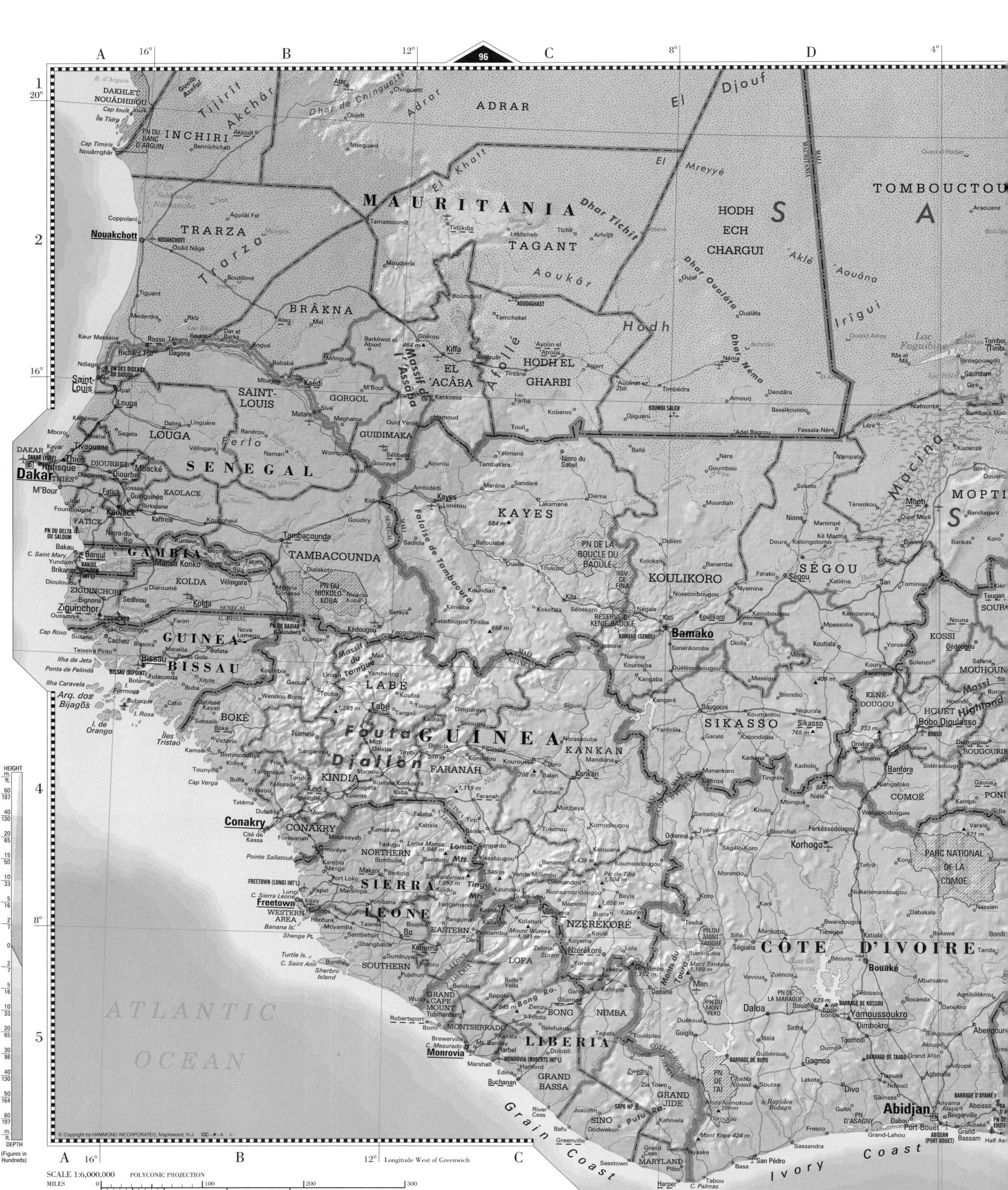

Southern West Africa

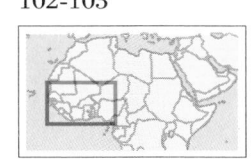

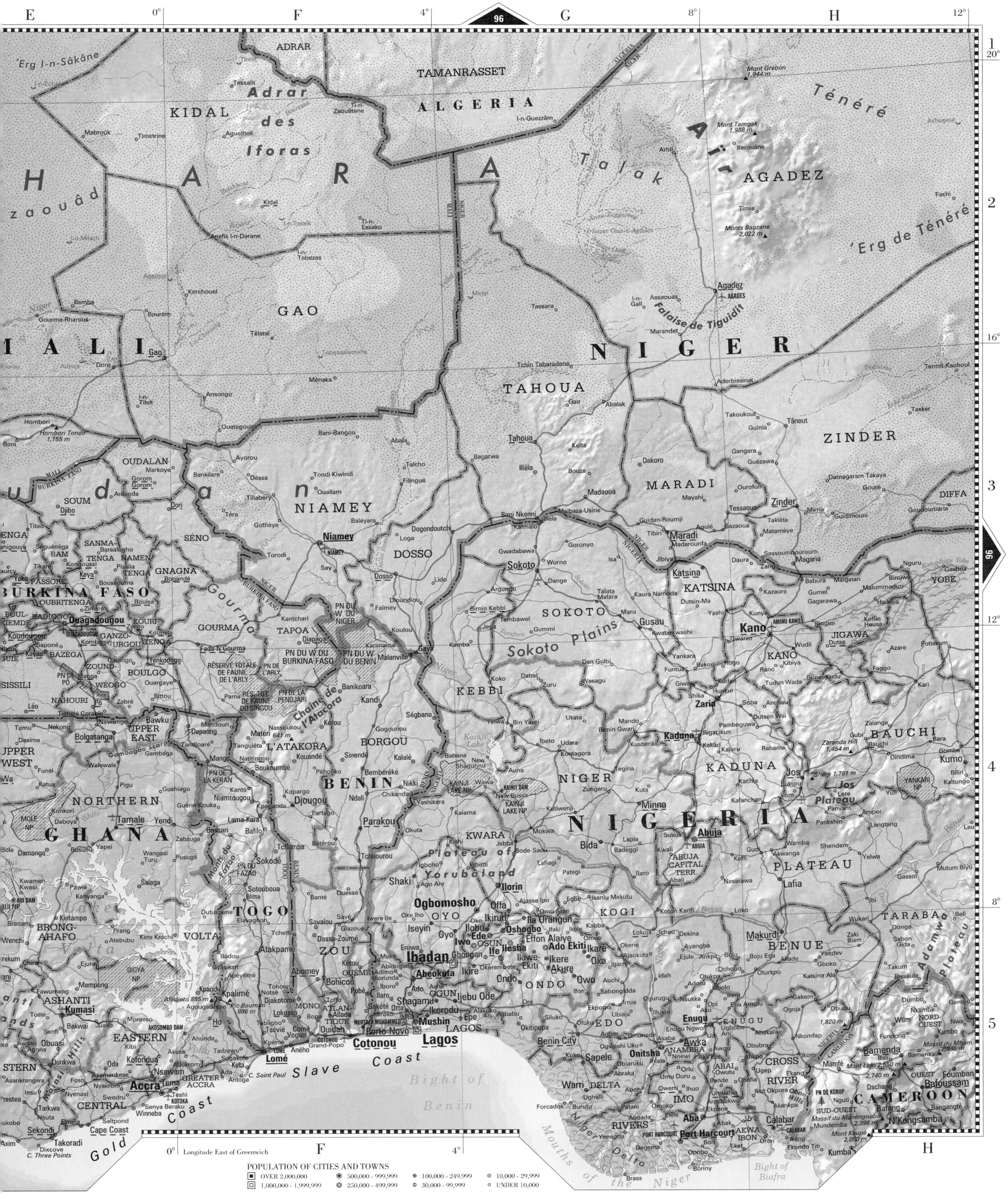

POPULATION OF CITIES AND TOWNS
- ■ OVER 2,000,000
- ● 500,000 - 999,999
- ◉ 100,000 - 249,999
- ○ 10,000 - 29,999
- □ 1,000,000 - 1,999,999
- ◉ 250,000 - 499,999
- ◎ 30,000 - 99,999
- ○ UNDER 10,000

0° Longitude East of Greenwich

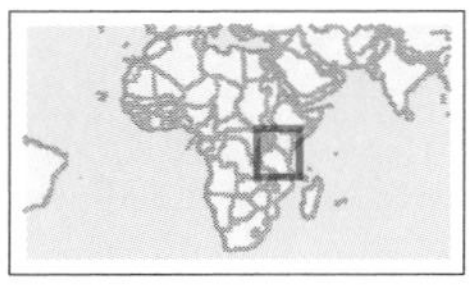

East Africa

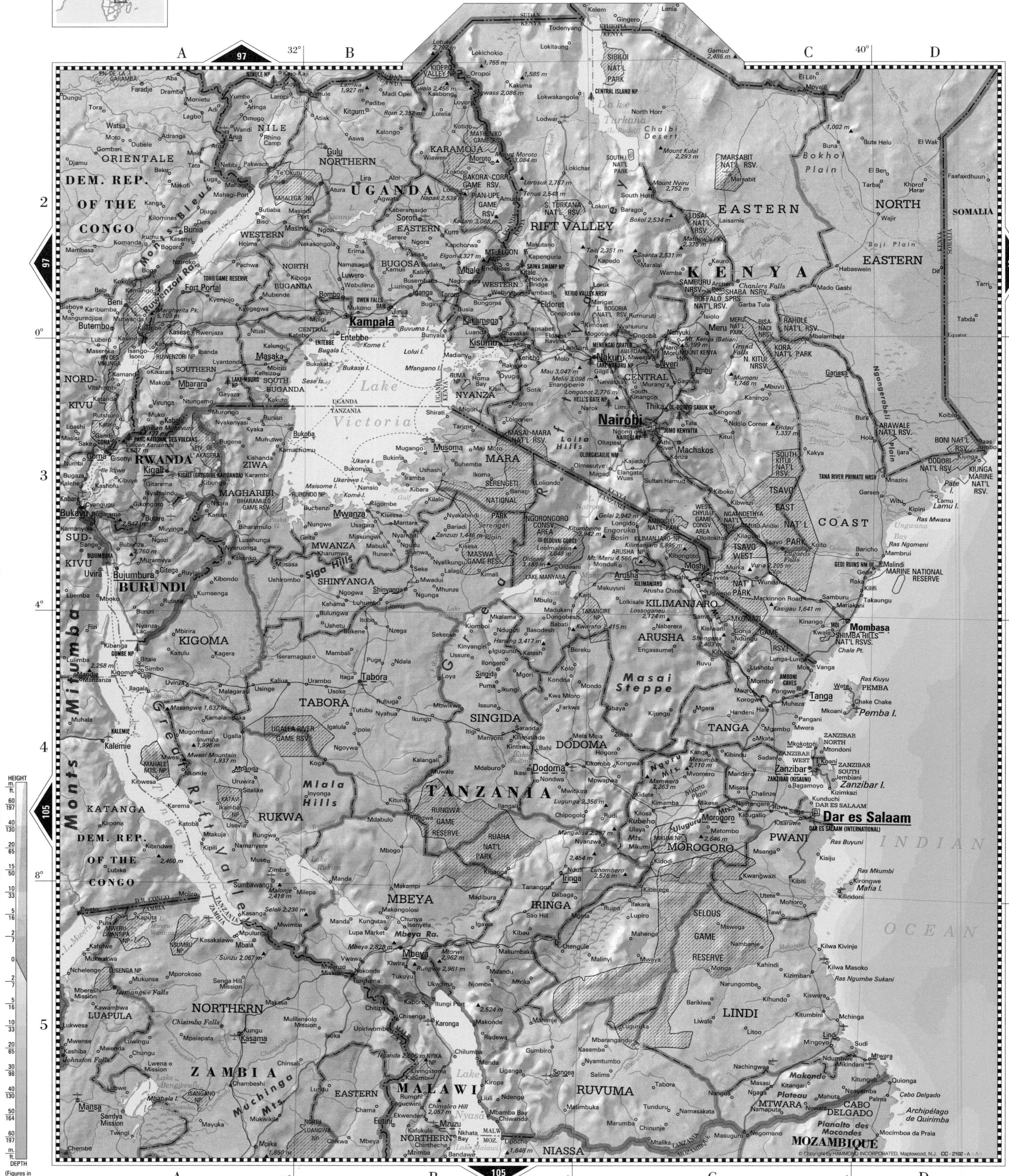

DEM. REP. OF THE CONGO

ORIENTALE

UGANDA
NORTHERN
KARAMOJA
NILE
WESTERN
BUGANDA
EASTERN
WESTERN
CENTRAL
NORTH
SOUTH BUGANDA
SOUTHERN

Kampala
Entebbe

KENYA
RIFT VALLEY
EASTERN
NORTH EASTERN
CENTRAL
NYANZA
WESTERN
COAST

Nairobi
Nakuru
Meru
Mombasa

SOMALIA

RWANDA
Kigali

BURUNDI
Bujumbura

TANZANIA
ZIWA MAGHARIBI
MWANZA
SHINYANGA
KIGOMA
TABORA
SINGIDA
DODOMA
ARUSHA
KILIMANJARO
TANGA
MARA
RUKWA
MBEYA
IRINGA
MOROGORO
PWANI
RUVUMA
LINDI
MTWARA

Dar es Salaam
Dodoma
Mwanza
Arusha
Moshi
Tanga
Zanzibar
Tabora
Mbeya
Morogoro

Lake Victoria
Lake Tanganyika
Lake Nyasa
Lake Turkana (L. Rudolf)

Mount Kenya (Batian) 5,199 m
Kilimanjaro 5,895 m
Mt. Meru 4,566 m
Margherita Pk. 5,109 m

ZAMBIA
LUAPULA
NORTHERN
Kasama

MALAWI
NORTHERN
Mzuzu

MOZAMBIQUE
NIASSA
CABO DELGADO

INDIAN OCEAN

Pemba I.
Zanzibar I.
Mafia I.

HEIGHT
DEPTH
(Figures in Hundreds)

SCALE 1:6,000,000   POLYCONIC PROJECTION
MILES
KILOMETERS
Longitude East of Greenwich

POPULATION OF CITIES AND TOWNS
- OVER 2,000,000
- 1,000,000 - 1,999,999
- 500,000 - 999,999
- 250,000 - 499,999
- 100,000 - 249,999
- 30,000 - 99,999
- 10,000 - 29,999
- UNDER 10,000

© Copyright by HAMMOND INCORPORATED, Maplewood, N.J.   CC - 2102 - A

Southern Africa

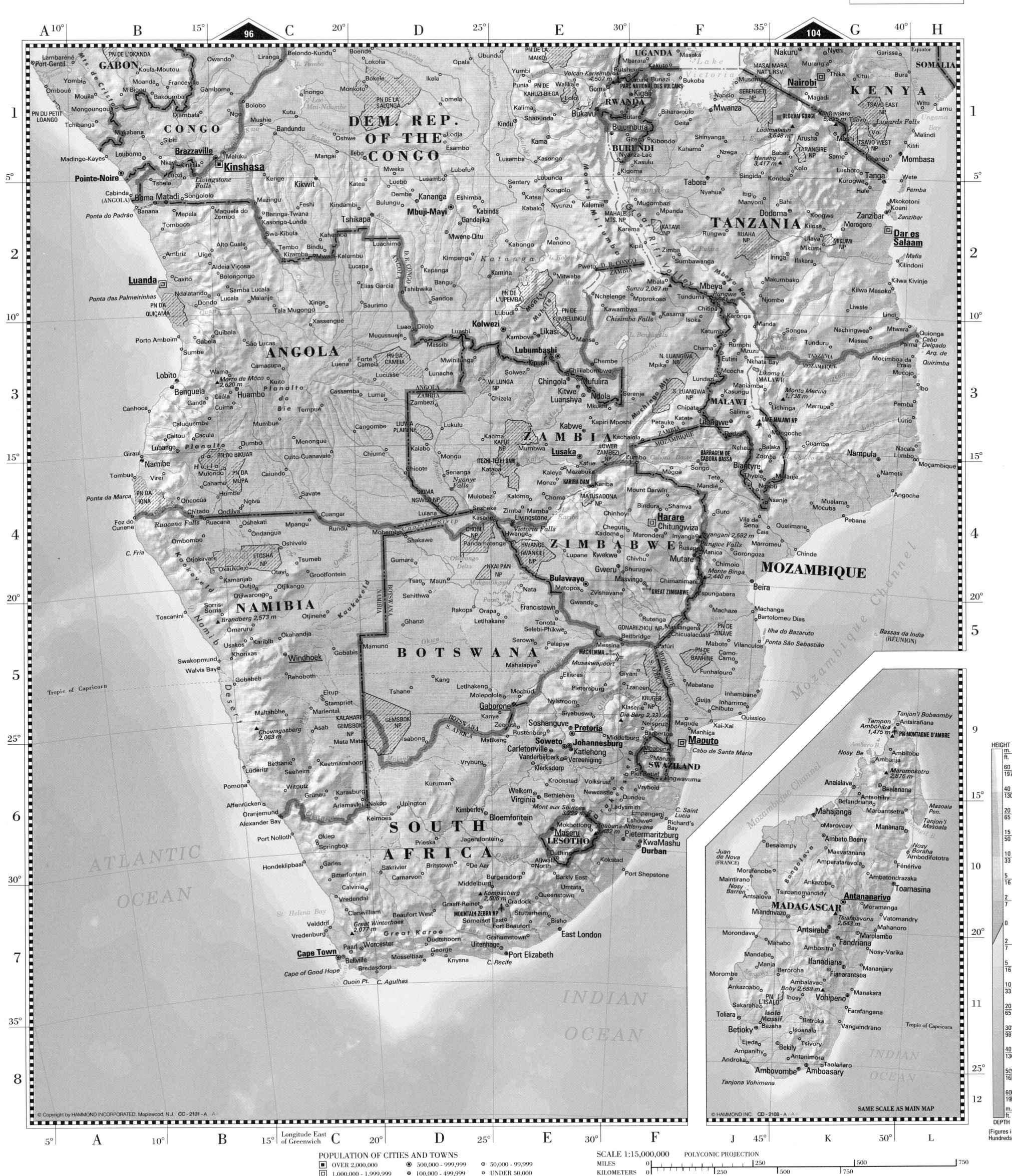

POPULATION OF CITIES AND TOWNS

■ OVER 2,000,000
▣ 1,000,000 - 1,999,999
◉ 500,000 - 999,999
● 100,000 - 499,999
● 50,000 - 99,999
○ UNDER 50,000

SCALE 1:15,000,000   POLYCONIC PROJECTION

MILES 0   250   500   750
KILOMETERS 0   250   500   750

HEIGHT

m.   ft.
60   197
40   130
15   50
10   33
5   16
0
2   7
5   16
10   33
20   65
30   98
50   164
60   197
m.   ft.

DEPTH

(Figures in Hundreds)

SAME SCALE AS MAIN MAP

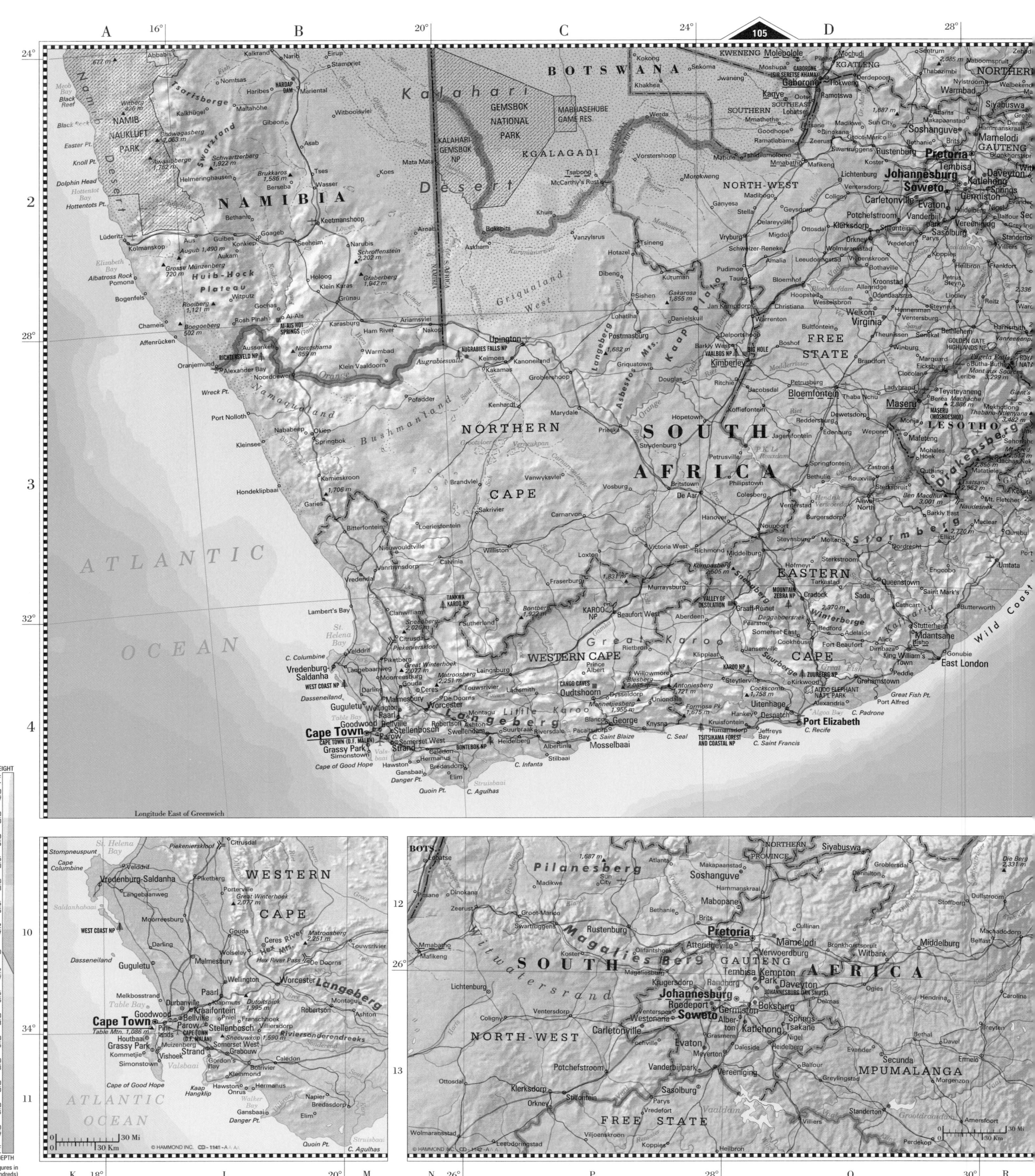

South Africa

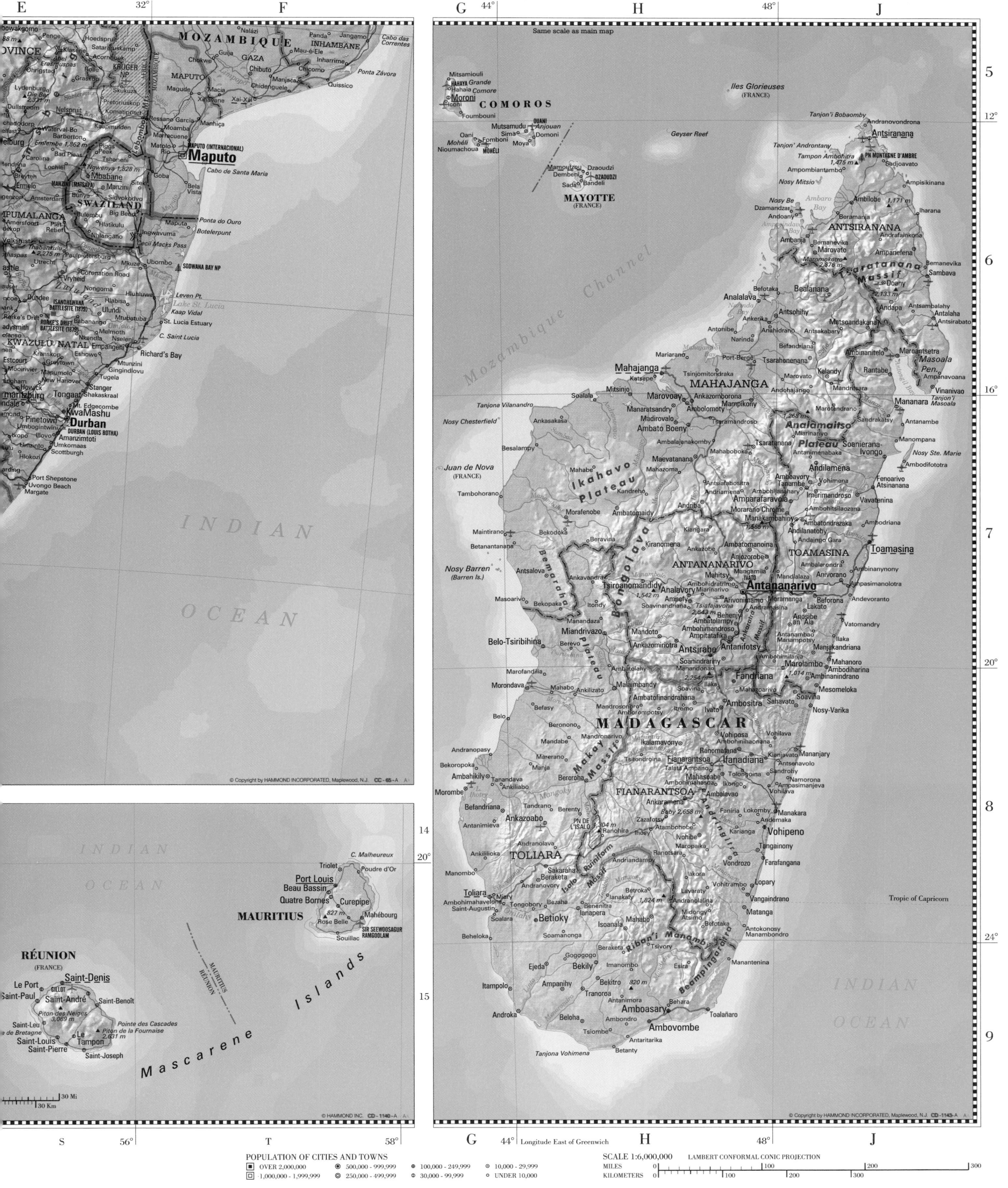

Australia

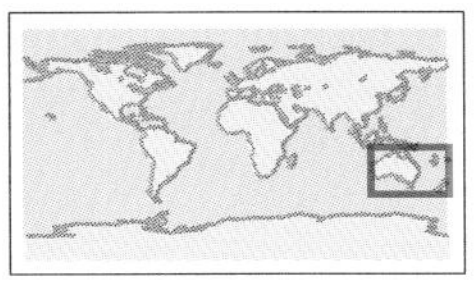

The Lake Eyre Basin is located in the arid interior of south central Australia. This basin is one of the largest areas of internal drainage in the world. It consists of two distinct, but interrelated basins: the north basin and the south basin. The much larger north basin shown here (the highly reflective areas) consists of two very large, normally dry lakebeds. The western lobe (bottom of the image) is Belt Bay, and the eastern lobe is Madigan Bay. The color change, especially in the Madigan Bay lobe, indicates that there was some water in this lobe at the time the image was taken.

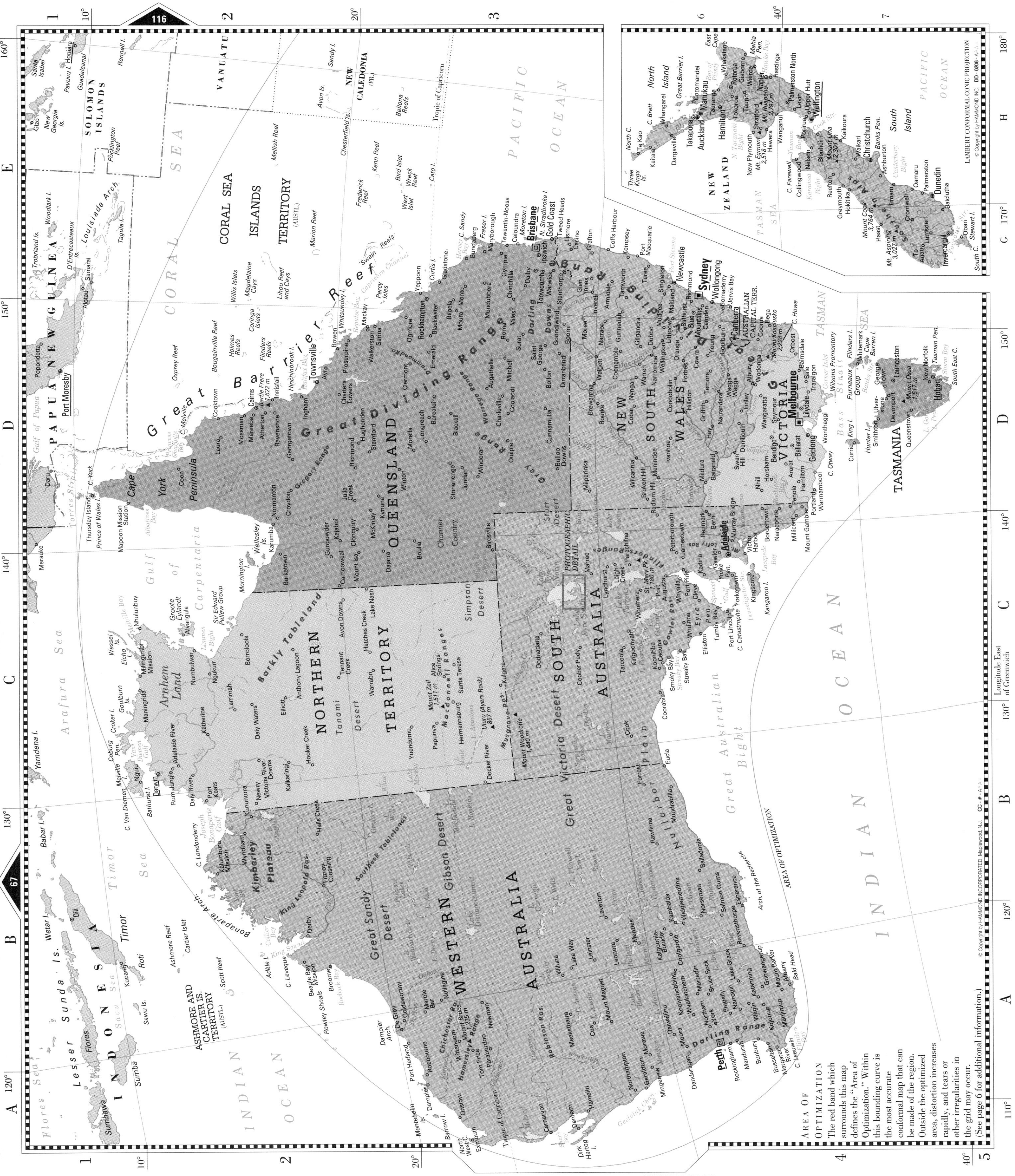

AREA OF OPTIMIZATION

The red band which surrounds this map defines the "Area of Optimization." Within this bounding curve is the most accurate conformal map that can be made of the region. Outside the optimized area, distortion increases rapidly, and tears or other irregularities in the grid may occur.

(See page 6 for additional information.)

POPULATION OF CITIES AND TOWNS

■ OVER 2,000,000	● 500,000 - 999,999	◦ 50,000 - 99,999
▣ 1,000,000 - 1,999,999	○ 100,000 - 499,999	• UNDER 50,000

SCALE 1:16,600,000   OPTIMAL CONFORMAL PROJECTION

MILES 0   250   500   750

KILOMETERS 0   250   500   750

LAMBERT CONFORMAL CONIC PROJECTION

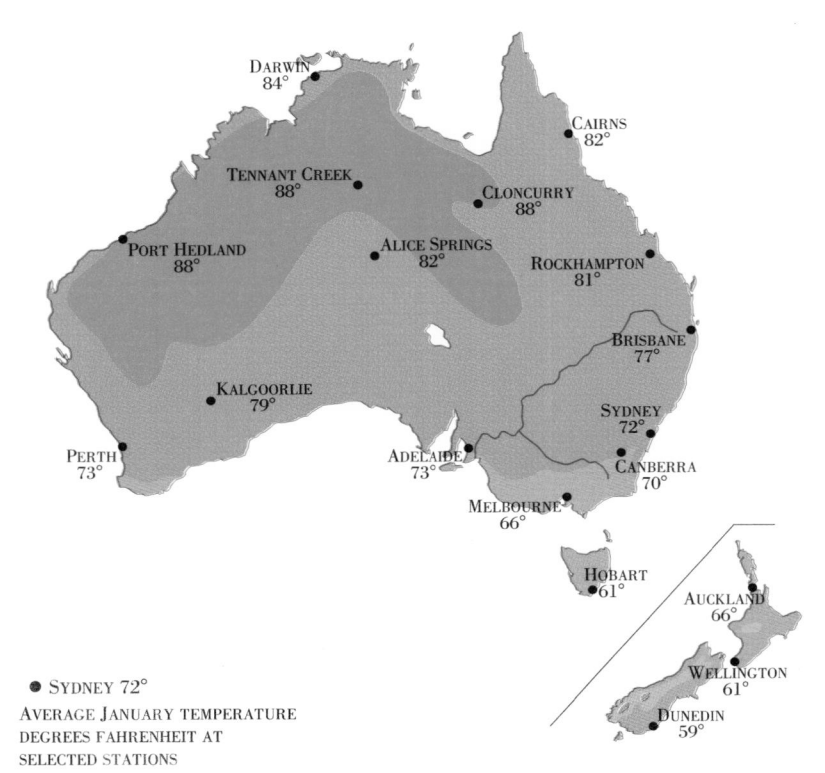

DARWIN
84°

CAIRNS
82°

TENNANT CREEK
88°

CLONCURRY
88°

PORT HEDLAND
88°

ALICE SPRINGS
82°

ROCKHAMPTON
81°

BRISBANE
77°

KALGOORLIE
79°

SYDNEY
72°

PERTH
73°

ADELAIDE
73°

CANBERRA
70°

MELBOURNE
66°

HOBART
61°

AUCKLAND
66°

WELLINGTON
61°

DUNEDIN
59°

● SYDNEY 72°
AVERAGE JANUARY TEMPERATURE
DEGREES FAHRENHEIT AT
SELECTED STATIONS

AVERAGE JANUARY TEMPERATURE

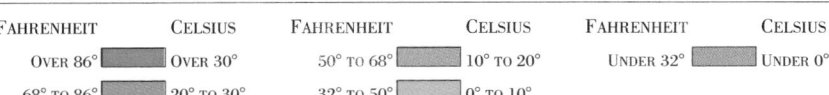

FAHRENHEIT	CELSIUS	FAHRENHEIT	CELSIUS	FAHRENHEIT	CELSIUS
OVER 86°	OVER 30°	50° TO 68°	10° TO 20°	UNDER 32°	UNDER 0°
68° TO 86°	20° TO 30°	32° TO 50°	0° TO 10°		

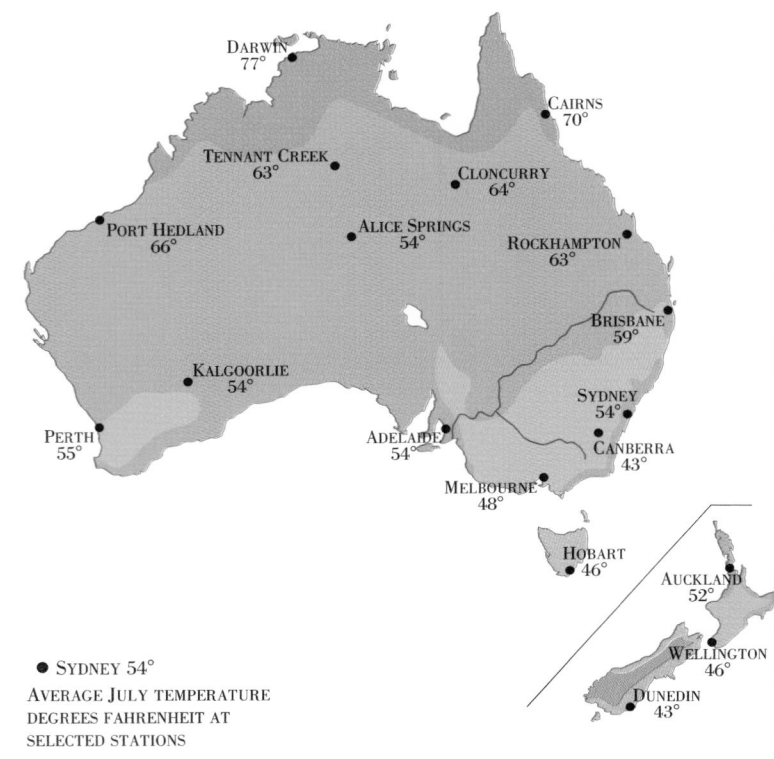

DARWIN
77°

CAIRNS
70°

TENNANT CREEK
63°

CLONCURRY
64°

PORT HEDLAND
66°

ALICE SPRINGS
54°

ROCKHAMPTON
63°

BRISBANE
59°

KALGOORLIE
54°

SYDNEY
54°

PERTH
55°

ADELAIDE
54°

CANBERRA
43°

MELBOURNE
48°

HOBART
46°

AUCKLAND
52°

WELLINGTON
46°

DUNEDIN
43°

● SYDNEY 54°
AVERAGE JULY TEMPERATURE
DEGREES FAHRENHEIT AT
SELECTED STATIONS

AVERAGE JULY TEMPERATURE

FAHRENHEIT	CELSIUS	FAHRENHEIT	CELSIUS
OVER 68°	OVER 20°	32° TO 50°	0° TO 10°
50° TO 68°	10° TO 20°	UNDER 32°	UNDER 0°

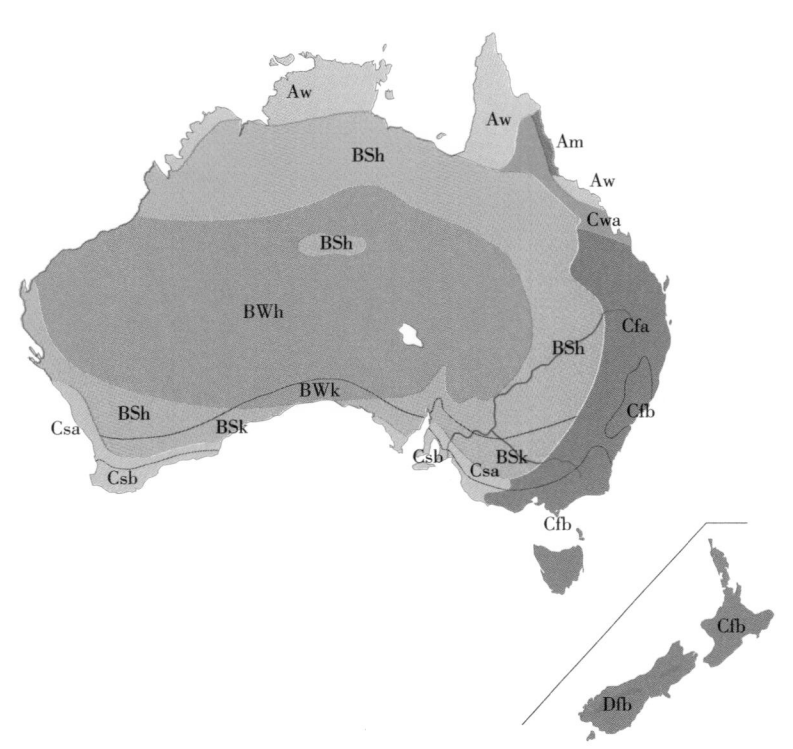

Aw
Aw
Am
BSh
Aw
Cwa
BSh
Cfa
BWh
BSh
BWk
Cfb
BSh
BSk
Csa
Csb
BSk
Csa
Cfb
Cfb
Dfb

CLIMATE

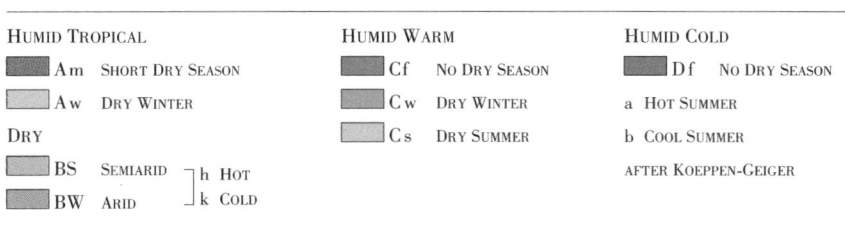

HUMID TROPICAL

Am SHORT DRY SEASON

Aw DRY WINTER

DRY

BS SEMIARID

BW ARID

⌉h HOT
⌋k COLD

HUMID WARM

Cf NO DRY SEASON

Cw DRY WINTER

Cs DRY SUMMER

HUMID COLD

Df NO DRY SEASON

a HOT SUMMER

b COOL SUMMER

AFTER KOEPPEN-GEIGER

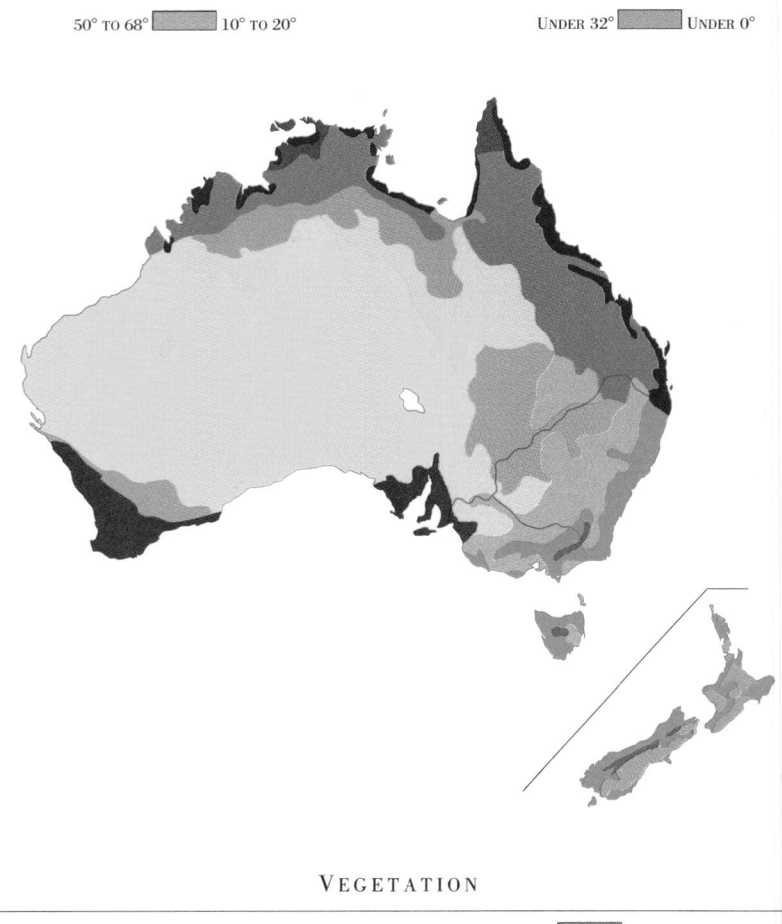

VEGETATION

TROPICAL FOREST

TROPICAL RAINFOREST

LIGHT TROPICAL FOREST

WOODLAND AND SHRUB

TROPICAL GRASSLAND

GRASS AND SHRUB
(SAVANNA)

WOODED SAVANNA

MID-LATITUDE FOREST

MIXED NEEDLELEAF AND
BROADLEAF FOREST

MIXED WOODLAND

WOODLAND AND SHRUB
(MEDITERRANEAN)

MID-LATITUDE
GRASSLAND

SCRUB AND FERNLANDS

DESERT AND DESERT
SHRUB

ALPINE

Australia, New Zealand - Geographical Comparisons

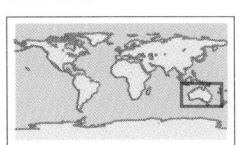

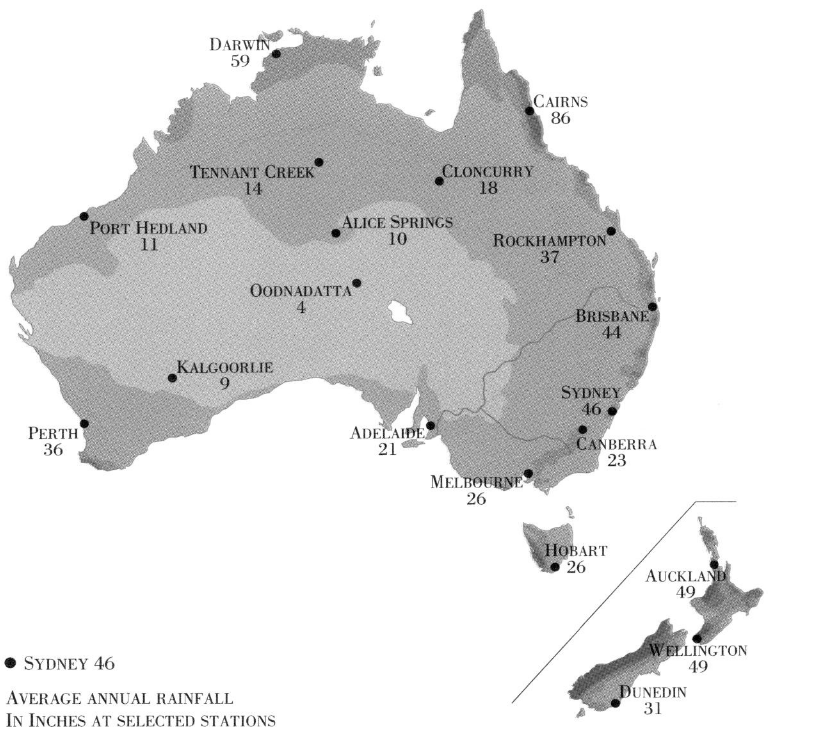

Map 1: Average Annual Rainfall

DARWIN 59
CAIRNS 86
TENNANT CREEK 14
CLONCURRY 18
PORT HEDLAND 11
ALICE SPRINGS 10
ROCKHAMPTON 37
OODNADATTA 4
BRISBANE 44
KALGOORLIE 9
SYDNEY 46
PERTH 36
ADELAIDE 21
CANBERRA 23
MELBOURNE 26
HOBART 26
AUCKLAND 49
WELLINGTON 49
DUNEDIN 31

● SYDNEY 46
AVERAGE ANNUAL RAINFALL
IN INCHES AT SELECTED STATIONS

AVERAGE ANNUAL RAINFALL

INCHES	CM	INCHES	CM	INCHES	CM
OVER 80	OVER 200	40 TO 60	100 TO 150	10 TO 20	25 TO 50
60 TO 80	150 TO 200	20 TO 40	50 TO 100	UNDER 10	UNDER 25

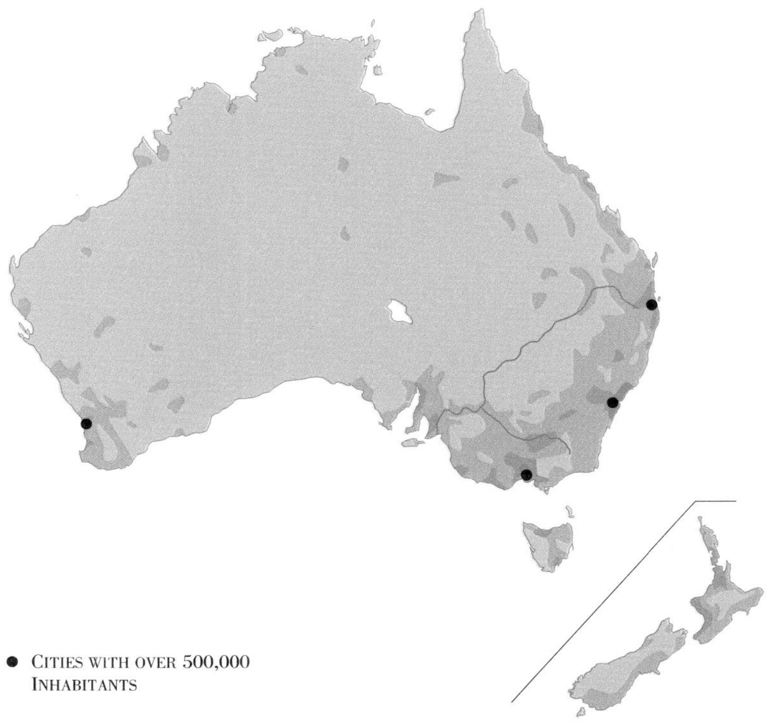

Map 2: Population Distribution

● CITIES WITH OVER 500,000
INHABITANTS

POPULATION DISTRIBUTION

DENSITY PER		SQ. MI.	SQ. KM.	SQ. MI.	SQ. KM.
SQ. MI.	SQ. KM.	25 TO 130	10 TO 50	UNDER 3	UNDER 1
OVER 130	OVER 50	3 TO 25	1 TO 10		

Map 3: Land Use

CATTLE
CATTLE
CATTLE
SUGARCANE
CATTLE
SHEEP
CATTLE
SHEEP
DAIRY
SHEEP
SHEEP
WHEAT
SHEEP
FRUIT
WHEAT
WHEAT
SHEEP
SHEEP
SHEEP

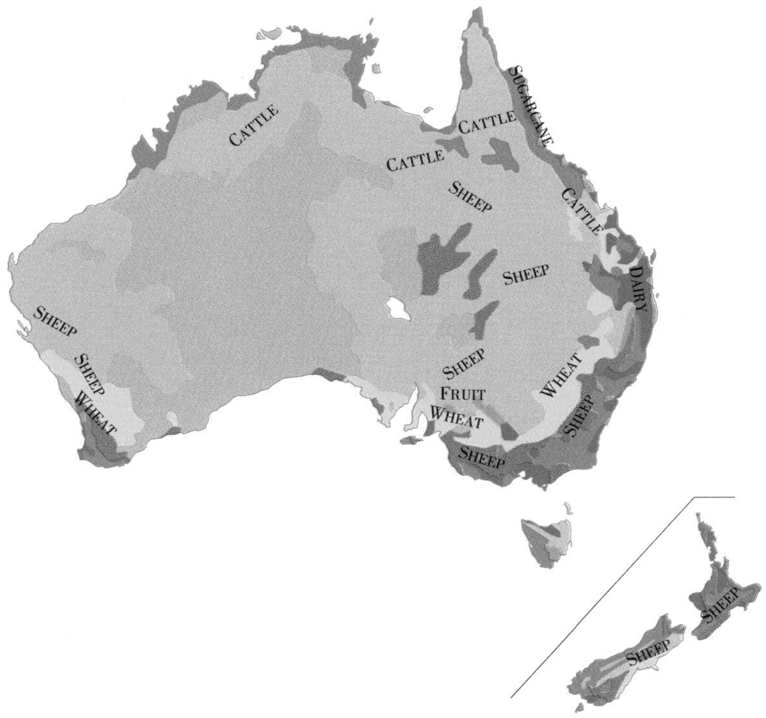

LAND USE

- CEREALS, LIVESTOCK
- PASTURE LIVESTOCK
- FORESTS
- LIVESTOCK RANCHING & HERDING
- CASH CROPS, MIXED FARMING
- NONPRODUCTIVE
- DAIRY, LIVESTOCK

Map 4: Mineral Resources

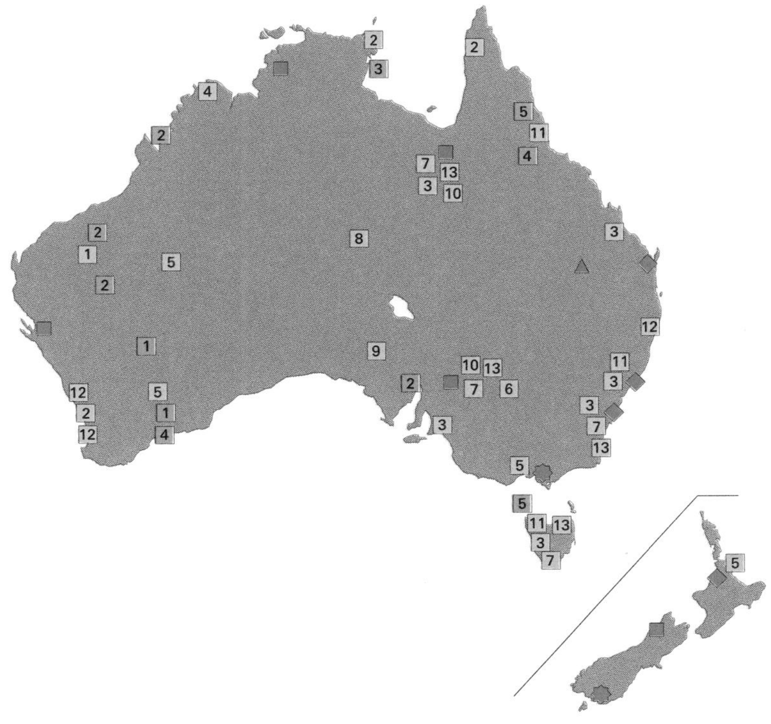

MINERAL RESOURCES

ENERGY & FUELS
- ◆ COAL
- LIGNITE
- ▲ NATURAL GAS
- URANIUM

IRON & FERROALLOYS
- 1 COBALT
- 2 IRON ORE
- 3 MANGANESE
- 4 NICKEL
- 5 TUNGSTEN

OTHER MAJOR RESOURCES
- 1 ASBESTOS
- 2 BAUXITE
- 3 COPPER
- 4 DIAMONDS
- 5 GOLD
- 6 GYPSUM
- 7 LEAD
- 8 MICA
- 9 OPALS
- 10 SILVER
- 11 TIN
- 12 TITANIUM
- 13 ZINC

This is a map of Western Australia showing the coastal and inland regions, with an inset map of the Perth metropolitan area.

Map Grid and Coordinates

Top border columns: B, 116°, C, 120°, D, 124°, E

Left border rows (latitude): 1, 20°, 2, Tropic of Capricorn, 24°, 3, 28°, 4, 5, 6, 32°, 7

Height / Depth Legend (left side)

HEIGHT
m. / ft.
60 / 197
40 / 130
20 / 65
15 / 50
10 / 33
2 / 7
0 / 0
2 / 7
5 / 16
10 / 33
20 / 65
30 / 98
40 / 130
50 / 164
60 / 197
m. / ft.
DEPTH
(Figures in Hundreds)

Major Labels

INDIAN OCEAN

WESTERN AUSTRALIA

Great Sandy Desert

Gibson Desert

Southesk Tablelands

Nullarbor

Place names (selected)

Poissonnier Point, De Grey, Pardoo, Goldsworthy, Shay Gap, Wallal Downs, Port Hedland, PORT HEDLAND, STRELLEY ABOR. LAND, CARLINDIE ABOR. LAND, COONGAN ABOR. LAND, Dooleena 346 m, Marble Bar, Mt. Edgar 371 m, Nullagine, 367 m, Percival Lakes, Tobin L., Lake Waukarlycarly, Lake Auld

Montebello Is., Cape Dupuy, BARROW I. NATURE RSV., Barrow I., Dampier Arch., Nickol B., Mundabullangana, Wickham, Karratha, Roebourne, Dampier, Cape Preston, PIPPINGARRA ABOR. LAND, LALLA ROOKH ABOR. LAND, KANGAN ABOR. LAND, YANDEEARRA ABORIGINAL RSV., NATURE RSV., MILLSTREAM-CHICHESTER NAT'L PARK, Mt. Welcome Abor. Land, Mt. Flora 613 m, Pannawonica, Onslow, PEEDAMULLA ABOR. LAND

North West Cape, Exmouth, Cape Range Nat'l Park, Mt. Hollister 315 m, Learmonth, Yanrey, Boolaloo, Mt. Elvire 673 m, Mt. Margaret 880 m, Mt. Brockman 1,132 m, Wittenoom, Mt. Bruce 1,235 m, Tom Price, Hamersley Range NP, Mt. Meharry 1,251 m, Roy Hill, Ethel Creek, Mt. Newman 1,056 m, Newman, Paraburdoo, Ophthalmia Ra., WALAGUNYA ABOR. LAND, JIGALONG ABOR. LAND, Lake Disappointment

Point Cloates, Chalyuwaardoo Bay, Point Maud, Winning, Mt. Alexander 418 m, Mt. Turner 1,013 m, Barlee Range Nature Rsv., Mt. Palgrave 704 m, Ashburton Downs, Deadman Hill 731 m, Mundiwindi

Tropic of Capricorn, Cape Farquhar, Lyndon, Minilya, Mount Vernon, Lofty Range, Collier Range Nat'l Park, Collier Ra., Wonyulgunna Hill 777 m, Mt. Essendon 906 m, Mt. Cecil Rhodes 702 m

Cape Cuvier, Lake Macleod, Cape Ronsard, Bernier I., Dorre I., Mt. Augustus 1,106 m, Mt. Gascoyne 789 m, Three Rivers, Robinson Ranges, Lake Nabberu, GIBSON DESERT NATURE RESERVE

Naturaliste Chan., Cape Inscription, Dirk Hartog Island, Denham, Peron, Faure I., Monkey Mia, Shark Bay, Gascoyne Junction, Mooloo Downs, Coordewandy 552 m, Mt. Gould 710 m, Peak Hill, Lake Gregory, Lake Carnegie, Warburton, WARBURTON RANGE ABOR. RSV.

Steep Point, Useless Loop, Hamelin Pool, Hamelin, Wooramel, Mt. Murchison 520 m, Meekatharra, Mt. Fraser 799 m, Mt. Hale 732 m, Glengarry Range, Wiluna, Lake Wells

Freycinet Har., Mt. Luke 530 m, Nicholson Range, Murgoo, Cue, Lake Austin, Murchison Downs, Nannine, Lake Way, BANDYA, Leinster, Lake Throssel, COSMO NEWBERRY ABORIGINAL RSV., YAMARNA ABOR. RSV., YEO LAKE NATURE RSV., Yeo Lake, Saunders Point 466 m

KALBARRI NAT'L PARK, Kalbarri, Bluff Point, Ajana, Poondarrie Hill 427 m, Mt. Charles 646 m, Mt. Dalgaranger 652 m, Mount Magnet, Sandstone, Agnew, Mt. Redcliffe 576 m, Laverton, YAMARNA ABOR. RSV., POINT SALVATION ABOR. RSV., NATURE RESERVE, Raeson Lake

Shoal Point, Northampton, Yuna, Mullewa, Tallering Pk. 453 m, Yalgoo, Leonora, Mt. East 565 m, Lake Carey

Houtman Abrolhos, Geraldton, Waggrakine, Canning Hill 543 m, Lake Annean, Lake Raeside, Lake Minigwal, PLUMRIDGE LAKES NATURE RESERVE

Dongara, Irwin, Minnenew, Morawa, Paynes Find, Mangaroon Lake, Lake Ballard, Menzies, Lake Rebecca, GOONGARRIE NAT'L PARK, Leander Point, Perenjori, Three Springs, Carnamah, Mt. Singleton 678 m, Lake Barlee, Broad Arrow, Kalgoorlie-Boulder, QUEEN VICTORIA SPRING NATURE RESERVE, Streich Mound 351 m, Knobby Head, Coorow, Wubin, Lake Moore, NATURE RESERVE, COONANA ABOR. LAND, CUNDEELEE ABOR. RSV., Zanthus, Rawlinna

Leeman, Eneabba, Watheroo, Dalwallinu, Koorda, Bencubbin, Bullfinch, Koolyanobbing, Coolgardie, Kambalda, North Head, WATHEROO NP, BADGINGARRA NP, Moora, Wongan Hills, Mukinbudin, Nungarin, Southern Cross, Mt. Burges 555 m, Widgiemooltha, Lake Lefroy, Jurien, Cervantes, Dandaragan, NAMBUNG NP, New Norcia, Wyalkatchem, Lake Yindarlgooda, Lancelin, MOORE R. NP, Goomalling, Dowerin, BOGRABBIN NATIONAL PARK, Ledge Point, Bindoon, Toodyay, Cunderdin, Merredin, Lake Cowan, NATURE RESERVE, Guilderton, Gingin, AVON VALLEY NP, Northam, Mt. Stirling 376 m, Kellerberrin, Mt. Thirsty 431 m, YANCHEP NP, JOHN FORREST NP, York, Quairading, Bruce Rock, Norseman, Wyralinu Hill 569 m, Mt. Ragged 585 m, CAPE ARID NP

Perth, PERTH INT'L, Rottnest I., Rockingham, Kwinana, Mt. Cooke 571 m, Beverley, Narembeen, Lake Johnston, NATURE RESERVE, Balladonia, Point Dover, Mandurah, North Dandalup, Brookton, Corrigin, Kondinin, Hyden, Lake Hope, Mt. Charles 658 m, PEAK CHARLES NP, Point Culver, Cape Bouvard, Pinjarra, Pingelly, Wickepin, Kulin, Lake King, FRANK HAHN NAT'L PARK, Salmon Gums, YALGORUP NP, Waroona, Wandering, Buddington, Narrogin, Lake Grace, Newdegate, Gibson, Mt. Ragged 585 m, Harvey, Williams, Highbury, Wagin, Dumbleyung, Nyabing, Ravensthorpe, Esperance, Cape Le Grand, Cape Arid, Australind, Brunswick Junction, Allanson, Darkan, Kojonup, Borden, NATURE RSV., Stokes NP, Dalyup, C. LE GRAND NP, Cape Pasley, Geographe Bay, Bunbury, Boyanup, Collie, Duranillin, Tambellup, FITZGERALD RIVER NAT'L PARK, Hopetoun, Stokes NP, Mississippi Pt., Archipelago of the Recherche, Cape Naturaliste, Capel, Donnybrook, Boyup Brook, Kojonup, Gnowangerup, Jerramungup, Esperance B., Doubtful Island B., Cape Le Grand, Dunsborough, Busselton, LEEUWIN-NATURALISTE NP, Margaret River, Cowaramup, Greenbushes, Bridgetown, Cranbrook, Bluff Knoll 1,109 m, STIRLING RANGE NP, Hood Point, LEEUWIN-NATURALISTE NP, SCOTT NP, Nannup, Manjimup, Mount Barker, PORONGURUP NP, Augusta, Deanmill, SIR JAMES MITCHELL NP, Northcliffe, Cape Leeuwin, Flinders Bay, Pemberton, Mt. Lindsay 448 m, Mt. Barker, Denmark, Albany, Cape Vancouver, Bald Head, Point D'Entrecasteaux, Walpole, WALPOLE-NORNALUP NP, WILLIAM BAY NP, WEST CAPE HOWE NP, TORNDIRRUP NP, C. Riche, Cape Knob

Inset Map (Perth)

© HAMMOND INC., CC-1124-A, 10 Mi, 10 Km, Bullsbrook East, NEERABUP NP, Quinns Rocks, WALYUNGA NP, Joondalup Lake, Woonoloo Bk., SCARBOROUGH, STIRLING, CITY BEACH, BAYSWATER, MIDLAND, JOHN FORREST NP, Mundaring, INDIAN OCEAN, KINGS PARK, NEDLANDS, Perth, PERTH ZOO, PERTH INT'L, COTTESLOE, SOUTH PERTH, MELVILLE, FREMANTLE, JANDAKOT, COHUNU NP, Cockburn Sound, Garden Island, ELIZABETHIAN VILLAGE, ARMADALE, PIONEER WORLD, Byford, Thompson L., Mangles Bay, Kwinana, Rockingham

Bottom border: K, 116°, L, B, 116°, C, 120°, Longitude East of Greenwich, D, 124°, E

Western and Central Australia

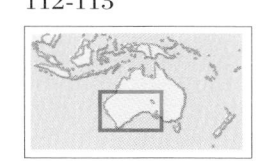

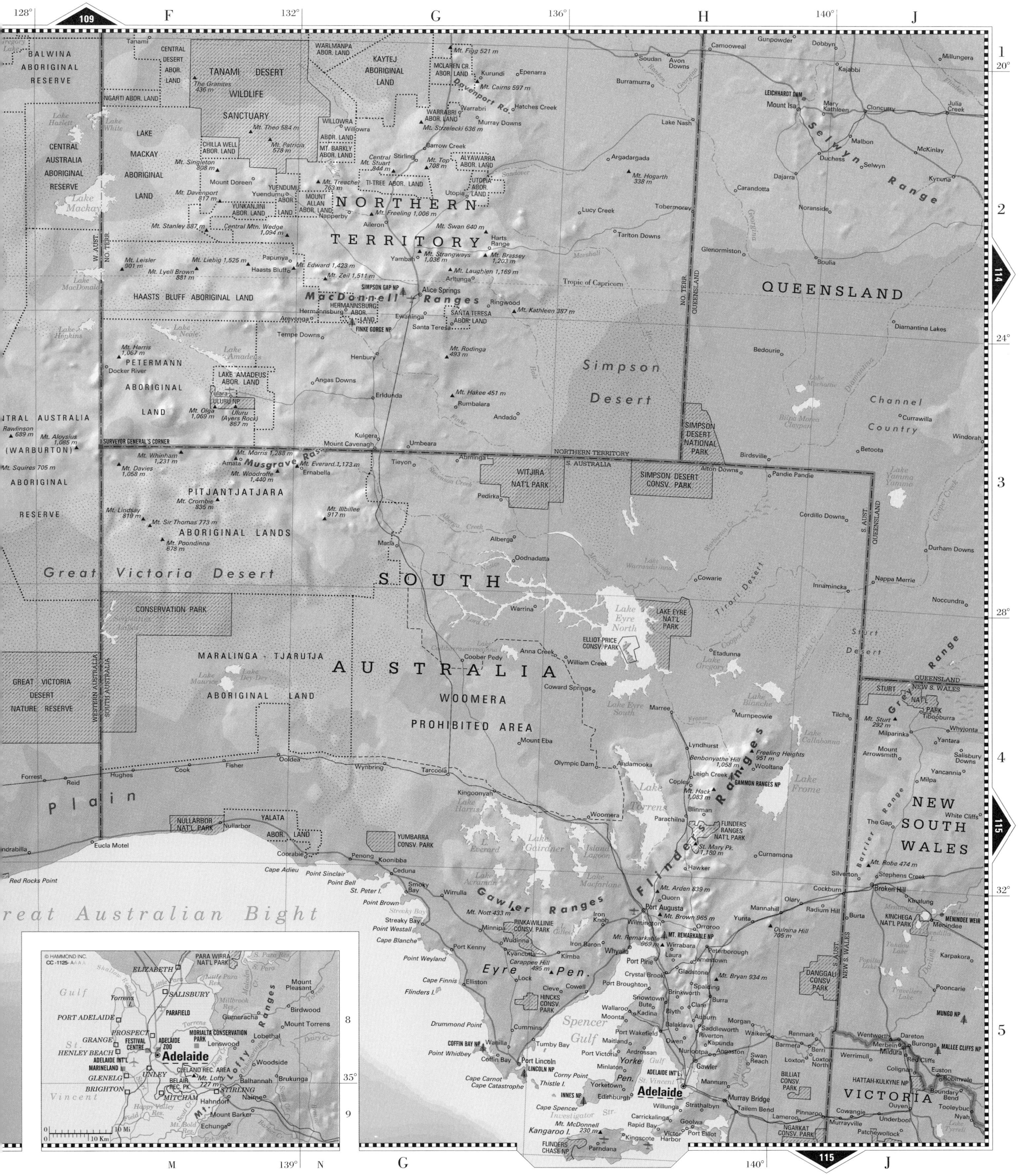

POPULATION OF CITIES AND TOWNS

■ OVER 2,000,000 ● 500,000 - 999,999 ◉ 100,000 - 249,999 ○ 10,000 - 29,999
□ 1,000,000 - 1,999,999 ◎ 250,000 - 499,999 ◌ 30,000 - 99,999 ○ UNDER 10,000

SCALE 1:6,000,000   LAMBERT CONFORMAL CONIC PROJECTION

MILES 0   100   200   300

KILOMETERS 0   100   200   300

© HAMMOND INC.
CC-1125-AAAA

Northeastern Australia

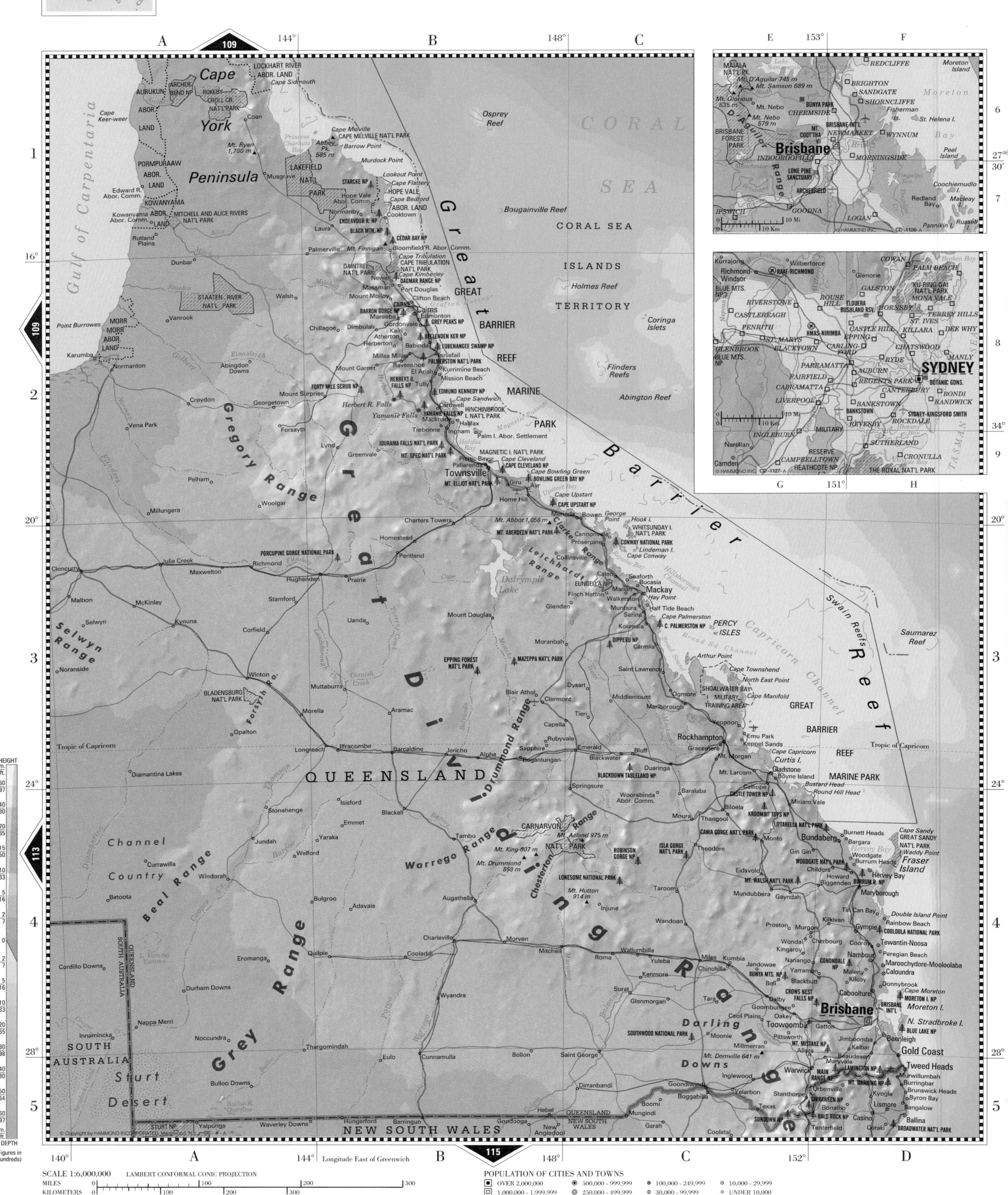

SCALE 1:6,000,000   LAMBERT CONFORMAL CONIC PROJECTION

MILES 0 ——————— 100 ——————— 200 ——————— 300

KILOMETERS 0 ——————— 100 ——————— 200 ——————— 300

POPULATION OF CITIES AND TOWNS

■ OVER 2,000,000   ● 500,000 - 999,999   ⊙ 100,000 - 249,999   ⊙ 10,000 - 29,999

▣ 1,000,000 - 1,999,999   ▢ 250,000 - 499,999   ⊙ 30,000 - 99,999   ∘ UNDER 10,000

Southeastern Australia

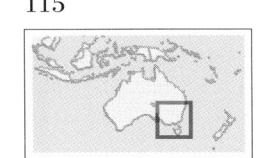

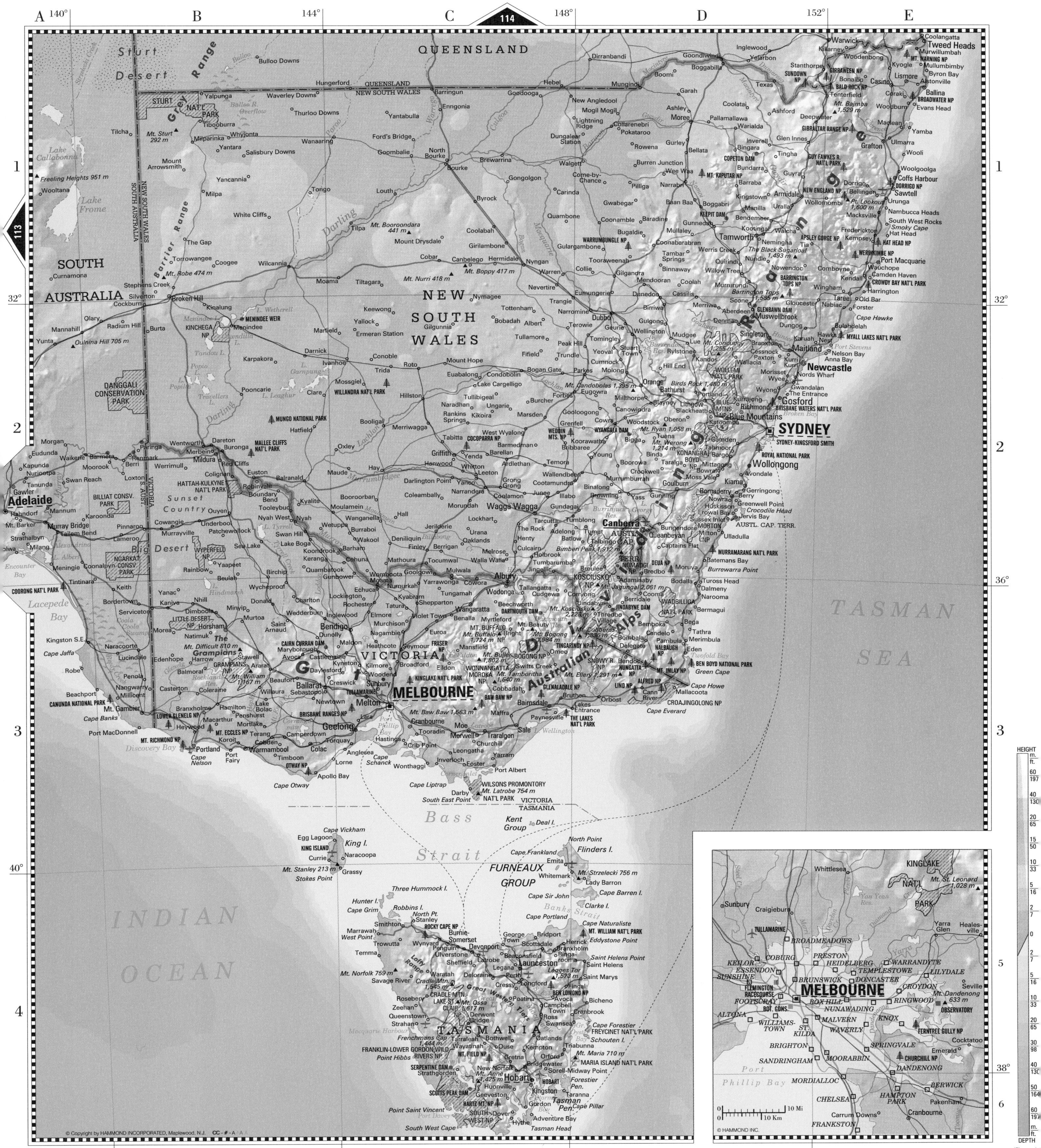

POPULATION OF CITIES AND TOWNS

■ OVER 2,000,000 ◉ 500,000 - 999,999 ⊕ 100,000 - 249,999 ⊙ 10,000 - 29,999
□ 1,000,000 - 1,999,999 ◉ 250,000 - 499,999 ⊕ 30,000 - 99,999 ○ UNDER 10,000

SCALE 1:6,000,000   LAMBERT CONFORMAL CONIC PROJECTION

© Copyright by HAMMOND INCORPORATED, Maplewood, N.J.

© HAMMOND INC.

Central Pacific Ocean, New Zealand

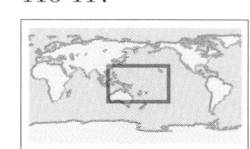

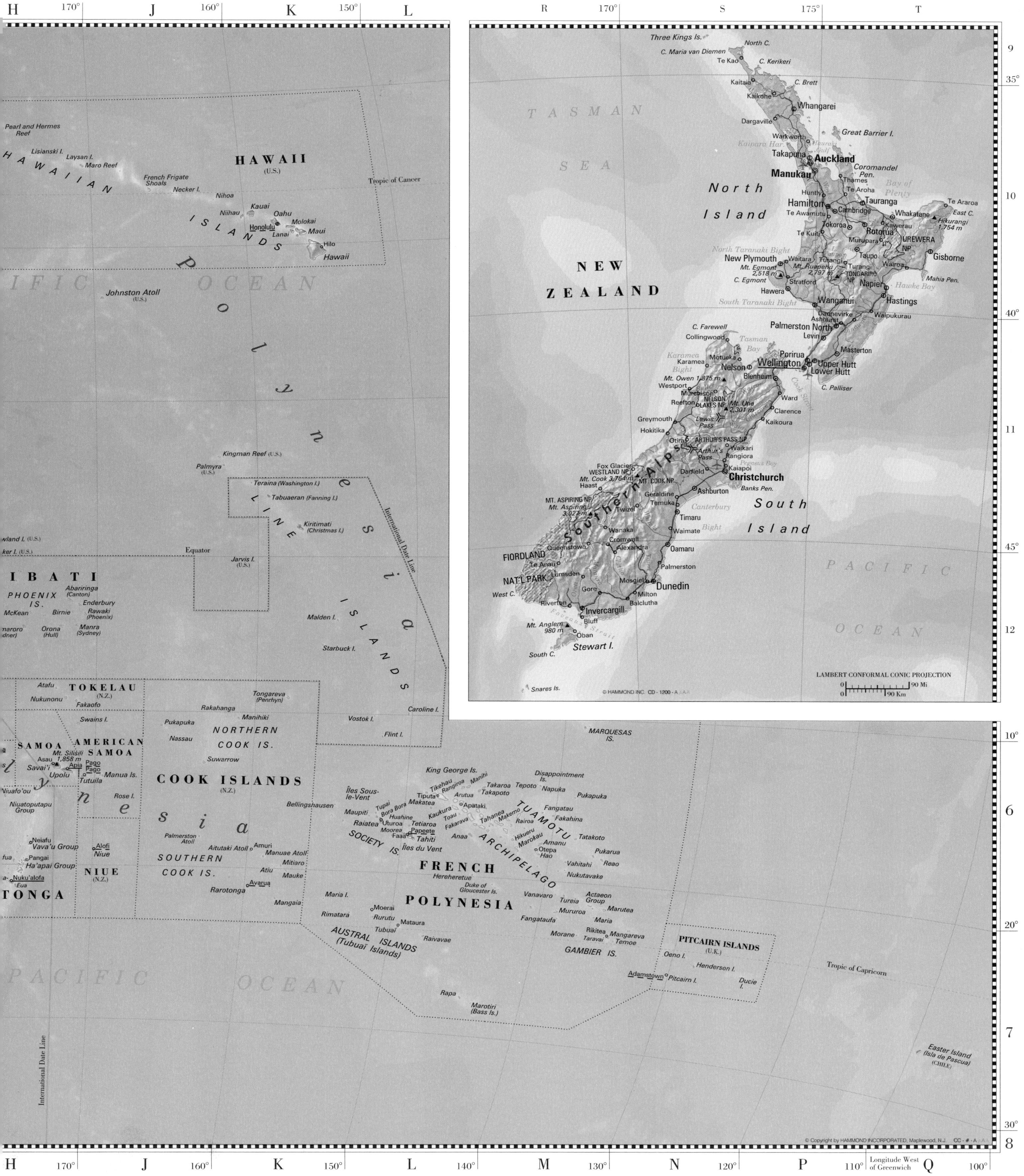

HAWAII (U.S.)

Pearl and Hermes Reef · Lisianski I. · Laysan I. · Maro Reef · French Frigate Shoals · Necker I. · Nihoa · Niihau · Kauai · Oahu · Molokai · Maui · Lanai · Honolulu · Hilo · Hawaii

HAWAIIAN ISLANDS

Tropic of Cancer

Johnston Atoll (U.S.)

P A C I F I C   O C E A N

P o l y n e s i a

Kingman Reef (U.S.) · Palmyra (U.S.) · Teraina (Washington I.) · Tabuaeran (Fanning I.) · Kiritimati (Christmas I.)

LINE ISLANDS

Equator · Jarvis I. (U.S.)

International Date Line

...wland I. (U.S.) · ...ker I. (U.S.)

IBATI

PHOENIX IS. · McKean · Birnie · Abariringa (Canton) · Enderbury · Rawaki (Phoenix) · ...naroro (...dner) · Orona (Hull) · Manra (Sydney)

Malden I. · Starbuck I. · Vostok I. · Flint I. · Caroline I.

TOKELAU (N.Z.) · Atafu · Nukunonu · Fakaofo · Swains I.

Rakahanga · Manihiki · Tongareva (Penrhyn)

Pukapuka · Nassau · Suwarrow · NORTHERN COOK IS.

SAMOA · Mt. Silisili 1,858 m · Asau · Savai'i · Apia · Upolu · **AMERICAN SAMOA** · Pago Pago · Tutuila · Manua Is. · Rose I.

Niuafo'ou · Niuatoputapu Group · Neiafu · Vava'u Group · Alofi · Niue (N.Z.) · ...fua · Ha'apai Group · Pangai · Nuku'alofa · ...a-Eua

TONGA

COOK ISLANDS (N.Z.) · Palmerston Atoll · Aitutaki Atoll · Manuae Atoll · Amuri · Mitiaro · Atiu · Mauke · Avarua · SOUTHERN COOK IS. · **NIUE** (N.Z.) · Rarotonga · Mangaia

P o l y n e s i a

P A C I F I C   O C E A N

International Date Line

MARQUESAS IS.

King George Is. · Disappointment Is. · Tepoto · Napuka · Pukapuka · Takaroa · Manihi · Takapoto · Fangatau · Fakahina

Îles Sous-le-Vent · Tikehau · Rangiroa · Arutua · Apataki · Toau · Kaukura · Fakarava · Makatea · Tupai · Bora Bora · Huahine · Tahanea · Makemo · Raroia · Tatakoto

Maupiti · Raiatea · Uturoa · Tetiaroa · Hikueru · Marokau

Moorea · Faaa · Papeete · Tahiti · Anaa · Reao · Pukarua · Amanu · Otepa · Vahitahi · Nukutavake

SOCIETY IS. · Îles du Vent

TUAMOTU ARCHIPELAGO

FRENCH POLYNESIA

Hereheretue · Duke of Gloucester Is. · Vanavaro · Tureia · Vahitahi · Actaeon Group · Marutea

Maria I. · Moerai · Rurutu · Mataura · Rimatara · Tubuai · Mururoa · Maria · Rikitea · Mangareva · Temoe

AUSTRAL ISLANDS (Tubuai Islands) · Raivavae · Morane · Fangataufa · Taravai · **GAMBIER IS.**

PITCAIRN ISLANDS (U.K.) · Oeno I. · Henderson I. · Adamstown · Pitcairn I. · Ducie I.

Rapa · Marotiri (Bass Is.)

Tropic of Capricorn

Easter Island (Isla de Pascua) (CHILE)

NEW ZEALAND

T A S M A N   S E A

Three Kings Is. · North C. · C. Maria van Diemen · Te Kao · C. Kerikeri · Kaitaia · Kaikohe · C. Brett · Whangarei · Dargaville · Great Barrier I. · Warkworth · Kaipara Har. · Takapuna · **Auckland** · Coromandel Pen. · **Manukau** · Thames · Bay of Plenty · Te Aroha · Huntly · Te Araroa · Hamilton · Te Awamutu · Cambridge · Tauranga · Whakatane · East C. · Kawerau · Hikurangi 1,754 m · Te Kuiti · Tokoroa · Rotorua · **UREWERA** NP · Murupara · Gisborne · Taupo · Turangi · TONGARIRO NP · Wairoa · New Plymouth · Waitara · Tangi · Mt. Egmont 2,518 m · Mt. Ruapehu 2,797 m · Mahia Pen. · Napier · Stratford · Hawera · C. Egmont · Wanganui · Hastings · North Taranaki Bight · Waipukurau · South Taranaki Bight · Dannevirke · Ashhurst · Palmerston North · C. Farewell · Collingwood · Levin · Motueka · Tasman Bay · Masterton · Karamea Bight · Karamea · Nelson · Porirua · Upper Hutt · Westport · Mt. Owen 1,875 m · Blenheim · **Wellington** · Lower Hutt · Murchison · NELSON LAKES NP · Ward · C. Palliser · Reefton · Mt. Una 2,301 m · Clarence · Greymouth · Lewis Pass · Kaikoura · Hokitika · Otira · ARTHUR'S PASS NP · Waikari · Arthur's Pass · Rangiora · Fox Glacier · WESTLAND NP · Mt. Cook 3,764 m · Darfield · Kaiapoi · Haast · MT. COOK NP · **Christchurch** · Banks Pen. · MT. ASPIRING NP · Geraldine · Ashburton · Mt. Aspiring 3,027 m · Temuka · **FIORDLAND** · Twizel · Canterbury Bight · **NAT'L PARK** · Wanaka · Timaru · Te Anau · Cromwell · Alexandra · Waimate · Lumsden · Queenstown · Oamaru · West C. · Mosgiel · Palmerston · Gore · **Dunedin** · Riverton · Milton · Balclutha · Invercargill · Bluff · Oban · Mt. Anglem 980 m · Stewart I. · South C. · Snares Is.

NEW ZEALAND

North Island · *South Island* · Southern Alps

P A C I F I C   O C E A N

LAMBERT CONFORMAL CONIC PROJECTION

0 _____ 90 Mi
0 _____ 90 Km

© HAMMOND INC. CD-1200-A

POPULATION OF CITIES AND TOWNS
- ▪ OVER 3,000,000
- ◻ 1,000,000 - 2,999,999
- ● 500,000 - 999,999
- ◉ 100,000 - 499,999
- ○ UNDER 100,000

SCALE 1:27,000,000   LAMBERT AZIMUTHAL EQUAL-AREA PROJECTION

MILES 0 ___ 400 ___ 800 ___ 1200
KILOMETERS 0 ___ 400 ___ 800 ___ 1200

Longitude West of Greenwich

North
America

The Grand Canyon, one of the deepest canyons in the world, with a depth of 1 mile (1.6 km.), can be seen in this spectacular, west-looking, low-oblique image. The Colorado River cut through rocks billions of years old to create this canyon. The Grand Canyon is 277 miles (466 km.) long and averages nearly 10 miles (16 km.) in width. The snow-covered, forested Kaibab Plateau (north of the canyon) and the Coconino Plateau (south of the canyon) are visible. Western portions of the Painted Desert can be seen east of the canyon where the Little Colorado joins the Colorado River.

AREA OF OPTIMIZATION

The red band which surrounds this map defines the "Area of Optimization." Within this bounding curve is the most accurate conformal map that can be made of the region. Outside the optimized area, distortion increases rapidly, and tears or other irregularities in the grid may occur. (See page 6 for additional information.)

© Copyright by HAMMOND INCORPORATED, Maplewood, N.J.

POPULATION OF CITIES AND TOWNS

■ OVER 3,000,000	◉ 500,000 - 999,999	○ UNDER 100,000
▣ 1,000,000 - 2,999,999	◉ 100,000 - 499,999	

SCALE 1:30,000,000   OPTIMAL CONFORMAL PROJECTION

MILES   0   500   1000   1500
KILOMETERS   0   500   1000   1500

Longitude   West of 100°   Greenwich

[Map of North America showing Canada, United States, Mexico, Central America, the West Indies, Greenland, and portions of Russia and South America, with the Pacific Ocean, Atlantic Ocean, Arctic Ocean, Gulf of Mexico, Caribbean Sea, Hudson Bay, and Bering Sea labeled. Grid references 3, 2, 1 across the top and F, G, H, J, L across the bottom; numbers 4–9 along the sides. Page markers 67 and 147.]

- FAIRBANKS -11°
- NUUK 18°
- JUNEAU 28°
- EDMONTON 7°
- VANCOUVER 37°
- WINNIPEG 0°
- QUÉBEC 12°
- DENVER 30°
- CHICAGO 27°
- NEW YORK 34°
- LOS ANGELES 55°
- PHOENIX 52°
- NEW ORLEANS 55°
- LA PAZ 63°
- TAMPICO 64°
- HAVANA 72°
- SAN JUAN 75°
- MEXICO 54°
- BELIZE CITY 73°
- COLÓN 81°

● NEW YORK 34°
AVERAGE JANUARY TEMPERATURE
DEGREES FAHRENHEIT AT
SELECTED STATIONS

AVERAGE JANUARY TEMPERATURE

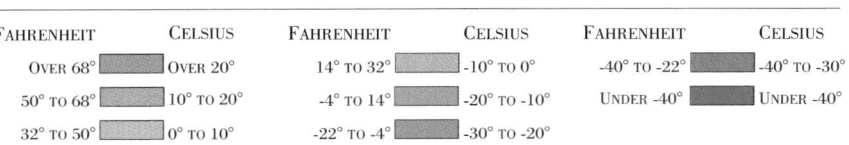

FAHRENHEIT	CELSIUS	FAHRENHEIT	CELSIUS	FAHRENHEIT	CELSIUS
OVER 68°	OVER 20°	14° TO 32°	-10° TO 0°	-40° TO -22°	-40° TO -30°
50° TO 68°	10° TO 20°	-4° TO 14°	-20° TO -10°	UNDER -40°	UNDER -40°
32° TO 50°	0° TO 10°	-22° TO -4°	-30° TO -20°		

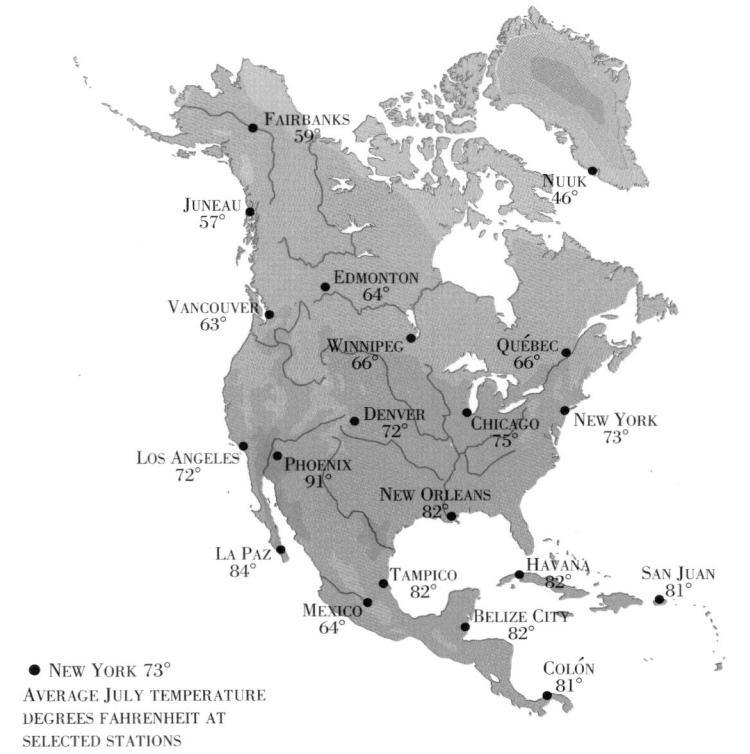

- FAIRBANKS 59°
- NUUK 46°
- JUNEAU 57°
- EDMONTON 64°
- VANCOUVER 63°
- WINNIPEG 66°
- QUÉBEC 66°
- DENVER 72°
- CHICAGO 75°
- NEW YORK 73°
- LOS ANGELES 72°
- PHOENIX 91°
- NEW ORLEANS 82°
- LA PAZ 84°
- TAMPICO 82°
- HAVANA 82°
- SAN JUAN 81°
- MEXICO 64°
- BELIZE CITY 82°
- COLÓN 81°

● NEW YORK 73°
AVERAGE JULY TEMPERATURE
DEGREES FAHRENHEIT AT
SELECTED STATIONS

AVERAGE JULY TEMPERATURE

FAHRENHEIT	CELSIUS	FAHRENHEIT	CELSIUS	FAHRENHEIT	CELSIUS
OVER 86°	OVER 30°	50° TO 68°	10° TO 20°	14° TO 32°	-10° TO 0°
68° TO 86°	20° TO 30°	32° TO 50°	0° TO 10°	UNDER 14°	UNDER -10°

ET, Dfc, ET, Cfc, ET, Dfc, ET, Cfb, Csa, Dsb, Dfb, BSk, Dfb, Dfa, Cfb, BWk, Dfb, Cfa, BWh, BSk, BSh, BWh, BSh, Cw, Aw, Aw, Am, Af, Af, BSh, EF

CLIMATE

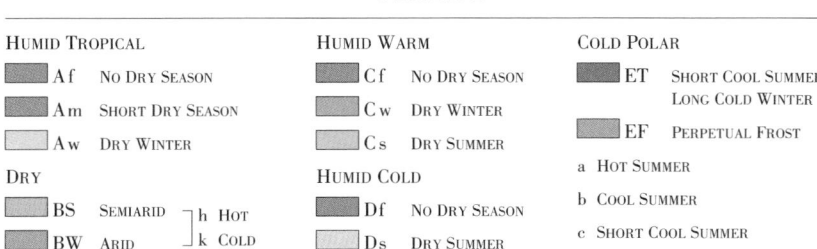

HUMID TROPICAL
- Af NO DRY SEASON
- Am SHORT DRY SEASON
- Aw DRY WINTER

DRY
- BS SEMIARID
- BW ARID

h HOT
k COLD

HUMID WARM
- Cf NO DRY SEASON
- Cw DRY WINTER
- Cs DRY SUMMER

HUMID COLD
- Df NO DRY SEASON
- Ds DRY SUMMER

COLD POLAR
- ET SHORT COOL SUMMER, LONG COLD WINTER
- EF PERPETUAL FROST

a HOT SUMMER
b COOL SUMMER
c SHORT COOL SUMMER

AFTER KOEPPEN-GEIGER

VEGETATION

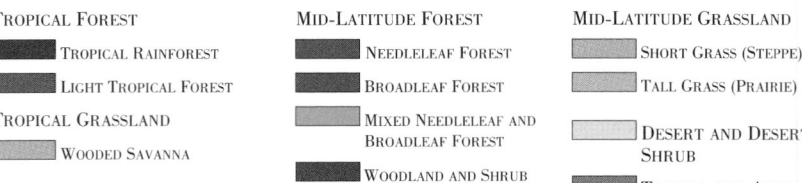

TROPICAL FOREST
- TROPICAL RAINFOREST
- LIGHT TROPICAL FOREST

TROPICAL GRASSLAND
- WOODED SAVANNA

MID-LATITUDE FOREST
- NEEDLELEAF FOREST
- BROADLEAF FOREST
- MIXED NEEDLELEAF AND BROADLEAF FOREST
- WOODLAND AND SHRUB (MEDITERRANEAN)

MID-LATITUDE GRASSLAND
- SHORT GRASS (STEPPE)
- TALL GRASS (PRAIRIE)
- DESERT AND DESERT SHRUB
- TUNDRA AND ALPINE
- PERMANENT ICE COVER

North America - Geographical Comparisons

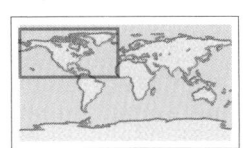

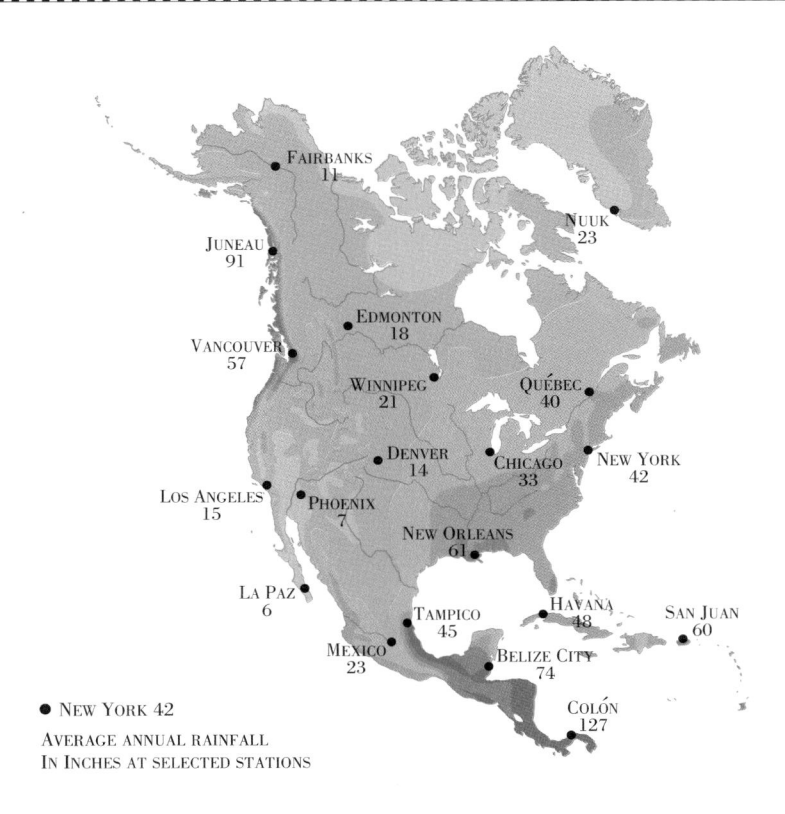

FAIRBANKS 11
NUUK 23
JUNEAU 91
EDMONTON 18
VANCOUVER 57
WINNIPEG 21
QUÉBEC 40
DENVER 14
CHICAGO 33
NEW YORK 42
LOS ANGELES 15
PHOENIX 7
NEW ORLEANS 61
LA PAZ 6
TAMPICO 45
HAVANA 48
SAN JUAN 60
MEXICO 23
BELIZE CITY 74
COLÓN 127

● NEW YORK 42
AVERAGE ANNUAL RAINFALL
IN INCHES AT SELECTED STATIONS

AVERAGE ANNUAL RAINFALL

INCHES	CM	INCHES	CM	INCHES	CM
OVER 80	OVER 200	40 TO 60	100 TO 150	10 TO 20	25 TO 50
60 TO 80	150 TO 200	20 TO 40	50 TO 100	UNDER 10	UNDER 25

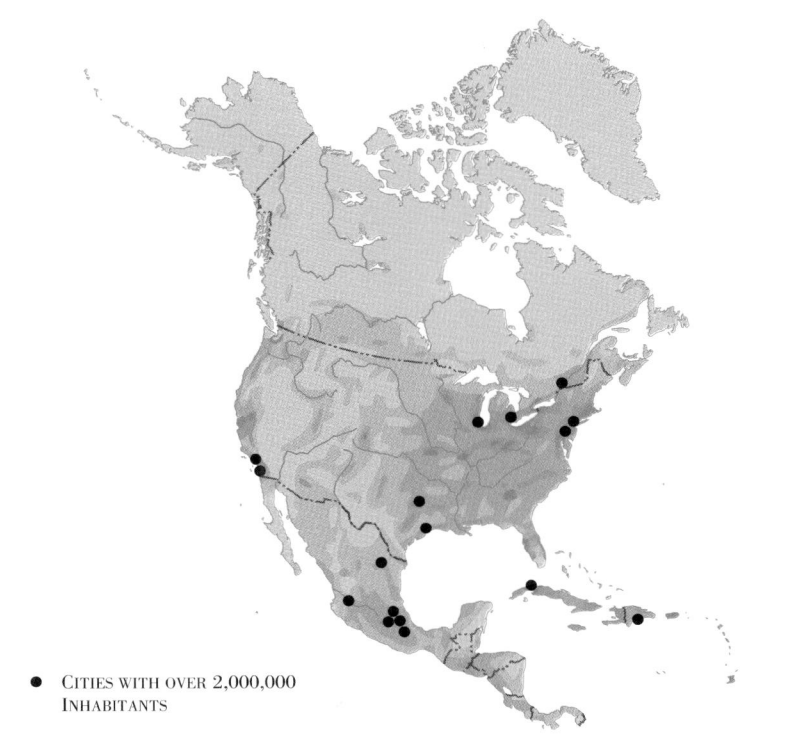

● CITIES WITH OVER 2,000,000 INHABITANTS

POPULATION DISTRIBUTION

DENSITY PER		SQ. MI.	SQ. KM.	SQ. MI.	SQ. KM.
SQ. MI.	SQ. KM.	130 TO 260	50 TO 100	3 TO 25	1 TO 10
OVER 260	OVER 100	25 TO 130	10 TO 50	UNDER 3	UNDER 1

FURS
FURS
BARLEY
OATS FLAX
WHEAT OATS
WINE
SHEEP
FRUIT
CATTLE CORN CORN
WHEAT
CATTLE SOYBEANS
TOBACCO
COTTON
COTTON
PEANUTS
GOATS
FRUIT
CORN
CATTLE
SUGARCANE
HOGS
COFFEE

LAND USE

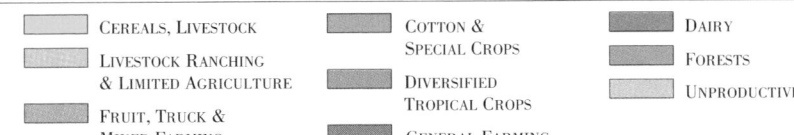

CEREALS, LIVESTOCK	COTTON & SPECIAL CROPS	DAIRY
LIVESTOCK RANCHING & LIMITED AGRICULTURE	DIVERSIFIED TROPICAL CROPS	FORESTS
FRUIT, TRUCK & MIXED FARMING	GENERAL FARMING	UNPRODUCTIVE

MINERAL RESOURCES

ENERGY & FUELS
◆ COAL
▲ NATURAL GAS
● PETROLEUM
■ URANIUM

IRON & FERROALLOYS
1 COBALT
2 IRON ORE
3 MANGANESE
4 MOLYBDENUM
5 NICKEL
6 TUNGSTEN
7 VANADIUM

OTHER MAJOR RESOURCES
1 ANTIMONY
2 ASBESTOS
3 BAUXITE
4 BORAX
5 COPPER
6 FLUORSPAR
7 GOLD
8 GRAPHITE
9 LEAD
10 MERCURY
11 MICA
12 PHOSPHATES
13 PLATINUM
14 POTASH
15 SILVER
16 SULFUR
17 TITANIUM
18 ZINC

Canada

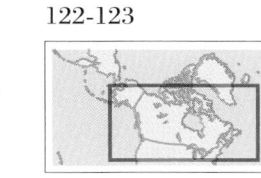

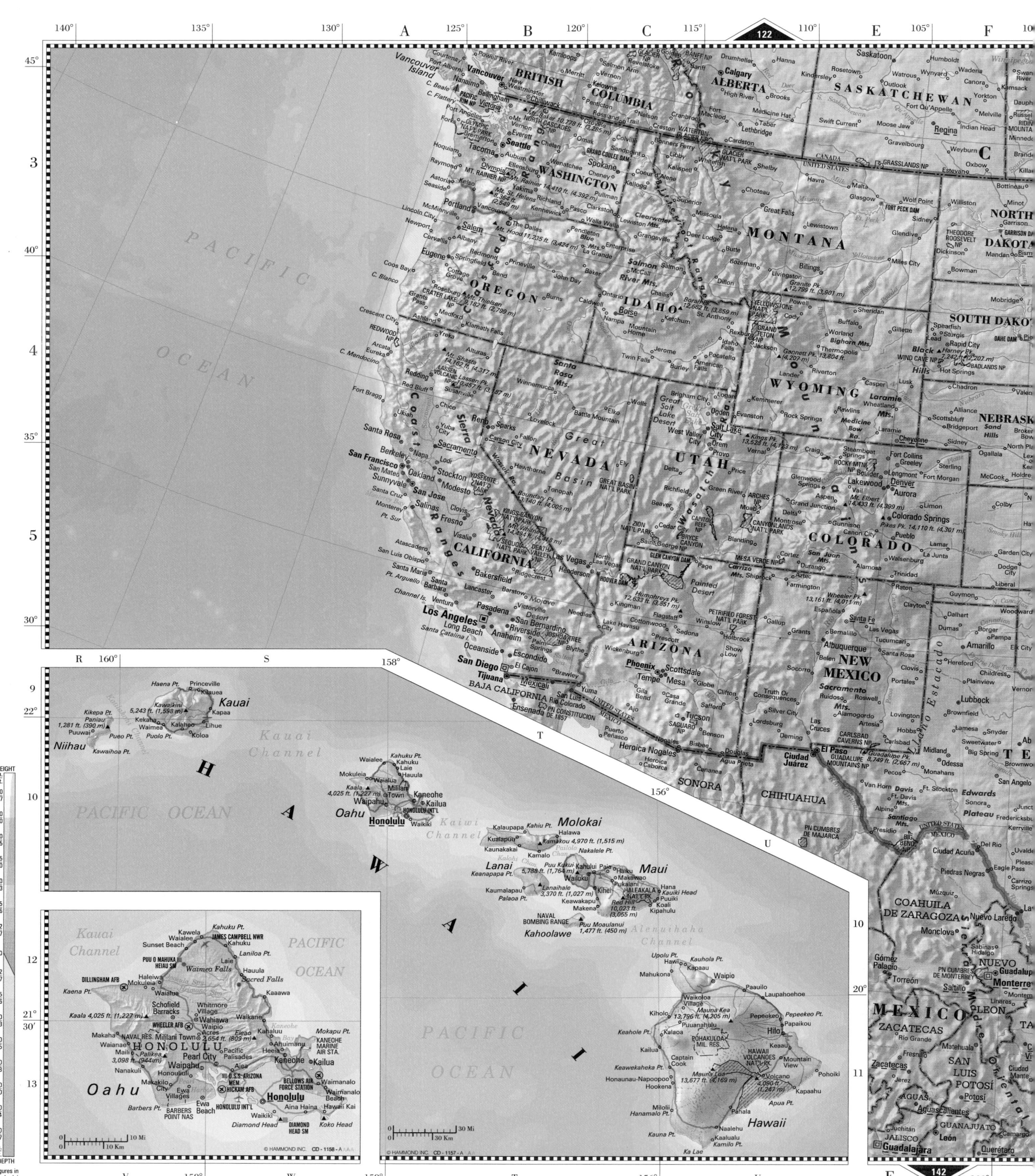

POPULATION OF CITIES AND TOWNS

■ OVER 2,000,000   ● 500,000 - 999,999   ◉ 50,000 - 99,999
▣ 1,000,000 - 1,999,999   ● 100,000 - 499,999   ○ UNDER 50,000

SCALE 1:12,000,000   LAMBERT CONFORMAL CONIC PROJECTION

Longitude West of Greenwich

© Copyright by HAMMOND INCORPORATED, Maplewood, N.J.   CD - 1079 - A - A

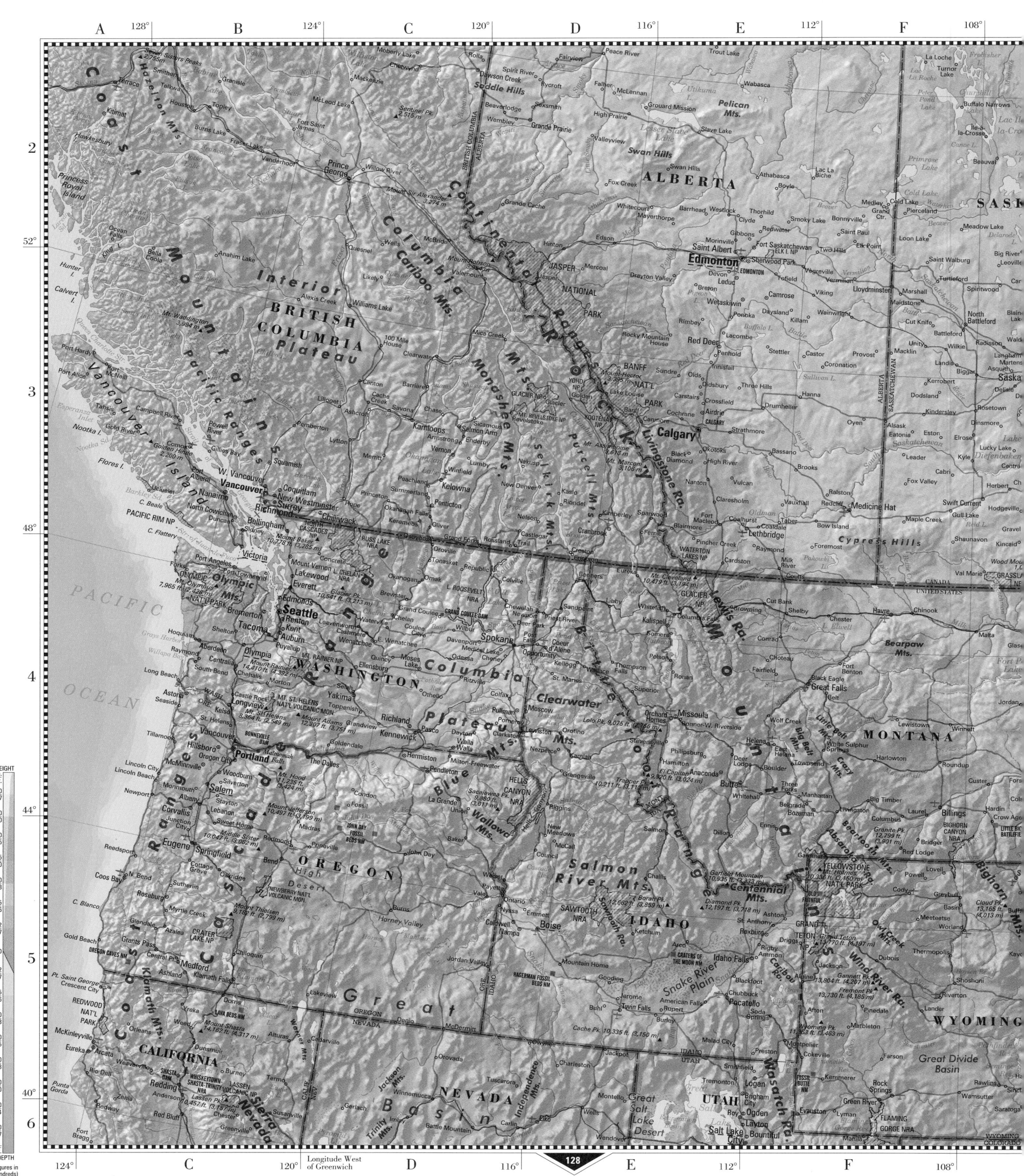

Southwestern Canada, Northwestern United States

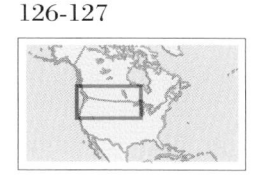

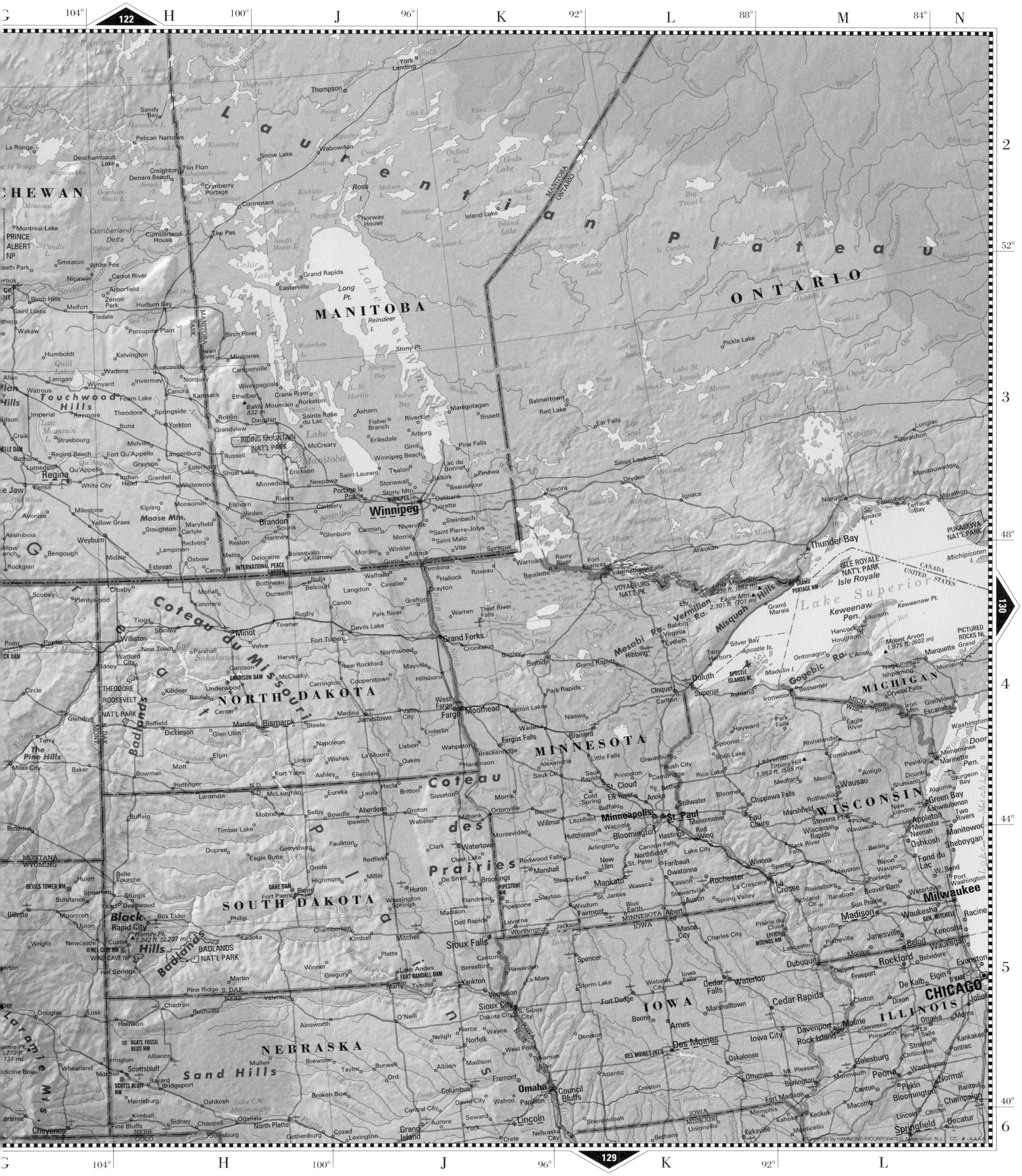

POPULATION OF CITIES AND TOWNS

- ■ OVER 2,000,000
- □ 1,000,000 - 1,999,999
- ● 500,000 - 999,999
- ◉ 250,000 - 499,999
- ◎ 100,000 - 249,999
- ⊙ 30,000 - 99,999
- ○ 10,000 - 29,999
- ○ UNDER 10,000

SCALE 1:6,000,000   LAMBERT CONFORMAL CONIC PROJECTION

MILES 0   100   200   300
KILOMETERS 0   100   200   300

Copyright by HAMMOND INCORPORATED, Maplewood, N.J.   CC- # -AAA

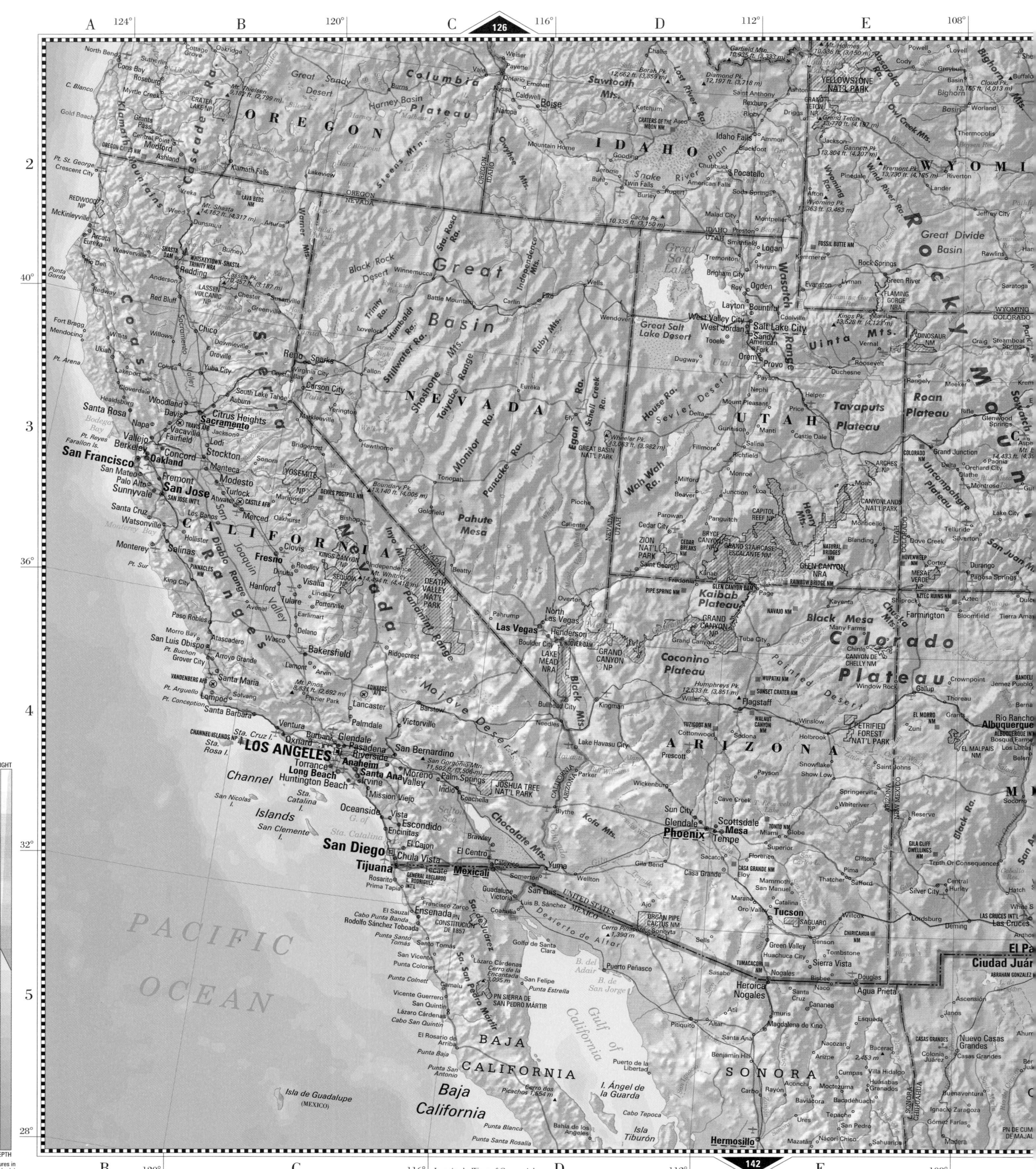

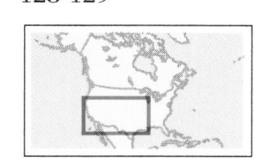

POPULATION OF CITIES AND TOWNS

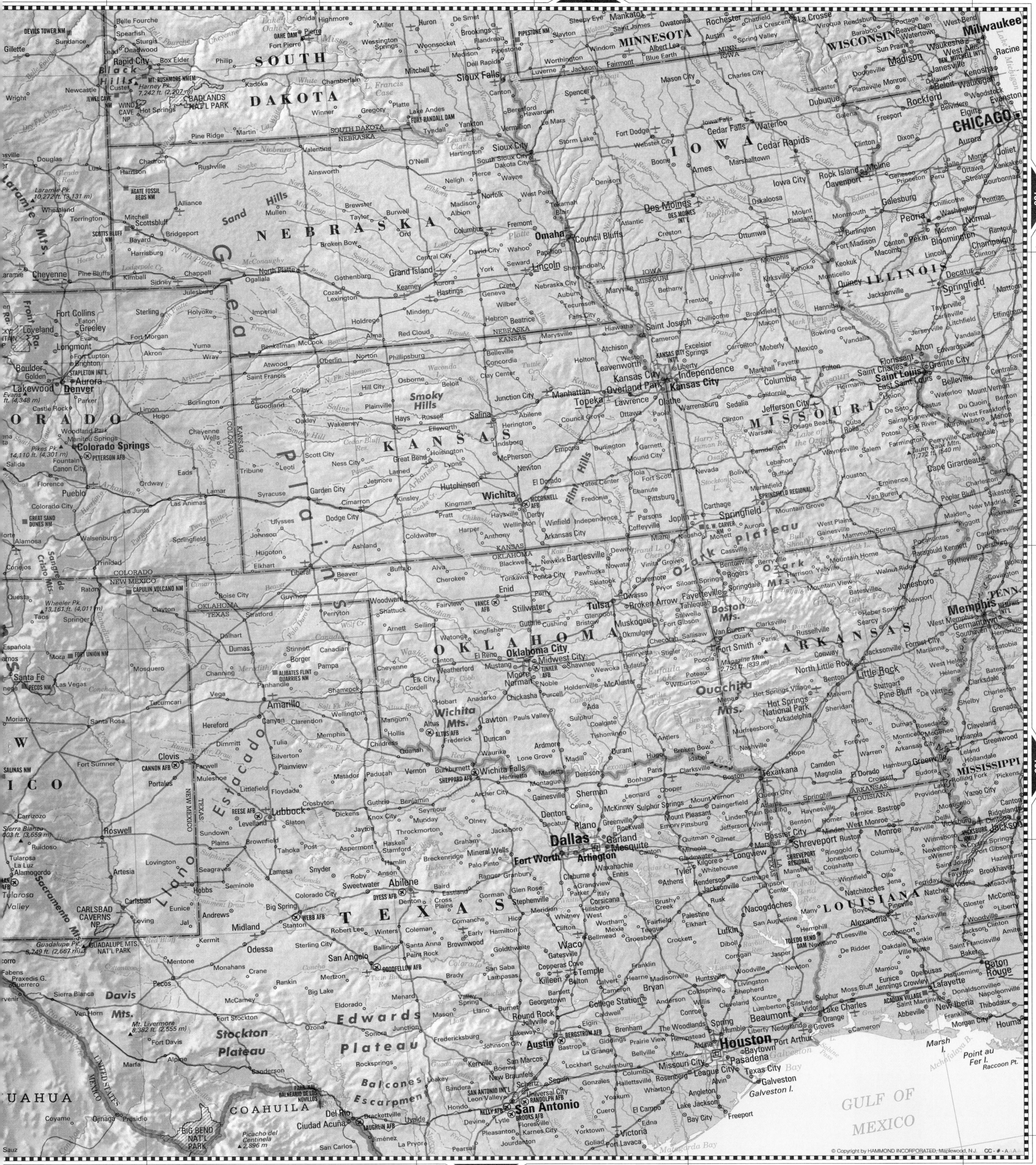

■ OVER 2,000,000 ● 500,000 - 999,999 ● 100,000 - 249,999 ○ 10,000 - 29,999
□ 1,000,000 - 1,999,999 ● 250,000 - 499,999 ○ 30,000 - 99,999 ○ UNDER 10,000

SCALE 1:6,000,000 LAMBERT CONFORMAL CONIC PROJECTION

MILES 0   100   200   300

KILOMETERS 0   100   200   300

© Copyright by HAMMOND INCORPORATED, Maplewood, N.J.

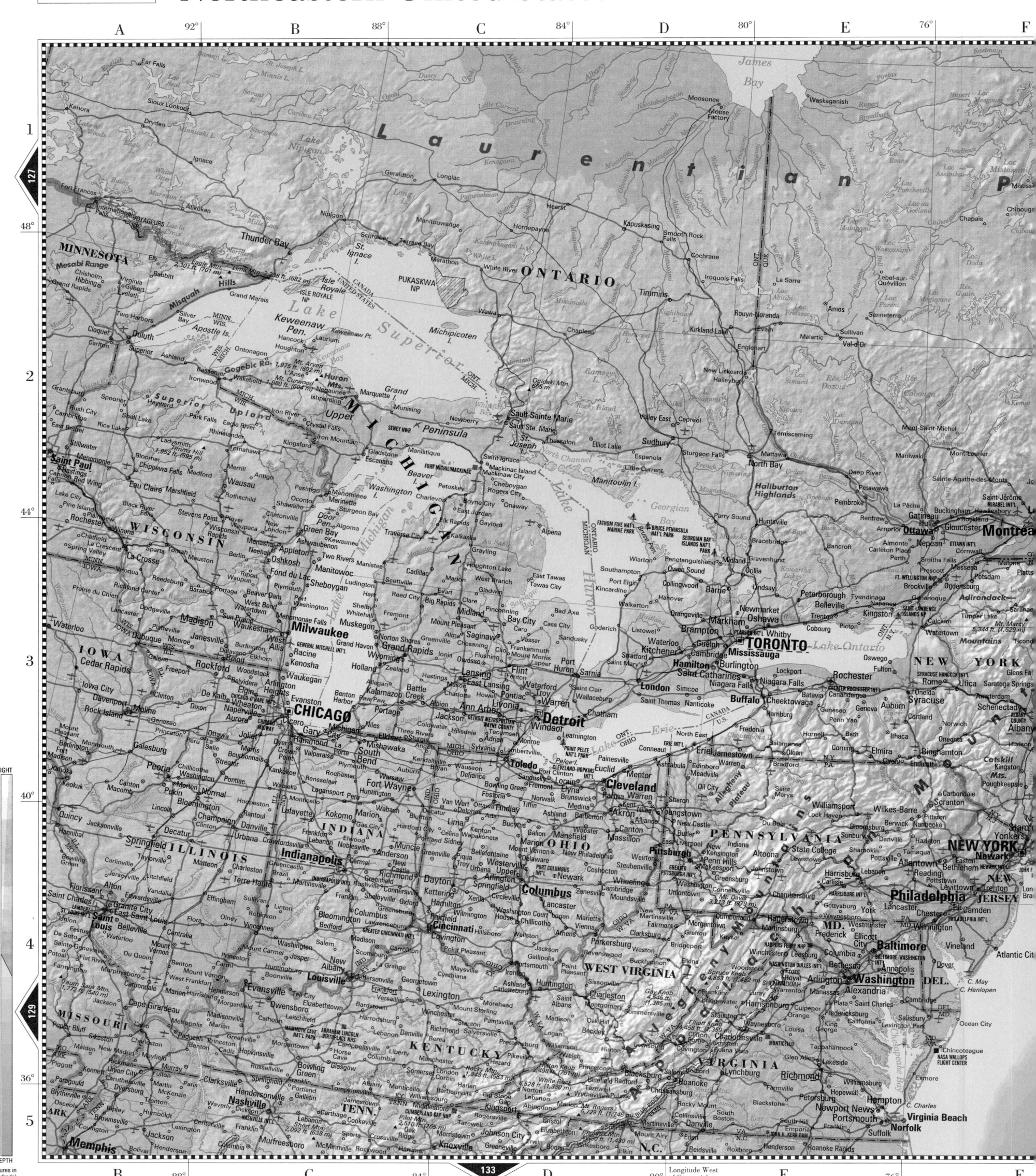

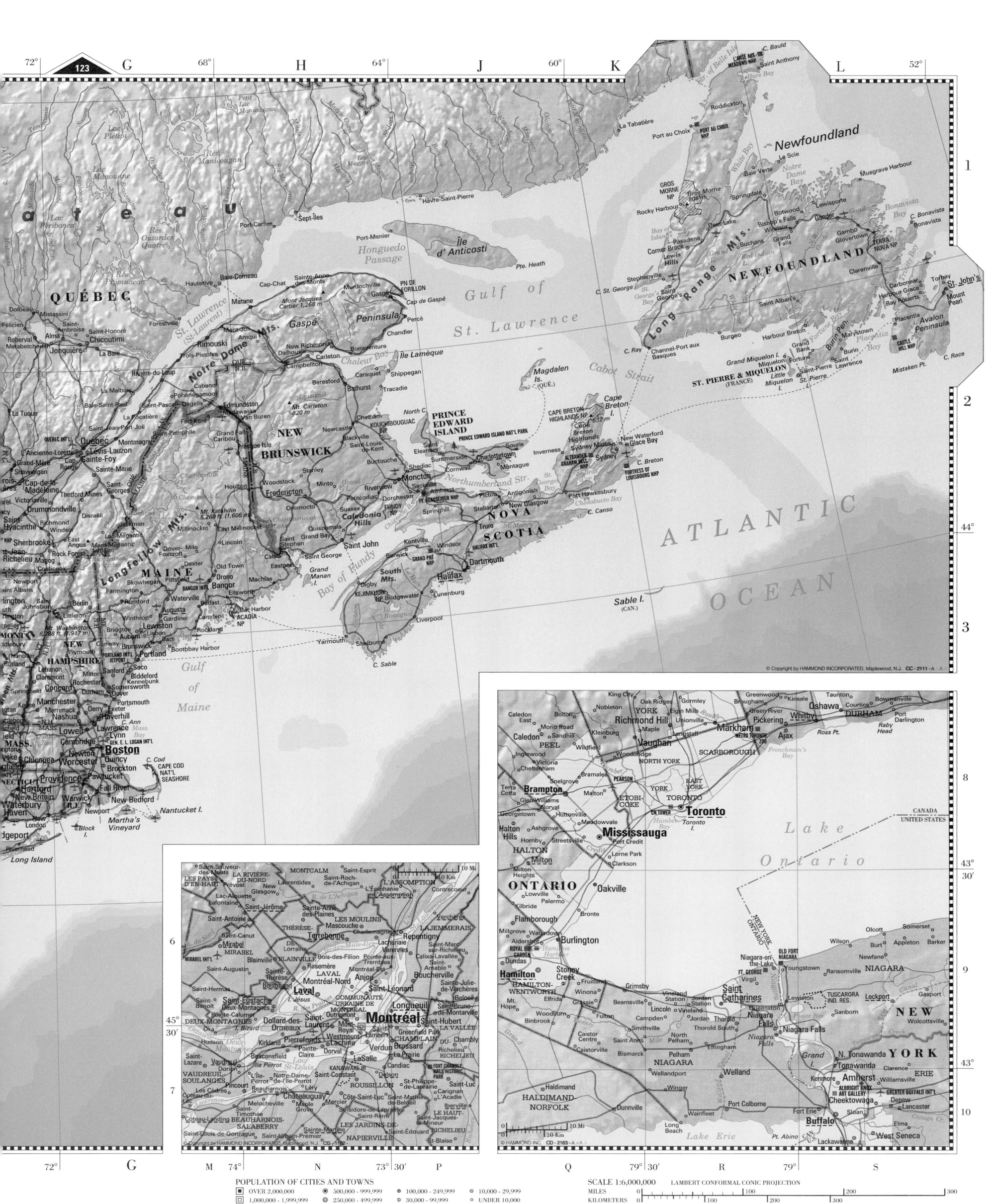

Southeastern United States

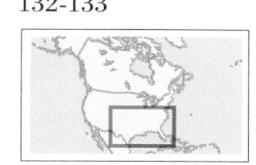

POPULATION OF CITIES AND TOWNS

- ■ OVER 2,000,000
- □ 1,000,000 - 1,999,999
- ⊛ 500,000 - 999,999
- ⊙ 250,000 - 499,999
- ● 100,000 - 249,999
- ⊙ 30,000 - 99,999
- ⊙ 10,000 - 29,999
- ⊙ UNDER 10,000

SCALE 1:6,000,000   LAMBERT CONFORMAL CONIC PROJECTION

MILES 0   100   200   300
KILOMETERS 0   100   200   300

Alaska

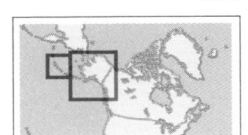

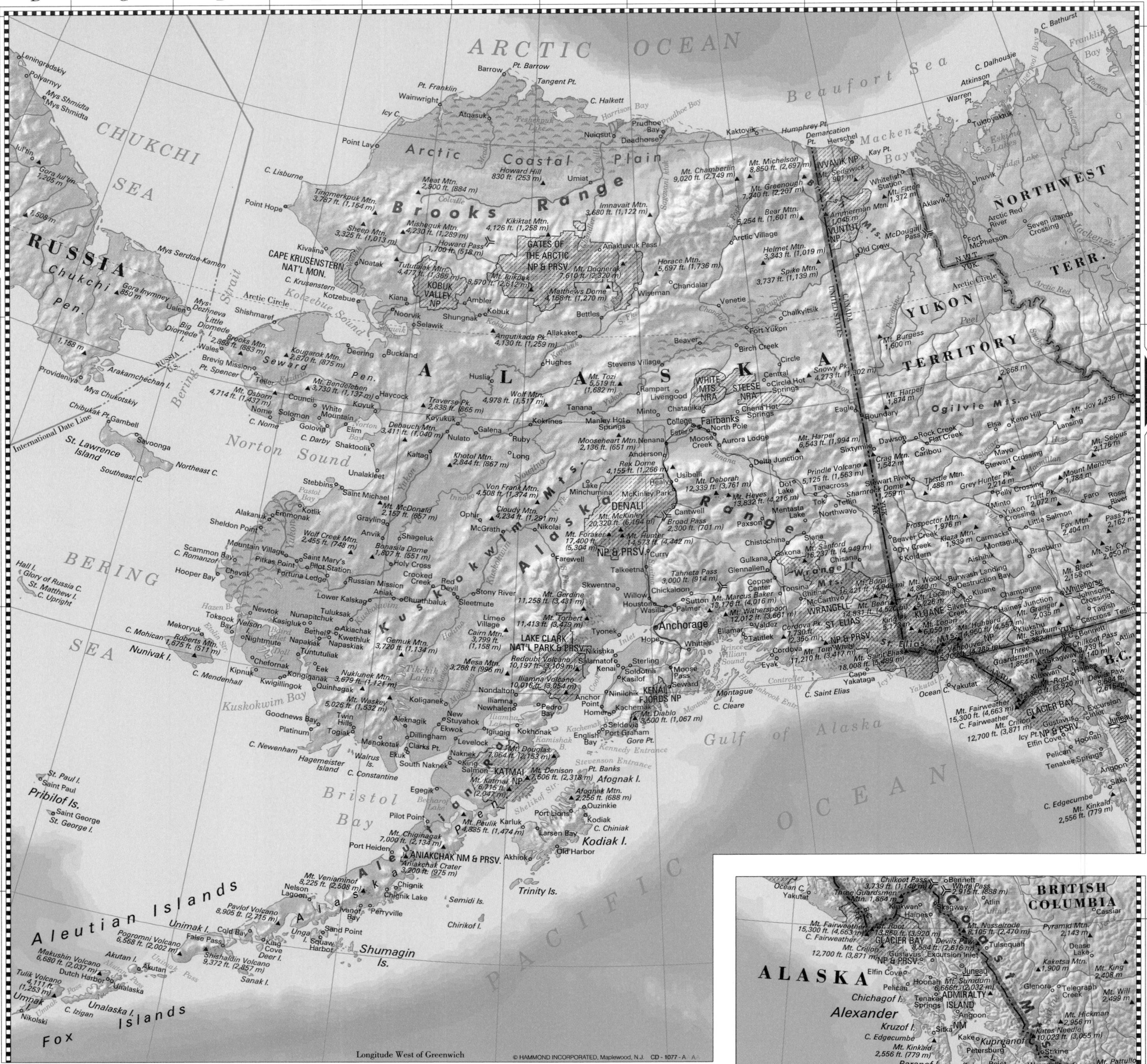

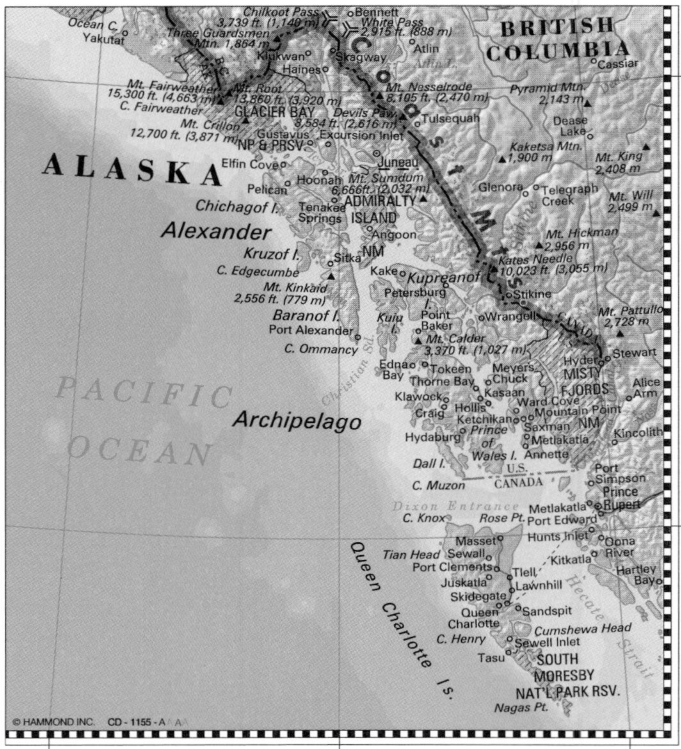

SCALE 1:9,000,000 LAMBERT CONFORMAL CONIC PROJECTION

MILES 0   150   300   450

KILOMETERS 0   150   300   450

POPULATION OF CITIES AND TOWNS

- ◻ OVER 2,000,000
- ◻ 1,000,000 - 1,999,999
- ● 500,000 - 999,999
- ● 250,000 - 499,999
- ● 100,000 - 249,999
- ● 30,000 - 99,999
- ○ 10,000 - 29,999
- ○ UNDER 10,000

© HAMMOND INCORPORATED, Maplewood, N.J.   CD - 1077 - A

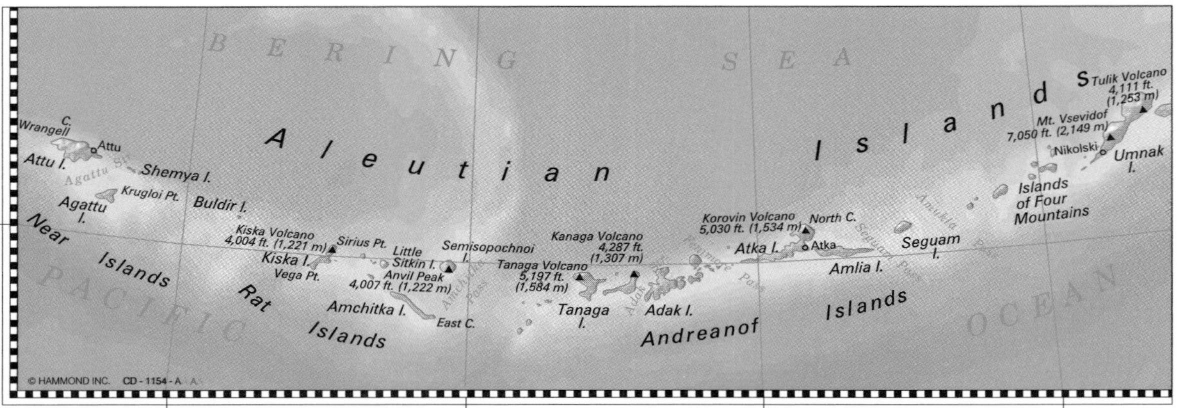

Seattle, San Francisco, Detroit, Chicago

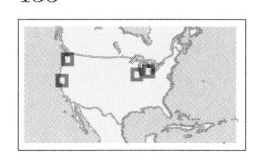

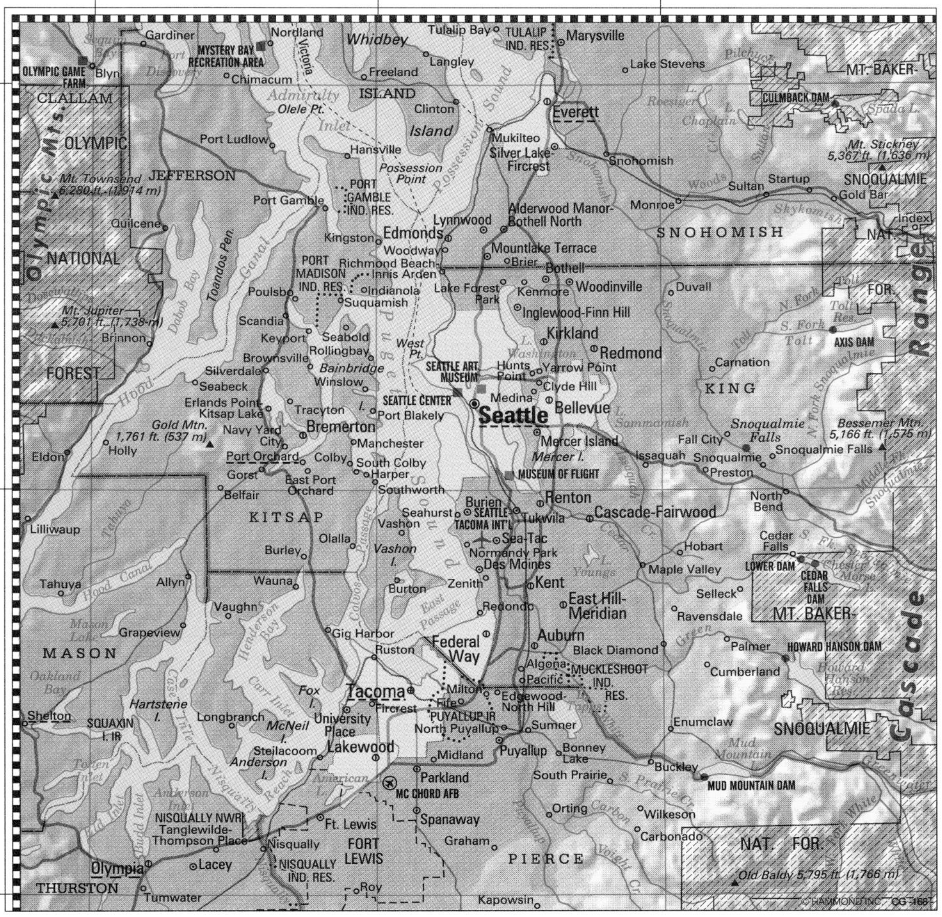

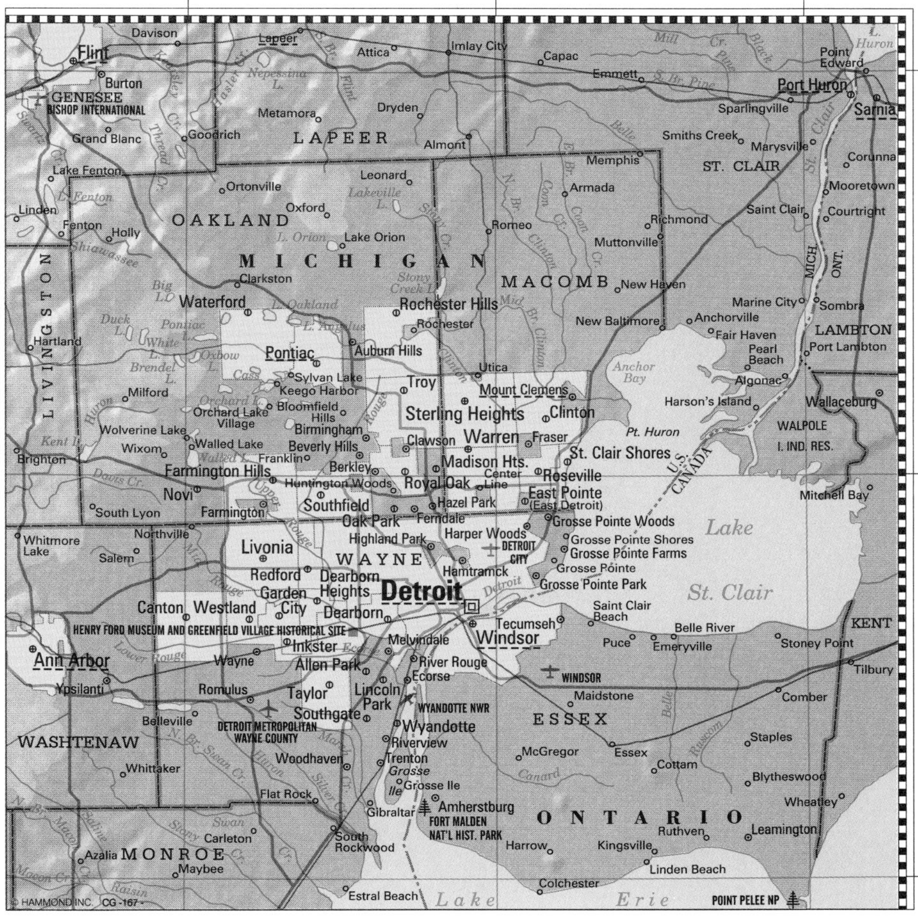

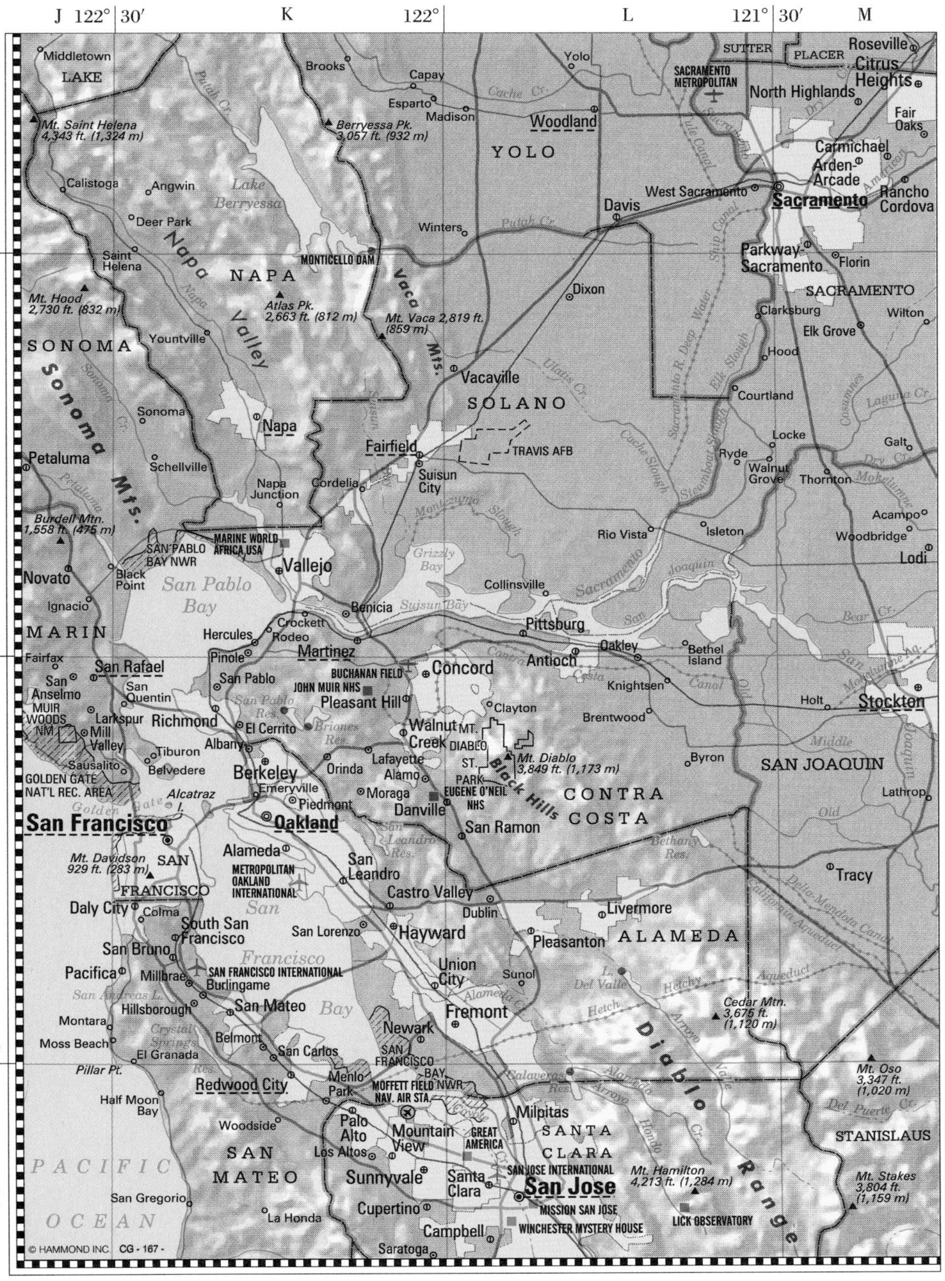

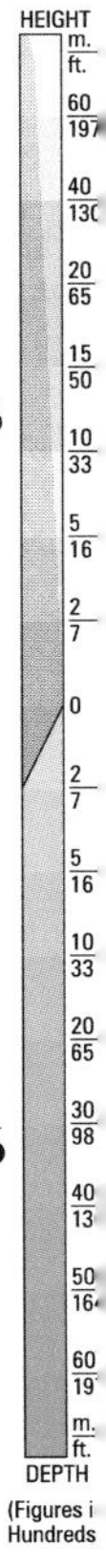

Los Angeles-San Diego

Longitude West of Greenwich 117°

SCALE 1:1,000,000   LAMBERT CONFORMAL CONIC PROJECTION

MILES

KILOMETERS

POPULATION OF CITIES AND TOWNS

◼ OVER 2,000,000	⊙ 500,000 - 999,999	◉ 100,000 - 249,999	⊙ 10,000 - 29,999
◻ 1,000,000 - 1,999,999	⊙ 250,000 - 499,999	◉ 30,000 - 99,999	○ UNDER 10,000

HEIGHT
m. ft.

DEPTH
(Figures in Hundreds)

PACIFIC OCEAN

Phoenix, Salt Lake City, Denver, Oklahoma City, Kansas City, St. Louis, San Antonio, New Orleans

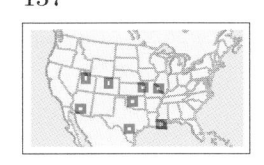

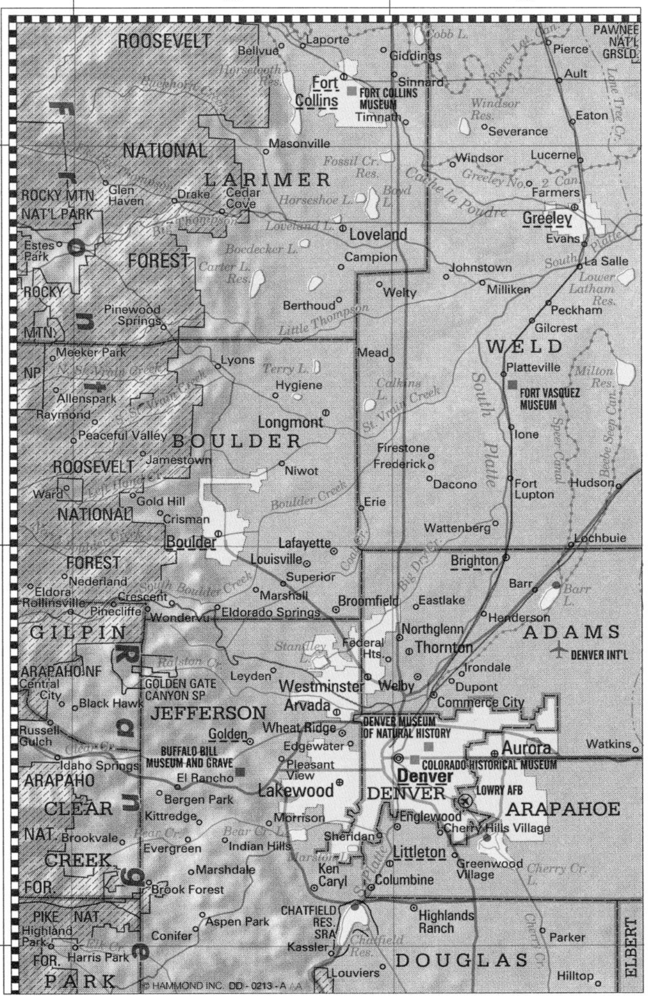

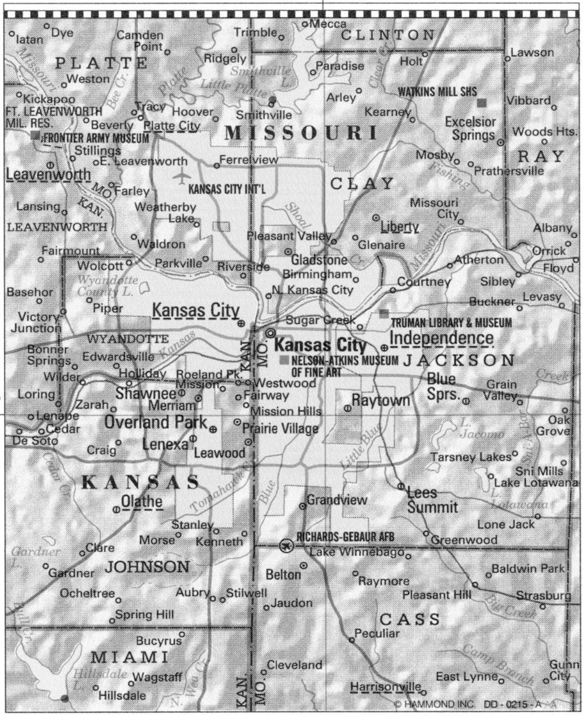

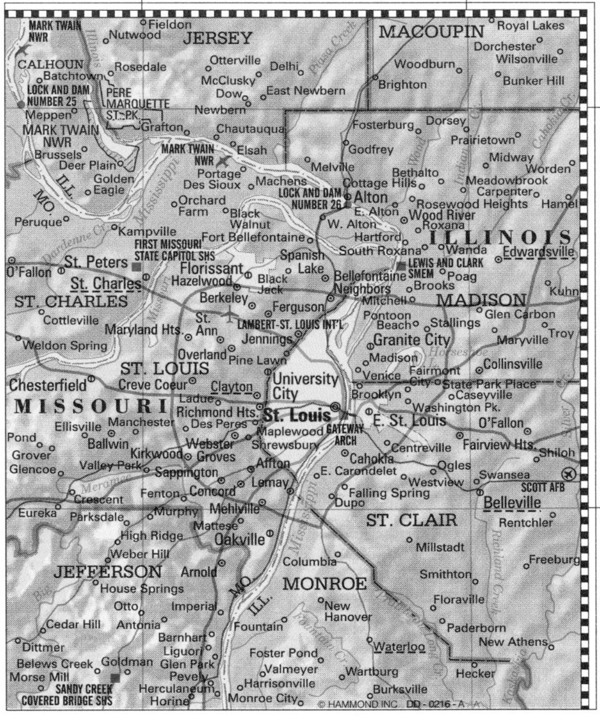

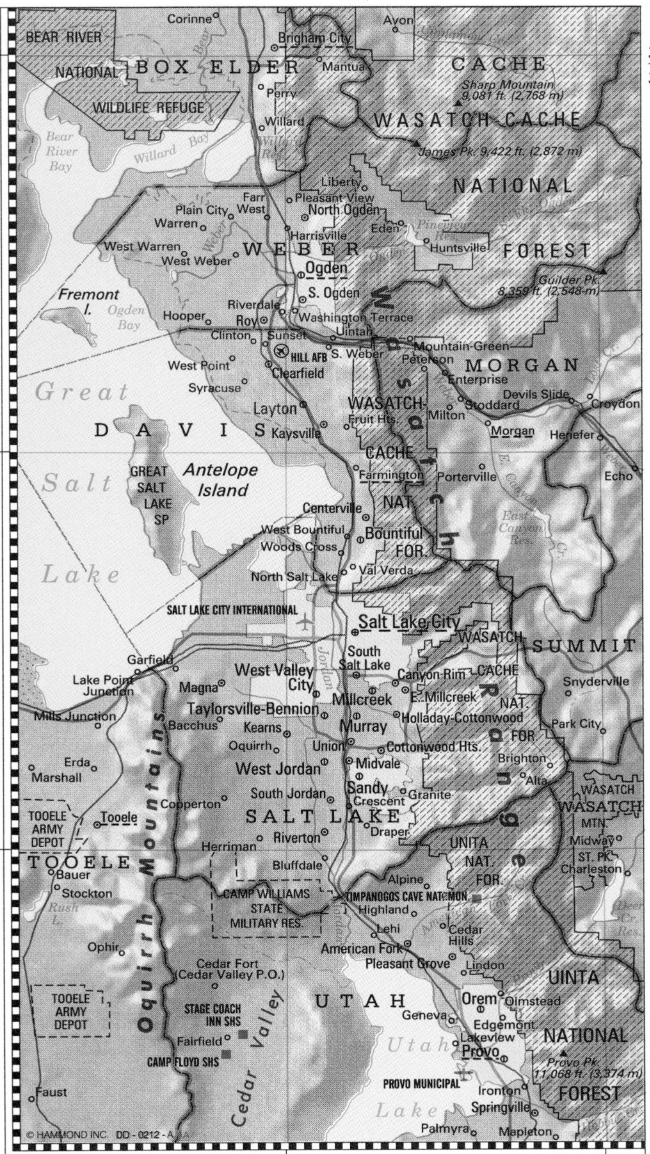

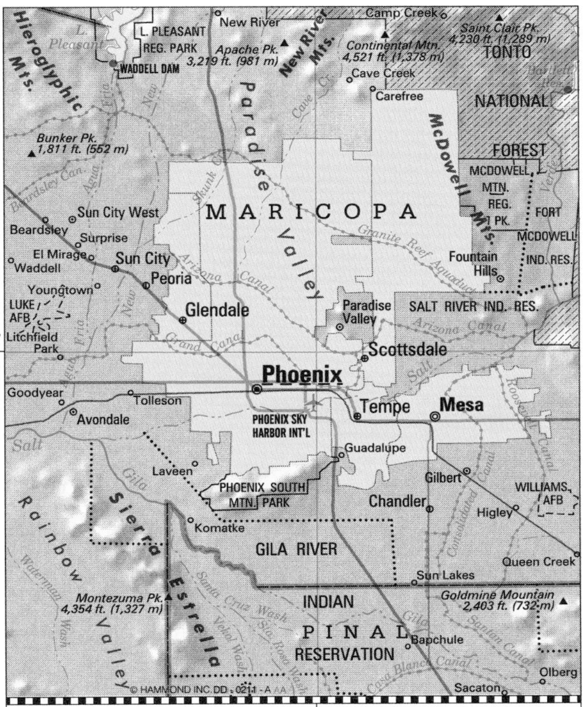

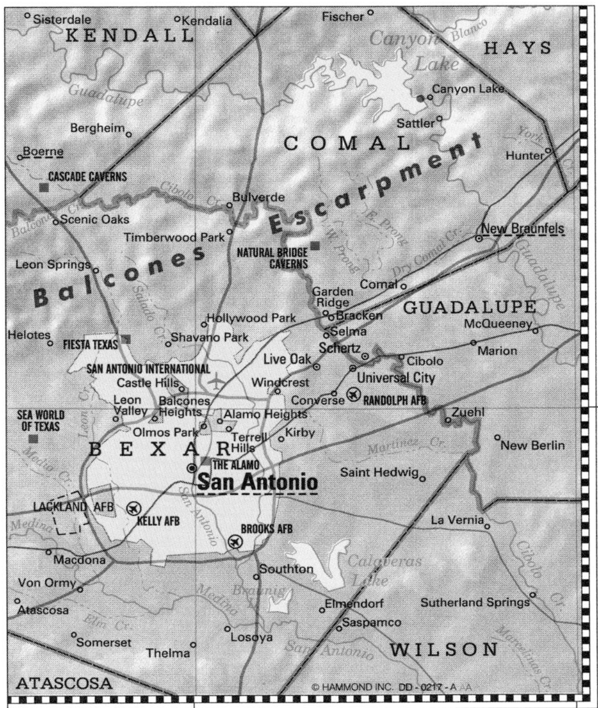

Denver area (B–C, 1–4): ROOSEVELT, NATIONAL, LARIMER, Fort Collins, Loveland, Greeley, Evans, WELD, BOULDER, Boulder, Longmont, ROOSEVELT NATIONAL FOREST, GILPIN, JEFFERSON, ADAMS, Westminster, Arvada, Wheat Ridge, Lakewood, **Denver**, Aurora, LOWRY AFB, ARAPAHOE, Englewood, Littleton, CLEAR CREEK NAT. FOR., PIKE NAT. FOREST, DOUGLAS, Highlands Ranch, Parker, ELBERT, ROCKY MTN. NAT'L PARK, DENVER INT'L

Kansas City area (D–E, 5–6): PLATTE, CLINTON, MISSOURI, CLAY, RAY, Leavenworth, LEAVENWORTH, Liberty, Excelsior Springs, **Kansas City**, Independence, WYANDOTTE, JACKSON, Raytown, KANSAS, Olathe, Overland Park, Lenexa, Leawood, JOHNSON, Grandview, Lees Summit, MIAMI, CASS, Harrisonville, TRUMAN LIBRARY & MUSEUM, NELSON-ATKINS MUSEUM OF FINE ART, RICHARDS-GEBAUR AFB

St. Louis area (F–H, 7–9): MACOUPIN, JERSEY, CALHOUN, ILLINOIS, MADISON, ST. CHARLES, St. Charles, St. Peters, Florissant, Hazelwood, MISSOURI, ST. LOUIS, **St. Louis**, Chesterfield, University City, Clayton, Kirkwood, Webster Groves, Ballwin, E. St. Louis, ST. CLAIR, Belleville, JEFFERSON, MONROE, Arnold, GATEWAY ARCH, MARK TWAIN NWR, MARK TWAIN STATE CAPITOL SHS

Salt Lake City area (J–L, 10–13): BEAR RIVER NATIONAL WILDLIFE REFUGE, BOX ELDER, Brigham City, CACHE, WASATCH CACHE NATIONAL FOREST, WEBER, Ogden, HILL AFB, MORGAN, Great Salt Lake, DAVIS, Bountiful, Antelope Island, GREAT SALT LAKE SP, **Salt Lake City**, SUMMIT, West Valley City, Murray, West Jordan, South Jordan, Sandy, SALT LAKE, TOOELE, Tooele, UINTA NAT. FOR., WASATCH NAT. FOR., American Fork, Orem, Provo, UTAH, Oquirrh Mountains

Oklahoma City area (M–N, 14–15): KINGFISHER, LOGAN, Guthrie, Edmond, OKLAHOMA, LINCOLN, The Village, Bethany, Warr Acres, Nichols Hills, **Oklahoma City**, CANADIAN, Del City, Midwest City, TINKER AFB, Moore, GRADY, CLEVELAND, Norman, Lake Thunderbird, POTTAWATOMIE, McCLAIN, WILL ROGERS WORLD, NATIONAL COWBOY HALL OF FAME AND WESTERN HERITAGE CENTER

New Orleans area (P–Q, 16–17): TANGIPAHOA, ST. TAMMANY, Ponchatoula, Madisonville, Mandeville, Slidell, Lake Pontchartrain, ST. JOHN THE BAPTIST, ORLEANS, Kenner, Metairie, **New Orleans**, Chalmette, JEFFERSON, Gretna, Harvey, Marrero, ST. BERNARD, ST. CHARLES, PLAQUEMINES, LAFOURCHE, Lake Salvador, NEW ORLEANS INT'L

Phoenix area (R–S, 18–19): New River, Apache Pk., Camp Creek, TONTO NATIONAL FOREST, MARICOPA, McDOWELL MTN. REG. PK., FORT McDOWELL IND. RES., Sun City West, Sun City, Peoria, Glendale, SALT RIVER IND. RES., Scottsdale, **Phoenix**, Tempe, **Mesa**, Fountain Hills, Paradise Valley, PHOENIX SKY HARBOR INT'L, Guadalupe, Gilbert, Chandler, Avondale, Goodyear, Tolleson, LUKE AFB, WILLIAMS AFB, GILA RIVER INDIAN RESERVATION, PINAL, Sierra Estrella, Goldmine Mountain 2,403 ft. (732 m), Montezuma Pk. 4,354 ft. (1,327 m)

San Antonio area (T–U, 20–21): KENDALL, HAYS, Canyon Lake, COMAL, Boerne, Balcones Escarpment, New Braunfels, GUADALUPE, Schertz, Universal City, Converse, RANDOLPH AFB, Live Oak, BEXAR, Castle Hills, Alamo Heights, **San Antonio**, THE ALAMO, LACKLAND AFB, KELLY AFB, BROOKS AFB, WILSON, ATASCOSA, NATURAL BRIDGE CAVERNS, CASCADE CAVERNS, SEA WORLD OF TEXAS, FIESTA TEXAS

POPULATION OF CITIES AND TOWNS

- ■ OVER 2,000,000
- ◻ 1,000,000 – 1,999,999
- ⊠ 500,000 – 999,999
- ⊙ 250,000 – 499,999
- ⊕ 100,000 – 249,999
- ⊙ 30,000 – 99,999
- ⊙ 10,000 – 29,999
- ○ UNDER 10,000

SCALE 1:1,000,000 LAMBERT CONFORMAL CONIC PROJECTION

MILES 0 10 20 30 40 50
KILOMETERS 0 10 20 30 40 50

HEIGHT / DEPTH (Figures in Hundreds)

Longitude West of Greenwich

© HAMMOND INC.

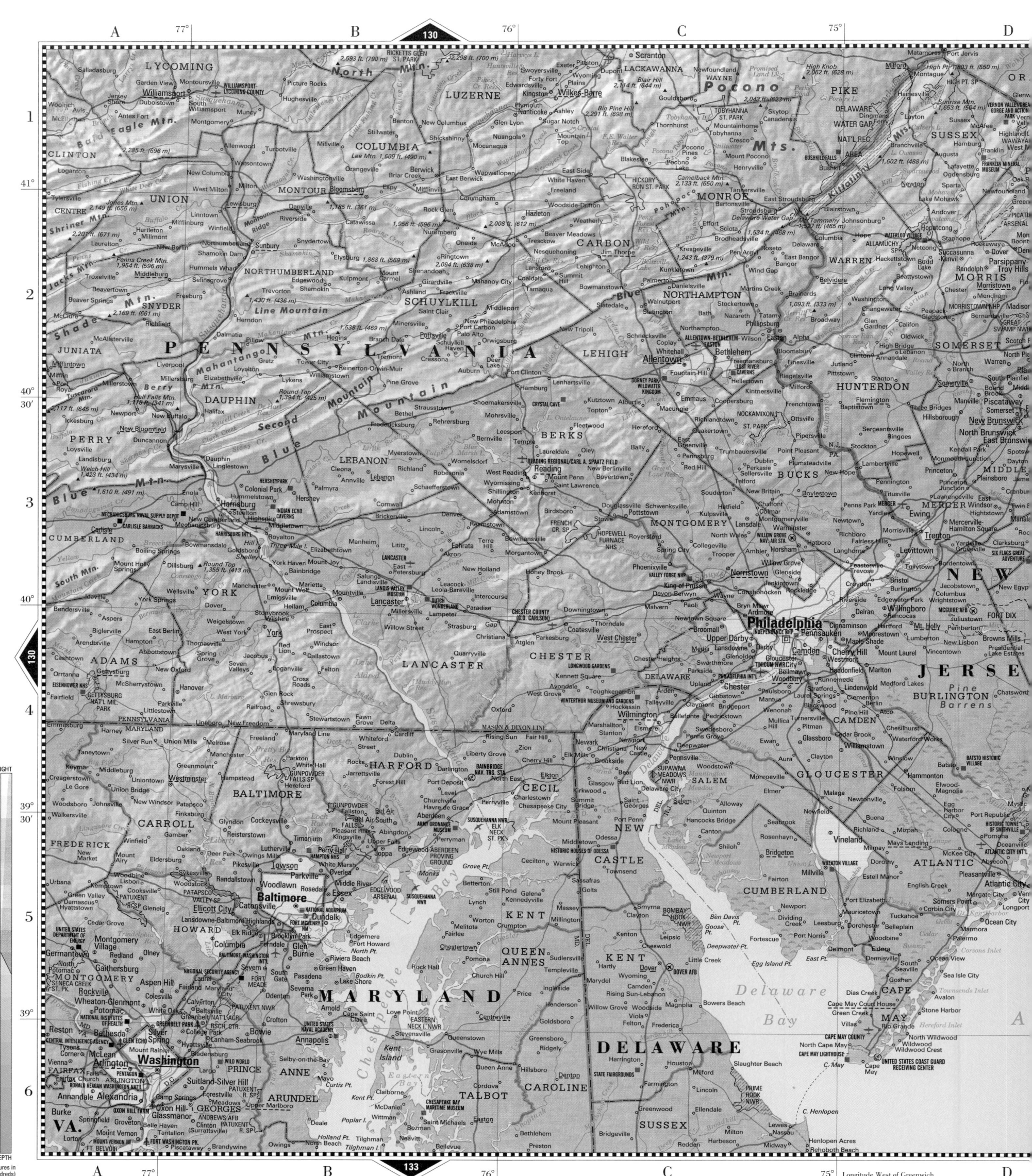

New York-Philadelphia-Washington

POPULATION OF CITIES AND TOWNS
- ■ OVER 2,000,000
- ◉ 500,000 - 999,999
- ● 100,000 - 249,999
- ◉ 10,000 - 29,999
- ◻ 1,000,000 - 1,999,999
- ◉ 250,000 - 499,999
- ● 30,000 - 99,999
- ○ UNDER 10,000

SCALE 1:1,000,000   LAMBERT CONFORMAL CONIC PROJECTION

MILES 0 10 20 30 40 50
KILOMETERS 0 10 20 30 40 50

© Copyright by HAMMOND INCORPORATED, Maplewood, N.J.   CC - # - A A A ▪

© HAMMOND INC.   CG - 1171 -

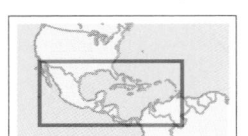

Middle America

MEXICO
① DISTRITO FEDERAL
② MÉXICO
③ MORELOS
④ TLAXCALA
⑤ QUERÉTARO DE ARTEAGA
⑥ AGUASCALIENTES

Longitude West of Greenwich

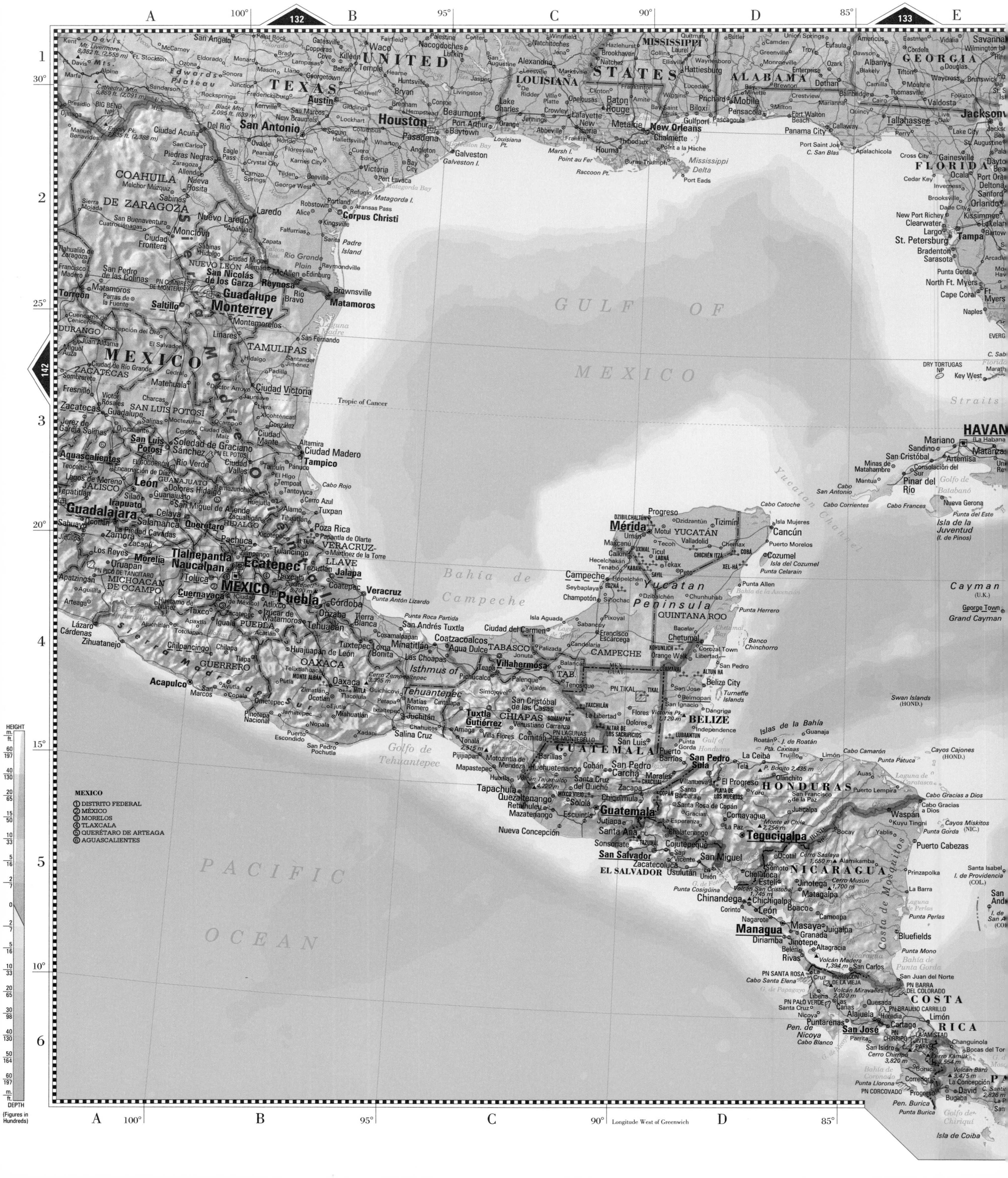

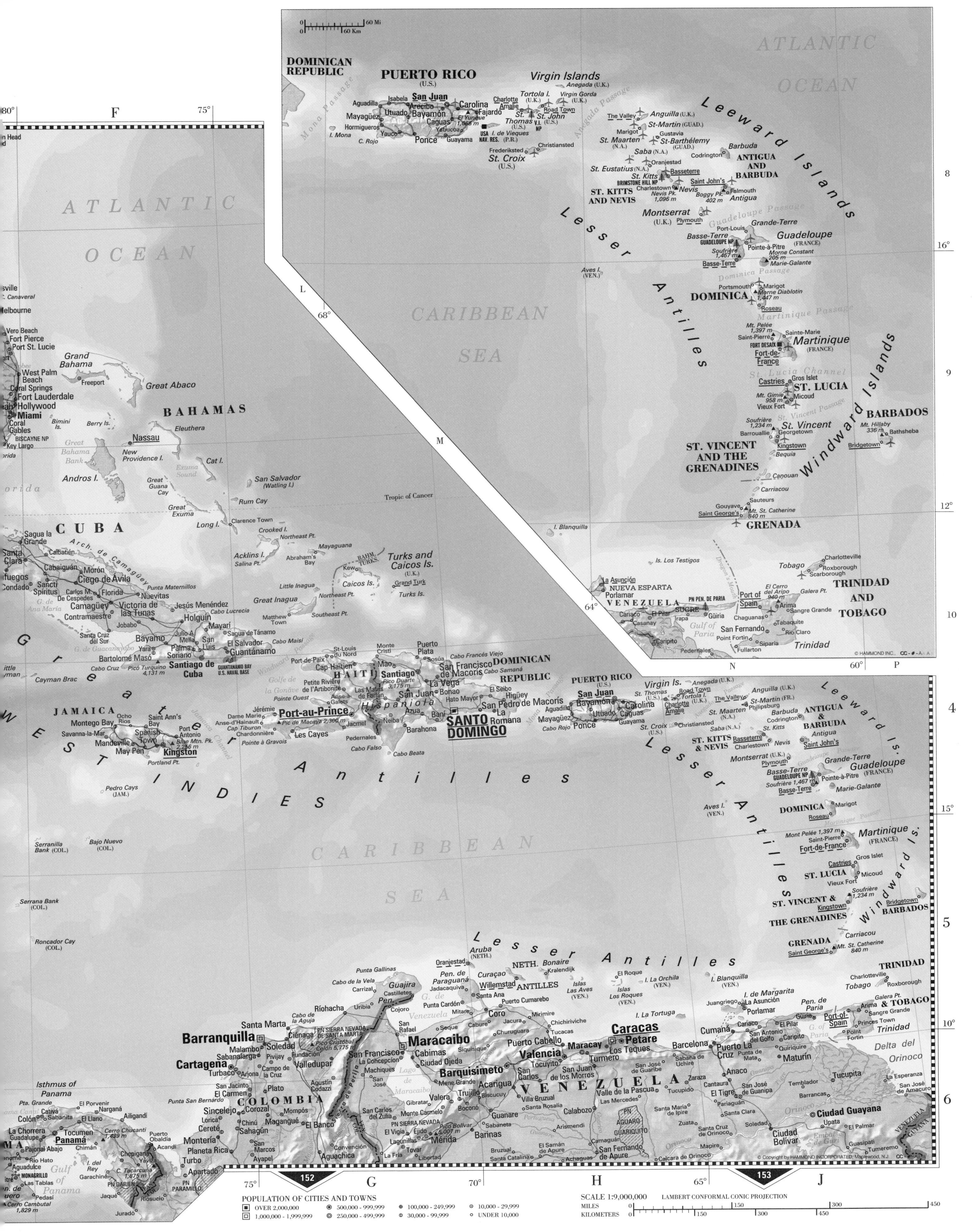

ATLANTIC OCEAN

DOMINICAN REPUBLIC

PUERTO RICO

Virgin Islands (U.K.)

0   60 Mi
0   60 Km

Aguadilla   Isabela   Arecibo
Mayagüez   Utuado   Bayamón   Carolina   Charlotte   Tortola I. (U.K.)   Virgin Gorda (U.K.)
Hormigueros   Caguas   Amalie   St. Thomas   Road Town
I. de Vieques   C. Rojo   Yauco   Ponce   Guayama   V.I. (U.S.)   St. John NP
I. Mona   San Juan   El Yunque 1,065 m   USN & NAV. RES. (P.R.)   Anguilla (U.K.)   St-Martin (GUAD.)
Mona Passage   Frederiksted   St. Croix (U.S.)   Christiansted   St. Maarten (N.A.)   Gustavia   St-Barthélemy (GUAD.)
Saba (N.A.)   Codrington   **Barbuda**
St. Eustatius (N.A.)   Basseterre   **ANTIGUA AND BARBUDA**
ST. KITTS AND NEVIS   Charlestown   Nevis   Saint John's   Boggy Pk. 402 m   Antigua   Falmouth
Nevis Pk. 1,096 m
Montserrat (U.K.)   Plymouth   **Leeward Islands**
Port-Louis   Grande-Terre
Basse-Terre   GUADELOUPE NP   Pointe-à-Pitre   **Guadeloupe** (FRANCE)
Soufrière 1,467 m   Morne Constant 205 m   Marie-Galante
Basse-Terre   **Lesser Antilles**
Aves I. (VEN.)
Portsmouth   Marigot
Morne Diablotin 1,447 m   **DOMINICA**
Roseau
Dominica Passage
Martinique Passage
Mt. Pelée 1,397 m   Sainte-Marie
Saint-Pierre   **Martinique** (FRANCE)
FORT DESAIX NM   Fort-de-France
St. Lucia Channel
Castries   Gros Islet
Mt. Gimie 958 m   **ST. LUCIA**   Micoud
Vieux Fort
Soufrière 1,234 m   St. Vincent Passage
Barrouallie   Georgetown   **BARBADOS**
Mt. Hillaby 336 m   Bathsheba
ST. VINCENT AND THE GRENADINES   Kingstown   Bridgetown
Bequia
Canouan
Carriacou
Sauteurs
Gouyave   Mt. St. Catherine 840 m   **Windward Islands**
I. Blanquilla   Saint George's   **GRENADA**

CARIBBEAN SEA

La Asunción   Is. Los Testigos   Tobago   Charlotteville
NUEVA ESPARTA   Roxborough   Scarborough
Porlamar   PN PEN. DE PARIA   Port of Spain   El Cerro del Aripo 940 m   Galera Pt.   **TRINIDAD AND TOBAGO**
VENEZUELA   SUCRE   El Pilar   Arima   Sangre Grande
Cariaco   Irapa   Güiria   Chaguanas   Tabaquite
Casanay   Point Fortin   Río Claro
Caripito
Gulf of Paria   San Fernando
Pedernales   Fullarton   **Trinidad**

© HAMMOND INC.   CC - # - A-x A

ATLANTIC OCEAN

Canaveral
Melbourne
Vero Beach
Fort Pierce
Port St. Lucie
West Palm Beach   Grand Bahama   Freeport   Great Abaco
Coral Springs
Fort Lauderdale
Hollywood   **BAHAMAS**
Miami   Bimini Is.   Berry Is.   Eleuthera
Coral Gables   Great Bahama Bank   New Providence I.   Cat I.
Key Largo   **Nassau**
BISCAYNE NP   Andros I.   Great Exuma Sound   San Salvador (Watling I.)
florida   Great Exuma   Rum Cay
Long I.   Clarence Town   Tropic of Cancer
Santa Clara   **CUBA**   Arch. de Camagüey   Crooked I.   Northeast Pt.
Sagua la Grande   Calbarién   Acklins I.   Mayaguana   Turks and Caicos Is. (U.K.)
Cabaiguán   Morón   Salina Pt.   Abraham's Bay
Cienfuegos   Ciego de Ávila   Kew   Caicos Is.   Grand Turk
Condado   Sancti Spíritus   Carlos M. de Céspedes   Little Inagua   Turks Is.
Florida   Punta Maternillos
Camagüey   Victoria de las Tunas   Jesús Menéndez   Cabo Lucrecia   Great Inagua   Matthew Town   Northeast Pt.
Contramaestre   Nuevitas   Holguín   Mayarí   Southeast Pt.
Santa Cruz del Sur   G. de Guacanayabo   Julio A.   Mella   Sagua de Tánamo   Cabo Maisí
Bayamo   Yara   Palma   Soriano   San Luis
Bartolomé Masó   Pico Turquino 4,131 m   **Santiago de Cuba**   GUANTANAMO BAY U.S. NAVAL BASE
Cabo Cruz   Guantánamo
Cayman Brac   St-Louis du Nord   Monte Cristi   Puerto Plata   Sosúa   Cabo Francés Viejo
Windward Passage   Port-de-Paix   Cap-Haïtien   Mao   San Francisco de Macorís   Cabo Samaná
Golfe de la Gonâve   Petite Rivière de l'Artibonite   **HAITI**   **Santiago**   Pico Duarte 3,175 m   La Vega
JAMAICA   Ocho Rios   Saint Ann's   Pointe Ouest   Gonaïves   Las Matas de Farfán   San Juan   Bonao   Hato Mayor   **DOMINICAN REPUBLIC**
Montego Bay   Port Antonio   Jérémie   Dame Marie   **Port-au-Prince**   **Hispaniola**   Azua   El Seibo   San Pedro de Macorís
Spanish Town   Anse-d'Hainault   Cap Tiburon   Chardonnières   La   **SANTO DOMINGO**   Higüey
Mandeville   May Pen   **Kingston**   Les Cayes   Pedernales   Neiba   Barahona   Romana
Savanna-la-Mar   Blue Mtn. Pk. 2,256 m   Pic de Macaya 2,300 m   Jacmel   Cabo Falso   Cabo Beata
Portland Pt.   Pointe à Gravois
Pedro Cays (JAM.)

WEST INDIES

Lesser Antilles

Puerto Rico (U.S.)   Virgin Is. (U.S.)   Anegada (U.K.)
San Juan   Bayamón   St. Thomas   Road Town   Tortola I. (U.K.)   Anguilla (U.K.)   Leeward Is.
Mayagüez   Utuado   Carolina   Charlotte   Amalie   St-Martin (FR.)   **ANTIGUA & BARBUDA**
Ponce   Guayama   Caguas   St. Croix   Christiansted   Saba (N.A.)   Philipsburg   Barbuda   Codrington
Cabo Rojo   St. Maarten (N.A.)   St. Kitts   Antigua
Aves I. (VEN.)   **ST. KITTS & NEVIS**   Basseterre   Saint John's
Charlestown   Nevis
Montserrat   Plymouth   Grande-Terre
Basse-Terre   GUADELOUPE NP   Pointe-à-Pitre   **Guadeloupe** (FRANCE)
Soufrière 1,467 m   Basse-Terre   Marie-Galante
DOMINICA   Marigot
Roseau
Mont Pelée 1,397 m   Saint-Pierre   **Martinique** (FRANCE)
Fort-de-France
Castries   Gros Islet
ST. LUCIA   Micoud
Vieux Fort
Soufrière 1,234 m
ST. VINCENT &   Kingstown   Bridgetown   **BARBADOS**
THE GRENADINES
GRENADA   Carriacou
Saint George's   Mt. St. Catherine 840 m   Windward Is.
TRINIDAD

CARIBBEAN SEA

Serranilla Bank (COL.)
Bajo Nuevo (COL.)
Serrana Bank (COL.)
Roncador Cay (COL.)

Aruba (NETH.)   I. Blanquilla (VEN.)
Oranjestad   NETH.   Bonaire   Charlotteville
Pen. de Paraguaná   **Curaçao**   Kralendijk   Tobago   Roxborough
Punta Gallinas   Jadacaquiva   Willemstad   **ANTILLES**   El Roque   I. La Orchila (VEN.)   I. de Margarita   **TRINIDAD & TOBAGO**
Cabo de la Vela   Carrizal   Santa Ana   Islas Las Aves (VEN.)   Juangriego   La Asunción   Galera Pt.
Riohacha   Uribia   Punta Cardón   Puerto Cumarebo   Islas Los Roques (VEN.)   Porlamar   Pen. de Paria   Arima
Santa Marta   Cabo de la Aguja   Cojoro   Coro   Mirimire   I. La Tortuga (VEN.)   Cariaco   El Pilar   Güiria   **Port-of-Spain**   Sangre Grande
PN SIERRA NEVADA DE SANTA MARTA   Maicao   Sabaneta   Jacura   Chichiriviche   Cumaná   El Pilar   Princes Town
Barranquilla   Ciénaga   Cristóbal Colón 5,775 m   Medanos   Puerto Cabello   Caracas   Petare   Barcelona   San Antonio del Golfo   Caripito   Trinidad
Soledad   San Francisco   **Maracaibo**   Siquisique   **Valencia**   Los Teques   **Maracay**   Puerto La Cruz   Punta de Mata   **Delta del Orinoco**
Cartagena   Sabanalarga   Cabimas   Churuguara   Puerto La   Maturín
Turbaco   Pivijay   Ciudad Ojeda   Mene Grande   **Barquisimeto**   Tucuyito   Sabana de Uchire   Quiriquire
San Jacinto   Fundación   Lago de Maracaibo   Trujillo   **Acarigua**   San Juan de los Morros   Zaraza   Anaco   Barrancas
El Carmen   Valledupar   Campo de la Cruz   Agustín Codazzi   Villa Bruzual   Las Mercedes   El Tigre
COLOMBIA   Sincelejo   Corozal   Magangué   San Carlos del Zulia   Gibraltar   Guanare   **VENEZUELA**   Santa María de Ipire   San José de Guanipa   San José de Amacuro
Punta San Bernardo   Plato   El Banco   San Carlos   Mene Grande   Calabozo   Cantaura   Tembladór   La Esperanza
Lorica   Chinú   El Vigía   Tovar   Arismendi   PN AGUARO   Ciudad Guayana
Isthmus of Panama   Montería   Sahagún   Mompós   Sierra Nevada   Pico Bolívar 5,007 m   Mérida   Barinas   GUARIQUITO   Tucupita
Planeta Rica   Cereté   Lagunillas   Ejido   San Fernando de Apure   Santa Cruz de Orinoco   Ciudad Bolívar
Panamá   Cerro Chucanti 1,439 m   San Marcos   Convención   La Fría   Bruzual   Achaguas   Calcara de Orinoco   Soledad   El Palmar
Colón   Puerto Escondido   Aguachica   Aguaclara   San Fernando de Apure   Mapire   Tumeremo
Cativá   Marcos   Apure
Pedasí   Aguadulce   Las Tablas   PN DARIEN   **COLOMBIA**   Jurado   Guasipati
Chimán   I. del Rey   Guadalupe   Acandí   Riosucio   Chepigana
C. Tacarcuna 1,875 m   Jaqué   PN PARAMILLO
Cerro Cambutal 1,829 m   Garachiné   Turbo   Apartadó
Gulf of Panama

POPULATION OF CITIES AND TOWNS

☐ OVER 2,000,000   ● 500,000 - 999,999   ● 100,000 - 249,999   ● 10,000 - 29,999
☐ 1,000,000 - 1,999,999   ● 250,000 - 499,999   ● 30,000 - 99,999   ● UNDER 10,000

SCALE 1:9,000,000   LAMBERT CONFORMAL CONIC PROJECTION

MILES   0   150   300   450
KILOMETERS   0   150   300   450

◄ 152   ► ◄ 153

Copyright by HAMMOND INCORPORATED, Maplewood, N.J.

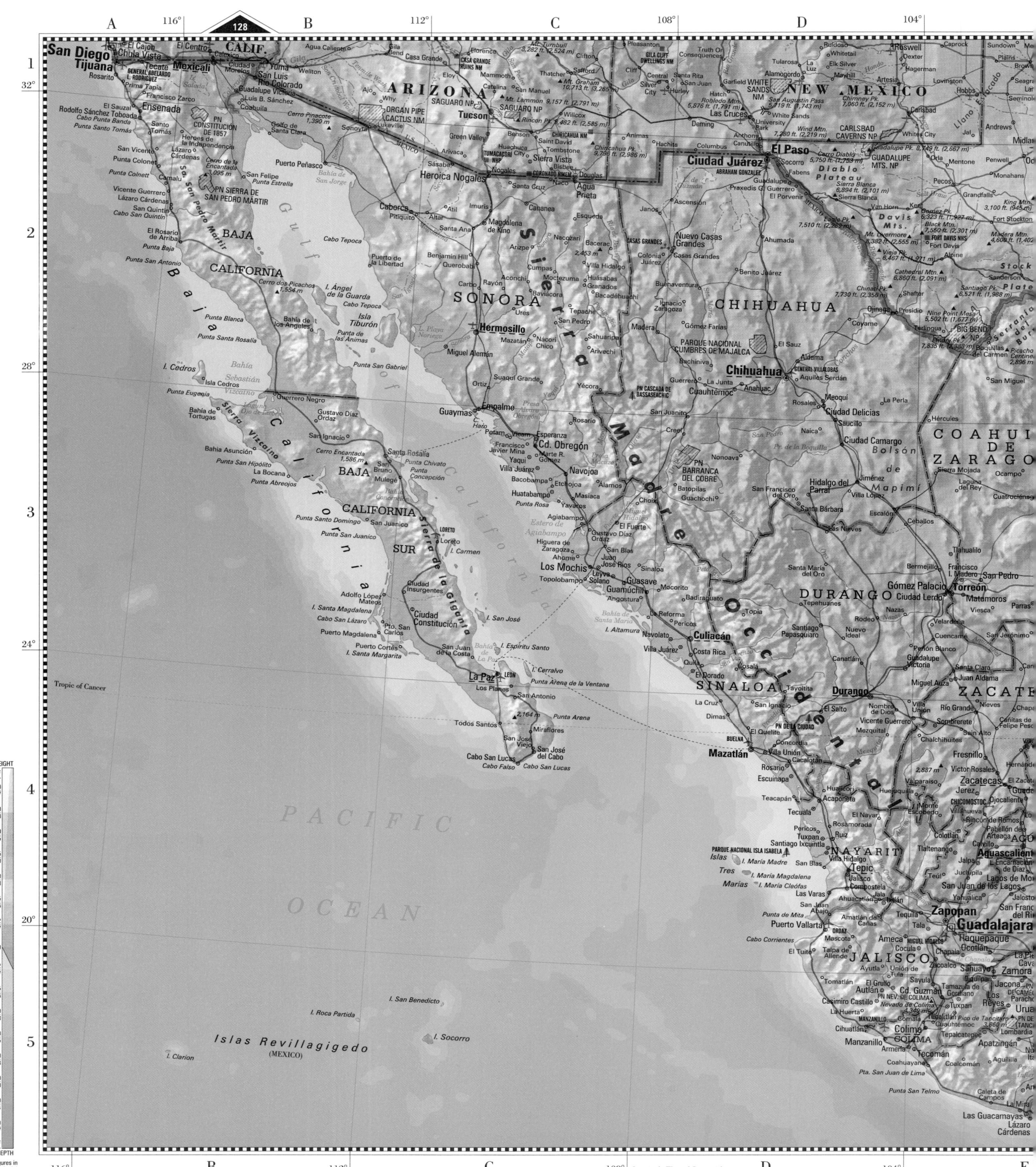

A 116° **B** 112° **C** 108° **D** 104°

1

32°

2

28°

3

24°

Tropic of Cancer

4

20°

5

HEIGHT
m.
ft.
60 / 197
40 / 130
20 / 65
15 / 50
10 / 33
5 / 16
2 / 7
0
2 / 7
5 / 16
10 / 33
20 / 65
30 / 98
40 / 130
50 / 164
60 / 197
m.
ft.
DEPTH
(Figures in
Hundreds)

PACIFIC

OCEAN

Islas Revillagigedo
(MEXICO)

I. Clarion

I. Roca Partida

I. San Benedicto

I. Socorro

San Diego
Tijuana

El Cajon
Chula Vista
El Centro
Mexicali
Tecate
General Abelardo L. Rodriguez
Prima Tapia
Rosarito
El Sauzal
Rodolfo Sánchez Toboada
Cabo Punta Banda
Ensenada
Punta Santo Tomás
Maneadero
San Vicente
Punta Colnett
Vicente Guerrero
Lázaro Cárdenas
Cabo San Quintín

CALIF.
Calexico
Ciudad Morelos
San Luis Río Colorado
Luis B. Sánchez
Coahuila
Golfo de Santa Clara

ARIZONA
Agua Caliente
Gila Bend
Casa Grande
Florence
Eloy
Mammoth
Why
Ajó
Lukeville
Sonoyta
Organ Pipe Cactus NM
SAGUARO NP
Tucson
Green Valley
Benson
Arivaca
Tumacacori NHP
Sierra Vista
Nogales
Heroica Nogales
Naco
Agua Prieta
Douglas

BAJA

CALIFORNIA

SONORA

Sierra Madre

NEW MEXICO

El Paso
Ciudad Juárez

CHIHUAHUA

Chihuahua

COAHUILA DE ZARAGOZA

DURANGO

Torreón
Gómez Palacio

Durango

SINALOA

Culiacán

Mazatlán

Los Mochis

La Paz

ZACATECAS

Zacatecas

Aguascalientes

NAYARIT
Tepic

JALISCO

Zapopan
Guadalajara
Tlaquepaque

COLIMA
Colima

116° **B** **112°** **C** **108°** Longitude West of Greenwich **D** **104°** **E**

Northern and Central Mexico

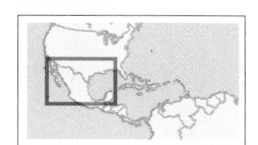

POPULATION OF CITIES AND TOWNS
- ■ OVER 2,000,000
- □ 1,000,000 - 1,999,999
- ● 500,000 - 999,999
- ⊙ 250,000 - 499,999
- ● 100,000 - 249,999
- ⊙ 30,000 - 99,999
- ○ 10,000 - 29,999
- ○ UNDER 10,000

SCALE 1:6,000,000   LAMBERT CONFORMAL CONIC PROJECTION

MILES 0   100   200   300

KILOMETERS 0   100   200   300

SCALE 1:6,000,000   LAMBERT CONFORMAL CONIC PROJECTION

MILES

KILOMETERS

POPULATION OF CITIES AND TOWNS

■ OVER 2,000,000   ◉ 500,000 - 999,999   ◉ 100,000 - 249,999   ○ 10,000 - 29,999

▣ 1,000,000 - 1,999,999   ◉ 250,000 - 499,999   ◉ 30,000 - 99,999   ○ UNDER 10,000

© Copyright by HAMMOND INCORPORATED, Maplewood, N.J. CD-1067-A·A

Southern Mexico, Central America, Western Caribbean

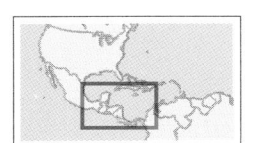

South America

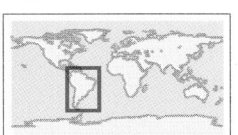

The highest mountain peak in the Americas, Mount Aconcagua, at 22,831 feet (6959 m.) above sea level, is visible in this northeast-looking, low-oblique image. Several major snow-covered peaks with summits exceeding 20,000 feet (6100 m.) rise along the north-south axis of the cohesive and massive structure of the Andes Mountains through this area of Argentina and Chile. The narrow east-west valley immediately south of Mount Aconcagua contains a section of the American Highway that connects Mendoza, Argentina, with Santiago, Chile.

AREA OF OPTIMIZATION The red band which surrounds this map defines the "Area of Optimization." Within this bounding curve is the most accurate conformal map that can be made of the region. Outside the optimized area, distortion increases rapidly, and tears or other irregularities in the grid may occur. (See page 6 for additional information.)

119

POPULATION OF CITIES AND TOWNS

■ OVER 3,000,000
■ 1,000,000 - 2,999,999
● 500,000 - 999,999
○ 100,000 - 499,999
○ UNDER 100,000

SCALE 1:24,000,000   OPTIMAL CONFORMAL PROJECTION

MILES 0   400   800   1200
KILOMETERS 0   400   800   1200

© Copyright by HAMMOND INCORPORATED, Maplewood, N.J.

CARIBBEAN SEA
ATLANTIC OCEAN
PACIFIC OCEAN
ATLANTIC OCEAN

COSTA RICA
PANAMA
Panama Canal
Gulf of Panama

VENEZUELA
COLOMBIA
ECUADOR
PERU
BOLIVIA
BRAZIL
GUYANA
SURINAME
FRENCH GUIANA
PARAGUAY
CHILE
ARGENTINA
URUGUAY

NETHERLANDS ANTILLES
TRINIDAD AND TOBAGO

Guiana Highlands
Selvas
Meseta del Mato Grosso
Brazilian Highlands
Caatingas
Altiplano Mountains
Atacama Desert

Equator
Tropic of Capricorn

Bogotá
Caracas
Quito
Lima
La Paz
Sucre
Brasília
Asunción
Santiago
Buenos Aires
Montevideo

Medellín
Cali
Maracaibo
Valencia
Barranquilla
Guayaquil
Trujillo
Callao
Arequipa
São Paulo
Río de Janeiro
Belo Horizonte
Salvador
Recife
Fortaleza
Manaus
Belém
Córdoba
Rosario
Santa Cruz
Campo Grande
Porto Alegre
Curitiba
Mar del Plata
La Plata

Pico Bolívar 5,007 m
Alto Ritacuba 5,493 m
Nevado del Huila 5,750 m
Pico de la Neblina 3,014 m
Mt. Roraima 2,772 m
Chimborazo 6,310 m
Nevado Huascarán 6,768 m
Nevado Ancohuma 6,550 m
Volcán Misti 5,822 m
Volcán Llullaillaco 6,723 m
Cerro Ojos del Salado 6,880 m
Cerro Aconcagua 6,959 m
Pico da Bandeira 2,890 m
Pico Cristóbal Colón 5,775 m

Isla de Malpelo (COL.)
I. de San Félix (CHILE)
I. San Ambrosio (CHILE)
Is. Juan Fernández (CHILE)
I. Robinson Crusoe
I. Alejandro Selkirk
I. Fernando de Noronha (BRAZIL)
Falkland Islands (U.K.) (Claimed by Arg.)
West Falkland
East Falkland
Stanley
Isla de Chiloé
Arch. de Los Chonos
Pen. de Taitao
Cabo Tres Montes
Isla Wellington
Arch. Reina Adelaida
Tierra del Fuego
Cape Horn
C. San Diego
Strait of Magellan
Punta Arenas
Ushuaia

PHOTOGRAPHIC DETAIL

AREA OF OPTIMIZATION

Longitude West of Greenwich

AVERAGE JANUARY TEMPERATURE

FAHRENHEIT	CELSIUS	FAHRENHEIT	CELSIUS	FAHRENHEIT	CELSIUS
OVER 86°	OVER 30°	50° TO 68°	10° TO 20°	UNDER 32°	UNDER 0°
68° TO 86°	20° TO 30°	32° TO 50°	0° TO 10°		

AVERAGE JULY TEMPERATURE

FAHRENHEIT	CELSIUS	FAHRENHEIT	CELSIUS	FAHRENHEIT	CELSIUS
OVER 86°	OVER 30°	50° TO 68°	10° TO 20°	UNDER 32°	UNDER 0°
68° TO 86°	20° TO 30°	32° TO 50°	0° TO 10°		

CLIMATE

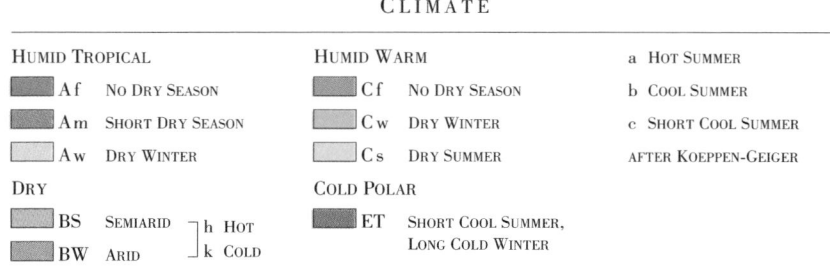

HUMID TROPICAL
- Af NO DRY SEASON
- Am SHORT DRY SEASON
- Aw DRY WINTER

DRY
- BS SEMIARID
- BW ARID
  - h HOT
  - k COLD

HUMID WARM
- Cf NO DRY SEASON
- Cw DRY WINTER
- Cs DRY SUMMER

COLD POLAR
- ET SHORT COOL SUMMER, LONG COLD WINTER

a HOT SUMMER
b COOL SUMMER
c SHORT COOL SUMMER

AFTER KOEPPEN-GEIGER

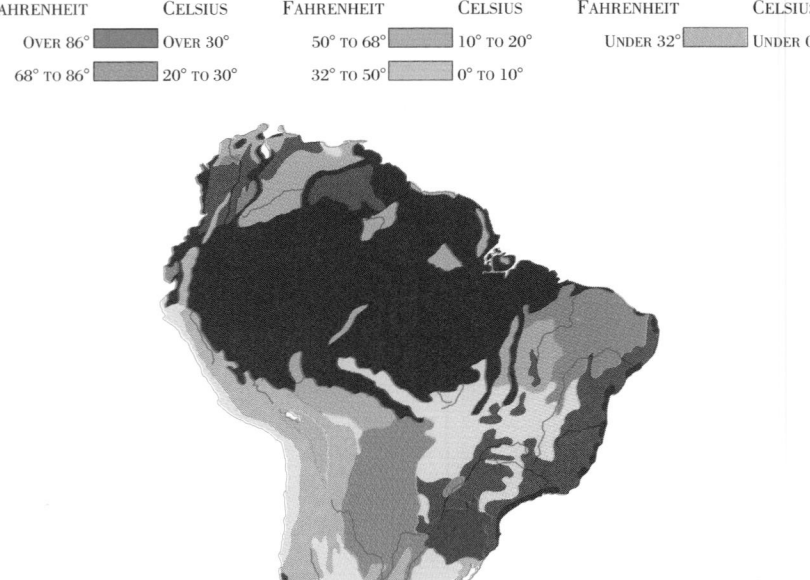

VEGETATION

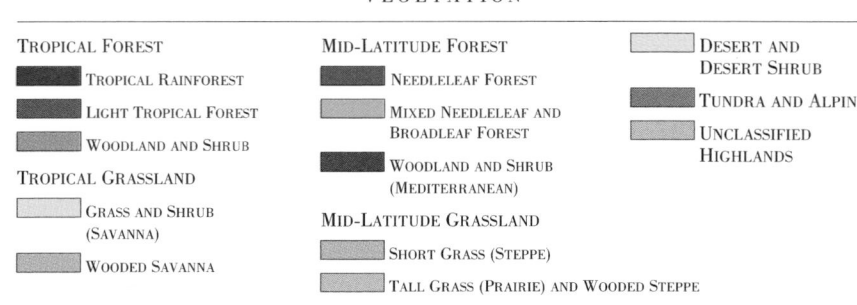

TROPICAL FOREST
- TROPICAL RAINFOREST
- LIGHT TROPICAL FOREST
- WOODLAND AND SHRUB

TROPICAL GRASSLAND
- GRASS AND SHRUB (SAVANNA)
- WOODED SAVANNA

MID-LATITUDE FOREST
- NEEDLELEAF FOREST
- MIXED NEEDLELEAF AND BROADLEAF FOREST
- WOODLAND AND SHRUB (MEDITERRANEAN)

MID-LATITUDE GRASSLAND
- SHORT GRASS (STEPPE)
- TALL GRASS (PRAIRIE) AND WOODED STEPPE

- DESERT AND DESERT SHRUB
- TUNDRA AND ALPINE
- UNCLASSIFIED HIGHLANDS

South America - Geographical Comparisons

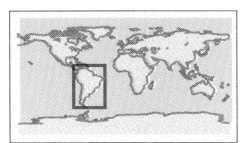

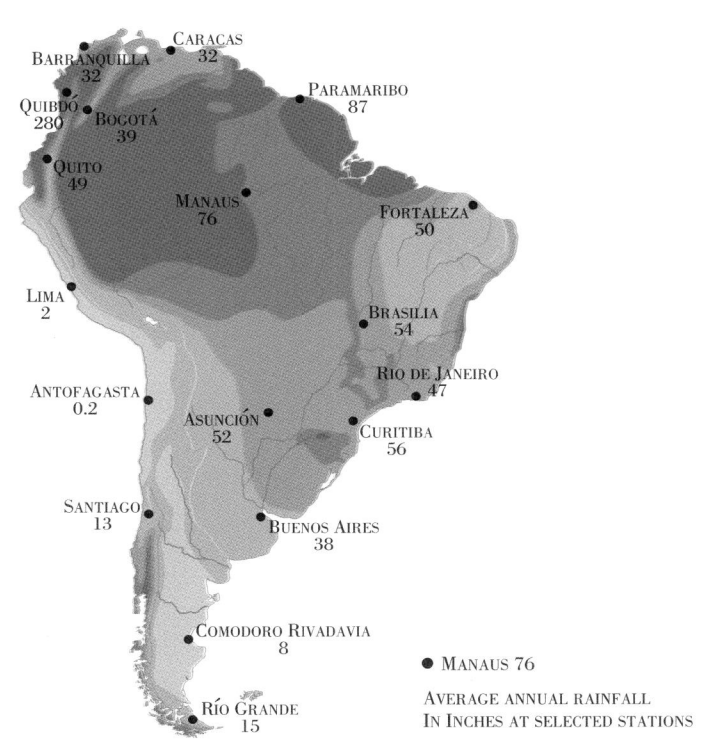

BARRANQUILLA 32
CARACAS 32
QUIBDÓ 280
BOGOTÁ 39
PARAMARIBO 87
QUITO 49
MANAUS 76
FORTALEZA 50
LIMA 2
BRASILIA 54
ANTOFAGASTA 0.2
RIO DE JANEIRO 47
ASUNCIÓN 52
CURITIBA 56
SANTIAGO 13
BUENOS AIRES 38
COMODORO RIVADAVIA 8
RÍO GRANDE 15

● MANAUS 76
AVERAGE ANNUAL RAINFALL
IN INCHES AT SELECTED STATIONS

AVERAGE ANNUAL RAINFALL

INCHES	CM	INCHES	CM	INCHES	CM
OVER 80	OVER 200	40 TO 60	100 TO 150	10 TO 20	25 TO 50
60 TO 80	150 TO 200	20 TO 40	50 TO 100	UNDER 10	UNDER 25

● CITIES WITH OVER 1,000,000 INHABITANTS

POPULATION DISTRIBUTION

DENSITY PER		SQ. MI.	SQ. KM.	SQ. MI.	SQ. KM.
SQ. MI.	SQ. KM.	130 TO 260	50 TO 100	3 TO 25	1 TO 10
OVER 260	OVER 100	25 TO 130	10 TO 50	UNDER 3	UNDER 1

RICE
HOGS
COCOA
CATTLE COFFEE
COFFEE CATTLE
VANILLA
BANANAS
BANANAS
BRAZIL NUTS
CORN
COTTON
WILD RUBBER
SISAL
SHEEP
CATTLE
SHEEP CORN
TOBACCO
SUGARCANE
CATTLE
CATTLE
HOGS
CITRUS
COCOA SUGARCANE
COTTON
TOBACCO
COTTON
COFFEE
TOBACCO
BANANAS SUGARCANE
TEA
CATTLE HOGS
TOBACCO
QUEBRACHO SOYBEANS
CORN SHEEP RICE CORN
WINE
FLAX CORN
CATTLE
WHEAT
SHEEP
SHEEP

LAND USE

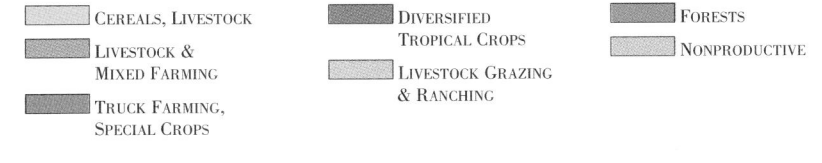

CEREALS, LIVESTOCK

LIVESTOCK & MIXED FARMING

TRUCK FARMING, SPECIAL CROPS

DIVERSIFIED TROPICAL CROPS

LIVESTOCK GRAZING & RANCHING

FORESTS

NONPRODUCTIVE

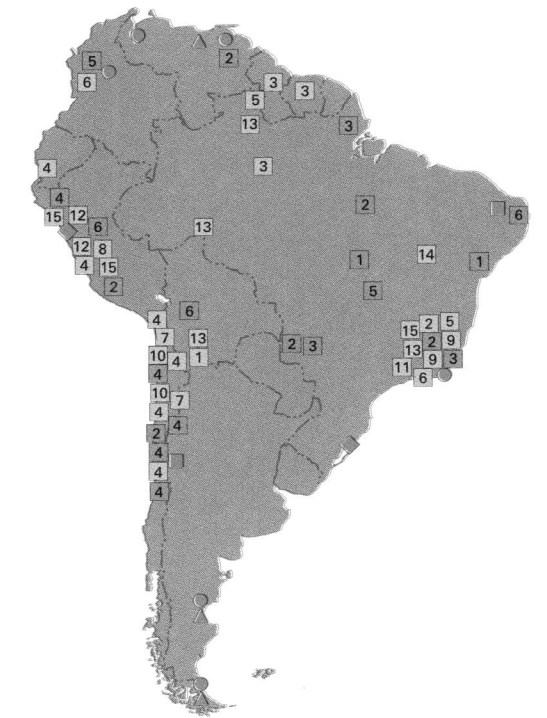

MINERAL RESOURCES

ENERGY & FUELS
◆ COAL
▲ NATURAL GAS
● PETROLEUM
■ URANIUM

IRON & FERROALLOYS
1 CHROMIUM
2 IRON ORE
3 MANGANESE
4 MOLYBDENUM
5 NICKEL
6 TUNGSTEN

OTHER MAJOR RESOURCES
1 ANTIMONY
2 ASBESTOS
3 BAUXITE
4 COPPER
5 DIAMONDS
6 GOLD
7 IODINE
8 LEAD
9 MICA
10 NITRATES
11 PHOSPHATES
12 SILVER
13 TIN
14 TITANIUM
15 ZINC

Northern South America

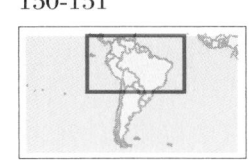

POPULATION OF CITIES AND TOWNS

- ■ OVER 2,000,000
- □ 1,000,000 - 1,999,999
- ⊛ 500,000 - 999,999
- ⊙ 100,000 - 499,999
- ⊙ 50,000 - 99,999
- ○ UNDER 50,000

SCALE 1:13,000,000   LAMBERT CONFORMAL CONIC PROJECTION

MILES 0 | 200 | 400 | 600

KILOMETERS 0 | 200 | 400 | 600

© Copyright by HAMMOND INCORPORATED, Maplewood, N.J. CD - 2107 - A

Colombia, Venezuela, Ecuador

E 64° F 60° G 56° H

CARIBBEAN SEA

ATLANTIC OCEAN

DEPENDENCIAS FEDERALES (VEN.)

I. Las Aves (VEN.)
El Roque
Is. Los Roques (VEN.)
I. La Orchila (VEN.)
I. La Blanquilla (VEN.)
I. La Tortuga (VEN.)
Is. Los Testigos (VEN.)

GRENADA
Carriacou
Victoria
Sauteurs
Saint George's
Mt. St. Catherine 840 m
POINT SALINES

Tobago 576 m
Charlotteville
Roxborough
CROWN POINT
Scarborough

NUEVA ESPARTA I. Margarita
Juangriego La Asunción
PN LAGUNA DE LA RESTINGA Porlamar
GRAL. S. MARIÑO
PN CERRO EL COPEY
I. Cubagua I. Coche

Maiquetía Caracas
Petare
Los Teques MIRANDA
La Victoria
Aragua
Cúa
San Juan de los Morros

C. Codera
Cumaná Cariaco
PN MOCHIMA
Puerto La Cruz
Barcelona SUCRE
Pozuelos
GRAL. J. A. ANZOÁTEGUI

Carúpano
PN PENÍNSULA DE PARIA
Pta. de Araya
Casanay
San Antonio del Golfo

Blanchisseuse
Toco Pta. Galera
936 m El Cerro del Aripo 940 m
Arima
Port-of-Spain
Chaguanas PIARCO
San Fernando Couva
Fullarton Río Claro
Siparia Tabaquite
Pta. Galeota

TRINIDAD AND TOBAGO
Trinidad
Gulf of Paria
Dragon's Mouth
Serpent's Mouth

Pedernales
Tucupita
La Horqueta
DELTA
Delta del Orinoco
AMACURO
San José de Amacuro

MONAGAS
Maturín
ANZOÁTEGUI
El Tigre San Tomé
San José de Guanipa

VENEZUELA
GUÁRICO
Calabozo

Ciudad Guayana
Ciudad Bolívar
PRESA GURI
Cerro Bolívar 802 m
Ciudad Piar
El Manteco

BARIMA-WAINI
Charity
POMEROON-SUPENAAM
Anna Regina
Queenstown
Suddie
ESSEQUIBO IS.-W. DEMERARA
Georgetown
Vreed-en-Hoop Paradise
TIMEHRI Mahaica
DEMERARA-MAHAICA
MAHAICA-BERBICE
Fort Wellington
New Amsterdam

VENEZUELA
Guiana
BOLÍVAR
Highlands
Salto Pará
PARQUE
Salto del Ángel (Angel Falls)
Auyán-Tepui 2,100 m
Uruyén 2,950 m
NACIONAL
Uriman Chimantá-Tepui 2,342 m
Apatarén
CANAIMA

La Gran Sabana
Cerro Yaví 2,441 m
Cerro Guaiquinima 2,100 m
Sierra Pacaraima
Monte Roraima 2,772 m
Peraí-tepuí
Santa Elena de Uairén
Icabarú
Guaná

CUYUNI-MAZARUNI
Tumereng
Cataratas de Surukwaima
Kamarang
Monte Ayanganna 2,042 m
Kangaruma
PN KAIETEUR
Cataratas de Kaieteur
POTARO-SIPARUNI
Kurupukari
GUYANA

SURINAME
SARAMACCA
PARAMARIBO
COMMEWIJNE
Nieuw-Amsterdam
Paramaribo
NICKERIE CORONIE
PARA
BROKOPONDO
PRESA AFOBAKA
FRENCH GUIANA
Grand Santi

AMAZONAS
PN DUIDA MARAHUACA
Cerro Marahuaca 2,579 m
Cerro Duida 2,400 m
La Esmeralda
PN YAPACANA

Sa. Parima
Serra Pacaraima

RORAIMA
Boa Vista
Caracaraí

Montes Kanuku
Wichabai
UPPER TAKUTU-UPPER ESSEQUIBO
Isherton

EAST BERBICE-CORENTYNE

SIPALIWINI
Mtes. Bakhuis
Montes Wilhelmina
Juliana Top 1,230 m
Montes Kayser
Mtes. Eilerts de Haan
Montes Orange
Tumuc-Humac Mts.
AMAPÁ

PARQUE NACIONAL SERRANÍA DE LA NEBLINA
Pico de la Neblina 3,014 m
PARQUE NACIONAL DO PICO DA NEBLINA

BRAZIL
PARÁ
Equator

AMAZONAS
Barcelos
PARQUE NACIONAL DO RIO JAÚ

EDUARDO GOMES
Manaus

Santarém
Óbidos
Monte Alegre
Alenquer
Parintins
Itacoatiara

© Copyright by HAMMOND INCORPORATED, Maplewood, N.J.

E 64° F 60° G 56° H

POPULATION OF CITIES AND TOWNS
■ OVER 2,000,000
□ 1,000,000 - 1,999,999
● 500,000 - 999,999
◉ 250,000 - 499,999
◍ 100,000 - 249,999
⊙ 30,000 - 99,999
○ 10,000 - 29,999
∘ UNDER 10,000

SCALE 1:6,000,000 LAMBERT CONFORMAL CONIC PROJECTION
MILES 0 100 200 300
KILOMETERS 0 100 200 300

Northeastern Brazil

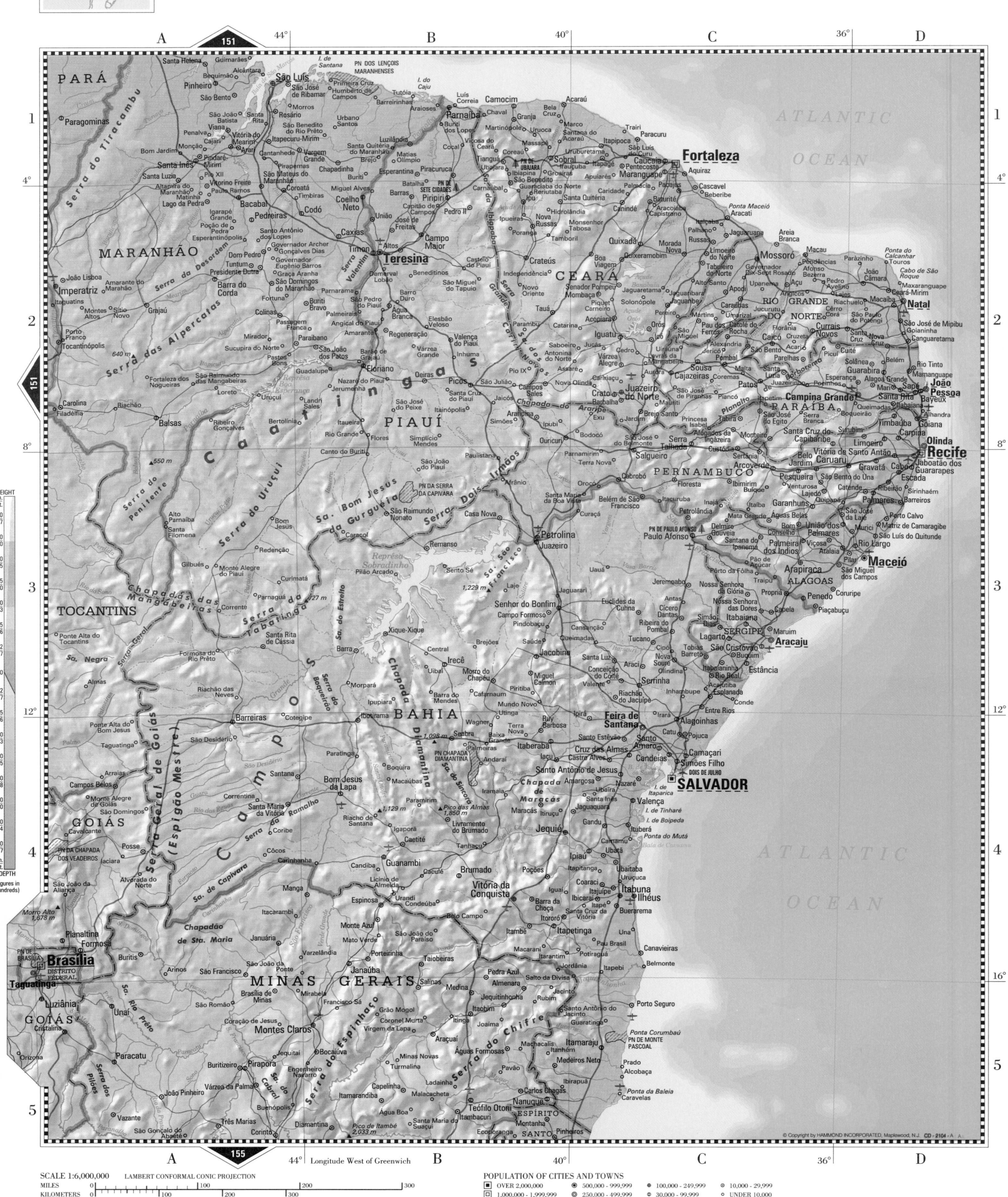

SCALE 1:6,000,000 LAMBERT CONFORMAL CONIC PROJECTION

MILES 0 | 100 | 200 | 300

KILOMETERS 0 | 100 | 200 | 300

POPULATION OF CITIES AND TOWNS

■ OVER 2,000,000
□ 1,000,000 – 1,999,999
⊡ 500,000 – 999,999
⊙ 250,000 – 499,999
● 100,000 – 249,999
◉ 30,000 – 99,999
○ 10,000 – 29,999
○ UNDER 10,000

HEIGHT
m. ft.
60 197
40 130
15 50
10 33
2 7
0
2 7
10 33
20 65
30 98
40 130
50 164
60 197
m. ft.
DEPTH
(Figures in Hundreds)

154

ATLANTIC OCEAN

Tropic of Capricorn

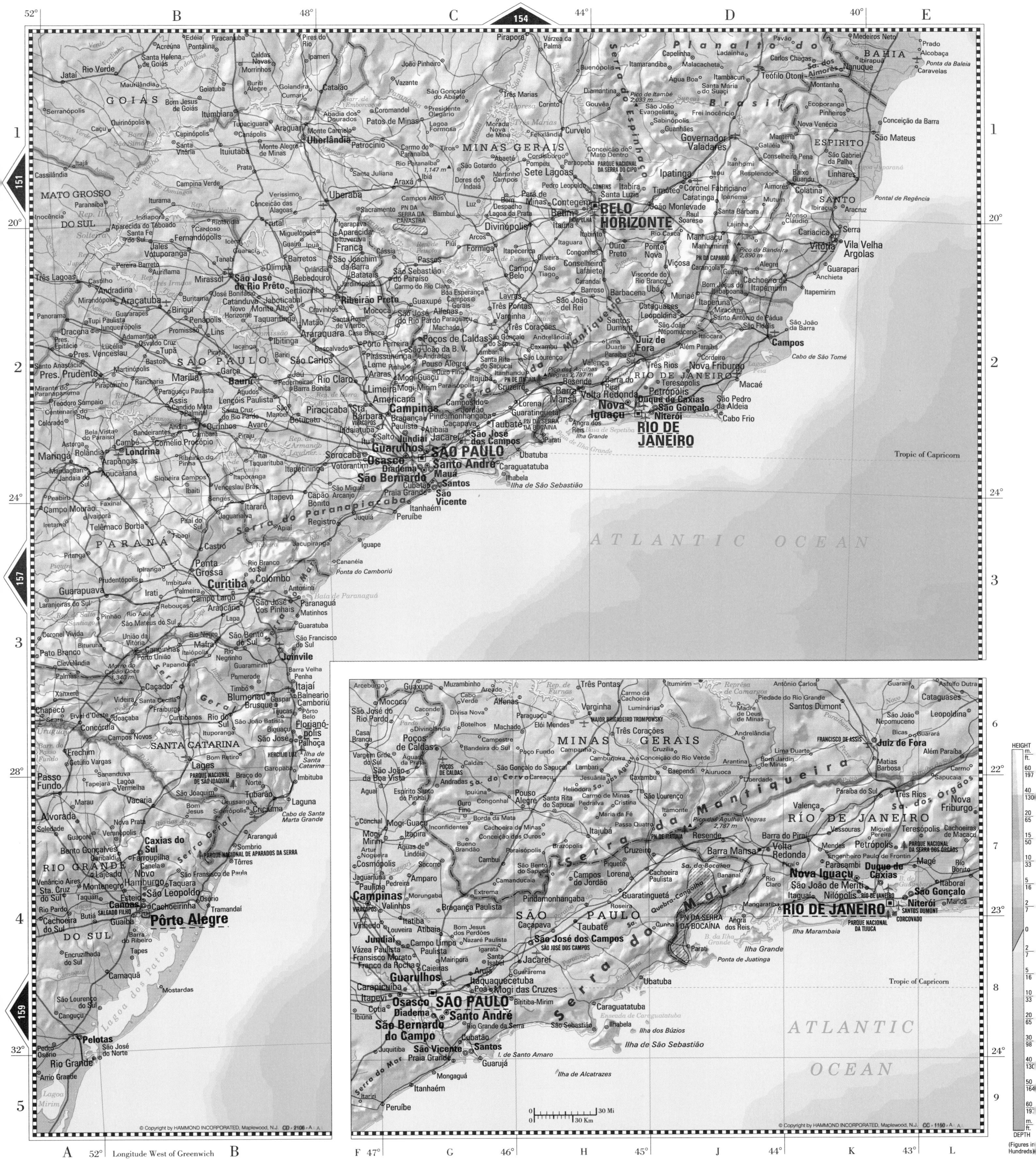

POPULATION OF CITIES AND TOWNS

■ OVER 2,000,000	● 500,000 - 999,999	● 100,000 - 249,999	⊙ 10,000 - 29,999
▣ 1,000,000 - 1,999,999	● 250,000 - 499,999	⊙ 30,000 - 99,999	○ UNDER 10,000

SCALE 1:6,000,000   LAMBERT CONFORMAL CONIC PROJECTION

MILES 0 — 100 — 200 — 300
KILOMETERS 0 — 100 — 200 — 300

HEIGHT

Longitude West of Greenwich

© Copyright by HAMMOND INCORPORATED, Maplewood, N.J. CD-2106-A-A

© Copyright by HAMMOND INCORPORATED, Maplewood, N.J. CC-1150-A-A

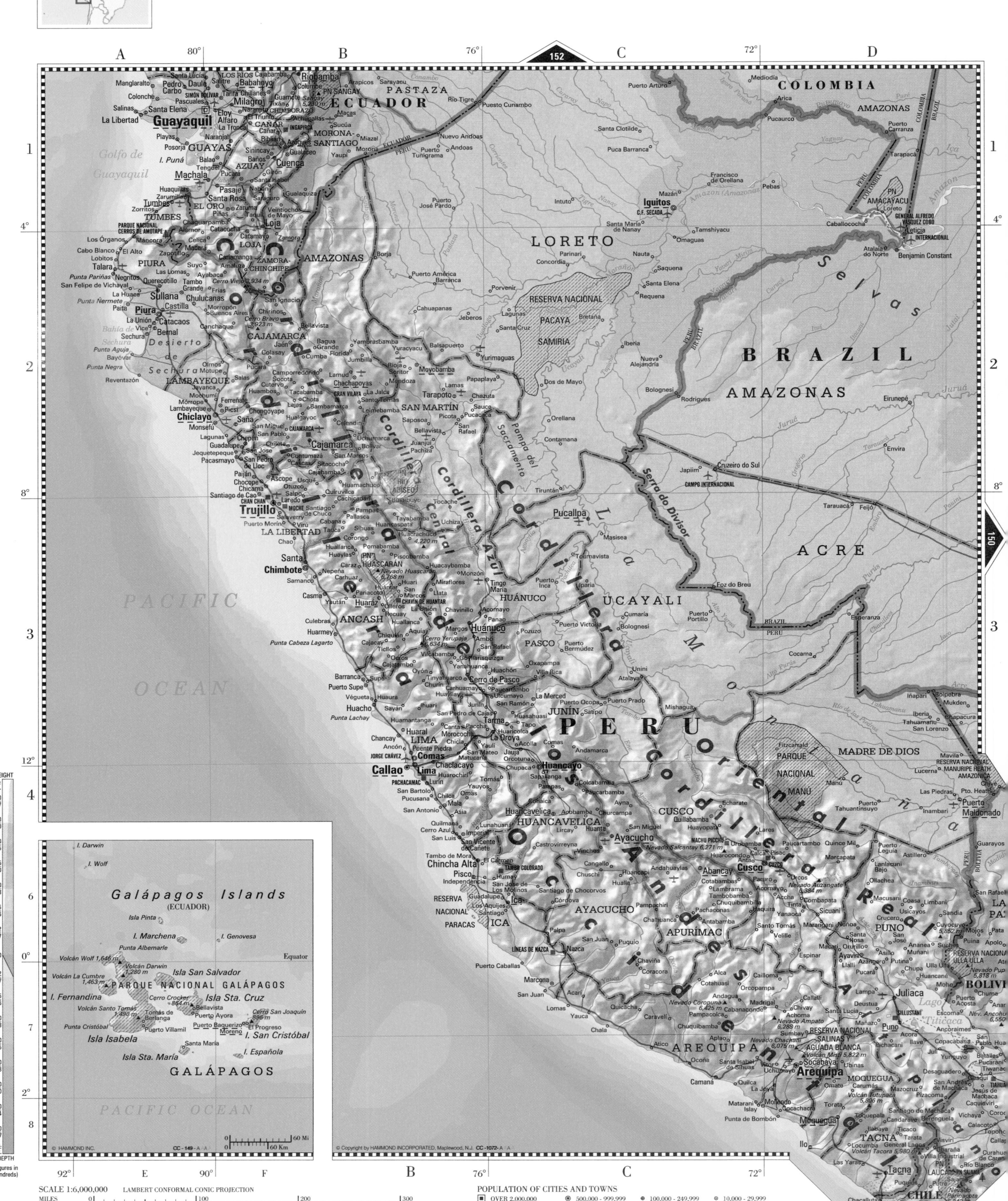

Southern South America

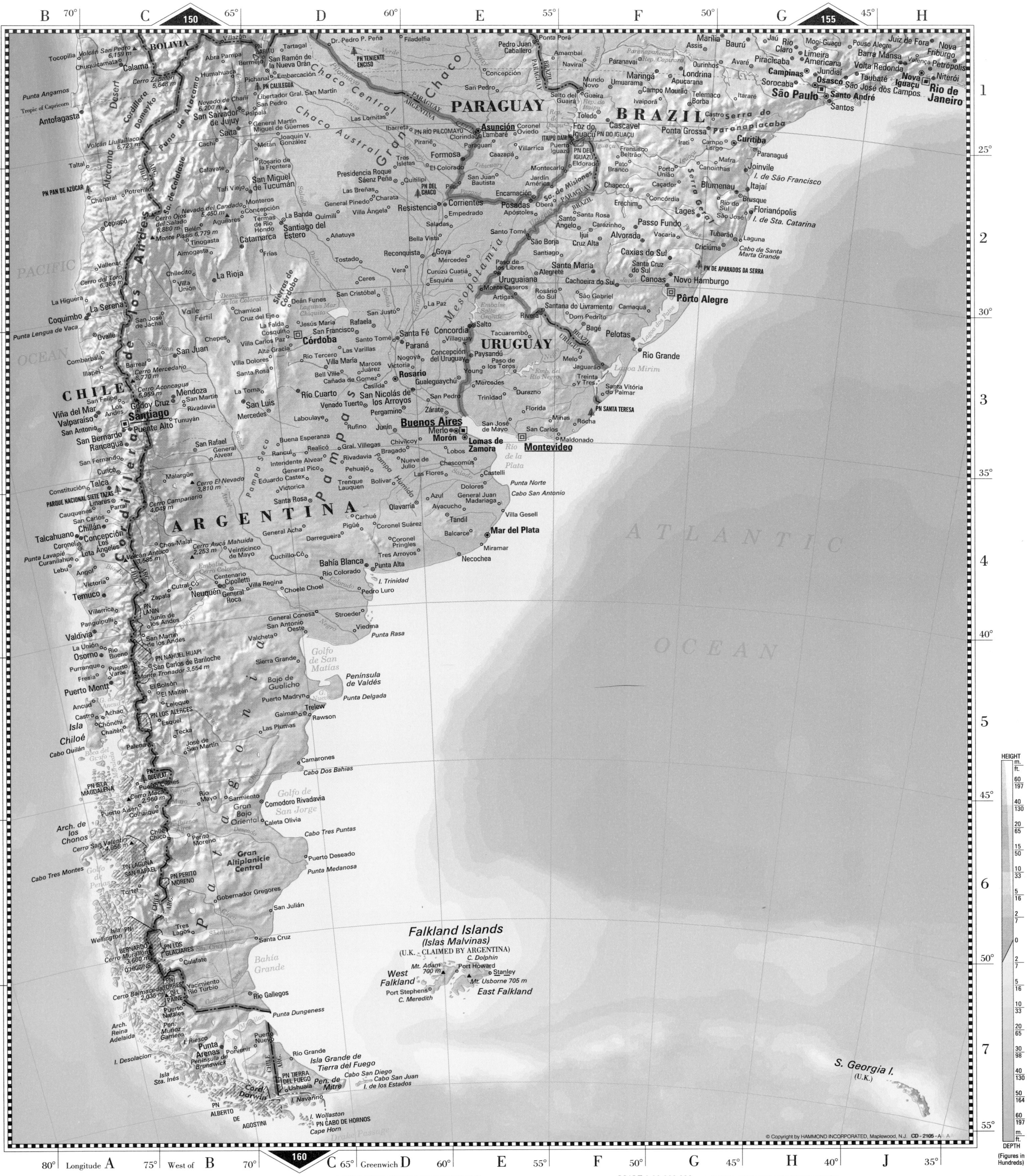

BOLIVIA

PARAGUAY

BRAZIL

ARGENTINA

CHILE

URUGUAY

PACIFIC OCEAN

ATLANTIC OCEAN

Asunción · Buenos Aires · Montevideo · Santiago · São Paulo · Rio de Janeiro · Córdoba · Rosario · Pôrto Alegre · Curitiba · Campinas · Osasco · Santo André · Santos

Falkland Islands
(Islas Malvinas)
(U.K. - CLAIMED BY ARGENTINA)
West Falkland · East Falkland
Mt. Adam 700 m. · Mt. Usborne 705 m.
Port Howard · Stanley · Port Stephens · C. Meredith · C. Dolphin

S. Georgia I. (U.K.)

Cape Horn · PN CABO DE HORNOS · Drake Passage

Tierra del Fuego · Isla Grande de Tierra del Fuego · Ushuaia · Punta Arenas

© Copyright by HAMMOND INCORPORATED, Maplewood, N.J. CD-2105-A-A

POPULATION OF CITIES AND TOWNS
■ OVER 2,000,000
■ 1,000,000 - 1,999,999
● 500,000 - 999,999
● 100,000 - 499,999
◉ 50,000 - 99,999
○ UNDER 50,000

SCALE 1:13,000,000 LAMBERT CONFORMAL CONIC PROJECTION
MILES 0 · 200 · 400 · 600
KILOMETERS 0 · 200 · 400 · 600

HEIGHT
m. / ft.
60/197 · 40/130 · 20/65 · 15/50 · 10/33 · 5/16 · 0 · 2/7 · 5/16 · 10/33 · 20/65 · 30/98 · 40/130 · 50/164 · 60/197 m. / ft.
DEPTH
(Figures in Hundreds)

Southern Chile and Argentina

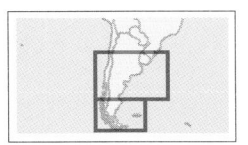

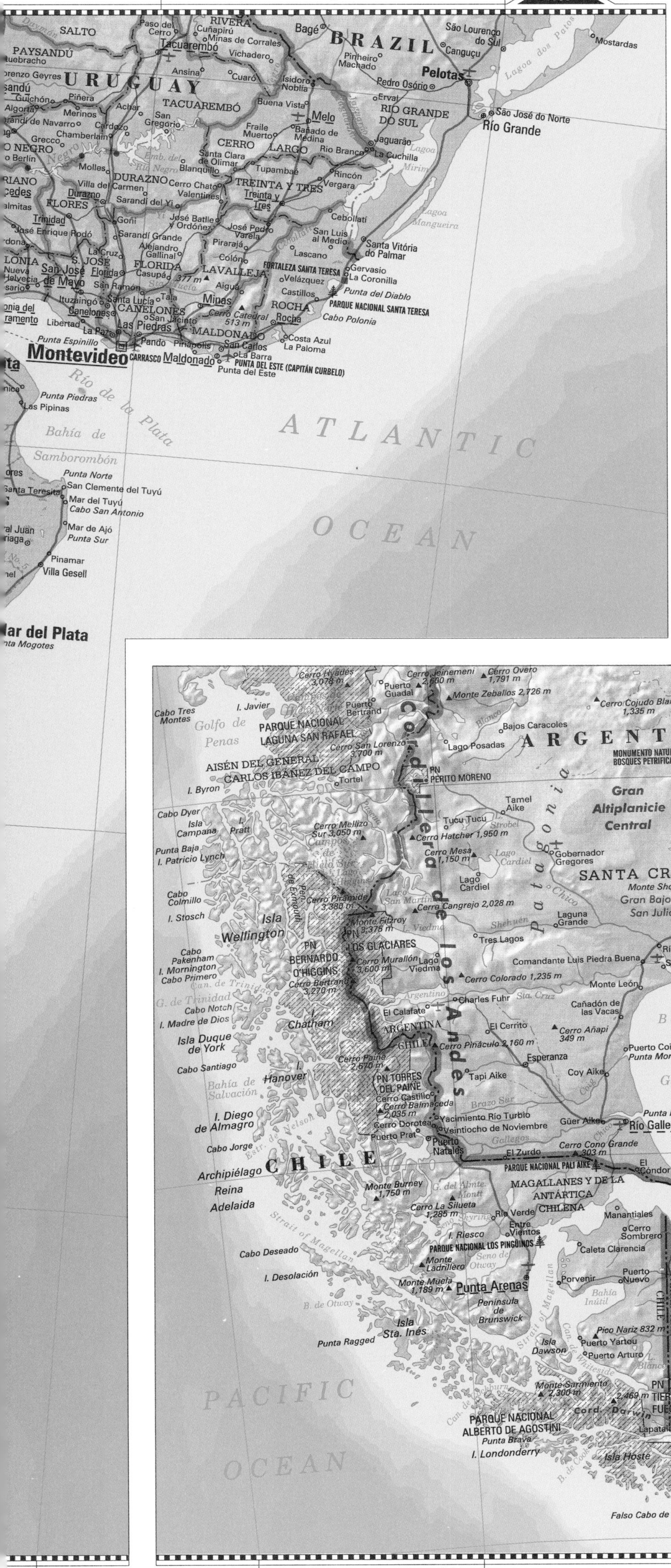

POPULATION OF CITIES AND TOWNS

- ■ OVER 2,000,000
- ◉ 500,000 - 999,999
- ● 100,000 - 249,999
- ⊙ 10,000 - 29,999
- ▣ 1,000,000 - 1,999,999
- ◉ 250,000 - 499,999
- ⊙ 30,000 - 99,999
- ○ UNDER 10,000

SCALE 1:6,000,000   LAMBERT CONFORMAL CONIC PROJECTION

MILES 0   100   200   300
KILOMETERS 0   100   200   300

Same scale as main map

© Copyright by HAMMOND INCORPORATED, Maplewood, N.J. CD-153-A-A

© HAMMOND INC. CD-1175-A-AA

0   30 Mi
0   30 Km

Arctic Regions, Antarctica

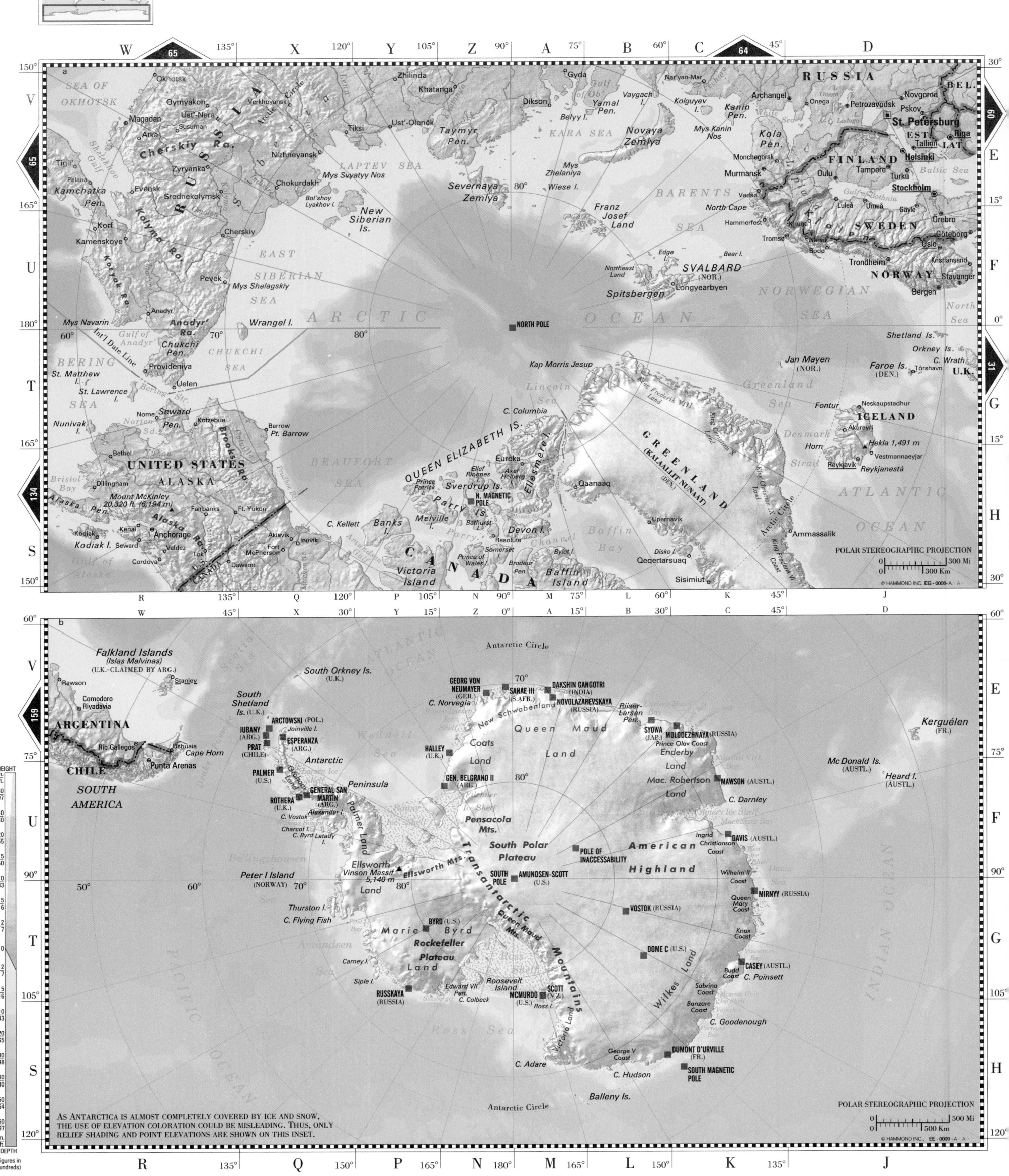

Statistical Tables and Index

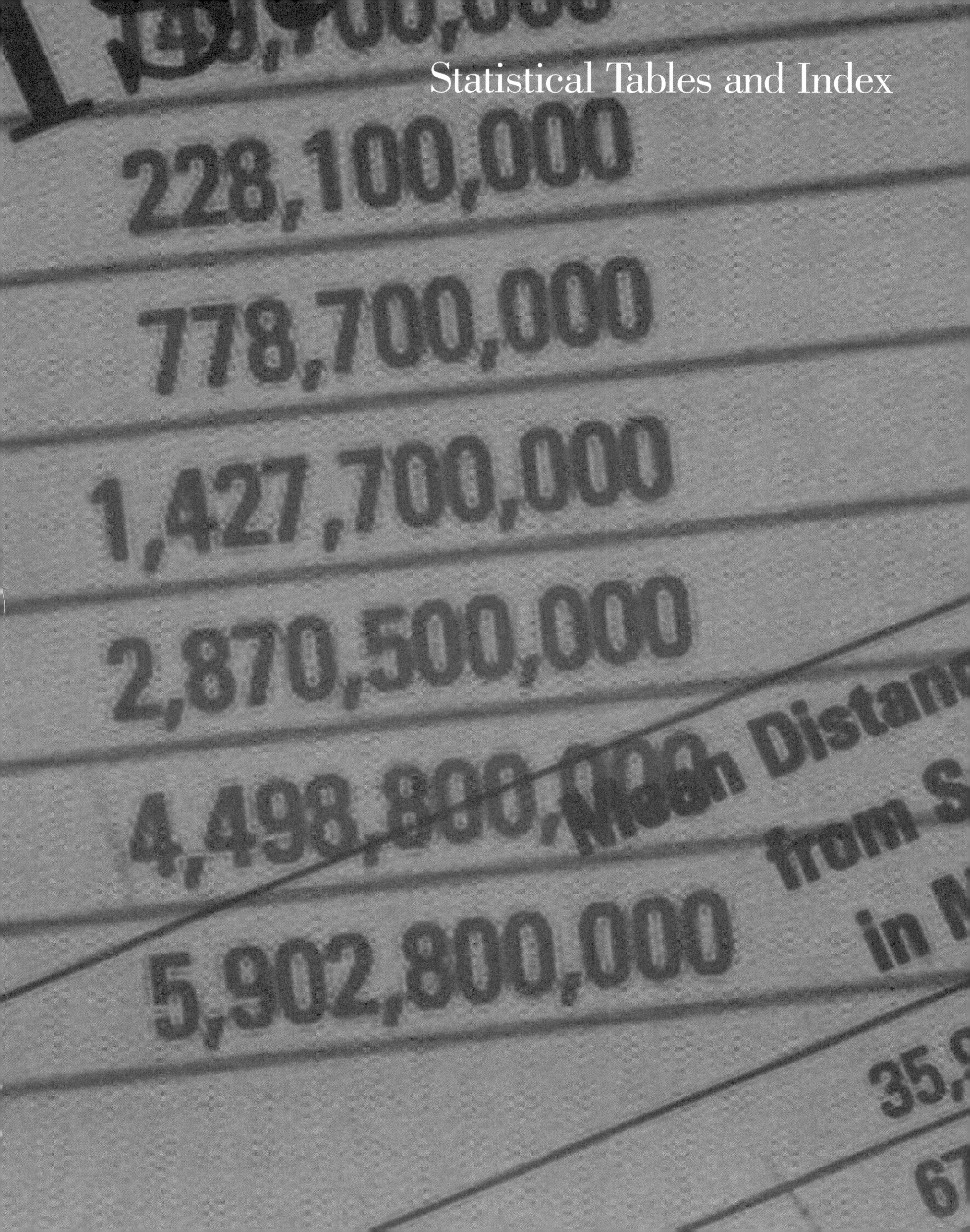

World Statistics

ELEMENTS OF THE SOLAR SYSTEM

	Mean Distance from Sun: in Miles	in Kilometers	Period of Revolution around Sun	Period of Rotation on Axis	Equatorial Diameter in Miles	in Kilometers	Surface Gravity (Earth = 1)	Mass (Earth = 1)	Mean Density (Water = 1)	Number of Satellites
Mercury	35,990,000	57,900,000	87.97 days	58.7 days	3,032	4,880	0.38	0.055	5.4	0
Venus	67,240,000	108,200,000	224.70 days	243.7 days†	7,521	12,104	0.91	0.815	5.2	0
Earth	93,000,000	149,700,000	365.26 days	23h 56m	7,926	12,755	1.00	1.00	5.5	1
Mars	141,610,000	227,900,000	686.98 days	24h 37m	4,221	6,794	0.38	0.107	3.9	2
Jupiter	483,675,000	778,400,000	11.86 years	9h 55m	88,846	142,984	2.36	317.8	1.3	16
Saturn	886,572,000	1,426,800,000	29.46 years	10h 30m	74,898	120,536	0.92	95.2	0.7	18
Uranus	1,783,957,000	2,871,000,000	84.01 years	17h 14m†	31,763	51,118	0.89	14.5	1.3	15
Neptune	2,795,114,000	4,498,300,000	164.79 years	16h 6m	30,778	49,532	1.13	17.1	1.6	8
Pluto	3,670,000,000	5,906,400,000	247.70 years	6.4 days†	1,413	2,274	0.07	0.002	2.1	1

† Retrograde motion

Source: NASA, National Space Science Center

DIMENSIONS OF THE EARTH

	Area in: Sq. Miles	Sq. Kilometers
Superficial area	196,939,000	510,072,000
Land surface	57,506,000	148,940,000
Water surface	139,433,000	361,132,000

	Distance in: Miles	Kilometers
Equatorial circumference	24,902	40,075
Polar circumference	24,860	40,007
Equatorial diameter	7,926.4	12,756.4
Polar diameter	7,899.8	12,713.6
Equatorial radius	3,963.2	6,378.2
Polar radius	3,949.9	6,356.8

Volume of the Earth	2.6×10^{11} cubic miles	10.84×10^{11} cubic kilometers
Mass or weight	6.6×10^{21} short tons	6.0×10^{21} metric tons
Maximum distance from Sun	94,600,000 miles	152,000,000 kilometers
Minimum distance from Sun	91,300,000 miles	147,000,000 kilometers

OCEANS AND MAJOR SEAS

	Area in: Sq. Miles	Sq. Kms.	Greatest Depth in: Feet	Meters
Pacific Ocean	63,855,000	165,384,000	36,198	11,033
Atlantic Ocean	31,744,000	82,217,000	28,374	8,648
Indian Ocean	28,417,000	73,600,000	25,344	7,725
Arctic Ocean	5,427,000	14,056,000	17,880	5,450
Caribbean Sea	970,000	2,512,300	24,720	7,535
Mediterranean Sea	969,000	2,509,700	16,896	5,150
South China Sea	895,000	2,318,000	15,000	4,600
Bering Sea	875,000	2,266,250	15,800	4,800
Gulf of Mexico	600,000	1,554,000	12,300	3,750
Sea of Okhotsk	590,000	1,528,100	11,070	3,370
East China Sea	482,000	1,248,400	9,500	2,900
Yellow Sea	480,000	1,243,200	350	107
Sea of Japan	389,000	1,007,500	12,280	3,740
Hudson Bay	317,500	822,300	846	258
North Sea	222,000	575,000	2,200	670
Black Sea	185,000	479,150	7,365	2,245
Red Sea	169,000	437,700	7,200	2,195
Baltic Sea	163,000	422,170	1,506	459

THE CONTINENTS

	Area in: Sq. Miles	Sq. Kms.	Percent of World's Land
Asia	17,128,500	44,362,815	29.5
Africa	11,707,000	30,321,130	20.2
North America	9,363,000	24,250,170	16.2
South America	6,879,725	17,818,505	11.9
Antarctica	5,405,000	14,000,000	9.4
Europe	4,057,000	10,507,630	7.0
Australia	2,967,893	7,686,850	5.1

MAJOR SHIP CANALS

	Length in: Miles	Kms.	Minimum Depth in: Feet	Meters
Volga-Baltic, Russia	225	362	–	–
Baltic-White Sea, Russia	140	225	16	5
Suez, Egypt	100.76	162	42	13
Albert, Belgium	80	129	16.5	5
Moscow-Volga, Russia	80	129	18	6
Volga-Don, Russia	62	100	–	–
Göta, Sweden	54	87	10	3
Kiel (Nord-Ostsee), Germany	53.2	86	38	12
Panama Canal, Panama	50.72	82	41.6	13
Houston Ship, U.S.A.	50	81	36	11

LARGEST ISLANDS

	Area in: Sq. Miles	Sq. Kms.		Area in: Sq. Miles	Sq. Kms.		Area in: Sq. Miles	Sq. Kms.
Greenland	840,000	2,175,600	Hispaniola, Haiti & Dom. Rep.	29,399	76,143	Somerset, Canada	9,570	24,786
New Guinea	305,000	789,950	Banks, Canada	27,038	70,028	Sardinia, Italy	9,301	24,090
Borneo	286,000	740,740	Ceylon, Sri Lanka	25,332	65,610	Shikoku, Japan	6,860	17,767
Madagascar	226,656	587,040	Tasmania, Australia	24,600	63,710	New Caledonia, France	6,530	16,913
Baffin, Canada	195,928	507,454	Svalbard, Norway	23,957	62,049	Nordaustlandet, Norway	6,409	16,599
Sumatra, Indonesia	164,000	424,760	Devon, Canada	21,331	55,247	Samar, Philippines	5,050	13,080
Honshu, Japan	88,000	227,920	Novaya Zemlya (north isl.), Russia	18,600	48,200	Negros, Philippines	4,906	12,707
Great Britain	84,400	218,896	Marajó, Brazil	17,991	46,597	Palawan, Philippines	4,550	11,785
Victoria, Canada	83,896	217,290	Tierra del Fuego, Chile & Argentina	17,900	46,360	Panay, Philippines	4,446	11,515
Ellesmere, Canada	75,767	196,236	Alexander, Antarctica	16,700	43,250	Jamaica	4,232	10,961
Celebes, Indonesia	72,986	189,034	Axel Heiberg, Canada	16,671	43,178	Hawaii, United States	4,038	10,458
South I., New Zealand	58,393	151,238	Melville, Canada	16,274	42,150	Viti Levu, Fiji	4,010	10,386
Java, Indonesia	48,842	126,501	Southampton, Canada	15,913	41,215	Cape Breton, Canada	3,981	10,311
North I., New Zealand	44,187	114,444	New Britain, Papua New Guinea	14,100	36,519	Mindoro, Philippines	3,759	9,736
Cuba	42,803	110,860	Taiwan	13,836	35,835	Kodiak, Alaska, U.S.A.	3,670	9,505
Newfoundland, Canada	42,031	108,860	Kyushu, Japan	13,770	35,664	Cyprus	3,572	9,251
Luzon, Philippines	40,420	104,688	Hainan, China	13,127	33,999	Puerto Rico, U.S.A.	3,435	8,897
Iceland	39,768	103,000	Prince of Wales, Canada	12,872	33,338	Corsica, France	3,352	8,682
Mindanao, Philippines	36,537	94,631	Spitsbergen, Norway	12,355	31,999	New Ireland, Papua New Guinea	3,340	8,651
Ireland	32,589	84,406	Vancouver, Canada	12,079	31,285	Crete, Greece	3,218	8,335
Hokkaidô, Japan	30,436	78,829	Timor, Indonesia	11,527	29,855	Anticosti, Canada	3,066	7,941
Sakhalin, Russia	29,500	76,405	Sicily, Italy	9,926	25,708	Wrangel, Russia	2,819	7,301

Principal Mountains

	Height in : Feet	Meters		Height in : Feet	Meters		Height in : Feet	Meters
Everest, Nepal-China	29,028	8,848	Pissis, Argentina	22,241	6,779	Margherita (Ruwenzori), Africa	16,795	5,119
K2 (Godwin Austen), Pakistan-China	28,250	8,611	Mercedario, Argentina	22,211	6,770	Kazbek, Georgia-Russia	16,558	5,047
Kânchenjunga, Nepal-India	28,208	8,598	Huascarán, Peru	22,205	6,768	Puncak Jaya, Indonesia	16,503	5,030
Lhotse, Nepal-China	27,923	8,511	Llullaillaco, Chile-Argentina	22,057	6,723	Blanc, France	15,771	4,807
Makalu, Nepal-China	27,789	8,470	Nevada Ancohuma, Bolivia	21,489	6,550	Klyuchevskaya Sopka, Russia	15,584	4,750
Dhaulagiri, Nepal	26,810	8,172	Chimborazo, Ecuador	20,561	6,267	Fairweather, Br. Col., Canada	15,300	4,663
Nanga Parbat, Pakistan	26,660	8,126	McKinley, Alaska	20,320	6,194	Dufourspitze (Mte. Rosa), Italy-Switzerland	15,203	4,634
Annapurna, Nepal	26,504	8,078	Logan, Yukon, Canada	19,524	5,951	Ras Dashen, Ethiopia	15,157	4,620
Nanda Devi, India	25,645	7,817	Cotopaxi, Ecuador	19,347	5,897	Matterhorn, Switzerland	14,691	4,478
Rakaposhi, Pakistan	25,550	7,788	Kilimanjaro, Tanzania	19,340	5,895	Whitney, California, U.S.A.	14,494	4,418
Kongur Shan, China	25,325	7,719	El Misti, Peru	19,101	5,822	Elbert, Colorado, U.S.A.	14,433	4,399
Tirich Mir, Pakistan	25,230	7,690	Pico Cristóbal Colón, Colombia	18,947	5,775	Rainier, Washington, U.S.A.	14,410	4,392
Gongga Shan, China	24,790	7,556	Huila, Colombia	18,865	5,750	Shasta, California, U.S.A.	14,162	4,317
Communism Peak, Tajikistan	24,590	7,495	Citlaltépetl (Orizaba), Mexico	18,700	5,700	Pikes Peak, Colorado, U.S.A.	14,110	4,301
Pobedy Peak, Kyrgyzstan	24,406	7,439	Damavand, Iran	18,605	5,671	Finsteraarhorn, Switzerland	14,022	4,274
Chomo Lhari, Bhutan-China	23,997	7,314	El'brus, Russia	18,510	5,642	Mauna Kea, Hawaii, U.S.A.	13,796	4,205
Muztag, China	23,891	7,282	St. Elias, Alaska, U.S.A.-Yukon, Canada	18,008	5,489	Mauna Loa, Hawaii, U.S.A.	13,677	4,169
Cerro Aconcagua, Argentina	22,831	6,959	Dykh-tau, Russia	17,070	5,203	Jungfrau, Switzerland	13,642	4,158
Ojos del Salado, Chile-Argentina	22,572	6,880	Batian (Kenya), Kenya	17,058	5,199	Grossglockner, Austria	12,457	3,797
Bonete, Chile-Argentina	22,546	6,872	Ararat, Turkey	16,946	5,165	Fujiyama, Japan	12,389	3,776
Tupungato, Chile-Argentina	22,310	6,800	Vinson Massif, Antarctica	16,864	5,140	Cook, New Zealand	12,349	3,764

Longest Rivers

	Length in: Miles	Kms.		Length in: Miles	Kms.		Length in: Miles	Kms.
Nile, Africa	4,145	6,671	Rio Grande, Mexico-U.S.A.	1,885	3,034	Kama, Russia	1,252	2,031
Amazon, S. America	4,007	6,448	Syrdarïya-Naryn, Asia	1,859	2,992	Don, Russia	1,222	1,967
Mississippi-Missouri-Red Rock, U.S.A.	3,710	5,971	Indus, Asia	1,800	2,897	Red, U.S.A.	1,222	1,966
Chang Jiang (Yangtze), China	3,500	5,633	Danube, Europe	1,775	2,857	Columbia, U.S.A.-Canada	1,214	1,953
Ob'-Irtysh, Russia-Kazakhstan	3,362	5,411	Brahmaputra, Asia	1,700	2,736	Tigris, Asia	1,181	1,901
Yenisey-Angara, Russia	3,100	4,989	Tocantins, Brazil	1,677	2,699	Darling, Australia	1,160	1,867
Huang He (Yellow), China	2,950	4,747	Salween, Asia	1,675	2,696	Angara, Russia	1,135	1,827
Congo, Africa	2,780	4,474	Euphrates, Asia	1,650	2,655	Sungari, Asia	1,130	1,819
Amur-Shilka-Onon, Asia	2,744	4,416	Xi (Si), China	1,650	2,655	Pechora, Russia	1,124	1,809
Lena, Russia	2,734	4,400	Amu Darya, Asia	1,616	2,601	Snake, U.S.A.	1,038	1,670
Mackenzie-Peace-Finlay, Canada	2,635	4,241	Nelson-Saskatchewan, Canada	1,600	2,575	Churchill, Canada	1,000	1,609
Paraná-La Plata, S. America	2,630	4,232	Orinoco, S. America	1,600	2,575	Pilcomayo, S. America	1,000	1,609
Mekong, Asia	2,610	4,200	Paraguay, S. America	1,584	2,549	Uruguay, S. America	994	1.600
Niger, Africa	2,580	4,152	Kolyma, Russia	1,562	2,514	Platte-N. Platte, U.S.A.	990	1,593
Missouri-Red Rock, U.S.A.	2,564	4,125	Ganges, Asia	1,550	2,494	Ohio, U.S.A.	981	1,578
Yenisey, Russia	2,500	4,028	Zhayyq (Ural), Kazakhstan-Russia	1,509	2,428	Magdalena, Colombia	956	1,538
Mississippi, U.S.A.	2,348	3,778	Japurá, S. America	1,500	2,414	Pecos, U.S.A.	926	1,490
Murray-Darling, Australia	2,310	3,718	Arkansas, U.S.A.	1,450	2,334	Oka, Russia	918	1,477
Volga, Russia	2,290	3,685	Colorado, U.S.A.-Mexico	1,450	2,334	Canadian, U.S.A.	906	1,458
Madeira, S. America	2,013	3,240	Negro, S. America	1,400	2,253	Colorado, Texas, U.S.A.	894	1,439
Purus, S. America	1,995	3,211	Dnepr (Dnyapro, Dnipro), Russia-Belarus-Ukraine	1,368	2,202	Dnister (Nistru), Ukraine-Moldova	876	1,410
Yukon, Alaska-Canada	1,979	3,185	Orange, Africa	1,350	2,173	Fraser, Canada	850	1,369
Zambezi, Africa	1,950	3,138	Ayeyarwady, Myanmar	1,325	2,132	Rhine, Europe	820	1,319
São Francisco, Brazil	1,930	3,106	Brazos, U.S.A.	1,309	2,107	Northern Dvina, Russia	809	1,302
St. Lawrence, Canada-U.S.A.	1,900	3,058	Ohio-Allegheny, U.S.A.	1,306	2,102	Ottawa, Canada	790	1,271

Principal Natural Lakes

	Area in: Sq. Miles	Sq. Kms.	Max. Depth in: Feet	Meters		Area in: Sq. Miles	Sq. Kms.	Max. Depth in: Feet	Meters
Caspian Sea, Asia	143,243	370,999	3,264	995	Lake Titicaca, Peru-Bolivia	3,200	8,288	1,000	305
Lake Superior, U.S.A.-Canada	31,820	82,414	1,329	405	Lake Nicaragua, Nicaragua	3,100	8,029	230	70
Lake Victoria, Africa	26,628	69,215	270	82	Lake Athabasca, Canada	3,064	7,936	400	122
Lake Huron, U.S.A.-Canada	23,010	59,596	748	228	Reindeer Lake, Canada*	2,568	6,651	–	–
Lake Michigan, U.S.A.	22,400	58,016	923	281	Lake Turkana (Rudolf), Africa	2,463	6,379	240	73
Aral Sea, Kazakhstan-Uzbekistan	15,830	41,000	213	65	Ysyk-Köl, Kyrgyzstan	2,425	6,281	2,303	702
Lake Tanganyika, Africa	12,650	32,764	4,700	1,433	Lake Torrens, Australia*	2,230	5,776	–	–
Lake Baykal, Russia	12,162	31,500	5,316	1,620	Vänern, Sweden	2,156	5,584	328	100
Great Bear Lake, Canada	12,096	31,328	1,356	413	Nettilling Lake, Canada*	2,140	5,543	–	–
Lake Nyasa (Malawi), Africa	11,555	29,928	2,320	707	Lake Winnipegosis, Canada	2,075	5,374	38	12
Great Slave Lake, Canada	11,031	28,570	2,015	614	Lake Albert, Africa	2,075	5,374	160	49
Lake Erie, U.S.A.-Canada	9,940	25,745	210	64	Kariba Lake, Zambia-Zimbabwe	2,050	5,310	295	90
Lake Winnipeg, Canada	9,417	24,390	60	18	Lake Nipigon, Canada	1,872	4,848	540	165
Lake Ontario, U.S.A.-Canada	7,540	19,529	775	244	Lake Mweru, Africa	1,800	4,662	60	18
Lake Balkhash, Kazakhstan	7,081	18,340	87	27	Lake Manitoba, Canada	1,799	4,659	12	4
Lake Chad, Africa*	7,000	18,130	25	8	Lake Taymyr, Russia	1,737	4,499	85	26
Lake Ladoga, Russia	6,900	17,871	738	225	Lake Khanka, China-Russia	1,700	4,403	33	10
Lake Maracaibo, Venezuela	5,120	13,261	100	31	Lake Kioga, Uganda	1,700	4,403	25	8
Lake Onega, Russia	3,761	9,741	377	115	Lake of the Woods, U.S.A.-Canada	1,679	4,349	70	21
Lake Eyre, Australia*	3,500-0	9,065-0	–	–					

* Figures subject to great seasonal variations.

Time Zones of the World

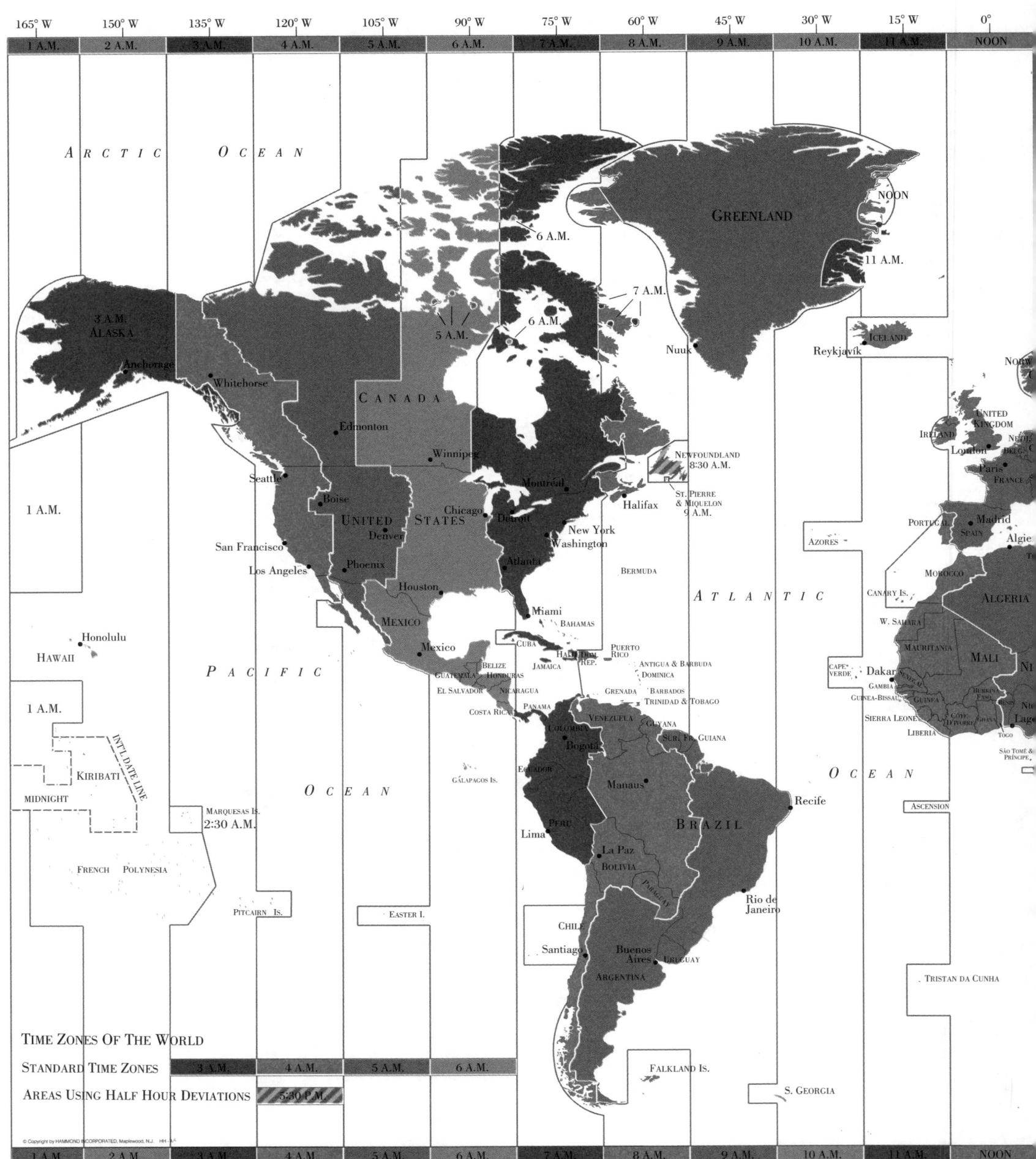

165° W	150° W	135° W	120° W	105° W	90° W	75° W	60° W	45° W	30° W	15° W	0°
1 A.M.	2 A.M.	3 A.M.	4 A.M.	5 A.M.	6 A.M.	7 A.M.	8 A.M.	9 A.M.	10 A.M.	11 A.M.	NOON

ARCTIC OCEAN

3 A.M.
ALASKA
Anchorage

GREENLAND
NOON
11 A.M.

6 A.M.
7 A.M.
6 A.M.
5 A.M.
Nuuk

ICELAND
Reykjavík
Norv

Whitehorse

CANADA

Edmonton

Winnipeg

IRELAND
UNITED
KINGDOM
London
Paris
FRANCE

1 A.M.

Seattle
Boise
UNITED STATES
Denver
San Francisco
Phoenix
Los Angeles
Houston

Chicago
Detroit
Montréal
Halifax

Montréal
New York
Washington
Atlanta

NEWFOUNDLAND
8:30 A.M.
ST. PIERRE
& MIQUELON
9 A.M.

AZORES

PORTUGAL
SPAIN
Madrid
Algie

MOROCCO

Honolulu
HAWAII

BERMUDA

ATLANTIC

CANARY IS.

W. SAHARA
MAURITANIA
ALGERIA

MEXICO
Miami
BAHAMAS
CUBA
HAITI DOM.
REP.
PUERTO
RICO
ANTIGUA & BARBUDA
DOMINICA

Mexico
BELIZE
GUATEMALA
HONDURAS
JAMAICA
EL SALVADOR
NICARAGUA
Costa Rica
PANAMA

CAPE
VERDE
Dakar
GAMBIA
GUINEA-BISSAU
SIERRA LEONE
LIBERIA

MALI
Ni

BURKINA
GUINEA
CÔTE
D'IVOIRE
TOGO
Lag

PACIFIC

1 A.M.

INTL DATE LINE

KIRIBATI

MIDNIGHT

MARQUESAS IS.
2:30 A.M.

FRENCH POLYNESIA

OCEAN

GÁLAPAGOS IS.

Bogotá
COLUMBIA
VENEZUELA
GUYANA
SURI. FR. GUIANA

Manaus

ECUADOR

Lima
PERU

BRAZIL
Recife

ASCENSION

OCEAN
São Tomé &
Príncipe

GRENADA
BARBADOS
TRINIDAD & TOBAGO

La Paz
BOLIVIA

PARAGUAY

Rio de
Janeiro

PITCAIRN IS.

EASTER I.

CHILE
Santiago

Buenos
Aires
URUGUAY
ARGENTINA

FALKLAND IS.

TRISTAN DA CUNHA

S. GEORGIA

TIME ZONES OF THE WORLD

STANDARD TIME ZONES	3 A.M.	4 A.M.	5 A.M.	6 A.M.
AREAS USING HALF HOUR DEVIATIONS	5:30 P.M.			

© Copyright by HAMMOND INCORPORATED, Maplewood, N.J. HH-

1 A.M.	2 A.M.	3 A.M.	4 A.M.	5 A.M.	6 A.M.	7 A.M.	8 A.M.	9 A.M.	10 A.M.	11 A.M.	NOON

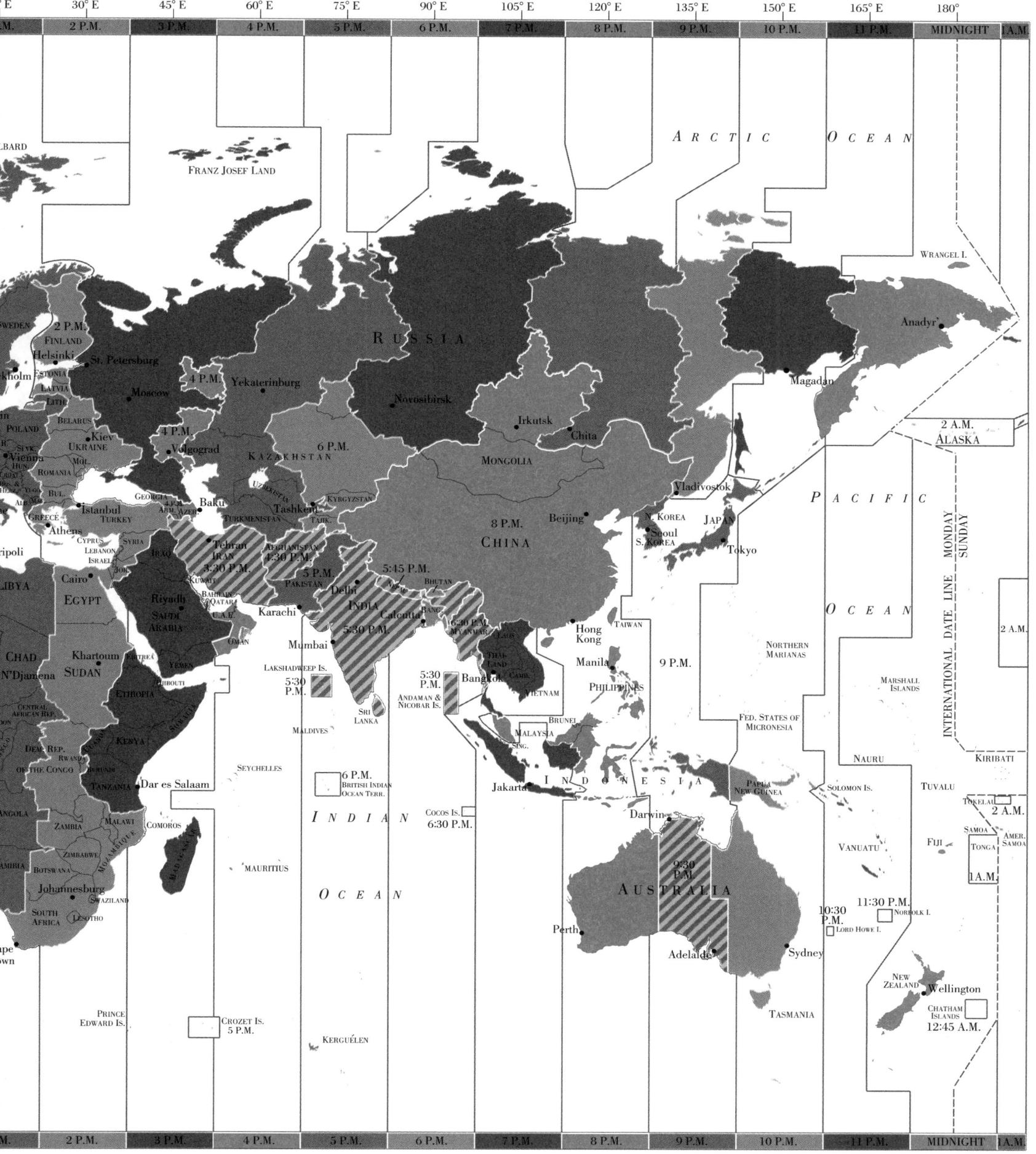

Index of the World

This index is a comprehensive listing of the places and geographic features found in the atlas. Names are arranged in strict alphabetical order, without regard to hyphens or spaces. Every name is followed by the country or area to which it belongs. Except for cities, towns, countries and cultural areas, all entries include a reference to feature type, such as province, river, island, peak, and so on. The page number and alpha-numeric code appear in blue to the right of each listing. The page number directs you to the largest scale map on which the name can be found. The code refers to the grid squares formed by the horizontal and vertical lines of latitude and longitude on each map. Following the letters from left to right and the numbers from top to bottom helps you to locate quickly the square containing the place or feature. Inset maps have their own alpha-numeric codes. Names that are accompanied by a point symbol are indexed to the symbol's location on the map. Other names are indexed to the initial letter of the name. When a map name contains a subordinate or alternate name, both names are listed in the index. To conserve space and provide room for more entries, many abbreviations are used in this index. The primary abbreviations are listed below.

Index Abbreviations

A Ab,Can	Alberta	**C** (cont.) Canl.	Canary Islands
Abor.	Aboriginal	Cap.	Capital
Acad.	Academy	Cap. Dist.	Capital District
ACT	Australian Capital Territory	Cap. Terr.	Capital Territory
A.F.B.	Air Force Base	Cay.	Cayman Islands
Afld.	Airfield	C.d'Iv.	Côte d'Ivoire
Afg.	Afghanistan	C.G.	Coast Guard
Afr.	Africa	Chan.	Channel
Ak,US	Alaska	Chl.	Channel Islands
Al,US	Alabama	Co.	County
Alb.	Albania	Co,US	Colorado
Alg.	Algeria	Col.	Colombia
Amm. Dep.	Ammunition Depot	Com.	Comoros
And.	Andorra	Cont.	Continent
Ang.	Angola	CpV.	Cape Verde Islands
Angu.	Anguilla	CR	Costa Rica
Ant.	Antarctica	Cr.	Creek
Anti.	Antigua and Barbuda	Cro.	Croatia
Ar,US	Arkansas	CSea.	Coral Sea Islands Territory
Arch.	Archipelago	Ct,US	Connecticut
Arg.	Argentina	Ctr.	Center
Arm.	Armenia	Ctry.	Country
Arpt.	Airport	Cyp.	Cyprus
Aru.	Aruba	Czh.	Czech Republic
ASam.	American Samoa	**D** DC,US	District of Columbia
Ash.	Ashmore and Cartier Islands	De,US	Delaware
Aus.	Austria	Den.	Denmark
Austl.	Australia	Depr.	Depression
Aut.	Autonomous	Dept.	Department
Az,US	Arizona	Des.	Desert
Azer.	Azerbaijan	DF	Distrito Federal
Azor.	Azores	Dist.	District
B Bahm.	Bahamas, The	Djib.	Djibouti
Bahr.	Bahrain	Dom.	Dominica
Bang.	Bangladesh	Dpcy.	Dependency
Bar.	Barbados	D.R.Congo	Democratic Republic of the Congo
BC,Can	British Columbia	DRep.	Dominican Republic
Bela.	Belarus	**E** Ecu.	Ecuador
Belg.	Belgium	Emb.	Embankment
Belz.	Belize	Eng.	Engineering
Ben.	Benin	Eng,UK	England
Berm.	Bermuda	EqG.	Equatorial Guinea
Bfld.	Battlefield	Erit.	Eritrea
Bhu.	Bhutan	ESal.	El Salvador
Bol.	Bolivia	Est.	Estonia
Bor.	Borough	Eth.	Ethiopia
Bosn.	Bosnia and Herzegovina	Eur.	Europe
Bots.	Botswana	**F** Falk.	Falkland Islands
Braz.	Brazil	Far.	Faroe Islands
BrIn.	British Indian Ocean Territory	Fed. Dist.	Federal District
Bru.	Brunei	Fin.	Finland
Bul.	Bulgaria	Fl,US	Florida
Burk.	Burkina Faso	For.	Forest
Buru.	Burundi	Fr.	France
BVI	British Virgin Islands	FrAnt.	French Southern and Antarctic Lands
C Ca,US	California	FrG.	French Guiana
CAfr.	Central African Republic	FrPol.	French Polynesia
Camb.	Cambodia	**G** Ga,US	Georgia
Camr.	Cameroon	Galp.	Galapagos Islands
Can.	Canada	Gam.	Gambia, The
Can.	Canal	Gaza	Gaza Strip

Abbr.	Meaning	Abbr.	Meaning
G (cont.) GBis.	Guinea-Bissau	**M** (cont.) Malw.	Malawi
Geo.	Georgia	Mart.	Martinique
Ger.	Germany	May.	Mayotte
Gha.	Ghana	Mb,Can	Manitoba
Gib.	Gibraltar	Md,US	Maryland
Glac.	Glacier	Me,US	Maine
Gov.	Governorate	Mem.	Memorial
Govt.	Government	Mex.	Mexico
Gre.	Greece	Mi,US	Michigan
Grld.	Greenland	Micr.	Micronesia, Federated States of
Gren.	Grenada	Mil.	Military
Grsld.	Grassland	Mn,US	Minnesota
Guad.	Guadeloupe	Mo,US	Missouri
Guat.	Guatemala	Mol.	Moldova
Gui.	Guinea	Mon.	Monument
Guy.	Guyana	Mona.	Monaco
H Har.	Harbor	Mong.	Mongolia
Hi,US	Hawaii	Monts.	Montserrat
Hist.	Historic(al)	Mor.	Morocco
Hon.	Honduras	Moz.	Mozambique
Hts.	Heights	Mrsh.	Marshall Islands
Hun.	Hungary	Mrta.	Mauritania
I Ia,US	Iowa	Mrts.	Mauritius
Ice.	Iceland	Ms,US	Mississippi
Id,US	Idaho	Mt.	Mount
Il,US	Illinois	Mt,US	Montana
IM	Isle of Man	Mtn., Mts.	Mountain, Mountains
In,US	Indiana	Mun. Arpt.	Municipal Airport
Ind. Res.	Indian Reservation	**N** NAm.	North America
Indo.	Indonesia	Namb.	Namibia
Int'l	International	NAnt.	Netherlands Antilles
Ire.	Ireland	Nat'l	National
Isl., Isls.	Island, Islands	Nav.	Naval
Isr.	Israel	NB,Can	New Brunswick
Isth.	Isthmus	Nbrhd.	Neighborhood
It.	Italy	NC,US	North Carolina
J Jam.	Jamaica	NCal.	New Caledonia
Jor.	Jordan	ND,US	North Dakota
K Kaz.	Kazakhstan	Ne,US	Nebraska
Kiri.	Kiribati	Neth.	Netherlands
Ks,US	Kansas	Nf,Can	Newfoundland
Kuw.	Kuwait	Nga.	Nigeria
Ky,US	Kentucky	NH,US	New Hampshire
Kyr.	Kyrgyzstan	NI,UK	Northern Ireland
L La,US	Louisiana	Nic.	Nicaragua
Lab.	Laboratory	NJ,US	New Jersey
Lag.	Lagoon	NKor.	North Korea
Lakesh.	Lakeshore	NM,US	New Mexico
Lat.	Latvia	NMar.	Northern Mariana Isl.
Lcht.	Liechtenstein	Nor.	Norway
Ldg.	Landing	NP	National Park
Leb.	Lebanon	NS,Can	Nova Scotia
Les.	Lesotho	Nv,US	Nevada
Libr.	Liberia	NW,Can	Northwest Territories
Lith.	Lithuania	NWR	National Wildlife Refuge
Lux.	Luxembourg	NY,US	New York
M Ma,US	Massachusetts	NZ	New Zealand
Macd.	Macedonia	**O** Obl.	Oblast
Madg.	Madagascar	Oh,US	Ohio
Madr.	Madeira	Ok,US	Oklahoma
Malay.	Malaysia	On,Can	Ontario
Mald.	Maldives	Or,US	Oregon
		P Pa,US	Pennsylvania
		PacUS	Pacific Islands, U.S.

Abbr.	Meaning	Abbr.	Meaning
P (cont.) Pak.	Pakistan	**S** (cont.) StP.	Saint Pierre and Miquelon
Pan.	Panama	StV.	Saint Vincent and the Grenadines
Par.	Paraguay	Sur.	Suriname
Par.	Parish	Sval.	Svalbard
PE,Can	Prince Edward Island	Swaz.	Swaziland
Pen.	Peninsula	Swe.	Sweden
Phil.	Philippines	Swi.	Switzerland
Phys. Reg.	Physical Region	**T** Tah.	Tahiti
Pitc.	Pitcairn Islands	Tai.	Taiwan
Plat.	Plateau	Taj.	Tajikistan
PN	National Park	Tanz.	Tanzania
PNG	Papua New Guinea	Ter.	Terrace
Pol.	Poland	Terr.	Territory
Port.	Portugal	Thai.	Thailand
Poss.	Possession	Tn,US	Tennessee
Pkwy.	Parkway	Tok.	Tokelau
PR	Puerto Rico	Trg.	Training
Pref.	Prefecture	Trin.	Trinidad and Tobago
Prov.	Province	Trkm.	Turkmenistan
Prsv.	Preserve	Trks.	Turks and Caicos Islands
Pt.	Point	Tun.	Tunisia
Q Qu,Can	Quebec	Tun.	Tunnel
R Rec.	Recreation(al)	Turk.	Turkey
Ref.	Refuge	Tuv.	Tuvalu
Reg.	Region	Twp.	Township
Rep.	Republic	Tx,US	Texas
Res.	Reservoir, Reservation	**U** UAE	United Arab Emirates
Reun.	Réunion	Ugan.	Uganda
RI,US	Rhode Island	UK	United Kingdom
Riv.	River	Ukr.	Ukraine
Rom.	Romania	Uru.	Uruguay
Rsv.	Reserve	US	United States
Rus.	Russia	USVI	U.S. Virgin Islands
Rvwy.	Riverway	Ut,US	Utah
Rwa.	Rwanda	Uzb.	Uzbekistan
S SAfr.	South Africa	**V** Va,US	Virginia
Sam.	Samoa	Val.	Valley
SAm.	South America	Van.	Vanuatu
SaoT.	São Tomé and Príncipe	VatC.	Vatican City
SAr.	Saudi Arabia	Ven.	Venezuela
Sc,UK	Scotland	Viet.	Vietnam
SC,US	South Carolina	Vill.	Village
SD,US	South Dakota	Vol.	Volcano
Seash.	Seashore	Vt,US	Vermont
Sen.	Senegal	**W** Wa,US	Washington
Sey.	Seychelles	Wal,UK	Wales
SGeo.	South Georgia and Sandwich Islands	Wall.	Wallis and Futuna
Sing.	Singapore	WBnk.	West Bank
Sk,Can	Saskatchewan	Wi,US	Wisconsin
SKor.	South Korea	Wild.	Wildlife, Wilderness
SLeo.	Sierra Leone	WSah.	Western Sahara
Slov.	Slovenia	WV,US	West Virginia
Slvk.	Slovakia	Wy,US	Wyoming
SMar.	San Marino	**Y** Yem.	Yemen
Sol.	Solomon Islands	Yk,Can	Yukon Territory
Som.	Somalia	Yugo.	Yugoslavia
Sp.	Spain	**Z** Zam.	Zambia
Spr., Sprs.	Spring, Springs	Zim.	Zimbabwe
SrL.	Sri Lanka		
Sta.	Station		
StH.	Saint Helena		
Str.	Strait		
StK.	Saint Kitts and Nevis		
StL.	Saint Lucia		

A

100 Mile House,
BC, Can. 126/C3
Aa (riv.), Ger. 50/D5
Aach (riv.), Ger. 57/F2
Aach, Ger. 57/E2
Aachen, Ger. 53/F2
Aalbach (riv.), Ger. 54/C3
Aalborg
(int'l arpt.), Den. 38/C3
Aalburg, Neth. 50/C5
Aalen, Ger. 54/D5
Aalsmeer, Neth. 50/B4
Aalst, Aus. 54/D5
Aalst, Belg. 52/D2
Aalten, Neth. 50/D5
Aalter, Belg. 52/C1
Aar (riv.), Ger. 53/H3
Aarberg, Swi. 56/E3
Aarburg, Swi. 56/D3
Aardenburg, Neth. 52/C1
Aare (riv.), Swi. 43/H3
Aargau (canton), Swi. 57/E3
Aarred (lake), WSah. 98/B4
Aarschot, Belg. 53/D2
Aartselaar, Belg. 53/D1
Aarwangen, Swi. 56/D3
Aba, D.R. Congo 104/A2
Aba, China 70/H5
Aba, Nga. 103/G5
Abā as Su'ūd, SAr. 88/D5
Abacaxis (riv.), Braz. 150/G5
Abadab (peak), Sudan 101/C5
Ābādān, Iran 88/F2
Ābādeh, Iran 88/F2
Abadia dos Dourados,
Braz. 155/C1
Abadla, Alg. 99/E3
Abádszalók, Hun. 48/E2
Abaeté, Braz. 155/C1
Abaetetuba, Braz. 151/J4
Abaiang (isl.), Kiri. 116/G4
Abakan, Rus. 64/K4
Abancay, Peru 156/C4
Abano Terme, It. 59/E2
Abar Kūh, Iran 88/F2
Abarán, Sp. 44/E3
Abashiri (lake),
Japan 76/C2
Abashiri, Japan 76/D1
Abasolo, Mex. 143/E4
Abasolo, Mex. 143/F3
Abay, Kaz. 87/F3
Ābaya Hayk (lake), Eth. 97/N6
Abbadia Lariana, It. 57/F6
Abbadia San Salvatore,
It. 43/J5
Abbeville, La, US 129/J5
Abbeville, SC, US 133/H3
Abbeville, Fr. 52/A3
Abbey (peak),
Austl. 114/B1
Abbeyfeale, Ire. 31/P10
Abbeyleix, Ire. 31/Q10
Abbiategrasso, It. 58/B2
Abbot (mt.), Austl. 114/B3
Abbotsinch (int'l arpt.),
Sc, UK 36/B5
Abbottābād, Pak. 86/B2
Abbottstown,
Pa, US 138/B4
Abcoude, Neth. 50/B4
Abdul Hakīm, Pak. 86/B4
Abdulino, Rus. 63/K1
Abéché, Chad 97/K5
Abemama (isl.), Kiri. 116/G4
Abenberg, Ger. 54/D4
Abengourou, C.d'Iv. 102/E5
Åbenrå, Den. 38/C4
Abens (riv.), Ger. 40/F4
Abensberg, Ger. 55/E5
Abeokuta, Nga. 103/F5
Abercarn, Wal, UK 32/C3
Aberchirder,
Sc, UK 36/D1
Aberdare, Wal, UK 32/C3
Aberdare NP,
Kenya 104/C3
Aberdeen, Austl. 115/D2
Aberdeen, SD, US 127/J4
Aberdeen, Wa, US 126/C4
Aberdeen, Ms, US 133/F3
Aberdeen, SAfr. 106/D4
Aberdeen (lake),
NW, Can. 122/F2
Aberdeen, Md, US 138/B5
Aberdeen, Sc, UK 36/D2
Aberdeen Proving Ground,
Md, US 138/B5
Aberdour, Sc, UK 36/C4
Aberdour (bay),
Sc, UK 36/D1
Aberfeldy, Sc, UK 36/C3
Aberfoyle, Sc, UK 36/B4
Abergavenny,
Wal, UK 32/C3
Abergele, Wal, UK 34/E5
Aberlour, Sc, UK 36/C2
Abernethy, Sc, UK 36/C4
Abert (lake),
Or, US 126/C5
Abertillery,
Wal, UK 32/C3
Aberystwyth,
Wal, UK 32/B2
Abhā, SAr. 88/D5
Abhar, Iran 88/E1
Abhayāpuri, India 85/H2
Abhe Bad (lake),
Djib. 97/P5
Abia (prov.), Nga. 103/G5
Abidjan, C.d'Iv. 102/D5
Abiko, Japan 77/E2
Abilene, Tx, US 129/H4
Abilene, Ks, US 129/H3
Abingdon, Eng, UK 33/E3
Abingdon, Md, US 138/B5
Abington (reef),
Austl. 114/C2
Abington, Sc, UK 36/C4
Abino (pt.), Can. 131/R10
Abiquiu, NM, US 132/B2
Abitibi (lake),
On,Qu, Can. 123/H4
Abitibi (riv.), Can. 123/H4
On, Can. 123/H4
Abkhazia Aut. Rep.,
Geo. 63/G4
Ableiges, Fr. 30/G4
Abnūb, Egypt 101/B3
Åbo (Turku), Fin. 39/K1
Abohar, India 86/C4
Aboisso, C.d'Iv. 102/E5

Abomey, Ben. 103/F5
Abondance, Fr. 56/C5
Abony, Hun. 48/D2
Aboyne, Sc, UK 36/D2
Abra (riv.), Phil. 79/D4
Abra Pampa, Arg. 157/C1
Abraham Gonzalez
(int'l arpt.), Mex. 128/F5
Abrantes, Port. 44/A3
Abreojos (pt.), Mex. 142/B3
Abrud, Rom. 49/F2
Abruzzi (prov.), It. 43/K5
Abruzzo, PN de, It. 46/C2
Absam, Aus. 55/J3
Absaroka (range), US 126/F4
Abscon, NJ, US 138/D5
Abtsgmünd, Ger. 54/D5
Abu al-Husein (well),
Egypt 101/B4
Abū Ḥammād,
Egypt 101/B4
Abu Hashim (well),
Egypt 91/B4
Abū Ḥummuṣ, Egypt 91/B4
Abū Kabīr, Egypt 91/B4
Abū Kamāl, Syria 90/E3
Abū Qashsh,
WBnk. 91/G8
Abu Shagara (cape),
Sudan 101/D5
Abu Simbel (ruin),
Egypt 101/B4
Abū Ẓaby (Abu Dhabi) (cap.),
UAE 89/F4
Abuja (cap.), Nga. 103/G4
Abuja (int'l arpt.),
Nga. 103/G4
Abuja Capital Territory,
Nga. 103/G4
Abukuma (riv.), Japan 75/G2
Abukuma (plat.), Japan 75/G2
Abunā, Phil. 79/D4
Abunā (riv.), Braz. 150/E6
Abuye Meda (peak),
Eth. 97/N5
Abuyog, Phil. 79/F5
Åby, Swe. 38/G2
Abydos (ruin), Egypt 101/B3
Acacías, Col. 150/C3
Acacoyagua, Mex. 144/C3
Acadia NP, Me, US 131/G2
Acadian Village,
La, US 129/J5
Acajutiba, Braz. 154/C3
Acámbaro, Mex. 143/E4
Acampo, Ca, US 135/M10
Acandí, Col. 152/B2
Acaponeta (riv.),
Mex. 142/D4
Acaponeta, Mex. 142/D4
Acapulco de Juárez,
Mex. 140/B4
Acarai, Braz. 150/G3
Acaraú (riv.), Braz. 154/B1
Acaraú, Braz. 154/B1
Acari (riv.), Braz. 150/G5
Acari, Braz. 154/C2
Acarí, Peru 156/C4
Acarigua, Ven. 152/D3
Acatlán de Osorio,
Mex. 140/B4
Acatlán de Pérez Figueroa,
Mex. 143/M7
Acatzingo, Mex. 143/M7
Acayucan, Mex. 144/C2
Accha, Peru 156/C4
Acciaroli, It. 46/D2
Accra (cap.), Gha. 103/E5
Accrington,
Eng, UK 35/F4
Aceuchal, Sp. 44/B3
Ach (riv.), Aus. 55/G6
Achacachi, Bol. 150/F7
Achaguas, Ven. 152/D3
Achao, Chile 158/B4
Achar, Uru. 159/K10
Achegour (well),
Niger 96/H4
Achen (pass), Ger. 57/H2
Acheng, China 71/N2
Achères, Fr. 30/J5
Achhnera, India 84/A2
Achicourt, Fr. 52/B3
Achill (isl.), Ire. 30/N10
Achill Head (pt.),
Ire. 30/N9
Achiltibuie, Sc, UK 31/R7
Achinsk, Rus. 64/K4
Achmim (well),
Egypt 91/B4
Achinsk, Rus. 64/K4
Achmim (well),
Mor. 100/D2
Achnasheen, Sc, UK 36/A1
Achoma, Peru 156/C4
A'chralaig (peak),
Sc, UK 36/A2
Achuapa, Nic. 144/E3
Achupallas, Ecu. 156/B1
Acireale, It. 46/D4
Acklins (isl.), Bahm. 119/K7
Acland (mt.),
Austl. 114/C4
Acobamba, Peru 156/C4
Acolla, Peru 156/C3
Acolman, Mex. 143/P6
Acomayo (riv.), Japan 77/J5
Acomayo, Peru 156/C4
Aconcagua (peak),
Arg. 158/C2
Aconchi, Mex. 142/C2
Acopiara, Braz. 154/C2
Açores, Braz. 154/C2
Ádoni, India 82/C4
Adour (riv.), Fr. 42/C5
Adra, India 85/F4
Adra, Sp. 44/D4
Adrano, It. 46/D4
Adrar (phys. reg.),
Mrta. 96/C3
Adrar, Alg. 99/E3
Adrar (pol. reg.),
Mrta. 96/C3
Adrar (reg.),
Mrta. 102/C1
Adrar bou Nasser (peak),
Mor. 98/D2
Adrar Sotuf (mts.),
WSah. 98/B5
Adria, It. 59/F2
Adrian, Mi, US 130/D3
Adriatic (sea), Eur. 27/F4

Adro, It. 58/C1
Aduana del Sásabe,
Mex. 128/E5
Adulis (ruin), Erit. 88/C5
Adur (riv.),
Eng, UK 35/G4
Adwa, Eth. 88/C6
Adwick le Street,
Eng, UK 35/G4
Adycha (riv.), Rus. 65/P3
Adygea Aut. Rep.,
Rus. 63/G4
Adz'va (riv.), Rus. 61/P2
Aegean (sea),
Gre.,Turk 62/C5
Aero (isl.), Den. 38/D4
Aeron (riv.),
Wal, UK 32/B2
Aesch, Swi. 56/D3
Aeschi bei Spiez,
Swi. 56/D4
Aetsä, Fin. 39/K1
Afadjoto (peak),
Gha. 103/F5
'Afak, Iraq 88/E2
Áfándou, Gre. 62/B2
Aff (riv.), Fr. 42/B3
Affoltern im Emmental,
Swi. 56/D3
Affric (lake), Sc, UK 36/A2
Affton, Mo, US 137/G8
Afghanistan (ctry.) 67/F6
Afmadow, Som. 99/P7
Afogados da Ingàzeira,
Braz. 154/C2
Afognak (mtn.),
Ak, US 134/H4
Afognak (isl.),
Ak, US 134/H4
Afolé (phys. reg.),
Mrta. 102/C2
Afonso Bezerra,
Braz. 154/C2
Afonso Cláudio,
Braz. 155/C2
Afragola, It. 46/D2
Afrânio, Braz. 154/B3
Africa (cont.) 93
Afrin (riv.), Turk. 91/E1
'Afrīn, Syria 91/E1
Afrique (peak), Fr. 56/A3
Afsluitdijk (dam),
Neth. 50/C2
Afte (riv.), Ger. 50/E4
Afton, Wy, US 126/F5
Afuidich (lake), WSah. 98/B5
'Afula, Isr. 91/G6
Afyon, Turk. 62/C5
Afyon (prov.), Turk. 62/D5
Afzalgarh, India 84/B1
Agades (int'l arpt.),
Niger 103/G2
Agadez, Niger 103/G2
Agadez (dept.), Niger 99/H5
Agadir, Mor. 98/C2
Agago (riv.),
Ugan. 104/B2
Agamor (well), Mali 103/F2
Agaña (cap.), Guam 116/D3
Agano (riv.), Japan 75/F2
Agassiz Ice Cap (ice field),
NW, Can. 123/T6
Agattu (str.), Ak, US 134/A5
Agattu (isl.), Ak, US 65/T4
Agbabu, Nga. 103/G5
Agboville, C.d'Iv. 102/D5
Ağdam, Azer. 63/H5
Agde, Fr. 42/E5
Agen, Fr. 42/D4
Ageo, Japan 77/D2
Ager (riv.), Aus. 55/G7
Agerbæk, Den. 38/C4
Agerisee (lake), Swi. 57/E3
Agger (riv.), Ger. 51/F2
Aggteleki NP, Slvk. 48/E1
Ághá Járí, Iran 88/F2
Aghagalon, NI, UK 34/B3
Aghagower, Ire. 31/P10
Agiabampo, Mex. 142/C3
Ağın, Turk. 90/D2
Agia Gol (riv.),
China 72/B2
Aginskoye, Rus. 71/K1
Agliana, It. 59/D3
Ağlıköy, Turk. 62/E4
Ağlı (riv.), Fr. 42/E5
Agna, It. 59/E2
Aganderón, Ven. 156/D1
Agnita, Rom. 49/G3
Agno (riv.), It. 59/E1
Agno (int'l arpt.), Swi. 57/E6
Agnone, It. 46/D2
Ago, Japan 77/L7
Agogna (riv.), It. 58/B2
Agordo, It. 43/K3
Agout (riv.), Fr. 42/D4
Agra (peak), Fr. 56/B4
Agra, India 84/B2
Agraciada, Uru. 159/J10
Agri (riv.), It. 42/F4
Agri, India 85/F4
Ağrı (peak), Turk. 63/H5
Ağrı (prov.), Turk. 63/H5
Agri Decumates (hist.)...
Ağrı, Turk. 63/H5
Agrigento, It. 46/C4
Agrinion, Gre. 47/H3
Agrínion, Gre. 62/C5
Agryz, Rus. 61/M4
Agsumal (dry lake),
WSah. 98/B5
Agua Boa, Braz. 154/B5
Agua Branca, Braz. 154/B5
Agua Dulce,
Ca, US 135/M6
Agua Dulce, Mex. 144/C2
Agua Fria (riv.),
Az, US 137/R19
Agua Hedionda (lake),
Ca, US 136/C4
Agua Larga, Ven. 152/D2
Agua Prieta, Mex. 128/E5
Aguachica, Col. 150/C2
Aguadilla, PR 141/M8
Aguadulce, Pan. 152/A2
Aguaí, Braz. 211/G7
Agualva-Cacém,
Port. 45/P10
Aguan (riv.), Hon. 140/D4
Aguanus (riv.),
Can. 131/J1
Aguapeí, Braz. 155/B2
Aguarico (riv.),
Peru 156/C1
Águas Belas, Braz. 154/B5

Aguas Corrientes,
Uru. 159/K11
Águas da Prata,
Braz. 211/G6
Águas de Lindóia,
Braz. 211/G7
Águas Formosas,
Braz. 154/B5
Águas, Serra das (hills),
Braz. 211/H7
Aguasay, Ven. 153/F2
Aguascalientes,
Mex. 142/E4
Aguascalientes (state),
Mex. 140/A3
Aguavermelha, Reprêsa (res.),
Braz. 155/B1
Aguaytía (riv.), Peru 156/C3
Agudos, Braz. 155/B2
Águeda (riv.), Sp. 44/B2
Águeda, Port. 44/A2
Aguéraktem (well),
Mali 98/D5
Agugliano, It. 59/G5
Aguijan (isl.),
NMar. 116/D3
Aguilar, Sp. 44/C4
Aguilar de Campóo,
Sp. 44/C1
Aguilares, Arg. 157/C2
Aguilas, Sp. 44/E4
Aguililla, Mex. 142/E5
Aguja (pt.), Peru 156/A2
Aguja (cape),
SAfr. 106/M11
Agulhas Negras, Pico das
(peak),
Braz. 211/J7
Agung (vol.), Indo. 81/E5
Agusan (riv.), Phil. 79/E6
Agustín Codazzi,
Col. 152/C2
Ahaggar (plat.),
Arg. 96/F3
Ahaggar (mts.),
Alg. 99/G5
Ahal (pol. reg.),
Trkm. 87/C5
Aham, Ger. 55/F5
Ahar, Iran 63/H5
Ahaus, Ger. 50/E4
Ahfir, Mor. 100/C2
Ahirli, Turk. 90/C2
Ahlat, Turk. 90/D2
Ahlen, Ger. 51/F5
Ahlerstedt, Ger. 51/G2
Ahmadābād, India 89/K4
Ahmadnagar, Pak. 86/A5
Ahmadpur East, Pak. 86/A4
Ahmadpur Siāl, Pak. 86/A4
Ahmar, 'Erg el (des.),
Mali 99/P6
Ahmed (well), WSah. 98/B5
Ahmeyine (well),
Mrta. 98/B5
Ahoghill, NI, UK 34/B2
Ahome, Mex. 142/C3
Ahoskie, NC, US 133/L2
Ahraurá, India 84/D3
Ahrensburg, Ger. 51/H1
Ahse (riv.), Ger. 51/F5
Ahuacatitlán, Mex. 143/K8
Ahuachapán, ESal. 144/D3
Ahualulco, Mex. 143/E4
Ahuimanu, Hi, US 124/W13
Ahumada, Mex. 128/F5
Ahun, Fr. 42/E3
Ahus, Swe. 38/F4
Ahväz, Iran 88/E2
Aiea, Hi, US 124/W13
Aiffres, Fr. 42/C3
Aigen im Mühlkreis,
Aus. 55/G5
Aigle, Pic de l' (peak),
Fr. 56/B4
Aigle, Swi. 56/C4
Aignan, Fr. 42/C5
Aigoual (peak), Fr. 42/E4
Aiguá, Uru. 159/G2
Aigüestortes y Lago de San
Mauricio, PN de, Sp. 45/F1
Aiguillón, Cap de l' (cape),
Fr. 42/C3
Aiguillon, Fr. 42/D4
Aigurande, Fr. 42/E3
Aikawa, Japan 75/F1
Aiken, SC, US 133/H3
Ailigandí, Pan. 152/B2
Ailinglapalap (isl.),
Mrsh. 116/H4
Aillevillers-et-Lyaumont,
Fr. 56/C2
Ailly-sur-Noye, Fr. 52/B4
Ailsa Craig (isl.),
Sc, UK 36/A6
Ailuk (isl.), Mrsh. 116/G3
Aimen (pass), China 72/C5
Aimogasta, Arg. 157/C2
Aimorés, Braz. 155/D1
Aimorés, Serra dos (mts.),
Braz. 155/D1
'Aïn Beida, Alg. 100/K7
'Aïn Beniau, Alg. 100/G4
'Aïn Bessem, Alg. 100/G4
Aïn Chok-Hay Mohammadia
(prov.),
Mor. 100/A2
Aïn Defla, Alg. 100/F4
Aïn Defla (prov.),
Alg. 100/F4
Aïn el Aouda, Mor. 100/A3
'Aïn el Bey (int'l arpt.),
Alg. 100/K6
'Aïn el Hammam,
Alg. 100/H4
'Aïn el Turk, Alg. 100/D2

'Aïn Fakroun, Alg. 100/K6
'Aïn M'lila, Alg. 100/K6
'Aïn Oulmene, Alg. 100/H5
'Aïn Oussersa,
Alg. 100/G5
'Aïn Sefra, Alg. 99/E2
Aïn Taoujdat,
Mor. 100/B3
'Aïn Taya, Alg. 100/G4
'Aïn Temouchent,
Alg. 100/D2
'Aïn Touta, Alg. 100/H5
Aina Haina, Hi, US 124/W13
Ainos (peak), Gre. 47/G3
Ainos NP, Gre. 47/G3
Aipe, Col. 152/C4
Air (plat.), Niger 96/G4
Air Force (riv.),
NW, Can. 123/J2
Airaines, Fr. 52/A4
Airdrie, Ab, Can. 126/E3
Airdrie, Sc, UK 36/C5
Aire (riv.), Fr. 42/F2
Aire, Canal d' (canal),
Fr. 52/B2
Aire-sur-la-Lys, Fr. 52/B2
Aire-sur-l'Adour, Fr. 42/C5
Airolo, Swi. 57/E4
Airuno, It. 58/C1
Airvault, Fr. 42/C3
Aisch (riv.), Ger. 43/J2
Aisén del General Carlos
Ibáñez del Campo (pol. reg.),
Chile 158/B5
Aisne (riv.), Fr. 40/B4
Aïssa (peak), Alg. 99/E2
Aist (riv.), Aus. 55/H6
Aitape, PNG 116/D5
Aitö, Japan 77/K5
Aitolikón, Gre. 47/G3
Aitrach, Ger. 57/G2
Aitutaki Atoll (isl.),
Cook Is. 117/J6
Aiud, Rom. 49/F2
Aiuruoca, Braz. 211/J6
Aiuruoca (riv.),
Braz. 211/J6
Aix-en-Provence, Fr. 42/F5
Aiya, Gre. 47/H4
Aiyinion, Gre. 47/H2
Aizawl, India 83/F3
Aizu-Wakamatsu,
Japan 75/F2
Ajaigarh, India 84/C3
Ajalpan, Mex. 143/M8
Ajaria Aut. Rep., Geo. 63/G4
Ajax, On, Can. 131/R8
Ajdābiyā, Libya 97/L1
Ajdovščina, Slov. 43/K4
Ajigasawa, Japan 76/B3
'Ajjah, WBnk. 91/G7
Ajka, Hun. 48/C2
Ajlūn, Jor. 91/G7
Ajmer, India 84/B2
Ajo, Az, US 128/D4
Ajo (cape), Sp. 44/D1
Ajuchitlán del Progreso,
Mex. 140/A4
Ajusco (vol.), Mex. 143/Q10
Aka (riv.), Japan 75/F1
Akabira, Japan 76/C2
Akaishi-dake (peak),
Japan 75/F3
Akaltara, India 84/D4
Akan NP, Japan 76/D2
Akarp, Swe. 38/E4
Akarsu, Turk. 62/F5
Akashi, Japan 76/H3
Akashi (str.), Japan 77/G6
Akbarpur, India 84/B2
Akbarpur, India 84/D2
Akbaytal (pass), Taj. 87/F5
Akbou, Alg. 100/H4
Akçakale, Turk. 90/D2
Akçakoca, Turk. 49/J5
Akçaova, Turk. 62/C5
Akdağmadeni, Turk. 62/E5
Akechi, Japan 77/M5
Akeno, Japan 77/E1
Akeno, Japan 77/M5
Akershus (co.), Nor. 37/D3
Akersberga, Swe. 38/H2
Akershus, Swe. 38/H2
Aketi, D.R. Congo 97/K7
Akhalts'ikhe, Geo. 63/G4
Akharnaí, Gre. 47/N8
Akhelóos (riv.), Gre. 47/G3
Akhiok, Ak, US 134/H4
Akhisar, Turk. 62/C5
Akhmīm, Egypt 101/B3
Akhtopol, Bul. 49/H4
Akhtubinsk, Rus. 63/H2
Aki, Japan 74/C4
Akiachak, Ak, US 134/F3
Akimiski (isl.),
Can. 123/H3
Akimovka, Ukr. 63/F3
Akincı (pt.), Turk. 91/D1
Akita, Japan 75/G3
Akita (pref.), Japan 76/B4
Akiyama, Japan 77/C2
Akjoujt, Mrta. 102/B2
Akka, Mor. 98/C3
Akkaraipattu, SrL. 82/D6
Akkerhaugen, Nor. 38/C2
Akkeshi, Japan 76/D2
Akkō, Isr. 91/D3
Aklavik, NW, Can. 122/C2
Akō, Japan 74/D3
Akora, Pak. 86/B2
Ak'ordat, Erit. 88/C5
Akören, Turk. 90/C2

Akosombo (dam),
Gha. 103/F5
Akpatok (isl.),
Qu, Can. 123/K2
Akpınar, Turk. 49/J5
Akqi, China 87/G4
Akranes, Ice. 37/M7
Akrathos (cape), Gre. 47/J2
Åkrehamn, Nor. 37/B3
Akritas (cape), Gre. 47/G4
Akron, Co, US 129/G2
Akron, Oh, US 130/D3
Akron, Pa, US 138/B3
Aksai Chin (reg.),
China,Ind 70/C4
Aksaray, Turk. 90/C2
Aksaray (prov.), Turk. 90/C2
Aksay Kazakzu Zizhixian,
China 70/F4
Akşehir, Turk. 90/B2
Akşehir Lake (lake),
Turk. 90/B2
Akseki, Turk. 91/B1
Aksoran (peak), Kaz. 70/D3
Aksu, China 70/D3
Aksu (riv.), Turk. 91/B1
Aksu, Turk. 91/B1
Aksum, Eth. 88/C6
Aktepe, Turk. 91/E1
Akto, China 87/F4
Akune, Japan 74/B4
Akure, Nga. 103/G5
Akureyri, Ice. 37/N6
Akuse, Gha. 103/F5
Akutan (isl.),
Ak, US 134/E5
Akutan, Ak, US 134/E5
Akutan Pass (chan.),
Ak, US 134/E5
Akwa Ibom (state),
Nga. 103/G5
Akyab (Sittwe), Myan. 82/F4
Akyazı, Turk. 49/K5
Al 'āl, Jor. 91/D4
Al, Nor. 38/C1
Al 'Amārah, Iraq 88/E2
Al Anbār (gov.), Iraq 90/E3
Al 'Arīsh, Egypt 91/A4
Al 'Ayn, UAE 89/F4
Al 'Azīzīyah, Libya 96/H1
Al 'Azīzīyah,
Iraq 90/F3
Al Bāb, Syria 91/E1
Al Badrashayn,
Egypt 91/B5
Al Baḥr Al Aḥmar (gov.),
Egypt 101/C3
Al Bājūr, Egypt 91/B4
Al Balqā' (gov.),
Jor. 91/D4
Al Balyanā, Egypt 101/B3
Al Başrah, Iraq 88/E2
Al Batrūn, Leb. 91/D3
Al Baydā, Libya 97/K1
Al Biqā' (valley), Leb. 91/D3
Al Birah, WBnk. 91/D3
Al Birkah, Libya 99/H4
Al Buḥayrah (gov.),
Egypt 101/B3
Al Fāshir, Sudan 97/L5
Al Fathah, Iraq 90/E3
Al Fāw, Iraq 88/E3
Al Fayyūm (gov.),
Egypt 101/B3
Al Fayyūm, Egypt 91/B5
Al Ghurdaqah,
Egypt 101/C3
Al Hadīthah, Iraq 90/E3
Al Hadr, Iraq 90/E3
Al Haffah, Syria 91/E2
Al Hajar ash Sharqī (mts.),
Oman 89/G4
Al Hamādah al Ḥamrā (upland),
Libya 96/H2
Al Hammām, Egypt 91/A4
Al Hasakah, Syria 90/E2
Al Hasakah (prov.),
Syria 90/E2
Al Ḥawāmidīyah,
Egypt 91/B5
Al Hayy, Iraq 88/E2
Al Ḥillah, Iraq 90/E3
Al Hindīyah, Iraq 90/E3
Al Hirmil, Leb. 91/E2
Al Hoceima,
Mor. 100/C2
Al Hoceima, Mor. 100/C2
Al Hufūf, SAr. 88/E3
Al Ḥusayn (riv.), Syria 91/E2
Al Iskandarīyah, Iraq 90/E3
Al Iskandarīyah (int'l arpt.),
Egypt 91/A4
Al Iskandarīyah (gov.),
Egypt 91/A4
Al Ismā'īlīyah,
Egypt 91/C4
Al Ismā'īlīyah (gov.),
Egypt 91/C4
Al Jabal Akdar (mts.),
Oman 89/G4
Al Jaghbūb, Libya 97/L2
Al Jamm, Tun. 46/B5
Al Janub (gov.), Leb. 91/D3
Al Jifārah (plain),
Libya 99/H2
Al Jīzah, Egypt 91/B5
Al Junaynah, Sudan 97/K5
Al Kāf (gov.), Tun. 100/L6
Al Kāf, Tun. 100/L6
Al Karak (gov.), Jor. 91/D4
Al Karak, Jor. 91/D4
Al Khābūrah, Oman 89/G4
Al Khalīl (Hebron),
WBnk. 91/D4
Al Khāliṣ, Iraq 90/F3
Al Khānkah, Egypt 91/B4
Al Khārijah, Egypt 101/B3
Al Khartūm Baḥrī (Khartoum
North), Sudan 97/M4
Al Khubar, SAr. 88/E3
Al Khums, Libya 96/H1
Al Kiswah, Syria 91/E3
Al Kūfah, Iraq 90/E3
Al Kufrah, Libya 97/K3
Al Lādhiqīyah (Latakia),
Syria 91/D2
Al Lādhiqīyah (prov.),
Syria 91/D2
Al Madīnah, SAr. 88/D4

Gha. 103/F5
Al Madīnah al Fikrīyah,
Egypt 88/B3
Al Mafraq (gov.),
Jor. 91/E3
Al Mafraq, Jor. 91/E3
Al Maghrib (reg.),
Mor. 96/E1
Al Maḥallah al Kubrá,
Egypt 91/B4
Al Maḥdīyah, Tun. 46/B5
Al Mahdīyah (prov.),
Tun. 100/M7
Al Maḥmūdīyah,
Egypt 91/B4
Al Mālikīyah, Syria 90/E2
Al Mansūrah, Egypt 91/B4
Al Manzilah, Egypt 91/B4
Al Marāghah,
Egypt 101/B3
Al Marj, Libya 97/K1
Al Marsá, Tun. 46/B4
Al Maṭarīyah, Egypt 91/C4
Al Mawṣil (Mosul),
Iraq 90/E2
Al Mayādin, Syria 90/E2
Al Mazra'ah, Jor. 91/D4
Al Minyā, Egypt 101/B2
Al Miqdādīyah, Iraq 90/F3
Al Mubarraz, SAr. 88/E3
Al Mudawwarah, Jor. 91/D5
Al Mukallā, Yem. 88/E6
Al Muknīn, Tun. 46/B5
Al Munastīr, Tun. 46/B5
Al Munastīr (prov.),
Tun. 46/B5
Al Murnāqīyah, Tun. 46/A5
Al Musayyib, Iraq 90/F3
Al Muthanná (gov.),
Iraq 90/F4
Al Qābil, Oman 89/G4
Al Qadārif, Sudan 88/C6
Al Qadīsīyah (gov.),
Iraq 90/F3
Al Qāhirah (gov.),
Egypt 91/B5
Al Qāhirah (Cairo) (cap.),
Egypt 91/B5
Al Qā'im, Iraq 90/E3
Al Qāmishlī, Syria 90/E2
Al Qanāṭir al Khayrīyah,
Egypt 91/B4
Al Qanṭarah, Egypt 91/C4
Al Qaṣr, Jor. 91/D4
Al Qaṭrayn (gov.),
Tun. 100/L7
Al Qaṣrayn, Tun. 100/L7
Al Qaṭṭārah (prov.),
Syria 91/D3
Al Qunayṭirah, Syria 91/D3
Al Qurnah, Iraq 88/E2
Al Quṣayr, Syria 91/E3
Al Quṭayfah, Syria 91/E3
Al Qurayyāt, Jor. 91/D4
Al Ubayyid, Sudan 97/M5
Al 'Uwaynāt (peak),
Sudan 97/L3
Al Wādī al Jadīd (gov.),
Egypt 101/B3
Al Wāḥāt al Baḥrīyah (oasis),
Egypt 101/B2
Al Wāḥāt al Khārijah (oasis),
Egypt 101/B3
Al Wāsiṭah, Egypt 101/B3
Al Yāmūn, WBnk. 91/G7
Ala (riv.), It. 46/B1
Ala, It. 59/E1
Ala,Ga, US 125/J5
Alabama (riv.), US 125/J5
Alabama (state), US 125/J5
Alabaster, Al, US 133/G3
Alaca, Turk. 62/E5
Alacalı, Turk. 49/J5
Alaçam, Turk. 62/E4
Alaçatı, Turk. 47/J3
Alaçam, Turk. 62/E4
Alacrán (reef), Mex. 144/D1
Alacranes (res.),
Cuba 145/F1
Aladağ, Turk. 91/D1
Alaejos, Sp. 44/C2
Alagir, Rus. 63/H4
Alagna Valsesia, It. 58/A1
Alagoa Grande,
Braz. 154/D2
Alagoas (state),
Braz. 154/C3
Alagoinhas, Braz. 154/C2
Alagón, Sp. 45/E2
Alagón (riv.), Sp. 44/B2
Alajärvi, Fin. 60/D3
Alajuela, CR 145/E4
Alakanak, Ak, US 134/F3
Alakol' (lake), Kaz. 70/D2
Alalaú (riv.), Braz. 153/F5
Alamagan (isl.),
NMar. 116/D2
Alameda, Ca, US 135/K11
Alaminos, Phil. 79/C4
Alamo (lake), Az, US 128/D4
Alamo, Mex. 143/M4
Alamo, Mex. 135/K11
Alamo Heights,
Tx, US 137/U21
Alamogordo, NM, US 132/B3
Alamor, Ecu. 156/A2
Alamos, Mex. 142/C3
Åland (isl.), Fin. 37/G3
Åland (riv.), Ger. 40/F1
Alanya, Turk. 91/C1
Alaotra (lake), Madg. 107/J7
Alapaha (riv.), US 133/H4
Alapli, Turk. 49/K4
Alarcón, Embalse de
(res.), Sp. 44/D3
Alaşehir, Turk. 62/C5
Alaska (gulf), US 134/D4
Alaska (range),
Ak, US 134/D3
Alaska (state), US 134/D3
Alaska (pen.), Ak, US 134/E4
Alaska (gulf of (gulf),
US
Alaska, Gulf of (gulf),
Ak, US 134/C4
Alaska Maritime NWR,
Ak, US 134/D3
Alaska Peninsula NWR,
US 134/G4

Alassio, It. 58/B5
Alatyr', Rus. 61/K5
Alaverdi, Arm. 63/H4
Alavus, Fin. 60/D3
Alaw, Llyn (lake),
Wal, UK 34/D5
Alayor, Sp. 44/G3
Alayskiy (mts.), Kyr. 87/F5
Alazeya (riv.), Rus. 65/Q3
Alba, It. 43/H4
Alba (prov.), Rom. 49/F2
Alba de Tormes, Sp. 44/C2
Alba Fucens (ruin), It. 46/C1
Alba Iulia, Rom. 49/F2
Albacete, Sp. 44/E3
Albaida, Sp. 45/E3
Albairate, It. 58/B2
Albal, Sp. 45/E3
Ålbæk, Den. 38/D3
Albalate del Arzobispo,
Sp. 45/E2
Alban, Fr. 42/E5
Albanel (lake), Can. 130/F1
Albania (ctry.) 27/F4
Albania, Or, US 126/C4
Albany, Ky, US 130/C4
Albany (cap.),
NY, US 130/F3
Albany, Ga, US 133/G4
Albany, Mo, US 137/E5
Albany, Austl. 112/C5
Albany (riv.), On, Can. 122/H3
Albany, Ca, US 135/K11
Albany County (int'l arpt.),
NY, US 130/F3
Albaredo d'Adige, It. 59/E2
Albarine (riv.), Fr. 56/B5
Albarracín, Sp. 45/E2
Albatross (bay),
Nga. 109/D2
Albatross Rock (pt.),
Namb. 106/A2
Albbruck, Ger. 56/E2
Albemarle (sound),
NC, US 133/J2
Albemarle, NC, US 133/H3
Albemarle (isl.), Ecu. 156/E6
Alben, It. 43/H4
Albenga, It. 58/B4
Albergaria-a-Velha,
Port. 44/A2
Alberhill, Ca, US 136/C3
Alberndorf in der Riedmark,
Aus. 55/H6
Alberschwende, Aus. 57/F3
Albersdorf, Ger. 38/C4
Albersweiler, Ger. 54/B4
Albert (lake),
Austl. 115/A2
Albert (lake),
Ugan.,D.R. 93/E4
Albert (riv.), Austl. 114/B2
Albert Kanaal (riv.),
Belg. 53/E2
Albert Nile (riv.),
Ugan. 97/M7
Alberta (prov.), Can. 122/E3
Alberti, Arg. 158/E2
Albertirsa, Hun. 48/D2
Alberto de Agostini, PN,
Chile 157/B7
Alberton, SAfr. 106/C14
Albertshofen, Ger. 54/D3
Albertville, Al, US 133/G3
Albertville, Fr. 43/G4
Albeuve, Swi. 56/D4
Albi, It. 42/E5
Albia, Ia, US 137/F5
Albina (prov.), Can. 122/E3
Albina, Sur. 151/H2
Albinea, It. 58/D3
Albino, It. 58/C1
Albion, Mi, US 130/C3
Albisola Marina, It. 58/B4
Albisola Superiore, It. 58/B4
Albla, Fin. 60/D3
Albox, Sp. 44/E4
Alborg (bay), Den. 38/D3
Albox, Sp. 44/D4
Albright-Knox Art Gallery,
NY, US 131/S10
Albristhorn (peak),
Swi. 56/D5
Albufeira, Port. 44/A4
Albula (riv.), Swi. 43/H3
Albuñol, Sp. 44/D4
Albuquerque (int'l arpt.),
NM, US 128/F4
Albuquerque,
NM, US 132/B3
Albuquerque, Cayos de (isls.),
Col. 145/F3
Alburquerque, Sp. 44/B3
Alburtis, Pa, US 138/C3
Albury, Austl. 115/C3
Alby-sur-Chéran, Fr. 56/B5
Alca, Peru 156/C4
Alcabideche, Port. 45/P10
Alcácer do Sal, Port. 44/A3
Alcalá de Chivert,
Sp. 45/F2
Alcalá de Guadaira,
Sp. 44/C4
Alcalá de Henares, Sp. 45/N9
Alcalá de los Gazules,
Sp. 44/C4
Alcalá la Real, Sp. 44/D4
Alcamo, It. 46/C4
Alcanar, Sp. 45/F2
Alcañices, Sp. 44/B2
Alcântara, Sp. 44/B3
Alcántara, Embalse de
(res.), Sp. 44/B3
Alcantarilla, Sp. 44/E4
Alcaraz, Sp. 44/D3
Alcaraz, Sierra de
(range), Sp. 44/D3
Alcatraz (isl.),
Ca, US 135/K11
Alcázar de San Juan,
Sp. 44/D3
Alcira, Sp. 45/E3

Alcir – Anton

Alcira, Arg. 158/D2
Alçıtepe, Turk. 47/K2
Alcoa, Tn, US 133/H3
Alcobaça, Braz. 154/C5
Alcobaça, Port. 44/A3
Alcobendas, Sp. 45/N8
Alcochete, Port. 45/Q10
Alcora, Sp. 45/E2
Alcorcón, Sp. 45/N9
Alcorisa, Sp. 45/E3
Alcoutim, Port. 44/B4
Alcoy, Sp. 45/E3
Alcúdia, Sp. 45/G5
Aldama, Mex. 132/B4
Aldama, Mex. 143/F4
Aldan (plat.), Rus. 65/N4
Aldan, Rus. 65/N4
Aldan (riv.), Rus. 67/N3
Alde (riv.), Eng, UK 33/H2
Aldeburgh, Eng, UK 33/H2
Aldeia Nova de São Bento, Port. 44/B4
Alden, Il, US 135/N15
Aldenhoven, Ger. 53/F2
Aldeno, It. 57/H6
Aldergrove (int'l arpt.), NI, UK 34/B2
Aldergrove, NI, UK 34/B2
Alderley Edge, Eng, UK 35/F5
Alderney (isl.), ChI, UK 42/B2
Aldershot, Eng, UK 33/F4
Alderwood Manor-Bothell North, Wa, US 135/C2
Aldine, Tx, US 129/J5
Aldingen, Ger. 57/E1
Aldred (lake), Pa, US 138/B4
Aldridge, Eng, UK 33/E1
Ale Water (riv.), Sc, UK 36/D6
Aleg, Mrta. 102/B2
Alegre, Braz. 155/D2
Alegrete, Braz. 157/E2
Alejandro Gallinal, Uru. 159/G2
Alejandro Roca, Arg. 158/E2
Alejandro Selkirk (isl.), Chile 147/A6
Alejo Ledesma, Arg. 158/E2
Aleknagik, Ak, US 134/G4
Aleksandrov, Rus. 60/H4
Aleksandrovac, Yugo. 48/E4
Aleksandrovsk, Rus. 61/N4
Aleksandrów Kujawski, Pol. 41/K2
Aleksandrów Łódzki, Pol. 41/K3
Alekseyevka, Kaz. 87/F2
Alekseyevka, Kaz. 87/E2
Alekseyevka, Rus. 62/F2
Aleksin, Rus. 60/H5
Aleksinac, Yugo. 48/E4
Além Paraíba, Braz. 211/L6
Alençon, Fr. 42/D2
Alenquer, Braz. 151/H4
Alenuihaha (chan.), US 124/T10
Alerce Andino, PN, Chile 158/B4
Aléria, Fr. 46/A1
Alert (pt.), NW, Can. 123/S6
Aleşd, Rom. 48/F2
Alessandria (prov.), It. 58/B3
Alessandria, It. 58/B3
Ålestrup, Den. 38/C3
Ålesund, Nor. 37/C3
Aletschhorn (peak), Swi. 56/D5
Aleutian (range), Ak, US 134/G4
Aleutian (isls.), Ak, US 119/A4
Alexander (mt.), Austl. 112/B2
Alexander (arch.), Ak, US 119/D4
Alexander (isl.), Ant. 160/V
Alexander Bay, SAfr. 106/B3
Alexander City, Al, US 133/G3
Alexander Nevsky Abbey, Rus. 61/T7
Alexandra, NZ 117/R12
Alexandria, La, US 129/J5
Alexandria, Braz. 154/C2
Alexandria, Mn, US 127/K4
Alexandria, SAfr. 106/D4
Alexándria, Gre. 47/H2
Alexandria, Rom. 49/G4
Alexandria (int'l arpt.), Egypt 91/A4
Alexandria, Va, US 138/A6
Alexandria, Sc, UK 36/B5
Alexandrina (lake), Austl. 109/C4
Alexandroúpolis, Gre. 47/J2
Alexis Creek, BC, Can. 126/C2
Alfaro, Sp. 44/E1
Alfatar, Bul. 49/H4
Alfbach (riv.), Ger. 53/F3
Alfeld, Ger. 51/G5
Alfenas, Braz. 211/H6
Alfiós (riv.), Gre. 47/G4
Alfonsine, It. 59/F3
Alfonso Bonilla Aragón (int'l arpt.), Col. 152/B4
Alfred NP, Austl. 115/D3
Alfreton, Eng, UK 35/G5
Alfter, Ger. 53/E2
Alga, Kaz. 63/L2
Ålgård, Nor. 38/B1
Algarrobo, Chile 158/N8
Algarve (reg.), Port. 44/A4
Algeciras, Col. 152/C4
Algemesí, Sp. 45/E3
Alger (wil.), Alg. 100/G4
Algeria (ctry.) 93/B2
Algermissen, Ger. 51/G4
Algete, Sp. 45/N8
Alghero, It. 46/A2

Algiers (El Djezair) (cap.), Alg. 100/G4
Algoa (bay), SAfr. 106/D4
Algodón (riv.), Peru 150/D4
Algodonales, Sp. 44/C4
Algoma, Wi, US 127/M4
Algona, Wa, US 135/C4
Algonac, Mi, US 135/G6
Algonquin, Il, US 135/P14
Algorta, Uru. 159/K10
Algorta (Lagundo), It. 57/H4
Alhama de Granada, Sp. 44/D4
Alhama de Murcia, Sp. 44/E4
Alhambra, Ca, US 136/F7
Alhandra, Braz. 154/D2
Alhandra, Port. 45/P10
Alhaurín el Grande, Sp. 44/C4
'Alī al Gharbī, Iraq 88/E2
'Alī ash Sharqī, Iraq 88/E2
Ali Bayramlı, Azer. 63/J5
Alia, Sp. 44/C3
Alia, It. 46/C4
Aliağa, Turk. 62/C5
Aliákmon (riv.), Gre. 47/G2
Aliákmonos (lake), Gre. 47/G2
Aliártos, Gre. 47/H3
Alicudi (isl.), It. 46/D3
Alicurá (res.), Arg. 158/C4
Alife, It. 46/D2
Alíganj, India 84/B2
Alijó, Port. 44/B2
Alima (riv.), Congo 96/J8
Alpe di Poti (peak), It. 59/E6
Alīgarh, Afg. 86/A2
Aligsås, Swe. 38/E3
Alīpur, Pak. 86/B2
Alīpur Duār, India 85/G2
Alīrājpur, India 89/K4
Alisos (riv.), Mex. 128/E5
Alistráti, Gre. 47/H2
Alivérion, Gre. 47/H3
Aliwal North, SAfr. 106/D3
Aljezur, Port. 44/A4
Aljustrel, Port. 44/A4
Alken, Belg. 53/E2
Alkmaar, Neth. 50/B3
Alkoum (well), Alg. 99/H4
Alkoven, Aus. 55/H6
Allada, Ben. 103/F5
Allahābād, India 84/C3
Allakaket, Ak, US 134/H2
Allaman, Swi. 56/C5
Allan (hills), Can. 127/G3
Allan, Sc, UK 127/G3
Alland, Aus. 49/N7
Allanmyo, Myan. 83/G4
Allanridge, SAfr. 106/D2
Allanson, Austl. 112/C5
Allatoona (lake), Ga, US 140/E1
Allauch, Fr. 45/D5
Allegan, Mi, US 135/E6
Allegheny (plat.), US 130/E3
Allegheny (riv.), US 138/B3
Allegheny (mts.), US 125/K4
Allen (riv.), Eng, UK 32/B5
Allen, Arg. 158/C3
Allen Park, Mi, US 135/F7
Allendale, SC, US 133/H3
Allendale, NJ, US 139/J7
Allende, Mex. 132/C4
Allende, Mex. 143/E3
Allendorf, Ger. 51/F6
Allendorf, Ger. 57/F2
Allenspark, Co, US 137/A2
Allentown, Pa, US 138/C2
Allentsteig, Aus. 55/J6
Allenwood, Pa, US 138/B1
Aller (riv.), Ger. 51/H3
Allerkanal (canal), Ger. 51/H4
Allersberg, Ger. 57/F3
Allershausen, Ger. 55/E6
Allgäu Alps (range), Aus.,Ger. 57/E6
Alliance, Ne, US 127/G5
Alliance, Oh, US 130/D3
Allier (riv.), Fr. 42/E3
Allied War Cemetery, Myan. 78/B2
Allier (riv.), Fr. 42/E3
Alligator (lake), Fl, US 137/Q16
Allingåbro, Den. 38/D3
Allinges, Fr. 56/C6
Alloa, Sc, UK 36/C4
Alloa (vol.), Ecu. 152/B5
Allora, Austl. 114/C5
Allos, Fr. 43/G4
Alloway, NJ, US 138/C4
Allschwil, Swi. 56/D2
Alm (riv.), Aus. 55/G7
Alma, Mi, US 130/C3
Alma, Qu, Can. 131/G1
Almacelles, Sp. 45/F2
Almada, Port. 45/P10
Almadén, Sp. 44/C3
Almafuerte, Arg. 158/D2
Almagro, Sp. 44/D3
Almanor (lake), Ca, US 128/B3
Almansa, Sp. 45/E3
Almansor, Pico de (peak), Sp. 44/C2
Almanzora (riv.), Sp. 44/D4
Almas (riv.), Braz. 151/J6
Almas, Pico das (peak), Braz. 154/D4
Almaty (int'l arpt.), Kaz. 87/G2
Almaty, Kaz. 87/G2
Almazán, Sp. 44/D2
Almazora, Sp. 45/E3
Almeida, Port. 44/B2

Almeirim, Braz. 151/H4
Almelo, Neth. 50/D4
Almenara, Braz. 154/D3
Almenara (peak), Sp. 44/D3
Almendra, Embalse de (res.), Sp. 44/B2
Almendralejo, Sp. 44/B3
Almere, Neth. 50/C4
Almería, Sp. 44/D4
Almería, Golfo de (gulf), Sp. 44/D4
Al'met'yevsk, Rus. 61/M5
Almhult, Swe. 38/F3
Almina (pt.), Sp. 100/B2
Almirós, Gre. 47/G3
Almirou (gulf), Gre. 47/J5
Almodóvar, Port. 44/A4
Almodóvar del Campo, Sp. 44/C3
Almodóvar del Río, Sp. 44/C4
Almoharín, Sp. 44/B3
Almond (riv.), Sc, UK 36/C4
Almont (riv.), Fr. 30/L6
Almonte, On, Can. 130/E2
Almonte, Sp. 44/B4
Almora, India 84/B1
Almoradí, Sp. 45/E3
Almorox, Sp. 44/C2
Almte. Montt (gulf), Chile 159/B7
Almudévar, Sp. 45/E1
Almuñécar, Sp. 44/D4
Almus, Turk. 62/F4
Alness, Sc, UK 36/B1
Alness (riv.), Sc, UK 36/B1
Alnwick, Eng, UK 36/E6
Alofi (isl.), Wall. 116/H6
Alofi, NZ 117/X16
Along, India 85/G2
Alónnisos (isl.), Gre. 47/H3
Alor (isls.), Indo. 81/F5
Alor (isl.), Indo. 116/B5
Alor Setar, Malay. 83/H6
Álora, Sp. 44/C4
Alotau, PNG 116/E6
Aloysius (mt.), Austl. 113/F3
Alpachiri, Arg. 158/C3
Alpe di Poti (peak), It. 59/E6
Alpedrete, Sp. 45/M8
Alpen, Ger. 50/D5
Alpena, Mi, US 130/D2
Alpercatas (riv.), Braz. 151/J5
Alpercatas, Serra das (mts.), Braz. 151/J5
Alperschällihorn (peak), Swi. 57/F4
Alpes de Provence (range), Fr. 43/G5
Alpha, Austl. 114/B3
Alpha, NJ, US 138/C2
Alphen aan de Rijn, Neth. 50/B4
Alpi Apuane (range), It. 43/J4
Alpi Dolomitiche (range), It. 43/J4
Alpi Orobie (range) It. 43/J3
Alpiarça, Port. 44/A3
Alpine, Wy, US 137/A3
Alpine, Ut, US 137/K13
Alpine, Ca, US 136/F7
Alpirsbach, Ger. 57/E1
Alpnach, Swi. 57/E4
Alps (mts.), Eur. 27/E4
Alqosh, Iraq 88/E1
Als (isl.), Den. 40/E1
Alsace (pol. reg.), Fr. 40/D5
Alsager, Eng, UK 35/F5
Alsask, Sk, Can. 126/F3
Alsasua, Sp. 44/D1
Alsdorf, Ger. 53/F2
Alsenz (riv.), Ger. 53/G4
Alsenz, Ger. 53/G4
Alsfeld, Ger. 43/H1
Alsip, Il, US 135/Q16
Alstahaug, Nor. 37/D2
Alsten, Al, Sc, UK 36/C3
Alston, Eng, UK 33/E5
Alstonville, Austl. 115/E1
Alta (riv.), Ger. 43/K2
Alta, Ut, US 137/K13
Alta, Nor. 37/G1
Alta Floresta, Braz. 151/G6
Alta Gracia, Arg. 157/D3
Altach, Aus. 57/F3
Altadena, Ca, US 136/F7
Altagracia, Nic. 144/E4
Altai (mts.), Asia 70/E2
Altamaha (riv.), Ga, US 140/E1
Altamira, Braz. 151/H4
Altamira, Mex. 144/A2
Altamira do Maranhão, Braz. 154/A2
Altamont Springs, Fl, US 133/H4
Altamura, It. 46/F2
Altamura, Port. 45/P10
Altar, Mex. 128/E5
Altar (riv.), Ecu. 152/B5
Altar de los Sacrificios (ruin), Guat. 144/D2
Altar, Desierto de (des.), Mex. 128/D5
Altare, It. 58/B4
Altavilla Vicentina, It. 59/E1
Altay, Mong. 70/E2
Altay, Mong. 70/G2
Altay, China 70/G2
Altay Kray, Rus. 87/G2
Altdorf, Swi. 57/E4
Altdorf bei Nürnberg, Ger. 55/E4
Altea, Sp. 45/E3
Altedo, It. 59/E3
Altena, Ger. 51/E6
Altenau, Ger. 51/H5
Altenbeken, Ger. 51/F5
Altenberg bei Linz, Aus. 55/H6
Altenburg, Ger. 52/N6
Altenfelden, Aus. 55/G6
Altenglan, Ger. 53/G4
Altengottern, Ger. 51/H6
Altenkirchen, Ger. 51/F6
Altenmünster, Ger. 54/D6

Altenstadt, Ger. 57/G1
Altenstadt, Ger. 54/B2
Altensteig, Ger. 54/B5
Altentreptow, Ger. 38/E5
Alter Rhein (riv.), Ger. 50/D5
Altes Land (phys. reg.), Ger. 51/G1
Altheim, Aus. 55/G6
Althengstett, Ger. 54/B5
Althofen, Aus. 43/L3
Althütte, Ger. 54/C5
Altindere NP, Turk. 46/D1
Altınözü, Turk. 91/E1
Altıntaş, Turk. 62/D5
Altınyala, Turk. 91/B1
Altınyayla, Turk. 91/A1
Altiplano (plat.), Bol.,Peru 147/C4
Altkirch, Fr. 56/D2
Altlandsberg, Ger. 40/Q6
Altmark (phys. reg.), Ger. 40/F2
Altmühl (riv.), Ger. 43/J2
Altmünster, Aus. 55/G7
Altnaharra, Sc, UK 31/R7
Alto (peak), Braz. 154/B4
Alto (peak), It. 57/G4
Alto Araguaia, Braz. 151/H7
Alto de Tamar (peak), Col. 152/C3
Alto Garças, Braz. 151/H7
Alto Lucero, Mex. 143/N7
Alto Parnaíba, Braz. 154/A3
Alto Purús (riv.), Peru 150/D6
Alto Santo, Braz. 154/C2
Alto Yuruá (riv.), Braz. 150/D5
Altomünster, Ger. 54/E6
Alton, La, US 137/Q16
Alton, Eng, UK 33/F4
Alton, Il, US 137/G8
Altona, Mb, Can. 127/J3
Altoona, Pa, US 138/B3
Altopascio, It. 59/D5
Altos, Braz. 154/B2
Altos de Camapana NP, Pan. 152/E6
Altotonga, Mex. 143/M7
Altötting, Ger. 55/F6
Altrincham, Eng, UK 35/F5
Altrip, Ger. 54/B4
Altun (mts.), China 67/H6
Altun Ha (ruin), Belz. 144/D2
Alturas, Ca, US 126/C5
Altus (lake), Ok, US 129/H4
Altus, Ok, US 129/H4
Altzayanca, Mex. 143/M7
Alucra, Turk. 62/F4
Aluminé, Arg. 158/C3
Alūksne, Lat. 42/G5
Alunda, Swe. 38/H1
Aluš, Iraq 90/E3
Alushta, Ukr. 62/E3
Alva (riv.), Port. 44/B2
Alva, Ok, US 129/H3
Alva, Sc, UK 36/C4
Alvalade, Port. 44/A4
Alvängen, Swe. 38/E1
Alvarado, Mex. 143/P8
Alvarado, Ar, US 158/E2
Alvarez, Arg. 158/E2
Alvaro Obregón, Presa (dam), Mex. 142/C2
Alvdal, Nor. 37/D3
Alvdalen, Swe. 38/F1
Alverca, Port. 45/P10
Alveringem, Belg. 52/B1
Alvesta, Swe. 38/F3
Alvik, Nor. 38/B1
Alvin, Tx, US 129/J5
Alvito, Port. 44/B3
Alvkarleby, Swe. 38/G1
Alvorada, Braz. 155/A4
Alvorada do Norte, Braz. 154/A4
Alvsborg (co.), Swe. 37/E4
Alvsbyn, Swe. 37/G2
Alwen (riv.), Wal, UK 34/E5
Alxa Zuoqi, China 70/A4
Alxa Youqi, China 70/H4
Alzano Lombardo, It. 58/C1
Alzenau in Unterfranken, Ger. 54/C2
Alzette (riv.), Lux. 53/F4
Alzey, Ger. 54/B3
Am Timan, Chad 97/K6
Ama, US, UK 137/P17
Amacayacú, PN, Col. 150/D4
Amadeus (lake), Austl. 109/C3
Amadjuak (lake), NW, Can. 123/J2
Amadora, Port. 45/P10
Amagansett, NY, US 139/F2
Amagansett NWR, NY, US 139/F2
Amagasaki, Japan 77/H6
Amagi, Japan 74/B4
Amagi-san (peak), Japan 75/F3
Amaguaña, Ecu. 152/B5
Amajac (riv.), Mex. 143/N7
Åmål, Swe. 38/E2
Amala (riv.) Kenya 104/B3
Amalfi, It. 46/D2
Amaliás, SAfr. 106/D2
Amaluza, Ecu. 156/B2
Amambaí (riv.), Braz. 151/H8

Amapá, Braz. 151/H3
Amapá (state), Braz. 153/H4
Amarante, Braz. 154/B2
Amarante, Port. 44/A2
Amarante do Maranhão, Braz. 154/A2
Amareleja, Port. 44/A3
Amargosa, Braz. 154/C4
Amargosa (riv.), Ca, US 128/D3
Amarillo, Tx, US 129/G4
Amaro (peak), It. 46/D1
Amarapura, Myan. 83/G3
Amarpātan, India 84/C3
Amarwāra, India 84/C4
Amasra, Turk. 49/L5
Amasya, Turk. 62/E4
Amasya (prov.), Turk. 62/E4
Amata, Austl. 113/F3
Amatlán de Cañas, Mex. 142/D4
Amatukominato, Japan 77/E3
Amawalk (res.), NY, US 139/E1
Amay, Belg. 52/M7
Amayuca, Mex. 143/L8
Amazon (Amazonas) (riv.), Braz.,Per 156/C1
Amazonas, Cuba 145/G1
Amazonas (state), Braz. 152/C5
Amazonas (Amazon) (riv.), Braz. 152/C5
Amazônia, PN da (Tapajós), Braz. 151/G4
Ambāh, India 84/B2
Ambahikily, Madg. 107/G8
Ambajogai, India 89/L5
Ambala Sadar, India 86/D4
Ambalangoda, SrL. 82/D6
Ambalavao, Madg. 107/H8
Ambam, Camr. 96/H7
Ambanja, Madg. 107/J6
Ambaro (bay), Madg. 107/J6
Ambato, Ecu. 152/B5
Ambato Boeny, Madg. 107/H7
Ambatofinandrahana, Madg. 107/H8
Ambatolampy, Madg. 107/H8
Ambatomainty, Madg. 107/H7
Ambatomanoina, Madg. 107/H7
Ambatondrazaka, Madg. 107/H7
Ambatosoratra, Madg. 107/H7
Ambazac, Fr. 42/D4
Ambelau (isl.), Indo. 81/G4
Ámbelos (cape), Gre. 47/H3
Amberg, Ger. 55/E4
Ambergris Cay (isl.), Belz. 144/E2
Ambérieu-en-Bugey, Fr. 56/B6
Amberloup, Belg. 53/E3
Ambikāpur, India 84/D4
Ambinanindrano, Madg. 107/H8
Ambinda, Swe. 38/H1
Ambjörnarp, Swe. 38/E3
Amblainville, Fr. 30/B5
Ambler, Ak, US 134/G2
Ambler, Pa, US 138/C3
Ambleside, Eng, UK 32/B5
Amblève (riv.), Belg. 40/C3
Amblève, Belg. 53/F3
Ambo, Peru 156/B3
Amboasary, Madg. 107/H9
Amboavory, Madg. 107/J7
Ambodifototra, Madg. 107/J7
Ambodiharina, Madg. 107/J8
Ambohidratrimo, Madg. 107/H7
Ambohijanahary, Madg. 107/H8
Ambohimahasoa, Madg. 107/H8
Ambohimandroso, Madg. 107/H8
Ambohinihaonana, Madg. 107/H8
Ambohitsilaozana, Madg. 107/H7
Ambolomoty, Madg. 107/H7
Ambon (isl.), Indo. 81/G4
Ambon, Indo. 81/G4
Ambondro, Madg. 107/H9
Amboni Caves, Tanz. 104/C4
Amborompotsy, Madg. 107/H8
Ambositra, Madg. 107/H8
Ambovombe, Madg. 107/H9
Ambrym (isl.), Van. 116/F6

Amesbury, Eng, UK 33/E4
Amet, India 89/K3
Amethi, India 84/C2
Amfíklia, Gre. 47/H3
Amfilokhía, Gre. 47/G3
Amfissa, Gre. 47/H3
Amga (riv.), Rus. 65/N3
Amga, Rus. 65/N3
Amgu, Rus. 65/T3
Amgun' (riv.), Rus. 65/P4
Amherst, Mex. 131/H2
Amherst, NS, Can. 131/H2
Amherst, NY, US 131/S10
Amherstburg, On, Can. 135/F7
Ami, Japan 77/E1
Amiata (peak), It. 43/J5
Amiens, Fr. 52/B4
Amik (lake), Turk. 90/D2
Amilcar Cabral (int'l arpt.), CpV 93/K10
Amillis, Fr. 30/M5
Aminu Kano (int'l arpt.), Nga. 103/H3
Amisk (lake), Can. 127/H2
Amistad Nat'l Rec. Area, Tx, US 129/G5
Amistad (res.), Mex.,US 140/A2
Amla, India 84/B5
Amlāgora, India 85/F4
Amli, Nor. 38/C2
Amlwch, Wal, UK 32/E4
'Ammān (gov.), Jor. 91/E4
'Ammān (Amman) (cap.), Jor. 91/D4
'Ammān ('Ammān) (cap.), Jor. 91/D4
'Anāta, WBnk. 91/G8
Ammanford, Wal, UK 32/C3
Ammarfjället (peak), Swe. 37/E2
Ammassalik, Grld 160/U
Ammer (riv.), Ger. 54/B5
Ammerman (mtn.), Can. 134/K2
Ammersee (lake), Ger. 43/J3
Ammon, Iran 88/F1
Amol, Iran 88/F1
Amora, Port. 45/P10
Amorbach, Ger. 54/C3
Amorgós, Gre. 47/J4
Amorgós (isl.), Gre. 47/J4
Amory, Ms, US 133/F3
Amos, Qu, Can. 130/E1
Amotfors, Swe. 38/E2
Amozoc, Mex. 143/L7
Ampachi, Japan 77/L5
Ampanefena, Madg. 107/J6
Ampanihy, Madg. 107/G8
Amparafaravola, Madg. 107/H7
Amparai, SrL. 82/D6
Amparo, Braz. 211/G2
Ampasindava (bay), Madg. 107/J6
Ampato (peak), Peru 156/C4
Ampefy, Madg. 107/H7
Amper (riv.), Ger. 55/E6
Ampfing, Ger. 55/F6
Ampflwang im Hausruckwald, Aus. 55/G6
Ampitatafika, Madg. 107/H7
Amposta, Sp. 45/F2
Amqui, Qu, Can. 131/H1
Amravati, India 82/C4
Amreli, India 89/K4
'Amrit (ruin), Syria 91/D2
Amritsar, India 86/C4
Amroha, India 84/B1
Amrum (isl.), Ger. 40/E1
Amstel (riv.), Neth. 50/B4
Amstelveen, Neth. 50/B4
Amsterdam, NY, US 130/F3
Amsterdam, SAfr. 107/E2
Amsterdam (cap.), Neth. 50/B4
Amsterdam (isl.), Fr. 23/N7
Amsterdam Rijnkanaal (riv.), Neth. 50/C4
Amsterdam (Schipol) (int'l arpt.), Neth. 50/B4
Amstetten, Aus. 43/L2
Amu Darya (riv.), Asia 86/A2
Amudat, Ugan. 104/B2
Amukta Pass (chan.), Ak, US 134/D5
Amuku (mts.), Guy. 153/G4
Amund Ringnes (isl.), NW, Can. 123/S7
Amundsen (gulf), NW, Can. 122/D2
Amundsen (inlet), NW, Can. 123/S7
Amundsen (bay), Ant. 160/S
Amundsen (sea), Ant. 160/S
Amundsen-Scott, US, Ant. 160/S
Amunge (lake), Swe. 38/F1
Amur (riv.), Rus. 71/P2
Amur Oblast, Rus. 65/N4
Amuri, NKor. 73/D3
Amūyūn, Leb. 91/D2

Anadyr' (riv.), Rus. 67/S3
Anadyr' (gulf), Rus. 67/T3
Anadyr', Rus. 65/T3
Anadyr' (pt.), Turk. 91/C1
Anáfi (isl.), Gre. 47/J4
Anaheim, Ca, US 136/F8
Anahim Lake, BC, Can. 126/B2
Anahuac, Mex. 132/C5
Anahuac, Tx, US 132/E4
Anak, NKor. 73/C3
Anakāpalle, India 82/D4
Anaktuvuk Pass, Ak, US 134/H2
Analalava, Madg. 107/H6
Analavory, Madg. 107/H7
Anambas (isls.), Indo. 80/C3
Anambra (state), Nga. 103/G5
Anamizu, Japan 77/E1
Anamur (int'l arpt.), Nga. 103/H3
Anamur (pt.), Turk. 91/C1
Anamur, Turk. 91/C1
Anan, Japan 74/D4
Anand, India 89/K4
Ananea, Peru 156/D4
Ananea, Bol. 156/D4
Anantapur, India 82/C5
Anantnag, India 86/C3
Anápa, Rus. 62/F3
Anápolis, Braz. 151/J7
Anapu (riv.), Braz. 151/H4
Anār, Iran 88/G2
Anārak, Iran 88/F2
Anastácio, Braz. 151/G7
Anatahan (isl.), NMar. 116/D3
Anatolia (reg.), Turk. 62/D5
Añatuya, Arg. 157/D2
Anaua (riv.), Braz. 150/F3
Ancash (dept.), Peru 156/B3
Anchieta, Braz. 155/D2
Anchor (bay), Mi, US 135/G6
Anchor Point, Ak, US 134/H4
Anchorage, Ak, US 134/J3
Anchorville, Mi, US 135/G6
Anchovy, Jam. 145/G2
Ancient City of Oc-Eo, Viet. 78/D4
Ancoeur (riv.), Fr. 30/L6
Ancohuma (peak), Bol. 156/D4
Ancón, Peru 156/B3
Ancón de Sardinas (bay), Col. 152/B4
Ancona (prov.), It. 59/G5
Ancona, It. 59/G5
Ancre (riv.), Fr. 52/B3
Ancud, Chile 158/B4
Ancud, Golfo de (gulf), Chile 157/B5
Anda, China 71/N2
Andacollo, Arg. 158/C3
Andacollo, Chile 158/B2
Andahuaylas, Peru 156/C4
Andal, India 85/F4
Andalnes, Nor. 37/C3
Andalucía (aut. comm.), Sp. 44/C4
Andalusia (reg.), Sp. 44/C4
Andalusia, Al, US 133/G4
Andaman (sea), Asia 67/J8
Andaman (isls.), India 67/H8
Andaman and Nicobar (isls.), India 83/F5
Andaman and Nicobar (isls.), India 83/F5
Andamarca, Peru 156/D4
Andamooka, Austl. 113/H4
Andapa, Madg. 107/J6
Andarai, Braz. 154/B4
Andau, Aus. 40/M3
Andebu, Nor. 38/D2
Andechs, Ger. 57/F1
Andeer, Swi. 57/F4
Andelfingen, Swi. 57/E2
Andelle (riv.), Fr. 52/A5
Andelot-Blancheville, Fr. 56/B1
Andelsbach (riv.), Ger. 57/F2
Andelu, Fr. 30/H5
Andemaka, Madg. 107/H8
Andenes, Nor. 37/E1
Andenne, Belg. 52/D2
Anderlues, Belg. 53/D2
Andermatt, Swi. 57/E4
Andernach, Ger. 53/G3
Andeer, Japan 76/B4
Anderson, Ak, US 134/J3
Anderson, SC, US 133/H3
Anderson, In, US 130/C4
Anderson, Ca, US 128/B3
Anderson (inlet), Wa, US 135/B3
Anderson (riv.), NW, Can. 122/D2
Anderson (mts.), Wa, US 135/B3
Andes, Cordillera de los (mts.), SAm. 147/C5
Andevoranto, Madg. 107/J7
Andfjorden (chan.), Nor. 37/F1
Andijk, Neth. 50/C3
Andijon (pol. reg.), Uzb. 87/F4
Andijon, Uzb. 87/F4
Andikíthira (isl.), Gre. 47/H5
Andírin, Turk. 91/E1
Andizhan, Uzb. 87/F4
Andkhvoy, Afg. 86/A1
Andoany, Madg. 107/J6
Andohajango, Madg. 107/H7
Andol, India 82/C4
Andong, SKor. 74/A2
Andorf, Aus. 55/G6
Andorra (ctry.) 27/E4
Andorra, Sp. 45/F2
Andorra la Vella, (cap.), And. 42/D5
Andover, Eng, UK 33/E4
Andover, NJ, US 138/C2
Andøya (isl.), Nor. 37/E1

Andradas, Braz. 211/G7
Andradina, Braz. 155/B2
Andraitx, Sp. 45/G3
Andramasina, Madg. 107/H8
Andranolava, Madg. 107/H8
Andranomavo (riv.), Madg. 107/H7
Andranopasy, Madg. 107/G8
Andreanof (isls.), Ak, US 134/C6
Andrelândia, Braz. 211/H6
Andrespol, Pol. 41/K3
Andrésy, Fr. 30/A5
Andrezel, Fr. 30/L6
Andria, It. 46/E2
Andriba, Madg. 107/H7
Andringitra (mts.), Madg. 107/H8
Andritsaina, Gre. 47/G4
Androka, Madg. 107/H9
Androntany (cape), Madg. 107/J6
Andros, Gre. 47/J4
Andros (isl.), Gre. 47/J4
Andros (isl.), Bahm. 119/K7
Androscoggin (riv.), US 131/G2
Andújar, Sp. 44/C3
Aneby, Swe. 38/F3
Anécon Grande (peak), Arg. 158/C4
Anegada (isl.), UK 141/J4
Anegada (bay), Arg. 158/E4
Anegada Passage (chan.), NAm. 141/J4
Aného, Togo 103/F5
Aneityum (isl.), Van. 116/F7
Añelo, Arg. 158/C3
Aneto, Pico de (peak), Sp. 45/F1
Ang Nam Ngum (res.), Laos 83/H4
Ang Thong, Thai. 78/B3
Angamos (pt.), Chile 157/B1
Angaston, Austl. 113/H5
Ångel (riv.), Sc, UK 51/E5
Angel (mt.), Austl. 115/C4
Angel (falls), Ven. 153/F3
Angeles National Forest, Ca, US 136/F7
Ängelholm, Swe. 38/E3
Ängelholm (int'l arpt.), Swe. 38/E3
Angelina (riv.), Tx, US 129/J5
Angelus (lake), Mi, US 135/F6
Angera, It. 58/C1
Ångermanälven (riv.), Swe. 37/E2
Ångermünde, Ger. 41/H2
Angers, Fr. 42/C3
Anghiari, It. 59/F5
Angical do Piauí, Braz. 154/B2
Angicos, Braz. 154/C2
Anglem (mt.), NZ 117/R12
Anglesea, Austl. 115/C3
Anglesey (isl.), Wal, UK 34/D5
Angleton, Tx, US 129/J5
Anglure, Fr. 42/E2
Angoche, Moz. 105/G4
Angol, Chile 158/B3
Angola, Afr. 105/B2
Angola, In, US 130/C3
Angoon, Ak, US 134/M4
Angoram, PNG 116/D5
Angostura (res.), Mex. 140/C4
Angostura, Mex. 142/C3
Angoulême, Fr. 42/D4
Angra do Heroísmo, Azor., Port. 45/S12
Angra dos Reis, Braz. 211/J7
Angren, Uzb. 87/F4
Anguilla, UK 141/N8
Anguillara Veneta, It. 59/E2
Angul, India 85/E4
Anhée, Belg. 53/D3
Anholt (isl.), Den. 38/D3
Anhui (prov.), China 71/L5
Anhumas, Braz. 151/H4
Ani, Japan 76/B4
Anina, Rom. 48/E3
Aniva (cape), Rus. 71/R2
Aniva (bay), Rus. 76/C1
Anivorano, Madg. 107/J7
Anizy-le-Château, Fr. 52/C4
Anjar, India 89/K4
Anjō, Japan 77/M5
Anjou, Fr. 42/C3
Anjou, Qu, Can. 131/N6
Anjouan, Com. 105/H2
Anjozorobe, Madg. 107/H7
Ankang, China 70/J5
Ankara (cap.), Turk. 62/E5
Ankaratra (mass.), Madg. 107/H8
Ankarsrum, Swe. 38/G3
Ankavandra, Madg. 107/H7
Ankazoabo, Madg. 107/H8
Ankazomiriotra, Madg. 107/H8
Ankeny, Ia, US 135/M9
Ankerika, Madg. 107/H7
Anklilioka, Madg. 107/H8
Anklam, Ger. 38/F5
Ankober, Eth. 104/D2
Ankum, Ger. 51/E3

Anlong, China 83/J2
Anloo, Neth. 50/D2
Anlu, China 72/C5
Ann (cape), Ma, US 131/G3
Ann (lake), Va, US 130/E4
Ann Arbor, Mi, US 130/D3
Anna Bay, Austl. 115/E2
Anna Pink (bay), Chile 158/B5
Anna Regina, Guy. 153/G3
Annaba, Alg. 100/K6
Annaba (prov.), Alg. 100/K6
Annaberg-Buchholz, Ger. 55/G1
Annaclone, NI, UK 34/B3
Annai, Guy. 153/G4
Annaka, Japan 77/B1
Annalong, NI, UK 34/C3
Annam (reg.), Viet. 78/E2
Annan, Sc, UK 36/C6
Annan (riv.), Sc, UK 36/C6
Annandale, Va, US 138/A6
Annandale, NJ, US 138/D2
Annapolis (cap.), Md, US 138/B6
Annapurna (peak), Nepal 84/D1
Annbank Station, Sc, UK 36/B6
Anne (mt.), Austl. 115/C4
Anne Arundel (co.), Md, US 138/B6
Annecy, Fr. 56/C6
Annecy (lake), Fr. 56/C6
Annecy-le-Vieux, Fr. 56/C6
Annemasse, Fr. 56/C5
Annet-sur-Marne, Fr. 30/L5
Annezin, Fr. 52/B2
Annette, Al, US 134/M4
Anniston, Al, US 133/G3
Annonay, Fr. 42/F4
Annweiler, Ger. 53/G5
Ano, Japan 77/K6
Ano Víannos, Gre. 47/J5
Anoia, Sp. 45/K7
Anō, Japan 77/K6
Anosibe An' Ala, Madg. 107/J7
Añou-Zeggarene, Niger 103/G2
Anould, Fr. 56/C1
Anóyia, Gre. 47/J5
Anping, China 72/C3
Anqing, China 72/D3
Anqiu, China 72/D3
Anren, China 83/K2
Anröchte, Ger. 51/F5
Ans, Belg. 53/E2
Ansai, China 72/B3
Ansan, SKor. 73/F7
Ansbach, Ger. 54/D4
Anse-d'Hainault, Haiti 145/H2
Anse-à-Galets, Haiti 145/H2
Anse Rouge, Haiti 145/H1
Ansfelden, Aus. 55/H6
Anshan, China 73/B2
Anshun, China 83/J2
Anson, Tx, US 129/H4
Anson (bay), SKor. 73/D4
Ansongo, Mali 103/F3
Ant (riv.), Eng, UK 33/H1
Ant (isls.), Anti. 116/E4
Anta (riv.), Peru 156/C4
Antabamba, Peru 156/C4
Antakya, Turk. 91/E1
Antalaha, Madg. 107/J6
Antalya (int'l arpt.), Turk. 91/B1
Antalya, Turk. 91/B1
Antalya, Gulf of (gulf), Turk. 91/B1
Antambao Manampotsy, Madg. 107/J7
Antananarivo (prov.), Madg. 107/H7
Antananarivo (cap.), Madg. 107/H7
Antanifotsy, Madg. 107/H8
Antanimieva, Madg. 107/H8
Antanimora, Madg. 107/H9
Antar (peak), Alg. 99/C3
Antarctic (pen.), Ant. 160/W
Antarctic Circle 160/C
Antarctica (cont.) 160
Antas, Braz. 155/B4
Antas, Rio das (riv.), Braz. 155/B4
Antella, It. 59/E5
Antelope (isl.), Ut, US 137/J12
Antelope Center, Ca, US 136/C1
Antequera, Sp. 44/C4
Antes Fort, Pa, US 138/A1
Anthering, Aus. 55/F7
'Anīn, Isr. 91/G6
Anthony, NM, US 128/F5
Anthony, Ks, US 129/H3
Anti-Atlas (mts.), Mor. 96/C2
Anti-Lebanon (mts.), Leb. 91/D3
Antibes, Fr. 43/G5
Anticosti, Île d' (isl.), Qu, Can. 123/K4
Antifer, Cap d' (cape), Fr. 42/D2
Antigo, Wi, US 127/L4
Antigonish, NS, Can. 131/J2
Antigua, Sp. 98/B3
Antigua and Barbuda (ctry.) 119/N8
Antigua Guatemala, Guat. 144/D3
Antiguo Morelos, Mex. 143/F3
Antilly, Fr. 30/M4
Antilla, Cuba 145/H1
Antioquia (dept.), Col. 145/H5
Antioquia, Col. 152/C3
Antipodes (isls.), NZ 117/S
Antisana (vol.), Ecu. 152/B5
Antlers, Ok, US 129/J4
Antofagasta, Chile 157/B1
Antoing, Belg. 52/C2
Antokonosy Manambondro, Madg. 107/H9
Antón Lizardo, Mex. 143/P8
Antón Lizardo (pt.), Mex. 143/P7

Column 1

Antongil (bay), Madg. 105/K10
Antonia, Mo, US 137/G9
Antonibe, Madg. 107/H6
Antoniesberg (peak), SAfr. 106/C4
Antonina, Braz. 155/B3
Antonina do Norte, Braz. 154/C2
Antônio Carlos, Braz. 211/K6
Antonito, Co, US 132/B2
Antonovo, Bul. 49/H4
Antony, Fr. 30/J5
Antrim, NI, UK 34/B1
Antrim (dist.), NI, UK 34/B2
Antronapiana, It. 56/E5
Antsalova, Madg. 107/H7
Antsambalahy, Madg. 107/J6
Antsenavolo, Madg. 107/J6
Antsirabe, Madg. 107/H7
Antsirañana, Madg. 107/J6
Antsiranana (prov.), Madg. 107/J6
Antsohihy, Madg. 107/H6
Antuco (vol.), Chile 158/C3
Antulai (mtn.), Malay. 81/E3
Antwerp (Deurne) (int'l arpt.), Belg. 50/B6
Antwerpen, Belg. 50/B6
Anūpgarh, India 86/B5
Anūpshahr, India 84/B1
Anuradhapura, SrL. 82/D6
Anvik, Ak, US 134/F3
Anvil Peak (vol.), Ak, US 134/B6
Anxi, China 79/C2
Anxi, China 70/G3
Anyang, China 72/C3
Anyang, SKor. 73/F7
A'nyêmaqên (mts.), China 70/G4
Anyi, China 72/B4
Anyuan, China 79/C2
Anza (riv.), It. 56/E6
'Anzah, WBnk. 91/G7
Anze, China 72/C3
Anzegem, Belg. 52/C2
Anzhero-Sudzhensk, Rus. 64/J4
Anzin, Fr. 52/C3
Anzing, Ger. 55/E6
Anzio, It. 46/C2
Anzoátegui, Ven. 152/D2
Anzoátegui (state), Ven. 153/E2
Anzoátegui (int'l arpt.), Ven. 153/E2
Anzola dell'Emilia, It. 59/E3
Ao Kham (pt.), Thai. 78/B4
Ao Phangnga NP, Thai. 78/B4
Aoba (isl.), Van. 116/H6
Aoga (isl.), Japan 75/F4
Aogaki, Japan 77/H5
Aoiz, Sp. 44/E1
Aomori, Japan 76/B3
Aomori (pref.), Japan 76/B3
Aonla, India 84/B1
Aoral (peak), Camb. 78/D3
Aos, Gre. 47/J4
Aosta, It. 43/G4
Aosta, Valle d' (valley), It. 58/A1
Aoudaghast (ruin), Mrta. 102/C2
Aouk, Bahr (riv.), Chad 93/D4
Aoukar (pol. reg.), Mrta. 96/D4
Aoyama, Japan 77/K6
Apache (mts.), US 132/B4
Apache (head.), Az, US 137/R18
Apalachicola, Fl, US 133/G4
Apaporis (riv.), Col. 150/D3
Aparados da Serra, PN de, Braz. 155/B4
Aparecida, Braz. 155/C2
Aparecida do Taboado, Braz. 155/B2
Aparición, Ven. 152/D2
Aparri, Phil. 79/D4
Apartadó, Col. 152/B3
Apatin, Yugo. 48/D3
Apatity, Rus. 60/G2
Apatzingán de la Constitución, Mex. 142/E5
Apaxco, Mex. 143/K7
Apaxtla de Castrejon, Mex. 143/F5
Apeldoorn, Neth. 50/C4
Apelern, Ger. 51/G4
Apen, Ger. 51/E2
Apennines (mts.), It. 27/F4
Apennino Ligure (mts.), It. 43/H4
Apennino Tosco-Emiliano (mts.), It. 43/J4
Apennino Umbro-Marchigiano, It. 43/K5
Appenweier, Ger. 56/D1

Column 2

Appenzell, Swi. 57/F3
Appenzell (canton), Swi. 57/F3
Appignano, It. 59/G6
Appingedam, Neth. 50/D2
Apple Valley, Ca, US 136/C1
Appleton, NY, US 131/S9
Aprica, Passo dell' (pass), It. 57/G5
Aprilia, It. 46/C2
Apriltsi, Bul. 47/J1
Apsheronsk, Rus. 63/J4
Apsley Gorge NP, Austl. 115/E1
Apua (pt.), Hi, US 124/U11
Apucarana, Braz. 155/G2
Apuiarés, Braz. 154/C1
Apure (riv.), Ven. 150/E2
Apure (prov.), Ven. 152/D3
Apurímac (dept.), Peru 156/C5
Apurímac (riv.), Peru 147/B4
Aqaba (gulf), Asia 67/E3
Aqmola (vol.), Chile 158/C3
'Aqrah, WBnk. 91/G7
'Aqrah, Iraq 90/E2
Aqsay, Kaz. 63/K2
Aqtaū, Kaz. 63/J4
Aqtöbe (int'l arpt.), Kaz. 87/C2
Aqtöbe (obl.), Kaz. 87/C3
Aqtöbe, Kaz. 63/L2
Aquanaval (riv.), Mex. 142/E3
Aquaro-Guariquito, PN, Ven. 150/E2
Aquia, Peru 156/B3
Aquidauana, Braz. 151/G8
Aquidauana (riv.), Braz. 151/G8
Aquileia, It. 59/G1
Aquiles Serdán, Mex. 132/B4
Aquin, Haiti 145/H2
Aquiraz, Braz. 154/C1
Aquitaine (pol. reg.), Fr. 42/C4
Ar-Asgat, Mong. 70/J2
Ar Horqin Qi, China 72/E2
Ar Ramādī, Iraq 90/E3
Ar Ramthā, Iraq 91/D3
Ar Raqqah, Syria 90/D2
Ar Raqqah (prov.), Syria 90/D2
Ar Rastan, Syria 91/D3
Ar Rayyān, Qatar 88/F3
Ar Riyāḍ (Riyadh) (cap.), SAr. 88/B4
Ar Rumaythah, Iraq 90/F4
Ar Ruşayfah, Jor. 91/E3
Ar Ruṭbah, Iraq 90/E3
Ara (riv.), Japan 75/F2
Arab, Al, US 133/G3
'Arab, Bahr al (riv.), Sudan 93/B3
Araban, Turk. 90/D2
Arabi, La, US 137/Q17
Arabian (des.), Egypt 97/M2
Arabian (pen.), SAr. 88/D3
Arabian (sea), Asia 88/D3
Arabian (sea), Asia 67/F5
Araç (riv.), Turk. 62/E4
Araç, Turk. 62/E4
Araça (riv.), Braz. 153/F4
Aracaju, Braz. 154/C4
Aracati, Braz. 152/C2
Araçatuba, Braz. 155/B2
Aracena, Sp. 44/B4
Aračinovo, Macd. 47/G1
Aracruz, Braz. 155/D1
Araçuaí, Braz. 155/D1
Araçuaí (riv.), Braz. 154/B5
Arad, Rom. 48/E2
Arad (prov.), Rom. 48/E2
'Arad, Isr. 91/D4
Ārādān, Iran 88/F1
Arafura (sea), Austl.,Ind 116/C5
Aragarças, Braz. 151/H6
Aragón (aut. comm.), Sp. 45/E2
Aragón (riv.), Sp. 45/E1
Aragua (state), Ven. 153/E2
Araguaia (riv.), Braz. 147/D3
Araguaia, PN do, Braz. 151/H6
Araguaína, Braz. 151/H7
Araguari, Braz. 155/B1
Araguari (riv.), Braz. 155/B1
Araguatins, Braz. 151/H5
Arai, Japan 75/F2
Araioses, Braz. 154/B1
Arāk, Iran 88/F2
Arakamchechan (isl.), Rus. 65/T3
Arakan (mts.), Myan. 70/F7
Arakawa, Japan 77/L3
Arakhthos (riv.), Gre. 47/G3
Araklı, Turk. 62/G4
Aral (sea), Asia 87/D3
Aral, Kaz. 86/D2
Aralık, Turk. 63/H5
Aralsor (lake), Kaz. 63/H2
Aramac, Austl. 114/B3
Arāmbāgh, India 85/F4
Aran (isls.), Ire. 31/P10
Aran Fawddwy (peak), Wal, UK 34/E6
Aranda de Duero, Sp. 44/D2
Arandelovac, Yugo. 48/E3
Arani, India 82/C5
Aranjuez, Sp. 44/D2
Aransas Pass, Tx, US 132/D5
Arantina, Braz. 141/M8
Aranuka (isl.), Kiri. 116/G5
Arapaho NWR, Co, US 137/T13
Arapiraca, Braz. 152/C2
Arapiuns (riv.), Braz. 153/H5
Arapongas, Braz. 155/B2
Araquari, Braz. 155/B3
'Ar'ara, Isr. 91/G7
Araranguá, Braz. 155/B4
Araraquara, Braz. 155/B2
Araras, Braz. 159/C7
Ararat, Austl. 115/B3
Arari, Braz. 154/A1

Column 3

Arãria, India 85/F2
Araripe, Chapada do (uplands), Braz. 154/B2
Araripina, Braz. 154/B2
Aras (riv.), Iran 88/E1
Aratane (well), Mrta. 102/C2
Aratoca, Col. 150/D2
Arauá (riv.), Braz. 150/F4
Arauca, Col. 150/D2
Arauca (riv.), Col.,Ven. 153/E3
Arauca (dept.), Col. 150/D2
Araucária, Braz. 155/B3
Arauco, Chile 158/B3
Arauquita, Col. 150/D3
Araure, Ven. 152/D2
Aravis, Col des (pass), Fr. 56/C6
Arawa, PNG 116/E5
Arawale Nat'l Rsv., Kenya 104/D3
Araxá, Braz. 155/C1
Árba Minch', Eth. 97/N6
Arbeca, Sp. 45/F2
Arbīl (gov.), Iraq 90/E2
Arboga, Swe. 56/B4
Arbois, Fr. 56/B3
Arbois, Mont d' (peak), Fr. 56/C6
Arboletes, Col. 152/B2
Arbon, Swi. 57/F2
Arborfield, Sk, Can. 127/H2
Arbrå, Swe. 38/G1
Arbroath, Sc, UK 36/D3
Arbuckle, Ca, US 128/B4
Arc (riv.), Fr. 42/F5
Arc-en-Barrois, Fr. 56/B2
Arc-et-Senans, Fr. 56/B3
Arc-lès-Gray, Fr. 56/B3
Arc-sur-Tille, Fr. 56/B3
Arcachon, Fr. 42/C4
Arcachon, Bassin d' (lag.), Fr. 42/C4
Arcachon, Pointe d' (pt.), Fr. 42/C4
Arcadia, Fl, US 133/H5
Arcadia, Ok, US 137/N14
Arcadia, Ca, US 136/F7
Arcas, Cayos (isl.), Mex. 144/D1
Arcata, Ca, US 126/B5
Arceburgo, Braz. 211/G6
Arcene, It. 58/C1
Arceto, It. 59/D3
Archena, Sp. 44/E3
Archer City, Tx, US 129/K4
Arches, Fr. 56/C1
Arches NP, Ut, US 128/E3
Archidona, Sp. 44/C4
Archman, Trkm. 63/L5
Arcipelago Toscano (isl.), It. 43/H5
Arcisate, It. 57/G6
Arco, It. 57/G6
Arco, Paso del (pass), Arg. 158/C3
Arcola, It. 58/D3
Arcole, It. 59/E2
Arcos, Braz. 211/G6
Arcos de Jalón, Sp. 44/D2
Arcos de la Frontera, Sp. 44/C4
Arcos de Valdevez, Port. 44/A2
Arcoverde, Braz. 154/C3
Arctic (plain), US 134/F2
Arctic (ocean) 160/J
Arctic Bay, NW, Can. 123/H1
Arctic Circle 160/J
Arctic NWR, US 134/J2
Arctic Red (riv.), Can. 134/M2
Arctic Village, Ak, US 134/J2
Arctowski, Pol., Ant. 160/W
Arda (riv.), Bul. 62/C4
Ardabīl, Iran 63/J5
Ardahan, Turk. 63/G4
Ardabīl, Iran 63/J5
Ardal, Iran 88/F1
Ardalstangen, Nor. 38/B1
Ardanuç, Turk. 63/G4
Ardèche (riv.), Fr. 42/F4
Ardee, Ire. 34/B4
Arden, It., Austl. 113/H5
Arden, De, US 138/C3
Arden, Den. 38/C3
Arden-Arcade, Ca, US 135/M9
Ardennes (for.), Belg. 42/F1
Ardennes, Canal des (canal), Fr. 53/D4
Ardenno, It. 57/F5
Ardersier, Sc, UK 36/B1
Ardeşen, Turk. 63/G4
Ardesio, It. 57/F6
Ardestān, Iran 88/F2
Ardez, Swi. 57/F6
Ardila (riv.), Sp. 44/B3
Ardino, Bul. 49/G5
Ardivachar (pt.), Sc, UK 31/O8
Ardle (riv.), Sc, UK 36/C3
Ardlethan, Austl. 115/C2
Ardmore, Ok, US 137/N5
Ardmore, Pa, US 138/C4
Ardnamurchan (pt.), Sc, UK 31/O8
Ardon, Belg. 56/D5
Ardooie, Belg. 52/C1
Ardrahan, Ire. 31/P10
Ardrossan, Austl. 113/H5
Ardrossan, Sc, UK 36/B5
Ards (pen.), NI, UK 34/C3
Ardsley, NY, US 139/K7
Åre, Swe. 38/G2
Areado, Braz. 211/G6
Arealva, Braz. 211/G1
Areia Branca, Braz. 154/C1
Arena de la Ventana Punta (pt.), Chile 158/N8
Arena, It. 47/F5
Arena, Punta (pt.), Ca, US 130/C3
Arendal, Nor. 41/L4
Arendonk, Belg. 50/C6

Column 4

Arendtsville, Pa, US 138/A4
Arenig Fawr (peak), Wal, UK 34/E6
Arenys de Mar, Sp. 45/L6
Arenzano, It. 58/B4
Areo, Ven. 153/F2
Areópolis, Gre. 47/H4
Ares, Sc, UK 36/C5
Aresing, Ger. 55/E5
Arévalo, Sp. 44/C2
Arezzo, It. 59/E6
Arezzo (prov.), It. 59/E6
Arga (riv.), Sp. 45/E1
Argalasti, Gre. 47/H3
Argamasilla de Alba, Sp. 44/D3
Argamasilla de Calatrava, Sp. 44/C3
Arganda, Sp. 45/N9
Argegno, It. 57/F6
Argelès-Gazost, Fr. 42/C5
Argelès-sur-Mer, Fr. 42/E5
Argen (riv.), Ger. 57/F2
Argenbühl, Ger. 57/F2
Argens (riv.), Fr. 43/G5
Argenta, It. 59/E3
Argentan, Fr. 42/C2
Argentat, Fr. 42/D4
Argentera (peak), It. 58/B3
Argenteuil, Fr. 30/J5
Argentière, Aiguille d' (peak), Swi. 56/D6
Argentina (ctry.), Arg. 150/E8
Argentina, It. 58/A5
Argentino (lake), Arg. 159/B6
Argenton-sur-Creuse, Fr. 42/D3
Argentona, Sp. 45/L6
Arghandab (riv.), Afg. 89/J2
Argthani, Turk. 90/B2
Argolis (gulf), Gre. 47/H4
Argonne National Laboratory, Il, US 135/P16
Argos, Gre. 47/H4
Argos Orestikón, Gre. 47/G2
Argostólion, It. 47/G3
Arguin, Cap d' (cape), Mrta. 98/A5
Argun' (riv.), Rus. 65/M4
Argun', Mong. 70/H2
Argungu, Nga. 101/G3
Argyle (lake), Austl. 109/B2
Argyll (reg.), Sc, UK 36/A4
Arhangay (prov.), Mong. 70/G2
Arhavi (co.), Den. 38/D3
Århus, It. 38/D3
Ariano Irpino, It. 46/D5
Ariari (riv.), Col. 152/C4
Arica, Chile 156/D5
Arid (cape), Austl. 112/D5
Aridaía, Gre. 47/H2
Aridol (lake), Ca, US 136/A1
Ariège (riv.), Fr. 42/D5
Arifiye, Turk. 49/K5
Arīḥā, Syria 91/E2
Arikaree (riv.), Co, US 129/G3
Arilje, Yugo. 48/E4
Arima, Trin. 153/F2
Arinos (riv.), Braz. 151/G6
Arinos, Braz. 154/A4
Ariñján, Pan. 152/B2
Arinthod, Fr. 56/B5
Ario de Rosales, Mex. 143/E5
Aripao, Ven. 153/E3
Aripuanã, Braz. 150/G6
Aripuanã (riv.), Braz. 147/C3
Ariquemes, Braz. 150/F6
Arish, Austl. 114/B2
Arismendi, Ven. 152/D2
Arivechi, Mex. 142/C2
Arivonimamo, Madg. 107/H7
Ariza, Sp. 44/D2
Arizona (canal), Az, US 137/R18
Arizona (state), US 128/D4
Arizona, Arg. 158/D2
Arizona, It. 58/B4
Årjäng, Swe. 38/E2
Arjeplog, Swe. 37/F2
Arjona, Sp. 44/C4
Arjona, Col. 152/C2
Arkadelphia, Ar, US 129/J4
Arkaig (riv.), Sc, UK 36/A3
Arkalokhórion, Gre. 47/J5
Arkansas (riv.), US 119/G6
Arkansas (state), US 125/H4
Arkansas City, Ks, US 129/K4
Arkanü (peak), Libya 97/K3
Arkhángelos, Gre. 90/B2
Arta (gulf), Sp. 45/G3
Artá, Sp. 45/G3
Arkhángel'sk (int'l arpt.), Rus. 60/J2
Arkhángel'sk (Arkhangel), Rus. 60/J2
Arkhángel'skoye, Rus. 60/H3
Arkhyz, Rus. 61/V9
Arklow, Ire. 34/B6
Arkona (cape), Ger. 38/E4
Arkonam, India 82/C5
Arkticheskiy Institut (isls.), Rus. 64/H2
Årla, Swe. 38/G2
Arlanza (riv.), Sp. 44/C1
Arlanza (riv.), Sp. 44/D1
Arlberg (pass), Aus. 57/G3
Arles, Fr. 42/F5
Arlesheim, Swi. 56/D3
Arley, Mo, US 137/S12
Arlington, Tx, US 137/J18
Arlington, Mn, US 127/K4
Arlington, Va, US 133/G4
Arlington, NJ, US 138/A6
Arlington Heights, Il, US 135/P15
Arlon, Belg. 53/E4

Column 5

Arluno, It. 58/B1
Arly (riv.), Fr. 56/C6
Arly, PN de l', Burk. 100/E2
Arly, Réserve Totale de Faune de l', Burk. 103/F4
Armada, Mi, US 135/G6
Armadale, Sc, UK 36/C5
Armadale (dist.), NI, UK 34/B3
Armagh, NI, UK 34/B3
Armagh (dist.), NI, UK 34/B3
Armant, Egypt 101/C3
Armavir, Rus. 63/G3
Armenia, Col. 150/C3
Armenia (ctry.) 67/D5
Armenia (ctry.) 63/G4
Armentières-en-Brie, Fr. 30/M5
Armería, Mex. 142/D5
Armidale, Austl. 115/D1
Armilla, Sp. 44/D4
Armstrong, BC, Can. 126/D3
Armstrong, Arg. 158/E2
Armthorpe, Eng, UK 35/G4
Armūr, India 82/C4
Army Ordnance Museum, Md, US 138/B5
Arnage, Fr. 42/D3
Arnager (int'l arpt.), Den. 38/F4
Arnaía, Gre. 47/H2
Arnaud (riv.), Qu, Can. 123/J3
Arnauti (cape), Cyp. 91/C2
Arnedo, Sp. 44/D1
Arnett, Ok, US 129/H3
Arnhem, Neth. 50/C5
Arnhem Land (reg.), Austl. 109/C2
Arno (riv.), It. 43/J5
Arno (isl.), Mrsh. 116/G4
Arnold, Mo, US 137/G9
Arnold, Md, US 138/B5
Arnold, Eng, UK 35/G6
Arnoldstein, Aus. 43/K3
Arnon (riv.), Fr. 42/E3
Arnouville-lès-Gonesse, Fr. 30/J4
Arnprior, On, Can. 130/E2
Arnsberg, Ger. 51/F6
Arnstadt, Ger. 43/J1
Arnstein, Ger. 54/C3
Aro Usu (cape), Indo. 81/H5
Aroab, Namb. 106/B2
Aroche, Sp. 44/B4
Arolsen, Ger. 51/G6
Aron (riv.), Fr. 42/E3
Arona, Canl. 45/X16
Arona, It. 57/F6
Arorae (isl.), Kiri. 116/G5
Arosa, Swi. 57/F4
Aroser Rothern (peak), Swi. 57/F4
Arpajon, Fr. 30/J6
Arpajon-sur-Cère, Fr. 42/E4
Arquata Scrivia, It. 58/B3
Arques, Fr. 52/B2
Arques-la-Bataille, Fr. 30/H4
Arrah, India 85/E3
Arraias (riv.), Braz. 151/H6
Arraias, Braz. 154/A4
Arraiján, Pan. 152/B2
Arran (isl.), Sc, UK 31/R8
Arras, Fr. 52/B3
Arreau, Fr. 42/D5
Arrecife, Sp. 98/B3
Arrecifes, Arg. 158/E2
Arrée, Monts d' (hills), Fr. 42/B2
Arriaga, Mex. 144/C2
Arriondas, Sp. 44/C1
Arrochar, Sc, UK 36/B4
Arroio Grande, Braz. 155/B4
Arronville, Fr. 30/J4
Arroux (riv.), Fr. 42/F3
Arrow (riv.), Eng, UK 32/C2
Arrowbear Lake, Ca, US 136/C2
Arroyo de la Luz, Sp. 44/B3
Arroyo Grande, Ca, US 128/B4
Arroyo Hondo (riv.), Ca, US 135/L12
Arroyo Trabuco (riv.), Ca, US 136/C4
Ars, Den. 38/C3
Ars-Moselle, Fr. 53/F5
Ars-en-Ré, Fr. 42/C3
Arsen'yev, Rus. 71/P3
Arsiero, It. 59/E1
Arslanköy, Turk. 91/D1
Arta (gulf), Gre. 47/G3
Arta, Gre. 47/G3
Arteaga, Mex. 142/E5
Arteixo, Sp. 44/A1
Artem, Rus. 71/P3
Artemisa, Cuba 145/F1
Artemivs'k, Ukr. 60/H3
Artesia, NM, US 129/G5
Artesia, Ca, US 136/C4
Arth, Swi. 57/E3
Arthies, Fr. 30/H4
Arthur (pt.), Austl. 114/C3
Arthur (riv.), Austl. 115/S11
Arthur Kill (riv.), US 139/J9
Arthur's (pass), NZ 117/S11
Arthur's Pass NP, NZ 117/S11
Artigas, Uru. 158/E2
Artogne, It. 57/F6
Artois (uplands), Fr. 38/G2
Artova, Turk. 62/F4
Arturo Merino Benítez (Santiago) (int'l arpt.), Chile 158/N8
Artux, China 86/A3
Artvin, Turk. 63/G4
Artvin (prov.), Austl. 117/S11
Arua, Ugan. 104/B3
Aruba (isl.), Aru., Neth. 147/B1
Arucas, Sp. 98/A3
Arudy, Fr. 42/C5
Arujá, Braz. 211/J7

Column 6

Arun (riv.), China 85/F2
Arunāchal Pradesh (state), India 70/F6
Arundel, Eng, UK 33/F5
Aruppukkottai, India 82/C6
Arus (cape), Indo. 81/F3
Arusha, Tanz. 104/C4
Arusha NP, Tanz. 104/C4
Arusha (gov.), Egypt 101/C4
Arusi (pol. reg.), Eth. 97/N6
Arutua (isl.), FrPol. 117/L6
Aruwimi (riv.), D.R. Congo 93/E4
Arvada, Co, US 137/B3
Arvayheer, Mong. 70/H2
Arve (riv.), Fr. 56/C6
Arvidsjaur, Swe. 37/F2
Arvika, Swe. 38/E2
Arvon (mt.), Mi, US 127/L4
Arxan, China 72/E2
Arys', Kaz. 87/E4
Arz (riv.), Fr. 42/B3
Arzachena, It. 46/A2
Arzamas, Rus. 61/K5
Arzbach, Ger. 53/G2
Arzdale, Iran 88/F2
Arzignano, It. 59/E1
Arzl im Pitztal, Aus. 57/G3
Arzúa, Sp. 44/A1
Ås, Nor. 38/D2
Ås, Belg. 53/E1
Aš, Czh. 53/G3
As Sabkhah, Syria 90/D3
As Şafī, Jor. 91/D4
As Sālimīyah, Kuw. 88/E3
As Sallūm, Egypt 97/L1
As Salmān, Iraq 90/F4
As Salt, Jor. 91/D3
As Santah, Egypt 91/B4
As Sarīḥ, Jor. 91/E3
As Sinbillāwayn, Egypt 91/B4
As Sulaymānīyah, Iraq 90/F3
As Sulaymānīyah (gov.), Iraq 90/F3
As Suwaydā' (prov.), Syria 91/E3
As Suwaydā', Syria 91/E3
As Şuwayrah, Iraq 90/F3
As Suways (Suez), Egypt 91/C4
Aşkale, Turk. 101/C2
Asaba, Nga. 103/G5
Asadābād, Afg. 86/A2
Asadābād, Iran 88/F2
Asagny, PN d', C.d'Iv. 100/E5
Asahan (peak), Indo. 80/A3
Asahi, Japan 74/C4
Asahi, Japan 77/C3
Asahi, Japan 77/F1
Asahi, Japan 77/L5
Asahi-dake (peak), Japan 76/C2
Asahikawa, Japan 76/C2
Asai, Japan 77/K5
Asaka, Japan 77/K2
Asama-yama (peak), Japan 75/F2
Asan (bay), SKor. 73/D4
Asansol, India 85/E3
Ásosa, Eth. 97/M5
Asoteriba (peak), Sudan 101/D4
Aspach, Aus. 55/G6
Aspe, Sp. 45/E3
Aspen, Co, US 128/F3
Aspen Hill, Md, US 138/B3
Aspen Park, Co, US 137/D3
Aspendos (ruin), Turk. 91/B1
Aspermont, Tx, US 129/G4
Aspers (head.), Gre. 47/J2
Aspropírgos, Gre. 47/H3
Asquith, Sk, Can. 126/G2
Assa, Mor. 98/C3
Assa Aguiene (peak), Alg. 99/G5
Assab, Erit. 88/D6
'Assāba (mass.), Mrta. 102/C2
Assam (state), India 70/F6
Assedjrad, Alg. 96/H4
Assemini, It. 46/A3
Assen, Neth. 50/D3
Assens, Den. 38/D3
Assentoft, Den. 38/D3
Assesse, Belg. 53/E2
Assiniboia, Sk, Can. 126/G2
Assiniboine (mt.), BC, Can. 126/D2
Assinika (lake), Can. 130/F1
Assis, Braz. 155/B2
Assling, Ger. 55/E6
Assomada, CpV. 93/K10
Atakós, Gre. 47/G3

Column 7

Ashdod, Isr. 91/F8
Asheboro, NC, US 133/J3
Asheville, NC, US 133/H3
Asheweig (riv.), Can. 127/K2
Ashford, Austl. 115/D1
Ashford, Eng, UK 33/G5
Ashford, Eng, UK 30/B2
Ashgabat (cap.), Trkm. 89/G1
Ashhurst, NZ 117/T11
Ashibetsu, Japan 76/C2
Ashigawa, Japan 77/B2
Ashikaga, Japan 77/C1
Ashington, Eng, UK 35/G1
Ashino (lake), Japan 77/B3
Ashiwada, Japan 77/B3
Ashiya, Japan 77/H6
Ashizuri-misaki (cape), Japan 74/C4
Ashkal (lake), Tun. 100/H6
Ashkāsham, Afg. 86/B1
Ashland, Ks, US 129/H3
Ashland, Or, US 126/C5
Ashland, Ky, US 130/D3
Ashland, Oh, US 130/D3
Ashland, Wi, US 127/L4
Ashland, Pa, US 138/C3
Ashley, ND, US 127/J4
Ashley, Pa, US 138/C2
Ashmore (reef), Austl. 109/B2
Ashmore and Cartier Islands Territory (dpcy.), Austl. 109/B2
Ashmūn, Egypt 91/B4
Ashoro, Japan 76/C2
Ashqelon, Isr. 91/F8
Ashta, India 82/C3
Ashtabula, Oh, US 130/D3
Ashton, Id, US 126/F4
Ashton-In-Makerfield, Eng, UK 35/F5
Ashton-under-Lyne, Eng, UK 35/F5
Asia, Peru 156/B4
Asia (cont.) 12
Asiago, It. 57/H6
Asikkala, Fin. 39/L1
Asilah, Mor. 100/A2
Asilo, Peru 156/D4
Asinara (isl.), It. 46/A2
Asinara, Golfo dell' (gulf), It. 46/A2
Asino, Rus. 64/J4
Asipovichy, Bela. 62/D1
'Asīr (mts.), SAr. 88/D6
Asis (cape), Sudan 101/D5
Aşkale, Turk. 90/E2
Askeaton, Ire. 31/P10
Asker, Nor. 38/D2
Askersund, Swe. 38/F2
Askim, Nor. 38/D2
Askim, Swe. 38/E3
Askion (peak), Gre. 47/G2
Askja (crater), Ice. 37/P6
Askov, Den. 38/C4
Askvoll, Nor. 37/C3
Asmara (cap.), Erit. 88/C5
Asmera (cap.), Erit. 88/C5
Asni, Mor. 98/C2
Asnières-sur-Oise, Fr. 30/J4
Asnières-sur-Seine, Fr. 30/J5
Asō, Japan 77/E2
Aso NP, Japan 74/B4
Aso-san (peak), Japan 74/B4
Asola, It. 59/E1
Asolo, It. 57/H6
Ásosa, Eth. 97/M5
Aspach, Aus. 55/G6

Column 8

Asunción Ixtaltepec, Mex. 140/B4
Asunden (lake), Swe. 38/F3
Aswa (riv.), Ugan. 97/M7
Aswān (gov.), Egypt 101/C4
Aswān, Egypt 101/C4
Aswan High (dam), Egypt 101/C4
Asyūṭ, Egypt 101/B3
Asyūṭ (gov.), Egypt 101/B3
Aţ Ţafīlah, Jor. 91/D4
At Tall, Syria 91/E3
At Tall al Kabīr, Egypt 91/B4
Aţ Ta'mīn (gov.), Iraq 90/E3
Aţ Ţūr, WBnk. 91/G8
Atabapo (riv.), Ven. 153/E4
Atacama (des.), Chile 147/B4
Atacames, Ecu. 150/B3
Atafu (isl.), Tok. 117/H5
Atakpamé, Togo 103/F5
Atalaia, Braz. 154/C3
Atalaia do Norte, Braz. 156/C3
Ataláni, Gre. 47/H3
Atalaya, Peru 156/C3
Atami, Japan 75/F3
Atar, Mrta. 96/C3
Atarfe, Sp. 44/D4
Atarra, India 84/C3
Atas Bogd (peak), Mong. 70/G3
Atascadero, Ca, US 128/B4
Atascosa, Tx, US 137/T21
Atatürk (dam), Turk. 90/D2
Atatürk (int'l arpt.), Turk. 49/J5
Atbara (riv.), Eth. 97/N4
Atbara, Sudan 97/M4
Atbasar, Kaz. 87/E2
Atchafalaya (riv.), US 129/K5
Atchafalaya (bay), US 137/Q17
Atchison, Ks, US 129/J3
Atebubu, Gha. 103/E5
Ateelva (riv.), Nor. 37/G1
Atena, It. 46/D5
Atencingo, Mex. 143/L8
Atenco, Mex. 143/Q10
Atengo (riv.), Mex. 142/D4
Atessa, It. 46/D1
Atglen, Pa, US 138/C4
Ath, Belg. 52/C2
Athabasca, Ab, Can. 122/E3
Athabasca (lake), Can. 122/E3
Athapapuskow (lake), Can. 127/H2
Athboy, Ire. 31/Q10
Athenry, Ire. 31/P10
Athens, Tx, US 129/J4
Athens, Ga, US 133/H3
Athens, Al, US 133/G3
Athens, Tn, US 133/G3
Athens (Athens) (cap.), Gre. 47/N9
Atherstone, Eng, UK 33/E1
Atherton, Eng, UK 35/F5
Atherton, Austl. 114/B2
Athgarh, India 82/E3
Athi (riv.), Kenya 104/C3
Athina (Athens) (cap.), Gre. 47/N9
Atholl (for.), Sc, UK 36/B3
Athos (peak), Gre. 47/J2
Athy, Ire. 31/Q10
Ati, Chad 96/J5
Atibaia (riv.), Braz. 211/G2
Atibaia, Braz. 211/G8
Atico, Peru 156/C5
Atienza, Sp. 44/D2
Atikokan, On, Can. 127/L3
Atil, Mex. 142/C2
Atitlán (lake), Guat. 144/C3
Atka (isl.), Ak, US 134/C5
Atka, Rus. 64/H3
Atkarsk, Rus. 61/J3
Atkinson (pt.), Can. 134/M2
Atlacomulco de Fabela, Mex. 143/K7
Atlanta (cap.), Ga, US 133/H3
Atlanta (ocean) 22/G3
Atlantic Beach, NY, US 139/L9
Atlantic City, NJ, US 138/D5
Atlantic Highlands, NJ, US 139/J10
Atlantic (dept.), Col. 145/H4
Atlántida (dept.), Uru. 159/L11
Atlántico (dept.), Col. 145/H4
Atlántique (prov.), Ben. 103/F5
Atlas (mts.), Mor. 96/D4
Atlas Saharien (mts.), Alg. 96/F1
Atlatlahuaca, Mex. 143/Q10
Atlin, BC, Can. 134/M3
Atlin (lake), Can. 134/M3
'Atlit, Isr. 91/G7
Atlixco, Mex. 143/L8
Atmore, Al, US 133/G4
Atocha, Bol. 150/E8
Atotonilco, Mex. 143/L6
Atotonilco el Alto, Mex. 142/E4
Atoyac, Mex. 143/Q10
Atoyac (riv.), Mex. 143/L8
Atrai (riv.), Bang. 85/F3
Atran (riv.), Swe. 38/E3
Åtran (riv.), Swe. 38/E3
Atrato (riv.), Col. 150/C2

Rightmost Column

Atrauli, India 84/B1
Atsugi, Japan 77/C3
Atsumi, Japan 77/M6
Atsumi (pen.), Japan 77/M6
Attalens, Swi. 56/C4
Attalla, Al, US 133/G3
Attapu, Laos 78/D3
Attawapiskat (lake), On, Can. 127/L2
Attawapiskat (riv.), On, Can. 123/H3
Attendorn, Ger. 51/F6
Attersee (lake), Aus. 43/K3
Atterridgeville, SAfr. 106/C12
Attica, It. 135/F5
Attica, Oh, US 135/F5
Attigny, Fr. 53/D5
Attleboro, Mass. 155/K2
Attock, Pak. 86/B3
Attu (isl.), Ak, US 134/A5
Attu (isl.), Ak, US 65/T4
Atuel (riv.), Arg. 157/C4
Atuntaqui, Ecu. 152/B4
Åtvidaberg, Swe. 38/G2
Atwater, Ca, US 128/B3
Atyraū (obl.), Kaz. 87/B3
Atyraū, Kaz. 63/J3
Atyraū (int'l arpt.), Kaz. 63/J3
Au, Aus. 57/F3
Au, Swi. 57/F3
Au in der Hallertau, Ger. 55/E5
Au Sable (riv.), Mi, US 130/C2
Auari (riv.), Braz. 153/E3
Aubange, Belg. 53/E4
Aube (dept.), Fr. 53/D6
Aube (riv.), Fr. 40/C4
Aubenas, Fr. 42/F4
Aubepierre-Ozouer-le-Repos, Fr. 30/L6
Aubergenville, Fr. 30/H5
Aubervilliers, Fr. 30/K5
Aubetin (riv.), Fr. 30/L6
Aubette (riv.), Fr. 52/A5
Aubette de Magny (riv.), Fr. 30/H4
Aubigny-en-Artois, Fr. 52/B3
Aubigny-sur-Nère, Fr. 42/E3
Aubin, Fr. 42/E4
Aubonne, Swi. 56/C5
Auboué, Fr. 53/E5
Aubrac, Monts du (mts.), Fr. 42/E4
Aubrives, Fr. 53/D3
Aubry, Sc, US 137/D6
Auburn, Wa, US 126/C4
Auburn, Ne, US 129/J2
Auburn, Ca, US 128/B3
Auburn, NY, US 130/E3
Auburn, In, US 130/C3
Auburn, Al, US 133/G3
Auburn, Austl. 113/H5
Auburn Hills, Mi, US 135/F6
Aubusson, Fr. 42/E4
Aucá Mahuida (peak), Arg. 158/C3
Auch, Fr. 42/D5
Auchel, It. 52/B3
Auchinleck, Sc, UK 36/C6
Auchtermuchty, Sc, UK 36/C4
Auchy-lès-Hesdin, Fr. 52/B3
Auckland, NZ 117/S10
Auckland (int'l arpt.), NZ 117/S10
Auckland (isls.), NZ 23/T8
Audenarde, Belg. 52/D2
Audeux (riv.), Fr. 56/C3
Audierne, Fr. 42/A2
Audincourt, Fr. 56/C3
Audo (range), Eth. 97/P6
Audruicq, Fr. 52/B2
Audun-le-Roman, Fr. 53/E5
Audun-le-Tiche, Fr. 53/E5
Aue, Ger. 51/E2
Auer (Ora), It. 57/H5
Auerbach, It. 55/F1
Auerbach in der Oberpfalz, Ger. 55/E5
Auersberg (peak), Ger. 55/F2
Aufess, Fr. 30/H5
Auffargis, Fr. 30/H5
Augathella, Austl. 114/B4
Augher, NI, UK 34/A3
Aughnacloy, NI, UK 34/B6
Aughrim, Ire. 31/Q10
Augrabies Falls NP, SAfr. 106/C3
Augrabiesvalle (falls), SAfr. 106/C3
Augsburg, Ger. 54/D6
Augub (peak), Namb. 106/A2
Augusta, Ga, US 133/H3
Augusta, Me, US 131/G2
Augusta, It. 46/D4
Augusta, Austl. 112/B5
Augusta (cap.), Me, US 131/G2
Augusta, Golfo di (gulf), It. 46/D4
Augustdorf, Ger. 51/F5
Augustenborg, Den. 38/D4
Augusto César Sandino (int'l arpt.), Nic. 144/E3
Augustów, Pol. 27/K5
Augustus (mt.), Austl. 108/B3
Auk Bok (riv.), Myan. 78/B3
Auki, Sol. 116/F6
Aukstaitija NP, Lith. 39/M4
Auld (lake), Austl. 109/B3
Aulencia (riv.), Sp. 45/M9
Aulendorf, Ger. 57/F2
Aulla, It. 58/C4
Aulnay-sous-Bois, Fr. 30/K5
Aulnay-sur-Mauldre, Fr. 30/H5
Aulne (riv.), Fr. 42/A2
Aulnoy, Fr. 30/M5
Aulnoye-Aymeries, Fr. 52/D3
Aulnut (int'l arpt.), Fr. 42/E4
Ault, Co, US 137/C1

Ault (peak), Swi.	57/F4
Ault, Fr.	52/A3
Aumale, Fr.	52/A4
Aumetz, Fr.	53/E5
Aumühle, Ger.	51/H1
Aunay-sur-Odon, Fr.	42/C2
Aunette (riv.), Fr.	52/B5
Auneuil, Fr.	52/B5
Auning, Den.	38/D3
Aur (isl.), Mrsh.	116/G4
Aura, NJ, US	138/C4
Aurach, Ger.	54/D4
Aurach (riv.), Ger.	54/D4
Auraiya, India	84/B2
Aurangābād, India	85/L3
Aurangābād, India	89/L5
Auray, Fr.	42/B3
Aureilhan, Fr.	42/D5
Aurich, Ger.	51/E2
Auriflama, Braz.	155/B2
Aurillac, Fr.	42/E4
Aurisina, It.	59/G1
Aurland, Nor.	38/B1
Aurolzmünster, Aus.	55/G6
Aurora, Braz.	155/B2
Aurora, Mo, US	129/J3
Aurora, Il, US	129/K2
Aurora, Co, US	137/C3
Aurora, Guy.	153/G3
Aurora Lodge, Ak, US	134/J3
Aus, Namb.	106/B2
Ausa (riv.), It.	59/G1
Aussillon, Fr.	42/E5
Aust-Agder (co.), Nor.	37/C4
Austin, Nv, US	128/C3
Austin (lake), Austl.	109/A3
Austin (isl.), NW, Can.	122/G2
Austral (Tubuai Islands) (isls.), FrPol.	117/K7
Australia (cont.)	109
Australian Alps (range), Austl.	115/C3
Australian Capital Territory (cap. terr.), Austl.	109/D4
Australind, Austl.	112/B5
Austria (ctry.)	27/F4
Austurhorn (pt.), Ice.	37/P7
Auterive, Fr.	42/D5
Authie (riv.), Fr.	42/D1
Autlán de Navarro, Mex.	142/D5
Automne (riv.), Fr.	52/B5
Autreppe, Belg.	52/C3
Autun, Fr.	42/F3
Auvergne (pol. reg.), Fr.	42/E4
Auvers-sur-Oise, Fr.	30/J4
Auvézère (riv.), Fr.	42/D4
Aux Sables (riv.), Can.	130/D2
Auxerre, Fr.	42/E3
Auxonne, Fr.	56/B3
Auyán-Tepuí (peak), Ven.	153/F3
Auyuittuq NP, NW, Can.	123/K2
Auzangate (peak), Peru	156/D4
Avaj, Iran	88/E1
Avallon, Fr.	42/E3
Avalon, Ca, US	136/B4
Avalon, NJ, US	138/D5
Avalon (pen.), Nf, Can.	123/L4
Avanne-Aveney, Fr.	56/B3
Avaré, Braz.	155/B2
Avarua, NZ	117/K7
Avdat (ruin), Isr.	91/D4
Avebury Stone Circle, Eng, UK	30/E4
Aveiro, Port.	44/A2
Aveiro (dist.), Port.	44/A2
Aveley, Eng, UK	30/D2
Avelgem, Belg.	52/C2
Avellaneda, Arg.	159/J11
Avellino, It.	46/D2
Avelon (riv.), Fr.	52/A5
Avenal, Ca, US	136/C3
Avenches, Swi.	56/D4
Avenel, NJ, US	139/H9
Avernes, Fr.	30/H4
Aversa, It.	46/D2
Aves (isl.), Ven.	141/J4
Avesnes-le-Comte, Fr.	52/B3
Avesnes-sur-Helpe, Fr.	52/C3
Avesta, Swe.	38/G1
Aveyron (riv.), Fr.	42/D4
Avezzano, It.	46/C1
Avich (lake), Sc, UK	36/A4
Aviemore, Sc, UK	36/C2
Avignon, Fr.	42/F5
Avihayil, Isr.	91/F7
Avila de los Caballeros, Sp.	44/C2
Avilés, Sp.	44/C1
Avio, It.	59/D1
Avion, Fr.	52/B3
Avis, Pa, US	138/A1
Avisio (riv.), It.	57/H5
Avize, Fr.	52/D6
Avlum, Den.	38/B3
Avoca, Austl.	115/C4
Avoca, Austl.	115/B3
Avoca, Mi, US	135/E7
Avoca, Ire.	34/B6
Avoch, Sc, UK	36/B1
Avola, It.	46/D4
Avon, Fr.	42/E2
Avon (riv.), Eng, UK	32/C6
Avon (co.), Eng, UK	32/F4
Avon (riv.), Eng, UK	30/L6
Avon, Sc, UK	36/C1
Avon Valley NP, Austl.	112/C4
Avon Water (riv.), Sc, UK	36/B6
Avonbeg (riv.), Ire.	34/B6
Avondale, Az, US	137/R19
Avondale, Pa, US	138/C4
Avonlea, Sk, Can.	127/G3
Avonmore (riv.), Ire.	34/B5
Avranches, Fr.	42/C2
Avre (riv.), Fr.	40/B4
Avrillé, Fr.	42/C3
Awa-shima (isl.), Japan	76/A4
A'waj (riv.), Syria	91/E3
Awaji, Japan	77/H6
Awans, Belg.	53/E2
Āwasa, Eth.	97/N6
Āwash, Eth.	97/P6
Awash Wenz (riv.), Eth.	97/P5
Awaso, Gha.	103/E5
Awat, China	70/D3
Awbārī, Libya	96/H2
Awbārī (des.), Libya	96/H2
Awe (lake), Sc, UK	36/A4
'Awjilah, Libya	97/K2
Awka, Nga.	103/G5
Awsim, Egypt	91/B4
Ax-les-Thermes, Fr.	42/D5
Axamo (int'l arpt.), Swe.	38/F2
Axams, Aus.	57/H3
Axarfjördhur (inlet), Ice.	37/N6
Axel, Neth.	50/A6
Axel Heiberg (isl.), Can.	119/H2
Axim, Gha.	103/E5
Axios (riv.), Gre.	47/H2
Axis (dam), Wa, US	135/D2
Axminster, Eng, UK	32/D5
Axochiapan, Mex.	143/L8
Ay (riv.), Rus.	61/N5
Ay, Fr.	52/C5
Ayabaca, Peru	156/B2
Ayabe, Japan	77/H5
Ayacucho, Peru	156/C4
Ayacucho (dept.), Peru	156/C4
Ayacucho, Arg.	158/F3
Ayagöz, Kaz.	70/D2
Ayaguz (riv.), Kaz.	70/C2
Ayamé I, Barrage d' (dam), C.d'Iv.	102/E5
Ayamé II, Barrage d' (dam), C.d'Iv.	102/E5
Ayamonte, Sp.	44/B4
Ayancık, Turk.	62/C4
Ayanganna (mtn.), Guy.	153/G3
Ayapel, Col.	152/C2
Ayaş, Turk.	62/E4
Ayase, Japan	77/C3
Ayaviri, Peru	156/D4
Aybak, Afg.	87/E5
'Aybāl, Jabal (peak), WBnk.	91/G7
Aybaşt, Turk.	62/F4
Aydar Köli (lake), Trkm.	87/E4
Aydın, Turk.	90/A2
Aydın (prov.), Turk.	90/B2
Aydıncık, Turk.	62/E4
Aydıncık, Turk.	91/C1
Ayer, Swi.	56/D5
Ayers Rock (Uluru) (peak), Austl.	113/F3
Ayeyarwady (state), Myan.	83/F4
Ayeyarwady (Irrawaddy) (riv.), Myan.	67/J7
Ayiá, Gre.	47/H3
Ayía Paraskeví, Gre.	47/K3
Ayiásos, Gre.	47/K3
Ayios Ioánnis (cape), Gre.	47/J5
Ayios Kírikos, Gre.	47/K4
Ayios Konstandínos, Gre.	47/H3
Ayios Matthaíos, Gre.	47/F3
Ayios Nikólaos, Gre.	47/J5
Aylesbury, Eng, UK	33/F3
Aylesford, Eng, UK	33/G4
Aylmer (lake), NW, Can.	122/F2
'Ayn al 'Arab, Syria	90/D2
'Ayn Zuwayyah (well), Libya	97/L3
Ayna, Peru	156/C4
Ayora, Sp.	45/E3
Ayotzintepec, Mex.	144/B2
'Ayoûn 'Abd el Mâlek (well), Mrta.	98/D4
'Ayoûn el 'Atroûs, Mrta.	102/C2
Ayr, Austl.	114/B2
Ayr, Sc, UK	36/B6
Ayr (riv.), Sc, UK	36/B5
Ayre (pt.), IM, UK	42/C3
Aytré, Fr.	42/C3
Ayubia NP, Pak.	86/B3
Ayutla, Mex.	142/D4
Ayutla de los Libres, Mex.	144/B3
Ayutthaya (ruin), Thai.	78/C3
Ayvacık, Turk.	47/K3
Ayvalık, Turk.	62/C5
Aywaille, Belg.	53/E3
Az Zabadānī, Syria	91/E3
Az Zāhirīyah, WBnk.	91/F8
Az Zaqāzīq, Egypt	91/B4
Az Zarqā' (gov.), Jor.	91/E3
Az Zarqā', Jor.	91/E3
Az Zāwiyah, Libya	96/H1
Az Zaydīyah, Yem.	88/D5
Azad Kashmir (terr.), Pak.	86/B3
Azahar (coast), Sp.	45/F3
Azalea, Or, US	126/C5
Azalia, Mi, US	135/E7
Azamgarh, India	84/D2
Azángaro, Peru	156/D4
Azángaro, Peru	156/D4
Avon, Fr.	99/H4
Azaouâd (phys. reg.), Mali	96/E4
Azaouak (riv.), Mali	98/D2
Āzārān, Iran	88/E1
Āzarbāyjān-E Gharbī (prov.), Iran	90/F2
Az'zāz, Syria	91/E1
Azemmour, Mor.	98/C2
Azerbaijan (ctry.)	67/D5
Azilal, Mor.	98/D3
Azimganj, India	85/G3
Azogues, Ecu.	152/B5
Azores (dpcy.), Port.	45/H12
Azouri, Mor.	98/D3
Azov, Rus.	63/F3
Azov (sea), Ukr.,Rus.	64/D5
Azpeitia, Sp.	44/D1
Aztec, NM, US	128/E3
Aztec Ruins Nat'l Mon., NM, US	128/E3
Azua de Compostela, DRep.	141/G4
Azuaga, Sp.	44/C3
Azuara, Sp.	45/E2
Azuchi, Japan	77/K5
Azuero, Peninsula de (pen.), Pan.	150/B2
Azuga, Rom.	49/G3
Azul (mtn.), CR	144/E4
Azul, Arg.	158/F3
Azul, Cordillera (mts.), Peru	156/B2
Azuma, Japan	77/E2
Azuma-san (peak), Japan	75/G2
Azumaya-san (peak), Japan	75/F2
Azur, Côte d' (coast), Fr.	43/G5
Azusa, Ca, US	136/C2
Azzaba, Alg.	100/K6
Azzano Decimo, It.	59/G1
Azzano San Paolo, It.	58/C1
Azzate, It.	58/B1
'Azzūn, WBnk.	91/G7

B

B (riv.), Viet.	79/A5
Ba (riv.), Viet.	83/J5
Ba Lang An (cape), Viet.	78/E3
Ba Quan (cape), Viet.	78/D4
Baar, Swi.	56/E4
Baarle-Hertog, Belg.	50/B6
Baarle-Nassau, Neth.	50/B6
Baarn, Neth.	50/C4
Bab el Mandeb (str.), Asia	88/D6
Baba (peak), Bul.	47/H1
Baba (riv.), Ecu.	47/K3
Baba (mts.), Afg.	89/J2
Baba Burnu (pt.), Turk.	47/K3
Babadag, Rom.	49/J3
Babaeski, Turk.	49/H5
Babahoyo, Ecu.	152/B5
Babai Khola (riv.), Nepal	84/C1
Babakale, Turk.	47/K3
Babar (isl.), Indo.	116/B5
Babatorun, Turk.	91/E1
Babatpur (int'l arpt.), India	84/D3
Babbacombe (bay), Eng, UK	32/C6
Babbitt, Mn, US	127/L4
B'abdā, Leb.	91/D3
Babelthuap (isl.), Palau	116/C4
Babenhausen, Ger.	51/G1
Babenhausen, Ger.	54/B3
Babenham, Ger.	55/F6
Baberu, India	84/C3
Babia (peak), Pol.	62/A2
Babian (riv.), China	83/H3
Bābil (gov.), Iraq	90/F3
Bābil (Babylon) (ruin), Iraq	90/F3
Babina, India	84/B3
Babinda, Austl.	114/B2
Babine (riv.), BC, Can.	122/D3
Bābol, Iran	88/F1
Babruysk, Bela.	63/G4
Babuyan (isl.), Phil.	67/M8
Babylon, NY, US	139/E2
Bac Giang, Viet.	78/D1
Bac Lieu, Viet.	78/D4
Bac Ninh, Viet.	83/J3
Bacabal, Braz.	154/A2
Bacadéhuachi, Mex.	142/C2
Bacajá (riv.), Braz.	151/H4
Bacalar, Mex.	144/D2
Bacalar (lag.), Mex.	144/D2
Bacan (isl.), Indo.	81/G4
Bacău, Rom.	49/H2
Baccarat, Fr.	53/E5
Bacchiglione (riv.), It.	59/E2
Bacchus, Ut, US	137/J12
Bacerac, Mex.	53/G3
Bacharach, Ger.	53/G3
Bachhraon, India	84/B1
Bachiniva, Mex.	142/D4
Back (riv.), Md, US	138/B5
Back (riv.), NW, Can.	119/H3
Bačka (reg.), Yugo.	48/D3
Bačka Palanka, Yugo.	48/D3
Bačka Topola, Yugo.	48/D3
Bäckefors, Swe.	38/E2
Backnang, Ger.	54/C5
Bacobampo, Mex.	142/C3
Bacolod, Phil.	81/F1
Bács-Kiskun (prov.), Hun.	40/D2
Bácsalmás, Hun.	40/D2
Bacup, Eng, UK	35/F4
Bad Abbach, Ger.	55/F5
Bad Axe, Mi, US	130/D3
Bad Bellingen, Ger.	56/D2
Bad Bergzabern, Ger.	54/A4
Bad Berneck, Ger.	55/E2
Bad Bocklet, Ger.	54/D2
Bad Brambach, Ger.	55/F2
Bad Breisig, Ger.	53/G3
Bad Buchau, Ger.	57/F1
Bad Camberg, Ger.	54/B2
Bad Doberan, Ger.	38/D4
Bad Driburg, Ger.	51/G5
Bad Dürkheim, Ger.	54/B4
Bad Dürrheim, Ger.	57/E1
Bad Endorf, Ger.	55/F7
Bad Essen, Ger.	51/F4
Bad Freienwalde, Ger.	41/H2
Bad Gandersheim, Ger.	51/H5
Bad Goisern, Aus.	56/G5
Bad Grund, Ger.	51/H5
Bad Hall, Aus.	55/H6
Bad Harzburg, Ger.	51/H5
Bad Herrenalb, Ger.	54/B5
Bad Hersfeld, Ger.	43/H1
Bad Hofgastein, Aus.	43/K3
Bad Homburg vor der Höhe, Ger.	54/B2
Bad Honnef, Ger.	53/G3
Bad Hönningen, Ger.	53/G2
Bad Ischl, Aus.	43/K3
Bad Karlshafen, Ger.	51/G5
Bad Kissingen, Ger.	54/D2
Bad Kohlgrub, Ger.	57/H2
Bad Königshofen, Ger.	54/D2
Bad Kreuznach, Ger.	53/G4
Bad Krozingen, Ger.	56/D2
Bad Langensalza, Ger.	51/H6
Bad Lauterberg, Ger.	51/H5
Bad Leonfelden, Aus.	55/H5
Bad Liebenzell, Ger.	54/B5
Bad Lippspringe, Ger.	51/F3
Bad Marienberg, Ger.	53/G2
Bad Mergentheim, Ger.	54/C4
Bad Munder am Deister, Ger.	51/G4
Bad Nauheim, Ger.	54/B2
Bad Nenndorf, Ger.	51/G4
Bad Neuenahr-Ahrweiler, Ger.	53/G3
Bad Neustadt an der Saale, Ger.	54/D2
Bad Oeynhausen, Ger.	51/F4
Bad Orb, Ger.	54/C2
Bad Peterstal-Griesbach, Ger.	56/E1
Bad Plaas, SAfr.	107/E2
Bad Pyrmont, Ger.	51/G5
Bad Ragaz, Swi.	57/F4
Bad Rappenau, Ger.	54/C4
Bad Reichenhall, Ger.	43/K3
Bad Rothenfelde, Ger.	51/F4
Bad Sachsa, Ger.	51/H5
Bad Salzdetfurth, Ger.	51/G4
Bad Salzschlirf, Ger.	54/C1
Bad Salzuflen, Ger.	51/F4
Bad Salzungen, Ger.	54/D2
Bad Sankt-Leonhard im Lavanttal, Aus.	43/L3
Bad Sassendorf, Ger.	51/F5
Bad Schallerbach, Aus.	55/G6
Bad Schwalbach, Ger.	53/H3
Bad Schwartau, Ger.	38/D5
Bad Segeberg, Ger.	38/D5
Bad Soden-Salmünster, Ger.	54/C2
Bad Sooden-Allendorf, Ger.	54/C2
Bad Tölz, Ger.	57/H2
Bad Vilbel, Ger.	54/B2
Bad Vöslau, Aus.	43/M3
Bad Waldsee, Ger.	57/F2
Bad Wildungen, Ger.	51/G6
Bad Wimpfen, Ger.	54/C4
Bad Wimsbach-Neydharting, Aus.	55/H6
Bad Windsheim, Ger.	54/D3
Bad Wörishofen, Ger.	57/G1
Bad Wurzach, Ger.	57/F2
Bad Zell, Aus.	55/H6
Bad Zwischenahn, Ger.	51/F2
Badagara, India	82/C5
Badain Jaran (des.), China	70/H3
Badajoz, Sp.	44/B3
Badalona, Sp.	45/L7
Badalucco, It.	58/A5
Badbergen, Ger.	51/F4
Baddeckenstedt, Ger.	51/H4
Baddomalhi, Pak.	84/C2
Baden, Aus.	43/M3
Baden, Swi.	56/E3
Baden-Baden, Ger.	54/B5
Baden-Württemberg (state), Ger.	72/D5
Badenoch (reg.), Sc, UK	36/B3
Badenweiler, Ger.	56/D2
Badgastein, Aus.	43/K3
Badgingarra NP, Austl.	112/B4
Badia Polesine, It.	59/E2
Badin, Pak.	89/J4
Badiraguato, Mex.	142/D3
Badlands (plat.), SD, US	127/H5
Badlands NP, SD, US	127/H5
Badou, Togo	103/F5
Badovinci, Yugo.	48/D3
Bādrāh, India	89/J3
Badrah, Iraq	88/E2
Badulla, SrL.	82/D6
Badūriā, India	85/G4
Baena, Sp.	44/C4
Baependi, Braz.	211/J6
Baerenkopf (peak), Fr.	53/F3
Baesweiler, Ger.	53/F2
Baeza, Sp.	44/D3
Baffa, Pak.	86/B2
Baffin (bay), Tx, US	132/D4
Baffin (bay), Can.	119/K2
Baffin (isl.), Can.	119/K2
Baffin Naval Training Sta., Md, US	138/B4
Bafia, Camr.	96/H6
Bafing (riv.), Gui.	102/C3
Bafoulabé, Mali	102/C3
Bafoussam, Camr.	96/H6
Bāfq, Iran	88/G2
Bafra, Turk.	62/E4
Bafra (cape), Turk.	62/E4
Bāft, Iran	89/G3
Bag Salt (lake), China	70/H4
Bagaces, CR	144/E4
Bagadó, Col.	152/B3
Bagaha, India	85/E2
Bagamoyo, Tanz.	97/H4
Baganga, Phil.	81/G2
Bagda (mts.), China	70/B3
Bagé, Braz.	157/F2
Bagenkop, Den.	38/D4
Baggao, Phil.	79/D4
Baggy (pt.), Eng, UK	32/B4
Bāgh, Pak.	86/B4
Baghain (riv.), India	84/C3
Baghdād (Baghdad) (cap.), Iraq	90/F3
Bagheria, It.	46/C3
Baghlān, Afg.	89/J1
Baghpat, India	86/D5
Bagley, Mn, US	127/K4
Bagnara Calabra, It.	46/D3
Bagnères-de-Bigorre, Fr.	42/D5
Bagnères-de-Luchon, Fr.	42/D5
Bagneux, Fr.	30/J5
Bagni di Lucca, It.	58/D4
Bagno a Ripoli, It.	59/E5
Bagnolet, Fr.	30/K5
Bagnoli Irpino, It.	46/D2
Bagnolo Cremasco, It.	58/C2
Bagnolo in Piano, It.	59/D3
Bagnolo Mella, It.	58/D2
Bagnolo San Vito, It.	59/D2
Bagnols-sur-Cèze, Fr.	42/F4
Bagnone, It.	58/C4
Bagô, Phil.	79/D5
Bago (div.), Myan.	78/B2
Bago (Pegu), Myan.	83/G4
Bagoé (riv.), Mali	96/D5
Bagolino, It.	58/D1
Bagshot, Eng, UK	30/A3
Bagua Grande, Peru	156/B2
Baguio, Phil.	79/D4
Baguirmi (reg.), Chad	96/J5
Bagzane (peak), Niger	103/H2
Bahādurganj, India	85/F2
Bahādurgarh, India	86/D5
Bahamas (ctry.)	119/K7
Bahāwalnagar, Pak.	86/B5
Bahāwalpur, Pak.	86/A5
Bahçesaray, Turk.	90/E2
Baheri, India	84/B1
Bahi (swamp), Tanz.	104/B4
Bahia (state), Braz.	154/B4
Bahia Asunción, Mex.	142/B3
Bahía Blanca, Arg.	158/E3
Bahia de Caráquez, Ecu.	152/A5
Bahía de los Angeles, Mex.	142/B2
Bahia de Tortugas, Mex.	142/B2
Bahia, Islas de la (isls.), Hon.	140/D4
Bahia Solano, Col.	152/B3
Bahir Dar, Eth.	97/N5
Bāhla, Oman	89/G4
Bahlah, Oman	89/G4
Bahr al 'Arab (riv.), Sudan	97/L6
Bahr al Milḥ (lake), Iraq	90/E3
Bahraich, India	84/C2
Bahrain (ctry.)	67/E7
Bahrain, Gulf of (gulf), Asia	88/F3
Baia de Aramă, Rom.	49/F3
Baia Mare, Rom.	49/F2
Baia Sprie, Rom.	49/F2
Baïboukoum, Chad	96/J6
Baicheng, China	71/M2
Bāicoi, Rom.	49/G3
Baidoa, Braz.	147/D3
Baie-Comeau, Qu, Can.	131/G1
Baie-Saint-Paul, Qu, Can.	131/G2
Baienfurt, Ger.	57/F2
Baiersbronn, Ger.	54/B5
Baiersdorf, Ger.	54/E3
Baigorrita, Arg.	158/E2
Baigou (riv.), China	72/G7
Baihar, India	84/C4
Baihua (mtn.), China	72/G7
Baikunthpur, India	84/D4
Bailadores, Ven.	152/D2
Baildon, Eng, UK	35/G4
Bailén, Sp.	44/D3
Baileborough, Ire.	31/Q10
Bailleul, Fr.	52/B2
Bailong (riv.), China	70/H5
Bailundo (riv.), China	72/C4
Baima, China	70/H5
Bain (riv.), UK	35/G3
Bainang, China	85/G3
Bains-les-Bains, Fr.	53/E5
Baïraïgnia, India	85/E2
Bairin Youqi, China	71/L3
Bairnsdale, Austl.	115/C3
Baïse (riv.), Fr.	42/D5
Baixa da Banheira, Port.	45/P10
Baixa Grande, Braz.	154/B4
Baixiang, China	72/F5
Baixo Guandu, Braz.	155/D1
Baiyin, China	70/H4
Baiyu (mts.), China	72/B3
Baiyun (int'l arpt.), China	73/N9
Baja (pt.), Mex.	142/B2
Baja, Hun.	48/D2
Baja (pt.), Chile	159/B6
Baja California (state), Mex.	142/B2
Baja California (pen.), Mex.	119/F6
Baja California Sur (state), Mex.	142/B3
Bājah (gov.), Tun.	46/A4
Bajah, Tun.	46/A4
Bajapuraa (peak), Turk.	90/E2
Bajánsenye, Hun.	40/M3
Bajestān, Iran	89/G2
Bajil, Yem.	88/D5
Bajina Bašta, Yugo.	48/D4
Bājmat (zone), Nepal	85/E2
Bajmok, Yugo.	48/D3
Bajo Boquete, Pan.	145/F4
Bajo de Gualicho (plain), Arg.	157/C5
Bajram Curri, Alb.	47/G1
Bakanas, Kaz.	87/G3
Bakau, Gam.	102/A3
Bakayan (peak), Indo.	81/E3
Bakel, Sen.	102/B3
Baker, Mt, US	127/G4
Baker, La, US	129/K5
Baker (mt.), Wa, US	126/C3
Baker (isl.), Pac., US	117/H4
Baker (lake), NW, Can.	122/G2
Baker, Or, US	126/D4
Baker, Ca, US	136/D3
Baker Lake, NW, Can.	122/G2
Bakersfield, Ca, US	136/C3
Bakhchysaray, Ukr.	62/E2
Bakhmach, Ukr.	62/E2
Bākhtarān, Iran	88/E2
Bakhtiyārpur, India	85/E3
Bakhuis (mts.), Sur.	153/G3
Bakkaflói (bay), Ice.	37/P6
Baklan, Turk.	90/B2
Bakonyszombathely, Hun.	48/C2
Bakora Corridor Game Rsv., Uga.	104/B2
Bakoye (riv.), Gui.	102/C4
Baku (int'l arpt.), Azer.	63/J4
Baku, Azer.	63/J4
Baku (cap.), Azer.	63/J4
Balā, India	84/C2
Bala, Wal, UK	34/E6
Balabac, Phil.	81/E2
Balabac (str.), Malay.,Ph	81/E2
Ba'labakk, Leb.	91/E2
Balâgaht, India	84/C5
Balaguer, Sp.	45/F2
Balaïtous (peak), Fr.	42/C5
Balakhna, Rus.	61/J4
Balakovo, Rus.	63/H1
Bal'amā, Jor.	91/E3
Bālan, Rom.	49/G2
Balancán, Mex.	144/D2
Balashikha, Rus.	61/W9
Balashov, Rus.	63/G2
Balasore (Baleshwar), India	82/E3
Balassagyarmat, Hun.	41/K4
Balaton (lake), Hun.	48/C2
Balatonföldvár, Hun.	48/C2
Balatonfüred, Hun.	48/C2
Balatonszabadi, Hun.	48/C2
Balatonszentgyörgy, Hun.	48/C2
Balbina (riv.), Braz.	158/F3
Balcarce, Arg.	158/F3
Balchik, Bul.	49/J4
Balclutha, NZ	117/R12
Balcones Escarpment (plat.), Tx, US	137/T20
Balcones Heights, Tx, US	137/T21
Bald Eagle Mtn. (mtn.), Pa, US	138/A1
Bald Rock NP, Austl.	115/E1
Baldock, Eng, UK	33/F3
Baldwin Harbour, NY, US	139/L9
Baldwin Park, Ca, US	136/C7
Baldy (mtn.), Mb, Can.	127/H3
Baldy Beacon (peak), Belz.	144/D2
Bale Mountains NP, Eth.	97/N6
Baleares (Balearic) (isls.), Sp.	45/G3
Baleia, Ponta da (pt.), Braz.	155/D1
Baleine, Grand Rivière de la (riv.), Qu, Can.	123/J2
Baleine, Petite Rivière de la (riv.), Qu, Can.	123/J2
Baleine, Rivière à (riv.), Qu, Can.	123/K2
Baleni, China	70/E5
Balen, Belg.	53/E1
Bāler, Rus.	79/F6
Balernà, Swi.	57/F6
Bāleshwar (Balasore), India	82/E3
Balfour, SAfr.	106/E2
Balfron, Sc, UK	36/B4
Balgatay, Mong.	70/G2
Balharshah, Austl.	113/M8
Bali (sea), Indo.	80/D5
Bali, Indo.	67/L10
Bāli Chak, India	84/C3
Balice (int'l arpt.), Pol.	41/J4
Baliem (riv.), Indo.	81/J4
Baliguian, Phil.	79/F6
Balıkesir, Turk.	49/H5
Balıkesir (prov.), Turk.	62/C5
Balikpapan, Indo.	81/E4
Balimbing, Phil.	81/E2
Baling, Malay.	83/H6
Balingasag, Phil.	79/D6
Balingen, Ger.	38/G2
Balingen, Swe.	57/E1
Balk, Neth.	50/D3
Balkan (pol. reg.), Trkm.	87/B4
Balkan (mts.), Bul.	49/H4
Balkanabat, Turk.	49/H5
Balkans (reg.), Eur.	48/E3
Balkh (gov.), Afg.	87/E5
Balkhash (lake), Kaz.	67/G5
Ballachulish, Sc, UK	36/A4
Ballaghadereen, Ire.	31/P10
Ballangen, Nor.	37/F1
Ballantrae, Sc, UK	36/A6
Ballarat, Austl.	115/B3
Ballard (lake), Austl.	109/B3
Ballater, Sc, UK	36/C2
Ballaugh, IM, UK	34/C3
Balleny (isls.), Ant.	160/L
Ballia, India	85/E3
Ballina, Austl.	115/E1
Ballina (isls.), Indo.	84/E4
Ballinamallard, NI, UK	31/Q9
Ballinasloe, Ire.	31/P10
Ballinderry (riv.), NI, UK	34/B2
Ballinger, Tx, US	129/H5
Ballingry, Sc, UK	36/C4
Ballinrobe, Ire.	31/P10
Ballon, Col du (pass), Fr.	56/C2
Ballon d'Alsace (peak), Fr.	56/C2
Ballon de Sevance (peak), Fr.	56/C2
Ballwin, Mo, US	137/F8
Bally, Pa, US	138/C3
Ballycarry, NI, UK	34/C2
Ballycastle, Ire.	31/P9
Ballyclare, NI, UK	34/C2
Ballyeaston, NI, UK	34/B2
Ballygawley, NI, UK	34/B3
Ballygeary, Ire.	31/Q10
Ballygowan, NI, UK	34/C2
Ballyhaunis, Ire.	31/P10
Ballyheigue, Ire.	30/P10
Ballyliffin, Ire.	34/A1
Ballymena (dist.), NI, UK	34/B2
Ballymena, NI, UK	34/B2
Ballymoney (dist.), NI, UK	34/B1
Ballymoney, NI, UK	34/B1
Ballynahinch, NI, UK	34/C2
Ballynure, NI, UK	34/C2
Ballyquintin (pt.), NI, UK	34/D2
Balmaceda, Chile	159/B6
Balmedie, Sc, UK	36/D2
Balmoral, Austl.	115/B3
Balmoral Castle, Sc, UK	36/C2
Balneário Camboriú, Braz.	155/B2
Balneario Claromecó, Arg.	158/E3
Balneario de los Novillos, PN, Mex.	129/G5
Balochistān (reg.), Pak.	89/J3
Balonne (riv.), Austl.	109/D3
Balotra, India	89/J3
Balqash, Kaz.	67/G5
Balrāmpur, India	84/D2
Balranald, Austl.	115/B2
Bals, Rom.	49/G3
Bálsamo (riv.), Ecu.	156/B2
Balsapuerto, Peru	156/B2
Balsas, Braz.	154/B3
Balsas (riv.), Mex.	119/G8
Balsthal, Swi.	56/D3
Baltanás, Sp.	44/C2
Bălți, Mol.	49/J2
Baltic (sea), Eur.	37/F5
Baltim, Egypt	91/B4
Baltimore, Md, US	138/B5
Baltimore (co.), Md, US	138/B5
Baltimore-Washington (int'l arpt.), Md, US	138/B5
Baltiysk, Rus.	39/H4
Baltrum (isl.), Ger.	51/E1
Bālurghāt, India	85/G3
Balve, Ger.	51/F6
Balya, Turk.	62/C5
Balykchy, Kyr.	63/J3
Balzar, Ecu.	152/B5
Balzers, Lcht.	57/F3
Bam (prov.), Burk.	103/E3
Bam, Iran	89/G3
Bama Yaozu Zizhixian, China	70/G5
Bamaji (lake), Can.	127/K3
Bamako (Senou) (int'l arpt.), Mali	102/C3
Bambamarca, Peru	156/B2
Bambana (riv.), Nic.	145/F4
Bambari, CAfr.	97/K7
Bamberg, SC, US	132/C4
Bamberg, Ger.	54/D3
Bambuí, Braz.	155/C2
Bamenda, Camr.	96/H6
Bāmīān, Afg.	87/E5
Bananal, Ilha do (isl.), Braz.	151/H6
Banar (riv.), Bang.	85/H3
Banarli, Turk.	49/H5
Banās (pt.), Egypt	101/C4
Banās (riv.), India	89/L3
Banat (reg.), Yugo.	48/E3
Banatsko Novo Selo, Yugo.	48/E3
Banbar, China	70/G5
Banbridge (dist.), NI, UK	34/B3
Banbridge, NI, UK	34/B3
Banbury, Eng, UK	33/E2
Banchory, Sc, UK	36/D2
Banco Chinchorro (isls.), Mex.	140/D4
Bancroft, On, Can.	131/E2
Bānda, India	84/C3
Banda (isl.), Indo.	81/H4
Banda (sea), Indo.	67/M10
Banda Aceh, Indo.	80/A2
Bandama (riv.), C.d'Iv.	96/D6
Bandama Blanc (riv.), C.d'Iv.	102/D4
Bandama Rouge (riv.), C.d'Iv.	102/D4
Bandar Beheshtī, Iran	89/H3
Bandar-e 'Abbās, Iran	89/G3
Bandar-e Anzalī, Iran	88/E1
Bandar-e Deylam, Iran	88/F2
Bandar-e Lengeh, Iran	89/G3
Bandar-e Māshahr, Iran	88/F2
Bandar-e Torkeman, Iran	88/F1
Bandar Seri Begawan (cap.), Bru.	81/E2
Bande, Sp.	44/B1
Bandeira do Sul, Braz.	211/G6
Bandeira, Pico da (peak), Braz.	155/D2
Bandeirantes, Braz.	155/B2
Bandelier Nat'l Mon., NM, US	129/F4
Banderilla, Mex.	143/N7
Bandhavgarh NP, India	84/C4
Bandholm, Den.	38/D4
Bandiagara, Mali	102/D3
Bandirma (gulf), Turk.	49/H5
Bandon, Ire.	31/P11
Bandon, Or, US	126/C4
Bandundu, D.R. Congo	105/C1
Bandung, Indo.	80/C5
Banes, Cuba	141/H1
Banff, Ab, Can.	126/E3
Banff, Sc, UK	36/D1
Banff NP, Can.	126/E3
Banfora, Burk.	102/D4
Banga, Phil.	79/D6
Banga, India	84/D2
Bangalore, India	82/C5
Bangalow, Austl.	114/D5
Bangassou, CAfr.	97/K7
Bangau (cape), Malay.	80/D3
Banggai (isls.), Indo.	81/F4
Banghiang (riv.), Laos	78/D2
Bangka (str.), Indo.	80/B4
Bangka (isl.), Indo.	67/K10
Bangkok (Krung Thep) (cap.), Thai.	78/C3
Bangladesh (ctry.)	82/E3
Bangor (int'l arpt.), Me, US	131/G2
Bangor, Me, US	131/G2
Bangor, Pa, US	138/C2
Bangor, Wal, UK	34/D5
Bangor, NI, UK	34/C2
Bangued, Phil.	79/D4
Bangweulu (swamp), Zam.	104/A5
Banhā, Egypt	91/B4
Banhine, PN de, Moz.	105/D5
Bani, DRep.	141/G4
Bani (riv.), Mali	96/D5
Bani Mazār, Egypt	101/B4
Banī Suhaylah, Gaza	91/D4
Banī Suwayf, Egypt	101/B4
Bánica, DRep.	145/J2
Banihāl (pass), India	86/C2
Banikoara, Ben.	103/F4
Banister (riv.), Va, US	133/J2
Bāniyās, Syria	91/D2
Banja Koviljača, Yugo.	48/D3
Banja Luka, Bosn.	48/D3
Banjar (riv.), India	84/C4
Banjarmasin, Indo.	80/D4
Banjul (cap.), Gam.	102/A3
Bānka, India	85/F3
Bankas, Mali	102/D3
Bankfoot, Sc, UK	36/C4
Bānkura, India	85/F4
Banks (pt.), Ak, US	134/H4
Banks (lakes), Wa, US	126/D3
Banks (isl.), Van.	116/F6
Banks (isl.), NW, Can.	119/G2
Banks (pen.), NZ	109/H7
Bānkura, India	85/F4
Bankya, Bul.	47/H1
Banmankhi, India	85/F3
Bann (riv.), NI, UK	34/B3
Bannockburn, Sc, UK	36/C4
Bannockburn Battlesite, Sc, UK	36/C4
Bannu, Pak.	86/B2
Baños, Ecu.	156/B1
Banpo Ruins, China	72/B4
Bansberia, India	85/G4
Bānsi, India	85/E3
Bānsi, India	84/D2
Banská Bystrica, Slvk.	62/A2
Banská Štiavnica, Slvk.	48/D1
Bansko, Bul.	47/H2
Banstead, Eng, UK	30/C3
Bānswāra, India	89/K4
Bantayan, Phil.	79/D5
Bāntī, India	84/C3
Bantenan (cape), Indo.	80/D5
Bantong Group (isls.), Thai.	78/B5
Bantry, Ire.	31/P11
Bāñuelo (peak), Sp.	44/C3
Banyak (isl.), Indo.	80/A3
Banyoles, Sp.	45/G1
Banyuwangi, Indo.	80/D5
Banzare (coast), Ant.	160/J
Banzart (Bizerte), Tun.	46/A4
Baode, China	72/B3
Baoding, China	72/G7
Baofeng, China	72/C4
Baoji, China	70/J5
Baojing, China	83/J2
Baoruco (mts.), DRep.	145/J2
Baoshan, China	83/G2
Baoshan, China	72/L4
Baotou, China	72/B2
Baoulé (riv.), Mali	96/D5
Baoying, China	72/D4
Bapaume, Fr.	52/B3
Baptistown, NJ, US	138/C2
Baqên, China	70/F5
Bā'qūbah, Iraq	90/F3
Bar, Yugo.	47/F1
Bar (riv.), Fr.	40/C4
Bar Bigha, India	85/E3
Bar Harbor, Me, US	131/G2
Bar-sur-Aube, Fr.	42/F2
Bar-sur-Seine, Fr.	42/F2
Bara, Swe.	38/E4
Bārā Lācha La (pass), India	86/D1
Barabai, Indo.	80/E4
Barabinsk, Rus.	87/G1
Baraboo, Wi, US	127/L5
Baracaldo, Sp.	44/D1
Baracoa, Cuba	141/H1
Barada (riv.), Syria	91/E3
Baradero, Arg.	159/J10
Baradine, Austl.	115/D1
Baragoi, Kenya	104/C2
Baraguá, Cuba	145/G1
Barahona, DRep.	141/G4
Barajas (int'l arpt.), Sp.	45/N8
Barak (riv.), India	85/H3
Barākī Barak, Afg.	87/J2
Baralaba, Austl.	114/C4
Baram (cape), Malay.	80/D3
Baram (riv.), Guy.	150/F2
Baramula, India	86/C2
Baran, India	86/C2
Baranagar, India	85/G4
Baranavichy, Bela.	62/C1
Baranof (isl.), Ak, US	122/C3
Baranya (prov.), Hun.	48/C3
Barão de Cocais, Braz.	155/D1
Barão de Grajaú, Braz.	154/B2
Baraque de Fraiture (hill), Belg.	53/E3
Barat Daya (isls.), Indo.	81/G5
Barataria, La, US	137/P17
Barauli, India	85/E2
Baraut, India	86/D5
Baraya, Col.	152/C3
Barbacena, Col.	155/D2
Barbacoas, Col.	152/B3
Barbados (ctry.)	119/M8
Barbalha, Braz.	154/C2
Barbaros, Turk.	49/H5
Barbas (cape), Mor.	98/A5
Barbate de Franco, Sp.	44/C4
Barbeau (peak), NW, Can.	123/K2
Barberà del Vallès, Sp.	45/L6
Barberino di Mugello, It.	59/E4
Barbers (pt.), Hi, US	124/V13
Barberton, Oh, US	130/D3
Barberton, SAfr.	107/F2
Barbezieux, Fr.	42/C4
Barbourville, Ky, US	130/D4
Barbuda (isl.), Anti.	119/L8
Barcaldine, Austl.	114/B3
Barcarrota, Sp.	44/B3
Barcellona Pozzo di Gotto, It.	46/D3
Barcelona, Sp.	45/L7
Barcelona, Ven.	153/F2
Barcelona (int'l arpt.), Sp.	45/L7
Barcelona (prov.), Sp.	45/L6
Barcelos, Port.	44/A2
Barcelos, Braz.	153/F5
Barcin, Pol.	41/J2
Barco (riv.), Austl.	109/D3

Barcs, Hun. 48/C3
Barczewo, Pol. 39/J5
Bardejov, Slvk. 41/L4
Bardi, It. 58/C3
Bardīyah, Libya 97/L1
Bardoli, India 89/K4
Bardonia, NY, US 139/K7
Bardsdale, Ca, US 136/B2
Bardsey (isl.), Wal, UK 34/D6
Bardstown, Ky, US 58/B2
Bareggio, It. 58/B2
Bareli, India 115/C2
Barellan, Austl. 115/C2
Barendrecht, Neth. 50/B5
Barentin, Fr. 42/D2
Barents (sea), Eur. 27/H1
Barentu, Erit. 88/C5
Bäretswil, Swi.
Barfleur, Pointe de (pt.), Fr. 42/C2
Barga, It. 58/D4
Bargara, Austl. 114/D4
Bargarh, India 82/D3
Bargfeld-Stegen, Ger. 51/H1
Bargi, India 84/B4
Bargo, Austl. 115/C2
Bargteheide, Ger. 51/H1
Bärh, India 85/E3
Barhaj, India 84/D2
Barhalganj, India 84/D2
Barham, Austl. 115/C2
Barhiya, India 85/F3
Bāri, India 84/A2
Bari, It. 46/E2
Bari Sardo, It. 46/A3
Bariano, It. 58/C1
Baricella, It. 59/E3
Barichara, Col. 152/C3
Barigazzo (peak), It. 58/D4
Barika, Alg. 100/H5
Barillas, Guat. 144/D3
Barima (riv.), Guy. 153/G2
Barima-Waini (pol. reg.), Guy. 153/F3
Barinas (state), Ven. 152/D2
Barinas, Ven. 152/D2
Barinitas, Ven. 152/D2
Bariri, Braz. 155/B2
Barīsāl (pol. reg.), Bang. 85/H4
Barisan Mountains (mts.), Indo. 80/B4
Barito (riv.), Indo. 80/D4
Baritu, PN, Arg. 157/D1
Bark (lake), Can.
Bark (riv.), Wi, US 135/N13
Barka Kāna, India
Barker, NY, US 131/S9
Barki Saria, India
Barking and Dagenham (bor.), Eng, UK 30/D2
Barkley (sound), Can. 126/B3
Barkley (lake), US 130/C4
Barkly East, SAfr. 106/D3
Barkly Tableland (plat.), Austl. 109/C2
Barkly West, SAfr. 106/D3
Barkol Kazak Zizhixian, China 70/F3
Barlee (lake), Austl. 109/A3
Barlee (range), Austl. 112/B2
Barlee Range Nature Rsv., Austl. 112/B2
Barletta, It. 46/E2
Barlin, Fr. 52/B3
Barlinek, Pol. 41/H2
Barmedman, Austl. 115/C2
Barmera, Austl. 113/J5
Barmstedt, Ger. 51/G1
Barnāla, India 86/C4
Bärnbach, Aus. 43/L3
Barnegat (inlet), NJ, US 138/D4
Barnegat (bay), NJ, US 138/D4
Barnegat, NJ, US 138/D4
Barnegat Light, NJ, US 138/D4
Barneveld, Neth. 50/C4
Barnhart, Mo, US 137/G9
Barnoldswick, Eng, UK 35/F4
Barnsley, Eng, UK 35/G4
Barnstaple, Eng, UK 32/B4
Barnstaple (Bideford) (bay), Eng, UK 32/B4
Barnstorf, Ger. 51/F3
Barntrup, Ger. 51/G5
Barnwell, SC, US 133/H3
Baroghil (pass), Pak. 87/F5
Baron, Fr. 30/L4
Barone (peak), It. 58/B1
Barow (riv.), Ire. 34/A5
Barowghīl (pass), Afg. 87/F1
Barquisimeto, Ven. 152/D2
Barquisimeto (int'l arpt.), Ven. 152/D2
Barr (lake), Co, US 137/C3
Barr, Co, US 137/C3
Barr, Fr. 56/D1
Barra, Braz. 154/B3
Barra (isl.), Sc, UK 31/08
Barra Bonita, Braz. 155/B2
Barra Bonita, Represa de (res.), Braz. 155/B2
Barra da Choça, Braz. 154/B4
Barra del Colorado, PN, CR 140/E5
Barra do Bugres, Braz. 150/G7
Barra do Corda, Braz. 154/A2
Barra do Garças, Braz. 151/H7
Barra do Mendes, Braz. 154/B3
Barra do Pirai, Braz. 211/K7
Barra do Ribeiro, Braz. 155/B4
Barra Head (pt.), Sc, UK 31/08
Barra Mansa, Braz. 211/J7
Barra Velha, Braz. 155/B3
Barraba, Austl. 115/D1
Barrackpur, India 85/G4
Barrage de Lagdo (dam), Camr. 96/H6
Barranca, Peru 156/B2
Barranca, Peru 156/B2

Barranca de Upía, Col. 152/C3
Barranca del Cobre PN, Mex. 142/D3
Barrancabermeja, Col. 152/C3
Barrancas, Ven. 153/F2
Barrancas, Col. 152/C2
Barrancas, Chile 158/N8
Barrancas, Col. 152/C2
Barranco de Loba, Col. 152/C2
Barrancos, Port. 44/B3
Barranquilla, Col. 152/C2
Barras, Braz. 154/B2
Barreiras, Braz. 154/B2
Barreirinhas, Braz. 154/B1
Barreiro, Port. 45/P10
Barren (isls.), Madg. 105/J10
Barren (isl.), It. 107/G7
Barren, Nosy (Barren Islands) (isls.), Madg. 107/G7
Barretal, Mex. 143/F3
Barretos, Braz. 155/B2
Barrhead, Ab, Can. 126/E2
Barrhead, Sc, UK 36/B5
Barrie, On, Can. 130/E2
Barrier (range), Austl. 113/J4
Barrington, Il, US 135/P15
Barrington Hills, Il, US 135/P15
Barrington Tops (peak), Austl. 115/D1
Barrington Tops NP, Austl. 115/D1
Barro Duro, Braz. 154/B2
Barron Gorge NP, Austl. 114/B2
Barros, Braz. 155/D2
Barrouallie, StV. 141/N9
Barrow, Ak, US 134/G1
Barrow (riv.), Ak, US 134/G1
Barrow (isl.), Austl. 109/A3
Barrow (pt.), Ire. 31/Q10
Barrow (pt.), Austl. 114/B1
Barrow (isls.), Phil. 67/M7
Barrow (isl.), NW, Can. 122/G1
Barrow-in-Furness, Eng, UK 35/E3
Barrow Island, Austl. 112/B2
Barrowford, Eng, UK 35/F4
Barrueco de Santullán, Sp. 44/C1
Barry, Wal, UK 32/C4
Barsa-Kel'mes (lake), Kaz. 87/C3
Barsakel'mes (lake), Uzb. 87/C4
Barsinghausen, Ger. 51/G4
Barssel, Ger. 51/E2
Barstow, Ca, US 128/C4
Bartang (riv.), Taj. 87/F5
Bartenheim, Fr. 56/D2
Barth, Ger. 38/E4
Bartholomä, Ger. 54/C5
Bartholomäberg, Aus. 57/F3
Bartica, Guy. 153/G3
Bartın, Turk. 49/L5
Bartle Frere (peak), Austl. 109/D2
Bartlesville, Ok, US 129/J3
Bartlett, Tx, US 129/H5
Bartlett (dam), NW, Can. 122/F2
Bartlett Inlet, NW, Can. 122/F2
Bartlett, II, US 137/S18
Bartlett, Az, US 137/S18
Bartlett, II, US 135/P16
Bartolomé Masó, Cuba 145/G1
Bartolomeu Dias, Moz. 105/G5
Bartonsville, Pa, US 138/C2
Bartoszyce, Pol. 39/J4
Bartow, Fl, US 133/H5
Bartow, Fl, US 38/E5
Barú (vol.), Pan. 145/F4
Barúipur, India 85/G4
Barumun (riv.), Indo. 80/B3
Barus, Indo. 80/A3
Baruun-Urt, Mong. 71/K2
Barwa Sāgar, India 84/B3
Barwāha, India 89/L4
Barwāla, India 86/C5
Barwon (riv.), Austl. 109/D3
Barycz (riv.), Pol. 41/J3
Barysaw, Bela. 39/N4
Barysh, Rus. 63/H1
Barzanö, It. 58/B1
Bas-Rhin (dept.), Fr. 56/D1
Basaldella, It. 59/G1
Basauri, Sp. 44/D1
Basavilbaso, Arg. 159/J10
Baschurch, Eng, UK 33/G5
Bascharage, Lux. 53/E4
Basehor, Ks, US 137/D5
Basel, Swi. 56/D2
Basel/Mulhouse (int'l arpt.), Fr. 56/D2
Baselga di Pinè, It. 57/H5
Baselland (canton), Swi.
Bashee (riv.), SAfr. 106/C3
Bashi (chan.), Phil.,Tai. 116/A2
Bashi Channel (chan.), Phil.Tai. 79/C3
Bashkortostan Aut. Rep., Rus. 64/Q6
Bāshtīn, Iran 88/F2
Basilan (isl.), Phil. 81/F2
Basilan, Phil.
Malay. 80/B3
Basildon, Eng, UK 33/G3
Basilica di Fieschi, It. 58/C4
Basilicata (reg.), It.
Basingstoke, Eng, UK 33/G4
Basingstoke (canal), Eng, UK 30/A4
Basīrhāt, India 85/G4
Baṣīrpur, Pak. 86/B4
Başkale, Turk. 103/H4
Baskatong (res.), Can. 130/F2
Baskil, Turk.
Başkomutan NP, Turk. 62/D5
Bāsoda, India 84/A4
Basodino (peak), It. 57/E5
Basoko, D.R. Congo 97/K7
Basoli, India 86/C3
Bass (str.), Austl. 109/D4

Bass Rock (isl.), Sc, UK 36/D4
Bassae (Vassés) (ruin), Gre. 47/G4
Bassano, Ab, Can. 126/E3
Bassano del Grappa, It. 57/H5
Bassari, Togo 103/F4
Bassas da India (isl.), Reun. 105/G5
Basse-Normandie (pol. reg.), Fr. 42/C2
Basse Santa Su, Gam. 102/B3
Basse-Terre (isl.), Guad. 141/J4
Basse-Terre, Fr. 141/N8
Bassecourt, Swi. 56/D3
Bassenheim, Ger. 53/G3
Bassenthwaite (lake), Eng, UK 35/E2
Basseterre (cap.), StK. 141/N8
Bassum, Ger. 51/F3
Basswood (lake), US,Can. 130/J5
Båstad, Swe. 38/E3
Bastam, Iran 89/G1
Baştām, Iran 89/G1
Bastelicaccia, Fr. 46/A2
Bastheim, Ger. 54/D2
Basti, India 84/D2
Bastì, India 84/D2
Bastia, Fr. 46/A1
Bastia, It. 43/K5
Bastogne, Belg. 53/E4
Bastos, Braz. 155/B2
Bastrop, Tx, US 129/H5
Basyūn, Egypt 91/B4
Bat Shelomo, Isr. 91/F6
Bat Yam, Isr. 91/F7
Bata, EqG. 96/G7
Batabanó (gulf), Cuba 145/F1
Batac, Phil. 79/D4
Batagay, Rus. 65/P3
Batai (pass), Pak. 86/A3
Batalha, Braz. 154/B2
Batalha, Port. 44/A3
Batang, China 70/G6
Batangafo, CAfr. 96/J6
Batangas, Phil. 79/D5
Batarasa, Phil. 79/C6
Batatais, Braz. 155/C2
Batavia, NY, US 130/E3
Batavia, Il, US 135/P16
Batavsk, Rus. 62/F3
Batchtown, Il, US 137/F7
Bātdâmbang, Camb. 83/C3
Bate (bay), Austl. 114/H9
Batéké (plat.), Congo 96/H8
Batemans Bay, Austl. 115/D2
Batesburg-Leesville, SC, US 133/H3
Batesville, Ms, US 129/K4
Bath, Me, US 131/G3
Bath, Eng, UK 32/D4
Bath, Pa, US 138/C2
Bathgate, Sc, UK 36/C5
Bathmen, Neth. 50/D4
Bathurst, Austl. 115/D2
Bathurst (cape), Can. 134/N1
Bathurst, NB, Can. 131/H2
Bathurst (isl.), Can. 119/G2
Bathurst (inlet), NW, Can. 122/F2
Batian (Mt. Kenya) (peak), Kenya 104/C3
Batiquitos (lag.), Ca, US 136/C5
Batiscan (riv.), Can. 131/F2
Batley, Eng, UK 35/G4
Batlow, Austl. 115/D2
Batman, Turk. 90/E2
Batman (dam), Turk. 90/E2
Batna (prov.), Alg. 99/G2
Batna, Alg. 100/J5
Baton Rouge (cap.), La, US 129/K5
Batopilas, Mex. 142/D3
Batoti, India 86/C3
Batouri, Camr. 96/H7
Baṭrā' (ruin), Jor. 91/D4
Båtsfjord, Nor. 37/J1
Batsto (riv.), NJ, US 138/D4
Batsto, NJ, US 138/D4
Batsto Historic Village, NJ, US 138/D4
Battambang, Camb. 83/C3
Battenberg, Ger. 51/F6
Bätterkinden, Swi. 56/D3
Batticaloa, SrL. 82/D6
Battipaglia, It. 46/D2
Battle (riv.), Ab,Sk, Can. 126/E2
Battle Creek, Mi, US 130/C3
Battle Mountain, Nv, US 126/C3
Battlefield (nat'l bfld.), Sc, UK
Battlefield, Sk, Can. 126/F2
Battle, Eng, UK 33/K5
Battock (mt.), Sc, UK
Batu (bay), Malay. 80/D3
Batu (peak), Malay. 80/D3
Batu (isls.), Indo. 80/A4
Batu (riv.), Eth. 97/N6
Batu (cape), Indo. 81/E3
Batu Gajah, Malay. 80/B3
Batu Puteh (peak), Malay. 80/B3
Batudaka (isl.), Indo. 81/F4
Batuensambang (peak), Indo. 80/D3
Bat'umi (int'l arpt.), Geo. 63/G4
Bat'umi, Geo. 63/G4
Baturaja, Indo. 80/B4
Baturité, Braz. 154/C2
Batys Qazaqstan, Kaz. 64/E5
Bauchi (state), Nga. 96/H6
Baudette, Mn, US 127/K3
Baudó (mts.), Col. 145/G5
Baudó (riv.), Col. 152/C3
Bauld (cape), Can. 131/L1
Baulmes, Swi. 56/C4
Bauman (peak), Togo 103/F5

Baume-les-Dames, Fr. 56/C3
Baumholder, Ger. 53/G4
Baunach, Ger. 54/D3
Baunatal, Ger. 51/G6
Baunei, It. 46/A2
Baurú, Braz. 155/B2
Bautzen, Ger. 41/H3
Bavans, Fr. 56/C3
Bavarian Alps (mts.), Aus.,Ger. 57/G3
Bavay, Fr. 52/C3
Bavāria (riv.), India 84/B4
Baveno, It. 57/E6
Bavispe, Rio de (riv.), Mex. 142/C2
Bawa de Segura, Sp. 44/D1
Bawal, India 84/C3
Bawang (cape), Indo. 80/C4
Bawang (isl.), Indo. 80/D5
Bawku, Gha. 103/E4
Baxoi, China 83/G2
Bay Bassin-Rose Hill, Mrts. 107/T15
Bay City, Tx, US 129/J5
Bay City, Mi, US 130/D3
Bay Minette, Al, US 133/G4
Bay Roberts, Nf, Can. 131/L2
Bay Saint Louis, Ms, US 133/F4
Bayamo, Cuba 145/G1
Bayamón, PR 141/M8
Bayan, Mong. 70/G2
Bayan Har (mts.), China 70/G5
Bayan-Hongor (prov.), Mong. 70/G2
Bayan-ölgiy (prov.), Mong. 70/G2
Bayan-Ulaan, Mong. 70/H2
Bayanhongor, Mong. 70/H2
Bayanhushuu, Mong. 70/F2
Bayannuur, Mong. 70/F2
Bayano (lake), Pan. 145/G4
Bayanterem, Mong. 71/K2
Bayantsagaan, Mong. 70/H2
Bayard, Ne, US 127/H5
Bayat, Turk. 62/F4
Bayawan, Phil. 81/F2
Baybach (riv.), Ger. 53/G3
Baybay, Phil. 79/D5
Bayburt, Turk. 62/G4
Bayburt (prov.), Turk. 62/F4
Baydaratskaya (bay), Rus. 64/G2
Baydhabo (Baidoa), Som. 97/P7
Bayel, Fr. 56/A1
Bayerischer Wald (hills), Ger. 43/K2
Bayerischer Wald, NP, Mb, Can. 127/J3
Bayerischer Wald NP, Ger. 43/K2
Bayern (state), Ger. 55/G5
Bayeux, Sk, Can. 126/G2
Bayeux, Fr. 42/C2
Baygorria (res.), Uru. 159/K10
Baykal (mts.), Rus. 128/G3
Baykal (lake), Rus. 67/L4
Baykan, Turk. 90/E2
Bayombong, Phil. 79/D4
Bayon, Fr. 56/C1
Bayonet Point, Fl, US 133/H4
Bayonne, Fr. 42/C5
Bayonne, NJ, US 139/J9
Bayport, NY, US 139/E2
Bayramaly, Trkm. 89/H1
Bayramiç, Turk. 47/K3
Bayreuth, Ger. 55/F3
Bayrūt (cap.), Leb. 91/D3
Bays, Lake of (lake), Can. 130/E2
Bebedouro, Braz. 155/B2
Bayşehir (lake), Turk. 90/B2
Bayt Ḥanīnā, WBnk. 91/G8
Bayt Ḥānūn, Gaza 91/G8
Bayt Laḥm (Bethlehem), WBnk. 91/G8
Bayt Ṣāḥūr, WBnk. 91/G8
Baytik Shan (mts.), China,Mon 70/E2
Bayudha (des.), Sudan 101/C5
Bayugan, Phil. 79/E6
Bayville, NY, US 139/F2
Bayville, Fr. 44/D2
Baza, Sp. 44/D4
Bazaine, Fr. 30/L6
Bazardüzü (peak), Az. 63/H4
Bazaruto, Ilha do (isl.), Moz. 105/G5
Bazège (prov.), Burk. 103/E4
Bazemont, Fr. 30/H5
Bazet, Fr. 42/D5
Bazhong, China 70/J5
Bazin (riv.), Can. 130/F2
Båzpur, India 84/B1
Bazzano, It. 59/E3
Be, Nosy (isl.), Madg. 107/H6
Beach Haven, NJ, US 138/D4
Beachport, Austl. 115/B3
Beachwood, NJ, US 138/D4
Beachy (head), Eng, UK 33/G5
Beachy Head (pt.), Eng, UK 42/D1
Beacon (riv.), Wal, UK 32/C2
Beaconsfield, Eng, UK 33/F3
Beaconsfield, Qu, Can. 131/N7
Beal (range), Austl. 109/C2
Bealanana, Madg. 107/J6
Beampingaratra (ridge), Madg. 107/H9
Beamsville, On,Can. 130/E3
Bear (mtn.), Ak, US 134/K3
Bear (mtn.), Ak, US 134/K2
Bear (isl.), Col. 126/F5
Bear (riv.), Ut, US 137/C2
Bear (lake), Ut, US 128/E2
Bear (riv.), Nor. 160/E
Bear, De, US 138/C4
Bear, Ut, US 137/C2

Bear Creek (lake), Co, US 137/B3
Bear River (bay), Ut, US 137/J11
Bear River Migratory Bird Refuge (nat'l wild. ref.), Ut, US 137/J10
Beardsley, Az, US 137/R18
Beardsley (canal), Az, US 137/R18
Beardstown, NJ, US 138/B1
Béarn (mtn.), NJ, US 139/H7
Beas (lake), NI, UK 34/B2
Beas (riv.), India 84/B4
Beata (cape), DRep. 141/G4
Beata (isl.), Thai. 145/J2
Beata (cape), DRep. 145/J2
Beatenberg, Swi. 56/D4
Beattystown, NJ, US 138/C3
Beaucaire, Fr. 42/F5
Beauchamp, Fr. 30/J4
Beaucourt, Fr. 56/C3
Beaudesert, Austl. 114/D4
Behren-lès-Forbach, Fr. 53/F5
Beaufort, SC, US 133/H3
Beaufort (sea), Can.,US 119/C2
Beaufort West, SAfr. 106/C4
Beaufort, Lux. 53/F4
Beaufort, It. 58/B4
Beaugency, Fr. 42/D3
Beaujolais, Monts du (mts.), Fr. 42/F4
Beauly (riv.), Sc, UK 36/B2
Beauly Firth (lake), Sc, UK 36/B2
Beaumaris, Wal, UK 34/D5
Beaumont, Tx, US 129/J5
Beaumont, Ca, US 136/D3
Beaumont, Belg. 52/C3
Beaumont-de-Lomagne, Fr. 42/D5
Beaumont-sur-Oise, Fr. 30/J4
Beaupréau, Fr. 42/C3
Beauquesne, Fr. 52/B3
Beauraing, Belg. 53/D3
Beaurainville, Fr. 52/A3
Beaurevoir, Fr. 52/C4
Beausejour, Mb, Can. 127/J3
Beautheil, Fr. 30/M5
Beautor, Fr. 52/C4
Beauvais, Fr. 52/B5
Beauval, Sk, Can. 126/G2
Beauvoir, Fr. 52/B3
Beaver, Ak, US 134/J2
Beaver (riv.), Ok, US 128/G3
Beaver (riv.), Pa, US 127/L2
Beaver, Ut, US 128/D3
Beaver (isl.), Mi, US 130/C2
Beaver (riv.), Yk, Can. 122/D2
Beaver Creek, Yk, Can. 134/K3
Beaver Meadows, Pa, US 138/C2
Beaver Springs, Pa, US 138/C3
Beaverhead (riv.), US 126/E4
Beaverlodge, Ab, Can. 126/D2
Beaverton, Pa, US 138/C2
Bebedouro, Braz. 155/B2
Beberibe, Braz. 154/C2
Bebington, Eng, UK 35/E5
Becal, Mex. 144/D1
Beccles, Eng, UK 33/H2
Beceened, Yugo. 48/E3
Becerreá, Sp. 44/B1
Béchar (prov.), Alg. 98/E2
Béchar, Alg. 99/E3
Becharof (lake), Ak, US 134/G4
Becharof NWR, Ak, US 134/G4
Bechhofen, Ger. 53/G5
Bechtheim, Ger. 54/B3
Bechynĕ, Czh. 51/G2
Beckenried, Swi. 56/E4
Beckingen, Ger. 53/F5
Beckley, WV, US 130/D4
Beckum, Ger. 51/F5
Beclean, Rom. 49/G2
Becs de Bosson (peak), Swi. 56/D5
Bédarieux, Fr. 42/E5
Bedburg, Ger. 53/D2
Bedburg-Hau, Ger. 50/D5
Beder, Den. 38/D3
Bedford, In, US 130/C4
Bedford, Qu, Can. 130/F2
Bedford, SAfr. 106/D4
Bedford, Eng, UK 33/F2
Bedford (cape), Austl. 114/B1
Bedford Hills, NY, US 139/E1
Bedford Level (phys. reg.), Eng, UK 33/F2
Bedford Park, Il, US 135/Q16
Bedfordshire (co.), Eng, UK 33/F2
Bedlington, Eng, UK 35/G1
Bedonia, It. 58/C4
Bédouaram (well), Niger 96/H4
Bedretto, Swi. 57/E5
Bedsted, Den. 38/C3
Bedum, Neth. 50/D2
Bedworth, Eng, UK 33/F2
Beebe Seep (canal), Ct, US 137/C2
Beechwood, Austl. 115/D1
Beechworth, Austl. 115/C3
Beecroft (head), Austl. 115/D2
Beek, Neth. 53/E2
Beelitz, Ger. 40/P7
Beenleigh, Austl. 114/D4

Beer (pt.), Eng, UK 32/C5
Be'er Sheva', Isr. 91/D4
Beerfelden, Ger. 54/B3
Beernem, Belg. 52/C1
Beerzel, Belg. 53/D1
Beesel, Neth. 50/D6
Beeville, Tx, US 132/D4
Befandriana, Madg. 107/J6
Befandriana, Madg. 107/G8
Beforona, Madg. 107/J6
Befotaka, Madg. 107/J6
Beg (lake), NI, UK 34/B2
Bega, Austl. 115/D3
Bega (riv.), Ger. 51/F5
Bega Veche (riv.), Cro. 48/E3
Begamganj, Bang. 85/H4
Begamganj, India 84/B4
Begejski (riv.), Rus. 65/M2
Begejci, Yugo. 48/E3
Begichev (isl.), Rus. 65/M2
Begna (riv.), Nor. 37/D3
Begusarai, India 85/F3
Béhague (pt.), FrG. 151/H3
Behala (str.), India 80/B4
Behāla, India 82/E3
Behat, India 86/D4
Behbahān, Iran 88/F2
Behenjy-Afovany, Madg. 107/H7
Behror, India 84/C2
Béhoust, Fr. 30/H5
Behren-lès-Forbach, Fr. 53/F5
Behri (riv.), Nepal 84/C1
Behshahr, Iran 88/F1
Bei (riv.), China 79/A2
Bei (riv.), China 64/K5
Bei'an, China 71/N2
Beierfeld, Ger. 55/F1
Beigua (peak), It. 58/B4
Beijing (mun.), China 71/J3
Beijing (cap.), China 72/H7
Beijing Capital (int'l arpt.), China 72/H6
Beilen, Neth. 50/D3
Beiliu, China 83/K3
Beilngries, Ger. 55/E4
Beilstein, Ger. 54/C4
Beilun (pass), China 79/A3
Bein Tharsuinn (peak), Sc, UK 36/B1
Beindersheim, Ger. 54/B4
Beinn a' Chuallaich (peak), Sc, UK 36/B3
Beinn a' Ghlò (peak), Sc, UK 36/C3
Beinn a' Mheadhoin (lake), Sc, UK 36/B2
Beinn Bhàn (peak), Sc, UK 36/A3
Beinn Bheula (peak), Sc, UK 36/B4
Beinn Bhrotain (peak), Sc, UK 36/C2
Beinn Bhuidhe (peak), Sc, UK 36/B4
Beinn Bhuidhe Mhór (peak), Sc, UK 36/A3
Beinn Dearg (peak), Sc, UK 36/B1
Beinn Dearg (peak), Sc, UK 36/C3
Beinn Dòrain (peak), Sc, UK 36/B4
Beinn Eighe (peak), Sc, UK 36/A1
Beinn Heasgarnich (peak), Sc, UK 36/B3
Beinn Mholach (peak), Sc, UK 36/B3
Beinn Mhór (peak), Sc, UK 31/08
Beinwil am See, Swi. 56/E3
Beipiao, China 72/E2
Beira, Moz. 105/F4
Beirut (int'l arpt.), Leb. 91/D3
Beiseker, Ab, Can. 126/E2
Beith, Sc, UK 36/B5
Beiuş, Rom. 48/F2
Beizhen, China 73/A2
Beja, Port. 44/B3
Beja (dist.), Port. 44/A4
Béja (prov.), Alg. 100/H4
Beja (prov.), Tun. 100/J5
Bejaïa (prov.), Alg. 100/H4
Bejaïa, Alg. 100/H4
Béjar, Sp. 44/C2
Bejhi (riv.), Pak. 89/J3
Bekabad, Uzb. 87/D4
Bekasi, Indo. 80/D5
Békés, Hun. 48/E2
Békés (prov.), Hun. 48/F2
Békéscsaba, Hun. 48/F2
Bekilli, Turk. 90/B2
Bekily, Madg. 107/H9
Bekitro, Madg. 107/H9
Bel Air, Md, US 138/B5
Bel Air South, Md, US 138/B5
Bela, Pak. 89/J3
Belā, India 84/C3
Bela Crkva, Yugo. 48/E3
Bela Palanka, Yugo. 47/H1
Bêlá pod Bezdězem, Czh. 55/H1
Belā Pratāpgarh, India 84/C3
Bela Vista, Braz. 151/G8
Bela Vista, Moz. 107/F2
Bela Vista do Paraíso, Braz. 155/B2
Belang, Indo. 81/F4
Belaya (riv.), Rus. 64/F4
Belbo (riv.), It.
Bełchatów, Pol. 41/K3
Belchen, Ger.
Belcher (chan.),
Belcher (isls.), On, Can. 51/J4
Belcourt, ND, US 127/H3
Beldānga, India 85/G4
Belem (riv.), Rus. 64/F4
Belel, India 84/B4?
Belz.
Belmopan (cap.), Belz. 144/D2
Bele Weyne, Som. 97/Q7
Beled Weyne, Som. 97/Q7
Belz 144/D2
Bengal (bay), Asia 67/H7
Belém, Braz. 151/J4
Beenleigh, Austl. 114/D4

Belém, Braz. 154/D2
Belem de São Francisco, Braz. 154/C3
Belem Tower, Port. 45/P10
Belén, Arg. 157/C2
Belén, NM, US 128/F4
Belén, Chile 156/D5
Belén, Nic. 140/D5
Belén, Turk. 91/E1
Belén, Turk. 91/C1
Belén de Escobar, Arg. 159/J11
Belene, Bul. 48/G4
Beles Wenz (riv.), Eth. 97/N5
Belesar, Embalse de (res.), Sp. 44/B1
Belev, Rus. 62/F1
Belews Creek, Mo, US 137/F9
Belfair, Wa, US 135/B3
Belfast, SAfr. 107/E2
Belfast (cap.), NI, UK 34/B2
Belfast, NI, UK 34/C2
Belfast Lough (bay), NI, UK 34/C2
Belfaux, Swi. 56/D4
Belfield, ND, US 127/H4
Belfort (dept.), Fr. 56/C3
Belfort, Fr. 56/C2
Belgioioso, It. 58/C2
Belgium (ctry.) 27/E3
Belgorod, Rus. 63/F2
Belgorod Oblast, Rus. 62/F2
Belgrade, Mt, US 126/E4
Belgrade (Beograd) (cap.), Yugo. 48/E3
Belgy, It. 40/G2
Belice (isl.), It. 43/K6
Beli Drim (riv.), Yugo. 47/G3
Beli Manastir, Cro. 48/D3
Beli Timok (riv.), Yugo. 48/F4
Belitsa, Bul. 47/H2
Belitung (isl.), Indo. 80/C4
Beljanica (peak), Yugo. 48/E3
Belk (pt.), Austl. 113/G5
Bell, Austl. 114/C4
Bell (riv.), Qu, Can. 123/H2
Bell, Ca, US 136/F8
Bell Gardens, Ca, US 136/F8
Bell Rock (Inchcape) (isl.), Sc, UK 36/D4
Bell Ville, Arg. 157/D3
Bella Coola, BC, Can. 126/B2
Bella Vista, Arg. 157/E2
Bellac, Fr. 42/D4
Bellaghy, NI, UK 34/B2
Bellagio, It. 57/F6
Bellano, It. 57/F5
Bellary, India 82/C4
Bellavista, Peru 156/B2
Bellavista (cape), It. 46/A3
Bellavista, Ecu. 156/E7
Belle (riv.), Can. 135/G7
Belle-Anse, Haiti 141/H4
Belle Chasse, La, US 137/Q17
Belle Fourche (riv.), Wy, US 127/G5
Belle Glade, Fl, US 133/H5
Belle Haven, Va, US 138/A6
Belle-Ile (isl.), Fr. 42/B3
Belle Isle (str.),
Belle Terre, NY, US 139/M4
Belleek, NI, UK 34/B2
Bellefontaine, Oh, US 130/D3
Bellefonte, De, US 138/C4
Bellegarde-sur-Valserine, Fr. 56/B5
Bellenberg, Ger. 57/G1
Bellenden Ker NP, Austl. 114/B2
Belleplain, NJ, US 138/D5
Bellerose, NY, US 139/L9
Bellerose-sur-Allier, Fr. 42/E3
Belleville, On, Can. 130/E2
Belleville, Il, US 137/H8
Belleville, Mi, US 135/F7
Bellevue, Ne, US 137/J5
Bellevue, Wa, US 135/C3
Bellevue, Id, US
Belley, Fr. 56/B6
Bellflower, Ca, US 136/F8
Bellheim, Ger. 54/B4
Bellingat, Fr. 56/B3
Bellinge, Den. 38/D4
Bellingham, Wa, US 135/C3
Bellingshausen, FrPol. 117/K6
Bellingshausen (sea), Ant. 160/U
Bellingwolde, Neth. 51/E2
Bellinzago Novarese, It. 58/B1
Bellinzona, Swi. 57/F5
Bellmawr, NJ, US 138/C4
Bellmead, Tx, US 129/H5
Bellmore, NY, US 139/L9
Bello, Col. 150/C2
Bellona Reefs (reef), NCal. 116/E7
Bellot (str.), NW, Can. 122/G1
Bellport, NY, US 139/F2
Bellshill, Sc, UK 36/C5
Belluno (prov.), It. 59/E1
Belluno, It. 43/K4
Bellville, Tx, US 129/H5
Bellville, SAfr. 106/L10
Belchów, Pol. 41/K3
Bellwood, Il, US 135/P16
Belmez, Sp. 44/C3
Belmont, Ca, US 136/K11
Belmont, NC, US 133/H3
Belmont (dept.), Fr. 56/C1
Belmont, Ms, US 133/G3
Belmont, Austl. 114/D5
Belmont, NY, US 130/E3
Belmont, Port. 44/B2
Belmonte, Braz. 154/C4
Belmopan (cap.), Belz. 144/D2
Belmullet, Ire. 31/P9

Belo Campo, Braz. 154/B4
Belo Horizonte, Braz. 155/D1
Belo-Tsiribihina, Madg. 107/H7
Beloeil, Qu, Can. 131/P6
Beloeil, Belg. 52/C2
Belogorsk, Rus. 71/N1
Beloha, Madg. 107/H9
Beloit, Wi, US 127/L5
Beloit, Ks, US 127/H3
Belomorsk, Rus. 60/G2
Belorechensk, Rus. 62/F3
Beloretsk, Rus. 61/N5
Belovo, Bul. 47/J1
Belovo, Rus. 64/J4
Beloye (lake), Rus. 64/F3
Belper, Eng, UK 33/F1
Belsand, India 85/E2
Belt, Mt, US 126/F4
Belterwijde (lake), Neth. 50/D3
Belton, Mo, US 137/D6
Belton, Mo, US 137/D6
Beltsville, Md, US 138/B5
Beltzville (lake), Pa, US 138/C2
Belukha (peak), Rus. 70/E2
Belvedere, Ca, US 135/K11
Belvidere, NJ, US 138/C3
Belvidere, Il, US
Belyando (riv.), Austl. 109/D3
Belyy (isl.), Rus. 160/A
Belz, Ukr. 41/M3
Belzig, Ger. 40/G2
Bemaraha (plat.), Madg. 107/H7
Bemarivo (riv.), Madg. 107/H7
Bembéréké, Ben. 103/F4
Bembibre, Sp. 44/B1
Bemboka, Austl. 115/D3
Bemetāra, India 82/D3
Bemidji, Mn, US 127/K4
Bemmel, Neth. 50/C5
Ben Aigan (hill), Sc, UK 36/C1
Ben Alder (peak), Sc, UK 36/B3
Ben Améra (well), Mrta. 98/B5
Ben Avon (peak), Sc, UK 36/C2
Ben Boyd NP, Austl. 115/D3
Ben Chonzie (peak), Sc, UK 36/C3
Ben Cleuch (peak), Sc, UK 36/C4
Ben Cruachan (peak), Sc, UK 36/B4
Ben Davis (pt.), NJ, US 138/C5
Ben Gurion (int'l arpt.), Isr. 91/F7
Ben Hope (peak), Sc, UK 31/R7
Ben Ime (peak), Sc, UK 36/B4
Ben Lawers (peak), Sc, UK 36/B3
Ben Ledi (peak), Sc, UK 36/B4
Ben Lomond (peak), Sc, UK 36/B4
Ben Lomond NP, Austl. 115/C4
Ben Lui (peak), Sc, UK 36/B4
Ben Macdui (peak), Sc, UK 36/C2
Ben More (peak), Sc, UK 36/C2
Ben More (peak), Sc, UK 31/Q8
Ben More Assynt (peak), Sc, UK 31/R7
Ben Msik-sidi Othmane (prov.), Mor. 100/A2
Ben Nevis (peak), Sc, UK 36/B3
Ben Rinnes (peak), Sc, UK 36/C2
Ben Slimane, Mor. 98/D2
Ben Slimane (prov.), Mor. 100/A2
Ben Starav (peak), Sc, UK 36/B4
Ben Tee (peak), Sc, UK 36/B3
Ben Tirran (peak), Sc, UK 36/C3
Ben Tre, Viet. 78/D4
Ben Vane (peak), Sc, UK 36/B4
Ben Vorlich (peak), Sc, UK 36/B4
Ben Vrackie (peak), Sc, UK 36/C3
Ben Wyvis (peak), Sc, UK 36/B1
Ben Zohra (well), Alg. 95/F1
Benabarre, Sp. 45/F1
Benahmed, Mor. 98/D2
Benalla, Austl. 115/C3
Benalmádena, Sp. 44/C4
Benavente, Sp. 44/C1
Benbane (pt.), NI, UK 34/B1
Benbecula (isl.), Sc, UK 31/Q8
Benbonyathe (peak), Austl. 113/H4
Benburb, NI, UK 34/B2
Bend, Or, US 126/C4
Bendel (str.), NW, Can. 122/G1
Bendeleben (mt.), Ak, US 134/F2
Bendemeer, Austl. 115/D1
Bendigo, Austl. 115/C3
Bene Beraq, Isr. 91/F7
Benedict, Md, US 138/B6
Benediktbeuern, Ger. 57/H2
Benediktenwand (peak), Ger. 57/H2
Benešov, Czh. 55/H1
Beneuvitra, Madg. 107/H8
Benevento (prov.), It. 42/D6
Benevento, It. 42/D6
Benfeld, Fr. 56/D1
Bengal (bay), Asia 67/H7

Bengal, Bay of (gulf), Asia 70/E7
Bengbu, China 72/D4
Benghāzī, Libya 96/K1
Bengkalis, Indo. 80/B3
Bengkalis (isl.), Indo. 80/B3
Bengkayang, Indo. 80/C3
Bengkulu, Indo. 80/B4
Bengough, Sk, Can. 122/G3
Bengtsfors, Swe. 38/E2
Benguela, Ang. 105/B3
Benguerir, Mor. 98/D2
Benha, D.R. Congo 104/A2
Beni, D.R. Congo 104/A2
Beni (riv.), Bol. 147/C4
Beni Abbes, Alg. 99/E3
Beni Bouayach, Mor. 100/C2
Beni Ensar, Mor. 100/C2
Beni Khiar, Tun. 100/M6
Beni Mellal, Mor. 99/E2
Beni Ounif, Alg. 99/E2
Benicarló, Sp. 45/F2
Benicia, Ca, US 135/K10
Benidorm, Sp. 45/E3
Benifayó, Sp. 45/E3
Benin (ctry.) 93/C3
Benin, Bight of (bay), Afr. 93/C4
Benin City, Nga. 103/G5
Benisa, Sp. 45/F3
Benito Juárez, Mex. 142/D2
Benjamin, Tx, US 129/H4
Benjamin Constant, Braz. 156/D2
Benjamin Hill, Mex. 142/C2
Benjamin, Isla (isl.), Chile 158/B5
Benkei-misaki (cape), Japan 76/B2
Benkelman, Ne, US 129/G2
Bennachie (hill), Sc, UK 36/D2
Bennan (pt.), Sc, UK 36/A6
Bennett (isl.), Rus. 65/Q2
Bennett (isl.), Rus. 65/G2
Bennettsville, SC, US 133/J3
Bennington, Vt, US 130/F3
Bénoue, PN de la, Camr. 96/H6
Bensenville, Il, US 135/Q16
Bensheim, Ger. 54/B3
Benson, Mn, US 127/K4
Benson, Az, US 128/E5
Benta (riv.), Hun. 49/Q10
Benthem, Ger. 51/E4
Bentley, Eng, UK 35/G4
Bento Gonçalves, Braz. 155/B4
Benton, La, US 129/J4
Benton, Ar, US 129/K4
Benton Harbor, Mi, US 130/C3
Bentong, Malay. 80/B3
Benue (state), Nga. 103/H5
Benue (riv.), Nga. 93/C4
Benxi, China 73/B2
Benxi, China 73/C2
Beočin, Yugo. 48/D3
Beograd (int'l arpt.), Yugo. 48/E3
Beohāri, India 84/C3
Beppu, Japan 74/B4
Bequia (isl.), StV. 141/N9
Bequimão, Braz. 154/A1
Beraber (well), Alg. 96/E1
Beragh, NI, UK 34/A2
Beraketa, India 107/H8
Berasia, India 84/A4
Berat, Alb. 47/F2
Beratus (peak), Indo. 81/E4
Beratzhausen, Ger. 55/E4
Berau (riv.), Indo. 81/E3
Berau (bay), Indo. 116/C3
Berbenno di Valtellina, It. 57/F5
Berbera, Som. 97/C5
Berbérati, CAfr. 96/J7
Berbice (riv.), Guy. 150/G2
Berceto, It. 58/C3
Berchem, Belg. 50/B6
Bercher, Swi. 56/C4
Berching, Ger. 55/E4
Berchtesgaden, Ger. 43/K3
Berchtesgaden, NP, Ger. 43/K3
Berck, Fr. 52/A3
Berdorf, Lux. 53/F4
Berdsk, Rus. 87/H2
Berdyans'k, Ukr. 62/F3
Berdychiv, Ukr. 62/D2
Berea, Ky, US 130/C4
Bereguardo, It. 58/C2
Berehove, Ukr. 41/M4
Berekum, Gha. 103/E5
Berenguela, Bol. 156/D5
Berenice (ruins), Egypt 101/C4
Beresford, SD, US 127/J5
Beresford, NB, Can. 131/H2
Bereşti, Rom. 49/H2
Berevo, Madg. 107/H7
Berezina (riv.), Bela. 62/D1
Berezniki, Rus. 61/N4
Berezovo, Rus. 64/H3
Berg, Swi. 57/F3
Berg, Lux. 53/F4
Berg, Nor. 54/D1
Berg bei Rohrbach, Aus. 55/G5
Berga, Sp. 45/F1
Berga, Turk. 62/C5
Bergama, Turk. 58/C1
Bergamo (prov.), It.
Bergamo, It.
Bergara, Sp. 44/D1
Bergen, Neth. 50/B3
Bergen op Zoom, Neth. 50/B5
Bergen, Nor. 38/A1
Bergen, Ger. 38/E4
Bergenfield, NJ, US 139/J8
Bergerac, Fr. 42/D4
Bergeyk, Neth. 50/C6
Bergheim, Fr.
Bergheim, Ger. 53/D2
Bergheim, Aus.
Bergheim, Ger. 53/F2

Bergisch Gladbach, Ger. 53/G2
Bergkamen, Ger. 51/E5
Bergnäset, Swe. 60/D2
Bergneustadt, Ger. 53/G1
Bergrheinfeld, Ger. 40/F4
Bergse Maas (riv.), Neth. 50/B5
Bergshamra, Swe. 38/H2
Bergsviken, Swe. 37/G2
Bergtheim, Ger. 54/D3
Berguent, Mor. 100/C2
Bergues, Fr. 52/B2
Bergum, Neth. 50/D2
Bergumermeer (lake), Neth. 50/D2
Bergün-Bravuogn, Swi. 57/F4
Bergviken (lake), Swe. 38/G1
Berh, Mong. 71/K2
Berikat (cape), Indo. 80/C4
Bering (isl.), Rus. 65/S4
Bering (sea), Asia,NAm. 65/U4
Bering (str.), Rus.,US 67/U3
Bering Land Bridge Nat'l Prsv., Ak, US 134/E2
Beringen, Belg. 53/E1
Beritarikap (cape), Indo. 80/B4
Berja, Sp. 44/D4
Berkel (riv.), Ger. 40/D2
Berkel, Neth. 50/B5
Berkeley, Ca, US 128/B3
Berkeley, Mo, US 137/G8
Berkeley Heights, NJ, US 139/H9
Berkhamsted, Eng, UK 30/B1
Berkheim, Ger. 57/G1
Berkhout, Neth. 50/B3
Berkley, Mi, US 135/F6
Berkovitsa, Bul. 47/H1
Berks (co.), Pa, US 138/C3
Berkshire (co.), Eng, UK 30/E6
Berkshire Downs (hills), Eng, UK 33/E3
Berlaimont, Fr. 52/C3
Berlanga de Duero, Sp. 44/D2
Berlare, Belg. 52/C2
Berleburg, Ger. 51/F6
Berlicum, Neth. 50/C5
Berlin, Wi, US 127/L5
Berlin, NH, US 131/G2
Berlin (cap.), Ger. 40/Q6
Berlin (state), Ger. 40/Q6
Berlin, NJ, US 138/D4
Bermagui, Austl. 115/D2
Bermejo (riv.), Arg. 147/C5
Bermeo, Sp. 44/D1
Bermillo de Sayago, Sp. 44/B2
Bermuda (isl.), UK 119/L6
Bern (canton), Swi. 56/D5
Bern (cap.), Swi. 56/D4
Bern-Belp (int'l arpt.), Swi. 56/D4
Bernal, Peru 156/A2
Bernalda, It. 46/E2
Bernalillo, NM, US 128/F4
Bernard (riv.), NW, Can. 122/D1
Bernardo O'Higgins, PN, Chile 157/B6
Bernardsville, NJ, US 138/D2
Bernau, Ger. 40/Q6
Bernau, Ger. 57/G2
Bernay, Fr. 52/C2
Bernbeuren, Ger. 57/G2
Bernburg, Ger. 40/F3
Berne (riv.), India 84/B3
Bernes-sur-Oise, Fr. 30/J4
Bernese Alps (mtn.), Swi. 43/G3
Bernhardswald, Ger. 55/F4
Bernice, La, US 137/H4
Bernier (riv.), Austl. 112/B3
Bernier (bay), NW, Can. 122/G1
Bernina (peak), Swi. 57/F5
Bernina (mtn.), Swi. 57/F5
Bernina, Passo del (pass), Swi. 57/G5
Bernissart, Belg. 52/C3
Bernkastel-Kues, Ger. 53/G4
Bernsbach, Ger. 55/F1
Bernville, Pa, US 138/C3
Beromünster, Swi. 56/D5
Beroroha, Madg. 107/H8
Beroun, Czh. 55/H3
Berounka (riv.), Czh. 41/G4
Berovo, Macd. 47/H2
Berra, It. 59/E3
Berre, Étang de (lake), Fr. 42/F5
Berrechid, Mor. 100/C2
Berri, Austl. 113/J5
Berriane, Alg. 99/F2
Berridale, Austl. 115/D3
Berriedale, Sc, UK 31/S7
Berrigan, Austl. 115/D2
Berriozábal, Mex. 144/C2
Berrotarán, Arg. 158/D2
Berrouaghia, Alg. 100/G4
Berry, Austl. 115/D2
Berry (isls.), Bahm. 141/F2
Berry (reg.), Fr. 42/D3
Berry (pt.), Eng, UK 32/C6
Berry (mtn.), Pa, US 138/C3
Berryessa (lake), Ca, US 135/K9
Bersenbrück, Ger. 51/F2
Berthoud, Co, US 137/B2
Bertinoro, It. 59/G1
Bertogne, Belg. 53/E3
Bertolinia, Braz. 154/B2
Bertoua, Camr. 96/H6
Bertrand (peak), Arg. 159/B6
Bertrandville, La, US 137/Q17
Bertrix, Belg. 53/E4
Bertry, Fr. 52/C3
Beru (isl.), Kiri. 116/G5
Beruit (isl.), Malay. 80/D3
Bervie Water (riv.), Sc, UK 36/D3
Berwick, NS, Can. 131/H2

Berwick, Pa, US 138/B1
Berwick-Upon-Tweed, Eng, UK 36/D5
Berwyn, Il, US 135/Q16
Berwyn (mts.), Wal, UK 34/E6
Berzence, Hun. 48/C2
Bès (riv.), Fr. 42/F2
Besalampy, Madg. 107/H7
Besançon, Fr. 56/C3
Besar (peak), Indo. 81/E4
Besbre (riv.), Fr. 42/E3
Beşiri, Turk. 90/E2
Beška, Yugo. 48/E3
Beskids (mts.), Pol. 41/L4
Beskonak, Turk. 91/B1
Beslan, Rus. 63/H4
Besna Kobila (peak), Yugo. 47/H1
Besozzo, It. 58/B1
Bessacarr, Eng, UK 35/G5
Bessancourt, Fr. 30/J4
Bessarabia (reg.), Mol. 49/J2
Bessbrook, NI, UK 34/B3
Bessemer, Al, US 133/G3
Bessemer (mtn.), Wa, US 135/D2
Bessines-sur-Gartempe, Fr. 42/D3
Best, Neth. 50/C5
Bestensee, Ger. 40/Q7
Bestwig, Ger. 51/F6
Bet She'an, Isr. 91/D3
Bet Shemesh, Isr. 91/F8
Betanantana, Madg. 107/H7
Betanzos, Sp. 44/A1
Beth She'arim (ruin), Isr. 91/G6
Bethal, SAfr. 106/E2
Bethalto, Il, US 137/G8
Bethanie, Namb. 106/B2
Bethany, Mo, US 127/K5
Bethany, Ok, US 137/M14
Bethany (riv.), Sc, UK 36/A1
Bethany, Ak, US 134/F3
Bethel, SAfr. 106/D2
Bethel Acres, Ok, US 137/N15
Bethel Island, Ca, US 135/L10
Béthéniville, Fr. 53/D5
Bethesda, Md, US 138/A6
Bethesda, Wal, UK 34/D5
Béthisy-Saint-Pierre, Fr. 52/B5
Bethlehem, SAfr. 106/D2
Bethlehem, Pa, US 138/C2
Bethlehem, WBnk. 62/E1
Bethlehem NP, Pol. 62/E1
Bethlehem, Md, US 138/C6
Bethoncourt, Fr. 56/C2
Bethpage, NY, US 139/M9
Bethulie, SAfr. 106/D3
Bethune, Sk, Can. 127/G3
Béthune, Fr. 52/B2
Béthune (riv.), Fr. 52/B2
Betim, Braz. 155/C1
Betioky, Madg. 107/H8
Betpaqala (plain), Kaz. 70/A2
Betroka, Madg. 107/H8
Betschdorf, Fr. 54/A5
Betsiamites (riv.), Can. 131/G1
Betsiboka (riv.), Madg. 107/H7
Bettancourt-la-Ferrée, Fr. 53/D6
Bette (peak), Libya 97/J3
Bettembourg, Lux. 53/F4
Betterton, Md, US 138/B5
Bettiah, India 85/E2
Bettlach, Swi. 56/D3
Bettles, Ak, US 134/H2
Betuwe (phys. reg.), Neth. 50/C5
Betwa (riv.), India 84/B3
Betz, Fr. 30/L4
Betzdorf, Ger. 53/G2
Betzenstein, Ger. 55/E3
Beulah, Austl. 115/B2
Beulah, ND, US 127/H4
Beulah (lake), Wi, US 135/P14
Beulakerwijde (lake), Neth. 50/C3
Beuningen, Neth. 50/C5
Beure, Fr. 56/C3
Beuvray (peak), Fr. 42/F3
Beuvron (riv.), Fr. 42/D3
Beuvronne (riv.), Fr. 30/L5
Beuvry, Fr. 52/B2
Bevensen, Ger. 51/H2
Bever (riv.), Ger. 51/E4
Beveren (peak), Swi. 57/F4
Beverley, Austl. 112/C5
Beverley, Eng, UK 35/H4
Beverly Hills, Ca, US 136/F7
Beverly Hills, Mi, US 135/F6
Beverstedt, Ger. 51/F2
Beverungen, Ger. 51/G5
Beverwijk, Neth. 50/B4
Bewar, India 84/B3
Bewl Bridge (res.), Eng, UK 33/G4
Bex, Swi. 56/D5
Bexar (co.), Tx, US 137/T21
Bexbach, Ger. 53/G5
Bexhill, Eng, UK 33/G5
Bexley (bor.), Eng, UK 30/D2
Beyçayırı, Turk. 49/H5
Beycuma, Turk. 49/K5
Beyne-Heusay, Belg. 53/E2
Beyoneisu-Retsugan (isl.), Japan 75/H5
Beypazarı, Turk. 49/K5
Beyşehir, Turk. 90/B2
Bezaha, Madg. 107/H8
Bezau, Aus. 57/F3
Bezdan, Yugo. 48/D3
Bezděčin, Czh. 55/H1
Bezdrev (lake), Czh. 55/H4
Bezhetsk, Rus. 60/H4
Béziers, Fr. 42/E5
Bhabua, India 84/D3
Bhadarwāh, India 86/C3
Bhadohī, India 84/D3
Bhādra, India 86/B5
Bhadreswar, India 82/A3
Bhāgalpur, India 85/F3

Bhāi Pheru, Pak. 86/B4
Bhairab (riv.), Bang. 85/G4
Bhairab Bāzār, Bang. 85/H3
Bhakkar, Pak. 86/A4
Bhākra (dam), India 86/A4
Bhaktapur, Nepal 85/E2
Bhalwāl, Pak. 86/B3
Bhamo, Myan. 83/G3
Bhānder, Myan. 83/G3
Bhānrer (range), India 84/B4
Bhānwad, India 82/A3
Bharatpur, Nepal 85/E2
Bharatpur, India 84/B2
Bhārātpur, India 84/D2
Bharthana, India 84/B4
Bharuch, India 89/K4
Bhasāwar, India 84/A2
Bhātapāra, India 82/D3
Bhatinda, India 86/C4
Bhatkal, India 89/K6
Bhātpāra, India 85/G4
Bhavāni, India 82/C5
Bhavnagar, India 86/B4
Bhawāna Mandi, India 89/L4
Bhera, Pak. 86/B3
Bheri (zone), Nepal 84/C1
Bhilai, India 82/D3
Bhilwāra, India 89/K3
Bhīma (riv.), India 89/L5
Bhimavaram, India 82/D4
Bhimunipatnam, India 82/D4
Bhinga, India 84/C2
Bhiwandi, India 89/K5
Bhiwāni, India 86/D5
Bhojpur, Nepal 85/F2
Bhokardan, India 82/C3
Bhola, India 85/H4
Bhongaon, India 84/B2
Bhopāl, India 89/K5
Bhor, India 89/K5
Bhraoin (lake), Sc, UK 36/A1
Bhuban, India 82/E3
Bhumibol (dam), Thai. 78/B2
Bhusawal, India 89/L5
Bhutan (ctry.) 67/J7
Bi Doup (peak), Viet. 78/E3
Biá (riv.), Braz. 150/E4
Biá (riv.), Braz. 102/E5
Biafra, Bight of (bay), Camr. 102/B4
Biak (isl.), Indo. 81/J4
Biak (int'l arpt.), Indo. 81/J4
Biała Podlaska (prov.), Pol. 41/M3
Biała Podlaska, Pol. 41/M2
Białobrzegi, Pol. 41/L3
Biafogard, Pol. 38/G4
Białowieski NP, Pol. 62/E1
Białowieski NP, Pol. 41/M2
Białystok (prov.), Pol. 41/M2
Białystok, Pol. 41/M2
Bianca (peak), It. 57/G4
Biancavilla, It. 46/D4
Biandrate, It. 58/B2
Biandronno, It. 58/B1
Bianze, It. 58/B2
Biarritz, Fr. 42/C5
Biasca, Swi. 57/E5
Bibā, Egypt 101/B2
Bibai, Japan 76/B2
Bibbiano, It. 58/D3
Bibbiena, It. 59/E5
Biberach, Ger. 56/E1
Biberach an der Riss, Ger. 57/F1
Biberist, Swi. 56/D3
Bibione, It. 59/G1
Biblián, Ecu. 152/B5
Biblis, Ger. 54/B3
Bicas, Braz. 211/K6
Bicaz, Rom. 49/H2
Bicester, Eng, UK 33/E3
Bicheno, Austl. 115/D4
Bicknacre, Eng, UK 30/E1
Bicske, Hun. 48/D2
Bida, Nga. 103/G4
Bīdar, India 89/K5
Biddeford, Me, US 131/G3
Biddiyā, WBnk. 91/G7
Biddu, WBnk. 91/G8
Biddulph, Eng, UK 35/F5
Bidean nam Bian (peak), Sc, UK 36/A4
Bideford, Eng, UK 32/C4
Bidente (riv.), It. 59/F4
Bidhūna, India 84/B2
Bīdokht, Iran 89/G2
Biebesheim am Rhein, Ger. 54/B3
Biebrza (riv.), Pol. 41/M2
Biel, Swi. 56/D3
Bielawa, Pol. 41/J3
Bieldside, Sc, UK 36/H4
Bielefeld, Ger. 51/F4
Bieler (lake), Swi. 56/D5
Bieler (lake), NW, Can. 123/J1
Biella, It. 58/B1
Bielsk Podlaski, Pol. 41/M2
Bielsko (prov.), Pol. 41/K4
Bielsko-Biała, Pol. 41/K4
Bien Hoa, Viet. 78/D4
Bienenbüttel, Ger. 51/H2
Bienne (riv.), Fr. 56/B5
Bienno, It. 57/G6
Bientina, It. 58/D5
Bienville, Fr. 42/C5
Bière, Swi. 56/C4
Bierset (int'l arpt.), Belg. 53/E2
Bierum, Neth. 50/D2
Bierutów, Pol. 41/J3
Biesbosch, Neth. 50/B5
Biesental, Ger. 40/Q6
Biesles, Fr. 56/B1
Biesme (riv.), Fr. 53/D5
Bieszczadzki NP, Pol. 62/B2
Bieszczadzki NP, Pol. 41/M4
Bietigheim, Ger. 54/C5
Bietschhorn (peak), Swi. 56/D5
Bièvre (riv.), Fr. 30/J5
Bièvre, Belg. 53/E4
Bièvres, Fr. 30/J5
Biga (des.), Austl. 115/B2
Big (isl.), Mo, US 137/F9
Big (isl.), On, Can. 122/G4
Bhādra, India 86/B5
Bilsi, India 84/B1

Big (lake), Mi, US 135/E6
Big Belt (mts.), Mt, US 126/F4
Big Bend, Swaz. 107/E2
Big Bend, Wi, US 135/P14
Big Bend NP, Tx, US 140/A2
Big Blue (riv.), US 134/C2
Big Diomede (isl.) 134/E2
Big Fork, US 127/K4
Big Hole (riv.), US 126/F4
Big Hole, SAfr. 106/D3
Big Lake, Tx, US 129/G5
Big Lost (riv.), Id, US 128/D2
Big Muskego (lake), Wi, US 135/P14
Big Pine (hill), Pa, US 138/C1
Big Pines, Ca, US 136/C3
Big Rapids, Mi, US 130/C3
Big River, Sk, Can. 126/G2
Big Rock, Il, US 135/N16
Big Sandy, Wy, US 128/E2
Big Sioux (riv.), US 127/J5
Big Spring, Tx, US 129/G4
Big Stone (lake), US 127/G2
Big Thompson (riv.), Co, US 137/B2
Big Thompson, North Fork (riv.), Co, US 137/A2
Big Timber, Mt, US 126/F4
Big Trout (lake), On, Can. 122/H3
Big Tujunga Canyon (canyon), Ca, US 136/B2
Big Wood (riv.), US 128/D2
Biga, Turk. 49/H5
Bigadiç, Turk. 62/D5
Bigbury (bay), Eng, UK 32/C6
Biggar, It. 58/A2
Biggar, Sc, UK 36/C5
Biggenden, Austl. 114/D4
Biggleswade, Eng, UK 33/F2
Bighorn (basin), Wy, US 126/F4
Bighorn (mts.), Wy, US 124/C3
Bighorn (lake), US 126/F4
Bighorn (riv.), Wy, US 122/F4
Biglerville, Pa, US 138/A4
Bignona, Sen. 102/A3
Biguaçu, Braz. 155/B3
Bihać, Bosn. 43/L4
Bihar, India 85/E3
Biharamulo, Tanz. 104/A3
Biharamulo Game Rsv., Tanz. 104/A3
Bihāriganj, India 85/F3
Biharkeresztes, Hun. 48/E2
Bihor (co.), Rom. 41/M5
Bihorel, Fr. 42/D2
Bihoro, Japan 76/D2
Bijagós (arch.), GBis. 93/A3
Bijagós, Arquipélago do (isl.) 96/B5
Bijar, Iran 88/E1
Bijāwar, India 84/B3
Bijbiara, India 86/C3
Bijeljina, Bosn. 48/D3
Bijelo Polje, Yugo. 47/F1
Bijiang, China 83/G2
Bijie, China 83/J2
Bijni, India 85/H2
Bijnor, India 84/B1
Bīkaner, India 89/K3
Bikar (isl.), Mrsh. 116/G3
Bikin, Rus. 71/P2
Bikin (riv.), Rus. 71/Q2
Bikini (isl.), Mrsh. 116/F3
Bikramganj, India 85/E3
Bikuar, PN do, Ang. 105/C4
Bila Tserkva, Ukr. 62/D2
Bilāra, India 82/B2
Bilāri, India 84/B1
Bilāsipāra, India 85/H2
Bilāspur, India 84/B1
Bilāspur, India 86/D4
Bilauktaung (range), Myan. 83/G5
Bilauktaung (range), Myan.,Thai 78/B3
Bilba Morea Claypan (lake), Austl. 109/C3
Bilbao, Sp. 44/D1
Bilbays, Egypt 91/B4
Bileća, Bosn. 47/F1
Bilecik (prov.), Turk. 49/J5
Bilecik, Turk. 62/D4
Bifgoraj, Pol. 41/M3
Bilgrām, India 84/C2
Bilhaur, India 84/C2
Bilhorod-dnistrovs'kyy, Ukr. 49/K2
Bilin, Myan. 83/G4
Bilibino, Rus. 65/S3
Bilin (riv.), Myan. 78/B2
Bilina, Czh. 55/G1
Biliu (riv.), China 73/B3
Bill of Portland (pt.), Eng, UK 32/D5
Bill Williams (riv.), Az, US 128/D4
Bille (riv.), Ger. 51/H1
Billerbeck, Ger. 50/D5
Billère, Fr. 42/C5
Billericay, Eng, UK 30/D2
Billiat Conservation Park, Austl. 115/B2
Billiat Consv. Park, Austl. 113/J5
Billigheim, Ger. 54/C4
Billingham, Eng, UK 35/G2
Billings, Mt, US 126/F4
Billingsfors, Swe. 38/E2
Billiton, Indo. 67/K10
Billund (int'l arpt.), Den. 38/D1
Billund, Den. 38/D1
Bilma, Niger 96/H4
Biloela, Austl. 114/C4
Biloku, Guy. 153/G4
Biloxi, Ms, US 133/F4
Bilpa Morea Claypan (lake), Austl. 113/H3
Bilqas Qism Awwal, Egypt 91/B4
Bilsi, India 84/B1

Bilthar, India 84/D2
Biltine, Chad 97/K5
Bilzen, Belg. 53/E2
Bīshah (riv.), SAr. 88/D4
Bimberi (peak), Austl. 115/D2
Bima, Indo. 81/E5
Bimbo, CAfr. 97/J7
Bimini (isls.), Bahm. 141/F2
Bin 'Arūs, Tun. 46/B4
Bin 'Arūs (gov.), Tun. 46/B4
Bin (riv.), Ger. 55/F6
Bina-Etāwa, India 84/B3
Binalong, Austl. 115/D2
Binasco, It. 58/C2
Binbrook, On, Can. 131/Q9
Binche, Belg. 53/D3
Binchuan, China 83/G2
Bindki, India 84/C2
Bindura, Zim. 105/F4
Binéfar, Sp. 45/F2
Binga (mtn.), Moz. 105/F4
Bingara, Austl. 115/D1
Bingen, Austl. 115/D1
Bingen, Ger. 53/G4
Bingerville, C.d'Iv. 102/E5
Binghamton, NY, US 130/F3
Bingley, Eng, UK 35/G3
Bingöl (prov.), Turk. 90/E2
Bingöl, Turk. 90/E2
Binh Son, Viet. 78/E3
Binhai, China 72/D4
Binhe (peak), Myan. 83/G4
Binisalem, Sp. 45/G3
Biniştea (riv.), Rom. 49/G2
Binkılıç, Turk. 49/J5
Binnaway, Austl. 115/D1
Binningen, Swi. 56/D2
Binongko (isl.), Indo. 81/F5
Bintan (peak), Indo. 80/B2
Bintang (peak), Malay. 80/B2
Bintimani (peak), Gabon 96/H7
Bintulu, Malay. 80/D2
Binyamina, Isr. 91/F6
Binz, Ger. 51/E3
Biograd, Cro. 48/B4
Bioko (isl.), EqG. 93/C4
Biougra, Mor. 98/C3
Bipont (Bissau) (int'l arpt.), GBis. 102/B4
Bir, Indo. 81/G3
Bippen, Ger. 51/E3
Bîr, India 89/L5
Bir Abu Minqār (well), Egypt 91/B4
Bir Aïdiat (well), Mrta. 98/C4
Bir Bel Guerdâne (well), Mrta. 98/C4
Bi'r Ghadir (well), Egypt 101/C3
Bir Ounâne (well), Mali 98/E5
Bi'r Zayt, WBnk. 91/G8
Birak, Libya 96/H2
Birao, CAfr. 97/K5
Birātnagar, Nepal 85/F2
Bijuv, Swe. 38/F4
Biratori, Japan 76/C2
Birch (mt.), Ab, Can. 122/E3
Birch Creek, Ak, US 134/J2
Birch Hills, Sk, Can. 127/G2
Birch River, Mb, Can. 127/H2
Birchip, Austl. 115/B2
Bird Islet, Austl. 109/E3
Birds Rock (peak), Austl. 115/D2
Birdsboro, Pa, US 138/C3
Birdwood, SAfr. 113/M8
Bikar (riv.), Mrsh. 116/G3
Birganj, Nepal 85/E2
Birganj, Nepal 85/E2
Biritiba-Mirim, Braz. 211/G8
Birigui, Braz. 155/B2
Bikaner, India 89/K3
Birjand, Iran 89/G2
Birkat Qārūn (lake), Egypt 90/B4
Birken-Honigsessen, Ger. 53/G2
Birkenau, Ger. 54/B3
Birkenfeld, Ger. 54/B3
Birkenfeld, Ger. 57/E5
Birkenhead, Eng, UK 35/E5
Birkenheide, Ger. 54/B4
Birkenwerder, Ger. 40/Q6
Birkirkara, Malta 46/L7
Birkkarspitze (peak), Aus. 57/H3
Birlad, Rom. 49/H2
Birmingham, Al, US 133/C3
Birmingham, Mo, US 137/E5
Birmingham (int'l arpt.), Eng, UK 33/E2
Birmingham, Mi, US 135/F6
Birmitrapur, India 85/E4
Birnam, Sc, UK 36/C3
Birnin Nkonni, Niger 96/G5
Birnie (isl.), Kiri. 117/H5
Birnin Kebbi, Nga. 96/G5
Birobijan, Rus. 71/P2
Bîrpur, India 85/F3
Birr, Ire. 31/Q10
Birs (riv.), Swi. 56/D2
Birsay, Sc, UK 36/K10
Birsk, Rus. 61/M5
Birstein, Ger. 54/C2
Biruaca, Ven. 153/E2
Biržai, Lith. 39/L3
Birżebbuġa, Malta 46/M7
Bisa (isl.), Indo. 81/G4
Bisaccia, It. 40/B5
Bisalpur, India 84/C1
Bisamberg, Aus. 49/N7
Bisauli, India 84/B1
Bisbee, Az, US 128/F5
Bisbee Douglas (int'l arpt.), Az, US 142/C2
Biscarrosse, Fr. 42/C4
Biscarrosse, Étang de (lake), Fr. 42/C4
Biscay (bay) 43/G4
Biscayne NP, Fl, US 133/H6
Bisceglie, It. 46/E2
Bischberg, Ger. 54/D3
Bischheim, Fr. 53/G6
Bischofsgrün, Ger. 55/F2
Bischofsheim, Ger. 54/B3
Bischofsheim an der Rhön, Ger. 54/D2
Bischofszell, Swi. 57/F3
Bischwiller, Fr. 56/D2

Biscubio (riv.), It. 59/F5
Biscucuy, Ven. 152/D2
Bishop, Ca, US 128/C3
Bishop Auckland, Eng, UK 35/G2
Bishopbriggs, Sc, UK 36/B5
Bishopville, NB, Can. 131/H2
Bishop's Falls, Nf, Can. 131/L1
Bishop's Stortford, Eng, UK 33/G3
Bishopton, Sc, UK 36/B5
Bisingen, Ger. 54/B6
Biskra, Alg. 100/H5
Biskupiec, Pol. 39/J5
Bislig, Phil. 81/G2
Bismarck (cap.), ND, US 127/H4
Bismarck, On, Can. 131/Q9
Bismarck (arch.), PNG 116/C5
Bismarck (sea), PNG 116/C5
Bismil, Turk. 90/E2
Bispgarden, Swe. 37/F3
Bispingen, Ger. 51/G2
Bissau (cap.), GBis. 102/B4
Bissau, India 86/C5
Bissendorf, Ger. 51/F4
Bissett, Mb, Can. 127/K3
Bissingen, Ger. 54/D5
Bistrița (riv.), Rom. 49/G2
Bistrița, Rom. 49/G2
Bitam, Gabon 96/H7
Bitburg, Ger. 53/F4
Bitche, Fr. 53/G5
Bitkin, Chad 96/J5
Bitlis (prov.), Turk. 90/E2
Bitlis, Turk. 90/E2
Bitola, Macd. 47/G2
Bitonto, It. 46/E2
Bitterfeld, Ger. 51/G5
Bitterfontein, SAfr. 106/B3
Bitterroot (range), US 126/E4
Bitti, It. 46/A2
Bitung, Indo. 81/G3
Biwa, Japan 77/K5
Biwabik, Mn, US 127/K4
Biyalā, Egypt 91/B4
Biyang, China 72/C4
Bizard (isl.), Qu, Can. 131/M7
Bizerte, Tun. 38/E4
Björbo, Swe. 38/F1
Bjelovar, Cro. 48/C3
Bjerkvik, Nor. 37/F1
Bjerringbro, Den. 38/C3
Björklinge, Swe. 38/G1
Björnafjorden (estu.), Nor. 38/A1
Bjørne (pen.), NW, Can. 123/S7
Bjugn, Nor. 37/D3
Blå Jungfrun NP, Swe. 38/G3
Black (mtn.), Ab, Can. 122/E3
Blachownia, Pol. 41/K3
Black (mt.), Can. 134/M3
Black (isl.), Sc, UK 36/B1
Black (range), NM, US 128/F4
Black (mesa), Az, US 128/E3
Black (bay), Can. 127/L3
Black (mts.), Az, US 128/D4
Black (mtn.), Wal, UK 32/C3
Black (pt.), China,Vie 70/V7
Black (mtn.), Wal, UK 32/C3
Black (sea), Asia,Eur. 49/F1
Black (pt.), Ct, US 139/F1
Black (hills) 124/G3
Black Canyon of the Gunnison Nat'l Mon., US 124/F3
Black Diamond, Wa, US 135/C3
Black Diamond, Ab, Can. 126/E3
Black Eagle, Mt, US 126/F4
Black Forest (Schwarzwald) (for.), Ger. 54/B6
Black Hawk, Co, US 137/B3
Black Jack, Mo, US 137/G8
Black Mountain NP, Austl. 114/B1
Black Mtn. (mtn.), Wal, UK 32/C3
Black Point, Ca, US 135/K10
Black River, Jam. 145/G2
Black River Falls, Wi, US 127/L4
Black Rock (peak), SAfr. 106/C4
Black Rock (pt.), RI, US 139/G1
Black Sea Lowland (reg.), Ukr. 49/J3
Black Sugarloaf (peak), Austl. 115/D1
Black Volta (riv.), Burk. 93/D3
Black Walnut, Mo, US 137/G8
Black Warrior (riv.), Al, US 133/G3
Blackadder Water (riv.), Sc, UK 36/D5
Blackall, Austl. 114/B4
Blackburn, Sc, UK 36/C5
Blackburn, Eng, UK 35/F4
Blackburn (mtn.), Ak, US 134/H3
Blackcraig (peak), Sc, UK 36/B6
Blackdown (hills), Eng, UK 32/C3
Blackdown Tableland NP, Austl. 114/C4
Blackfoot, Id, US 126/E4
Blackfoot (res.), Id, US 126/E5

Blackheath, Austl. 115/D2
Blackmoor (upland), Eng, UK 35/E4
Blackpool, Eng, UK 35/E4
Blackrod, Eng, UK 35/F4
Blackshear (lake), Ga, US 133/H3
Blackstone, Va, US 130/E4
Blackville, NB, Can. 131/H2
Blackwater, Mo, US 137/G5
Blackwater, Ire. 31/P10
Blackwater, Austl. 114/C3
Blackwater (res.), Sc, UK 36/B3
Blackwell, Ok, US 129/H3
Blackwood (riv.), Austl. 112/B5
Blackwood, NJ, US 138/C4
Blackwood, NJ, US 138/D4
Bladensburg NP, Austl. 114/A3
Bladnoch (riv.), Sc, UK 34/D2
Blaenau, Fr. 52/A2
Blaenavon, Wal, UK 32/C3
Blagnac, Fr. 42/D5
Blagnac (int'l arpt.), Fr. 42/D5
Blagny, Fr. 53/E4
Blagoevgrad, Bul. 47/H1
Blagoveshchensk, Rus. 71/N1
Blaine Lake, Sk, Can. 126/G2
Blainville, Qu, Can. 131/N6
Blair, Ne, US 127/J5
Blair Atholl, Sc, UK 36/C3
Blairstown, NJ, US 138/D2
Blaise (riv.), Fr. 42/F2
Blaj, Rom. 49/G2
Blakely, Ga, US 133/G4
Blakeslee, Pa, US 138/C2
Blamont, Fr. 56/C3
Blanc (cape), Mrta. 150/A4
Blanc (cape), Mrta. 96/A4
Blanc, Fr. 42/G5
Blanc (cape), Tun. 46/A4
Blanc, Cap (cape), Tun. 46/A4
Blanc-Nez (cape), Fr. 52/A2
Blanca (peak), NM, US 129/F4
Blanca (pt.), Mex. 142/B2
Blanca, Cordillera (mts.), Peru 150/C5
Blanca, Costa (coast), Sp. 45/E3
Blanchard, Ok, US 137/M15
Blanche (lake), Austl. 109/D3
Blanche (peak), Swi. 56/D5
Blanche (lake), Austl. 113/H5
Blanco (cape), Peru 150/A4
Blanco (pen.), NW, Can. 123/S7
Blanco, Tx, US 129/H5
Blanco (cape), Mor. 98/B4
Blanco (cape), CR 145/E4
Blanco, Or, US 128/A2
Blandford, Eng, UK 32/D5
Blanding, Ut, US 128/F3
Blandy, Fr. 30/L6
Blanes, Sp. 45/G2
Blangenberge, Belg. 52/C1
Blangy-sur-Bresle, Fr. 52/A3
Blankenberge, Belg. 52/C1
Blankenburg, Ger. 51/H5
Blankenfelde, Ger. 40/Q7
Blankenheim, Ger. 53/F3
Blanquilla (isl.), Ven. 150/F1
Blanquillo, Uru. 159/F2
Blansko, Czh. 41/J4
Blantyre, Malw. 105/G4
Blantyre, Sc, UK 36/B5
Blanzy, Fr. 42/F3
Blaricum, Neth. 50/C4
Blas (pt.), Swi. 56/D5
Blatná, Czh. 55/G4
Blato, Cro. 46/E1
Blatten, Swi. 56/D5
Blau (riv.), Ger. 57/F4
Blaubeuren, Ger. 54/C6
Blauen (peak), Ger. 57/E4
Blaustein, Ger. 54/C6
Blauvelt, NY, US 139/K7
Blåvands (pt.), Den. 38/C4
Blavet (riv.), Fr. 42/B3
Blaye, Fr. 42/C4
Blayney, Austl. 115/D2
Bleckede, Ger. 51/H2
Bled, Slov. 40/B5
Bledjell, Nor. 38/C2
Blégny, Belg. 53/E2
Bléharies, Belg. 52/C2
Bleiburg, Aus. 40/B5
Bleik, Nor. 37/F1
Bleicherode, Ger. 51/H5
Bleiswijk, Neth. 50/B4
Blekinge (co.), Swe. 38/F4
Blendecques, Fr. 52/B2
Blender, Ger. 51/G3
Blenheim, NZ. 117/S11
Blénod-lès-Pont-à-Mousson, Fr. 53/E6
Blessington, Ire. 31/Q10
Bletterans, Fr. 56/B4
Bleury, Fr. 30/H6
Blewett, Ar, US 133/C3
Bligh Sound, RI, US 139/G1
Blies (riv.), Ger. 53/G5
Blieskastel, Ger. 53/G5
Blik (mt.), Phil. 81/F2
Blinnenhorn (peak), Swi. 56/D5
Blithe, Ca, US 128/D4
Blithfield (res.), Eng, UK 35/G6
Block (isl.), RI, US 138/E3
Block Island C. G. Sta., RI, US 139/G1
Block Island (New Shoreham), RI, US 139/G1
Block Island NWR, RI, US 139/G1
Blodelsheim, Fr. 56/D2
Bloemendaal, Neth. 50/B4
Bloemfontein, SAfr. 106/D3
Bloemhof, SAfr. 106/D2

Bloemhofdam (res.), SAfr. 106/D2
Blois, Fr. 42/D3
Blomberg, Ger. 51/E1
Blomberg, Ger. 51/G5
Blomstermåla, Swe. 38/G3
Blonay, Swi. 56/C5
Blönduós, Ice. 37/N6
Bloodvein (riv.), Mb,On, Can. 122/G3
Bloody Foreland (pt.), Ire. 31/P9
Bloomfield, NM, US 128/F3
Bloomfield, NJ, US 139/J8
Bloomfield Hills, Mi, US 135/F6
Bloomingdale, NJ, US 139/H7
Bloomingdale, Il, US 135/P16
Bloomington, Mn, US 127/K5
Bloomington, Il, US 127/L5
Bloomington, Ca, US 136/C2
Bloomsburg, Pa, US 138/B2
Bloomsbury, NJ, US 138/C2
Blora, Indo. 80/D5
Blotzheim, Fr. 57/E5
Blountstown, Fl, US 133/G4
Blovice, Czh. 55/G3
Bišanka (riv.), Czh. 43/K1
Bludenz, Aus. 57/F3
Bludov, Czh. 41/J4
Blue (mtn.), India 83/F3
Blue (mts.), US 124/C2
Blue Head (pt.), Jam. 145/G2
Blue Island, Il, US 135/Q16
Blue Lake NP, Austl. 114/D4
Blue Marsh Lake (res.), Pa, US 138/C3
Blue Mesa (res.), Co, US 128/F3
Blue Mountain (peak), Jam. 145/G2
Blue Mountain (ridge), Pa, US 138/A3
Blue Mountains, Jam. 145/G2
Blue Mountains, Austl. 115/D2
Blue Mountains NP, Austl. 115/D2
Blue Nile (riv.), Sudan, Et 97/M5
Blue Ridge (mts.), US 133/H3
Blue Ridge Parkway, US 133/H3
Blue Springs, Mo, US 137/E5
Bluefield, WV, US 130/D4
Bluefields, Nic. 145/F4
Bluefields (bay), Nic. 145/F4
Bluejoint (lake), Or, US 128/C2
Bluenose (lake), NW, Can. 122/E2
Bluff, NZ. 117/R12
Bluff (pt.), Austl. 112/B3
Bluff, Austl. 114/C4
Bluff (peak), Austl. 112/C5
Bluffdale, Ut, US 137/K13
Bluffton, In, US 130/C3
Blumberg, Ger. 57/E2
Blümlisalp (peak), Swi. 56/D5
Blumenau, Braz. 155/B3
Blyn, US 135/B1
Blyth, On, Can. 131/Q9
Blyth (riv.), Eng, UK 33/H2
Blyth, Eng, UK 35/G1
Blyth, Austl. 113/H5
Blythe, Ca, US 128/D4
Blytheville, Ar, US 129/K4
Bnom Mhai (peak), Viet. 78/E3
Bo, SLeo. 102/C5
Bo Hai (Chihli) (gulf), China 72/D3
Bo Hai (Gulf of Chihli) (gulf), China 71/L4
Boa Esperança, Braz. 155/C2
Boa Esperança, Represa (res.), Braz. 151/J5
Boa Vista, Braz. 153/F4
Boa Vista (int'l arpt.), Braz. 153/F4
Boac, Phil. 79/D5
Boaco, Nic. 144/E3
Boadilla del Monte, Sp. 45/N9
Bo'ai, China 72/C4
Boano (isl.), Indo. 81/G4
Boas (riv.), NW, Can. 123/H2
Boavita, Col. 150/D2
Boaz, Al, US 133/G3
Boba, Hun. 40/C2
Bobai, China 83/J3
Boaomby (cape), Madg. 107/J5
Bobbili, India 82/D4
Bobbio, It. 58/B2
Bobenheim-Roxheim, Ger. 54/B4
Bobigny, Fr. 30/K5
Bobingen, Ger. 57/G1
Böblingen, Ger. 54/C5
Bobo Dioulasso, Burk. 102/D4
Boboshevo, Bul. 47/H1
Bobotov Kuk, Yugo. 47/H1
Bobovdol, Bul. 47/H1
Bóbr (riv.), Pol. 41/H3
Bobrov, Rus. 62/G2
Bobures, Ven. 150/D2
Boby (peak), Madg. 107/H8
Boca de Aroa, Ven. 152/D2
Boca del Guafo (chan.), Chile 158/B4
Boca del Río, Mex. 143/N7
Bôca do Acre, Braz. 150/E5
Boca Raton, Fl, US 133/H5
Bocaina, Serra da (mts.), Braz. 211/J7
Bocairente, Sp. 45/E3
Bocas del Toro, Pan. 145/F4
Bocay (riv.), Nic. 145/E3
Bochil, Mex. 144/C2
Bochnia, Pol. 41/L4
Bocholt, Belg. 50/D5
Bocholt, Ger. 50/D5
Bochum, Ger. 51/E6
Bockau, Ger. 55/F1
Bockenem, Ger. 51/H4

Bockenheim an der Weinstrasse, Ger. 53/H4
Bockhorn, Ger. 51/F2
Bockhorn, Ger. 55/E6
Boconó, Ven. 152/D2
Boda, Fr. 56/B4
Boda, CAfr. 96/J7
Bodajbo, Rus. 65/M4
Bodalla, Austl. 115/D3
Boddam, Sc, UK 36/E2
Boddington, Austl. 112/C5
Bode (riv.), Ger. 40/F3
Bode, Nor. 37/F1
Bodega Bay, Ca, US 128/B3
Bodegraven, Neth. 50/B4
Bodenheim, Ger. 54/B3
Bodenkirchen, Ger. 55/F6
Bodenmais, Ger. 55/G4
Bodensee (Constance) (lake), Swi 43/H3
Bodenteich, Ger. 51/H3
Bodh Gaya, India 85/E3
Bodhan, India 82/C4
Bodināyakkanūr, India 82/C5
Bodo, Nor. 80/D5
Bodø, Nor. 37/E2
Bodocó, Braz. 154/C2
Bodrog (riv.), Hun.,Slvk. 41/L4
Bodrum, Turk. 90/A2
Bódvaszilas, Hun. 41/L4
Boège, Fr. 56/C5
Boegoeberg (peak), Namb. 106/A2
Boekel, Neth. 50/C5
Boende, D.R. Congo 97/K8
Boerne, Tx, US 137/T20
Boeuf (riv.), La, US 129/K4
Bog of Allen (swamp), Ire. 34/A3
Bogalusa, La, US 133/F4
Bogan (riv.), Austl. 109/D4
Bogan Gate, Austl. 115/C2
Bogandé, Burk. 103/E3
Bogatić, Yugo. 48/D3
Bogatynia, Pol. 41/H3
Boğazkale-Alacahöyük NP, Turk. 62/F2
Boğazlıyan, Turk. 62/F5
Bogdanci, Macd. 47/H2
Bogen, Ger. 55/F5
Bogen, Nor. 37/F1
Bogense, Den. 38/D4
Boggabilla, Austl. 114/C5
Boggabri, Austl. 115/D1
Boggeragh (mts.), Ire. 31/N10
Boggy (peak), Anti. 141/N8
Bogia, Sc, UK 36/E2
Boglárlelle, Hun. 48/C2
Bognor Regis, Eng, UK 33/F5
Bogny-sur-Meuse, Fr. 53/E4
Bogo, Phil. 81/G2
Bogo, Cmr. 96/H5
Bogong (mt.), Austl. 115/C3
Bogong NP, Austl. 115/C3
Bogor, Indo. 80/C5
Bogorodsk, Rus. 63/G1
Bogotá (cap.), Col. 150/D3
Bogoso, NJ, US 139/J8
Bogovina, Yugo. 47/G2
Bogra (pol. reg.), Bang. 85/G3
Bogué, Mrta. 102/B2
Boguchany, China 72/D3
Bohain-en-Vermandois, Fr. 52/C4
Bohemia (reg.), Czh. 41/G4
Bohemian (for.), Czh.,Ger. 40/G4
Bohen, It. 103/F3
Böhl-Iggelheim, Ger. 54/B4
Böhmenkirch, Ger. 51/G3
Böhmenkirch, Ger. 54/C5
Bohners Lake, Wi, US 135/P14
Bohol (isl.), Phil. 116/D4
Böhönye, Hun. 48/C2
Bohu, China 70/E3
Boiling Springs, Pa, US 138/A3
Boipeba, Ilha de (isl.), Braz. 154/C4
Boí, Braz. 155/N1
Bois-d'Amont, Fr. 56/C4
Bois-d'Arcy, Fr. 30/K5
Bois de Boulogne (dept.), Fr. 30/J5
Bois de Vincennes (dept.), Fr. 30/K5
Bois-des-Filion, Qu, Can. 131/N6
Bois, Rio dos (riv.), Braz. 155/B1
Boisbriand, Qu, Can. 131/N6
Boise (cap.), Id, US 126/D5
Boise City, Ok, US 129/G3
Boissevain, Mb, Can. 127/H3
Boissy-Fresnoy, Fr. 30/L4
Boissy-l'Aillerie, Fr. 30/H4
Boissy-le-Châtel, Fr. 30/M5
Boissy-Saint-Léger, Fr. 30/K5
Boissy-Sans-Avoir, Fr. 30/H5
Boizenburg, Ger. 51/H2
Bojador (cape), Mor. 96/C2
Bojano, It. 40/B5
Bojonegoro, Indo. 80/D5
Bojkovice, Czh. 41/J4
Bojnūrd, Iran 89/G1
Bokaro Steel City, India 85/E3
Boké (pol. reg.), Gui. 102/B3
Boké, Gui. 102/B3
Bokhol (plain), Kenya 104/C2
Boknafjorden (estu.), Nor. 37/C4
Bokol (peak), Kenya 104/C2
Bokoro, Chad 96/J5
Bokoro, Myan. 78/B2
Boksburg, SAfr. 106/Q13
Boksitogorsk, Rus. 60/G4
Bol, Chad 96/H5
Bolama, GBis. 102/B4
Bolān (pass), Pak. 89/J3
Bolaños de Calatrava, Sp. 44/D3
Bolayır, Turk. 47/K2

Bolbec, Fr. 42/D2
Boldeşti-scăeni, Rom. 49/H3
Boldon, Eng, UK 35/G2
Bole, China 70/D3
Bole, Gha. 103/E4
Bolesławiec, Pol. 41/H3
Bolgatanga, Gha. 103/E4
Boli, China 71/P2
Boliden, Swe. 37/G2
Bolinao, Phil. 79/C4
Bolívar, Mo, US 129/J3
Bolívar, Peru 156/B2
Bolívar (dept.), Col. 152/C2
Bolívar (peak), Ven. 152/D2
Bolívar, Col. 152/C2
Bolívar, Ven. 153/F3
Bolívar (state), Ven. 158/E3
Bolívar, Arg. 158/E3
Bolivia (ctry.), Bol. 152/C1
Bollate, It. 58/C1
Bollène, Fr. 56/D4
Bolligen, Swi. 56/D4
Bollin (riv.), Eng, UK 35/F5
Bollnäs, Swe. 38/G1
Bollullos Par del Condado, Sp. 44/B4
Bolmen (lake), Swe. 38/F3
Bolobo, D.R. Congo 96/J8
Bologna, It. 59/E4
Bologna (prov.), It. 59/E3
Bologne, Fr. 56/B1
Bolognesi, Peru 156/C3
Bologoye, Rus. 60/G4
Bolomba, D.R. Congo 97/J7
Bolonchén de Rejón, Mex. 144/D2
Bolovens (plat.), Laos 78/D3
Bolpur, India 85/F4
Bolsena, It. 46/B1
Bolsena (lake), It. 46/B1
Bol'shaya Khobda (riv.), Kaz. 63/K2
Bol'shaya Kinel' (riv.), Rus. 63/K1
Bol'shaya Rogovaya (riv.), Rus. 61/P2
Bol'shaya Synya (riv.), Rus. 61/N2
Bol'shevik (isl.), Rus. 67/H2
Bol'shezemel'skaya (tundra), Rus. 61/M2
Bol'shoy Bolvanskiy Nos (pt.), Rus. 64/F2
Bol'shoy Irgiz (riv.), Rus. 63/J1
Bol'shoy Lyakhov (isl.), Rus. 67/P2
Bol'shoy Lyakhovskiy (isl.), Rus. 65/Q2
Bol'shoy Uzen' (riv.), Rus. 63/J2
Bolsover, Eng, UK 35/G5
Bolsward, Neth. 50/C2
Bolt (pt.), Sc, UK 32/C6
Boltaña, Sp. 45/F1
Boltigen, Swi. 56/D4
Bolton, Eng, UK 35/F4
Bolu, Turk. 49/K5
Bolu (prov.), Turk. 115/D2
Bolungavík, Ice. 37/M6
Bolus Head (pt.), Ire. 30/N11
Bolvadin, Turk. 90/B2
Bóly, Hun. 40/D3
Bolzano, It. 57/H5
Bolzano-Bozen (prov.), It. 57/H5
Bom Conselho, Braz. 154/C3
Bom Despacho, Braz. 155/C1
Bom Jardim, Braz. 154/A1
Bom Jardin de Minas, Braz. 211/J6
Bom Jesus, Braz. 155/B3
Bom Jesus, Braz. 155/B3
Bom Jesus da Gurguéia, Serra (mts.), Braz. 151/K5
Bom Jesus de Goiás, Braz. 155/B1
Bom Jesus do Itabapoana, Braz. 155/D2
Bom Jesus dos Perdões, Braz. 211/G8
Bom Retiro, Braz. 155/B3
Boma, D.R. Congo 105/B2
Bomaderry, Austl. 115/D2
Bombala, Austl. 115/D3
Bombay Hook NWR, De, US 138/C5
Bombay (Mumbai), India 89/K5
Bomberai (pen.), Indo. 81/H4
Bombo, Ugan. 104/B2
Bomi, China 83/G2
Bomlitz, Ger. 51/G3
Bømlo (isl.), Nor. 38/A2
Bomu (riv.), D.R. Congo 93/E4
Bon-Encontre, Fr. 42/D4
Bona (mt.), Ak, US 134/K3
Bonaduz, Swi. 57/F4
Bonaire (isl.), NAnt. 119/L8
Bonalbo, Austl. 115/E1
Bonampak (ruin), Mex. 144/D2
Bonao, DRep. 141/G4
Bonaparte (isls.), Austl. 109/B2
Bonaparte (arch.), Austl. 116/B6
Bonasila (mtn.), Ak, US 134/F3
Bonaventure, Qu, Can. 131/H1
Bonaventure (riv.), Can. 131/H1
Boncourt, Swi. 56/D3
Bondeno, It. 59/E3
Bondo, D.R. Congo 97/K7
Bondoukou, C.d'Iv. 102/E4
Bondowoso, Indo. 67/M10
Bönen, Ger. 51/E5
Bonerate (isls.), Indo. 81/F5
Bonfol, Swi. 56/D3
Bonfouca, La, US 137/Q16
Bong (range), Libr. 96/C6
Bong (co.), Libr. 102/C5
Bongabong, Phil. 81/F1
Bongandanga, D.R. Congo 97/K7
Bongao, Phil. 81/E3

Bonggi (isl.), Malay. 81/E2
Bongka (riv.), Indo. 81/F4
Bongo, Massif des (plat.), CAfr. 97/K6
Bongolava (uplands), Madg. 105/K10
Bongor, Chad 96/J5
Bonham, Tx, US 129/H4
Bonheiden, Belg. 53/D1
Bonhill, Sc, UK 36/B5
Bonholzhausen, Ger. 51/F4
Bonhorst, Ger. 51/E4
Bonibon, Braz. 211/L6
Bonifacio, Fr. 46/A2
Bonifacio (str.), It. 46/A2
Bonifay, Fl, US 133/G4
Bönigen, Swi. 56/D4
Bonin (isls.), Japan 116/C2
Bonita Springs, Fl, US 133/H5
Bonito (peak), Hon. 144/E3
Bonn, Fr. 56/C5
Bonnelles, Fr. 30/J6
Bonnes, Sc, UK 36/B5
Bonner Springs, Ks, US 137/D5
Bonner-West Riverside, Mt, US 126/E4
Bonners Ferry, Id, US 126/D3
Bonnet Carré Spillway, La, US 137/P16
Bonnet, Lac du (lake), Can. 127/K3
Bonneuil-sur-Marne, Fr. 30/K5
Bonneval, Fr. 42/D2
Bonneville (dam), Wa,Or, US 126/C4
Bonneville, Fr. 56/C5
Bonney Lake, Wa, US 135/C3
Bonnigheim, Ger. 54/C4
Bonnybridge, Sc, UK 36/C5
Bonorva, It. 46/A2
Bons-en-Chablais, Fr. 56/C5
Bonsall, Ca, US 136/C4
Bontberg (mts.), SAfr. 106/C4
Bontebok NP, SAfr. 106/C4
Bonthain, Indo. 81/E5
Bonthe, SLeo. 102/B5
Bontoc, Phil. 79/D4
Bonyhád, Hun. 48/D2
Bonzart (chan.), Tun. 100/L6
Booker T. Washington Nat'l Mon., Va, US 133/J2
Boone, Belg. 53/D1
Boone, Ia, US 127/K5
Boone, NC, US 130/D4
Booneville, Ms, US 133/F3
Boonton, NJ, US 139/H8
Boorabin NP, Austl. 112/D4
Booroama, Som. 97/P6
Booroondara (mt.), Austl. 35/F4
Boorowa, Austl. 115/D2
Boos (int'l arpt.), Fr. 42/D2
Boos, Ger. 57/G1
Boosaaso (Bender Cassim), Som. 97/Q5
Boostedt, Ger. 38/D4
Boothbay Harbor, Me, US 131/G3
Boothia (pen.), NW, Can. 122/G1
Boothia (gulf), Can. 119/H2
Bootle, Eng, UK 35/E5
Booué, Gabon 96/H8
Bopa, Ben. 103/F5
Bopfingen, Ger. 54/D5
Boppard, Ger. 53/G3
Boppy (mt.), Austl. 115/C1
Boqueirão, Braz. 154/C2
Boqueirão, Serra do (mts.), Braz. 154/B3
Boquete (peak), Arg. 158/C4
Boquilla, Presa de la (lake), Mex. 142/D3
Boquillas del Carmen, Mex. 132/C4
Boquira, Braz. 154/B4
Bor, CR 145/F4
Bor, Yugo. 48/F3
Bor, Rus. 61/K4
Bor, Czh. 55/F3
Bor UI (mts.), China 64/B5
Bora Bora (isl.), FrPol. 117/K6
Borah (peak), Id, US 126/E3
Borås, Swe. 38/E3
Borāzjān, Iran 88/F3
Borba, Braz. 150/G4
Borba, Port. 44/B3
Borbera (riv.), It. 58/B3
Borbore (riv.), It. 58/B3
Borborema, Planalto da (plat.), Braz. 151/L5
Borça, Yugo. 48/E3
Borcea Branch (riv.), Rom. 49/H3
Borchen, Ger. 51/F5
Borça, Turk. 63/G4
Borculo, Neth. 50/D4
Borda da Mata, Braz. 211/G7
Bordeaux, Fr. 42/C4
Borden (isl.), NW, Can. 123/R7
Borden (pen.), Can. 123/H1
Bordentown, NJ, US 138/D3
Bordertown, Austl. 115/B3
Bordj Bou Arreridj, Alg. 100/H4
Bordj Bou Arreridj (prov.), Alg. 100/H4
Bordj el Kiffan, Alg. 100/G4
Bordj Manaïel, Alg. 100/G4
Bordj Moktar, Alg. 100/G2
Bordj Omar Driss, Alg. 99/G3
Bordj Sainte-Marie, Alg. 98/E4
Borello, It. 58/D2
Boretto, It. 58/D1
Borgå (Porvoo), Fin. 39/L1
Borgaretto, It. 58/A2
Borgarnes, Ice. 37/N7
Borgaro Torinese, It. 58/A2
Bergefjell NP, Nor. 37/F5
Borger, Tx, US 129/G4

Börger, Ger. 51/E3
Borger, Neth. 50/D3
Borgerhout, Belg. 50/B6
Borges Blanques, Sp. 45/F2
Borghetto Lodigiano, It. 58/C2
Borghetto Santo Spirito, It. 58/B4
Borgholm, Swe. 38/G3
Borgholzhausen, Ger. 51/F4
Borghorst, Ger. 51/E4
Borgloon, Belg. 53/E2
Borgo (int'l arpt.), Fr. 46/A1
Borgo, It. 57/H5
Borgo a Mozzano, It. 57/E5
Borgo San Dalmazzo, It. 43/G4
Borgo San Giacomo, It. 58/C2
Borgo San Lorenzo, It. 59/E5
Borgo Tossignano, It. 59/E5
Borgo Val di Taro, It. 58/C2
Borgo Vercelli, It. 58/B2
Borgofranco d'Ivrea, It. 58/A1
Borgomanero, It. 58/B1
Borgonovo Val Tidone, It. 58/C2
Borgosatollo, It. 58/D2
Borgosesia, It. 58/B1
Borgund, Nor. 38/B1
Borio, India 85/F3
Borisoglebsk, Rus. 63/G2
Borispol' (int'l arpt.), Ukr. 62/D2
Borja, Peru 156/B2
Borja, Sp. 44/E2
Borken, Ger. 50/D5
Borken, Ger. 51/G6
Børkop, Den. 38/C4
Borkum, Ger. 50/D1
Borkum (isl.), Ger. 50/D1
Borlänge, Swe. 38/F1
Bormida (riv.), It. 43/H4
Bormida, It. 58/B4
Bormida di Millesimo (riv.), It. 58/B4
Bormio, It. 57/G5
Born, Neth. 53/E1
Borna, Ger. 40/G3
Borndiep (chan.), Neth. 50/C2
Borne, Neth. 50/D4
Borne (riv.), Fr. 56/C6
Bornel, Fr. 30/K5
Bornem, Belg. 53/D1
Borneo (isl.), Indo.,Mala 80/D4
Bornheim, Ger. 53/G2
Bornholm (isl.), Den., Swe. 27/F3
Bornholm (co.), Den. 38/F4
Bornholmsgat (chan.), Den.,Swi. 41/H1
Borno, It. 57/G6
Bornos, Sp. 44/C4
Börnsen, Ger. 51/H2
Bornu (plain), Nga. 96/H5
Boro (riv.), Sudan 97/L6
Borohoro (mts.), China 70/D3
Borongan, Phil. 79/E5
Borough Green, Eng, UK 30/D3
Borovany, Czh. 55/H5
Borovichi, Rus. 60/G4
Borovo, Cro. 40/D3
Borovo, Bul. 49/G4
Borre, Nor. 38/D2
Borrisokane, Ire. 31/P10
Borrnida (riv.), It. 58/B3
Borşa, Rom. 49/F2
Borsec, Rom. 49/G2
Borso del Grappa, It. 57/H6
Borsod-Abaúj-Zemplén (prov.), Hun. 40/E3
Borsod-Abaúj-Zemplén (co.), Hun. 41/L4
Borssele, Neth. 50/A6
Borstel, Ger. 51/G3
Bort-les-Orgues, Fr. 42/E4
Borūjerd, Iran 88/E2
Boryslav, Ukr. 41/M4
Borzonasca, It. 58/C4
Borzya, Rus. 71/L1
Bosa, It. 46/A2
Bosanska Dubica, Bosn. 48/C3
Bosanska Gradiška, Bosn. 48/D3
Bosanska Kostajnica, Bosn. 48/C3
Bosanska Krupa, Bosn. 48/C3
Bosanski Brod, Bosn. 48/D3
Bosanski Petrovac, Bosn. 48/C3
Bosanski Šamac, Bosn. 48/D3
Bosco Mesola, It. 59/F3
Bosconero, It. 58/A2
Boshof, SAfr. 106/D3
Boskovice, Czh. 41/J4
Bosna (riv.), Bosn. 48/D3
Bosnia and Herzegovina (ctry.) 27/F4
Bošnjaci, Cro. 48/D3
Böso (pen.), Japan 75/G3
Bosobolo, D.R. Congo 97/J7
Bosporus (str.), Turk. 62/D4
Bosque Farms, NM, US 128/F4
Bosques Petrificados, Mon. Natural, Arg. 159/C5
Bossangoa, CAfr. 96/J6
Bossier City, La, US 129/J4
Bostān, Iran 88/E2
Bostānābād-e Bālā, Iran 88/E1
Boston (mts.), Ar, US 129/J4

Boston (cap.), Ma, US 131/G3
Boston, Eng, UK 35/H6
Bosut (riv.), Cro. 48/D3
Boswil, Swi. 57/F3
Botād, India 89/K4
Boteler (peak), NC, US 133/H3
Botelerpunt (pt.), SAfr. 107/F2
Botev (peak), Bul. 47/J1
Botevgrad, Bul. 47/H1
Bothaspas (pass), SAfr. 106/D2
Bothaville, SAfr. 106/D2
Bothel, Ger. 51/G2
Bothell, Wa, US 135/C2
Bothnia (gulf), Swe.,Fin. 160/E
Bothwell, Austl. 115/C4
Botoşani (prov.), Rom. 49/H2
Botoşani, Rom. 49/H2
Botou, China 72/D3
Botrange (peak), Belg. 53/F3
Botrivier, SAfr. 106/L11
Botsford, Ct, US 139/E1
Botswana (ctry.) 93/E7
Botte Donato (peak), It. 46/E3
Botticino, It. 58/D1
Bottineau, ND, US 127/H3
Bottisham, Eng, UK 33/H2
Botucatu, Braz. 155/B2
Botwood, Nf, Can. 131/L1
Bou (riv.), Fr. 30/J6
Bou Arfa, Mor. 99/E2
Boû Djébéha (well), Mali 102/E2
Bou Hamdane, Oued (riv.), Alg. 100/K6
Bou Ismaïl, Alg. 100/G4
Bou Izakarn, Mor. 98/C3
Bou Kadir, Alg. 100/F4
Bou Laber (well), Alg. 98/D4
Bou Nacuer (peak), Mor. 100/C3
Bou Regreg (riv.), Mor. 100/A3
Bou Salem, Tun. 100/L6
Bou Sellam, Oued (riv.), Alg. 100/H4
Bouaflé, C.d'Iv. 102/D3
Bouafle, Fr. 30/H5
Bouaké, C.d'Iv. 102/D3
Bouar, CAfr. 96/J6
Bouarfa, Alg. 100/G4
Bouaye, Fr. 42/B3
Boubín (peak), Czh. 55/G5
Bouca, CAfr. 96/J6
Bouchain, Fr. 52/C3
Bouchegouf, Alg. 100/K6
Boucherville, Qu, Can. 131/P6
Boucle du Baoulé, PN de la, Mali 96/D5
Boucle Du Baoulé, PN de la, Mali 102/C3
Boudry, Swi. 56/C4
Boufarik, Alg. 100/G4
Bouffémont, Fr. 30/J4
Bougainville (reef), Austl. 109/D2
Bougainville (isl.), PNG 116/E5
Bougainville (cape), UK 159/F6
Bougara, Alg. 100/G4
Bougar'oûn (cape), Alg. 100/K6
Bough Beech (res.), Eng, UK 30/D3
Bougouni, Mali 102/D4
Bougouriba (prov.), Burk. 102/E4
Bouguenais, Fr. 42/C3
Bouhachem (peak), Mor. 100/B2
Bouillante, Fr. 105/G3
Bouillancy, Fr. 30/L4
Bouillon, Belg. 53/E4
Bouira (prov.), Alg. 100/G4
Bouira, Alg. 100/G4
Boujad, Mor. 98/D2
Boukhalf (Tangier) (int'l arpt.), Mor. 100/B2
Boukoumbé, Ben. 103/F4
Boulaide, Lux. 53/E4
Boulaouane, Mor. 98/C2
Boulay-Moselle, Fr. 53/F5
Boulazac, Fr. 42/D4
Boulder, Mt, US 126/E4
Boulder (co.), Co, US 137/B2
Boulder, Co, US 137/B2
Boulder City, Nv, US 128/D4
Boulder Hill, Il, US 135/P16
Boulemane, Mor. 98/D2
Boulemane (prov.), Mor. 100/C3
Bouleurs, Fr. 30/L5
Boulga (prov.), Burk. 103/E4
Boulia, Austl. 113/H2
Boullarre, Fr. 30/M4
Boulogne, Fr. 42/D3
Boulogne-Billancourt, Fr. 30/J5
Boulogne-sur-Mer, Fr. 42/D2
Boulsworth (hill), Eng, UK 35/F4
Boumahra, Mor. 98/D3
Boumalne, Mor. 98/D3
Boumerdas, Alg. 100/G4
Boumerdas (prov.), Alg. 100/G4
Boun Nua, Laos 78/D3
Bouna, C.d'Iv. 102/E4
Bozcaada, Turk. 47/K3
Bozcaada (isl.), Turk. 47/K3
Bozkir, Turk. 90/C2
Bozman, Md, US 138/B5
Bozoum, CAfr. 96/J6
Bozova, Turk. 90/D2
Bozüyük, Turk. 91/C1
Bozyazı, Turk. 91/C1
Bozzolo, It. 58/D2
Bra, It. 58/A3
Braan (riv.), Sc, UK 36/C3
Brač (isl.), Cro. 46/E1
Bracciano (lake), It. 46/B1
Bound Brook, NJ, US 138/D2
Boundary (peak), Nv, US 128/C3
Boundiali, C.d'Iv. 102/D4
Bountiful, Ut, US 137/K12
Bouquet (res.), Ca, US 136/B3
Bouquet (canyon), Ca, US 136/B2

Bourbon l'Archambault, Fr. 42/E3
Bourbonnais (reg.), Fr. 42/D3
Bourbonne-les-Bains, Fr. 56/B2
Bourbourg, Fr. 52/B2
Bourdonné, Fr. 30/G5
Bourem, Mali 103/F2
Bouressa (riv.), Mali 103/F2
Bourg-en-Bresse, Fr. 56/B5
Bourg-lès-Valence, Fr. 42/F4
Bourg-Saint-Andéol, Fr. 42/F4
Bourg-Saint-Maurice, Fr. 43/G4
Bourg-Saint-Pierre, Swi. 56/D6
Bourganeuf, Fr. 42/E3
Bourges, Fr. 42/E3
Bourget (lake), Fr. 56/B6
Bourgneuf (bay), Fr. 42/F3
Bourgogne (reg.), Fr. 42/F3
Bourgogne (canal), Fr. 56/B3
Bourgoin-Jallieu, Fr. 42/F4
Bourke, Austl. 115/C1
Bourmont, Fr. 56/B1
Bourne (riv.), Eng, UK 33/E4
Bourne End, Eng, UK 30/F3
Bourne, The (riv.), Eng, UK 33/F3
Bournemouth, Eng, UK 33/E5
Bournezeau, Fr. 42/C3
Bourscheid, Lux. 53/F4
Bourtanger Moor (reg.), Ger. 51/E3
Bousbecque, Fr. 52/C2
Bousso, Chad 96/J5
Boussois, Fr. 52/D3
Boutte, La, US 137/P17
Bouvard (cape), Austl. 112/A3
Bouvet (isl.), Nor. 23/K8
Bouxières-aux-Dames, Fr. 53/F6
Bouxwiller, Fr. 53/G6
Bouznika, Mor. 100/A3
Bouzonville, Fr. 53/F5
Bovalino, It. 46/E3
Bovegno, It. 58/D1
Boven Tapanahoni (riv.), Sur. 153/H4
Bovenwijde (lake), Neth. 50/D3
Bovenden, Ger. 51/G5
Boves, Fr. 52/B4
Boves, It. 43/G4
Bovezzo, It. 58/D1
Bovigdon, Eng, UK 30/F3
Bovino, It. 40/B5
Bovolone, It. 59/E2
Bovril, Arg. 158/E2
Bow (riv.), Sc, UK 36/A1
Bow Island, Ab, Can. 126/F3
Bowdle, SD, US 127/J4
Bowdon, Eng, UK 35/F5
Bowen, Austl. 113/H2
Bowen, Arg. 158/D2
Bowers Beach, De, US 138/D2
Bowie, Az, US 128/E5
Bowie, Md, US 138/B6
Bowling Green, NJ, US 138/D1
Bowling Green, Ct, US 139/E1
Bowling Green, Ky, US 130/C4
Bowling Green, Braz. 147/C2
Bowling Green (cape), Austl. 114/B2
Bowling Green Bay NP, Austl. 114/H2
Bowman, ND, US 127/H4
Bowman (bay), NW, Can. 123/J2
Bowmansdale, Pa, US 138/B3
Bowmanstown, Pa, US 138/C2
Bowmansville, Pa, US 138/C2
Bowmore, Sc, UK 31/Q9
Bowokan (isls.), Indo. 81/F4
Bowral, Austl. 115/D2
Bowron, Fr. 126/C2
Box Elder (co.), Ut, US 137/J11
Boxberg, Ger. 54/C4
Boxholm, Swe. 38/F2
Boxing, China 72/D3
Boxmeer, Neth. 50/C5
Boxtel, Neth. 50/C5
Boyabat, Turk. 62/E4
Boyacá (dept.), Col. 152/C3
Boyang, Austl. 112/B5
Boyarka, Ukr. 41/N4
Boychinovtsi, Bul. 49/F4
Boyd (lake), Co, US 137/B2
Boye, China 72/C3
Boyer (riv.), Fr. 56/A5
Boyertown, Pa, US 138/C3
Boyle, Ab, Can. 126/E2
Boyle, Ire. 31/P10
Boyne (riv.), Ire. 31/Q10
Boyne City, Mi, US 130/C2
Boynton Beach, Fl, US 133/H5
Boysen (res.), Wy, US 126/F5
Boyup Brook, Austl. 112/C5
Boz (pt.), Turk. 90/J5
Bozcaada, Turk. 47/K3

Bracebridge, On, Can. 130/E2
Brackel, Ger. 51/H2
Bracken, Tx, US 137/U20
Brackenheim, Ger. 54/C4
Brackettville, Tx, US 129/G5
Bracknell, Eng, UK 33/F4
Braço do Norte, Braz. 155/B3
Brad, Rom. 49/F2
Bradano (riv.), It. 48/B5
Bradda (pt.), IM, UK 34/D3
Bradenton, Fl, US 133/H5
Bradford, Pa, US 130/E3
Bradford, Eng, UK 35/G4
Bradley (int'l arpt.), Ct, US 131/F3
Bradley Beach, NJ, US 138/D3
Braemar (reg.), Sc, UK 36/C2
Braeriach (peak), Sc, UK 36/C2
Braga (dist.), Port. 44/A2
Braga, Port. 44/A2
Bragança, Braz. 158/E2
Bragança (dist.), Port. 44/B2
Bragança, Port. 44/B2
Bragança Paulista, Braz. 211/H7
Brahmanbaria, Bang. 85/H4
Brahmaputra (riv.), Asia 67/J7
Braich-y-Pwll (pt.), Wal, UK 34/D6
Braidwood, Il, US 135/P17
Braine, Fr. 52/C5
Braine-l'Alleud, Belg. 53/D2
Braine-le-Comte, Belg. 53/D2
Brainerd, Mn, US 127/K4
Braintree, Eng, UK 33/G3
Braithwaite, La, US 137/Q17
Brak (riv.), SAfr. 106/C3
Brake, Ger. 51/F2
Brakel, Ger. 51/G5
Brakel, Neth. 50/C5
Brakna (pol. reg.), Mrta. 102/B2
Brålanda, Swe. 38/E2
Bram, Fr. 42/E5
Bramdrupdam, Den. 38/C4
Bramley, Eng, UK 30/B3
Brampton, On, Can. 131/Q8
Bramsche, Ger. 51/F4
Bramstedt, Ger. 51/G2
Bran (riv.), Sc, UK 36/A1
Brancaleone-Marina, It. 46/E4
Branch Dale, Pa, US 138/B6
Branchville, NJ, US 138/D1
Branchville, Ct, US 139/E1
Branco (riv.), Braz. 147/C2
Brand, Aus. 57/F3
Brandberg (peak), Namb. 105/B5
Brandbu, Nor. 38/D1
Brande, Den. 38/C4
Brandenburg (state), Ger. 40/F2
Brandenburg, Ger. 40/G2
Brandizzo, It. 58/A2
Brandon, Mb, Can. 127/J3
Brandon, Fl, US 133/H5
Brandon, Ms, US 133/F3
Brandsen, Arg. 159/J11
Brandýs nad Labem, Czh. 55/H2
Brandywine, Md, US 138/B6
Brandywine (riv.), Md, US 138/B6
Branford, Ct, US 139/E1
Braniewo, Pol. 39/H4
Brannenburg, Ger. 43/K3
Brant Beach, NJ, US 138/D4
Branxholm, Austl. 115/C4
Branzoll (Bronzolo), It. 57/H4
Bras d'Or (lake), Can. 131/J2
Brasiléia, Braz. 150/E6
Brasília de Minas, Braz. 154/A5
Brasília, PN de, Braz. 151/J7
Braşov, Rom. 49/G3
Braşov (prov.), Rom. 49/G3
Brasschaat, Belg. 50/B6
Brassey (mt.), Austl. 113/G2
Brasstown Bald (peak), Ga, US 133/H3
Brastad, Swe. 38/D2
Bratislava (cap.), Slvk. 40/D2
Bratislava (pol. reg.), Slvk. 41/J4
Bratislava (Ivanka) (int'l arpt.), Slvk. 40/C2
Bratsk, Rus. 65/J4
Brattleboro, Vt, US 131/F3
Bratunac, Bosn. 40/D3
Braubach, Ger. 53/G3
Braunau am Inn, Aus. 55/G6
Braunfels, Ger. 54/B1
Braunig (lake), Tx, US 137/U21
Braunlage, Ger. 51/H5

Bräunlingen, Ger. 57/E2
Braunschweig, Ger. 51/H4
Brava, It. CpV. 93/J11
Brava (pt.), Chile 159/C7
Brava (pt.), Uru. 159/K11
Brava, Costa (coast), Sp. 45/G2
Bravo (peak), Bol. 150/F7
Bravo (peak), Peru 156/B2
Bravo del Norte (riv.), Mex. 140/A2
Brawley, Ca, US 128/D4
Bray, NW, Can. 123/J2
Bray, Ire. 34/B5
Bray (pt.), Ire. 34/B5
Bray-Dunes, Fr. 52/B1
Braye (riv.), Fr. 42/D3
Brazey-en-Plaine, Fr. 56/B3
Brazil (ctry.) 147/D3
Brazilian Highlands (uplands), Braz. 147/K6
Brazo Casiquiare (riv.), Ven. 153/E4
Brazo Sur (riv.), Arg. 159/C6
Brazópolis, Braz. 211/H7
Brazos (riv.), Tx, US 129/G5
Brazos, Salt Fork (riv.), Tx, US 132/C3
Brazos (dist.), Tx, US 132/C3
Brazzaville (cap.), Congo 105/C1
Brčko, Bosn. 48/D3
Brda (riv.), Pol. 38/G5
Brdy (mts.), Czh. 41/G4
Brea, Ca, US 136/C8
Breadalbane (dist.), Sc, UK 36/B4
Breamish (riv.), Eng, UK 34/B2
Breaza, Rom. 49/G3
Brebbia, It. 58/B1
Brèche (riv.), Fr. 52/B5
Brechen, Ger. 54/B2
Brechin, Sc, UK 36/D3
Brecht, Belg. 50/B6
Breckenridge, Mn, US 127/K4
Breckenridge, Tx, US 129/G4
Breckerfeld, Ger. 51/E6
Breckland (phys. reg.), Eng, UK 33/H1
Brecknock (pen.), Chile 159/C7
Brecon, Wal, UK 32/C3
Brecon Beacons (mts.), Wal, UK 32/C2
Breda, Neth. 50/B5
Bredaryd, Swe. 38/E3
Bredasdorp, SAfr. 106/M11
Bredbro, Den. 38/C4
Bredene, Belg. 52/B1
Bredstedt, Ger. 38/C4
Bree, Belg. 53/E1
Breg (riv.), Ger. 40/E5
Bregagno (peak), It. 57/F5
Bregalnica (riv.), Macd. 47/H2
Breganze, It. 59/E1
Bregenz, Aus. 57/F3
Bregenzer Ache (riv.), Aus. 57/F3
Bregovo, Bul. 48/F3
Brégy, Fr. 30/L4
Breidhafjördhur (bay), Ice. 37/M6
Breil-Brigels, Swi. 57/F4
Breisach, Ger. 56/D1
Breitbrunn am Chiemsee, Ger. 55/F7
Breitenauriegel (peak), Ger. 55/G5
Breitenbach, Swi. 56/D3
Breitenbrunn, Ger. 55/F7
Breitenfurt bei Wien, Aus. 49/N7
Breitenworbis, Ger. 51/H6
Breithorn (peak), Swi. 56/D5
Brejo, Braz. 154/C3
Brejo Santo, Braz. 154/C3
Brejões, Braz. 154/C4
Brembate di Sopra, It. 58/C1
Brembilla, It. 58/C1
Brembio, It. 58/C2
Bremen (int'l arpt.), Ger. 51/F2
Bremen (state), Ger. 40/E2
Bremen, Ger. 51/F2
Bremen, NJ, US 138/C2
Bremer (riv.), Austl. 114/C5
Bremerhaven, Ger. 51/F2
Bremerton, Wa, US 126/C4
Bremervörde, Ger. 51/G2
Bremgarten bei Bern, Swi. 56/D4
Bremnes, Nor. 38/A2
Brend (lake), It. 58/D1
Brendel (lake), Mi, US 137/E7
Brendola, It. 59/E2
Brendon (hills), Eng, UK 32/C4
Brenham, Tx, US 132/D4
Brenig, Llyn (lake), Wal, UK 34/E5
Brenner (pass), Aus. 43/J3
Brenner (riv.), Austl. 113/N9
Breno, It. 57/G6
Brent (bor.), Eng, UK 30/C2
Brent (res.), Eng, UK 30/C2
Brenta (riv.), It. 43/J4
Brentwood, Eng, UK 33/G3
Brentwood, NY, US 139/E2
Brentwood, Ca, US 135/K11

Brentwood, Eng, UK 135/L11
Brenz (riv.), Ger. 54/D5
Brescello, It. 58/D3
Brescia, It. 58/D1
Brescia (prov.), It. 57/G6
Bresle (riv.), Fr. 42/D1
Bresles, Fr. 52/B5
Bressana, It. 58/C2
Bressanone, It. 43/J3
Bressay (isl.), Sc, UK 31/W13
Bressuire, Fr. 42/C3
Brest, Fr. 42/A2
Brest, Bela. 41/M2
Brest (int'l arpt.), Bela. 41/M2
Brestskaya (prov.), Bela. 62/C1
Bretagne (pol. reg.), Fr. 42/B2
Bretagne, Monts de (mts.), Fr. 42/B2
Bretagne, Pointe de (pt.), Reun. 107/S15
Bretaña, Peru 156/C2
Breteuil, Fr. 42/D2
Brétigny-sur-Orge, Fr. 30/J6
British Columbia (prov.), Can. 122/D3
British Empire (range), Ak, Can. 123/S6
British Indian Ocean Territory (dpcy.), UK 67/G10
British Museum, Eng, UK 30/C2
Britstown, SAfr. 106/C3
Brittany (reg.), Fr. 42/B3
Britton, SD, US 127/J4
Britz, Ger. 40/F2
Brive-la-Gaillarde, Fr. 42/D4
Brives-Charensac, Fr. 42/E4
Briviesca, Sp. 44/D1
Brivio, It. 58/C1
Brno, Czh. 41/J4
Brno (int'l arpt.), Slov. 43/L3
Broa (bay), Cuba 145/F1
Broad (pass), Ak, US 134/J3
Broad (riv.), SC, US 133/H3
Broad Law (peak), Sc, UK 36/C6
Broad Sound (isls.), Austl. 114/C2
Broadback (riv.), Can. 130/E1
Broadford, Austl. 115/C3
Broadkill, De, US 138/C6
Broads NP, The, Eng, UK 33/H1
Broadstairs, Eng, UK 33/H4
Broadus, Mt, US 126/F4
Broadwater NP, Austl. 115/E1
Broadway (hill), Eng, UK 33/E3
Broadway, NJ, US 138/C2
Broadway, It. 56/D4
Briar Creek, Pa, US 138/B1
Bricketwood, Eng, UK 30/B4
Brickerville, Pa, US 138/B3
Bricktown, NJ, US 138/D3
Bride, Ire. 31/P10
Bride, IM, UK 34/D3
Brochet, Mb, Can. 122/F2
Brockman (mt.), Austl. 112/B2
Brockton, Ma, US 131/G3
Brockville, On, Can. 130/F2
Brodeur (pen.), NW, Can. 122/G1
Brodheadsville, Pa, US 138/C2
Brodnica, Pol. 41/K2
Broek in Waterland, Neth. 50/B4
Broek Op Langedijk, Neth. 50/B4
Bröhn (peak), Ger. 51/G4
Broken (riv.), Austl. 115/D2
Broken Arrow, Ok, US 129/J3
Broken Bow (lake), Ok, US 129/J4
Broken Bow, Ok, US 129/J4
Broken Bow, Ne, US 127/J5
Broken Hill, Austl. 115/B1
Brokeoff (mts.), NM, US 132/B3
Brokopondo, Sur. 151/G2
Brokopondo, Sur. 153/H3
Brome, Ger. 40/E2
Bromölla, Swe. 38/F3
Bromsgrove, Eng, UK 32/D2
Bromskirchen, Ger. 51/F6
Bron, Fr. 56/A6
Brønderslev, Den. 38/C3
Brong-Ahafo (pol. reg.), Gha. 103/E5
Broni, It. 58/C2
Bronkhorstspruit, SAfr. 106/E2
Brønøy, Nor. 38/C4
Brønshøj, Den. 38/D4
Bronschhofen, Swi. 57/F3
Bronte, It. 46/D4
Bronx (bor.), NY, US 139/E2
Bronx Zoo, NY, US 139/E2
Bronxville, NY, US 139/E2
Brook Forest, Co, US 137/B3
Brooke's Point, Phil. 81/E2
Brookfield, Il, US 135/Q16
Brookhaven, Ms, US 129/K5
Brooklyn (bor.), NY, US 138/D2
Brooklyn(lovejoy), Il, US 137/G8
Brooklyn Park, Md, US 138/B5
Brookmans Park, Eng, UK 30/C1
Brooks (mtn.), Ak, US 134/E2
Brooks, Ab, Can. 126/F3
Brooks, Il, US 137/G8
Brooks (range), Ak, US 119/B3
Brookside, De, US 138/C4
Brooksville, Fl, US 133/H4
Brookton, Austl. 112/C5

Brookvale, Co, US 137/B3
Brookville, NY, US 139/L8
Broomall, Pa, US 138/C4
Broomfield, Co, US 137/C3
Brørup, Den. 38/C4
Brösarp, Swe. 38/F4
Brossard, Qu, Can. 131/P7
Brough (pt.), Sc, UK 31/V14
Broughshane, NI, UK 34/B2
Broughton Island, NW, Can. 123/K2
Brousseval, Fr. 56/A1
Brouwersdam (dam), Neth. 50/A5
Brouwershaven, Neth. 50/A5
Brovst, Den. 38/C3
Brown (mt.), Austl. 113/H5
Brown (pt.), Austl. 113/G5
Brown Clee (hill), Eng, UK 32/D2
Brown Shoal (bar) 79/C5
Brownfield, Tx, US 129/G4
Brownhills, Eng, UK 33/E1
Browning, Mt, US 126/E3
Browns Mills, NJ, US 138/D4
Brownsea (isl.), Eng, UK 33/E5
Brownsville, Tn, US 130/B5
Brownsville, Tx, US 132/D5
Brownsville, Wa, US 135/B2
Broxborn, Sc, UK 36/C5
Broye (riv.), Swi. 56/C4
Brozas, Sp. 44/B3
Bruay-la-Buissière, Fr. 52/B3
Bruay-sur-L'Escaut, Fr. 52/C3
Bruce (pen.), Can. 130/D2
Bruce (mt.), Austl. 112/C2
Bruce Rock, Austl. 112/C4
Bruchberg (peak), Ger. 51/H5
Bruche (riv.), Fr. 53/G2
Bruchhausen-Vilsen, Ger. 51/G3
Bruchköbel, Ger. 54/B2
Bruchmühlbach-Miesau, Ger. 53/G5
Bruchsal, Ger. 54/B3
Brucht (riv.), Ger. 50/D3
Bruck, Aus. 49/P7
Bruck an der Grossglocknerstrasse, Aus. 43/K3
Bruck an der Mur, Aus. 43/L3
Bruckberg, Ger. 55/F5
Bruckmühl, Ger. 43/J2
Brue (riv.), Eng, UK 32/D4
Bruflat, Nor. 38/C1
Brügg, Swi. 56/D2
Brugg, Swi. 56/E3
Brugge, Belg. 52/C1
Brüggen, Ger. 50/D6
Brugnera, It. 59/F1
Brühl, Ger. 53/F2
Bruinisse, Neth. 50/B5
Brukkaros (peak), Namb. 106/B2
Brukunga, Austl. 113/M8
Brumath, Fr. 53/G4
Brummen, Neth. 50/D4
Brumunddal, Nor. 38/D1
Brune (riv.), Fr. 52/C4
Bruneau (riv.), US 126/E3
Brunei (ctry.) 67/L9
Brunete, Sp. 45/M9
Brunflo, Swe. 37/E3
Brunico, It. 43/J3
Brünigpass (pass), Swi. 56/E4
Brunn am Gebirge, Aus. 49/N7
Brunoy, Fr. 30/K5
Brunsbüttel, Ger. 51/G1
Brunssum, Neth. 53/E2
Brunstatt, Fr. 53/G4
Brunswick, Ga, US 133/H4
Brunswick, Me, US 131/G3
Brunswick, Oh, US 130/D3
Brunswick Heads, Austl. 114/D5
Brunswick Junction, Austl. 112/B5
Brunswick, Península de (pen.), Chile 157/B7
Brus, Laguna de, Nic. 145/E3
Brusartsi, Bul. 48/F4
Brushy Creek, Tx, US 129/J5
Brusio, Swi. 57/F5
Brussels, Il, US 137/F8
Brussels (int'l arpt.), Belg. 53/D2
Brussels (Bruxelles) (cap.), Belg. 53/D2
Brusson, It. 58/A1
Bruthen, Austl. 115/C3
Bruyères, Fr. 56/C1
Bruyères-le-Châtel, Fr. 30/J6
Bruyères-sur-Oise, Fr. 30/J4
Bruz, Fr. 42/C2
Bruzual, Ven. 152/D2
Bryan, Tx, US 129/H5
Bryan, Oh, US 130/C3
Bryan (mt.), Austl. 113/H5
Bryansk, Rus. 62/E1
Bryansk Oblast, Rus. 62/E1
Bryce Canyon NP, Ut, US 128/D3
Bryn Brawd (peak), Wal, UK 32/C2
Bryn Mawr, Pa, US 138/C3
Bryne, Nor. 38/A2
Brzeg Dolny, Pol. 41/J3
Brzesko, Pol. 41/L4
Brzozów, Pol. 41/M4
Bua, Swe. 38/A4
Buala, Sol. 116/E5
Buba, GBis. 102/B4
Bubaque, GBis. 102/B4
Bubendorf, Swi. 56/D3
Bubikon, Swi. 57/E3

Bubu (riv.), Tanz. 104/B4
Buc, Fr. 30/J5
Bucak, Turk. 90/B2
Bucakkışla, Turk. 91/C1
Bucaramanga, Col. 152/C3
Bucasia, Austl. 114/C3
Bucelas, Port. 45/P10
Buch, Ger. 57/G1
Buchan (gulf), NW, Can. 123/J1
Buchan (reg.), Sc, UK 36/D1
Buchan Ness (pt.), Sc, UK 36/E2
Buchanan (lake), Tx, US 129/H5
Buchanan, Libr. 102/C5
Buchans, Nf, Can. 131/K1
Bucharest (Bucureşti) (cap.), Rom. 49/H4
Buchbach, Ger. 55/F6
Büchen, Ger. 51/H2
Buchen, Ger. 54/C3
Buchenbach, Ger. 57/G2
Buchholz, Ger. 53/G3
Buchholz in der Nordheide, Ger. 51/G2
Buchloe, Ger. 57/G1
Büchlerzell, Ger. 54/C5
Buchon (pt.), Ca, US 128/B4
Buchs, Swi. 57/F3
Bucine, It. 59/E6
Buck, The (peak), Sc, UK 36/D2
Buckden Pike (peak), Eng, UK 33/E5
Bückeburg, Ger. 51/G4
Buckie, Sc, UK 36/D1
Buckingham, Qu, Can. 130/F2
Buckingham, Eng, UK 33/F3
Buckingham Palace, Eng, UK 30/C2
Buckland, Ak, US 134/F2
Buckley, Wa, US 135/C3
Buckley, Wal, UK 35/E5
Buckner, Mo, US 137/K6
Bucks (co.), Pa, US 138/C3
Bucksburn, Sc, UK 36/D2
Bucksport, Me, US 131/G3
Bucquoy, Fr. 52/B3
Buctouche, NB, Can. 131/H2
Bucureşti (co.), Rom. 49/G3
Bucyrus, Oh, US 130/D3
Bucyrus, Ks, US 137/D6
Budai hegy (hill), Hun. 49/Q9
Budakeszi, Hun. 49/Q10
Budaörs, Hun. 49/R10
Budapest (cap.), Hun. 49/R9
Budaun, India 84/B1
Budd (coast), Ant. 160/H
Budd (inlet), Wa, US 135/B3
Budd Lake, NJ, US 138/D2
Buddon Ness (pt.), Sc, UK 36/D4
Buddusò, It. 46/A2
Bude, Eng, UK 32/B5
Bude (bay), Eng, UK 32/B5
Budel, Neth. 50/C6
Büdelsdorf, Ger. 38/C4
Budge-Budge, India 85/G4
Budhāna, India 86/D5
Budhanilantha, Nepal 86/C4
Budhlāda, India 86/C5
Budia, Sp. 44/D2
Büdingen, Ger. 54/C2
Budrio, It. 59/E3
Budva, Yugo. 47/F1
Budzhak (reg.), Mol. 49/J2
Buea, Camr. 96/G7
Buelna (int'l arpt.), Mex. 142/D4
Buena, NJ, US 138/D4
Buena Esperanza, Arg. 158/D2
Buena Fe, Ecu. 152/B5
Buena Park, Ca, US 136/G8
Buena Vista, Co, US 129/F3
Buenaventura, Mex. 142/D2
Buenaventura, Col. 152/B4
Buenavista, Phil. 79/E6
Buenavista, Mex. 143/Q9
Bueno Brandão, Braz. 211/G7
Buenópolis, Braz. 154/A5
Buenos Aires, Peru 156/B2
Buenos Aires, Co, US 152/B4
Buenos Aires (lake), Arg.,Chile 147/B7
Buenos Aires (prov.), Arg. 158/E3
Buenos Aires (cap.), Arg. 159/J11
Buenos Aires (Jorge Newbery) (int'l arpt.), Arg. 159/J11
Buenos Aires (Ministro Pistarini) (int'l arpt.), Arg. 159/J11
Buerarema, Braz. 154/C4
Buesaco, Col. 152/B4
Buet (peak), Fr. 56/C5
Bueu, Sp. 44/A1
Buffalo (mt.), Austl. 115/C3
Buffalo, Ok, US 129/H3
Buffalo, Mn, US 127/K4
Buffalo, Wy, US 126/E3
Buffalo (lake), Can. 126/E2
Buffalo, SD, US 127/H4
Buffalo, NY, US 131/S10
Buffalo, Ar, US 132/E3
Buffalo Bill Museum and Grave, Co, US 137/B3
Buffalo Narrows, Sk, Can. 126/F2
Buffalo Springs Nat'l Rsv., Kenya 104/C2
Buffelsrivier (riv.), SAfr. 106/B3
Buford, Ga, US 133/G3
Buftea, Rom. 49/G3
Bug (riv.), Pol. 64/C4

Buga, Col. 152/B4
Bugaba, Pan. 145/F4
Bugac, Hun. 48/D2
Bugala (isl.), Ugan. 104/B3
Bugalagrande, Col. 152/B3
Bugat, Mong. 70/F2
Buğdaylı, Turk. 49/H5
Bugel (riv.), Indo. 80/D5
Buggenhout, Belg. 53/D1
Bugojno, Bosn. 48/C3
Bugosa (prov.), Ugan. 104/B2
Bugsuk (isl.), Phil. 81/E2
Bugul'ma, Rus. 61/M5
Buguruslan, Rus. 63/K1
Buh (riv.), Ukr. 41/M3
Buhayrat al Asad (lake), Syria 90/D2
Buhayrat ath Tharthār (res.), Iraq 90/E3
Buhayrat Banzart (lake), Tun. 46/A4
Buhi, Phil. 79/D5
Buhl, Fr. 56/D2
Buhl, Ger. 40/F2
Buhuši, Rom. 49/H2
Bui (dam), Gha. 103/E4
Bui Gorge (res.), Gha. 103/E4
Bui NP, Gha. 103/E4
Buicine, It. 59/E6
Buin (peak), Swi. 57/G4
Buin, Chile 158/N8
Buique, Braz. 154/C3
Bujalance, Sp. 44/C4
Bujanovac, Yugo. 47/G1
Bujumbura (cap.), Buru. 104/A3
Bujumbura (int'l arpt.), Buru. 104/A3
Buk, Pol. 41/J2
Buka (isl.), PNG 116/E5
Bukadaban (peak), China 70/F4
Būkān, Iran 88/E1
Bukasa (isl.), Ugan. 104/B3
Bukavu, D.R. Congo 104/A3
Bukene, Tanz. 104/B4
Buket Bubat (peak), Malay. 83/H6
Bukhoro (pol. reg.), Uzb. 87/D4
Bukhoro, Uzb. 87/D5
Bukhovo, Bul. 47/H1
Bukittinggi, Indo. 80/B4
Bükki NP, Hun. 62/B2
Bukoba, Tanz. 104/A3
Buku (cape), Indo. 80/B4
Būlach, Swi. 57/E2
Bulahdelah, Austl. 115/E2
Bulancak, Turk. 62/F4
Bulandshahr, India 84/A1
Bulanık, Turk. 90/E2
Bulawa (peak), Indo. 81/F5
Bulawayo, Zim. 105/E5
Buldan, Turk. 90/B2
Buldibuyo, Peru 156/B3
Bulgan, Mong. 70/H2
Bulgan (prov.), Mong. 70/H2
Bulgan, Mong. 70/H1
Bulgan, Mong. 70/H3
Bulgaria (ctry.) 27/G4
Bŭlgarovo, Bul. 49/H4
Bulgheria (peak), It. 46/D4
Buliluyan (cape), Phil. 81/E2
Bulkley (riv.), BC, Can. 126/B2
Bull (isl.), NI, UK 34/B1
Bull Shoals (lake), US 129/J3
Bullange, Belg. 53/F3
Bullas, Sp. 44/E3
Bulle, Swi. 56/D4
Buller (isl.), NZ 117/S11
Bullfontein, SAfr. 106/D3
Bullhead City, Az, US 128/D4
Bullion, Fr. 30/H6
Bulloo (riv.), Austl. 114/B3
Bulloo River Overflow (swamp), Austl. 114/B3
Bully-les-Mines, Fr. 52/B3
Bulnayn (mts.), Mong. 70/G2
Bulnes, Chile 158/A6
Bulverde, Tx, US 137/U20
Bumba, D.R. Congo 97/K7
Bumtang (riv.), Bhu. 85/F2
Bumthang, Bhu. 85/F2
Bunaga-take (peak), Japan 77/J5
Bunbury, Austl. 112/B5
Bundaberg, Austl. 114/D4
Bundarra, Austl. 115/D1
Bünde, Ger. 51/F4
Bunde, Ger. 51/E2
Bundoran, Ire. 31/P9
Būndu, India 85/E4
Bungendore, Austl. 115/D3
Bunguran (isl.), Indo. 80/C3
Bunia, D.R. Congo 104/A2
Bunker (peak), Austl. 137/R18
Bunker Hill, Il, US 137/H7
Bunkie, La, US 129/J5
Bunnell, Fl, US 133/H4
Bunnik, Neth. 50/C4
Bunschoten, Neth. 50/C3
Bunya, Austl. 114/E6
Buñol, Sp. 45/E3
Bunya Mountains NP, Austl. 114/C4
Bünyan, Turk. 90/C2
Bunyu (isl.), Indo. 81/E3
Buochs, Swi. 57/E3
Buon Me Thuot, Viet. 78/E3
Buonconvento, It. 59/E4
Buquim, Braz. 154/C3
Buronga, Austl. 115/B2
Buronzo, It. 58/B2
Burâq, WBnk. 91/G7
Bür Sa'īd (gov.), Egypt 91/A4
Bür Sa'īd (Port Said), Egypt 91/A4
Bür Sūdân (Port Sudan), Sudan 101/D5
Burang, China 86/D2
Buranga (pass), Ugan. 97/M7
Burano, It. 59/F2
Burano (riv.), It. 59/F2
Buras-Triumph, La, US 133/K8
Burauen, Phil. 79/D5
Buraydah, SAr. 88/D3

Burbach, Ger. 53/H2
Burbank, Ca, US 136/F7
Burbure, Fr. 52/B2
Burco (Burao), Som. 97/Q6
Burdekin (riv.), Austl. 109/D2
Burdell (mtn.), Ca, US 135/J10
Burdur (lake), Turk. 90/B2
Burdur (prov.), Turk. 90/B2
Burdur, Turk. 90/B2
Burdwān, India 85/F4
Bure (riv.), Eng, UK 33/H1
Büren, Neth. 50/C5
Büren an der Aare, Swi. 56/D3
Bureya (riv.), Rus. 65/P4
Bürewāla, Pak. 86/B4
Burg, Ger. 38/C4
Burg, Ger. 51/H2
Burgas (prov.), Bul. 47/K1
Burgas (bay), Bul. 49/H4
Burgas (int'l arpt.), Bul. 49/H4
Burgaw, NC, US 133/J3
Burgberg im Allgäu, Ger. 57/G2
Burgbernheim, Ger. 54/D4
Burgbrohl, Ger. 53/G3
Burgdorf, Ger. 51/H4
Burgdorf, Swi. 56/D3
Burgebrach, Ger. 54/D3
Burgenland (prov.), Aus. 41/J5
Burgeo, Nf, Can. 131/K2
Burgersdorp, SAfr. 106/D3
Burges (mt.), Austl. 112/D4
Burgess Hill, Eng, UK 33/F5
Burgfjället (peak), Swe. 37/E2
Burghaslach, Ger. 54/D3
Burghausen, Ger. 55/F6
Burghead (bay), Sc, UK 36/C1
Burghead, Sc, UK 36/C1
Burgkirchen an der Alz, Ger. 55/F6
Burgkunstadt, Ger. 54/E3
Burglengenfeld, Ger. 55/E4
Burgos (prov.), Sp. 44/D1
Burgos, Sp. 44/D1
Burgsinn, Ger. 54/C3
Burgstall (Postal), It. 57/H4
Burgsteinfurt, Ger. 51/E4
Burgsvik, Swe. 38/H3
Burgundy (reg.), Fr. 56/B1
Burgwedel, Ger. 51/G3
Burhābalang (riv.), India 85/F4
Burhan Budai (mts.), China 70/F4
Burhaniye, Turk. 62/C5
Burhānpur, India 89/L4
Burhar-Dhanpuri, India 84/C4
Burhi Gandak (riv.), India 85/E3
Burica (pen.), Pan. 140/E6
Burica (pt.), Pan. 145/G7
Burin (pen.), Nf, Can. 131/L2
Buriram, Thai. 78/C3
Buritama, Braz. 155/B2
Buriti, Braz. 154/B1
Buriti Alegre, Braz. 155/B1
Buriti Bravo, Braz. 154/B1
Buriti dos Lopes, Braz. 154/B1
Buritis, Braz. 154/A4
Buritizeiro, Braz. 154/A5
Burjasot, Sp. 45/E3
Burke (chan.), BC, Can. 126/B2
Bürkelkopf (peak), Aus. 57/G4
Burkina Faso (ctry.) 93/B3
Burksville, Il, US 137/G8
Burladingen, Ger. 57/F1
Burlenworth, Malay. 80/B2
Burley, Wa, US 135/B3
Burlingame, Ca, US 135/K11
Burlington, Ia, US 127/L5
Burlington (bay), On, Can. 131/J2
Burlington, Ks, US 129/J3
Burlington, Wi, US 130/B3
Burlington, NC, US 133/J2
Burlington, Vt, US 131/N15
Burlington, Il, US 135/N15
Burlington, On, Can. 131/Q9
Burlington (co.), NJ, US 138/D4
Burma (Myanmar) (ctry.) 70/H7
Bürmoos, Aus. 55/F7
Burnas, Ukr. 49/K3
Burnet, Tx, US 129/H5
Burnett Heads, Austl. 114/D4
Burney, Ca, US 128/B2
Burney (peak), Chile 159/B7
Burnham, Il, US 136/Q16
Burnham-on-Sea, Eng, UK 32/D4
Burnie-Somerset, Austl. 115/C4
Burnley, Eng, UK 35/F4
Burns, Or, US 126/C3
Burns Lake, BC, Can. 126/B2
Burnside (riv.), NW, Can. 122/D2
Burntisland, Sc, UK 36/C4
Burntwood, Eng, UK 33/E1
Burntwood (riv.), Mb, Can. 122/G3

Burrinjuck (res.), Austl. 115/D2
Burrowes (pt.), Austl. 114/A2
Burrow (pt.), Sc, UK 34/D2
Burrow Heads, Austl. 114/D4
Burrum River NP, Austl. 114/D4
Burry (inlet), Wal, UK 32/B3
Bursa (prov.), Turk. 62/D5
Bursa, Turk. 62/D4
Burscheid, Ger. 53/G1
Burt, NY, US 131/S9
Burtenbach, Ger. 54/D6
Burton, Wa, US 135/C3
Burton Latimer, Eng, UK 33/F2
Burton upon Trent, Eng, UK 33/E1
Buru (isl.), Indo. 67/M10
Burullus, Buhayrat al (lake), Egypt 91/B4
Burundi (ctry.) 93/E5
Bururi, Buru. 104/A3
Buruticupu (riv.), Braz. 154/A2
Burwash Landing, Yk, US 134/L3
Bury, Eng, UK 35/F4
Bury, Fr. 52/B5
Bury Saint Edmunds, Eng, UK 33/G2
Buryatiya (aut. rep.), Rus. 63/J3
Busalla, It. 58/B3
Busembatia, Ugan. 104/B2
Busenberg, Ger. 53/G5
Bush (riv.), Md, US 138/B5
Bush Kill (riv.), Pa, US 138/C1
Bushey, Eng, UK 30/B2
Bushkill, Pa, US 138/C1
Bushkill Falls, Pa, US 138/C1
Bushmanland (reg.), SAfr. 106/B3
Bushmills, NI, UK 34/B1
Busigny, Fr. 52/C3
Businga, D.R. Congo 97/K7
Buskerud (co.), Nor. 37/D3
Busko-Zdrój, Pol. 41/L3
Buss Craig (res.), NM, US 128/F4
Busselton, Austl. 112/B5
Busseri (riv.), Sudan 97/L6
Busseto, It. 59/D2
Bussolengo, It. 59/D2
Bussum, Neth. 50/C4
Bustamante, Mex. 132/C5
Bustamante, Mex. 143/F4
Bustamante (pt.), Arg. 159/C6
Bustard (pt.), Austl. 114/C4
Busto Arsizio, It. 58/B1
Busto Garolfo, It. 58/B1
Busuanga (isl.), Phil. 79/C5
Büsum, Ger. 38/C4
Buta, D.R. Congo 97/K7
Buta Ranquil, Arg. 158/C3
Butare, Rwa. 104/A3
Butaritari (isl.), Kiri. 116/G4
Butawal, Nepal 84/D2
Bute (inlet), Can. 126/B3
Bute (isl.), Sc, UK 34/A5
Bute, Sound of (sound), Sc, UK 36/A5
Büteelyn (mts.), Mong. 70/H2
Butembo, D.R. Congo 104/A2
Butgenbach, Belg. 53/F3
Buti, It. 58/D5
Butiama, Tanz. 104/B3
Butiaba, Ugan. 104/A2
Butler, Pa, US 130/D3
Butler, NJ, US 138/H8
Butmir (int'l arpt.), Bosn. 48/D4
Butsier-sur-Oise, Fr. 30/J4
Bütschelegg (peak), Swi. 56/D4
Bütschwil, Swi. 57/F3
Butt of Lewis (pt.), Sc, UK 31/Q7
Buttapietra, It. 59/D2
Butte-Silver Bow County, Mt, US 126/D4
Butte, Mt, US 126/D4
Büttelborn, Ger. 54/B3
Butterworth, Malay. 80/B2
Buttes, Swi. 56/C4
Buttevant, Ire. 31/P10
Buttrio, It. 59/G1
Butuan, Phil. 79/E6
Butung (isl.), Indo. 67/M10
Buturlinovka, Rus. 63/G2
Butzbach, Ger. 54/B2
Bützow, Ger. 38/D5
Buulo Berde, Som. 97/Q7
Buvuma (isl.), Ugan. 104/B2
Buxar, India 84/D3
Buxheim, Ger. 57/G1
Buxtehude, Ger. 51/G2
Buxton, Eng, UK 35/G5
Buy, Rus. 60/J4
Buyant-Uhaa, Mong. 71/K3
Buynaksk, Rus. 63/H4
Buyo, Barrage de (dam), C.d'Iv. 102/D5
Büyük Anafarta, Turk. 47/K2
Büyükarmutlu, Turk. 62/F5
Büyükçekmece, Turk. 49/L5
Büyükkarıştıran, Turk. 49/H5
Büyükyurt, Turk. 90/D2
Buyun Shan (peak), China 73/B2
Buzachi (pen.), Kaz. 63/J3
Buzançais, Fr. 42/D3
Buzău, Rom. 49/H3
Buzău (riv.), Rom. 49/H3
Buzaymah, Libya 101/J2
Búzios, Ilha dos (isl.), Braz. 211/H8
Buz'kyy Lyman (estu.), Ukr. 49/K2
Buzuluk, Rus. 63/K1
Byala, Bul. 49/H4
Byala, Bul. 49/H4
Byala Slatina, Bul. 49/F4
Byam Martin (chan.), NW, Can. 123/H1

Byam Martin (isl.), NW, Can. 123/R7
Byarezina (riv.), Bela. 60/E5
Bydgoszcz, Pol. 41/J2
Bydgoszcz (prov.), Pol. 41/J2
Byfleet, Eng, UK 30/B3
Byford, Austl. 112/L7
Bygland, Nor. 38/B2
Bykhov, Bela. 39/P5
Bykle, Nor. 38/B2
Bylot (isl.), NW, Can. 123/J1
Bynum Run (riv.), Md, US 138/B5
Byram (riv.), Ct, US 139/F1
Byram (pt.), Ct, US 139/L7
Byram (lake), NY, US 139/L7
Byrd, US, Ant. 160/S
Byrd (cape), Ant. 160/U
Byremo, Nor. 38/B2
Byron, Ca, US 135/L11
Byron (isl.), Chile 159/B5
Byron Bay, Austl. 114/D5
Byrranga (mts.), Rus. 64/K2
Bystrice, Czh. 55/F2
Bystrá (peak), Slvk. 41/K4
Bystřice, Czh. 55/H3
Bytantay (riv.), Rus. 65/N3
Bytom, Pol. 41/K3
Bytów, Pol. 38/G4

C

C.F. Secada (int'l arpt.), Peru 156/C1
Ca (riv.), Viet. 83/J4
Ca Mau, Viet. 78/D4
Ca Mau (cape), Viet. 78/D4
Caála, Ang. 105/C3
Caatingas (phys. reg.), Braz. 147/E3
Caazapá, Par. 157/E2
Cabadbaran, Phil. 79/E6
Cabanaconde, Peru 156/D4
Cabañaquinta, Sp. 44/C1
Cabanatuan, Phil. 79/D4
Cabanes, Sp. 45/F2
Cabella Ligure, It. 58/C3
Cabeza del Buey, Sp. 44/C3
Cabeza Lagarto (pt.), Peru 156/B3
Cabezón de la Sal, Sp. 44/D1
Cabildo, Arg. 158/E3
Cabildo, Chile 158/B2
Cabimas, Ven. 152/D2
Cabinda, Ang. 105/B2
Cabinda (prov.), Ang. 105/B2
Cabo Corrientes, Cabo (cape), Mex. 142/E4
Cabo de Hornos, PN (Cape Horn Nat'l Park), Chile 157/C8
Cabo Delgado (prov.), Moz. 104/C5
Cabo Frio, Braz. 155/D2
Cabo Gracias a Dios, Nic. 145/F3
Cabo Orange, PN do, Braz. 151/H3
Cabo San Lucas, Mex. 142/C4
Cabo Verde, Braz. 211/G6
Cabonga (res.), Qu, Can. 123/J4
Cabora Bassa (lake), Moz. 105/F4
Cabora Bassa, Barragem de (dam), Moz. 105/F4
Cabot (str.), NS,Nf, Can. 123/K4
Cabra, Sp. 44/C4
Cabra de Santo Cristo, Sp. 44/D4
Cabral, Serra do (range), Braz. 154/A5
Cabrera, Isla de (isl.), Sp. 45/G3
Cabri, Sk, Can. 126/F3
Cabrillo Nat'l Mon., Ca, US 136/C5
Cabrobó, Braz. 154/C3
Cabudare, Ven. 152/D2
Cabugao, Phil. 79/D4
Cabure, Ven. 152/D2
Caçador, Braz. 155/B3
Čačak, Yugo. 48/E4
Cacalotán, Mex. 142/D4
Caccia (cape), It. 46/A2
Cáceres, Braz. 150/G7
Cáceres, Sp. 44/B3
Cachari, Arg. 159/J12
Cache (peak), Id, US 126/E5
Cache (pt.), Ut, US 137/K11
Cache Creek, BC, Can. 126/C3
Cache la Poudre (riv.), Co, US 137/B4
Cache Slough (riv.), Ca, US 135/L10
Cacheu, GBis. 102/A3
Cachí, Arg. 157/C2
Cachicadán, Peru 156/B3
Cachimbo, Serra do (mts.), Braz. 150/G5
Cachoeira, Braz. 153/E2
Cachoeira de Minas, Braz. 211/H7
Cachoeira do Sul, Braz. 155/A4
Cachoeira Paulista, Braz. 211/H7
Cachoeiras de Macacu, Braz. 211/L7
Cachoeirinha, Braz. 155/B4
Caconde, Braz. 211/G6
Caçu, Braz. 155/B1
Caculé, Braz. 154/B4
Čadca, Slvk. 41/K4
Caddo (mts.), Ar, US 132/E3

Cadelbosco di Sopra, It. 58/D3
Cadelle (peak), It. 57/F5
Cadenberge, Ger. 51/G1
Cader Idris (peak), Wal, UK 32/C1
Cadibarrawirracanna (lake), Austl. 113/G4
Cadillac, Mi, US 130/C2
Cadiz, Phil. 81/F1
Cadiz, Ky, US 130/C4
Cádiz, Sp. 44/B4
Cádiz, Golfo de (gulf), Port.,Sp. 44/B4
Cadolzburg, Ger. 54/D4
Cadria (peak), It. 57/G6
Caen, Fr. 42/C2
Caerano di San Marco, It. 59/F1
Caernarfon (bay), Wal, UK 34/D5
Caernarfon, Wal, UK 34/D5
Caernarfon Castle, Wal, UK 34/D5
Caerphilly, Wal, UK 32/D3
Caesarea (ruin), Isr. 91/G6
Caesarea (ruin), Isr. 91/G6
Caetité, Braz. 154/B4
Cafarnaum, Braz. 154/B3
Cafayate, Arg. 157/C2
Cagayan Sulu (isl.), Phil. 79/D6
Cagli, It. 59/F5
Cagliari, It. 46/B3
Cagliari, Golfo di (gulf), It. 46/A3
Cagnes-sur-Mer, Fr. 43/G5
Caguán (riv.), Col. 150/D3
Caguas, PR 141/M8
Caher, Ire. 31/Q10
Cahirsiveen, Ire. 30/N11
Cahokia, Il, US 137/G8
Cahore (pt.), Ire. 31/Q10
Cahors, Fr. 42/D4
Cahuapanas, Peru 156/B2
Cahuinari (riv.), Col. 152/D5
Cahuita, PN, CR 145/F4
Cahul, Mol. 49/J3
Cai (riv.), Braz. 155/B4
Caia, Moz. 105/G4
Caiapó (riv.), Braz. 151/H7
Caiapó, Serra (mts.), Braz. 151/H7
Caibarién, Cuba 145/G1
Caicara, Ven. 153/E2
Caicó, Braz. 154/C2
Caicos (isls.), UK 141/G3
Caicos Passage (chan.), Bahm. 145/H1
Cailloma, Peru 156/D4
Cailly (riv.), Fr. 52/A4
Caio (peak), It. 58/D4
Cairate, It. 58/B1
Cairn (mtn.), Ak, US 134/G3
Cairn Curran (dam), Austl. 115/D3
Cairn Gorm (peak), Sc, UK 36/C2
Cairn Table (peak), Sc, UK 36/B6
Cairn Toul (peak), Sc, UK 36/C2
Cairndow, Sc, UK 36/B4
Cairngorm (mts.), Sc, UK 36/B2
Cairns (int'l arpt.), Austl. 114/B2
Cairns (mt.), Austl. 113/G2
Cairns, Austl. 114/B2
Cairnsmore of Carsphairn (peak), Sc, UK 36/B6
Cairo, Ga, US 133/G4
Cairo (int'l arpt.), Egypt 91/B4
Cairo Montenotte, It. 58/B3
Caister Centre, On, Can. 131/Q10
Caistorville, On, Can. 131/Q9
Caizi (lake), China 72/D5
Cajabamba, Peru 156/B2
Cajabamba, Ecu. 152/B5
Cajamarca, Peru 156/B3
Cajamarca (dept.), Peru 156/B2
Cajapió, Braz. 154/B1
Cajari, Braz. 154/B1
Cajatambo, Peru 156/B3
Cajazeiras, Braz. 154/C2
Cajibío, Col. 152/B4
Cajon Junction, Ca, US 136/C3
Cajón (pt.), Cuba 145/E1
Cajuru, Braz. 211/G6
Čakovec, Cro. 40/C5
Çakmak NP, Turk. 62/E5
Çalköy, Turk. 62/E5
Çal, Turk. 90/B2
Cala d'Oliva, It. 46/A2
Calabar (int'l arpt.), Nga. 103/H5
Calabar, Nga. 103/H5
Calabasas, Ca, US 136/F7
Calabozo, Ven. 153/E2
Calabria, PN della, It. 46/D3
Calaburras (pt.), Sp. 44/C4
Calaceite, Sp. 45/F2
Calacoto, Bol. 156/D5
Calafat, Rom. 48/F4
Calahorra, Sp. 44/E1
Calais, Me, US 131/G2
Calais, Fr. 52/A2
Calais, Canal de (canal), Fr. 52/A2
Calalaste, Sierra de (mts.), Arg. 157/C2
Calama, Chile 157/C2
Calamar, Col. 152/C2

Calaveras (lake), Tx, US 137/U21
Calaveras (res.), Ca, US 135/L12
Calayan (isl.), Phil. 79/D4
Calayan (isl.), Phil. 116/B3
Calbayog, Phil. 81/F1
Calberlah, Ger. 51/H4
Calbuco, Chile 158/B4
Calca, Peru 156/D4
Calcanhar, Ponta do (pt.), Braz. 154/D2
Calcasieu (riv.), La, US 129/J5
Calceta, Ecu. 152/A5
Calci, It. 58/D5
Calcinate, It. 58/C1
Calcinato, It. 58/C1
Calcinelli, It. 59/F5
Calcio, It. 58/C1
Calcium, NY, US 130/F2
Calcutta, India 85/G4
Calcutta (int'l arpt.), India 85/G4
Calcutta, Sur. 153/H3
Caldaro (Kaltern), It. 43/J3
Caldas (dept.), Col. 152/C3
Caldas da Rainha, Port. 44/A3
Caldas Novas, Braz. 155/B1
Calder (mt.), Ak, US 134/M4
Calder (riv.), Eng, UK 35/F4
Caldera de Taburiente, PN de la, Sp. 98/A3
Caldera di Reno, It. 59/E3
Caldercruix, Sc, UK 36/C5
Caldes de Montbui, Sp. 45/L6
Caldicot, Wal, UK 32/D3
Caldiero, It. 59/E2
Caldonazzo, It. 57/H6
Caldono, Col. 152/B4
Caldwell, Tx, US 129/H5
Caldwell, NJ, US 139/H8
Caldwell, Wi, US 135/P14
Caldy (isl.), Eng, UK 32/B3
Caledon (riv.), SAfr. 106/D3
Caledon, On, Can. 131/Q8
Caledon, SAfr. 106/L11
Caledon, NI, UK 34/B3
Caledonia (hills), Can. 131/H2
Caledonia, Wi, US 135/P14
Caledonian (canal), Sc, UK 36/B2
Calella, Sp. 45/G2
Calen, Austl. 114/C3
Calenzana, It. 46/A1
Calenzano, It. 59/E5
Calera de Tango, Chile 158/N8
Calestano, It. 58/D3
Caleta de Campos, Mex. 142/E5
Caleta Olivia, Arg. 158/D5
Calexico, Ca, US 128/D4
Calf of Man (isl.), IM, UK 34/C3
Calf, The (peak), Eng, UK 35/F3
Calgary (int'l arpt.), Can. 126/E3
Calgary, Ab, Can. 126/E3
Calheta, Azor., Port. 45/S12
Calhoun, Ga, US 133/G3
Calhoun, Ky, US 130/C4
Calhoun (co.), Austl. 115/E1
Cali, Col. 152/B4
Calicut (Kozhikode), India 82/C0
Calida, Costa (coast), Sp. 44/E4
Caliente, Nv, US 128/D3
Califon, NJ, US 138/D2
California, Md, US 138/B6
California (state), US 128/C2
California (gulf), Mex. 119/F6
California, Tx, US 129/H5
Calilegua, PN, Arg. 157/D1
Călimăneşti, Rom. 49/G3
Calimaya, Mex. 143/Q10
Calimera (pt.), India 82/C5
Calimesa, Ca, US 136/D4
Calitri, It. 46/D2
Calixá-Lavallée, Qu, Can. 131/P6
Calizzano, It. 58/B4
Calkiní, Mex. 144/D1
Calkins (lake), Co, US 137/B4
Callabonna (lake), Austl. 115/A1
Callac, Fr. 42/B2
Callahonna (lake), Austl. 115/A1
Callander, Sc, UK 36/B4
Callantsoog, Neth. 50/B3
Callao, Peru 156/B4
Callaway, Fl, US 133/G4
Calliope, Austl. 114/C4
Callosa de Segura, Sp. 45/E3
Calne, Eng, UK 32/E4
Calolziocorte, It. 58/C1
Colonne-Ricouart, Fr. 52/B3
Calore (riv.), It. 46/D2
Caloundra, Austl. 114/D4
Calpe, Sp. 45/E3
Calpulálpan, Mex. 143/L7
Caltagirone, It. 46/D4
Caltanissetta, It. 46/D4
Caltavuturo, It. 46/D4
Calumet, Il, US 135/Q16
Calumet Sag (chan.), Il, US 135/Q16
Caluso, It. 58/A2
Calvello, It. 46/D2
Calvert, Tx, US 129/H5
Calvenzano, It. 58/C2
Călăraşi (prov.), Rom. 49/H3
Călăraşi, Rom. 49/H3
Calasparra, Sp. 44/E3
Calatafimi, It. 46/C4
Calatayud, Sp. 44/E2
Calatorao, Sp. 44/E2
Calauag, Phil. 79/D5

Calvillo, Mex. 142/E4
Calvinia, SAfr. 106/B3
Calvisano, It. 58/D2
Calw, Ger. 54/B5
Calzada de Calatrava, Sp. 44/D3
Cam or Rhee (riv.), Eng, UK 33/G2
Cam Pha, Viet. 79/A3
Cam Ranh, Viet. 78/E4
Camaçari, Braz. 154/C4
Camacupa, Ang. 105/C3
Camaguán, Ven. 153/E2
Camagüey (arch.), Cuba 141/F3
Camagüey, Cuba 145/G1
Camaiore, It. 58/D5
Camajuaní, Cuba 145/G1
Camalú, Mex. 142/A2
Camamu, Braz. 154/C4
Camamu, Baía de (bay), Braz. 154/C4
Camaná, Peru 156/C5
Camanducaia, Braz. 211/G7
Camapuã, Braz. 155/A4
Camaquã, Braz. 155/A4
Camaquã (riv.), Braz. 155/A4
Camargo, Sp. 44/D1
Camargos, Reprêsa de (res.), Braz. 211/J6
Camariñas, Sp. 44/A1
Camarillo, Ca, US 136/F7
Camarón (cape), Hon. 145/E3
Camarones, Arg. 158/D5
Camarones (riv.), Arg. 158/D5
Camas, Sp. 44/B4
Cambados, Sp. 44/A1
Cambará, Braz. 155/B2
Cambay, Gulf of (gulf), India 82/B3
Cambé, Braz. 155/B2
Camberley, Eng, UK 30/A3
Cambiano, It. 58/A3
Cambodia (ctry.) 67/K8
Camboriú, Ponta do (pt.), Braz. 155/C3
Cambrai, Fr. 52/C3
Cambrian (mts.), Wal, UK 34/E6
Cambridge, Ma, US 131/G3
Cambridge, Oh, US 130/D3
Cambridge, On, Can. 130/D3
Cambridge, Md, US 130/E4
Cambridge (int'l arpt.), Eng, UK 33/G2
Cambridge, Eng, UK 33/G2
Cambridge Bay, NW, Can. 122/F2
Cambridgeshire (co.), Eng, UK 33/F2
Cambrils, Sp. 45/F2
Cambui, Braz. 211/G7
Cambuquira, Braz. 211/H6
Cambuslang, Sc, UK 36/B5
Cambutal (mtn.), Pan. 152/A3
Camden, Me, US 131/G2
Camden, NJ, US 138/C4
Camden, Al, US 133/G3
Camden, De, US 138/C4
Camden (co.), NJ, US 138/C4
Camden, Eng, UK 30/C2
Camden, Austl. 114/G9
Camden Haven, Austl. 115/E1
Camden Point, Mo, US 137/D5
Camdenton, Mo, US 129/K3
Cameia, PN da, Ang. 105/D3
Camel (riv.), Eng, UK 32/B6
Camelback (mtn.), Az, US 137/C18
Camelford, Eng, UK 32/B5
Camerano, It. 59/G5
Cameri, It. 58/B2
Camerino, It. 59/F5
Cameron, Mo, US 129/J3
Cameron, Tx, US 129/H5
Cameron (isl.), NW, Can. 123/R7
Cameroon (ctry.) 93/D4
Cametá, Braz. 154/A1
Camiguin (isl.), Phil. 79/E6
Camiguin (isl.), Phil. 79/D4
Camilla, Ga, US 133/G4
Camiña, Chile 156/D5
Camilo Aldao, Arg. 158/E2
Caminha, Port. 44/A2
Camiri, Bol. 150/F8
Camisano Vicentino, It. 59/E2
Camlidere, Turk. 62/E4
Çamlık NP, Turk. 62/E5
Çamlıyayla, Turk. 91/D1
Camogli, It. 58/C3
Camooweal, Austl. 114/A2
Camorta (isl.), India 83/F6
Camp Angelus (Angelus Oaks), Ca, US 136/D3
Camp Creek, Az, US 137/S18
Camp Hill, Pa, US 138/B3
Camp Lake, Wi, US 135/P14
Camp Springs, Md, US 138/B6
Campagna Lupia, It. 59/F2
Campagnola Emilia, It. 59/E2
Campana, Arg. 159/J11
Campana (isl.), Chile 159/B6
Campana, It. 46/D2
Campana, PN de la, Chile 158/N8
Campanario (peak), Chile 158/C2
Campanella (cape), It. 46/D2
Campánia (prov.), It. 46/D2
Campánia, It. 46/D2
Campbell, Ca, US 135/L12
Campbell (isl.), NZ 23/B8
Campbell River, BC, Can. 126/B3
Campbell Town, Austl. 115/C4
Campbellsville, Ky, US 130/C4
Campbellton, NB, Can. 131/H1
Campbeltown, Sc, UK 31/R9
Campden, On, Can. 131/R9

Campeche (state), Mex. 140/C4
Campeche, Mex. 144/D2
Campeche (bay), Mex. 144/D2
Camperdown, Austl. 115/B3
Camperville, Mb, Can. 127/H4
Campestre, Braz. 211/G6
Campi Bisenzio, It. 59/E5
Campidano (range), It. 46/A3
Campillo de Altobuey, Sp. 44/C4
Campillos, Sp. 44/C4
Campina Verde, Braz. 155/B5
Campinas, It. 155/C2
Campion, Co, US 137/B2
Campione d'Italia, It. 57/E6
Campo (int'l arpt.), Braz. 156/C2
Campo Belo, Braz. 155/C2
Campo de Criptana, Sp. 44/D3
Campo de la Cruz, Col. 152/C1
Campo dei Fiori (peak), It. 58/B1
Campo Grande, Braz. 151/H8
Campo Ligure, It. 58/B3
Campo Limpo Paulista, Braz. 211/G8
Campo Maior, Port. 44/B3
Campo Mourão, Braz. 155/A3
Campo Tencia (peak), Swi. 57/E5
Campoalegre, Col. 152/C4
Campobasso, It. 46/D2
Campodarsego, It. 59/E2
Campodolcino, It. 57/F5
Campomorone, It. 58/B3
Camponogara, It. 59/F2
Camporosso, It. 58/A5
Camporredondo, Peru 156/B2
Camporredondo, Embalse de (res.), Sp. 44/C1
Campos (phys. reg.), Braz. 147/D5
Campos Altos, Braz. 155/C1
Campos Belos, Braz. 154/A4
Campos de Hielo Norte (glacier), Chile 159/B5
Campos de Hielo Sur (glacier), Chile 159/B6
Campos del Puerto, Sp. 45/G3
Campos do Jordão, Braz. 211/H7
Campos Gerais, Braz. 155/C2
Campos Novos, Braz. 155/B3
Campos Sales, Braz. 154/B2
Camposampiero, It. 59/E1
Camposanto, It. 59/E3
Campsie Fells (hills), Sc, UK 36/B4
Campti, La, US 132/E4
Camrose, Ab, Can. 126/E2
Çan, Turk. 49/H5
Can (riv.), Eng, UK 30/E1
Can Tho, Viet. 78/D4
Canaçari (lake), Braz. 153/G5
Canada (ctry.) 119/G4
Cañada de Gómez, Arg. 158/E2
Cañada Nieto, Uru. 159/J10
Cañada Rosquín, Arg. 158/E2
Canadensis, Pa, US 138/C1
Canadian, Tx, US 129/G4
Canadian (co.), Ok, US 137/M15
Canadian (riv.), US 119/G6
Canadian, North (riv.), Ok, US 124/F4
Cañadon Grande (mts.), Arg. 158/C5
Cañadón Seco, Arg. 158/B6
Canaima, PN, Ven. 150/F2
Çanakkale, Turk. 47/K2
Çanakkale (prov.), Turk. 62/C5
Canal de Moraleda (chan.), Chile 157/B6
Canalbianco (riv.), It. 59/E2
Canale, It. 58/B2
Canale Cavour (canal), It. 58/B2
Canals, Sp. 45/E3
Canals, Arg. 158/E2
Canandaigua, NY, US 130/E3
Cananea, Mex. 142/C2
Cananéia, Braz. 155/C3
Canápolis, Braz. 155/B1
Cañar, Ecu. 156/B1
Cañar (dept.), Ecu. 152/B5
Canard (riv.), On, Can. 135/G7
Canary (isl.), Sp. 93/A2
Cañas, CR 144/E5
Cañasgordas, Col. 152/C2
Canatlán de las Manzanas, Mex. 142/D3
Canaveral (cape), Fl, US 133/H4
Canberra, Austl. 115/D2
Canchaque, Peru 156/B5
Canche (riv.), Fr. 42/E1
Cancún, Mex. 144/E1
Cancún (int'l arpt.), Mex. 144/E1
Candado, Nevado del (peak), Arg. 157/C2
Candarave, Peru 156/D5
Çandarlı (gulf), Gre.,Turk. 62/C5
Candás, Sp. 44/C1
Candeias, Braz. 154/C4
Candelaria, Mex. 144/D2
Candelaria (riv.), Mex. 144/D2
Candelaria, Arg. 159/D2
Candeleda, Sp. 44/C2
Candelo, Austl. 115/D3
Candelo, It. 58/B1
Candia Lomellina, It. 58/B2
Candiac, Qu, Can. 131/N7
Candiba, Braz. 154/C2
Cândido Mota, Braz. 155/B2

Canding (cape), Indo. 80/D5
Çandır, Turk. 62/E5
Candlewood, NJ, US 138/D3
Cando, ND, US 127/J3
Candon, Phil. 79/D4
Canea, Braz. 155/B4
Canelli, It. 58/B3
Canelones (dept.), Uru. 159/F2
Canelones, Uru. 159/K11
Cañete, Sp. 44/E2
Cañete, Rio de (riv.), Peru 156/B4
Caney (riv.), Ks,Ok, US 143/F2
Cangallo, Peru 156/C4
Cangas, Sp. 44/A1
Cangas de Narcea, Sp. 44/B1
Cangas de Onís, Sp. 44/C1
Cangkuang (cape), Indo. 80/C5
Cangshan, China 72/D4
Canguaretama, Braz. 154/D2
Canguçu, Braz. 155/A4
Cangwu, China 83/K3
Cangyuan (Cangyuan Vazu Zizhixian), China 83/G3
Cangzhou, China 72/D3
Canh Cuoc (isl.), Viet. 78/D1
Cania Gorge NP, Austl. 114/C4
Caniapiscau (lake), Qu, Can. 123/K3
Caniapiskau (riv.), Qu, Can. 123/J3
Canicattì, It. 46/C4
Canik (mts.), Turk. 90/C1
Caniles, Sp. 44/D4
Canindé (riv.), Braz. 151/K5
Canino, It. 46/B1
Canistear (res.), NJ, US 139/H7
Cañitas de Felipe Pescador, Mex. 142/E4
Cañjayar, Sp. 44/D4
Çankırı, Turk. 62/E4
Çankırı (prov.), Turk. 62/E4
Canlaon (vol.), Phil. 81/F1
Canmore, Ab, Can. 126/E3
Cann River, Austl. 115/D3
Canna (isl.), Sc, UK 31/Q8
Cannanore, India 82/C5
Canne (riv.), Fr. 53/F9
Cannes, Fr. 43/G5
Canneto sull'Oglio, It. 58/D2
Canning, Austl. 112/C4
Canning (dam), Austl. 112/L7
Canning (riv.), Austl. 112/K7
Cannobio, It. 57/E5
Cannock, Eng, UK 32/D1
Cannon Falls, Mn, US 127/K4
Cannonball (riv.), ND, US 127/H4
Cannondale, Ct, US 139/E1
Cannonvale, Austl. 114/C3
Caño Guaritico (riv.), Ven. 152/D3
Caño Negro NWF, CR 145/E4
Canoas (riv.), Braz. 155/B4
Canoas, Braz. 155/B3
Canobolas (mt.), Austl. 115/D2
Canoinhas, Braz. 155/B3
Cañón de Rio Blanco, PN, Mex. 143/M8
Cañón del Sumidero, PN, Mex. 144/C2
Canora, Sk, Can. 127/H3
Canosa di Puglia, It. 46/E2
Canouan (isl.), 159/J11
Canowindra, Austl. 115/D2
Cansanção, Braz. 154/C3
Canso (cape), Can. 131/J2
Canta, Peru 156/B3
Cantabria (aut. comm.), Sp. 44/C1
Cantabria, Cordillera (mts.), Sp. 44/B1
Cantal, Massif du (mass.), Fr. 42/E4
Cantalejo, Sp. 44/D2
Cantanhede, Braz. 154/A1
Cantanhede, Port. 44/A2
Cantaura, Ven. 153/E2
Canterbury, Eng, UK 33/H4
Canterbury Bight (bay), NZ 109/H7
Canterbury Cathedral, Eng, UK 33/H4
Cantillana, Sp. 44/C4
Canto do Buriti, Braz. 154/B3
Canton, Ms, US 129/K4
Canton, Ok, US 132/D2
Canton, Oh, US 130/D3
Canton, NY, US 130/F2
Canton, NJ, US 138/C5
Canton, Mi, US 135/E7
Canton (Abariringa) (isl.), Kiri. 117/H5
Cantoria, Sp. 44/D4
Cantù, It. 58/C1
Cantwell, Ak, US 134/F2
Cañuelas, Arg. 159/J11
Canyon, Tx, US 129/F4
Canyon de Chelly Nat'l Mon., Az, US 128/E3
Canyon Lake, Tx, US 137/U20
Canyonlands NP, Ut, US 128/E3
Cao (riv.), China 73/C2
Cao Bang, China 83/J3
Cao Lanh, Viet. 78/D4
Cao Xian, China 72/C4
Caodu (riv.), China 79/A2
Caorle, It. 59/F1
Caorso, It. 58/C2
Cap-Chat, Qu, Can. 131/H1

Cap d'Agde (cape), Fr. 42/E5
Cap-de-la-Madeleine, Qu, Can. 131/F2
Cap-Haïtien, Haiti 145/H2
Cap Rock Escarpment (cliff), Tx, US 132/C3
Cap-Rouge, Qu, Can. 131/G2
Cap Roux, Pointe du (pt.), Fr. 43/G5
Capac, Mi, US 135/D6
Capanaparo (riv.), Ven. 150/E2
Capanema, Braz. 151/J4
Capanne (peak), It. 46/B1
Capannoli, It. 59/D5
Capannori, It. 58/D5
Capão Bonito, Braz. 155/B3
Capão Doce, Morro do (hill), Braz. 155/B3
Caparaó, PN do, Braz. 155/D2
Cappee Hill (peak), Austl. 113/H5
Caparo (riv.), Ven. 152/D3
Capay, Ca, US 135/K9
Capbreton, Fr. 42/C5
Capdenac-Gare, Fr. 42/E4
Capdepera, Sp. 45/G3
Cape Arid NP, Austl. 112/D5
Cape Barren (isl.), Austl. 109/D5
Cape Breton (isl.), NS, Can. 119/L5
Cape Breton Highlands (uplands), Can. 131/J2
Cape Breton Highlands NP, Can. 131/J2
Cape Cleveland NP, Austl. 114/B2
Cape Coast, Gha. 100/E5
Cape Cod Nat'l Seashore, Ma, US 131/G3
Cape Coral, Fl, US 133/H5
Cape Dorset, NW, Can. 123/J2
Cape Fear (riv.), NC, US 133/J3
Cape Hatteras Nat'l Seashore, NC, US 133/K3
Cape Krusenstern Nat'l Mon., Ak, US 134/C2
Cape Le Grand NP, Austl. 112/D5
Cape Lookout Nat'l Seashore, NC, US 133/J3
Cape May (co.), NJ, US 138/D6
Cape May, NJ, US 138/D6
Cape May Court House, NJ, US 138/D6
Cape May Lighthouse, NJ, US 138/D6
Cape Melville NP, Austl. 114/B1
Cape Palmerston NP, Austl. 114/C3
Cape Range NP, Austl. 112/B2
Cape Saint Claire, Md, US 138/B5
Cape Town (cap.), SAfr. 106/U10
Cape Town (D.F. Malan) (int'l arpt.), SAfr. 106/L10
Cape Tribulation NP, Austl. 114/B2
Cape Upstart NP, Austl. 114/B2
Cape Verde (ctry.) 93/J9
Cape Yakataga, Ak, US 134/K3
Cape York (pen.), Austl. 109/D2
Capel, Austl. 112/B5
Capela, Braz. 154/C3
Capela, Braz. 154/C3
Capelinha, Braz. 154/B5
Capella, Austl. 114/C3
Capelladas, Sp. 45/K6
Capestang, Fr. 42/E5
Capicciola (pt.), Fr. 46/A2
Capilla del Señor, Arg. 159/J11
Capim (riv.), Braz. 151/J4
Capinópolis, Braz. 155/B1
Capirara (res.), Braz. 157/F1
Capistrano, Braz. 154/C2
Capistrello, It. 46/C2
Capitan (mts.), NM, US 132/B3
Capitán de Campos, Braz. 154/B2
Capitão Poço, Braz. 151/J4
Capitol Reef NP, Ut, US 128/E3
Capivara, Reprêsa (res.), Braz. 155/H8
Capivara, Serra de (range), Braz. 154/A4
Capivari (riv.), Braz. 211/J6
Čapljina, Bosn. 47/E1
Caplone (peak), It. 58/D1
Capo di Ponte, It. 57/G5
Capo d'Orlando, It. 46/D3
Capodichino (int'l arpt.), It. 46/D2
Capolona, It. 59/E5
Capoterra, It. 46/B3
Cappella Maggiore, It. 59/F1
Cappoquin, Ire. 31/Q10
Capraia (isl.), It. 46/A1
Caprarola, It. 46/C2
Capreol, On, Can. 130/D2
Capri (isl.), It. 46/D2
Capricorn (chan.), Austl. 109/E3
Capricorn (cape), Austl. 114/C3
Caprino Veronese, It. 58/D1
Capriolo, It. 58/C1
Caprivi Strip (reg.), Namb. 105/D4
Captain Cook, Hi, US 124/U11
Captainganj, India 84/D2
Captains Flat, Austl. 115/D2
Capua, It. 48/B5
Capulhuac, Mex. 143/Q10
Capulhuac, Mex. 143/Q10
Caputh, Ger. 50/E3
Caquetá (riv.), Col. 150/D3
Caquetá (dept.), Col. 152/C4
Caquiaviri, Bol. 152/D5
Car Nicobar (isl.), India 83/F6
Carabobo (state), Ven. 152/D2

Caracal, Rom. 49/G3
Caracaraí, Braz. 153/F4
Caracas (cap.), Ven. 152/D2
Carache, Ven. 152/D2
Caracol, Braz. 154/B3
Caracolí, Col. 152/C3
Carácuaro de Morelos, Mex. 143/F5
Caradon (hill), Eng, UK 32/B5
Caraguatatuba, Braz. 211/H8
Caraguatatuba, Enseada de (bay), Braz. 211/H8
Carahue, Chile 158/B3
Carajás, Serra dos (mts.), Braz. 151/H5
Caranavi, Bol. 150/E7
Carandaí, Braz. 155/D2
Carangola, Braz. 155/D2
Caransebeş, Rom. 48/F3
Carapicuíba, Braz. 211/G8
Caraquet, NB, Can. 131/H2
Carasco, It. 58/C3
Carataca (lag.), Hon. 140/E4
Carate Brianza, It. 58/C1
Caratinga, Braz. 155/D1
Carauari, Braz. 150/E4
Caraúbas, Braz. 154/C2
Caravaca de la Cruz, Sp. 44/D3
Caravaggio, It. 58/C2
Caravela, Ilha (isl.), GBis. 102/A4
Caravelas, Braz. 154/C5
Caravelí, Peru 156/C4
Caraz, Peru 156/B3
Carazinho, Braz. 157/F2
Carballino, Sp. 44/A1
Carballo, Sp. 44/A1
Carberry, Mb, Can. 127/J3
Carbo, Mex. 142/C2
Carbon (cape), Alg. 106/H4
Carbon (co.), Pa, US 138/C2
Carbon (riv.), Wa, US 135/C3
Carbonara (cape), It. 46/B3
Carbondale, Pa, US 130/F3
Carbonear, Nf, Can. 131/L2
Carbonera, It. 59/F1
Carboneras, Mex. 143/F3
Carbonia, It. 46/A3
Carbonne, Fr. 42/D5
Carbost, Sc, UK 31/Q8
Carcagente, Sp. 45/E3
Carcarañá, Arg. 158/E2
Carcare, It. 58/B4
Carcassonne, Fr. 42/E5
Carche (peak), Sp. 44/E3
Carchi (dept.), Ecu. 152/B4
Carcross, Yk, Can. 134/M3
Çardak, Turk. 49/H5
Cardal, Uru. 159/K11
Cardedeu, Sp. 45/L6
Cárdenas, Mex. 143/F4
Cárdenas, Cuba 145/F1
Cardenden, Sc, UK 36/C4
Cardiel (lake), Arg. 159/C6
Cardiff (cap.), Wal, UK 32/C4
Cardiff, Md, US 138/B4
Cardiff by the Sea, Ca, US 136/C4
Cardigan, Wal, UK 32/B2
Cardona, Uru. 159/K10
Cardona, Sp. 45/L6
Cardozo, Uru. 159/K10
Cardston, Ab, Can. 126/E3
Cardwell, Austl. 114/B2
Care Alto (peak), It. 57/G5
Carenero, Az, US 31/Q10
Carei, Rom. 41/M5
Carentan, Fr. 42/C2
Carev vrh (peak), Arg. 159/J11
Carey (lake), Austl. 109/B3
Carhaix-Plouguer, Fr. 42/B2
Carhuamayo, Peru 156/B3
Carhuaz, Peru 156/B3
Carhué, Arg. 158/E3
Cariaco, Ven. 153/F2
Cariamanga, Ecu. 152/B4
Cariati, It. 46/E3
Caribbean (sea), NAm.,SAm. 119/L8
Cariboo (mts.), Can. 126/C2
Caribou (range), Id, US 126/F5
Caribou (lake), Can. 127/L2
Caribou, Me, US 131/G2
Caribou (riv.), Ab, Can. 122/E3
Caridade, Braz. 154/C2
Carigara, Phil. 79/D5
Carignan, Fr. 53/E4
Carignan, Qu, Can. 131/P7
Carignano, It. 58/A2
Cariñena, Sp. 44/E2
Carinhanha, Braz. 154/C4
Carinhanha (riv.), Braz. 154/A4
Carini, It. 46/C3
Caripito, Ven. 153/F2
Caririaçu, Braz. 154/C2
Cariris Novos, Serra dos (mts.), Braz. 154/B2
Carirubana, Ven. 152/D1
Carleton, Qu, Can. 131/H2
Carleton (hill), Ct, US 139/E1
Carleton, Mi, US 135/F7
Carleton Place, On, Can. 130/E2
Carletonville, SAfr. 106/P13
Carlin, Nv, US 126/D5
Carlisle Abor. Land, Austl. 112/C2
Carling, Fr. 53/F5
Carlingford, Ire. 34/B3
Carlingford (lake), Ire. 34/B3
Carlingford (mtn.), Ire. 34/B3
Carlinville, Il, US 129/E3
Carlisle, Pa, US 130/E3
Carlisle, La, US 132/J17
Carlisle, Eng, UK 35/F7
Carlisle Barracks, Mil. Res., Pa, US 138/A3

Carlos Casares, Arg. 158/E2
Carlos Chagas, Braz. 154/B5
Carlos M. de Cespedes, Cuba 145/G1
Carlow, Ire. 31/Q10
Carlow (co.), Ire. 34/B6
Carloway, Sc, UK 31/Q7
Carlsbad, NM, US 132/C4
Carlsbad Caverns NP, NM, US 132/C4
Carlsberg, Ger. 54/B3
Carlton, Eng, UK 35/G6
Carlton, Sc, UK 36/C5
Carlyle, Il, US 129/K3
Carlyle (lake), Il, US 129/K3
Carlyle, Sk, Can. 127/H3
Carmagnola, It. 58/A3
Carman, Mb, Can. 127/J3
Carmarthen, Wal, UK 32/B3
Carmarthen (bay), Wal, UK 32/B3
Carmaux, Fr. 42/E4
Carmel (pt.), Wal, UK 34/D5
Carmelo, Uru. 159/J11
Carmen (riv.), Mex. 132/B4
Carmen, Mex. 144/C2
Carmen de Patagones, Arg. 158/D3
Carmensa, Arg. 158/D2
Carmo, Braz. 211/L6
Carmo (peak), It. 58/B4
Carmo da Cachoeira, Braz. 211/H6
Carmo de Minas, Braz. 211/H7
Carmo do Paranaíba, Braz. 155/C1
Carmo do Rio Claro, Braz. 155/C2
Carmona, CR 145/F4
Carn Ban (peak), Sc, UK 36/B2
Carn Easgann Bàna (peak), Sc, UK 36/B2
Càrn Eige (peak), Sc, UK 36/A2
Carn Glas-choire (peak), Sc, UK 36/C2
Carn Kitty (hill), Sc, UK 36/C2
Carn Mairg (peak), Sc, UK 36/B3
Carn Mòr (peak), Sc, UK 36/C2
Carn na Cailliche (hill), Sc, UK 36/C1
Carn na Saobhaidhe (peak), Sc, UK 36/B2
Carnac, Fr. 42/B3
Carnamah, Austl. 112/B4
Carnarvon, SAfr. 106/C3
Carnarvon NP, Austl. 114/B4
Carnarvon, Austl. 109/A3
Carnaxide, Port. 45/P10
Carncastle, NI, UK 34/A1
Carndonagh, Ire. 34/A1
Carnduff, Sk, Can. 127/H3
Carned Llewelyn (peak), Wal, UK 34/E5
Carnegie (lake), Austl. 109/B3
Carney, Ok, US 137/N14
Carney (riv.), Ant. 160/S
Carnforth, Eng, UK 35/F3
Carnlough, NI, UK 34/B2
Carnot, CAfr. 96/J7
Carnot (cape), Austl. 113/G5
Carnoustie, Sc, UK 36/D4
Carnsore (pt.), Ire. 31/Q10
Carnwath, Sc, UK 36/C5
Caro, Mi, US 130/D3
Carol Stream, Il, US 135/P16
Carolina, Braz. 154/A2
Carolina, SAfr. 107/E2
Carolina, PR 141/M8
Carolina Beach, NC, US 133/J3
Caroline (isl.), Kiri. 117/K5
Caroline (isls.), Micr. 116/D4
Caroni (riv.), Ven. 147/C2
Carora, Ven. 152/D2
Carouge, Swi. 56/C5
Carpaneto Piacentino, It. 58/C3
Carpathian (mts.), Eur. 27/G4
Carpegna (peak), It. 59/F5
Carpegna, It. 59/F5
Carpenedolo, It. 58/D2
Carpentaria, Gulf of (gulf), Austl. 109/C2
Carpenter, Il, US 137/H8
Carpentersville, Il, US 135/P15
Carpentras, Fr. 42/F4
Carpi, It. 59/D3
Carpina, Braz. 154/D2
Carpinteria, Ca, US 136/C4
Carpio, Va, US 126/D4
Carquefou, Fr. 42/C3
Carr (inlet), Wa, US 135/B3
Carra (lake), Ire. 31/P10
Carrabelle, Fl, US 133/G4
Carrantuohill (peak), Ire. 31/P10
Carrara, It. 58/D4
Carrasquero, Ven. 152/D2
Carrboro, NC, US 133/H2
Carreg Ddu (pt.), Wal, UK 34/D6
Carriacou (isl.), Gren. 150/F1
Carrick on Shannon, Ire. 31/P10
Carrick on Suir, Ire. 31/Q10
Carrickfergus, NI, UK 34/C2
Carrickfergus (dist.), NI, UK 34/C2
Carrickmacross, Ire. 31/Q10
Carrickmore, NI, UK 34/A2
Carrières-sous-Poissy, Fr. 30/J5

Carrigaholt, Ire. 31/P10
Carrigaline, Ire. 31/P11
Carrington, ND, US 127/J4
Carrión (riv.), Sp. 44/C1
Carrión de los Condes, Sp. 44/C1
Carrizo (mts.), Az, US 124/D4
Carrizo Springs, Tx, US 132/D4
Carrizo Wash, Az, US 128/E4
Carrizozo, NM, US 132/B4
Carroll (co.), US 138/A5
Carrollton, Ky, US 130/C4
Carrollton, Ga, US 133/G3
Carron (lake), Sc, UK 36/A2
Carron (riv.), Sc, UK 36/A2
Carrot (riv.), Sk, Can. 127/H2
Carrot River, Sk, Can. 127/H2
Carrowkeel, Ire. 34/A1
Carrù, It. 58/A4
Carrum Downs, Austl. 115/C6
Çarşamba, Turk. 62/F4
Çarşamba (riv.), Turk. 62/E4
Carse of Forth (plain), Sc, UK 36/B4
Carse of Gowrie (plain), Sc, UK 36/C4
Carson (riv.), Nv, US 128/C3
Carson, Ca, US 136/F8
Carson City (cap.), Nv, US 128/C3
Carson Sink (dry lake), Nv, US 128/C3
Carstairs, Ab, Can. 126/E3
Cartagena, Col. 152/C2
Cartagena, Sp. 44/E4
Cartago, Col. 152/C3
Cartago, CR 145/F4
Cártama, Sp. 44/C4
Cartaxo, Port. 44/A3
Cartaya, Sp. 44/B4
Carteret, NJ, US 139/J9
Carterton, Eng, UK 33/E3
Cartersville, Ga, US 133/G3
Carthage, Tx, US 129/J4
Carthage, Mo, US 129/J3
Carthage, Tn, US 130/C4
Carthage, Ms, US 133/F3
Carthage, Isr. 91/G8
Carthage (int'l arpt.), Tun. 48/B4
Carthage (Qarṭājannah) (ruin), Tun. 48/B4
Carti (mts.), Pan. 152/B2
Cartier Islet (isl.), Austl. 109/B2
Cartwright, Nf, Can. 123/L3
Carumás, Peru 156/D5
Carúpano, Ven. 153/F2
Caruthersville, Mo, US 129/K3
Carvico, It. 58/C1
Carvin, Fr. 30/B2
Carvoeiro (cape), Port. 44/A3
Cary, NC, US 133/J3
Cary, Il, US 135/P15
Casa Blanca (canal), Az, US 137/S19
Casa Branca, Braz. 211/F6
Casa de Piedra (res.), Arg. 158/D3
Casa Grande, Az, US 128/E4
Casa Grande Nat'l Mon., Az, US 128/E4
Casa Nova, Braz. 154/B3
Casablanca, Chile 158/N8
Casablanca-Anfa (int'l arpt.), Mor. 100/A2
Casal di Principe, It. 46/D2
Casalbordino, It. 46/D1
Casalbuttano ed Uniti, It. 58/C2
Casale di Scodosia, It. 59/E2
Casale Monferrato, It. 58/B2
Casale sul Sile, It. 59/F1
Casalecchio di Reno, It. 59/E3
Casaleone, It. 59/E2
Casalmaggiore, It. 58/D3
Casalpusterlengo, It. 58/C2
Casalserugo, It. 59/E2
Casamance (riv.), Sen. 102/A3
Casanare (dept.), Col. 152/D3
Casanay, Ven. 153/F2
Casar de Cáceres, Sp. 44/B3
Casarano, It. 47/F2
Casarsa della Delizia, It. 59/F1
Casarza Ligure, It. 58/C4
Casas Grande (riv.), Ab, Can. 122/E3
Casas-Ibáñez, Sp. 44/E3
Casazza, It. 58/C1
Cascade de Bassaseachic, PN, Mex. 142/C2
Cascade (res.), Id, US 126/D4
Cascade (range), Or,Wa, US 124/D4
Cascade Caverns, Tx, US 137/T20
Cascade-Fairwood, Wa, US 135/C3
Cascais, Port. 45/P10
Cascavel, Braz. 157/F1
Cascavel, Braz. 154/C2
Casciago, It. 58/B1
Casciana Terme, It. 59/D5
Cascina, It. 58/D5
Case (inlet), Wa, US 135/B3
Casella, It. 58/B3
Caselle, It. 58/A2
Casentino (valley), It. 59/E5
Caserta, It. 46/D2
Casey (bay), Ant. 160/D
Casey, Austl. 160/L
Caseyr (cape), Som. 97/R5
Caseyville, Il, US 137/G8

Cashel, Ire. 31/Q10
Cashion, Ok, US 137/M14
Cashmere, Wa, US 126/C4
Cashtown, Pa, US 138/A4
Casiguia, Ven. 152/C2
Casilda (pt.), Cuba 145/F1
Casilda, Arg. 158/E2
Casimiro Castillo, Mex. 142/D5
Casina, It. 58/D3
Casinalbo, It. 59/D3
Casino, Austl. 115/E1
Casino and Opera House, Mona. 58/A8
Casitas (lake), Ca, US 136/A2
Casitas Springs, Ca, US 136/A2
Casma, Peru 156/B3
Casnigo, It. 58/C1
Casole d'Elsa, It. 59/E6
Casorate Primo, It. 58/C2
Casorate Sempione, It. 58/C1
Caspe, Sp. 45/E2
Casper, Wy, US 124/F3
Caspian (sea), Asia 67/E5
Cass (riv.), Mi, US 130/D3
Cass (co.), Mo, US 137/E6
Cass City, Mi, US 130/D3
Cass Lake, Mi, US 135/H6
Cassano allo Ionio, It. 46/E3
Cassano d'Adda, It. 58/C2
Cassano Magnago, It. 58/B1
Cassano Spinola, It. 58/B3
Cassel, Fr. 52/B2
Cássia, Braz. 211/F5
Cassiar, BC, Can. 134/N3
Cassiar (mts.), BC, Can. 122/C3
Cassine, It. 58/B3
Cassino, It. 46/C2
Cassolnovo, It. 58/B2
Cassopolis, Mi, US 135/E8
Cassville, Mo, US 129/J3
Castagnaro, It. 59/E2
Castagneto Carducci, It. 43/D5
Castagnole delle Lanze, It. 58/B3
Castaic, Ca, US 136/B2
Castalla, Sp. 45/E3
Castanet-Tolosan, Fr. 42/D5
Castanhal, Braz. 151/J4
Castaños, Mex. 132/C5
Casteggio, It. 58/C2
Castegnato, It. 58/D1
Castel Bolognese, It. 59/E3
Castel d'Ario, It. 59/D2
Castel di Sangro, It. 46/D2
Castel Goffredo, It. 58/D2
Castel Mella, It. 58/D1
Castel San Giovanni, It. 58/C2
Castel San Pietro Terme, It. 59/E3
Castelbuono, It. 46/D4
Castelcovati, It. 58/C1
Castelfidardo, It. 59/G6
Castelfranco di Sopra, It. 59/E5
Castelfranco Emilia, It. 59/E3
Castelfranco Veneto, It. 59/E1
Castelgomberto, It. 59/E1
Casteljaloux, Fr. 42/D4
Castell de Montjuïc, Sp. 45/L7
Castell'Arquato, It. 58/C3
Castellabate, It. 46/D2
Castellammare di Stabia, It. 46/D2
Castellammare, Golfo di (gulf), It. 46/C3
Castellamonte, It. 58/A1
Castellana Grotte, It. 46/E2
Castellane, Fr. 43/G4
Castellaneta, It. 46/E2
Castellanza, It. 58/B1
Castell del Vallès, Sp. 45/G2
Castellarano, It. 58/D3
Castelldefels, Sp. 45/K7
Castelleone, It. 58/C2
Castelli, Arg. 159/K12
Castellina in Chianti, It. 59/E6
Castello di Godego, It. 59/E1
Castello di Miramare, It. 59/G1
Castello Eurialo (ruin), It. 46/D4
Castello, Monte il (peak), It. 58/B2
Castellón de la Plana, Sp. 45/E2
Castellote, Sp. 45/E2
Castelluccio, It. 59/E3
Castelmassa, It. 59/E2
Castelnau-le-Lez, Fr. 42/E5
Castelnaudary, Fr. 42/D5
Castelnovo di Sotto, It. 58/D3
Castelnovo ne'Monti, It. 58/C3
Castelnuovo Berardenga, It. 59/E5
Castelnuovo di Garfagnana, It. 58/D3
Castelnuovo Don Bosco, It. 58/B2
Castelnuovo Scrivia, It. 58/B3
Castelo Branco, Port. 44/B3
Castelo Branco (dist.), Port. 44/B3
Castelo de Vide, Port. 44/B3
Castelo do Piauí, Braz. 154/B2
Castelsardo, It. 46/A2
Castelsarrasin, Fr. 42/D4
Castelverde, It. 58/C2
Castelvetrano, It. 46/C4
Castelvetro di Modena, It. 59/D3
Castelvetro Piacentino, It. 58/C2
Castenaso, It. 59/E3
Castenedolo, It. 58/D2
Casterton, Austl. 115/B3
Castets, Fr. 42/C4
Castiadas, It. 46/B3
Castiglion Fiorentino, It. 59/E5
Castiglione d'Adda, It. 58/C2
Castiglione dei Pepoli, It. 59/E3
Castiglione delle Stiviere, It. 58/D2
Castiglione Torinese, It. 58/A2

Castilla-La Mancha (aut. comm.), Sp. 44/C3
Castilla y León (aut. comm.), Sp. 44/D2
Castilla y León Treviño, Sp. 44/D1
Castillo (peak), Arg. 158/C4
Castillo de San Marcos Nat'l Mon., Fl, US 133/H4
Castine, Me, US 131/G2
Castione della Presolana, It. 57/G6
Castions, It. 59/F1
Castions di Strada, It. 59/F1
Castle Dale, Ut, US 128/E3
Castle Douglas, Sc, UK 34/F2
Castle Hills, Tx, US 137/D20
Castle Rock, Co, US 129/F3
Castle Rock, Wa, US 126/C4
Castle Rock (lake), Wi, US 127/L5
Castle Tower NP, Austl. 114/C4
Castlebar, Ire. 31/P10
Castlebay, Sc, UK 31/Q8
Castlebellingham, Ire. 34/B4
Castlebridge, Ire. 31/Q10
Castlecaulfield, NI, UK 34/B3
Castlecomer, Ire. 31/Q10
Castledawson, NI, UK 34/B2
Castleford, Eng, UK 35/G4
Castlegar, BC, Can. 126/D3
Castlegregory, Ire. 30/N10
Castleisland, Ire. 31/P10
Castlemaine, Austl. 115/C3
Castletown, IM, UK 34/D3
Castlereagh, Ire. 31/P10
Castlewellan, NI, UK 34/C3
Castor, Ab, Can. 126/F2
Castor (riv.), Libr. 96/D6
Castres, Fr. 42/E5
Castries (cap.), StL. 141/N9
Castro, Braz. 155/B3
Castro, Chile 158/B4
Castro Alves, Braz. 154/C4
Castro Daire, Port. 44/B2
Castro de Rey, Sp. 44/B1
Castro-Urdiales, Sp. 44/D1
Castro Verde, Port. 44/A4
Castrojeriz, Sp. 44/C1
Castrop-Rauxel, Ger. 51/E5
Castropol, Sp. 44/B1
Castrovillari, It. 46/E3
Castrovirreyna, Peru 156/C4
Castuera, Sp. 44/C3
Casupá, Uru. 159/G2
Cat (lake), Can. 127/K3
Çat, Turk. 63/G5
Catacamas, Hon. 144/E3
Catacaos, Peru 156/A2
Catacocha, Ecu. 156/B2
Cataduanes (isl.), Phil. 116/B3
Cataguases, Braz. 211/L6
Çatak, Turk. 90/E2
Çatalağzı, Turk. 49/K5
Çatalca, Turk. 62/F5
Çatalçam, Turk. 90/E2
Catalina, Az, US 128/E4
Catalonia (reg.), Sp. 45/L6
Cataluña (aut. comm.), Sp. 44/C3
Catamarca, Arg. 157/C2
Catamayo, Ecu. 156/B1
Catanduanes (isl.), Phil. 79/D5
Catanduva, Braz. 155/B2
Catania, It. 46/D4
Catania, Golfo di (gulf), It. 46/D4
Catanzaro, It. 46/E3
Catarina (lake), It. 46/E3
Catarman, Phil. 81/F1
Catastrophe (cape), Austl. 113/G5
Catatumbo (riv.), Col. 141/G6
Catatungan (mtn.), Phil. 81/E1
Catawba (riv.), US 133/H2
Catawba, Wi, US 133/H2
Catbalogan, Phil. 79/D5
Catedral (peak), Uru. 159/G2
Catemaco, Mex. 144/C2
Catemaco (lake), Mex. 144/C2
Catende, Braz. 154/D3
Caterham, Eng, UK 36/E5
Caterham and Warlingham, Eng, UK 33/F4
Cathcart, SAfr. 106/D4
Cathédrale de Reims, Fr. 52/D5
Catherine (Kätrinä),
Catherine Palace, Rus. 61/T7
Ca'Tiepolo, It. 59/F2
Cativá, Pan. 141/G6
Catlettsburg, Ky, US 130/D4
Catlin, Il, US 137/J13
Cato (isl.), Austl. 109/E3
Catoche, Cabo (cape), Mex. 144/E1
Catolé do Rocha, Braz. 154/C2
Catonsville, Md, US 138/B5
Catria (peak), It. 59/F6
Catrilo, Arg. 158/E3
Catrimani (riv.), Braz. 150/F3
Catskill, NY, US 130/F3
Catskill (mts.), NY, US 130/F3
Cattolica, It. 59/F5
Catu, Braz. 154/C4
Cauayan, Phil. 79/D4
Cauayan, Phil. 79/D6
Cauca (dept.), Col. 152/C3
Cauca (riv.), Col. 147/B2
Caucaia, Braz. 154/C1

Caucasia, Col. 152/C3
Caucasus (mts.), Geo. 64/F6
Caudete, Sp. 45/E3
Caudry, Fr. 52/C3
Cauldcleuch Head (peak), Sc, UK 36/D6
Cauquenes, Chile 158/B2
Caura (riv.), Ven. 150/F2
Caussade, Fr. 42/D4
Cauterets, Fr. 42/C5
Cauto (riv.), Cuba 145/G1
Cauvery (riv.), India 82/C5
Cava d'Ispica (ruin), It. 46/D4
Cávado (riv.), Port. 44/A2
Cavaglià, It. 58/B2
Cavaillon, Fr. 42/F5
Cavalaire-sur-Mer, Fr. 43/G5
Cavalcante, Braz. 154/A4
Cavalese, It. 57/H5
Cavalier, ND, US 127/J3
Cavalli (isls.), Libr. 96/D6
Cavallermaggiore, It. 58/A3
Cavallino, It. 59/F2
Cavallo, Capo al (cape), Fr. 46/A1
Cavally (riv.), C.d'Iv. 102/C5
Cavan, Ire. 31/Q10
Cavan (co.), Ire. 31/Q10
Cavarzere, It. 59/F2
Cave Creek, Az, US 137/S18
Cave of Ten Thousand Buddhas, Myan. 78/B2
Cavezzo, It. 59/E3
Caviana (isl.), Braz. 151/J3
Cavite, Phil. 79/D5
Cavour, It. 58/A3
Cawdor, Sc, UK 36/C1
Cawndilla (lake), Austl. 115/B2
Caxias, Braz. 154/B2
Caxias do Sul, Braz. 155/B4
Caxinas (pt.), Hon. 144/E2
Caxito, Ang. 105/B2
Çay, Turk. 90/B2
Cayambe, Ecu. 152/B4
Cayambe (vol.), Ecu. 152/B4
Cayce, SC, US 133/H3
Çaycuma, Turk. 49/L5
Çayeli, Turk. 63/G4
Cayenne (cap.), FrG. 151/H3
Cayeux-sur-Mer, Fr. 52/A3
Çayırhan, Turk. 49/K5
Çaylar, Turk. 90/E2
Cayman Brac (isl.), UK 141/F4
Cayman (isls.), UK 119/J8
Cazalla de la Sierra, Sp. 44/C4
Cazères, Fr. 42/D5
Cazin, Bosn. 43/L4
Cazis, Swi. 57/F4
Cazones (riv.), Mex. 144/B1
Cazorla, Sp. 44/D4
Cazzago San Martino, It. 58/D1
Cea (riv.), Sp. 44/C1
Ceanannus Mór (kells), Ire. 31/Q10
Ceará (state), Braz. 154/B2
Cébaco (isl.), Pan. 145/F5
Ceballos, Mex. 142/D3
Cebollar (riv.), Uru. 159/G2
Cebollatí, Uru. 159/G2
Cebollatí (riv.), Uru. 159/G2
Cebreros, Sp. 44/C2
Cebu, Phil. 81/F1
Cebu (int'l arpt.), Phil. 79/D5
Cebu (isl.), Phil. 116/B3
Ceccano, It. 46/C2
Cecil (co.), Md, US 138/C4
Cecil Macks (pass), Swaz. 107/E2
Cecil Plains, Austl. 114/C4
Cecil Rhodes, It. 112/D3
Cecilton, Md, US 138/C5
Cecina, It. 43/J5
Cecina (riv.), It. 59/D6
Ceclavín, Sp. 44/B3
Cedar, Ks, US 137/D6
Cedar (valley), Ut, US 137/J13
Cedar (mtn.), Ca, US 135/L11
Cedar (mtn.), Fla. 114/B1
Cedar Bay NP, Austl. 114/B1
Cedar Bluff (res.), Ks, US 129/G3
Cedar Breaks Nat'l Mon., Ut, US 128/D3
Cedar Brook, NJ, US 138/D4
Cedar City, Ut, US 128/D3
Cedar Cove, Or, US 137/B2
Cedar Creek (res.), Tx, US 143/F1
Cedar Falls (dam), Wa, US 135/D3
Cedar Falls, Wa, US 135/D3
Cedar Fort (Cedar Valley), Ut, US 137/J13
Cedar Glen, Ca, US 136/C2
Cedar Grove, Md, US 138/A5
Cedar Grove, NJ, US 139/J8
Cedar Hill, Mo, US 137/R9
Cedar Hills, Ut, US 137/K13
Cedar Key, Fl, US 133/H4
Cedarhurst, NY, US 139/L9
Cedartown, Ga, US 133/G3
Cedarville, Ca, US 126/C5
Cedegolo, It. 57/G5
Cedeira, Sp. 44/A1
Cedral, Mex. 143/E4
Cedral, Braz. 154/C2
Cedros (isl.), Mex. 119/F7
Cedros, Braz. 154/C2
Ceduna, Austl. 113/G5
Cee, Sp. 44/A1
Cefalù, It. 46/D3
Cefni (riv.), Wal, UK 34/D5
Cega (riv.), Sp. 44/C2
Ceggia, It. 59/F1
Cehegín, Sp. 44/D3
Çekerek (riv.), Turk. 62/F4
Čelákovice, Czh. 55/H2
Celanova, Sp. 44/B1

Celaya, Mex. 143/E4
Celebes (isl.), Indo. 67/L10
Celebes (sea), Asia 67/M9
Celendín, Peru 156/B2
Celestún, Mex. 144/D1
Celica, Ecu. 156/B2
Céligny, Swi. 56/C5
Celina, Tx, US 129/H4
Celina, Oh, US 130/C3
Celje, Slov. 43/L3
Cella, Sp. 44/E2
Celldömölk, Hun. 48/C2
Celle, Ger. 51/H3
Celle (riv.), Fr. 40/B4
Celle Ligure, It. 58/B4
Celles, Belg. 52/C2
Čelopek, Macd. 48/E5
Celorico da Beira, Port. 44/B2
Celtic (sea), Eur. 31/P11
Cemaes (pt.), Wal, UK 32/B2
Cemaru (peak), Indo. 80/D3
Cembra, It. 57/H5
Cenajo, Embalse del (res.), Sp. 44/E3
Cenderawasih (bay), Indo. 116/C5
Cene, It. 58/C1
Cenepa (riv.), Peru 156/B1
Cengong, China 83/J2
Cenia, Sp. 45/F2
Ceno (riv.), It. 58/C3
Centenario, Arg. 157/C4
Centenario do Sul, Braz. 155/B2
Centennial (mts.), Id, US 126/E4
Center, ND, US 127/H4
Center Moriches, NY, US 139/F2
Center Point, Al, US 133/G3
Centerbrook, Ct, US 139/F1
Centereach, NY, US 139/E2
Centerville, Tn, US 130/C5
Centerville, Tx, US 132/E4
Centerville, Ut, US 137/K12
Cento, It. 59/E3
Cento Croci, Passo di (pass), It. 58/C4
Central, Ak, US 134/K2
Central (prov.), Ugan. 104/A2
Central (prov.), Kenya 104/C3
Central, NM, US 128/E4
Central, Braz. 154/B3
Central (pol. reg.), Gha. 103/E5
Central (int'l arpt.), Ukr. 49/K2
Central (peak), Arg. 158/C4
Central (pol. reg.), Sc, UK 36/B4
Central African Republic (ctry.) 93/D4
Central Australia Abor. Land, Austl. 113/F2
Central Australia (Warburton) Abor. Rsv., Austl. 113/E3
Central Butte, Sk, Can. 126/G3
Central City, Ne, US 127/J5
Central City, Co, US 137/A3
Central, Cordillera (mts.), Peru 150/C5
Central Desert Abor. Rsv., Austl. 113/F2
Central Intelligence Agency Fed. Govt. Res., Va, US 138/A6
Central Island NP, Kenya 104/C2
Central Islip, NY, US 139/E2
Central Makrān (range), Pak. 89/H3
Central, Massif (mass.), Fr. 42/E4
Central Mount Stuart (peak), Austl. 113/G2
Central Mount Wedge (peak), Austl. 113/F2
Central Park, NY, US 139/K8
Central, Planalto (plat.), Braz. 151/J7
Central Point, Or, US 126/C5
Central Siberian (plat.), Rus. 65/L3
Central Ural (mts.), Rus. 61/N4
Central Valley, NY, US 138/D1
Centralia, Wa, US 126/C4
Centralia, Il, US 129/K3
Centre (pol. reg.), Mor. 98/D2
Centre (pol. reg.), Fr. 42/D3
Centre (co.), Pa, US 138/A2
Centre Island, NY, US 139/L8
Centre Nord (pol. reg.), Mor. 98/D2
Centre-Nord (pol. reg.), Mor. 100/B2
Centre Sud (pol. reg.), Mor. 98/D3
Centre-Sud (pol. reg.), Mor. 100/B2
Centreville, Al, US 133/G3
Centreville, Il, US 137/G8
Centreville, Md, US 138/B5
Cenxi, China 83/K3
Čepin, Cro. 48/D3
Ceram (isl.), Indo. 67/N10
Ceram (sea), Indo. 116/B5
Cerano, It. 58/B2
Ceraso (cape), It. 46/A2
Cerbère, Fr. 42/E5
Cercal, Port. 44/A4
Cercedilla, Sp. 45/M8
Čerchov (peak), Czh. 55/F4
Cerdanyola del Vallès, Sp. 45/L7
Cère (riv.), Fr. 42/E4
Cerea, It. 59/E2
Ceres, Arg. 157/D2
Ceres, Braz. 151/J7
Ceres, SAfr. 106/L10
Cerese, It. 59/D2
Céret, Fr. 42/E5
Cereté, Col. 152/C2
Cerfone (riv.), It. 59/E6
Cerfontaine, Belg. 53/D3
Cergy, Fr. 30/J4
Ceriale, It. 58/B4
Cerignola, It. 46/D2
Çerkeş, Turk. 62/E4
Çerkezköy, Turk. 49/J5
Çermik, Turk. 90/D2
Černá (riv.), Czh. 55/H5
Černá (peak), Czh. 55/G5
Cernavodă, Rom. 49/J3
Cernay, Fr. 56/D2
Cernay-la-Ville, Fr. 30/H5
Cernier, Swi. 56/C3
Cérou (riv.), Fr. 42/D4
Cerralvo, Mex. 132/D5
Cerralvo (isl.), Mex. 142/C3
Cerreto Guidi, It. 59/D5
Cerreto, Passo del (pass), It. 58/D4
Cërrik, Alb. 47/F2
Cerritos, Mex. 143/E4
Cerritos, Ca, US 136/F8
Cerro Azul, Peru 156/B4
Cerro Azul, Mex. 144/B1
Cerro Castillo, Chile 159/B6
Cerro Chato, Uru. 159/G2
Cêrro Corá, Braz. 154/C2
Cerro de la Estrella, PN, Mex. 143/Q10
Cerro de las Campanas, PN, Mex. 143/E4
Cerro de Pasco, Peru 156/B3
Cerro de San Antonio, Col. 152/C2
Cerro El Copey, PN, Ven. 153/F2
Cerro Maggiore, It. 58/B1
Cerro Nanchital, Mex. 144/C2
Cerro Pinacate (peak), Mex. 128/D5
Cerros Colorados (res.), Arg. 157/C4
Cerros de Amotape, PN, Peru 156/A2
Certaldo, It. 59/E5
Certosa di Pavia, It. 58/C2
Certosa di Pisa, It. 58/D5
Cervantes, Austl. 112/B4
Cervaro (riv.), It. 48/B5
Cervati (peak), It. 46/D2
Cervellino (peak), It. 58/D3
Cervera, Sp. 45/F2
Cervera de Pisuerga, Sp. 44/C1
Cervera del Río Alhama, Sp. 44/E1
Cervia, It. 59/F4
Cervialto (peak), It. 46/D2
Cervignano del Friuli, It. 59/G1
Cervina (peak), It. 57/H4
Cervione, Fr. 46/A1
Cervo (riv.), It. 58/B1
Cervo, Sp. 44/B1
Cervo, It. 58/B5
Cervo, Serra do (hills), Braz. 211/G7
Cesano (riv.), It. 59/F6
Cesano Boscone, It. 58/C2
Cesano Maderno, It. 58/C1
César (riv.), Col. 141/G5
Cesar (prov.), Col. 145/H4
César (dept.), Col. 152/C2
Cesen (peak), It. 59/F1
Cesena, It. 59/F4
Cesenatico, It. 59/F4
Cēsis, Lat. 39/L3
České Budějovice, Czh. 55/H5
Ceské Středohoří (mts.), Czh. 55/G2
Českomoravská Vysočina (mts.), Czh. 41/H4
Český Brod, Czh. 55/H2
Český Krumlov, Czh. 55/H5
Český Les Sumava (mts.), Czh. 55/F3
Česma (riv.), Cro. 48/C3
Çeşme, Turk. 47/K3
Cesson, Fr. 30/K6
Cesson-Sévigné, Fr. 42/C2
Cestos (riv.), Libr. 102/C5
Cetinje, Yugo. 47/F1
Çetinkaya, Turk. 90/D2
Ceurda del Pozo, Embalse de la (res.), Sp. 44/D2
Ceuta, Sp. 100/B2
Ceva, It. 58/B4
Cevedale (peak), It. 57/G5
Cévennes (mts.), Fr. 42/E4
Cevio, Swi. 57/E5
Ceyhan, Turk. 91/D1
Ceylânpınar, Turk. 90/E2
Ceylon (isl.), SrL. 67/H9
Ceyzériat, Fr. 56/B5
Cèze (riv.), Fr. 42/F4
Cha Da (cape), Viet. 78/E4
Chabás, Arg. 158/E2
Chabjuwardoo (bay), Austl. 112/B2
Chablé, Mex. 144/D2
Chacabuco, Arg. 158/E2
Chachani (peak), Peru 156/D5
Chachapoyas, Peru 156/B2
Chachoengsao, Thai. 78/C3
Chaclacayo, Peru 156/B3
Chaco (riv.), NM, US 128/F3
Chaco (mesa), NM, US 132/B3
Chaco Austral (plain), Arg. 157/D1
Chaco Boreal (plain), Par. 150/F8
Chaco Central (plain), Arg. 157/D1
Chaco, PN, Arg. 157/E2
Chacujal (ruin), Guat. 144/D3
Chad (lake), Niger 93/D3
Chad (ctry.) 93/D3
Chafarinas (isl.), Sp. 100/C2
Chagang-do (prov.), NKor. 73/D2
Chagda, Rus. 65/P4
Chaghcharān, Afg. 87/E6
Chagny, Fr. 42/F3
Chagos (arch.), BIOT, UK 67/G10
Chaguanas, Trin. 153/F2
Chaguarpamba, Ecu. 156/B1
Chahuites, Mex. 144/C2
Chaibāsā, India 85/E4
Chailly-en-Brie, Fr. 30/M5
Chain, SKor. 73/E5
Chainat, Thai. 78/C3
Chaîne Annamitique (mts.), Laos 83/H4
Chaine de la Selle (peak), Haiti 145/J2
Chaîne de l'Atacora (mts.), Ben. 103/F4
Chaitén, Chile 157/B5
Chaiyaphum, Thai. 78/C3
Chākdaha, India 85/G4
Chake Chake, Tanz. 104/C4
Chākia, India 84/D3
Chakradharpur, India 85/E4
Chakrāta, India 86/D4
Chakwāl, Pak. 86/B3
Chala, Peru 156/C4
Chalain (lake), Fr. 56/B4
Chalais, Swi. 56/D5
Chālakudi, India 82/C5
Chalaronne (riv.), Fr. 56/A5
Chalatenango, ESal. 144/D3
Chalbi (des.), Kenya 97/N7
Chalchihuites, Mex. 142/E4
Chalco, Mex. 143/R10
Chale (pt.), Kenya 104/C4
Chaleur (bay), Can. 131/H2
Chalfont, Pa, US 138/C3
Chalfont Saint Giles, Eng, UK 30/B2
Chalfont Saint Peter, Eng, UK 30/B2
Chalhuanca, Peru 156/C4
Chalifert (canal), Fr. 30/L5
Chalindrey, Fr. 56/B2
Chalk (mts.), Tx, US 132/C4
Chalkyitsik, Ak, US 134/K2
Challans, Fr. 42/C3
Challapata, Bol. 150/E7
Challenger (mts.), NW, Can. 123/T6
Chalmette, La, US 137/Q17
Chālna Port, Bang. 85/G4
Chalon-sur-Saône, Fr. 56/A4
Châlons-sur-Marne, Fr. 53/D6
Châlonvillars, Fr. 56/C2
Chālūs, Iran 88/F1
Cham, Swi. 57/E3
Cham, Ger. 55/F4
Cham (riv.), Ger. 55/F4
Chama, Zam. 104/B5
Chama (riv.), NM, US 128/F3
Chamah (peak), Malay. 80/B2
Chaman, Pak. 89/J2
Chamba, India 86/D3
Chambal (riv.), India 89/L3
Chambaran, Plateau de (plat.), Fr. 42/F4
Chambas, Cuba 145/G1
Chamberlain (lake), Me, US 131/G2
Chamberlin (mt.),]Ak, US 134/K2
Chambersburg, Pa, US 130/E4
Chambéry, Fr. 42/F4
Chambeshi (riv.), Zam. 105/F3
Chambly, Qu, Can. 131/P7
Chambly, Fr. 30/J4
Chambourcy, Fr. 30/J5
Chambry, Fr. 30/L5
Chamchamāl, Iraq 88/D1
Chamechaude (peak), Fr. 42/F4
Chamical, Arg. 157/C3
Chamigny, Fr. 30/M5
Chamizal Nat'l Mem., Tx, US 132/B4
Chamizo, Uru. 159/L11
Chamonix-Mont-Blanc, Fr. 56/C6
Champagne, Yk, Can. 134/L3
Champagne (reg.), Fr. 40/C4
Champagne-Ardenne (pol. reg), Fr. 42/F2
Champagne-sur-Oise, Fr. 30/J4
Champagney, Fr. 56/C2
Champagnole, Fr. 56/B4
Champasak, Laos 78/D3
Champawat, India 84/C1
Champdeuil, Fr. 30/L6
Champeaux, Fr. 30/L6
Champéry, Swi. 56/C5
Champigneulles, Fr. 53/F6
Champigny-sur-Marne, Fr. 30/K5
Champlain (lake), NY,Vt, US 125/M3
Champlitte, Fr. 56/B2
Champotón, Mex. 144/D2
Champotón (riv.), Mex. 144/D2
Champs-sur-Marne, Fr. 30/K5
Champsevraine, Fr. 56/B2
Champvans, Fr. 56/B3
Chamusca, Port. 44/A3
Chan Chan (ruin), Peru 156/B3
Chan May Dong (cape), Viet. 78/E2
Chañaral, Chile 157/B2
Chança (riv.), Port. 44/B4
Chancay, Peru 156/B3
Chanco, Chile 158/B2
Chancy, Swi. 56/B5
Chandalar, Ak, US 134/J2
Chandalar (riv.), Ak, US 134/J2
Chandalar, East Fork (riv.), Ak, US 134/J2
Chandannagar, India 85/G4
Chandausi, India 84/B1
Chanderi, India 84/B3
Chandīgarh, India 86/D4
Chandīgarh (state), India 86/D4
Chandlees (riv.), Braz. 150/D6
Chandler (riv.), Ak, US 134/H2
Chandler, Ok, US 132/D3
Chandler, Qu, Can. 131/H1
Chandler, Az, US 137/S19
Chandolin, Swi. 56/D5
Chāndpur, Bang. 85/H4
Chāndpur, India 84/B1
Chandrapur, India 82/C4
Chanduy, Ecu. 152/A5
Chang (riv.), China 67/L6
Chang (lake), China 72/C5
Changan, SKor. 73/E5
Changbai (peak), China 73/E2
Changbai Chaoxianzu Zizhixian, China 73/E2
Changchun, China 71/N3
Changdang (lake), China 72/D5
Changdao, China 72/E3
Changde, China 79/B2
Changé, Fr. 42/D3
Changewater, NJ, US 138/D2
Changfeng, China 72/D4
Changge, China 72/C4
Changgi-ap (cape), SKor. 74/A2
Changhai, China 73/B3
Changhang, SKor. 73/D4
Changhowŏn, SKor. 73/D4
Changhua, Tai. 79/D3
Changhŭng, SKor. 73/D5
Changis-sur-Marne, Fr. 30/M5
Changji, China 70/E3
Changjiang, China 83/J4
Changjin (res.), NKor. 73/D2
Changjin (lake), NKor. 73/D2
Changle, China 72/D3
Changli, China 72/D3
Changling, China 72/E1
Changning, China 83/H2
Changning, China 83/G3
Ch'angnyŏng, SKor. 73/E5
Changping, China 72/H6
Changqing, China 72/D3
Changsan-got (cape), NKor. 73/C3
Changsha, China 83/K2
Changshou, China 79/A2
Changshu, China 72/L8
Changshun, China 83/J2
Changsŏng, SKor. 73/D5
Changsu, SKor. 73/D5
Changsŭngp'o, SKor. 73/E5
Changtai, China 79/C3
Changtu, China 72/F2
Changuinola, Pan. 145/F4
Ch'angwŏn, SKor. 73/E5
Changxing, China 72/K8
Changyang, China 79/B1
Changyi, China 72/D3
Changyŏn, NKor. 73/C3
Changyuan, China 72/C4
Changzhi, China 72/C3
Changzhou, China 72/K8
Chañi, Nevado de (peak), Arg. 157/C1
Chanlers (falls), Kenya 104/C2
Channel (isls.), UK 27/D4
Channel Country (phys. reg.), Austl. 109/C3
Channel Islands NP, Ca, US 128/C4
Channel-Port aux Basques, Nf, Can. 131/K2
Channel Tunnel, Eng, Fr.,UK 33/H5
Channing, Tx, US 129/G4
Chantada, Sp. 44/B1
Chanteloup-les-Vignes, Fr. 30/J5
Chanthaburi, Thai. 78/C3
Chantilly, Fr. 52/B5
Chantraine, Fr. 56/C1
Chantrey (inlet), NW, Can. 122/G2
Chao (lake), China 72/D5
Chao Phraya (riv.), Thai. 78/C3
Chaoyang, China 79/C3
Chaoyang, China 72/E2
Chapacura, Bol. 156/D3
Chapada Diamantina, PN, Braz. 151/K6
Chapada dos Veadeiros, PN da, Braz. 151/J6
Chapadinha, Braz. 154/B1
Chapais, Qu, Can. 130/F1
Chapala (lake), Mex. 142/E4
Chapala, Mex. 142/E4
Chaparral, Col. 152/C4
Chaparrosa, Mex. 142/E4
Chapayevsk, Rus. 63/J1
Chapel Hill, NC, US 133/J3
Chapel Ness (pt.), Sc, UK 36/D4
Chapelfell Top (peak), Eng, UK 35/F2
Chapelle-lez-Herlaimont, Belg. 53/D3
Chapeltown, Eng, UK 35/G5
Chaplain (lake), Wa, US 135/D2
Chapleau, On, Can. 130/D2
Chaplin, Sk, Can. 126/G3
Chāpra, India 85/E3
Char (well), Mrta. 98/B5
Chara (riv.), Rus. 65/M4
Charambirá (pt.), Col. 152/B3
Charaña, Bol. 156/D5
Charandra (riv.), Gre. 47/N8
Charata, Arg. 157/D2
Charcas, Mex. 143/E4
Charcot (isl.), Ant. 160/U
Chardonnière, Haiti 145/H2
Charente (riv.), Fr. 42/C4
Chari (riv.), Chad 93/D3
Chārīkār, Afg. 89/J1
Chariton (riv.), US 127/K5
Charity, Guy. 153/G3
Chärjew, Trkm. 87/D5
Charkhāri, India 84/B3
Charkhi Dādri, India 86/D5
Charlemagne, Qu, Can. 131/P6
Charlemont, NI, UK 34/B3
Charleroi, Belg. 53/D3
Charleroi à Bruxelles, Canal de (canal), Belg. 53/D2
Charles (peak), Austl. 112/D5
Charles (mt.), Austl. 112/C3
Charles (isl.), Qu, Can. 123/J2
Charles City, Ia, US 127/K5
Charles de Gaulle (int'l arpt.), Fr. 30/K4
Charleston, Nv, US 126/E5
Charleston, Ms, US 129/K4
Charleston (cap.), WV, US 130/D4
Charleston, SC, US 133/J3
Charleston, Ut, US 137/L13
Charlestown, StK. 141/N8
Charlestown, Md, US 138/C4
Charleville, Austl. 114/B4
Charleville-Mézières, Fr. 53/D4
Charlevoix, Mi, US 130/C2
Charlotte (lake), BC, Can. 126/B2
Charlotte, Mi, US 130/C3
Charlotte, NC, US 133/H3
Charlotte Amalie, USVI 141/M8
Charlotte/Douglas (int'l arpt.), NC, US 133/H3
Charlottenberg, Swe. 38/E2
Charlottenburg, Ger. 40/Q6
Charlottetown (cap.), PE, Can. 131/J2
Charlton, Austl. 115/B3
Charlton (isl.), On, Can. 123/H3
Charlton Kings, Eng, UK 32/D3
Charly, Fr. 52/C6
Charmes (res.), Fr. 56/B2
Charmes, Fr. 56/C1
Charmey, Swi. 56/D4
Charnay-lès-Mâcon, Fr. 42/F3
Charny, Fr. 30/L5
Charny-sur-Meuse, Fr. 53/E5
Charolais, Monts du (mts.), Fr. 42/F3
Charouine, Alg. 99/E3
Charquemont, Fr. 56/C3
Chars, Fr. 30/H4
Chārsadda, Pak. 86/A2
Charters Towers, Austl. 114/B3
Charthāwāl, India 86/D5
Chartres, Fr. 42/D2
Chās, India 85/F4
Chaschauna (peak), Swi. 57/G4
Chascomús, Arg. 158/F2
Chase, BC, Can. 126/D3
Chasŏng, NKor. 73/D2
Chassezac (riv.), Fr. 42/F4
Chastre-Villeroux-Blanmont, Belg. 53/D2
Chatanika, Ak, US 134/J2
Château Bougon (int'l arpt.), Fr. 42/C3
Chateau de Versailles, Fr. 30/J5
Château-d'Olonne, Fr. 42/C3
Château-du-Loir, Fr. 42/D3
Château-Porcien, Fr. 53/D4
Château-Renault, Fr. 42/D3
Château-Salins, Fr. 53/F6
Château-Thierry, Fr. 52/C5
Châteaubriant, Fr. 42/C3
Châteaudun, Fr. 42/D2
Châteauguay, Qu, Can. 131/N7
Châteauneuf-sur-Charente, Fr. 42/C4
Châteaurenard, Fr. 42/F5
Châteauroux, Fr. 42/D3
Châteauvillain, Fr. 56/A1
Châtel-Saint-Denis, Swi. 56/C4
Châtelaillon-Page, Fr. 42/C3
Châtelet, Belg. 53/D3
Châtellerault, Fr. 42/D3
Châtenay-Malabry, Fr. 30/J5
Châtenois, Fr. 56/B1
Châtenois-les-Forges, Fr. 56/C2
Chatfield (res.), Co, US 137/B3
Chatham, On, Can. 130/D3
Chatham, NB, Can. 131/H2
Chatham, Eng, UK 33/G4
Chatham (isls.), Chile 159/B6
Chatham, NJ, US 139/H9
Châtillon, It. 43/G4
Châtillon, Fr. 30/J5
Châtillon-sur-Chalaronne, Fr. 56/A5
Châtillon-sur-Marne, Fr. 52/C5
Châtillon-sur-Seine, Fr. 42/F3
Chatkal (riv.), Kyr. 87/F4
Chatou, Fr. 30/J5
Chatra, India 85/E3
Chatrapur, India 82/E4
Châtres, Fr. 30/L5
Chatsworth (res.), Ca, US 136/B2
Chatsworth, NJ, US 138/D4
Chattahoochee (riv.),US 133/G4
Chattahoochee, Fl, US 133/G4
Chattanooga, Tn, US 133/G3
Chatteris, Eng, UK 33/G2
Chau Doc, Viet. 78/D4
Chaucey, Îles (isls.), Fr. 42/C2
Chauconin-Neufmontiers, Fr. 30/L5
Chaudfontaine, Belg. 53/E2
Chaudière (riv.), Can. 131/G2
Chauk, Myan. 83/F3
Chaukan (pass), India 83/G2
Chaumes-en-Brie, Fr. 30/L5
Chaumont, Fr. 56/B1
Chaumont-en-Vexin, Fr. 52/A5
Chaunskaya (bay), Rus. 65/T3
Chauny, Fr. 52/C4
Chaussin, Fr. 56/B4
Chaussy, Fr. 30/H4
Chautauqua (lake), NY, US 130/E3
Chautauqua, Il, US 137/G8
Chauvigny, Fr. 42/D3
Chaval, Braz. 154/B1
Chavanoz, Fr. 56/B6
Chaves, Port. 44/B2
Chavín de Huantar (ruin), Peru 156/B3
Chaviña, Peru 156/C4
Chavinillo, Peru 156/B3
Chavornay, Swi. 56/C4
Chawinda, Pak. 86/C3
Chay (riv.), Viet. 78/D1
Chayana (riv.), Bol. 150/E7
Chaykovskiy, Rus. 61/M4
Chazuta, Peru 156/B2
Cheadle, Eng, UK 35/G6
Cheaha (mtn.), Al, US 133/G3
Cheb, Czh. 55/F2
Cheboksary, Rus. 61/K4
Cheboksary (res.), Rus. 61/K4
Cheboygan, Mi, US 130/C2
Chechaouene, Mor. 100/B2
Chechaouene (prov.), Mor. 100/B2
Chechen' (isl.), Rus. 63/H3
Chechnya Aut. Rep., Rus. 64/Q6
Chech'ŏn, SKor. 73/E4
Checotah, Ok, US 129/J4
Chedabucto (bay), Can. 131/J2
Cheduba (isl.), Myan. 83/F4
Cheektowaga, NY, US 131/S10
Cheepash (riv.), Can. 130/D1
Cheepay (riv.), Can. 130/D1
Chefornak, Ak, US 134/F3
Chegutu, Zim. 105/F4
Chehalis, Wa, US 126/C4
Cheïkh (well), Alg. 99/F3
Cheju, SKor. 71/N5
Cheju (str.), SKor. 71/N5
Cheju (isl.), SKor. 71/N5
Cheka (peak), Rus. 87/C2
Chelan, Wa, US 126/C4
Chelan (lake), Wa, US 126/C4
Chelghoum El Aïd, Alg. 100/J4
Chelles, Fr. 30/K5
Chełm (prov.), Pol. 41/M3
Chełm, Pol. 41/M3
Chełmno, Pol. 41/K2
Chelmsford, Eng, UK 33/G3
Chełmża, Pol. 41/K2
Cheltenham, Eng, UK 32/D3
Chelva, Sp. 45/E3
Chelyabinsk (int'l arpt.), Rus. 61/P5
Chelyabinsk, Rus. 61/P5
Chelyabinsk Oblast, Rus. 87/D2
Chelyuskina (cape), Rus. 65/L2
Chemaïa, Mor. 98/C2
Chemax, Mex. 144/E1
Chemnitz, Ger. 40/G3
Chen (riv.), China 79/A2
Chena Hot Springs, Ak, US 134/J2
Chenāb (riv.), Pak. 89/K2
Chenachane (well), Alg. 98/D4
Cheney, Wa, US 126/D4
Cheng'anpu, China 72/C3
Chengbu Miaozu Zizhixian, China 83/K2
Chengde, China 72/D2
Chengdu, China 70/H5
Chengkou, China 70/J5
Chengmai, China 83/J4
Chengshan Jiao (cape), China 73/B4
Chengwu, China 72/C4
Cheniménil, Fr. 56/C1
Chennai (Madras), India 82/D5
Chennevières-lès-Louvres, Fr. 30/K4
Chenòve, Fr. 56/A3
Chenxi, China 83/K2
Chenzhou, China 83/K2
Chep Lak Kok (int'l arpt.), China 71/T10
Chepelare, Bul. 47/J2
Chepén, Peru 156/B2
Chepes, Arg. 157/C3
Chépica, Chile 158/C2
Chepigana, Pan. 152/B2
Chepo, Pan. 152/B2
Chepstow, Wal, UK 32/D3
Cheptsa (riv.), Rus. 61/M4
Cher (riv.), Fr. 42/E3
Chéran (riv.), Fr. 56/C6
Cherasco, It. 58/A3
Cherāt, Pak. 86/A3
Cheraw, SC, US 133/J3
Cherbourg, Fr. 42/C2
Cherbourg, Austl. 114/C4
Cherchell, Alg. 100/G4
Cherepovets, Rus. 60/H4
Cherf, Oued (riv.), Alg. 100/K6
Cheria, Alg. 100/K7
Cherkas'ka (obl.), Ukr. 62/D2
Cherkasy, Ukr. 62/E2
Cherkessk, Rus. 63/G3
Chermignon, Swi. 56/D5
Chernaya (riv.), Rus. 61/N1
Cherni Lom (riv.), Bul. 49/H4
Cherni Vrŭkh (peak), Bul. 47/H1
Chernihiv, Ukr. 62/D2
Chernivets'ka (obl.), Ukr. 62/C2
Chernivtsi, Ukr. 49/G1
Chernushka, Rus. 61/N4
Cherokee, Ok, US 129/H3
Cherry Creek (dam), Co, US 137/C3
Cherry Creek (lake), Co, US 137/C3
Cherry Hill, Md, US 138/C4
Cherry Hill, NJ, US 138/C4
Cherry Valley, Ca, US 136/D3
Cherski (range), Rus. 67/P3
Chertsey, Eng, UK 30/B2
Cherven Bryag, Bul. 49/G4
Chervonohrad, Ukr. 62/C2
Cherwell (riv.), Eng, UK 33/E3
Chesaning, Mi, US 130/C3
Chesapeake (bay), US 125/L4
Chesapeake and Delaware (canal), De,Md, US 138/C4
Chesapeake Bay Maritime Museum, Md, US 138/B6
Chesapeake City, Md, US 138/C4
Chesham, Eng, UK 33/F3
Cheshire (co.), Eng, UK 35/F5
Cheshire (plain), Eng, UK 35/F5
Cheshskaya (bay), Rus. 64/E3
Cheshunt, Eng, UK 30/C1
Chesilhurst, NJ, US 138/D4
Chester, Mt, US 126/F3
Chester, Ca, US 126/C5
Chester, SC, US 133/H3
Chester, Pa, US 138/C4
Chester, NJ, US 138/D2
Chester (co.), Pa, US 138/C4
Chester (riv.), Md, US 138/B5
Chester, Eng, UK 35/F5
Chester Heights, Pa, US 138/C4
Chester-le-Street, Eng, UK 35/G2
Chester Morse (lake), Wa, US 135/D3
Chesterfield, Mo, US 137/F8
Chesterfield (isls.), NCal. 116/E6
Chesterfield (inlet), NW, Can. 119/H3
Chesterfield, Eng, UK 35/G5
Chesterfield Inlet, NW, Can. 122/G2
Chesterfield, Nosy (isl.), Madg. 107/G7
Chesterton (range), Austl. 114/B4
Chestertown, Md, US 138/B5
Chesuncook (lake), Me, US 131/G2
Cheswold, De, US 138/C5
Chetumal (bay), Mex. 140/D4
Chetumal, Mex. 144/D2
Chetwynd, BC, Can. 126/C2
Cheung Chau (isl.), China 71/T11
Chevak, Ak, US 134/E3
Cheval Blanc (pt.), Haiti 145/H2
Chevigny-Saint-Sauveur, Fr. 56/B3
Cheviot (hills), Sc, UK 36/D6
Cheviot, The (peak), Eng, UK 36/D6
Chevreuse, Fr. 30/J5
Chevry-Cossigny, Fr. 30/K5
Chew (riv.), Eng, UK 32/D4
Chew Valley (lake), Eng, UK 32/D4
Chewelah, Wa, US 126/D3
Chexbres, Swi. 56/C5
Cheyenne (riv.), US 127/H5
Cheyenne (cap.), Wy, US 127/G5
Cheyenne, Ok, US 129/H4
Cheyenne Wells, Co, US 129/G3
Cheyres, Swi. 56/C4
Chhabra, India 84/A3
Chhaprauli, India 86/D5
Chhāta, India 84/A2
Chhatarpur, India 84/B3
Chhibrāmau, India 84/B2
Chhindwāra, India 84/B4
Chi (riv.), Thai. 83/H4
Chiai, Tai. 79/D3
Ch'iak-san NP, SKor. 73/E4
Chiampo, It. 59/E1
Chianciano Terme, It. 43/J5
Chiang Kai Shek (int'l arpt.), Tai. 79/D2
Chiang Mai, Thai. 83/G4
Chiang Rai, Thai. 83/G4
Chianti (reg.), It. 59/E5
Chianti, Monti del (mts.), It. 59/E5
Chiapa de Corzo, Mex. 144/C2
Chiapas (state), Mex. 140/C4
Chiappa (pt.), It. 58/C4
Chiaravalle, It. 59/G5
Chiari, It. 58/C1
Chiasso, Swi. 57/F6
Chiat'ura, Geo. 63/G4
Chiautempan, Mex. 143/L7
Chiautla, Mex. 143/R9
Chiautla de Tapia, Mex. 144/B2
Chiavari, It. 58/C4
Chiavenna, It. 57/F5
Chiba, Japan 75/G3
Chibougamau (riv.), Can. 130/E1
Chibougamau, Qu, Can. 130/F1
Chibougamau (lake), Can. 130/F1
Chibukak (pt.), Ak, US 134/D3
Chibuto, Moz. 105/F5
Chicago, Il, US 127/M5
Chicago Heights, Il, US 135/Q16
Chicago Midway (int'l arpt.), Il, US 129/L2
Chicago, North Branch (riv.), Il, US 135/Q15
Chicago-O'Hare (int'l arpt.), Il, US 127/M5
Chicago Ridge, Il, US 135/Q16
Chicago Sanitary and Ship Canal, Il, US 135/P16
Chicama, Peru 156/B2
Chichagof (isl.), Ak, US 122/C3
Chichaoua, Mor. 98/C3
Chīchāwatni, Pak. 86/B4
Chichén Itzá (ruin), Mex. 144/D1
Chicheng, China 71/L3
Chichester (range), Austl. 109/A3
Chichester, Eng, UK 33/F5
Chichibu, Japan 75/F3
Chichicastenango, Guat. 144/D3
Chichigalpa, Nic. 144/E3
Chichihualco, Mex. 143/F5
Chichiriviche, Ven. 152/D2
Chichishima (isls.), Japan 116/D2
Chickaloon, Ak, US 134/J3
Chickamauga (lake), Tn, US 133/G3
Chickasaw Nat'l Rec. Area, Ok, US 129/H4
Chickasha, Ok, US 129/H4
Chicla, Peru 156/B3
Chiclana de la Frontera, Sp. 44/B4
Chiclayo, Peru 156/B2
Chico, Ca, US 128/B3
Chico (riv.), Arg. 147/B7
Chicoloapan, Mex. 143/R10
Chicomostoc (ruin), Mex. 142/E4
Chicomuselo, Mex. 144/C3
Chiconcuac, Mex. 143/R9
Chicontepec de Tejeda, Mex. 144/B1
Chicopee, Ma, US 131/F3
Chicoutimi, Qu, Can. 131/G1
Chicualacuala, Moz. 105/F5
Chidley (cape), Nf, Can. 123/K2
Chido, SKor. 73/D5
Chiefland, Fl, US 133/H4
Chiemsee (lake), Ger. 43/K3
Chieo Lan (res.), Thai. 83/G6
Chieri, It. 58/A2
Chierry, Fr. 52/C5
Chiers (riv.), Fr. 53/E5
Chiesa in Valmalenco, It. 57/F5
Chiese (riv.), It. 43/J3
Chieti, It. 46/D1
Chietla, Mex. 143/L8
Chièvres, Belg. 52/C2
Chifeng, China 71/L3
Chifre, Serra do (mts.), Braz. 151/K7
Chigasaki, Japan 75/F3
Chiginagak (mt.), Ak, US 134/G4
Chignahuapan, Mex. 143/L7
Chignecto (bay), Can. 131/H2
Chignik, Ak, US 134/G4
Chignik Lake, Ak, US 134/G4
Chigorodó, Col. 152/B3
Chigu (lake), China 85/H1
Chigwell, Eng, UK 30/D2
Chihayaakasaka, Japan 77/J7
Chihuahua, Mex. 132/B4
Chihuahua (state), Mex. 142/D2
Chikaskia (riv.), US 129/H3
Chikballāpur, India 82/C5
Chikhli, India 89/L4
Chikmagalūr, India 89/L6
Chikoy (riv.), Rus. 65/L5
Chikugo (riv.), Japan 74/B4
Chikuma (riv.), Japan 75/F2
Chilac, Mex. 143/M8
Chilaw, SrL. 82/C6
Chilbo-san (peak), NKor. 73/E2
Chilca, Peru 156/B4
Chilcotin (riv.), BC, Can. 122/D3
Childers, Austl. 114/D4
Childersburg, Al, US 133/G3
Childress, Tx, US 129/G4
Chile (ctry.) 157/B3
Chile Chico, Chile 158/C5
Chile, Monte el (peak), Hon. 144/E3
Chilecito, Arg. 157/C2
Chilete, Peru 156/B2
Ch'ilgap-san NP, SKor. 73/D4
Chililabombwe, Zam. 105/E3
Chilka (lake), India 82/E4
Chilko (lake), BC, Can. 122/D3
Chilkoot (pass), Can. 134/L4
Chilkoot (pass), Ak, US 134/L3
Chilla Well Abor. Land, Austl. 113/F2
Chillán, Chile 158/B3
Chillanes, Ecu. 156/B1
Chillicothe, Il, US 127/L5
Chilliwack, BC, Can. 126/C3
Chillon, Swi. 56/C5
Chilly-Mazarin, Fr. 30/J5
Chiloé (isl.), Chile 147/B7
Chiloé, PN, Chile 158/B4
Chiloquin, Or, US 126/C5
Chilpancingo de los Bravos, Mex. 143/F5
Chiltern (hills), Eng, UK 33/E3
Chiltern Hundreds (reg.), Eng, UK 30/A2
Chilung La (pass), India 86/D3
Chilwa (lake), Malw. 105/G4
Chimacum, Wa, US 135/B1
Chimalhuacán, Mex. 143/R10
Chimaliro (hill), Malw. 104/B5
Chimaltenango, Guat. 144/D3
Chimán, Pan. 152/B2
Chimanimani, Zim. 105/F4
Chimantá-Tepuí (peak), Ven. 153/F3
Chimay, Belg. 53/D3
Chimbay, Uzb. 87/C4
Chimborazo (dept.), Ecu. 152/B5
Chimborazo (vol.), Ecu. 152/B5
Chimbote, Peru 156/B3
Chimichaqua, Col. 152/C2
Chimoio, Moz. 105/F4
Chimtarga (peak), Taj. 87/E5
Chin (state), Myan. 70/F7
China, Mex. 143/F3
China (ctry.) 67/J6
China, Mex. 144/D2
Chinácota, Col. 152/C3
Chinan, SKor. 73/D5
Chinandega, Nic. 144/E3
Chinati (mts.), Tx, US 132/B4
Chincha Alta, Peru 156/B4
Chinchaga (riv.), Ab,BC, Can. 122/E3
Chinchilla, Sp. 44/E3
Chinchilla, Austl. 114/C4
Chinch'ŏn, SKor. 73/D4
Chinchón, Sp. 44/D2
Chincoteague, Va, US 130/F4
Chinde, Moz. 105/G4
Chindo, SKor. 73/D5
Chindrieux, Fr. 56/B6
Chindu, China 70/G4
Chindwin (riv.), Myan. 70/F7
Chingaza, PN, Col. 152/C3
Chingleput, India 82/C5
Chingola, Zam. 105/E3
Chinguetti, Dhar de (cliff), Mrta. 98/B5
Chinhae, SKor. 73/E5
Chinhoyi, Zim. 105/F4
Chiniak (cape), Ak, US 134/H4
Chiniot, Pak. 86/B4
Chinit (riv.), Camb. 78/D3
Chinju, SKor. 73/E5
Chinko (riv.), CAfr. 97/K6
Chinle, Az, US 128/E3
Chinnor, Eng, UK 33/F3
Chino, Japan 75/F3
Chino, Ca, US 136/C2
Chino (hills), Ca, US 136/G8
Chinook, Mt, US 126/F3
Chinsali, Zam. 104/B5
Chinú, Col. 152/C2
Chiny, Belg. 53/E4
Chinyŏng, SKor. 73/E5
Chioggia, It. 59/F2
Chipata, Zam. 105/F3
Chipatá, Col. 152/C3
Chiping, China 72/D3
Chipiona, Sp. 44/B4
Chipley, Fl, US 133/G4
Chiplūn, India 89/K5
Chippenham, Eng, UK 32/D4
Chippewa (riv.), Wi, US 127/L4
Chippewa (co.), Wi, US 127/L4
Chipping Ongar, Eng, UK 30/D1
Chiprovtsi, Bul. 48/F4
Chiputneticook (lakes), US,Can. 131/H2
Chiquián, Peru 156/B3
Chiquimula, Guat. 144/D3
Chiquimulilla, Guat. 144/D3
Chiquinquirá, Col. 150/D2
Chiquita (sea), Arg. 147/C6
Chīrāla, India 82/D4
Chirāwa, India 86/C5
Chirchiq, Uzb. 87/E4
Chīrgaon, India 84/B3
Chiri-san (peak), SKor. 73/D5
Chiri-san NP, SKor. 73/D5
Chiricahua Nat'l Mon., Az, US 142/C1
Chiriguaná, Col. 152/C2
Chirikof (isl.), Ak, US 134/G4
Chirinos, Peru 156/B2
Chirip (peak), Rus. 76/E1
Chiripa (peak), Nic. 145/E4
Chiriquí (lag.), Pan. 145/F4
Chiriquí, Golfo de (gulf), Pan. 150/B2
Chirkunda, India 85/F4
Chirnside, Sc, UK 36/D5
Chironico, Swi. 57/E5
Chirpan, Bul. 47/J1
Chirripó (mtn.), CR 145/F4
Chirripó, PN, CR 140/E6
Chiryu, Japan 77/M6
Chisana, Ak, US 134/K3
Chisasibi (Fort-George), Qu, Can. 123/J3
Chisholm, Mn, US 130/A2
Chishtiān Mandi, Pak. 86/B5
Chisimba (falls), Zam. 104/A5
Chişinău (cap.), Mol. 49/J2
Chişinău (int'l arpt.), Mol. 49/J2
Chişineu Criş, Rom. 48/E2
Chistochina, Ak, US 134/K3
Chistopol', Rus. 61/L5
Chita, Col. 152/C3
Chita (bay), Japan 77/L6
Chita, Japan 77/L6
Chita (pen.), Japan 77/L6
Chitina, Ak, US 134/K3
Chitipa, Malw. 104/B5
Chitose (int'l arpt.), Japan 76/B2
Chitose, Japan 76/B2
Chitradurga, India 82/C5
Chitrakut, India 84/C3
Chitral Gol NP, Pak. 86/A2
Chitré, Pan. 152/A3
Chittagong (pol. div.), Bang. 85/H4
Chittagong, Bang. 83/F3
Chittaranjan, India 85/F4
Chittoor, India 82/C5
Chitungwiza, Zim. 105/F4
Chiuduno, It. 58/C1
Chiuppano, It. 59/E1
Chiusa di Pesio, It. 58/A4
Chiusella (riv.), It. 58/A1
Chiusi, It. 43/J5
Chivacoa, Ven. 152/D2
Chivasso, It. 58/A2
Chivato (pt.), Mex. 142/C3
Chivay, Peru 156/D4
Chivé, Bol. 156/D4
Chivhu, Zim. 105/F4
Chivilcoy, Arg. 158/E2
Chixoy (riv.), Guat. 144/D3
Chiyoda, Japan 77/C1
Chiyoda, Japan 77/E1
Chiyokawa, Japan 77/D1
Chizela, Zam. 105/E3
Chlef (riv.), Alg. 100/F4
Chlef (prov.), Alg. 100/F4
Chlef, Alg. 100/F4
Chlum (peak), Czh. 55/H5
Chno Dearg (peak), Sc, UK 36/B3
Ch'o (isl.), NKor. 73/C3
Cho Oyu (peak), Nepal 85/F1

Chobe NP, Bots. 105/D4
Chobham, Eng, UK 30/B3
Chocen, Czh. 41/J4
Choch'iwon, SKor. 73/D4
Chocianów, Pol. 41/H3
Chocó (dept.), Col. 145/G5
Chocolate (mts.), Ca, US 128/D4
Chocontá, Col. 152/C3
Chocope, Peru 156/B2
Choctaw, Ok, US 137/N15
Chodavaram, India 82/D4
Chodziez, Pol. 41/J2
Choele Choel, Arg. 158/D3
Chofu, Japan 75/F3
Choiseul (isl.), Sol. 116/E5
Choisy-au-Bac, Fr. 30/B5
Choisy-le-Roi, Fr. 30/K5
Choix, Mex. 142/C3
Chojna, Pol. 41/H2
Chojnice, Pol. 41/J2
Chojnów, Pol. 41/H3
Chokai-san (peak), Japan 76/B4
Choke Canyon (res.), Tx, US 132/D4
Chola (mts.), China 70/C5
Cholet, Fr. 42/C3
Cholila, Arg. 158/C4
Chŏlla-bukto (prov.), SKor. 73/D5
Ch'ŏlla-namdo (prov.), SKor. 73/D5
Cholula de Rivadabia, Mex. 143/L7
Choluteca (riv.), Hon. 140/D5
Choluteca, Hon. 144/E3
Choma, Zam. 105/E4
Chŏmch'on, SKor. 73/E4
Chomo Lhari (peak), Bhu. 85/G2
Chomutov, Czh. 55/G2
Chomutovka (riv.), Czh. 55/G2
Chon Buri, Thai. 78/C3
Ch'ŏnan, SKor. 73/D4
Chŏnan, Japan 77/E3
Chonchi, Chile 158/B4
Ch'ŏnch'ŏn, NKor. 73/D2
Chone, Ecu. 152/A5
Ch'ŏng-yang, SKor. 73/D4
Ch'ŏngch'ŏn (lake), Sk, Can. 122/F3
Chong'an, China 79/C2
Ch'ŏngch'ŏn (riv.), NKor. 73/D2
Ch'ŏngdo, SKor. 73/E5
Ch'ŏngjin, NKor. 73/E2
Ch'ŏngjin -si (prov.), NKor. 73/E2
Chŏngju, SKor. 73/D5
Chŏngju, NKor. 73/D4
Chŏngju, NKor. 73/C3
Chongli, China 72/C2
Chongmyo Shrine, SKor. 73/D4
Chongoyape, Peru 156/B2
Ch'ŏngsŏn, SKor. 73/E4
Ch'ŏngsong, SKor. 74/A2
Chongyi, China 83/K2
Chongzuo, China 83/J3
Chŏnju, SKor. 73/D5
Ch'ŏnma-san (peak), SKor. 73/G6
Chonos, Archipelago de los (arch.), Chile 157/A6
Chonos, Archipiélago de los (arch.), Chile 158/B5
Chopan, India 84/D3
Chorcha (mtn.), Pan. 145/F4
Chorley, Eng, UK 35/F4
Chorleywood, Eng, UK 30/B2
Choroszcz, Pol. 41/M2
Chortkiv, Ukr. 62/C2
Ch'ŏrwŏn, SKor. 73/D3
Chorzele, Pol. 41/L2
Chorzów, Pol. 41/K3
Chos-Malal, Arg. 158/C2
Ch'osan, NKor. 73/C2
Chōsei, Japan 77/E3
Chōshi, Japan 75/G3
Choszczno, Pol. 41/H2
Chota, Peru 156/B2
Chota Nagpur (plat.), India 82/D3
Chota Nagur (plat.), India 70/D7
Choteau, Mt, US 126/E4
Chott el Rharbi (depr.), Alg. 100/D3
Chotysanka (riv.), Czh. 55/H3
Chowagasberg (peak), Namb. 105/C6
Chowan (riv.), NC, US 133/J2
Choybalsan, Mong. 71/K2
Choyr, Mong. 70/J2
Chreirik (well), Mrta. 98/B5
Christchurch (int'l arpt.), NZ 117/S11
Christchurch, NZ 117/S11
Christchurch (bay), Eng, UK 33/E5
Christchurch, Eng, UK 33/E5
Christian (sound), Ak, US 134/M4
Christiana, SAfr. 106/D2
Christiana, Jam. 145/G2
Christiana, De, US 138/C4
Christiana, Pa, US 138/C4
Christiansfeld, Den. 38/C4
Christiansted, USVI 141/M8
Christina (riv.), De, US 138/C3
Christmas (isl.), Austl. 67/K11
Chrudim, Czh. 41/H4
Chryston, Sc, UK 36/B5
Chrzanów, Pol. 41/K3
Chu Yang Sin (peak), Viet. 78/E3
Chuadanga, Bang. 85/G4
Chuanshan, China 72/L8
Chuathbaluk, Ak, US 134/G3
Chubut (riv.), Arg. 147/C7
Chubut (prov.), Arg. 158/C4
Chucanti (peak), Pan. 152/B2

Chūgoku (mts.), Japan 74/C3
Chūgoku (prov.), Japan 74/B4
Chūhar Kāna, Pak. 86/B4
Chukai, Malay. 80/B3
Chukchi (sea), Rus. 67/T3
Chukchi (pen.), Rus. 67/T3
Chukotka Aut. Okrug, Rus. 65/S3
Chukotskiy (cape), Rus. 134/D3
Chula Vista, Ca, US 136/C5
Chulucanas, Peru 156/A2
Chulym (riv.), Rus. 64/J4
Chulym (riv.), Rus. 156/D4
Chuma, Bol. 156/D4
Chumerna (peak), Bul. 47/J1
Chumphon, Thai. 78/B4
Chuna (riv.), Rus. 64/K4
Chunar, India 84/D3
Ch'unch'ŏn, SKor. 73/D4
Ch'ungch'ŏng-bukto (prov.), SKor. 73/D4
Ch'ungch'ŏng-namdo (prov.), SKor. 73/D4
Ch'ungju, SKor. 73/D4
Ch'ungman (riv.), SKor. 73/C2
Ch'ungmu, SKor. 73/E5
Chüngsan, NKor. 73/C3
Chunhuhub, Mex. 144/D2
Ch'unian, Pak. 86/B4
Chunya, Tanz. 104/B5
Chunya (riv.), Rus. 65/L3
Ch'unyang, SKor. 73/E4
Chupa, Peru 156/D4
Chupaca, Peru 156/C4
Chuquibamba, Peru 156/C4
Chuquibambilla, Peru 156/C4
Chuquicamata, Chile 157/C1
Chur, Swi. 57/F4
Churachandpur, India 83/F3
Churcampa, Peru 156/C4
Church, Eng, UK 35/F4
Church Hill, Md, US 138/C5
Churchill, Austl. 115/C3
Churchill (lake), Sk, Can. 122/F3
Churchill, Mb, Can. 122/G3
Churchill (riv.), Mb, Can. 122/G3
Churchill, Mb, Sk, Can. 122/F3
Churchill (cape), Mb, Can. 122/G3
Churchill (peak), BC, Can. 122/D3
Churchill Falls, Nf, Can. 123/K3
Churchill NP, Austl. 115/G5
Churchville, Md, US 138/B4
Churia Ghats (mts.), Nepal 85/E2
Churín, Peru 156/B3
Churnet (riv.), Eng, UK 35/G5
Churu, India 86/C5
Churuguara, Ven. 152/D2
Churumuco de Morelos, Mex. 143/E5
Churwalden, Swi. 57/F4
Chuschi, Peru 156/C4
Chuska (mts.), US 128/E3
Chusovaya (riv.), Rus. 61/N4
Chusovoi, Rus. 61/N4
Chutung, Tai. 79/D3
Chuvashia Aut. Rep., Rus. 64/Q6
Chuwang-san NP, SKor. 74/A2
Chuxiong, China 83/H2
Chùy (obl.), Kyr. 87/F4
Chuzhou, China 71/L5
Chūzu, Japan 77/K5
Ci Xian, China 72/C3
Ciadîr-lunga, Mol. 49/J2
Ciamis, Indo. 80/C5
Ciampino (int'l arpt.), It. 46/C2
Ciampino, It. 46/C2
Cianjur, Indo. 80/C5
Cibolo, Tx, US 137/U20
Cicagna, It. 58/C4
Cicero, Il, US 130/C3
Cicero Dantas, Braz. 154/C3
Cicevac, Yugo. 48/E4
Cide, Turk. 62/E4
Ciechanow (prov.), Pol. 41/L2
Ciechanów, Pol. 41/L2
Ciechocinek, Pol. 41/K2
Ciego de Ávila, Cuba 145/G1
Ciénaga, Col. 152/C2
Ciénaga de Oro, Col. 152/C2
Cienfuegos, Cuba 145/F1
Cieplice Śląskie Zdrój, Pol. 41/H3
Cieszyn, Pol. 41/K4
Cieza, Sp. 44/E3
Cifteler, Turk. 62/D5
Cifuentes, Sp. 44/D2
Cifuentes, Cuba 145/G1
Cigánd, Hun. 41/L4
Cigliano, It. 58/B3
Cigüela (riv.), Sp. 44/D3
Cihanbeyli, Turk. 62/C5
Cihuatlán, Mex. 142/D5
Cijara, Embalse de (res.), Sp. 44/C3
Cijulang, Indo. 80/C5
Cilacap, Indo. 80/C5
Cilavegna, It. 58/B2
Çıldır (lake), Turk. 63/G4
Cilfaesty (peak), Wal, UK 32/C5
Cili, China 79/B2
Cilleros, Sp. 44/B2
Cima della Laurasca (peak), It. 57/F5
Cima de'Piazzi (peak), It. 57/H4
Cima la Casina (peak), It. 57/G4
Cimarron (range), NM, US 132/B2

Cimarron (riv.), Ks, Ok, US 124/G4
Cime du Cheiron (peak), Fr. 43/G5
Cime du Diable (peak), Fr. 43/G5
Cimone (peak), It. 59/D4
Cîmpeni, Rom. 49/F2
Cîmpia Turzii, Rom. 49/F2
Cîmpina, Rom. 49/G3
Cîmpulung, Rom. 49/G3
Cîmpulung Moldovenesc, Rom. 49/G2
Çınar, Turk. 90/E2
Çınarcık, Turk. 49/J5
Cizur, Sp. 44/E1
Çine, Turk. 90/B2
Ciney, Belg. 52/C5
Cingia de'Botti, It. 58/D2
Cingoli, It. 59/G6
Ciniselló Balsamo, It. 58/C1
Cinnaminson, NJ, US 138/C4
Cintalapa de Figueroa, Mex. 144/C2
Cinto (peak), Fr. 46/A1
Cinto Caomaggiore, It. 59/F1
Cintruénigo, Sp. 44/E1
Ciovo (isl.), Cro. 48/C4
Cipó, Braz. 154/C3
Cipolletti, Arg. 158/D3
Circeo, PN del, It. 46/C2
Circle, Ak, US 134/K2
Circle, Mt, US 127/G4
Circle Hot Springs, Ak, US 134/K2
Cirebon, Indo. 80/C5
Cirencester, Eng, UK
Cires-lès-Mello, Fr. 52/B5
Cirò Marina, It. 47/E3
Ciron (riv.), Fr. 42/C4
Ciserano, It. 58/C1
Cisnádie, Rom. 49/G3
Cisneros, Col. 152/C3
Cisnes (riv.), Chile 158/B5
Cisse (riv.), Fr. 42/D3
Cisterna di Latina, It. 46/C2
Cistierna, Sp. 44/C1
Citlaltépetl (vol.), Mex. 143/M7
Citrus Heights, Ca, US 135/K11
Citrusdal, SAfr. 106/L10
Città del Vaticano (Vatican City) (cap.), VatC. 46/C2
Città di Castello, It. 59/F6
Citta di Torino (int'l arpt.), It. 43/G4
Cittadella, It. 59/E1
Cittanova, It. 46/E3
Cittiglio, It. 57/E6
City (isl.), NY, US 139/K8
City (int'l arpt.), NI, UK 34/C2
Ciudad Acuña, Mex. 129/G5
Ciudad Altamirano, Mex. 143/E5
Ciudad Bolívar, Ven. 153/G2
Ciudad Bolivia, Ven. 152/D2
Ciudad Camargo, Mex. 142/C3
Ciudad Constitución, Mex. 142/C3
Ciudad Cortés, CR 145/F4
Ciudad Cuauhtémoc, Mex. 144/B1
Ciudad de Dolores Hidalgo, Mex. 143/E4
Ciudad de México (Mexico) (cap.), Mex. 143/Q10
Ciudad de Nutrias, Ven. 152/D2
Ciudad del Carmen, Mex. 144/D2
Ciudad del Maíz, Mex. 143/F4
Ciudad Delicias, Mex. 132/B4
Ciudad Fernández, Mex. 143/E4
Ciudad Frontera, Mex. 132/C3
Ciudad Guayana, Ven. 153/F2
Ciudad Guzmán, Mex. 142/E5
Ciudad Hidalgo, Mex. 143/E5
Ciudad Hidalgo, Ca, US 128/D3
Ciudad Insurgentes, Mex. 142/C4
Ciudad Ixtepec, Mex. 144/C2
Ciudad Juárez, Mex. 128/F5
Ciudad Lerdo, Mex. 142/E3
Ciudad Madero, Mex. 143/F4
Ciudad Mante, Mex. 143/F4
Ciudad Mendoza, Mex. 143/M8
Ciudad Miguel Alemán, Mex. 132/C3
Ciudad Obregón, Mex. 142/C3
Ciudad Ojeda, Ven. 152/D2
Ciudad Pemex, Mex. 144/C2
Ciudad, PN de la, Mex. 143/Q10
Ciudad Real, Sp. 44/D3
Ciudad Rodrigo, Sp. 44/B2
Ciudad Serdán, Mex. 143/M8
Ciudad Valles, Mex. 144/B1
Ciudad Victoria, Mex. 143/F4
Ciudatella de Menorca, Sp. 45/G3
Civa Burnu (pt.), Turk. 62/F4
Civate, It. 57/H5
Cividale del Friuli, It. 43/K3

Cividate Camuno, It. 57/G6
Civita Castellana, It. 46/C1
Civitavecchia, It. 46/B1
Civray, Fr. 42/D3
Çivril, Turk. 90/B2
Cixi, China 72/L9
Cize, Fr. 56/B4
Cizre, Turk. 90/E2
Cizre (dam), Turk. 90/E2
Cizur, Sp. 44/E1
Clackmannan, Sc, UK 36/C4
Claerwen (res.), Wal, UK 32/C2
Clain (riv.), Fr. 42/D3
Clair Engle (lake), Ca, US 128/B2
Claire (lake), Ab, Can. 122/E3
Clairefontaine-en-Yvelines, Fr. 30/H6
Clairvaux-les-Lacs, Fr. 56/B4
Clallam (co.), Wa, US 135/A2
Clamart, Fr. 30/J5
Clamecy, Fr. 42/E3
Clane, Ire. 31/Q10
Clanton, Al, US 133/G3
Clanwilliam, SAfr. 106/B4
Clara, Ire. 31/Q10
Clara (pt.), Arg. 158/C4
Clara (isl.), Mex. 130/C3
Clare, Ks, US 137/D6
Clare, Austl. 113/H5
Clare (isl.), Ire. 30/N10
Clare (co.), Ire. 31/P10
Claremont, NH, US 131/F3
Claremont (riv.), NZ 117/S11
Claremore, Ok, US 129/J3
Claremorris, Ire. 31/P10
Clarence, BC, Can. 126/C3
Clarence, Ia, US 127/L5
Clarence, NY, US 131/S9
Clarence, Mo, US 129/K4
Clarence, La, US 129/K4
Clarence (pt.), NW, Can. 123/T7
Clarence Town, Bahm. 141/G3
Clarendon, Tx, US 129/G4
Clareville, Nf, Can. 123/L1
Claresholm, Ab, Can. 126/E3
Clarion (isl.), Mex. 142/B5
Clark, SD, US 127/J4
Clark (isl.), Austl. 115/C5
Clark Fork (riv.), Mt, US 126/E4
Clark Fork (riv.), Id, US 122/E4
Clarke (isl.), Austl. 115/D4
Clarke (lake), Pa, US 138/B4
Clarks Point, Ak, US 134/G4
Clarksburg, WV, US 130/D4
Clarksburg, NJ, US 138/C3
Clarksdale, Ms, US 129/K4
Clarkston, Wa, US 126/D4
Clarkston, Mi, US 135/G6
Clarksville, Tx, US 129/J4
Clarksville, Ar, US 129/J4
Clarksville, Tn, US 130/C4
Claro (riv.), Braz. 151/H7
Claro, Swi. 57/F5
Clatteringshaws Loch (lake), Sc, UK 34/D1
Claudy, NI, UK 34/A1
Clausen, Ger. 53/G5
Clausthal-Zellerfeld, Ger. 51/H3
Claveria, Phil. 79/D4
Clawson, Mi, US 135/F6
Clay (co.), Mo, US 137/J5
Clay (pt.), IM, UK 34/A3
Clay Center, Ks, US 129/H3
Clay Cross-North Wingfield, Eng, UK 35/G5
Claye-Souilly, Fr. 30/L5
Claymont, De, US 138/C4
Clayton, NM, US 129/G3
Clayton, Ok, US 129/J4
Clayton, Ga, US 133/H3
Clayton, Mo, US 137/G8
Clayton, De, US 138/C4
Clayton, NJ, US 138/D4
Clayton-le-Moors, Eng, UK 35/F4
Clear (lake), Ca, US 128/B3
Clear (hills), Ab, Can. 122/E3
Clear (cape), Ire. 31/P11
Clear Fork (riv.), Tx, US 137/E1
Clear Fork Brazos (riv.), Tx, US 137/E1
Clear Lake, SD, US 127/J4
Clearwater (riv.), Mn, US 127/K4
Clearwater, BC, Can. 122/D3
Clearwater, Fl, US 133/H5
Clearwater (mts.), Id, US 122/C2
Clearwater, Tx, US 129/H4
Cleburne, Tx, US 129/H4
Cleethorpes, Eng, UK 35/H4
Cleeve (hill), Eng, UK
Cleland Rec. Area, Mex. 143/M8
Clementon, NJ, US 138/D4
Clemson, SC, US 133/H3
Cleona, Pa, US 138/B3
Cleopatra Needle (peak), Phil. 81/E1
Clermont, Austl. 114/B3
Clermont, Fr. 52/B5
Clermont-en-Argonne, Fr. 53/E5
Clermont-Ferrand, Fr. 42/E4

Clerval, Fr. 56/C3
Clervaux, Lux. 53/F3
Cles, It. 57/H5
Cleve, Austl. 113/H5
Clevedon, Eng, UK 32/D4
Cleveland, Tx, US 129/J5
Cleveland (mt.), Mt, US 126/E3
Cleveland, Tn, US 129/K4
Cleveland, Oh, US 130/D3
Cleveland, Mo, US 137/D6
Cleveland (co.), Ok, US 137/N15
Cleveland (cape), Austl. 114/B2
Cleveland (hills), Eng, UK 35/G3
Cleveland (co.), Eng, UK 35/G2
Cleveland-Hopkins (int'l arpt.), Oh, US 130/D3
Cleveland National Forest, Ca, US 127/K4
Clevelândia, Braz. 155/B3
Clew (bay), Ire. 31/P10
Clewiston, Fl, US 133/H5
Clichy, Fr. 30/J5
Clichy-sous-Bois, Fr. 30/K5
Cliffdale Park, NJ, US 139/J10
Cliffside Park, NJ, US 139/K8
Clifden, Ire. 31/N10
Cliffwood, NJ, US 139/J10
Clifton, Az, US 128/E4
Clifton, NJ, US 139/J8
Clifton Beach, Austl. 114/B2
Clifton Forge, Va, US 133/J2
Clingmans (peak), US 133/H3
Clinton, BC, Can. 126/C3
Clinton, Ia, US 127/L5
Clinton, Ok, US 129/H4
Clinton, Mo, US 129/K4
Clinton, La, US 129/K5
Clinton, NC, US 133/J3
Clinton, SC, US 133/H3
Clinton (co.), Mo, US 137/D1
Clinton, Ut, US 137/J11
Clinton, NJ, US 138/D2
Clinton (res.), NJ, US 138/D1
Clinton, Ct, US 139/F1
Clinton, Md, US 138/B5
Clinton, Mi, US 135/G6
Clinton-Colden (lake), NW, Can. 122/F2
Clinton, Middle Branch (riv.), Mi, US 135/G6
Clinton, North Branch (riv.), Mi, US 135/G6
Clintonville, Wi, US 130/B2
Clints Dod (hill), Sc, UK 36/D5
Clitheroe, Eng, UK 35/F4
Cliza, Bol. 156/D5
Cloates (pt.), Austl. 112/B2
Clocolan, SAfr. 106/D3
Clodomira, Arg. 158/D3
Clogherhead, Ire. 34/B4
Clonakilty, Ire. 31/P11
Cloncurry, Austl. 114/A3
Clones, Ire. 34/A4
Clonmany, Ire. 34/A1
Clonmel, Ire. 31/Q10
Cloppenburg, Ger. 51/F3
Clorinda, Arg. 157/E2
Clos-Fontaine, Fr. 30/M6
Closter, NJ, US 139/K8
Cloud Peak, Wy, US 126/F4
Cloudcroft, NM, US 132/B3
Cloverdale, Ca, US 128/B3
Clovis, NM, US 129/G4
Clovis, Ca, US 128/C3
Cluain Meala (Clonmel), Ire. 31/Q10
Cluanie (lake), Sc, UK 36/A2
Cluj (co.), Rom. 49/F2
Cluj-Napoca, Rom. 49/F2
Clusone, It. 57/G5
Cluses, Fr. 56/C5
Clutha (riv.), NZ 109/G7
Clwyd (riv.), Wal, UK 35/E5
Clwyd (co.), Wal, UK 35/E5
Clwydian (range), Wal, UK 35/E5
Clyde (riv.), Can. 131/H2
Clyde (riv.), Sc, UK 36/B5
Clyde, Firth of (inlet), Sc, UK 31/R8
Clyde Hill, Wa, US 135/C2
Clydesdale (valley), Sc, UK 36/C5
Clywedog (riv.), Wal, UK 32/C2
Cn Tower, Co, Can. 131/R8
Co Loa Citadel, Viet. 78/D1
Côa (riv.), Port. 44/B2
Coacalco, Mex. 143/Q9
Coachella, Ca, US 128/C4
Coahuayana de Hidalgo, Mex. 142/E5
Coahuila (state), Mex. 142/B1
Coahuila, Mex. 142/B1
Coalcomán de Matamoros, Mex. 142/E5
Coaldale, Ab, Can. 126/E3
Coalgate, Ok, US 129/H4
Coalhurst, Ab, Can. 126/E3
Coalinga, Ca, US 128/B3
Coalisland, NI, UK 34/B2
Coalville, Eng, UK 35/F1
Coalville, Ut, US 137/J11
Coamo, PR 141/N8

Coast (ranges), Ca, US 126/C5
Coast (mts.), Can.,US 119/D4
Coast (range), US 119/E6
Coast (mts.), US 119/D4
Coatbridge, Sc, UK 36/B5
Coatepec, Mex. 143/N7
Coatepec Harinas, Mex. 143/K8
Coatesville, Pa, US 138/C4
Coatetelco, Mex. 143/K8
Coaticook, Qu, Can. 131/G2
Coats (isl.), NW, Can. 123/H2
Coats Land (pol. reg.), Ant. 160/V
Coatzacoalcos, Mex. 144/C2
Coatzingo, Mex. 143/L8
Coba (ruin), Mex. 144/D1
Coba de Serpe, Sierra de (peak), Sp. 44/B1
Cobán, Guat. 144/D3
Cobar, Austl. 115/C1
Cobb (lake), Co, US 137/C1
Cobberas (mt.), Austl. 115/C3
Cobblestone (mtn.), Ca, US 136/B1
Cobden, Austl. 115/B3
Cobden (dist.), Can.,US 119/E5
Cobh, Ire. 31/P11
Cobham (riv.), Can. 127/K2
Cobourg, On, Can. 131/S8
Cobourg (pen.), Austl. 109/C2
Coburg (isl.), NW, Can. 123/T7
Coburg, Ger. 54/D2
Coca (riv.), Ecu. 152/B5
Coca, Sp. 44/D2
Cocachacra, Peru 156/D5
Cocaglio, It. 58/C1
Cocentaina, Sp. 45/E3
Cochabamba, Bol. 150/E7
Coche (isl.), Ven. 153/F2
Cochem, Ger. 53/G3
Cocherel, Fr. 30/M4
Cochin, India 82/C6
Cochrane, Ga, US 133/H3
Cochrane, Ab, Can. 126/E3
Cochrane, On, Can. 130/D1
Cochrane (co.), Mo, US 137/J5
Cock Cairn (mt.), Sc, UK 36/D3
Cockatoo, Austl. 115/G5
Cockburn, NJ, US 138/D2
Cockburn (sound), Austl. 112/K7
Cockburn (chan.), Pa, US 138/A1
Cockeysville, Md, US 138/B3
Cockscomb (peak), SAfr. 106/D4
Coclé del Norte, Pan. 145/F4
Coco (riv.), Hon. 140/E5
Coco, Isla del (isl.), CR 150/A2
Cocoa, Fl, US 133/H4
Coconino (plat.), Az, US 128/D4
Cocoparra NP, Austl. 115/C2
Cocorocuma, Cayo (isl.), Hon. 145/F3
Côcos, Braz. 154/A4
Cocos (isls.).
Cocula, Mex. 142/E4
Codajás, Braz. 150/F4
Codegua, Chile 158/N9
Codigoro, It. 59/F3
Codlea, Rom. 49/G3
Codogno, It. 58/C2
Codsall, Eng, UK 35/F1
Coelemu, Chile 158/B3
Coelho Neto, Braz. 154/B2
Coesfeld, Ger. 51/E5
Coeur d'Alene (lake), Id, US 126/D4
Coeur d'Alene, Id, US 126/D4
Coevorden, Neth. 50/D3
Coffin Bay, Austl. 113/G5
Coffin Bay NP, Austl. 113/G5
Coffs Harbour, Austl. 115/E1
Cofre de Perote, PN, Mex. 143/M7
Coggiola, It. 58/B1
Coghinas (lake), It. 46/A2
Cognac, Fr. 42/C4
Cogolin, Fr. 43/G5
Cogollo del Cengio, It. 59/E1
Cogolludo, Sp. 44/D2
Cohansey (riv.), NJ, US 138/C5
Cohasset, Ma, US 138/G6
Cohocton (riv.), NY, US 131/R10
Cohoes, NY, US 139/M2
Cohuna, Austl. 115/B3
Cohunu NP, Austl. 112/L7
Coiba, Isla de (isl.), Pan. 150/B2
Coig (riv.), Arg. 157/C7
Coignières, Fr. 30/H5
Coihaique, Chile 158/B5
Coihueco, Chile 158/C3
Coimbatore, India 82/C5
Coimbra (dist.), Port. 44/A2
Coimbra, Port. 44/A2
Coin, Sp. 44/C4
Coina (riv.), Port. 45/P10
Coise (riv.), Fr. 42/F4
Cojedes (state), Ven. 152/D2
Cojedes (riv.), Ven. 152/D2
Cojímies, Ecu. 152/A4
Cojudo Blanco (peak), Arg. 157/C6
Cojutepeque, ESal. 144/D3
Coka, Yugo. 48/E3
Cokeville, Wy, US 126/F5
Col d'Ispéguy (pass), Fr. 42/C5
Colac, Austl. 115/B3
Colares, Port. 45/P10
Colasay, Peru 156/B2
Colatina, Braz. 155/D1

Colbeck (cape), Ant. 160/P
Colby, Wa, US 135/B2
Colca, Peru 156/D4
Colcabamba, Peru 156/C4
Colchester, Eng, UK 33/G3
Cold Bay, Ak, US 134/F4
Cold Fell (peak), Eng, UK 35/F2
Cold Lake, Ab, Can. 126/F2
Cold Spring, Mn, US 127/K4
Cold Spring Harbor, NY, US 139/M8
Coldwater, Ks, US 129/H3
Coldwater, Mi, US 130/C3
Cole, Ok, US 137/M15
Cole (riv.), Eng, UK 33/E3
Coleambally, Austl. 115/C2
Coleman, Tx, US 129/H5
Colenso, SAfr. 107/E3
Coleraine, NI, UK 34/B1
Coleraine (dist.), NI, UK 34/B1
Coleraine, Austl. 115/B3
Coleridge (lake), Can.,US 119/E5
Colesberg, SAfr. 106/D3
Colesville, Md, US 138/A5
Colfax, Wa, US 126/D4
Colgate (cape), NW, Can. 123/S8
Colgong, India 85/F3
Colhué Huapi (lake), Arg. 158/C5
Colico, It. 57/F5
Coligny, SAfr. 106/D2
Coligny, Fr. 56/B5
Colima, Mex. 142/E5
Colima (state), Mex. 142/D5
Colima, Nevado de (peak), Mex. 142/E5
Colina, Chile 158/N8
Coll (isl.), Sc, UK 31/Q8
Collado-Villalba, Sp. 45/N8
Collagna, It. 58/D4
Collarenebri, Austl. 115/C1
Colle di Val d'Elsa, It. 59/E6
Collecchio, It. 58/D3
College, Ak, US 134/J3
College Park, Md, US 138/B5
College Station, Tx, US 129/H5
Collegeville, Pa, US 138/C3
Collegno, It. 43/G4
Collesalvetti, It. 58/D5
Colletorto, It. 46/D2
Collie, Austl. 112/C5
Collier (bay), Austl. 109/B2
Collier (range), Austl. 112/C3
Collier Range NP, Austl. 112/C3
Collierville, Tn, US 129/K4
Colliford (res.), Eng, UK 32/B6
Collingwood, On, Can. 130/C2
Collins, Ms, US 133/F4
Collinstown (int'l arpt.), Ire. 34/B1
Collinsville, Pa, US 132/D2
Collinsville, Il, US 137/H8
Collinsville, Austl. 114/B3
Collinsville, Ca, US 135/L10
Collo, Alg. 100/K6
Collombey, Swi. 56/C5
Collon, Ire. 34/B4
Collonges, Fr. 56/C5
Colma, Ca, US 135/K11
Colmar, Fr. 56/D1
Colmar, Pa, US 138/C3
Colmberg, Ger. 54/D4
Colmenar de Oreja, Sp. 44/D2
Colmenar Viejo, Sp. 45/N8
Colmillo (cape), Chile 159/B6
Colne (riv.), Eng, UK 35/G4
Colne, Eng, UK 35/F4
Cologne, Ger. 51/E2
Cologne, NJ, US 138/D5
Cologne/Bonn (int'l arpt.), Ger. 51/E2
Cologno Monzese, It. 58/C1
Colombey-les-Belles, Fr. 56/B1
Colombia, Col. 152/C4
Colombia (ctry.) 147/A2
Colombine (lake), Swi. 56/C4
Colombo (cap.), SrL. 82/C6
Colomoncagua, Hon. 144/D3
Colón (mts.), Hon. 145/F4
Colón, Pan. 145/G4
Colón, Uru. 159/G2
Colonelganj, India 84/C2
Colonia, Micr. 116/C4
Colonia (dept.), Uru. 158/G2
Colonia Barón, Arg. 158/D3
Colonia del Sacramento, Uru. 159/K11
Colonia Juárez, Mex. 128/F5
Colonia Las Heras, Arg. 157/C6
Colonial Park, Pa, US 138/B3

Colorado (peak), Arg. 159/C6
Colorado City, Tx, US 129/G4
Colorado Historical Museum, Co, US 137/C3
Colorado Springs, Co, US 129/F3
Colorno, It. 58/D3
Colotlán, Mex. 142/E4
Colquiri, Bol. 150/E7
Colson (pt.), Belz. 144/D2
Colt (hill), Sc, UK 36/B6
Coltauco, Chile 158/N9
Colton, Ca, US 136/C2
Colts Neck, NJ, US 139/J2
Coluene (riv.), Braz. 147/D4
Columbia, La, US 129/J4
Columbia (plat.), US 126/C4
Columbia (cap.), SC, US 133/H3
Columbia, Tn, US 130/C5
Columbia, Ky, US 130/C4
Columbia (riv.), Can.,US 119/E5
Columbia (co.), Or, US 126/C4
Columbia, Mo, US 129/K4
Columbia, Il, US 137/G9
Columbia, NJ, US 138/D2
Columbia, Md, US 138/B4
Columbia, Pa, US 138/B3
Columbia Falls, Mt, US 126/E3
Columbine (cape), SAfr. 106/K10
Columbus, Ne, US 127/J5
Columbus, Tx, US 129/H5
Columbus, Mt, US 126/F4
Columbus, NM, US 132/B4
Columbus, In, US 130/C4
Columbus (cap.), Oh, US 130/D4
Columbus, Ms, US 133/F3
Columbus, Ga, US 133/G3
Colunga, Sp. 44/C1
Colusa, Ca, US 128/B3
Colville (riv.), Ak, US 134/H2
Colville, Wa, US 126/D3
Colville (cape), NW, Can. 122/D2
Colville (riv.), Wa, US 126/D3
Colwyn Bay, Wal, UK 34/E5
Comacchio, It. 59/F3
Comacchio, Valli di (lag.), It. 59/F3
Comai, China 85/H1
Comal (co.), Tx, US 137/U20
Comal, Tx, US 137/U20
Comala, Mex. 142/D5
Comalcalco, Mex. 144/C2
Comanche, Tx, US 129/H5
Comandante Luis Piedra Buena, Arg. 159/C6
Comandante Nicanor Otamendi, Arg. 159/...
Comänesti, Rom. 49/H2
Comarnic, Rom. 49/G3
Comas, Peru 156/C3
Comas, Peru 156/B3
Combarbalá, Chile 157/B3
Combeaufontaine, Fr. 56/B2
Comber, NI, UK 34/C2
Combin (peak), Swi. 57/E4
Comblain-au-Pont, Belg. 52/E3
Combloux, Fr. 56/C6
Combs-la-Ville, Fr. 30/K6
Comé, Ben. 96/A4
Comines, Fr. 52/C2
Comines, Belg. 52/C2
Comino (isl.), Malta 46/L6
Comitán de Domínguez, Mex. 144/C2
Commack, NY, US 139/E2
Commentry, Fr. 42/E3
Commerce, Ga, US 133/H3
Commerce, Ca, US 136/F7
Commerce City, Co, US 137/C3
Commercy, Fr. 53/E5
Commewijne (dist.), Sur. 153/H3
Como (lake), It. 57/F5
Como, It. 58/B1
Como, Wi, US 135/P14
Comodoro Rivadavia, Arg. 158/D5
Comorin (cape), India 82/C6
Comox, BC, Can. 126/B3
Comrie, Sc, UK 36/C4
Con Son (isl.), Viet. 83/J6
Connemara NP, Ire. 31/P10
Conakry (cap.), Gui. 102/B4
Conakry (pol. reg.), Gui. 102/B4
Conakry (int'l arpt.), Gui. 102/B4
Conambo (riv.), Ecu. 152/B5
Conca, Peru 156/C3
Concarneau, Fr. 42/B3
Conceição da Barra, Braz. 155/E1

Conceição das Alagoas, Braz. 155/B1
Conceição do Araguaia, Braz. 151/J5
Conceição do Coité, Braz. 154/C3
Conceição do Mato Dentro, Braz. 155/D1
Conceição do Rio Verde, Braz. 211/H6
Conceição dos Ouros, Braz. 211/H7
Concepción (lake), Bol. 150/F7
Concepción (lake), Arg. 157/D2
Concepción, Arg. 157/E1
Concepción, Bol. 150/C6
Concepción, Peru 150/C6
Concepción (pt.), Mex. 142/C3
Concepción (bay), Mex. 142/B3
Concepción, Chile 158/B3
Concepción de La Vega, DRep. 141/G4
Concepción del Oro, Mex. 143/E3
Concepción del Uruguay, Arg. 159/J10
Conception (pt.), Ca, US 128/B4
Concesio, It. 58/D1
Conchal, Braz. 211/F7
Conchas (lake), NM, US 129/F4
Conches, Fr. 30/L5
Conchillas, Uru. 159/J11
Concho (riv.), Tx, US 129/G5
Conchos (riv.), Mex. 119/G7
Concord, Ca, US 128/B3
Concord, NC, US 133/H3
Concord (cap.), NH, US 131/G3
Concord, Wi, US 135/N13
Concordia, SAfr. 106/B3
Concórdia, Peru 156/C2
Concordia, Mex. 142/D4
Concordia Sagittaria, It. 59/F1
Concordia sulla Secchia, It. 59/D3
Concrete, Wa, US 126/C3
Condado, Cuba 145/G1
Condamine (riv.), Austl. 109/E3
Condamine, Austl. 114/C3
Conde, Braz. 154/C3
Condé-sur-l'Escaut, Fr. 52/C3
Condé-sur-Noireau, Fr. 42/C2
Condé-sur-Vesgre, Fr. 30/G5
Condé-sur-Vire, Fr. 42/C2
Condécourt, Fr. 30/H4
Condeúba, Braz. 154/B4
Condino, It. 57/H5
Condobolin, Austl. 115/C2
Condom, Fr. 42/D5
Condon, Or, US 126/C4
Condroz (plat.), Belg. 40/C3
Conecuh (riv.), Al, US 133/G4
Conegliano, It. 59/F1
Conejos, Co, US 129/F3
Conesa, Arg. 158/E2
Conestoga (riv.), Pa, US 138/B3
Conewago (lake), Pa, US 138/A3
Confins (int'l arpt.), Braz. 155/E1
Conflans-en-Jarnisy, Fr. 53/E5
Conflans-Sainte-Honorine, Fr. 30/H5
Congaree Swamp Nat'l Mon., SC, US 133/H3
Congleton, Eng, UK 35/F5
Congjiang, China 83/J2
Congo (basin), D.R. Congo 97/K7
Congo (ctry.) 105/B1
Congo, Dem. Republic of the (ctry.), Afr. 93/D4
Congo, Democratic Republic of the (ctry.) 96/D4
Congonhal, Braz. 211/G7
Congonhas, Braz. 155/D2
Congonhas (int'l arpt.), Braz. 211/G8
Conguillio, PN, Chile 158/C3
Conic (hill), Sc, UK 36/B4
Cónico (peak), Arg. 158/C4
Conifer, Co, US 137/C3
Conil de la Frontera, Sp. 44/B4
Conisbrough, Eng, UK 35/G5
Conlig, NI, UK 34/C2
Conn (lake), Ire. 31/P10
Connacht (reg.), Ire. 31/P10
Connah's Quay, Wal, UK 35/E5
Connaught, Ire. 52/C6
Conneaut, Oh, US 130/D3
Connecticut (riv.), US 131/G2
Connecticut (state), US 125/M3
Connellsville, Pa, US ...
Connemara NP, Ire. 31/P10
Connersville, In, US 130/C4
Cono Grande (peak), Arg. 159/C6
Conococha, Peru 156/B3
Conocoto, Ecu. 152/B5
Conon, Falls of (falls), Sc, UK 36/B1
Cononbridge, Sc, UK 36/B1
Conondale NP, Austl. 114/...
Conoplja, Yugo. 48/D3
Conrad, Mt, US 126/E3
Conroe, Tx, US 129/J5

Consandolo, It. 59/E3
Conscience Point NWR, NY, US 139/F2
Consdorf, Lux. 53/F4
Conselheiro Pena, Braz. 155/D1
Conselice, It. 59/E2
Conselve, It. 59/E2
Conservation Park, Austl. 113/F4
Consett, Eng, UK 35/G2
Conshohocken, Pa, US 138/C3
Consolación del Sur, Cuba 145/F1
Consolidated (canal), Az, US 137/S19
Constance (lake), Swi. 43/H3
Constance (Bodensee) (lake), Swi. 43/H3
Constant (mtn.), Fr. 141/N9
Constanța (prov.), Rom. 49/H3
Constanța, Rom. 49/J3
Constantí, Sp. 45/F2
Constantina, Sp. 44/C3
Constantine (cape), Ak, US 134/G4
Constantine, Alg. 100/K6
Constitución, Chile 158/B3
Constitució (res.), Uru. 159/K10
Constitución de 1857, PN, Mex. 128/C5
Consuegra, Sp. 44/D3
Contai, India 85/F5
Contamana, Peru 156/B2
Contarina, It. 59/F2
Contas, Rio de (riv.), Braz. 151/K6
Contegem, Braz. 155/C1
Contes, Fr. 56/D5
Conthey, Swi. 56/D5
Continental (range), Can. 126/C2
Continental (mtn.), Az, US 137/S18
Contoy (isl.), Mex. 144/E1
Contra Costa (canal), Ca, US 135/L10
Contra Costa (co.), Ca, US 135/L11
Contramaestre, Cuba 145/G1
Contratación, Col. 152/C3
Contrecoeur, Qu, Can. 131/P6
Contreras, Embalse de (res.), Sp. 44/E3
Contrexéville, Fr. 56/B1
Controller (bay), Ak, US 134/J3
Contulmo, Chile 158/B2
Contumazá, Peru 156/B2
Contwig, Ger. 53/G5
Contwoyto (lake), NW, Can. 122/F2
Conty, Fr. 52/B4
Convención, Col. 152/C2
Conversano, It. 47/E2
Converse, Tx, US 137/U20
Conway, Ar, US 129/J4
Conway, SC, US 131/G3
Conway, NH, US 131/G3
Conway (cape), Austl. 114/C3
Conway NP, Austl. 114/C3
Conwy (bay), Wal, UK 34/D5
Conwy (riv.), Wal, UK 34/E5
Conwy, Vale of (valley), Wal, UK 34/E5
Conyngham, Pa, US 138/B2
Coober Pedy, Austl. 113/G4
Cooch Behār, India 85/G2
Coochiemudlo (isl.), Austl. 114/F7
Cook (mt.), NZ 117/S11
Cook (inlet), Ak, US 122/A3
Cook (co.), Il, US 135/Q16
Cook (bay), Chile 159/C7
Cook (str.), NZ 109/H7
Cook Islands (dpcy.), NZ 117/J6
Cooke (mt.), Austl. 112/C5
Cookeville, Tn, US 130/C4
Cookham, Eng, UK 30/A2
Cookhouse, SAfr. 106/D4
Cookstown, NI, UK 34/B2
Cookstown (dist.), NI, UK 34/B2
Cooksville, Md, US 138/A5
Cooktown, Austl. 114/B2
Coola Coola (swamp), Austl. 115/B3
Coolah, Austl. 115/D1
Coolamon, Austl. 115/C2
Coolangatta, Austl. 115/E1
Cooley (pt.), Ire. 34/B4
Coolgardie, Austl. 112/D4
Cooloola NP, Austl. 114/D4
Cooloongup (lake), Austl. 112/K7
Cooma, Austl. 115/D3
Coonabarabran, Austl. 115/B3
Coonalpyn, Austl. 115/A2
Coonamble, Austl. 115/D1
Coonana Abor. Land, Austl. 112/D4
Coondapoor (Kundapura), India 89/K6
Coongan Abor. Land, Austl. 112/C2
Coonoor, India 82/C5
Cooper, Tx, US 129/J4
Coopersburg, Pa, US 138/C2
Cooperstown, ND, US 127/J4
Coordewandy (peak), Austl. 112/C3
Coorong NP, Austl. 115/A3
Coorow, Austl. 112/C4

Cooroy, Austl. 114/D4
Coosa (riv.), Al, US 133/G3
Cootamundra, Austl. 115/D2
Coot'tha (mt.), Austl. 114/E6
Copacabana, Bol. 156/D5
Copahué (vol.), Chile 158/C3
Copainalá, Mex. 144/C2
Copala, Mex. 140/B4
Copala, Mex. 143/P8
Copán (ruin), Hon. 144/D3
Cope (gulf), Sp. 44/E4
Copeland (isl.), NI, UK 34/C2
Copenhagen (København) (cap.), Den. 38/E4
Copertino, It. 47/F2
Copeton (dam), Austl. 115/D1
Copiague, NY, US 139/M9
Copiapó, Chile 157/B2
Coplay, Pa, US 138/C2
Copparo, It. 59/E3
Coppename (riv.), Sur. 153/H3
Coppenbrügge, Ger. 51/G4
Copper (riv.), Ak, US 122/B2
Copper Center, Ak, US 134/J3
Copperas Cove, Tx, US 129/H5
Coppermine, NW, Can. 122/E2
Coppermine (riv.), NW, Can. 122/E2
Copperton, Ut, US 137/J12
Coppet, Swi. 56/C5
Copşa Mică, Rom. 49/G2
Coqen, China 70/E5
Coquet (riv.), Eng, UK 36/D6
Coquet Dale (valley), Eng, UK 35/G1
Coquimbo, Chile 157/B2
Coquitlam, BC, Can. 126/C3
Corabia, Rom. 49/G4
Coração de Jesus, Braz. 154/A5
Coracora, Peru 156/C4
Corail, Haiti 145/H2
Coraki, Austl. 115/E1
Coral (sea) 109/D2
Coral Gables, Fl, US 133/H5
Coral Harbour, NW, Can. 123/H2
Coral Sea Islands Territory (dpcy.), Austl. 109/E2
Coral Springs, Fl, US 133/H5
Corales del Rosario, PN, Col. 152/C2
Coram, NY, US 139/E2
Corato, It. 46/E2
Corbeil-Essonnes, Fr. 30/K6
Corbelin (cape), Alg. 100/H4
Corbenay, Fr. 56/C2
Corbet (peak), Swi. 57/F5
Corbett NP, India 84/B1
Corbetta, It. 58/B2
Corbie, Fr. 52/B4
Corbieres (mts.), Fr. 42/E5
Corbin, Ky, US 130/C4
Corbin City, NJ, US 138/D5
Corby, Eng, UK 33/F2
Corcoran, Ca, US 135/K10
Corcovado, Braz. 211/K7
Corcovado, CR 145/E4
Corcovado (vol.), Chile 158/B4
Corcovado (gulf), Chile 158/B4
Corcovado, PN, CR 140/E6
Cordeiro, Braz. 155/D2
Cordele, Ga, US 133/H4
Cordelia, Ca, US 135/K10
Cordell, Ok, US 129/H4
Cordenons, It. 43/K4
Cordignano, It. 59/F1
Cordillera de Los Picachos, PN, Col. 150/D3
Cordillera Oriental (mts.), SAm. 152/B5
Cordisburgo, Braz. 155/C1
Córdoba, Braz. 157/D3
Córdoba, Sp. 44/C4
Córdoba, Mex. 143/N8
Córdoba (dept.), Col. 145/H4
Córdoba (plain), SAm. 158/E2
Córdoba, Sierra de (mts.), Arg. 157/D3
Cordova, Ak, US 134/J3
Cordova (peak), Ak, US 134/J3
Cordova, Md, US 138/C6
Coreaú, Braz. 154/B1
Corella, Sp. 44/E1
Coremas, Braz. 154/C2
Corentyne (riv.), Guy. 153/G3
Corfu (Kérkira) (isl.), Gre. 47/F3
Corgémont, Swi. 56/D3
Corgo, Sp. 44/B1
Coria, Sp. 44/B3
Coria del Río, Sp. 44/B4
Coriano, It. 59/F5
Coribe, Braz. 154/A4
Coricudgy (mt.), Austl. 115/D2
Corigliano Calabro, It. 46/E3
Corinaldo, It. 59/G5
Corinth (gulf), Gre. 47/H3
Corinth, Ms, US 133/F3
Corinth (Kórinthos) (ruin), Gre. 47/H4
Corinto, Nic. 144/E3
Cork, Ire. 31/P11
Corleone, It. 46/C4
Corleto Perticara, It. 46/E2
Corlu, Turk. 49/H5
Cormeilles-en-Vexin, Fr. 30/J4
Cormons, It. 59/G1
Cormontreuil, Fr. 30/J5
Cormorant, Mb, Can. 127/H2
Cormorant (lake), Can. 127/H2
Cornacchia (peak), It. 46/D2
Cornaredo, It. 58/C2
Cornberg, Ger. 51/G6

Corndon (peak), Wal, UK 32/C1
Corneto Vicentino, It. 59/E1
Cornélio Procópio, Braz. 155/B2
Cornelius Grinnel (bay), NW, Can. 123/K2
Cornell, Ca, US 136/B2
Cornella, Sp. 45/L7
Corner (inlet), Austl. 109/D4
Corner Brook, Nf, Can. 131/K1
Cornetto (peak), It. 57/H6
Cornfield (pt.), Ct, US 139/F1
Corniglio, It. 58/D4
Cornimont, Fr. 56/C2
Corning, NY, US 130/E3
Corno alle Scale (peak), It. 43/J4
Corno di Rosazzo, It. 59/G1
Cornone di Blumone (peak), It. 57/G6
Cornú (peak), Arg. 159/D7
Cornuda, It. 59/F1
Cornwall, PE, Can. 131/J2
Cornwall, On, Can. 130/F2
Cornwall (isl.), NW, Can. 123/S7
Cornwall (cape), Eng, UK 32/A6
Cornwall (co.), Eng, UK 32/A6
Cornwall, Pa, US 138/B3
Cornwallis (isl.), NW, Can. 123/S7
Corny (pt.), Austl. 113/H5
Coro, Ven. 152/D2
Coroatá, Braz. 154/A2
Corocoro, Bol. 156/D5
Coromandel, Braz. 155/C1
Coromandel (pen.), NZ 117/T10
Coromandel (coast), India 82/D3
Coron, Phil. 81/F1
Corona, Ca, US 136/C3
Corona (bay), CR 140/E6
Coronado, Ca, US 136/C5
Coronation, Ab, Can. 126/F2
Coronation (gulf), NW, Can. 122/E2
Coronel, Chile 158/B3
Coronel Dorrego, Arg. 158/E3
Coronel Fabriciano, Braz. 155/D1
Coronel Moldes, Arg. 158/D2
Coronel Murta, Braz. 154/B5
Coronel Oviedo, Par. 157/E2
Coronel Pringles, Arg. 158/E3
Coronel Suárez, Arg. 158/E3
Coronel Vidal, Arg. 158/F3
Coronel Vivida, Braz. 155/A3
Corongo, Peru 156/B3
Coronie (dist.), Sur. 153/G3
Coropuna (peak), Peru 156/C4
Corovodë, Alb. 47/G2
Corozal, Col. 152/C2
Corozal, Belz. 144/D2
Corpach, Sc, UK 36/A3
Corpus Christi, Tx, US 132/D5
Corpus Christi (int'l arpt.), Tx, US 143/F3
Corral, Chile 158/B3
Corral de Almaguer, Sp. 44/D3
Corral de Bustos, Arg. 158/E3
Corrales, Col. 152/C3
Corralillo, Cuba 145/F1
Corre, Fr. 56/C2
Correa, Arg. 158/E2
Corredor, CR 145/F4
Correggio, It. 59/D3
Corrente (riv.), Braz. 154/A4
Corrente, Braz. 154/A4
Corrib (lake), Ire. 31/P10
Corrientes (riv.), Peru 150/C4
Corrientes, Arg. 157/E2
Corrientes (cape), Cuba 145/E1
Corrientes (pt.), Col. 152/B3
Corrigan, Tx, US 129/J5
Corrigin, Austl. 112/C5
Corriverton, Guy. 153/G3
Corryhabbie (peak), Sc, UK 36/C2
Corryong, Austl. 115/C3
Corse (dept.), Fr. 43/H5
Corse (cape), Fr. 52/B1
Corse (hill), Sc, UK 36/B5
Corserine (peak), Sc, UK 34/C1
Corsewall (pt.), NI, UK 34/C1
Corsham, Eng, UK 32/E4
Corsica (isl.), Fr. 27/E4
Corsicana, Tx, US 129/H5
Corsico, It. 58/C2
Corsons (inlet), NJ, US 138/D5
Cortaillod, Swi. 56/C3
Cortegana, Sp. 44/B4
Cortemaggiore, It. 58/C3
Cortemilia, It. 58/B3
Cortez, Co, US 129/H3
Cortina d'Ampezzo, It. 43/K3
Cortines, Arg. 159/J11
Cortland, NY, US 130/E3

Corve (riv.), Eng, UK 32/D2
Corvo (peak), It. 46/C1
Corvo (isl.), Azor., Port. 45/R12
Corzoneso, Swi. 57/E5
Cosalá, Mex. 142/D3
Cosamaloapan, Mex. 143/P8
Cosautlán, Mex. 143/N7
Coscomatepec, Mex. 143/M7
Cosenza, It. 46/E3
Coshocton, Oh, US 130/D3
Cosigüina (pt.), Nic. 144/E3
Coslada, Sp. 45/N9
Cosmo Newberry Abor. Rsv., Austl. 112/D3
Cosmópolis, Braz. 211/F7
Cosne-Cours-sur-Loire, Fr. 42/E3
Cosne d'Allier, Fr. 42/E3
Cosolapa, Mex. 143/N8
Cospeito, Sp. 44/B1
Cosquín, Arg. 157/D3
Cossato, It. 58/B1
Cossonay, Swi. 56/C4
Costa Azul, Uru. 159/G2
Costa Brava (int'l arpt.), Sp. 45/G2
Costa da Caparica, Port. 45/P10
Costa de Mosquitos (phys. reg.), Nic. 145/E4
Costa di Rovigo, It. 59/E3
Costa Masnaga, It. 58/C1
Costa Mesa, Ca, US 136/G8
Costa Rica (ctry.) 119/J8
Costa Smeralda (int'l arpt.), It. 46/B2
Costa Volpino, It. 58/D1
Costabissara, It. 59/E1
Costeşti, Rom. 49/G3
Costigliole d'Asti, It. 58/B3
Cotabambas, Peru 156/C4
Cotabato, Phil. 81/F2
Cotacachi (peak), Ecu. 152/B4
Cotahuasi, Peru 156/C4
Cotatumbo (riv.), Col. 145/H4
Côte d'Azur (int'l arpt.), Fr. 43/G5
Côte de Hautmont (hill), Fr. 56/B1
Côte d'Ivoire (ctry.) 93/B4
Côte d'Or (uplands), Fr. 42/F3
Côte du Rif (Al Hoceima) (int'l arpt.), Mor. 100/C2
Côte-Saint-Luc, Qu, Can. 131/N7
Coteau des Prairies (plat.), SD, US 127/J4
Coteau-du-Lac, Qu, Can. 131/M7
Coteau du Missouri (plat.), ND, US 127/H3
Coteau-Landing, Qu, Can. 131/M7
Cotegipe, Braz. 154/A4
Cotentin (pen.), Fr. 32/C2
Côtes de Meuse (uplands), Fr. 42/F2
Cothi (riv.), Wal, UK 32/C3
Cotia, Braz. 211/G8
Cotignola, It. 59/E4
Cotonou, Ben. 103/F5
Cotonou (int'l arpt.), Ben. 103/F5
Cotopaxi (dept.), Ecu. 152/B5
Cotopaxi (vol.), Ecu. 152/B5
Cotopaxi, PN, Ecu. 152/B5
Cotswolds (hills), Eng, UK 32/D3
Cottage Grove, Or, US 126/C5
Cottage Hills, Il, US 137/G8
Cottam, On, Can. 135/G7
Cottbus, Ger. 41/H3
Cottian Alps (mts.), Fr. 43/G4
Cottleville, Mo, US 137/F8
Cotton River, Austl. 114/A2
Cottonport, La, US 129/J5
Cottonwood, Az, US 128/D4
Cottonwood (riv.), US 129/F5
Cotulla, Tx, US 129/H6
Coubert, Fr. 30/L6
Coubre, Pointe de la (pt.), Fr. 42/C4
Couchey, Fr. 56/A3
Coudekerque-Branche, Fr. 52/B1
Couëron, Fr. 42/C3
Couesnon (riv.), Fr. 32/C3
Coulee City, Wa, US 126/D3
Coulee Dam Nat'l Rec. Area, Wa, US 126/D3
Coulogne, Fr. 52/A2
Coulombs-en-Valois, Fr. 30/M4
Coulommes, Fr. 30/L5
Coulommiers, Fr. 52/C6
Coulonge (riv.), Can. 130/E2
Coulounieix-Chamiers, Fr. 42/D4
Council, Ak, US 134/F3
Council, Id, US 126/D4
Council Grove, Ks, US 129/H3
Coupar Angus, Sc, UK 36/C3
Coupvray, Fr. 30/L5
Courantyne (riv.), Guy., Sur. 153/G3
Courcelles, Belg. 52/C2
Courchevel, Fr. 43/G4
Courcouronnes, Fr. 30/K6

Coursan, Fr. 42/E5
Courtelary, Swi. 56/D4
Courtice, On, Can. 131/S8
Courtisols, Fr. 53/D6
Courtmacsherry, Ire. 31/P11
Courtomer, Fr. 32/D3
Courtown, Mo, US 137/E6
Cousance, Fr. 56/B4
Coushatta, La, US 129/J4
Coussolre, Fr. 52/D2
Coutances, Fr. 42/C2
Coutevroult, Fr. 30/L5
Coutts, Ab, Can. 126/E3
Coutras, Fr. 42/C4
Couva, Trin. 153/F2
Couvet, Swi. 56/C4
Couvin, Belg. 52/C2
Couzeix, Fr. 42/D4
Covadonga NP, Sp. 44/C1
Covasna, Rom. 49/H3
Covasna (prov.), Rom. 49/G3
Covelo, Ca, US 135/J9
Covington, Mo, US 137/K8
Covina, Ca, US 136/G7
Covington, Tn, US 129/K4
Covington, La, US 133/H3
Covington, Pa, US 138/C1
Covo, It. 58/C2
Cow Green (res.), Eng, UK 35/F2
Cowal (reg.), Sc, UK 36/A4
Cowan (lake), Austl. 109/B4
Cowdenbeath, Sc, UK 36/C1
Cowell, Austl. 113/H5
Cowes, Eng, UK 33/E5
Cowlitz (riv.), Wa, US 126/C3
Cowra, Austl. 115/D2
Cox, Braz. 151/H7
Cox's Bāzār, Bang. 83/F3
Coyame, Mex. 129/F5
Coye-la-Forêt, Fr. 30/K4
Coyotepec, Mex. 143/K7
Coyuca de Benítez, Mex. 143/M6
Coyutla, Mex. 143/M6
Cozad, Ne, US 127/H5
Cozumel (int'l arpt.), Mex. 144/E1
Cozumel (isl.), Mex. 144/E1
Cradle (mtn.), Austl. 115/C4
Cradle Mountain-Lake Saint Clair NP, Austl. 115/C4
Cradock, SAfr. 106/D4
Crag (mtn.), Can. 134/K3
Crag (peak), US 135/F3
Craig, Co, US 128/F2
Craig, Ak, US 134/M4
Craig, Ks, US 137/D6
Craigavon (dist.), NI, UK 34/B3
Craigavon, NI, UK 34/B3
Craigieburn, Austl. 115/F5
Craik, Sk, Can. 127/G3
Craiova, Rom. 49/F3
Cramalina (peak), Swi. 57/E5
Cramlington, Eng, UK 35/G1
Cran-Gevrier, Fr. 56/C6
Crana (riv.), Ire. 34/A1
Cranberry Portage, Mb, Can. 127/H2
Cranborne Chase (for.), Eng, UK 32/D5
Cranbourne, Austl. 115/G6
Cranbrook, BC, Can. 126/E3
Cranbrook, Austl. 112/C5
Cranbury, NJ, US 138/D3
Crane, Tx, US 132/C4
Crane Neck (pt.), NY, US 139/E2
Crane River, Austl. 114/A2
Cranleigh, Eng, UK 33/F4
Cranston, RI, US 139/H2
Craponne, Fr. 42/F4
Crater (lake), Or, US 128/B2
Crater Lake NP, Or, US 128/B2
Craters of the Moon Nat'l Mon., Id, US 128/D2
Cratéus, Braz. 154/B2
Crati (riv.), It. 46/E3
Crato, Port. 44/B3
Cravinhos, Braz. 155/C2
Crawfordsville, In, US 130/C3
Crawfordville, Fl, US 133/G4
Crawley, Eng, UK 33/F4
Cray (riv.), Eng, UK 30/D2
Crazy (mts.), Mt, US 128/E2
Creag Meagaidh (peak), Sc, UK 36/B3
Creagorry, Sc, UK 36/A3
Creasy (Mifflinville), Pa, US 138/B1
Creazzo, It. 59/E2
Crèches-sur-Saône, Fr. 56/A5
Crécy-sur-Serre, Fr. 52/C4
Credit (riv.), On, Can. 131/Q8
Credit, Eng, UK 35/F5
Cree (lake), Sk, Can. 122/F3
Cree (riv.), Sk, Can. 122/F3
Cree City, Fl, US 133/H5
Cree Fell (peak), Eng, UK 35/F2
Creetown, Sc, UK 34/C2
Cregy-lès-Meaux, Fr. 30/L5
Creighton, Sk, Can. 127/H2
Creil, Fr. 52/B5

Crema, It. 58/C2
Crémieu, Fr. 56/B6
Cremlingen, Ger. 51/H4
Cremona (prov.), It. 58/C2
Cremona, It. 58/D2
Crépy, Fr. 52/C4
Crépy-en-Valois, Fr. 30/K4
Creran (riv.), Sc, UK 36/A3
Crescent, Mo, US 137/F8
Crescent, Co, US 137/B3
Crescent, Ut, US 137/K12
Crescent City, Ca, US 126/B5
Crescentino, It. 58/B2
Crespano del Grappa, It. 59/E1
Crespellano, It. 59/E3
Crespières, Fr. 30/H5
Crespin, Fr. 52/C3
Cresskill, NJ, US 139/L8
Cressona, Pa, US 138/B2
Cressy, Austl. 115/C4
Crest, Fr. 42/F4
Crest Hill, Il, US 135/P16
Crestline, Ca, US 136/C2
Creston, Ia, US 127/K5
Creston, BC, Can. 126/D3
Crestview, Fl, US 133/G4
Crestwood Village, NJ, US 138/D4
Crete (sea), Gre. 47/J4
Crete (isl.), Gre. 27/G5
Créteil, Fr. 30/K5
Creuch (hill), Sc, UK 36/B5
Creuse (riv.), Fr. 42/D3
Creus (cape), Sp. 45/G1
Creussen, Ger. 55/F3
Creutzwald-la-Croix, Fr. 53/F5
Creuzburg, Ger. 51/H6
Crevalcore, It. 59/E3
Crevacoure, It. 58/B1
Creve Coeur, Mo, US 137/G8
Crèvecœur-le-Grand, Fr. 52/B4
Crevillente, Sp. 45/E3
Crevoladossola, It. 57/E5
Crewe, Eng, UK 35/F5
Crib Point, Austl. 115/C3
Criciúma, Braz. 155/B4
Crieff, Sc, UK 36/C4
Criffell (hill), Sc, UK 34/E2
Crikvenica, Cro. 48/B3
Crillon (mt.), Ak, US 134/L4
Crimea (pen.), Ukr. 49/L3
Crimean (pen.), Ukr. 62/E3
Crimond, Sc, UK 36/E1
Criseney, Fr. 30/L6
Crisman, Co, US 137/B2
Crissier, Swi. 56/C4
Cristal, Monts de (mts.), Gabon 105/B1
Cristalina, Braz. 154/A5
Cristina, Braz. 211/H7
Cristóbal (pt.), Ecu. 156/E7
Cristóbal Colón (peak), Col. 152/C2
Cristoforo Colombo (int'l arpt.), It. 58/B4
Cristuru Secuiesc, Rom. 49/G2
Crişul Alb (riv.), Rom. 48/F2
Crişul Negru (riv.), Rom. 48/E2
Crixás-Açu (riv.), Braz. 151/H6
Crna Reka (riv.), Macd. 47/G2
Črnomelj, Slov. 43/L4
Croajingolong NP, Austl. 115/D3
Croatia (ctry.) 27/F4
Croce (beach), It. 57/H5
Croce, Pico di (peak), It. 57/H4
Croche (riv.), Can. 131/F2
Croche (peak), Fr. 56/C6
Crocker (range), Malay. 81/E3
Crocker (peak), Ecu. 156/E7
Crockett, Tx, US 129/J5
Crockett, Ca, US 135/K10
Crocodile Head (pt.), Austl. 114/B2
Crodo, It. 57/E5
Crofton, Md, US 138/B6
Croghan (mtn.), Ire. 34/B6
Croisette (cape), Fr. 42/F5
Croisilles, Fr. 52/B3
Croissy-Beaubourg, Fr. 30/K5
Croker (isl.), Austl. 109/C2
Cromarty Firth (bay), Sc, UK 36/B1
Crombie (mt.), Austl. 114/F3
Cromdale (hills), Sc, UK 36/C2
Cromwell, NZ 117/R12
Crong A Na (riv.), Viet. 78/D3
Crooked (isl.), Bahm. 141/G3
Crooked Creek, Ak, US 134/G3
Crooked Island Passage (chan.), Bahm. 145/H1
Crookston, Mn, US 127/H3
Crookwell, Austl. 115/D2
Croom, Ire. 31/P10
Crosby, ND, US 127/H3
Crosby, Eng, UK 35/E5
Crosbyton, Tx, US 129/F4
Cross (lake), Sk, Can. 122/F3
Cross (riv.), Sk, Can. 127/G2
Cross City, Fl, US 133/H5
Cross Fell (peak), Eng, UK 35/F2
Cross Lake, Mb, Can. 127/H2
Cross Plains, Tx, US 129/H4
Cross River (state), Nga. 103/H5
Cross River (res.), NY, US 139/E1

Cross Roads, Pa, US 138/B4
Crossfield, Ab, Can. 126/E3
Crossford, Sc, UK 36/C5
Crosshouse, Sc, UK 36/B5
Crossroads, Ire. 31/P9
Crossville, Tn, US 133/G3
Crostolo (riv.), It. 58/D3
Croton-On-Hudson (Croton-Harmon), NY, US 139/K8
Crotone, It. 47/E3
Crottendorf, Ger. 55/F1
Croult (riv.), Fr. 30/K5
Crouy, Fr. 52/C5
Crouy-sur-Ourcq, Fr. 30/M4
Crow Agency, Mt, US 126/F4
Crowborough, Eng, UK 33/G4
Crowdy Bay NP, Austl. 115/E1
Crowe (riv.), Can. 130/E2
Crowley, La, US 129/J5
Crowley's (ridge), US 133/F3
Crown Point, In, US 130/C3
Crown Point, La, US 137/P17
Crown Point (int'l arpt.), Trin. 153/F2
Crown Prince Frederik (isl.), NW, Can. 123/H1
Crownpoint, NM, US 128/E4
Crows Nest Falls NP, Austl. 114/D4
Cruden Bay, Sc, UK 36/E2
Cruick Water (riv.), Sc, UK 36/D3
Crumlin, NI, UK 34/B2
Crummock Water (lake), Eng, UK 35/E2
Crumpton, Md, US 138/C6
Cruseilles, Fr. 56/C5
Crusnes (riv.), Fr. 53/E5
Cruz (cape), Cuba 145/G2
Cruz Alta, Arg. 158/E2
Cruz Alta, Braz. 157/F2
Cruz Alta (peak), Port. 45/P10
Cruz das Almas, Braz. 154/C4
Cruz del Eje, Arg. 157/D3
Cruz Grande, Mex. 144/B2
Cruzeta, Braz. 154/C2
Cruzeiro, Braz. 211/J8
Cruzeiro do Sul, Braz. 156/C2
Cruzília, Braz. 211/J6
Crvenka, Yugo. 48/D3
Cryn-y-Brain (peak), Wal, UK 35/E5
Csenger, Hun. 41/M5
Cseprog, Hun. 43/M3
Csongrád, Hun. 48/E2
Csorna, Hun. 48/E2
Csorvás, Hun. 48/E2
Csóványos (peak), Hun. 48/E2
Csurgó, Hun. 48/C2
Cu Lao (isl.), Viet. 79/A5
Cuajinicuilapa, Mex. 144/B2
Cualedro, Sp. 44/B2
Cuamba, Moz. 105/G3
Cuando (riv.), Ang. 105/D4
Cuango (riv.), Ang. 105/C2
Cuanza (riv.), Ang. 93/D6
Cuarto (riv.), Arg. 158/D2
Cuatrociénagas de Carranza, Mex. 132/C5
Cuauhtémoc, Mex. 142/D3
Cuauhtémoc, Mex. 142/D2
Cuautepec, Mex. 143/L6
Cuautitlán, Mex. 143/P9
Cuautitlán Izcalli, Mex. 143/P9
Cuautla, Mex. 143/L8
Cuba, Mo, US 129/K3
Cuba, Port. 44/B3
Cuba (ctry.) 119/J7
Cubagua (isl.), Ven. 153/E2
Cuballing, Austl. 112/C5
Cubango (riv.), Ang. 93/D6
Cubuk, Turk. 62/E4
Cucamonga (Rancho Cucamonga), Ca, US 136/C2
Cuchi (riv.), Ang. 105/C4
Cuchivero (riv.), Ven. 152/E2
Cuchumatanes (mts.), Guat. 144/D3
Cuckmere (riv.), Eng, UK 30/D5
Cucq, Fr. 42/D1
Cúcuta, Col. 152/C2
Cucuyagua, Hon. 144/D3
Cudahy, Wi, US 135/P13
Cudalbi, Rom. 49/H3
Cuddalore, India 82/C5
Cuddapah, India 82/C4
Cudgewa, Austl. 115/C3
Cudillero, Sp. 44/B1
Cudrefin, Swi. 56/D4
Cudworth, Eng, UK 35/G4
Cue, Austl. 112/C3
Cuéllar, Sp. 44/C2

Cuéllar-Baza, Sp. 44/D4
Cuenca, Sp. 44/D2
Cuenca, Ecu. 152/B5
Cuenca, Sierra de (range), Sp. 44/E2
Cuencamé de Ceniceros, Mex. 142/D3
Cuernavaca, Mex. 143/K8
Cuero, Tx, US 129/H5
Cuers, Fr. 42/G5
Cueto, Cuba 145/H1
Cuetzalan, Mex. 143/M7
Cueva de los Guácharos, PN, Col. 150/C3
Cuevas de Vinromá, Sp. 45/F2
Cuevas del Almanzora, Sp. 44/E4
Cuffley, Eng, UK 30/C1
Cufré, Uru. 159/K11
Cugir, Rom. 49/F3
Cuglieri, It. 46/A2
Cugnaux, Fr. 42/D5
Cuiabá (riv.), Braz. 151/G7
Cuiabá, Braz. 151/G7
Cuicas, Ven. 152/D2
Cuijk, Neth. 50/C5
Cuilapa, Guat. 144/D3
Cuillin (sound), Sc, UK 36/A2
Cuilo (riv.), Ang. 105/C2
Cuisance (riv.), Fr. 56/B4
Cuise-la-Motte, Fr. 52/C5
Cuiseaux, Fr. 56/B5
Cuisery, Fr. 56/A4
Cuité, Braz. 154/C2
Cuitláhuac, Mex. 143/N8
Cuito (riv.), Ang. 105/C4
Cuito Cuanavale, Ang. 105/C4
Cuiuni (riv.), Braz. 150/F4
Culcairn, Austl. 115/C2
Culdaff (riv.), Ire. 34/A1
Culebra (isl.), PR 145/N8
Culemborg, Neth. 50/C5
Culgoa (riv.), Austl. 109/D3
Culiacán Rosales, Mex. 142/D3
Culion (isl.), Phil. 79/D5
Cullen, Sc, UK 36/D1
Cullera, Sp. 45/E3
Culleredo, Sp. 44/A1
Cullman, Al, US 133/G3
Culloden Battlesite, Sc, UK 36/B2
Cullompton, Eng, UK 32/D5
Cully, Swi. 56/C5
Cullybackey, NI, UK 34/B2
Culmback (dam), Wa, US 135/D2
Culmore, NI, UK 34/A1
Culoz, Fr. 56/B6
Culpeper, Va, US 130/E4
Culross, Sc, UK 36/C5
Cults, Sc, UK 36/D2
Culver (pt.), Austl. 112/D5
Culver City, Ca, US 136/F7
Culvers (lake), NJ, US 138/D2
Cuttal-Có, Arg. 158/C3
Cumaná, Ven. 153/E2
Cumari, Braz. 155/B1
Cumba, Braz. 156/B2
Cumbal, Col. 152/B4
Cumbal, Nevado de (peak), Col. 152/B4
Cumberland (lake), Can. 127/H2
Cumberland (lake), Ky, US 130/C4
Cumberland (plat.), US 133/G3
Cumberland Cave, Md, US 130/D4
Cumberland (falls), Ky, US 133/G2
Cumberland (pen.), NW, Can. 123/K2
Cumberland (co.), NJ, US 138/C5
Cumberland (sound), NW, Can. 123/K2
Cumberland, Wa, US 135/D3
Cumberland, Md, US 130/D4
Cumberland House, Sk, Can. 127/H2
Cumbernauld, Sc, UK 36/C5
Cumbres Bastonal, Cerro (peak), Mex. 144/C2
Cumbres de Majalca, PN, Mex. 142/D2
Cumbres de Monterrey, PN, Mex. 144/D2
Cumbres de Monterrey, PN de, Mex. 144/D2
Cumbria (co.), Eng, UK 35/E2
Cumbrian (mts.), Eng, UK 35/E2
Cumbum, India 82/C4
Cumins, Austl. 113/G5
Cummings, Austl. 115/C2
Cummins, Austl. 115/G5
Cumnock, Austl. 115/D2
Cumpas, Mex. 142/C2
Cumra, Turk. 90/C2
Cumshewa (pt.), Can. 134/M5
Cunaviche, Ven. 153/E3
Cunco, Chile 158/B3
Cundeelee Abor. Rsv., Austl. 112/D4
Cundinamarca (dept.), Col. 152/C3
Cunduacán, Mex. 144/C2
Cunene (riv.), Ang. 93/D6
Cuneo (prov.), It. 58/A3
Cuneo, It. 58/A3
Cunha, Braz. 211/J8
Cunnamulla, Austl. 114/B5
Cununurú (riv.), It. 59/G6
Cupar, Sc, UK 36/C4
Cupertino, Ca, US 135/K12
Cupira, Braz. 154/D2
Cupramontana, It. 59/G6
Cuprija, Yugo. 48/E4

Cuquenán (riv.), Ven. 153/F3
Curaçá, Braz. 154/C3
Curaçao (isl.), NAnt. 150/E1
Curacautín, Chile 158/C3
Curacaví, Chile 158/N8
Curahuara de Carangas, Bol. 156/D5
Curanilahue, Chile 158/C2
Curaray (riv.), Ecu. 150/C4
Curaray (riv.), Ecu.,Peru 152/C5
Curaumín, Hon. 144/E3
Curarrehue, Chile 158/N8
Curcubăta (peak), Rom. 49/F2
Cure (riv.), Fr. 40/B5
Curecanti Nat'l Rec. Area, 132/B2
Curepipe, Mrts. 107/T15
Curepto, Chile 158/C2
Curicó, Chile 158/C2
Curimatá, Braz. 154/A3
Curitibanos, Braz. 155/B3
Curno, It. 58/C1
Curral Velho, CpV. 93/K10
Current (riv.), US 129/K3
Currie, Austl. 115/B3
Currie, Sc, UK 36/C5
Curry, Ak, US 134/H3
Curtea de Argeş, Rom. 49/G3
Curtici, Rom. 48/E2
Curtis (isl.), NZ 117/L7
Curtis (riv.), Austl. 114/D4
Curtis, Md, US 138/B6
Curú NWR, CR 145/E4
Curuá (riv.), Braz. 151/G4
Curuá Una (riv.), Braz. 153/H5
Curuçá (riv.), Braz. 150/D5
Curup, Indo. 80/B4
Cururupu, Braz. 151/K4
Curuzú Cuatiá, Arg. 157/E2
Curvelo, Braz. 155/C1
Cusco (dept.), Peru 156/C4
Cusco, Peru 156/C4
Cusher (riv.), NI, UK 34/B3
Cushet Law (peak), Eng, UK 36/D6
Cushing, Ok, US 129/H4
Cusna (peak), It. 58/D4
Cusset, Fr. 42/E3
Cusseta, Ga, US 133/G3
Custer, Mt, US 126/G4
Custer, SD, US 127/H5
Cústines, Fr. 53/F6
Custódia, Braz. 154/C3
Cut Bank, Mt, US 126/E3
Cut Knife, Sk, Can. 126/F2
Cutchogue, NY, US 139/F2
Cutervo, Peru 156/B2
Cuthbert, Ga, US 133/G4
Cutler, Ca, US 135/L11
Cutro, It. 47/E3
Cuttack, India 82/E3
Cuvergnon, Fr. 30/L4
Cuvier (cape), Austl. 112/B3
Cuxhaven, Ger. 51/F1
Cuyabeno, Ecu. 152/C5
Cuyama (riv.), Ca, US 135/L11
Cuyo (isls.), Phil. 81/F1
Cuyo, Phil. 81/F1
Cuyo (isl.), Phil. 81/F1
Cuyotenango, Peru 156/D4
Cuyuní (riv.), Ven. 150/F2
Cuyuni (riv.), Guy., Ven. 153/F2
Cuyuni-Mazaruni (pol. reg.), Guy. 153/F3
Cuzco (ruin), Peru 156/D4
Cwmbran, Wal, UK 32/C3
Cyangugu, Rwa. 104/A3
Cyclades (isls.) 27/J4
Cypress (hills), Can. 126/F3
Cypress, Ca, US 136/F8
Cypress (riv.), Can. 126/F3
Cyrenaica (reg.), Libya 97/K1
Cysoing, Fr. 52/C2
Czarna Białostocka, Pol. 41/M2
Czarnków, Pol. 41/J2
Czech Republic (ctry.) 27/F4
Częstochowa, Pol. 41/K3
Częstochowa (prov.), Pol. 41/K3
Człuchów, Pol. 38/G5

D

D (riv.), China 79/D2
Da Hinggang (mts.), China 67/M5
Da Lat, Viet. 78/E4
Da Nang (cape), Viet. 78/E2
Da Nang, Viet. 78/E2
Da Xian, China 70/H4
Da'an, China 71/M2
Daanbantayan, Phil. 79/D5
Daba (mts.), China 70/J5
Dabakala, C.d'Iv. 102/D4
Dabas, Hun. 48/D2
Dabba, China 79/C3
Dabbāgh, Jabal (peak), SAr. 88/C3
Dabeiba, Col. 152/C2
Dabie (peak), Pol. 53/G6
Dabob (bay), Wa, US 135/B2
Daboya, Gha. 103/E4
Dabra, India 84/B3
Dąbrowa Białostocka, Pol. 39/G3
Dąbrowa Górnicza, Pol. 41/K3
Dabu, China 79/C3
Dachang Huizu Zizhixian, China 72/H7

Dachau, Ger. 55/E6
Dacono, Co, US 137/C2
Dade City, Fl, US 133/H4
Dades, Oued (riv.), Mor. 98/D3
Dadi (cape), Indo. 81/H4
Dādra and Nagar Haveli (state), India 82/B4
Dādri, India 86/D5
Dādu, Pak. 82/C6
Daduru (riv.), SrL. 82/C6
Daen Noi (peak), Thai. 78/B4
Daet, Phil. 79/D5
Dafang, China 83/J2
Dafeng, China 72/E4
Dagana, Sen. 102/B2
Dağardı, Turk. 90/D2
Dağbaşı, Turk. 90/D2
Dagestan Aut. Rep., Rus. 63/H4
Dagestan Aut. Rep., Rus. 64/Q6
Daggaboersnek (pass), SAfr. 106/D4
Dagmar Range NP, Austl. 114/B2
Dagneux, Fr. 56/B6
Dagny, Fr. 30/M5
Dagu, China 72/H7
Daguan, China 83/H2
D'Aguilar (mt.), Austl. 114/E6
D'Aguilar (mt.), Austl. 114/E6
Dagupan, Phil. 79/D4
Dahana (des.), SAr. 67/D7
Daharki, Pak. 82/A2
Dahei (riv.), China 72/B2
Dahlak (arch.), Erit. 97/N4
Dahlem, Ger. 53/F3
Dahlenburg, Ger. 51/H2
Dahlonega, Ga, US 133/H4
Dahme (riv.), Ger. 41/G3
Dahn, Ger. 53/G5
Dahūk, Iraq 90/E2
Dahūk (gov.), Iraq 90/E2
Dahuofang (res.), China 72/D2
Dai (lake), China 72/C2
Dai-segen-dake (peak), Japan 76/B3
Dai-sen (peak), Japan 74/C3
Dai Xian, China 72/C3
Daian, China 77/L5
Daicheng, China 72/D3
Daigo, Japan 75/G2
Dailekh, Nepal 84/C1
Dailly, Sc, UK 36/B6
Daimiao, China 72/D3
Daimiel, Sp. 34/D3
Daingerfield, Tx, US 129/J4
Daiō-zaki (pt.), Japan 75/E3
Dāira Dīn Panāh, Pak. 86/A4
Daireaux, Arg. 158/E3
Daisen-Oki NP, Japan 74/C3
Daisetsuzan NP, Japan 76/C2
Daishan, China 73/M9
Daito (isl.), Japan 67/N7
Daitō, Japan 77/J6
Daiyun (peak), China 71/L6
Dajabón, DRep. 145/J2
Dakar (cap.), Sen. 102/A3
Dakar (pol. reg.), Sen. 102/A3
Dākhilah, Wāḩāt ad (oasis), Egypt 101/B3
Dakhin Shāhbāzpur (isl.), Bang. 85/H4
Dakhlet Nouadhibou (pol. reg.), Mrta. 98/A5
Dakoro, Niger 103/G3
Dakota City, Ne, US 127/J5
Dakovica, Yugo. 47/J1
Dakovo, Cro. 48/D3
Dakshin Gangotri, India, Ant. 160/A
Dal (falls), Sudan 64/B3
Dal (riv.), Swe. 38/F1
Dalaas, Aus. 57/F3
Dalad Qi, China 72/B2
Dalaman, Turk. 90/B2
Dalaman (int'l arpt.), Turk. 90/B2
Dalandzadgad, Mong. 70/H3
Dalandzadgad, Mong. 65/L5
Dalarna (reg.), Swe. 37/E3
Dalatangi (pt.), Ice. 37/Q6
Dalbeattie, Sc, UK 34/E2
Dalby, Austl. 115/H5
Dalby, Swe. 38/E4
Dalcour, La, US 137/Q17
Dalcross (int'l arpt.), Sc, UK 36/B1
Dale, Ok, US 137/N15
Dale, Nor. 38/B4
Dalen, Neth. 50/D3
Dalen, Nor. 38/C2
Dalfsen, Neth. 50/D3
Dalgaranger (mt.), Austl. 112/C3
Dalhart, Tx, US 129/G3
Dalhousie (cape), Can. 134/N1
Dalhousie, NB, Can. 131/H1
Dalhousie, India 86/C3
Dali, China 83/H2
Dali, China 72/B4
Dalian (bay), China 73/A3
Dalian, China 73/A3
Dalian (int'l arpt.), China 72/E3
Dalias, Sp. 34/D4
Dalidag (peak), Azer. 91/G4
Dāliyat el Karmil, Isr. 91/G6
Dalj, Cro. 48/D3
Dalkeith, Sc, UK 36/C5
Dalkola, India 85/F3
Dall (lake), Ak, US 134/F3
Dall (isl.), Ak, US 122/C3
Dallas, Tx, US 129/H4
Dallas-Fort Worth (int'l arpt.), Tx, US 129/H4
Dallastown, Pa, US 138/B4

Dallgow, Ger. 40/Q6
Dallol Bosso (riv.), Niger,Mali 103/F3
Dalmatia, Pa, US 138/B2
Dalmatia (reg.), Cro. 48/B3
Dalmellington, Sc, UK 36/B6
Dalmeny, Austl. 115/D3
Dalmine, It. 58/C1
Dal'negorsk, Rus. 71/G3
Dal'nerechensk, Rus. 71/P2
Daloa, C.d'Iv. 102/D5
Dalry, Sc, UK 36/B5
Dalrymple (lake), Austl. 109/D3
Dalrymple, Sc, UK 36/B6
Dals Långed, Swe. 38/E2
Dalsingh Sarai, India 85/E3
Dalsjöfors, Swe. 38/E3
Dalton, Ga, US 133/G3
Daltonganj, India 85/E3
Dalvík, Ice. 37/N6
Dalwallinu, Austl. 112/C4
Daly (riv.), Austl. 109/C2
Daly (bay), NW, Can. 122/G2
Damak, Nepal 85/F2
Daman, It. 82/B3
Damān and Diu (state), India 82/B3
Damanhûr, Egypt 91/B4
Damar (isl.), Indo. 81/G5
Dame Marie (cape), Haiti 145/H2
Dame Marie, Haiti 145/H2
Dāmghān, Iran 89/F1
Damietta (Dumyāṭ), Egypt 91/B4
Damietta (Dumyāṭ), Egypt 71/B4
Damion, China 72/C3
Dammam, Fr. 37/M4
Dammartin-en-Goële, Fr. 30/L4
Dammastock (peak), Swi. 57/E4
Damme, Ger. 51/F3
Damme, Belg. 52/C1
Damoh, India 84/B4
Damongo, Gha. 103/E4
Damparis, Fr. 56/B3
Dampier (str.), Indo. 81/H4
Dampier (arch.), Austl. 109/A2
Dampier, Austl. 112/C2
Dampierre, Fr. 56/B3
Dampierre-sur-Salon, Fr. 56/B2
Damprichard, Fr. 56/C3
Damrei (mts.), Camb. 78/C4
Damsterdiep (riv.), Neth. 50/D2
Damvant, Swi. 56/C3
Damxung, China 70/F5
Dan (riv.), US 133/H2
Dan Xian, China 83/J4
Dana Point, Ca, US 136/C4
Dānā, Jor. 91/D4
Danao, Phil. 79/D5
Danba, China 70/H5
Danbury, Eng, UK 33/G3
Dancheng, China 72/C4
Dandaragan, Austl. 112/B4
Dandenong (mt.), Austl. 115/C2
Danderhall, Sc, UK 36/C5
Dandong, China 73/C2
Danger (pt.), SAfr. 106/L11
Danggali Conservation Park, Austl. 115/B2
Dangriga, Belz. 144/D2
Dangshan, China 72/D4
Dangtu, China 72/D5
Dangyang, China 71/K5
Danielskuil, SAfr. 106/C3
Danielsville, US 133/H3
Danilov, Rus. 60/J4
Daning, China 72/B3
Danjoutin, Fr. 56/C2
Dankaur, India 86/D5
Dankov, Rus. 62/F1
Dankova (peak), Kyr. 87/G4
Danli, Hon. 144/E3
Dannelly (res.), Al, US 133/G3
Dannemora, Swe. 38/G1
Dannenberg, Ger. 40/F2
Dannes, Fr. 52/A2
Dannevirke, NZ 117/T11
Danube, Delta of the (delta), Rom. 49/J3
Danube (Donau) (riv.), Ger. 43/F2
Danube, Mouths of the (delta), Rom.,Ukr. 62/D3
Danville, Il, US 130/C3
Danville, Ky, US 130/C4
Danville, Pa, US 138/B2
Dao Xian, China 83/K2
Daosa, C.d'Iv. 102/C5
Dapaong, Togo 103/E4
Dapitan, Phil. 79/D6
Datu (cape), Indo. 80/B3

Dar'ā (prov.), Syria 91/E3
Dar'ā, Syria 91/E3
Dārāb, Iran 89/F3
Darabani, Rom. 49/H1
Daraga, Phil. 81/F1
Daram, Phil. 79/D5
Dārān, Iran 88/F2
Daravica (peak), Yugo. 47/J1
Dārayyā, Syria 91/E3
Darbhanga, India 85/E2
Darby (cap), Ak, US 134/F3
Darby, Pa, US 138/C4
Darda, Cro. 48/D3
Dardanelle (lake), Ar, US 129/J4
Dardanelles (str.), Turk. 62/C4
Darent (riv.), Eng, UK 30/D3
Dareton, Austl. 115/B2
Darfield, NZ 117/S11
Darfo, It. 57/G6
Dārfūr (state), Sudan 101/A5
Dargaville, NZ 117/S10
Dargle (riv.), Ire. 34/B5
Darhan, Mong. 70/J2
Darie (hills), Som. 97/G6
Darien, Ga, US 133/H4
Darien, PN, Pan. 139/M7
Darien, Il, US 135/P16
Darién, PN, Pan. 150/C2
Darién, Serranía del (mts.), Pan. 150/C2
Darkan, Austl. 112/C5
Darlag, China 70/G5
Darling (range), Austl. 109/A4
Darling (riv.), Austl. 109/D4
Darling, SAfr. 106/L10
Darling Downs (reg.), Austl. 109/D3
Darling Downs (range), Austl. 114/C3
Darlington, SC, US 133/J3
Darlington, Md, US 138/B4
Darlington, US 138/B4
Darlington, Eng, UK 35/G2
Darlington Point, Austl. 115/C2
Darłowo, Pol. 38/G4
Darmstadt, Ger. 54/B3
Darnah, Libya 97/K1
Darney, Fr. 56/C1
Darnley (bay), NW, Can. 122/D2
Darnley (cape), Ant. 160/E
Daroca, Sp. 44/E2
Darregueira, Arg. 158/E3
Darsser (cape), Ger. 38/E4
Dart (riv.), Eng, UK 32/C6
Dart, West (riv.), Eng, UK 32/C6
Dartford, Eng, UK 30/D2
Dartmoor (upland), Eng, UK 32/B5
Dartmoor NP, Eng, UK 32/B5
Dartmouth (dam), Austl. 115/C3
Dartmouth (res.), Austl. 115/C3
Dartmouth, NS, Can. 131/J2
Dartmouth, Eng, UK 32/C6
Darton, Eng, UK 35/G4
Dartuch (cape), Sp. 45/G3
Daruvar, Cro. 48/C3
Darvel (bay), Malay. 81/E3
Darvel, Sc, UK 36/B5
Darwen, Eng, UK 35/F4
Darwin (bay), Chile 158/B5
Darwin (int'l arpt.), Austl. 109/C2
Darwin, Austl. 109/C2
Darwin (vol.), Ecu. 156/E7
Darwin, Cordillera (mts.), Chile 157/B7
Darya Khan, Pak. 86/A4
Daryābād, India 84/C2
Dashennongjia (peak), China 72/B5
Dashhowuz, Trkm. 87/C4
Dashhowuz (pol. reg.), Trkm. 87/C4
Dashhowuz (int'l arpt.), Trkm. 87/C4
Dasht-e Kavīr (des.), Iran 64/F6
Dasht-e Lūt (des.), Iran 64/F6
Dasht-e Mārgow (des.), Afg. 89/H2
Dasht Kaur (riv.), Pak. 89/H3
Dasing, Ger. 54/E6
Dassa-Zoumé, Ben. 103/F5
Dassel, Ger. 51/G5
Dassendorf, Ger. 51/H1
Dasseneiland (isl.), SAfr. 106/B4
Dasūya, India 86/C4
Dātāganj, India 84/B1
Datchet, Eng, UK 30/B2
Date, Japan 76/B2
Datia, India 84/B3
Datian, China 79/C2
Datil, NM, US 132/B3
Datong (mts.), China 70/G4
Datong, China 70/H4
Datong, China 70/H4
Datteln, Ger. 51/E5
Datu (cape), Indo. 80/B3
Datuk (cape), Indo. 80/B3
Dauphin (co.), Pa, US 138/B3
Dauphin, Pa, US 138/B3
Dar'ā (prov.), Syria 90/E3

Dauphiné (reg.), Fr. 42/F4
Dauphiné, Alpes du (range), Fr. 42/F4
Dāvangere, India 89/L6
Davao, Phil. 81/G2
Davao (gulf), Phil. 81/G2
Davel, SAfr. 107/E2
Davenport, Wa, US 126/D4
Davenport, Ia, US 127/L5
Davenport (pt.), Austl. 113/F2
Daventry, Eng, UK 33/F2
Daverdisse, Belg. 53/E3
Davézieux, Fr. 42/A4
Daveyton, SAfr. 106/E2
David, Pan. 145/F4
David City, Ne, US 127/J5
Davidson, Sk, Can. 127/G3
Davidson (mt.), Ca, US 135/J11
Davie, Fl, US 133/H5
Davies (mt.), Austl. 113/F2
Davis (mt.), Pa, US 130/E4
Davis, Ca, US 128/B3
Davis (riv.), Tx, US 124/F5
Davis (str.), Can.,Grld. 123/L2
Davis, Ant. 160/F
Davis, Il, US 135/P16
Davis (sea), Ant. 160/F
Davlekanovo, Rus. 61/M5
Davos, Swi. 57/F4
Dawa (riv.), China 73/B2
Dawa Wenz (riv.), Eth. 97/N7
Dawei (isl.), China 73/B3
Dawo, China 73/B2
Dawson, Yk, Can. 134/L3
Dawson, Ga, US 133/G4
Dawson (isl.), Chile 159/C7
Dawson, Austl. 109/D3
Dawson Creek, BC, Can. 126/C2
Dawu, China 70/H5
Dawu (mtn.), China 72/C5
Dawu, China 72/C5
Dax, Fr. 42/C5
Daxing, China 72/H7
Daxue (mts.), China 73/B2
Dayao, China 83/H2
Daye, China 79/B1
Daying (riv.), China 83/G3
Daylesford, Austl. 115/C3
Dayong, China 79/B2
Dayr al Balaḥ, Gaza 91/D4
Dayr al Ghuṣūn, WBnk. 91/G7
Dayr az Zawr (prov.), Syria 90/E2
Dayr Ballūṭ, WBnk. 91/G7
Dayr Sharaf, WBnk. 91/G7
Dayrūt, Egypt 101/B3
Daysland, Ab, Can. 126/E2
Dayton, Wa, US 126/D4
Dayton, Tn, US 133/G3
Dayton, NJ, US 138/D3
Daytona Beach, Fl, US 133/H4
Dayu, China 83/K2
Dazhizhu Dau (isl.), China 71/T11
De Aar, SAfr. 106/D3
De Bilt, Neth. 50/C4
De Doorns, SAfr. 106/L10
De Funiak Springs, Fl, US 133/G4
De Grey (riv.), Austl. 109/A3
De Haan, Belg. 52/C1
De Hart, Belg. 52/C1
De Kalb, Il, US 135/N16
De Land, Fl, US 133/H4
De Leijen (lake), Neth. 50/D2
De Lier, Neth. 50/B5
De Luz, Ca, US 136/C4
De Panne, Belg. 52/B1
De Peel (phys. reg.), Neth. 50/C5
De Pinte, Belg. 52/C2
De Ridder, La, US 129/J5
De Soto, Mo, US 129/K3
De Soto, Ks, US 137/D6
De Wijk, Neth. 50/D3
Dead Sea (sea), Jor.,Isr. 91/D4
Deadhorse, Ak, US 134/J1
Deadman (pt.), Austl. 112/C2
Deadwood, SD, US 127/H4
Deal (isl.), Austl. 115/C3
Deal, NJ, US 138/D3
Deale, Md, US 138/B6
Dean (riv.), BC, Can. 126/C2
Dean (chan.), BC, Can. 126/B2
De'an, China 79/C2
Dean (for.), Eng, UK 33/E3
Deán Funes, Arg. 157/D3
Deanmill, Austl. 112/C5
Dearborn Heights, Mi, US 135/F7
Dearne, Eng, UK 35/G4
Dease (str.), NW, Can. 119/F3
Dease (riv.), BC, Can. 122/C3
Dease Lake, BC, Can. 134/M4
Death Valley NP, Ca, US 128/D3
Debar, Macd. 47/G2
Debauch (mtn.), Ak, US 134/G3
Debe Nao, Myan. 78/B3
Debelets, Bul. 47/H3
Deben (riv.), Eng, UK 33/H2
Dębica, Pol. 41/L3
Dęblin, Pol. 41/L3
Dębno, Pol. 41/H2

Deborah (mt.), Ak, US 134/J3
Debre Birhan, Eth. 97/N6
Debre Mark'os, Eth. 97/N5
Debre Tabor, Eth. 97/N5
Debre Zeyit, Eth. 97/N6
Debrecen, Hun. 41/L5
Decatur, Il, US 127/L6
Decatur, Tx, US 129/H4
Decatur, Al, US 133/G3
Decatur, Ga, US 133/G3
Decatur, In, US 130/C3
Decazeville, Fr. 42/E4
Deccan (plat.), India 82/C5
Deception (isl.), Chile 159/T6
Décines-Charpieu, Fr. 56/A6
Decize, Fr. 42/E3
Dedo (peak), Arg. 158/C5
Dédougou, Burk. 102/E3
Dedza, Malw. 105/F3
Dee (riv.), Sc, UK 36/C3
Deel (riv.), Ire. 34/A4
Deep Fork (riv.), Ok, US 137/N14
Deep River, On, Can. 130/E2
Deepcut, Eng, UK 30/B3
Deepwater, Austl. 115/D1
Deepwater, NJ, US 138/C5
Deer (isl.), Ak, US 134/F5
Deer Creek (res.), Ut, US 137/L13
Deer Lake, Nf, Can. 131/K1
Deer Lake, Pa, US 138/C2
Deer Lodge, Mt, US 126/E4
Deer Park, Wa, US 126/D4
Deer Park, NY, US 139/E2
Deer Park, Il, US 135/P15
Deer Plain, Il, US 135/P15
Deerfield, Il, US 135/P15
Deerkirkent, Turk. 90/C2
Deering, Ak, US 134/F2
Deeside (valley), Sc, UK 36/C3
Deex Nugaaleed (riv.), Som. 97/Q6
Defensores del Chaco, PN, Par. 150/F8
Defiance, Oh, US 130/C3
Dégelis, Qu, Can. 131/G2
Degerfors, Swe. 38/F2
Degersheim, Swi. 57/F3
Deggendorf, Ger. 55/F5
Deggingen, Ger. 54/C5
Dego, It. 58/B4
Deh Bīd, Iran 88/F2
Dehalak (isl.), Erit. 97/P4
Dehalak Marine NP, Erit. 97/P4
Dehaq, Iran 88/F2
Dehaqan, Iran 88/F2
Dehra Dūn, India 89/L2
Dehri, India 85/E3
Dehua, China 79/C2
Deidesheim, Ger. 54/B4
Deinste, Ger. 51/G1
Deinze, Belg. 52/C2
Deister (mts.), Ger. 51/G4
Deiva Marina, It. 58/C4
Dej, Rom. 49/F2
Deje, Swe. 38/E2
Dejiang, China 83/J2
Dejima, Japan 77/E1
Dek'emhāre, Erit. 88/C5
Del Campillo, Arg. 158/D3
Del Carril, Arg. 159/J11
Del City, Ok, US 137/N15
Del Dios, Ca, US 136/C5
Del Gran Paraíso, It. 58/A2
Del Mar, Ca, US 136/C5
Del Norte, Co, US 129/F3
Del Rio, Tx, US 129/G5
Del Valle, Arg. 158/E2
Del Valle (lake), Ca, US 135/L12
Delacroix, La, US 137/Q17
Delafield, Wi, US 135/P13
Delano, Ca, US 128/C3
Delano (peak), Ut, US 137/N14
Delareyville, SAfr. 106/D2
Delaware, Oh, US 130/D3
Delaware (bay), NJ, US 138/D4
Delaware, NJ, US 138/D2
Delaware (state), US 125/L4
Delaware (riv.), US 138/D2
Delaware (co.), Pa, US 138/C4
Delaware City, De, US 138/C4
Delaware Water Gap Nat'l Rec. Area, US 138/D2

Delligsen, Ger. 51/G5
Delmas, SAfr. 107/E2
Delme, Fr. 51/F3
Delmenhorst, Ger. 51/F2
Delmiro Gouveia, Braz. 154/C3
Delmont, NJ, US 138/D5
Deloraine, Cro. 48/B3
Deloraine, Austl. 115/C4
Delphi (Delfoi) (ruin), Gre. 47/H3
Delportshoop, SAfr. 106/D3
Delray Beach, Fl, US 133/H5
Delson, Qu, Can. 131/N7
Delta, Ut, US 128/D3
Delta (state), Nga. 103/G5
Delta del Tigre, Uru. 159/N11
Delta do Saloum, PN du, Sen. 102/A3
Delta Junction, Ak, US 134/J3
Delta-Mendota (canal), Ca, US 135/M11
Deltona, Fl, US 133/H4
Delvinë, Alb. 47/G3
Delvino (riv.), Rus. 61/P2
Demanda, Sierra de la (range), Sp. 44/D1
Demarcation (pt.), Ak, US 134/K2
Demarest, NJ, US 139/K8
Demba, D.R. Congo 105/D2
Dembī Dolo, Eth. 97/M6
Demer (riv.), Belg. 40/C3
Demerara (riv.), Guy. 153/G3
Demerara-Mahaica (pol. reg.), Guy. 153/G3
Demerval Lobão, Braz. 154/B2
Demini (riv.), Braz. 153/F3
Demirci, Turk. 62/D5
Demirkent, Turk. 90/C2
Demirköprü (dam), Turk. 90/C2
Demirköy, Turk. 49/H5
Demirtaş, Turk. 49/J5
Demmin, Ger. 38/E5
Democratic Republic of the Congo (ctry.) 105/D1
Demone (valley), It. 46/D4
Demopolis, Al, US 133/G3
Dempo (peak), Indo. 80/B4
Den Burg, Neth. 50/B2
Den Ham, Neth. 50/D3
Den Helder, Neth. 50/B3
Den Oever, Neth. 50/C3
Denain, Fr. 52/C3
Denali NP and Prsv., Ak, US 134/H3
Denare Beach, Sk, Can. 127/H2
Denbigh, Wal, UK 35/E5
Dender (riv.), Belg. 40/B3
Denderleeuw, Belg. 52/D2
Dendermonde, Belg. 52/D1
Deng Xian, China 72/C4
Dengfeng, China 72/C4
Dengkou, China 70/J3
Dengta, China 79/B3
Denham (sound), Austl. 112/B3
Denham, Austl. 112/B3
Denholme, Eng, UK 35/G4
Deniliquin, Austl. 115/C2
Denio, Nv, US 126/D5
Denison, Ia, US 127/K5
Denison, Tx, US 129/H4
Denizli, Turk. 90/B2
Denizli (prov.), Turk. 90/B2
Denkendorf, Ger. 55/E5
Denkendorf, Ger. 57/G2
Denman, Austl. 115/D2
Denmark (str.) 37/P6
Denmark (ctry.) 27/E3
Denmark, Austl. 112/C5
Dennison, NJ, US 138/D5
Dennisville, NJ, US 138/D5
Denpasar, Indo. 80/E5
Dent de Lys (peak), Swi. 56/D4
Dent d'Hérens (peak), It. 56/C6
Dentergem, Belg. 52/C2
Dentlein am Forst, Ger. 54/D4
Denton, Tx, US 129/H4
Denton, Md, US 138/C6
Denton, Eng, UK 35/F5
Denver (co.), Co, US 137/C3
Denver, Pa, US 138/B3
Denver, Co, US 137/C3
Denver International (int'l arpt.), Co, US 137/C3
Denver Museum of Natural History, Co, US 151/H2
Denville, NJ, US 138/D2
Denzlingen, Ger. 56/D1
Deoband, India 86/D5
Deogarh, India 82/D3
Deoghar, India 85/F3
Deohā (riv.), India 84/B1
Deolāli, India 89/K5
Deoli, India 89/L4
Deols, Fr. 42/D3
Deori, India 84/B4
Deoria, India 84/C2
Depew, NY, US 131/N10
Depok, Indo. 80/C5
Deqing, China 79/B3

Deqing, China 72/L9
Dera Ghāzi Khān, Pak. 86/A4
Dera Gopipur, India 86/D4
Dera Ismāīl Khān, Pak. 86/A4
Derbent, Rus. 63/J4
Derby, Ct, US 139/E1
Derby, Eng, UK 35/G6
Derbyshire (co.), Eng, UK 35/G6
Derdap NP, Yugo. 62/B3
Derecske, Hun. 48/E2
Derendingen, Swi. 56/D3
Derg, Lough (lake), Ire. 31/P10
Derik, Turk. 90/E2
Derinkuyu, Turk. 90/C2
Dernau, Ger. 53/G2
Déroute, Passage de la (chan.), Fr. 42/B2
Derravaragh (lake), Ire. 34/A4
Derry, NH, US 131/G3
Derryboy, NI, UK 34/C3
Dervaig, Sc, UK 31/Q8
Derventa, Bosn. 48/C3
Dervio, It. 57/F5
Derwent (riv.), Austl. 115/C4
Derwent (riv.), Bang. 85/E2
Derwent (riv.), Eng, UK 35/E2
Derwent (riv.), Eng, UK 35/F2
Derwent Water (lake), Eng, UK 35/E2
Des Allemands, La, US 137/P17
Des Moines (cap.), Ia, US 127/K5
Des Moines (riv.), Ia,Mn, US 125/H3
Des Peres, Mo, US 137/G8
Desaguadero (riv.), Bol. 150/E7
Desaguadero, Peru 156/D5
Desagües de los Colorados (dry lake), Arg. 157/C2
Descabezado Grande (vol.), Chile 157/B2
Descalvado, Braz. 155/C2
Descartes, Fr. 42/D3
Descham-Bault (lake), Can. 127/H2
Deschambault Lake, Sk, Can. 127/H2
Deschutes (riv.), Or, US 126/C4
Dese, Eth. 97/N5
Dese (riv.), It. 59/F2
Deseado (riv.), Arg. 147/C7
Deseado (cape), Chile 159/B7
Desengaño (pt.), Arg. 159/D6
Desenzano del Garda, It. 58/D2
Desio, It. 58/C1
Desolación (isl.), Chile 157/A7
Desordem, Serra da (range), Braz. 154/A2
Despatch, SAfr. 106/D4
Dessau, Ger. 40/G3
Dessel, Belg. 50/C6
Dessoubre (riv.), Fr. 56/C3
Destelbergen, Belg. 52/C1
Destrehan, La, US 137/P17
Destruction Bay, Yk, Can. 134/L3
Desulo, It. 46/A2
Desvres, Fr. 52/A2
Deta, Rom. 48/E3
Detern, Ger. 51/E2
Detmold, Ger. 51/F5
Detroit (riv.), Can.,US 135/F7
Detroit Lakes, Mn, US 127/K4
Detroit Metropolitan Wayne County (int'l arpt.), Mi, US 130/D3
Dettelbach, Ger. 54/D3
Dettifoss (falls), Ice. 37/P6
Dettwiller, Fr. 53/G6
Deua NP, Austl. 115/D3
Deuil-la-Barre, Fr. 30/J5
Deûle (riv.), Fr. 52/B2
Deurne, Neth. 50/C6
Deurne, Belg. 50/C6
Deustua, Peru 156/D7
Deutsch Evern, Ger. 51/H2
Deutsch Wagram, Aus. 57/P1
Deutschkreutz, Aus. 57/P3
Deutschlandsberg, Aus. 43/L3
Deux-Montagnes, Qu, Can. 131/N6
Deux-Montagnes (co.), Qu, Can. 131/N6
Deux-Montagnes, Lac des (lake), Qu, Can. 131/M7
Deva, Rom. 48/F3
Dévaványa, Hun. 48/E2
Develi, Turk. 90/C2
Deventer, Neth. 50/D4
Deveron (riv.), Sc, UK 36/D1
Devil's (isl.), Mex. 143/E2
Devil's Elbow (pass), Sc, UK 36/C3
Devils Lake, ND, US 127/J4
Devils Paw (peak), Ak, US 134/M4
Devils Postpile Nat'l Mon., Ca, US 128/C3
Devils Slide, Ut, US 137/K11
Devine, Tx, US 129/H5
Devizes, Eng, UK 32/E4
Devoll (riv.), Alb. 47/G2
Devon, Ab, Can. 126/E2

Devon (co.), Eng, UK 32/C5
Devon (isl.), NW, Can. 123/S7
Devon, Pa, US 138/C3
Devon (isl.), Sc, UK 36/C4
Devon-Berwyn, Pa, US 138/C3
Devonport, Austl. 115/C4
Devore, Ca, US 136/C2
Devrek, Turk. 62/D4
Devrek (riv.), Turk. 62/E4
Devrez (riv.), Turk. 62/E4
Dewa (pt.), Indo. 76/B4
Dewa (mts.), Japan 89/L4
Dewās, India 84/B4
Dewetsdorp, SAfr. 106/D3
Dewsbury, Eng, UK 35/G4
Dey-Dey (lake), Austl. 109/C3
Deyang, China 70/H5
Dez (riv.), Iran 64/E6
Dezful, Iran 88/E2
Dezhou, China 72/D3
Dhāka (div.), Bang. 85/H3
Dhāka, Bang. 85/E2
Dhaleswari (riv.), Bang. 85/E2
Dhāli, Cyp. 91/C2
Dhāmpur, India 84/B1
Dhamtari, India 82/D3
Dhanaula, India 86/C4
Dhanaura, India 84/B1
Dhangadhī, Nepal 84/C1
Dhankutā, Nepal 85/F2
Dhār, India 84/B4
Dharampur, India 89/K4
Dharan, Nepal 85/F2
Dhāri, India 89/K4
Dhāriwāl, India 86/C4
Dharmapuri, India 82/C5
Dharmavaram, India 82/C5
Dharmjaygarh, India 84/D3
Dharmsāla, India 86/D4
Dhasan (riv.), India 84/B3
Dhaulāgiri (peak), Nepal 84/D1
Dhaulāgiri (zone), Nepal 84/D1
Dhaurahra, India 84/C1
Dhaurahra, India 84/C1
Dhekiājuli, India 85/G2
Dhemāji, India 85/G2
Dhenkānāl, India 82/D3
Dhībān, Jor. 91/D4
Dhidhimótikhon, Gre. 47/K2
Dhikaia, Gre. 47/K2
Dhílos (ruin), Gre. 47/J4
Dhimitsána, Gre. 47/H4
Dhírfis (peak), Gre. 47/H3
Dhistomon, Gre. 47/H3
Dhofar (reg.), Oman 88/F5
Dhokímion, Gre. 47/H3
Dhokós (isl.), Gre. 47/H3
Dholka, India 89/K4
Dhomokós, It. 47/H3
Dhonoúsa (isl.), Gre. 47/J4
Dhorāji, India 89/K4
Dhronbach (riv.), Ger. 53/F4
Dhūlia, India 89/K4
Dhuliān, India 85/F3
Dhulikhel, Nepal 85/E2
Dhupgāri, India 85/G2
Dhūri, India 86/C4
Di Linh, Viet. 78/E4
Dia (isl.), Gre. 47/J5
Diablo (mt.), Ca, US 135/L12
Diablo (range), Ca, US 124/B3
Diablo, Punta del (pt.), Uru. 159/G2
Diablotin (peak), Dom. 141/N9
Diademá, Braz. 211/G8
Diadema Argentina, Arg. 158/C5
Diamante, Arg. 158/E2
Diamante (riv.), Arg. 158/D3
Diamantina (riv.), Austl. 109/D3
Diamantina, Braz. 154/B5
Diamantina, Chapada (hills), Braz. 151/K6
Diamantino, Braz. 151/G7
Diamond Bar, Ca, US 136/C2
Diamond Harbour, India 85/G3
Diamond Head (pt.), Hi, US 124/W13
Dianbai, China 83/K3
Dianjiang, China 79/A1
Diano Marina, It. 58/B5
Dianshan (lake), China 72/L8
Diapaga, Burk. 103/F4
Dias Creek, NJ, US 138/D5
Diavolezza, Swi. 57/F5
Dibeng, SAfr. 106/C2
Dibib (well), Egypt 101/B4
Dibis, Iraq 90/E2
Dickens, Tx, US 129/G4
Dickinson, ND, US 127/H4
Dickson, Tn, US 130/C4
Dicle (riv.), Turk. 90/E2
Dicomano, It. 59/E5
Didam, Neth. 50/D4
Didcot, Eng, UK 33/E3
Didsbury, Ab, Can. 126/E3
Dīdwāna, India 89/K3
Die, Fr. 42/F4
Die Berg (peak), SAfr. 105/F5
Dieburg, Ger. 54/C3
Diedersdorf, Ger. 40/Q7
Diefenbaker (lake), Can. 126/F2

Diego de Almagro (isl.), Chile 159/B6
Diego Garcia (isl.) 67/G10
Diekirch (dist.), Lux. 53/F4
Diekirch, Lux. 53/F4
Diemen, Neth. 50/B4
Diemtigen, Swi. 56/D4
Diepenbeek, Belg. 53/E2
Diepenveen, Neth. 50/D4
Diepholz, Ger. 51/F3
Diepoldsau, Swi. 57/F3
Dierdorf, Ger. 53/G2
Diespeck, Ger. 54/D4
Diessen am Ammersee, Ger. 57/F1
Diest, Belg. 53/E2
Dietenheim, Ger. 57/G1
Dietenhofen, Ger. 54/D4
Dietersheim, Ger. 54/D4
Dietfurt an der Altmühl, Ger. 55/E4
Dietikon, Swi. 57/E3
Dietmannsried, Ger. 57/G2
Dietzenbach, Ger. 54/B2
Dieue-sur-Meuse, Fr. 53/E5
Dieulouard, Fr. 53/F6
Dieuze, Fr. 53/F6
Diever, Neth. 50/D3
Diez, Ger. 54/B2
Diffa, Niger 96/H5
Diffa (dept.), Niger 103/H3
Differdange, Lux. 53/E4
Difficult (mt.), Austl. 115/B3
Dīg, India 84/A2
Digboi, India 83/G2
Digby, NS, Can. 131/H2
Digby, Eng, UK 35/J5
Digne-les-Bains, Fr. 43/G4
Digoin, Fr. 42/E3
Digor, Turk. 63/G4
Digos, Phil. 81/K4
Digya NP, Gha. 103/E4
Dijon, Fr. 56/B2
Dikhil, Dji. 97/N5
Dikili, Turk. 90/A2
Diklosmta (peak), Geo. 63/H4
Díla, Eth. 97/N6
Dilbeek, Belg. 52/D2
Dilek Yarımadası NP, Turk. 90/A2
Dili, Indo. 81/G5
Dillenburg, Ger. 53/F5
Dillingen, Ger. 53/F5
Dillingen an der Donau, Ger. 54/D5
Dillingham, Ak, US 134/G4
Dillon, Mt, US 126/E4
Dillon, SC, US 133/J3
Dillsburg, Pa, US 138/A3
Dilsen, Belg. 53/E2
Dimāpur, India 83/G3
Dimaro, It. 57/G5
Dimas, Mex. 142/D4
Dimashq (cap.), Syria 90/D3
Dimbokro, C.d'Iv. 102/D5
Dimbulah, Austl. 114/B2
Dimitriya Lapteva (str.), Rus. 65/P2
Dimitrovgrad, Rus. 47/J1
Dimitrovgrad, Yugo. 47/H1
Dimitrovgrad, Bul. 47/J5
Dimlang (peak), Nga. 96/H6
Dimmitt, Tx, US 129/G4
Dimona, Isr. 91/D4
Dimovo, Bul. 49/F4
Dina, Pak. 86/B3
Dinagat (isl.), Phil. 81/G1
Dinagat, Phil. 79/E6
Dīnājpur (pol. reg.), Bang. 85/G3
Dinan, Fr. 42/B2
Dīnānagar, India 86/C3
Dinant, Belg. 53/E3
Dinar, Turk. 90/B2
Dinard, Fr. 42/B2
Dinaric Alps (mts.), 48/B3
Dinas (pt.), Wal, UK 32/B2
Dinder NP, Sudan 97/N5
Dindigul, India 82/C5
Dindori, India 84/C4
Dinga, Pak. 86/B3
Ding'an, China 83/K4
Dingbian, China 72/B3
Dingelstädt, Ger. 51/H6
Dinggyê, China 85/F1
Dingle (bay), Ire. 30/N10
Dingmans Ferry, Pa, US 138/D1
Dingnan, China 79/C3
Dingolfing, Ger. 55/F5
Dingtao, China 72/C4
Dingxi, China 70/H4
Dingxiang, China 72/C3
Dinguiraye, Gui. 102/C4
Dingyuan, China 72/D5
Dinkel (riv.), Ger. 51/E4
Dinkelsbühl, Ger. 54/D4
Dinkelscherben, Ger. 54/D5
Dinklage, Ger. 51/F3
Dinosaur Nat'l Mon., US 128/E2
Dinslaken, Ger. 50/D5
Dinsmore, Sk, Can. 126/G3
Dinté Mark (riv.), Neth. 50/B5
Dinuba, Ca, US 128/C3
Dinxperlo, Neth. 50/D5
Dion (riv.), Gui. 102/C4
Diósd, Hun. 49/Q10
Diourbel, Sen. 102/A3
Diourbel (pol. reg.), Sen. 102/A3
Dipalpur, Pak. 86/B4
Diphu, India 83/G3
Dipni (dam), Turk. 90/E2
Dipperu NP, Austl. 114/C3

Dipperz, Ger. 54/C1
Dique (canal), Col. 145/H4
Diré, Mali 102/E2
Dirē Dawa, Eth. 97/P6
Diriamba, Nic. 144/E4
Dirj, Libya 99/H3
Dirk Hartog (isl.), Austl. 109/A3
Dirksland, Neth. 50/B5
Dirlewang, Ger. 57/G2
Dirranbandi, Austl. 114/C5
Dirrington Great Law (hill), Sc, UK 36/D5
Dirty Devil (riv.), Ut, US 128/E3
Disappointment (lake), Austl. 109/B3
Disappointment (isls.), FrPol. 117/L6
Discovery (bay), Austl. 115/B3
Discovery Bay, Jam. 145/G2
Disentis-Mustér, Swi. 57/E4
Disgrazi (peak), It. 57/F5
Disko (isl.), Grld. 119/M3
Disko (Qeqertarsuaq) (isl.), Grld. 123/L2
Disneyland, Ca, US 136/G8
Dison, Belg. 53/E2
Dispur, India 83/F2
Disraëli, Qu, Can. 131/G2
Dissen am Teutoburger Wald, Ger. 51/F4
Distrito Féderal (fed. dist.), Braz. 154/A4
Distrito Federal (fed. dist.), Mex. 140/A5
Distrito Federal (fed. dist.), Ven. 153/E2
Distrito Federal (fed. dist.), Col. 152/C3
Disūq, Egypt 91/B4
Ditchling Beacon (hill), Eng, UK 33/F5
Dittaino (riv.), It. 46/D4
Dittelbrunn, Ger. 54/D2
Dittmer, Mo, US 137/F9
Ditzingen, Ger. 54/C5
Diu, India 82/B3
Diva (riv.), Yugo. 48/D4
Dive (riv.), Fr. 42/D3
Dividing Creek, NJ, US 138/C5
Divinolândia, Braz. 211/G6
Divinópolis, Braz. 155/C2
Divisa Nova, Braz. 211/G6
Divisor, Serra do (mts.), Braz. 150/D5
Divo, C.d'Iv. 102/D5
Divonne-les-Bains, Fr. 56/C5
Divriği, Turk. 62/F5
Dix (lake), Swi. 56/D5
Dixmoor, Il, US 135/Q16
Dixon, Il, US 127/L5
Dixon Entrance (str.), Can.,US 134/M4
Dixon Entrance (chan.), Can.,US 119/D4
Diyadin, Turk. 63/G5
Diyāla (gov.), Iraq 90/F3
Diyarb Najm, Egypt 91/B4
Diyarbakir (prov.), Turk. 90/E2
Diyarbakır, Turk. 90/E2
Djado (plat.), Niger 93/D2
Djakotomé, Ben. 103/F5
Djamaa, Alg. 99/G2
Djambala, Congo 96/H8
Djanet, Alg. 99/H4
Djebel-Amrag (mtn.), Alg. 100/D3
Djebel Tichka (peak), Mor. 98/C3
Djedi, Oued (riv.), Alg. 99/G2
Djelfa, Alg. 96/F1
Djema, CAfr. 97/L6
Djemila (ruin), Alg. 100/H4
Djénné, Mali 102/D3
Djibo, Burk. 103/E3
Djibouti (cap.), Djib. 97/P5
Djibouti (ctry.) 93/G3
Djougou, Ben. 103/F4
Djúpivogur, Ice. 37/P7
Dnepr (riv.), Rus. 62/D1
Dnipro (riv.), Ukr. 27/H3
Dniprodzerzhyns'k, Ukr. 62/E2
Dnipropetrovs'k, Ukr. 62/E2
Dnipropetrovs'ka (obl.), Ukr. 62/E2
Dniprovs'kyy Lyman (estu.), Ukr. 49/K2
Dnister (riv.), Ukr. 40/M4
Dnistrovs'kyy Lyman (estu.), Ukr. 49/K2
Dnyapro (riv.), Bela. 39/P4
Do (lake), Mali 103/E3
Do Rāh (pass), Afg. 89/K1
Do Son, Viet. 78/D1
Doany, Madg. 107/J6
Doba, Chad 96/J6
Dobbs Ferry, NY, US 139/K7
Dobele, Lat. 39/K3
Döbeln, Ger. 40/G3
Doberai (pen.), Indo. 81/H4
Dobiegniew, Pol. 41/H2
Dobogó-kó (peak), Hun. 49/Q9
Doboj, Bosn. 48/D3
Dobřany, Czh. 55/G3
Dobre Miasto, Pol. 39/J5
Dobrich, Bul. 49/H4
Dobříš, Czh. 55/H3
Dobruja (reg.), Bul. 49/H4
Dobrush, Bela. 62/D1
Dobryanka, Rus. 61/N4
Doce (riv.), Braz. 151/K7
Dochart (riv.), Sc, UK 36/B4
Dock Junction, Ga, US 133/H4
Docker River, Austl. 113/F3
Doctor Arroyo, Mex. 143/E4
Doctor Pedro P. Peña, Par. 157/D1
Doctor Petru Groza, Rom. 48/F2
Doda (lake), Can. 130/F1
Doda, India 86/C3
Doda (riv.), India 86/D3
Dodder (riv.), Ire. 34/B5
Doddinghurst, Eng, UK 30/D2
Dodecanese (isl.), Gre. 90/A2
Dodge City, Ks, US 129/G3
Dodger Stadium, Ca, US 136/F7
Dodgeville, Wi, US 127/L5
Dodman (pt.), Eng, UK 32/B6
Dodoma, Tanz. 104/B4
Dodoma (pol. reg.), Tanz. 104/B4
Dodori Nat'l Rsv., Kenya 104/D3
Dodsland, Sk, Can. 126/F3
Dodworth, Eng, UK 35/G4
Doesburg, Neth. 50/D4
Doetinchem, Neth. 50/D5
Doğanhisar, Turk. 90/B2
Doğankent (riv.), Turk. 62/F4
Doğanşar, Turk. 90/D1
Doğanşehir, Turk. 90/D2
Doğanyurt, Turk. 62/E4
Doğer, Turk. 62/D5
Dogliani, It. 58/A3
Dogondoutchi, Niger 103/G3
Doğubayazıt, Turk. 63/H5
Doğukaradeniz (mts.), Turk. 90/D1
Dohad, India 89/K4
Dohrīghāt, India 84/D2
Doi Khun Tan NP, Thai. 78/B2
Doilungdêqên, China 82/F2
Doiras, Embalse de (res.), Sp. 44/B1
Dois de Julho (int'l arpt.), Braz. 154/C4
Dois Irmãos, Serra (mts.), Braz. 151/K5
Doische, Belg. 53/D3
Dokka, Nor. 38/D1
Dokkum, Neth. 50/D2
Dokkumer Ee (riv.), Neth. 50/C2
Doksy, Czh. 55/H1
Dolbeau, Qu, Can. 131/F1
Dolcedorme (peak), It. 46/E3
Dole, Fr. 56/B3
Dolent (peak), Swi. 56/D6
Dolgellau, Wal, UK 32/C1
Dolgoprudnyy, Rus. 61/W9
Dolianova, It. 46/A3
Dolinsk, Rus. 71/R2
Dolj (prov.), Rom. 49/F3
Dollar, Sc, UK 36/C4
Dollar Law (peak), Sc, UK 36/C5
Dollard-des-Ormeaux, Qu, Can. 131/N7
Dollard (Dollart) (bay), Neth.,Ger. 51/E2
Doller (riv.), Fr. 40/D5
Dollnstein, Ger. 54/E5
Dolmar (peak), Ger. 54/D1
Dolmen (ruin), It. 46/E2
Dolna Banya, Bul. 47/H1
Dolni Dŭbnik, Bul. 49/G4
Dolo, Eth. 97/P7
Dolo, It. 59/F2
Dolo (riv.), It. 58/D4
Dolon, Mong. 70/J3
Dolores (riv.), US 128/E3
Dolores, Co, US 132/A2
Dolores, Guat. 144/D2
Dolores, Ven. 152/D2
Dolores, Arg. 158/F3
Dolores, Uru. 159/J10
Dolphin (cape), UK 159/F6
Dolphin and Union (str.), NW, Can. 122/E2
Dölsach, Aus. 43/K3
Dolton, Il, US 135/Q16
Dom (peak), Swi. 56/D5
Dom (peak), Indo. 81/J4
Dom Noi (res.), Thai. 78/D3
Dom Pedrito, Braz. 157/F3
Dom Pedro, Braz. 154/A2
Domat-Ems, Swi. 57/F4
Domažlice, Czh. 55/F4
Dombasle-sur-Meurthe, Fr. 53/F6
Dombay-Ul'gen (peak), Geo. 63/G4
Dombes (lake), Fr. 56/B5
Dombóvár, Hun. 48/D2
Dombrád, Hun. 48/E1
Domburg, Neth. 50/A5
Dome C, US, Ant. 160/J
Domérat, Fr. 42/E3
Domeyko, Cordillera (mts.), Chile 157/C1
Dominica (ctry.) 119/L8
Dominica Passage (chan.), Dom.,Guad. 141/N9
Dominican Republic (ctry.) 119/K8
Dommartin-lès-Remiremont, Fr. 56/C2
Dommartin-lès-Toul, Fr. 53/E6
Dommel (riv.), Belg. 53/E1
Domodedovo (int'l arpt.), Rus. 61/W9
Domodossola, It. 57/E5
Domohāni, India 85/G2
Domont, Fr. 30/J4
Dompu, Indo. 81/E5
Domrémy-la-Pucelle, Fr. 56/B1
Dömsöd, Hun. 48/D2
Domusnovas, It. 46/A3
Domuyo (vol.), Arg. 158/C3
Domvilk (mt.), Austl. 114/C5
Domžale, Slov. 43/L3
Don (ridge), Rus. 64/E5
Don (riv.), Rus. 27/J4
Don (riv.), Eng, UK 35/G5
Don Benito, Sp. 44/C3
Donabate, Ire. 34/B5
Donada, It. 59/F2
Donaghadee, NI, UK 34/C2
Donaghmore, NI, UK 34/B2
Donald, Austl. 115/B3
Donaldsonville, La, US 129/K5
Doñana NP, Sp. 44/B4
Donath, Swi. 57/F4
Donau (Danube) (riv.), Ger. 43/H2
Donaueschingen, Ger. 57/E2
Donauwörth, Ger. 54/D5
Doncaster, Eng, UK 35/G4
Donchery, Fr. 53/D4
Dondra Head (pt.), SrL. 82/D6
Donegal, Ire. 31/P9
Donegal (dist.), Ire. 34/A1
Donegal (bay), Ire. 31/P9
Donets (riv.), Ukr. 64/D5
Donets'k, Ukr. 62/F2
Donets'k (int'l arpt.), Ukr. 62/F2
Donets'ka (obl.), Ukr. 62/F3
Dong (riv.), Viet. 83/J5
Dong Ha, Viet. 78/D2
Dong Hoi, Viet. 78/D2
Dong Noi (riv.), Viet. 79/A5
Donga (riv.), Nga. 103/H4
Dongar Parāsia, India 84/B4
Dongara, Austl. 112/B4
Dongbei (plain), China 72/E2
Dongchuan, China 83/H2
Dong'e, China 72/D3
Dongen, Neth. 50/B5
Dongfang, China 83/J4
Donggou, China 73/C3
Dongguan, China 83/K3
Dongguang, China 72/D3
Donghai, China 72/D4
Dongio, Swi. 57/E5
Dongkya (pass), China 85/G2
Donglan, China 79/A3
Dongliao (riv.), China 72/F2
Dongming, China 72/C4
Dongo, It. 57/F5
Dongping, China 72/D4
Dongsha (isl.), China 79/C3
Dongshan, China 79/C3
Dongtai, China 72/E4
Dongtiao (riv.), China 72/L9
Dongting (lake), China 79/B2
Dongzhi, China 79/C1
Donihue, Chile 158/N9
Donjek (riv.), Yk, Can. 122/C2
Donji Komren, Yugo. 47/G1
Donji Vakuf, Bosn. 48/C3
Donnas, It. 58/A1
Donnersberg (peak), Ger. 53/G4
Donnybrook, Austl. 114/D4
Donnybrook, Austl. 112/B5
Donon (peak), Fr. 56/D1
Donoratico, It. 43/J5
Donzdorf, Ger. 54/C5
Donzy, Fr. 42/E3
Dooleena (peak), Austl. 112/C2
Doon (riv.), Sc, UK 36/B6
Doon (lake), Sc, UK 36/B6
Doonbeg, Ire. 31/P10
Doonerak (mt.), Ak, US 134/H2
Door (pen.), Wi, US 127/M4
Doorn (riv.), SAfr. 106/B3
Doorn, Neth. 50/C4
Doppo (peak), It. 58/D1
Doqên (lake), China 85/G1
Dora (lake), Austl. 109/B3
Dora Riparia (riv.), It. 43/G4
Dorada (coast), Sp. 45/F2
Dorchester, NB, Can. 131/H2
Dorchester, Il, US 137/H7
Dorchester, Eng, UK 32/D5
Dorchester (cape), NW, Can. 123/J2
Dorchester, NJ, US 138/D5
Dordogne (riv.), Fr. 42/D4
Dordrecht, SAfr. 106/D3
Dordrecht, Neth. 50/B5
Dore (lake), Can. 126/G2
Dore, Monts (mts.), Fr. 42/E4
Dores do Indaiá, Braz. 155/C1
Dorfen, Ger. 55/F6
Dorfen (riv.), Ger. 55/E6
Dorgali, It. 46/A2
Dori, Burk. 103/E3
Dorion, Qu, Can. 131/M7
Dorking, Eng, UK 30/C3
Dorlisheim, Fr. 56/D1
Dormagen, Ger. 53/F1
Dormans, Fr. 52/C5
Dornach, Swi. 56/D3
Dornbirn, Aus. 57/F3
Dorney Park/ Wildwater Kingdom, Pa, US 138/C2
Dornhan, Ger. 57/E1
Dorno, It. 58/B2
Dornoch Firth (inlet), Sc, UK 36/B1
Dornod (prov.), Mong. 71/K2
Dornogovĭ (prov.), Mong. 71/J3
Dornstadt, Ger. 54/C6
Dornstetten, Ger. 54/B6
Dorog, Hun. 49/Q9
Dorothy, NJ, US 138/D5
Dörpen, Ger. 51/E3
Dorre (isl.), Austl. 112/B3
Dorrigo, Austl. 115/E1
Dorrigo NP, Austl. 115/E1
Dorsale (mts.), Tun. 46/A5
Dorsbach (riv.), Ger. 54/B2
Dorset (co.), Eng, UK 32/D5
Dorsey, Il, US 137/G8
Dorsten, Ger. 50/D5
Dortan, Fr. 56/B5
Dortmund, Ger. 51/E5
Dortmund-Ems (canal), Ger. 51/E4
Dortmund (Wickede) (int'l arpt.), Ger. 51/E5
Dörtyol, Turk. 91/E1
Dorum, Ger. 51/F1
Dorval, Qu, Can. 131/N7
Dörverden, Ger. 51/G3
Dos Bahías (cape), Arg. 158/D5
Dos de Mayo, Peru 156/C2
Dos Hermanas, Sp. 44/C4
Döşemealtı, Turk. 91/B1
Dosewallips (riv.), Wa, US 135/A2
Dōshi, Japan 77/C2
Dōshi (riv.), Japan 77/C2
Dosse (riv.), Ger. 40/G2
Dosso, Niger 103/F3
Dosso (dept.), Niger 103/F3
Dosson, It. 59/F1
Dossor, Kaz. 63/K3
Dot Lake, Ak, US 134/K3
Dothan, Al, US 133/G4
Dötlingen, Ger. 51/F3
Döttingen, Swi. 57/E2
Douai, Fr. 52/C3
Douala, Camr. 96/G7
Douar el Cäid el Gueddara, Mor. 100/A2
Douar Toulal, Mor. 100/B3
Douarnenez, Fr. 42/A2
Douarnenez, Baie de (bay), Fr. 42/A2
Double Island (pt.), Austl. 114/D4
Double Mountain Fork Brazos (riv.), Tx, US 129/G4
Double Mtn. Fork (riv.), Tx, US 143/E1
Doubs (riv.), Fr. 42/F3
Doubs (dept.), Fr. 56/C3
Doubs, Fr. 56/C4
Doubtful Island (bay), Austl. 112/C5
Douchy-les-Mines, Fr. 52/C3
Doue, Fr. 30/M5
Doué-la-Fontaine, Fr. 42/C3
Douentza, Mali 102/E3
Dougga (ruin), Tun. 100/L6
Douglas (mt.), Ak, US 134/H4
Douglas, Wy, US 127/G5
Douglas, Ga, US 133/H4
Douglas, SAfr. 106/C3
Douglas (co.), Co, US 137/C4
Douglas, Sc, UK 36/C5
Douglas (cap.), IM, UK 34/D3
Douglassville, Pa, US 138/C3
Doulaincourt-Saucourt, Fr. 56/B1
Doullens, Fr. 52/B3
Doune, Sc, UK 36/B4
Doune (peak), Sc, UK 36/B4
Doupovské Hory (mts.), Czh. 43/K1
Dour, Belg. 52/C3
Dourados, Braz. 151/H8
Dourdan, Fr. 30/J6
Dourdou (riv.), Fr. 42/E4
Dourh (peak), Mor. 99/E2
Douro (riv.), Port. 44/B2
Dousman, Wi, US 135/P13
Doussard, Fr. 56/C6
Douvaine, Fr. 56/C5
Douvrin, Fr. 52/B2
Doux (riv.), Fr. 42/F4
Douze (riv.), Fr. 42/C4
Dove Creek, Co, US 128/E3
Dover, Austl. 115/C4
Dover, Eng, UK 33/H4
Dover (pt.), Austl. 112/E5
Dover, Pa, US 138/B4
Dover, NJ, US 138/D2
Dover (cap.), De, US 138/C5
Dover-Foxcroft, Me, US 131/G2
Dover, Strait of (str.), Fr.,UK 42/D1
Dovrefjell NP, Nor. 37/D3
Dow, Il, US 137/G7
Dowerin, Austl. 112/C4
Dowlatābād, Iran 89/G3
Down (dist.), NI, UK 34/C3
Downers Grove, Il, US 135/P16
Downey, Ca, US 136/F8
Downieville, Ca, US 128/B3
Downingtown, Pa, US 138/C4
Downpatrick, NI, UK 34/C3
Doylestown, Pa, US 138/C3
Dōzen (isl.), Japan 74/C3
Dozois (res.), Can. 130/E2
Drâa (cape), Mor. 98/C3
Drâa, Oued (riv.), Mor. 93/B2
Drac (riv.), Fr. 42/F4
Dracena, Braz. 155/B2
Drachten, Neth. 50/D2
Drăgănești-Olt, Rom. 49/G3
Dragoman, Bul. 47/H1
Dragon's Mouth (str.), Trin.,Ven. 153/F2
Draguignan, Fr. 43/G5
Drake (passg.) 157/C8
Drake, Co, US 137/B2
Drake (passg.), SAm. 159/D8
Drakensberg (mts.), SAfr. 93/E8
Dráma, Gre. 47/J2
Drammen, Nor. 38/D2
Drance (riv.), Swi. 56/D5
Drancy, Fr. 30/K5
Drangedal, Nor. 38/C2
Dranse (riv.), Fr. 56/C5
Dransfeld, Ger. 51/G5
Draper, Ut, US 137/K12
Drau (riv.), Aus. 43/K3
Drava (riv.), Slov. 43/L3
Dráva (riv.), Aus. 48/C3
Draveil, Fr. 30/K5
Drawa (riv.), Pol. 41/H2
Drawieński NP, Pol. 41/H2
Drawsko Pomorskie, Pol. 41/H2
Drayton, ND, US 127/J3
Drayton Valley, Ab, Can. 126/E2
Dreghorn, Sc, UK 36/B5
Drei Zinnen (peak), PNG 81/K4
Dreiesselberg (peak), Ger. 55/G5
Dreisam (riv.), Ger. 56/D2
Drensteinfurt, Ger. 51/E5
Drenthe (prov.), Neth. 50/D3
Drentse Hoofdvaart (riv.), Neth. 50/D3
Drentwede, Ger. 51/F3
Dresano, It. 58/C2
Dresden, Ger. 64/B4
Drezdenko, Pol. 41/H2
Driebergen, Neth. 50/C4
Driedorf, Ger. 53/H2
Drigh Road, Pak. 89/J4
Drimoleague, Ire. 31/P11
Drin (gulf), Alb. 47/F2
Drin (riv.), Alb. 47/F1
Drina (riv.), Bosn. 48/D4
Drniš, Cro. 48/C4
Dro, It. 57/G6
Drøbak, Nor. 38/D2
Drobeta-Turnu Severin, Rom. 48/F3
Drochtersen, Ger. 51/G1
Drocourt, Fr. 30/H4
Drogheda, Ire. 34/B4
Drohobych, Ukr. 62/B2
Droitwich, Eng, UK 32/D2
Drolshagen, Ger. 53/G1
Dromiskin, Ire. 34/B4
Dromore (riv.), Ire. 34/A3
Dromore, NI, UK 34/B3
Dronero, It. 43/G4
Dronfield, Eng, UK 35/G5
Drongan, Sc, UK 36/B6
Dronne (riv.), Fr. 42/D4
Dronten, Neth. 50/C3
Dropt (riv.), Fr. 42/D4
Drouette (riv.), Fr. 52/A6
Drowning (riv.), Can. 130/C1
Drumbeg, NI, UK 34/C2
Drumcar, Ire. 34/B4
Drumheller, Ab, Can. 126/E3
Drumleck (pt.), Ire. 34/B5
Drummond (range), Austl. 109/D3
Drummond (pt.), Austl. 113/G5
Drummond (mt.), Austl. 114/B4
Drummondville, Qu, Can. 131/F2
Drumochter, Pass of (pass), Sc, UK 36/B3
Drunen, Neth. 50/C5
Druridge (bay), Eng, UK 35/G1
Drusenheim, Fr. 53/G6
Druskininkai, Lith. 39/K4
Druten, Neth. 50/C5
Drvar, Bosn. 48/C3
Drwęca (riv.), Pol. 41/K2
Dry Fork Cheyenne (riv.), Wy, US 129/F2
Dry Tortugas (isl.), Fl, US 133/H5
Dry Tortugas NP, Fl, US 133/H5
Dry Tortugas NP, Fl, US 140/E3
Dryanovo, Bul. 47/J1
Dryden, On, Can. 127/K3
Dryden, Tx, US 132/C4
Dryden, Mi, US 135/F6
Drygarn Fawr (peak), Wal, UK 32/C2
Du Bois, Pa, US 130/E3
Du Page (riv.), Il, US 135/P16
Du Page (co.), Il, US 135/P16
Du Page, East Br. (riv.), Il, US 135/P16
Du Quoin, Il, US 129/K3
Duaringa, Austl. 114/C3
Duarte (peak), DRep. 141/G4
Duarte, Ca, US 136/G7
Dubawnt (riv.), NW, Can. 122/F2
Dubawnt (lake), NW, Can. 122/F2
Dubayy, UAE 89/G3
Dubbo, Austl. 115/D2
Dübendorf, Swi. 57/E3
Dübener Heide (phys. reg.), Ger. 40/G3
Dubino, It. 57/F5
Dublin, Ga, US 133/H3
Dublin, Pa, US 138/C3
Dublin, Md, US 138/B4
Dublin, Ca, US 135/L11
Dublin (co.), Ire. 34/B5
Dublin (cap.), Ire. 34/B5
Dubna, Rus. 60/H4
Dubnica nad Váhom, Slvk. 41/K4
Dubno, Ukr. 62/C2
Dubois, Wy, US 126/F5
Duboistown, Pa, US 138/A1
Dubossary (res.), Mol. 49/J2
Dubrājpur, India 85/F4
Dubrovnik, Cro. 47/F1
Dubrovnik (int'l arpt.), Cro. 47/F1
Dubuque, Ia, US 127/L5
Duchang, China 79/C2
Duchcov, Czh. 55/G1
Duchesne (riv.), Ut, US 128/E2
Duchesne, Ut, US 128/E2
Ducie (isl.), Pitc. 117/N7
Duck (riv.), Tn, US 130/C5
Duck (lake), Mi, US 135/E7
Duckabush (riv.), Wa, US 135/A2
Duda (riv.), Col. 152/C4
Duddon (riv.), Eng, UK 35/E3
Dudelange, Lux. 53/F5
Dudenhofen, Ger. 54/B4
Duderstadt, Ger. 51/H5
Dudh Kosi (riv.), Nepal 85/F2
Dūdhi, India 84/D3
Dudhwa NP, India 84/C1
Dudignac, Arg. 158/E2
Düdingen, Swi. 56/D4
Dudinka, Rus. 64/J3
Dudley, Eng, UK 32/D1
Dueñas, Sp. 44/C2
Duero (riv.), Sp. 44/C2
Dueville, It. 59/E1
Dufaja (riv.), Kenya 104/C3
Duff (isls.), Sol. 116/F5
Duffel, Belg. 53/D1
Dufftown, Sc, UK 36/C2
Dufour (Dufourspitze) (peak), Swi. 58/A1
Dufourspitze (peak), Swi. 43/G4
Dugi Otok (isl.), Cro. 48/B3
Dugny-sur-Meuse, Fr. 53/E5
Dugo Selo, Cro. 48/C3
Dugway, Ut, US 128/D2
Duich (lake), Sc, UK 36/A2
Duida (peak), Ven. 153/E4
Duida Marahuaca, PN, Ven. 150/E3
Duingen, Ger. 51/G4
Duisburg, Ger. 50/D6
Duitama, Col. 152/C3
Duiven, Neth. 50/D5
Duke of Gloucester (isls.), FrPol. 117/L7
Duke's (pass), Sc, UK 36/B4
Dukielska (Dukla Pass) (pass), Pol. 41/L4
Dulan, China 70/G4
Dulce (riv.), Arg. 157/D2
Dulce, NM, US 128/F3
Dulce (gulf), Pan. 145/F4
Dulce Nombre de Culmí, Hon. 144/E3
Duleek, Ire. 34/B4
Dulgopol, Bul. 49/H4
Duliu (riv.), China 83/J2
Dullewāla, Pak. 86/A4
Dülmen, Ger. 51/E5
Dulnain (riv.), Sc, UK 36/C2
Dulovo, Bul. 49/H4
Dumalinao, Phil. 79/D6
Dumaran (isl.), Phil. 81/E1
Dumaresq (riv.), Austl. 115/D1
Dumas, Ar, US 129/K4
Dumas, Tx, US 129/G4
Dumbarton, Sc, UK 36/B5
Ďumbier (peak), Slvk. 41/K4
Dumbleyung, Austl. 112/C5
Dumbrăveni, Rom. 49/G2
Dume (pt.), Ca, US 136/B2
Dumfries, Sc, UK 34/E1
Dumfries and Galloway (pol. reg.), Sc, UK 36/C6
Dumka, India 85/F3
Dumlu, Turk. 63/G4
Dümmer (lake), Ger. 51/F3
Dumoine (riv.), Can. 130/E2
Dumoine (lake), Qu, Can. 123/J4
Dumont, NJ, US 139/K8
Dumont d'Urville, Fr., Ant. 160/K
Dumraon, India 85/E3
Dumyāt (gov.), Egypt 101/B1
Dún Laoghaire, Ire. 34/B5
Dun Rig (peak), Sc, UK 36/C5
Dunaföldvár, Hun. 48/D2
Dunaharaszti, Hun. 49/R10
Dunajec (riv.), Pol. 41/L4
Dunakeszi, Hun. 49/R9
Dunany (pt.), Ire. 34/B4
Dunaszekcső, Hun. 48/D2
Dunaújváros, Hun. 48/D2
Dunavecse, Hun. 48/D2
Dunavtsi, Bul. 48/F4
Dunbar, Sc, UK 36/D5
Dunblane, Sc, UK 36/C4
Dunboyne, Ire. 34/B5
Duncan, BC, Can. 126/C3
Duncan, Ok, US 129/H4
Duncannon, Pa, US 138/A3
Duncansby Head (pt.), Sc, UK 31/V14
Duncanville, Tx, US 132/D3
Dund-Us, Mong. 70/F2
Dundalk (bay), Ire. 31/Q10
Dundalk, Md, US 138/B5
Dundalk, Ire. 34/B4
Dundas (lake), Austl. 109/B4
Dundas, On, Can. 131/Q9
Dundas (pen.), NW, Can. 123/R7
Dundee, SAfr. 107/E3
Dundee, Sc, UK 36/D4
Dundgovĭ (prov.), Mong. 70/J2
Dundonald, Sc, UK 36/B5
Dundrum, NI, UK 34/C3
Dundrum (bay), NI, UK 34/C3
Dundurn, Sk, Can. 126/G3
Dundwa (range), Nepal 84/D2
Dundwārāganj, India 84/B2
Dunedin, Fl, US 133/H4
Dunedin, NZ 117/S12
Dunedoo, Austl. 115/D2
Dunellen, NJ, US 139/H9
Dunfanaghy, Ire. 31/Q9
Dunfermline, Sc, UK 36/C4
Dunga Bunga, Pak. 86/B5
Dungannon (co.), NI, UK 34/B3
Dungannon, NI, UK 34/B3
Dungarpur, India 89/K4
Dungarvan, Ire. 31/Q10
Dungau (reg.), Ger. 55/F5
Dungeness (pt.), Eng, UK 33/G5
Dungeness (pt.), Arg. 159/C7
Dungiven, NI, UK 34/B2
Dunglow, Ire. 31/P9
Dungog, Austl. 115/D2
Dungu, D.R. Congo 104/A2
Dungu (riv.), D.R. Congo 104/A2
Dunhua, China 71/N3
Dunhuang, China 70/F3
Dunkeld, Sc, UK 36/C3
Dunkerque (Dunkirk), Fr. 42/E1
Dunkery (hill), Eng, UK 32/C4
Dunkirk (Dunkerque), Fr. 42/E1
Dunkwa, Gha. 103/E5
Dunleer, Ire. 34/B4
Dunloy, NI, UK 34/B2
Dunmanway, Ire. 31/P11
Dunmurry, NI, UK 34/B2
Dunn, NC, US 133/J3
Dunnamanagh, NI, UK 34/A2
Dünnern (riv.), Swi. 56/D3
Dunnet Head (pt.), Sc, UK 31/V14
Dunningen, Ger. 57/E1
Dunnville, On, Can. 131/Q10
Dunolly, Austl. 115/B3
Dunoon, Sc, UK 36/B5
Dunqulah, Sudan 101/B5
Duns, Sc, UK 36/D5
Dunsborough, Austl. 112/B5
Dunseith, ND, US 127/H3
Dunshaughlin, Ire. 34/B4
Dunsmuir, Ca, US 128/B2
Dunstable, Eng, UK 33/F3
Dunyāpur, Pak. 86/A5
Duolun, China 71/L3
Dupo, Il, US 137/G8
Dupont, Pa, US 138/C1
Dupree, SD, US 127/H4
Dupuy (cape), Austl. 112/B2
Duque de Caxias, Braz. 211/K7
Duque de York (isl.), Chile 159/A6
Dūrā, WBnk. 91/D4
Durağan, Turk. 62/E4
Durak, Turk. 91/D1
Durance (riv.), Fr. 42/F5
Durango (state), Mex. 140/A3
Durango, Sp. 44/D1
Durango de Victoria, Mex. 142/D3
Durant, Ok, US 129/H4
Durazno (dept.), Uru. 159/F2
Durazno, Uru. 159/K10
Durban, SAfr. 107/E3
Durbanville, SAfr. 106/L10
Durbion (riv.), Fr. 56/C1
Durbuy, Belg. 53/E3
Dúrcal, Sp. 44/D4
Durdevac, Cro. 48/C2
Durdevo, Yugo. 48/E3
Düren, Ger. 53/F2
Durg, India 84/D4
Durgāpur, India 85/F4
Durham, NH, US 131/G3
Durham, NC, US 133/J3
Durham (co.), Eng, UK 35/F2
Durham, Eng, UK 35/G2
Durlston (pt.), Eng, UK 32/E5
Durmitor NP, Yugo. 47/F1
Durnford (pt.), WSah. 98/B5
Dürrenroth, Swi. 56/D3
Durrës, Alb. 47/F2
Dürrlauingen, Ger. 54/D6
Dürrwangen, Ger. 54/D4
Dursunbey, Turk. 62/D5
Durūz (peak), Syria 91/E3
D'Urville (cape), Indo. 81/J4
Dusanovo, Yugo. 47/G1
Dusey (riv.), Can. 127/M3
Dushan, China 83/J2
Dushanbe (cap.), Taj. 87/E5
Dushanbe (int'l arpt.), Taj. 87/E5
Düsseldorf (int'l arpt.), Ger. 50/D6
Düsseldorf, Ger. 50/D6
Duszniki-Zdrój, Pol. 41/J3
Dutch (riv.), Eng, UK 35/H4
Dutch Harbor, Ak, US 134/E5
Dutch Wonderland, Pa, US 138/B3
Dutoitspiek (peak), SAfr. 106/L10
Dutse, Nga. 103/H4
Duvall, Wa, US 135/D2
Duvno, Bosn. 48/C4
Duyun, China 83/J2
Düzce, Turk. 49/K5
Düzici, Turk. 90/D2
Dve Mogili, Bul. 49/G4
Dvina (bay), Rus. 60/H2
Dvořiště (lake), Czh. 55/H4
Dwārka, India 89/J4
Dwārkeswar (riv.), India 85/F4
Dworshak (res.), Id, US 126/D4
Dwyfor (riv.), Wal, UK 34/D6
Dwyka (riv.), SAfr. 106/C4
Dyat'kovo, Rus. 62/E1
Dybvad, Den. 38/D3
Dyce (int'l arpt.), Sc, UK 36/D2
Dyce, Sc, UK 36/D2
Dye, Mo, US 137/D5
Dyer, In, US 130/C3
Dyer (cape), NW, Can. 123/K2
Dyer (cape), Chile 159/B6
Dyfed (co.), Wal, UK 32/B2
Dyfi (riv.), Wal, UK 32/C1
Dyje (riv.), Czh. 41/J4
Dykh-tau (peak), Rus. 63/G4
Dyle (riv.), Belg. 40/C3
Dyleň (peak), Czh. 55/F3
Dylewska (peak), Pol. 41/K2
Dysart, Austl. 114/C3
Dysselsdorp, SAfr. 106/C4
Dyul'tydag (peak), Rus. 63/H4
Dzaoudzi (int'l arpt.), May. 107/H6
Dzaoudzi (cap.), May. 107/H6
Dzavhan (prov.), Mong. 70/G2
Dzavhan (riv.), Mong. 70/F2
Dzenzik (pt.), Ukr. 62/F3
Dzerzhinsk, Rus. 60/J4
Dzhankoy, Ukr. 62/E3
Dzharylgach (gulf), Ukr. 49/L2
Dzhebel, Bul. 47/J2
Dzhugdzhur (range), Rus. 67/N4
Działdowo, Pol. 41/L2
Dzibalchén, Mex. 144/D2
Dzibilchaltún (ruin), Mex. 144/D1
Dzidzantún, Mex. 144/D1
Dzierżoniów, Pol. 41/J3
Dzitbalché, Mex. 144/D1
Dziuché, Mex. 144/D2
Dzukija NP, Lith. 39/L4
Dzungarian (basin), China 64/J5
Dzur, Mong. 70/G2
Dzüünbayan, Mong. 71/K3
Dzüünbulag, Mong. 71/K2
Dzüünharaa, Mong. 70/J2
Dzuunmod, Mong. 70/J2

E

Eads, Co, US 129/G3
Eagle, Ak, US 134/K3
Eagle (lake), Wi, US 127/K3
Eagle (mtn.), Mn, US 127/L4
Eagle (lake), Ca, US 126/C5
Eagle, Co, US 128/F3
Eagle (lake), Can. 130/A1
Eagle (riv.), Nf, Can. 123/L3
Eagle, Wi, US 135/P14
Eagle Butte, SD, US 127/H4
Eagle Pass, Tx, US 132/C4
Eagle River, Wi, US 127/L4
Eaglesham, Sc, UK 36/B5
Ealing (bor.), Eng, UK 30/B2
Ear Falls, On, Can. 127/K3
Earle Naval Weapons Center, NJ, US 138/D3
Earlimart, Ca, US 128/C4
Earl's Seat (peak), Sc, UK 36/B4
Earlston, Sc, UK 36/D5
Earn (riv.), Sc, UK 36/C4
Earn (lake), Sc, UK 36/B4
Easley, SC, US 133/H3
East (cape), NZ 117/T10
East (cape), Ak, US 134/B6
East (mt.), Austl. 112/D4
East (pt.), NJ, US 138/C5
East (passg.), Wa, US 135/C3
East (riv.), NY, US 139/K8
East Alton, Il, US 137/G8
East Anglia (reg.), Eng, UK 33/H2
East Angus, Qu, Can. 131/G2
East Bangor, Pa, US 138/C2
East Berbice-Corentyne (pol. reg.), Guy. 153/G3
East Berlin, Pa, US 138/B4
East Berwick, Pa, US 138/B1
East Brunswick, NJ, US 139/H10
East Caicos (isl.), UK 145/J1
East Canyon (res.), Ut, US 137/K12
East Carondelet, Il, US 137/G8
East China (sea), Asia 67/M6
East Dart (riv.), Eng, UK 32/C5
East Dereham, Eng, UK 33/G1
East Falkland (isl.), UK 147/D8
East Farmingdale, NY, US 139/M9
East Frisian (isls.), Ger. 40/D2
East Glen (riv.), Eng, UK 35/H6
East Greenville, Pa, US 138/C3
East Grinstead, Eng, UK 33/F4
East Hampton, NY, US 139/F2
East Haven, Ct, US 139/F1
East Helena, Mt, US 126/F4
East Hill-Meridian, Wa, US 135/C3
East Hills, NY, US 139/L8
East Jordan, Mi, US 130/C2
East Kilbride, Sc, UK 36/B5
East Korea (bay), NKor. 71/N4
East Lamma (chan.), China 71/U11
East Lansing, Mi, US 130/C3
East Leavenworth, Mo, US 137/D5
East Linton, Sc, UK 36/D5
East Liverpool, Oh, US 130/D3
East London, SAfr. 106/D4
East Los Angeles, Ca, US 136/F7
East Lynne, Mo, US 137/E6
East Meadow, NY, US 139/L9
East Midlands (int'l arpt.), Eng, UK 35/G6
East Millcreek, Ut, US 137/K12
East Millinocket, Me, US 131/G2
East Newark, NJ, US 139/J9
East Newbern, Il, US 137/G7
East Nishnabotna (riv.), US 129/J2
East Northport, NY, US 139/E2
East Orange, NJ, US 139/J8
East Peckham, Eng, UK 30/E3
East Petersburg, Pa, US 138/B3
East Point, Ga, US 133/G3
East Pointe (East Detroit), Mi, US 135/G7
East Port Orchard, Wa, US 135/B2
East Prospect, Pa, US 138/B4
East Quogue, NY, US 139/F2
East Retford, Eng, UK 35/H5
East Rockaway, NY, US 139/L9
East Rutherford, NJ, US 139/J8
East Saint Louis, Il, US 137/G8
East Siberian (sea), Rus. 65/S2
East Side, Pa, US 138/C1
East Stroudsburg, Pa, US 138/C2
East Sussex (co.), Eng, UK 33/G5
East Tawas, Mi, US 130/D2
East Troy, Wi, US 135/P14
East Wemyss, Sc, UK 36/C4
East Wenatchee, Wa, US 126/C4
East Windsor, NJ, US 138/D3
East York, Can. 131/R8
Eastbourne, Eng, UK 33/G5
Eastern (prov.), Zam. 104/B5
Eastern (pol. reg.), Gha. 103/E5
Eastern (chan.), Japan 74/A4
Eastern (prov.), SLeo. 102/C4
Eastern (bay), Md, US 138/B6
Eastern (plain), Eng, UK 35/H4
Eastern Ghats (mts.), India 82/C5
Eastern Neck Island NWR, Md, US 138/B5
Eastern Sayans (mts.), Rus. 64/K4
Easterville, Mb, Can. 127/J2
Eastlake, Co, US 137/C3
Eastleigh (int'l arpt.), Eng, UK 33/E5
Eastleigh, Eng, UK 33/E5
Eastmain (riv.), Qu, Can. 123/J3
Eastman, Ga, US 133/H3
Easton (res.), Ct, US 139/E1
Easton, Pa, US 138/C2
Easton, Ct, US 139/E1
Eastport, Me, US 131/H2
Eastport, NY, US 139/F2
Eastriggs, Sc, UK 35/E2
Eastwood, Eng, UK 35/G6
Eaton, Co, US 137/C1
Eatonia, Sk, Can. 126/F3
Eatons Neck (pt.), NY, US 139/M8
Eatontown, NJ, US 138/D3
Eau (riv.), Eng, UK 35/H5
Eau Claire (lake), Qu, Can. 123/J3
Eau d'Heure (riv.), Belg. 53/D3
Eau d'Heure, Barrage de l' (dam), Belg. 53/D3
Eaubonne, Fr. 30/J5
Eaulne (riv.), Fr. 52/A4
Eauripik (isl.), Micr. 116/D4
Eauze, Fr. 42/D5
Ebano, Mex. 144/B1
Ebble (riv.), Eng, UK 33/E4
Ebbw Vale, Wal, UK 32/C3
Ebebiyín, EqG. 96/H7
Ebeggi (well), Alg. 99/G5
Ebeleben, Ger. 51/H6
Ebeltoft, Den. 38/D3
Ebensee, Aus. 43/K3
Eberbach, Ger. 54/B4
Ebergassing, Aus. 49/P7
Ebergötzen, Ger. 51/H5
Ebermannstadt, Ger. 54/E3
Ebern, Ger. 54/D2
Ebersbach an der Fils, Ger. 54/C5
Ebersberg, Ger. 55/E6
Eberschwang, Aus. 55/G6
Ebersheim, Fr. 56/D1
Eberswalde-Finow, Ger. 41/G2
Ebetsu, Japan 76/B2
Ebian, China 83/H2

Ebina, Japan 77/C3
Ebnat-Kappel, Swi. 57/F3
Ebo (lake), Mali 102/E3
Eboli, It. 46/D2
Ebolowa, Camr. 96/H7
Ebon (isl.), Mrsh. 116/F4
Ebrach, Ger. 54/D3
Ebreichsdorf, Aus. 49/N8
Ebro (riv.), Sp. 27/D4
Ebstorf, Ger. 51/H2
Ecatepec, Mex. 143/Q9
Ecclefechan, Sc, UK 35/E1
Eccles, Eng, UK 35/F5
Eceabat, Turk. 49/H5
Echallens, Swi. 56/C4
Echarate, Peru 156/C4
Echaz (riv.), Ger. 54/C6
Éché Fadadinga (riv.), Niger 103/H3
Echigawa, Japan 77/K5
Eching, Ger. 55/E6
Échirolles, Fr. 42/F4
Echo, Ut, US 137/L12
Echo (lake), NJ, US 138/D1
Echoing (riv.), Can. 127/L2
Echt, Neth. 53/E1
Echterdingen (int'l arpt.), Ger. 54/C5
Echternach, Lux. 53/F4
Echuca, Austl. 115/C3
Echunga, Austl. 113/M9
Echzell, Ger. 54/B2
Écija, Sp. 44/C4
Ečka, Yugo. 48/E3
Eckernförde, Ger. 38/C4
Eckerö (isl.), Fin. 39/H1
Eckerö, Fin. 39/H1
Eclipse Sound (bay), NW, Can. 123/H1
Écommoy, Fr. 42/D3
Ecoporanga, Braz. 154/B5
Ecorse (riv.), Mi, US 135/F7
Ecorse, Mi, US 135/F7
Écouen, Fr. 30/K4
Ecquevilly, Fr. 30/H5
Ecrins, PN des, Fr. 43/G4
Ecrosnes, Fr. 30/H6
Écrouves, Fr. 53/E6
Ecuador (ctry.) 147/A2
Ecublens, Swi. 56/C4
Ed, Swe. 38/D2
Eday (isl.), Sc, UK 31/V14
Eddystone (pt.), Austl. 115/D4
Eddystone Rocks (isls.), Eng, UK 32/B6
Ede, Nga. 103/G5
Ede, Neth. 50/C4
Edéa, Camr. 96/H7
Edegem, Belg. 53/D1
Edehin Ouarene (des.), Alg. 99/G4
Edéia, Braz. 155/B1
Edelény, Hun. 41/L4
Edemissen, Ger. 51/H4
Eden, Austl. 115/D3
Eden, NC, US 130/E4
Eden, Ut, US 137/K11
Eden (riv.), Sc, UK 36/D4
Edenbridge, Eng, UK 30/D3
Edenburg, SAfr. 106/D3
Edendale, SAfr. 107/E3
Edenhope, Austl. 115/B3
Edenkoben, Ger. 54/B4
Edenside (valley), Eng, UK 35/F2
Edenton, NC, US 133/J2
Eder (riv.), Ger. 40/E3
Eder-Stausee (lake), Ger. 51/F6
Edewecht, Ger. 51/E2
Edgar (mt.), Austl. 112/D2
Edge (isl.), Sval. 160/E
Edgecumbe (cape), Ak, US 134/L4
Edgell (isl.), NW, Can. 123/K2
Edgemere, Md, US 138/B5
Edgemont, Ut, US 137/K13
Edgerton, Wy, US 127/G5
Edgewater, Co, US 137/B3
Edgewater Park, NJ, US 138/D3
Edgewood, Pa, US 138/B2
Edgewood, Md, US 138/B5
Edgewood Arsenal, Md, US 138/B5
Edgewood-North Hill, Wa, US 135/C3
Édhessa, Gre. 47/H2
Edinboro, Pa, US 130/D3
Edinburg, Tx, US 132/D5
Edinburgh (cap.), Sc, UK 36/C5
Edirne (prov.), Turk. 62/C4
Edirne, Turk. 47/K2
Edison, NJ, US 139/H9
Edison International Field, Ca, US 136/G8
Edison Nat'l Hist. Site, NJ, US 139/J8
Edisto Island, SC, US 133/H3
Edisto, South Fork (riv.), SC, US 133/H3
Edithburgh, Austl. 113/H5
Édjérir (riv.), Mali 103/F2
Edmond, Ok, US 137/N14
Edmonds, Wa, US 126/C4
Edmonton (int'l arpt.), Can. 126/E2
Edmonton (cap.), Ab, Can. 126/E2
Edmund Kennedy NP, Austl. 114/B2
Edmundston, NB, Can. 131/G2
Edna, Tx, US 129/H5
Edna Bay, Ak, US 134/M4
Edo (state), Nga. 103/G5
Edo (riv.), Japan 77/D2
Edolo, It. 57/G5
Edosaki, Japan 77/E2
Edremit, Turk. 62/C5
Edremit (gulf), Gre.,Turk 62/C5
Edsbyn, Swe. 38/F1
Edson, Ab, Can. 126/D2
Eduardo Castex, Arg. 158/D2
Edward (mt.), Austl. 113/F2
Edward (lake), D.R. Congo 93/E5
Edward River Aboriginal Community, Austl. 114/A1
Edward VII (pen.), Ant. 160/P
Edward VIII (bay), Ant. 160/D
Edwards (riv.), Il, US 129/K2
Edwards (plat.), Tx, US 124/F5
Edwardsville, Il, US 137/H8
Edwardsville, Ks, US 137/D5
Edwardsville, Pa, US 138/C1
Edzell, Sc, UK 36/D3
Edzná (ruin), Mex. 144/D2
Eek, Ak, US 134/F3
Eeklo, Belg. 52/C1
Eel (riv.), Ca, US 128/B3
Eelde-Paterswolde, Neth. 50/D2
Eem (riv.), Neth. 50/C4
Eemenes, Neth. 50/C4
Eems (Ems) (riv.), Ger., Neth 50/D2
Eemshaven (har.), Neth. 50/D2
Eemskanaal (riv.), Neth. 50/D2
Eersel, Neth. 50/C6
Efate (isl.), Van. 116/F6
Eferding, Aus. 55/H6
Effigy Mounds Nat'l Mon., Ia, US 127/L5
Effingham, Il, US 129/K3
Effingham, On, Can. 131/R9
Effon Alaiye, Nga. 103/G5
Effort, Pa, US 138/C2
Eforie, Rom. 49/J3
Efringen-Kirchen, Ger. 56/D2
Efyrnwy, Llyn (lake), Wal, UK 34/E6
Egadi (isls.), It. 46/B3
Egan (range), Nv, US 128/D3
Egan (riv.), Ger. 54/D5
Egaña, Uru. 159/K10
Egegik, Ak, US 134/G4
Eger (riv.), Ger. 40/G3
Eger, Hun. 41/L5
Egeskov, Den. 38/D4
Egestorf, Ger. 51/H2
Egg, Aus. 57/F3
Egg, Swi. 57/E3
Egg Harbor City, NJ, US 138/D4
Egg Island (pt.), NJ, US 138/C5
Eggebek, Ger. 38/C4
Eggegebirge (ridge), Ger. 51/F5
Eggelsberg, Aus. 55/F6
Eggenburg, Aus. 43/L2
Eggenfelden, Ger. 55/F6
Eggenstein-Leopoldshafen, Ger. 54/B4
Eggesin, Ger. 38/F5
Eggiwil, Swi. 56/D4
Egglescliffe, Eng, UK 35/G3
Eggstätt, Ger. 55/F7
Egham, Eng, UK 30/B2
Éghezée, Belg. 53/D2
Egilsstadhir, Ice. 37/P6
Égletons, Fr. 42/E4
Eglinton (isl.), NW, Can. 123/R7
Eglinton, NI, UK 34/A1
Eglisau, Swi. 57/E2
Égly, Fr. 30/J6
Egmond aan Zee, Neth. 50/B3
Egmont (cape), NZ 117/S10
Egmont (mt.), NZ 117/S10
Egna (Neumarkt), It. 57/H5
Egnach, Swi. 57/F2
Eğridir, Turk. 90/B2
Eğridir (lake), Turk. 90/B2
Éguas, Rio das (riv.), Braz. 154/A4
Egypt (ctry.) 93/E2
Ehebach (riv.), Ger. 54/D3
Ehekirchen, Ger. 54/D5
Ehime (pref.), Japan 74/C4
Ehingen, Ger. 57/F1
Ehingen, Ger. 54/D4
Ehringshausen, Ger. 54/B1
Ehrwald, Aus. 57/G3
Eibar, Sp. 44/D1
Eibelstadt, Ger. 54/C3
Eibenstock, Ger. 55/F1
Eibergen, Neth. 50/D4
Eich, Ger. 54/B3
Eichel (riv.), Fr. 53/G6
Eichenau, Ger. 54/E6
Eichenbühl, Ger. 54/C3
Eichendorf, Ger. 55/F5
Eichenzell, Ger. 54/C2
Eichstätt, Ger. 54/E5
Eichwalde, Ger. 40/Q7
Eicklingen, Ger. 51/H3
Eid, Nor. 37/C3
Eidfjord, Nor. 38/B1
Eidsvold, Austl. 114/C4
Eidsvoll, Nor. 38/D1
Eifel (plat.), Ger. 40/D3
Eiffel Tower, Fr. 30/J5
Eigenji, Japan 77/K5
Eiger (peak), Swi. 56/D4
Eigersund, Nor. 38/A2
Eigg (isl.), Sc, UK 31/Q8
Eight Degree (chan.), India,Mal 82/B6
Eijerlandse Gat (chan.), Neth. 50/B2
Eijsden, Neth. 53/E2
Eikelandsosen, Nor. 38/A1
Eil, Loch (inlet), Sc, UK 36/A3
Eildon (lake), Austl. 115/C3
Eildon, Austl. 115/C3
Eilerts de Haan (mts.), Sur. 153/G4
Einbeck, Ger. 51/G5
Eindhoven (int'l arpt.), Neth. 50/C6
Eindhoven, Neth. 50/C6
Einsiedeln, Swi. 57/E3
Einville-au-Jard, Fr. 53/F6
Eirunepé, Braz. 156/D2
Eisch (riv.), Lux. 53/E4
Eisenach, Ger. 51/H7
Eisenberg, Ger. 54/B3
Eisenhower Nat'l Hist. Site, Pa, US 138/A4
Eisenhüttenstadt, Ger. 41/H2
Eiserfeld, Ger. 53/G2
Eisfeld, Ger. 54/D2
Eisingen, Ger. 54/C3
Eislingen, Ger. 54/C5
Eitelborn, Ger. 53/G3
Eiter (riv.), Ger. 51/F3
Eitorf, Ger. 53/G2
Eitting, Ger. 55/E6
Ejea de los Caballeros, Sp. 45/E1
Ejeda, Madg. 107/H9
Ejido, Ven. 152/D2
Ejin Horo Qi, China 72/B3
Ejin Qi, China 70/H3
Ejutla de Crespo, Mex. 144/B2
Ekeby, Swe. 38/E3
Ekenäs (Tammisaari), Fin. 39/K2
Ekeren, Belg. 50/B6
Ekhínos, Gre. 47/J2
Ekibastuz, Kaz. 87/G2
Eksjö, Swe. 38/F3
Ekuk, Ak, US 134/G4
Ekwan (riv.), On, Can. 123/H3
Ekwok, Ak, US 134/G4
El Aaiún, WSah. 98/B4
El Aatf (reg.), WSah. 98/B5
El Abiodh Sidi Chrikh, Alg. 99/F2
El 'Acâba (pol. reg.), Mrta. 102/C2
El Affroun, Alg. 100/G4
El Águila, Mex. 132/B5
El Aïoun, Mor. 100/C2
El Alto, Peru 156/A2
El Amparo de Apure, Ven. 152/D3
El Anegado, Ecu. 152/A5
El Aouinet, Alg. 100/K7
El Arahal, Sp. 44/C4
El Arhlaf (well), Mrta. 102/D2
El Astillero, Sp. 44/D1
El Bagre, Col. 152/C3
El Banco, Col. 152/C2
El Barco, Sp. 44/B1
El Barco de Ávila, Sp. 44/C2
El Baúl, Ven. 152/D2
El Bayadh (prov.), Alg. 99/F2
El Bayadh, Alg. 99/F2
El Bolsón, Arg. 158/C4
El Bonillo, Sp. 44/D3
El Borouj, Mor. 98/D2
El Burgo de Osma, Sp. 44/D2
El Cajon, Ca, US 136/D5
El Cajón (res.), Hon. 144/E3
El Calafate, Arg. 159/B6
El Callao, Ven. 153/F3
El Capitan (peak), Mt, US 126/E4
El Carmen, Peru 156/B4
El Carmen, Chile 158/B3
El Carmen, Col. 152/B3
El Carmen de Bolívar, Col. 152/C2
El Casar de Talamanca, Sp. 45/N8
El Centro, Ca, US 128/D4
El Cerrito, Col. 152/B4
El Cerrito, Ca, US 135/K11
El Cerro del Aripo (peak), Trin. 153/F2
El Cerrón (peak), Ven. 152/D2
El Chico, PN, Mex. 143/L6
El Cocuy, Col. 152/C3
El Cocuy, PN, Col. 150/D2
El Colorado, Arg. 157/E2
El Difícil, Col. 152/C2
El Djouf (des.), Mrta. 96/D3
El Dorado, Ks, US 129/H3
El Dorado, Ar, US 129/J4
El Dorado, Mex. 142/D3
El Dorado, Ven. 153/F3
El Eglab (plat.), Alg. 96/D2
El Empedrado, Ven. 152/D2
El Escorial, Sp. 45/M8
El Espinar, Sp. 44/C2
El Eulma, Alg. 100/H4
El Fahs, Tun. 100/L6
El Ferrol, Sp. 44/A1
El Fuerte, Mex. 142/C3
El Fureidīs, Isr. 91/F6
El Gogorrón, PN, Mex. 140/A3
El Golea, Alg. 99/F3
El Golfete (lake), Guat. 144/D3
El Granada, Ca, US 135/K11
El Grullo, Mex. 142/D5
El Guachara, PN, Ven. 153/F2
El Hajeb, Mor. 100/B3
El Hank (cliff), Mali, 98/D4
El Harino, Pan. 152/A2
El Harta (well), Alg. 99/E4
El Higo, Mex. 144/B1
El Indio, Tx, US 132/C4
El Jadida, Mor. 98/C2
El Kelaâ des Srarhna, Mor. 98/D2
El Khatt (cliff), Mrta. 96/C3
El Khatt (depr.), Mrta. 102/C2
El Khnâchîch (cliff), Mali 98/E5
El Kroub, Alg. 100/K6
El Kseur, Alg. 100/H4
El Libertador General Bernardo O'Higgins (pol. reg.), Chile 158/N8
El Limón, Mex. 143/F4
El Mahia (phys. reg.), Mali 99/E5
El Maitén, Arg. 158/C4
El Malpais Nat'l Mon., NM, US 128/F4
El Manteco, Ven. 153/F3
El-Menzel, Mor. 100/B3
El Miamo, Ven. 153/F3
El Milia, Alg. 100/J4
El Mirage, Az, US 137/R18
El Mirage, Ca, US 136/C1
El Montcau (peak), Sp. 45/K6
El Monte, Ca, US 136/F7
El Morrito (pt.), Chile 158/C1
El Mrâyer (well), Mrta. 98/C5
El Mreyyé (phys. reg.), Mrta. 102/C2
El Mzereb (well), Mali 98/D4
El Naranjo de Carlos Sarabia, Mex. 143/F4
El Nayar, Mex. 142/D4
El Nevado (peak), Arg. 158/C2
El Nido, Phil. 81/E1
El Olivar Alto, Chile 158/N9
El Oro (prov.), Ecu. 156/A1
El Oued (prov.), Alg. 99/G2
El Oued, Alg. 99/G2
El Palmar, Ven. 153/F3
El Pao, Ven. 153/F2
El Pao, Ven. 153/E2
El Paraíso, Mex. 143/E5
El Paraíso, Hon. 144/E3
El Paso, Tx, US 128/F5
El Paso International (int'l arpt.), Tx, US 129/F5
El Pilar, Ven. 153/F2
El Porvenir, Mex. 129/F5
El Porvenir, Pan. 152/B2
El Potosí, Mex. 143/E3
El Potosí, PN, Mex. 140/B3
El Prat de Llobregat, Sp. 45/L7
El Progreso, Hon. 144/E3
El Progreso, Guat. 144/D3
El Progreso, Ecu. 156/F7
El Progreso Industrial, Mex. 143/Q9
El Puerto de Santa María, Sp. 44/B4
El Quelite, Mex. 142/D4
El Quisco, Chile 158/N8
El Rama, Nic. 145/E3
El Rancho, Co, US 137/B3
El Reno, Ok, US 129/H4
El Rio, Ca, US 136/A2
El Roble, Pan. 152/A2
El Rosario de Arriba, Mex. 142/B2
El Sacromonte, PN, Mex. 143/L7
El Salto, Mex. 142/D4
El Salvador, Mex. 143/E3
El Salvador, Cuba 145/H1
El Salvador (int'l arpt.), ESal. 144/D3
El Salvador (ctry.) 119/H8
El Samán de Apure, Ven. 152/D3
El Sauz, Mex. 129/F5
El Sauzal, Mex. 142/A2
El Segundo, Ca, US 136/F8
El Shab (well), Egypt 101/B4
El Tabo, Chile 158/N8
El Tajín (ruin), Mex. 143/M6
El Tama, PN, Ven. 152/C3
El Tambo, Ecu. 152/B5
El Tarf (prov.), Alg. 100/K6
El Tarf, Alg. 100/L6
El Teleno (peak), Sp. 44/B1
El Tepozteco, PN, Mex. 143/R10
El Tiemblo, Sp. 44/C2
El Tigre, Ven. 153/E2
El Tocuyo, Ven. 152/D2
El Toro, Ca, US 136/C3
El Triunfo, Ecu. 152/B5
El Triunfo, Mex. 144/D2
El Tucuche (peak), Trin. 153/F2
El Tuito, Mex. 142/D4
El Tuparro, PN, Col. 150/E3
El Valle, Pan. 152/A2
El Venado (isl.), Nic. 145/F4
El Viejo, Nic. 144/E3
El Viejo (peak), Col. 152/C3
El Vigía, Ven. 152/D2
El Yagual, Ven. 152/D3
El Yunque (peak), PR 141/M8
El Zacatón, Mex. 142/E4
Elan (riv.), Wal, UK 32/C2
Élancourt, Fr. 30/H5
Elandsrivier (riv.), SAfr. 106/Q12
Elassón, Gre. 47/H3
Elat (int'l arpt.), Isr. 91/D5
Elat, Isr. 91/D5
Elátia, Gre. 47/H3
Elato (isl.), Micr. 116/D4
Elazığ, Turk. 90/D2
Elazig (prov.), Turk. 90/D2
Elba, Al, US 133/G4
Elba (isl.), It. 43/H5
Elbasan, Alb. 47/G2
Elbbach (riv.), Ger. 53/G2
Elbe (riv.), Ger. 27/F3
Elbe (Labe) (riv.), Czh.,Ger. 41/H2
Elbe-Seitenkanaal (canal), Ger. 51/H2
Elbert (co.), Co, US 137/C4
Elberton, Ga, US 133/H3
Elbeuf, Fr. 42/D2
Elbigenalp, Aus. 57/G3
Elbląg, Pol. 39/H4
Elblag (prov.), Pol. 39/H4
Elbow, Sk, Can. 126/G3
El'brus (peak), Rus. 63/G4
Elburg, Neth. 50/C4
Elburn, Il, US 135/N16
Elburz (mts.), Iran 64/E6
Elche, Sp. 45/E3
Elche de la Sierra, Sp. 44/D3
Elchingen, Ger. 54/D6
Elcho (isl.), Austl. 109/C2
Eld (inlet), Wa, US 135/A3
Elda, Sp. 45/E3
Elde (riv.), Ger. 40/G2
Eldersburg, Md, US 138/B5
Eldivan, Turk. 62/E4
Eldon, Wa, US 135/A2
Eldora, Co, US 137/A3
Eldora, NJ, US 138/D5
Eldorado, Arg. 157/F2
Eldorado, Tx, US 129/G5
Eldorado Springs, Co, US 137/B3
Eldoret, Kenya 104/B2
Eleao (peak), Hi, US 124/W13
Elefsís, Gre. 47/H3
Elek, Hun. 48/E2
Elektrostal', Rus. 61/X9
Elena, Arg. 158/D2
Elesbão Veloso, Braz. 154/B2
Eleşkirt, Turk. 63/G5
Eleuthera (isl.), Bahm. 119/K7
Eleven Point (riv.), Mo, US 129/K3
Elevsís (ruin), Gre. 47/N8
Elevtheroúpolis, Gre. 47/J2
Elfershausen, Ger. 54/C2
Elgg, Swi. 57/E3
Elgin, ND, US 127/H4
Elgin, Il, US 127/L5
Elgin, Tx, US 129/H5
Elgin, Sc, UK 36/C1
Elgóibar, Sp. 44/D1
Elgon (Wagagai) (peak), Ugan. 104/B2
Elida, NM, US 132/C3
Elim, Ak, US 134/F3
Elimäki, Fin. 39/M1
Elista, Rus. 63/H3
Elixhausen, Aus. 55/G7
Elizabeth (bay), Namb. 106/A2
Elizabeth, NJ, US 139/J9
Elizabeth City, NC, US 133/J2
Elizabethan Village Hist. Site, Austl. 112/L7
Elizabethton, Tn, US 130/D4
Elizabethtown, Pa, US 138/B3
Elizabethville, Pa, US 138/B2
Elk (mts.), Co, US 132/B2
Elk (riv.), WV, US 133/H2
Eľk, Pol. 39/K5
Elk City, Ok, US 129/H4
Elk Grove, Ca, US 135/M10
Elk Grove Village, Il, US 135/P16
Elk Island NP, Can. 126/E2
Elk Mills, Md, US 138/C4
Elk Point, Ab, Can. 126/F2
Elk Rapids, Mi, US 130/C2
Elk Ridge, Md, US 138/B5
Elk River, Mn, US 127/K4
Elk Slough (riv.), Ca, US 135/L10
Elkenroth, Ger. 53/G2
Elkhart, In, US 130/C3
Elkhart, Ks, US 129/G3
Elkhart, Tx, US 129/J5
Elkhorn, Mb, Can. 127/H3
Elkhorn, Wi, US 130/B3
Elkhorn (riv.), Ne, US 125/G3
Elkhovo, Bul. 47/K1
Elkin, NC, US 130/D4
Elko, Nv, US 126/E5
Elkton, Md, US 138/C4
Ellamar, Ak, US 134/J3
Elland, Eng, UK 35/G4
Elle (riv.), Ger. 53/F2
Ellef Ringnes (isl.), Can. 123/R7
Ellefeld, Ger. 55/F2
Ellen (riv.), Eng, UK 35/E2
Ellenberg, Ger. 54/D4
Ellendale, ND, US 127/J4
Ellendale, De, US 138/C6
Ellensburg, Wa, US 126/C4
Eller (riv.), Ger. 51/H5
Ellerbach (riv.), Ger. 53/G4
Ellero (riv.), It. 58/A4
Ellery (mt.), Austl. 115/D3
Ellesmere (isl.), Can. 119/J2
Ellesmere Island NP, NW, Can. 123/T6
Ellesmere Port, Eng, UK 35/F5
Ellezelles, Belg. 52/C2
Ellice (riv.), NW, Can. 122/F2
Ellicott City, Md, US 138/B5
Ellinikón (int'l arpt.), Gre. 47/N9
Elliot, SAfr. 106/D3
Elliot Lake, On, Can. 130/D2
Elliot Price Consv. Park, Austl. 113/H4
Elliott (peak), Va, US 133/J2
Ellis Island, NJ,NY, US 139/J9
Ellisras, SAfr. 105/E5
Elliston, Austl. 113/G5
Ellisville, Mo, US 137/F8
Ellon, Sc, UK 36/D2
Ellrich, Ger. 51/H5
Ellsworth, Me, US 131/G2
Ellsworth, Wi, US 130/A2
Ellsworth, Ks, US 129/H3
Ellsworth (mts.), Ant. 160/U
Ellsworth Land (phys. reg.), Ant. 160/U
Ellwangen, Ger. 54/D5
Elm, Swi. 57/F4
Elm Grove, Wi, US 135/P13
Elma, NY, US 131/S10
Elmadağ, Turk. 62/E5
Elmalı, Turk. 91/A1
Elmas (int'l arpt.), It. 46/A3
Elmendorf, Tx, US 137/U21
Elmer, NJ, US 138/C4
Elmhurst, Il, US 135/Q16
Elmina, Gha. 103/E5
Elmira, NY, US 130/E3
Elmont, NY, US 139/L9
Elmore, Austl. 115/C3
Elmsford, NY, US 139/K7
Elmshorn, Ger. 51/G1
Elmstein, Ger. 53/G5
Elmwood Park, Wi, US 135/Q14
Elmwood Park, NJ, US 139/J8
Elmwood Park, Il, US 135/Q16
Elne, Fr. 42/E5
Elói Mendes, Braz. 211/H6
Élorn (riv.), Fr. 42/A2
Elortondo, Arg. 158/E2
Elorza, Ven. 152/D3
Elouera Nat'l Rsv., Austl. 114/H8
Eloy, Az, US 128/E4
Eloy Alfaro, Ecu. 152/B5
Éloyes, Fr. 56/C1
Elpitiya, SrL. 82/D6
Elrose, Sk, Can. 126/F3
Elsa, Yk, Can. 134/L3
Elsa (riv.), It. 43/J5
Elsa, Embalse de (res.), Sp. 44/B2
Elsah, Il, US 137/G8
Elsdorf, Ger. 51/G2
Elsdorf, Ger. 53/F2
Else (riv.), Ger. 51/F4
Elsenfeld, Ger. 54/C3
Elsenz (riv.), Ger. 54/B4
Elsfleth, Ger. 51/F2
Elsinore (lake), Ca, US 136/C3
Elsmere, De, US 138/C4
Elst, Neth. 50/C5
Elstal, Ger. 40/Q6
Elstead, Eng, UK 33/F4
Elsterberg, Ger. 55/F1
Eltmann, Ger. 54/D3
El'ton (lake), Rus. 63/H2
Eltville am Rhein, Ger. 54/B2
Elūrū, India 82/D4
Elvanlı, Turk. 91/D1
Elvas, Port. 44/B3
Elverum, Nor. 38/D1
Elvire (mt.), Austl. 112/C2
Elvo (riv.), It. 58/B2
Elwell (lake), Mt, US 126/F3
Elwood, In, US 130/C3
Elwood-Magnolia, NJ, US 138/D4
Elwy (riv.), Wal, UK 34/E5
Ely, Nv, US 128/D3
Ely, Eng, UK 33/G2
Elyaqim, Isr. 91/G6
Elyashiv, Isr. 91/F7
Elyria, Oh, US 130/D3
Elysburg, Pa, US 138/B2
Elysian Park, Ca, US 136/F7
Elz (riv.), Ger. 54/B6
Elz, Ger. 54/B2
Elzach, Ger. 56/E1
Elzbach (riv.), Ger. 53/G3
Elze, Ger. 51/G4
Emajõgi (riv.), Est. 39/M2
Emāmshahr (Shāhrūd), Iran 89/F1
Emån (riv.), Swe. 38/F3
Emancé, Fr. 30/H6
Emas, PN das, Braz. 151/H7
Emba (riv.), Kaz. 62/K3
Embarcación, Arg. 157/D1
Embarras (riv.), Il, US 133/F2
Embi, Kaz. 63/L2
Embi (riv.), Kaz. 64/F5
Embira (riv.), Braz. 150/D5
Emborcação, Barragem de (res.), Braz. 155/C1
Embrach, Swi. 57/E3
Embrun, Fr. 43/G4
Embsen, Ger. 51/H2
Embu, Kenya 104/C3
Emden, Ger. 51/E2
Emeishan, China 83/H2
Emerald, Austl. 114/C3
Emerald, Austl. 115/G5
Emerson, Mb, Can. 127/J3
Emerson, NJ, US 139/J8
Emeryville, Ca, US 135/K11
Emet, Turk. 62/D5
Emigsville, Pa, US 138/B3
Emilia-Romagna (pol. reg.), It. 43/J4
Emiliano Zapata, Mex. 144/D2
Emin, China 70/D2
Eminābād, Pak. 86/C3
Eminence, Mo, US 129/K3
Emir Pasha (gulf), Tanz. 104/A3
Emirdağ, Turk. 62/D5
Emirgazi, Turk. 90/C2
Emlembe (peak), Swaz. 107/E2
Emlichheim, Ger. 50/D3
Emma (riv.), Sur. 153/H4
Emmaboda, Swe. 38/F3
Emmanuel Head (pt.), Eng, UK 36/E5
Emmaus, Pa, US 138/C2
Emme (riv.), Swi. 56/D4
Emmeloord, Neth. 50/C3
Emmen, Neth. 50/D3
Emmendingen, Ger. 56/D1
Emmental (valley), Swi. 56/D3
Emmer (riv.), Ger. 51/G4
Emmerbach (riv.), Ger. 51/E5
Emmerich, Ger. 50/D5
Emmett, Mi, US 135/G6
Emmingen-Liptingen, Ger. 57/E2
Emmitsburg, Md, US 138/A4
Emmonak, Ak, US 134/F3
Emneth, Eng, UK 33/G1
Emőd, Hun. 48/E2
Emory, Tx, US 129/J4
Emosson (lake), Swi. 56/C5
Empalme, Mex. 142/C3
Empangeni, SAfr. 107/E3
Empedrado, Arg. 157/E2
Empedrado, Chile 158/B2
Empoli, It. 59/D5
Emporia, Ks, US 129/H3
'Emrānī, Iran 89/G2
Ems (Eems) (riv.), Ger.,Neth. 50/D2
Ems-Jade (canal), Ger. 51/E2
Emsbüren, Ger. 51/E4
Emsdetten, Ger. 51/E4
Emskirchen, Ger. 54/D3
Emsland (reg.), Ger. 40/D2
Emstek, Ger. 51/F3
Emu Park, Austl. 114/C3
Emumägi (hill), Est. 39/M2
Emyvale, Ire. 34/B3
Ena, Japan 75/E3
Enbetsu, Japan 76/B1
Encantada, Cerro (peak), Mex. 142/B3
Encantada, Cerro de la (peak), Mex. 142/B2
Encarnación, Par. 157/E2
Encarnación de Díaz, Mex. 142/E4
Enchi, Gha. 102/E5
Encinitas, Ca, US 136/C4
Enciso, Col. 152/C3
Encontrados, Ven. 152/C2
Encounter (bay), Austl. 115/A2
Encruzilhada do Sul, Braz. 155/A4
Encs, Hun. 41/L4
Endau (peak), Kenya 104/C3
Ende, Indo. 81/F5
Endeavour River NP, Austl. 114/B1
Enderbury (isl.), Kiri. 117/H5
Enderby, BC, Can. 126/D3
Enderby Land (phys. reg.), Ant. 160/D
Enderlin, ND, US 127/J4
Endicott, NY, US 130/E3
Endingen, Ger. 56/D1
Ene (riv.), Peru 150/D6
Eneabba, Austl. 112/B4
Enebakk, Nor. 38/D2
Enewetak (isl.), Mrsh. 116/F3
Enez, Turk. 47/K2
Enfield (bor.), Eng, UK 30/C2
Engaño (cape), Phil. 79/D4
Engaru, Japan 76/C1
Engaruka (basin), Tanz. 104/B3
Engelberg, Swi. 57/E4
Engelhartszell, Aus. 55/G5
Engel's, Rus. 63/H2
Engelskirchen, Ger. 53/G2
Engelsmanplaat (isl.), Neth. 50/D2
Engen, Ger. 57/E2
Engenheiro Navarro, Braz. 154/B5
Engenheiro Paulo de Frontin, Braz. 211/K7
Enger, Ger. 51/F4
Engerwitzdorf, Aus. 55/H6
Enggano (isl.), Indo. 80/B5
Enghershatu (peak), Erit. 88/C5
Enghien, Belg. 52/D2
Engi, Swi. 57/F4
England, UK 32/D2
Englefontaine, Fr. 52/C3
Englehart, On, Can. 130/E2
Englewood, Co, US 137/C3
Englewood, NJ, US 139/K8
Englewood Cliffs, NJ, US 139/K8
English (riv.), Can. 127/K3
English (chan.), UK,Fr. 27/D4
English Bay, Ak, US 134/H4
English Bāzār, India 85/G3
English Creek, NJ, US 138/D5
Englishtown, NJ, US 138/D3
Énguera, Sp. 45/E3
Enguri (riv.), Geo. 63/G4
Enhtal, Mong. 70/J2
Enid, Ok, US 129/H3
Eniwa, Japan 76/B2
Enkenbach-Alsenborn, Ger. 53/G5
Enkhuizen, Neth. 50/C3
Enkirch, Ger. 53/G4
Enköping, Swe. 38/G2
Enna, It. 46/D4
Ennedi (plat.), Chad 97/K4
Ennepe (riv.), Ger. 51/E6
Ennepetal, Ger. 51/E6
Ennery, Fr. 30/J4
Enningerloh, Ger. 51/F5
Ennis, Mt, US 126/F4
Ennis, Tx, US 129/H4
Ennis, Ire. 31/P10
Enniscorthy, Ire. 31/Q10
Enniskerry, Ire. 34/B5
Enniskillen, NI, UK 31/Q9
Ennistimon, Ire. 31/P10
Enns, Aus. 55/H6
Enns (riv.), Aus. 41/H5
Enogger (res.), Austl. 114/E6
Enola, Pa, US 138/B3
Enontekiö, Fin. 37/G1
Enoree (riv.), SC, US 133/H3
Enping, China 83/K3
Enrick (riv.), Sc, UK 36/B2
Enrique Carbó, Arg. 159/J10
Enriquillo, DRep. 145/J2
Enschede, Neth. 50/D4
Ensdorf, Ger. 55/E4
Ense, Ger. 51/E5
Enseleni, SAfr. 107/F3
Ensenada, Mex. 142/A2
Ensenada, Arg. 159/K11
Enshi, China 79/A1
Ensisheim, Fr. 56/D2
Entebbe (int'l arpt.), Ugan. 104/B2
Entebbe, Ugan. 104/B2
Entenbühl (peak), Ger. 55/F3
Enterprise, Al, US 133/G4
Enterprise, Ut, US 137/K11
Entlebuch, Swi. 56/E4
Entre Rios, Braz. 154/C3
Entre Ríos (mts.), Hon. 144/E3
Entroncamento, Port. 44/A3
Entzheim, Fr. 56/D1
Enugu, Nga. 103/G5
Enugu (state), Nga. 103/G5
Enumclaw, Wa, US 135/D3
Enushū (sea), Japan 77/M6
Envira, Braz. 156/D2
Enz (riv.), Ger. 43/H2
Enza (riv.), It. 58/D4
Enzan, Japan 75/F3
Enzbach (riv.), Ger. 53/F4
Enzersdorf an der Fischa, Aus. 49/P7
Enzklösterle, Ger. 54/B5
Epalinges, Swi. 56/C4
Epáno Arkhánai, Gre. 47/J5
Epanomí, Gre. 47/H2
Epe, Nga. 103/F5
Epe, Neth. 50/C4
Épehy, Fr. 52/C3
Épernay, Fr. 52/C5
Epfig, Fr. 56/D1
Ephrata, Pa, US 138/B3
Epi (isl.), Van. 116/F6
Épiais-Rhus, Fr. 30/J4
Epídhavros (Epidaurus) (ruin), Gre. 47/H4
Épinal, Fr. 56/C1
Épinay-sur-Orge, Fr. 30/J6
Épinay-sur-Seine, Fr. 30/J5
Epira, Guy. 153/G3
Epirus (reg.), Gre. 47/G3
Épône, Fr. 52/A6
Eppelborn, Ger. 53/F5
Eppelheim, Ger. 54/B4
Eppenbrunn, Ger. 53/G5
Eppeville, Fr. 52/C4
Epping (for.), Eng, UK 30/D2
Epping, Eng, UK 30/D1
Epping Forest NP, Austl. 114/B3
Eppingen, Ger. 54/B4
Eppishausen, Ger. 57/G1
Epsom, Eng, UK 30/C3
Epsom and Ewell, Eng, UK 33/F4
Epte (riv.), Fr. 52/A4
Equator (fall), Ecu. 152/A4
Equatorial Guinea (ctry.) 93/C4
Équihen-Plage, Fr. 52/A2
Er (lake), China 83/H2
Er Rachidia, Mor. 98/D3
Er Reina, Isr. 91/G6
Er Rif (mts.), Mor. 96/D1
Era (riv.), It. 59/D6
Eraclea, It. 59/F1
Eraclea (ruin), It. 46/E2
Eraclea Minoa (ruin), It. 46/C4
Éragny, Fr. 30/J4
Erandique, Hon. 144/D3
Eravur, SrL. 82/D6
Erawan NP, Thai. 78/B3
Erba, It. 58/C1
Erbaa, Turk. 62/F4
Erbach, Ger. 54/B3
Erbendorf, Ger. 55/F3
Erbeskopf (peak), Ger. 53/G4
Ercan (int'l arpt.), Cyp. 91/C2
Erçek, Turk. 90/E2
Erçek (lake), Turk. 90/E2
Ercilla, Chile 158/B3
Erciş, Turk. 90/E2
Erciyes (peak), Turk. 90/C2
Erclin (riv.), Fr. 52/C3
Érd, Hun. 49/Q10
Erda, Ut, US 137/J12
Erdek (gulf), Turk. 49/H5
Erdek, Turk. 49/H5
Erdemli, Turk. 91/D1
Erdenet, Mong. 70/H2
Erdi-Ma (plat.), Chad 97/K4
Erding, Ger. 55/E6
Erdre (riv.), Fr. 42/C3
Erdweg, Ger. 54/E6
Erechim, Braz. 155/A3
Ereen Davaanï (mts.), Mong. 71/K2
Ereğli, Turk. 90/C2
Ereğli, Turk. 49/K5
Eremo di Camaldoli, It. 59/E5
Erenhaberga (mts.), China 70/D3
Erenhot, China 71/K3
Erenler, Turk. 49/K5
Erentepe, Turk. 90/E2
Erepecu, Lago do (lake), Braz. 151/G4
Eresma (riv.), Sp. 44/C2
Erétria, Gre. 47/H3
Ereymentaū, Kaz. 87/F2
Érezée, Belg. 53/E3
Erfa (riv.), Ger. 54/C3
Erfoud, Mor. 98/D3
Erft (riv.), Ger. 40/D3
Erftstadt, Ger. 53/F2
Erfurt, Ger. 40/F3
'Erg Chech (des.), Mali,Alg. 93/B2
'Erg Iguidi (des.), Alg.,Mrta. 98/D4
Ergene Nehri (riv.), Turk. 49/H5
Erguig (riv.), Chad 96/J5
Ergun Youqi, China 71/M1
Ergun Zuoqi, China 71/M1
Ericeira, Port. 45/P10
Ericht (lake), Sc, UK 36/B3
Ericht (riv.), Sc, UK 36/B3
Erickson, Mb, Can. 127/J3
Erickson, BC, Can. 126/D3
Erie (int'l arpt.), Pa, US 130/D3
Erie, Pa, US 130/D3
Erie, Co, US 137/B2
Erie (co.), NY, US 131/S10
Erie (canal), NY, US 131/S9
Erie (lake), Can.,US 119/J5
Eriksdale, Mb, Can. 127/J3
Eriksmalå, Swe. 38/F3
Erikub (isl.), Mrsh. 116/F4
Erímanthos (peak), Gre. 47/G4
Erimo, Japan 76/C2
Erimo-misaki (cape), Japan 76/C3
Erithraí, Gre. 47/H3
Eritrea (ctry.) 93/F3
Erkelenz, Ger. 53/F1
Erken (isl.), Swe. 39/H1
Erkheim, Ger. 57/G1
Erkner, Ger. 40/Q7
Erkrath, Ger. 50/D6
Erlach, Swi. 56/D3
Erlands Point-Kitsap Lake, Wa, US 135/B2
Erlangen, Ger. 54/E3
Erlau (riv.), Ger. 55/G5
Erlenbach (riv.), Ger. 54/B4
Erlenbach am Main, Ger. 54/C3
Erlenbach bei Marktheidenfeld, Ger. 54/C3
Erlenbach im Simmental, Swi. 56/D4
Erlinsbach, Swi. 56/E3
Erlongshan (res.), China 72/F2
Erme (riv.), Eng, UK 32/C6
Ermelo, SAfr. 107/E2
Ermelo, Neth. 50/C4
Ermenek (riv.), Turk. 91/C1
Ermenek, Turk. 91/C1
Ermenonville, Fr. 30/L4
Ermióni, Gre. 47/H4
Ermont, Fr. 30/J5
Ermoúpolis, Gre. 47/J4
Erms (riv.), Ger. 54/C6
Erndtebrück, Ger. 53/H2
Ernée (riv.), Fr. 42/C2
Ernée, Fr. 42/C2
Ernesto Cortissoz (int'l arpt.), Col. 152/C2
Ernsthofen, Aus. 55/H6
Erode, India 82/C5
Erolzheim, Ger. 57/G1
Erowal Bay, Austl. 115/D2
Erpel, Ger. 53/G2
Erquelinnes, Belg. 53/D3
Errigal (mtn.), Ire. 31/P9
Erris Head (pt.), Ire. 31/P9
Erro (riv.), It. 58/B4
Errochty (lake), Sc, UK 36/B3
Erromango (isl.), Van. 116/F6
Erse (riv.), Ger. 51/H4
Ersekë, Alb. 47/G2
Erstein, Fr. 56/D1
Erstfeld, Swi. 57/E4
Ertingen, Ger. 57/F1
Ertis (riv.), Kaz. 64/H4
Ertix (riv.), China 70/E2
Eruh, Turk. 90/E2
Eruwa, Nga. 103/F5
Erwin, Tn, US 130/D4
Erwitte, Ger. 51/F5
Eryuan, China 83/G2
Erzegebirge (Krušné Hory) (mts.), Czh.,Ger. 43/K1
Erzen (riv.), Alb. 47/F2
Erzhausen, Ger. 54/B3
Erzincan, Turk. 62/F5
Erzurum (prov.), Turk. 63/G4
Erzurum, Turk. 63/G5
Es Senia (int'l arpt.), Alg. 100/E5
Esan-misaki (cape), Japan 76/B3
Esashi, Japan 76/C1
Esashi, Japan 76/B3
Esashi, Japan 76/B4
Esbiye, Turk. 62/F4
Esbjerg, Den. 38/C4
Esbjerg (int'l arpt.), Den. 38/C4
Esbly, Fr. 30/L5
Esbo (Espoo), Fin. 39/L1
Escada, Braz. 154/D3
Escalante (riv.), Ut, US 128/E3
Escalón, Mex. 142/D3
Escalona, Sp. 44/C2
Escambia (riv.), Fl, US 133/G4
Escaudain, Fr. 52/C3
Escaut (riv.), Fr. 40/B3
Esch (riv.), Fr. 53/E6
Esch-sur-Alzette, Lux. 53/E4
Esch-sur-Sure, Lux. 53/E4
Eschach (riv.), Ger. 57/E1
Eschau, Fr. 56/D1
Eschborn, Ger. 54/B2
Eschede, Ger. 51/H3
Eschen, Lcht. 57/F3
Eschenbach, Ger. 54/C5
Eschenbach in der Oberpfalz, Ger. 55/E3
Eschershausen, Ger. 51/G5
Esches (riv.), Fr. 52/B5
Escholzmatt, Swi. 56/D4
Eschwege, Ger. 51/H6
Eschweiler, Ger. 53/F2
Escobedo (int'l arpt.), Mex. 132/C5
Escoma, Bol. 156/D4
Escondido, Ca, US 136/C4
Escuinapa de Hidalgo, Mex. 142/D4
Escuintla, Guat. 144/D3
Esdraelon, Plain of (plain), Isr. 91/G6
Eséka, Camr. 96/H7
Esenboga (int'l arpt.), Turk. 62/E4
Esence (peak), Turk. 62/F5
Esens, Ger. 51/E1
Esera (riv.), Sp. 45/F1
Eşfahān, Iran 88/F2
Esfandak, Iran 89/H3

Esgair Ddu (peak), Wal, UK 32/C1
Esha Ness (cape), Sc, UK 31/W13
Esher, Eng, UK 30/B2
Eshowe, SAfr. 107/E3
Esil, Kaz. 87/E2
Esil (riv.), Kaz. 67/F4
Esine, It. 57/G6
Esino (riv.), It. 59/G6
Esk (riv.), Eng, UK 35/E2
Eskdale (valley), Sc, UK 36/C6
Eskifjördhur, Ice. 37/Q6
Eskil, Turk. 90/C2
Eskilstuna, Swe. 38/G2
Eskimalatya, Turk. 90/D2
Eskimo (lakes), NW, Can. 122/C2
Eskimo Point, NW, Can. 122/G2
Eskipazar, Turk. 62/E4
Eskişehir, Turk. 62/D5
Eskişehir (prov.), Turk. 62/D5
Esla (riv.), Sp. 44/C1
Eslāmābād, Iran 88/E2
Eslohe, Ger. 51/F6
Eslöv, Swe. 38/E4
Eşme, Turk. 90/B2
Esmeralda, Cuba 145/G1
Esmeraldas, Ecu. 152/B4
Esmeraldas (dept.), Ecu. 152/B4
Esneux, Belg. 53/E2
Espada (pt.), Col. 152/D1
Espalion, Fr. 42/E4
Española, NM, US 129/F4
Espanola, On, Can. 130/D2
Española (isl.), Ecu. 156/F7
Esparraguera, Sp. 45/K6
Esparta, Hon. 144/E3
Esparto, Ca, US 135/K9
Espejo, Sp. 44/C4
Espelkamp, Ger. 51/F4
Esperança, Braz. 154/D2
Esperance (bay), Austl. 112/D5
Esperance, Austl. 112/D5
Esperantina, Braz. 154/B1
Esperantinópolis, Braz. 154/A2
Esperanza (inlet), Can. 126/B3
Esperanza, Peru 156/D3
Esperanza, Mex. 142/C3
Esperanza, Mex. 143/M8
Esperanza (mts.), Hon. 144/E3
Esperanza, Arg., Ant. 160/W
Espichel (cape), Port. 45/P11
Espinal, Mex. 143/M6
Espinal, Col. 152/C3
Espinar, Peru 156/D4
Espinhaço, Serra do (mts.), Braz. 151/K7
Espinho, Port. 44/A2
Espinillo (pt.), Uru. 159/F2
Espinosa, Braz. 154/B4
Espírito Santo (state), Braz. 155/D2
Espiritu Santo (isl.), Van. 116/F6
Espíritu Santo (bay), Cuba 144/E2
Espita, Mex. 144/D1
Esplanada, Braz. 154/C3
Espluga de Francolí, Sp. 45/E2
Espluges, Sp. 45/L7
Esposende, Port. 44/A2
Espungabera, Moz. 105/F5
Espy, Pa, US 138/B1
Esqueda, Mex. 142/C2
Esquel, Arg. 158/C4
Esquina, Arg. 157/E3
Essaouira, Mor. 98/C3
Esse (riv.), Ger. 51/G5
Essen, Belg. 50/B6
Essen, Ger. 50/E6
Essen, Ger. 51/E3
Essenbach, Ger. 55/F5
Essendon (mt.), Austl. 112/D3
Essenheim, Ger. 53/H4
Essequibo (riv.), Guy. 147/D2
Essequibo Island-West Demerara (pol. reg.), Guy. 153/G3
Essex (co.), NJ, US 138/D2
Essex, Md, US 138/B5
Essex (co.), On, Can. 135/G7
Essex, On, Can. 135/G7
Essex (co.), Eng, UK 30/E1
Essex Fells, NJ, US 139/H8
Esslingen, Ger. 54/C5
Essômes-sur-Marne, Fr. 52/C5
Essonne (riv.), Fr. 42/E2
Est, Canal de l' (canal), Fr. 53/E5
Estaca de Bares, Punta de la (cape), Sp. 44/B1
Estación Santa Engracia, Mex. 143/F3
Estados, Isla de los (isl.), Arg. 157/D7
Eştahbān, Iran 88/F3
Estaires, Fr. 52/B2
Estância, Braz. 154/C3
Estats, Pico de (peak), Sp. 45/F1
Estavayer-le-Lac, Swi. 56/C4
Estcourt, SAfr. 107/E3
Este, It. 59/E2
Este, Punta del (pt.), Cuba 140/E3
Este Sudeste, Cayos del (isls.), Col. 145/F3
Esteio, Braz. 155/B4
Estelí, Nic. 144/E3
Estell Manor (Risley), NJ, US 138/D5
Estella, Sp. 44/D1
Estelle (mtn.), Ca, US 136/C3
Estelle, La, US 137/P17
Estepa, Sp. 44/C4
Estepona, Sp. 44/C4
Ester, Ak, US 134/J3
Esterhazy, Sk, Can. 127/H3
Esterias (cape), Gabon 96/G7
Esternay, Fr. 52/C6
Estero de Agiabampo (lag.), Mex. 142/C3
Estéron (riv.), Fr. 43/G5
Esterwegen, Ger. 51/E3
Estes Park, Co, US 137/A2
Estevan, Sk, Can. 127/H3
Estinnes-au-Mont, Belg. 53/D3
Eston, Sk, Can. 126/F3
Eston and South Bank, Eng, UK 35/G2
Estonia (ctry.) 27/G3
Estoril, Port. 45/P10
Estral Beach, Mi, US 135/F8
Estrées-Saint-Denis, Fr. 52/B5
Estrela, Serra da (mts.), Port. 44/A3
Estrela, Serra da (peak), Port. 44/B2
Estrella (pt.), Mex. 142/B2
Estrelto, Serra do (range), Braz. 154/B3
Estremoz, Port. 44/B3
Estrondo, Serra do (mts.), Braz. 151/J5
Esztergom, Hun. 48/D2
Eţ Taiyiba, Isr. 91/G7
Eţ Tīra, Isr. 91/F7
Etah, India 84/B2
Étain, Fr. 53/E5
Etal (isl.), Micr. 116/E4
Étalle, Belg. 53/E4
Étaples, Fr. 52/A2
Etāwah, India 84/B2
Etāwah Branch (riv.), India 84/B2
Etchojoa, Mex. 142/C3
Ethelbert, Mb, Can. 127/H3
Ethiopia (ctry.) 93/F4
Ethiopian (plat.), Eth. 93/F4
Eti (riv.), Japan 77/K5
Etili, Turk. 49/H6
Étival-Clairefontaine, Fr. 56/C1
Etive, Loch (inlet), Sc, UK 36/A4
Etna (peak), It. 46/D4
Etna, Monte (Mount Etna) (vol.), It. 46/D4
Etne, Nor. 38/A2
Etobicoke, Can. 131/Q8
Etolin (str.), Ak, US 134/E3
Eton, Eng, UK 30/B2
Etorofu (isl.), Japan 71/S2
Etorofu (isl.), Rus. 67/P5
Etosha (salt pan), Namb. 105/C4
Etosha NP, Namb. 105/C4
Etowah, Ok, US 137/N15
Étrépilly, Fr. 30/L4
Etropole, Bul. 47/J1
Etroubles, It. 56/D6
Ettadhamen Douarhicher, Tun. 100/M6
Ettelbruck, Lux. 53/F4
Etten-Leur, Neth. 50/B5
Ettenheim, Ger. 56/D1
Etterbeek, Belg. 53/D2
Etters (Goldsboro), Pa, US 138/B3
Ettlingen, Ger. 54/B5
Ettrick Pen (peak), Sc, UK 36/C6
Ettrick Water (riv.), Sc, UK 36/C5
Ettringen, Ger. 57/G1
Eu, Fr. 52/A3
'Eua (isl.), Tonga 117/H7
Eubenangee Swamp NP, Austl. 114/B2
Euclid, Oh, US 130/D3
Euclides da Cuhna, Braz. 154/C3
Eudora, Ar, US 129/K4
Eudunda, Austl. 115/A2
Euerbach, Ger. 54/D2
Eufaula, Al, US 133/G4
Eufaula (lake), Ok, US 125/G4
Eugendorf, Aus. 55/G7
Eugene, Or, US 126/C4
Eugene O'Neill NHS, Ca, US 135/L11
Eugenia (pt.), Mex. 142/B3
Eugowra, Austl. 115/D2
Eume, Embalse de (res.), Sp. 44/B1
Eungella NP, Austl. 114/C3
Eunice, La, US 129/J5
Eunice, NM, US 129/G4
Eupen, Belg. 53/F2
Euphrates (riv.), Iraq,Syria 67/D6
Eura, Fin. 39/K1
Eurajoki, Fin. 39/J1
Eure (riv.), Fr. 42/D2
Eure (dept.), Fr. 52/A5
Eure-et-Loir (dept.), Fr. 52/A6
Eureka, SD, US 127/J4
Eureka, Mt, US 126/E3
Eureka, Ca, US 126/B5
Eureka, Nv, US 128/D3
Eureka, Mo, US 137/F9
Eureka (sound), NW, Can. 123/S7
Euroa, Austl. 115/C3
Eurodisney, Fr. 30/L5
Euron (riv.), Fr. 56/C1
Europa (pt.), Gib. 44/C4
Europabrücke, Aus. 57/H3
Europe (cont.) 27
Europoort, Neth. 50/B5
Euskirchen, Ger. 53/F2
Eussenheim, Ger. 54/C3
Eustis, Fl, US 133/H4
Euston, Austl. 115/B2
Eutin, Ger. 38/D4
Eutini, Malw. 104/B5
Eutsuk (lake), BC, Can. 126/B2
Euville, Fr. 53/E6
Évain, Qu, Can. 130/E1
Evander, SAfr. 106/E2
Evans (mt.), Co, US 129/F3
Evans (lake), Can. 130/E1
Evans, Co, US 137/C2
Evans (str.), NW, Can. 123/H2
Evans Head, Austl. 115/E1
Evanston, Wy, US 126/F5
Evansville, Wy, US 129/F2
Evansville, In, US 130/C4
Evaporation (basin), Ut, US 126/E5
Evart, Mi, US 130/C3
Evaton, SAfr. 106/D2
Evaz, Iran 88/F3
Ève, Fr. 30/L4
Even Yehuda, Isr. 91/F7
Evenlode (riv.), Eng, UK 33/E3
Everard (cape), Austl. 115/D3
Everard (lake), Austl. 109/C4
Everard (mt.), Austl. 113/G3
Everest (peak), China, Ne 82/E2
Everest (Sagarmatha) (mtn.), China,Nepa 85/F2
Everett, Wa, US 126/C4
Evergem, Belg. 52/C1
Everglades (swamp), Fl, US 133/H5
Everglades NP, Fl, US 133/H5
Evergreen, Al, US 133/G4
Evergreen, Co, US 137/B3
Evergreen Park, Il, US 135/Q16
Everswinkel, Ger. 51/E5
Evesham, Eng, UK 33/E2
Evesham, Vale of (valley), Eng, UK 32/D2
Évian-les-Bains, Fr. 56/C5
Évinos (riv.), Gre. 47/G3
Evje, Nor. 38/B2
Evolène, Swi. 56/D5
Évora, Port. 44/B3
Évora (dist.), Port. 44/A3
Évreux, Fr. 42/D2
Évron, Fr. 42/C2
Evrótas (riv.), Gre. 47/H4
Évry, Fr. 30/K6
Évvoia (isl.), Gre. 47/H3
Évvoia (gulf), Gre. 47/H3
Evvoia (gulf), Gre. 62/B5
Evvoia (isl.), Gre. 62/B5
Evxinoúpolis, Gre. 47/H3
Ewa Beach, Hi, US 124/V13
Ewa Villages, Hi, US 124/V13
Ewan, NJ, US 138/C4
Ewarton, Jam. 145/G2
Ewaso Ng'iro (riv.), Kenya 104/C2
Ewell, Eng, UK 30/C3
Ewing, NJ, US 138/D3
Exaplátanos, Gre. 47/H2
Excelsior Springs, Mo, US 137/E5
Excursion Inlet, Ak, US 134/L4
Exe (riv.), Eng, UK 32/C4
Exeter, NH, US 131/G3
Exmoor (upland), Eng, UK 32/C4
Exmoor NP, Eng, UK 32/C4
Exmore, Va, US 133/K2
Exmouth, Austl. 112/B2
Exmouth (gulf), Austl. 112/B2
Exmouth (pen.), Chile 159/B6
Extrema, Braz. 211/G7
Extremadura (reg.), Sp. 44/B3
Exu, Braz. 154/C2
Exuma (sound), Bahm. 141/F3
Eyach (riv.), Ger. 54/B6
Eyak, Ak, US 134/J3
Eyasi (lake), Tanz. 105/F1
Eyb (riv.), Ger. 54/C5
Eydehamn, Nor. 38/C2
Eyemouth, Sc, UK 36/D5
Eyguières, Fr. 42/F5
Eyn Hemed (ruin), Isr. 91/G8
Eyre (pen.), Austl. 109/C4
Eyre (lake), Austl. 116/C7
Eyre North (lake), Austl. 109/C3
Eyre South (lake), Austl. 109/C3
Ézanville, Fr. 30/K4
Ezequiel Ramos Mexía (res.), Arg. 158/C3
Ezhou, China 79/B1
Ezine, Turk. 47/K3
Ezzane (well), Alg. 96/H3

F

F.E. Walter (res.), Pa, US 138/C1
Fabbrico, It. 59/D3
Fabens, Tx, US 132/B4
Fabero, Sp. 44/B1
Fåborg, Den. 38/D4
Fabriano, It. 43/K5
Facatativá, Col. 150/D3
Faches-Thumesnil, Fr. 52/C2
Fada (lake), Sc, UK 36/A1
Fada-N'Gourma, Burk. 103/F3
Faenza, It. 59/E4
Fafa (riv.), CAfr. 97/J6
Fafe, Port. 44/A2
Fafen Shet' (riv.), Eth. 97/P6
Făgăraş, Rom. 49/G3
Fagersta, Swe. 38/F2
Faggiola (peak), It. 59/E4
Fagnano (lake), Arg. 159/D7
Fagnano Olona, It. 58/B1
Fagnières, Fr. 53/D6
Faguibine (lake), Mali 96/D4
Fahl (well), Alg. 99/F3
Fahrenzhausen, Ger. 55/E6
Faial (isl.), Azor., Port. 45/S12
Faido, Swi. 57/E5
Failsworth, Eng, UK 35/F4
Fains-Véel, Fr. 53/E6
Fair Haven, Vt, US 130/F3
Fair Haven, Mi, US 135/G6
Fair Hill, Md, US 138/C4
Fair Isle (isl.), Sc, UK 31/W14
Fair Lawn, NJ, US 139/J8
Fair Oaks, Ca, US 135/M9
Fairbanks, Ak, US 134/J3
Fairfax (co.), Va, US 138/A6
Fairfax, Va, US 138/A6
Fairfax, Ca, US 135/J11
Fairfield, Mt, US 126/F4
Fairfield, Tx, US 129/H5
Fairfield, Ca, US 128/B3
Fairfield, Ut, US 137/J13
Fairfield, Pa, US 138/A4
Fairfield, Ct, US 139/E1
Fairfield (co.), Ct, US 139/L7
Fairfield, NJ, US 139/H8
Fairland, Md, US 138/B5
Fairlee, Md, US 138/B5
Fairless Hills, Pa, US 138/D3
Fairlie, Sc, UK 36/B5
Fairmont, WV, US 130/D4
Fairmont City, Il, US 137/G8
Fairmount, Ks, US 137/D5
Fairplay, Co, US 132/B2
Fairton, NJ, US 138/C5
Fairview, Ok, US 129/H3
Fairview, NJ, US 139/K8
Fairview Heights, Il, US 137/G8
Fairway, Ks, US 137/D5
Fairweather (mt.), Ak, US 134/L4
Fairweather (cape), Ak, US 134/L4
Fairweather (mt.), BC, Can. 122/C3
Faisalābad, Pak. 86/B4
Faistós (ruin), Gre. 47/J5
Faizābād, India 84/D2
Fajardo, PR 141/M8
Fakahina (isl.), FrPol. 117/M6
Fakaofo (isl.), Tok. 117/H5
Fakarava (isl.), FrPol. 117/L6
Fako (peak), Camr. 96/G7
Fakse, Den. 38/E4
Fakse Ladeplads, Den. 38/E4
Faku, China 72/E2
Fal (riv.), Eng, UK 32/B6
Fālākāta, India 85/G2
Falāmah, WBnk. 91/G7
Fálanna, Gre. 47/H3
Falcon (res.), Mex.,US 140/B2
Falcon (cape), Alg. 100/D2
Falcón (state), Ven. 152/D2
Falconara Marittima, It. 59/G5
Falémé (riv.), Mali 96/C5
Falfurrias, Tx, US 132/D5
Falher, Ab, Can. 126/D2
Falkenberg, Swe. 38/E3
Falkensee, Ger. 40/Q6
Falkenstein, Ger. 55/F4
Falkenstein, Ger. 55/F2
Falkirk, Sc, UK 36/C5
Falkland (isls.), UK 147/C8
Falkland, Sc, UK 36/C4
Falkland Sound (str.), UK 159/E7
Falköping, Swe. 38/E2
Fall City, Wa, US 135/D2
Fall River, Ma, US 131/G3
Fallbrook, Ca, US 136/C4
Fallere (peak), It. 56/D6
Falling Spring, Il, US 137/G8
Fallingbostel, Ger. 51/G3
Fallis, Ok, US 137/N14
Fallon, Nv, US 128/C3
Falls Church, Va, US 138/A6
Fallston, Md, US 138/B4
Falmouth, Anti. 141/N8
Falmouth, Eng, UK 32/A6
Falmouth (bay), Eng, UK 32/A6
False Pass, Ak, US 134/F5
Falshöft (pt.), Ger. 38/C4
Falso (cape), Hon. 145/F3
Falso, Cabo (cape), Mex. 142/C4
Falso Cabo de Hornos (cape), Chile 159/C7
Falster (isl.), Den. 37/E5
Falterona (peak), It. 59/E5
Fălticeni, Rom. 49/H2
Falun, Swe. 38/F1
Famagusta (bay), Cyp. 91/C2
Famagusta (dist.), Cyp. 91/C2
Famagusta, Cyp. 91/C2
Fameck, Fr. 53/F5
Famenne (reg.), Belg. 53/E3
Fammau, Moel (peak), Wal, UK 35/E5
Fan Si Pan (peak), Viet. 83/H3
Fana, Nor. 38/A1
Fanchang, China 72/D5
Fandriana, Madg. 107/H8
Fang Xian, China 72/B4
Fangatau (isl.), FrPol. 117/L6
Fangataufa (isl.), FrPol. 117/L7
Fangcheng, China 72/C4
Fangcheng Gezu Zizhixian, China 83/J3
Fangshan, China 72/B3
Fanjing (peak), China 83/J2
Fannich (lake), Sc, UK 36/A1
Fanning (Tabuaeran) (isl.), Kiri. 117/K4
Fano, It. 59/G5
Fanø (isl.), Den. 38/C4
Fanshi, China 72/C3
Fanwood, NJ, US 139/H9
Faqīrwāli, Pak. 86/B5
Fāqūs, Egypt 91/B4
Fara Novarese, It. 58/B1
Faradje, D.R. Congo 104/A2
Farafangana, Madg. 107/H8
Farāfirah, Wāḩāt al (oasis), Egypt 101/A3
Farāh, Afg. 64/G6
Farāh (riv.), Afg. 64/G6
Farallon (isls.), Ca, US 128/B3
Farallon de Medinilla (isl.), NMar. 116/D3
Farallon de Pajaros (isl.), NMar. 116/D2
Farallones de Cali, PN, Col. 150/C3
Faranah (pol. reg.), Gui. 102/C4
Faranah, Gui. 102/C4
Farángi Samariás NP, Gre. 47/H5
Faraony (riv.), Madg. 107/H8
Faraulep (isl.), Micr. 116/D4
Farciennes, Belg. 53/D3
Fareham, Eng, UK 33/E5
Faremoutiers, Fr. 52/C6
Farewell, Ak, US 134/H3
Farewell (cape), NZ 117/S11
Färgelanda, Swe. 38/D2
Farghona (pol. reg.), Uzb. 87/F4
Farghona, Uzb. 87/F4
Fargo, ND, US 127/J4
Faribault, Mn, US 127/K4
Farīdābād, India 86/D5
Farīdkot, India 86/C4
Farīdpur, Bang. 85/G4
Farīdpur (pol. reg.), Bang. 85/G4
Farīdpur, India 84/B1
Fāriskūr, Egypt 91/B4
Färjestaden, Swe. 38/G3
Farkadhón, Gre. 47/H3
Farkasgyepü, Hun. 48/C2
Farley, Mo, US 137/D5
Farmers, Co, US 137/C2
Farmingdale, NJ, US 138/D3
Farmingdale, NY, US 139/M9
Farmington, Me, US 131/G2
Farmington, NM, US 128/E3
Farmington, Mo, US 129/K3
Farmington, Ut, US 137/K12
Farmington, De, US 138/C6
Farmington, Mi, US 135/F7
Farmington Hills, Mi, US 135/E6
Farnborough, Eng, UK 33/F4
Farnham, Eng, UK 33/F4
Farnham Royal, Eng, UK 30/B2
Farnworth, Eng, UK 35/F4
Faro, Yk, Can. 134/M3
Faro (dist.), Port. 44/A4
Faro, Port. 44/B4
Faro (int'l arpt.), Port. 44/B4
Faro, PN du, Camr. 96/H6
Faroe (isls.), Den. 160/G
Fåron (isl.), Swe. 39/H3
Farösund, Swe. 39/H3
Farquhar (cape), Austl. 112/B2
Farr West, Ut, US 137/J11
Farroupilha, Braz. 155/B4
Farrukhābād, India 84/B2
Fársala, Gre. 47/H3
Farsø, Den. 38/C3
Farson, Wy, US 126/F5
Farsund, Nor. 38/B2
Fartak, Ras (pt.), Yem. 88/F5
Farwell, Tx, US 129/G4
Fasā, Iran 88/F3
Fasano, It. 47/E2
Faşıkan (pass), Turk. 91/C1
Fassberg, Ger. 51/H3
Fast Castle (pt.), Sc, UK 36/D5
Fastiv, Ukr. 62/D2
Fatagar Tuting (cape), Indo. 81/H4
Fatahjang, Pak. 86/B3
Fatehābād, India 86/C5
Fatehpur, India 84/C3
Fatehpur, India 84/C2
Fatehpur, India 89/K3
Fatick (pol. reg.), Sen. 102/A3
Fatick, Sen. 102/A3
Fátima, Port. 44/A3
Fatsa, Turk. 62/F4
Fatu Hiva (isl.), FrPol. 117/M6
Faucille, Col de la (pass), Fr. 56/C5
Faucilles (mts.), Fr. 40/C4
Faughan (riv.), NI, UK 34/A2
Fauglia, It. 58/D5
Fauldhouse, Sc, UK 36/C5
Faulkton, SD, US 127/J4
Faulquemont, Fr. 53/F5
Faure (isl.), Austl. 112/B3
Făurei, Rom. 49/H3
Fauske, Nor. 37/E2
Faust, Ut, US 137/J13
Fauvillers, Belg. 53/E4
Faux, Tête de (peak), Fr. 56/D1
Favalto (peak), It. 59/F6
Favara, It. 46/C4
Fave (riv.), Fr. 56/C1
Faverges, Fr. 56/C6
Faverney, Fr. 56/C2
Faversham, Eng, UK 33/G4
Favières, Fr. 30/L5
Favignana, It. 46/C4
Favria, It. 58/A2
Favrieux, Fr. 30/G5
Fawn (riv.), US 127/L2
Fawn (riv.), On, Can. 122/H3
Fawn Grove, Pa, US 138/B4
Faxaflói (bay), Ice. 37/M7
Faxinal, Braz. 155/B2
Faya-Largeau, Chad 97/J4
Fayette, Al, US 133/G3
Fayette, Ms, US 129/K5
Fayetteville, Tn, US 133/G3
Fayetteville, Ga, US 133/G3
Fayetteville, NC, US 133/J3
Fayl-la-Forêt, Fr. 56/B2
Fazao, Monts du (mts.), Togo 103/F4
Fazao, PN du, Togo 103/F4
Fdérik, Mrta. 98/B5
Feale (riv.), Ire. 31/P10
Fear (cape), NC, US 133/J3
Feasterville-Trevose, Pa, US 138/D3
Feather (riv.), Ca, US 128/B3
Featherstone, Eng, UK 35/G4
Fécamp, Fr. 42/D2
Fecht (riv.), Fr. 56/D1
Federal Hall Nat'l Mem., NY, US 139/K9
Federal Heights, Co, US 137/B3
Federally Admin. Tribal Areas, Pak. 86/A2
Federsee (lake), Ger. 54/C6
Fedje, Nor. 38/A1
Feeny, NI, UK 34/A2
Fegersheim, Fr. 54/A6
Fehérgyarmat, Hun. 48/F2
Fehmarn (isl.), Den. 38/D4
Fehmarn Belt (str.), Den. 40/F1
Fei Huang (riv.), China 72/D4
Fei Xian, China 72/D4
Feia, Lagoa (lake), Braz. 155/D2
Feicheng, China 72/D3
Feidong, China 72/D5
Feignies, Fr. 52/C3
Feijó, Braz. 156/D3
Feillans, Fr. 56/A5
Feira, Port. 44/A2
Feira de Santana, Braz. 154/C4
Feistritz (riv.), Aus. 43/L3
Feixi, China 72/D5
Fejér (co.), Hun. 48/D2
Fejø (isl.), Ger. 38/D4
Feke, Turk. 90/C2
Feketić, Yugo. 48/D3
Felanitx, Sp. 45/G3
Feldafing, Ger. 57/H2
Feldaist (riv.), Aus. 55/H6
Feldberg (peak), Ger. 56/E2
Feldkirch, Aus. 57/F3
Feldkirchen an der Donau, Aus. 55/H6
Feldkirchen bei Graz, Aus. 48/B2
Feldkirchen in Kärnten, Aus. 43/L3
Feletto, It. 58/A2
Feletto Umberto, It. 59/G1
Felino, It. 58/D3
Felipe Carillo Puerto, Mex. 144/D2
Felixdorf, Aus. 48/C2
Felixlândia, Braz. 155/C1
Felixstowe, Eng, UK 33/H3
Felizzano, It. 58/B3
Fell, Ger. 53/F4
Fellbach, Ger. 54/C5
Felling, Eng, UK 35/G2
Felsberg, Ger. 51/G6
Felsberg, Swi. 57/F4
Felton, Pa, US 138/B4
Felton, De, US 138/C5
Fema (peak), It. 43/K5
Femø (isl.), Den. 38/D4
Femundsmarka NP, Nor. 37/D3
Fénay, Fr. 56/B3
Fene, Sp. 44/A1
Fener (pt.), Turk. 91/D1
Fénérive, Madg. 105/K10
Feng Xian, China 72/D4
Fengári (peak), Gre. 47/J2
Fengcheng, China 71/L6
Fengcheng, China 73/C2
Fenghuang, China 83/J2
Fengle (riv.), China 72/D5
Fengnan, China 72/J7
Fengning, China 72/D2
Fengqing, China 83/G3
Fengqiu, China 72/C4
Fengrun, China 72/J7
Fengshan, Tai. 79/D3
Fengtai, China 72/H7
Fengxian, China 72/L9
Fengyang, China 72/D4
Fengyüan, Tai. 79/D3
Fengzhen, China 72/C2
Fenimore Pass (chan.), Ak, US 134/C5
Fenoarivo Atsinanana, Madg. 107/J7
Fens (phys. reg.), Eng, UK 33/G1
Fensmark, Den. 38/D4
Fensterbach (riv.), Ger. 55/F4
Fenton, Mi, US 130/D3
Fenton, Mo, US 137/G8
Fenton (lake), Mi, US 135/E7
Fenxi, China 72/B3
Feodosiya, Ukr. 62/E3
Fer, Cap de (cape), Alg. 100/K6
Ferbane, Ire. 31/Q10
Ferdinandshof, Ger. 41/G2
Fère-Champenoise, Fr. 52/C6
Fère-en-Tardenois, Fr. 52/C5
Ferentino, It. 46/C2
Ferento (ruin), It. 46/C1
Fergus Falls, Mn, US 127/J4
Ferguson, Mo, US 137/G8
Ferguson (lake), NW, Can. 122/F2
Ferihegy (int'l arpt.), Hun. 48/D2
Ferkéssédougou, C.d'Iv. 102/D4
Ferlach, Aus. 43/L3
Fermanagh (dist.), NI, UK 34/A3
Fermi National Accelerator Laboratory, Il, US 135/P16
Fermignano, It. 59/F5
Fermin (pt.), Ca, US 136/F8
Fermo, It. 43/K5
Fermoselle, Sp. 44/B2
Fermoy, Ire. 31/P10
Fernán-Núñez, Sp. 44/C4
Fernandina (isl.), Ecu. 156/E7
Fernandina Beach, Fl, US 133/H4
Fernando de Noronha (isl.), Braz. 147/F3
Fernandópolis, Braz. 155/B2
Ferndale, Md, US 138/B5
Ferndale, Mi, US 135/F7
Ferney-Voltaire, Fr. 56/C5
Fernie, BC, Can. 126/E3
Fernpass (pass), Aus. 57/G3
Ferntree Gully NP, Austl. 115/G5
Ferrandina, It. 46/E2
Ferrara (prov.), It. 59/E3
Ferrara, It. 59/E3
Ferrat (cape), Alg. 100/E5
Ferreira do Alentejo, Port. 44/A3
Ferrelview, Mo, US 137/D5
Ferreñafe, Peru 156/B2
Ferret (cape), Fr. 42/C4
Ferrette, Fr. 56/D3
Ferriday, La, US 129/K5
Ferriere, It. 58/C3
Ferrière-la-Grande, Fr. 52/D3
Ferrières, Belg. 53/E3
Ferryden, Sc, UK 36/D3
Ferryfield (int'l arpt.), Eng, UK 33/G5
Ferryhill, Eng, UK 35/G2
Fertő (Neusiedler See) (lake), Aus. 43/M3
Ferté-Bernard, Fr. 42/D2
Fértil (valley), Arg. 157/C3
Ferwerd, Neth. 50/C2
Fès, Mor. 100/B2
Fès (prov.), Mor. 100/B3
Fesches-le-Châtel, Fr. 56/C2
Feshie (riv.), Sc, UK 36/C2
Fessenheim, Fr. 56/D2
Festival Centre, Austl. 113/M8
Feteşti, Rom. 49/H3
Fethaland (pt.), Sc, UK 31/W13
Fethiye, Turk. 90/B2
Feucherolles, Fr. 30/H5
Feucht, Ger. 54/E4
Feuchtwangen, Ger. 54/D4
Feuilles (lake), Qu, Can. 123/J3
Feuilles, Rivière aux (riv.), Qu, Can. 119/K4
Feuquières, Fr. 52/A4
Feuquières-en-Vimeu, Fr. 52/A3
Feurs, Fr. 42/F4
Fevzipaşa, Turk. 91/E1
Feyzābād, Afg. 89/K1
Fez (Saiss) (int'l arpt.), Mor. 100/B3
Fezzan (reg.), Libya 96/H2
Fferna, Moel (peak), Wal, UK 35/E6
Ffestiniog, Wal, UK 34/E6
Fianarantsoa (prov.), Madg. 107/H8
Fianarantsoa, Madg. 107/H8
Fianga, Chad 96/J6
Ficarolo, It. 59/E3
Fichtelberg (peak), Ger. 55/F2
Fichtelgebirge (mts.), Ger. 40/F3
Fichtelnaab (riv.), Ger. 55/E3
Ficksburg, SAfr. 106/D3
Fidenza, It. 58/D3
Fié (riv.), Gui. 102/C4
Field (riv.), Austl. 113/M9
Fieldon, Il, US 137/G7
Fieni, Rom. 49/G3
Fier (riv.), Fr. 56/B6
Fierzë (lake), Alb. 47/G1
Fiesch, Swi. 56/E5
Fiesole, It. 59/E5
Fiesso, It. 59/F2
Fiesso Umbertiano, It. 59/E3
Fiesta Texas, Tx, US 137/T20
Fife, Wa, US 135/C3
Fife (pol. reg.), Sc, UK 36/D4
Fife Ness (pt.), Sc, UK 36/D4
Fifth Cataract (falls), Sudan 101/C5
Figalo (cape), Alg. 100/D2
Figari, Fr. 46/A2
Figeac, Fr. 42/E4
Figline Valdarno, It. 59/E5
Figueira da Foz, Port. 44/A2
Figueres, Sp. 45/G1
Figuig, Mor. 99/E2
Figuig (prov.), Mor. 100/C3
Fiherenana (riv.), Madg. 107/G8
Fiji (ctry.) 116/G6
Filadelfia, Par. 157/D1
Filadélfia, Braz. 154/A2
Filattiera, It. 58/C4
Filchner Ice Shelf, Ant. 160/Y
Filey (bay), Eng, UK 35/H3
Filí, Gre. 47/N8
Filiaşi, Rom. 49/F3
Filiatái, Gre. 47/G3
Filiatrá, Gre. 47/G4
Filicudi (isl.), It. 46/D3
Filingué, Niger 103/F3
Filippiás, Gre. 47/G3
Fílippoi (ruin), Gre. 47/J2
Filipstad, Swe. 38/F2
Filisur, Swi. 57/F4
Fillière (riv.), Fr. 56/C6
Fillmore, Ut, US 128/D3
Fillmore, Ca, US 136/B2
Filomeno Mata, Mex. 143/M6
Filótion, Gre. 47/J4
Filottrano, It. 59/G6
Fils (riv.), Ger. 54/C5
Filsum, Ger. 51/E2
Fimi (riv.), D.R. Congo 96/J8
Fina, Rsv. de, Mali 102/C3
Finale Emilia, It. 59/E3
Finale Ligure, It. 58/B4
Fiñana, Sp. 44/D4
Finch Hatton, Austl. 114/C3
Findel (int'l arpt.), Lux. 53/F4
Findhorn (riv.), Sc, UK 36/B2
Findhorn, Sc, UK 36/C1
Findlay, Oh, US 130/D3
Findochty, Sc, UK 36/D1
Finesville, NJ, US 138/C2
Fingal, Austl. 115/C4
Finger (lake), On, Can. 127/K2
Finhaut, Swi. 56/C5
Finike, Turk. 91/B1
Finisterre, Sp. 44/A1
Finisterre (cape), Sp. 44/A1
Finke (riv.), Austl. 113/G3
Finke Gorge NP, Austl. 113/G3
Finkenstein, Aus. 43/K3
Finksburg, Md, US 138/B5
Finland (gulf), Eur. 64/C4
Finlay (mts.), US 132/B4
Finlay (riv.), BC, Can. 122/D3
Finley, Austl. 115/C2
Finn (riv.), Ire. 31/Q9
Finnentrop, Ger. 51/E6
Finnigan (mt.), Austl. 114/B1
Finnis (cape), Austl. 113/G5
Finnmark (co.), Nor. 37/G1
Fino Mornasco, It. 58/C1
Finsing, Ger. 55/E6
Finspång, Swe. 38/F2
Finsteraarhorn (peak), Swi. 56/E4
Finström, Fin. 39/H1
Fintel, Ger. 51/G2
Fintona, NI, UK 34/A3
Fionn Loch (lake), Sc, UK 36/A1
Fiora (riv.), It. 43/J5
Fiorano, It. 59/D3
Fiordland NP, NZ 117/R12
Fiorenzuola d'Arda, It. 58/C3
Fircrest, Wa, US 135/C3
Fire Island Nat'l Seashore, NY, US 139/E2
Firenze (prov.), It. 59/E5
Firenze (Florence), It. 59/E5
Firenzuola, It. 59/E4
Firestone, Co, US 137/C2
Firmat, Arg. 158/E2
Firmi, Fr. 42/E4
Firminy, Fr. 42/F4
Firozābād, India 84/B2
Firozpur, India 86/C4
First Cataract (falls), Egypt 101/C3
Fīrūz Kūh, Iran 88/F1
Fīrūzābād, Iran 88/F3
Fischa (riv.), Aus. 49/P7
Fischach, Ger. 57/G1
Fischamend Markt, Aus. 49/P7
Fischbacher Alpen (mts.), Aus. 43/L3
Fischen im Allgäu, Ger. 57/G3
Fischer, Tx, US 137/U20
Fish (riv.), Namb. 105/C5
Fisher (bay), Can. 127/J3
Fisher (str.), NW, Can. 123/H2
Fisher Branch, Mb, Can. 127/J3
Fisherman (isl.), Austl. 114/F6
Fishers (isl.), NY, US 139/G1
Fishguard, Wal, UK 32/B3
Fisht (peak), Rus. 62/F4
Fismes, Fr. 52/C5
Fitful Head (pt.), Sc, UK 31/W14
Fitjar, Nor. 38/A2
Fitton (mt.), Can. 134/L2
Fitzgerald, Ga, US 133/H4
Fitzgerald River NP, Austl. 112/C5
Fitzroy (riv.), Austl. 109/B2
Fitzroy (peak), Arg. 159/B6
Fitzwilliam (str.), NW, Can. 123/R7
Fiume Veneto, It. 59/F1
Fiumicino, It. 46/C2
Five Sisters (peak), Sc, UK 36/A2
Fivemiletown, NI, UK 34/A3
Fivizzano, It. 58/D4
Fjell, Nor. 38/A1
Fjerritslev, Den. 38/C3
Fjugesta, Swe. 38/F2
Flå, Nor. 38/C1
Flachslanden, Ger. 54/D4
Fladungen, Ger. 54/D1
Flagler, Co, US 132/C2
Flagler Beach, Fl, US 133/H4
Flagstaff, Az, US 128/E4
Flambeau (riv.), Wi, US 127/L4
Flamborough, On, Can. 131/Q9
Flamborough Head (pt.), Eng, UK 35/H3
Fläming (hills), Ger. 40/G2
Flaming Gorge (res.), US 126/F5
Flaming Gorge Nat'l Rec. Area, US 128/E2
Flamingo Field (int'l arpt.), NAnt. 152/D1
Flanagan (riv.), Can. 127/K2
Flanders (reg.), Fr. 42/E1
Flanders, NY, US 139/F2
Flat Holm (isl.), Eng, UK 32/C4
Flat River, Mo, US 129/K3
Flathead (riv.), Mt, US 126/E4
Flathead (lake), Mt, US 126/E4
Flathead, South Fork (riv.), Mt, US 126/E3
Flattery (cape), Wa, US 126/B3
Flattery (cape), Austl. 114/B1
Flavio Alfaro, Ecu. 152/B5
Flawil, Swi. 57/F3
Flaxlanden, Fr. 56/D2
Fleet, Eng, UK 33/F4
Fleetwood, Pa, US 138/C3
Fleetwood, Eng, UK 35/E4
Flekkefjord, Nor. 38/B2
Flemington, NJ, US 138/D2
Flemington Racecourse, Austl. 115/F5
Flemish Brabant (prov.), Belg. 53/D2
Flen, Swe. 38/G2
Flensburg, Ger. 38/C4
Flero, It. 58/D2
Fleron, Belg. 53/E2
Flers, Fr. 42/C2
Flesland (int'l arpt.), Nor. 38/A1
Fletschhorn (peak), Swi. 56/D5
Fleurance, Fr. 42/D5
Fleurier, Swi. 56/C4
Fleurus, Belg. 53/D3
Fleury-les-Aubrais, Fr. 42/D3
Flevoland (prov.), Neth. 50/C4
Flevoland (isl.), Neth. 40/C2
Flexenpass (pass), Aus. 57/G3
Flieden, Ger. 54/C2
Flieden (riv.), Ger. 54/C2
Fliess, Aus. 57/G3
Flims, Swi. 57/F4
Flin Flon, Mb, Can. 127/H2
Flinders (ranges), Austl. 109/C4
Flinders (bay), Austl. 109/A4
Flinders (reef), Austl. 109/D2
Flinders (riv.), Austl. 109/D2
Flinders (reefs), Austl. 109/D4
Flinders (range), Austl. 113/H5
Flinders Chase NP, Austl. 113/H5
Flinders Ranges NP, Austl. 113/H4
Flinders Reefs (isls.), Austl. 114/C2
Flines-lez-Raches, Fr. 52/C3
Flint (hills), US 129/H3
Flint (riv.), Ga, US 133/G4
Flint, Mi, US 130/D3
Flint (isl.), Kiri. 117/K6
Flint (lake), NW, Can. 123/J2
Flint, Wal, UK 35/E5
Flint, South Branch (riv.), Mi, US 135/F5
Flintbek, Ger. 38/D4
Flisa, Nor. 38/E1
Flix, Sp. 45/F2
Flixecourt, Fr. 52/B3
Flize, Fr. 53/D4
Floby, Swe. 38/E2
Floda, Swe. 38/E3
Flögelner See (riv.), Ger. 51/F1
Flöha (riv.), Ger. 41/G3
Floing, Fr. 53/D4
Flonheim, Ger. 54/B3
Flora, Il, US 129/K3
Flora (mt.), Austl. 112/C2
Flora, Nor. 37/C3
Floral Park, NY, US 139/L9
Florange, Fr. 53/F5
Florânia, Braz. 154/C2
Floraville, Il, US 137/G9
Floreffe, Belg. 53/D3
Florence, SC, US 133/J3
Florence, Al, US 133/G3
Florence, Az, US 128/E4
Florence (Firenze), It. 43/J5
Florence-Graham, Ca, US 136/F8
Florencia, Col. 152/C4
Florennes, Belg. 53/D3
Florenville, Belg. 53/E4
Flores (sea), Indo. 67/L10
Flores (isl.), Indo. 67/M10
Flores, Guat. 144/D2
Flores (dept.), Uru. 159/F2
Flores do Piauí, Braz. 154/B2
Floresta, Braz. 154/C3
Florham Park, NJ, US 139/H8
Floriano, Braz. 154/B2
Florianópolis, Braz. 155/B3
Florida, Peru 156/B2
Florida (bay), Fl, US 133/H5
Florida, Hon. 144/D3
Florida, Cuba 145/G1
Florida, Col. 152/B4
Florida (dept.), Uru. 159/F2
Florida, NY, US 138/D1
Florida (state), US 125/K6
Florida (str.), Cuba,US 125/K7
Florida, Uru. 159/K11
Florida Keys (isl.) 133/H5
Florida Keys (isls.), Fl, US 119/J7
Floridablanca, Col. 152/C3
Floridia, It. 46/D4
Florin, Ca, US 135/M10
Flórina, Gre. 47/G2
Florissant, Mo, US 137/G8

Florissant Fossil Beds
Nat'l Mon., Co, US 132/B2
Flörsbachtal, Ger. 54/C2
Flörsheim am Main, Ger. 54/B2
Flörsheim-Dalsheim, Ger. 54/B3
Florstadt, Ger. 54/B2
Flossenbürg, Ger. 55/F3
Floyd, Mo, US 137/E5
Floydada, Tx, US 129/G4
Fluchthorn (peak), Aus. 57/G4
Flüelapass (pass), Swi. 57/F4
Flüelen, Swi. 57/E4
Fluessen (lake), Neth. 50/C3
Flums, Swi. 57/F3
Flushing, Mi, US 130/D3
Fly (riv.), PNG 116/D5
Flying Fish (cape), Ant. 160/T
Fnjóská (riv.), Ice. 37/P6
Foam Lake, Sk, Can. 127/H3
Foča, Bosn. 48/D4
Fochabers, Sc, UK 36/C1
Fochville, SAfr. 106/P13
Fockbek, Ger. 38/C4
Focşani, Rom. 49/H3
Fogang, China 83/K3
Foggia, It. 46/D2
Foglia (riv.), It. 59/F5
Foglizzo, It. 58/A2
Föglö (isl.), Fin. 39/J3
Fogo (isl.), CpV. 93/J10
Fohnsdorf, Aus. 43/L3
Föhren, Ger. 53/F4
Foix, Fr. 42/D5
Folarskardnuten (peak), Nor. 38/B1
Folda (inlet), Nor. 37/E2
Földeák, Hun. 48/E2
Folégandros (isl.), Gre. 47/J4
Folembray, Fr. 52/C4
Foley (isl.), NW, US 123/J2
Folgaria, It. 57/H6
Foligno, It. 43/K5
Folkestone, Eng, UK 33/H4
Folkston, Ga, US 133/H4
Follainville-Dennemont, Fr. 30/H4
Follonica, Golfo di (gulf), It. 43/J5
Folschviller, Fr. 53/F5
Folsom, NJ, US 138/D4
Fomboni, Com. 107/G6
Fond du Lac, Wi, US 127/L5
Fond du Lac, Sk, Can. 122/F3
Fond du Lac (riv.), Sk, Can. 122/F3
Fondi, It. 46/C2
Fondo, It. 57/H5
Fongen (peak), Nor. 37/D3
Fonni, It. 46/A2
Fonsagrada, Sp. 44/B1
Fonseca (gulf), Nic. 140/D5
Fonseca, Col. 152/C2
Font Sancte, Pic de la (peak), Fr. 43/G4
Fontaine, Fr. 52/C4
Fontaine-Châalis, Fr. 30/L4
Fontaine-lès-Dijon, Fr. 56/A3
Fontaine-lès-Luxeuil, Fr. 56/C2
Fontaine-l'Evêque, Belg. 53/D3
Fontana, Ca, US 136/C2
Fontanarossa (int'l arpt.), It. 46/D4
Fontanella, It. 58/C2
Fontanellato, It. 58/D3
Fontaniva, It. 59/E1
Fonte Boa, Braz. 153/E5
Fontenailles, Fr. 30/L6
Fontenais, Swi. 56/C4
Fontenay-en-Parisis, Fr. 30/K4
Fontenay-le-Comte, Fr. 42/C3
Fontenay-le-Fleury, Fr. 30/J5
Fontenay-les-Briis, Fr. 30/J6
Fontenay-Saint-Père, Fr. 30/H4
Fontenay-sous-Bois, Fr. 30/K5
Fontenelle (res.), Wy, US 126/F5
Fontoy, Fr. 53/F5
Fontur (pt.), Ice. 37/P6
Foping, China 70/L5
Foraker (mt.), Ak, US 134/H3
Forbach, Fr. 53/F5
Forbach, Ger. 54/B5
Forbes, Austl. 115/D2
Forbesganj, India 85/F2
Forchheim, Ger. 54/E3
Forclaz, Col de la (pass), Swi. 56/D5
Førde, Nor. 37/C3
Fords, NJ, US 139/H9
Foreland (pt.), Eng, UK 32/C4
Foreland, The (pt.), Eng, UK 33/E5
Foremost, Ab, Can. 126/F3
Foreness (pt.), Eng, UK 33/H4
Forest, Ms, US 133/F3
Forest Hill, Md, US 138/B4
Forest Park, Ok, US 137/N14
Forestier (pen.), Austl. 115/D4
Forestville (cap.), Can. 131/G1
Forestville, Md, US 138/B6
Forez, Monts du (mts.), Fr. 42/E4
Forfar, Sc, UK 36/D2
Forges-les-Bains, Fr. 30/J6
Forggensee (lake), Ger. 57/G2
Forillon NP, Can. 131/H1
Forked River, NJ, US 139/K8
Forkill, NI, UK 34/B3
Forks, Wa, US 126/B4

Forlì, It. 59/F4
Forlì (prov.), It. 59/F4
Forlimpopoli, It. 59/F4
Formartine (reg.), Sc, UK 36/D2
Formby, Eng, UK 35/E4
Formby (pt.), Eng, UK 35/E4
Formentera, Isla de (isl.), Sp. 45/F3
Formentor (cape), Sp. 45/G3
Formerie, Fr. 52/A4
Formia, It. 46/C2
Formigine, It. 59/D3
Formignana, It. 59/E3
Formosa, Braz. 154/A4
Formosa, Arg. 157/E2
Formosa (peak), SAfr. 106/C4
Formosa, Braz. 154/A3
Formosa do Rio Prêto, Braz. 154/A3
Formosa, Serra (mts.), Braz. 151/G6
Formoso (riv.), Braz. 151/J6
Fornacelle, It. 59/E5
Fornaci di Barga, It. 59/E5
Fornæs (cape), Den. 38/D3
Fornebu (int'l arpt.), Nor. 38/D2
Fornovo di Taro, It. 58/D3
Forres, Sc, UK 36/C1
Forrest City, Ar, US 129/K4
Forsand, Nor. 38/B2
Forshaga, Swe. 38/E2
Forssa, Fin. 39/K1
Forstern, Ger. 55/E6
Forstinning, Ger. 55/E6
Forsyth, Mt, US 126/G4
Forsyth, Ga, US 133/H3
Forsyth (range), Austl. 114/A3
Forsythe NWR, NJ, US 138/D5
Fort Abbās, Pak. 86/B5
Fort Augustus, Sc, UK 36/B2
Fort Beaufort, SAfr. 106/D4
Fort Belvoir, Va, US 138/A6
Fort Benton, Mt, US 126/F4
Fort Bragg, Ca, US 126/C6
Fort Chambly Nat'l Hist. Park, Qu, Can. 131/P7
Fort Chipewyan, Ab, Can. 122/E3
Fort Cobb (res.), Ok, US 129/H4
Fort Collins, Co, US 137/B1
Fort Collins Museum, Co, US 137/B1
Fort Davis, Tx, US 129/G5
Fort de Douaumont, Fr. 53/E5
Fort-de-France, Guad. 141/N9
Fort de Vaux, Fr. 53/E5
Fort Desaix Mil. Res., Fr. 141/N9
Fort Erie, On, Can. 131/S10
Fort Frances, On, Can. 127/K5
Fort Franklin, NW, Can. 122/D2
Fort Frederica Nat'l Mon., Ga, US 133/H4
Fort George Nat'l Hist. Park, On, Can. 131/R9
Fort Gibson (lake), Ok, US 137/E2
Fort Good Hope, NW, Can. 122/D2
Fort Hancock, NJ, US 139/J10
Fort Howard, Md, US 138/B5
Fort Kent, Me, US 131/G2
Fort Lauderdale, Fl, US 133/H5
Fort Lauderdale-Hollywood (int'l arpt.), Fl, US 133/H5
Fort Lee, NJ, US 139/K8
Fort Lewis, Wa, US 135/B3
Fort Liard, NW, Can. 122/D2
Fort Liberté, Haiti 141/J2
Fort Lupton, Co, US 137/C2
Fort Macleod, Ab, Can. 126/E3
Fort Madison, Ia, US 127/L5
Fort-Mahon-Plage, Fr. 52/A3
Fort Malden Nat'l Hist. Park, On, Can. 135/F7
Fort-Mardyck, Fr. 52/B1
Fort Matanzas Nat'l Mon., Fl, US 133/H4
Fort McDowell Ind. Res., Az, US 137/S18
Fort McHenry Nat'l Mon., Md, US 138/B5
Fort McMurray, Ab, Can. 122/E3
Fort Mcpherson, NW, Can. 134/M2
Fort Meade, Md, US 138/B5
Fort Morgan, Co, US 129/G2
Fort Myers, Fl, US 133/H5
Fort Nelson, BC, Can. 124/AA13
Fort Nelson (riv.), BC, Can. 122/D3
Fort Norman, NW, Can. 122/D2
Fort Nottingham, SAfr. 107/F3
Fort Payne, Al, US 133/G3
Fort Peck (dam), Mt, US 126/G4
Fort Peck (lake), Mt, US 119/G5
Fort Pierce, Fl, US 133/H5
Fort Portal, Ugan. 104/A2
Fort Providence, NW, Can. 122/E2
Fort Qu'appelle, Sk, Can. 127/H3

Fort Randall (dam), SD, US 127/J5
Fort Resolution, NW, Can. 122/E2
Fort Saint James, BC, Can. 126/B2
Fort Saint John, BC, Can. 122/D3
Fort Saskatchewan, Ab, Can. 126/E2
Fort Scott, Ks, US 129/J3
Fort-Shevchenko, Kaz. 63/J3
Fort Simpson, NW, Can. 122/D2
Fort Smith, Ar, US 129/J4
Fort Smith, NW, Can. 122/E2
Fort Stanwix Nat'l Mon., NY, US 130/F3
Fort Stockton, Tx, US 129/G5
Fort Sumner, NM, US 129/G4
Fort Tilden, NY, US 139/K9
Fort Totten, ND, US 127/J4
Fort Vasquez Museum, Co, US 137/C2
Fort Vermilion, Ab, Can. 122/E3
Fort Wadsworth, NY, US 139/J9
Fort Walton Beach, Fl, US 133/G4
Fort Wayne, In, US 130/C3
Fort Wellington Nat'l Hist. Park, Can. 130/F2
Fort William, Sc, UK 36/A3
Fort Yates, ND, US 127/H4
Fort Yukon, Ak, US 134/J2
Fortaleza, Braz. 154/C1
Fortaleza dos Nogueiras, Braz. 154/A2
Fortaleza Santa Teresa, Uru. 159/G2
Forte dei Marmi, It. 58/D5
Fortescue (riv.), Austl. 116/A7
Fortescue, NJ, US 138/C5
Forth, Sc, UK 36/C4
Forth (riv.), Sc, UK 36/B4
Forth, Firth of (inlet), Sc, UK 36/C4
Fortin, Mex. 143/N8
Fortore (riv.), It. 46/D2
Fortrose, Sc, UK 36/B1
Fortuna, Braz. 154/A2
Fortuna, Arg. 158/D2
Fortuna Ledge, Ak, US 134/F3
Fortune (bay), Can. 131/L2
Fortune, Nf, Can. 131/L2
Forty Fort, Pa, US 138/C2
Forty Mile Scrub NP, Austl. 114/B2
Foshan, China 83/K3
Fosheim (pen.), NW, Can. 123/S7
Foss (riv.), Eng, UK 35/G4
Fossalta di Piave, It. 59/F1
Fossalta di Portogruaro, It. 59/F1
Fossano, It. 58/A3
Fosses, Fr. 30/K4
Fosses-la-Ville, Belg. 53/D3
Fossil, Or, US 126/C4
Fossil Creek (res.), Co, US 137/B2
Fossò, It. 59/F2
Fossombrone, It. 59/F5
Foster, Austl. 115/C3
Foster Pond, Il, US 137/G9
Fosterburg, Il, US 137/G8
Fostoria, Oh, US 130/D3
Fót, Hun. 49/R9
Foucarmont, Fr. 52/A4
Foucherans, Fr. 56/B3
Foug, Fr. 53/E6
Fougerolles, Fr. 56/C2
Fouilloy, Fr. 52/B3
Foul (bay), Egypt, Su 97/N3
Foulness (isl.), Sc, UK 31/V13
Foulness (isl.), Eng, UK 33/G3
Foulness (riv.), Eng, UK 35/G4
Foum Zguid, Mor. 98/D3
Foumban, Camr. 96/H6
Foundiougne, Sen. 102/A3
Fountain, Il, US 137/G9
Fountain Hill, Pa, US 138/C2
Fountain Hills, Az, US 137/S18
Fountain Valley, Ca, US 136/D8
Fountains Abbey, Eng, UK 35/G3
Fourchambault, Fr. 42/E3
Fourche La Fave (riv.), Ar, US 129/J4
Fourges, Fr. 30/G4
Fourmies, Fr. 52/D4
Fourth Cataract (falls), Sudan 101/C5
Fouta Djallon (phys. reg.), Gui. 96/C5
Foveaux (str.), NZ 109/G7
Fowey, Eng, UK 32/B6
Fowey (riv.), Eng, UK 32/B6
Fowler, Ca, US 136/C7
Fowlers (bay), Austl. 115/G6
Fowman, Iran 88/E1
Fox (isl.), Ak, US 134/D6
Fox (riv.), US 137/L5
Fox Creek, Ab, Can. 126/E3
Fox Glacier, NZ 117/S11
Fox Lake, BC, Can. 126/B2
Fox River Grove, Il, US 137/P15
Fox Valley, Sk, Can. 126/F3
Foxe (pen.), Can. 119/K3
Foxe (chan.), Can. 119/K3
Foxe Basin (basin), Can. 119/K3
Foxen (lake), Swe. 38/D2
Foyle (riv.), NI, UK 34/A2
Foz, Sp. 44/B1

Foz do Iguaçu, Braz. 157/F2
Frackville, Pa, US 138/B2
Fraga, Sp. 45/F2
Fragosa, Cayo (isl.), Cuba 145/G1
Fraiburgo, Braz. 155/B3
Frailes, Cordillera de los (mts.), Ven. 150/E7
Fraisans, Fr. 56/B3
Fraize, Fr. 56/D1
Frameries, Belg. 52/C3
Framlingham, Eng, UK 33/H2
Frammersbach, Ger. 54/C2
Franca, Braz. 155/C2
Francavilla al Mare, It. 46/D1
Francavilla Fontana, It. 47/F2
Francavilla in Sinni, It. 46/E2
France (ctry.) 27/E4
Frances (cape), Cuba 145/F1
Frances (lake), Yk, Can. 122/C2
Francés Viejo (cape), DRep. 141/H4
Franceville, Gabon 96/H8
Franche-Comté (pol. reg.), Fr. 56/B5
Franche-Comté (reg.), Fr. 43/G3
Francis Case (lake), SD, US 127/J5
Francisco de Orellana, Peru 156/C1
Francisco Escárcega, Mex. 144/D2
Francisco Javier Mina, Mex. 142/C3
Francisco Sá, Braz. 154/B5
Francisco Zarco, Mex. 142/A1
Francistown, Bots. 105/E5
Franco da Rocha, Braz. 211/G8
Francolino, It. 59/E3
Franconville, Fr. 30/J5
Franeker, Neth. 50/C2
Frang, Fr. 56/B5
Frank Hahn NP, Austl. 112/C5
Franken Wald (for.), Ger. 54/D3
Frankenau, Ger. 51/F6
Frankenberg-Eder, Ger. 51/F6
Frankenburg am Hausruck, Aus. 55/G6
Frankenhöhe (mts.), Ger. 54/D4
Frankenmarkt, Aus. 55/G7
Frankenmuth, Mi, US 130/D3
Frankenthal, Ger. 54/B3
Frankfort (cap.), Ky, US 130/C4
Frankfort, SAfr. 106/E2
Frankfurt, Ger. 41/H2
Frankfurt (int'l arpt.), Ger. 54/B2
Frankfurt am Main, Ger. 54/B2
Fränkische Alb (mts.), Ger. 40/F4
Fränkische Rezat (riv.), Ger. 54/D4
Fränkische Saale (riv.), Ger. 40/E3
Fränkische Schweiz (reg.), Ger. 43/J2
Fränkische Schweiz (reg.), Ger. 40/F4
Frankland (cape), Austl. 115/C3
Franklin (riv.), Austl. 115/C3
Franklin, NC, US 133/H3
Franklin, La, US 129/K5
Franklin, Ky, US 130/C4
Franklin, Tn, US 130/C5
Franklin, WV, US 130/E4
Franklin, In, US 130/B3
Franklin (mts.), NW, Can. 122/D2
Franklin (bay), NW, Can. 122/D2
Franklin, Mi, US 135/F6
Franklin D. Roosevelt (lake), Wa, US 126/D3
Franklin Lakes, NJ, US 139/J7
Franklin-Lower Gordon Wild Rivers NP, Austl. 115/C4
Franklin Mineral Museum, NJ, US 138/D1
Franklin Park, Il, US 135/O16
Franklin Square, NY, US 139/L9
Franksville, Wi, US 135/O14
Frankston, Austl. 115/N8
Franschhoek, SAfr. 106/L10
Fransisco Beltrão, Braz. 157/F2
Fransisco Morato, Braz. 211/G8
Františkovy Lázně, Czh. 55/F2
Franz Josef Land (isls.), Rus. 160/C
Franz Joseph Strauss (int'l arpt.), Ger. 43/J2
Franz Joseph Strauss (int'l arpt.), Ger. 55/E6
Fraser, Eng, UK 32/B6
Fraser (isl.), Austl. 109/E3
Fraser (mt.), Austl. 115/C3
Fraser, Mi, US 135/G6
Fraser Lake, BC, Can. 126/B2
Fraser NP, Austl. 115/C3
Fraserburg, SAfr. 106/C4
Fraserburgh, Sc, UK 36/D1
Frasne, Fr. 56/C3
Frassine (riv.), It. 59/E2
Frassino, It. 58/A3
Frastanz, Aus. 57/F3
Frazant, Fr. 42/D5

Frati, Monte dei (peak), It. 59/F5
Frauenfeld, Swi. 57/E2
Fraunberg, Ger. 55/F6
Fray Bentos, Uru. 159/J10
Fray Marcos, Uru. 159/L11
Frazier Park, Ca, US 128/C4
Frechen, Ger. 53/F2
Freckenhausen am Main, Ger. 54/B4
Fred (mt.), Les. 106/E3
Frederic, De, US 138/C6
Fredericia, Den. 38/C4
Frederick (reef), Austl. 109/E3
Frederick, Md, US 130/E4
Frederick, Ok, US 129/H4
Frederick (co.), Md, US 138/A5
Fredericksburg, Tx, US 129/H5
Fredericksburg, Pa, US 138/B3
Frederickton, Austl. 115/E1
Fredericton (cap.), Can. 131/G2
Frederik Willem IV (falls), Sur. 153/G4
Frederiks, Den. 38/C3
Frederiksberg (co.), Den. 38/E4
Frederiksborg Slot (Frederiksborg Castle), Den. 38/D3
Frederikshavn, Den. 38/D3
Fredersdorf bei Berlin, Ger. 40/Q7
Fredonia, Az, US 128/D3
Fredonia, NY, US 130/E3
Fredriksberg, Swe. 38/F1
Fredrikstad, Nor. 38/D2
Freeburg, Il, US 137/H9
Freeburg, Pa, US 138/B2
Freedom, Ok, US 132/D2
Freehold, NJ, US 138/D3
Freeland, Pa, US 138/C1
Freeland, Md, US 138/B4
Freeland, Wa, US 135/B1
Freeling (mt.), Austl. 113/G2
Freeling Heights (peak), Austl. 113/H4
Freemansburg, Pa, US 138/C2
Freeport, Il, US 127/L5
Freeport, NY, US 139/L9
Freeport, Tx, US 129/J5
Freeport, Bahm. 141/F2
Freeport, NY, US 139/L9
Freetown (cap.), SLeo. 102/B4
Fregenal de la Sierra, Sp. 44/B3
Fregonne, It. 42/D5
Fréhel (cape), Fr. 42/B2
Frei Inocêncio, Braz. 155/D1
Frei Mulde (riv.), Ger. 40/G3
Freiberg, Ger. 41/G3
Freiburg, Ger. 51/G1
Freiburg, Ger. 56/D2
Freienbach, Swi. 57/E3
Freihung, Ger. 55/E3
Freilassing, Ger. 55/F7
Fruška Gora NP, Cro. 46/D1
Freinsheim, Ger. 54/B3
Freire, Chile 158/B3
Freisen, Ger. 53/G4
Freising, Ger. 55/E6
Freistadt, Aus. 55/H5
Freital, Ger. 41/G3
Freixo de Espada à Cinta, Port. 44/B2
Frejorgues (int'l arpt.), Fr. 42/E5
Fréjus, Fr. 43/G5
Frekhaug, Nor. 38/A1
Fremainfille, Fr. 30/H4
Fremdingen, Ger. 54/D5
Frémécourt, Fr. 30/J4
Fremont (co.), Ut, US 128/E3
Fremont, Oh, US 130/D3
Fremont, Mi, US 130/C3
Fremont, Ca, US 128/B3
Fremont (isl.), Ut, US 137/J11
Fremont Lakes, NJ, US 139/J7
French (riv.), Can. 130/D2
French Creek State Park, Pa, US 138/C3
French Frigate Shoals (bar), Hi, US 117/J2
French Guiana (dpcy.), Fr. 151/H1
French Polynesia (terr.), Fr. 117/L6
Frenchman (isl.), Can., US 122/F4
Frenchman's (bay), Can. 131/R8
Frenchmans Cap (peak), Austl. 115/C4
Frenchtown, NJ, US 138/C2
Frenda, Alg. 100/F5
Frépillon, Fr. 30/J4
Freren, Ger. 51/E4
Fresco (riv.), Braz. 151/H5
Fresco, C.d'Iv. 102/D5
Fresia, Chile 158/B4
Fresnes, Fr. 71/L6
Fresnes-en-Woëvre, Fr. 53/E5
Fresnillo, Mex. 142/E4
Fresno, Ca, US 128/C3
Fresnoy-le-Grand, Fr. 52/C4
Fresse-sur-Moselle, Fr. 56/C2
Fressenneville, Fr. 52/A3
Fretin, Fr. 52/C2
Freuchie (lake), Sc, UK 36/C3
Freudenberg, Ger. 53/G2
Freudenberg, Ger. 54/C3
Freudenstadt, Ger. 57/F1
Frévent, Fr. 52/B3
Freycinet (har.), Austl. 112/B3
Freycinet NP, Austl. 115/D4
Freyming-Merlebach, Fr. 53/F5

Freystadt, Ger. 55/E4
Freyung, Ger. 55/G5
Fria (cape), Namb. 105/A4
Frias, Arg. 157/C2
Frias, Peru 156/B2
Fribourg, Swi. 56/D4
Fribourg (canton), Swi. 56/C4
Frick, Swi. 56/E2
Frickenhausen am Main, Ger. 54/D3
Fridingen an der Donau, Ger. 57/F1
Fridolfing, Ger. 55/F6
Friedberg, Ger. 54/B2
Friedberg, Ger. 54/D6
Friedeburg, Ger. 51/E2
Friedrichsdorf, Ger. 54/C2
Friedrichshafen, Ger. 57/F2
Friedrichstadt, Ger. 38/C4
Friedrichsthal, Ger. 53/G5
Friesenhagen, Ger. 53/G2
Friesenheim, Ger. 56/D1
Friesland (prov.), Neth. 50/C2
Friesoythe, Ger. 51/E2
Frignicourt, Fr. 53/D6
Frio, CR 143/F2
Friockheim, Sc, UK 36/D3
Friol, Sp. 44/B1
Frisange, Lux. 53/F4
Fristad, Swe. 38/E3
Fritsla, Swe. 38/E3
Fritzlar, Ger. 51/G6
Friuli-Venezia Giula (prov.), It. 43/K3
Frívitle-Escarbotin, Fr. 52/A3
Frobisher (bay), NW, Can. 123/C2
Frogmore, Eng, UK 30/A3
Frohavet (inlet), Nor. 37/D3
Frohnleiten, Aus. 43/L3
Froid-Chapelle, Belg. 53/D3
Froideconche, Fr. 56/C2
Froissy, Fr. 52/B4
Froland, Nor. 38/C2
Frolovo, Rus. 50/H3
Frome (lake), Austl. 109/D4
Frome, Eng, UK 32/D4
Frome (riv.), Eng, UK 32/D4
Froncles, Fr. 56/B1
Front (range), US 129/F2
Fronteira, Port. 44/B3
Frontenhausen, Ger. 55/F5
Frontera, Mex. 144/C3
Frontera Comalapa, Mex. 144/C3
Frontier Army Museum, Ks, US 137/D5
Frontignan, Fr. 42/E5
Fronton, Fr. 42/D5
Frosinone, It. 46/C2
Frösö, Swe. 37/D3
Frotey-lès-Vesoul, Fr. 56/C2
Frouard, Fr. 53/F6
Frövi, Swe. 38/F2
Froya (isl.), Nor. 37/D3
Frozen (str.), NW, Can. 123/H2
Fruges, Fr. 52/B2
Fruit Heights, Ut, US 137/K11
Frutal, Braz. 155/B1
Frutigen, Swi. 56/D4
Frutillar, Chile 158/B4
Fryazino, Rus. 61/X9
Frýdek-Mistek, Czh. 41/K4
Fu'an, China 79/C2
Fucecchio, It. 59/D5
Fucheng, China 72/D3
Fuchskaute (peak), Ger. 43/H1
Fuchū, China 70/L5
Fuchū, Japan 74/C3
Fuchū, Japan 77/C2
Fuchuan, China 70/L5
Fuchun (riv.), China 72/D5
Fuding, China 79/D2
Fuxian (lake), China 83/H3
Fuxin, China 72/E2
Fuxin Monggolzu Zizhixian, China 72/E2
Fuente de Cantos, Sp. 44/B3
Fuente del Maestre, Sp. 44/B3
Fuente Obejuna, Sp. 44/C3
Fuentesaúco, Sp. 44/C2
Fuentes de Oñoro, Sp. 44/B2
Fuerte Olimpo, Par. 150/G8
Fuerteventura (isl.), Sp. 96/B3
Fuga (isl.), Phil. 79/D4
Fuglebjerg, Den. 38/D4
Fugong, China 83/G2
Fugou, China 72/C4
Fuhai, China 70/E2
Fuhne (riv.), Ger. 51/H4
Fuji, Japan 75/F3
Fuji (riv.), Japan 75/F3
Fuji-Hakone-Izu NP, Japan 75/F3
Fuji-san (peak), Japan 75/F3
Fujian (prov.), China 71/L6
Fujieda, Japan 75/F3
Fujijdera, Japan 77/J6
Fujikawa, Japan 75/F3
Fujimi, Japan 77/D2
Fujin, China 71/M3
Fujinomiya, Japan 77/B3
Fujioka, Japan 77/D1
Fujioka, Japan 77/M5
Fujisawa, Japan 75/F3
Fujishiro, Japan 77/K5
Fujiwara, Japan 77/K5
Fujiyoshida, Japan 77/B3
Fukagawa, Japan 76/C2
Fukang, China 70/E3
Fukaya, Japan 77/C1
Fukiage, Japan 77/C1

Fukuchiyama, Japan 77/H5
Fukue, Japan 74/A4
Fukue (pref.), Japan 74/E3
Fukui, Japan 74/E3
Fukuoka, Japan 74/B4
Fukuoka (int'l arpt.), Japan 74/B4
Fukuoka (pref.), Japan 74/B4
Fukuoka, Japan 77/M4
Fukuroi, Japan 75/E3
Fukushima, Japan 75/G2
Fukushima (pref.), Japan 75/F2
Fukushima, Japan 76/B3
Fukuyama, Japan 74/C3
Fūlādī (mtn.), Afg. 89/J2
Fulda (riv.), Ger. 40/E3
Fulda, Ger. 54/C1
Fully, Swi. 56/D5
Fulpmes, Aus. 57/H3
Fulton, Mo, US 129/K3
Fulton, NY, US 130/E3
Fulton, Ky, US 130/B4
Fuluffjället (peak), Swe. 38/E1
Fumay, Fr. 53/D4
Fumel, Fr. 42/D4
Fumin, China 83/H2
Funabashi, Japan 77/D2
Funafuti (cap.), Tuv. 116/G5
Funafuti (isl.), Tuv. 116/G5
Funchal, Port. 98/A2
Funchal (int'l arpt.), Port. 98/A2
Fundación, Col. 152/C2
Fundão, Port. 44/B2
Fundy (bay), US, Can. 131/G2
Fundy NP, Can. 131/H2
Funing, China 83/J3
Funing, China 47/F2
Funing, China 72/D4
Funing, China 72/C3
Fuping, China 72/C3
Fuqing, China 79/D2
Fuquan, China 83/J2
Fur (riv.), China 73/C2
Furan (riv.), Fr. 56/B6
Furano, Japan 76/C2
Fürfeld, Ger. 53/G4
Furmanov, Rus. 61/G3
Furnas (res.), Braz. 147/E5
Furneaux Group (isls.), Austl. 109/D4
Fürstenau, Ger. 51/E3
Fürstenfeld, Aus. 43/M3
Fürstenfeldbruck, Ger. 54/E6
Fürstenwalde, Ger. 41/H2
Fürth, Ger. 54/B3
Fürth, Ger. 54/D3
Furth, Ger. 55/F5
Furth im Wald, Ger. 55/F4
Furtwangen im Schwarzwald, Ger. 56/D1
Furudal, Swe. 38/F1
Furukawa, Japan 76/B4
Fury and Hecla (str.), NW, Can. 123/H2
Fushan, China 72/E4
Fushan, China 72/D4
Fushun, China 72/D4
Fushun, China 73/B2
Fushun, China 83/J2
Fusio, Swi. 57/E5
Fuso, Japan 77/L5
Fusong, Japan 77/C2
Füssen, Ger. 57/G2
Fusui, China 78/D1
Futaba, Japan 75/G2
Futaleufú, Chile 158/C4
Futami, Japan 77/L7
Futog, Yugo. 48/D3
Futrono, Chile 158/B4
Futtsu, Japan 77/D2
Futuna (isl.), 116/H6
Fuwah, Egypt 91/B4
Fuyang, China 79/D2
Fuyuan, China 70/E2
Fuyun, China 70/E2
Fuyu, China 71/M2
Fuyu, China 71/M2
Fuzhou, China 72/E2
Fyn (co.), Den. 38/D4
Fyn (isl.), Den. 37/D5
Fyne, Loch (inlet), Sc, UK 36/A5
Fyresdal, Nor. 38/C2

Gagarin, Rus. 60/G5
Gaggenau, Ger. 54/B5
Gaggio Montano, It. 59/D4
Gaglianico, It. 58/B1
Gagnoa, C.d'Iv. 102/D5
Gagny, Fr. 30/K5
Gagra, Geo. 62/G4
Gagret, India 86/D4
Gai Xian, China 73/B2
Gaichtpass (pass), Aus. 57/G3
Gail (riv.), Aus. 43/K3
Gaildorf, Ger. 54/C5
Gaillac, Fr. 42/D5
Gailtaler (mts.), Aus. 43/K3
Gaiman, Arg. 158/D4
Gaimersheim, Ger. 55/E5
Gainesville, Tx, US 129/H4
Gainesville, Ga, US 133/H3
Gainesville, Fl, US 133/H4
Gainsborough, Eng, UK 35/H5
Gairdner (lake), Austl. 109/C4
Gairn (riv.), Sc, UK 36/C2
Gaiserwald, Swi. 57/F3
Gaizina (peak), Lat. 39/L3
Gakarosa (peak), SAfr. 106/C2
Galana (riv.), Kenya 104/C3
Galand, Iran 89/G1
Galanta, Slvk. 48/D2
Galápagos (isls.), Ecu. 156/E6
Galápagos (dept.), Ecu. 156/E7
Galápagos, PN, Ecu. 156/E7
Galashiels, Sc, UK 36/D5
Galati (prov.), Rom. 49/H3
Galati, Rom. 49/J3
Galatina, Gre. 47/G2
Galátiste, Gre. 47/H2
Galatone, It. 47/F2
Galb Azefal (hill), WSah. 98/B5
Goldácano, Sp. 44/D1
Gáldar, Sp. 98/B3
Galeana, Mex. 143/E3
Galeana, Indo. 81/G3
Galena, Ak, US 134/G3
Galena, Md, US 138/C5
Galena, Il, US 127/L5
Galeota (pt.), Trin. 153/F2
Galera (pt.), Ecu. 152/A4
Galera (pt.), Trin. 153/F2
Galera (riv.), Braz. 151/F7
Galesburg, Il, US 127/L5
Galesville, Md, US 138/B6
Galga (riv.), Hun. 49/R9
Galgorm, NI, UK 34/B2
Galich, Rus. 60/J4
Galicia (aut. comm.), Sp. 44/A1
Galičica NP, Macd. 47/G2
Galileo Galilei (int'l arpt.), It. 58/D5
Galinakopf (peak), Aus. 57/F3
Galion, Oh, US 130/D3
Gallan Head (pt.), Sc, UK 31/G7
Gallarate, It. 58/B1
Gallatin, Tn, US 130/C4
Gallatin, SrL. 82/D6
Gallego (riv.), Sp. 44/E1
Gallican, It. 58/D2
Galliera Veneta, It. 59/E1
Gallinas (mts.), NM, US 132/B3
Gallinas (pt.), Col. 152/D1
Gallipoli, It. 47/E2
Gallipoli (pen.), Tur. 49/H5
Gällivare, Swe. 37/G3
Gallneukirchen, Aus. 55/H6
Gallo (lake), It. 46/C2
Gallo (lake), It. 57/G4
Gallspach, Aus. 55/G6
Galluis, Fr. 30/H5
Gallup, NM, US 128/E4
Gallur, Sp. 44/E2
Gally (riv.), Fr. 30/H5
Galston, Sc, UK 36/B5
Galten, Den. 38/C3
Galva, La, US 137/F16
Galva, Swi. 31/P10
Galvarino, Chile 158/B3
Galveston, Tx, US 129/J5
Galveston (bay), Tx, US 129/J5
Galveston (isl.), Tx, US 140/C2
Gálvez, Sp. 44/C3
Galway, Ire. 31/P10
Galway (bay), Ire. 31/P10
Galzignano, It. 59/E2
Gam (riv.), Viet. 83/J3

G

Ga Vache (isl.), Haiti 141/H2

Gambsheim, Fr. 54/A5
Gaming, Aus. 43/L3
Gamka (riv.), SAfr. 106/C4
Gamkab (riv.), Namb. 106/B3
Gamleby, Swe. 38/G3
Gammelstad, Swe. 60/D2
Gammertingen, Ger. 57/F1
Gammon Ranges NP, Austl. 113/H4
Gamo, Japan 77/K5
Gampern, Aus. 55/G7
Gamud (peak), Eth. 104/C1
Gan, Fr. 42/C5
Gananoque, On, Can. 130/E2
Gânca, Azer. 63/H4
Ganda, Ang. 105/B3
Gandajika, D.R. Congo 105/D2
Gandak (riv.), India 85/E2
Gandaki (zone), Nepal 84/D1
Gander (lake), Can. 131/L1
Gander, Nf, Can. 131/L1
Genderkesee, Ger. 51/F2
Gandesa, Sp. 45/F2
Gāndhi Sāgar (res.), India 82/B3
Gandhīdhām, India 89/K4
Gandhinagar, India 89/K4
Gandia, Sp. 45/E3
Gandino, It. 58/C1
Gandoca-Manzanillo NWR, CR 145/F4
Gandu, Braz. 154/C4
Ganelo (well), Mrta. 102/C2
Ganesh (mtn.), China 85/E1
Gangapur, India 89/L3
Gangārāmpur, India 85/G3
Gangaw, Myan. 83/F3
Gangdisê (mts.), China 70/D5
Gangelt, Ger. 53/F2
Ganges, Fr. 42/E5
Ganges (Ganga) (riv.), India 84/B1
Ganges, Mouths of the (delta), Bang. 70/E7
Gangi, It. 46/D4
Gangkofen, Ger. 55/F6
Gangoh, India 86/D5
Gangtok, India 85/G2
Ganluo, China 83/H2
Gannat, Fr. 42/E3
Gansbaai, SAfr. 106/L11
Gänserndorf, Aus. 49/P7
Gansu (prov.), China 71/H4
Gantrisch (peak), Swi. 70/H4
Ganyu, China 72/D4
Ganzhou, China 79/B2
Ganzlin, Ger. 40/G2
Ganzourgou (prov.), Burk. 103/E3
Gao (pol. reg.), Mali 103/F2
Gao, Mali 103/F2
Gao'an, China 79/C2
Gaocheng, China 72/D5
Gaochun, China 72/D5
Gaoping, China 72/C4
Gaoqiao, China 72/D3
Gaotai, China 70/H4
Gaotang, China 72/D3
Gaoua, Burk. 102/E4
Gaoyang, China 72/C3
Gaoyou, China 72/D4
Gaozhou, China 83/K3
Gap, Fr. 43/G4
Gap, Pa, US 138/B4
Gar, China 70/C5
Garabogazköl Aylagy (gulf), Trkm. 63/K4
Garachiné, Pan. 152/B2
Garachiné (pt.), Pan. 145/G4
Garai (riv.), Bang. 85/G3
Garajonay PN de, Sp. 98/A3
Garamba, PN de la, D.R. Congo 97/L7
Garancières, Fr. 52/A6
Garanhuns, Braz. 154/C2
Garbsen, Ger. 51/G4
Garça, Braz. 155/B2
Garças (riv.), Braz. 155/H7
Garching an der Alz, Ger. 55/F6
García de Sota, Embalse de (res.), Sp. 44/C3
Gard (riv.), Fr. 42/F4
Garda (lake), It. 43/J3
Garda, It. 59/D1
Garde, Cap de (cape), Alg. 100/K6
Gardelegen, Ger. 51/H3
Garden (isl.), Austl. 112/K7
Garden City, Ks, US 129/H3
Garden City, NY, US 139/L9
Garden City, Mi, US 135/F7
Garden City Park, NY, US 139/L9
Garden Grove, Ca, US 136/D8
Garden Ridge, Tx, US 137/U20
Garden View, Pa, US 138/A1
Gardena, Ca, US 136/F8
Gardenstown, Sc, UK 36/D1
Gardez, Afg. 89/J2
Gardiner, Mt, US 126/F4
Gardiner, Me, US 131/G2
Gardiner (riv.), US 135/B1

Gardi – Goryn

Gardiners (isl.), NY, US 139/F1
Gardiners (bay), NY, US 139/F1
Gardner (lake), Ks, US 137/D6
Gardner, Ks, US 137/D6
Gardone val Trompia, It. 58/D1
Gare Loch (inlet), Sc, UK 36/B4
Gareat el Tarf (salt pan), Alg. 100/K7
Garelochhead, Sc, UK 36/B4
Garessio, It. 58/B4
Garet el Djenoun (peak), Alg. 99/G4
Garfield (mtn.), Mt, US 126/E4
Garfield, NJ, US 139/J8
Garfield, Ut, US 137/J12
Garforth, Eng, UK 35/G4
Gargaliánoi, Gre. 47/G4
Gargan (peak), Fr. 42/D4
Gargenville, Fr. 52/A6
Garges-lès-Gonesse, Fr. 30/K5
Gargnano, It. 59/D1
Garh Mahārāja, Pak. 86/A4
Garhākotā, India 84/B4
Garhbeta, India 85/F4
Garhmuktesar, India 84/B1
Garibaldi, Braz. 155/B4
Garies, SAfr. 106/B3
Garioch (reg.), Sc, UK 36/D2
Garissa, Kenya 104/C3
Garland, Tx, US 129/H4
Garlasco, It. 58/B2
Garmisch-Partenkirchen, Ger. 57/H3
Garmsār, Iran 88/F1
Garnpung (lake), Austl. 115/B2
Garonne (riv.), Fr. 42/D4
Garopaba, Braz. 155/B4
Garou (lake), Mali 103/E2
Garoua, Camr. 96/H6
Garphyttan, Swe. 38/F2
Garraf (mts.), Sp. 45/K7
Garrel, Ger. 54/D1
Garrison (dam), ND, US 127/H4
Garrison, ND, US 127/H4
Garron (pt.), NI, UK 34/C1
Garrovillas, Sp. 44/B3
Garry (bay), NW, Can. 122/G2
Garry (lake), Sc, UK 36/B2
Garry (riv.), Sc, UK 36/A2
Gars am Inn, Ger. 55/F6
Garsten, Ger. 55/H6
Garte (riv.), Ger. 51/H6
Gartempe (riv.) Fr. 42/D3
Gärtringen, Ger. 54/B5
Garut, Indo. 80/C5
Garvagh, NI, UK 34/B2
Garwa, India 84/D3
Garwolin, Pol. 41/L3
Gary, In, US 130/C3
Garza García, Mex. 143/E3
Garzê, China 70/H5
Garzón, Col. 152/C4
Gas, Fr. 30/G6
Gas City, In, US 130/C3
Gas-san (peak), Japan 76/B4
Gæsafjöll (peak), Ice. 37/P6
Gaschurn, Aus. 57/G4
Gasconade (riv.), Mo, US 129/J3
Gascony (reg.), Fr. 42/C5
Gascoyne (riv.), Austl. 109/A3
Gascoyne (mt.), Austl. 112/C3
Gaspar (str.), Indo. 80/C4
Gaspar, Braz. 155/B3
Gaspé, Qu, Can. 131/H1
Gaspé (pen.), Qu, Can. 123/K4
Gaspé, Cap de (cape), Can. 131/H1
Gaspoltshofen, Aus. 55/G6
Gasport, NY, US 131/S9
Gassino Torinese, It. 58/A2
Gastins, Fr. 30/M6
Gaston (lake), US 133/J2
Gastonia, NC, US 133/H3
Gastoúni, Gre. 47/G4
Gata (cape), Sp. 44/D4
Gata (cape), Cyp. 91/C2
Gata de Gorgos, Sp. 45/F3
Gata, Sierra de (mts.), Sp. 44/B2
Gatchina, Rus. 39/P2
Gatehouse-Of-Fleet, Sc, UK 34/D2
Gates of the Arctic NP and Prsv., Ak, US 134/G2
Gateshead (isl.), NW, Can. 122/F1
Gateshead, Eng, UK 35/G2
Gatesville, Tx, US 132/D4
Gateway Arch (arch), Mo, US 137/G8
Gateway NRA, NJ,NY, US 139/K9
Gatineau, Qu, Can. 130/F2
Gatineau (riv.), Qu, Can. 123/J4
Gatow, Ger. 40/Q7
Gattaran, Phil. 79/D4
Gattendorf, Aus. 43/M2
Gattianara, It. 58/B1
Gatton, Austl. 114/C4
Gatún (dam), Pan. 145/G4
Gatún (lake), Pan. 145/G4
Gatwick (int'l arpt.), Eng, UK 30/C3
Gau Algesheim, Ger. 54/B3
Gau Bischofsheim, Ger. 54/B3
Gau Odernheim, Ger. 54/B3
Gaubickelheim, Ger. 53/H4
Gauchy, Fr. 52/C4
Gaucín, Sp. 44/C4
Gauja (riv.), Est.,Lat. 39/L3
Gauja NP, Lat. 39/L3

Gaukönigshofen, Ger. 54/C3
Gaunless (riv.), Eng, UK 35/G2
Gaupne, Nor. 37/C3
Gaur (riv.), Sc, UK 36/B3
Gauri Sankar (peak), Nepal 85/F2
Gauripur, India 85/G2
Gausta (peak), Nor. 38/C2
Gauting, Ger. 55/E6
Gavà, Sp. 45/L7
Gávdhos (isl.), Gre. 47/J5
Gavere, Belg. 52/C2
Gavi, It. 58/B3
Gavião, Port. 44/B3
Gavirate, It. 58/B1
Gävle, Swe. 38/G1
Gävleborg (co.), Swe. 37/E3
Gawler (ranges), Austl. 109/C4
Gawler, Austl. 113/H5
Gay (peak), WV, US 130/D4
Gay, Rus. 63/L2
Gaya, Niger 103/F4
Gayaza, Ugan. 104/A3
Gaylord, Mi, US 130/C2
Gayndah, Austl. 114/C4
Gazaren, It. 58/D1
Gazelle (riv.), Sd. 30/H6
Gaziantep (prov.), Turk. 90/D2
Gaziantep, Turk. 90/D2
Gaziköy, Turk. 49/H5
Gazipaşa, Turk. 91/C1
Gazon de Faing (peak), Fr. 56/D1
Gazzaniga, It. 58/C1
Gbadolite, D.R. Congo 97/K7
Gbarnga, Libr. 102/C5
Gbongan, Nga. 103/G5
Gdansk (gulf), Pol. 41/K1
Gdańsk, Pol. 38/H4
Gdańsk (prov.), Pol. 38/H4
Gdynia, Pol. 38/H4
Ge (lake), China 72/D5
Geal Charn (peak), Sc, UK 36/C3
Geal Charn (peak), Sc, UK 36/A3
Gebaberg (peak), Ger. 54/D1
Gebe (isl.), Indo. 81/G3
Gebhardshain, Ger. 53/G2
Gebiz, Turk. 91/B1
Gebze, Turk. 49/J5
Gede (peak), Indo. 80/C5
Gedikbulak, Turk. 90/E2
Gedinne, Belg. 53/D4
Gediz, Turk. 49/B3
Gediz (riv.), Turk. 62/D5
Gedser (cape), Den. 38/D4
Gedser, Den. 38/D4
Gedsted, Den. 38/C3
Geel, Belg. 53/E1
Geelong, Austl. 115/C3
Geelvink (chan.), Austl. 109/A3
Geertruidenberg, Neth. 50/B5
Geeste (riv.), Ger. 51/F1
Geeste, Ger. 51/E2
Geesthacht, Ger. 51/H2
Geeveston, Austl. 115/C4
Gefrees, Ger. 55/E2
Gê'gyai, China 70/D5
Gehrde, Ger. 51/F3
Gehrden, Ger. 51/G4
Geifas (peak), Wal, UK 32/C2
Geikie (riv.), Sk, Can. 122/F3
Geilenkirchen, Ger. 53/F2
Geilo, Nor. 38/C1
Geinō, Japan 77/K6
Geiselhöring, Ger. 55/F5
Geiselwind, Ger. 54/D3
Geisenfeld, Ger. 55/E5
Geisenhausen, Ger. 55/F6
Geisenheim, Ger. 53/G4
Geislingen, Ger. 57/E1
Geislingen an der Steige, Ger. 54/C5
Geita, Tanz. 104/B3
Gejiu, China 70/H4
Gela, It. 46/D4
Gela, Golfo di (gulf), It. 46/D4
Gelai (peak), Tanz. 104/C3
Gelderland (prov.), Neth. 50/C4
Geldermalsen, Neth. 50/C5
Geldern, Ger. 50/D5
Geldrop, Neth. 50/C6
Geleen, Neth. 53/E2
Gelendost, Turk. 90/B2
Gelendzhik, Rus. 62/F3
Gelibolu (Gallipoli), Turk. 47/K2
Gelibolu Yarımadası NP, Turk. 47/K2
Gelincik (peak), Turk. 91/B2
Gelligaer, Wal, UK 32/C3
Gelnhausen, Ger. 54/C2
Gelsenkirchen, Ger. 50/E5
Geltendorf, Ger. 57/H1
Gelterkinden, Swi. 56/D3
Gelting, Ger. 38/C4
Gemas, Malay. 80/B3
Gembloux, Belg. 53/D2
Gemena, D.R. Congo 97/J7
Gemert, Neth. 50/C5
Gemlik (gulf), Turk. 49/J5
Gemlik, Turk. 49/J5
Gemona del Friuli, It. 43/K3
Gemsbok NP, Bots. 105/D6
Gemuk (mtn.), Ak, US 134/G3
Gemünden am Main, Ger. 54/C2
Genalē Wenz (riv.), Eth. 97/N6
Genappe, Belg. 53/D2
Genay, Fr. 56/A6
Gençay, Fr. 42/D3
Genç, Turk. 90/E2
Gendringen, Neth. 50/D5
Gendt, Neth. 50/C5
Genemuiden, Neth. 50/C5

General Abelardo L. Rodriguez (int'l arpt.), Mex. 128/C4
General Acha, Arg. 158/D3
General Alfredo Vasquez Cobo (int'l arpt.), Col. 156/D2
General Alvear, Arg. 158/E2
General Alvear, Arg. 158/E3
General Arenales, Arg. 158/E2
General Belgrano, Arg. 158/F2
General Belgrano II, Arg., Ant. 160/X
General Cabrera, Arg. 158/E2
General Carrera (lake), Chile 157/B6
General Cepeda, Mex. 143/E3
General Conesa, Arg. 158/D4
General Deheza, Arg. 158/E2
General Edward Lawrence Logan (Logan Int'l) (int'l arpt.), Ma, US 131/G3
General Enrique Godoy, Arg. 158/D3
General Francisco Villa, Mex. 143/F3
General Galarza, Arg. 159/J10
General Grant Nat'l Mem., NY, US 139/K8
General Juan Álvarez, Pk., Mex. 143/F5
General Juan José Ríos, Mex. 142/C3
General Juan Madariaga, Arg. 159/F3
General La Madrid, Arg. 158/E3
General Lagos, Chile 156/D5
General Las Heras, Arg. 159/J11
General Lavalle, Arg. 159/K12
General Martín Miguel de Güemes, Arg. 157/C1
General Pico, Arg. 158/E2
General Pinedo, Arg. 158/E1
General Pinto, Arg. 158/E2
General Roca, Arg. 158/D3
General San Martín, Arg. 158/E3
General San Martín, Arg. 159/J11
General San Martín, Arg., Ant. 160/X
General Santiago Marino (int'l arpt.),Ven. 153/F2
General Terán, Mex. 143/F3
General-Toshevo, Bul. 49/J2
General Viamonte, Arg. 158/E2
General Villalobos (int'l arpt.), Mex. 132/B4
General Villegas, Arg. 158/E2
General Zaragoza, Mex. 143/E3
Generoso (peak), Swi. 57/F6
Genesee (riv.), NY, US 130/E3
Genesee (co.), Mi, US 135/E6
Genesee, Wi, US 135/P14
Genesee Depot, Wi, US 135/P14
Geneseo, Il, US 127/L5
Geneseo, NY, US 130/E3
Geneva, Al, US 133/G4
Geneva, NY, US 130/E3
Geneva, Ne, US 129/H2
Geneva, Ut, US 137/K13
Geneva (int'l arpt.), Swi. 56/C5
Geneva (Genève), Swi. 56/C5
Geneva (Léman) (lake), Fr. 43/G3
Genève (canton), Swi. 56/C5
Genève, Swi. 56/C5
Gengenbach, Ger. 56/E1
Génicourt, Fr. 30/J4
Genk, Belg. 53/E2
Genlis, Fr. 56/B3
Gennach (riv.), Ger. 57/G2
Gennargentu (mts.), It. 155/A3
Gennep, Neth. 50/C5
Gennevilliers, Fr. 30/J5
Genoa City, Wi, US 135/P14
Genoa (Genova), It. 43/H4
Genoa (prov.), It. 58/B4
Genoa (Genoa), It. 58/B4
Genoa, Golfo di (gulf), It. 43/H4
Genovesa (isl.), Ecu. 153/F6
Gensingen, Ger. 53/G4
Gent-Brugge Kanaal (canal), Belg. 52/C1
Gent (Ghent), Belg. 52/C1
Genteng (cape), Indo. 80/C5
Genteng, Indo. 80/D5
Geographe (bay), Austl. 112/B3
Geographe (chan.), Austl. 112/B3
Georg von Neumayer, Ger., Ant. 160/Z
George (lake), Ugan. 104/A3
George (lake), Fl, US 133/H4
George, SAfr. 106/C4
George (lake), NY, US 130/F3
George (riv.), Can. 119/L4
George Land (isl.), Rus. 64/A2
George Town, Malay. 80/B3
George Town, Austl. 115/C4
George Town (cap.), Cay. 145/F2
George V (coast), Ant. 160/L
George Washington Birthplace Nat'l Mon., Va, US 138/C4
George West, Tx, US 132/D4
Georgensmünd, Ger. 54/E4
Georges (riv.), Austl. 114/C4
Georgetown, Ga, US 133/H4

Georgetown, SC, US 133/J3
Georgetown, Tx, US 129/H5
Georgetown, Ky, US 130/C4
Georgetown, StV. 141/N9
Georgetown (cap.), Guy. 153/G3
Georgetown, Austl. 114/B2
Georgetown, Ct, US 139/E1
Georgi Traykov, Bul. 49/H2
Georgia (ctry.) 49/H2
Georgia (state), US 125/K5
Georgia, Strait of (str.), Can. 126/B3
Georgian (bay), On, Can. 123/H4
Georgian Bay Islands NP, Can. 130/D2
Georgina (riv.), Austl. 109/C3
Georgsmarienhütte, Ger. 51/F4
Gepatsch (lake), Aus. 57/G4
Gera, Ger. 55/F2
Geraardsbergen, Belg. 52/C2
Geral de Goiás, Serra (mts.), Braz. 151/J6
Geral, Serra (mts.), Braz. 157/F2
Geraldine, NZ 117/S11
Geraldton, Austl. 112/B4
Gérardmer, Fr. 56/C1
Gerasdorf bei Wien, Aus. 49/N7
Gerbéviller, Fr. 56/C1
Gerbier de Jonc (peak), Fr. 42/F4
Gerbrunn, Ger. 54/C3
Gerdau (riv.), Ger. 51/H3
Gerdine (mt.), Ak, US 134/H3
Gerede, Turk. 49/L5
Geretsried, Ger. 57/H2
Gérgal, Sp. 44/D4
Gerger, Turk. 90/D2
Gerlach, Nv, US 126/D5
Gerlachovský Štít (peak), Slvk. 41/L4
Gerlafingen, Swi. 56/D3
Germantown, Tn, US 129/K4
Germantown, Md, US 138/A5
Germany (ctry.) 27/E3
Germering, Ger. 55/E6
Germersheim, Ger. 54/B4
Germigny-l'Evêque, Fr. 30/L5
Germiston, SAfr. 106/E2
Gernsbach, Ger. 54/B5
Geroldsgrün, Ger. 55/E2
Gerolsbach, Ger. 55/E5
Gerolstein, Ger. 53/F3
Gerolzhofen, Ger. 54/D3
Gerpinnes, Belg. 53/D3
Gerra (Verzasca), Swi. 57/E5
Gerrongong, Austl. 115/D2
Gers (riv.), Fr. 42/D5
Gersau, Swi. 57/E4
Gersfeld, Ger. 54/C2
Gersheim, Ger. 53/G5
Gerspenz (riv.), Ger. 54/B3
Gerstetten, Ger. 54/D5
Gerstheim, Fr. 56/D1
Gersthofen, Ger. 54/D5
Gerstungen, Ger. 51/H7
Gêrzê, China 70/D5
Gerze, Turk. 62/E4
Geseke, Ger. 51/F5
Gespunsart, Fr. 53/D4
Gessertshausen, Ger. 54/D6
Gestro Wenz (riv.), Eth. 97/P6
Gesves, Belg. 53/E2
Geta, Fin. 39/H1
Getafe, Sp. 45/N9
Gete (riv.), Belg. 53/E2
Getinge, Swe. 38/E3
Gettorf, Ger. 38/D4
Gettysburg, SD, US 127/J4
Gettysburg, Pa, US 138/A4
Gettysburg Nat'l Mil. Park, Pa, US 138/A4
Getúlio Vargas, Braz. 155/A3
Geul (riv.), Neth. 53/E2
Geureudong (peak), Indo. 80/A3
Geurie, Austl. 115/D2
Gevas, Turk. 90/D2
Gevelsberg, Ger. 51/E6
Gevgelija, Macd. 47/H2
Gex, Fr. 56/C5
Geyer, Fr. 55/F1
Geyersberg (peak), Ger. 54/C3
Geyikli, Turk. 49/G3
Geyser (reef), Madg. 107/H6
Geyve, Turk. 49/K5
Gez (riv.), China 87/F5
Ghadāmis, Libya 99/H3
Ghaghara (riv.), India 84/C5
Ghaghara (riv.), India 84/D3
Ghakhar, Pak. 86/C3
Ghana (ctry.) 93/B4
Ghanzi, Bots. 105/D5
Gharaunda, India 84/D5
Ghardaïa, Alg. 99/F2
Ghardaïa (prov.), Alg. 99/F2
Ghardimaou, Tun. 100/L6
Gharghoda, India 84/D4
Gharyān, Libya 99/H2
Ghāt, Libya 99/H4
Ghātāl, India 85/F4
Ghātampur, India 84/C2
Ghātsīla, India 85/F4
Ghazal, Bahr el (riv.), Chad 96/J5
Ghazaouet, Alg. 100/D2
Ghāzīpur, India 84/D3
Ghazni, Afg. 89/J2
Ghedi, It. 58/D2
Gheens, La, US 137/P17
Ghemme, It. 58/B1
Ghenghis Khan, Wall of, Mong. 71/K2
Gheorghe Gheorghiu-Dej, Rom. 49/H2

Gheorgheni, Rom. 49/G2
Gherla, Rom. 49/F2
Ghilarza, It. 46/A2
Ghimbav (Ghinda), Erit. 88/C5
Ghio (lake), Arg. 158/C5
Ghirārah (gulf),
Ghisalba, It. 58/C1
Ghisonaccia, Fr. 46/A1
Ghotki, Pak. 82/A2
Ghugri (riv.), India 85/F3
Ghūriān, Afg. 89/H2
Ghuzayyil, Bi'r al (well), Libya 96/H2
Giannutri (isl.), It. 46/B1
Giant's Castle (peak), SAfr. 106/E3
Giant's Causeway, NI, UK 34/B1
Giarre, It. 46/D4
Gistel, Belg. 52/B1
Gibbons, Ab, Can. 126/E2
Gibbstown, NJ, US 138/C4
Gibloux (peak), Swi. 56/D4
Gibraleón, Sp. 44/B4
Gibraltar, Ven. 141/G6
Gibraltar (res.), Ca, US 136/K1
Gibraltar (cap.), Gib. 44/C4
Gibraltar (str.), Mor.,Sp. 27/D5
Gibraltar, Mi, US 135/F7
Gibraltar (pt.), Eng, UK 35/J5
Gibraltar Range NP, Austl. 115/E1
Gibson (is.), Austl. 109/B3
Gibson Desert Nature Reserve, Austl. 109/B3
Giddarbāha, India 86/C4
Giddings, Tx, US 129/H5
Giddings, Co, US 137/B1
Gidi (pass), Egypt 91/C4
Giebelstadt, Ger. 54/C3
Gieboldehausen, Ger. 51/H5
Gien, Fr. 42/E3
Giengen an der Brenz, Ger. 54/D5
Giessbachfälle (falls), Swi. 56/E4
Giessen (riv.), Fr.,Ger. 56/D1
Giessendam, Neth. 50/B5
Gieten, Neth. 50/D2
Gif-sur-Yvette, Fr. 30/J5
Gīfān, Iran 63/L5
Gifford, Fl, US 133/H5
Gifford, Fr. 57/C5
Gifhorn, Ger. 51/H4
Gifu, Japan 77/L5
Giganta, Sierra de la (mts.), Mex. 142/C3
Gigante, Col. 152/C4
Giglio (isl.), It. 46/B1
Gijón, Sp. 44/C1
Gil de Vilches, PN, Chile 158/C2
Gila (riv.), US 128/D4
Gila Bend, Az, US 128/D4
Gila Cliff Dwellings Nat'l Mon., NM, US 128/E4
Gila River Ind. Res., Az, US 137/R19
Gilbert, Mn, US 130/A2
Gilbert, Az, US 137/S19
Gilbert (isls.), Kiri. 116/G5
Gilberts, Il, US 135/P15
Gilbués, Braz. 154/A3
Gilching, Ger. 54/E6
Gilcrest, Co, US 137/C2
Gilford, NI, UK 34/B2
Gilford Park, NJ, US 138/D4
Gilgandra, Austl. 115/D1
Gilgil, Kenya 104/C3
Gilgit (riv.), Pak. 87/F5
Gilgit, Pak. 87/F5
Gilles (lake), Austl. 113/H5
Gillette, Wy, US 127/G4
Gillies Bay, BC, Can. 126/B3
Gilly, Swi. 56/C5
Gilman Hot Springs, Ca, US 136/D3
Gilman, Tx, US 129/J4
Gilpin, Co, US 137/A3
Gilqit (riv.), Pak. 89/K1
Gilze, Neth. 50/C5
Gimbī, Eth. 97/N6
Gimbsheim, Ger. 54/B3
Gimel, Swi. 56/C5
Gimie (mt.), StL. 141/N9
Gimli, Mb, Can. 127/J3
Gimo, Swe. 38/H1
Gin Gin, Austl. 114/C4
Ginan, Japan 77/L5
Gingelom, Belg. 53/E2
Gingin, Austl. 112/B4
Gingindlovu, SAfr. 107/E3
Gingoog, Phil. 81/G2
Gingst, Ger. 38/E4
Ginosa, It. 46/E2
Ginowan, Japan 75/J7
Gioia (gulf), It. 46/E3
Gioia del Colle, It. 46/E2
Gioia Tauro, It. 46/D3
Gíornico, Swi. 57/E5
Gioùra (isl.), Gre. 47/J3
Gioveretto (peak), It. 57/G5
Giovi (riv.), It. 58/B3
Gippsland (riv.), Eng, UK 35/E5
Girardot, Col. 150/D3
Girardville, Pa, US 138/B2
Giraumont, Fr. 53/E4
Girdle Ness (pt.), Sc, UK 36/E2
Gireoun, Fr. 52/A2
Giresun, Turk. 62/F4
Giresun (prov.), Turk. 62/F4
Girga, Egypt 91/C4
Girgasco, It. 58/B1
Giridīh, India 85/F3

Girifalco, It. 46/E3
Girling (res.), Eng, UK 30/C2
Giromagny, Fr. 56/C2
Girón, Ecu. 152/B5
Girona, Sp. 45/G2
Gironcourt-sur-Vraine, Fr. 56/B1
Gironde (riv.), Fr. 42/C4
Gironella, Sp. 45/F1
Giru, Austl. 114/B2
Girvan, Sc, UK 34/D1
Gisborne, NZ 117/T10
Gisenyi, Rwa. 104/A3
Gisors, Fr. 52/A5
Gistrup, Den. 38/D3
Gitega, Buru. 104/A3
Giubiasco, Swi. 57/E5
Giugliano in Campania, It. 48/B5
Giulianova, It. 43/K5
Giurgiu (prov.), Rom. 49/G3
Giurgiu, Rom. 49/G4
Giussano, It. 58/C1
Giv'at Brenner, Isr. 91/F8
Giv'at Hayyim, Isr. 91/F7
Giv'atayim, Isr. 91/F7
Give, Den. 38/C4
Givet, Fr. 53/D3
Givine, Col de la (pass), Swi. 56/C5
Givors, Fr. 42/F4
Gizo, Sol. 116/F5
Gizhiga (bay), Rus. 65/R3
Gizo, Sol. 116/F5
Gjøl, Den. 38/C3
Gjoa Haven, NW, Can. 122/G2
Gjøvik, Nor. 38/D1
Glabbeek, Belg. 53/E2
Glace Bay, NS, Can. 131/K2
Glacier (peak), Wa, US 126/C3
Glacier NP, Can. 126/D3
Glacier Bay NP and Prsv., Ak, US 134/L4
Gladbeck, Ger. 50/D5
Gladewater, Tx, US 129/J4
Gladstone, Fl, US 137/D5
Gladstone, Austl. 114/C3
Gladstone, Austl. 113/H5
Gladstone, Mo, US 137/G6
Glafsfjorden (lake), Swe. 38/D2
Glåma (riv.), Nor. 37/D3
Glamis, Sc, UK 36/D3
Glamsbjerg, Den. 38/D4
Glan (riv.), Ger. 54/A4
Glan (riv.), Aus. 40/D4
Glan, Phil. 81/G2
Glanamman, Wal, UK 32/C3
Gland, Swi. 56/C5
Gland (riv.), Fr. 53/D4
Glärnisch (range), Swi. 57/E3
Glarus, Swi. 57/F3
Glarus (canton), Swi. 57/E4
Glarus Alps (range), Swi. 43/H3
Glas Maol (peak), Sc, UK 36/D3
Glasgow, Mt, US 126/G3
Glasgow, Ky, US 130/C4
Glasgow, De, US 138/C4
Glasgow, Sc, UK 36/B5
Glashütten, Ger. 54/B2
Glaslyn (riv.), Wal, UK 34/D6
Glass (mts.), Ok, US 132/D2
Glass (lake), Sc, UK 36/B1
Glass (riv.), Sc, UK 36/B1
Glassboro, NJ, US 138/C4
Glastonbury, Eng, UK 32/C4
Glatt (riv.), Swi. 54/B6
Glattbach, Ger. 54/C3
Glattfelden, Swi. 57/E2
Glavinitsa, Bul. 49/H4
Glazoué, Ben. 103/F5
Glazov, Rus. 61/M4
Glemms (riv.), Ger. 54/C5
Glen Burnie, Md, US 138/B5
Glen Canyon (dam), US 128/D3
Glen Canyon Nat'l Rec. Area, US 128/D3
Glen Carbon, Il, US 137/H8
Glen Coe (pass), Sc, UK 36/B3
Glen Cove, NY, US 139/L8
Glen Gardner, NJ, US 138/D2
Glen Haven, Co, US 137/B2
Glen Innes, Austl. 115/D1
Glen Lyon, Pa, US 138/B1
Glen Môr (valley), Sc, UK 36/B2
Glen Park, Mo, US 137/G9
Glen Ridge, NJ, US 139/J8
Glen Rock, Pa, US 138/B4
Glen Rock, NJ, US 139/J7
Glen Ullin, ND, US 127/H4
Glenaire, Mo, US 137/E5
Glenarm, NI, UK 34/C2
Glenavy, NI, UK 34/B2
Glenboig, Sc, UK 36/B5
Glenboro, Mb, Can. 127/J3
Glencoe, SAfr. 107/E3

Glencoe, Mo, US 137/F8
Glencoe, Il, US 135/Q15
Glencoe, Sc, UK 36/B3
Glencoe, Or, US 136/C5
Glendale, Ca, US 136/K1
Glendale, Az, US 137/R18
Glendale, Ca, US 136/F7
Glendale Heights, Il, US 135/P16
Glenden, Austl. 114/C3
Glendive, Mt, US 127/G4
Glendo (res.), Wy, US 127/G5
Glendora, Ca, US 136/C2
Glendun (riv.), Sc, UK 34/B1
Gleneagles, Sc, UK 36/C4
Glenelg, Austl. 113/H5
Glenelg (riv.), Austl. 115/B3
Glenelg, Sc, UK 31/B8
Glenelly (riv.), NI, UK 34/A2
Glengarry (range), Austl. 112/C3
Glenluce, Sc, UK 34/D2
Glenmere (lake), NY, US 138/D1
Glennallen, Ak, US 134/J3
Glenolden, Pa, US 138/C4
Glenorie, Austl. 114/H8
Glenpool, Ok, US 129/H4
Glenrothes, Sc, UK 36/C4
Glens Falls, NY, US 130/F3
Glenshane (pass), NI, UK 34/B2
Glenside, Pa, US 138/C3
Glenties, Ire. 31/P9
Glenveagh NP, Ire. 31/Q9
Glenview, Il, US 135/Q15
Glenwood, NJ, US 138/D1
Glenwood Springs, Co, US 128/B3
Gleouraich (peak), Sc, UK 36/A2
Glifádha, Gre. 47/N9
Glimåkra, Swe. 38/E3
Glina, Cro. 48/C3
Glinde, Ger. 51/H1
Glindow, Ger. 40/P7
Gliwice, Pol. 41/K3
Globe, Az, US 128/E4
Glockturm (peak), Aus. 57/G4
Gloggnitz, Aus. 41/H5
Głogów, Pol. 41/J3
Głogówek, Pol. 41/J3
Glonn (riv.), Ger. 54/E6
Glonn, Ger. 57/H1
Gloria (bay), Can. 145/G1
Glorieuses, Îles (isls.), Reun. 107/H5
Glorious (mt.), BC, Can. 126/B3
Glory of Russia (cape), Ak, US 134/D3
Glossop, Eng, UK 35/G5
Gloster, Ms, US 129/K5
Gloucester, BC, Can. 126/B3
Gloucester, Austl. 115/D1
Gloucester, On, Can. 130/F2
Gloucester, Eng, UK 32/D3
Gloucester (co.), NJ, US 138/C4
Gloucester City, NJ, US 138/C4
Gloucestershire (co.), Eng, UK 32/D3
Glovers Reef (reef), Belz. 144/E2
Glovertown, Nf, Can. 131/L1
Głowno, Pol. 41/K3
Głubczyce, Pol. 41/J3
Głuchołazy, Pol. 41/J3
Glücksburg, Ger. 38/C4
Glückstadt, Ger. 51/G1
Glyndon, Md, US 138/B5
Glyngøre, Den. 38/C3
Glynn, NI, UK 34/C2
Gmünd, Aus. 41/H4
Gmünd, Aus. 40/D4
Gmunden, Aus. 55/G7
Gnagna (prov.), Burk. 103/E3
Gnarrenburg, Ger. 51/G2
Gniew, Pol. 39/H5
Gniezno, Pol. 41/J2
Gnjilane, Yugo. 47/G1
Gnowangerup, Austl. 112/C5
Gō (riv.), Japan 74/D3
Go Cong, Viet. 78/D4
Goa (state), India 85/H2
Goālpāra, India 85/G2
Goat Fell (peak), Sc, UK 34/C1
Goba, Eth. 97/N6
Gobabis, Namb. 105/C5
Gobernador Castro, Arg. 158/F2
Gobernador Costa, Arg. 157/B5
Gobernador Gregores, Arg. 157/B7
Gobernador Mansilla, Arg. 159/J10
Gobi (des.), China,Mon 67/K3
Göblberg (peak), Aus. 55/G6
Gobō, Japan 74/D4
Goch, Ger. 50/D5
Gochsheim, Ger. 54/D2
Godalming, Eng, UK 33/F4
Godāvari (riv.), India 67/G9
Goddā, India 85/F3
Godeanu (peak), Rom. 48/F3
Godech, Bul. 47/H1
Godfrey, Il, US 137/H8
Gōdo, Japan 77/L5
Gödöllő, Hun. 49/K5
Godoy Cruz, Arg. 158/C2
Gods (riv.), Mb, Can. 122/H3
Gods (lake), Mb, Can. 122/H3
Gods Mercy (bay), NW, Can. 123/H3
Godthåb (Nuuk), Grld. 119/N3
Godwin Austen (K2) (peak), Pak. 86/D2
Goéland (lake), Can. 130/E1

Goeree (isl.), Neth. 50/A5
Goes, Neth. 50/A5
Gogebice (range), US 127/L4
Göggingen, Ger. 54/D6
Gogland (isl.), Rus. 39/M1
Gogōme, Japan 76/B4
Gogounou, Ben. 103/F4
Gogra (riv.), India 82/D2
Gohad, India 84/B2
Gohāna, India 86/D5
Gohbach (riv.), Ger. 51/G3
Goiana, Braz. 154/D2
Goiandira, Braz. 155/B1
Goiânia, Braz. 151/J7
Goianinha, Braz. 154/D2
Goiás, Braz. 151/H7
Goiás (state), Braz. 154/A5
Goiatuba, Braz. 155/B1
Goil (lake), Sc, UK 36/B4
Goirle, Neth. 50/C5
Góis, Port. 44/A2
Goito, It. 58/D2
Gojō, Japan 74/D3
Gojra, Pak. 86/B4
Gok (riv.), Turk. 62/E4
Goka, Japan 77/D1
Gokase (riv.), Japan 74/B4
Gokashō, Japan 77/K5
Gokasho, (bay), Japan 77/L7
Gökçeada (isl.), Turk. 49/H3
Gökçebey, Turk. 49/L5
Gökçekaya (dam), Turk. 49/K5
Gökçen, Turk. 90/B2
Göksun, Turk. 90/D2
Göksu (riv.), Turk. 90/C2
Göktepe, Turk. 91/C1
Gol, Nor. 38/C1
Gola Gokarannāth, India 84/C1
Golan Hts. (reg.), Syria 91/G7
Golasecca, It. 58/B1
Gölbaşı, Turk. 90/D2
Gölcük, Mt, US 135/F6
Golbey, Fr. 56/C1
Gölcük, Turk. 49/J5
Gölcük, Turk. 49/K5
Gold (riv.), Mb, Can. 122/G3
Gold (mtn.), US 137/R19
Gold (coast), Gha. 96/E7
Gold Bar, Wa, US 135/B2
Gold Beach, Or, US 126/B5
Gold Coast, Austl. 114/D5
Gold Hill, Co, US 137/B2
Gold River, BC, Can. 126/B3
Goldach, Swi. 57/F3
Goldbach, Ger. 54/C3
Goldberg, Ger. 38/E5
Golden, BC, Can. 126/D3
Golden, Co, US 137/B3
Golden Eagle, Il, US 137/F8
Golden Gate (chan.), Ca, US 135/J11
Golden Gate Highlands NP, SAfr. 106/E2
Golden Hinde (peak), BC, Can. 126/B3
Golden Temple, India 86/C4
Goldendale, Wa, US 126/C4
Goldene Aue (reg.), Ger. 51/H5
Goldenstedt, Ger. 51/F3
Goldkronach, Ger. 55/E2
Goldman, Mo, US 137/F9
Goldmine (mtn.), Az, US 137/S19
Goldsboro, NC, US 133/J3
Goldsboro, Md, US 138/C5
Goldsby, Ok, US 137/N15
Goldsworthy, Austl. 112/C2
Goldthwaite, Tx, US 132/D4
Göle, Turk. 63/G4
Goleniów, Pol. 41/H2
Golfito NWR, CR 145/F4
Golfo Aranci, It. 46/A2
Golfo de Santa Clara, Mex. 142/B2
Gölhısar, Turk. 91/A1
Göliad, Tx, US 129/H5
Gölköy, Turk. 62/F4
Gollach (riv.), Ger. 54/D3
Göllheim, Ger. 54/B3
Gölmarmara, Turk. 62/C5
Golmud, China 70/F4
Golovin, Ak, US 134/F3
Golovnina (peak), Rus. 76/D2
Golpāyegān, Iran 88/F2
Gölpazarı, Turk. 49/K5
Gols, Austl. 43/M3
Golts, Md, US 138/C5
Golub-Dobrzyń, Pol. 41/K2
Golubovci (int'l arpt.), Yugo. 47/F1
Golyam Perelik (peak), Bul. 49/F2
Golyama Kamchiya (riv.), Bul. 49/H4
Golyama Syutkya (peak), Bul. 47/J2
Goma, D.R. Congo 104/A3
Goma (int'l arpt.), D.R. Congo 104/A3
Gomati (riv.), India 84/C6
Gombe, Nga. 103/G4
Gombe NP, Tanz. 104/A4
Gomera (isl.), Sp. 96/A3
Gómez Farías, Mex. 143/E3
Gómez Palacio, Mex. 142/E3
Gomishān, Iran 88/F1
Gommern, Ger. 40/F2
Gomoh, India 85/F3
Goms (valley), Swi. 56/E5
Gonābād, Iran 89/G2
Gonaïves, Haiti 145/H3
Gonam (riv.), Rus. 65/N4
Gonave (gulf), Haiti 141/G4
Gonbad-e Qābūs, Iran 89/G1

Gonbadlī, Iran 87/K2
Gönc, Hun. 41/L4
Gonçalves Dias, Braz. 154/A2
Gondelsheim, Ger. 54/B4
Gonder, Eth. 97/N5
Gondia, India 85/B3
Gondomar, Sp. 44/A1
Gondomar, Port. 44/A2
Gondrecourt-le-Château, Fr. 56/B1
Gonesse, Fr. 30/K5
Gong Xian, China 83/H2
Gong Xian, China 72/C4
Gong'an, China 83/K3
Gongbo'gyamda, China 83/F2
Gongcheng, China 79/D3
Gongga (peak), China 83/H2
Gonggar, China 85/H1
Gonghe, China 70/G3
Gongliu, China 70/D3
Gongola (riv.), Nga. 96/H5
Gongshan Drungzu Nuzu Zizhixian, China 83/G2
Gongzhuling, China 72/C4
Goñi, Uru. 159/K10
Gonjo, China 70/G5
Gónnoi, Gre. 47/H3
Gonubie, SAfr. 106/D4
Gonyü, Hun. 48/C2
Gonzaga, It. 59/D3
Gonzales, Tx, US 129/H5
González, Mex. 143/F4
Good Hope, La, US 137/P17
Good Hope, Cape of (cape), SAfr. 106/L11
Goodenough (cape), Ant. 160/J
Goodnews Bay, Ak, US 134/F4
Goodooga, Austl. 115/C1
Goodrich, Mi, US 135/F6
Goodwick, Wal, UK 32/B2
Goodwood, SAfr. 106/L10
Goodyear, Az, US 137/R19
Gooimeer (lake), Neth. 50/C4
Goole, Eng, UK 35/H4
Goolgowi, Austl. 115/C2
Gooloogong, Austl. 115/D2
Goolwa, Austl. 113/H5
Goomalling, Austl. 112/C4
Goombungee, Austl. 114/C4
Goondiwindi, Austl. 114/C5
Goongarrie NP, Austl. 112/D4
Goor, Neth. 50/D4
Goose (lake), Can. 127/H2
Goose (pt.), La, US 137/Q16
Goose (lake), Ca, US 124/B3
Goose (pt.), De, US 138/C5
Gopālganj, India 85/E2
Gopālpur, Bang. 85/G3
Gopat (riv.), India 84/D3
Göppingen, Ger. 54/C5
Góra Kalwaria, Pol. 41/L3
Góra, Pol. 41/J3
Gorakhpur, India 84/D2
Goražde, Bosn. 48/D4
Gorczański NP, Pol. 41/L4
Gorda (pt.), Nic. 145/F4
Gorda (pt.), Cuba 145/F1
Gorda (pt.), Cuba 145/F4
Gordevio, Swi. 57/E5
Gording, Den. 38/C4
Gordola, Swi. 57/E5
Gordon, Austl. 115/C4
Gordon (lake), Austl. 109/D5
Gordonsbaai, SAfr. 106/L11
Gordonvale, Austl. 114/B2
Gore (pt.), Ak, US 134/H4
Goré, Chad 96/J6
Gore, Eth. 97/N6
Gore, NZ 117/R12
Gorebridge, Sc, UK 36/C5
Görele, Turk. 62/F4
Goresbridge, Ire. 31/Q10
Gorey, Chl, UK 42/B2
Gorey, Ire. 31/Q10
Gorgān, Iran 89/F1
Gorge du Loup, Fr. 53/F4
Gorges du Ziz, Mor. 98/D2
Gorgol (prol. reg.), Mrta. 102/B3
Gorgol (riv.), Mrta. 102/B2
Gorgona, Isola di (isl.), It. 58/C5
Gorgonza, It. 58/C1
Gori, Geo. 63/H4
Gorinchem, Neth. 50/B5
Gorizia, It. 59/G1
Gorizia (prov.), It. 59/G1
Gorj (prov.), Rom. 49/F3
Gorki, Bela. 62/D1
Gor'kiy (res.), Rus. 60/J4
Gorlice, Pol. 41/L4
Görlitz, Ger. 41/H3
Gorllwyn (peak), Wal, UK 32/C2
Gorman, Tx, US 129/H4
Gormanstown, Ire. 34/B3
Gormī, India 84/B2
Gorner (glacier), Swi. 56/D6
Gornji Milanovac, Yugo. 48/E3
Gornji Vakuf, Bosn. 48/C4
Gorno-Altay Aut. Rep., Rus. 64/J4
Goro, It. 59/F3
Gorodets, Rus. 60/J4
Gorom Gorom, Burk. 103/E3
Gorontalo, Indo. 81/F3
Goroka, PNG 114/B1
Gorongoza, Moz. 105/F4
Gorseinon, Wal, UK 32/B3
Gorssel, Neth. 50/D4
Gort, Ire. 31/P10
Gortin, NI, UK 34/A2
Görwihl, Ger. 56/E2
Goryn' (riv.), Ukr. 52/C2

Gorzano (peak), It. 43/K5
Gorzów Wielkopolski, Pol. 41/H2
Gosainganj, India 84/D2
Göschenen, Swi. 57/E4
Göse, Japan 77/J7
Gosen, Japan 75/F2
Gosford, Austl. 115/D2
Gosforth, Eng, UK 35/G2
Goshen, NJ, US 138/D5
Goshogawara, Japan 76/B3
Goslar, Ger. 51/H5
Gospić, Cro. 48/B3
Gosport, Eng, UK 33/E5
Gossas, Sen. 102/A3
Gossau, Swi. 114/B2
Gosserweiler-Stein, Ger. 53/G5
Gostivar, Macd. 47/G2
Gostyń, Pol. 41/J3
Gostynin, Pol. 41/K2
Göta (riv.), Swe. 38/G2
Götaland (reg.), Swe. 38/E3
Göteborg, Swe. 38/D3
Göteborg Och Bohus (co.), Swe. 37/D4
Gotel (mts.), Nga. 96/H6
Gotemba, Japan 75/F3
Götene, Swe. 38/E2
Gotha, Ger. 51/H7
Gotland (isl.), Swe. 64/B4
Gotland (co.), Swe. 37/F4
Gotse Delchev, Bul. 47/H2
Gotska Sandön (isl.), Swe. 39/H2
Gotska Sandön NP, Swe. 39/H2
Gōtsu, Japan 74/C3
Gottenheim, Ger. 56/D1
Göttingen, Ger. 51/G5
Gottmadingen, Ger. 57/E2
Gottolengo, It. 58/D2
Gouda, Neth. 50/B4
Gouda, SAfr. 106/L10
Gough (isl.), StH 22/J7
Gouin (res.), Qu, Can. 123/J4
Goulais (riv.), Can. 130/C2
Goulburn (riv.), Austl. 115/D2
Goulburn, Austl. 115/D2
Goulburn (riv.), Austl. 109/C2
Gould, Ar, US 132/F3
Gould (mt.), Austl. 112/C3
Gouldsboro, Pa, US 138/C1
Goulimine, Mor. 98/C3
Goulmima, Mor. 98/D3
Goundam, Mali 102/E2
Goupillières, Fr. 30/H5
Gourdon, Fr. 42/D4
Gouré, Niger 103/H3
Gourin, Fr. 42/B2
Gourits (riv.), SAfr. 106/C4
Gourma (phys. reg.), Burk. 103/F3
Gourma (prov.), Burk. 103/F3
Gourma Rharous, Mali 103/E2
Gournay-en-Bray, Fr. 52/A5
Gourock, Sc, UK 36/B5
Goussainville, Fr. 30/K4
Gouvêa, Braz. 155/D1
Gouveia, Port. 44/B2
Gouvieux, Fr. 30/K4
Gouvy, Belg. 53/E3
Gouyave, Gren. 141/N9
Govardhan, India 84/A2
Goverla (peak), Ukr. 49/G1
Governador Archer, Braz. 154/A2
Governador Dix-Sept Rosado, Braz. 154/C2
Governador Eugênio Barros, Braz. 154/A2
Governador Valadares, Braz. 155/D1
Governor Generoso, Phil. 79/E6
Governors (isl.), NY, US 139/J9
Govi-Altay (prov.), Mong. 70/F2
Govĭ Altayn (mts.), Mong. 65/K5
Govind Sāgar (res.), India 86/D4
Govindgarh, India 84/C3
Gower (pen.), Wal, UK 32/B3
Goya, Arg. 157/E2
Goyllarisquizga, Peru 156/B3
Göynük, Turk. 49/K5
Goyt (riv.), Eng, UK 35/F5
Gozaisho-yama (peak), Japan 77/K5
Gözeli, Turk. 90/D2
Gozo (isl.), Malta 46/D4
Gozzano, It. 58/B1
Graaff-Reinet, SAfr. 106/D4
Graafschap (phys. reg.), Neth. 50/D4
Graben, Ger. 57/G1
Graberg (peak), Namb. 106/B2
Grabouw, SAfr. 106/L11
Grabow, Ger. 40/F2
Graça Aranha, Braz. 154/A2
Gračac, Cro. 48/B3
Gračanica, Bosn. 48/D3
Gracemere, Austl. 114/C3
Graceville, Fl, US 133/G4
Grächen, Swi. 56/D5
Gracias, Hon. 144/D3
Gracias a Dios (cape), Hon. 145/F3
Graciosa (isl.), Azor., Port. 45/S12
Grad Sofiya (prov.), Bul. 47/H1
Gradačac, Bosn. 48/D3
Gradisca d'Isonzo, It. 59/G1
Grado, It. 59/G1
Grado, Sp. 44/B1
Grady (co.), Ok, US 137/M15
Graefelfing, Ger. 55/E6
Grafenau, Ger. 55/G5

Gräfenberg, Ger. 54/E3
Grafenrheinfeld, Ger. 54/D3
Gräfentonna, Ger. 51/H6
Grafenwöhr, Ger. 55/E3
Graffignana, It. 58/C2
Grafing bei München, Ger. 55/E6
Grafton, Austl. 115/E1
Grafton, ND, US 127/J3
Grafton, WV, US 130/D4
Grafton, Il, US 137/G8
Grafton Passage, Austl. 114/C2
Graham, Tx, US 129/H4
Graham (isl.), NW, Can. 123/S7
Graham (isl.), BC, Can. 122/C3
Graham Bell (isl.), Rus. 64/G1
Graham Land (phys. reg.), Ant. 160/V
Grahamstown, SAfr. 106/D4
Graian Alps (range), It. 43/G4
Grain (coast), Libr. 96/D6
Grain Valley, Mo, US 137/E5
Grainau, Ger. 57/H3
Grajaú (riv.), Braz. 151/J5
Grajaú, Braz. 155/C2
Grajewo, Pol. 39/K5
Gram, Den. 38/C4
Gramada, Bul. 48/F4
Gramastetten, Aus. 55/H6
Gramat, Fr. 42/D4
Gramat, Causse de (plat.), Fr. 42/D4
Gramatneusiedl, Aus. 49/N7
Grampian (pol. reg.), Sc, UK 36/C2
Grampian (mts.), Sc, UK 36/C3
Grampians NP, Austl. 115/B3
Grampians, The (phys. reg.), Austl. 115/B3
Gramsbergen, Neth. 50/D3
Gramsh, Alb. 47/G2
Gran, Nor. 38/D1
Gran Altiplanicie Central (plat.), Arg. 157/C2
Gran Bajo de San Julián (plain), Arg. 157/C6
Gran Bajo Oriental (plain), Arg. 157/C6
Gran Canaria (isl.), Sp. 96/B2
Gran Canaria (int'l arpt.), Sp. 98/B4
Gran Chaco (plain), SAm. 147/C5
Gran Isla del Maíz (isl.), Nic. 145/F3
Gran Laguna Salada (lag.), Arg. 158/C5
Gran Paradiso, PN del, It. 43/G4
Gran Piedra (hill), Cuba 145/H2
Gran Pilastro (peak), It. 43/J3
Gran Vilaya (ruin), Peru 156/B2
Granada, Sp. 44/D4
Granada, Nic. 144/E4
Granada, Col. 152/C4
Granadilla de Abona, Sp. 98/A3
Granados, Mex. 142/C2
Granard, Ire. 31/Q10
Granarolo dell'Emilia, It. 59/E3
Granbury, Tx, US 129/H4
Grand (riv.), Kenya 104/C3
Grand (isl.), SD, US 127/H4
Grand (isl.), NY, US 127/M4
Grand (isl.), Mi, US 130/C2
Grand (riv.), US 132/E2
Grand (canal), China 72/D3
Grand (lake), Nf, Can. 123/L4
Grand Bahama (isl.), Bahm. 119/K7
Grand Bank, Nf, Can. 131/L2
Grand Bassa (co.), Libr. 102/C3
Grand-Bassam, C.d'Iv. 102/E3
Grand Bay, NB, Can. 131/H2
Grand Canal d'Alsace (canal), Fr. 56/G1
Grand Canyon, Az, US 128/D3
Grand Canyon NP, Az, US 128/D3
Grand Cape Mount (co.), Libr. 102/C5
Grand Cayman (isl.), Cay. 140/E4
Grand Centre, Ab, Can. 126/F2
Grand-Charmont, Fr. 56/C2
Grand Colombier (peak), Fr. 56/B6
Grand Combine (peak), Swi. 56/D6
Grand Coulee, Wa, US 126/D4
Grand Coulee (dam), Wa, US 126/D4
Grand Drumont (peak), Fr. 56/C2
Grand Erg de Bilma (des.), Niger 96/H4
Grand Erg Occidental (des.), Alg. 93/C1
Grand Erg Oriental (des.), Alg. 93/C1
Grand Falls, Nf, Can. 131/L2
Grand Falls, Nf, Can. 131/L1
Grand Forks, ND, US 127/J4
Grand Forks, BC, Can. 126/D3
Grand-Fort-Philippe, Fr. 52/B2
Grand Goâve, Haiti 145/H2
Grand Haven, Mi, US 130/C3
Grand Isle, La, US 133/F4
Grand Jide (co.), Libr. 102/D5

Grand Junction, Co, US 128/E3
Grand-Iahou, C.d'Iv. 102/D3
Grand Lake o' the Cherokees (lake), Ok, US 129/J3
Grand Manan (isl.), Can. 131/H2
Grand-Mère, Qu, Can. 131/F2
Grand Mont Ruan (peak), Fr. 56/C5
Grand Muveran (peak), Swi. 56/D5
Grand-Popo, Ben. 103/F5
Grand Portage Nat'l Mon., Mn, US 127/L4
Grand Rapids, Mb, Can. 127/J2
Grand Rapids, Mi, US 130/C3
Grand Rhône (riv.), Fr. 42/F5
Grand Saint-Bernard, Col du (pass), Swi. 56/C4
Grand Staircase-Escalante Nat'l Mon., Ut, US 128/E3
Grand Taureau (peak), Fr. 56/C4
Grand Teton NP, Wy, US 128/E2
Grandcour, Swi. 56/C4
Grande (isl.), Braz. 150/A7
Grande (riv.), Braz. 155/C2
Grande (peak), It. 46/C1
Grande (peak), It. 46/C4
Grande (riv.), Pan. 145/G4
Grande (bay), Arg. 147/C8
Grande Cache, Ab, Can. 126/D2
Grande Comore (isl.), Com. 93/G6
Grande de Gurupá, Ilha (isl.), Braz. 150/D5
Grande de Manacapuru, Lago (lake), Braz. 150/D5
Grande de Matagalpa (riv.), Nic. 140/D5
Grande de Santiago (riv.), Mex. 142/C4
Grande de Tierra del Fuego (isl.), Arg.,Chil 157/C7
Grande Dixence, Barrage de la (dam), Swi. 56/D5
Grande do Curuaí (lake), Braz. 150/D5
Grande Miquelon (isl.), Can. 131/K2
Grande Prairie, Ab, Can. 126/D2
Grande Saline, Haiti 145/H2
Grande, Serra (mts.), Braz. 153/F4
Grande-Synthe, Fr. 52/B1
Grande-Terre (isl.), Guad. 141/J4
Grandes Jorasses (peak), It. 56/D4
Grandfresnoy, Fr. 52/B5
Grândola, Port. 44/A3
Grandpuits-Bailly-Carrois, Fr. 30/L6
Grandson, Swi. 56/C4
Grandview, Wa, US 126/D4
Grandview, Mb, Can. 127/H3
Grandview, Tx, US 129/H4
Grandview, Mo, US 137/D6
Grandvillars, Fr. 56/C2
Grandvilliers, Fr. 52/A4
Graneros, Chile 158/N9
Granfjället (peak), Swe. 38/E1
Grange, Mont de (peak), Fr. 56/C5
Grangemouth, Sc, UK 36/C4
Granger (mt.), Can. 134/C3
Granges-sur-Vologne, Fr. 56/C1
Grängesberg, Swe. 38/F1
Grangeville, Id, US 126/D4
Granisle, BC, Can. 126/B2
Granite (peak), Mt, US 126/F4
Granite, Ut, US 137/K12
Granite City, Il, US 137/G8
Granite Reef Aquaduct, Az, US 137/S18
Granites, The (peak), Austl. 113/F2
Granja, Braz. 154/B1
Granollers, Sp. 45/L6
Grantham, Eng, UK 35/H6
Grantown-on-Spey, Sc, UK 36/C2
Grants, NM, US 128/F4
Grants Pass, Or, US 126/C5
Granville, Fr. 42/C2
Granville (lake), Mb, Can. 122/H3
Grão Mogol, Braz. 154/B5
Grapeview, Wa, US 135/B3
Gras-Ellenbach, Ger. 54/D6
Grasberg, Ger. 51/F2
Grasbrunn, Ger. 55/E6
Grasø (isl.), Swe. 38/H1
Grasonville, Md, US 135/P15
Grasse, Fr. 43/G5
Grassie, On, Can. 131/Q9
Grasslands NP, Can. 127/G3
Grassy Park, SAfr. 106/L11
Gråstorp, Swe. 38/E2
Gratkorn, Aus. 43/L3
Gratz, Pa, US 138/B2
Graubünden (canton), Swi. 57/F4
Graulhet, Fr. 42/E5
Graus, Sp. 45/G2
Gravatá, Braz. 154/D3
Grave, Neth. 50/C5
Gravedona, It. 58/C1
Gravelbourg, Sk, Can. 126/G3
Gravelines, Fr. 52/B2
Gravellona Toce, It. 58/B1
Gravenhurst, On, Can. 130/E2

Grävenwiesbach, Ger. 54/B2
Gravesend, Eng, UK 30/E2
Gravina di Puglia, It. 46/E2
Gravois (pt.), Haiti 145/H2
Gray, Fr. 56/B3
Grayling, Ak, US 134/F3
Grayling, Mi, US 130/C2
Grays (har.), Wa, US 126/B4
Grays (lake), Id, US 126/F5
Grays, Eng, UK 30/E2
Grayslake, Il, US 139/P15
Grayson, Sk, Can. 127/H3
Graz, Aus. 43/L3
Grazalema, Sp. 44/C4
Grecco, Uru. 159/K10
Grecia (plain), Austl. 115/C4
Greco (peak), It. 46/C2
Greco (cape), Cyp. 91/D2
Greding, Ger. 55/E4
Gredos, Sierra de (mts.), Sp. 44/C2
Grée (riv.), Fr. 160/G
Greeley, Co, US 137/C2
Greeley Number 2 (canal), Co, US 137/C2
Greely (fjord), NW, Can. 123/S6
Green (cape), Austl. 115/D3
Green (bay), US 127/M4
Green (riv.), Ky, US 130/C4
Green (riv.), Wy, US 130/C4
Green (mts.), Vt, US 130/F3
Green (riv.), Ut,Wy, US 124/E4
Green Cove Springs, Fl, US 133/H4
Green Creek, NJ, US 138/D5
Green Haven, Md, US 138/B5
Green Lane (res.), Pa, US 138/C3
Green Lowther (peak), Sc, UK 36/C6
Green Pond, NJ, US 138/D1
Green River, Wy, US 126/F5
Green Valley, Az, US 128/E5
Green Valley, Ca, US 136/B1
Green Valley Lake, Ca, US 136/C2
Green Village, NJ, US 139/H9
Greenbelt, Md, US 138/B4
Greenbushes, Austl. 112/C5
Greencastle, In, US 130/C4
Greencastle, Ire. 34/B1
Greendale, Wi, US 135/Q14
Greeneville, Tn, US 130/D4
Greenfield, Ma, US 131/F3
Greenfield, In, US 130/C4
Greenfield Park, Eng, UK 35/F4
Great Himalaya (range), Asia 70/D6
Greenisland, NI, UK 34/C2
Greenland (sea) 119/R2
Greenmount, Md, US 138/B4
Greenock, Sc, UK 36/B5
Greenough (mt.), Ak, US 134/K2
Greenough (riv.), Austl. 112/B4
Greenport, NY, US 139/F1
Greensboro, NC, US 133/J2
Greensboro, Al, US 133/G3
Greensboro, Md, US 138/C6
Greensburg, In, US 130/C4
Greensburg, Pa, US 130/E3
Greenvale, Austl. 114/B2
Greenville, Ca, US 126/C5
Greenville, SC, US 133/H3
Greenville, Al, US 133/G4
Greenville, Mi, US 130/C3
Greenville, NC, US 133/J3
Greenville, Tx, US 129/H4
Greenville, Ms, US 129/K4
Greenville, Oh, US 130/C3
Greenville, Libr. 102/C5
Greenwater (riv.), Wa, US 135/D3
Greenwell Point, Austl. 115/D2
Greenwich (bor.), Eng, UK 30/D2
Greenwich (pt.), Ct, US 139/L7
Greenwich Observatory, Eng, UK 30/D2
Greenwood (lake), SC, US 133/H3
Greenwood, SC, US 133/H3
Greenwood, Ms, US 129/K4
Greenwood, Mo, US 137/G6
Greenwood, De, US 138/C6
Greenwood Lake, Wa, US 135/D3
Greers Ferry (lake), Ar, US 129/J4
Grefrath, Ger. 50/D6
Gregório, Braz. 150/D5
Gregory, SD, US 127/J5
Gregory (range), Austl. 114/A2
Gregory (lake), Austl. 109/B3
Greifswald, Ger. 38/F4
Greifswalder Bodden (bay), Ger. 41/G1
Greimberg (peak), Austl. 43/L3
Greiz, Ger. 54/B3
Gremyachinsk, Rus. 61/N4
Grenå, Den. 38/D3
Grenada, Ms, US 129/K4
Grenada (ctry.) 119/L8
Grenade, Fr. 42/D5
Grenay, Fr. 52/B2
Grenchen, Swi. 56/C5
Grenfell, Austl. 115/D2
Grenfell, Sk, Can. 127/H3
Grenoble, Fr. 42/F4
Grenville, Gren. 141/N9
Grenzach-Wyhlen, Ger. 56/D2
Gressåmoen NP, Nor. 37/E2
Greta (riv.), Eng, UK 35/E2

Greater Buffalo (int'l arpt.), NY, US 131/S10
Greater Cincinnati (int'l arpt.), Ky, US 130/C4
Greater London (co.), Eng, UK 30/D2
Greater Manchester (co.), Eng, UK 35/F4
Greater Pittsburgh (int'l arpt.), Pa, US 130/D3
Greater Rochester (int'l arpt.), NY, US 130/E3
Greater Sunda (isls.), Indo. 80/C4
Grebenhain, Ger. 54/C2
Grebenstein, Ger. 51/G6
Grébon (peak), Niger 103/H2
Grecco, Uru. 159/K10
Great (plain), Austl. 115/C4
Great (basin), Nv, US 124/C4
Great (falls), NJ, US 139/J8
Great Abaco (isl.), Bahm. 119/K7
Great Alföld (plain), Yugo. 48/D2
Great America, Ca, US 135/L12
Great Australian Bight (bay), Austl. 109/B4
Great Barrier (reef), Austl. 109/D2
Great Barrier (isl.), NZ 109/H6
Great Basin NP, US 128/D3
Great Bear (lake), NW, Can. 122/D2
Great Bend, Ks, US 129/H3
Great Bitter (lake), Egypt 91/C4
Great Brak (riv.), SAfr. 106/C3
Great Britain (isl.), UK 27/D3
Great Cedar (swamp), Pa, US 138/C3
Great Coco (isl.), Myan. 83/F5
Great Cumbrae (isl.), Sc, UK 36/B5
Great Divide (basin), Wy, US 126/F5
Great Dividing (range), Austl. 109/D2
Great Egg (har.), NJ, US 138/D5
Great Egg Harbor (riv.), NJ, US 138/D5
Great Exuma (isl.), Bahm. 119/K7
Great Falls, Mt, US 126/F4
Great Fish (riv.), SAfr. 106/D4
Great Fish (pt.), SAfr. 106/D4
Great Guana Cay (isl.), Bahm. 119/K7
Great Harwood, Eng, UK 35/F4
Great Inagua (isl.), Bahm. 119/K7
Great Indian (des.), India, Pa 82/D2
Great Karoo (plat.), SAfr. 105/D7
Great Kei (riv.), SAfr. 106/D4
Great Mis Tor (hill), Eng, UK 32/B5
Great Missenden, Eng, UK 33/E2
Great Neck, NY, US 139/L8
Great Nicobar (isl.), India 83/F6
Great Ouse (riv.), Eng, UK 33/E2
Great Oyster (bay), Austl. 115/D4
Great Palace, Rus. 61/T7
Great Palace, Rus. 61/S7
Great Peconic (bay), NY, US 139/F2
Great Pee Dee (riv.), SC, US 133/J3
Great Piece Meadows (swamp), NJ, US 139/H8
Great Rift (valley), Afr. 105/F1
Great Ruaha (riv.), Tanz. 105/F2
Great Salt (lake), Ut, US 119/F5
Great Salt Lake (des.), Ut, US 124/D3
Great Salt Lake (lake), Ut, US 119/F5
Great Sand Sea (des.), Egypt, Li 97/K2
Great Sandy (des.), Austl. 109/B3
Great Scarcies (riv.), SLeo. 102/B4
Great Shunner Fell (peak), Eng, UK 35/F3
Great Slave (lake), NW, Can. 119/F3
Great Smoky Mountains NP, US 133/H3
Great South (bay), NY, US 139/F2
Great Stour (riv.), Eng, UK 33/H4
Great Tenasserim (riv.), Myan. 83/G4
Great Victoria (des.), Austl. 109/B3
Great Victoria Desert Nature Rsv., Austl. 113/E4
Great Wall, China 70/J4
Great Western Tiers (mts.), Austl. 115/C4
Great Winterhoek (peak), SAfr. 106/L10
Great Yarmouth, Eng, UK 33/H1
Great Zab (riv.), Iraq 90/E2
Great Zimbabwe (ruin), Zim. 105/F5
Greater Accra (pol. reg.), Gha. 103/F5
Greater Antilles (isls.), NAm. 119/J7
Greater Barsuki (des.), Kaz. 87/D3

Gretna, Mb, Can. 127/J3
Gretna, La, US 137/P17
Gretna, Sc, UK 35/E2
Grettstadt, Ger. 54/D3
Gretz-Armainvilliers, Fr. 30/L5
Greve, Fr. 53/E5
Greve in Chianti, It. 59/E5
Greven, Ger. 51/E4
Grevená, Gre. 47/G2
Grevenbroich, Ger. 53/F1
Grevenmacher (dist.), Lux. 53/F4
Grevesmühlen, Ger. 40/F2
Grevlingen (chan.), Neth. 50/A5
Grey (range), Austl. 109/D3
Grey (riv.), Austl. 131/K2
Grey (riv.), NI, UK 34/C2
Grey Abbey, NI, UK 34/C2
Grey Hunter (peak), Can. 134/L3
Grey Peaks NP, Austl. 114/B2
Greybull, Wy, US 126/F4
Greylingstad, SAfr. 106/E2
Greymouth, NZ 117/S11
Greystones, Ire. 34/B5
Greytown, SAfr. 107/E3
Grez-Doiceau, Belg. 53/D2
Grezzana, It. 59/E1
Gribbin (pt.), Eng, UK 32/B6
Griefensee (lake), Swi. 57/E3
Griekwastad, SAfr. 106/C3
Griend (isl.), Neth. 50/C2
Gries am Brenner, Aus. 57/H3
Griesheim, Ger. 54/B3
Grieskirchen, Aus. 55/G6
Griesskogel (peak), Aus. 57/H3
Griesstätt, Ger. 55/F7
Griffin, Ga, US 133/G3
Griffith, Austl. 115/C2
Griffith, In, US 135/R16
Griffith Park, Ca, US 136/F7
Grigna (peak), It. 57/F6
Grignano Polesine, It. 59/F2
Grigny, Fr. 30/K6
Grijalva (riv.), Mex. 144/C2
Grijpskerk, Neth. 50/D2
Grim (cape), Austl. 115/C4
Grimbergen, Belg. 53/D2
Grimisuat, Swi. 56/D5
Grimmen, Ger. 38/F4
Grimsby, On, Can. 131/Q9
Grimsby, Eng, UK 35/H4
Grimsel (riv.), Swi. 57/E4
Grimstad, Nor. 38/C2
Grindavík, Ice. 37/N6
Grindelwald, Swi. 56/E4
Grindsted, Den. 38/C4
Grinnell (pen.), NW, Can. 123/S7
Grintavec (peak), Slov. 43/L3
Griqualand East (reg.), SAfr. 106/C4
Griqualand West (reg.), SAfr. 106/C2
Gris-Nez (cape), Fr. 52/A2
Grise Fiord, Can. 123/S7
Grisslehamn, Swe. 39/H1
Grisy-les-Plâtres, Fr. 30/J4
Grisy-Suisnes, Fr. 30/L6
Grivette (riv.), Fr. 30/L4
Grizzly (bay), Ca, US 135/K10
Grmeč (mts.), Bosn. 48/C3
Groairas, Braz. 154/B1
Grobbendonk, Belg. 53/D1
Gröbenzell, Ger. 55/E6
Groblershoop, SAfr. 106/C3
Grodków, Pol. 41/J3
Grodzisk Wielkopolski, Pol. 41/J2
Groenlo, Neth. 50/D4
Groesbeck, Tx, US 129/H5
Groesbeek, Neth. 50/C5
Groix, Fr. 42/B3
Grójec, Pol. 41/L3
Grömitz, Ger. 38/D4
Gromo, It. 57/F6
Gronau, Ger. 50/E4
Groningen, Neth. 50/D2
Groningen (prov.), Neth. 50/D2
Grönlait (peak), It. 57/H5
Grono, Swi. 57/F5
Groot (riv.), SAfr. 106/C4
Groot-Marico (riv.), SAfr. 106/Q13
Grootdraaidam (res.), SAfr. 106/E2
Groote Eylandt (isl.), Austl. 109/C2
Grootegast, Neth. 50/D2
Grootfontein, Namb. 105/C4
Grootvloer (salt pan), SAfr. 106/C3
Grone (salt pan), It. 57/G2
Gropello Cairoli, It. 58/B2
Gros Islet, StL. 141/N9
Gros Morne (peak), Austl. 131/K1
Gros Morne NP, Can. 131/K1
Gros-Gerungs, Aus. 49/H4
Gross Oesingen, Ger. 51/H3
Gross Unstadt, Ger. 54/B3
Gross-Zimmern, Ger. 54/B3
Grossalmerode, Ger. 51/G6
Grossbeeren, Ger. 54/D3
Grossbottwar, Ger. 54/C4
Grossbreitenbach, Ger. 54/D1
Grossenzersdorf, Aus. 49/N7
Grosse (isl.), Mi, US 135/F7

Grosse Aue (riv.), Ger. 51/F4
Grosse Ile, Mi, US 135/F7
Grosse Laber (riv.), Ger. 55/F5
Grosse Mühl (riv.), Aus. 55/H6
Grosse Münzenberg (peak), Namb. 106/A2
Grosse Nister (riv.), Ger. 53/G2
Grosse Pointe, Mi, US 135/G7
Grosse Pointe Farms, Mi, US 135/G7
Grosse Pointe Park, Mi, US 135/G7
Grosse Pointe Shores, Mi, US 135/G7
Grosse Pointe Woods, Mi, US 135/G7
Grosse Rodl (riv.), Aus. 55/H6
Grossengottern, Ger. 51/H6
Grossenkneten, Ger. 51/F4
Grossenlüder, Ger. 54/C1
Grossenwiehe, Ger. 38/C4
Grosser Ahrensberg (peak), Ger. 51/G5
Grosser Aletsch (glacier), Swi. 56/D5
Grosser Arber (peak), Ger. 55/G4
Grosser Beer-Berg (peak), Ger. 43/J1
Grosser Bösenstein (peak), Aus. 57/H3
Grosser Daumen (peak), Ger. 57/G3
Grosser Feldberg (peak), Ger. 54/B2
Grosser Gleichberg (peak), Ger. 54/D2
Grosser Heuberg (mts.), Ger. 54/B6
Grosser Knechtsand (isl.), Port.,Sp. 44/B3
Grosser Peilstein (peak), Aus. 41/H4
Grosser Plessower (lake), Ger. 40/P7
Grosser Priel (peak), Aus. 43/L3
Grosser Rachel (peak), Ger. 55/G5
Grosser Seddiner (lake), Ger. 40/P7
Grosser Selchower (lake), Ger. 40/Q7
Grosses Meer (lake), Ger. 51/E2
Grosses Moor (swamp), Ger. 51/F2
Grosseto, It. 43/J5
Grossgerau, Ger. 54/B3
Grossglienicke (lake), Ger. 40/Q7
Grossglockner (peak), Aus. 43/K3
Grosshansdorf, Ger. 51/H1
Grossheubach, Ger. 54/C3
Grosskrotzenburg, Ger. 54/B2
Grossmaischeid, Ger. 53/G2
Grossrosseln, Ger. 53/F5
Grossschönau, Ger. 41/H3
Grosswangen, Swi. 56/D3
Grosuplje, Slov. 43/L4
Grote Gete (riv.), Belg. 53/D2
Groton, SD, US 127/J4
Grotta Gigante, It. 59/G1
Grottaglie, It. 47/E2
Grottammare, It. 43/K5
Grotte de Han, Belg. 53/E3
Grouard Mission, Ab, Can. 126/D2
Groundhog (riv.), Can. 130/D1
Grouw, Neth. 50/C2
Grovdageaidnu-Kautokeino, Nor. 37/G1
Grove, Ok, US 129/J3
Grove (pt.), Md, US 138/B5
Grover, Mo, US 137/F8
Grover City, Ca, US 128/C4
Groveton, Va, US 138/A5
Groznyy, Rus. 63/H4
Grudovo, Bul. 48/H3
Grudziądz, Pol. 41/K2
Grumeti (riv.), Tanz. 104/B3
Grums, Swe. 38/E2
Grünau im Almtal, Aus. 55/G7
Grünberg, Ger. 54/C2
Gründau, Ger. 54/C2
Grune (pt.), Eng, UK 35/E2
Grünsfeld, Ger. 54/C3
Grünwald, Ger. 55/E6
Gruyères, Swi. 56/D5
Gryazi, Rus. 62/F1
Gryckebo, Swe. 38/H1
Gryfice, Pol. 38/F5
Gryfino, Pol. 41/H2
Gryon, Swi. 56/D5
Grytviken, UK 160/W
Gstaad, Swi. 56/D5
Gua, India 85/E4
Guabún (pt.), Chile 158/B4
Guaca, Col. 152/C3
Guacanayabo (gulf), Cuba 141/G4
Guacara, Col. 152/D3
Guachochi, Mex. 142/D3
Guácimo, CR 145/F5
Guaçuí, Braz. 155/D2
Guadalajara, Mex. 142/D4
Guadalajara, Sp. 44/D2
Guadalcanal, Sp. 44/C3
Guadalcanal (isl.), Sol. 116/E6
Guadalentín (riv.), Sp. 44/D4

Guadalimar (riv.), Sp. 44/D3
Guadalix (riv.), Sp. 45/N8
Guadalope (riv.), Sp. 45/E2
Guadalquivir (riv.), Sp. 44/D4
Guadalupe, Peru 156/C4
Guadalupe, Peru 156/B2
Guadalupe (peak), Braz. 211/K6
Guadalupe, Tx, US 129/F5
Guadalupe, Braz. 154/D2
Guadalupe, Mex. 143/E3
Guadalupe (co.), Tx, US 137/U20
Guadalupe (riv.), Tx, US 143/E3
Guadalupe, Tx, US 140/B2
Guadalupe, Pan. 152/B2
Guadalupe, Ca, US 152/C4
Guadalupe (isl.), Braz. 150/D5
Guadalupe, Mex. 119/E7
Guadalupe Mountains NP, Tx, US 129/F5
Guadalupe Mountains NP, Tx, US 142/D2
Guadalupe, Sierra de (mts.), Sp. 44/C3
Guadalupe Victoria, Mex. 142/B1
Guadalupe Victoria, Mex. 142/D3
Guadalupe Victoria, Mex. 143/M7
Guadalupe, Sp. 45/N8
Guadarrama (riv.), Sp. 44/D2
Guadarrama, Ven. 152/D2
Guadarrama, Sierra de (mts.), Sp. 44/C2
Guadeloupe NP, Fr. 119/L8
Guadeloupe (dept.), Fr. 141/N8
Guadeloupe Passage (chan.), Fr. 141/J4
Guadiana (riv.), Port.,Sp. 44/B3
Guadiana Menor (riv.), Sp. 44/D4
Guadix, Sp. 44/D4
Guafo, Boca del (mouth) 157/B5
Guafo, Isla (isl.), Chile 157/B5
Guagua Pichincha (peak), Ecu. 152/B5
Guaíba, Braz. 155/B4
Guáimaro, Cuba 145/G1
Guainía (dept.), Col. 152/D4
Guainía (riv.), Col. 143/F4
Guaiquinima (peak), Ven. 153/F3
Guaira, Braz. 157/F1
Guaíra, Braz. 155/B2
Guaiteca (isl.), Chile 158/B4
Guaitecas (isls.), Chile 157/B5
Guajará-Mirim, Braz. 150/E6
Guajira (pen.), Col. 147/B1
Gualaceo, Ecu. 152/B5
Gualaco, Hon. 144/E3
Gualán, Guat. 144/D3
Gualaquiza, Ecu. 156/B1
Gualeguay, Arg. 159/J10
Gualeguaychú, Arg. 158/D3
Gualtieri, It. 59/D3
Guam (isl.), Pac., US 116/D3
Guamal, Col. 152/C2
Guamblin, Isla (isl.), Chile 158/A5
Guamote, Ecu. 156/B1
Guamúchil, Mex. 142/C3
Gu'an, China 72/H7
Guan Xian, China 70/H5
Guanabacoa, Cuba 145/F1
Guanabara (bay), Braz. 211/K7
Guanacaste (gulf), CR 144/E1
Guanacevi, Mex. 142/D3
Guanaja, Hon. 144/E2
Guanaja (isl.), Hon. 144/E2
Guanajay, Cuba 145/F1
Guanajuato, Mex. 143/E4
Guanajuato (state), Mex. 140/A3
Guanambi, Braz. 154/B4
Guanare, Ven. 150/D2
Guanare, Ven. 152/D2
Guanarito, Ven. 152/D2
Guanay (peak), Ven. 153/E3
Guanay (mtn.), China 72/B3
Guangchang, China 79/C2
Guangde, China 72/D5
Guangdong (prov.), China 71/K7
Guangling, China 79/C2
Guangnan, China 83/J3
Guangning, China 79/C2
Guangrao, China 72/C3
Guangxi (aut. reg.), China 70/J7
Guangyuan, China 70/J5
Guangyun, China 72/D4
Guanhães, Braz. 155/D1
Guanipa (riv.), Ven. 150/F2
Guanta, Ven. 150/F2
Guantánamo, Cuba 145/H1
Guantánamo Bay U.S. Naval Base, Cuba 141/G4
Guanting (res.), China 72/G6
Guanyun, China 72/D4
Guapi, Col. 152/B4
Guapiles, CR 145/F5
Guápo (riv.), Braz. 155/B4
Guaporé, Braz. 155/B4
Guaporé (riv.) 147/C4
Guaqui, Bol. 156/D5
Guara, Braz. 154/D2

Guaraci, Braz. 155/B2
Guaraciaba do Norte, Braz. 154/D4
Guarai, Braz. 151/J5
Guaramirim, Braz. 155/B3
Guarani, Braz. 211/K6
Guarapari, Braz. 155/D2
Guarapuava, Braz. 155/B3
Guaraní, Braz. 211/K6
Guararapes (int'l arpt.), Braz. 154/D3
Guararapes, Braz. 155/D3
Guararema, Braz. 211/G8
Guaratinga, Braz. 154/C5
Guaratinguetá, Braz. 211/H7
Guaratuba, Braz. 155/B3
Guarda (dist.), Port. 44/B2
Guarda, Port. 44/B2
Guardamar, Sp. 45/E3
Guardamiglio, It. 58/C2
Guardarrama (riv.), Sp. 45/N8
Guardia Alta (peak), Arg. 157/H4
Guardia Mitre, Arg. 158/E4
Guardia Sanframondi, It. 46/B5
Guaregna, Sp. 44/B3
Guárico (riv.), Ven. 141/H6
Guárico (state), Ven. 153/E2
Guárico (riv.), Cuba 145/H1
Guárico, Embalse de (res.), Ven. 150/E2
Guarujá, Braz. 211/G9
Guarulhos (int'l arpt.), Braz. 211/G8
Guarulhos, Braz. 211/G8
Guarumal, Pan. 152/A3
Guasave, Mex. 142/C3
Guasdualito, Ven. 152/D2
Guasimal, Cuba 145/G1
Guaspati, Ven. 153/F3
Guastalla, It. 58/D3
Guatemala (cap.), Guat. 144/D3
Guatemala (ctry.) 119/H8
Guatemala (state), Mex. 144/C3
Guaviare (dept.), Col. 152/C4
Guaviare (riv.), Col. 147/C2
Guaxupé, Braz. 211/G6
Guayabero (riv.), Col. 152/C4
Guayabo, Cayo (isl.), Cuba 145/G1
Guayalejo (riv.), Mex. 143/F4
Guayama, PR 141/M8
Guayaquil, Ecu. 144/C2
Guayaquil (gulf), Ecu.,Peru 147/A3
Guayaramerín, Bol. 150/E6
Guayas, Ecu. 152/B5
Guayas (prov.), Ecu. 152/A5
Guayas (riv.), Ecu. 152/C4
Gubakha, Rus. 61/N4
Gubbio, It. 59/F6
Guben, Ger. 41/H3
Gubin, Pol. 41/H3
Gubkin, Rus. 62/F2
Gucheng, China 72/C3
Gucheng, China 72/C3
Gúdar, Sierra de (range), Sp. 45/E2
Gudenå (riv.), Den. 38/D3
Gudensberg, Ger. 51/G6
Gudermes, Rus. 63/H4
Gudiváda, India 82/D4
Gudow, Ger. 51/H1
Güdúl, Turk. 49/L5
Gudvangen, India 82/C5
Güdül, Turk. 49/L5
Guebli (lake), Mrta. 98/B5
Guebwiller, Fr. 56/D2
Guecho, Sp. 44/D1
Guelb Azefal (hill), Mrta. 98/B5
Guelb er Richât (peak), Mrta. 98/C5
Guelma, Alg. 100/K6
Guelma (prov.), Alg. 100/K6
Guelph, On, Can. 130/D3
Guémené-Penfao, Fr. 42/C3
Guénange, Fr. 53/F5
Guérande, Fr. 42/B3
Guerara, Alg. 99/G2
Guercif, Mor. 100/C2
Guéret, Fr. 42/D3
Guernes, Fr. 30/G5
Guernsey (int'l arpt.), ChI, UK 42/B2
Guernsey, ChI, UK 42/B2
Guerrero (state), Mex. 140/B4
Guerrero, Mex. 142/D2
Guerrero Negro, Mex. 119/D7
Guerville, Fr. 30/H5
Guesle (riv.), Fr. 30/H6
Gueugnon, Fr. 42/F3
Gueydan, La, US 137/N16
Gughè (peak), Eth. 97/N6
Guggisberg, Swi. 56/D4
Guglielmo Marconi (int'l arpt.), It. 59/E3
Güglingen, Ger. 54/B4
Gugguan (isl.), NMar. 116/D3
Guguletu, SAfr. 106/L10
Gui (riv.), China 73/B3
Guichen, Fr. 42/C3
Guichón, Uru. 159/K10
Guidder, Camr. 96/H6
Guidimaka (pol. reg.), Mrta. 102/B3
Guiding, China 83/J2
Guidizzolo, It. 58/D2
Guidong, China 83/K2
Guidonia, It. 46/C2
Guiglo, C.d'Iv. 102/D5
Guignes-Rabutin, Fr. 30/L6
Guihulngan, Phil. 81/F1

Guija – Hazle

Guija, Moz. 105/F5
Guijuelo, Sp. 44/C2
Guilder (peak), Ut, US 137/L11
Guilderton, Austl. 112/B4
Guildford, Eng, UK 30/B3
Guilherand, Fr. 42/F4
Guilin (int'l arpt.), China 79/B2
Guilin, China 83/K2
Guillaume-Delisle (lake), Qu, Can. 123/J3
Guillena, Sp. 44/B3
Guimarães, Braz. 154/A1
Guimarães, Port. 44/A2
Guimba, Phil. 79/D4
Guimeng (mtn.), China 72/D4
Guinan, China 72/D4
Guinard (riv.), Sc, UK 36/A1
Guinea (ctry.) 93/A3
Guinea (gulf), Afr. 93/C4
Guinea-Bissau (ctry.) 93/A3
Guînes, Fr. 52/A2
Guingamp, Fr. 42/B2
Guinguinéo, Sen. 102/B3
Guiones (pt.), CR 144/E4
Guipavas, Fr. 42/A2
Guipavas (int'l arpt.), Fr. 42/A2
Guir, Oued (riv.), Alg. 98/E2
Guiratinga, Braz. 151/H7
Güiria, Ven. 153/F2
Guisborough, Eng, UK 35/G2
Guiscard, Fr. 52/C4
Guise, Fr. 52/C4
Guitiriz, Sp. 44/B1
Guitrancourt, Fr. 30/H4
Guiuan, Phil. 79/E5
Güiza (riv.), Col. 152/B4
Guizhou (prov.), China 70/J6
Gujan-Mestras, Fr. 42/C4
Gujar Khān, Pak. 86/B3
Gujarāt (state), India 82/B3
Gujrānwāla, Pak. 86/C3
Gujrāt, Pak. 86/C3
Gukovo, Rus. 62/F2
Gulaothi, India 84/A1
Gulargambone, Austl. 115/D1
Gulbarga, India 82/C4
Guldenbach (riv.), Ger. 53/G3
Güldüzü, Turk. 91/E1
Gulen, Nor. 38/A1
Gulf (coast. pl.), Tx, US 143/F2
Gulf Coastal (plain), US 132/D5
Gulf Islands Nat'l Seashore, US 133/F4
Gulf Shores, Al, US 133/G4
Gulfport, Ms, US 133/F4
Gulgong, Austl. 115/D2
Guliston, Uzb. 87/E4
Gulkana, Ak, US 134/J3
Gull Lake, Sk, Can. 126/F3
Gulladuff, NI, UK 34/B2
Gullane, Sc, UK 36/D4
Gullane (Hellam), Sc, UK 36/D4
Gullspång, Swe. 38/E2
Güllükdağı (Termessos) NP, Turk. 91/B1
Gulmarg, India 86/C2
Gülnar, Turk. 91/C1
Gulpen, Neth. 53/E2
Gülpınar, Turk. 47/K3
Gulu, Ugan. 104/B2
Gulyantsi, Bul. 49/G4
Gumal (riv.), Pak. 86/A4
Gumare, Bots. 105/D4
Gumbrechtshoffen, Fr. 53/G6
Gumdag, Trkm. 62/G5
Gumeracha, Austl. 113/M8
Gumia, India 85/E4
Gumla, India 85/E4
Gumma (pref.), Japan 75/F2
Gummersbach, Ger. 53/G1
Gumpoldskirchen, Aus. 49/N7
Gumti (riv.), India 85/H4
Gümüşhacıköy, Turk. 62/E4
Gümüşhane, Turk. 62/F4
Gümüşhane (prov.), Turk. 62/F4
Guna (peak), Eth. 97/N5
Gunbower, Austl. 115/C2
Gundagai, Austl. 115/D2
Gundelfingen, Ger. 54/D5
Gundelfingen an der Donau, Ger. 54/D5
Gundelsheim, Ger. 54/C4
Gundersheim, Ger. 54/B3
Gundershoffen, Fr. 53/G6
Gündoğmuş, Turk. 91/C1
Güneydogu Toroslar (mts.), Turk. 90/D2
Gunisao (riv.), Can. 127/J2
Gunisao (lake), Can. 127/J2
Gunja, Cro. 48/D3
Gunn City, Mo, US 137/G6
Gunnar, India 84/B1
Gunnebo, Swe. 38/G3
Gunnedah, Austl. 115/D2
Gunning, Austl. 115/D2
Gunnison (riv.), Co, US 128/F3
Gunnison, Ut, US 128/E3
Gunpowder (riv.), Md, US 138/B5
Gunpowder Falls State Park, Md, US 138/B4
Gunskirchen, Aus. 55/G6
Guntersblum, Ger. 54/B3
Guntersville, Al, US 133/G3
Guntersville (lake), Al, US 133/G3
Guntramsdorf, Aus. 49/N7
Guntūr, India 82/D4
Günz (riv.), Ger. 40/F4
Günzburg, Ger. 54/D6
Gunzenhausen, Ger. 54/D4
Guoyang, China 72/D4
Gura Humorului, Rom. 49/G2
Guragë (peak), Eth. 97/N6

Gurbantünggut (des.), China 70/E2
Gurdāspur, India 86/C3
Gurgaon, India 86/D5
Gürgentepe, Turk. 62/F4
Gurguéia (riv.), Braz. 151/K6
Guri (res.), Ven. 147/C2
Guri (dam), Ven. 153/F3
Gurk (riv.), Aus. 49/K3
Gürkhaler Alpen (mts.), Aus. 43/K3
Gurnee, Il, US 135/Q15
Guro, Moz. 105/F4
Gürpınar, Turk. 90/C2
Gürpınar, Turk. 84/B3
Gürsu, Turk. 62/D4
Guru Sikhar (peak), India 89/K4
Gürün, Turk. 90/D2
Gurupi, Braz. 151/K3
Gurupi (riv.), Braz. 151/K4
Gurupi, Serra do (mts.), Braz. 151/J4
Gus'-Khrustal'nyy, Rus. 60/J5
Gusau, Nga. 103/G3
Gushi, China 72/C4
Gushikawa, Japan 75/J7
Gusinje, Yugo. 47/F1
Guskhara, India 85/F4
Guspini, It. 46/A3
Gussola, It. 58/D3
Gustavo Díaz Ordaz, Mex. 142/C3
Gustavo Díaz Ordaz, Mex. 142/B3
Gusterath, Ger. 53/F4
Güstrow, Ger. 38/E5
Gusum, Swe. 38/G2
Gutau, Aus. 55/H6
Gütersloh, Ger. 51/F5
Guthrie, Tx, US 129/G4
Guthrie, Ok, US 137/N14
Gutiérrez Zamora, Mex. 143/M6
Guttannen, Swi. 57/E4
Guttenberg, NJ, US 139/K8
Guttingen, Swi. 57/F2
Gutulia NP, Nor. 37/E3
Guwāhāti, India 83/F2
Guxhagen, Ger. 51/G6
Guxian, China 72/B3
Guy Fawkes River NP, Austl. 115/E1
Guyana (ctry.) 147/D2
Guyancourt, Fr. 30/J5
Guyandotte (riv.), WV, US 133/H2
Guyang, China 72/B2
Guyenne (reg.), Fr. 42/C4
Guymon, Ok, US 129/G3
Guyra, Austl. 115/D1
Guyuan, China 70/J4
Güzelbağ, Turk. 91/C1
Güzelsu, Turk. 91/B1
Guzhang, China 83/J2
Guzhen, China 72/D4
Guzmán (lake), Mex. 142/D2
Gwādar, Pak. 89/H3
Gwaii Haanas NP, BC, Can. 122/C3
Gwalia, Austl. 84/B2
Gwalior, India 84/B2
Gwanda, Zim. 105/E5
Gwandalan, Austl. 115/D2
Gwash (riv.), Eng, UK 33/F1
Gwaunceste (peak), Wal, UK 32/C2
Gwda (riv.), Pol. 41/J2
Gwent (co.), Wal, UK 32/C3
Gwersyllt, Wal, UK 35/E5
Gwydir (riv.), Austl. 115/D1
Gwynedd (co.), Wal, UK 34/D5
Gwyrfai (riv.), Wal, UK 34/D5
Gy, Fr. 56/B3
Gya (pass), China 85/E1
Gyaca, China 83/F2
Gyál, Hun. 49/R10
Gyarados, Gha. 103/F5
Gyda (pen.), Rus. 67/G2
Gyhum, Ger. 51/G2
Gyirong, China 85/E1
Gyldenløveshøj (peak), Den. 38/D2
Gympie, Austl. 114/D4
Gyöda, Japan 77/C1
Gyoma, Hun. 48/E2
Gyömrő, Hun. 49/R10
Győr, Hun. 48/D2
Győr-Moson-Sopron (co.), Hun. 48/C2
Győrújbarát, Hun. 48/C2
Gyumri, Arm. 63/G4
Gyzylarbat, Trkm. 63/L5
Gżira, Malta 46/L7

H

Ha, Nor. 38/A2
Ha Giang, Viet. 83/H3
Ha Noi (Hanoi) (cap.), Viet. 83/J3
Haacht, Belg. 52/D2
Haag, Aus.
Haag am Hausruck, Aus.
Haag an der Amper, Ger. 55/E6
Haag in Oberbayern, Ger. 55/F6
Haaksbergen, Neth. 50/D4
Haaltert, Belg. 52/C2
Haamstede, Neth. 50/A5
Haan, Ger. 53/G1
Ha'apai Group (isl.), Tonga 117/H7
Haapavesi, Fin. 60/H2
Haapsalu, Est. 39/K2
Haar, Ger. 55/E6
Haardt (mts.), Ger. 43/G2
Haarlem, Neth. 50/B4
Haast, NZ 117/R11
Haasts Bluff Abor. Land, Austl. 113/C2
Hab (riv.), Pak. 89/J3
Habahe, China 83/K2
Habartov, Czh. 55/F2
Habbānīyah, Iraq 90/E3

Habicht (peak), Aus. 57/H3
Habiganj, Bang. 85/H3
Habikino, Japan 77/K6
Habomai (isls.), Rus. 76/D2
HaBonim, Isr. 91/F7
Haboro, Japan 76/B1
Hābra, India 85/G4
Habsheim, Fr. 56/C5
Hacha (falls), Ven. 153/F3
Hache (riv.), Ger. 51/F3
Hachenburg, Ger. 53/G2
Hachijō, Japan 75/F4
Hachikai, Japan 77/L5
Hachimori, Japan 76/B3
Hachinohe, Japan 76/B3
Hachiōji, Japan 75/F3
Hacıbektaş, Turk. 90/C2
Hacienda Heights, Ca, US 136/G8
Haclar, Turk. 90/C2
Hack (mt.), Austl. 113/H4
Hackensack, NJ, US 139/J8
Hackensack (riv.), NJ, US 139/J8
Hackettstown, NJ, US 138/D2
Hackney (bor.), Eng, UK 30/C2
Hadabat al Jilf al Kabīr (plat.), Egypt 101/A4
Hadali, Pak. 86/B3
Hadamar, Ger. 54/B2
Hadano, Japan 75/F3
Hadarba (cape), Sudan 101/D4
Hadd, Ra's al (pt.), Oman 89/G4
Haddenham, Eng, UK 33/F3
Haddington, Sc, UK 36/D5
Haddonfield, NJ, US 138/D3
Hadejia (riv.), Nga. 93/C3
Hadelner (canal), Ger. 51/F1
Hadera, Isr. 91/F7
Haderslev, Den. 38/C4
Hadhramaut (reg.), Yem. 88/D5
Hadim, Turk. 91/C1
Hadjout, Alg. 100/A4
Hadleigh, Eng, UK 30/D1
Hadley (bay), NW, Can. 122/E1
Hadrian's Wall, Eng, UK 35/F1
Hadselfjorden (inlet), Nor. 37/E1
Hadsten, Den. 38/D3
Hadsund, Den. 38/D3
Haeju (bay), NKor. 73/C4
Haeju, NKor. 73/C4
Haena (pt.), Hi, US 124/S9
Haenam, SKor. 73/D5
Hafik, Turk. 62/F5
Hāfizābād, Pak. 86/B3
Haflong, India 83/F2
Hafnarfjördhur, Ice. 37/N7
Hafnarhreppur, Ice. 37/N7
Haft Gel, Iran 88/E2
Hafun (pt.), Som. 97/R5
Hagelstadt, Ger. 55/F5
Hagemeister (isl.), Ak, US 134/E4
Hagen, Ger. 51/E6
Hagen am Teutoburger Wald, Ger. 51/F4
Hagen im Bremischen, Ger. 51/F2
Hagenow, Ger. 38/D5
Hagerman, NM, US 132/B4
Hagerstown, Md, US 138/A4
Hagetmau, Fr. 42/C5
Hagfors, Swe. 38/E1
Hagi, Japan 74/B3
Hagnau am Bodensee, Ger. 57/F3
Hags (pt.), Ire. 31/P10
Hague, Sk, Can. 127/G2
Hague, Cap de la (cape), Fr. 42/C2
Haguenau, Fr. 53/G6
Hahashima (isls.), Japan 116/A3
Hahaya (int'l arpt.), Com. 107/G5
Hahle (int'l arpt.), Eng, UK 33/H3
Hahndorf, Austl. 113/M9
Hahnbach, Ger. 54/E4
Hahnstätten, Ger. 54/B2
Hahnville, La, US 137/P17
Hahót, Hun. 48/C3
Haian, China 72/E4
Haibach, Ger. 54/C3
Haibara, Japan 77/J6
Haicheng, China 73/B2
Haidenaab (riv.), Ger.
Haidershofen, Aus. 55/H6
Haifa (dist.), Isr. 91/D3
Haifeng, China 79/C3
Haiger, Ger. 54/B1
Haigerloch, Ger. 54/B5
Haikou (int'l arpt.), China 79/B3
Haikou, China 83/K3
Haiku-Pauwela, Hi, US 124/T10
Ha'il, SAr. 88/D3
Hailākāndi, India 85/H4
Hailar, China 71/L2
Hailey, Id, US 126/E2
Haileybury, On, Can. 130/E2
Hailsham, Eng, UK 33/G5
Hailun, China 71/N2
Haimen, China 72/E5
Haimhausen, Ger. 55/E6
Haiming, China 57/H3
Haina, Ger. 51/G6
Hainan (prov.), China 79/B3
Hainan (isl.), China 83/K3
Hainan (str.), China 83/K3
Hainaut (prov.), Belg. 52/B2

Hainburg, Ger. 54/C1
Haines, Ak, US 134/L3
Haines City, Fl, US 133/H4
Haines Junction, Yk, Can. 134/L3
Hainesville, NJ, US 138/D1
Hainesville, Il, US 135/P15
Hainich (mts.), Ger. 40/F3
Haiti (ctry.) 119/K8
Haixia (str.), China 71/K7
Haixing, China 72/D3
Haiyan, China 79/B3
Haiyang, China 70/H4
Haiyang (isl.), China 71/H4
Haiyuan, China 70/J4
Haizhou (bay), China 72/D4
Háj (peak), Czh. 55/F2
Hajdú-Bihar (co.), Hun. 70/E7
Hajdúboszormény, Hun. 41/L5
Hajdúdorog, Hun. 41/L5
Hajdúhadház, Hun. 48/E2
Hajdúnánás, Hun. 41/L5
Hajdúszoboszló, Hun. 41/L5
Hajiki-zaki (pt.), Japan 75/F1
Hājjpur, India 85/E3
Hajjah, Yem. 88/D5
Hajnówka, Pol. 41/M2
Hājo, India 85/G3
Hajós, Hun. 48/D2
Haka, Myan. 83/F3
Hakee (mt.), Austl. 113/G3
Hakkari (prov.), Turk. 90/E2
Hakken-san (peak), Japan 74/D4
Hakkōda-san (peak), Japan 76/B3
Hakodate, Japan 76/B3
Hakone, Japan 77/C3
Hakone-yama (peak), Japan 77/C3
Haku-san (peak), Japan 77/C3
Hakui, Japan 75/E2
Hakusan, Japan 75/E2
Hakusan NP, Japan 75/E2
Hakushū, Japan 77/A2
Häla, Pak. 89/J3
Halab (prov.), Syria 90/D2
halab (Aleppo), Syria 91/E1
Halabja, Iraq 88/E1
Halachó, Mex. 143/M6
Halawa, Hi, US 124/T10
Halcon (mt.), Phil. 81/F1
Halden, Nor. 38/D2
Haldensleben, Ger. 40/D5
Haldenwang, Ger. 57/G2
Haldia, India 85/G4
Haldimand, On, Can. 131/Q10
Haldimand-Norfolk (co.), On, Can. 131/Q10
Hale (bay), NW, Can. 122/E1
Hale (mt.), Austl. 113/C2
Haleakala NP, US 124/T10
Haleiwa, Hi, US 124/V12
Hales Corners, Wi, US 135/P14
Halesowen, Eng, UK 33/E2
Haleyville, Al, US 133/G3
Half Assini, Gha. 102/E5
Half Falls (mtn.), Pa, US 138/B2
Half Moon Bay, Ca, US 135/K12
Half Tide Beach, Austl. 114/C3
Halfing, Ger. 55/F7
Halfweg, Neth. 50/B4
Haliburton Highlands (uplands), Can. 130/E2
Halifax (cap.), NS, Can. 131/J2
Halifax (int'l arpt.), Can. 131/J2
Halifax (bay), Austl. 114/B2
Halifax, Austl. 114/B2
Halifax, Sc, UK 35/G4
Halifax, Pa, US 138/B3
Halifax, Eng, UK 35/G4
Halikko, Fin. 39/K1
Halīl (riv.), Iran 89/G3
Haliun, Mong. 70/G2
Halkett (cape), Ak, US 134/H1
Hall, Austl. 115/C2
Hall (riv.), China 72/D3
Hall (isls.), Micr. 134/D3
Hall (pen.), NW, Can. 123/K2
Hall Beach, NW, Can. 123/H2
Hall Park, Ok, US 137/N15
Halladale (riv.), Sc, UK 31/S7
Hallam (Hellam), Pa, US 138/B4
Halland (co.), Swe. 38/E4
Hallbybrunn, Swe. 38/G2
Halle, Ger. 51/H4
Halle, Belg. 64/B4
Halle, Belg. 52/D1
Halle-Neustadt, Ger. 40/F3
Hällefors, Swe. 38/F2
Hälleforsnäs, Swe. 38/G2
Hallein, Aus. 43/K3
Hallenberg, Ger. 51/F6
Hallettsville, Tx, US 129/H5
Halley, Uk, Ant. 160/Y
Hallingdalselvi (riv.), Nor. 38/C1
Hallock, Mn, US 127/J3
Hallstahammar, Swe. 38/G2
Hallstatt, Aus. 55/H7
Halluin, Fr. 40/H1
Hallway, Ks, US 137/J5
Hallwilersee (lake), Swi. 56/D3
Hallyo Haesang NP, SKor. 74/A3
Halmahera (sea), Indo. 81/G4

Halmahera (isl.), Indo. 67/M9
Halmstad, Swe. 38/E3
Hälsingborg (Helsingborg), Swe. 38/E3
Halsteren, Neth. 50/B5
Haltern, Ger. 51/E5
Halton (co.), Can. 131/Q8
Halton Hills, On, Can. 131/Q8
Halver, Ger. 51/E6
Halverder Aa (riv.), Ger. 51/E4
Ham, Fr. 52/C4
Ham, Oued El (riv.), Alg. 100/G5
Hamada de Tinrhert (plat.), Alg. 99/G4
Hamada du Drâa (plat.), Alg. 96/D2
Hamada du Tinrhert (plat.), Alg. 96/G2
Hamada Safia (plat.), Mali 98/D1
Hamadān, Iran 88/E2
Hamadāt Marzūq (plat.), Libya 99/H4
Hamadat Tinghert (plat.), Libya 99/H2
Hamadat Tinghert (uplands), Libya 99/H3
Hamāh (prov.), Syria 91/E2
Hamajima, Japan 77/L7
Hamakita, Japan 75/E3
Hamamatsu, Japan 75/E3
Hamami (reg.), Mrta. 98/B2
Hamanaka, Japan 76/D2
Hamar, Nor. 38/D1
Hamāṭah (peak), Egypt 101/C3
Hambantota, SrL. 82/D6
Hambergen, Ger. 51/F2
Hambleton (hills), Eng, UK 35/G3
Hambühren, Ger. 51/G3
Hamburg, NY, US 130/E3
Hamburg, Ger. 51/G1
Hamburg, NJ, US 138/D1
Hamburg, SAfr. 106/D4
Hamburg (state), Ger. 38/D5
Hamburg (Fuhlsbüttel) (int'l arpt.), Ger. 51/G1
Hamburg Park, Il, US 135/P16
Hämeenkyrö, Fin. 39/K1
Hämeenlinna, Fin. 39/L1
Häme (prov.), Fin. 37/G3
Hämelerwald, Ger. 51/H4
Hamelin Pool (bay), Austl. 112/B3
Hameln, Ger. 51/G4
Hamersley (range), Austl. 112/B2
Hamersley Range NP, Austl. 112/C2
Hamford Water (inlet), Eng, UK 33/H3
Hamgyöng-bukto (prov.), NKor. 73/E2
Hamgyöng-namdo (prov.), NKor. 73/D2
Hamh, Syria 90/D3
Hamhüng, NKor. 73/D3
Hamhüng-si (prov.), NKor. 73/D3
Hami, China 70/F3
Hamilton, Austl. 115/B3
Hamilton, Mt, US 126/E4
Hamilton, Tx, US 129/H5
Hamilton, Sc, UK 36/C5
Hamilton, On, Can. 131/Q9
Hamilton, NZ 117/T10
Hamilton (inlet), Can. 131/M4
Hamilton (mt.), Ca, US 135/L12
Hamilton (har.), Can.
Hamilton, NZ 117/T10
Hamilton-Wentworth (co.), Can. 131/Q9
Hamina, Fin. 39/M1
Hamīrpur, India 84/C3
Hamlin, Tx, US 129/G4
Hamm, Ger. 51/E5
Hamm, Ger. 51/G4
Hamma-Bouziane, Alg. 100/K6
Hammām Al Anf, Tun. 46/B4
Hammāmāt (gulf), Tun.
Hammarland, Fin. 39/H1
Hammarön (isl.), Swe. 38/F2
Hammarstrand, Swe. 37/F3
Hamont-Achel, Belg. 50/C5
Hampshire Downs (hills), Eng, UK
Hampstead, Md, US 138/A4
Hampton, NY, US 139/L8
Hampton (co.), NS, Can. 131/J2
Hampton, Eng, UK 30/B2
Hampton Bays, NY, US 139/F2
Hampton Court, Eng, UK 30/B2

Hampton Nat'l Hist. Site, 138/B5
Hamp'yöng, SKor. 73/D5
Hamra, al Wādī, Tun. 46/B4
Hamra, Japan 77/C2
Hamyang, SKor. 73/D5
Hamyöl, SKor. 73/D4
Han (riv.), China 67/M6
Han (riv.), China 84/C5
Hana, Hi, US 124/U10
Hanak, Turk. 63/G4
Hanamaki, Japan 76/B4
Hanamalo (pt.), Hi, US 124/U11
Hanang (peak), Tanz. 104/B4
Hanau, Ger. 54/B2
Hanazono, Japan 77/C1
Handa, Japan 77/L6
Handawور, India 86/C2
Handeloh, Ger. 51/G2
Handiā, India 84/D3
Hanford, Ca, US 128/C3
Hangayn (mts.), Mong. 64/K5
Hangingstone (hill), Eng, UK 32/C5
Hangklip (cape), SAfr. 106/L11
Hangu, Pak. 86/A3
Hangzhou, China 72/L9
Hangzhou (bay), China 72/E5
Hanhöfen, Ger. 54/B4
Hanhöhiy (mts.), Mong. 70/F2
Hani, Turk. 90/E2
Haninge, Swe. 38/H2
Hankensbüttel, Ger. 51/H3
Hankey, SAfr. 106/C4
Hankinson, ND, US 127/J4
Hanko (Hangö), Fin. 39/K2
Hanley, Sk, Can. 127/G3
Hanley, Eng, UK 33/E1
Hanna, Ab, Can. 126/F3
Hannan, Japan 77/H7
Hannibal, Mo, US 137/K5
Hannover (int'l arpt.), Ger. 51/G4
Hannover, Ger. 51/G4
Hannut, Belg. 52/D2
Hanöbukten (bay), Swe. 37/E5
Hanover, NH, US 131/F3
Hanover, On, Can. 130/D2
Hanover, PA, US 138/B4
Hanover, SAfr. 106/C3
Hanover (isl.), Chile 159/B6
Hanover Park, Il, US 135/P16
Hanshan, China 72/D5
Hanshou, China 79/B2
Hänsi, India 86/C5
Hanstedt, Ger. 51/H2
Hanstholm, Den. 38/C3
Hansville, Wa, US 135/B2
Hantzsch (riv.), NW, Can. 123/J2
Hanumāngarh, India 86/C5
Hanwood, Austl. 115/C2
Hanyū, Japan 77/D1
Hanyuan, China 83/H2
Hanzhong, China 70/J5
Hao (isl.), FrPol. 117/L6
Haparanda, Swe. 60/E2
Hapch'on, SKor. 73/D5
Happy Valley, Austl. 113/M9
Happy Valley-Goose Bay, Nf, Can. 123/K3
Haptök, SKor. 73/D4
Häpur, India 84/A1
Haquira, Peru 156/C4
Har (riv.), Japan 77/J7
Har-Ayrag, Mong. 71/L3
Har Karmel (Mount Carmel) (mt.), Isr. 91/G6
Har Meron (peak), Isr. 91/D3
Har Ramon (peak), Isr. 91/M4
Hara, Japan 77/A2
Harahan, La, US 137/P17
Haramachi, Japan 75/G2
Harappa (ruin), Pak. 86/B4
Harash, Bi'r al (well), Libya 97/K2
Haravilliers, Fr. 30/J4
Harbel, Libr. 102/C5
Harbeson, De, US 138/C6
Harbin, China 71/N2
Harbiye, Turk. 91/E1
Harbonnières, Fr. 52/B4
Harbour Breton, Nf, Can. 131/L2
Harbour Grace, Nf, Can. 131/L2
Hårby, Den. 38/D4
Hard, Aus. 57/F3
Hardā, India 89/L4
Hardangervidda NP, Nor. 38/B1
Hardau (riv.), Ger. 51/H3
Hardegsen, Ger. 51/G5
Hardenberg, Neth. 50/D3
Harderwijk, Neth. 50/C4
Hardheim, Ger. 54/C4
Hardin, Mt, US 126/G4
Harding, SAfr. 107/E3
Hardoi Branch (riv.), India 84/C2
Hardricourt, Fr. 30/H4
Hardy, De, US 138/C5
Hardy (riv.), Mex. 142/C1
Hare (bay), Can. 131/L1
Hare Dimona (peak), Isr. 91/D4
Harefield, Eng, UK 30/B1
Harelbeke, Belg. 52/C2
Haren, Ger. 50/E3
Haren, Neth. 50/D2
Härer, Eth. 97/P6
Harford (co.), Md, US 138/B4
Hargeisa, Som. 97/P6
Hargeville, Fr. 30/H5
Hargeyca, Som. 97/P6
Harghita (prov.), Rom. 49/G2

Harghita (peak), Rom. 49/G2
Hari (riv.), Indo. 80/B4
Hari (str.), Est. 39/K2
Harihar, India 89/K4
Härim, Syria 91/E1
Harīmā (sea), Japan 74/D3
Harima, Japan 77/G6
Harima (bay), Japan 77/G6
Haringey (bor.), Eng, UK 30/C2
Haringhāta (riv.), Bang. 85/G4
Haringvliet (chan.), Neth. 50/B5
Haringvlietdam (dam), Neth. 50/B5
Harīpur, Pak. 86/C2
Harīrūd (riv.), Afg. 67/F6
Häris, WBnk. 91/G7
Harjavalta, Fin. 39/K1
Harlan, Ky, US 130/D4
Harlech, Wal, UK 34/D6
Harlingen, Tx, US 132/D5
Harlingen, Neth. 50/C2
Harlow, Eng, UK 30/D1
Harlowton, Mt, US 126/F4
Harmanli, Bul. 49/N7
Harmelen, Neth. 50/B4
Harmony, It. 52/B3
Harney (basin), Or, US 128/C2
Harney (lake), Or, US 126/D5
Harney (peak), SD, US 127/H5
Harney (valley), Or, US 126/D5
Haro (cape), Mex. 142/C3
Haro, Sp. 44/D1
Harold, Ca, US 136/G7
Harpenden, Eng, UK 33/F3
Harper (mt.), Ak, US 134/K3
Harper, Ks, US 129/H3
Harper, Libr. 102/D5
Harper, Wa, US 135/B2
Harper Woods, Mi, US 136/G6
Harpstedt, Ger. 51/F3
Harqin Zuoyi Monggolzu Zizhixian, China 72/D2
Harrah, Ok, US 137/N15
Harrai, India 84/B4
Harran, Turk. 90/D2
Harricana (riv.), Qu, Can. 123/J4
Harriman, Tn, US 130/C5
Harrington, NY, US 139/L8
Harrington, Austl. 115/E1
Harrington Park, NJ, US 139/K8
Harris (mt.), Austl. 113/F4
Harris, Ne, US 129/H2
Harris (isl.), Sc, UK 31/Q8
Harris Park, Co, US 135/B3
Harrisburg, Ne, US 127/H5
Harrisburg (cap.), Pa, US 138/B3
Harrislee, Ger. 38/C4
Harrismith, SAfr. 106/E3
Harrison (bay), Ak, US 134/H1
Harrison (lake), Can. 126/C3
Harrison, Ar, US 129/J3
Harrison, Mi, US 130/C2
Harrison (cape), Can. 131/M3
Harrison, NY, US 139/L8
Harrisonville, Mo, US 137/G6
Harrisville, Ut, US 137/K11
Harrogate, Eng, UK 35/G4
Harrow (bor.), Eng, UK 30/B1
Harry S Truman (res.), Mo, US 137/J6
Harsefeld, Ger. 51/G2
Harsewinkel, Ger. 51/F5
Harson's Island, Mi, US 136/F6
Hart (lake), Or, US 128/C2
Hart, Mi, US 130/C3
Hart (riv.), Yk, Can. 122/C2
Hart (isl.), NY, US 139/K8
Hart Fell (mt.), Sc, UK 36/C5
Hartford (cap.), Ct, US 131/F3
Hartford, NJ, US 138/B4
Hartford City, In, US 130/C3
Hartheim, Ger. 56/C4
Hartland, Ne, US 129/J2
Hartland, Eng, UK 32/B4
Hartlepool, Eng, UK 35/G2
Hartley Wintney, Eng, UK 30/A2
Hartly, De, US 138/C5
Hartola, Fin. 39/L1
Harts (riv.), SAfr. 106/D3
Hartsdale, NY, US 139/K7
Hartshill, Eng, UK 33/F1
Hartstene (isl.), Wa, US 135/A3
Hartwell, In, US 135/D7
Hartwell (lake), US 133/H3
Hartz Mountain NP, Austl. 115/H5
Harun (peak), Indo. 81/E3
Hārūnābād, Pak. 86/B5

Harvey, ND, US 127/J4
Harvey, La, US 137/P17
Harvey, Austl. 112/B5
Harvey, Il, US 135/Q16
Harveys (lake), Pa, US 138/B1
Harwich, Eng, UK 33/H3
Haryana (state), India 82/C2
Harz (mts.), Ger. 51/H5
Haut-Rhin (dept.), Fr. 56/D2
Hasan (peak), Turk. 90/C2
Hasan Abdāl, Pak. 86/B2
Hasanpur, India 84/B1
Hasbrouck Heights, NJ, US 139/J8
Hase (riv.), Ger. 40/D2
Haselünne, Ger. 51/E3
Haslemere, Eng, UK 33/F4
Haslev, WBnk. 91/G7
Hasselt, Belg. 53/E2
Hasselt, Neth. 50/D3
Hassloch, Ger. 54/B4
Hassfurt, Ger. 54/D2
Hassi Bahbah, Alg. 100/G5
Hassi bou Zid (well), Alg. 99/F3
Hassi el Hadjar (well), Alg. 99/G3
Hassi el Mislane (well), Alg. 99/H4
Hassi er Rebib (well), Alg. 99/G2
Hässleholm, Swe. 38/E3
Hasslo (int'l arpt.), Swe. 38/F3
Haste, Ger. 51/G4
Hastings, Austl. 115/C3
Hastings, Ne, US 129/H2
Hastings, Mi, US 130/C3
Hastings, NZ 117/T10
Hastings Battlesite, Eng, UK 33/G5
Hastings-On-Hudson, NY, US 139/K7
Hasuda, Japan 77/D1
Hasunuma, Japan 77/E2
Hasvik, Nor. 37/G1
Hat Chao Mai NP, Thai. 78/B5
Hat Head, Austl. 115/E1
Hat Head NP, Austl. 115/E1
Hat Nai Yang NP, Thai. 78/B5
Hat Yai, Thai. 78/C5
Hat Yai (int'l arpt.), Thai. 78/C5
Hatashō, Japan 77/K5
Hatay (prov.), Turk. 90/C2
Hatboro, Pa, US 138/C3
Hatch, NM, US 132/B4
Hatcher (peak), Arg. 159/B6
Hateg, Rom. 48/F3
Hatfield, Pa, US 138/C3
Hatfield, Eng, UK 30/C1
Hatfield Peverel, Eng, UK 33/G3
Hatgal, Mong. 70/H1
Hāthras, India 84/B2
Hātia (riv.), Bang. 85/H4
Hātia, North (isl.), Bang. 85/H4
Hātia, South (isl.), Bang. 85/H4
Hātjoel, Ras (pt.), Ab,BC, Can. 122/E3
Hay River, NW, Can. 122/E3
Hayachine-san (mt.), Japan 76/B3
Hayakawa, Japan 77/A3
Hato Corozal, Col. 152/D3
Hato Mayor, DRep. 141/H4
Hatogaya, Japan 77/D2
Hatoyama, Japan 77/D2
Hatsu (isl.), Japan 77/D2
Hatta, India 84/B3
Hattah-Kulkyne NP, Austl. 113/J5
Hattem, Neth. 50/D3
Hatten, Fr. 53/G6
Hatteras, NC, US 133/J3
Hatteras (cape), NC, US 133/J3
Hattersheim am Main, Ger. 54/B2
Hattingen, Ger. 51/E6
Hattiesburg, Ms, US 133/F4
Hattieville, Belz. 144/D2
Hattula, Fin. 39/L1
Hatvan, Hun. 48/E2
Hatzenbühl, Ger. 54/B4
Hatzfeld, Ger. 51/F6
Hau Giang, Viet. 78/D4
Haubourdin, Fr. 52/B2
Haud (reg.), Eth. 97/P6
Hauge, Nor. 38/B2
Haugesund, Nor. 38/A2
Haukipudas, Fin. 60/H2
Haukivesi (lake), Fin. 60/G3
Haunsberg (peak), Aus. 55/F7
Hauppauge, NY, US 139/F2
Hauraki (gulf), NZ 117/S10

Haus, Nor. 38/A1
Hausach, Ger. 56/E1
Hausen, Ger. 54/E1
Hausjärvi, Fin. 39/L1
Hausleiten, Aus. 49/N7
Hausstock (peak), Swi. 57/F4
Haut Atlas (mts.), Mor. 96/D1
Haut-Rhin (dept.), Fr. 56/D2
Haute-Normandie (pol. reg.), Fr. 42/D2
Haute-Saône (dept.), Fr. 56/B2
Haute-Savoie (dept.), Fr. 56/C5
Hautefeuille, Fr. 30/L5
Hautes Fagnes (uplands), Belg. 53/E3
Hauteville-Lompnes, Fr. 56/B6
Hautmont, Fr. 52/C3
Hauts (plat.), Alg. 99/E2
Hauula, Hi, US 124/W12
Havana, Il, US 137/L5
Havant, Eng, UK 33/F5
Havasu (lake), US 128/D4
Havdhem, Swe. 38/H3
Havel (canal), Ger. 40/P6
Havel (riv.), Ger. 41/G2
Havelange, Belg. 53/E3
Havelberg, Ger. 41/F2
Haveli, Pak. 86/B4
Havelian, Pak. 86/B2
Havelock, NC, US 133/J3
Havelte, Neth. 50/D3
Havenore, Eng, UK 33/G3
Haverfordwest, Wal, UK 32/B3
Haverhill, Ma, US 131/G3
Haverhill, Eng, UK 33/G2
Havering (bor.), Eng, UK 30/D2
Havířov, Czh. 41/K4
Havlíčkuv Brod, Czh. 41/H4
Havneby, Den. 38/C4
Havre, Mt, US 126/F3
Havre de Grace, Md, US 138/B4
Havre-Saint-Pierre, Qu, Can. 131/J2
Havsa, Turk. 47/K2
Havza, Turk. 62/E4
Haw (riv.), NC, US 133/J3
Hawaii (state), US 124/S10
Hawaii (isl.), US
Hawaii Kai, Hi, US 124/W13
Hawaii Volcanoes NP, US 124/U11
Hawaiian (isls.), US 117/H2
Hawaiian Gardens, Ca, US 136/F8
Hawalli, Kuw. 88/E3
Hawarden, Wal, UK 35/E5
Hawera, NZ 117/S10
Haweswater (res.), Eng, UK 35/F2
Hawi, Hi, US 124/U10
Hawick, Sc, UK 36/D6
Hawke (cape), Austl. 115/E2
Hawke (bay), NZ 109/H6
Hawker, Austl. 113/H4
Hawkesbury (isl.), BC, Can. 126/A2
Hawkesbury, On, Can. 130/F2
Hawkesbury, Austl. 115/D2
Hawkes Nest, Austl. 115/E2
Hawkhurst, Eng, UK 33/G4
Hawsh 'Isá, Egypt 91/A4
Hawston, SAfr. 106/L11
Hawthorn Woods, Il, US 135/P15
Hawthorne, Nv, US 128/C3
Hawthorne, Ca, US 136/F8
Hawthorne, NY, US 139/K8
Hawwārah, Jor. 91/D3
Haxby, Eng, UK 35/G3
Hay (pt.), Austl. 114/C3
Hay River, NW, Can. 122/E3
Hayachine-san (mt.), Japan 76/B3
Hayakawa, Japan 77/A3
Hayange, Fr. 53/F4
Haybes, Fr. 53/E4
Haycock, Ak, US 134/F2
Haydock, Eng, UK 35/F5
Hayes (mt.), Ak, US 134/J3
Hayes (riv.), Mb, Can. 122/G3
Hayingen, Ger. 57/F1
Haylaastay, Mong. 71/K2
Hayle, Eng, UK 32/A6
Hayling (isl.), Eng, UK 33/F5
Haynesville, La, US 129/J4
Hayrabolu, Turk. 49/H5
Hays, Ks, US 129/H3
Haysyn, Ukr. 62/D2
Hayward, Wi, US 127/K4
Hayward, Ca, US 135/L12
Hazārībāg, India 85/E4
Hazebrouck, Fr. 52/B2
Hazel Park, Mi, US 136/F6
Hazelwood, Mo, US 137/P7
Hazen
Hazlehurst, Ms, US 129/K5
Hazlemere, Eng, UK 30/A2
Hazlet, NJ, US 139/J10
Hazleton (mts.), BC, Can. 126/A2
Hazleton, Pa, US 138/C2

Hazlett (lake), Austl. 113/F2
Hazratbal Mosque, India 86/C2
Hazro, Pak. 86/B3
Hazu, Japan 77/M6
He (riv.), China 79/B3
He Xian, China 72/D5
Headcorn, Eng, UK 33/G4
Heads of Ayr (pt.), Sc, UK 36/B6
Healdsburg, Ca, US 128/B3
Healesville, Austl. 115/G5
Healy, Ak, US 134/J3
Heanor, Eng, UK 35/G6
Heard (isl.), Austl. 160/E
Hearst, On, Can. 130/D1
Heart (riv.), ND, US 127/H4
Heart Law (hill), Sc, UK 36/D5
Heath (pt.), Can. 131/J1
Heathcote, Austl. 115/C3
Heathcote NP, Austl. 114/G9
Heathrow (int'l arpt.), Eng, UK 30/B2
Hebbronville, Tx, US 138/B5
Hebei (prov.), China 71/K4
Hebertshausen, Ger. 55/E6
Hebrides (isls.), UK 27/D3
Hebrides (sea), Sc, UK 31/Q8
Hebron, NE, US 129/H2
Hebron, Il, US 135/P15
Heby, Swe. 38/G2
Hecate (str.), BC, Can. 119/D4
Hecelchakán, Mex. 144/D1
Hechi, China 83/J3
Hechingen, Ger. 54/B6
Hechtel, Belg. 53/E1
Hechthausen, Ger. 51/G1
Hecker, Il, US 137/H9
Hecla, SD, US 127/J4
Hecla and Griper (bay), NW, Can. 123/R7
Hector (mt.), Ab, Can. 126/D3
Heddal, Nor. 38/C2
Hedel, Neth. 50/C5
Hedemora, Swe. 38/F1
Hedensted, Den. 38/C4
Hedmark (co.), Nor. 37/D3
Hedo-misaki (cape), Japan 75/K7
Hédouville, Fr. 30/J4
Heede, Ger. 51/E3
Heeia, Hi, US 124/W13
Heek, Ger. 51/E4
Heemskerk, Neth. 50/B3
Heemstede, Neth. 50/B4
Heerde, Neth. 50/D4
Heerenveen, Neth. 50/C3
Heerhugowaard, Neth. 50/B3
Heerlen, Neth. 53/E2
Heers, Belg. 53/E2
Heesch, Neth. 50/C5
Heeslingen, Ger. 51/G2
Heeze, Neth. 50/C6
Hefa (Haifa), Isr. 91/F6
Hefei, China 72/D5
Hefeng Tujiazu Zizhixian, China 79/B2
Hefner (lake), Ok, US 137/M14
Hegang, China 71/P2
Hegau (mts.), Ger. 43/H3
Hegau (reg.), Ger. 40/E5
Heggenes, Nor. 38/C1
Hegins, Pa, US 138/B2
Heguri, Japan 77/J6
Hei (riv.), Japan 76/B4
Heide, Ger. 38/C4
Heideck, Ger. 54/E4
Heidelberg, Ms, US 133/F4
Heidelberg, SAfr. 106/C4
Heidelberg, Ger. 54/B4
Heiden, Ger. 50/D5
Heiden, Swi. 57/F3
Heidenheim, Ger. 54/D4
Heidenreichstein, Aus. 41/H4
Heiderscheid, Lux. 53/E4
Heigenbrücken, Ger. 54/C2
Heihe, China 71/N1
Heikendorf, Ger. 51/H1
Heilbron, SAfr. 106/D2
Heilbronn, Ger. 54/C4
Heiligenberg, Ger. 57/F2
Heiligenblut, Aus. 43/K3
Heiligenhafen, Ger. 38/D4
Heiligenhaus, Ger. 50/D6
Heiligenstadt, Ger. 51/H5
Heilong (Amur) (riv.), China, Rus. 65/N5
Heilongjiang (prov.), China 71/N2
Heiloo, Neth. 50/B3
Heimaey (isl.), Ice. 37/N7
Heimberg, Swi. 56/D4
Heimsheim, Ger. 54/B5
Heino, Neth. 50/D4
Heinsberg, Ger. 53/F1
Heishan, China 73/B2
Heist-op-den-Berg, Belg. 53/D1
Heitersheim, Ger. 56/D2
Heiwa, Japan 77/L5
Hejian, China 72/D3
Hejin, China 72/B4
Hejing, China 70/E3
Hekimhan, Turk. 90/D2
Hekinan, Japan 77/L6
Hekla (vol.), Ice. 37/N7
Hekou, China 83/H3
Hel, Pol. 39/H4
Helan, China 70/J4
Helbe (riv.), Ger. 51/H6
Helden, Neth. 50/D6
Helena (cap.), Mt, US 126/E4
Helena (riv.), Austl. 112/L6
Helensburgh, Sc, UK 36/B4
Helgasjön (lake), Swe. 38/F3
Helgoland (isl.), Ger. 38/B4

Helgoländer (bay), Wa, US 135/B3
Helgoländer (bay), Ger. 38/C5
Heliodora, Braz. 211/H7
Heliopolis (int'l arpt.), Swe. 38/E3
Hellas (see Greece)
Hellen (riv.), Iran 88/F3
Hellendoorn, Neth. 50/D4
Hellenthal, Ger. 53/F3
Hellertown, Pa, US 138/C2
Hellevoetsluis, Neth. 50/B5
Hellin, Sp. 44/E3
Hells Canyon Nat'l Rec. Area, US 126/D4
Hell's Gate NP, Kenya 104/C3
Helmand (riv.), Afg. 67/F6
Helmbrechts, Ger. 55/E2
Helmet (mtn.), Ak, US 134/K2
Helmetta, NJ, US 139/H10
Helmond, Neth. 50/C6
Helmstadt, Ger. 54/C3
Helmstedt, Ger. 40/F2
Hèrlèn Gol (Kerulen) (riv.), Mong. 71/K2
Helotes, Tx, US 137/T20
Helper, Ut, US 128/E3
Helsenhorn (peak), Swi. 56/E5
Helsingør, Den. 38/E3
Helsinki (Helsingfors) (cap.), Fin. 37/H3
Helsinki-Vantaa (int'l arpt.), Fin. 39/L1
Hem (riv.), Fr. 52/B2
Hemau, Ger. 55/E4
Hemel Hempstead, Eng, UK 30/B1
Hemer, Ger. 51/E6
Hemet, Ca, US 136/D3
Hemmingen, Ger. 51/G4
Hemmoor, Ger. 51/G1
Hemphill, Tx, US 132/E4
Hempstead (har.), NY, US 139/L8
Hempstead, NY, US 139/L9
Hemsedal, Nor. 38/C2
Hemse, Swe. 38/H3
Hemsworth, Eng, UK 35/G4
Henan (prov.), China 71/K5
Henán, Swe. 38/D2
Henares (riv.), Sp. 44/D2
Henashi-zaki (pt.), Japan 76/A3
Hendaye, Fr. 42/C5
Hendek, Turk. 49/K5
Henderson, NC, US 130/E4
Henderson, Nv, US 128/D3
Henderson, Tn, US 130/B5
Henderson, Ky, US 130/C4
Henderson, Co, US 137/C3
Henderson (isl.), Pitc. 117/N7
Henderson, Arg. 158/E3
Henderson, Md, US 138/C5
Hendersonville, Tn, US 130/C4
Hendersonville, NC, US 133/H3
Hendrik-Ido-Ambacht, Neth. 50/B5
Hendrik Verwoerdam (res.), SAfr. 106/D3
Hendrina, SAfr. 107/E2
Henefer, Ut, US 137/L11
Heng (mtn.), China 72/C3
Heng (isl.), China 72/L8
Heng Xian, China 83/J3
Hengduan (mts.), China 70/G6
Hengelo, Neth. 50/D4
Hengersberg, Ger. 55/G5
Hengshan, China 79/B2
Hengshan, China 72/B3
Hengshui, China 72/C3
Hengyang, China 79/B2
Hengyang, China 83/K2
Heniches'k, Ukr. 44/H4
Hénin-Beaumont, Fr. 52/B2
Henley-on-Thames, Eng, UK 33/F3
Henlopen (cape), De, US 138/C6
Henlopen Acres, De, US 138/C6
Henndorf am Wallersee, Aus. 55/G7
Henne, Den. 38/C4
Hennebont, Fr. 42/B3
Hennef, Ger. 54/B3
Hennenman, SAfr. 106/D2
Henniggsdorf, Ger. 40/G6
Henrietta, Tx, US 129/H4
Henrietta Maria (cape), On, Can. 123/H3
Henry (mts.), Ut, US 128/E3
Henry (cape), Can. 134/M5
Henry Ford Museum and Greenfield Village Historical Site, Mi, US 135/E7
Henryetta, Ok, US 129/J4
Henryville, Pa, US 138/C1
Hensies, Belg. 52/C3
Hentiy (riv.), Mong. 71/J2
Hentiyn (mts.), Mong. 70/J2
Henty, Austl. 115/C2
Henzada, Myan. 83/G4
Heping, China 79/B3
Heppenheim an der Bergstrasse, Ger. 54/B3
Hepu, China 83/J3
Hequ, China 72/B3

Herálio Luz (int'l arpt.), Braz. 155/B3
Herculaneum, Mo, US 137/G9
Herculaneum (ruin), It. 46/D2
Hercules, Ca, US 135/K10
Herdecke, Ger. 51/E6
Herdorf, Ger. 51/G2
Heredia, CR 145/E4
Hereford, Tx, US 129/G4
Hereford, Eng, UK 32/D2
Hereford, Pa, US 138/C3
Hereford (inlet), NJ, US 138/D3
Hereford, Md, US 138/B4
Hereford and Worcester (co.), Eng, UK 32/D2
Herehereteue (isl.), FrPol. 117/L7
Hereke, Turk. 49/J5
Herencia, Sp. 44/C3
Herentals, Belg. 50/B6
Herford, Ger. 51/F4
Hergiswil, Swi. 57/E4
Héricourt, Fr. 56/C2
Hérimoncourt, Fr. 56/C3
Herington, Ks, US 129/H3
Herisau, Swi. 57/F3
Herk-de-Stad, Belg. 53/E2
Herlen (riv.), Belg. 53/E2
Herleshausen, Ger. 51/H5
Herma Ness (cape), Sc, UK 31/W13
Hermann, Mo, US 129/K3
Hermannsburg, Ger. 51/H3
Hermannsburg Abor. Land, Austl. 113/G2
Hermanus, SAfr. 106/L11
Hermeray (riv.), Fr. 30/G6
Hermersberg, Ger. 53/G5
Hermes, Fr. 52/B5
Hermeskeil, Ger. 53/F4
Herminston, Or, US 126/D4
Hermitage, Rus. 61/T7
Hermosa Beach, Ca, US 136/F8
Hermosillo, Mex. 142/C2
Hermsdorf, Ger. 40/G6
Hernández, Mex. 142/E4
Hernando, Ms, US 129/K4
Hernani, Sp. 44/E1
Hernando, Pa, US 138/B2
Hieroglyphic (mts.), Az, US 137/R18
Hierro (isl.) 96/B2
Hieve (lake), Ger. 51/E2
Higashi-Chichibu, Japan 77/C1
Higashi-Matsuyama, Japan 77/C1
Higashi-ōsaka, Japan 77/J6
Higashikurume, Japan 77/T6
Higashimurayama, Japan 77/C2
Higashine, Japan 76/B4
Higashiura, Japan 77/G6
Higashiyoshino, Japan 77/J7
High (isl.), Or, US 126/C5
High (hill), Pa, US 138/C1
High (isl.), China 71/V10
High Bridge, NJ, US 138/D2
High Island, Tx, US 132/E4
High Level, Ab, Can. 122/E3
High Point, NC, US 133/H3
High Ridge, Mo, US 137/F9
High River, Ab, Can. 126/E3
High Street (peak), Eng, UK 35/F3
High Willhays (hill), Eng, UK 32/B5
High Wycombe, Eng, UK 33/F2
Higham, Eng, UK 30/E2
Higham Ferrers, Eng, UK 33/F2
Highland, Ca, US 136/C2
Highland, Ut, US 137/K13
Highland, In, US 135/R16
Highland (pol. reg.), Sc, UK 36/A2
Highland Lakes, NJ, US 138/D1
Highland Park, Co, US 137/A4
Highland Park, NJ, US 139/H10
Highland Park, Mi, US 135/F7
Highlands, NJ, US 139/K10
Highrock (lake), Can. 127/H2
Highspire, Pa, US 138/B3
Hightstown, NJ, US 138/D2
Highwood, Il, US 135/Q15
Higley, Az, US 137/S19
Higuera de Zaragoza, Mex. 142/D3
Hirlău, Rom. 49/H2
Hiro'o, Japan 76/C2
Hirosaki, Japan 76/B3
Hiroshima, Japan 74/C3
Hiroshima (pref.), Japan 74/C3
Hirschaid, Ger. 54/D3
Hirschau, Ger. 55/E3
Hirschhorn, Ger. 54/B4
Hirson, Fr. 53/D4
Hîrşova, Rom. 49/H3
Hirtshals, Den. 38/C3
Hirtop, Japan 77/M4
Hirukawa, Japan 77/K6
Hirwaun (pail), NZ 117/T10
Hisarcık, Turk. 62/D5
Hisdal, Ind. 84/A2
Hispania (isl.), 145/J7
Hişn al 'Abr, Yem. 88/E5

Heubach, Ger. 54/C5
Heuchelheim, Ger. 54/B1
Heukuppe (peak), Aus. 41/H5
Heusden, Neth. 50/C5
Heusden-Zolder, Belg. 53/E1
Heusenstamm, Ger. 54/B1
Heusweiler, Ger. 53/F5
Hève (cape), Fr. 42/D2
Heves, Hun. 41/L5
Heves (co.), Hun. 41/L5
Hewett, NY, US 139/L9
Hewitt (pt.), NY, US 139/L8
Hewlett, NY, US 139/L9
Hex River (mts.), SAfr. 106/L10
Hex River (pass), SAfr. 106/L10
Hexenkopf (peak), Aus. 57/G3
Heyerode, Ger. 51/H6
Heythuysen, Neth. 50/C6
Heywood, Austl. 115/B3
Heywood, Eng, UK 35/F4
Heze, China 72/C4
Hialeah, Fl, US 133/H5
Hiawatha, Ks, US 129/J3
Hibbing, Mn, US 127/K4
Hibbs, (pt.), Austl. 115/C4
Hicacos (pt.), Cuba 145/F1
Hichisō, Japan 77/C1
Hickman, Can. 134/M4
Hickory, NC, US 133/H3
Hickory, La, US 137/Q16
Hickory Run State Park, Pa, US 138/C1
Hicksville, NY, US 139/L8
Hico, Tx, US 129/H5
Hidaka (riv.), Japan 74/D4
Hidaka, Japan 76/C2
Hidaka (mts.), Japan 76/C2
Hidalgo, Mex. 143/F3
Hidalgo (state), Mex. 140/B3
Hidalgo del Parral, Mex. 142/D3
Hidrolândia, Braz. 154/B2
Hierapolis (ruin), Turk. 90/B2
Hidalgo de Zaragoza, Mex. 142/D3
Higüey, DRep. 145/J2
Hiidenportin NP, Fin. 60/F3
Hiiumaa (isl.), Est. 60/D4
Híjar, Sp. 45/E2
Hijāz, Jabal al (mts.), SAr. 88/C3
Hiji, Japan 74/B4
Hijuelas de Conchalí, Chile 158/N8
Hikami, Japan 77/H5
Hikari, Japan 77/F2
Hikone, Japan 74/D3
Hikueru (isl.), FrPol. 117/L6
Hikurangi (mtn.), NZ 117/T10
Hildburghausen, Ger. 54/D2
Hilden, Ger. 53/F1
Hildesheim, Ger. 51/H4
Hilders, Ger. 54/C1
Hilgermissen, Ger. 51/G3
Hill City, Ks, US 129/H3
Hill of Fare (hill), Sc, UK 36/D2
Hill of Stake (hill), Sc, UK 36/B5
Hillaby (mt.), Bar. 141/P9
Hillburn, NY, US 139/J7
Hillcrest, NY, US 139/J7
Hille, Ger. 51/F4
Hillegom, Neth. 50/B4
Hillerød, Den. 38/E3
Hillesheim, Ger. 53/F3
Hillingdon (bor.), Eng, UK 30/A1
Hillsboro, ND, US 127/J4
Hillsboro, Or, US 126/C4

Hillsboro, Tx, US 129/H4
Hillsboro, Oh, US 130/D4
Hillsboro, Md, US 138/C6
Hillsborough (chan.), Austl. 114/C3
Hillsborough, NJ, US 138/D3
Hillsborough, Ca, US 135/K11
Hillsdale, Mi, US 130/C3
Hillsdale, Ks, US 137/D6
Hillsdale (lake), Ks, US 137/D6
Hillsdale, NJ, US 139/J7
Hillside, NJ, US 139/J9
Hillside, Sc, UK 36/D3
Hillswick, Sc, UK 31/W13
Hillston, Austl. 115/C2
Hilltop, Co, US 137/C4
Hilltown, NI, UK 34/B3
Hilo, HI, US 124/U11
Hilonghilong (mt.), Phil. 81/G2
Hilpoltstein, Ger. 54/E4
Hilpsford (pt.), Eng, UK 35/E3
Hilsa, India 85/E3
Hilterfingen, Swi. 56/D4
Hilton Head (isl.), SC, US 133/H3
Hilton Head Island, SC, US 133/H3
Hilvarenbeek, Neth. 50/C6
Hilversum, Neth. 50/C4
Hilzingen, Ger. 57/F3
Himáchal Pradesh (state), India 70/C5
Himalaya (range), Asia 67/G6
Himālchuli (peak), Nepal 85/E1
Himamaylan, Phil. 79/D5
Himanka, Fin. 60/D2
Himeji, Japan 74/D3
Himeji Castle, Japan 74/D3
Himeji, Japan 75/E2
Himmelpforten, Ger. 51/G1
Himş (prov.), Syria 90/D3
Himş, Syria 91/E2
Hinche, Haiti 145/H2
Hinchinbrook (isl.), Austl. 114/C3
Hinchinbrook Entrance (chan.), 134/J3
Hinchinbrook Island, Ak, US 134/J3
Hinckley, Eng, UK 33/E1
Hincks Conservation Park, Austl. 113/H5
Hindaun, India 84/A1
Hindelang, Ger. 57/F4
Hindeloopen, Neth. 50/C3
Hindley, Eng, UK 35/F4
Hindmarsh, Austl. 115/B3
Hindu Kush (mts.), Asia 67/F6
Hinesville, Ga, US 133/H4
Hinganghāt, India 82/C3
Hingol (riv.), Pak. 89/J3
Hingoli, India 82/C4
Hinigaran, Phil. 89/J3
Hinis, Turk. 63/G5
Hinnøya (isl.), Nor. 37/F1
Hino, Japan 77/K5
Hino (riv.), Japan 77/K5
Hino-misaki (cape), Japan 74/C3
Hinohara, Japan 77/C2
Hinojosa del Duque, Sp. 44/C3
Hinsdale, Il, US 135/Q16
Hinterbrühl, Aus. 49/N7
Hinterrhein, Swi. 57/F4
Hinterrugg (peak), Swi. 57/F3
Hinterweidenthal, Ger. 53/G5
Hinton, Ab, Can. 126/D2
Hinton, WV, US 130/D4
Hinwil, Swi. 57/E3
Hippolyte Bouchard, Arg. 158/E2
Hippolytushoef, Neth. 50/B3
Hipswell, Eng, UK 35/G3
Hira Highlands (uplands), Japan 77/J5
Hirakata, Japan 74/J6
Hirakud (res.), India 82/D3
Hiraman (riv.), Kenya 104/C3
Hirara (riv.), India 84/B4
Hiranai, Japan 76/B3
Hiranai, Japan 75/H8
Hirata, Japan 74/C3
Hirata, Japan 77/L5
Hiratsuka, Japan 77/J5
Hirfanli (dam), Turk. 62/E5
Hiro'o, Japan 76/C2
Hirosaki, Japan 76/B3
Hirtop, Japan 77/M4
Hisai, Japan 77/M4
Hisar, India 85/E3
Hişn al 'Abr, Yem. 88/E5
Historic Houses of Odessa, De, US 138/C6
Historic Towne of Smithville, NJ, US 138/D3
Hīt, Iraq 90/D3
Hitachi, Japan 75/G2
Hitachi-ōta, Japan 75/G2
Hitoyoshi, Japan 74/B4
Hitra (isl.), Nor. 37/D3
Hitzacker, Ger. 51/H2
Hitzkirch, Swi. 57/E3
Hiyoshi, Japan 77/J5
Hizan, Turk. 90/F2
Hjälmaren (lake), Swe. 38/G2

Hjartfjellet (peak), Nor. 37/E2
Hjelmeland, Nor. 38/B2
Hjerm, Den. 38/C3
Hjo, Swe. 38/F2
Hjørring, Den. 38/C3
Hka (riv.), Myan. 78/B1
Hkakabo (peak), Myan. 78/B1
Habisa, SAfr. 107/E3
Hlohovec, Slvk. 48/C1
Hluboká nad Vltavou, Czh. 55/H4
Hluhluwe, SAfr. 107/F3
Hlukhiv, Ukr. 62/E2
Hmawbi, Myan. 83/G4
Ho, Gha. 103/F5
Ho Chi Minh, Viet. 78/D1
Hoa Binh, Viet. 78/D1
Hoare (bay), NW, Can. 123/K3
Hobart, Wa, US 135/D3
Hobart, Austl. 115/C4
Hobbs, NM, US 129/G4
Hoboken, Belg. 50/B6
Hoboken, NJ, US 139/J9
Hoboksar Monggol Zizhixian, China 70/E2
Hobro, Den. 38/C3
Hochalmspitze (peak), Aus. 43/K3
Höchberg, Ger. 54/C3
Hochdorf, Ger. 57/F1
Hochfelden, Fr. 53/G6
Hochgrat (peak), Ger. 57/F3
Hochheim am Main, Ger. 54/B1
Hochkönig (peak), Aus. 43/K3
Hoch'ŏn (riv.), NKor. 73/D2
Hochschwab (peak), Aus. 43/L3
Hochsimmer (peak), Ger. 53/G3
Hochspeyer, Ger. 53/G5
Höchst, Aus. 57/F3
Höchst im Odenwald, Ger. 54/C3
Hochstadt am Main, Ger. 54/D2
Höchstadt an der Aisch, Ger. 54/D3
Höchstädt an der Donau, Ger. 54/D5
Hochstetten-Dhaun, Ger. 53/G4
Hochvogel (peak), Ger. 57/G3
Hochwang (peak), Swi. 57/F4
Hockenheim, Ger. 54/B4
Hockessin, De, US 138/C4
Hod Hasharon, Isr. 91/F7
Hodal, India 84/A2
Hoddesdon, Eng, UK 30/D1
Hodenhagen, Ger. 51/G3
Hodges (lake), Ca, US 136/C5
Hodgeville, Sk, Can. 126/G3
Hodh El Gharbi (pol. reg.), Mrta. 102/C2
Hodh ech Chargui (pol. reg.), Mrta. 102/C2
Hódmezővásárhely, Hun. 48/E2
Hodonín, Czh. 41/J4
Hoek van Holland, Neth. 50/B5
Hoeksche Waard (isl.), Neth. 50/B5
Hoensbroek, Neth. 53/E2
Hoeselt, Belg. 53/E2
Hoevelaken, Neth. 50/C4
Hoeven, Neth. 50/B5
Hoeybuktmoen (int'l arpt.), Nor. 37/J1
Hof, Ger. 55/E2
Hofbieber, Ger. 54/C1
Höfðhakaupstadhur, Ice. 37/N6
Hoffman Estates, Il, US 135/P15
Hofgeismar, Ger. 51/G5
Hofheim am Taunus, Ger. 54/B2
Hofheim in Unterfranken, Ger. 54/D2
Hofmeyr, SAfr. 106/D3
Hofong Qagan Salt (lake), China 72/B3
Hofors, Swe. 38/G1
Hofsá (riv.), Ice. 37/P6
Hofsjökull (glacier), Ice. 37/N7
Höfu, Japan 74/B3
Hogarth (mt.), Austl. 113/H2
Hoh Xil (mts.), China 70/E4
Höhbirö, Mong. 70/H2
Hohe Acht (peak), Ger. 53/G3
Hohe Geige (peak), Aus. 43/K3
Hohe Tauern (mts.), Aus. 43/K3
Hohe Tauern, NP, Aus. 43/K3
Hohe Tauern NP, Aus. 43/K3
Hohen Neuendorf, Ger. 40/G6
Hohenbrunn, Ger. 55/E6
Hohenems, Aus. 57/F3
Hohenhameln, Ger. 51/H4
Hohenlinden, Ger. 55/E6
Hohenlockstedt, Ger. 40/E2
Hohenlohe Ebene (plain), Ger. 57/G2
Hohenpeissenberg, Ger. 57/G2
Hohenroth, Ger. 54/D2
Hoher Dachstein (peak), Aus. 43/K3
Hoher Ifen (peak), Aus. 57/G3
Hoher Randen (mt.), Ger. 57/F3
Hohhot, China 72/B2
Höhn, Ger. 53/G3
Hohneck (peak), Fr. 56/D1
Hohnstorf, Ger. 51/H2
Hohokam Pima Nat'l Mon., Az, US 137/R18

Höhr-Grenzhausen, Ger. 53/G3
Hoi An, Viet. 78/E3
Hoima, Ugan. 104/A2
Hoisington, Ks, US 129/H3
Højby, Den. 38/D4
Højer, Den. 38/C4
Hōjō, Japan 74/C4
Hokitika, NZ 117/S11
Hokkaidō (isl.), Japan 67/P3
Hokksund, Nor. 38/D2
Hokota, Japan 75/G2
Hol, Nor. 38/C1
Holbox (isl.), Mex. 144/E1
Holbrook, SAfr. 107/E3
Holbrook, Az, US 128/E4
Holbrook, NY, US 139/E2
Holderness (pen.), Eng, UK 35/H4
Holdorf, Ger. 51/F3
Holdrege, Ne, US 129/H2
Holeby, Den. 38/D4
Holguín, Cuba 145/G1
Holiday Hills, Il, US 135/P15
Holitna (riv.), Ak, US 134/G3
Höljes, Swe. 38/E1
Holladay-Cottonwood, Ut, US 137/K12
Holland, Mi, US 130/C3
Hollandale, Ms, US 129/K4
Hollandse IJssel (riv.), Neth. 50/B5
Hollandstoun, Sc, UK 31/V14
Hollenstedt, Ger. 51/G2
Hollfeld, Ger. 54/E3
Holliday, Ks, US 137/D5
Hollis, Ok, US 129/H4
Hollis, NY, US 134/M4
Hollister, Ca, US 128/B3
Hollister (mt.), Austl. 112/B2
Hollogne-aux-Pierres, Belg. 53/E2
Höllviksnäs, Swe. 38/E4
Holly, Wa, US 135/B2
Holly Springs, Ms, US 133/F3
Hollywood, Fl, US 133/H5
Hollywood Bowl, Ca, US 136/F7
Hollywood Park, Tx, US 137/U20
Holm, Ger. 51/G2
Holman, NW, Can. 122/E1
Hólmavik, Ice. 37/N6
Holmdel, NJ, US 138/D3
Holmes (reefs), Austl. 109/D2
Holmesdale (valley), Eng, UK 30/E
Holmestrand, Nor. 38/D2
Holmfirth, Eng, UK 35/G4
Holmsjön (lake), Swe. 37/F3
Holmsund, Swe. 37/G3
Holon, Isr. 91/F7
Holopedale, Nf, Can. 123/K3
Holstebro, Den. 38/C3
Holston (riv.), Tn, US 133/H2
Holt, Ca, US 135/M11
Holt, Eng, UK 30/H4
Holtälen, Nor. 37/D3
Holten, Neth. 50/D4
Holtland, Ger. 51/E2
Holton, Ks, US 129/J3
Holtsville, NY, US 139/E2
Holy (isl.), Sc, UK 36/A5
Holy Cross, Ak, US 134/G3
Holyhead, Wal, UK 34/D4
Holyoke, Co, US 129/G2
Holyoke, Ma, US 131/F3
Holywell, Wal, UK 35/E5
Holywood, NI, UK 34/C2
Holzkirchen, Ger. 55/E6
Holzminden, Ger. 51/G5
Holzwickede, Ger. 51/E5
Hom (riv.), Namb. 106/B3
Homberg, Ger. 53/E2
Homberg, Ger. 51/G5
Hombori Tondo (peak), Mali 103/E3
Homburg-Haut, Fr. 53/E5
Homburg, Ger. 53/G5
Home (bay), NW, Can. 123/K2
Home Hill, Austl. 114/B2
Homécourt, Fr. 53/E5
Homeland, Ca, US 136/C3
Homer, Ak, US 134/H4
Homer, La, US 129/J5
Homestead, Fl, US 133/H5
Homestead Nat'l Mon. of America, Ne, US 129/J2
Homewood, Al, US 133/G3
Homewood, Il, US 135/Q16
Homib (riv.), Erit. 88/E
Hommersåk, Nor. 38/A2
Homochitto (riv.), Ms, US 132/F4
Homyel' (pol. reg.), Bela. 62/D1
Homyel', Bela. 62/D1
Homyel'skaya (prov.), Bela. 62/D1
Hon Quan, Viet. 78/D1
Honaunau-Napoopoo, Hi, US 124/U11
Honbetsu, Japan 76/C2
Hondo (riv.), Wal, UK 32/C2
Hondeklipbaai, SAfr. 106/B3
Hondo, Tx, US 129/H5
Hondo, Japan 74/B4
Hondo, Belz. 144/D2
Hondschoote, Fr. 52/B2
Hondsrug (reg.), Neth. 50/D3
Hondsrug (hills), Neth. 40/D2
Honduras (gulf), NAm. 144/D2
Honduras (ctry.) 119/J8
Honey (lake), Ca, US 128/C3
Honey Brook, Pa, US 138/C3
Honey Creek, Wi, US 135/P13
Honfleur, Fr. 42/D2
Hong (riv.), China 72/C4
Hong Gai, Viet. 78/D1
Hong Kong (dpcy.), China 65/L7
Hong Kong (isl.), China 71/U10
Hong'an, China 72/C5
Hongch'ŏn, SKor. 73/D4
Hongch'ŏn, China 72/B2
Hongde, China 72/A3
Honghu, China 72/C5
Hongjiang, China 83/J2

Hongqiao (int'l arpt.), China 72/L9
Hongshui (riv.), China 70/J6
Hongsŏng, SKor. 73/D4
Hongtong, China 72/B3
Honguedo (passg.), Can. 131/H1
Hongwŏn, NKor. 73/D2
Hongze, China 72/D4
Hønefoss, Nor. 38/D2
Honiara (cap.), Sol. 116/E5
Honjō, Japan 76/B4
Honjō, Japan 77/C1
Honolulu (cap.), Hi, US 124/T10
Honolulu (int'l arpt.), Hi, US 124/W13
Honolulu Co. (isl.), Hi, US 124/V13
Honouliuli, Hi, US 124/V13
Hönow, Ger. 40/G6
Honshū (isl.), Japan 65/Q6
Honshū (isl.), Japan 67/P6
Honton (mt.), Or, US 122/D2
Heruphav, Den. 38/C4
Horusický Rybník (lake), Czh. 55/H4
Herve, Den. 38/D4
Horvot Dor, Isr. 91/F6
Wa, US 126/C4
Horw, Swi. 57/E3
Horwich, Eng, UK 35/F4
Horwood (lake), Can. 130/D2
Hösbach, Ger. 54/C2
Hosenfeld, Ger. 54/C1
Hoshiārpur, India 86/C4
Hooghly (riv.), India 85/F5
Hooghly-Chinsura, India 85/G4
Hosszúpereszteg, Hun. 48/C2
Hoste (isl.), Chile 159/C7
Hot Springs, SD, US 127/H5
Hot Springs NP, Ar, US 129/J4
Hotaka, Japan 75/E2
Hotaka-dake (peak), Japan 75/E2
Hotan, China 70/C4
Hotan (riv.), China 70/D4
Hotazel, SAfr. 106/C2
Hotont, Mong. 70/H2
Hottah (lake), NW, Can. 122/E2
Hottentot (bay), Namb. 106/A2
Hotton, Belg. 53/E3
Houari Boumedienne (int'l arpt.), Alg. 100/G4
Houdain, Fr. 52/B3
Houdan, Fr. 30/G5
Houet (prov.), Burk. 102/D4
Houffalize, Belg. 53/E3
Houilles, Fr. 30/H5
Houlton, Me, US 131/H2
Houma, China 72/B4
Houma, La, US 132/F5
Houplines, Fr. 52/B2
Hourdel (pt.), Fr. 52/A3
Hourn, Loch (inlet), Sc, UK 36/A2
Hourtin, Fr. 42/C4
Housatonic (riv.), Ct, US 139/E1
House (range), Ut, US 128/D3
House Springs, Mo, US 137/F9
Housesteads Roman Fort, Eng, UK 35/F1
Houssen, Fr. 56/D1
Houston, BC, Can. 126/B2
Houston, Mo, US 129/K3
Houston, De, US 138/C6
Houston, Tx, US 132/E4
Houten, Neth. 50/C4
Houthulst, Belg. 52/B2
Houtman Abrolhos (isl.), Austl. 112/B4
Houtribdijk (dam), Neth. 50/C3
Houtskär (isl.), Fin. 39/J1
Houyet, Belg. 53/E3
Hov, Nor. 38/D1
Hova, Swe. 38/F2
Hovd (prov.), Mong. 70/F2
Hövelhof, Ger. 51/F5
Hovenweep Nat'l Mon., Ut, US 128/E3
Hovfjället (peak), Swe. 38/E1
Hovmantorp, Swe. 38/F3
Hövsgöl (prov.), Mong. 70/H2
Hövsgöl (lake), Mong. 70/H1
Hovsta, Swe. 38/F2
Howard (lake), Ak, US 134/G2
Howard, Austl. 114/D4
Howard (hill), Ak, US 134/G2
Howard Hanson (res.), Wa, US 135/D3
Howard Hanson (dam), Wa, US 135/D3
Howe (cape), Austl. 115/D3
Howe of the Mearns (reg.), Sc, UK 36/D3
Howell, Mi, US 130/D3
Howell, NJ, US 138/D3
Howick, SAfr. 107/E3
Howland (isl.), Pac., US 117/H4
Höxter, Ger. 51/G5
Hoxud, China 70/E3
Hoy (isl.), Sc, UK 31/V14
Hoya, Ger. 51/G3
Hōya, Japan 77/D2
Hoyland Nether, Eng, UK 35/G4
Hoyerswerda, Ger. 41/H3
Hoylake, Eng, UK 35/E5
Hoyos, Azor., Port. 45/S12
Hoyo de Manzanares, Sp. 45/N8
Hoyos, Sp. 44/B2
Hoyoux (riv.), Belg. 53/E2
Hozumi, Japan 77/L5
Hracholusky (lake), Cz. 55/F3
Hradec Králové, Czh. 41/H3
Hradiště (peak), Czh. 55/F2
Hrasnica, Bosn. 48/D4

Hrastnik, Slov. 43/L3
Hrazdan, Arm. 63/H4
Hrodna, Bela. 39/K5
Hrodzyenskaya (prov.), Bela. 60/E5
Hrolleifsborg (peak), Ice. 37/M6
Hron (riv.), Slvk. 62/A2
Hronov, Czh. 41/J3
Hrubieszów, Pol. 41/M3
Hrubý Jeseník (mts.), Czh.,Pol. 41/J3
Hrútafjöll (peak), Ice. 37/P6
Hsinchu, Tai. 79/D3
Hua (reg.), China 72/B4
Hua Hin, Thai. 78/B3
Hua Xian, China 72/C4
Hua'an, China 79/C2
Huacaybamba, Peru 156/B3
Huacho, Peru 156/B3
Huachón, Peru 156/C3
Huachuca City, Az, US 128/E5
Huacrachuco, Peru 156/B3
Huade, China 71/K3
Huahine (isl.), FrPol. 117/K6
Huai (riv.), China 72/D4
Huai'an, China 72/C4
Huai'an, China 72/D4
Huaibei, China 71/L5
Huaibin, China 72/C5
Huaiji, China 83/K3
Huailai, China 72/G6
Huainan, China 72/D4
Huairen, China 72/C3
Huairou, China 72/H6
Huaiyang, China 72/C4
Huaiyin, China 72/D4
Huaiyuan, China 72/D4
Huajicori, Mex. 142/D4
Huajuapan de León, Mex. 144/B2
Hualahuises, Mex. 143/F3
Hualañé, Chile 158/C2
Hualgayoc, Peru 156/B2
Hualien, Tai. 79/D3
Hualla, Peru 156/C4
Huallaga (riv.), Peru 147/B3
Huallanca, Peru 156/B3
Huallanca, Peru 156/B3
Huamachuco, Peru 156/B2
Huamantanga, Peru 156/B3
Huamantla, Mex. 143/M7
Huambo, Ang. 105/C3
Huambos, Peru 156/B2
Huan (riv.), China 72/C5
Huan Xian, China 70/J4
Huancané, Peru 156/D4
Huancapi, Peru 156/C4
Huancaspata, Peru 156/B3
Huancavelica (dept.), Peru 156/C4
Huancavelica, Peru 156/C4
Huancayo, Peru 156/C4
Huanchaca (peak), Bol. 150/E8
Huang (riv.), China 67/L6
Huangchuan, China 72/C4
Huanggang (peak), China 79/C2
Huanghua, China 72/D3
Huangling, China 72/B4
Huanglong, China 72/B4
Huangping, China 83/J2
Huangqi (lake), China 72/C2
Huangshan, China 79/C2
Huangtang (lake), China 72/C5
Huangtu (plat.), China 72/B3
Huanguelén, Arg. 158/E3
Huangyan, China 79/D2
Huangzhong, China 70/H4
Huanren, China 73/C2
Huanta, Peru 156/C4
Huantai, China 72/D3
Huánuco (dept.), Peru 156/C3
Huánuco, Peru 156/B3
Huanuni, Bol. 150/E7
Huapi (mts.), Nic. 144/E3
Huaquechula, Mex. 143/L8
Huaquillas, Ecu. 156/A1
Huaral, Peru 156/B3
Huaraz, Peru 156/B3
Huari, Peru 156/B3
Huaricolca, Peru 156/C3
Huarina, Peru 156/D5
Huarmey, Peru 156/B4
Huarochirí, Peru 156/B4
Huarocondo, Peru 156/C4
Huarong, China 79/B2
Huásabas, Mex. 142/C2
Huasahuasi, Peru 156/C3
Huascarán (peak), Peru 156/B3
Huatabampo, Mex. 162/C3
Huatunas (lake), Bol. 150/E6
Huatuxco, Mex. 143/N7
Huauchinango, Mex. 143/F3
Huaura, Peru 156/B3
Huautla de Jiménez, Mex. 144/B2
Huayacocotla, Mex. 143/L6
Huaying, China 79/A1
Huaylas, Peru 156/B3
Huayllay, Peru 156/C4
Huayopata, Peru 156/C4
Huayuan, China 83/J2
Huazhou, China 83/K3
Hubbard (mt.), Ak, US 134/L3
Hubbard Creek (res.), Tx, US 129/H4
Hubei (prov.), China 71/K5
Hubei (pass), China 72/B4
Hubli-dhārwār, India 89/L5
Huch'ang, NKor. 73/D2
Hückelhoven, Ger. 53/F1
Hückeswagen, Ger. 53/G1
Hucknall, Eng, UK 35/G5
Huddersfield, Eng, UK 35/G4
Huddinge, Swe. 38/G2
Hude, Ger. 51/F2
Hudiksvall, Swe. 38/G1
Hudson (riv.), US 130/F3
Hudson, NY, US 130/G3
Hudson, Co, US 137/C2

Hudson (str.), NW,Qu,Can. 123/J2
Hudson (bay), Can. 119/J3
Hudson, Qu, Can. 131/M7
Hudson (cape), Ant. 160/L
Hudson (co.), US 139/J9
Hudson's Hope, BC, Can. 122/D3
Hue, Viet. 78/E2
Huedin, Rom. 49/F2
Huehuetenango, Guat. 144/D3
Huehuetla, Mex. 143/L6
Huehuetlán, Mex. 143/L8
Huehuetlán Park, US 136/G8
Huejotzingo, Mex. 143/L7
Huejuquilla el Alto, Mex. 142/E4
Huejutla de Reyes, Mex. 144/B1
Huelma, Sp. 44/D4
Huelva, Sp. 44/B4
Huelva (riv.), Sp. 44/B4
Huequi (vol.), Chile 158/B4
Huercal-Overa, Sp. 44/E4
Huérfano (riv.), Co, US 129/F3
Huesca, Sp. 45/E1
Huéscar, Sp. 44/D4
Huetamo de Nuñez, Mex. 143/E5
Hunucmá, Mex. 144/D1
Hünxe, Ger. 50/D5
Hunyuan, China 72/C3
Huo (mtn.), China 72/D2
Huo (mtn.), China 72/D5
Huocheng, China 70/D3
Huojia, China 72/C4
Huolin Gol, China 71/L2
Huoqiu, China 72/D4
Huoshan, China 72/D4
Huozhou, China 72/B3
Hurdal, Nor. 38/D1
Hure Qi, China 72/D2
Hurepoix (reg.), Fr. 30/H6
Hurley, NM, US 128/E4
Hurley, Eng, UK 30/A2
Hurley (riv.), Ire. 36/A4
Hurlford, Sc, UK 36/B5
Hurlford, Sc, UK 36/B5
Huron (mts.), Mi, US 130/C2
Huron (lake), Can.,US 119/J5
Huron (riv.), Mi, US 135/G7
Huron (pt.), Mi, US 135/G6
Hurricane, WV, US 133/D4
Hurtaut (riv.), Fr. 52/D4
Hürtgenwald (reg.), Ger. 53/F2
Hürth, Ger. 53/F2
Hurup, Den. 38/C3
Husainābād, India 85/E3
Húsavík, Ice. 37/P6
Huscarán, PN, Peru 156/B3
Husher, Wi, US 135/Q14
Huşi, Rom. 49/J2
Huskisson, Austl. 115/D2
Huslia, Ak, US 134/G2
Husnes, Nor. 38/A2
Hussigny-Godbrange, Fr. 53/E5
Husum, Ger. 38/C4
Husum, Swe. 37/F3
Hutag, Mong. 70/H2
Hutchinson, Mn, US 127/K4
Hutchinson, Ks, US 129/H3
Hüttisheim, Ger. 57/F1
Hüttlingen, Ger. 54/D5
Hutton (mt.), Austl. 114/C4
Hutton, Neth. 50/C4
Huttwil, Swi. 56/D3
Hutuo (riv.), China 71/N2
Huwwārah, WBnk. 91/G7
Huy, Belg. 53/E2
Huyton-with-Roby, Eng, UK 35/G5
Huzhou, China 72/L9
Hvammstangi, Ice. 37/N6
Hvannadalshnúkur (peak), Ice. 37/P7
Hvar (isl.), Cro. 46/C1
Hvide Sande, Den. 37/N7
Hvítá (riv.), Ice. 37/M6
Hvolsvöllur, Ice. 37/L5
Hwange (Wankie) NP, Zim. 105/E4
Hwanghae-bukto (prov.), NKor. 73/D3
Hwanghae-namdo (prov.), NKor. 73/C3
Hwangju, NKor. 73/C3
Hwangju (riv.), NKor. 73/C3
Hwasun, SKor. 73/D5
Hyades (peak), Chile 158/B5
Hyattstown, Md, US 138/A5
Hyattsville, Md, US 138/B6
Hydaburg, Ak, US 134/M4
Hyde, Eng, UK 35/F5
Hyder, Ak, US 134/M4
Hyderābād, India 82/C4
Hyderābād, Pak. 89/J3
Hyères, Fr. 43/G5
Hyères, Îles d' (isls.), Fr 43/G5
Ide, Japan 75/J6
Ideles, Alg. 99/G5
Ideok, NKor. 73/D2
Idfū, Egypt 101/C3
Idhra, Gre. 47/H4
Idice (riv.), It. 59/E4
Idiwe, Île (isl.), D.R. Congo 104/A3
Idkū, Egypt 91/B4
Idle (riv.), Eng, UK 35/H5
Idlib (prov.), Syria 50/D3
Idnah, WBnk. 91/D4
Idrija, Slov. 40/B3
Idriss I (dam), Mor. 100/D2
Idriss I, Barrage (res.), Mor. 100/D2
Idro, Lago d' (lake), It. 58/D1
Idstein, Ger. 54/B2
Ie (isl.), Japan 75/J7
Ieper, Belg. 52/B2
Ierápetra, Gre. 47/J5
Ierissós, Gre. 47/H2
Iesolo, It. 59/F1
Ifakis (isl.), Micr. 116/D4
Ifanadiana, Madg. 107/H8
Ife, Nga. 103/G5
Ifèrfes (well), Libya 99/H3
Iffezheim, Ger. 54/B5
Iforas, Adrar des (upland), Mali 96/F4
Ifrane, Mor. 98/D2

Hunterdon (co.), NJ, US 138/C2
Huntingburg, In, US 133/G2
Huntingdon, Eng, UK 33/F2
Huntington, WV, US 130/D4
Huntington, In, US 130/C3
Huntington, NY, US 139/M8
Huntington (bay), NY, US 139/M8
Huntington Bay, NY, US 139/M8
Huntington Beach, Ca, US 136/G8
Huntington Park, Ca, US 136/G8
Huntington Station, NY, US 139/M8
Huntington Woods, Mi, US 135/F7
Huntley, Il, US 135/P15
Huntly, NZ 117/T10
Huntly, Sc, UK 36/D2
Hunts Inlet, BC, Can. 134/D4
Hunts Point, Wa, US 134/D3
Huntsville, Al, US 133/G3
Huntsville, On, Can. 130/E2
Huntsville, Ut, US 137/K11
Huntsville (res.), Pa, US 138/B1
Hunucmá, Mex. 144/D1
Hünxe, Ger. 50/D5
Hunyuan, China 72/C2
Huo (mtn.), China 72/D2
Huo (mtn.), China 72/D5
Huocheng, China 70/D3
Huojia, China 72/C4
Huolin Gol, China 71/L2
Huoqiu, China 72/D4
Huoshan, China 72/D4
Huozhou, China 72/B3

I-n-Sákâne, 'Erg (des.), Mali 103/E1
I-n-Salah, Alg. 99/F4
I-n-Tassik (well), Mali 103/E1
Iacanga, Braz. 155/B2
Iaciara, Braz. 154/A4
Iaco (riv.), SAm. 150/E6
Iaçu, Braz. 155/B3
Iáf di Montasio (peak), It. 43/K3
Iakora, Madg. 107/H8
Ialomiţa (riv.), Rom. 62/C3
Ialomiţa (prov.), Rom. 49/H3
Ianapera, Madg. 107/H8
Iapu, Braz. 155/D1
Iaşi (prov.), Rom. 49/H2
Iaşi, Rom. 49/H2
Iasmos, Gre. 47/J2
Iba, Phil. 79/C4
Ibadan, Nga. 103/F5
Ibagué, Col. 150/C3
Ibaiti, Braz. 155/B2
Ibajay, Phil. 79/D5
Ibapah, Serra da (range), Braz. 154/B1
Ibar (riv.), Yugo. 62/E4
Ibara, Japan 74/C3
Ibaraki (pref.), Japan 75/F2
Ibaraki, Japan 77/L6
Ibaraki, Japan 75/J5
Ibarra, Ecu. 152/B4
Ibarreta, Arg. 157/D2
Ibb, Yem. 88/D6
Ibba (riv.), Sudan 97/L6
Ibbenbüren, Ger. 51/F4
Ibdekkene (riv.), Mali 103/F2
Ibéria, Peru 150/D3
Ibéria, Peru 147/D5
Ibérico, Sistema (range), Sp. 44/D2
Ibi, Sp. 45/E3
Ibiá, Braz. 155/C1
Ibiapina, Braz. 155/B2
Ibicaraí, Braz. 154/C2
Ibicuy, Arg. 159/J10
Ibigawa, Japan 77/L5
Ibirapuã, Braz. 155/D1
Ibirapuã, Braz. 155/B2
Ibitinga, Braz. 155/B2
Ibiúna, Braz. 211/F8
Ibiza (isl.), Sp. 45/F3
Ibiza, Sp. 45/F3
Ibo, Moz. 105/H3
Ibo (riv.), Japan 74/D3
Iboro, Nga. 103/F5
Ibotirama, Braz. 155/C3
Iboundji (peak), Gabon 96/H8
Ibrány, Hun. 41/L4
Ibshawāy, Egypt 91/B5
Ibuki, Japan 77/K5
Ibuki-yama (peak), Japan 75/K5
Ibusuki, Japan 74/B4
Icabarú, Braz. 150/F3
Icaraí, Braz. 154/C2
Içana (riv.), SAm. 147/D3
Içana, Braz. 152/D2
Icel (prov.), Turk. 90/C2
Icém, Braz. 155/B2
Ichalkaranji, India 89/K5
Ichāmati (riv.), Bang. 85/G3
Ichāpuram, India 85/D4
Ichenhausen, Ger. 54/D6
Ichihara, Japan 77/H5
Ichijima, Japan 74/D4
Ichikawa, Japan 77/H5
Ichikawa, Japan 77/H5
Ichikawadani, Japan 77/K5
Ichinohe, Japan 75/G2
Ichinomiya, Japan 77/M6
Ichinomiya, Japan 77/J6
Ichinomiya, Japan 77/L5
Ichinoseki, Japan 76/B4
Ichishi, Japan 77/K6
Ich'ön, SKor. 73/D4
Ichtegem, Belg. 52/C1
Ickesburg, Pa, US 138/A3
Icó, Braz. 154/C2
Icod de los Vinos, Sp. 98/A3
Icy (cape), Ak, US 134/F1
Icy (pt.), Ak, US 134/K3
Icy (bay), Ak, US 122/A2
Icy (bay), Ak, US 134/K3
Ida, Japan 77/K7
Idaho, Sk, Can. 127/J3
Idaho (state), US 124/C3
Idaho Springs, Co, US 137/A3
Idanha-a-Nova, Port. 44/B3
Idar, India 82/B3
Idar-Oberstein, Ger. 53/G4
Idarkopf (peak), Ger. 53/G4
Idaville, Pa, US 138/A3

Iga (riv.), Japan 77/K6
Iga, Japan 77/K6
Igal, Hun. 48/C2
Iganga, Ugan. 104/B2
Igaporã, Braz. 154/B4
Igara Paraná (riv.), Col. 152/C5
Igarapava, Braz. 155/C2
Igarapé Grande, Braz. 154/A2
Igarapé-Miri, Braz. 151/J4
Igaratá, Braz. 211/G8
Igarka, Rus. 59/K2
Igatpuri, India 82/B4
Igbeti, Nga. 103/F4
Igbetti (peak), Mor. 98/C3
Iğdır, Turk. 63/H5
Iğdır (dam), Turk. 90/E2
Igdir, Turk. 90/E2
Igesund, Swe. 38/G1
Igham, Eng, UK 30/D3
Igikpak (mt.), Ak, US 134/H2
Iğis, Swi. 57/F4
Iglesias, It. 46/A3
Igli, Alg. 99/E3
Igloolik, NW, Can. 123/H2
Ignacio, Ca, US 135/J10
Ignacio de la Llave, Mex. 143/P8
Ignacio Zaragoza, Mex. 142/D2
Iğneada Burnu (cape), Turk. 49/J5
Ignalina (lake), Lith. 63/G3
Igney, Fr. 56/C1
Ignon (riv.), Fr. 56/A2
Igny, Fr. 30/J5
Igombe (riv.), Tanz. 104/B4
Igra, Rus. 61/M4
Igreja, Morro da (peak), Braz. 155/B4
Iguaçu (riv.), Braz. 147/D5
Iguaçu, PN do, Braz. 157/F2
Iguala, Mex. 143/K8
Igualada, Sp. 45/F2
Iguape, Braz. 155/C3
Iguatama, Braz. 155/B3
Iguatu, Braz. 154/C2
Iguela Parc Nat., Col. 156/C1
Igueñi (lake), Mrta. 98/C4
Iguidi, 'Erg (des.), Alg. 99/H4
Ihklakrantu (riv.), Rus. 63/P3
Iho, Peru 156/D5
Iiobu, Nga. 103/G5
Iida, Japan 75/F3
Iide-san (peak), Japan 75/F3
Iijoki (riv.), Fin. 60/F2
Iisalmi, Fin. 42/E1
Iitti, Fin. 39/M1
Iiyama, Japan 75/F2
Iizuka, Japan 74/B4
Ijebu Ode, Nga. 103/F5
Ijevan, Arm. 63/H4
Ijíll (peak), Mrta. 98/B5
Ijill (lake), Mrta. 98/B5
Ijira, Japan 77/L4
IJmeer (bay), Neth. 50/C4
IJmuiden, Neth. 50/B4
ljoki (riv.), Fin. 77/H2
ljoubbane, 'Erg (des.), Mali 98/D5
IJssel (riv.), Neth. 50/D3
IJsselmeer (lake), Neth. 40/C2
IJsselmuiden, Neth. 50/C3
IJsselstein, Neth. 50/C4
Ik (riv.), Rus. 61/M5
Ikakamavony, Madg. 107/H8
Ikalamavony, Madg. 107/H8
Ikare, Nga. 103/G5
Ikaria (isl.), Gre. 90/A2
Ikaria (isl.), Gre. 47/J4
Ikeda, Japan 74/C3
Ikeda, Japan 76/C2
Ikeda, Japan 77/H6
Ikenokoya-yama (peak), Japan 77/K7
Ikerre, Nga. 103/G5
Ikhtiman, Bul. 47/H1
Iki (isl.), Japan 74/A4
Iki (chan.), Japan 74/A4
Ikire, Nga. 103/G5
Ikirun, Nga. 103/G5
Ikizce, Turk. 62/C5
Ikko, Japan 77/J6
Ikongo, Madg. 107/H8
Ikopa (riv.), Madg. 107/H7
Ikorodu, Nga. 103/F5
Ikuno, Japan 74/D3
Ilabaya, Peru 156/D5
Ilagan, Phil. 79/D4
Ilām, Nepal 85/F2
Ilām, Iran 88/E2
Ilan, Tai. 79/D3
Ilanz, Swi. 57/F4
Ilaro, Nga. 103/F5
Ilave, Peru 156/D5
Ilawa, Pol. 41/K2
Ilawe-Ekiti, Nga. 103/G5
Ilbi, China,.Ka 79/D5
Ile-à-la-Crosse, Sk, Can. 126/G2
Ile-à-la-Crosse (lake), Sk, Can. 126/G2
Ile-de-France (pol. reg.), Fr. 52/A6
Ilebo, D.R. Congo 104/C2
Ilek (riv.), Rus. 63/K2
Iles Ehotilés, PN des, C.d'Iv. 102/E5
Iles Tristao, Res. (isls.), Gui. 102/B4
Ilesha, Braz. 103/G5
Ilfov (prov.), Rom. 49/H3
Ilgaz, Turk. 90/B2
Ilgın, Turk. 49/C1
Ilha Grande (bay), Braz. 211/G8
Ilha Grande, Baía de (bay), Braz. 155/C2

Ilha Solteira, Reprêsa (res.), Braz. 151/H7
Ilhabela, Braz. 211/H8
Ilhavo, Port. 44/A2
Ilhéus, Braz. 154/C4
Ilíamna (lake), Ak, US 134/H4
Iliamna (vol.), Ak, US 134/H3
Ilic, Turk. 62/F5
Ilica, Turk. 63/G5
Iligan, Phil. 79/D6
Iliniza (peak), Ecu. 152/B5
Ilirska Bistrica, Slov. 46/B2
Iljir, Turk. 90/C2
Ilium (Troy) (ruin), Turk. 47/J3
Ilkeston, Eng, UK 35/G6
Ilkley, Eng, UK 35/G4
Ill (riv.), Aus. 43/G3
Ill (riv.), Fr. 56/C2
Illana, Sp. 44/D2
Illapel, Chile 157/B3
Illela, Niger 103/G3
Iller (riv.), Ger. 43/J2
Illertissen, Ger. 57/G1
Illescas, Sp. 44/C2
Illiers-Combray, Fr. 42/D2
Illimani (peak), Bol. 150/E7
Illingen, Ger. 53/G5
Illinois (riv.), US 137/F2
Illinois (state), US 125/J4
Illizi, Alg. 99/H4
Illkirch-Graffenstaden, Fr. 56/D1
Illmensee, Ger. 57/F2
Illnau, Swi. 57/E3
Illora, Sp. 44/D4
Illovo, SAfr. 107/E3
Illzach, Fr. 56/D2
Ilm (riv.), Ger. 40/H3
Ilmajoki, Fin. 37/G3
Ilmen (lake), Rus. 64/D4
Ilmenau, Swi. 54/C4
Ilmenau (riv.), Ger. 51/J2
Ilo, Peru 156/D5
Ilobu, Nga. 103/G5
Ilorin, Nga. 103/G4
Ilovlya (riv.), Rus. 63/H2
Ilsede, Ger. 51/H4
Ilsenburg, Ger. 51/H5
Ilsfeld, Ger. 54/C4
Ilshofen, Ger. 54/C4
Ilyas Burnu (pt.), Turk. 49/K5
Ilych (riv.), Rus. 61/N3
Ilz (riv.), Ger. 41/G4
Imabari, Japan 74/C4
Imaichi, Japan 75/F2
Imaloto (riv.), Madg. 107/H8
Imamoğlu, Turk. 90/C2
Imandra (lake), Rus. 37/J2
Imari, Japan 74/A4
Imatra, Fin. 39/N1
Imazu, Japan 77/K5
Imba (lake), Japan 77/H5
Imbabura (prov.), Ecu. 152/B4
Imbituba, Braz. 155/B4
Imbituva, Braz. 155/B3
Imeni Moskvy (canal), Rus. 61/W9
Imerimandroso, Madg. 107/H7
Imi n'tanout, Mor. 98/C3
Imişli, Azer. 63/J5
Imittós (peak), Gre. 47/H4
Imja (isl.), SKor. 73/D5
Imlay, Nv, US 128/C2
Immendingen, Ger. 57/E2
Immenhausen, Ger. 51/G5
Immenstaad am Bodensee, Ger. 57/F2
Immenstadt im Allgäu, Ger. 57/F3
Immingham, Eng, UK 35/H4
Immokalee, Fl, US 133/H5
Imnavait (mtn.), Ak, US 134/J2
Imo (state), Nga. 103/G5
Imola, It. 59/E4
Imouzzèr-Kandar, Mor. 98/D2
Imperatriz, Braz. 154/A2
Imperia, It. 45/H2
Imperial, Sk, Can. 127/G2
Imperial, Ne, US 129/G2
Imperial (riv.), Rus. 65/M4
Imperial Beach, Ca, US 136/C5
Imperial Palace, Japan 77/D2
Impero (riv.), It. 45/H3
Imperoz, Congo 96/J7
Imphāl, India 83/F3
Imphy, Fr. 42/E3
Imralı (isl.), Turk. 49/B1
Imranlı, Turk. 62/F5
Imroz, Gre. 47/J3
Imshil, SKor. 73/D5
Imst, Aus. 57/H3
Imuris, Mex. 142/C2
Ina, Japan 75/F3
Inabe, Japan 77/L5
Inabu, Japan 77/L5
Inagawa, Japan 77/J5
Inagi, Japan 77/D2
Inambari (riv.), Peru 156/D4
Inami, Japan 77/K5
Inaouene (riv.), Mor. 100/D2
Iñapari, Peru 150/E6
Inarijärvi (lake), Fin. 37/H1
Inäu (peak), Rom. 49/G2
Inawashiro (lake), Japan 75/F2
Inawashiro, Japan 77/H1
Inca, Sp. 45/F2
Incekum (pt.), Turk. 91/C1
Incheville, Fr. 30/G3
Inchinnan, Sc, UK 36/B5
Inchkeith (isl.), Sc, UK 36/C4
Inchnadamph, Sc, UK 31/R7

Ilha Solteira, Reprêsa (res.), Braz. 151/H7
Inch'ön, SKor. 73/F7
Inch'on-jikhalsi (prov.), SKor. 73/D4
Incirliova, Turk. 90/A2
Incisa in Val d'Arno, It. 59/E5
Inconfidentes, Braz. 211/G3
Incudine, Mont l' (peak), Fr. 46/A2
Indaiá (riv.), Braz. 155/C1
Indaiatuba, Braz. 211/F7
Indalsälven (riv.), Swe. 37/E3
Indanan, Phil. 81/F2
Inde (riv.), Ger. 53/F2
Inde, Ger. 53/F2
Independence, Nv, US 126/E5
Independence, Ks, US 129/J3
Independence, Ca, US 128/C3
Independence, Mo, US 137/F3
Independence, Belz. 144/D2
Independence Nat'l Hist. Park, Pa, US 138/C4
Independência, Braz. 154/B2
Independencia, Peru 156/B3
Inder (lake), Kaz. 63/K2
Index, Wa, US 135/D2
India (ctry.) 89/L4
Indian (ocean) 23/N6
Indian Echo Caverns, Pa, US 138/B3
Indian Head, Sk, Can. 127/H3
Indian Hills, Co, US 137/B3
Indian Peaks Wilderness Area, Co, US 137/A2
Indiana, Pa, US 130/E3
Indiana (state), US 125/J4
Indianapolis (int'l arpt.), In, US 130/C4
Indianola, Ms, US 129/K4
Indianola, Wa, US 135/B2
Indiaporã, Braz. 155/B1
Indigirka (riv.), Rus. 65/P3
Indija, Yugo. 48/E3
Indio, Ca, US 124/C4
Indira Gandhi (int'l arpt.), India 86/D5
Indochina (reg.), Laos 83/H4
Indonesia (ctry.) 87/K10
Indore, India 89/L4
Indragiri (riv.), Indo. 80/B4
Indramayu (cape), Indo. 80/C5
Indravati (riv.), India 89/H4
Indre (riv.), Fr. 42/D3
Indre Arna, Nor. 38/A1
Indre-et-Loire (dept.), Fr. 42/D3
Indrois (riv.), Fr. 42/D3
Induno Olona, It. 57/E6
Indus (riv.), Asia 90/C2
Industry, Ca, US 136/G7
Inebolu, Turk. 90/B2
Inece, Turk. 49/H5
Inecik, Turk. 49/H5
Inedbirenne (int'l arpt.), Alg. 99/H4
Inegöl, Turk. 62/D4
Iner (riv.), Rus. 61/W8
Ineu, Rom. 48/E2
Inezgane, Mor. 98/B3
Inezgane (Agadir) (int'l arpt.), Mor. 47/G3
Infanta (cape), SAfr. 106/C4
Infernillo (riv.), Mex. 143/E5
Infernillo, Presa del (dam), Mex. 142/E5
Infiesto, Sp. 44/C1
Ingapirca (ruin), Ecu. 152/B5
Ingatestone, Eng, UK 30/E2
Ingelmunster, Belg. 52/C2
Ingeniero Jacobacci, Arg. 158/C4
Ingeniero Luiggi, Arg. 158/D3
Ingersheim, Fr. 56/D1
Ingettolgoy, Mong. 70/H2
Ingham, Austl. 114/B2
Ingleside, Md, US 138/C4
Inglewood, Austl. 115/B3
Inglewood, Ca, US 136/F8
Inglewood-Finn Hill, Wa, US 134/C1
Inglis, Fl, US 133/H4
Ingoda (riv.), Rus. 65/M4
Ingolstadt, Ger. 55/E5
Ingrid Christianson (coast), Ant. 160/F
Ingushetia Aut. Rep., Rus. 63/H4
Ingwavuma, SAfr. 107/E2
Ingwiller, Fr. 53/G6
Inhambane, Moz. 105/F6
Inhambupe, Braz. 154/C3
Inharrime, Moz. 105/G6
Inhumas, Braz. 151/J7
Iniesta, Sp. 44/D3
Inírida (riv.), Col. 150/D3
Inishbofin (isl.), Ire. 30/A10
Inishowen (pen.), Ire. 34/A1
Inishowen (head), Ire. 32/B1
Inje, SKor. 73/E3
Injune, Austl. 114/C4
Inkster, Mi, US 135/F7
Inland (sea), Japan 74/C4
Inle (lake), Myan. 83/G3
Inn (riv.), Aus. 43/J3
Innamincka, Austl. 115/B1
Innbach (riv.), Aus. 55/M6
Innellan, Sc, UK 36/B5
Inner (chan.), Belz. 144/D3
Inner (sound), Sc, UK 31/S8
Inner Hebrides (isls.), Sc, UK 31/R8
Inner Mongolia (reg.), China 67/L5
Innerdouny (hill), Sc, UK 36/C4
Innerleithen, Sc, UK 36/C5
Innerste (riv.), Ger. 51/H4
Innerkirchen, Swi. 57/E4
Innes NP, Austl. 113/H5

Inch'ön (San Candito), It. 43/K3
Inch'on-jikhalsi (prov.), SKor. 73/D4
Innichen (San Candito), It. 43/K3
Innisfail, Ab, Can. 122/F3
Innisfail, Austl. 114/B2
Innoko (riv.), Ak, US 134/G3
Innoko NWR, US 134/G3
Innsbruck, Aus. 57/H3
Inntal (reg.), Aus. 55/G6
Inny (riv.), Eng, UK 32/B5
Ino, Japan 74/C4
Inocência, Braz. 155/B1
Inongo, D.R. Congo 97/J8
Inönü, Turk. 62/D5
Inowrocław, Pol. 41/K2
Insch, Sc, UK 36/D2
Inscription (cape), Austl. 112/B3
Insein, Myan. 83/G4
Inside (passg.), BC, Can. 126/A2
Insjön, Swe. 38/F1
Inta, Rus. 61/N2
Intendente Alvear, Arg. 158/D2
Intercourse, Pa, US 138/C3
Interior (plat.), BC, Can. 126/B2
Interlaken, Swi. 56/D4
Internacional (int'l arpt.), Braz. 156/D2
Internacional (int'l arpt.), Mex. 143/E5
International Peace Garden, ND, US 127/H3
Inthanon (peak), Thai. 83/G4
Intorsura Buzăului, Rom. 49/H3
Intracoastal Waterway, La, US 137/P17
Intragna, Swi. 57/E5
Introbio, It. 57/F6
Inubō-zaki (pt.), Japan 75/G3
Inukjuak, Qu, Can. 123/H3
Inútil (bay), Chile 159/C7
Inuvik, NW, Can. 134/M2
Inuyama, Japan 77/L5
Inveraray, Sc, UK 36/A4
Inverbervie, Sc, UK 36/D3
Invercargill, NZ 117/R12
Inverell, Austl. 115/D1
Invergordon, Sc, UK 36/B1
Inverie, Sc, UK 31/R8
Inverkeithing, Sc, UK 36/C4
Inverloch, Austl. 115/C3
Inverness, Fl, US 133/H4
Inverness, Al, US 133/G3
Inverness, Sc, UK 36/B2
Inverurie, Sc, UK 36/D2
Investigator (str.), Austl. 109/H7
Inworio, It. 58/B1
Inwood, NY, US 139/L9
Inyanga (peak), Zim. 105/F4
Inyangani (peak), Zim. 105/F4
Inyo (mts.), Ca, US 128/C3
Inza, Rus. 63/H1
Inzai, Japan 77/H5
Inzigkofen, Ger. 57/F1
Inzing, Aus. 57/H3
Iō-shima (isl.), Japan 74/B5
Ioánnina (int'l arpt.), Gre. 47/G3
Ioánnina, Gre. 47/G3
Iona (isl.), Sc, UK 31/R8
Iona, PN da, Ang. 105/C2
Ione, Ca, US 135/C2
Ionia, Mi, US 130/C3
Ionian (sea), Gre. 47/F3
Ionian (isls.), Gre. 47/F4
Ios (isl.), Gre. 47/J4
Iouík (cape), Mrta. 102/A2
Iowa (state), US 125/H3
Iowa (riv.), Ia, US 125/H3
Iowa Falls, Ia, US 127/L5
Ipameri, Braz. 155/B1
Ipanema, Braz. 155/D1
Iparia, Peru 156/C3
Ipatinga, Braz. 155/D1
Ipel' (riv.), Slvk. 41/K4
Iphofen, Ger. 54/D3
Ipiales, Col. 152/B4
Ipiaú, Braz. 152/B4
Ipil, Phil. 79/D6
Ipirá, Braz. 155/B3
Ipiranga, Braz. 155/B3
Ipoh, Malay. 80/B3
Ipoly (riv.), Hun. 41/K4
Ipora, Braz. 151/H7
Ipsala, Turk. 49/H5
Ipsheim, Ger. 54/D3
Ipswich, SD, US 127/J4
Ipswich, Eng, UK 33/H2
Ipuã, Braz. 155/B2
Ipuêiras, Braz. 154/B2
Ipueira, Braz. 154/C2
Ipuiúna, Braz. 211/G7
Ipupiara, Braz. 154/B3
Iqaluit, NW, Can. 123/J2
Iquique, Chile 150/D8
Iquitos, Peru 156/C1
Irago (chan.), Japan 77/L6
Irago-misaki (cape), Japan 77/M6
Iraí, Braz. 155/B3

Iretama, Braz. 155/B3
Irfon (riv.), Wal, UK 32/C2
Irharhar, Oued (riv.), Alg. 99/G4
Irhazer Oua-n-Agadez (riv.), Alg. 103/G2
Iri, SKor. 73/D5
Irian Jaya (reg.), Indo. 81/H4
Iricoume (mts.), Braz. 153/G4
Iriga, Yugo. 48/D3
Iringa (phys. reg.), Tanz. 104/B4
Iringa (prov.), Tanz. 104/B5
Iriní (riv.), Braz. 151/H4
Iriomote (isl.), Japan 79/D3
Iriri (riv.), Braz. 151/H4
Iriklinskiy (res.), Rus. 63/L2
Iriri, Braz. 211/G3
Irish (sea), Ire.,UK 34/C4
Irlam, Eng, UK 35/F5
Irō-zaki (pt.), Japan 75/F3
Iron (riv.), Fr. 42/E2
Iron Baron, Austl. 113/H5
Iron Knob, Austl. 113/H5
Iron Mountain, Mi, US 127/L4
Irondale, Co, US 137/C3
Ironton, Oh, US 130/D4
Ironton, Ut, US 137/K13
Ironwood, Mi, US 127/L4
Irpin' (riv.), Ukr. 62/E1
Irrawaddy (Ayeyarwady) (riv.), Myan. 67/J7
Irrawaddy, Mouths of the (delta), Myan. 83/F4
Irsch, Ger. 53/F3
Irsen (riv.), Ger. 53/F3
Irsina, It. 46/E2
Irt (riv.), Eng, UK 35/F1
Irthing (riv.), Eng, UK 35/F1
Irthlingborough, Eng, UK 33/F2
Irtysh (riv.), Rus. 67/G4
Iruma, Japan 77/C2
Irumu, D.R. Congo 104/A2
Irún, Sp. 44/E1
Irvine, Ca, US 136/G8
Irvine, Sc, UK 36/B5
Irvine (bay), Sc, UK 36/B5
Irving, Tx, US 132/D3
Irvington, NJ, US 139/J9
Irvington, NY, US 139/K7
Is-sur-Tille, Fr. 56/B2
Is (riv.), Rus. 61/N4
Isaac (riv.), Austl. 109/D3
Isabela, PR 141/M8
Isabela (isl.), Ecu. 156/E7
Isabela (mts.), Nic. 144/E3
Isabella, NW, Can.123/K2
Isaccea, Rom. 49/J3
Isachsen (cape), NW, Can. 123/H7
Isafjardhardjúp (inlet), Ice. 37/M6
Isafjördhur, Ice. 37/M6
Isahaya, Japan 74/B4
Isana (riv.), Col. 152/D4
Isandhlwana Battlesite, SAfr. 107/E3
Isanganno NP, Zam. 104/D5
Isaouanne-n-Irarraren (des.), Alg. 99/G4
Isaouanne-n-Tifernine (des.), Alg. 99/G4
Isar (riv.), Ger. 43/J3
Isarco (riv.), It. 57/H4
Isarco (Eisack) (riv.), It. 57/H4
Isaszeg, Hun. 49/R9
Isawa, Japan 77/B2
Isbergues, Fr. 52/B2
Iscar, Sp. 44/C2
Ischgl, Aus. 57/G3
Ischia, It. 48/L6
Ischia (isl.), It. 48/L6
Ise (bay), Japan 75/F3
Ise, Eng, UK 33/F2
Ise-Shima NP, Japan 75/F3
Isehara, Japan 75/F3
Iselin, NJ, US 139/J9
Isen, Ger. 55/F6
Isen (riv.), Ger. 40/G4
Iseo, It. 57/E6
Iseo (lake), It. 43/J4
Iseo, Lago d' (lake), It. 58/C1
Isère (riv.), Fr. 43/F4
Isère (dept.), Fr. 43/B6
Iserlohn, Ger. 51/E6
Isernia, It. 46/D2
Isesaki, Japan 75/F2
Iset (riv.), Rus. 61/P4
Ishpeming, Mi, US 130/C2
'Isfiyā, Isr. 91/G6
Ishasha (riv.), Rus. 104/B3
Ishibashi, Japan 77/F1
Ishidoriya, Japan 76/B3
Ishige, Japan 77/G2
Ishigaki (isl.), Japan 79/D3
Ishikari (riv.), Japan 76/C2
Ishikari (bay), Japan 76/C2
Ishikari (mts.), Japan 76/D2
Ishikawa (pref.), Japan 75/E2
Ishiki, Japan 77/L6
Ishim (riv.), Kaz. 64/H4
Ishim, Rus. 61/P4
Ishimbay, Rus. 63/L1
Ishinomaki, Japan 75/G2
Ishizuchi-san (peak), Japan 74/C4
Ishikawa, Japan 75/E2
Isiboro Sécure, PN, Bol. 150/E7
Isigny-sur-Mer, Fr. 42/C2
Isil'kul', Rus. 61/P4
Isiolo, Kenya 104/C2
Isiro, D.R. Congo 97/L7
Isisford, Austl. 114/B4
Iskenderun, Gulf of (gulf), Turk. 91/D2
İskenderun, Turk. 62/E4
İskilip, Turk. 90/B2
İskŭr (riv.), Bul. 47/H1
Iskŭr (res.), Bul. 47/H1
Iskŭr (lake), Bul. 49/F4
İsla, Mex. 144/C2

Isla (riv.), Sc, UK 36/C3
Isla Aguada, Mex. 144/D2
Isla Cabritos, PN, DRep. 145/J2
Isla Cedros, Mex. 142/B2
Isla Cristina, Sp. 44/B4
Isla de Maipo, Chile 158/N8
Isla de Salamanca, PN, Col. 152/C2
Isla de San Andrés (int'l arpt.), Col. 145/F3
Isla Gorge NP, Austl. 114/C4
Isla Guamblin, PN, Chile 158/B5
Isla Isabela, PN, Mex. 142/D4
Isla Magdalena, PN, Chile 157/B5
Isla Mujeres, Mex. 144/E1
İslâhiye, Turk. 91/E1
Islām Kot, Pak. 89/K4
Islāmābād (cap. terr.), Pak. 86/B3
Islāmābād (cap.), Pak. 86/B3
Islāmābād/Rāwalpindi (int'l arpt.), Pak. 86/B3
Islāmnagar, India 84/B1
Islamorada, Fl, US 133/H5
Islāmpur, India 85/G2
Islāmpur, India 85/E3
Island (lake), Mb, Can. 122/G3
Island (co.), Wa, US 135/B2
Island Beach State Park, NJ, US 138/D4
Island Lagoon (lake), Austl. 113/H4
Island Lake, Mb, Can. 127/K2
Island Lake, Il, US 135/P15
Island Park, NY, US 139/L9
Islands (bay), Can. 131/K1
Islay, Peru 156/C5
Islay (isl.), Sc, UK 31/Q9
Isle (riv.), Fr. 42/D4
Isle of Ely (phys. reg.), Eng, UK 33/G2
Isle of Portland (pen.), Eng, UK 32/D5
Isle of Thanet (phys. reg.), Eng, UK 33/H4
Isle of Wight (co.), Eng, UK 33/E5
Isle Royale NP, US 127/L3
Isle Royale NP, Mi, US 130/B2
Isleton, Ca, US 135/L10
Islington (bor.), Eng, UK 30/A1
Islip, NY, US 139/E2
Ismailovo Park, Rus. 61/W9
Ismaning, Ger. 55/E6
Isny, Ger. 57/G2
Isoanala, Madg. 107/H8
Isobe, Japan 77/L7
Isojärven NP, Fin. 39/L1
Isojärvi (lake), Fin. 39/J1
Isoka, Zam. 104/B5
Isola del Liri, It. 46/C2
Isola della Scala, It. 59/D2
Isola di Capo Rizzuto, It. 47/E3
Isola Vicentina, It. 59/E1
Isonzo (riv.), It. 59/G1
Isorella, It. 58/D2
Isparta, Turk. 90/B2
Isparta (prov.), Turk. 90/B2
Isperikh, Bul. 49/H4
İspir, Turk. 63/G4
Israel (ctry.) 67/C6
Issaquah, Wa, US 135/C2
Issel (riv.), Ger. 50/D5
Isselburg, Ger. 50/D5
Issenheim, Fr. 56/D2
Issia, C.d'Iv. 102/D5
Issoire, Fr. 42/E4
Issou, Fr. 30/H5
Issoudun, Fr. 42/E3
Issum, Ger. 50/D5
Issy-les-Moulineaux, Fr. 30/J5
Istállós-kő (peak), Hun. 48/E1
İstanbul (prov.), Turk. 62/D4
İstanbul, Turk. 49/J5
Istead Rise, Eng, UK 30/E2
Istiaía, Gre. 47/H3
Istmina, Col. 152/B3
Istok, Yugo. 47/G1
Istra (riv.), Rus. 61/W9
Istrana, It. 59/F1
Istranca (mts.), Turk. 49/H5
Istres, Fr. 42/F5
Istria (pen.), Cro. 48/A3
Isulan, Phil. 81/F2
Isumi, Japan 77/E3
Itabaiana, Braz. 154/C3
Itabaiana, Braz. 154/D2
Itabaianinha, Braz. 154/C3
Itabapoana (riv.), Braz. 155/D2
Itaberaba, Braz. 154/B4
Itabira, Braz. 155/D1
Itabirito, Braz. 155/D2
Itaboraí, Braz. 211/L7
Itabuna, Braz. 154/C4
Itacaiunas (riv.), Braz. 151/H5
Itacarambi, Braz. 154/A4
Itacoatiara, Braz. 150/G4
Itacuaí (riv.), Braz. 150/D5
Itacuruba, Braz. 154/C3
Itaguaí, Braz. 211/K7
Itaguara, Braz. 155/C2
Itaguatins, Braz. 154/A2
Itagüí, Col. 150/C2
Itaí, Braz. 155/B2
Itaíba, Braz. 154/C3
Itaiçaba, Braz. 154/C2
Itainópolis, Braz. 154/B2
Itaiópolis, Braz. 155/B3
Itaipú (dam), Par. 157/F2
Itaipu (res.), Braz.,Par. 147/D5
Itaipu, Represa do (res.), Braz. 157/F1
Itaituba, Braz. 151/G4
Itajá, Braz. 155/B1
Itajaí, Braz. 155/B3
Itajaí (riv.), Braz. 155/B3
Itajubá, Braz. 211/H7
Itajuípe, Braz. 154/C4
Itako, Japan 75/G3
Itakura, Japan 77/D1
Italy, Tx, US 129/H4
Italy (ctry.) 27/F4
Itamaraju, Braz. 154/C5
Itamarandiba, Braz. 154/B5
Itambacuri, Braz. 154/B5
Itambé, Braz. 154/B4
Itambé, Pico de (peak), Braz. 154/B5
Itami, Japan 77/H6
Itamonte, Braz. 211/J7
Itampolo, Madg. 107/G9
Itanhaém, Braz. 211/G9
Itanhandu, Braz. 155/C2
Itanhém, Braz. 154/B5
Itanhém (riv.), Braz. 155/D1
Itanhomi, Braz. 155/D1
Itaobim, Braz. 154/B5
Itaocara, Braz. 155/D2
Itapagé, Braz. 154/C1
Itaparica (isl.), Braz. 154/C4
Itapé, Braz. 154/C4
Itapebi, Braz. 154/C4
Itapecerica, Braz. 155/C2
Itapecuru-Mirim, Braz. 154/A1
Itapemirim, Braz. 155/D2
Itaperuna, Braz. 155/D2
Itapetim, Braz. 154/C2
Itapetinga, Braz. 154/B4
Itapetininga, Braz. 155/B2
Itapeva, Braz. 155/B2
Itapevi, Braz. 211/G8
Itapicuri (riv.), Braz. 154/C3
Itapicuru (riv.), Braz. 151/K5
Itapipoca, Braz. 154/C1
Itapira, Braz. 211/G7
Itapitanga, Braz. 154/C4
Itaporanga, Braz. 155/B2
Itaquaquecetuba, Braz. 211/G8
Itarantim, Braz. 154/B4
Itararé, Braz. 155/B3
Itariri, Braz. 211/F9
Itārsi, India 84/A4
Itatiaia, PN de, Braz. 211/J7
Itatiba, Braz. 211/G7
Itaueira (riv.), Braz. 151/K5
Itaueira, Braz. 154/B2
Itaúna, Braz. 155/C2
Itayanagi, Japan 76/B3
Itbayat, Phil. 79/D3
Itbayat (isl.), Phil. 116/B2
Itchen (riv.), Eng, UK 33/E4
Itéa, Gre. 47/H3
Iténez (riv.), Bol. 147/C4
Itezhi-Tezhi (dam), Zam. 105/E4
Ith (hills), Ger. 51/G4
Ithaca, NY, US 130/E3
Ithaca, (Itháki) (isl.), Gre. 47/G3
Itháki, Gre. 47/G3
Ithon (riv.), Wal, UK 32/C2
Itimbiri (riv.), D.R. Congo 97/K7
Itinga, Braz. 154/B5
Itiruçu, Braz. 154/B4
Itō, Japan 75/F3
Itogon, Phil. 79/D4
Itoigawa, Japan 75/E2
Itoman, Japan 75/J7
Iton (riv.), Fr. 42/D2
Itonuki, Japan 77/L5
Itororó, Braz. 154/B4
Itsukaichi, Japan 77/C2
Itter (riv.), Ger. 51/F6
Itterbeck, Ger. 50/D3
Ittiri, It. 46/A2
Itu, Braz. 155/C2
Ituango, Col. 152/C3
Ituberá, Braz. 154/C4
Ituí (riv.), Braz. 150/D5
Ituiutaba, Braz. 155/B1
Itumbiara, Braz. 155/B1
Itumbiara, Barragem (res.), Braz. 155/B1
Itumirim, Braz. 211/J6
Ituna, Sk, Can. 127/H3
Itupiranga, Braz. 151/J5
Ituporanga, Braz. 155/B3
Iturama, Braz. 155/B1
Ituri (riv.), D.R. Congo 104/A2
Itutinga, Represa de (res.), Braz. 155/C2
Ituverava, Braz. 155/C2
Ituxi (riv.), Braz. 150/E5
Ituzaingó, Uru. 159/K11
Ityāy al Bārūd, Egypt 91/B4
Itz (riv.), Ger. 40/F3
Iul'tin (peak), Rus. 134/C2
Iúna, Braz. 155/D2
Ivaí (riv.), Braz. 155/B3
Ivaiporã, Braz. 155/B3
Ivalojoki (riv.), Fin. 37/H1
Ivančice, Czh. 43/M2
Ivanec, Cro. 43/M3
Ivangrad, Yugo. 47/F1
Ivanhoe, Austl. 115/C2
Ivanhoe (riv.), Can. 130/D1
Ivanjica, Yugo. 48/E4
Ivanjska, Bosn. 48/C3
Ivankovo, Cro. 48/D3
Ivano-Frankivs'k, Ukr. 62/C2
Ivano-Frankivs'ka (obl.), Ukr. 62/C2
Ivanof Bay, Ak, US 134/G4
Ivanovo (dist.), Rus. 60/J4
Ivanovo, Rus. 60/J4
Ivato, Madg. 107/H8
Ivato (int'l arpt.), Madg. 107/H7
Ivaylovgrad (res.), Bul. 47/J2
Ivaylovgrad, Bul. 47/K2
Ivdel, Rus. 64/G3
Iveragh (pen.), Ire. 30/P11
Iverny, Fr. 30/L5
Ivindo (riv.), Gabon 96/H7
Ivohibe, Madg. 107/H8
Ivondro (riv.), Madg. 107/J7
Ivory (coast), C.d'Iv. 96/D7
Ivösjön (lake), Swe. 38/F3
Ivrea, It. 58/A2
İvrindi, Turk. 62/C5
Ivry-sur-Seine, Fr. 30/K5
Ivujivik, Qu, Can. 123/J2
Ivvavik NP, Yk, Can. 122/B2
Iwafune, Japan 77/D1
Iwai, Japan 75/F2
Iwaizumi, Japan 76/B4
Iwaki, Japan 75/G2
Iwaki-san (peak), Japan 76/B3
Iwakuni, Japan 74/C3
Iwakura, Japan 77/L5
Iwama, Japan 77/E1
Iwami, Japan 74/D3
Iwamizawa, Japan 76/B2
Iwamura, Japan 77/M5
Iwanai, Japan 76/B2
Iwanuma, Japan 75/G1
Iwasaki, Japan 76/A3
Iwata, Japan 75/E3
Iwataki, Japan 77/H4
Iwate (pref.), Japan 76/B4
Iwate, Japan 76/B4
Iwate-san (peak), Japan 76/B4
Iwatsuki, Japan 77/D2
Iwere Ile, Nga. 103/F5
Iwo, Nga. 103/G5
Iwo Jima (isl.), Japan 116/D2
Iwŏn, NKor. 73/E2
Iwuy, Fr. 52/C3
Ixcán (riv.), Guat. 144/D3
Ixelles, Belg. 53/D2
Ixmiquilpan, Mex. 143/K6
Ixopo, SAfr. 107/E3
Ixtapaluca, Mex. 143/L7
Ixtapan de la Sal, Mex. 143/K8
Ixtlán del Río, Mex. 142/D4
Iyo (sea), Japan 74/B4
Iyo, Japan 74/C4
Izabal (lake), Guat. 140/D4
Īzad Khvāst, Iran 88/F2
Izamal, Mex. 144/D1
Izberbash, Rus. 63/H4
Izegem, Belg. 52/C2
Izembek NWR 134/F4
Izhevsk, Rus. 61/M4
Izhma (riv.), Rus. 61/M2
Izhora (riv.), Rus. 61/T7
Izi (well), Alg. 99/F3
Izigan (cape), Ak, US 134/E5
Izkī, Oman 89/G4
Izmayil, Ukr. 49/J3
İzmir, Turk. 62/C5
İzmir (prov.), Turk. 62/C5
İzmit (gulf), Turk. 49/J5
İzmit, Turk. 49/J5
Iznájar, Sp. 44/C4
İznik, Turk. 49/J5
İznik (lake), Turk. 49/J5
Izola, Slov. 59/G1
Izra', Syria 91/E3
Izsák, Hun. 48/D2
Iztaccíhuatl-Popocatépetl, PN, Mex. 143/L7
Izu (pen.), Japan 75/F3
Izu (isls.), Japan 65/P6
Izúcar de Matamoros, Mex. 143/L8
Izuhara, Japan 74/A3
Izumi, Japan 74/B4
Izumi, Japan 76/B4
Izumi, Japan 77/H7
Izumi-Ōtsu, Japan 77/H7
Izumi-Sano, Japan 77/H7
Izumo, Japan 74/C3
Izunagaoka, Japan 77/B3
Izushi, Japan 77/G5
Izyum, Ukr. 62/F2

J

J. Paul Getty Museum, Ca, US 136/E7
Jääsjärvi (lake), Fin. 39/M1
Jaba', WBnk. 91/G7
Jabal 'Abd al 'Azāz (mts.), Syria 90/D2
Jabal Abu Rujmayn (mts.), Syria 90/D3
Jabal Abyad (plat.), Sudan 101/B5
Jabal al 'Arab (mts.), Syria 91/E3
Jabal an Nusayriyab (mts.), Syria 91/E2
Jabal ar Ruwaq (mts.), Syria 90/D3
Jabal as Sawdā' (hills), Libya 96/H2
Jabal ash Shaykh (peak), Leb. 91/D3
Jabāl Lubnān (gov.), Leb. 91/D2
Jabal Ramm (peak), Jor. 91/D5
Jabal 'Unāzah (peak), SAr. 90/D3
Jabalí (pt.), Pan. 145/F5
Jabalón (riv.), Sp. 44/D3
Jabalpur, India 84/B4
Jabālyah, Gaza 91/D4
Jabbeke, Belg. 52/C1
Jablah, Syria 91/D2
Jablanica (mts.), Alb. 47/G2
Jablonec nad Nisou, Czh. 41/H3
Jaboatão dos Guararapes, Braz. 154/D3
Jaboticabal, Braz. 155/B2
Jabuka, Yugo. 48/E3
Jabung (cape), Indo. 80/B4
Jaca, Sp. 45/E1
Jacaré (riv.), Braz. 154/B3
Jacareí, Braz. 211/H8
Jaceel (riv.), Som. 97/Q5
Jáchymov, Czh. 55/F2
Jacinto, Braz. 154/B5
Jacinto Arauz, Arg. 158/E3
Jackman, Me, US 131/G2
Jackpot, Nv, US 126/E5
Jacks Mountain (ridge), Pa, US 138/A2
Jacksboro, Tx, US 129/H4
Jackson (mts.), Nv, US 126/D5
Jackson (cap.), Ms, US 129/K4
Jackson, Wy, US 126/F5
Jackson (lake), Wy, US 128/E2
Jackson, Mi, US 130/C3
Jackson, Ca, US 128/B3
Jackson, Mo, US 129/K3
Jackson, La, US 129/K5
Jackson, Al, US 133/G4
Jackson, Tn, US 130/B5
Jackson (co.), Mo, US 137/E5
Jacksonville, Ar, US 129/J4
Jacksonville, Al, US 133/G3
Jacksonville, Fl, US 133/H4
Jacksonville, NC, US 133/J3
Jacksonville (int'l arpt.), Fl, US 133/H4
Jacksonville, Il, US 129/K3
Jacksonville Beach, Fl, US 133/H4
Jacktown, Ok, US 137/N14
Jacmel, Haiti 145/H2
Jacobābād, Pak. 89/J3
Jacobina, Braz. 154/B3
Jacobsdal, SAfr. 106/D3
Jacobstown, NJ, US 138/D3
Jacobus, Pa, US 138/B4
Jacomo (lake), Mo, US 137/E6
Jacona de Plancarte, Mex. 142/E5
Jacques-Cartier (riv.), Can. 131/G2
Jacques Cartier (peak), Can. 131/H1
Jacuí (riv.), Braz. 157/F2
Jacuípe (riv.), Braz. 151/L6
Jacupiranga, Braz. 155/B3
Jacura, Ven. 152/D2
Jadacaquiva, Ven. 152/D2
Jaddi (pt.), Pak. 89/H3
Jade, Ger. 51/F2
Jade (riv.), Ger. 51/F1
Jade (bay), Ger. 40/E2
Jadebusen (bay), Ger. 51/F2
Jaén, Peru 156/B2
Jaén, Sp. 44/D4
Jaffa (cape), Austl. 115/A3
Jaffna, SrL. 82/C6
Jagādhri, India 86/D4
Jagdīspur, India 85/E3
Jagersfontein, SAfr. 106/D3
Jægerspris, Den. 38/D4
Jagna, Phil. 79/D6
Jagraon, India 86/C4
Jagst (riv.), Ger. 43/J2
Jagtiāl, India 82/C4
Jaguaquara, Braz. 154/C4
Jaguarão, Braz. 157/F3
Jaguarão (riv.), Braz. 159/G2
Jaguarari, Braz. 154/B3
Jaguaretama, Braz. 154/C2
Jaguariaíva, Braz. 155/B3
Jaguaribara, Braz. 154/C2
Jaguaribe (riv.), Braz. 151/L5
Jaguaribe, Braz. 154/C2
Jaguariúna, Braz. 211/G7
Jaguaruana, Braz. 154/C2
Jagungal (mt.), Austl. 115/D3
Jahānābād, India 85/E3
Jahāngīra, Pak. 86/B3
Jahāngīrābād, India 84/B1
Jahrom, Iran 88/F3
Jaicós, Braz. 154/B2
Jailolo, Indo. 81/G3
Jailu (riv.), China 72/C4
Jainca, China 70/H4
Jāis, India 84/C2
Jaisalmer, India 89/K3
Jaisinghnagar, India 84/C4
Jājapur, India 82/E3
Jājarm, Iran 89/G1
Jajce, Bosn. 48/C3
Jakarta (cap.), Indo. 80/C5
Jakobstad (Pietarsaari), Fin. 60/D3
Jal, NM, US 129/G4
Jala, Mex. 142/D4
Jalacingo, Mex. 143/M7
Jalaid Qi, China 71/M2
Jalal-Abad, Kyr. 87/F4
Jalal-Abad (obl.), Kyr. 87/F4
Jalālābād, India 84/B2
Jalālābād, India 86/C4
Jalālābād, Afg. 86/A2
Jalālābād, India 86/D5
Jalāli, India 84/B2
Jalālpur, India 84/D2
Jalālpur, Pak. 86/C3
Jalālpur Pīrwāla, Pak. 86/A5
Jalamah, WBnk. 91/G6
Jalangi (riv.), India 85/G3
Jalapa, Mex. 143/N7
Jalapa, Mex. 144/C2
Jalapa, Guat. 144/D3
Jalatlaco, Mex. 143/Q10
Jālaun, India 84/B2
Jaldhāka (riv.), India 85/G2
Jales, Braz. 155/B2
Jalesar, India 84/B2
Jalingo, Nga. 96/H6
Jalisco, Mex. 142/D4
Jāliţah, Jazīrat (isl.), Tun. 46/A4
Jallouvre, Pic de (peak), Fr . 56/C6
Jalon (riv.), Sp. 44/E2
Jalostotitlán, Mex. 142/E4
Jalpa, Mex. 142/E4
Jalpa de Méndez, Mex. 144/C2
Jalpan de Serra, Mex. 143/F4
Jaltenango de la Paz, Mex. 144/C3
Jaltepec (riv.), Mex. 144/C2
Jáltipan de Morelos, Mex. 144/C2
Jālūd, WBnk. 91/G7
Jaluit (isl.), Mrsh. 116/F4
Jalūlā', Iraq 90/F3
Jam, Iran 88/F3
Jamaame, Som. 97/P7
Jamaare (riv.), Nga. 96/H5
Jamaica (chan.), Jam. 141/F4
Jamaica (ctry.) 119/K8
Jamaica (bay), NY, US 138/K9
Jamālpur, Bang. 85/G3
Jamanxim (riv.), Braz. 151/G5
Jamapa, Mex. 143/N7
Jamari (riv.), Braz. 150/F5
Jambi, Indo. 80/B4
Jambuair (cape), Indo. 80/A2
James (riv.), Va, US 127/J4
James (peak), Ut, US 137/K11
James (pt.), Chile 158/B5
James (bay), Qu, Can. 119/J4
James Campbell NWR, Hi, US 124/V12
James M. Cox Dayton (int'l arpt.), Oh, US 130/C4
James Ross (str.), NW, Can. 122/G1
Jamesburg, NJ, US 138/D3
Jamestown, ND, US 127/J4
Jamestown, NY, US 130/E3
Jamestown, Tn, US 130/C4
Jamestown, Co, US 137/B2
Jamestown, Austl. 113/H5
Jamīrāpāt (range), India 84/D4
Jāmke, Pak. 86/C3
Jammāl, Tun. 46/B5
Jammerbugt (bay), Den. 38/C3
Jammu and Kashmīr (state), India 70/C5
Jāmpur, Pak. 86/A5
Jāmtāra, India 85/F4
Jämtland (co.), Swe. 37/E3
Jamūi, India 85/F3
Jamuna (riv.), Bang. 85/G3
Jan (lake), Can. 127/H2
Jan Kempdorp, SAfr. 106/D2
Jan Mayen (isl.), Nor. 160/G
Jan Smuts (Johannesburg) (int'l arpt.), SAfr. 106/E2
Janakkala, Fin. 39/L1
Janakpur, Nepal 85/E2
Janakpur (zone), Nepal 85/E2
Janaúba, Braz. 154/B4
Janaucu, Ilha (isl.), Braz. 151/H3
Jandaia do Sul, Braz. 155/B2
Jandaq, Iran 89/F2
Jandowae, Austl. 114/C4
Jándula (riv.), Sp. 44/C4
Jangaon, India 82/C4
Jangipur, India 85/G3
Janikowo, Pol. 41/K2
Janīn, WBnk. 91/G7
Janja, Bosn. 48/D3
Janjevo, Yugo. 47/G1
Janos, Mex. 142/C2
Jánoshalma, Hun. 48/D2
Jánosháza, Hun. 48/C2
Janów Lubelski, Pol. 41/M3
Jansenville, SAfr. 106/D4
Januária, Braz. 154/A4
Janvry, Fr. 30/J6
Janzé, Fr. 42/C3
Japan (sea), Asia 67/N5
Japan (ctry.) 67/N6
Japan, Sea of (sea), Asia 71/P3
Japanese Alps NP, Japan 75/E2
Japurá (riv.), Braz. 147/C3
Jaqué, Pan. 152/B3
Jarābulus, Syria 90/D2
Jaraíz de la Vera, Sp. 44/C2
Jarama (riv.), Sp. 44/D2
Jaramānah, Syria 91/E3
Jarandilla de la Vera, Sp. 44/C2
Jarānwāla, Pak. 86/B4
Jarash, Jor. 91/D3
Jarbah (isl.), Tun. 96/H1
Järbo, Swe. 38/G1
Jarby (pt.), IM, UK 34/D3
Jardim, Braz. 154/C2
Jardín América, Arg. 157/E2
Jardines de la Reina (arch.), Cuba 145/G1
Jardinópolis, Braz. 155/C2
Jargalant, Mong. 70/G2
Jari (riv.), Braz. 147/D2
Jaridih, India 85/F4
Jarjīs, Tun. 96/H1
Jarmen, Ger. 38/E5
Järna, Swe. 38/G2
Jarny, Fr. 53/E5
Jarocin, Pol. 41/J3
Jaroměř, Czh. 41/H3
Jarosľaw, Pol. 41/M3
Jarrettsville, Md, US 138/B4
Jarrow, Eng, UK 35/G2
Jars (plain), Laos 78/C2
Jarud Qi, China 72/E1
Järvenpää, Fin. 39/L1
Jarville-la-Malgrange, Fr. 53/F6
Jarvis (isl.), Pac., US 117/J5
Järvsö, Swe. 38/G1
Jáse-Nagykun-Szolnok (prov.), Hun. 48/E2
Jashpurnagar, India 85/E4
Jasidih, India 85/F3
Jāsk, Iran 89/G3
Jasľo, Pol. 41/L4
Jason (isl.), Mald. 159/E6
Jasper, Ab, Can. 126/D2
Jasper, Al, US 133/G3
Jasper, Fl, US 133/H4
Jasper, Tx, US 129/J5
Jasper, Ga, US 133/G3
Jasper, In, US 130/C4
Jasper NP, Can. 126/D2
Jasper NP, Ab, Can. 122/E3
Jaspur, India 84/B1
Jastrebarsko, Cro. 48/B3
Jastrowie, Pol. 41/J2
Jastrzębie Zdroj, Pol. 41/K4
Jaswantnagar, India 84/B2
Jászapáti, Hun. 41/L5
Jászárokszállás, Hun. 48/D2
Jászberény, Hun. 41/K5
Jataí, Braz. 155/B1
Jatapu (riv.), Braz. 150/G3
Jatāra, India 84/B3
Jataté (riv.), Mex. 144/D2
Jāti, Pak. 89/J4
Jatibonico, Cuba 145/G1
Játiva, Sp. 45/E3
Jatoi Janūbi, Pak. 86/A5
Jaú (riv.), Braz. 150/F4
Jaú, Braz. 155/B2
Jaua Sarisarinama, PN, Ven. 150/F3
Jauaperi (riv.), Braz. 150/F3
Jauaperi (riv.), Braz. 153/F5
Jauaru, Serra (mts.), Braz. 151/H4
Jaudon, Mo, US 137/D6
Jauharābād, Pak. 86/B3
Jauja, Peru 156/C3
Jaumave, Mex. 143/F4
Jaun, Swi. 56/D4
Jaunay-Clan, Fr. 42/D3
Jaunpass (pass), Swi. 56/D4
Java (sea), Indo. 67/K10
Java (isl.), Indo. 67/K10
Javari (riv.), Braz. 150/D5
Jávea, Sp. 45/F3
Javier (isl.), Chile 159/B5
Javorie (peak), Slvk. 48/D1
Javornice (riv.), Czh. 55/G2
Javorník (peak), Czh. 55/G4
Javorová Skála (peak), Czh. 55/H3
Jawāla Mukhi, India 86/D4
Jawor, Pol. 41/J3
Jayanca, Peru 156/B2
Jayapura, Indo. 116/D5
Jaynagar, India 85/F2
Jaynagar, India 85/G4
Jayton, Tx, US 129/G4
Jbel Bani (mts.), Mor. 98/D3
Jean Lafitte, La, US 137/P17
Jeberos, Peru 156/B2
Jebjerg, Den. 38/C3
Jed Water (riv.), Sc, UK 36/D6
Jedburgh, Sc, UK 36/D6
Jedlicze, Pol. 41/L4
Jędrzejów, Pol. 41/L3
Jeetze (riv.), Ger. 40/F2
Jefferson (mt.), Or, US 126/C4
Jefferson, Tx, US 129/J4
Jefferson (co.), La, US 137/P17
Jefferson (riv.), La, US 137/P17
Jefferson (co.), Mo, US 137/F9
Jefferson (co.), Co, US 137/B3
Jefferson (co.), Wi, US 135/N14
Jefferson City (cap.), Mo, US 129/J3
Jeffersonville, In, US 130/C4
Jeffrey City, Wy, US 128/F2
Jeffreys Bay, SAfr. 106/D4
Jegenstorf, Swi. 56/D3
Jeinemeni (peak), Chile 158/B5
Jēkabpils, Lat. 39/L3
Jelcz-Laskowice, Pol. 41/J3
Jelenia Góra, Pol. 41/H3
Jelenia Gora (prov.), Czh.,Ger. 41/E2
Jelep (pass), China 82/E2
Jelgava, Lat. 39/K3
Jemaa Sahim, Mor. 98/C2
Jemappes, Belg. 52/C3
Jember, Indo. 80/D5
Jemez Pueblo, NM, US 128/F4
Jeminay, China 70/E2
Jempang (lake), Indo. 81/E4
Jena, La, US 129/J5
Jena, Ger. 40/F3
Jenaz, Swi. 57/F4
Jenbach, Aus. 43/J3
Jendouba, Tun. 100/L6
Jendouba (gov.), Tun. 100/L6
Jeneponto, Indo. 81/E5
Jengen, Ger. 57/G2
Jenkintown, Pa, US 138/C3
Jennings, La, US 129/J5
Jennings, Mo, US 137/G8
Jenny Lind (isl.), NW, Can. 122/F2
Jens Muck (isl.), NW, Can. 123/H2
Jeppener, Arg. 159/J11
Jequetepeque, Peru 156/B2
Jequié, Braz. 154/B4
Jequitaí, Braz. 154/A5
Jequitinhonha, Braz. 154/B5
Jequitinhonha (riv.), Braz. 147/E4
Jerada, Mor. 100/C2
Jérémie, Haiti 145/H2
Jeremoabo, Braz. 154/C3
Jerez de García Salinas, Mex. 142/E4
Jerez de la Frontera, Sp. 44/B4
Jerez de los Caballeros, Sp. 44/B3
Jericho, Austl. 114/B3
Jericho, NY, US 139/L8
Jericho (Arīḩā), Isr. 91/D4
Jericó, Braz. 154/C2
Jerilderie, Austl. 115/C2
Jerissa, Tun. 100/L7
Jerramungup, Austl. 112/C5
Jersey (isl.), Chl, UK 42/B2
Jersey (co.), Il, US 137/G7
Jersey City (res.), NJ, US 139/H8
Jersey City, NJ, US 139/J9
Jersey Shore, Pa, US 138/A1
Jerumenha, Braz. 154/B2
Jerusalem (dist.), Isr. 91/D4
Jerusalem (Yerushalayim) (cap.), Isr. 91/G8
Jervis (inlet), Can. 126/C3
Jervis Bay, Austl. 115/D2
Jerzu, It. 46/A3
Jesberg, Ger. 51/G6
Jesenice, Slov. 43/L3
Jesenice (res.), Czh. 55/F2
Jesi, It. 59/G5
Jessheim, Nor. 38/D1
Jessore (pol. reg.), Bang. 85/G4
Jesuânia, Braz. 211/H6
Jesup, Ga, US 133/H4
Jésus (isl.), Qu, Can. 131/N6
Jesús Carranza, Mex. 144/C2
Jesús de Machaca, Bol. 156/D5
Jesús María, Arg. 157/D3
Jesús Menéndez, Cuba 145/G1
Jeta, Ilha de (isl.), GBis. 102/A4
Jetmore, Ks, US 129/H3
Jetpur, India 89/K4
Jettingen-Scheppach, Ger. 54/D6
Jetzendorf, Ger. 55/E6
Jeumont, Fr. 53/D3
Jevenstedt, Ger. 40/E1
Jever, Ger. 51/E1
Jevnaker, Nor. 38/D1
Jewar, India 84/A1
Jewel Cave Nat'l Mon., SD, US 127/H5
Jezerce (peak), Alb. 47/F1
Jezerní Stěna (peak), Czh. 55/G4
Jeziorak (lake), Pol. 41/K2
Jhā Jhā, India 85/F3
Jhajjar, India 86/D5
Jhālawār, India 89/L4
Jhalida, India 85/E4
Jhālū, India 84/B1
Jhang Sadar, Pak. 86/B4
Jhanjhārpur, India 85/F2
Jhānsi, India 84/B3
Jhārgrām, India 85/F4
Jharia, India 85/F4
Jhārsuguda, India 85/E5
Jhawāriān, Pak. 86/B3
Jhelum, Pak. 86/B3
Jhelum (riv.), Pak. 89/K2
Jhenida, Bang. 85/G4
Jhumra, Pak. 86/B4
Ji-Paraná, Braz. 150/F6
Ji Xian, China 72/C4
Ji Xian, China 72/H6
Jia Xian, China 72/B3
Jiading, China 72/L8
Jiahe, China 83/K2
Jialing (riv.), China 67/K6
Jiamusi, China 71/P2
Jian (riv.), China 79/B3
Jianchang, China 72/D2
Jiang (riv.), China 78/E1
Jiang Xian, China 72/B4
Jiang'an, China 83/J2
Jiangcheng Hanizu Yizu Zizhixian, China 83/H3
Jiangchuan, China 83/H3
Jiangdu, China 72/D4
Jianghua Yaozu Zizhixian, China 83/K3
Jiangjin, China 83/J2
Jiangmen, China 83/K3
Jiangning, China 72/D5
Jiangsu (prov.), China 71/L5
Jiangxi (prov.), China 71/K6
Jiangyin, China 72/E5
Jiangyong, China 83/K2
Jiangyou, China 70/H5
Jianhe, China 83/J2
Jianhu, China 72/D4
Jianli, China 79/B2
Jian'ou, China 79/C2
Jianshi, China 71/J5
Jianshui, China 83/H3
Jianyang, China 79/C2
Jiaocheng, China 72/C3
Jiaohe, China 71/N3
Jiaojiang, China 79/D2
Jiaokou, China 72/C3
Jiaoling, China 79/C3
Jiaonan, China 72/D4
Jiaozuo, China 72/C4
Jiashan, China 72/D4
Jiashan, China 72/L9
Jiashi, China 87/G5
Jiaxiang, China 72/D4
Jiaxing, China 72/L9
Jiayin, China 71/P2
Jiayu, China 79/B2
Jiayuguan, China 70/G4
Jibou, Rom. 49/F2
Jibsh, Ra's (pt.), Oman 89/G4
Jicarón (isl.), Pan. 145/F5
Jičín, Czh. 41/H3
Jiddah, SAr. 88/C4
Jieshou, China 72/C4
Jiexiu, China 72/B3
Jieyang, China 79/C3
Jifnā, Isr. 91/G8
Jigalong Abor. Land, Austl. 112/D2
Jigawa (prov.), Nga. 103/H4
Jiguaní, Cuba 145/G1
Jigzhi, China 70/H5
Jihlava (riv.), Czh. 43/L2
Jihlava, Czh. 41/H4
Jihočeský (pol. reg.), Czh. 43/K2
Jihomoravský (pol. reg.), Czh. 43/M2
Jijel (prov.), Alg. 100/H4
Jijel, Alg. 100/H4
Jijia (riv.), Rom. 62/C3
Jijiga, Eth. 97/P6
Jijona, Sp. 45/E3
Jilhâ, Represa (res.), Braz. 155/B2
Jilhava (riv.), Czh. 41/H4
Jilib, Som. 97/P7
Jilin, China 71/N3
Jilin (prov.), China 71/N3
Jiloca (riv.), Sp. 44/E2
Jilotepec, Mex. 143/K7
Jílové u Prahy, Czh. 55/H3
Jim Thorpe, Pa, US 138/C2
Jīma, Eth. 97/N6
Jimaní, DRep. 145/J2
Jimbolia, Rom. 48/E3
Jimboomba, Austl. 114/D4
Jimena de la Frontera, Sp. 44/C4
Jiménez, Mex. 129/G5
Jiménez, Mex. 142/D3
Jimo, China 72/E3
Jimokuji, Japan 77/L5
Jimsar, China 70/E3
Jin (riv.), China 83/K2
Jin Xian, China 72/C3
Jinan, China 72/D3
Jinchang, China 70/H4
Jincheng, China 72/C4
Jinchuan, China 70/H5
Jinci Temple, China 72/C3
Jīnd, India 86/D5
Jindabyne (dam), Austl. 115/D3
Jindabyne, Austl. 115/D3
Jindřichuv Hradec, Czh. 41/H4
Jing Xian, China 71/L5
Jing Xian, China 83/J2
Jingbian, China 72/B3
Jingde, China 79/C1
Jingdezhen, China 79/C2
Jingdong, China 83/H3
Jinggangshan, China 83/K2
Jinghai, China 72/H7
Jinghe, China 70/D3
Jinghong, China 83/H3
Jingjiang, China 72/E4
Jingle, China 72/B3
Jingmen, China 72/C5
Jingshan, China 72/C5
Jingxi, China 83/J3
Jingyuan, China 70/H4
Jinhu, China 72/D4
Jinhua, China 79/C2
Jining, China 72/C2
Jining, China 72/D4
Jinja, Ugan. 104/B2
Jinkouhe, China 83/H2
Jinotega, Nic. 144/E3
Jinotepe, Nic. 144/E4
Jinping, China 83/J2
Jinsha, China 83/J2
Jinsha (riv.), China 67/J7
Jinshan, China 72/L9
Jinshi, China 83/K2
Jintan, China 72/D5
Jintotolo (chan.), Phil. 79/D5
Jintūr, India 89/L5
Jinxi, China 79/C2
Jinxi, China 72/E2
Jinxian, China 79/C2
Jinxiang, China 72/D4
Jinyun, China 79/D2
Jinzhai, China 72/C5
Jinzhou (bay), China 73/A3
Jinzhou, China 72/E2
Jiparana (riv.), Braz. 150/F5
Jipijapa, Ecu. 152/A5
Jiquilpan de Juárez, Mex. 142/E5
Jiquipilco, Mex. 143/Q9
Jiřkov, Czh. 55/G1
Jishan, China 72/B4
Jishou, China 83/J2
Jishui, China 79/C2
Jisr ash Shughūr, Syria 91/E2
Jiu (riv.), Rom. 62/B3
Jiujiang, China 79/C2
Jiujiang, China 79/C2
Jiulong, China 83/H2
Jiutai, China 71/N3
Jiutepec, Mex. 143/K8
Jiuwan (mts.), China 70/J6
Jixi, China 71/P2
Jixi, China 79/C1
Jiyang, China 72/D3
Jiyuan, China 72/C4
Jīzān, SAr. 88/D5
Jize, China 72/C3
Jizera (riv.), Czh. 41/H3
Jizō-zaki (pt.), Japan 74/C3
Jizzakh, Uzb. 87/E4
Jizzakh (pol. reg.), Uzb. 87/E4
Joaçaba, Braz. 155/B3
Joachín, Mex. 143/N8
Joaíma, Braz. 154/B5
João Câmara, Braz. 154/D2
João Lisboa, Braz. 154/A2
João Monlevade, Braz. 155/D1
João Pessoa, Braz. 154/D2
João Pinheiro, Braz. 154/A5
Joaquín V. González, Arg. 157/D2
Jobabo, Cuba 145/G1
Jockgrim, Ger. 54/B4
Jocón, Hon. 144/E3
Jódar, Sp. 44/D4
Jodhpur, India 89/K3
Jodoigne, Belg. 53/D2
Joensuu, Fin. 60/F3
Jōetsu, Japan 75/F2
Jogbani, India 85/F2
Johannesberg, Ger. 54/C2
Johannesburg, SAfr. 106/E2
Johanngeorgenstadt, Ger. 55/F2
Johilla (riv.), India 84/C4
John Day, Or, US 126/D4
John Day (riv.), Or, US 124/B2
John Day Fossil Beds Nat'l Mon., Or, US 126/C4
John Day, Middle Fork (riv.), Or, US 126/D4
John Day, North Fork (riv.), Or, US 126/D4
John F. Kennedy (int'l arpt.), NY, US 139/K9
John Forrest NP, Austl. 112/L6
John H. Kerr (Buggs Island Lake) (res.), US 133/J2
John Martin (res.), Co, US 132/C2
John Wayne/Orange County (int'l arpt.), Ca, US 136/G8
Johnson (co.), Ks, US 137/D6
Johnson City, Tn, US 130/D4
Johnsonburg, NJ, US 138/D2
Johnsons Crossing, Yk, Can. 134/M3
Johnston (falls), Zam. 104/A5
Johnston (lake), Austl. 109/B4
Johnston Atoll (isl.), Pac., US 117/J3
Johnstone, Sc, UK 36/B5
Johnstown, Pa, US 130/E3
Johnstown, Co, US 137/C2
Johnsville, Md, US 138/A4
Johor Baharu, Malay. 80/B3
Jöhstadt, Ger. 55/G1
Joigny, Fr. 42/E3
Joinvile, Braz. 155/B3
Joinville, Fr. 56/B1
Jojutla, Mex. 143/K8
Jokioinen, Fin. 39/K1
Jokkmokk, Swe. 37/F2
Jökulsargljufur NP, Ice. 37/P6
Jolanda di Savoia, It. 59/E3
Joliette, Qu, Can. 130/F2
Jollyville, Tx, US 129/H5
Jolo (isl.), Phil. 81/F2
Jolo, Phil. 81/F2
Jomala, Fin. 39/H1
Jombang, Indo. 80/D5
Jomda, China 70/G5
Jomo Kenyatta (int'l arpt.), Kenya 104/C3
Jona, Swi. 57/E3
Jonacatepec, Mex. 143/L8
Jonava, Lith. 39/L4
Jonchery-sur-Vesle, Fr. 52/C5
Jones, Ok, US 137/N14
Jones (sound), Can. 119/J2
Jones (mtn.), Pa, US 138/A2
Jones (inlet), NY, US 139/L9
Jones Beach State Park, NY, US 139/L9
Jonesboro, Ar, US 129/K4
Jonesboro, La, US 129/J4
Jönköping (co.), Swe. 37/E4
Jönköping, Swe. 38/F3
Jonquière, Qu, Can. 131/G1
Jonuta, Mex. 140/C4
Joondalup (lake), Austl. 112/K6
Joplin, Mo, US 129/J3
Joppatowne (Joppa), Md, US 138/B5
Jora, India 84/A2
Jordan, Mt, US 126/G4
Jordan, On, Can. 131/R9
Jordan (riv.), Isr.,Jor. 91/D4
Jordan (ctry.) 67/C6
Jordan Valley, Or, US 126/D5
Jordânia, Braz. 154/B4
Jorge (cape), Chile 159/B6
Jorge Chavez (int'l arpt.), Peru 156/B4
Jork, Ger. 51/G1
Jornada del Muerto (valley), NM, US 132/B3
Jørpeland, Nor. 38/B2
Jos (plat.), Nga. 96/G6
Jos, Nga. 103/H4
Jose Abad Santos, Phil. 81/G2
José Batlle y Ordóñez, Uru. 159/G2
José Bonifácio, Braz. 155/B2
José Cardel, Mex. 143/N7
José de Freitas, Braz. 154/B2
José de San Martín, Arg. 157/B5
José Enrique Rodó, Uru. 159/K10
José María Morelos, Mex. 144/D2
Jose Marti (int'l arpt.), Cuba 145/F1
José Pedro Varela, Uru. 159/G2
José, South (dept.), Uru. 159/F2
Josefa Camejo (int'l arpt.), Ven. 152/D2
Joseph Bonaparte (gulf), Austl. 109/B2
Joshin-Etsu Kogen NP, Japan 75/F2
Joshua (pt.), Ct, US 139/F1
Joshua Tree NP, Ca, US 128/D4
Jossa (riv.), Ger. 54/C2
Jotunheimen NP, Nor. 38/C1
Jouanne (riv.), Fr. 42/C2
Jouarre, Fr. 30/M5
Joué-lès-Tours, Fr. 42/D3
Jœuf, Fr. 53/F5
Jourama Falls NP, Austl. 114/B2
Jourdanton, Tx, US 129/H5
Joure, Neth. 50/C3
Joutseno, Fin. 39/N1
Joux (lake), Swi. 56/C4
Jouy-en-Josas, Fr. 30/J5
Jouy-le-Châtel, Fr. 30/M6
Jouy-le-Moutier, Fr. 30/J4
Jouy-sur-Morin, Fr. 52/C6
Jovellanos, Cuba 145/F1
Joveyn (riv.), Iran 89/G1
Jowai, India 83/F2
Joy (mt.), Can. 134/M3
Jōyō, Japan 77/J6
Jozankei Spa, Japan 76/B2
Ju Xian, China 72/D4
Juan Aldama, Mex. 142/E3
Juan de Fuca (str.), BC, Can.,US 122/D4
Juan de Fuca, Strait of (str.), US,Can. 126/B3
Juan de Nova (isl.), Fr. 93/G6
Juan Fernández (isls.), Chile 147/A6
Juan Fernández, Arg. 158/F3
Juan José Paso, Arg. 158/E2
Juan L. Lacaze, Uru. 159/K11
Juan Santamaria (int'l arpt.), CR 145/E4
Juancheng, China 72/C4
Juangriego, Ven. 153/F2
Juanjuí, Peru 156/B2
Juárez, Arg. 158/F3
Juarez, Sierra de (mts.), Mex. 128/D4
Juatinga, Ponta de (pt.), Braz. 211/J8
Juazeirinho, Braz. 154/C2
Juazeiro, Braz. 154/B3
Juazeiro do Norte, Braz. 154/C2
Juba, Sudan 97/M7
Jubany, Arg., Ant. 160/W
Jubba (riv.), Som. 97/P7
Jübek, Ger. 40/E1
Jubones (riv.), Ecu. 156/B1
Juby (cape), Mor. 98/B4
Júcar (riv.), Sp. 44/D3
Jucás, Braz. 154/C2
Jüchen, Ger. 53/F1
Juchipila, Mex. 142/E4
Juchique de Ferrer, Mex. 143/N7
Juchitán de Zaragoza, Mex. 144/C2
Juchitepec, Mex. 143/R10
Jucurutu, Braz. 154/C2
Judaberg, Nor. 38/A2
Judenburg, Aus. 43/L3
Judith (riv.), Mt, US 126/F4
Juelsminde, Den. 38/D4
Juhaynah, Egypt 101/B3
Juigalpa, Nic. 144/E3
Juilly, Fr. 30/L4
Juine (riv.), Fr. 42/E2
Juist (isl.), Ger. 50/D1
Juist, Ger. 50/E1
Juiz de Fora, Braz. 211/K6
Jujurieux, Fr. 56/B5
Julbach, Ger. 55/F6
Julesburg, Co, US 127/H5
Juli, Peru 156/D5
Julia Creek, Austl. 114/A3
Juliaca, Peru 156/D4
Julian Alps (mts.), It. 43/K3
Juliana Top (peak), Sur. 151/G3
Jülich, Ger. 53/F2
Julio A. Mella, Cuba 145/H1
Juliustown, NJ, US 138/D3
Jullundur, India 86/C4
Julu, China 72/C3
Jumbilla, Peru 156/B2
Jumeauville, Fr. 30/H5
Jumilla, Sp. 44/E3

Jumin – Keiho

Juminda (pt.), Est. 39/L2
Jumla, Nepal 84/D1
Jümme (riv.), Ger. 51/E2
Jūmonji, Japan 76/B4
Junagadh, India 89/K4
Junan, China 72/D4
Juncal (peak), Chile 158/N8
Junction, Ut, US 128/D3
Junction, Tx, US 129/H5
Junction City, Or, US 126/C4
Jundiaí, Braz. 211/G8
Jundu (mts.), China 72/H6
Juneda, Sp. 45/F2
Junee, Austl. 115/C2
Jungar Qi, China 72/B3
Jungfrau (peak), Swi. 56/D4
Jungfraujoch, Swi. 56/D4
Junglinster, Lux. 53/F4
Juniata (riv.), Pa, US 130/E3
Juniata (co.), Pa, US 138/A2
Junik, Yugo. 47/G1
Junín, Peru 156/B3
Junín (dept.), Peru 156/C3
Junín, Ecu. 152/A5
Junín, Arg. 158/C2
Junín, Arg. 158/E2
Junín de los Andes, Arg. 158/C3
Juniper Hills, Ca, US 136/C2
Junji (pass), China 72/C3
Juno Beach, Fl, US 133/H5
Junqueirópolis, Braz. 155/B2
Junsele, Swe. 37/F3
Juparanã, Lagoa (lake), Braz. 155/D2
Jupiter (riv.), Can. 131/J1
Jupiter, Fl, US 133/H5
Jupiter (mt.), Wa, US 135/A2
Juquiá, Braz. 155/C3
Juquitiba, Braz. 211/F8
Jur (riv.), Sudan 97/L6
Jur pri Bratislave, Slvk. 48/C1
Jura (mts.), Fr. 42/F3
Jura (dept.), Fr. 56/B4
Jura (pen.), Sc, UK 31/R8
Jura (isl.), Sc, UK 31/Q9
Juradó, Col. 152/B3
Jurançon, Fr. 42/C5
Jurbise, Belg. 52/C2
Jurien, Austl. 112/B4
Jürmala, Lat. 39/K3
Juruá (riv.), Braz. 147/C3
Juruena (riv.), Braz. 147/D4
Juruti, Braz. 151/G4
Jushiyama, Japan 77/L5
Juskatla, BC, Can. 134/M5
Jussey, Fr. 56/B2
Jussy, Swi. 56/C5
Jussy, Fr. 52/C4
Justo Daract, Arg. 158/D2
Jutaí, Braz. 150/E5
Jutaí (riv.), Braz. 146/D4
Jutiapa, Guat. 144/D3
Juticalpa, Hon. 144/E3
Jutland, NJ, US 138/D2
Jutland (pen.), Den. 37/D4
Juventud, La (isl.), Cuba 119/J7
Juye, China 72/D4
Juzhang (riv.), China 72/C5
Juziers, Fr. 30/H4
Južna Morava (riv.), Yugo. 48/E4
Juzur Qarqannah (isl.), Congo 99/H2
Jyderup, Den. 38/D4

K

Ka (riv.), Nga. 96/F5
Ka (isl.), NKor. 73/C3
Ka Lae (cape), Hi, US 124/U11
Kaaawa, Hi, US 124/W12
Kaabong, Ugan. 104/B2
Kaala (peak), Hi, US 124/U11
Kaalualu, Hi, US 124/U11
Kaap Plato (plat.), SAfr. 106/C3
Kaarina, Fin. 39/K1
Kaarst, Ger. 50/D6
Kaba, Hun. 48/E2
Kabadak (riv.), Bang. 85/G4
Kabaena (isl.), Indo. 116/B5
Kabah (ruin), Mex. 144/D1
Kabala, SLeo. 102/C4
Kabale, Ugan. 104/A3
Kabalega (falls), Ugan. 104/A2
Kabalega NP, Ugan. 97/M7
Kabalo, D.R. Congo 105/E2
Kabamba, Lac (lake), D.R. Congo 105/E2
Kabankalan, Phil. 81/F2
Kabardino-Balkaria Aut. Rep., Rus. 63/G4
Kabare, D.R. Congo 104/B2
Kaberamaido, Ugan. 104/B2
Kabinakagani (lake), Can. 130/C1
Kabinda, D.R. Congo 105/D2
Kabīr, Oued el (riv.), Alg. 100/H4
Kabīrwāla, Pak. 86/A4
Kabīyah, Sabkhat al (swamp), Tun. 46/A5
Kableshkovo, Bul. 49/H4
Kābol (Kabul) (cap.), Afg. 89/J2
Kabompo (riv.), Zam. 105/E2
Kabongo, D.R. Congo 105/E2
Kabrai, India 84/C3
Kabul (riv.), Afg. 89/J2
Kabul (Kābol) (cap.), Afg. 89/J2
Kaburuang (isl.), Indo. 81/G3
Kabwe, Zam. 105/E3
Kačanik, Yugo. 47/G1
Kachalola, Zam. 105/F3
Kachemak (bay), 134/H4
Kachemak, Ak, US 134/H4
Kachin (div.), Myan. 70/G6
Kaçkar Dai (peak), Turk. 63/G4
Kadaianallur, India 82/C6
Kadam (riv.), Ugan. 104/B2
Kadam (isl.), Myan. 83/G5

Kadan (isl.), Myan. 78/B3
Kadaň, Czh. 55/G2
Kadavu (isl.), Fiji 116/G6
Kadei (riv.), CAfr.,Cam 96/J7
Kadina, Austl. 113/H5
Kadınhanı, Turk. 90/C2
Kadiogo (prov.), Burk. 103/E3
Kadiolo, Mali 102/D4
Kadiri, India 82/C5
Kadirli, Turk. 90/D2
Kadışehri, Turk. 62/E5
Kadoka, SD, US 127/H5
Kadoma, Zim. 105/E4
Kadoma, Japan 77/J6
Kaduna (state), Nga. 103/G4
Kaduna, Nga. 103/G4
Kaduna, Nga. 103/G4
Kādugli, Sudan 97/L5
Kaech'ŏn, NKor. 73/C3
Kaédi, Mrta. 102/B2
Kaélé, Camr. 96/H5
Kaena (pt.), Hi, US 124/V12
Kaeng Krachan NP, Thai. 78/B3
Kaesŏng, NKor. 73/D3
Kaesŏng-si (prov.), NKor. 73/D3
Kafar Jar Ghar (mts.), Afg. 89/J2
Kaffraria (reg.), SAfr. 106/D4
Kaffrine, Sen. 102/B3
Kafr Ash Shaykh (gov.), Egypt 101/B1
Kafr ash Shaykh, Egypt 91/B1
Kafr az Zayyāt, Egypt 91/B4
Kafr Kannā, Isr. 91/G6
Kafr Mandā, Isr. 91/G6
Kafr Qari', Isr. 91/G6
Kafr Qāsim, Isr. 91/G6
Kafu (riv.), Ugan. 104/A2
Kafue (riv.), Zam. 105/E4
Kafue, Zam. 105/E4
Kafue NP, Zam. 105/E3
Kaga, Japan 74/E2
Kaga Bandoro, CAfr. 97/J6
Kāgān (valley), Pak. 86/D2
Kagawa (pref.), Japan 77/J6
Kagera (riv.), Tanz. 104/A3
Kağızman, Turk. 63/G4
Kagoshima (int'l arpt.), Japan 74/B5
Kagoshima, Japan 74/B5
Kagoshima (bay), Japan 74/B5
Kagoshima (dept.), Japan 74/B5
Kahaluu, Hi, US 124/W13
Kahama, Tanz. 104/B3
Kahayan (riv.), Indo. 80/D4
Kahlu (pt.), Hi, US 124/T10
Kahl am Main, Ger. 54/C2
Kāhna, Pak. 86/C4
Kahoka, Mo, US 127/L5
Kahoolawe (isl.), Hi, US 124/T10
Kahperusvaara (peak), Fin. 37/G1
Kahraman Maraş, Turk. 90/D2
Kahraman Maraş (prov.), Turk. 90/D2
Kahramanmaraş, Turk. 90/D2
Kahror Pakka, Pak. 86/A5
Kāhta, Turk. 90/D2
Kahuku, Hi, US 124/W12
Kahuku (pt.), Hi, US 124/W12
Kahului, Hi, US 124/T10
Kahuzi-Biega, PN de, D.R. Congo 105/E1
Kai (isls.), Indo. 116/C5
Kai Besar (isl.), Indo. 81/H5
Kai Kecil (isl.), Indo. 81/H5
Kaiapoi, NZ 117/S11
Kaibab (plat.), Az, US 128/D3
Kaibara, Japan 77/H5
Kaieteur (falls), Guy. 153/G3
Kaieteur NP, Guy. 153/G3
Kaifeng, China 71/K5
Kaihua, China 79/C2
Kaikohe, NZ 117/S10
Kaikoura, NZ 117/S11
Kaili, China 83/J2
Kailu, China 72/E2
Kailua, Hi, US 124/U11
Kailua, Hi, US 124/W13
Kaimganj, India 84/B2
Kaimur (range), India 84/C3
Kainab (riv.), Namb. 106/B2
Kainach (riv.), Aus. 48/B2
Kainan, Japan 74/D3
Kainji (dam), Nga. 103/G4
Kainji (lake), Nga. 93/C3
Kainji Lake NP, Nga. 103/F4
Kaipara (har.), NZ 117/S10
Kairāna, India 86/D5
Kairi, Austl. 114/B2
Kairouan, Tun. 46/B5
Kaiseregg (peak), Swi. 56/D4
Kaisersesch, Ger. 53/G3
Kaiserslautern, Ger. 53/G5
Kaisheim, Ger. 54/E4
Kaitaia, NZ 117/S10
Kaithal, India 86/D5
Kaiwi (chan.), US 124/T10
Kaiyuan, China 83/J2
Kaiyuan, China 83/H3
Kaizu, Japan 77/L5
Kaizuka, Japan 77/H7
Kajaani, Fin. 64/C3
Kaji-san (peak), SKor. 74/A3
Kajiado, Kenya 104/A3
Kajikazawa, Japan 77/A2
Kakamas, SAfr. 106/C3
Kakamega, Kenya 104/B2
Kakamigahara, Japan 77/L5
Kakanj, Bosn. 48/D3
Kake, Ak, US 134/M4

Kakiri, Ugan. 104/B2
Kako (riv.), Japan 77/G6
Kakogawa, Japan 77/G6
Kakori, India 84/C2
Kakrāla, India 84/B2
Kakrima (riv.), Gui. 102/B4
Kaktovik, Ak, US 134/K1
Kakuda, Japan 75/G2
Kakunodate, Japan 76/B4
Kala Kebira, Tun. 46/B5
Kalabo, D.R. Congo 105/E3
Kalabo, Zam. 105/D3
Kalach, Rus. 63/G2
Kalach-na-Donu, Rus. 63/G2
Kalachinsk, Rus. 87/F1
Kaladan (riv.), Myan. 83/F3
Kālāgarh, India 84/D2
Kalahari (des.), Namb. 93/D7
Kalahari-Gemsbok NP, SAfr. 105/C6
Kalahari-Gemsbok NP, SAfr. 106/C2
Kalaheo, Hi, US 124/S10
Kalaiya, Nepal 85/E2
Kalalé, Ben. 103/F4
Kalamákion, Gre. 47/N8
Kalamaloué, PN de, Camr. 96/H5
Kalamariá, Gre. 47/H2
Kalamáta, Gre. 47/H4
Kalamazoo, Mi, US 130/C3
Kalampáka, Gre. 47/G3
Kalandy, Madg. 107/J6
Kalaoa, Hi, US 124/U11
Kalasin, Thai. 78/C2
Kaláswāla, Pak. 86/C3
Kalāt, Pak. 89/J3
Kalaupapa, Hi, US 124/T10
Kalávrita, Gre. 47/H3
Kalbach, Ger. 54/B2
Kalbar, Austl. 113/G5
Kalbarri, Austl. 112/B3
Kalbarri NP, Austl. 112/B3
Kaldakvísl (riv.), Ice. 37/N2
Kale, Turk. 62/F4
Kale, Turk. 91/A1
Kalecik, Turk. 62/E4
Kalefeld, Ger. 51/H5
Kalemie (int'l arpt.), D.R. Congo 104/A4
Kalemie, D.R. Congo 104/A4
Kalemyo, Myan. 83/F3
Kalety, Pol. 41/K3
Kalewa, Myan. 83/F3
Kalewa, Zam. 105/E3
Kalgoorlie-Boulder, Austl. 112/D4
Kāli (riv.), India 84/B1
Kāli (riv.), India 84/B1
Kāli (riv.), Nepal 84/D2
Kalianda, Indo. 80/C5
Kalima, D.R. Congo 97/L8
Kalimantan (reg.), Indo. 80/D4
Kálimnos, Gre. 47/H4
Kálimnos (isl.), Gre. 90/A2
Kalimpong, India 85/G2
Kaliningrad, Rus. 39/J4
Kaliningrad Oblast, Rus. 39/J4
Kalininsk, Rus. 63/H2
Kalinkavichy, Bela. 63/H1
Kaliro, Ugan. 104/B2
Kalisizo, Japan 104/A3
Kalispell, Mt, US 126/E3
Kalisz, Pol. 41/K3
Kalix, Swe. 60/D2
Kalixälven (riv.), Swe. 37/G2
Kāliyāganj, India 85/F3
Kalkaska, Mi, US 130/C2
Kallham, Aus. 55/G6
Kallinge, Swe. 38/F3
Kallinge (int'l arpt.), Swe. 38/F3
Kallithéa, Gre. 47/N8
Kallsjön (lake), Swe. 37/E3
Kalmar Swe. [no val]
Kalmar, Swe. 38/G3
Kalmar, Swe. 38/G3
Kalmarsund (sound), Swe. 38/G3
Kalmthout, Belg. 50/B6
Kalmykia Aut. Rep., Rus. 64/G2
Kalna, India 85/F4
Kalni (riv.), Bang. 85/H3
Kalocsa, Hun. 48/D2
Kalofer, Bul. 47/J1
Kalohi (chan.), US 124/U10
Kalohkhórion, Gre. 47/H4
Kālol, India 89/K4
Kalomo, Zam. 105/E4
Kalongo, Japan 104/A3
Kalpi, India 84/B2
Kalpin, China 70/C3
Kālsdorf bei Graz, Aus. 43/L3
Kaltag, Ak, US 134/G3
Kaltbrunn, Swi. 57/F3
Kaltenleutgeben, Aus. 46/N7
Kaltennordheim, Ger. 54/D1
Kaltern (Caldaro), It. 43/J3
Kaluga, Rus. 60/H5
Kaluga Oblast, Rus. 60/H5
Kalundborg, Den. 38/D4
Kalungwishi (riv.), Zam. 105/E2
Kalür Kot, Pak. 86/B3
Kalutara, SrL. 82/C6
Kalyān, India 82/B4
Kalyani, India 85/F4
Kama, D.R. Congo 105/E1
Kama (riv.), Rus. 61/M4
Kama (riv.), Rus. 27/K3
Kamagaya, Japan 77/D2
Kamaishi, Japan 76/B4
Kamakou (peak), Hi, US 124/T10
Kamakura, Japan 77/D3
Kamālia, Pak. 86/B4
Kamalo, D.R. Congo 104/A4
Kāman, India 84/A4
Kaman, Turk. 62/E5

Kamango (lake), Mali 102/E2
Kamanjab, Namb. 105/B4
Kamarang, Guy. 153/F3
Kāmāreddi, India 82/C4
Kāmārhāti, India 82/E3
Kamaria (falls), Guy. 153/G3
Kambalda, Austl. 112/D4
Kambar, Pak. 82/A2
Kambara, Japan 77/B3
Kambia, SLeo. 102/B4
Kambove, D.R. Congo 105/E3
Kambuno (peak), Indo. 81/F4
Kamchatka (pen.), Rus. 67/Q4
Kamchatka Oblast, Rus. 65/R4
Kamchiya (riv.), Bul. 62/C4
Kamen, Ger. 51/E5
Kamen'-na-Obi, Rus. 87/H2
Kamenka, Rus. 63/H1
Kamensk-Shakhtinsky, Rus. 62/G2
Kamensk-Ural'skiy, Rus. 61/P4
Kameoka, Japan 77/J5
Kameyama, Japan 77/K6
Kami (isl.), Japan 77/M6
Kami-koshiki (isl.), Japan 74/A5
Kamiah, Id, US 126/D4
Kamien Pomorski, Pol. 38/F5
Kamieskroon, SAfr. 106/B3
Kamifukuoka, Japan 77/D2
Kamiiso, Japan 76/B3
Kamiishizu, Japan 77/K5
Kamiizumi, Japan 77/C1
Kamikawa, Japan 76/C2
Kamikuishiki, Japan 77/C3
Kamilo (pt.), Hi, US 124/U11
Kamina, D.R. Congo 105/E2
Kaminaka, Japan 77/J5
Kaminoho, Japan 77/K5
Kaminoyama, Japan 75/G1
Kamisato, Japan 77/C1
Kamishak (bay), Ak, US 134/H4
Kamiyahagi, Japan 77/M5
Kamiyaku, Japan 75/L5
Kamla (riv.), India 85/F3
Kamloops, BC, Can. 126/C3
Kammaki, Japan 77/J6
Kamnik, Slov. 43/L3
Kamo, Japan 75/F2
Kamo (riv.), Japan 77/D3
Kamogawa, Japan 77/G3
Kamojima, Japan 74/D3
Kamoke, Pak. 86/C4
Kamp (riv.), Aus. 41/H4
Kamp-Bornhofen, Ger. 53/G3
Kamp-Lintfort, Ger. 50/D5
Kampala (cap.), Ugan. 104/B2
Kampar, Malay. 80/B3
Kampar (riv.), Indo. 80/B3
Kampen, Neth. 50/D3
Kampen, Ger. 38/C4
Kamphaeng Phet, Thai. 78/C5
Kamphaeng Phet (ruin), Thai. 78/C5
Kampinoski NP, Pol. 62/B1
Kampo, SKor. 73/E5
Kampong Kuala Besut, Malay. 80/B2
Kampong Saom (bay), Camb. 80/B1
Kampong Saom, Camb. 80/B1
Kampville, Mo, US 137/F8
Kamsack, Sk, Can. 127/H3
Kamsdorf, Ger. 55/E1
Kamuchawie (lake), Can. 127/H1
Kamui-misaki (cape), Japan 76/B2
Kámuk (mtn.), CR 145/F4
Kamuli, Ugan. 104/B2
Kam'yanets'-Podil's'kyy, Ukr. 63/H2
Kamyshin, Rus. 63/H2
Kanaaupscow (riv.), Qu, Can. 130/G2
Kanab, Ut, US 128/D3
Kanab (riv.), Ut, US 128/D3
Kanaga (isl.), Ak, US 134/C6
Kanairiktok (riv.), Nf, Can. 131/H1
Kanan, D.R. Congo 105/D2
Kananga, D.R. Congo 105/D2
Kanangra-Boyd NP, Austl. 115/C2
Kanash, Mex. 144/D1
Kanawake Ind. Res., Qu, Can. 131/N7
Kanawha (riv.), WV, US 133/H2
Kanazawa, Japan 75/F2
Kanchanaburi, Thai. 78/B3
Kānchenjunga (peak), Nepal 82/E2
Kānchīpuram, India 82/C5

Kangaba, Mali 102/C4
Kangal, Turk. 90/D2
Kangān, Iran 88/F3
Kangan Abor. Land, Austl. 112/C2
Kanganpur, Pak. 86/C4
Kangaroo (isl.), Austl. 109/C4
Kangaroo Island, Austl. 113/G5
Kangasala, Fin. 39/L1
Kangavar, Iran 88/E2
Kangbao, China 71/K3
Kangding, China 70/H5
Kangean (isls.), Indo. 81/E5
Kanggye, NKor. 73/D2
Kanggyŏng, SKor. 73/D4
Kangiqcliniq (Rankin Inlet), NW, Can. 122/G2
Kangiqsualujjuaq, China 70/H3
Kangiqsujuaq, Qu, Can. 123/K3
Kangirsuk, Qu, Can. 123/J2
Kangjin, SKor. 73/D5
Kangmar, China 85/G1
Kangnam (mts.), NKor. 73/C2
Kangnŭng, SKor. 74/A2
Kangping, China 72/E2
Kāngra, India 86/D3
Kangrinboqê (peak), China 70/D5
Kangshan, Tai. 79/D3
Kangto (peak), China 83/F2
Kangwŏn-do (prov.), SKor. 74/A2
Kanha NP, India 84/C4
Kanhān (riv.), India 82/C3
Kani, Japan 77/M5
Kani, Japan 77/L5
Kanie, Japan 77/L5
Kanin (pen.), Rus. 160/C
Kanin Nos (pt.), Rus. 64/E3
Kanina, Austl. 115/B3
Kanjiža, Yugo. 48/E2
Kankakee (riv.), US 130/C3
Kankan (pol. reg.), NZ 109/H7
Kankan, Gui. 102/C4
Kanmuri-yama (peak), Japan 74/C3
Kannapolis, NC, US 133/H3
Kannauj, India 84/B2
Kannon-zaki (pt.), Japan 77/D3
Kannus, Fin. 60/D3
Kano (state), Nga. 103/H4
Kano, Nga. 103/H4
Kan'onji, Japan 74/C3
Kanouse (mtn.), NJ, US 139/H7
Kanoya, Japan 74/B5
Kanra, Japan 77/B1
Kansai (int'l arpt.), Japan 77/H7
Kansai (isl.), Japan 77/H7
Kansas (state), US 125/G4
Kansas (riv.), Ks, US 125/G4
Kansas City, Mo, US 129/J3
Kansas City, Ks, US 137/D5
Kansas City, Mo, US 137/D5
Kansasville, Wi, US 135/P14
Kansŏng, SKor. 73/E3
Kantābānji, India 82/D3
Kānth, India 84/B1
Kantō (prov.), Japan 75/F2
Kantunilkin, Mex. 144/E1
Kanuku (mts.), Guy. 150/G3
Kanuma, Japan 75/F2
Kanti NWR, US 134/H2
Kanye, Bots. 105/E5
Kaohsiung, Tai. 79/D3
Kaohsiung, Tai. 79/D3
Kaokoveld (mts.), Namb. 105/B4
Kaoma, Zam. 105/E3
Kapaahu, Hi, US 124/S9
Kapaau, Hi, US 124/U10
Kapadvanj, India 82/B2
Kapan, Arm. 63/H5
Kapchorwa, Ugan. 104/B2
Kapellen, Belg. 52/C1
Kapenguria, Kenya 104/B2
Kapidaği (pen.), Turk. 49/H5
Kapingamarangi (isl.), Micr. 116/E4
Kapiri Mposhi, Zam. 105/E3
Kapiskau (riv.), On, Can. 123/H3
Kaplice, Czh. 55/H5
Kapos (riv.), Hun. 48/C2
Kaposvár, Hun. 48/C2
Kappl, Aus. 57/G3
Kapsan, NKor. 73/D3
Kapuas (riv.), Indo. 80/C4
Kapuas Hulu (mts.), Indo.,Mal. 80/D3
Kapunda, Austl. 113/H5
Kapūrthala, India 86/C4
Kapuskasing, On, Can. 130/D1
Kaputar (peak), Austl. 115/D1
Kapydzhik (peak), Azer. 63/H5
Kara, Togo 103/F4
Kara (riv.), Rus. 61/N2
Kara (basin), Grld. 123/J3
Kara (sea), Rus. 160/A
Kara Abor. Res., Austl. 112/C2
Kara-saki (pt.), Japan 77/J5
Karabük, Turk. 62/E5
Karabük, Turk. 62/E5
Karaburun, Turk. 49/H5
Karaca (peak), Turk. 90/D2

Karacabey, Turk. 62/D4
Karacaköy, Turk. 49/J5
Karaçal (peak), Turk. 91/C1
Karachay-Cherkessia Aut. Rep., Rus. 63/G4
Karachev, Rus. 62/E1
Karāchi, Pak. 89/J4
Karadere, Turk. 49/K5
Karaginskiy (isl.), Rus. 67/R4
Karaj, Iran 88/F1
Karakax (riv.), China 89/L1
Karakaya (dam), Turk. 90/D2
Karakelong, Indo. 81/G3
Karakhoto (ruin), China 70/H3
Karakol, Kyr. 87/G4
Karakoram (range), India 70/C4
Karakoram (pass), India 86/D2
Karakoro (riv.), Mali 102/C3
Karakorum (ruin), Mong. 70/H2
Karakorum (pass), Mong. 87/G5
Karakorum (pass), China 89/L1
Karaköse, Turk. 63/G5
Karaköy, Turk. 90/C2
Karakul' (lake), Taj. 87/F5
Karakyon (peak), Trkm. 64/F5
Karam (riv.), Indo. 81/E4
Karaman (prov.), Turk. 90/C2
Karaman, Turk. 90/C2
Karamay, China 70/D2
Karamea Bight (bay), NZ 117/H7
Karamoja (prov.), Ugan. 104/B2
Karamürsel, Turk. 49/J5
Karanganem, Indo. 81/E5
Karaninskiy (isl.), Rus. 65/S4
Karaninskiy (bay), Rus. 65/S4
Kārān (riv.), Iran 88/C3
Kāranja, India 82/C3
Karanpur, India 86/B5
Karapınar, Turk. 90/C2
Karas (prov.), Namb. 106/B3
Karasabai, Guy. 153/G3
Karaşar, Turk. 49/L5
Karasu, Turk. 49/K5
Karasu, Rus. 87/F2
Karasuk, Rus. 87/G2
Karataş (lag.), Nic. 145/F3
Karataş, Turk. 91/D1
Karatoya (riv.), Bang. 85/G3
Karatsu, Japan 74/A4
Karauli, India 84/A2
Karaurgan, Turk. 63/G4
Karáva (peak), Gre. 47/G3
Karawang, Indo. 80/C5
Karayazı, Turk. 63/G5
Karazhal, Kaz. 87/F3
Karbalā' (gov.), Iraq 90/E3
Karbalā', Iraq 90/E3
Karben, Ger. 54/B2
Karcag, Hun. 48/E2
Kardhámila, Gre. 47/K3
Kardhitsa, Gre. 47/G3
Kārdlā, Est. 39/J2
Kardritsomagoúla, Gre. 47/G3
Kāshān, Iran 88/F2
Kareli, India 84/B4
Karelia Aut. Rep., Rus. 64/D3
Karera, India 84/B3
Kāresuando, Swe. 37/G1
Karēt (reg.), Mrta. 98/D4
Karf Ash Shaykh (gov.), Sen. 102/B3
Kargil, India 86/D2
Karhal, India 84/B2
Karhijärvi (lake), Fin. 39/H1
Kāria Ba Mohammed, Mor. 100/B2
Kariana, Madg. 107/H8
Kariba (dam), Zam. 105/E4
Kariba, Zim. 105/E4
Kariba (lake), Zim. 93/E6
Kariba-yama (peak), Japan 76/A2
Karībib, Namb. 105/B5
Karimama, Ben. 103/F3
Karīmnagar, India 82/C4
Karimunjawa (isls.), Indo. 80/D5
Karimganj, India 83/F3
Karin, Som. 95/R5
Karīsimbi (vol.), D.R. Congo 104/A3
Karīsimbi (vol.), Rwa. 104/A3
Kāristos, Gre. 47/J3
Kariya, Japan 77/L6
Kariaat (mts.), Alg. 43/M3
Kārkāl, India 82/B5
Karkar (isl.), PNG 116/D5
Karkinits'ka Zatoka (gulf), Ukr. 62/D3
Kārkkila, Fin. 39/L1
Karkonoski NP, Pol. 41/H3
Karla Marksa (peak), Taj. 89/K1
Karlholmsbruk, Swe. 38/G1
Karlı, Turk. 62/E5
Karlino, Pol. 38/G2
Karlovac, Cro. 48/B3
Karlovo, Bul. 47/H1
Karlovy Vary, Czh. 55/F2

Karlsdorf-Neuthard, Ger. 54/B4
Karlsfeld, Ger. 55/E6
Karlshamn, Swe. 38/F3
Karlshuld, Ger. 54/E5
Karlskoga, Swe. 38/F2
Karlskron, Ger. 55/E5
Karlskrona, Swe. 38/F3
Karlstad, Swe. 38/E2
Karlstadt, Ger. 54/C3
Karlstein am Main, Ger. 54/C2
Karluk, Ak, US 134/H4
Karmøla, India 89/L5
Karnali (riv.), Nepal 70/D6
Karnali (zone), Nepal 84/C1
Karnaphuli (res.), Bang. 85/H4
Karnataka (state), India 82/C4
Karnes City, Tx, US 129/H5
Karnobat, Bul. 47/K1
Kärnten (prov.), Aus. 43/K3
Karonga, Malw. 104/B5
Karoo NP, SAfr. 106/D4
Karoo NP, SAfr. 106/C4
Karoonda, Austl. 115/A2
Karor, Pak. 86/A4
Karoso (cape), Indo. 81/E5
Kárpathos, Gre. 90/A3
Kárpathos (isl.), Gre. 90/A3
Karpatskiy NP, Ukr. 49/G1
Karpenision, Gre. 47/G3
Karratha, Austl. 112/C2
Kars, Turk. 63/G4
Kars (prov.), Turk. 63/G4
Karsakuy, Ak, US 134/H4
Kārsämäki, Fin. 60/E3
Karsanti, Turk. 91/C1
Karshi (int'l arpt.), Uzb. 87/E5
Kartaly, Rus. 63/M1
Kartárpur, India 86/C4
Kartuzy, Pol. 38/M4
Karuah, Austl. 115/D2
Karuma (falls), Ugan. 104/A2
Karumba, Austl. 114/A2
Karün (riv.), Iran 88/C3
Karup, Den. 38/C3
Karvinā, Czh. 41/K4
Kārwār, India 82/B5
Karwendel (mts.), Ger. 55/E7
Kás, Den. 38/C3
Kasaan, Ak, US 134/M4
Kasabonika (lake), Can. 127/L2
Kasagi, Japan 77/J6
Kasahara, Japan 77/M5
Kāsai (riv.), India 85/F4
Kasai, Japan 74/D3
Kasai (riv.), D.R. Congo 93/D5
Kasama, Zam. 104/A5
Kasama, Japan 75/G2
Kasamatsu, Japan 77/L5
Kasane, Bots. 105/E4
Kasaoka, Japan 74/C3
Kasar (cape), Sudan 101/D5
Kasba (lake), NW, Can. 122/F2
Kasba Tadla, Mor. 98/D2
Kaseda, Japan 74/B5
Kasese, Ugan. 104/A2
Kashaf (riv.), Iran 89/H1
Kashi, China 89/K1
Kashiba, Japan 77/J6
Kashihara, Japan 77/J6
Kashima, Japan 75/G3
Kashima (bay), Japan 77/F1
Kashin, Rus. 64/D3
Kāshīpur, India 84/B1
Kashiwa, Japan 77/D2
Kashiwazaki, Japan 75/F2
Kāshmar, Iran 89/G1
Kashmir (reg.), India,Pak. 87/G5
Kāshmūnd Ghar (range), Afg. 86/A2
Kasigluk, Ak, US 134/F3
Kasilof, Ak, US 134/H4
Kasiruta (isl.), Indo. 81/H4
Kasiui (isl.), Indo. 81/H4
Kaskaskia (riv.), Il, US 137/D5
Kaslo, BC, Can. 126/E3
Kasongo, D.R. Congo 105/E1
Kásos (isl.), Gre. 90/A3
Kaspiysk, Rus. 64/G3
Kassala, Bul. 49/H6
Kassándra (pen.), Gre. 47/H2
Kassándria, Gre. 47/H2
Kassel, Ger. 51/G6
Kassikaityu (riv.), Guy. 153/G3
Kassler, Co, US 137/B4
Kasson, Mn, US 137/L4
Kastamonu, Turk. 62/E4
Kastélli, Gre. 47/H5
Kastéll Stari, Cro. 48/C4
Kaštel Sućurac, Cro. 48/C4
Kastéllaun, Ger. 53/G3
Kastéllion, Gre. 47/H5
Kasterlee, Belg. 50/C6
Kastl, Ger. 55/F4
Kastoría, Gre. 47/G2
Kastrakíou (lake), Gre. 47/G3
Kastrakíou, Gre. 47/G3

Kasugai, Japan 77/B2
Kasugai, Japan 77/L5
Kasukabe, Japan 75/F3
Kasumiga (lake), Japan 75/G2
Kasungu, Malw. 105/F3
Kasūr, Pak. 86/C4
Kat O Chau (isl.), China 71/V9
Katahdin (mt.), Me, US 131/G2
Katākolon, Gre. 47/G4
Katanga (reg.), China 77/J6
Katanga (pol. reg.), D.R. Congo 105/D2
Katanga, India 84/C4
Katanning, Austl. 112/C5
Katano, Japan 77/J6
Katavi NP, Tanz. 105/F2
Katchall (isl.), India 83/F6
Katerini, Gre. 47/H2
Kates Needle (peak), Ak, US 134/M4
Katete, Zam. 105/F3
Katghora, India 84/D4
Kāthgodām, India 84/B1
Kathiawar (pen.), India 89/K4
Kāthmāndu (cap.), Nepal 85/E2
Kathua, India 86/C3
Kati, Mali 102/C3
Katiola, C.d'Iv. 102/D4
Katlehong, SAfr. 106/E2
Katlenburg-Lindau, Ger. 51/H5
Katmai (vol.), Ak, US 134/H4
Katmai NP, US 134/H4
Kato Akhaïa, Gre. 47/G4
Katokhi, Gre. 47/G3
Katonah, NY, US 139/E1
Katouna, Gre. 47/G3
Katowice, Pol. 41/K3
Katra, India 86/C3
Kātrās, India 85/F4
Katrine (lake), Sc, UK 31/Q8
Katrineholm, Swe. 38/G2
Katsikás, Gre. 47/G3
Katsina (state), Nga. 103/G3
Katsina, Nga. 103/G3
Katsina Ala (riv.), Nga. 103/H5
Katsunuma, Japan 77/B2
Katsura (riv.), Japan 77/J6
Katsuragi, Japan 74/D3
Katsuragi-san (peak), Japan 77/H7
Katsuura, Japan 75/G3
Katsuyama, Japan 74/E2
Katsuyama, Japan 74/C3
Katsuura, Japan 75/G3
Kattakurgan, Uzb. 87/E5
Kattegat (str.), Den. 27/F3
Katumbi, Malw. 104/B5
Katwa, India 85/G4
Katwe-Kabatooro, Ugan. 104/A3
Katwijk aan Zee, Neth. 50/B4
Ke Ga (cape), Viet. 78/E3
Katy, Tx, US 129/J5
Katzenbach (riv.), Ger. 54/B4
Katzhütte, Ger. 54/D1
Katzwinkel, Ger. 53/G2
Kau-ye (isl.), Myan. 78/B4
Kauai (chan.), US 124/S10
Kauai (isl.), US 124/S10
Kaufbeuren, Ger. 57/G2
Kaufering, Ger. 55/E6
Kaufungen, Ger. 51/G6
Kauhola (pt.), Hi, US 124/U10
Kauiki (pt.), Hi, US 124/U10
Kaukauveld (uplands), Namb. 105/C5
Kaukura (isl.), FrPol. 117/L6
Kaulakahi (chan.), US 124/T10
Kaumalapau, Hi, US 124/T10
Kauna (pt.), Hi, US 124/U11
Kaunakakai, Hi, US 124/T10
Kaunas (int'l arpt.), Lith. 39/K4
Kaunas, Lith. 39/K4
Kaunas, Lith. 39/K4
Kaupanger, Nor. 38/N1
Kauttua, Fin. 39/K1
Kavadarci, Macd. 47/H2
Kavajë, Alb. 47/F2
Kāvali, India 82/C5
Kavalerovo, Rus. 71/Q3
Kavaratti, India 82/B5
Kavarna, Bul. 49/J4
Kavgolovskoye (lake), Rus. 64/J4
Kávos, Gre. 47/N8
Kavieng, PNG 116/E4
Kavīr-e Namak (dry lake), Iran 27/C6
Kávlinge, Swe. 38/E4
Kaw (lake), Ok, US 129/H3
Kaw (riv.), Sudan 76/B5
Kawabe, Japan 77/G3
Kāfar Sava, Isr. 91/F7
Kawachi (riv.), Japan 77/L6
Kawachi-nagano, Japan 77/J6
Kawage, Japan 77/L6
Kawagoe, Japan 75/F3
Kawaguchi, Japan 77/D2
Kawaguchiko, Japan 77/B2
Kawaguchi, Japan 77/K5

Kawai, Japan 77/J6
Kawaihoa (pt.), Hi, US 124/R10
Kawaikini (peak), Hi, US 124/S9
Kawakami, Japan 77/J7
Kawamata, Japan 75/G2
Kawambwa, Zam. 104/A5
Kawamoto, Japan 77/C1
Kawanishi, Japan 77/J6
Kawanishi, Japan 77/J6
Kawardha, India 84/C4
Kawartha (lakes), Can. 130/E2
Kawasaki, Japan 75/F3
Kawasato, Japan 77/D1
Kawashima, Japan 77/L5
Kawaue, Japan 77/M4
Kawela (Kawela Bay), Hi, US 124/V12
Kawerau, NZ 117/T10
Kawlin, Myan. 83/G3
Kawthaung, Myan. 78/B4
Kax (pt.), Can. 134/L2
Kaya, SKor. 73/E5
Kaya, India 77/H5
Kaya-san (peak), SKor. 73/D4
Kayadibi, Turk. 62/E5
Kayagangiri (peak), CAfr. 96/J6
Kayah (div.), Myan. 70/G6
Kayah (state), Myan. 83/G4
Kayanga (riv.), Sen. 102/B3
Kaycee, Wy, US 126/G5
Kayenta, Az, US 128/E3
Kayes, Mali 102/C3
Kayes (pol. reg.), Mali 102/C3
Kayin (state), Myan. 83/G4
Kayl, Lux. 53/F5
Kaymaz, Turk. 49/K5
Kaynaşlı, Turk. 49/K5
Kayoa (isl.), Indo. 81/G3
Kayser (mts.), Sur. 153/G4
Kayseri (prov.), Turk. 90/C2
Kaysersberg, Fr. 56/D1
Kaysville, Ut, US 137/K11
Kayuagung, Indo. 80/B4
Kazakh (uplands), Kaz. 64/H5
Kazakhstan (ctry.) 67/E4
Kazan (riv.), NW, Can. 122/F2
Kazan', Rus. 61/L5
Kazan (int'l arpt.), Rus. 61/L5
Kazanci, Turk. 91/C1
Kazanlŭk, Bul. 47/J1
Kazanlük, Bul. 47/J1
Kazanskaya, Rus. 62/C4
Kazanlük (beg.), Geo. 63/H4
Kazimierza Wielka, Pol. 41/L3
Kazincbarcika, Hun. 41/L4
Kâzımkarabekir, Turk. 90/C2
Kazincbarcika, Hun. 41/L4
Kazuno, Japan 76/B3
Kazuno, Japan 76/B3
Ké Macina, Mali 102/D3
Kéa (isl.), Gre. 47/J4
Kéa, Gre. 47/J4
Keaau, Hi, US 124/U11
Keady, NI, UK 34/B3
Keahole (pt.), Hi, US 124/T11
Keanapapa (pt.), Hi, US 124/T10
Keansburg, NJ, US 139/J10
Kearney, Ne, US 129/H2
Kearns, Ut, US 137/K12
Kearny, NJ, US 139/J8
Kearny (pt.), NI, UK 34/C3
Keawakapu, Hi, US 124/T10
Keawekaheka (pt.), Hi, US 124/U11
Keban (dam), Turk. 90/D2
Kebbi (state), Nga. 103/G4
Kébémer, Sen. 102/A3
Kebnekaise (peak), Swe. 37/F2
Kebumen, Indo. 80/C5
Kecel, Hun. 48/D2
Keçiborlu, Turk. 90/B2
Kecskemét, Hun. 48/D2
Kedah (state), Malay. 78/C5
Kédainiai, Lith. 39/K4
Kediri, Indo. 80/D5
Kédougou, Sen. 102/B3
Kędzierzyn-Koźle, Pol. 41/K3
Keego Harbor, Mi, US 135/F6
Keele (riv.), NW, Can. 124/AA12
Keele (mt.), Yk, US 134/M3
Keele (peak), Yk, Can. 122/C2
Keelung, Tai. 79/D2
Keelung, Tai. 75/G8
Keene (mt.), Sc, UK 36/D3
Keene, NH, US 131/F3
Keepit (dam), Austl. 115/D1
Keer-Weer (cape), Austl. 114/A1
Keetmanshoop, Namb. 106/C3
Kefallinía (isl.), Gre. 47/G3
Kefar Sava, Isr. 91/F7
Kefar Vitkin, Isr. 91/F7
Keflavík, Ice. 37/M7
Keflavík (int'l arpt.), Ice. 37/M7
Kehl, Ger. 56/D1
Kehoku, Japan 77/L5
Keighley, Eng, UK 35/G4
Keihoku, Japan 77/J5

Keimoes, SAfr. 106/C3
Kéita (riv.), Chad 97/J6
Keith, Austl. 115/B3
Keith, Sc, UK 36/D1
Kejimkujik NP, Can. 131/H2
Kekaha, Hi, US 124/S10
Kékes (peak), Hun. 41/K5
Kelan, China 72/B3
Kelang (isl.), Indo. 81/G4
Kelang, Malay. 80/B3
Kelberg, Ger. 53/F3
Keles, Turk. 62/D5
Kelheim, Ger. 55/E5
Kelkheim, Ger. 54/B2
Kelkıt (riv.), Turk. 90/D1
Kelkit, Turk. 62/F4
Kell, Ger. 53/F4
Kellenhusen, Ger. 38/D4
Keller (peak), Ca, US 136/C2
Keller (lake), NW, Can. 122/D2
Kellerberrin, Austl. 112/C4
Kellogg, Id, US 126/D4
Kells, NI, UK 34/B2
Kélo, Chad 96/J6
Kelowna, BC, Can. 126/D3
Kelsey (pt.), Eng, UK 32/A6
Kelso, Wa, US 126/C4
Kelso, Sc, UK 36/D5
Kelsterbach, Ger. 54/B2
Keluang, Malay. 80/B3
Kelvington, Sk, Can. 127/H2
Kem' (riv.), Rus. 64/D3
Kem', Rus. 60/G2
Kemah, Turk. 62/F5
Kemaliye, Turk. 90/D2
Kemalpaşa, Turk. 63/G4
Kemasik, Malay. 80/B3
Kematen an der Ybbs, Aus. 55/H6
Kematen in Tirol, Aus. 57/H3
Kembs, Fr. 56/D2
Kemecse, Hun. 41/L4
Kemena (riv.), Malay. 80/D3
Kemence, Hun. 41/K4
Kemer (dam), Turk. 90/B2
Kemer, Turk. 91/B1
Kemerhisar, Turk. 90/C2
Kemerovo, Rus. 64/J4
Kemi, Fin. 64/C3
Kemijärvi, Fin. 60/E2
Kemijoki (riv.), Fin. 37/H2
Kemmerer, Wy, US 126/F5
Kemnath, Ger. 55/E3
Kemnay, Sc, UK 36/D2
Kemp (lake), Tx, US 129/H4
Kempele, Fin. 60/E2
Kempen, Ger. 50/D6
Kempenich, Ger. 53/G3
Kempenland (phys. reg.), Belg. 50/C6
Kempisch Kanaal (canal), Belg. 53/E1
Kempsey, Austl. 115/E1
Kempston, Eng, UK 33/F2
Kempt (res.), Can. 130/F2
Kempten, Ger. 57/G2
Kempton, Austl. 115/C4
Kempton Park, SAfr. 106/Q13
Kemptown, Md, US 138/A5
Kemri, India 84/B1
Kemul (peak), Indo. 81/E3
Ken (riv.), India 84/C3
Ken (lake), Sc, UK 34/D1
Ken-zaki (pt.), Japan 77/D3
Kenadsa, Alg. 99/E3
Kenai, Ak, US 134/H3
Kenai Fjords NP, Ak, US 134/H4
Kenai NWR, US 134/H3
Kendal, Eng, UK 35/F3
Kendalia, Tx, US 137/T20
Kendall, Austl. 115/E1
Kendall, Fl, US 133/H5
Kendall (co.), Tx, US 137/T20
Kendall (co.), Il, US 135/P16
Kendall Park, NJ, US 138/D3
Kendallville, In, US 130/C3
Kendari, Indo. 81/F4
Kéndavros, Gre. 47/J2
Kendel (riv.), Ger. 50/D5
Kendrāpāra, India 82/E3
Kénédougou (prov.), Burk. 102/D4
Kenema, SLeo. 102/C5
Kenge, D.R. Congo 105/C1
Kenhardt, SAfr. 106/C3
Kenhorst, Pa, US 138/C3
Kenié-Baoulé, Réserve de, Mali 102/C3
Kenilworth, Eng, UK 33/E2
Kenilworth, NJ, US 139/H9
Kénitra (prov.), Mor. 100/A2
Kénitra, Mor. 100/A2
Kenli, China 72/D3
Kenmare, ND, US 127/H3
Kenmare, Ire. 31/P11
Kenmore, NY, US 131/S10
Kenmore, Wa, US 135/C2
Kenn (reef), Austl. 109/E3
Kenn, Ger. 53/F4
Kennebec (riv.), Me, US 131/G2
Kennebunk, Me, US 131/G3
Kennedy (chan.), NW, Can. 123/T6
Kennedy (range), Austl. 112/B3
Kennedy Entrance (chan.) 134/H4
Kennedyville, Md, US 138/C5
Kennelbach, Aus. 57/F3
Kennemerduinen, NP de, Neth. 50/B4
Kenner, La, US 137/P17
Kennet (riv.), Eng, UK 33/E4
Kennet and Avon (canal), Eng, UK 32/D4
Kenneth, Ks, US 137/D6
Kennett, Mo, US 129/K3
Kennett Square, Pa, US 138/C4
Kennewick, Wa, US 126/D4
Keno Hill, Yk, Can. 134/L3
Kenogami (riv.), On, Can. 123/H3
Kenora, On, Can. 127/K3
Kenosha (co.), Wi, US 135/P14
Kensico (res.), NY, US 139/K7
Kensington and Chelsea (bor.), Eng, UK 30/A1
Kent, Wa, US 126/C4
Kent, Oh, US 130/D3
Kent (pt.), Md, US 138/B6
Kent (pen.), NW, Can. 122/F2
Kent (isl.), Md, US 138/B6
Kent (lake), Mi, US 135/E7
Kent (co.), On, Can. 135/G6
Kent (riv.), Eng, UK 35/F3
Kent County (int'l arpt.), Mi, US 130/C3
Kent Group (isls.), Austl. 115/C3
Kentaū, Kaz. 87/E4
Kenton, Oh, US 130/D3
Kenton, De, US 138/C5
Kentucky (riv.), Ky, US 130/C4
Kentucky (state), US 125/J4
Kentucky (lake), Ky, US 125/J4
Kentville, NS, Can. 131/H2
Kenya (ctry.) 93/F4
Kenzingen, Ger. 56/D1
Keonjhar, India 82/E3
Kep i Gjuhëzës (cape), Alb. 47/F2
Kep i Rodonit (cape), Alb. 47/F2
Kępno, Pol. 41/J3
Keppel Sands, Austl. 114/C3
Kerala (state), India 82/C5
Kéran, PN de la, Togo 103/F4
Kerang, Austl. 115/B2
Keratéa, Gre. 47/N9
Kerava, Fin. 39/L1
Kerch' (str.), Rus.,Ukr. 62/F3
Kerch, Ukr. 62/F3
Keremeos, BC, Can. 126/D3
Kerempe (pt.), Turk. 62/E4
Kerempe Burnu (cape), Turk. 90/C1
Keren, Erit. 88/C5
Kerepestarcsa, Hun. 49/R9
Keret' (lake), Rus. 37/K2
Kerguélen (isl.), Fr. 23/N8
Kericho, Kenya 104/B3
Kerikeri (cape), NZ 117/S9
Kerinci (peak), Indo. 80/B4
Kerio (riv.), Kenya 104/C2
Kerio Valley Nat'l Rsv., Kenya 104/B2
Kerkdriel, Neth. 50/C5
Kerken, Ger. 50/D6
Kerki, Trkm. 87/E5
Kerkínis (lake), Gre. 47/H2
Kérkira, Gre. 47/F3
Kerkrade, Neth. 53/F2
Kerkwijk, Neth. 50/C5
Kermadec (isls.), NZ 116/G8
Kermān, Iran 89/G2
Kern (riv.), Ca, US 128/C4
Kern, South Kern (riv.), Ca, US 128/C4
Kerns, Swi. 57/E4
Kéros (isl.), Gre. 47/J4
Kérou, Ben. 103/F4
Kerr (lake), Ok, US 129/J4
Kerr (res.), US 130/E4
Kerrobert, Sk, Can. 126/F3
Kerrville, Tx, US 129/H5
Kert (riv.), Mor. 100/C2
Kerulen (riv.), Mong. 67/L5
Kerzaz, Alg. 99/E3
Kerzenheim, Ger. 53/H4
Kerzers, Swi. 56/D4
Kesagami (riv.), Can. 130/D1
Keşan, Turk. 47/K2
Kesch (peak), Swi. 57/F4
Kesen'numa, Japan 76/B4
Keshan, China 71/N2
Keshod, India 82/B3
Keski-Suomi (prov.), Fin. 37/H3
Keskin, Turk. 62/E5
Kesselbach (riv.), Ger. 54/D5
Kestel, Turk. 62/D4
Kesteren, Neth. 50/C5
Keszthely, Hun. 48/C2
Ket' (riv.), Rus. 64/J4
Keta, Gha. 103/F5
Keta (riv.), Rus. 64/K3
Ketchikan, Ak, US 134/M4
Kete Krachi, Gha. 103/E5
Ketelmeer (lake), Neth. 50/C3
Kétou, Ben. 103/F5
Kętrzyn, Pol. 39/J4
Ketsch, Ger. 54/B4
Kettering, Eng, UK 33/F2
Kettle (riv.), Mn, US 126/D3
Kettle Moraine State Forest, Wi, US 135/P14
Ketzin, Ger. 40/P7
Keukenhof, Neth. 50/B4
Kevelaer, Ger. 50/D5
Kewaunee, Wi, US 130/C2
Keweenaw (pen.), Mi, US 127/L4
Keweenaw (pt.), Mi, US 127/M4
Keweenaw (bay), Mi, US 127/L4
Key Largo, Fl, US 133/H5
Key West, Fl, US 133/H5
Keymar, Md, US 138/A4
Keyport, NJ, US 139/J10
Keyport, Wa, US 135/B2
Keystone (lake), Ok, US 129/H3
Kežmarok, Slvk. 41/L4
Khaanziir (cape), Som. 97/Q5
Khabarovsk, Rus. 71/Q2
Khabarovsk Kray, Rus. 65/P4
Khagaria, India 85/F3
Khair, India 84/A2
Khairābād, India 84/C2
Khairpur, Pak. 86/B5
Khairpur, Pak. 89/J3
Khalābat, Pak. 86/B2
Khalándrion, Gre. 47/N8
Khalīj al Hammāmāt (gulf), Tun. 46/B4
Khalīlābād, India 84/D2
Khalkhāl, Iran 88/E1
Khalkhidhikhi (pen.), Gre. 47/H2
Khalkidhón, Gre. 47/H2
Khalkís, Gre. 47/H3
Khamar-Daban (mts.), Rus. 70/H1
Khambhāliya, India 89/J4
Khambhat, India 89/K4
Khamīs Mushayţ, SAr. 88/D5
Khammam, India 82/D4
Khamr, Yem. 88/D5
Khān Yūnus, Gaza 91/D4
Khānābād, Afg. 89/J1
Khānaqīn, Iraq 90/F3
Khandwa, India 89/L4
Khanem (well), Alg. 99/F3
Khānewāl, Pak. 86/A4
Khāngāh Dogrān, Pak. 86/B4
Khāngarh, Pak. 86/A5
Khaniá, Gre. 47/J5
Khanka (lake), China,Rus 67/N5
Khanna, India 86/D4
Khānpur, Pak. 86/A5
Khanty-Mansiysk, Rus. 64/G3
Khao Chamao-Khao Wong NP, Thai. 78/C3
Khao Khitchakut NP, Thai. 78/C3
Khao Laem (res.), Thai. 83/G4
Khao Sam Roi Yot NP, Thai. 78/B3
Khao Yai NP, Thai. 78/C3
Kharagpur, India 85/F4
Kharagpur, India 85/F3
Kharak, Pak. 86/A3
Khārān, Pak. 89/J3
Kharar, India 85/F4
Kharar, India 86/D4
Kharbatā, Isr. 91/G8
Khargon, India 89/L4
Khāriān, Pak. 86/B3
Kharkiv (int'l arpt.), Ukr. 62/F2
Kharkiv, Ukr. 62/F2
Kharkivs'ka (obl.), Ukr. 62/F2
Kharmanli, Bul. 47/J2
Kharovsk, Rus. 60/J4
Kharrour (riv.), Mor. 100/B2
Kharsia, India 84/D5
Khartoum (Kharţūm) (cap.), Sudan 88/B5
Khasavyurt, Rus. 63/H4
Khāsh (riv.), Afg. 89/H2
Khashuri, Geo. 63/G4
Khasi (hills), India 85/H3
Khaskovo (pol. reg.), Bul. 47/J2
Khaskovo (prov.), Bul. 49/G5
Khatanga (riv.), Rus. 160/Z
Khatanga (gulf), Rus. 65/L2
Khatauli, India 86/D5
Khātegaon, India 84/A4
Khatīma, India 84/B1
Khatlon (obl.), Taj. 87/E5
Khatmia (pass), Egypt 91/C4
Khātra, India 85/F4
Khatt Atoui (riv.), Mrta. 96/B3
Khaur, Pak. 86/B3
Khaybar (pass), Afg. 86/A2
Khazzān Dūkān (res.), Iraq 90/F3
Khazzān Jabal Al Awliyā (dam), Sudan 97/M4
Khekra, India 86/D5
Khemis el Khechna, Alg. 100/G4
Khemis Miliana, Alg. 100/G4
Khémisset (prov.), Mor. 100/A3
Khémisset, Mor. 100/A3
Khenchela (prov.), Alg. 99/G2
Khenchela, Alg. 100/K7
Khénifra, Mor. 98/D2
Khepoyarvi (lake), Rus. 61/T6
Kheri, India 84/C2
Khersān (riv.), Iran 88/F2
Kherson, Ukr. 49/L2
Kherson (int'l arpt.), Ukr. 49/L2
Khersons'ka (obl.), Ukr. 62/E3
Khilok, Rus. 71/K1
Khimki, Rus. 61/W9
Khíos, Gre. 47/K3
Khíos (isl.), Gre. 62/C5
Khirpai, India 85/F4
Khisarya, Bul. 47/J1
Khiva, Uzb. 87/D4
Khlebarovo, Bul. 49/H4
Khmel'nyts'ka (obl.), Ukr. 62/C2
Khmel'nytskyy, Ukr. 62/C2
Kho Sawai (plat.), Thai. 83/H4
Khodzheyli, Uzb. 87/C4
Khojak (pass), Pak. 89/J2
Kholm, Afg. 89/J1
Kholmsk, Rus. 71/R2
Khomeynīshahr, Iran 88/F2
Khon Kaen, Thai. 78/C2
Khopër (riv.), Rus. 64/E4
Khor (riv.), Rus. 65/P5
Khóra Sfakíon, Gre. 47/J5
Khorazm (pol. reg.), Uzb. 87/D4
Khoríon, Gre. 90/A2
Khorramābād, Iran 88/E2
Khorramshahr, Iran 88/E2
Khorugh, Taj. 89/K1
Khotol (mtn.), Ak, US 134/G3
Khouribga, Mor. 98/D2
Khowai, India 83/F3
Khrisoúpolis, Gre. 47/J2
Khromtaū, Kaz. 63/L2
Khrysi (isl.), Gre. 47/J5
Khuan Ubon Ratana (lake), Thai. 78/C2
Khudiān, Pak. 86/C4
Khuis, Bots. 106/C2
Khujand, Taj. 87/E4
Khulna (pol. div.), Bang. 85/G4
Khūnjerāb (pass), Pak. 89/L1
Khunjerab NP, Pak. 87/G5
Khunti, India 85/E4
Khurai, India 84/B3
Khurda, India 82/E3
Khurja, India 84/A1
Khushāb, Pak. 86/B3
Khust, Ukr. 41/M4
Khūtār, India 84/C1
Khuzdār, Pak. 89/J3
Khvalynka, Rus. 71/P3
Khvonsār, Iran 88/F2
Khvor, Iran 89/G2
Khvoy, Iran 63/H5
Khwaja Rawash (int'l arpt.), Afg. 87/E6
Khyber (pass), Pak. 86/A2
Kia, Sol. 116/E5
Kiama, Austl. 115/D2
Kiamichi (mts.), Ok, US 132/E3
Kiana, Ak, US 134/F2
Kibæk, Den. 38/C3
Kibali (riv.), D.R. Congo 104/A2
Kibergneset (pt.), Nor. 37/J1
Kibo (Kilimanjaro) (peak), Tanz. 104/C3
Kiboga, Ugan. 104/A2
Kıbrısçık, Turk. 49/K5
Kibwezi, Kenya 104/C3
Kičevo, Macd. 47/G2
Kichha, India 84/B1
Kickapoo, Ks, US 137/D5
Kidal, Mali 103/F2
Kidal (pol. reg.), Mali 103/F2
Kidapawan, Phil. 81/G2
Kidderminster, Eng, UK 32/D2
Kidepo Valley NP, Ugan. 97/M7
Kidsgrove, Eng, UK 35/F5
Kiel (bay), Den. 37/D5
Kiel, Ger. 38/D4
Kielce, Pol. 41/L3
Kielder (res.), Eng, UK 35/F1
Kien An, Viet. 78/D1
Kierspe, Ger. 53/G1
Kiev (Kyyiv) (cap.), Ukr. 62/D2
Kiffa, Mrta. 102/C2
Kifisiá, Gre. 47/N8
Kigali (cap.), Rwa. 104/A3
Kigali (Gregoire Kayibanda) (int'l arpt.), Rwa. 104/A3
Kiği, Turk. 90/E2
Kigoma (pol. reg.), Tanz. 104/A4
Kigoma, Tanz. 104/A4
Kigye, SKor. 73/E4
Kihei, Hi, US 124/T10
Kihnu (isl.), Est. 39/L2
Kiholo, Hi, US 124/U11
Kihti (str.), Fin. 39/J1
Kii (chan.), Japan 74/D4
Kii (mts.), Japan 74/D4
Kijang, SKor. 73/E5
Kikai (isl.), Japan 75/L6
Kikepa (pt.), Hi, US 124/R9
Kikiktat (mtn.), Ak, US 134/H2
Kikinda, Yugo. 48/E3
Kikonai, Japan 76/B3
Kikwit, D.R. Congo 105/C2
Kil, Swe. 38/E2
Kilafors, Swe. 38/G1
Kilauea, Hi, US 124/S9
Kilbarchan, Sc, UK 36/B5
Kilberry, Ire. 31/Q10
Kilbirnie, Sc, UK 36/B5
Kilbrannan (sound), Sc, UK 36/A5
Kilchoan, Sc, UK 31/Q8
Kilchu, NKor. 73/E2
Kilcoole, Ire. 34/B5
Kilcormac, Ire. 31/Q10
Kilcoy, Austl. 114/D4
Kildare, Ire. 31/Q10
Kildeer, Il, US 135/P15
Kil'den (isl.), Rus. 60/G1
Kilembe Estates, Ugan. 104/A2
Kilgarvan, Ire. 31/P11
Kilgore, Tx, US 129/J4
Kilian (isl.), NW, Can. 122/E1
Kilifi, Kenya 104/C3
Kilimanjaro (pol. reg.), Tanz. 104/C3
Kilimanjaro (int'l arpt.), Tanz. 104/C3
Kilimanjaro NP, Tanz. 104/C3
Kilimli, Turk. 49/K5
Kilinochchi, SrL. 82/D6
Kilis, Turk. 91/E1
Kiliya, Ukr. 49/J3
Kilkee, Ire. 31/P10
Kilkeel, NI, UK 34/B3
Kilkenny, Ire. 31/Q10
Kilkenny (co.), Ire. 34/A6
Kilkís, Gre. 47/H2
Kilkivan, Austl. 114/D4
Kill, Ire. 31/Q10
Kill Van Kull (riv.), NJ,NY, US 139/J9
Killam, Ab, Can. 126/F2
Killarney, Austl. 115/E1
Killarney, Mb, Can. 127/J3
Killarney, Ire. 31/P10
Killarney NP, Ire. 31/P10
Killdeer, ND, US 127/H4
Killearn, Sc, UK 36/B4
Killeen, Tx, US 129/H5
Killenaule, Ire. 31/Q10
Killiecrankie, Pass of (pass), Sc, UK 36/C3
Killin, Sc, UK 36/B4
Killinchy, NI, UK 34/C3
Killinek (isl.), NW, Can. 123/K2
Killíni (peak), Gre. 47/H4
Killíni, Gre. 47/G4
Killough, NI, UK 34/C3
Killybegs, Ire. 31/P9
Killyclogher, NI, UK 34/A2
Killyleagh, NI, UK 34/C3
Kilmacanogue, Ire. 34/B5
Kilmacolm, Sc, UK 36/B5
Kilmacow, Ire. 31/Q10
Kilmallock, Ire. 31/P10
Kilmar Tor (hill), Eng, UK 32/B5
Kilmarnock, Sc, UK 36/B5
Kilmaurs, Sc, UK 36/B5
Kilmichael (pt.), Ire. 34/B6
Kilmore, Austl. 115/C3
Kilmore Quay, Ire. 31/Q10
Kilombero (riv.), Tanz. 104/C5
Kilosa, Tanz. 104/C4
Kilraghts, NI, UK 34/B1
Kilrea, NI, UK 34/B2
Kilrush, Ire. 31/P10
Kilsyth, Sc, UK 36/B5
Kilwa Kivinje, Tanz. 104/C5
Kilwinning, Sc, UK 36/B5
Kimba, Austl. 113/H5
Kimball, SD, US 127/J5
Kimbe, PNG 116/E5
Kimberley, BC, Can. 126/E3
Kimberley (plat.), Austl. 109/B2
Kimberley, SAfr. 106/D3
Kimberley (cape), Austl. 114/B2
Kimch'aek, NKor. 73/E2
Kimch'ŏn, SKor. 73/E4
Kimhae, SKor. 74/A3
Kimhae (int'l arpt.), SKor. 74/A3
Kími, Gre. 47/J3
Kímina, Gre. 47/H2
Kimitsu, Japan 75/F3
Kimje, SKor. 73/D5
Kimméria, Gre. 47/J2
Kímolos (isl.), Gre. 47/J4
Kimovsk, Rus. 62/F1
Kimp'o, SKor. 73/F6
Kimp'o (int'l arpt.), SKor. 73/F6
Kimpō-zan (peak), Japan 77/B2
Kimry, Rus. 60/H4
Kinabalu (peak), Malay. 81/E2
Kinabatangan (riv.), Malay. 81/E2
Kinango, Kenya 104/C4
Kinbasket (lake), Can. 126/D2
Kinbrace, Sc, UK 31/S7
Kincaid, Sk, Can. 126/G3
Kincardine, On, Can. 130/D2
Kincardine, Sc, UK 36/C4
Kinchega NP, Austl. 115/B2
Kinder Scout (peak), Eng, UK 35/G5
Kindersley, Sk, Can. 126/F3
Kindia, Gui. 102/B4
Kindia (pol. reg.), Gui. 102/B4
Kinding, Ger. 55/E5
Kindsbach, Ger. 53/G5
Kindu, D.R. Congo 105/E1
Kinel', Rus. 63/J1
Kineshma, Rus. 60/J4
King (peak), Can. 134/K3
King (isl.), BC, Can. 126/B2
King (sound), Austl. 109/B2
King (lake), Austl. 109/A4
King (mt.), Can. 134/N4
King (mt.), Austl. 114/B4
King (isl.), NZ 109/H6
King (co.), Wa, US 135/D2
King Christian (isl.), NW, Can. 123/R7
King Christian IX Land (reg.), Grld. 119/P3
King Christian X Land (reg.), Grld. 119/Q2
King City, Ca, US 128/B3
King Cove, Ak, US 134/F4
King Frederik VI Coast (reg.), Grld. 119/N3
King Frederik VIII Land (reg.), Grld. 119/Q2
King George (isls.), FrPol. 117/L6
King George Is. (isls.), Qu, Can. 123/J3
King George's (res.), Eng, UK 30/C2
King Leopold (ranges), Austl. 109/B2
King of Prussia, Pa, US 138/C3
King Salmon, Ak, US 134/G4
King William (isl.), NW, Can. 122/G2
King William's Town, SAfr. 106/D4
Kingaroy, Austl. 114/C4
Kingfisher, Ok, US 129/H4
Kingfisher (co.), Ok, US 137/M14
Kinghorn, Sc, UK 36/C4
Kinglake NP, Austl. 115/C3
Kinglake NP, Austl. 115/G5
Kingman, Ks, US 129/H3
Kingman, Az, US 128/D4
Kingman (reef), Pac., US 117/J4
Kings (peak), Ut, US 128/E2
Kings (riv.), Ca, US 128/C3
Kings (co.), NY, US 139/K9
Kings Canyon NP, Ca, US 128/C3
Kings Langley, Eng, UK 30/B1
King's Lynn, Eng, UK 33/G1
Kings Park, Austl. 112/K6
Kings Point, NY, US 139/L8
King's Seat (hill), Sc, UK 36/C4
Kingsbridge, Eng, UK 32/C6
Kingscote, Austl. 113/H5
Kingscourt, Ire. 31/Q10
Kingsford, Mi, US 130/B2
Kingsport, Tn, US 130/D4
Kingston, Austl. 115/C4
Kingston, On, Can. 130/E2
Kingston, NY, US 130/F3
Kingston, Austl. 116/F7
Kingston (cap.), Jam. 145/G2
Kingston, Pa, US 138/C1
Kingston, Wa, US 135/B2
Kingston S.E., Austl. 115/A3
Kingston upon Hull, Eng, UK 35/H4
Kingston upon Thames, Eng, UK 30/C2
Kingston Upon Thames (bor.), Eng, UK 30/C2
Kingstown (cap.), StV. 141/N9
Kingstree, SC, US 133/J3
Kingsville, Tx, US 132/D5
Kingsville, Md, US 138/B5
Kingswood, Eng, UK 32/D4
Kingussie, Sc, UK 36/B2
Kınık, Turk. 62/C5
Kinkaid (mt.), Ak, US 134/L4
Kinkala, Congo 105/B1
Kinki (prov.), Japan 74/D3
Kinlochewe, Sc, UK 36/A1
Kinlochleven, Sc, UK 36/B3
Kinloss, Sc, UK 36/C1
Kinna, Swe. 38/E3
Kinnairds (pt.), Sc, UK 36/D1
Kinnelon, NJ, US 139/H8
Kinnelon (lake), NJ, US 139/H8
Kinnitty, Ire. 31/Q10
Kino (riv.), Japan 74/D3
Kinoje (riv.), Can. 130/D1
Kinomoto, Japan 77/K5
Kinrooi, Belg. 53/E1
Kinross, Sc, UK 36/C4
Kinsach (riv.), Ger. 55/F4
Kinsale, Ire. 31/P11
Kinsarvik, Nor. 38/B1
Kinshasa (cap.), D.R. Congo 105/C1
Kinston, NC, US 133/J3
Kintampo, Gha. 103/E4
Kintnersville, Pa, US 138/C2
Kintore, Sc, UK 36/D2
Kintyre (isl.), Sc, UK 31/R8
Kintzheim, Fr. 56/D1
Kinu (riv.), Japan 75/F2
Kinvarra, Ire. 31/P10
Kinyeti (peak), Sudan 97/M7
Kinzig (riv.), Ger. 40/E4
Kipahulu, Hi, US 124/T10
Kiparissía (gulf), Gre. 47/G4
Kiparissía, Gre. 47/G4
Kipawa (lake), Can. 130/E2
Kipkarren (riv.), Kenya 104/B2
Kipling, Sk, Can. 127/H3
Kipnuk, Ak, US 134/F4
Kippel, Swi. 56/D5
Kippen, Sc, UK 36/B4
Kippure (peak), Ire. 34/B5
Kipushi, D.R. Congo 105/E3
Kira, Japan 77/M6
Kira Panayía (isl.), Gre. 47/H3
Kirakira, Sol. 116/F6
Kiranomena, Madg. 107/H7
Kīratpur, India 84/B1
Kirazlı, Turk. 47/K2
Kirby, Tx, US 137/U21
Kırcasalih, Turk. 47/K2
Kirchberg, Swi. 56/D3
Kirchberg, Swi. 57/F3
Kirchberg, Ger. 53/G4
Kirchberg, Ger. 55/F1
Kirchberg an der Iller, Ger. 57/G1
Kirchberg an der Jagst, Ger. 54/C4
Kirchdorf, Ger. 51/F3
Kirchdorf an der Krems, Aus. 55/H7
Kirchenlamitz, Ger. 55/E2
Kirchenthumbach, Ger. 55/E3
Kirchheim, Ger. 57/G1
Kirchheim bei München, Ger. 55/E6
Kirchheim unter Teck, Ger. 54/C5
Kirchheimbolanden, Ger. 54/B3
Kirchhundem, Ger. 51/F6
Kirchlengern, Ger. 51/F4
Kirchlinteln, Ger. 51/G3
Kirchsee (lake), Ger. 57/H2
Kirchseeon, Ger. 55/E6
Kirchweidach, Ger. 55/F6
Kirchzarten, Ger. 56/D2
Kirchzell, Ger. 54/C3
Kircudbright (bay), Sc, UK 34/D2
Kirensk, Rus. 65/L4
Kirgiz Steppe (upland), Kaz. 64/F5
Kirgizskiy (mts.), Kyr. 70/B3
Kiriákion, Gre. 47/H3
Kiribati (ctry.) 116/H5
Kırık, Turk. 63/G4
Kırıkhan, Turk. 91/E1
Kirikkale (prov.), Turk. 90/C2
Kırıkkale, Turk. 62/E5
Kirishi, Rus. 39/Q2
Kirishima-Yaku NP, Japan 74/B5
Kirishima-yama (peak), Japan 74/B5
Kiritimati (Christmas) (isl.), Kiri. 117/K4
Kırkağaç, Turk. 62/C5
Kirkby, Eng, UK 35/F5
Kirkby in Ashfield, Eng, UK 35/G5
Kirkcaldy, Sc, UK 36/C4
Kirkconnel, Sc, UK 36/C6
Kirkcudbright, Sc, UK 34/D2
Kirkee, India 89/K5
Kirkenær, Nor. 38/E1
Kirkintilloch, Sc, UK 36/B5
Kirkkonummi (Kyrkslätt), Fin. 39/L1
Kirkland, Qu, Can. 131/N7
Kirkland (hill), Sc, UK 36/C6
Kirkland Lake, On, Can. 130/D1
Kırklar (peak), Turk. 62/C5
Kırklareli, Turk. 49/H5
Kirklareli (prov.), Turk. 62/C4
Kirkliston, Sc, UK 36/C5
Kirkstone (pass), Eng, UK 35/F3
Kirkūk, Iraq 90/F3
Kirkwall, Sc, UK 31/V14
Kirkwood, SAfr. 106/D4
Kirkwood, De, US 138/C4
Kirn, Ger. 53/G4
Kirov, Rus. 62/E1
Kirov, Rus. 61/L4
Kirov Oblast, Rus. 61/L4
Kirovo-Chepetsk, Rus. 61/L4
Kirovohrad, Ukr. 62/E2
Kirovohrads'ka (obl.), Ukr. 62/D2
Kirovsk, Rus. 60/G2
Kirriemuir, Sc, UK 36/D3
Kirrweiler, Ger. 54/B4
Kirsanov, Rus. 63/G1
Kirşehir (prov.), Turk. 90/C2
Kırşehir, Turk. 62/E5
Kiruna, Swe. 37/G2
Kiryū, Japan 75/F2
Kisa, Swe. 38/F3
Kisai, Japan 77/D1
Kisakata, Japan 76/A4
Kisangani, D.R. Congo 97/L7
Kisarazu, Japan 75/F3
Kisber, Hun. 41/K5
Kisei, Japan 77/K7
Kiselevsk, Rus. 64/J4
Kishanganj, India 85/F2
Kishangarh, India 89/K3
Kishiwada, Japan 77/H7
Kishorganj, Bang. 85/H3
Kishtwar, India 86/C3
Kishwaukee (riv.), Il, US 135/N15
Kisigo (riv.), Tanz. 104/B4
Kisii, Kenya 104/B3
Kiska (vol.), Ak, US 134/B5
Kiska (isl.), Ak, US 65/T4
Kiskatinnaw (riv.), Can. 126/C2
Kiskitto (lake), Can. 127/J2
Kiskőrös, Hun. 48/D2
Kiskunfélegyháza, Hun. 48/D2
Kiskunhalas, Hun. 48/D2
Kiskunmajsa, Hun. 48/D2
Kiskunsági Nemzeti NP, Hun. 48/D2
Kislovodsk, Rus. 63/G4
Kismaayo (Chisimayu), Som. 97/P8
Kiso (riv.), Japan 75/E3
Kisogawa, Japan 77/L5
Kisozaki, Japan 77/L5
Kíssamos, Gre. 47/H5
Kissimmee (lake), Fl, US 133/H4
Kissimmee, Fl, US 133/H4
Kissing, Ger. 54/D6
Kississing (lake), Can. 127/H2
Kisslegg, Ger. 57/F2
Kist, Ger. 54/C3
Kisújszállás, Hun. 48/E2
Kisumu, Kenya 104/B3
Kisvárda, Hun. 41/M4
Kita, Mali 102/C3
Kita (lake), Japan 75/G2
Kita-ibaraki, Japan 75/G2
Kitaaiki, Japan 77/B1
Kitadaitō (isl.), Japan 75/L8
Kitagata, Japan 77/L5
Kitakami (mts.), Japan 76/B4
Kitakami (riv.), Japan 76/B4
Kitakami, Japan 76/B4
Kitakata, Japan 75/F2
Kitakawabe, Japan 77/D1
Kitakyūshū, Japan 74/B4
Kitale, Kenya 104/B2
Kitami, Japan 76/C2
Kitamimaki, Japan 77/A1
Kitamoto, Japan 77/D1
Kitan (str.), Japan 77/G7
Kitangiri (lake), Tanz. 104/B4
Kitaura, Japan 77/F1
Kitchener, On, Can. 130/D3
Kitgum, Ugan. 104/B2
Kíthira, Gre. 47/H4
Kíthira (isl.), Gre. 47/H4
Kíthnos, Gre. 47/J4
Kíthnos (isl.), Gre. 47/J4
Kitimat Arm (lake), BC, Can. 126/A2
Kitsap (co.), Wa, US 135/B3
Kittatinny (mts.), NJ, US 138/C1
Kittery, Me, US 131/G3
Kittredge, Co, US 137/B3
Kitui, Kenya 104/C3
Kitumbeine (peak), Tanz. 104/C3
Kitwe, Zam. 105/E3
Kitzbühel, Aus. 43/K3
Kitzingen, Ger. 54/D3
Kiunga Marine Nat'l Rsv., Kenya 104/D3
Kiuruvesi, Fin. 60/E3
Kiuyu (pt.), Tanz. 104/C4
Kivalina, Ak, US 134/F2
Kivalo (mts.), Fin. 37/H2
Kivijärvi (lake), Fin. 39/M1
Kiviõli, Est. 39/M2
Kivu (lake), D.R. Congo 93/E5
Kıyıköy, Turk. 49/J5
Kiyokawa, Japan 77/C3
Kiyosu, Japan 77/L5
Kizel, Rus. 61/N4
Kizil (riv.), China 64/H6
Kızılcadağ, Turk. 91/A1
Kızılcahamam, Turk. 62/E4
Kızıldag NP, Turk. 90/B2
Kızılhisar, Turk. 90/B2
Kızılırmak (riv.), Turk. 62/E4
Kızıltepe, Turk. 90/E2
Kızılyaka, Turk. 91/C1
Kizlyar, Rus. 63/H4
Kizu (riv.), Japan 74/E3
Kizu, Japan 77/J6
Kizukuri, Japan 76/B3
Kjerkestinden (peak), Nor. 37/F1
Kjevik (int'l arpt.), Nor. 38/C2
Kjølen (mts.), Nor. 37/E2
Klabava (riv.), Czh. 55/G3
Kladanj, Bosn. 48/D3
Kladno, Czh. 55/H2
Kladovo, Yugo. 48/F3
Klagenfurt, Aus. 43/L3
Klaipėda, Lith. 39/J4
Klamath (mts.), US 126/C5
Klamath (riv.), Ca, US 124/B3
Klamath Falls, Or, US 126/C5
Klangenan, Indo. 80/C5
Klar (riv.), Swe. 64/B4
Klarälven (riv.), Swe. 37/E3
Klarup, Den. 38/D3
Klášterec nad Ohři, Czh. 55/G2
Klatovy, Czh. 55/G4
Klaus, Aus. 57/F3
Klausen (Chiusa), It. 57/H4
Klausenpass (pass), Swi. 57/E4
Klawock, Ak, US 134/M4
Klaza (mtn.), Can. 134/L3
Klazienaveen, Neth. 50/E3
Kleinblittersdorf, Ger. 53/G5
Kleine Elster (riv.), Ger. 41/G3
Kleine Emme (riv.), Swi. 56/E4
Kleine Gete (riv.), Belg. 53/D2
Kleine Laber (riv.), Ger. 55/F5
Kleine Nete (riv.), Belg. 53/D1
Kleinheubach, Ger. 54/C3
Kleinlützel, Swi. 56/D3
Kleinmachnow, Ger. 40/Q7
Kleinmond, SAfr. 106/L11
Kleinolifants (riv.), SAfr. 106/Q12
Kleinrinderfeld, Ger. 54/C3
Kleinsee, SAfr. 106/B3
Kleinwallstadt, Ger. 54/C3
Kleinwinternheim, Ger. 54/B3
Kleppe, Nor. 38/A2
Kleppestø, Nor. 38/A1
Klerksdorp, SAfr. 106/D2
Klet' (peak), Czh. 55/H5
Kleve, Ger. 50/D5
Klina, Yugo. 47/G1
Klingenberg am Main, Ger. 54/C3
Klingenmünster, Ger. 54/B4
Klingenthal, Ger. 55/F2
Klínovec (peak), Czh. 55/F2
Klintehamn, Swe. 38/H3
Klintsy, Rus. 62/E1
Klip (riv.), SAfr. 106/E2
Klippan, Swe. 38/E3
Klipplaat, SAfr. 106/D4
Klisura, Bul. 47/J1
Klitmøller, Den. 38/C3
Kljajićevo, Yugo. 48/D3
Ključ, Bosn. 48/C3
Kłodawa, Pol. 41/K2
Kłodzko, Pol. 41/J3
Klöntaler-See (lake), Swi. 57/E3
Klosterbach (riv.), Ger. 51/F3
Klosterlechfeld, Ger. 57/G1
Klosterneuburg, Aus. 49/N7
Klosters, Swi. 57/F4
Klosterwappen (peak), Aus. 41/H5
Kloten, Swi. 57/E3
Klötze, Ger. 40/F2
Kluane NP, Can. 134/K3
Kluane NP, Yk, Can. 122/C2
Kluczbork, Pol. 41/K3
Klukwan, Ak, US 134/L3
Klundert, Neth. 50/B5
Klyaz'ma (riv.), Rus. 60/J4
Klyuchevskaya (peak), Rus. 65/S4
Knäred, Swe. 38/E3
Knaresborough, Eng, UK 35/G3
Knee (lake), Can. 127/K2
Knetzgau, Ger. 54/D3
Knezha, Bul. 49/G4
Knight (inlet), Can. 126/B3
Knighton, Wal, UK 32/C2
Knightsen, Ca, US 135/L11
Knin, Cro. 48/C3
Knittelfeld, Aus. 43/L3
Knittlingen, Ger. 54/B4
Knivsta, Swe. 38/G2
Knížecí Stolec (peak), Czh. 55/H5
Knížecí Strom (peak), Czh. 55/F3
Knjaževac, Yugo. 48/F4
Knob (peak), Phil. 81/F1
Knob (cape), Austl. 112/C5
Knobby (pt.), Austl. 112/B4
Knoch (hill), Sc, UK 36/D1
Knockcloghrim, NI, UK 34/B2
Knösen (pt.), Swe. 38/E4
Knøsen (peak), Den. 38/D3
Knosós (Knossos) (ruin), Gre. 47/J5
Knottingley, Eng, UK 35/G4
Knott's Berry Farm, Ca, US 136/G8
Knox (cape), Can. 134/M4
Knox (coast), Ant. 160/G
Knox City, Tx, US 129/H4
Knoxville, Tn, US 130/D5
Knutsford, Eng, UK 35/F5
Knysna, SAfr. 106/C4
Ko (riv.), Sen. 102/B3
Ko-saki (pt.), Japan 74/A3
Ko Samut NP, Thai. 78/C3
Koali, Hi, US 124/T10
Koani, Tanz. 104/C4
Koāth, India 85/E3
Kobayashi, Japan 74/B5
Kōbe, Japan 77/H6
København (int'l arpt.), Den. 38/E4
Kobern-Gondorf, Ger. 53/G3
Kobipato (peak), Indo. 81/G4
Koblach, Aus. 57/F3
Koblenz, Swi. 57/E2
Koblenz, Ger. 53/G3
Kobryn, Bela. 41/N2
Kobuchizawa, Japan 77/A2
Kobuk (riv.), Ak, US 134/G2
Kobuk, Ak, US 134/G2
Kobuk Valley NP, Ak, US 134/G2
Kobushi-ga-take (peak), Japan 75/F3
Kocába (riv.), Czh. 55/H3
Kocaeli (prov.), Turk. 62/D4
Koçalı, Turk. 90/D2
Kočani, Macd. 47/H2
Kocapınar, Turk. 90/E2
Kočevje, Slov. 43/L4
Koch (isl.), NW, Can. 123/J2
Koch'ang, SKor. 73/D5
Koch'ang, SKor. 73/D5
Kochel am See, Ger. 57/H2
Kochelsee (lake), Ger. 57/H2
Kocher (riv.), Ger. 43/H2
Kocherinovo, Bul. 47/H1
Kōchi, Japan 74/C4
Kōchi (pref.), Japan 74/C4
Kodaira, Japan 77/C2
Kodala, India 82/E4
Kodama, Japan 77/C1
Kodarmā, India 85/E3
Kodiak, Ak, US 134/H4
Kodiak (isl.), Ak, US 119/B4
Kodiak NWR, US 134/H4
Kodinār, India 89/K4
Kodomari, Japan 76/B3
Kodry (hills), Mol. 49/H2
Koekelare, Belg. 52/B1
Koel (riv.), India 82/D3
Koes, Namb. 106/B2
Koesan, SKor. 73/D4
Koetari (riv.), Sur. 153/G4
Kofa (mts.), Az, US 128/D4
Kofarnihon (riv.), Taj. 87/E5
Kofçaz, Turk. 49/H5
Koffiefontein, SAfr. 106/D3
Kofiau (isl.), Indo. 81/G4
Koforidua, Gha. 103/E5
Kōfu, Japan 75/F3
Koga, Japan 75/F2
Koganei, Japan 77/D2
Køge (bay), Den. 38/E4
Kogi, Nga. 103/G4
Kogon (riv.), Gui. 96/C5
Kŏgum (isl.), SKor. 73/D5
Kohāt, Pak. 86/A3
Kohīma, India 83/F2
Kohoku, Japan 77/K5
Kohout (peak), Czh. 55/H5
Kohtla-Järve, Est. 39/M2
Kohŭng, SKor. 73/D5
Kohunlich (ruin), Mex. 144/D2
Koímisis, Gre. 47/H2
Koito (riv.), Japan 77/D3
Koiva (riv.), Lat. 39/M3
Kŏje (isl.), SKor. 74/A3
Kojonup, Austl. 112/C5
Kojšovská (peak), Slvk. 41/L4
Kok (riv.), Myan. 78/B1
Kōka, Japan 77/K6
Kokai (riv.), Japan 77/E2
Kökar (isl.), Fin. 39/J3
Kokemäenjoki (riv.), Fin. 39/J1
Kokhonak, Ak, US 134/H4
Kokkola (Karleby), Fin. 60/D3
Koko Head (pt.), Hi, US 124/W13
Kokomo, In, US 130/C3
Kokrajhar, India 85/H2
Kokrines, Ak, US 134/H3
Koksan, NKor. 73/D3
Kökshetaū, Kaz. 87/E2
Kökshetaū (obl.), Kaz. 87/E2
Koksijde, Belg. 52/B1
Koksoak (riv.), Qu, Can. 123/K3
Kokstad, SAfr. 106/E3
Kokubu, Japan 74/B5

Kola (pen.), Rus. 160/D1
Kola (riv.), Rus. 60/G1
Kolaka, Indo. 81/F4
Kolår, India 82/C5
Kolåras, India 84/A3
Kolašin, Yugo. 47/F1
Kolbäck, Swe. 38/G2
Kol'bay (peak), Kaz. 87/B4
Kolbermoor, Ger. 43/K3
Kolbuszowa, Pol. 41/L2
Kolda, Sen. 102/B3
Kolda (pol. reg.), Sen. 102/B3
Kolding, Den. 38/C4
Kölen (mts.), Swe. 37/E2
Kolepom (isl.), Indo. 116/C5
Kolgompya (cape), Rus. 39/N2
Kolguyev (isl.), Rus. 160/C
Kolhåpur, India 89/K5
Koliba (riv.), Gui. 102/B3
Koliganek, Ak, US 134/G4
Kolín, Czh. 41/H3
Kolkasrags (pt.), Lat. 39/K3
Kollbach (riv.), Ger. 55/F5
Kollnburg, Ger. 55/F4
Kollum, Neth. 50/D2
Köln (Cologne), Ger. 53/F2
Kolno, Pol. 41/L2
Kofo, Pol. 62/A1
Koloa, Hi, US 124/S10
Kofobrzeg, Pol. 38/F4
Kolokani, Mali 102/C3
Kolomna, Rus. 60/H5
Kolomyya, Ukr. 49/G1
Kolondiéba, Mali 102/D4
Kolossa (riv.), Mali 102/D3
Kolpashevo, Rus. 64/J4
Kolpino, Rus. 61/T7
Kolsva, Swe. 38/F2
Kolubara (riv.), Yugo. 48/D3
Koluszki, Pol. 41/K3
Kolva (riv.), Rus. 61/N2
Kolwezi, D.R. Congo 105/E3
Kolyma (riv.), Rus. 67/Q3
Kolyma (range), Rus. 67/Q3
Kolyma Lowland (plain), Rus. 65/R2
Kom (peak), Bul. 47/H1
Koma (riv.), Japan 77/C2
Komádi, Hun. 44/E2
Komadugu Gana (riv.), Niger.,Ng 96/H5
Komadugu Yobe (riv.), Nga. 103/H3
Komae, Japan 77/D2
Komagane, Japan 75/E3
Komaki, Japan 77/L5
Komandorskiye (isls.), Rus. 67/R4
Komárno, Slvk. 48/D2
Komárom, Hun. 48/D2
Komárom-esztergom (prov.), Hun. 44/D2
Komatiriver (riv.), SAfr. 106/Q13
Komatke, Az, US 137/R19
Komatsu, Japan 74/E2
Komatsu (int'l arpt.), Japan 74/E2
Komatsushima, Japan 74/D3
Kombissiri, Burk. 103/E3
Kome (isl.), Tanz. 104/B3
Komi Aut. Rep., Rus. 61/M2
Komló, Hun. 48/D2
Kommetjie, SAfr. 106/L11
Kommunizma (peak), Taj. 87/F5
Komodo (isl.), Indo. 81/E5
Komodo Island NP, Indo. 81/E5
Komoé (riv.), C.d'Iv. 96/E6
Komono, Japan 77/L5
Komoran (isl.), Indo. 81/J5
Komoro, Japan 77/A1
Komotini, Gre. 47/J2
Kompasberg (peak), SAfr. 106/D3
Komsomolets (isl.), Rus. 67/J1
Komsomol'skiy, Rus. 61/P2
Kômûr (pt.), Turk. 47/K3
Kon Tum, Viet. 78/D3
Konakovo, Rus. 60/H4
Kônan, Japan 77/C1
Kônan, Japan 77/L5
Kônan, Japan 77/K6
Konár, India 85/E4
Konár (res.), India 85/E4
Konar (riv.), Afg. 86/A2
Konaweha (riv.), Indo. 81/F4
Konda, Japan 77/H6
Kondagaon, India 82/D4
Kondinin, Austl. 112/C5
Kondoa, Tanz. 104/B4
Kondopoga, Rus. 60/G3
Kondûz, Afg. 87/E5
Kong, C.d'Iv. 102/D4
Kong (riv.), Laos 78/D3
Kong (isl.), Camb. 78/C4
Kong Miao, China 72/D4
Kongiganak, Ak, US 134/F4
Kongju, SKor. 73/D4
Kongō-zan (peak), Japan 77/J7
Kongolo, D.R. Congo 105/E2
Kongoussi, Burk. 103/E3
Kongsberg, Nor. 38/C2
Kongsvinger, Nor. 38/E1
Kongur (peak), China 86/D2
Koniecpol, Pol. 41/K3

Königstein im Taunus, Ger. 54/B2
Königswinter, Ger. 53/G2
Konin, Pol. 41/K2
Kónitsa, Gre. 47/G2
Köniz, Swi. 56/D4
Konjic, Bosn. 48/C4
Könkämäeno (riv.), Fin. 60/D1
Konkouré (riv.), Gui. 102/B4
Konnevesi, Fin. 60/E3
Konolfingen, Swi. 56/D4
Kônosu, Japan 77/D1
Konotop, Ukr. 62/E2
Konqi (riv.), China 64/J5
Konsen (plat.), Japan 76/D2
Końskie, Pol. 41/L3
Konstancin-Jeziorna, Pol. 41/L2
Konstantynów Łódzki, Pol. 41/K3
Konstanz, Ger. 57/F2
Kontich, Belg. 53/D1
Kontiolahti, Fin. 60/F3
Konuralp, Turk. 49/K5
Kôny, Hun. 48/C2
Konya, Turk. 90/C2
Konya (prov.), Turk. 90/C2
Konz, Ger. 54/B4
Koondrook, Austl. 115/C2
Koorawatha, Austl. 115/D2
Koorda, Austl. 112/C4
Kootenai (riv.), Id, US 126/D2
Kootenay (lake), BC, Can. 122/C4
Kootenay NP, Can. 126/D3
Kootingal, Austl. 115/D1
Kop-Gejdi (pass), Turk. 63/G4
Kopåganj, India 84/D2
Kopargaon, India 89/K5
Kópavogur, Ice. 37/W6
Kope (peak), C.d'Iv. 102/D5
Köpenick, Ger. 40/Q7
Koper, Slov. 43/K4
Kopervik, Nor. 38/A2
Kopeysk, Rus. 61/P5
Kopfing im Innkreis, Aus. 55/G6
Köping, Swe. 38/G2
Kopondei (cape), Indo. 81/F5
Koporskiy (bay), Rus. 39/N2
Koppang, Nor. 38/D1
Kopparberg (co.), Swe. 37/E3
Kopparberg, Swe. 38/F2
Koppies, SAfr. 106/D2
Koprivnica, Cro. 48/C2
Koprivshtitsa, Bul. 47/J1
Köprü (riv.), Turk. 91/B1
Köprülü, Turk. 91/C1
Köprülü Kanyon NP, Turk. 90/B2
Kor (riv.), Iran 88/F2
Kora, India 84/C2
Kôra, Japan 77/K5
Kora NP, Kenya 104/C3
Korab (peak), Alb. 47/G2
Koráb (peak), Czh. 55/G4
Korakuen Garden, Japan 74/C3
Koraluk (riv.), Nf, Can. 123/K3
Korana (riv.), Cro. 43/L4
Koraput, India 82/D4
Korba, India 84/D4
Korbach, Ger. 51/F6
Korçë, Alb. 47/G2
Korčula (isl.), Cro. 46/E1
Korčulanski Kanal (chan.), Cro. 46/E1
Kord Küy, Iran 88/F1
Kordel, Ger. 54/B4
Korea (bay), China,NKor 65/N6
Korea (str.), Japan,Skor 65/P6
Korean Folk Village, SKor. 73/G7
Korenovsk, Rus. 62/F3
Korhogo, C.d'Iv. 102/D4
Korinós, Gre. 47/H2
Kórinthos (Corinth), Gre. 47/F1
Korizo, Passe de (pass), Chad 96/J3
Korkodon (riv.), Rus. 67/Q3
Korkuteli, Turk. 91/B1
Korla, China 70/E3
Körmend, Hun. 43/M3
Körner, Ger. 51/F6
Korneuburg, Aus. 49/N7
Korntal-Münchingen, Ger. 54/C5
Kornwestheim, Ger. 54/C5
Koro (sea), Fiji 116/G6
Köröğlu (peak), Turk. 49/K5
Korogwe, Tanz. 104/C4
Koroit, Austl. 115/B3
Koronadal, Phil. 81/F2
Korónia (lake), Gre. 47/H2
Koronowo, Pol. 41/J2
Koropion, Gre. 47/N9
Koror (cap.), Palau 116/C4
Körös (riv.), Hun. 48/E2
Korosten', Ukr. 62/D2
Korostyshiv, Ukr. 62/D2
Korotaikha (riv.), Rus. 61/P1
Korovin (vol.), Ak, US 134/H4
Korpo (Korppoo), Fin. 39/L2
Korsakov, Rus. 71/K2
Korschenbroich, Ger. 50/D4
Korsør, Den. 38/D4
Kortemark, Belg. 53/C2
Kortenaken, Belg. 53/E2
Kortenberg, Belg. 53/D2
Kortessem, Belg. 53/E2
Kortrijk, Belg. 53/C2
Korup, PN de, Camr. 103/H5
Koryak (range), Rus. 67/R3
Koryakia Aut. Okrug, Rus. 65/S3
Koryazhma, Rus. 61/K3

Kôryô, Japan 77/J6
Koryŏng, SKor. 73/E5
Kós (isl.), Gre. 90/A2
Kós, Gre. 90/A2
Kosai, Japan 75/E3
Kosai, Japan 77/J7
Kösching, Ger. 55/E5
Kościan, Pol. 41/J2
Kościerzyna, Pol. 38/G4
Kosciusko (riv.), Austl. 115/D3
Kosciusko, Ms, US 133/F3
Kosciusko (mt.), Austl. 115/D3
Kosciusko NP, Austl. 115/D3
Köse, Turk. 62/F4
Kosei, Japan 77/K6
Koshigaya, Japan 75/F3
Koshiki (isls.), Japan 75/K5
Kosi, India 84/A2
Kosi (zone), Nepal 85/F2
Kosi (riv.), India 82/E2
Košice, Slvk. 41/L4
Koskinoú, Gre. 90/B2
Kosoba (peak), Kaz. 87/G3
Kosŏng, SKor. 73/E5
Kosŏng, NKor. 73/E3
Kosovo (reg.), Yugo. 47/G1
Kosovo (prov.), Yugo. 48/E4
Kosovo Polje, Yugo. 47/G1
Kosovska Kamenica, Yugo. 47/G1
Kosovska Mitrovica, Yugo. 47/G1
Kosový (riv.), Czh. 55/F3
Kosrae (isl.), Micr. 116/F4
Kossi (prov.), Burk. 102/D3
Kossou, Barrage de (dam), C.d'Iv. 102/D5
Kossou, Lac de (lake), C.d'Iv. 96/D6
Kosta, Swe. 38/F3
Kostelec nad Černými Lesy, Czh. 55/J2
Koster, SAfr. 106/D2
Kostinbrod, Bul. 47/H1
Kostopil', Ukr. 62/C2
Kostroma, Rus. 60/J4
Kostroma, Rus. 60/J4
Kostroma Oblast, Rus. 60/J4
Kostrzyn, Pol. 41/H2
Kostrzyn, Pol. 41/J2
Kostyantynivka, Ukr. 62/F2
Kosuge, Japan 77/B2
Kos'va (riv.), Rus. 61/N4
Kos'yu (riv.), Rus. 61/N2
Koszalin, Pol. 38/G4
Koszalin (prov.), Pol. 38/F5
Kőszeg, Hun. 43/M3
Kot Addu, Pak. 86/A4
Kot Kapūra, India 84/B2
Kôt Mümin, Pak. 86/B3
Kot Rādha Kishan, Pak. 86/C4
Kot Samāba, Pak. 86/A5
Kota, India 84/D4
Kôta, Japan 77/M6
Kota Baharu, Malay. 80/B2
Kota Kinabalu, Malay. 81/E2
Kotaagung, Indo. 80/B5
Kotabaru, Indo. 81/E4
Kotabumi, Indo. 80/B4
Kotapād, India 82/D4
Kotdwāra, India 84/B1
Kotel, Bul. 47/K1
Kotel'nich, Rus. 61/L4
Kotel'nikovo, Rus. 63/G3
Kotel'nyy (isl.), Rus. 65/P2
Kothagūdem, India 82/D4
Kôthen, Ger. 40/F3
Kotido, Ugan. 104/B2
Kotka, Fin. 39/N1
Kotlas, Rus. 61/K3
Kotli Lohārān, Pak. 86/C3
Kotlik, Ak, US 134/F3
Kotlin, Rus. 61/S7
Kotō, Japan 77/K5
Kotoka (int'l arpt.), Gha. 103/E5
Kotor, Yugo. 47/F1
Kotor Varoš, Bosn. 48/C3
Kotovo, Rus. 63/H2
Kotovsk, Rus. 63/G1
Kotri, Pak. 89/J3
Kottayam, India 82/C6
Kotto (riv.), CAfr. 97/K6
Kôtu (riv.), Japan 77/K3
Kôtzebue, Ak, US 134/F2
Kotzebue (sound), Ak, US 134/E2
Kötzting, Ger. 55/F4
Kouandé, Ben. 103/F4
Kouchibouguac NP, Can. 131/H2
Koudougou, Burk. 103/E3
Koufonísion (isl.), Gre. 47/J5
Kougarok (mtn.), Ak, US 134/E2
Koukdjuak (riv.), NW, Can. 123/J2
Koula-Moutou, Gabon 96/H8
Kouliabo, Mali 102/D3
Koulikoro, Mali 102/C3
Koulikoro (pol. reg.), Mali 102/C3
Koulountou (riv.), Sen. 102/B3
Koumbi Saleh (ruin), Mrta. 96/D5
Koumi, Japan 77/A1
Koumra, Chad 96/J6
Koundara, Gui. 102/B3
Kounradskiy, Kaz. 87/G2
Kountze, Tx, US 129/J5
Koupela, Burk. 103/E3
Kourou, FrG. 151/H2
Koussi (peak), Chad 96/J4
Koutiala, Mali 102/D3
Kouvola, Fin. 39/N1
Kovačica, Yugo. 48/E3
Kovada Gölü NP, Turk. 90/B2
Kovashi (riv.), Rus. 61/S7
Kovdozero (lake), Rus. 37/J2
Kovel', Ukr. 62/E2
Kovilj, Yugo. 48/E3
Kovilpatti, India 82/C6

Kovrov, Rus. 60/J4
Kovûr, India 82/C5
Kovylkino, Rus. 63/G1
Kowanyama Aboriginal Community, Austl. 114/A1
Kowkcheh (riv.), Afg. 89/J1
Kowl-e Namaksār (lake), Afg. 87/D6
Kowloon, China 79/B3
Kowt-e 'Ashrow, Afg. 89/J2
Kôyaguchi, Japan 77/J7
Kôyama, Japan 74/B5
Koynare, Bul. 49/G4
Koyuk, Ak, US 134/F2
Koyukuk (riv.), Ak, US 134/H2
Koyukuk NWR, US 134/G3
Koyukuk, South Fork (riv.), Ak, US 134/H2
Kozakai, Japan 77/M6
Közaki, Japan 77/E2
Kozaklı, Turk. 62/E5
Kozan, Turk. 90/C2
Kozáni, Gre. 47/G2
Kozara NP, Aus. 48/C3
Kozhozero (lake), Rus. 60/H3
Kozhva (riv.), Rus. 61/M2
Kozienice, Pol. 41/L3
Kozloduy, Bul. 49/F4
Kozlu, Turk. 49/K5
Kozluk, Turk. 90/E2
Kozmin, Pol. 41/J3
Koznitsa (peak), Bul. 47/H1
Kôzu (isl.), Japan 75/F3
Kôzuchow, Pol. 41/H3
Kozyatyn, Ukr. 62/D2
Kpalimé, Togo 103/F5
Kpandu, Gha. 103/F5
Kpémé, Togo 103/F5
Kra (isth.), Myan. 83/G6
Kraai (riv.), SAfr. 106/D3
Kraaifontein, SAfr. 106/L10
Krabi, Thai. 78/B4
Kragerø, Nor. 38/C2
Kragujevac, Yugo. 48/E3
Kraiburg am Inn, Ger. 55/F6
Kraichbach (riv.), Ger. 54/B4
Kraichgau (reg.), Ger. 54/B4
Krailling, Ger. 43/H2
Krakatau (vol.), Indo. 80/C5
Kraków, Pol. 41/K3
Kraków (prov.), Pol. 41/K3
Kralendijk, NAnt. 152/D1
Kraljevo, Yugo. 48/E3
Kralkızı (dam), Turk. 90/E2
Kralovice, Czh. 55/G3
Kralupy nad Vltavou, Czh. 55/H3
Kramators'k, Ukr. 62/E2
Kramfors, Swe. 37/F3
Krammer (chan.), Neth. 50/B5
Kranéa Elassónos, Gre. 47/G3
Kranebitten (int'l arpt.), Aus. 57/H3
Kranenburg, Ger. 50/D5
Kranidhion, Gre. 47/H4
Kranj, Slov. 43/L3
Kranskop, SAfr. 107/E3
Krapkowice, Pol. 41/J3
Kraslice, Czh. 55/F2
Kraśnik, Pol. 41/M3
Kraśnik Fabryczny, Pol. 41/M3
Krasnoarmeysk, Rus. 63/H2
Krasnodar, Rus. 62/F3
Krasnodar Kray, Rus. 62/F3
Krasnogorsk, Rus. 61/W9
Krasnohrad, Ukr. 62/E2
Krasnokamensk, Rus. 71/L1
Krasnokamsk, Rus. 61/M4
Krasnoslobodsk, Rus. 63/G1
Krasnotur'insk, Rus. 61/P4
Krasnoural'sk, Rus. 61/P4
Krasnovodsk (int'l arpt.), Trkm. 62/F2
Krasnowodsk (Trkmenbashi), Trkm. 63/K5
Krasnoyarsk, Rus. 64/M4
Krasnyy Kut, Rus. 63/H2
Krasnyy Luch, Ukr. 62/G3
Krasnyy Sulin, Rus. 62/G3
Kratovo, Macd. 47/H1
Krautheim, Ger. 54/C4
Kravanh (mts.), Camb. 78/C3
Kreb en Nâga (cliff), Mali 102/D3
Kreck (riv.), Ger. 50/D6
Krefeld, Ger. 50/D6
Kreiensen, Ger. 51/G5
Kremastón (lake), Gre. 47/G3
Křemelna (riv.), Czh. 55/G3
Kremenchuts'ke Vodoskhovyshche (res.), Ukr. 62/E2
Kremlin, Rus. 61/W9
Kremmen, Ger. 40/D6
Kremmling, Co, US 128/F2
Krempe, Ger. 51/G1
Krems an der Donau, Aus. 41/H4
Kremsmünster, Aus. 55/K5
Kreševike, Pa, US 138/C3
Kressbronn am Bodensee, Ger. 57/F2
Kresta (gulf), Rus. 67/T3
Krestena, Gre. 47/G4
Kretinga, Lith. 39/J4
Kreuzau, Ger. 50/D6
Kreuzberg (peak), Ger. 54/C2
Kreuzlingen, Swi. 57/F2
Kreuztal, Ger. 53/G2
Kreuzwertheim, Ger. 54/C3
Kría Vrísi, Gre. 47/H2

Kribi, Camr. 96/G7
Krieglach, Aus. 43/L3
Kriens, Swi. 57/E3
Kriftel, Ger. 54/B2
Kril'on (pen.), Rus. 76/B1
Krimpen aan de IJssel, Neth. 50/B5
Krinidhes, Gre. 47/J2
Kriós (cape), Gre. 47/H5
Krishna (riv.), India 67/G8
Krishnagar, India 85/G4
Kristdala, Swe. 38/G3
Kristiansand, Nor. 38/B2
Kristianstad (int'l arpt.), Swe. 38/F4
Kristianstad, Swe. 38/F4
Kristiansund, Nor. 37/C3
Kristinehamn, Swe. 38/F2
Kriva Palanka, Macd. 47/H1
Krk (isl.), Cro. 48/B3
Krk, Cro. 48/B3
Krnov, Czh. 41/J3
Krokom, Swe. 37/F3
Krókos, Gre. 47/G2
Krolevets', Ukr. 62/E2
Krombach, Ger. 54/C2
Kroměříž, Czh. 41/J4
Kronach, Ger. 55/E2
Kronberg im Taunus, Ger. 54/B2
Kronoberg (co.), Swe. 37/E4
Kronshtadt, Rus. 61/S6
Kronstorf, Aus. 55/H6
Kroombit Tops NP, Austl. 114/C4
Kropotkin, Rus. 62/F3
Kropp, Ger. 38/C4
Krosno (prov.), Pol. 41/L4
Krosno Odrzańskie, Pol. 41/H2
Krotoszyn, Pol. 41/J3
Krottenkopf (peak), Ger. 57/G3
Krousón, Gre. 47/J5
Krško, Slov. 43/L4
Kruckau (riv.), Ger. 51/G1
Kruger NP, SAfr. 105/F5
Krugersdorp, SAfr. 106/P13
Kruglitsa (peak), Rus. 61/W9
Kruibeke, Belg. 50/B6
Kruisfontein, SAfr. 106/D4
Krujë, Alb. 47/F2
Krumbach, Ger. 57/G1
Krummenau, Swi. 57/F3
Krumovgrad, Bul. 47/J2
Krün, Ger. 57/H3
Krupina, Slvk. 48/D1
Krusá, Den. 38/C4
Krusenstern (cape), Ak, US 134/F2
Kruševac, Yugo. 48/E4
Kruševo, Macd. 47/G2
Krušné Hory (Erzgebirge) (mts.), Czh./Ger. 43/K1
Kruzof (isl.), Ak, US 134/L4
Krym Aut. Rep., Ukr. 62/E3
Krymsk, Rus. 62/F3
Krynica, Pol. 41/L4
Kryvyy Rih, Ukr. 49/L2
Krzna (riv.), Pol. 41/M2
Krzyż, Pol. 41/H2
Ksar el Kebir, Mor. 100/B2
Ksel (peak), Alg. 99/F2
Ktima, Cyp. 91/B2
Ku-Ring-Gai NP, Austl. 114/H8
Ku Sathan (peak), Thai. 78/C2
Kuah, Malay. 78/B5
Kuala Belait, Bru. 80/D3
Kuala Dungun, Malay. 80/B3
Kuala Kerai, Malay. 83/H6
Kuala Lipis, Malay. 80/B3
Kuala Lumpur (cap.), Malay. 80/B3
Kuala Pilah, Malay. 80/B3
Kuala Selangor, Malay. 80/B3
Kuala Terengganu, Malay. 83/H6
Kualapu'u, Hi, US 124/T10
Kuancheng, China 72/D2
Kuandian, China 73/C2
Kuantan, Malay. 80/B3
Kuban' (riv.), Rus. 62/F3
Kubaysah, Iraq 90/D4
Kubenskoye (lake), Rus. 60/H4
Kubrat, Bul. 49/H4
Kučevo, Yugo. 48/E3
Kuchen (peak), Ger. 54/C5
Kuching, Malay. 80/D3
Kuchino (isl.), Japan 75/K5
Kuchinoerabu (isl.), Japan 74/A5
Kuchl, Aus. 57/M3
Kücükbahçe, Turk. 47/J3
Kücükkuyu, Turk. 47/J3
Kudat, Malay. 80/D2
Kudus, Indo. 80/D5
Kudymkar, Rus. 61/M4
Kufrah (oasis), Libya 101/K4
Kufrinjah, Jor. 91/D3
Kufstein, Aus. 43/K3
Kuhardt, Ger. 54/B4
Kühmo, Fin. 60/F2
Kuhmoinen, Fin. 39/M1
Kuhn, II, US 137/P16
Kui Buri, Thai. 78/C3
Kuiu (isl.), Ak, US 122/C3

Kujawy (reg.), Pol. 41/K2
Kuji, Japan 76/B3
Kujū-san (peak), Japan 74/B4
Kujūkuri, Japan 77/E2
Kuki, Japan 75/F2
Kukizaki, Japan 77/E2
Kül (riv.), Iran 88/C3
Kula, Yugo. 48/D3
Kula, Bul. 48/F4
Kula Kangri (peak), Bhu. 85/H1
Kulachi, Pak. 86/A4
Kulai, Malay. 80/B3
Kulal (mt.), Kenya 104/C2
Kulaly (isl.), Kaz. 63/J3
Kuldīga, Lat. 39/J3
Kulgām, India 86/C3
Kulin, Austl. 112/C5
Kullen (cape), Swe. 38/E3
Kullu, India 86/D4
Kūlob, Taj. 89/J1
Kuloy (riv.), Rus. 61/J2
Kulpahār, India 84/B3
Kulpmont, Pa, US 138/B2
Kulpsville, Pa, US 138/C3
Kul'sary, Kaz. 63/K3
Kulsi (riv.), India 85/H2
Kulti, India 85/F4
Kulunda (lake), Rus. 87/G2
Kulunda, Rus. 87/G1
Küm (riv.), SKor. 73/D4
Kuma (riv.), Rus. 64/E5
Kumagaya, Japan 75/F2
Kumaishi, Japan 76/A2
Kumamoto (int'l arpt.), Japan 74/B4
Kumamoto, Japan 74/B4
Kumamoto (pref.), Japan 74/B4
Kumano (riv.), Japan 74/D4
Kumano, Japan 74/D4
Kumanovo, Macd. 47/G1
Kumār (riv.), Bang. 85/G4
Kumasi, Gha. 103/E5
Kumatori, Japan 77/H7
Kumba, Camr. 96/G7
Kumbia, Austl. 114/C4
Kumbo, Camr. 96/H6
Kûmch'on, SKor. 73/F6
Kumé (isl.), Japan 79/Z2
Kumen' (riv.), Rus. 61/K4
Kumertau, Rus. 63/K1
Kumgang-san (peak), NKor. 73/E3
Kûmho (riv.), SKor. 73/E5
Kumi, Ugan. 104/B2
Kumi, SKor. 73/D4
Kumihama, Japan 77/G4
Kumiyama, Japan 77/J6
Kumkale, Turk. 49/H6
Kûmköy, Turk. 49/J5
Kumla, Swe. 38/F2
Kumluca, Turk. 91/B1
Kümmersbruck, Ger. 55/E4
Kumo, Nga. 96/H5
Kumon (range), Myan. 70/G6
Kümsan, SKor. 73/D4
Kumta, India 89/K6
Kunashiri (isl.), Rus. 65/O5
Kûnch, India 84/B3
Kunda, Est. 39/M3
Kundapoor (Coondapoor), India 89/K6
Kundarkhi, India 84/B1
Kundelungu, PN de, D.R. Congo 105/E3
Kundiān, Pak. 86/A3
Kungälv, Swe. 38/D3
Kungsbacka, Swe. 38/D3
Kungshamn, Swe. 38/D2
Kungur, Rus. 61/M4
Kunhegyes, Hun. 48/E2
Kunimi-dake (peak), Japan 74/B4
Kunitachi, Japan 77/D2
Kunjāh, Pak. 86/B3
Kunjirap (pass), China 89/L1
Kunlun (mts.), China 70/D4
Kunmadaras, Hun. 41/L5
Kunsan, SKor. 73/D5
Kunshan, China 71/M6
Kunszentmárton, Hun. 48/E2
Kunu (riv.), India 84/B3
Kunwāri (riv.), India 84/A2
Kunwi, SKor. 73/E4
Kunya (mtn.), China 72/E3
Kuopio (lake), Fin. 60/F3
Kuopio (prov.), Fin. 37/H3
Kupa (riv.), Cro. 43/L4
Kupang, Indo. 81/F6
Kupino, Rus. 64/J4
Kuppenheim, Ger. 54/B5
Kupreanof (isl.), Ak, US 122/C3

Küre, Turk. 62/E4
Kure (isl.), Hi, US 116/H2
Kuressaare, Est. 39/K2
Kureyka (riv.), Rus. 64/K3
Kurgan, Rus. 61/O5
Kurgan Oblast, Rus. 87/D1
Kuri, SKor. 73/G6
Kuria (isl.), Kiri. 116/G4
Kuria Muria (isls.), Oman 67/F5
Kurīgrām, Bang. 85/G3
Kurihashi, Japan 77/D1
Kurikoma-yama (peak), Japan 76/B4
Kuril (isls.), Rus. 67/Q5
Kurilsk, Rus. 65/P5
Kurimoto, Japan 77/E2
Kurinwas (riv.), Nic. 145/E3
Kurisawa, Japan 76/B2
Kuriyama, Japan 76/B2
Kurkçü, Turk. 91/C1
Kurla, India 82/B4
Kurnool, India 82/C5
Kuro-shima (isl.), Japan 74/A5
Kurodashō, Japan 77/G6
Kuroishi, Japan 76/B3
Kuroiso, Japan 75/G2
Kuroso-yama (peak), Japan 77/K6
Kurotaki, Japan 77/J7
Kurrajong, Austl. 114/G8
Kurram (riv.), Afg.,Pak. 89/K2
Kurrimine Beach, Austl. 114/B2
Kurşénai, Lith. 39/K3
Kurseong, India 85/G2
Kuršumlija, Yugo. 47/G1
Kuršumlu, Turk. 62/E4
Kurtalan, Turk. 90/E2
Kuru (riv.), Sudan 97/L6
Kuruca (pass), Turk. 49/H5
Kürten, Ger. 53/G2
Kuruçay, Turk. 62/F5
Kurume, Japan 74/B4
Kurunegala, SrL. 82/D6
Kurupukari, Guy. 153/G3
Kurur (peak), Sudan 101/N4
Kurwongbah (lake), Austl. 114/E6
Kurye, SKor. 73/D5
Kuş Cenneti NP, Turk. 49/J5
Kuşadası, Turk. 90/A2
Kusatsu, Japan 77/J5
Kusel, Ger. 54/B4
Kushālgarh, India 89/K4
Kushida (riv.), Japan 77/K7
Kushigata, Japan 77/A2
Kushikino, Japan 74/B5
Kushima, Japan 74/B5
Kushimoto, Japan 74/D4
Kushiro, Japan 76/D2
Kushiro-Shitsugen NP, Japan 76/D2
Kushmurun (lake), Kaz. 87/C1
Kushtia (pol. reg.), Bang. 85/G4
Kushtia, Bang. 85/G4
Kusiyana (riv.), India 85/H3
Kuskokwim (bay), Ak, US 134/E4
Kuskokwim (mts.), Ak, US 134/G3
Kuskokwim, North Fork (riv.), Ak, US 134/H3
Kuskokwim, South Fork (riv.), Ak, US 134/H3
Küsnacht, Swi. 57/E3
Küssnacht am Rigi, Swi. 57/E3
Küstenkanal (canal), Ger. 51/F2
Kusterdingen, Ger. 54/C5
Kūstī, Sudan 101/N6
Kut (isl.), Thai. 78/C3
Kütahya, Turk. 62/D5
Kutch (reg.), India 89/J4
Kutch, Gulf of (gulf), India 89/J4
Kutchan, Japan 76/B2
Kutina, Cro. 48/C3
Kutno, Pol. 41/K2
Kutsuki, Japan 77/J5
Küttigen, Swi. 56/E3
Kutu, D.R. Congo 105/C1
Kutztown, Pa, US 138/C2
Kuujjua (riv.), NW, Can. 122/E1
Kuujjuaq, Qu, Can. 123/K3
Kuusamo, Fin. 60/F2
Kuusankoski, Fin. 39/N1

Kuvandyk, Rus. 63/L2
Kuwait (cap.), Kuw. 88/E3
Kuwait (ctry.) 67/D7
Kuwana (riv.), India 85/E3
Kuwana, Japan 77/L5
Kuybyshev (res.), Rus. 64/E4
Kuytun, China 70/E3
Kuyuwini (riv.), Guy. 153/G4
Kuze, Japan 77/K4
Kuzitrin (riv.), Ak, US 134/E2
Kuznetsk, Rus. 63/H1
Kuzucubelen, Turk. 91/D1
Kuzumaki, Japan 76/B3
Kvaløy (isl.), Nor. 37/F1
Kværndrup, Den. 38/D4
Kvarner (gulf), Cro. 48/B3
Kvarnerić (chan.), Cro. 48/B3
Kvigtinden (peak), Nor. 37/E2
Kvinesdal, Nor. 38/B2
Kvinnherad, Nor. 38/C2
Kwa (riv.), D.R. Congo 93/D5
Kwach'ŏn, SKor. 73/D3
Kwajalein (isl.), Mrsh. 116/F4
Kwale, Kenya 104/C4
KwaMashu, SAfr. 107/E3
Kwanak-san (peak), SKor. 73/F7
Kwangch'ŏn, SKor. 73/D4
Kwangju-jikhalsi (prov.), SKor. 73/D5
Kwangju, SKor. 73/G7
Kwangmyŏng, SKor. 73/F7
Kwango (riv.), D.R. Congo 93/D5
Kwangyang, SKor. 73/D5
Kwania (lake), Ugan. 97/M7
Kwansan, SKor. 73/D5
Kwara (state), Nga. 103/G4
Kwaraha (peak), Tanz. 104/B4
Kwatoboahegan (riv.), Can. 130/D1
Kwazulu Natal (prov.), SAfr. 107/E3
Kwekwe, Zim. 105/E4
Kwethluk, Ak, US 134/F3
Kwidzyn, Pol. 39/H5
Kwigillingok, Ak, US 134/F4
Kwilu (riv.), D.R. Congo 105/C1
Kwinana, Austl. 112/K7
Kyabé, Chad 97/J6
Kyabram, Austl. 115/C3
Kyaiktiyo Pagoda, Myan. 78/B2
Kyaikto, Myan. 83/G4
Kyancutta, Austl. 115/A2
Kyangin, Myan. 83/G4
Kyaukpadaung, Myan. 83/G3
Kyaukpyu, Myan. 83/F4
Kyaukse, Myan. 83/G3
Kyeryong-san NP, SKor. 73/D4
Kyjov, Czh. 41/J4
Kyle, Sk, Can. 126/F3
Kyle (riv.), Sc, UK 36/B5
Kyll (riv.), Eng, UK 40/D2 —
Kymijoki (riv.), Fin. 39/M1
Kymore, India 84/C3
Kyneton, Austl. 115/C3
Kyŏnggi (bay), SKor. 73/D4
Kyŏnggi-Do (prov.), SKor. 73/D3
Kyŏngju, SKor. 73/E5
Kyŏngsang-bukto (prov.), SKor. 73/E4
Kyŏngsang-namdo (prov.), SKor. 73/E5
Kyŏngbok Palace, SKor. 73/G7
Kyogle, Austl. 114/D5
Kyōga-misaki (cape), Japan 74/D3
Kyogle, Austl. 114/D5
Kyŏnggi-Do (prov.), SKor. 73/D3
Kyōto Imperial Palace, Japan 74/D3
Kyōto (pref.), Japan 74/D3
Kyōwa, Japan 77/E1
Kyrenia, Cyp. 91/C2
Kyrgyzstan (ctry.) 67/G5
Kyrkslätt, Fin. 39/K1
Kyšperk nad Orlicí, Czh. 55/G4 —
Kythera (isl.), Gre. 47/H5
Kythrea, Cyp. 91/C2
Kýthira, Gre. 47/H5 —
Kyŭshŭ Highlands (uplands), Japan 74/B4
Kyustendil, Bul. 47/H1
Kyūshū (isl.), Japan 74/B4
Kyyiv (cap.), Ukr. —
Kyyivs'ka (obl.), Ukr. 62/D2
Kyzyl, Rus. 70/F1

La Asunción, Ven. 153/F2
La Aurora (int'l arpt.), Guat. 144/D3
La Babia, Mex. 132/C4
La Baie, Qu, Can. 131/G1
La Banda, Arg. 157/D2
La Bañeza, Sp. 44/C1
La Bassée, Fr. 52/B2
La Baule-Escoublac, Fr. 42/B3
La Belle, Fl, US 133/H5
La Birse (riv.), Swi. 56/D3
La Blanquilla (isl.), Ven. 153/E2
La Bocana, Mex. 142/B3
La Bresse, Fr. 56/C2
La Broque, Fr. 56/C2
La Calera, Chile 158/N8
La Campana, Sp. 44/C4
La Cañada, Ca, US 145/F1
La Canada-Flintridge, Ca, US 136/F7
La Capelle, Fr. 52/C4
La Carlota, Sp. 44/C4
La Carlota, Arg. 158/E2
La Carolina, Sp. 44/D3
La Catedral (peak), Mex. 143/Q9
La Ceiba, Hon. 144/E3
La Ceiba (int'l arpt.), Hon. 144/E3
La Celle-les-Bordes, Fr. 30/H6
La Celle-Saint-Cloud, Fr. 30/J5
La Celle-sur-Morin, Fr. 30/M5
La Chapelle-de-Guinchay, Fr. 56/A5
La Chapelle-Saint-Luc, Fr. 42/F2
La Chaux-de-Fonds, Swi. 56/C3
La Chinata (int'l arpt.), Ven. 152/D2
La Chorrera, Pan. 150/C2
La Cienega, NM, US 129/K4
La Ciotat, Fr. 42/F5
La Clusaz, Fr. 56/C6
La Concepción, Ven. 152/D2
La Concepción, Nic. 144/E4
La Coronilla, Uru. 159/G2
La Coruña, Sp. 44/A1
La Couronne, Fr. 42/C3
La Crèche, Fr. 42/C3
La Crescenta-Montrose, Ca, US 136/F7
La Croix-en-Brie, Fr. 30/M6
La Croix, Lac (lake), Can. 127/L3
La Cruz, Mex. 142/D4
La Cruz, CR 144/E4
La Cruz, Chile 158/N8
La Cruz, Uru. 159/F1
La Cumbre (vol.), Ecu. 156/V7
La Dôle (peak), Swi. 56/C5
La Dorada, Col. 150/D2
La Dormida, Arg. 158/D2
La Esperanza, Hon. 144/D3
La Estrada, Sp. 44/A1
La Estrella, Chile 158/N9
La Falda, Arg. 157/D3
La Fayette, Ga, US 133/G3
La Fère, Fr. 52/C4
La Ferté-Gaucher, Fr. 52/C6
La Ferté-Macé, Fr. 42/C2
La Ferté-Milon, Fr. 30/M7
La Ferté-Sous-Jouarre, Fr. 52/C2
La Flèche, Fr. 42/C3
La Fria, Ven. 152/D2
La Garamba NP, D.R. Congo 104/A2
La Garita (mts.), US 132/B2
La Gineta, Sp. 44/E3
La Gloria, Col. 152/C2
La Gran Sabana (plain), Ven. 150/F2
La Grande, Or, US 126/D4
La Grande, Tx, US 130/H5
La Grita, Ven. 152/D2
La Gruyère (lake), Swi. 56/D4
La Guajira (dept.), Col. 150/D1
La Guajira (pen.), Col. 150/D1
La Guardia, Sp. 44/A2
La Guardia (int'l arpt.), NY, US 139/K8
La Habana (Havana) (cap.), Cuba 140/D2
La Habra, Ca, US 136/D8
La Have, Fr. 131/H2
La Higuera, Chile 157/B2
La Honda, Ca, US 135/K12
La Houssaye-en-Brie, Fr. 30/M5
La Huaca, Peru 156/B5
La Huacana, Mex. 142/E5
La Huerta, Mex. 142/D5
La Isla, Peru 143/Q10
La Jalca, Peru 156/C5
La Joya de los Sachas, Ecu. 152/B5
La Junta, Co, US 129/L3
La Laguna, Sp. 98/A3
La Libertad (dept.), Peru 156/C5
La Libertad, Hon. 144/E3
La Libertad, Guat. 144/C3
La Libertad, Ecu. 152/A5
La Ligua, Chile 158/C2
La Línea de la Concepción, Sp. 44/C4
La Loche, Sk, Can. 125/G3
La Loggia, It. 33/G2
La Louvière, Belg. 53/D3
La Luz, NM, US 129/F4
La Machine, Fr. 42/E3

La Maddalena, It. 46/A2
La Madeleine, Fr. 52/C2
La Malbaie, Qu., Can. 131/G2
La Martre (lake), NW, Can. 122/E2
La Masica, Hon. 144/E3
La Mauricie NP, Can. 130/F2
La Mensura (peak), Col. 152/C4
La Merca, Sp. 44/B1
La Merced, Peru 156/C3
La Mesa, Ca, US 136/C5
La Mesa (int'l arpt.), Hon. 144/E3
La Mesa, Ven. 152/D2
La Mira, Mex. 142/E5
La Mirada, Ca, US 136/F8
La Moine (riv.), Il, US 130/B3
La Montaña (phys. reg.), Peru 147/B3
La Moure, ND, US 127/J4
La Neuveville, Swi. 56/C3
La Norville, Fr. 30/J6
La Orchila (isl.), Ven. 141/H5
La Orotava, Sp. 98/A3
La Oroya, Peru 156/C3
La Palma, Pan. 145/G4
La Palma (isl.), Sp. 98/A3
La Paloma, Uru. 159/G2
La Pampa (prov.), Arg. 158/D3
La Paz, Arg. 158/D3
La Paz (cap.), Bol. 150/E7
La Paz (dept.), Bol. 156/D4
La Paz (bay), Mex. 142/C3
La Paz, Mex. 142/C3
La Paz, Hon. 144/E3
La Paz, Col. 152/C2
La Paz, Col. 152/C3
La Paz, Arg. 158/D2
La Paz, Uru. 159/K11
La Pêche, Qu, Can. 130/F2
La Peña, Pan. 140/E6
La Perla, Mex. 132/B4
La Pérouse (str.), Japan,Rus. 71/R2
La Perouse (str.), Japan,Rus. 67/P5
La Petite-Raon, Fr. 56/C1
La Piedad Cavadas, Mex. 142/E4
La Plata, Md, US 139/J4
La Plata, Col. 152/C3
La Plata, Arg. 159/K11
La Pobla de Lillet, Sp. 45/F1
La Pocatière, Qu, Can. 131/G2
La Pola de Gordón, Sp. 44/C1
La Ponge (lake), Can. 126/G2
La Porte, In, US 130/C3
La Prairie, Qu, Can. 131/P7
La Pryor, Tx, US 129/H5
La Puebla, Sp. 45/G3
La Puebla de Almoradiel, Sp. 44/D3
La Puebla de Cazalla, Sp. 44/C4
La Puebla de Montalbán, Sp. 44/C3
La Puente, Ca, US 136/G7
La Puntilla (pt.), Ecu. 152/A5
La Quebrada, Ven. 152/D2
La Queue-les-Yvelines, Fr. 52/A6
La Quiaca, Arg. 150/E8
La Rambla, Sp. 44/C3
La Reforma, Mex. 142/C3
La Rinconada, Sp. 44/C5
La'ri, Pak. 86/A3
La Rioja, Arg. 157/C2
La Rioja (aut. comm.), Sp. 44/D1
La Rioja (prov.), Sp. 44/C1
La Robla, Sp. 44/C1
La Roche, Can. 126/F1
La Roche, Swi. 56/D4
La Roche-en-ardenne, Belg. 53/E3
La Roche-sur-Foron, Fr. 56/C5
La Roche-sur-Yon, Fr. 42/C3
La Rochelle, Fr. 42/C3
La Roda, Sp. 44/D3
La Romana, DRep. 141/H4
La Ronge, Sk, Can. 127/G2
La Rúa, Sp. 44/B1
La Salle, Co, US 137/C2
La Sarraz, Swi. 56/C4
La Sarre, Qu, Can. 130/E1
La Sauvette (peak), Fr. 42/G5
La Scie, Nf, Can. 131/L1
La Serena, Chile 157/B2
La Seu d'Urgell, Sp. 45/F1
La Seyne-sur-Mer, Fr. 42/F5
La Sila (mts.), It. 46/E3
La Silueta (peak), Chile 159/B7
La Solana, Sp. 44/D3
La Souterraine, Fr. 42/D4
La Spezia, It. 58/C4
La Spezia (prov.), It. 58/C4
La Tabatière, Qu, Can. 131/K1
La Teste, Fr. 42/C4
La Tête à l'Ane (peak), Fr. 56/C6
La Tigra, PN, Hon. 144/E3
La Toma, Arg. 158/D2
La Tortue (isl.), Haiti 145/H1
La Tortuga (isl.), Ven. 150/E1
La Tortuga, Isla (isl.), Ven. 150/E1
La Tour-de-Peilz, Swi. 56/C5
La Tour-de-Trême, Swi. 56/C5
La Tremblade, Fr. 42/C4
La Trinitaria, Mex. 143/N4
La Troncal, Ecu. 152/B5
La Tuque, Qu, Can. 131/F2

La Turbie, Fr. 58/H8
La Unión, Peru 156/C3
La Unión, Peru 156/B3
La Unión, Mex. 143/E5
La Unión, Sp. 45/E4
La Unión, Chile 158/B4
La Unión, Col. 152/B4
La Unión, ESal. 144/E3
La Unión, Ven. 152/E2
La Vecilla, Sp. 44/C1
La Verna, Sp. 59/E5
La Verne, Ca, US 136/C2
La Vernia, Tx, US 137/U21
La Verrière, Fr. 30/H5
La Víbora, Mex. 132/C5
La Victoria, Ven. 150/E1
La Victoria, Ven. 152/D3
La Wantzenau, Fr. 53/G6
Laa an der Thaya, Aus. 43/M2
Laaber, Ger. 55/E4
Laage, Ger. 38/E5
Laakirchen, Aus. 55/G7
Laarne, Belg. 52/C1
Laatzen, Ger. 51/G4
Laax, Swi. 57/F4
Labason, Phil. 79/D6
L'Abbaye, Swi. 56/B4
Labdah (Leptis Magna) (ruin), Libya 96/H1
Labé (pol. reg.), Gui. 102/B4
Labe (Elbe) (riv.), Czh. 43/L1
Laberweinting, Ger. 55/F5
Labian (cape), Malay. 81/E2
Labin, Cro. 48/B3
Labinsk, Rus. 63/G3
Labis, Malay. 80/B3
Labná (ruin), Mex. 144/D1
Laboe, Ger. 51/F1
Laborec (riv.), Slvk. 41/L4
Laboulaye, Arg. 158/E2
Labrador (reg.), Can. 119/L4
Labrador (sea), Can.,NAm. 119/M4
Labrador City, Nf, Can. 123/K3
Lábrea, Braz. 150/F5
Labruguière, Fr. 42/E5
Labry, Fr. 53/E5
Labuk (riv.), Malay. 81/E2
Labuk (bay), Malay. 81/E2
Labunista, Macd. 47/G2
Labutta, Myan. 83/F4
Laç, Alb. 47/F2
Lac Afwein (riv.), Kenya 104/C2
Lac du Bonnet, Mb, Can. 127/J3
Lac La Biche, Ab, Can. 126/F2
Lac la Martre, NW, Can. 122/E2
Lac-Mégantic, Qu, Can. 131/G2
Lacantum (riv.), Mex. 144/D2
Lacaune, Fr. 42/E5
Laccadive (sea), India 82/B5
Lacchiarella, It. 58/C2
Lacepede (bay), Austl. 109/C4
Lach Dera (riv.), Som. 97/P7
Lachay (riv.), Peru 156/B3
Lachen, Swi. 57/E3
Lachenaie, Qu, Can. 131/N6
Lachendorf, Ger. 51/H3
Lachine, Qu, Can. 131/N7
Lachlan (riv.), Austl. 109/C4
Lachte (riv.), Ger. 51/H3
Lackawanna, NY, US 131/S10
Lackawanna (co.), Pa, US 138/C1
Läckö, Swe. 38/E2
Lacombe, Ab, Can. 126/E2
Lacombe, La, US 137/O16
Laconia, NH, US 131/G3
Lacroix-Saint-Ouen, Fr. 52/B5
Ladainha, Braz. 154/B5
Ladakh (mts.), India 89/L2
Ladbergen, Ger. 51/E4
Ladder (hills), Sc, UK 36/C2
Ladenburg, Ger. 54/B4
Ladera Heights, Ca, US 136/B2
Ladismith, SAfr. 106/C4
Ladispoli, It. 46/C2
Ladoga (lake), Rus. 60/D1
Ladoix-Serrigny, Fr. 56/A3
Ladrillero (mtn.), Chile 159/B7
Ladue, Mo, US 137/G8
Ladwa, India 86/D5
Lady Isle (isl.), Sc, UK 36/B5
Ladybank, Sc, UK 36/C4
Ladybower (res.), Eng, UK 35/G5
Ladybrand, SAfr. 106/D3
Ladysmith, SAfr. 107/E3
Ladysmith, Wi, US 130/A2
Laer, Ger. 51/E4
Lafayette, La, US 129/J5
Lafayette, In, US 130/C3
Lafayette, Co, US 137/B3
Lafayette, NJ, US 138/D1
Lafayette, Ca, US 135/K11
Lafia, Nga. 103/H4
Lafitte, La, US 137/P17
Lafnitz (riv.), Aus. 43/L3
Lafontaine, Qu, Can. 131/M6
Laga Balal (riv.), Kenya 104/D2
Laga Mado Gali (riv.), Kenya 104/C2

Laga Merille (riv.), Kenya 104/C2
Lagan (riv.), Swe. 38/E3
Lagan (riv.), Swe. 38/E3
Lagarto, Braz. 154/C3
Lagawe, Phil. 79/D4
Lagdo, Lac de (lake), Camr. 96/H6
Lage, Ger. 51/F5
Lage Vaart (canal), Neth. 50/C4
Lågen (riv.), Nor. 38/C1
Lages, Braz. 155/B3
Laggan (lake), Sc, UK 36/B3
Lagh Bogal (riv.), Kenya 104/C2
Lagh Bor (riv.), Kenya 97/N7
Lagh Kutulo (riv.), Kenya 104/D2
Laghouat (prov.), Alg. 99/F2
Laghouat, Alg. 99/F2
Lagnieu, Fr. 56/B6
Lagny-le-Sec, Fr. 30/L4
Lagny-sur-Marne, Fr. 30/L4
Lago da Pedra, Braz. 154/A2
Lago de Atitlán, PN, Guat. 144/D3
Lago Puelo, PN, Arg. 158/C4
Lago Verde, Chile 158/C5
Lagoa, Port. 44/A4
Lagoa da Prata, Braz. 155/C2
Lagoa Formosa, Braz. 155/C1
Lagoa Vermelha, Braz. 155/B4
Lagoda (lake), Rus. 37/J3
Lagonegro, It. 46/D2
Lagong (isl.), Indo. 80/B3
Lagos, Nga. 103/F5
Lagos (state), Nga. 103/F5
Lagos, Port. 44/A4
Lagos de Moreno, Mex. 142/E4
Lagosanto, It. 59/F3
Laguardia, Sp. 44/D1
Laguna, Braz. 155/B4
Laguna Beach, Ca, US 136/C3
Laguna Blanca, PN, Arg. 158/C3
Laguna de Duero, Sp. 44/C2
Laguna de la Restinga, PN, Ven. 153/E2
Laguna del Laja, PN, Chile 158/C3
Laguna del Rey, Mex. 142/E3
Laguna Hills, Ca, US 136/C3
Laguna San Rafael, PN, Chile 157/B6
Lagunas, Peru 156/B2
Lagunas de Chacahua, PN, Mex. 144/B2
Lagunas de Montebello, Mex. 140/C4
Lagunas de Zempoala, PN, Mex. 143/Q10
Lagunillas, Ven. 152/D2
Laguntara (lag.), Hon. 145/E3
Lahad Datu, Malay. 81/E2
Lahār, India 84/B2
Lāharpur, India 84/C2
Lahat, Indo. 80/B4
Lahaina, Hi, US 124/W12
Lahat, Indo. 80/B4
Lahemaa NP, Est. 39/L2
Lahij̄ān, Iran 88/F1
Lahn (riv.), Ger. 40/E3
Lahnstein, Ger. 53/G3
Laholm, Swe. 38/E3
Laholms (bay), Den. 38/F3
Lahore, Pak. 86/C4
Lahore (int'l arpt.), Pak. 86/C4
Lahr, Ger. 56/D1
Lahti, Fin. 39/L1
Lai Chau, Viet. 78/C1
Lai'an, China 72/D4
Laibin, China 79/A3
Laichingen, Ger. 55/F1
Laidon (lake), Sc, UK 36/B3
Laie, Hi, US 124/W12
Laifeng Tujiazu Zizhixian, China 79/A2
L'Aigle, Fr. 42/D2
Laigueglia, It. 58/B5
Laihia, Fin. 37/G3
Lainate, It. 58/C1
Laingsburg, SAfr. 106/C4
Lainioälven (riv.), Swe. 37/G1
Laishui, China 72/G7
Laisvall, Swe. 37/F2
Laitila, Fin. 39/J1
Laives (Leifers), It. 57/H5
Laiwu, China 72/D3
Laiyuan, China 72/G7
Laixi, China 72/E3
Laizhou (bay), China 72/D3
Laja (riv.), Chile 158/C3
Lajas, Peru 156/B2
Laje, Braz. 154/B3
Lajeado, Braz. 155/B4
Lajedo, Braz. 154/C2
Lajes, Braz. 154/C2
Lajes, Azor., Port. 45/S12
Lajes (int'l arpt.), Azor., Port. 45/S12
Lajing (pass), Nepal 85/E1
Lajinha, Braz. 155/D2
Lajosmizse, Hun. 48/D2
L'Akagera, PN de, Rwa. 104/A3
Lakato, Madg. 107/J7
Lake, Ok, US 135/P15
Lake Aluma, Ok, US 137/N14
Lake Amadeus Abor. Land, Austl. 112/C2
Lake Arrowhead, Ca, US 136/C2
Lake Barrington, Il, US 135/P15
Lake Beulah, Wi, US 135/P14
Lake Bluff, Il, US 135/Q15
Lake Boga, Austl. 115/C3
Lake Bogoria Nat'l Rsv., Kenya 104/C2
Lake Bolac, Austl. 115/B3

Lake Cargelligo, Austl. 115/C2
Lake Catherine, Il, US 135/P15
Lake Chany (lake), Rus. 87/G2
Lake Charles, La, US 129/J5
Lake Chelan Nat'l Rec. Area, Wa, US 128/C1
Lake City, Fl, US 133/H4
Lake Clark NP and Prsv., Ak, US 134/G3
Lake District NP, Eng, UK 35/E2
Lake Elsinore, Ca, US 136/C3
Lake Forest, Il, US 135/Q15
Lake Forest Park, Wa, US 135/C2
Lake Fork (res.), Tx, US 132/E3
Lake Grace, Austl. 112/C5
Lake Harbour, NW, Can. 123/K2
Lake Havasu City, Az, US 128/D4
Lake Hiwassee, Ok, US 137/N14
Lake in the Hills, Il, US 135/P15
Lake Jackson, Tx, US 129/J5
Lake Lotawana, Mo, US 137/E6
Lake Louise, Ab, Can. 126/D3
Lake Malawi NP, Malw. 105/F3
Lake Manyara NP, Tanz. 104/B3
Lake Mburo NP, Ugan. 104/A3
Lake Mead Nat'l Rec. Area, US 128/D4
Lake Meredith Nat'l Rec. Area, Tx, US 132/C3
Lake Minchumina, Ak, US 134/H3
Lake Mohawk, NJ, US 138/D1
Lake Nakuru NP, Kenya 104/C3
Lake of the Woods (lake), US,Can. 127/K3
Lake Orion, Mi, US 135/F6
Lake Point Junction, Ut, US 137/J12
Lake Providence, La, US 129/K4
Lake Ronkonkoma, NY, US 139/F2
Lake Shore, Md, US 138/B5
Lake Station, In, US 135/R16
Lake Success, NY, US 139/L8
Lake Villa, Il, US 135/P15
Lake Wales, Fl, US 133/H5
Lake Winnebago, Mo, US 137/F6
Lake Worth, Fl, US 133/H5
Lake Zurich, Il, US 135/P15
Lakehurst, NJ, US 138/D3
Lakehurst Naval Air Eng. Ctr., NJ, US 138/D3
Lakeland, Fl, US 133/H4
Lakeland Village, Ca, US 136/C3
Lakemoor, Il, US 135/P15
Lakeport, Ca, US 128/B3
Lakes Entrance, Austl. 115/C3
Lakes NP, The, Austl. 115/C3
Lakesfjorden (inlet), Nor. 37/H1
Lakeside, Ca, US 136/D5
Lakeview, Or, US 126/C5
Lakeview, Ut, US 137/K13
Lakeview, Ca, US 136/C3
Lakeville (lake), Mi, US 135/F6
Lakeway, Tx, US 129/H5
Lakewood, Wa, US 126/C3
Lakewood, Co, US 137/B3
Lakewood, NJ, US 138/D3
Lakewood, Ca, US 136/F8
Lakewood, Oh, US 130/D3
Lakhdenpokh'ya, Rus. 60/D1
Lakhemaa NP, Est. 39/L2
Lakhimpur, India 84/C2
Lakhnādon, India 84/C3
Laki (vol.), Ice. 37/N7
Lakki, Pak. 86/A3
Lakkion, Gre. 47/H4
Lakonia (gulf), Gre. 47/H4
Lakor (isl.), Indo. 67/F5
Lakota, Ivor.C. 102/C4
Laksefjord (inlet), Nor. 37/H1
Lakshadweep (terr.), India 82/B6
Lakshadweep (isls.), India 67/F7
Lal Suhanra NP, Pak. 86/B3
Lala Mūsa, Pak. 86/C2
Lalana (riv.), Madg. 107/H8
Lalang (riv.), Indo. 80/B4
Lalganj, India 84/E2
Lālgola, India 85/E3
Lālian, India 86/B4
Lalín, Sp. 44/A1
Lalinde, Fr. 42/D4
Lalitpur, India 84/B3
Lalitpur (Pāṭan), Nepal 85/E2
Lalla Rookh Abor. Land, Austl. 112/C2
Lamachan (peak), Sc, UK 34/...
Lamadrid, Mex. 132/C5
Lamanai (ruin), Belz. 144/D2
Lamandau (riv.), Indo. 80/C4
Lamar, Co, US 128/G4
Lamarche, Fr. 53/E6
Lamarche-sur-Saône, Fr. 56/A3
Lamarque, Arg. 158/D3
Lamas, Peru 156/B2
Lambach, Aus. 55/G6
Lamballe, Fr. 42/B2
Lambaré, Par. 157/E2
Lambaréné, Gabon 96/H8

Lambari, Braz. 211/H6
Lambay (isl.), Ire. 31/Q10
Lambayeque (dept.), Peru 156/A2
Lambayeque, Peru 156/B2
Lambé Coba (riv.), Mali 102/C3
Lambert-St. Louis (int'l arpt.), Mo, US 129/K3
Lambert's Bay, SAfr. 106/B4
Lambertville, Mi, US 130/D3
Lambertville, NJ, US 138/D2
Lambesc, Fr. 42/F5
Lambeth (bor.), Eng, UK 35/F...
Lambton (co.), On, Can. 135/H6
Lambunao, Phil. 79/D5
Lamego, Port. 44/B2
Lamèque (isl.), NB, Can. 131/H2
Lamesa, Tx, US 129/G4
Lamia, Gre. 47/H3
Lamington NP, Austl. 114/D5
Lamitan, Phil. 81/F2
Lamlash, Sc, UK 36/A5
Lamma (isl.), China 71/U11
Lammermuir (hills), Sc, UK 36/D5
Lammhult, Swe. 38/F3
Lammi, Fin. 39/L1
Lamon (riv.), It. 43/J4
Lamone (riv.), It. 59/E3
Lamont, Ca, US 136/C2
Lamont (int'l arpt.), La, US 129/K4
Lamorlaye, Fr. 30/K4
Lamotrek (isl.), Micr. 116/D4
Lampa, Peru 156/D4
Lampa, Chile 158/N8
Lampang, Thai. 78/B2
Lampasas, Tx, US 129/H5
Lampasas (riv.), Tx, US 143/F2
Lampazos de Naranjo, Mex. 132/C5
Lampedusa, It. 46/C5
Lampedusa (isl.), It. 27/F5
Lampertheim, Ger. 54/B3
Lampeter, Wal, UK 35/D5
Lamphun, Thai. 78/B2
Lampman, Sk, Can. 127/H3
Lamporecchio, It. 59/D3
Lampung, Indo. 80/B5
Lamu, Kenya 104/D3
Lamud, Peru 156/B2
Lamstedt, Ger. 51/G1
Lan Sang NP, Thai. 78/B2
Lana, It. 57/H4
Lana, Río de la (riv.), Mex. 144/C2
Lanai (isl.), Hi, US 117/K2
Lanaihale (peak), Hi, US 124/T10
Lanaken, Belg. 53/E2
Lanao (lake), Phil. 81/G5
Lanark, Sc, UK 36/C5
Lanark (co.), On, Can. 131/F2
Lancang Lahuzu Zizhixian, China 83/G3
Lancashire (plain), Eng, UK 35/E4
Lancashire (co.), Eng, UK 35/F4
Lancaster, SC, US 133/H3
Lancaster, Ca, US 128/C4
Lancaster, NY, US 131/S10
Lancaster (sound), NW, Can. 123/S7
Lancaster, Pa, US 138/C3
Lancaster, Eng, UK 35/F3
Lancaster Sound (bay), NW, Can. 123/H1
Lancelin, Austl. 112/B4
Lanciano, It. 46/D1
L'ancienne-Lorette, Qu, Can. 131/G2
Lanco, Chile 158/B3
Lancun, China 72/E3
Lancy, Swi. 56/C5
Land Kehdingen (reg.), Ger. 51/G1
Landau an der Isar, Ger. 55/F5
Landau in der Pfalz, Ger. 54/B4
Landeck, Aus. 55/K3
Lander, Wy, US 126/F5
Landerneau, Fr. 42/A2
Landes (dept.), Fr. 42/C4
Landes de Lanvaux (mts.), Fr. 42/B3
Landesbergen, Ger. 51/G3
Landisburg, Pa, US 138/A3
Landivisiau, Fr. 42/A2
Landrecies, Fr. 52/C3
Landri Sales, Braz. 154/B2
Landriano, It. 58/C2
Land's End (pt.), Eng, UK 32/A6
Landsberg, Ger. 57/G1
Landser, Fr. 56/D2
Landshut, Ger. 55/F5
Landskrona, Swe. 38/E4
Landsmeer, Neth. 50/B4
Landstuhl, Ger. 53/G5
Landvetter (int'l arpt.), Swe. 38/E3
Lane End, Eng, UK 30/A2
Lanett, Al, US 133/G3
Lang Craig (riv.), Sc, UK 36/C5
Lang Kha Tuk (peak), Thai. 78/B4
Lang Son, Viet. 83/J3
Lang Suan, Thai. 78/B4
Langadhás, Gre. 47/H2
Langdon, ND, US 127/J3

Langeac, Fr. 42/E4
Wy, US 124/E3
Langebaanweg, SAfr. 106/L10
Langeberg (mts.), SAfr. 106/L10
Langeland (isl.), Ger. 38/D4
Langen, Ger. 51/F1
Langen, Ger. 54/B3
Langenaltheim, Ger. 54/D5
Langenargen, Ger. 55/F2
Langenau, Ger. 54/D5
Langenbach, Ger. 55/E6
Langenberg, Ger. 51/E6
Langenburg, Ger. 54/D5
Längenfeld, Aus. 57/G3
Längenfeld, Ger. 53/F1
Langenhagen, Ger. 51/G4
Langenlois, Aus. 41/H4
Langenpreising, Ger. 55/E6
Langenselbold, Ger. 54/C2
Langenstein, Aus. 55/H6
Langenthal, Swi. 56/D3
Langenzersdorf, Aus. 49/N1
Langeoog, Ger. 51/E1
Langeoog (isl.), Ger. 51/E1
Langerringen, Ger. 57/G1
Langeskov, Den. 38/D4
Langesund, Den. 38/C2
Langeten (riv.), Swi. 56/D3
Langfang, China 72/H7
Langfurth, Ger. 54/D4
Langgam, Indo. 80/B3
Langham, Sk, Can. 126/G2
Langhirano, It. 58/D3
Langholm, Sc, UK 35/F1
Langhorne, Pa, US 138/D3
Langjökull (glacier), Ice. 37/N7
Langkawi (isl.), Malay. 83/G6
Langley, Wa, US 135/C1
Langnau im Emmental, Swi. 56/D4
Langney (pt.), Eng, UK 31/G5
Langogne, Fr. 42/E4
Langon, Fr. 42/C4
Langøya (isl.), Nor. 37/E1
Langquaid, Ger. 55/F5
Langres, Fr. 42/F3
Langres, Plateau de (plat.), Fr. 42/F3
Langsa, Indo. 80/A3
Langshyttan, Swe. 38/G1
Langtang Lirung (peak), Nepal 85/E1
Langtang NP, Nepal 85/E1
Langtry, Tx, US 132/C4
Languedoc (reg.), Fr. 42/E5
Languedoc-Roussillon (reg.), Fr. 42/E5
Langwedel, Ger. 51/G3
Langweid an Lech, Ger. 54/E6
Langxi, China 72/D5
Langwies, Swi. 57/F4
Lanham-Seabrook, Md, US 138/B5
Lanigan, Sk, Can. 127/G3
Lanin (vol.), Arg. 158/C3
Lanin, PN, Arg. 157/B4
Länkäran, Azer. 63/J5
Lanlacuni Bajo, Peru 156/D4
Lannemezan (plat.), Fr. 42/D5
Lannion (bay), Fr. 42/B2
Lannion, Fr. 42/B2
Lansdale, Pa, US 138/C3
Lansdowne, India 84/B1
Lansdowne, Pa, US 138/C4
Lansing-Baltimore-Highlands, Md, US 138/B5
Lansford, Pa, US 138/C3
Lanshan, China 83/K2
Lansing (riv.), Mi, US 130/C3
Lansing, Ks, US 137/D5
Lansing, Il, US 135/Q16
Lanta (isl.), Thai. 83/G6
Lantau (chan.), China 71/T11
Lantau (peak), China 71/T11
Lantau (isl.), China 71/T11
Lanterne (riv.), Fr. 56/C2
Lanús, Arg. 159/J11
Lanusei, It. 46/A3
Lanxi, China 79/C2
Lanzarote (int'l arpt.), Sp. 98/B3
Lanzarote (isl.), Sp. 98/B3
Lanzhot, Czh. 41/J4
Lanzhou, China 70/H4
Lao (mts.), China 73/D2
Lao Cai, Viet. 70/H7
Laoag, Phil. 79/E5
Laohekou, China 72/B4
Laojun (mtn.), China 73/B4
Laojunmiao, China 70/H4
Laon, Fr. 52/C4
Laos (ctry.) 67/K8
Laotuding (peak), China 73/C2
Laou (riv.), Mor. 100/B2
Lapa, Braz. 155/B3
Lapalisse, Fr. 42/E3
Lapeer (co.), Mi, US 135/F5
Lapeer, Mi, US 135/F5
Lapinlahti, Fin. 60/E3
Lapland (reg.), Swe. 37/G2
Laplume, Fr. 42/D4
Lappeenranta, Fin. 39/N1
Lappi (prov.), Fin. 37/H2
Laptev (sea), Rus. 67/M2
Lapua, Fin. 60/D3
Lapua (riv.), Fin. 37/G3
Lāpuš, Pol. 41/M2
L'Aquila, It. 46/C1
Lār, Iran 89/F3
Lara, Austl. 115/C3
Lara (state), Ven. 152/D2
Laracha, Sp. 44/A1
Larache, Mor. 100/B2
Laragne-Montéglin, Fr. 42/F4
Laramie, Wy, US 127/G5
Laramie (riv.), Wy, US 127/G5
Lathrop, Ca, US 135/M11

Laramie (mts.), Wy, US 124/E3
Latisana, It. 59/G1
Laranjeiras do Sul, Braz. 155/A3
Larat (isl.), Indo. 81/H5
Larba, Alg. 100/G4
Larchmont, NY, US 139/K4
Lærdalsøyri, Nor. 38/B1
Laredo, Peru 156/B3
Laredo, Tx, US 132/D5
Laredo, Sp. 44/D1
Laren, Neth. 50/C4
Lares, Peru 156/C4
Largo, Fl, US 133/H5
Largo, Md, US 138/B4
Largo (bay), Sc, UK 36/C4
Largo, Cayo (isl.), Cuba 145/F1
Largs, Sc, UK 36/B5
Largue (riv.), Fr. 56/D2
Lariang (riv.), Indo. 81/E4
Larino, It. 46/D2
Lárisa, Gre. 47/H3
Lark (riv.), Eng, UK 33/G2
Larkspur, Ca, US 135/J11
Larkhall, Sc, UK 36/C5
Larmor-Plage, Fr. 42/B3
Larnaca (int'l arpt.), Cyp. 91/C2
Larnaca (dist.), Cyp. 91/C2
Larne, NI, UK 34/C2
Larne Lough (inlet), NI, UK 34/C2
Larned, Ks, US 129/H3
Larochette, Lux. 53/F4
Laroque-d'Olmes, Fr. 42/D5
Larose, La, US 133/F4
Larreynaga, Nic. 144/E3
Larroque, Qu, Can. 159/J10
Larsen Bay, Ak, US 134/H4
Larsen Ice Shelf, Ant. 160/V
Larsen Sound (bay), NW, Can. 122/G1
Laura, Austl. 113/H5
Laureana di Borrello, It. 46/E3
Laurel, Mt, US 126/F4
Laurel, Ms, US 133/F4
Laurel, Md, US 138/B5
Laurel Springs, NJ, US 138/D3
Laureldale, Pa, US 138/C3
Laurelton, Pa, US 138/A2
Laurence Harbor, NJ, US 138/D2
Laurencekirk, Sc, UK 36/D3
Laurens, SC, US 133/H3
Laurentian (plat.), On, Can. 122/G3
Laurentides, Fr. 30/H5
Laurinburg, NC, US 133/J3
Laurium, Mi, US 127/L4
Lausanne, Swi. 56/C4
Lausche, Ger. 54/E2
Laut (isl.), Indo. 81/E4
Lautaro, Chile 158/B3
Lauter, Ger. 55/F1
Lauter (riv.), Ger. 40/E3
Lauterach, Aus. 55/F2
Lauterbach (riv.), Ger. 54/E2
Lauterbourg, Fr. 54/B4
Lauterbrunnen, Swi. 56/D4
Lauterecken, Ger. 53/G4
Lauve, Nor. 38/C2
Lauwe (chan.), Neth. 50/D1
Lauwersmeer (lake), Neth. 50/D1
Lava Beds Nat'l Mon., Ca, US 128/C3
Lavagna (riv.), It. 58/C4
Lavagna, It. 58/C4
Laval, Fr. 42/C2
Laval, Qu, Can. 131/N6
Lavalleja (dept.), Uru. 159/G2
Lavallette, NJ, US 138/D3
Lavans-lès-Saint-Claude, Fr. 56/B4
Lavant (riv.), Aus. 43/L3
Lavapié (pt.), Chile 158/B3
Lavaur, Fr. 42/D5
Laveen, Az, US 137/R19
Lavelanet, Fr. 42/D5
Lavello, It. 46/D2
Laveno, It. 57/E6
Laverton, Austl. 112/C4
Lavey, Swi. 56/C5
Lavezzola, It. 59/E3
Lavino (riv.), It. 58/D3
Lavis, It. 57/H4
Lávrion, Gre. 47/J4
Lavras, Braz. 155/C2
Lavras da Mangabeira, Braz. 154/C2
Lawa (riv.), FrG. 153/H4
Lawagamau (riv.), Can. 130/D1
Lāwar Khās, India 84/A1
Lawrai (pass), Pak. 86/A2
Lawit (peak), Malay. 80/B3
Lawit (peak), Malay. 83/H6
Lawn Hill, BC, Can. 134/M5
Lawra, Gha. 102/E3
Lawrence, Ma, US 131/G3
Lawrence, NY, US 139/L9
Lawrenceburg, In, US 130/C3
Lawrenceville, Il, US 130/C4
Lawrenceville, Ga, US 133/G3
Lawson, Mo, US 137/E5
Lawton, Ok, US 129/H4
Lawu (peak), Indo. 80/D5

Latina, It. 46/C2
Lawz, Jabal al (peak), SAr. 88/C3
Laxå, Swe. 38/F2
Laxey, IM, UK 34/D3
Laxou, Fr. 53/F6
Lay (riv.), Fr. 42/C3
Lay-Saint-Christophe, Fr. 53/F6
Layar (cape), Indo. 81/E4
Laylān, Iraq 90/F3
Layon (riv.), Fr. 42/C3
Laysan (isl.), HI, US 117/H2
Layton, Ut, US 137/K11
Layton, NJ, US 138/D1
Lazarevac, Yugo. 48/E3
Lázaro Cárdenas, Mex. 128/D5
Lázaro Cárdenas, Mex. 142/B2
Lázaro Cárdenas, Mex. 142/E5
Lazio (prov.), It. 43/J5
Llbriktepe, Turk. 47/K2
Le Ban-Saint-Martin, Fr. 53/E5
Le Blanc, Fr. 42/D3
Le Blanc-Mesnil, Fr. 30/K5
Le Breuil, Fr. 56/A3
Le Cannet, Fr. 43/G5
Le Cateau-Cambrésis, Fr. 52/C3
Le Chasseral (peak), Swi. 56/D3
Le Chasseron (peak), Swi. 56/C4
Le Chesnay, Fr. 30/J5
Le Chesne, Fr. 53/D4
Le Cheval Blanc (peak), Fr. 56/C5
Le Cheylard, Fr. 42/F4
Le Cornate (peak), It. 43/J5
Le Creusot, Fr. 42/F3
Le Croisy, Fr. 52/A3
Le Gore, Md, US 138/A4
Le Grammont (peak), Swi. 56/C5
Le Grand (cape), Austl. 112/D5
Le Grand Ballon (peak), Fr. 56/D2
Le Grau-du-Roi, Fr. 42/F5
Le Grazie, It. 58/C4
Le Havre, Fr. 42/D2
Le Landeron, Swi. 56/D3
Le Lavandou, Fr. 43/G5
Le Locle, Swi. 56/C3
Le Luc, Fr. 43/G5
Le Mans, Fr. 42/D2
Le Mée-sur-Seine, Fr. 30/K6
Le Mesnil-Amelot, Fr. 30/K4
Le Mesnil-Aubry, Fr. 30/K4
Le Mesnil-Esnard, Fr. 52/A5
Le Mesnil-le-Roi, Fr. 30/J5
Le Mesnil-Saint-Denis, Fr. 30/H5
Le Mesnil-sur-Oger, Fr. 52/D6
Le Môle (peak), Fr. 56/C5
Le Morond (peak), Fr. 56/C4
Le Moure de la Gardille (peak), Fr. 42/E4
Le Murge (mts.), It. 46/E2
Le Noirmont (peak), Swi. 56/C3
Le Noirmont, Swi. 56/C3
Le Nouvion-en-Thiérache, Fr. 52/C3
Le Palais, Fr. 42/B3
Le Palais-sur-Vienne, Fr. 42/D4
Le Passage, Fr. 42/D4
Le Perray-en-Yvelines, Fr. 30/H5
Le Petit Ballon (peak), Fr. 56/D2
Le Plessis-Belleville, Fr. 30/L4
Le Plessis-Feu-Aussoux, Fr. 30/M5
Le Plessis-Placy, Fr. 30/L4
Le Port, Reun. 107/S15
Le Portel, Fr. 52/A2
Le Puy-en-Velay, Fr. 42/E4
Le Quesnoy, Fr. 52/C3
Le Russey, Fr. 56/C3
Le Suchet (peak), Swi. 56/C4
Le Tampon, Reun. 107/S15
Le Teil, Fr. 42/F4
Le Tholy, Fr. 56/C1
Le Touquet-Paris-Plage, Fr. 52/A2
Le Tréport, Fr. 52/A2
Le Val-d'Ajol, Fr. 56/C2
Le Vésinet, Fr. 30/J5
Le Vigan, Fr. 42/E5
Lea (riv.), Eng, UK 33/F3
Leach (lake), Ca, US 137/K4
Leach (riv.), Eng, UK 33/E3
Leacock-Leola-Bareville, Pa, US 138/B3
Lead, SD, US 127/H4
Leader, Sk, Can. 126/F3
Leader Water (riv.), Sc, UK 36/D5
Leadon (riv.), Eng, UK 32/D3
Leadville, Co, US 132/B2
Leaf (riv.), Can. 130/D3
League City, Tx, US 129/H5
Leakey, Tx, US 129/H5
Leamington, On, Can. 130/D3
Leamington Spa, Eng, UK 35/E5
Le'an, China 79/C2
Leander (pt.), Austl. 112/A3
Leaota (peak), Rom. 49/G3
Learmonth, Austl. 112/A2
Leatherhead, Eng, UK 30/C3
Leavenworth, Wa, US 126/C4
Leavenworth (co.), Ks, US 137/D5
Leavenworth, Ks, US 137/D5
Leawood, Ks, US 137/D6
Lebak, Phil. 79/D6

Leban – Loeri

Lebane, Yugo. 47/G1
Lebanon, Or, US 126/C4
Lebanon, In, US 130/C3
Lebanon, Tn, US 130/C4
Lebanon, Ky, US 130/C4
Lebanon, NH, US 131/F3
Lebanon, Mo, US 129/J3
Lebanon (mts.), Leb. 91/D3
Lebanon (ctry.) 67/C6
Lebanon, NJ, US 138/D2
Lebanon, Pa, US 138/B3
Lebedyn, Ukr. 62/E2
Lebel-sur-Quévillon, Qu, Can. 100/B2
Lebene (riv.), Mor. 100/B1
Lébény, Hun. 48/C2
Lębork, Pol. 38/G4
Lebrija, Sp. 44/B4
Lebu, Chile 157/B4
Lebu, Chile 158/B3
Leça da Palmeira, Port. 44/A2
Lecce, It. 47/F2
Lecco, It. 43/H4
Lecco, Lago di (lake), It. 58/C1
Lech (riv.), Ger. 43/K2
Lech, Aus. 57/G3
Lechang, China 83/K2
Lechbruck, Ger. 57/G2
Leche (lake), Cuba 145/G1
Lechtaler Alps (mts.), Aus. 57/G3
Leck, Ger. 38/C4
Lectoure, Fr. 42/D5
Ledu (peak), It. 57/F5
Leduc, Ab, Can. 126/E2
Lee (riv.), Ire. 31/P11
Lee (mtn.), Pa, US 138/B1
Leech (lake), Mn, US 125/H2
Leeds, Eng, UK 35/G4
Leeds and Bradford (int'l arpt.), Eng, UK 35/G4
Leeds and Liverpool (canal), Eng, UK 35/G4
Leeds Point, NJ, US 138/D5
Leegebruch, Ger. 40/C6
Leek, Neth. 50/D2
Leek, Eng, UK 35/F5
Leeman, Austl. 112/B4
Leer, Ger. 51/E2
Leerdam, Neth. 50/C5
Leersum, Neth. 50/C4
Lees Summit, Mo, US 137/E6
Leesburg, Fl, US 133/H4
Leesburg, Va, US 138/D5
Leese, Ger. 51/G3
Leesport, Pa, US 138/C3
Leesville, La, US 129/J5
Leeton, Austl. 115/C2
Leeu (riv.), SAfr. 106/L10
Leeudoringstad, SAfr. 106/D2
Leeuwarden, Neth. 50/C2
Leeuwin (cape), Austl. 112/B5
Leeuwin-Naturaliste NP, Austl. 112/B5
Leeward (isls.), NAm. 141/J4
Leff (riv.), Fr. 42/B2
Lefka, Cyp. 91/C2
Lefo (peak), Camr. 103/H5
Lefroy (lake), Austl. 112/D4
Legana, Austl. 115/C4
Leganés, Sp. 45/N9
Legaspi, Phil. 79/D5
Legau, Ger. 57/G2
Legazpia, Sp. 44/D1
Legges Tor (peak), Austl. 115/C4
Legionowo, Pol. 41/L2
Léglise, Belg. 53/E4
Legnano, It. 59/E2
Legnano, It. 43/H4
Legnaro, It. 59/E2
Legnica, Pol. 41/J3
Legnone (peak), It. 57/F5
Leh, India 86/D2
Leh Palace, India 86/D2
Lehi, Ut, US 137/K13
Lehigh (co.), Pa, US 138/C2
Lehigh Acres, Fl, US 133/H5
Leighton, Pa, US 138/C2
Lehinch, Ire. 31/P10
Lehrberg, Ger. 54/D4
Lehrte, Ger. 51/G4
Lei (riv.), China 83/K2
Leiah, Pak. 86/A4
Leiblfing, Ger. 55/F5
Leibo, China 83/H2
Leicester, Eng, UK 33/E1
Leicester-Shire (co.), Eng, UK 35/H4
Leichhardt (riv.), Austl. 109/C2
Leichhardt (dam), Austl. 113/H2
Leichlingen, Ger. 53/G1
Leiden, Neth. 50/B4
Leiderdorp, Neth. 50/B4
Leidschendam, Neth. 50/B4
Leie (riv.), Belg. 42/E1
Leifers (Laives), It.
Leigh, Eng, UK 35/F5
Leigh Creek, Austl. 115/A1
Leimebamba, Peru 156/B2
Leimen, Ger. 54/B4
Leimersheim, Ger. 54/B4
Leine (riv.), Ger. 40/D3
Leinefelde, Ger. 51/H6
Leinfelden-Echterdingen, Ger. 54/C5
Leinster (mt.), Ire. 31/Q10
Leinster, Austl. 112/D3
Leinster (reg.), Ire. 34/A5

Leipheim, Ger. 54/D6
Leipsic, De, US 138/C5
Leipsic (riv.), De, US 138/C5
Leipzig, Ger. 64/B4
Leira, Nor. 38/C1
Leiria (dist.), Port. 44/A3
Leiria, Port. 44/A3
Leisler (mt.), Austl. 113/F2
Leith (hill), Eng, UK 30/B3
Leitha (riv.), Aus. 57/H5
Leixlip, Ire. 34/B5
Leizhou (pen.), China 83/J3
Lekkainá, Gre. 47/G4
Lek (riv.), Neth. 40/C3
Lekkerkerk, Neth. 50/B5
Lekki (lag.), Nga. 103/G5
Leksands-Noret, Swe. 38/F1
Leksozero (lake), Rus. 37/J3
Lelai (cape), Indo. 81/G3
Leland, Ms, US 129/K4
Lelâng (lake), Swe. 38/E2
Leling, China 72/D3
Lelystad, Neth. 50/C3
Lem, Den. 38/C3
Léman (Geneva) (lake), Fr. 43/G3
Lemberg (peak), Ger. 57/E6
Lemberg, Ger. 53/G5
Lembu (peak), Indo. 80/A3
Leme, Braz. 155/C2
Lemenjoen NP, Fin. 37/H1
Lemgo, Ger. 51/F4
Lemland (isl.), Fin. 39/H2
Lemland, Fin. 39/J1
Lemmer, Neth. 50/C3
Lemmon, SD, US 127/H4
Lemon Grove, Ca, US 136/C5
Lempa (riv.), ESal. 144/D3
Lempäälä, Fin. 39/K1
Lempdes, Fr. 42/E4
Lemvig, Den. 38/C3
Lemverder, Ger. 51/F2
Lena (riv.), Rus. 67/M3
Lena, Nor. 38/D1
Lenape, Ks, US 137/D6
Lenape (lake), NJ, US 138/D4
Lençóis Maranhenses, PN dos, Braz. 151/K4
Lençóis Paulista, Braz. 155/B2
Lendinara, It. 59/E2
Lenexa, Ks, US 137/D6
Lengau, Aus. 55/G6
Lengdorf, Ger. 55/F6
Lengede, Ger. 51/H4
Lengenfeld, Ger. 55/F1
Lengerich, Ger. 51/E4
Lenggries, Ger. 57/H2
Lengnau, Swi. 56/D3
Lengshuitan, China 83/K2
Lengua de Vaca (pt.), Chile 158/C3
Lenhartsville, Pa, US 138/C2
Lenina (peak), Taj. 87/F5
Leninabad (int'l arpt.), Taj. 87/E4
Leningrad Oblast, Rus. 60/G3
Leninobod (obl.), Taj. 87/E5
Leninogorsk, Rus. 61/M5
Leninsk-Kuznetskiy, Rus. 64/J4
Leninváros, Hun. 41/L5
Lenk, Swi. 56/D5
Lennestadt, Ger. 51/F6
Lennox (peak), Chile 159/D7
Lennox, Ca, US 136/F8
Lennox (hills), Sc, UK 36/B5
Leno, It. 58/D2
Lenoir, NC, US 133/H3
Lenoir City, Tn, US 133/G3
Lens, Swi. 56/D5
Lens, Fr. 52/B2
Lens, Belg. 52/C2
Lensahn, Ger. 38/D4
Lensk, Rus. 65/M3
Lenting, Ger. 55/E5
Lentini, It. 47/G6
Lenvik, Nor. 37/F1
Leny, Pass of (pass), Sc, UK 36/B4
Lenzburg, Swi. 56/E3
Lenzing, Aus. 55/G7
Lenzkirch, Ger. 57/E2
Léo, Burk. 103/E4
Leoben, Aus. 43/L3
Leográ (riv.), It. 59/E1
Leola, SD, US 127/J4
León, Mex. 143/E4
León (int'l arpt.), Mex. 142/C3
León, Sp. 44/C1
León, Nic. 144/E4
Leon (riv.), Tx, US 130/G4
Leon, Ia, US 137/F5
Léon, Étang de (lake), Fr. 42/C4
León-Guanajuato (int'l arpt.), Mex. 143/E4
Leon Springs, Tx, US 137/T20
Leon Valley, Tx, US 137/T21
Leonardo, NJ, US 138/B5
Leonard, Mi, US 129/H4
Leonardo da Vinci (int'l arpt.), It. 46/C2
Leonberg, Ger. 54/C5
Leonding, Aus. 55/H6
Leone (peak), It. 56/D5
Leonforte, It. 46/D4
Leongatha, Austl. 115/C4
Leonia, NJ, US 139/K8
Leonídhion, Gre. 47/H4
Leonora, Austl. 112/D4
Leopoldina, Braz. 211/L6
Leopoldkanaal (riv.), Belg. 52/C1
Leopoldsburg, Belg. 53/E1

Leopoldsdorf, Aus. 49/N7
Leopoldsdorf im Marchfelde, Aus. 49/P7
Leopoldshöhe, Ger. 51/F4
Leoville, Sk, Can. 126/G2
Lepaera, Hon. 144/D3
Lépanges-sur-Vologne, Fr. 53/F6
Lepe, Sp. 44/B4
Lepenoú, Gre. 47/G3
Lepontine Alps (mts.), Swi. 43/H3
Leptokariá, Gre. 47/H2
Léraba (riv.), Burk. 102/D4
Lercara Friddi, It. 46/C4
Lerdo de Tejada, Mex. 144/C2
Leribe, Les. 106/E3
Lerici, It. 58/C4
Lerín, Sp. 44/E1
Lerma, Sp. 44/D1
Lerma, Mex. 143/Q10
Lerma (riv.), Mex. 119/G7
Lermoos, Aus. 57/G3
Lérouville, Fr. 53/E6
Lerum, Swe. 38/E3
Lerwick, Sc, UK 31/W13
Lery (lake), La, US 137/Q17
Léry, Qu, Can. 131/N7
Les Alluets-le-Roi, Fr. 30/H5
Les Bois, Swi. 56/D3
Les Breuleux, Swi. 56/D3
Les Bréviaires, Fr. 30/H5
Les Cayes, Haiti 147/H4
Les Cèdres, Qu, Can. 131/M7
Les Clayes-sous-Bois, Fr. 30/H5
Les Contamines-Montjoie, Fr. 56/C6
Les Diablerets (range), Swi. 56/D5
Les Essarts-le-Roi, Fr. 30/H5
Les Gets, Fr. 56/C5
Les Herbiers, Fr. 42/C3
Les Islettes, Fr. 53/E5
Les Mesnuls, Fr. 30/H5
Les Molières, Fr. 30/J6
Les Mureaux, Fr. 52/A6
Les Ponts-de-Martel, Swi. 56/C4
Les Rousses, Fr. 56/C5
Les Sables-d'Olonne, Fr. 42/C3
Les Salines (int'l arpt.), Alg. 100/K6
Les Ulis, Fr. 30/J5
Les Verrières, Swi. 58/B1
Lesa, It. 58/B1
Leshan, China 83/H2
Lésigny, Fr. 30/K5
Lesima (peak), It. 58/C3
Lesja, Nor. 37/D3
Lesjöfors, Swe. 38/F2
Lesko, Pol. 41/M4
Leskovac, Yugo. 47/G1
Leslie, Sc, UK 36/C4
Lesmahagow, Sc, UK 36/B5
Lesneven, Fr. 42/A2
Leśnica, Yugo. 48/D3
Lesosibirsk, Rus. 68/H4
Lesotho (ctry.) 93/E7
Lesozavodsk, Rus. 71/P2
Lesparre-Médoc, Fr. 42/C4
Lesquin (int'l arpt.), Fr. 52/C2
Lesse (riv.), Belg. 40/C3
Lessebo, Swe. 38/F3
Lessines, Belg. 52/C2
Lesung (peak), Indo. 80/D3
Lésvos (isl.), Gre. 62/C5
Leszno, Pol. 41/J3
Létavértes, Hun. 48/E2
Letchworth, Eng, UK 33/F3
Letham, Sc, UK 36/D3
Lethbridge, Ab, Can. 126/E3
Lethem, Guy. 153/G4
Leti (isls.), Indo. 116/B5
Leticia, Col. 156/D2
Leting, China 73/B2
Letlhakane, Bots. 105/E5
Letlhakeng, Bots. 105/E5
Letnitsa, Bul. 49/G4
Letpadan, Myan. 83/G4
Letsôk-Aw (isl.), Myan. 80/A1
Letterkenny, Ire. 31/Q9
Leucate, Fr. 42/E5
Leuchars, Sc, UK 36/D4
Leuk, Swi. 56/D5
Leukerbad, Swi. 56/D5
Leusden-Zuid, Neth. 50/C4
Leuser (peak), Indo. 80/A3
Leutenhausen, Ger. 54/D4
Leutkirch im Allgäu, Ger. 57/G2
Leuze-en-Hainaut, Belg. 52/C2
Levádhia, Gre. 47/H3
Levallois-Perret, Fr. 30/J5
Levanger, Nor. 37/D3
Levante, Riviera di (coast), It. 58/C4
Levanto, It. 58/C4
Levanzo (isl.), It. 46/C4...

Levico Terme, It. 57/H5
Levier, Fr. 56/C4
Levin, NZ 117/T11
Lévis, Qu, Can. 131/G2
Lévis-Saint-Nom, Fr. 30/H5
Levittown, Pa, US 138/D3
Levittown, NY, US 139/L9
Levkás, Gre. 47/G3
Levkás (isl.), Gre. 47/G3
Levkímmi, Gre. 47/G3
Levoča, Slvk. 41/L4
Levroux (bay), Mrta. 98/A5
Levski, Bul. 49/G4
Lewes, Eng, UK 33/G5
Lewes (range), Mt, US 126/E3
Lewis (hills), Can. 131/J2
Lewis (pass), NZ 117/S11
Lewis and Clark (lake), Al, US 127/J5
Lewis Smith (lake), Al, US 133/G3
Lewisburg, Tn, US 133/G3
Lewisburg, WV, US 130/D4
Lewisburg, Pa, US 138/B2
Lewisham (bor.), Eng, UK 30/C2
Lewisport, Ky, US 130/C4
Lewiston, Id, US 126/D4
Lewiston, Me, US 131/G2
Lewiston, NY, US 131/R9
Lewistown, Mt, US 126/F4
Lewistown, Pa, US 138/B2
Lewisville, Tx, US 130/G3
Lewotobi (peak), Indo. 81/F5
Lexington, Ne, US 127/J5
Lexington, Tn, US 130/B5
Lexington, Ky, US 130/C4
Lexington, NC, US 133/H3
Lexington Park, Md, US 130/E4
Leyburn, Eng, UK 35/G3
Leyland, Eng, UK 35/F4
Leyte (isl.), Phil. 67/M8
Leysin, Swi. 56/D5
Leytron, Swi. 56/D5
Lez (riv.), Fr. 42/A5
Lézignan-Corbières, Fr. 42/E5
Leżajsk, Pol. 41/M3
Lezhê, Alb. 47/F2
L'gov, Rus. 62/E2
Lhanbryd, Sc, UK 36/C1
Lhari, China 70/F5
Lhasa, China 82/F2
Lhazê, China 85/F1
L'Hongrin (lake), Swi. 56/D5
Lhorong, China 70/G5
Lhozhag, China 85/H1
Lhünzê, China 83/G2
Li (riv.), China 79/B2
Li (riv.), China 83/K2
Li (mtn.), China 72/B4
Li Xian, China 79/B2
Lian Xian, China 83/K3
Liancourt, Fr. 52/B5
Liancourt Rocks (isl.), Asia 74/B2
Liangcheng, China 79/C2
Liangpran (peak), Indo. 80/D3
Lianhua, China 83/K2
Lianjiang, China 79/C2
Liannan Yaozu Zizhixian, China 83/K3
Lianshui, China 72/D4
Lianyuan, China 79/B2
Lianyungang, China 72/D4
Liao (riv.), China 67/M5
Liaocheng, China 72/D3
Liaodong (pen.), China 73/A3
Liaodong (isls.), China 72/E3
Liaodong, Gulf of (gulf), China 71/M3
Liaoning (prov.), China 71/M3
Liaoyang, China 73/B2
Liaoyuan, China 71/N3
Liaozhong, China 73/B2
Liāqatpur, Pak. 86/A5
Liauwwap, Wa, US 135/A3
Libby, Mt, US 126/E3
Libčhovice (riv.), Czh. 55/H2
Liberdade, Braz. 151/H6
Liberdade, Braz. 211/J7
Liberec, Czh. 41/H3
Liberia, CR 144/E4
Liberia (ctry.) 93/B4
Libertad, Belz. 144/D2
Libertad, Uru. 159/K11
Libertador General San Martín, Arg. 157/D1
Liberty, Tx, US 129/J5
Liberty, Ky, US 130/C4
Liberty, Ms, US 129/K5
Liberty, Mo, US 137/E5
Liberty, Ut, US 137/K11
Liberty (res.), Md, US 138/B5
Liberty Grove, Braz.
Libertyville, Il, US 135/P15
Libín, Belg. 53/E4
Libo, China 83/J2
Libobo (cape), Indo. 81/G4
Liboc (riv.), Czh. 41/G3
Libochovice, Czh. 55/H2
Libon, Phil. 79/D5
Librazhd, Alb. 47/G2
Libres, Mex. 143/M7
Libreville (cap.), Gabon 96/G7
Librilla, Sp. 44/E3
Libyan (ctry.) 93/D2
Libyan (plat.), Libya 97/K1

Libyan (des.), Egypt,Liby 93/E2
Licantén, Chile 158/B2
Licata, It. 46/C4
Lich, Ger. 54/B1
Licheng, China 72/C3
Licheng, China 72/D3
Lichinga, Moz. 105/G3
Lichtenau, Ger. 51/F5
Lichtenau, Ger. 54/D4
Lichtenau, Ger. 54/B5
Lichtenfels, Ger. 54/D2
Lichtenrade, Ger. 40/Q7
Lichtensteig, Swi. 57/F3
Lichtenvoorde, Neth. 50/D5
Lichtervelde, Belg. 52/C1
Licinio de Almeida, Braz. 154/B4
Lick Observatory, Ca, US 135/L12
Licking (riv.), Ky, US 130/C4
Licosa (cape), It. 46/D2
Licques, Fr. 52/A2
Lida, Bela. 39/L5
Liddel Water (riv.), Sc, UK 35/F1
Liden, Swe. 38/F1
Lidköping, Swe. 38/E2
Lidzbark, Pol. 41/K2
Lidzbark Warmiński, Pol. 39/J4
Liebenau, Aus. 55/H5
Liebenbergsvlei (riv.), SAfr. 106/L10
Liebig (mt.), Austl. 113/F2
Liechtenstein (ctry.) 27/E4
Liedekerke, Belg. 53/D2
Liège (prov.), Belg. 53/E3
Liège, Belg. 53/E3
Lieksa, Fin. 60/F3
Lienden, Neth. 50/C5
Lienen, Ger. 51/E4
Lienz, Aus. 43/K3
Liepāja, Lat. 39/J3
Lier, Belg. 53/D1
Lierneux, Belg. 53/E3
Lieser (riv.), Ger. 53/F3
Liesjärven NP, Fin. 39/K1
Liesse-Notre-Dame, Fr. 52/C4
Liestal, Swi. 56/D3
Liétor, Sp. 44/E3
Liévin, Fr. 52/B2
Lièvre (riv.), Can. 130/F2
Liezen, Aus. 43/L3
Liffey (riv.), Ire. 34/B5
Lifford, Ire. 31/Q9
Ligao, Phil. 81/F1
Lightning Ridge, Austl. 115/C1
Lightwater, Eng, UK 30/G8
Lignano Sabbiadoro, It. 59/G1
Ligny-en-Barrois, Fr. 53/E5
Ligonció (peak), It. 57/F5
Ligoúrion, Gre. 47/H4
Liguori, Mo, US 137/G9
Liguria (pol. reg.), It. 58/B4
Liguria (prov.), It. 43/H5
Ligurian (sea), Fr./It. 43/H5
Lihou (reefs), Austl. 109/E2
Lihue, Hi, US 124/S10
Lijiang Naxizu Zizhixian, China 83/H2
Likasi, D.R. Congo 105/E3
Likely, BC, Can. 126/C2
Likoma (isl.), Malw. 105/F3
Likouala (riv.), Congo 104/D2
Likova (riv.), Rus. 61/W9
Lili'āni, Pak. 86/B3
Lilienthal, Ger. 51/F2
Liling, China 83/K2
Lilla Edet, Swe. 38/E2
Lille, Belg. 50/B6
Lille, Fr. 52/C2
Lille Bælt (chan.), Ger. 38/D1
Lillehammer, Nor. 38/D1
Lillers, Fr. 52/B2
Lillesand, Nor. 38/C2
Lillestrøm, Nor. 38/D2
Lillo, Sp. 44/D3
Lilongwe (cap.), Malw. 105/F3
Liloy, Phil. 79/D6
Lim (riv.), Yugo. 47/F1
Lima (dept.), Peru 156/B3
Lima, Peru 156/B4
Lima (riv.), Port. 45/A2
Lima, Oh, US 130/C3
Lima, Arg. 159/J11
Lima Duarte, Braz. 211/K6
Limache, Chile 158/N8
Limanowa, Pol. 41/L4
Limassol, Cyp. 91/C2
Limassol (dist.), Cyp. 91/C2
Limavady (dist.), NI, UK 34/A2
Limavady, NI, UK 34/B1
Limay (riv.), Arg. 147/C7
Limbach, Ger. 54/C4
Limbang, Malay. 80/D3
Limbara (peak), It. 46/B2
Limbdi, India 86/A4
Limbé, Haiti 145/H2
Limbiate, It. 58/B2
Limbourg, Belg. 53/E2
Limburg (prov.), Belg. 53/E2
Limburg an der Lahn, Ger. 54/B1
Limburg (prov.), Neth. 53/E2
Limburgerhof, Ger. 54/B4
Lime Village, Ak, US 135/Q16
Limeil-Brévannes, Fr. 30/K5
Limeira, Braz. 155/C2
Limekilns, Sc, UK 36/C4
Limena, It. 59/E2

Limenária, Gre. 47/J2
Limerick, Ire. 31/P10
Limfjorden (chan.), Den. 38/C3
Limhamn, Swe. 38/E4
Limia (riv.), Sp. 44/B2
Limmared, Swe. 38/E3
Limmat (riv.), Swi. 57/E3
Limmen Bight (bay), Austl. 109/C2
Limni, Gre. 47/H3
Limnos (isl.), Gre. 62/C5
Limoeiro, Braz. 154/C2
Limoeiro do Norte, Braz. 154/C2
Limoges, Fr. 42/D4
Limogne, Causse de (plat.), Fr. 42/D4
Limón, Hon. 144/E3
Limón, CR 144/F4
Limon, Co, US 127/G5
Limours, Fr. 30/H6
Limousin (mts.), Fr. 42/D4
Limousin (pol. reg.), Fr. 42/D4
Limoux, Fr. 42/E5
Limpopo (riv.), Moz. 93/F7
Lin Xian, China 72/C3
Lin'an, China 79/C1
Linapacan (isl.), Phil. 79/C5
Linard (peak), Swi. 57/G4
Linares, Mex. 143/F3
Linares, Sp. 44/D3
Linares, Chile 158/C2
Linate (int'l arpt.), It. 58/C2
Lincang, China 83/H3
Lincheng, China 72/C3
Linchuan, China 79/C2
Lincoln, Il, US 130/C4
Lincoln (peak), Swi. 57/G4
Lincoln, Arg. 158/E2
Lincoln (sea), Can. 119/L1
Lincoln, Pa, US 138/B3
Lincoln, Eng, UK 35/H5
Lincoln, Me, US 131/G2
Lincoln (cap.), Ne, US 137/J5
Lincoln, ND, US 127/J4
Lincoln Beach, Or, US 126/B4
Lincoln City, Or, US 126/B4
Lincoln Heath (woodld.), Eng, UK 35/H5
Lincoln NP, Austl. 113/G5
Lincoln Park, NJ, US 139/H8
Lincoln Park, Mi, US 135/F7
Lincolnshire (co.), Eng, UK 35/H5
Lincolnshire Wolds (grsld.), Eng, UK 35/H4
Lincroft, NJ, US 138/D3
Lind, Den. 38/C2
Lind NP, Austl. 115/D3
Lindau, Ger. 57/F2
Lindau, Swi. 57/F3
Linde (riv.), Neth. 50/D3
Lindeman (chan.), Austl. 114/C3
Linden, Al, US 133/G3
Linden, Tx, US 129/J4
Linden, Guy. 153/G3
Linden, NJ, US 139/J9
Linden, Mi, US 135/E6
Linden, Ger. 54/B1
Linden Beach, Hi, US 135/G7
Lindenberg im Allgäu, Ger. 57/F2
Lindenfels, Ger. 54/B3
Lindenhurst, NY, US 139/F2
Lindenhurst, Il, US 135/P15
Lindenwold, NJ, US 138/D4
Lindern, Ger. 51/E3
Lindesnes (cape), Nor. 38/B2
Lindewitt, Ger. 38/D4
Lindi (pol. reg.), Tanz. 104/C3
Lindlar, Ger. 53/G1
Lindome, Swe. 38/E3
Lindon, Ut, US 137/K13
Lindre (riv.), Fr. 53/F6
Lindsay, Ca, US 136/C2
Lindsay, On, Can. 130/E2
Lindsay, Austl. 112/D4
Lindsdal, Swe. 38/G3
Line (isls.), Kiri. 117/J4
Line Mountain (mtn.), Pa, US 138/B2
Lineboro, Md, US 138/B5
Líneas de Nazca, Peru 156/C4
Linfen, China 72/B3
Ling Xian, China 83/K2
Lingao, China 83/J4
Lingayen, Phil. 79/D4
Lingbao, China 72/B4
Lingbi, China 72/D4
Lingchuan, China 83/K3
Lingen, Ger. 51/E3
Lingfield, Eng, UK 30/C4
Lingga, Indo. 80/B3
Linglestown, Pa, US 138/B3
Lingqiu, China 72/C3
Lingshan, China 72/C4
Lingshi, China 72/B3
Lingshou, China 72/C3
Lingshui, China 83/K4
Lingtou, China 72/C3
Lingue, Sen. 72/L9
Lingyin Si, China 72/L9
Lingyuan, China 73/A2
Linhai, China 79/D2
Linhares, Braz. 155/D1
Linhe, China 70/J3

Linköping, Swe. 38/F2
Linli, China 79/B2
Linlithgow, Sc, UK 36/C5
Linliu (mtn.), China 72/C3
Linnhe (lake), Sc, UK 36/A5
Linqing, China 72/C3
Linqu, China 72/D3
Linquan, China 72/C4
Linru, China 72/C4
Lins, Braz. 155/B2
Linschoten, Neth. 50/B4
Linshu, China 72/D4
Linta (riv.), Madg. 107/H9
Linth (riv.), Swi. 57/F3
Linthal, Swi. 57/F4
Linton, ND, US 127/H4
Linwood, Eng, UK 35/H5
Linwu, China 83/K2
Linxi, China 72/D2
Linxi, China 72/D3
Linxia, China 72/B3
Linying, China 72/C4
Linz, Aus. 55/H6
Linz am Rhein, Ger. 53/G2
Linzhang, China 72/C3
Lion (gulf), Fr.,Sp. 45/G1
Lipa, Phil. 79/D5
Lipari (isl.), It. 46/D3
Lipari (isls.), It. 46/D3
Lipari, It. 46/D3
Liperi, Fin. 60/F3
Lipetsk, Rus. 62/F1
Lipetsk (int'l arpt.), Rus. 62/F1
Lipetsk Oblast, Rus. 62/F1
Lipez (riv.), Bol. 150/E8
Lipez, Cordillera de (mts.), Bol. 150/E8
Liping, China 83/J2
Lipljan, Yugo. 47/G1
Lipno (res.), Czh. 55/H6
Lipno, Pol. 41/K2
Lipno, Údolní nádrž (lake), Czh. 43/L2
Lipova, Rom. 48/E2
Lippe (riv.), Ger. 40/D3
Lippstadt, Ger. 51/F5
Liptovský Svätý Mikuláš, Slvk. 41/K4
Liptrap (cape), Austl. 115/C4
Lira, Ugan. 104/B2
Lircay, Peru 156/C4
Liri (riv.), It. 46/C2
Liria, Sp. 44/E3
Liro (riv.), It. 57/F5
Lisboa (dist.), Port. 44/A3
Lisboa (int'l arpt.), Port. 45/P10
Lisboa (Lisbon) (cap.), Port. 45/P10
Lisbon, ND, US 127/J4
Lisbon, Me, US 131/G2
Lisbon, Md, US 138/A5
Lisburn, NI, UK 34/B2
Lisburn (dist.), NI, UK 34/B3
Lisburne (cape), Ak, US 119/C3
Lisdoonvarna, Ire. 31/P10
Liselund, Den. 38/D3
Lishu, China 72/F2
Lishui, China 79/C2
Lisianski (isl.), 117/H2
Lisieux, Fr. 42/D2
Liski, Rus. 62/F2
Lisle, Il, US 135/P16
Lismore, Austl. 115/E1
Lisnacree, NI, UK 34/B3
Lišov, Czh. 55/H4
Lispeszentadorján, Hun. 48/C2
Lisse, Neth. 50/B4
Lisses, Fr. 30/K6
Lissewege, Belg. 52/C1
List, Ger. 38/C4
Lister (riv.), Ger. 51/E6
Listowel, On, Can. 130/D3
Listowel (cape), Ire. 31/P10
Lit. Scarcies (riv.), SLeo. 102/B3
Litang, China 70/H6
Litang (riv.), China 83/H2
Lītāni (riv.), Leb. 91/D3
Litchfield, Mn, US 127/K4
Litchfield, Il, US 130/C4
Litchfield Park, Az, US 137/R19
Lith, US 50/C5
Lithgow, Austl. 115/D2
Lithuania (ctry.) 27/G3
Litija, Slov. 40/B3
Lititz, Pa, US 138/C3
Litókhoron, Gre. 47/H2
Litoměřice, Czh. 55/H1
Littau, Swi. 57/E3
Little (riv.), Ar, US 129/J4
Little (riv.), Tx, US 130/G4
Little (riv.), NC, US 133/H4

Little Creek, De, US 138/C5
Little Cumbrae (isl.), Sc, UK 36/A5
Little Current (riv.), Can. 127/M3
Little Current, On, Can. 130/D2
Little Desert NP, Austl. 115/B3
Little Diomede (isl.), Ak, US 134/E2
Little Egg (har.), NJ, US 138/D4
Little Falls, NJ, US 139/J8
Little Falls, Mn, US 127/K4
Little Ferry, NJ, US 139/J8
Little Fork (riv.), Mn, US 127/K3
Little Inagua (isl.), Bahm. 141/G3
Little Karoo (valley), SAfr. 106/C4
Little Lehigh (riv.), Pa, US 138/C3
Little Minch (str.), Sc, UK 31/Q8
Little Missouri (riv.), US 127/H4
Little Neck (bay), NY, US 139/K8
Little Nicobar (isl.), India 83/F6
Little Para (res.), Austl. 113/M8
Little Para (riv.), Austl. 113/M8
Little Patuxent (riv.), Md, US 138/B5
Little Peconic (bay), NY, US 139/F2
Little Platte (riv.), Mo, US 137/D5
Little Prairie, Wi, US 135/N14
Little Red (riv.), Ar, US 129/J4
Little Rock (cap.), Ar, US 129/J4
Little Schuylkill (riv.), Pa, US 138/B2
Little Sioux (riv.), Ia, US 125/G3
Little Smoky (riv.), Can. 126/D2
Little Snake (riv.), Co, US 128/E2
Little Stour (riv.), Eng, UK 33/H4
Little Wabash (riv.), Il, US 129/K3
Little White (riv.), SD, US 129/G2
Little Wood (riv.), Id, US 126/E5
Little Zab (riv.), Iraq 90/E3
Littleborough, Eng, UK 35/F4
Littlefield, Tx, US 129/G4
Littlehampton, Eng, UK 33/F5
Littlerock, Ca, US 136/C1
Littlestown, Pa, US 138/A4
Littleton, NH, US 131/G2
Litvinov, Czh. 55/G1
Liu (riv.), China 65/N6
Liu (riv.), China 70/J5
Liucheng, China 83/J3
Liulin, China 72/B3
Liuwa Plain NP, Zam. 105/D3
Liuyang, China 83/K2
Liuzhou, China 83/J3
Livádhion, Gre. 47/H2
Livanátai, Gre. 47/H3
Live Oak, Fl, US 133/H4
Live Oak, Ca, US 135/L10
Livengood, Ak, US 134/J2
Livenza (riv.), It. 59/F2
Liverdun, Fr. 53/F6
Liverley-en-Brie, Fr. 30/L5
Livermore, Ca, US 135/L11
Livermore, Mt, US 129/F5
Livermore Falls, Me, US 131/G2
Liverpool, NS, Can. 131/H2
Liverpool (cape), NW, Can. 123/J1
Liverpool (bay), NW, Can. 122/C1
Liverpool, Eng, UK 35/F5
Liverpool (bay), Wal, UK 35/E5
Livingston, Mt, US 126/F4
Livingston, Tx, US 129/J5
Livingston, NJ, US 139/H8
Livingston, Zam. 105/D4
Livingstone, Zam. 105/D4
Livingstone (falls), Congo 105/B2
Livingstone (range), Can. 126/E3
Livno, Bosn. 48/C4
Livny, Rus. 62/F1
Livojoki (riv.), Fin. 37/H2
Livonia, Mi, US 135/F7
Livorno (prov.), It. 58/D4
Livorno, It. 58/D4
Livorno Ferraris, It. 58/B2
Livramento do Brumado, Braz. 154/B4
Livron-sur-Drôme, Fr. 42/F4
Livry-Gargan, Fr. 30/K5
Lixin, China 72/D4
Lixoúrion, Gre. 47/G3
Liyang, China 72/D5
Lizard, The (pen.), Eng, UK 32/A6
Lizard (pt.), Eng, UK 32/A6
Lizy-sur-Ourcq, Fr. 52/C5

Ljubija, Bosn. 48/C5
Ljubinje, Bosn. 47/F1
Ljubljana (cap.), Slov. 43/L3
Ljubuški, Bosn. 47/E1
Ljungby, Swe. 38/E3
Ljungskile, Swe. 38/D2
Ljusdal, Swe. 38/G1
Ljusnan (riv.), Swe. 37/F3
Ljusne, Swe. 38/G1
Lkst (cap.), Mor. 98/C3
Llabanere (int'l arpt.), Fr. 42/E5
Llaillay, Chile 158/N8
Llaima (vol.), Chile 158/C3
Llallagua, Bol. 150/D4
Llanberis, Pass of (pass), Wal, UK 34/D5
Llancañelo (lake), Arg. 158/C2
Llandovery, Wal, UK 32/C2
Llandrindod Wells, Wal, UK 32/C2
Llandudno, Wal, UK 34/E5
Llanes, Sp. 44/C1
Llanfairfechan, Wal, UK 34/E5
Llangollen, Wal, UK 35/E6
Llanidloes, Wal, UK 32/C2
Llano (riv.), Tx, US 129/H5
Llano Estacado (plain), US 124/F5
Llanos (plain), Col.,Ven. 147/B2
Llanquihue (lake), Chile 158/B4
Llata, Peru 156/B3
Lleida (cap.), Sp. 45/F2
Llera de Canales, Mex. 143/F4
Llerena, Sp. 44/B3
Lleyn (pen.), Wal, UK 34/D6
Llívia, Sp. 45/F1
Llobregat (riv.), Sp. 45/F1
Llodio, Sp. 44/D1
Lloret de Mar, Sp. 45/G2
Llorona (pt.), CR 140/F4
Lloyd (pt.), NY, US 139/M8
Lloyd Harbor, NY, US 139/M8
Lloydminster, Sk, Can. 126/F2
Lloyds (riv.), Can. 131/K1
Lluchmayor, Sp. 45/G3
Llullaillaco (vol.), Arg.,Chil. 157/C1
Llwchwr (riv.), Wal, UK 32/C3
Llynfi (riv.), Wal, UK 32/C3
Loa, Ut, US 128/E3
Loa (riv.), Chile 147/C5
Loanhead, Sc, UK 36/C5
Loano, It. 58/B4
Loaoya (canal), Sp. 45/N8
Lobbes, Belg. 53/D3
Lobatse, Bots. 105/E4
Löbau, Ger. 41/H3
Lobería, Arg. 158/F3
Lobethal, Austl. 113/M8
Lobez, Pol. 41/H2
Lobito, Ang. 105/B3
Lobito, Peru 156/A2
Lobo (riv.), C.d'Iv. 102/D5
Lobos (isl.), Peru 156/A2
Lobos de Tierra, Isla (isl.), Peru 156/A2
Lobos, Punta de (pt.), Chile 158/M9
Locarno, Swi. 57/E5
Loch na Sealga (lake), Sc, UK 36/A1
Loch Raven (res.), Md, US 138/B5
Lochaber (reg.), Sc, UK 36/A3
Locharbriggs, Sc, UK 34/E1
Lochau, Aus. 57/F3
Lochboisdale, Sc, UK 31/Q8
Lochbuie, Co, US 137/C2
Lochem, Neth. 50/D4
Lochgelly, Sc, UK 36/C4
Lochgilphead, Sc, UK 36/A4
Lochindorb (lake), Sc, UK 36/C2
Lochmaben, Sc, UK 34/E1
Lochmaddy, Sc, UK 31/Q8
Lochów, Pol. 41/L2
Lochristi, Belg. 52/C1
Lochwinnoch, Sc, UK 36/B5
Lochy (lake), Sc, UK 36/B3
Lochy (riv.), Sc, UK 36/B3
Lock, Austl. 113/G5
Lock Haven, Pa, US 138/B2
Locke, Ca, US 135/L10
Lockerbie, Sc, UK 35/E1
Lockhart, Austl. 115/C2
Lockhart, Tx, US 130/G4
Lockington, Austl. 115/C3
Locknitz (riv.), Ger. 40/D2
Lockport, NY, US 131/S9
Lockport, Il, US 135/P16
Lockwood (res.), ...
Locon, Fr. 52/B2
Locri, It. 46/E3
Locumba, Peru 156/D4
Locust Fork (riv.), ...
Lod, Isr. 91/F8
Loddon (riv.), Austl. 115/C3
Loddon, Eng, UK 33/J1
Lodê, Eng, UK 33/H3
Lodenice (riv.), Czh. 55/H3
Lodeynoye Pole, Rus. 60/G3
Lodhrān, Pak. 86/A3
Lodi, Ca, US 135/L10
Lodi, It. 58/C2
Lodi, NJ, US 139/J8
Lodi Vecchio, It. 58/C2
Lodja, D.R. Congo 105/D1
Lodosa, Sp. 44/E1
Lodrino, Swi. 57/E5
Łódź, Pol. 41/K3
Łódź (prov.), Pol. 41/K3
Loei, Thai. 83/H4
Loenen, Neth. 50/C4
Loeriesfontein, SAfr. 106/B3

Lofa (co.), Libr. 102/C5
Lofa (riv.), Libr. 102/C5
Löffingen, Ger. 57/E2
Lofoten (isle.), Nor. 37/D2
Lofty (range), Austl. 112/C3
Lofty (mt.), Austl. 113/M8
Logan (mt.), Can. 134/K3
Logan, Ut, US 126/F5
Logan, WV, US 130/D4
Logan, NM, US 132/C3
Logan, Oh, US 130/D4
Logan (co.), Ok, US 137/N14
Logansport, In, US 130/C3
Loganton, Pa, US 138/A1
Loganville, Pa, US 138/B4
Logatec, Slov. 43/L4
Logone (riv.), Chad 93/D3
Lograto, It. 58/D2
Logroño, Sp. 44/D1
Logrosán, Sp. 44/C3
Løgstør, Den. 38/C3
Løgten, Den. 38/D3
Lohals, Den. 38/D4
Lohārdaga, India 85/E4
Lohfelden, Ger. 51/G6
Lohja, Fin. 39/L1
Lohjanjärvi (lake), Fin. 39/K1
Lohmar, Ger. 53/G2
Löhnberg, Ger. 54/B1
Lohne, Ger. 51/F3
Löhne, Ger. 51/F4
Lohr, Ger. 54/C3
Loi-kaw, Myan. 83/G4
Loi Lun (range), China,Mya 70/G7
Loing (riv.), Fr. 40/B5
Loir (riv.), Fr. 42/D3
Loire (riv.), Fr. 27/E4
Loisin (riv.), Fr. 53/E5
Loita (hills), Kenya 97/N8
Loja (prov.), Ecu. 156/B2
Loja, Ecu. 156/B2
Loja, Sp. 44/C4
Løjt Kirkeby, Den. 38/C4
Lokeren, Belg. 52/D1
Lokitaung, Kenya 104/B1
Løkken, Den. 38/C3
Lokoja, Nga. 103/G5
Lokolo (riv.), D.R. Congo 97/K8
Lokomby, Madg. 107/H8
Lokoro (riv.), D.R. Congo 97/J8
Lökösháza, Hun. 48/E2
Lokossa, Ben. 103/F5
Loks (isl.), NW, Can. 123/K2
Lol (riv.), Sudan 97/L6
Lolland (isl.), Den. 37/D5
Lollar, Ger. 54/B3
Lolo (peak), Mt, US 126/E4
Lolui (isl.), Ugan. 104/B3
Lom, Nor. 37/D3
Lom Sak, Thai. 78/C2
Loma (mts.), SLeo. 96/C6
Loma (pt.), Ca, US 136/C5
Loma Bonita, Mex. 144/C2
Loma Linda, Ca, US 136/C2
Loma Mansa (peak), SLeo. 102/C4
Loma Negra, Arg. 158/E3
Lomami (riv.), D.R. Congo 93/E5
Lomas de Zamora, Arg. 159/J11
Lomazzo, It. 58/C1
Lombard, Il, US 135/P16
Lombarda, Serra (mts.), Braz. 151/H3
Lombardia, Mex. 142/E5
Lombardia (pol. reg.), It. 43/H4
Lomblen (isl.), Indo. 81/F5
Lombok (isl.), Indo. 67/L10
Lomé (int'l arpt.), Togo 103/F5
Lomé (cap.), Togo 103/F5
Lomello, It. 58/B2
Lomita, Ca, US 136/F8
Lomma, Swe. 38/E4
Lomme, Fr. 52/B2
Lommel, Belg. 50/C6
Lomnice (riv.), Czh. 55/G4
Lomnice nad Lužnicí, Czh. 55/H4
Lomond (lake), Sc, UK 36/B4
Lomond (hills), Sc, UK 36/C4
Lomone (riv.), It. 59/E4
Lomonosov, Rus. 61/S7
Lompobatang (peak), Indo. 81/E5
Lompoc, Ca, US 128/B4
Łomża, Pol. 41/M2
Lonato, It. 58/D2
Lonāvale, India 89/K5
Loncoche, Chile 158/B3
Loncopué, Arg. 158/C3
Londerzeel, Belg. 53/D2
London, On, Can. 130/D3
London, Ky, US 130/C4
London (reef), Nic. 145/F3
London (cap.), UK 30/C2
London, City of (bor.), Eng, UK 30/A1
Londonderry (cape), Austl. 109/B2
Londonderry (isl.), Chile 159/C7
Londonderry (dist.), NI, UK 34/A2
Londonderry, NI, UK 34/A2
Londrina, Braz. 155/B2
Lone (riv.), Ger. 54/C5
Lone Grove, Ok, US 129/H4
Lone Jack, Mo, US 137/E6
Lone Pine Sanctuary, Austl. 114/E7
Lonesome NP, Austl. 114/C4
Long, Ak, US 134/G3
Long (lake), Can. 127/M3
Long (riv.), China 79/A3
Long (isl.), NY, US 131/F3
Long (mtn.), Wal, UK 32/C1
Long (str.), Rus. 65/T2
Long (isl.), Bahm. 119/K7
Long (lake), Sc, UK 36/A2
Long Beach, Wa, US 126/B4
Long Beach, On, Can. 131/R10
Long Beach (isl.), NJ, US 138/D4
Long Beach, Ca, US 136/F8
Long Beach, NY, US 139/L9
Long Branch, NJ, US 138/E3
Long Cay (isl.), India 145/H1
Long Crag (hill), Eng, UK 36/E6
Long Eaton, Eng, UK 35/G6
Long Grove, Il, US 135/P15
Long Hill, Ct, US 139/E1
Long, Loch (inlet), Sc, UK 36/B4
Long Mynd, The (hill), Eng, UK 32/D1
Long Neck (pt.), Ct, US 139/M7
Long Range (mts.), Can. 131/K2
Long Valley, NJ, US 138/D2
Long Xuyen, Viet. 78/D4
Longá (riv.), Braz. 154/B1
Longare, It. 59/E2
Longaví, Chile 158/C2
Longboat Key, Fl, US 133/H5
Longbranch, Wa, US 135/B3
Longchang, China 83/J2
Longchuan, China 79/C3
Longchuan, China 83/G3
Longde, China 70/J4
Longeau (riv.), Fr. 53/E5
Longeville-en-Barrois, Fr. 53/E6
Longeville-lès-Metz, Fr. 53/F5
Longeville-lès-Saint-Avold, Fr. 53/F5
Longfellow (mts.), Me, US 131/G2
Longfield, Eng, UK 30/D2
Longford, Austl. 115/C4
Longford, Ire. 31/Q10
Longhua, China 72/D2
Longhui, China 83/K2
Longjumeau, Fr. 30/J5
Longkou, China 72/E3
Longlac, On, Can. 127/M3
Longli, China 83/J2
Longmen, China 79/B3
Longmen Shiyao, China 72/C4
Longmont, Co, US 137/B2
Longnan, China 79/B3
Longniddry, Sc, UK 36/D5
Longonot (peak), Kenya 104/C3
Longperrier, Fr. 30/K4
Longpont-sur-Orge, Fr. 30/J6
Longport, NJ, US 138/D5
Longpré-les-Corps-Saints, Fr. 52/A3
Longquan, China 79/C2
Longreach, Austl. 114/B3
Longshan, China 79/A2
Longshou (mts.), China 70/H4
Longueau, Fr. 52/B4
Longueil-Annel, Fr. 52/B5
Longuenesse, Fr. 52/B2
Longuesse, Fr. 30/H4
Longueuil, Qu, Can. 131/P6
Longuyon, Fr. 53/E5
Longvic, Fr. 56/B3
Longview, Wa, US 126/C4
Longview, Tx, US 129/J4
Longwood Gardens, Pa, US 138/C4
Longwy, Fr. 53/E4
Longyan, China 79/C2
Longyearbyen, Nor. 64/B2
Longyou, China 79/C2
Longzhou, China 78/D1
Loni, India 86/D5
Lonigo, It. 59/E2
Löningen, Ger. 51/E3
Lonquimay, Arg. 158/E3
Lons, Fr. 42/C5
Lons-le-Saunier, Fr. 56/B4
Lönsboda, Swe. 38/F3
Lontzen, Belg. 53/F2
Lonza (riv.), Swi. 56/D5
Looe (isl.), Eng, UK 32/B6
Lookout (cape), NC, US 133/J3
Lookout (pt.), Austl. 114/B1
Loolmalasin (peak), Tanz. 104/B3
Loon Lake, Sk, Can. 126/F2
Loon op Zand, Neth. 50/C5
Loop Head (pt.), Ire. 30/P10
Loos, Fr. 52/C2
Lop Buri, Thai. 78/C3
Lopary, Madg. 107/H8
Lopez (cape), Gabon 96/G8
López Mateos, Mex. 143/Q9
Lopik, Neth. 50/B5
Lopori (riv.), D.R. Congo 97/K7
Lopphavet (bay), Nor. 37/G1
Loppi, Fin. 39/L1
Lora del Río, Sp. 44/C4
Lorain, Oh, US 130/D3
Loralai, Pak. 89/J2
Lorca, Sp. 44/E4
Lord Howe (isl.), Austl. 116/E8
Lordsburg, NM, US 128/E4
Lorelei, Ger. 53/G3
Lorena, Braz. 211/H7
Lorengau, PNG 116/D5
Lørenskog, Nor. 38/D2
Lorentz (riv.), Indo. 81/J5
Lorentzsluizen (dam), Neth. 50/C2
Loreo, It. 59/F2
Loreto, Braz. 154/A2
Loreto, It. 59/G6
Loreto, Mex. 142/C3
Loreto (int'l arpt.), Mex. 142/C3
Loreto, Mex. 142/E4
Loreto, Ecu. 152/B5
Loreto (state), Peru 152/C5
Lorette, Mb, Can. 127/J3
Lorgues, Fr. 43/G5
Lorian (swamp), Kenya 97/N7
Lorica, Col. 152/C2
Lorient, Fr. 42/B3
L'Oriental (pol. reg.), Mor. 99/E2
Lorillard (riv.), NW, Can. 122/G2
Lorinci, Hun. 41/K5
Loring, Ks, US 137/D5
Loriol-sur-Drôme, Fr. 42/F4
Lorn, Firth of (inlet), Sc, UK 31/Q8
Lorne, Austl. 115/B3
Lorosuk (peak), Kenya 104/B2
Lorquin, Fr. 53/G6
Lörrach, Ger. 56/D2
Lorrain (plat.), Fr. 40/D4
Lorraine (pol. reg.), Fr. 42/G2
Lorraine (pol. reg.), Fr. 56/C1
Lorraine, Qu, Can. 131/N6
Lorraine (reg.), Fr. 53/E5
Lorsch, Ger. 54/B3
Lorup, Ger. 51/E3
Los Alamitos, Ca, US 136/F8
Los Alamos, NM, US 129/F4
Los Alerces, PN, Arg. 157/B5
Los Altos, Ca, US 135/K12
Los Amates, Guat. 144/D3
Los Andes, Col. 152/B4
Los Andes, Chile 158/N8
Los Angeles (riv.), Ca, US 136/B2
Los Angeles (co.), Ca, US 136/B2
Los Ángeles, Chile 158/B3
Los Angeles, Ca, US 136/F7
Los Angeles (int'l arpt.), Ca, US 136/F8
Los Angeles Outer (har.), Ca, US 136/F8
Los Aquijes, Peru 156/C4
Los Aztecas, Mex. 143/F4
Los Banos, Ca, US 128/B3
Los Barrios, Sp. 44/C4
Los Canarreos (arch.), Cuba 145/F1
Los Cardales, Arg. 159/J11
Los Cerrillos, Uru. 159/K11
Los Chonos (arch.), Chile 147/B7
Los Corrales de Buelna, Sp. 44/C1
Los Glaciares, PN, Arg. 157/B6
Los Katios, PN, Col. 152/B3
Los Lagos, Chile 158/B3
Los Lagos (pol. reg.), Chile 158/B4
Los Llanos de Aridane, Sp. 98/A3
Los Lunas, NM, US 128/F4
Los Mármoles, PN, Mex. 144/B1
Los Menucos, Arg. 158/C4
Los Mochis, Mex. 142/C3
Los Mosquitos (gulf), Pan. 145/F4
Los Muermos, Chile 158/B4
Los Navalmorales, Sp. 44/C3
Los Navalucillos, Sp. 44/C3
Los Órganos, Peru 156/A2
Los Padres National Forest, Ca, US 136/A1
Los Palacios y Villafranca, Sp. 44/C4
Los Pingüinos, PN, Chile 159/C7
Los Planes, Mex. 142/C3
Los Reyes, Mex. 143/R10
Los Reyes de Salgado, Mex. 142/E5
Los Ríos (prov.), Ecu. 156/B1
Los Roques, Islas (isls.), Ven. 150/E1
Los Santos, Pan. 152/A3
Los Santos de Maimona, Sp. 44/B3
Los Sauces, Chile 158/B3
Los Taques, Ven. 152/D2
Los Teques, Ven. 150/E1
Los Testigos (isls.), Ven. 153/F2
Los Vilos, Chile 158/C1
Los Yébenes, Sp. 44/D3
Losai Nat'l Rsv., Kenya 104/C2
Losheim, Ger. 53/F4
Łosice, Pol. 41/M2
Lošinj (isl.), Cro. 48/B3
Losne, Fr. 56/B3
Losone, Swi. 57/E5
Losoya, Tx, US 137/U21
Lossburg, Ger. 57/E1
Losser, Neth. 50/E4
Lossie (riv.), Sc, UK 36/C1
Lössnitz, Ger. 55/F1
Lossoganeu (hill), Tanz. 104/C4
Lost River (range), Id, US 128/D1
Lost River Caverns, Pa, US 138/C2
Lostallo, Swi. 57/F5
Lot (riv.), Fr. 42/D4
Lota, Chile 158/B3
Lotawana (lake), Mo, US 137/E6
Løten, Nor. 38/D1
Lothian (pol. reg.), Sc, UK 36/C5
Lotte, Ger. 51/E4
Lotuke (peak), Sudan 104/B1
Lotung, Tai. 79/D3
Lou (riv.), China 72/B5
Louang Namtha, Laos 83/H3
Louangphrabang, Laos 83/H4
Loubomo, Congo 105/B1
Loudéac, Fr. 42/B2
Loudi, China 83/K2
Loudun, Fr. 42/D3
Loue (riv.), Fr. 42/F3
Loufan, China 72/B3
Louga (pol. reg.), Sen. 102/B3
Louga, Sen. 102/A3
Lough Foyle (lake), UK 34/A1
Loughborough, Eng, UK 33/E1
Loughbrickland, NI, UK 34/B3
Lougheed (isl.), NW, Can. 123/R7
Loughgall, NI, UK 34/B3
Loughrea, Ire. 31/P10
Loughton, Eng, UK 30/D2
Louhans, Fr. 56/B4
Louis Botha (Durban) (int'l arpt.), SAfr. 107/E3
Louisiade (arch.), PNG 116/E6
Louisiana (state), US 125/H5
Louisville, Ms, US 133/F3
Louisville, Ky, US 130/C4
Louisville, Co, US 137/B3
Loukkos (riv.), Mor. 100/A2
Loulé, Port. 44/A4
Louny, Czh. 55/G2
Loup (riv.), US 127/J5
Loup, Middle (riv.), Ne, US 127/H5
Loup, North (riv.), Ne, US 127/H5
Lourches, Fr. 52/C3
Lourdes, Fr. 42/C5
Lourdes/Tarbes (int'l arpt.), Fr. 42/D5
Loures, Port. 45/P10
Louriçal, Port. 44/A2
Lourinhã, Port. 44/A3
Lousã, Port. 44/A2
Lousa, Port. 45/Q10
Louth, Eng, UK 35/H5
Louth (co.), Ire. 34/B4
Louth, Ire. 34/B4
Loutrá Aidhipsoú, Gre. 47/H3
Loutrákion, Gre. 47/H4
Loútsa, Gre. 47/P9
Louvain (Leuven), Belg. 53/D2
Louveira, Braz. 211/G8
Louviers, Fr. 42/D2
Louviers, Co, US 137/B4
Louvigné-du-Désert, Fr. 42/C2
Louvres, Fr. 30/K4
Louvroil, Fr. 52/C3
Lovaart (riv.), Belg. 52/B1
Lovat' (riv.), Rus. 60/F4
Lovat' (riv.), Bela.,Rus. 39/P3
Lovćen NP, Yugo. 47/F1
Lovćenac, Yugo. 48/D3
Love Point, Md, US 138/B5
Lovech (prov.), Bul. 47/J1
Loveland, Co, US 137/B2
Loveland (lake), Co, US 137/B2
Lovell, Wy, US 126/F4
Lovelock, Nv, US 128/C2
Lovere, It. 58/D1
Loving, NM, US 129/F4
Lovington, NM, US 129/G4
Lovios, Sp. 44/A2
Lövő, Hun. 43/M3
Lovosice, Czh. 55/H1
Lovozero (lake), Rus. 60/G2
Low (cape), NW, Can. 123/H2
Lowa (riv.), D.R. Congo 93/E5
Lowell, Ma, US 131/G3
Löwen (riv.), Namb. 106/B2
Löwenstein, Ger. 54/C4
Lower (bay), NJ, US 138/D2
Lower (dam), Wa, US 135/D3
Lower Arrow (lake), Can. 126/D3
Lower Engadine (valley), Swi. 57/G4
Lower Ganges (canal), India 84/B2
Lower Glenelg NP, Austl. 115/B3
Lower Hutt, NZ 117/S11
Lower Kalskag, Ak, US 134/F3
Lower Latham (res.), Co, US 137/C2
Lower Otay (lake), Ca, US 136/D5
Lower Red (lake), Mn, US 127/K4
Lower Rhine (riv.), Neth. 50/C5
Lower Rouge (riv.), Mi, US 135/E7
Lower Trajan's Wall, Mol.,Ukr. 62/D3
Lower Tunguska (riv.), Rus. 67/J3
Lower Zambezi NP, Zam. 105/E4
Lowestoft, Eng, UK 33/H2
Lowi (riv.), D.R. Congo 105/E1
Łowicz, Pol. 41/K2
Lowther (hills), Sc, UK 36/C6
Loxstedt, Ger. 51/F2
Loxton, SAfr. 106/C3
Loxton, Austl. 113/J5
Loyalton, Pa, US 138/B2
Loyalty (isls.), NCal. 116/F7
Loyettes, Fr. 56/B6
Loyne (lake), Sc, UK 36/A2
Loysville, Pa, US 138/A3
Loznica, Yugo. 48/D3
Loznitsa, Bul. 49/H4
Lozova, Ukr. 62/F2
Lozovik, Yugo. 48/E3
Lu (mtn.), China 72/D3
Lu (riv.), China 72/C5
Lu Xian, China 83/J2
Lualaba (riv.), D.R. Congo 93/E5
Luan (riv.), China 65/M5
Lu'an, China 72/D5
Luan Xian, China 72/D3
Luanchuan, China 72/B4
Luanco, Sp. 44/C1
Luanda (cap.), Ang. 105/B2
Luang (peak), Thai. 78/B4
Luang Lagoon (lag.), Thai. 83/H6
Luangwa (riv.), Zam. 105/F2
Luangwe, Zam. 104/A5
Luanping, China 72/D2
Luanshya, Zam. 105/E3
Luapula (prov.), Zam. 104/A5
Luarca, Sp. 44/B1
Luba, EqG. 96/G7
Lubaantun (ruin), Belz. 144/D2
Lubaczów, Pol. 41/M3
Lubań, Pol. 41/H3
Lubango, Ang. 105/B3
Lubansenshi (riv.), Zam. 104/A5
Lubartów, Pol. 41/M3
Lubawa, Pol. 41/K2
Lübbecke, Ger. 51/F4
Lubbeek, Belg. 53/D2
Lubbock, Tx, US 129/G4
Lubelska (uplands), Pol. 41/M3
Lubero (riv.), D.R. Congo 104/A3
Lubień Kujawski, Pol. 41/K2
Lubin, Pol. 41/J3
Lublin (prov.), Pol. 41/M3
Lublin, Pol. 41/M3
Lubliniec, Pol. 41/K3
Lubmin, Ger. 38/E4
Lubnaig (lake), Sc, UK 36/B4
Lubny, Ukr. 62/E2
Luboń, Pol. 41/J2
Lubrín, Sp. 44/D4
Lubsko, Pol. 41/H3
Lubudi, D.R. Congo 105/E2
Lubuklinggau, Indo. 80/B4
Lubuksikaping, Indo. 80/B3
Lubumbashi, D.R. Congo 105/E3
Lucan, Ire. 34/B5
Lucania (mt.), Can. 134/K3
Lucas González, Arg. 159/J10
Lucca (prov.), It. 58/D5
Lucca, It. 58/D5
Lucciana, Fr. 46/A1
Luce (bay), Sc, UK 34/D2
Lucedale, Ms, US 133/F4
Lucélia, Braz. 155/B2
Lucena, Phil. 79/D5
Lucena, Sp. 44/C4
Lucena del Cid, Sp. 45/E2
Lučenec, Slvk. 41/K4
Lucens, Swi. 56/C4
Lucerne, Co, US 137/C2
Lucerne (lake), Swi. 43/H3
Lucerne (Vierwaldstättersee) (lake), Swi. 57/E3
Lucheng, China 72/C3
Lüchow, Ger. 40/F2
Lucindale, Austl. 115/B3
Luckeesarai, India 85/F3
Luckenwalde, Ger. 41/G2
Lucknow, India 84/C2
Lucky Lake, Sk, Can. 126/G3
Luco dei Marsi, It. 46/C2
Lucomagno, Passo del (pass), Swi. 57/E4
Lucrecia (cape), Cuba 145/H1
Lucrezia, It. 59/F5
Luda Kamchiya (riv.), Bul. 47/K1
Lüdenscheid, Ger. 51/E6
Lüderitz, Namb. 106/A2
Ludesch, Aus. 57/F3
Ludhiāna, India 86/C4
Ludian, China 83/H2
Ludinghausen, Ger. 51/E5
Ludington, Mi, US 130/C3
Ludogorie (reg.), Bul. 49/H4
Ludvika, Swe. 38/F1
Ludwigs (canal), Ger. 55/E4
Ludwigsburg, Ger. 54/C5
Ludwigsfelde, Ger. 40/Q7
Ludwigshafen, Ger. 57/F2
Ludwigshafen, Ger. 54/B4
Ludwigslust, Ger. 40/F2
Ludwigsstadt, Ger. 55/E2
Luebo, D.R. Congo 105/D2
Luena, Ang. 105/C3
Lufeng, China 79/C3
Lufkin, Tx, US 129/J5
Luga (bay), Rus. 39/N2
Luga, Rus. 39/N2
Luga (riv.), Rus. 39/N2
Lugagnano, It. 59/D2
Lugagnano Val d'Arda, It. 58/C3
Lugano, Swi. 57/E6
Lugano (lake), It. 57/E6
Luganville, Van. 116/F6
Lugards (falls), Kenya 104/C3
Lugavčina, Yugo. 48/E3
Lügde, Ger. 51/G5
Lugenda (riv.), Moz. 105/G3
Lugg (riv.), Eng, UK 32/D2
Lugg (riv.), Wal, UK 32/C2
Lugnaquillia (peak), Ire. 34/B6
Lugo, It. 59/E4
Lugo, Sp. 44/B1
Lugogo (riv.), Ugan. 104/B2
Lugoj, Rom. 48/E3
Lugrin, Fr. 56/C5
Lugunga (peak), Tanz. 104/C4
Luhan (int'l arpt.), Ukr. 62/F2
Luhans'k, Ukr. 62/F2
Luhans'ka (obl.), Ukr. 62/F2
Lühe (riv.), Ger. 51/H2
Luhe, China 72/D4
Luhe (riv.), Ger. 55/F3
Luhe-Wildenau, Ger. 55/F3
Luhombero (peak), Tanz. 104/C4
Luichart (lake), Sc, UK 36/B1
Luino, It. 57/E6
Luis B. Sánchez, Mex. 142/B1
Luís Correia, Braz. 154/B1
Luján, Arg. 159/J11
Lujiang, China 72/D5
Lukácsháza, Hun. 43/M3
Lukang, Tai. 79/D3
Lukavac, Bosn. 48/D3
Luke (mt.), Austl. 112/C3
Lukenie (riv.), D.R. Congo 105/C1
Lukovit, Bul. 47/J1
Łuków, Pol. 41/M3
Lukuga (riv.), D.R. Congo 104/A4
Lukulu, Zam. 105/D3
Lukulu (riv.), Zam. 104/A5
Lukunor (isl.), Micr. 116/E4
Luleå, Swe. 60/D2
Luleälven (riv.), Swe. 37/G2
Luliang, China 83/H2
Luling, La, US 137/P17
Luling (pass), China 72/B4
Lulong, China 72/D3
Lulonga (riv.), D.R. Congo 93/E4
Lulsgate (int'l arpt.), Eng, UK 32/D4
Lulua (riv.), D.R. Congo 93/E5
Lumangwe (falls), Zam. 104/A5
Lumberton, Tx, US 129/J5
Lumberton, NC, US 133/J3
Lumberton, NJ, US 138/D4
Lumbini (zone), Nepal 84/D2
Lumbo, Moz. 105/H4
Lumbrales, Sp. 44/B2
Lumbrein, Swi. 57/F4
Lumbres, Fr. 52/B2
Lumby, BC, Can. 126/D3
Lumding, India 83/F2
Lumigny-Nesles-Ormeaux, Fr. 30/L5
Luminárias, Braz. 211/J6
Lummen, Belg. 53/E2
Lumparland, Fin. 39/J1
Lumsden, Sk, Can. 127/G3
Lumsden, NZ 117/R12
Lumut, Malay. 80/B3
Luna (mtn.), Ca, US 136/C2
Lunahuaná, Peru 156/B4
Lund, Swe. 38/E4
Lundazi, Zam. 105/F3
Lundby, Den. 38/D4
Lundi (riv.), Zim. 105/F5
Lundy (isl.), Eng, UK 32/B4
Lune (riv.), Ger. 51/F2
Lune (riv.), Eng, UK 35/F2
Lüneburg, Ger. 51/H2
Lüneburger Heide (reg.), Ger. 40/F2
Lunel, Fr. 42/F5
Lünen, Ger. 51/E5
Lunenburg, NS, Can. 131/H2
Lunestedt, Ger. 51/F2
Lunéville, Fr. 43/G2
Lung Kwu Chau (isl.), China 71/T10
Lunga (riv.), Zam. 105/E3
Lungern, Swi. 56/E4
Lungi, SLeo. 102/B4
Lungi (Freetown) (int'l arpt.), SLeo. 102/B4
Lunglei, India 83/F3
Lungue-Bungo (riv.), Ang. 105/C3
Luni (riv.), India 89/K3
Lünne, Ger. 51/E4
Luocheng, China 83/J3
Luodian, China 83/J2
Luoding, China 83/K3
Luohe, China 72/C4
Luoma (lake), China 72/D4
Luongo (riv.), Zam. 104/A5
Luoning, China 72/B4
Luoshan, China 72/C4
Luoshuikan, China 79/A1
Luoyang, China 72/C4
Luoyuan, China 79/C2
Luozi, D.R. Congo 105/B1
Lupanshui, China 83/H2
Luqa (int'l arpt.), Malta 46/L7
Luqu, China 70/H5
Luquan, China 83/H2
Lūrah (riv.), Afg. 89/J2
Lure, Fr. 56/C2
Lurgan, NI, UK 34/B3
Luri, Fr. 43/H5
Lurín, Peru 156/B4
Lúrio, Moz. 105/H3
Lúrio (riv.), Moz. 93/F6
Lurnfeld, Aus. 43/K3
Lurøy, Nor. 37/E2
Lusaka (cap.), Zam. 105/E4
Lusambo, D.R. Congo 105/D1
Lusen (peak), Ger. 55/G5
Lusenga NP, Zam. 104/A5
Lushan, China 72/C4
Lushi, China 72/B4
Lushnjë, Alb. 47/F2
Lushoto, Tanz. 104/C4
Lushui, China 83/G2
Lusignan, Fr. 42/D3
Lusk, Wy, US 127/G5
Lusk, Ire. 34/B4
Lustenau, Aus. 57/F3
Lutanga (riv.), D.R. Congo 97/J7
Luther, Ok, US 137/N14
Luthern, Swi. 56/D3
Lutherville, Md, US 138/B5
Lütjehorn (isl.), Ger. 50/D1
Lütjenburg, Ger. 38/D4
Luton, Eng, UK 33/F3
Luton (int'l arpt.), Eng, UK 33/F3
Lutry, Swi. 56/C5
Luts'k, Ukr. 62/C2
Lutter (riv.), Ger. 51/F5
Lutterbach, Fr. 56/D2
Lutz (riv.), Aus. 57/F3
Lützow-Holm (bay), Ant. 160/C
Luumäki, Fin. 39/M1
Luverne, Mn, US 127/J5
Luvua (riv.), D.R. Congo 104/A4
Luwegu (riv.), Tanz. 105/G2
Luwero, Ugan. 104/B2
Luwingu, Zam. 104/A5
Lux, Fr. 56/A4
Luxembourg (prov.), Belg 53/E4
Luxembourg (ctry.) 27/E4
Luxembourg (cap.), Lux. 53/F4
Luxeuil-les-Bains, Fr. 56/C2
Luxi, China 83/H3
Luxi, China 83/K2
Luxi, China 83/G3
Luxor (int'l arpt.), Egypt 101/C3
Luyi, China 72/C4
Luz, Braz. 155/C1
Luz (coast), Port.,Sp. 44/B4
Luza (riv.), Rus. 61/L3
Luzarches, Fr. 30/K4
Luzein, Swi. 57/F4
Luzern (canton), Swi. 56/E3
Luzern, Swi. 57/E3
Luzerne (co.), Pa, US 138/B1
Luzhai, China 83/J3
Luzhi, China 83/J2
Luzhou, China 83/J2
Luziânia, Braz. 154/A5
Luzilândia, Braz. 154/B1
Lužnice (riv.), Czh. 41/H4
Luzon (isl.), Phil. 67/M8
Luzon (str.), Phil. 116/A3
Lužuice (riv.), Czh. 43/L2
Luzzara, It. 59/D3
Luzzi, It. 46/E3
L'viv, Ukr. 62/C2
L'vivs'ka (obl.), Ukr. 62/B2
L'vivs'ka (prov.), Ukr. 41/M4
Lwala (peak), Ugan. 104/B2
Lwi (riv.), Myan. 78/C1
Lyantonde, Ugan. 104/A3
Lyapin (riv.), Rus. 61/P2
Lycksele, Swe. 37/F2
Lycoming (co.), Pa, US 138/A1
Lyell Brown (mt.), Austl. 113/F2
Lykens, Pa, US 138/B2
Lyman, Wy, US 126/F5
Lyme (bay), Eng, UK 42/B1
Lymington, Eng, UK 33/E5
Lymm, Eng, UK 35/F5
Łyna (riv.), Pol. 41/L1
Lynas (pt.), Wal, UK 34/D5
Lynbrook, NY, US 139/L9
Lynch, Md, US 138/B5
Lynches (riv.), SC, US 133/H3
Lyndhurst, NJ, US 139/J8
Lyne (riv.), Eng, UK 35/F1
Lyngdal, Nor. 38/B2
Lyngen (inlet), Nor. 37/G1
Lynn, Ma, US 131/G3
Lynn Haven, Fl, US 133/G4
Lynn Lake, Mb, Can. 122/F3
Lynwood, Ca, US 136/F8
Lynx (lake), NW, Can. 122/F2
Lyon, Fr. 42/F4
Lyon (riv.), Sc, UK 36/B3
Lyon (lake), Sc, UK 36/B3
Lyon (Satolas) (int'l arpt.), Fr. 56/B6
Lyons, Ks, US 129/H3
Lyons, Co, US 137/B2
Lyons (riv.), Austl. 112/C3
Lyons, Wi, US 135/P14
Lype (hill), Eng, UK 32/C4
Lyra Reef (reef), PNG 116/E5
Lys (riv.), It. 58/A1
Lys (riv.), Fr. 42/E1
Lys-lez-Lannoy, Fr. 52/C2
Lysá (peak), Czh. 41/K4
Lysá nad Labem, Czh. 55/H2
Lysaker, Nor. 38/D2
Lysaya (hill), Bela. 39/M4
Lysekil, Swe. 38/D2
Łysica (peak), Pol. 41/L3
Lysina (peak), Czh. 55/F2
Lyss, Swi. 56/D3
Lystrup, Den. 38/D3
Lys'va, Rus. 61/N4
Lysychans'k, Ukr. 62/F2
Lytham Saint Anne's, Eng, UK 35/E4
Lytle, Tx, US 129/H5
Lytle Creek, Ca, US 136/C2
Lytton, BC, Can. 126/C3
Lyubertsy, Rus. 61/W9
Lyubotyn, Ukr. 62/E2
Lyudinovo, Rus. 62/E1
Lywd (riv.), Wal, UK 32/C3

M

M. Aleman (res.), Mex. 140/B4
Ma-Ubin, Myan. 83/G4
Ma'alot-Tarshiha, Isr. 91/D3
Ma'ān, Jor. 91/D4
Ma'an (gov.), Jor. 91/E4
Maanĭt, Mong. 70/H2
Maanĭt, Mong. 70/J2
Maanselkä (mts.), Fin. 37/H1
Ma'anshan, China 72/D5
Maarheeze, Neth. 50/C6
Maarianhamina (Mariehamn), Fin. 39/H1
Ma'arrat an Nu'mān, Syria 91/E2
Maarssen, Neth. 50/C4
Maartensdijk, Neth. 50/C4
Maas (riv.), Belg. 42/F1
Maasbracht, Neth. 53/E1
Maasbree, Neth. 50/D6
Maaseik, Belg. 53/E1
Maassluis, Neth. 50/B5
Maastricht, Neth. 53/E2
Maastricht (int'l arpt.), Neth. 53/E2
Mabalacat, Phil. 79/D4
Mabalane, Moz. 105/F5
Mabaruma, Guy. 153/G2
Mabechi (riv.), Japan 76/B3
Mabian, China 83/H2
Mabinay, Phil. 79/D6
Mabopane, SAfr. 106/Q12
Mabote, Moz. 105/F5
Mabule, Bots. 106/D2
Mac. Robertson Land (phys. reg.), Ant. 160/D
Macá (peak), Chile 158/B5
Macachín, Arg. 158/E3
Macaé, Braz. 155/D2
Macael, Sp. 44/D4
Macaíba, Braz. 154/D2
Mação, Port. 44/A3
Macapá, Braz. 151/H3
Macará, Ecu. 156/B2
Macarani, Braz. 154/B4
Macaravita, Col. 152/C3
Macari, Peru 156/D4
Macarthur, Austl. 115/B3
Macas, Ecu. 152/B5
Macau, Braz. 154/C2
Macau (cap.), Macau 83/K3
Macau (dpcy.), Port. 67/L7
Macaúbas, Braz. 154/B4
Macauley (isl.), NZ 116/G7
Macaya (riv.), Col. 150/D3
Macaya, Pic de (peak), Haiti 145/H2
Maccagno, It. 57/E5
Macclenny, Fl, US 133/H4
Macclesfield (canal), Eng, UK 35/F5
Macclesfield, Eng, UK 35/F5
Macdhui (peak), SAfr. 106/D3
Macdona, Tx, US 137/T21
MacDonald (lake), Austl. 109/B3
Macdonnell (ranges), Austl. 109/C3
Macduff, Sc, UK 36/D1
Maceda, Sp. 44/B1
Macedonia (reg.), Gre. 47/G2
Macedonía (int'l arpt.), Gre. 47/H2
Macedonia (ctry.) 62/B4
Macedonia (Former Yugoslav Republic of Macedonia) (ctry.) 27/G4
Maceió (pt.), Braz. 154/C2
Maceió, Braz. 154/D3
Macerata (prov.), It. 59/G6
Macerata, It. 43/K5
Macfarlane (lake), Austl. 113/H5
Machacalis, Braz. 154/B5
Machacamarca, Bol. 150/E7
Machache (peak), Les. 106/D3
Machachi, Ecu. 152/B5
Machado, Braz. 211/H6
Machado (swamp), Col. 145/H4
Machadodorp, SAfr. 107/E2
Machakos, Kenya 104/C3
Machala, Ecu. 156/B1
Machalí, Chile 158/N9
Machalilla, PN, Ecu. 152/A5
Machanga, Moz. 105/F5
Machaquilá (riv.), Guat. 144/D2
Machars, The (pen.), Sc, UK 34/D2
Machattie (lake), Austl. 113/H3
Machaze, Moz. 105/F5
Machecoul, Fr. 42/C3
Machemma (ruin), SAfr. 105/E5
Macheng, China 72/C5
Machens, Mo, US 137/G8
Machhlīshahr, India 84/D3
Machias, Me, US 131/H2
Machichaco (cape), Sp. 44/D1
Machida, Japan 77/C2
Machilipatnam, India 82/D4
Machiques, Ven. 152/C2
Machovo Jezero (lake), Czh. 55/H1
Machu Picchu (ruin), Peru 156/C4
Machupo (riv.), Bol. 150/F6
Machynlleth, Wal, UK 32/C1
Măcin, Rom. 49/J3
Macina (phys. reg.), Mali 96/E4
Macintyre (riv.), Austl. 109/E3
Mackay (lake), Austl. 109/B3
Mackay, Austl. 114/C3
Mackenzie, BC, Can. 126/C2
Mackenzie, Austl. 114/C3
Mackenzie (bay), NW,Yk, Can. 122/C2
Mackenzie (mts.), Can. 122/C2
Mackenzie (riv.), Can. 122/E2
Mackenzie King (isl.), NW, Can. 123/R7
Mackinac Island, Mi, US 130/C2
Mackinaw City, Mi, US 130/C2
Macklin, Sk, Can. 126/F2
Macknade, Austl. 114/B2
Macksville, Austl. 115/E1
Maclean, Austl. 115/E1
Maclear, SAfr. 106/E3
Macleay (isl.), Austl. 114/F7
Macleod (lake), Austl. 112/B3
Macmillan (riv.), Can. 134/L3
Macomb, Il, US 127/L5
Macomb, Ok, US 137/N15
Macomb (co.), Mi, US 135/G6
Macomer, It. 46/A2
Macon, Ga, US 133/H3
Macon, Mo, US 129/J3
Mâcon, Fr. 42/F3
Macondes, Planalto dos (plat.), Moz. 104/C5
Macosquin, NI, UK 34/B1
Macotera, Sp. 44/C2
Macoupin (co.), Il, US 137/G7
Macquarie (har.), Austl. 115/C4
Macquarie (riv.), Austl. 109/D4
Macquarie (isl.), Austl. 23/S8
Macroom, Ire. 31/P11
Macuelizo, Hon. 144/D3
Macuim (riv.), Braz. 150/F5
Macuira, PN, Col. 152/D1
Macuma (riv.), Ecu. 156/B1
Macumba (riv.), Austl. 109/C3
Macungie, Pa, US 138/C2
Macusani, Peru 156/D4
Macuspana, Mex. 144/C2
Macuzari, Presa (dam), Mex. 142/C3
Mādabā, Jor. 91/D4
Madagascar (ctry.) 93/G7
Madan, Bul. 47/J2
Madanapalle, India 82/C5
Madanīyīn, Tun. 96/H1
Madanīyīn (gov.), Tun. 99/H2
Madaoua, Niger 103/G3
Madaras, Hun. 48/D2
Madauk, Myan. 83/G4
Madawaska, Me, US 131/G2
Madawaska (riv.), Can. 130/E2
Madden (dam), Pan. 152/B2
Madeira (aut. reg.), Port. 45/U14
Madeira (riv.), Braz. 147/C3
Mädelegabel (peak), Ger. 57/G3
Madeleine, Îles de la (isls.), Qu, Can. 123/K4
Madeline (isl.), Wi, US 127/L4
Maden, Turk. 90/D2
Mäder, Aus. 57/F3
Madera, Mex. 142/C2
Maderas (vol.), Nic. 144/E4
Madgaon (Margao), India 89/K5
Madhipura, India 85/F3
Madhubani, India 85/F2
Madhumati (riv.), Bang. 85/G4
Madhupur, India 85/F3
Madhya Pradesh (state), India 70/D7
Madidi (riv.), Bol. 150/E6
Madīnat ath Thawrah, Syria 90/D3
Madirovalo, Madg. 107/H7
Madison, Ne, US 127/J5
Madison, SD, US 127/J4
Madison, Ms, US 133/F3
Madison, In, US 130/C4
Madison, Fl, US 133/H4
Madison, Al, US 133/G3
Madison, Il, US 137/G8
Madison (co.), Oh, US 137/G8
Madison (riv.), Mt, US 124/D2
Madison, Ct, US 139/F1
Madison, Ca, US 135/K9
Madison, NJ, US 139/H9
Madison Heights, Mi, US 135/F6
Madisonville, Tx, US 129/J5
Madisonville, Ky, US 130/C4
Madisonville, La, US 137/P16
Madiun, Indo. 80/D5
Mado Gashi, Kenya 104/C2
Madoi, China 70/G5
Madon (riv.), Fr. 40/D4
Madrakah, Ra's al (pt.), Oman 89/G5
Madre (lag.), Tx, US 140/B2
Madre de Deus de Minas, Braz. 211/J6
Madre de Dios (riv.), Bol. 150/E6
Madre de Dios (dept.), Peru 156/C4
Madre de Dios (isl.), Chile 159/A6
Madre del Sur, Sierra (mts.), Mex. 140/A4
Madre Occidental, Sierra (mts.), Mex. 119/G7
Madre Oriental, Sierra (mts.), Mex. 119/G7
Madrid (aut. comm.), Sp. 44/C2
Madrid (cap.), Sp. 45/N9
Madridejos, Sp. 44/D3
Madrigal, Peru 156/D4
Madrigal de las Altas Torres, Sp. 44/C2
Madrigalejo, Sp. 44/C3
Madrisahorn (peak), Swi. 57/F4
Madroñera, Sp. 44/C3
Madugula, India 82/D4
Madura (isl.), Indo. 67/L10
Madurai, India 82/C6
Mae Hong Son, Thai. 83/G4
Mae Ping NP, Thai. 78/B2
Mae Tho (peak), Thai. 78/B2
Mae Ya (mtn.), Thai. 78/B2
Maebashi, Japan 75/F2
Maella, Sp. 45/F2
Maep'o, SKor. 73/E4
Maerne, It. 59/F1
Maestra, Sierra (mts.), Cuba 145/G2
Maevatanana-Ambanivohitra, Madg. 107/H7
Maewo (isl.), Van. 116/F6
Mafeteng, Les. 106/D3
Maffra, Austl. 115/C3
Mafia (isl.), Tanz. 105/G2
Mafia (chan.), Tanz. 104/C5
Mafikeng, SAfr. 106/D2
Mafou (riv.), Gui. 102/C4
Mafra, Braz. 155/B3
Mafra, Port. 45/P10
Magadan, Rus. 65/R4
Magadino, Swi. 57/E5
Magalies Berg (mts.), SAfr. 106/P12
Magaliesburg, SAfr. 106/P12
Magallanes y Antártica Chilena (prov.), Chile 159/C7
Magangué, Col. 152/C2
Mağara, Turk. 91/C1
Magaria, Niger 103/H3
Magat (riv.), Phil. 79/D4
Magazine (mtn.), Ar, US 129/J4
Magdalena, Bol. 150/F6
Magdalena (peak), Malay. 81/E3

Magda – Markt

Magdalena (riv.), Col. 147/B2
Magdalena (dept.), Col. 145/H4
Magdalena, Arg. 159/K11
Magdalena de Kino, Mex. 142/C2
Magdeburg, Ger. 64/B4
Magdelaine Cays (isls.), Austl. 109/E2
Magé, Braz. 211/K7
Mage-shima (isl.), Japan 74/B5
Magee, Ms, US 133/F4
Magee (isl.), NI, UK 34/C2
Magelang, Indo. 80/D5
Magellan (str.), Arg.,Chile 147/B8
Magenta, It. 58/B2
Magenta (lake), Austl. 112/C5
Magerøya (isl.), Nor. 37/H1
Maggia, Swi. 57/E5
Maggia (riv.), Swi. 57/E5
Maggio (peak), It. 59/E6
Maggiorasca (peak), It. 58/C3
Maggiore (peak), It. 59/E5
Maggiore (lake), It. 43/H4
Maghāghah, Egypt 101/B2
Maghar, India 84/D2
Maghera, NI, UK 34/B2
Magherafelt (co.), NI, UK 34/B2
Magherafelt, NI, UK 34/B2
Maghīla (peak), Tun. 100/L7
Maghnia, Alg. 100/D2
Magilligan (pt.), NI, UK 34/B1
Maglaj, Bosn. 48/D3
Maglić (peak), Yugo. 47/F1
Maglie, It. 47/F2
Maglod, Hun. 49/R10
Magna, Ut, US 137/J12
Magnac-Laval, Fr. 42/D3
Magnetawan (riv.), Can. 130/D2
Magnetic North Pole 160/N
Magnetic Passage, Austl. 114/B2
Magnitogorsk, Rus. 61/N5
Magnitogorsk (int'l arpt.), Rus. 61/N5
Magnolia, Ar, US 129/J4
Magnolia, De, US 138/C5
Magny-en-Vexin, Fr. 52/A5
Magny-les-Hameaux, Fr. 30/J5
Mago NP, Eth. 97/N6
Mágoè, Moz. 105/F4
Magog, Qu, Can. 131/F2
Magpie (riv.), Can. 131/H1
Magpie (lake), Can. 131/H1
Magpie Ouest (riv.), Can. 131/H1
Magra (riv.), It. 58/C4
Magreta, It. 59/D3
Maguan, China 78/D1
Magude, Moz. 105/F6
Magugnano, It. 59/D1
Magway (div.), Myan. 70/F8
Magway (Magwe), Myan. 83/F3
Magwe (Magway), Myan. 83/F3
Maha Sarakham, Thai. 78/C2
Mahābād, Iran 88/E1
Mahabe, Madg. 107/H8
Mahābhārat (range), Nepal 84/C1
Mahabo, Madg. 107/H8
Mahaboboka, Madg. 107/H7
Mahād, India 89/K5
Mahadeo (range), India 84/A4
Mahaica, Guy. 153/G3
Mahaica-Berbice (pol. reg.), Guy. 153/G3
Mahaicony Village, Guy. 153/G3
Mahajamba (riv.), Madg. 107/H7
Mahajamba (bay), Madg. 107/H6
Mahajanga (prov.), Madg. 107/H6
Mahajanga, Madg. 107/H6
Mahajilo (riv.), Madg. 107/H7
Mahakali (zone), Nepal 84/C1
Mahakam (riv.), Indo. 81/E3
Mahalapye, Bots. 105/E5
Mahale Mountains NP, Tanz. 104/A4
Maḩallāt, Iran 88/F2
Maham, India 86/D5
Māhān (riv.), India 84/D4
Māhān, Iran 89/G2
Mahānadī (riv.), India 70/D7
Mahananda (riv.), India 85/F3
Mahandiabani (riv.), C.d'Iv. 102/D4
Mahanoro, Madg. 107/J7
Mahanoy City, Pa, US 138/B2
Mahantango (mtn.), Pa, US 138/B2
Mahārājganj, India 85/E2
Mahārājganj, India 84/D2
Mahārajpur, India 82/C2
Mahārāshtra (state), India 82/B4
Mahāsamund, India 82/D3
Mahāshān (ruin), Bang. 85/G3
Mahasoabe, Madg. 107/H8
Mahavavy (riv.), Madg. 107/H7
Mahawa (riv.), India 84/B1
Mahazoarivo, Madg. 107/H8
Mahazoma, Madg. 107/H7
Mahbubnagar, India 82/C4
Mahdia, Guy. 153/G3
Mahébourg, Mrts. 107/T15
Mahendranagar, Nepal 84/C1
Mahesāna, India 89/K4
Mahgawān, India 84/B2
Mahia (pen.), NZ 109/H6
Mahilyow (int'l arpt.), Bela. 39/P5
Mahilyow, Bela. 39/P5
Mahilyowskaya (prov.), Bela. 60/F5
Mahīshādal, India 85/F4
Mahitsy, Madg. 107/H7
Mahlaing, Myan. 83/G3
Mahlberg, Ger. 56/D1
Mahleur (lake), Or, US 126/D5
Mahlow, Ger. 40/Q7
Mahmel (peak), Alg. 96/G1
Maḩmūd-e 'Erāqī, Afg. 89/J1
Mahmūdābād, India 84/C2
Mahón, Sp. 45/H3
Mahroni, India 84/B3
Mahukona, Hi, US 124/U10
Mahuva, India 89/K4
Mahwah, India 84/A2
Mahwah, NJ, US 139/J7
Mai-Ndombe (lake), D.R. Congo 96/J8
Maia, Port. 44/A2
Maiala NP, Austl. 114/E6
Maials, Sp. 45/F2
Maiana (isl.), Kiri. 116/G4
Maicao, Col. 152/C2
Maîche, Fr. 56/C3
Maicuru (riv.), Braz. 151/H3
Maidenhead, Eng, UK 33/F3
Maidens, Sc, UK 36/B6
Maidstone, Sk, Can. 126/F2
Maidstone, Eng, UK 33/G4
Maidstone, On, Can. 135/G7
Maiduguri, Nga. 96/H5
Maienfeld, Swi. 57/F4
Maigue (riv.), Ire. 31/P10
Maihar, India 84/C3
Maihara, Japan 77/K5
Maikala (range), India 84/C4
Maiko, PN de la, D.R. Congo 97/L8
Maiko, PN de la, D.R. Congo 105/E1
Mailāni, India 84/C1
Maili, Hi, US 124/V13
Mailly-le-Camp, Fr. 53/D6
Mailsi, Pak. 86/B5
Main (riv.), NI, UK 34/B2
Main (riv.), Ger. 40/E4
Main-Donau (canal), Ger. 54/D3
Main Range NP, Austl. 114/C5
Maināguri, India 85/G2
Mainbernheim, Ger. 54/D3
Maincy, Fr. 30/L6
Maine (riv.), Ire. 31/P10
Maine (reg.), Fr. 42/C2
Maine (state), US 125/N2
Maine, Collines du (hills), Fr. 42/C2
Maine, Gulf of (gulf), Me, US 131/G3
Mainhardt, Ger. 54/C4
Mainhausen, Ger. 54/B2
Mainland (isl.), Sc, UK 31/V14
Mainling, China 83/F2
Mainpurī, India 84/B2
Mainstockheim, Ger. 54/D3
Maintirano, Madg. 107/H7
Mainz, Ger. 54/B3
Maio (isl.), CpV. 93/K10
Maipo (vol.), Chile 158/P9
Maipo (riv.), Chile 158/N8
Maipú, Arg. 158/F3
Maipú, Chile 158/N8
Maira (riv.), It. 43/G4
Maire (str.), Arg. 159/D7
Mairiporã, Braz. 211/G8
Mairwa, India 85/E2
Mais Gate (int'l arpt.), Haiti 145/H2
Maisach, Ger. 54/E6
Maisí (cape), Cuba 141/G3
Maisome (isl.), Tanz. 104/A3
Maison-Rouge, Fr. 30/M6
Maisons-Alfort, Fr. 30/K5
Maisons-Laffitte, Fr. 30/J5
Maithon (res.), India 85/F4
Maitland, Austl. 115/D2
Maitland (riv.), Can. 130/D3
Maitland, Austl. 113/H5
Maizhokunggar, China 83/F2
Maizières-lès-Metz, Fr. 53/F5
Maizuru, Japan 77/H5
Maizuru (bay), Japan 77/H4
Maja e Zezë (peak), Alb. 47/G2
Majadahonda, Sp. 45/N9
Majagual, Col. 152/C2
Majardah (mts.), Alg. 100/K6
Majāz Al Bāb, Tun. 100/L6
Majdanpek, Yugo. 48/E3
Majene, Indo. 81/E4
Majia (riv.), China 72/D3
Majiang, China 79/A2
Majorca (isl.), Sp. 45/G3
Majur, Yugo. 48/D3
Majuro (cap.), Mrsh. 116/G4
Makabe, Japan 77/E1
Makaha, Hi, US 124/V13
Makakilo City, Hi, US 124/V13
Makālu (peak), China 85/F2
Makālu (peak), Nepal 82/E2
Makarska, Cro. 47/E1
Makassar (str.), Indo. 67/L10
Makatea (isl.), FrPol. 117/L6
Makawao, Hi, US 124/T10
Makay (mass.), Madg. 107/H8
Makemo (isl.), FrPol. 117/L6
Makena, Hi, US 124/T10
Makeni, SLeo. 102/B4
Makgadikgadi (salt pans), Bots. 105/D5
Makhachkala, Rus. 63/H4
Makhdūmpur, Pak. 86/B4
Makhfar al Busayyah, Iraq 88/E2
Makhmūr, Iraq 90/E3
Makian (isl.), Indo. 81/G3
Makin (isl.), Kiri. 116/G4
Makino, Japan 77/K5
Makinsk, Kaz. 87/F2
Makioka, Japan 77/B2
Makiyivka, Ukr. 62/F2
Makkah, SAr. 88/C4
Makkovik, Nf, Can. 123/L3
Makó, Hun. 48/E2
Makokou, Gabon 96/H7
Makonde (plat.), Tanz. 104/C5
Maków Mazowiecki, Pol. 41/L2
Makrakómi, Gre. 47/H3
Makran (coast), Iran 89/G3
Makran (reg.), Iran 89/H3
Makrokhórion, Gre. 47/H2
Maksutlu, Turk. 47/K2
Makteir (reg.), Mrta. 98/C5
Makthar, Tun. 100/L7
Makurazaki, Japan 74/B5
Makurdi, Nga. 103/H5
Makushin (vol.), Ak, US 134/E5
Mal Abrigo, Uru. 159/K11
Mala, Peru 156/B4
Mala (pt.), CR 144/E4
Mala (pt.), Pan. 152/B3
Malabar (coast), India 82/B5
Malabata (pt.), Mor. 100/B2
Malabo (cap.), EqG. 96/G7
Malacacheta, Braz. 154/B5
Malacca (str.), Asia 67/J9
Malacky, Slvk. 41/J4
Maladers, Swi. 57/F4
Maladzyechna, Bela. 39/M4
Málaga (int'l arpt.), Sp. 44/C4
Málaga, Sp. 44/C4
Malaga, NJ, US 138/C4
Malaga Cove (bay), Ca, US 136/F8
Malagarasi (riv.), Tanz. 104/A4
Malagón, Sp. 44/D3
Malagueta (bay), Cuba 145/G1
Malahide, Ire. 34/B5
Malaimbandy, Madg. 107/H8
Malaita (isl.), Sol. 116/F5
Malakāl, Sudan 97/M6
Malakangiri, India 82/D4
Malakwāl, Pak. 86/B3
Malambo, Col. 152/C2
Malang, Indo. 80/D5
Malangawa, Nepal 85/E2
Malanje, Ang. 105/C2
Malans, Swi. 57/F4
Malanville, Ben. 103/F4
Malargüe, Arg. 158/C2
Malartic, Qu, Can. 130/E1
Malasoro (pt.), Indo. 81/E5
Malatya (prov.), Turk. 90/D2
Malatya, Turk. 90/D2
Malaut, India 86/C4
Malawi (ctry.) 93/F6
Malawi (Nyasa) (lake), Malw. 104/B5
Malay (pen.), Thai. 83/G6
Malaya (reg.), Malay. 80/B3
Malaya Vishera, Rus. 39/Q2
Malaybalay, Phil. 79/E6
Malāyer, Iran 88/E2
Malaysia (ctry.) 67/K9
Malazemel'skaya (tundra), Rus. 61/L2
Malazgirt, Turk. 90/E2
Malbaie (riv.), Can. 131/G1
Malbork, Pol. 39/H4
Malcesine, It. 59/D1
Malchin, Ger. 38/E5
Malcontenta, It. 59/F2
Maldegem, Belg. 52/C1
Malden, Mo, US 129/K3
Malden (isl.), Kiri. 117/K5
Maldive (isls.), Mald. 82/B6
Maldives (ctry.) 67/G9
Maldon, Austl. 115/C3
Maldon, Eng, UK 33/G3
Maldonado, Uru. 159/G2
Maldonado (dept.), Uru. 159/G2
Male (cap.), Mald. 67/G9
Maléa (cape), Gre. 47/H4
Mālegaon, India 89/K4
Malekula (isl.), Van. 116/F6
Malemort-sur-Corrèze, Fr. 42/D4
Malente, Ger. 38/D4
Maleny, Austl. 114/D4
Maleo, It. 58/C2
Malesína, Gre. 47/H3
Malfa, It. 46/D3
Malgobek, Rus. 63/H4
Malgrat de Mar, Sp. 45/G2
Malgrate, It. 58/C1
Malheur (lake), Or, US 128/C2
Malheur (riv.), Or, US 126/D5
Malheureux (cape), Mrts. 107/T14
Mali (riv.), Myan. 83/G2
Mali (isl.), Myan. 78/B3
Mali (ctry.) 93/B3
Mali Lošinj, Cro. 48/B3
Mália, Gre. 47/J5
Malibu, Ca, US 136/B2
Malīhābād, India 84/C2
Målilla, Swe. 38/F3
Malin Head (pt.), Ire. 31/Q9
Malinau, Indo. 81/E3
Malindang (mt.), Phil. 81/F2
Malindi, Kenya 104/D3
Maling (pass), China 72/C3
Malio (riv.), Madg. 107/H8
Malipo, China 78/D1
Malīr Cantonment, Pak. 89/J4
Malka Mari NP, Kenya 97/P7
Malkara, Turk. 49/H5
Malko Tŭrnovo, Bul. 49/H5
Mallacoota, Austl. 115/D3
Mallaig, Sc, UK 31/R8
Mallānwān, India 84/C2
Mallasvesi (lake), Fin. 39/K1
Mallee Cliffs NP, Austl. 115/B2
Mallén, Sp. 44/E2
Malleray, Swi. 56/D3
Mallero (riv.), It. 57/F5
Mallersdorf-Pfaffenberg, Ger. 55/F5
Malles (Mals), It. 57/G4
Malloa, Chile 158/N9
Mallow, Ire. 31/P10
Malmberget, Swe. 37/G2
Malmédy, Belg. 53/F3
Malmesbury, SAfr. 106/L10
Malmköping, Swe. 38/G2
Malmö, Swe. 38/E4
Malmöhus (co.), Swe. 37/E5
Malmslätt, Swe. 38/F2
Malnate, It. 58/B1
Malo, It. 59/E1
Maloelap (isl.), Mrsh. 116/G4
Malone, NY, US 130/F2
Malong, China 83/H2
Malonje (peak), Tanz. 104/A5
Malonno, It. 57/G5
Mal'opolska (uplands), Pol. 41/K3
Malpartida de Cáceres, Sp. 44/B3
Malpartida de Plasencia, Sp. 44/B3
Malpelo (isl.), Col. 147/A2
Malpensa (int'l arpt.), It. 58/B1
Malpica, Sp. 44/A1
Malsch (riv.), Aus. 55/H5
Malsch, Ger. 54/B5
Malše (riv.), Czh. 41/H4
Mälstek (peak), Czh. 55/G4
Malta, Mt, US 126/G3
Malta, Braz. 154/C2
Malta (chan.), Malta 46/C4
Malta (ctry.) 27/F5
Maltahöhe, Namb. 105/C5
Maltby, Eng, UK 35/G5
Malters, Swi. 56/E3
Maltorne (riv.), Fr. 30/G6
Malung, Swe. 38/E1
Malvaglia, Swi. 57/E5
Malvan, India 89/K5
Malveira, Port. 45/P10
Malvern, Pa, US 138/C3
Malverne, NY, US 139/L9
Malvinas (Falkland) (isls.), UK 160/W
Malvy Uzen' (riv.), Rus. 63/H2
Malyn, Ukr. 62/D2
Malyy Yenisey (riv.), Rus. 70/G1
Malzéville, Fr. 53/F6
Mamanguape, Braz. 154/D2
Mamaroneck, NY, US 139/L8
Mamba, Zam. 105/E4
Mamba, Japan 77/B1
Mambajao, Phil. 79/D6
Mambasa, D.R. Congo 104/A2
Mamberamo (riv.), Indo. 81/J4
Mambéré (riv.), CAfr. 96/J7
Mambij, Syria 90/D2
Mamburao, Phil. 81/F1
Mamer, Lux. 53/F4
Mamers, Fr. 42/D2
Mamfé, Camr. 103/H5
Mammendorf, Ger. 57/H1
Mamming, Ger. 55/F5
Mammoth, Az, US 128/E4
Mammoth Cave NP, Ky, US 133/G2
Mamoré (riv.), Braz. 150/E6
Mamou, La, US 129/J5
Mamoutzou, May. 107/H6
Mampikony, Madg. 107/H7
Mampong, Gha. 103/E5
Mamry (lake), Pol. 39/J4
Mamuju, Indo. 81/E4
Mamuri (riv.), Braz. 151/G4
Mamwera (peak), Tanz. 104/C4
Man, C.d'Iv. 102/D5
Man, Isle of (isl.), IM, UK 34/D3
Man Mia (peak), Thai. 78/B4
Mana (riv.), FrG. 153/H3
Manabl (prov.), Ecu. 152/A5
Manacapuru, Braz. 150/F4
Manacle (pt.), Eng, UK 32/A6
Manacor, Sp. 45/G3
Manado, Indo. 81/F3
Manage, Belg. 53/D3
Managua (lake), Nic. 140/D5
Managua (cap.), Nic. 144/E3
Manahawkin, NJ, US 138/D4
Manakambahiny, Madg. 107/J7
Manakara, Madg. 107/J8
Manalapan, NJ, US 138/D3
Manāli, India 86/D3
Manambaho (riv.), Madg. 107/H7
Manambolo (riv.), Madg. 107/H7
Manananantanana (riv.), Madg. 107/H8
Mananara, Madg. 107/J7
Mananara (riv.), Madg. 107/H8
Mananjary, Madg. 107/J8
Mananjary (riv.), Madg. 107/H8
Manara (pt.), It. 58/C4
Manaratsandry, Madg. 107/H7
Manas, China 70/E3
Manas (int'l arpt.), Kyr. 87/F4
Manas (peak), Kyr. 87/F4
Manās (riv.), India 85/H2
Manas (riv.), China 64/J5
Manāslu (peak), Nepal 85/E1
Manasquan, NJ, US 138/D3
Manasquan (riv.), NJ, US 138/D3
Manassa, Co, US 132/B2
Manastir Dečani, Yugo. 47/G1
Manastir Gračanica, Yugo. 47/G1
Manastir Sopoćani, Yugo. 47/G1
Manatsuru, Japan 77/C3
Manaus, Braz. 150/F4
Manawatu (riv.), NZ 117/T11
Mañazo, Peru 156/D4
Manazuru-misaki (cape), Japan 77/C3
Mance (riv.), Fr. 56/B2
Mancha Real, Sp. 44/D4
Mancheng, China 72/G7
Mancherāl, India 82/C4
Manchester, Ky, US 130/D4
Manchester, NH, US 131/G3
Manchester, Tn, US 133/G3
Manchester, Mo, US 137/F8
Manchester, Md, US 138/B4
Manchester, Pa, US 138/B3
Manchester (lake), Austl. 114/E7
Manchester, Wa, US 135/B2
Manchester, Eng, UK 35/F5
Manchester (Ringway) (int'l arpt.), Eng, UK 35/F5
Manchuria (reg.), China 65/N5
Mancieulles, Fr. 53/E5
Máncora, Peru 156/A2
Mand (riv.), Iran 89/F3
Manda, PN de, Chad 96/J6
Mandabe, Madg. 107/H8
Mandaguari, Braz. 155/B2
Mandal, India 82/B3
Mandal, Nor. 38/B2
Mandal-Ovoo, Mong. 70/H3
Mandala (peak), Indo. 81/K4
Mandalay (div.), Myan. 70/F7
Mandalay, Myan. 83/G3
Mandalgovĭ, Mong. 70/J2
Mandalī, Iraq 88/E2
Mandan, ND, US 127/H4
Mandasavu (peak), Indo. 81/F5
Mandaue, Phil. 79/D5
Mandeb (str.), Afr.,Asia 93/G3
Mandello del Lario, It. 57/F6
Mandera, Kenya 97/P7
Mandeure, Fr. 56/C3
Mandeville, La, US 137/P16
Mandeville, Jam. 145/G2
Mandi Bahāuddīn, Pak. 86/B3
Mandi Dabwāli, India 86/C5
Mandi Sādiqganj, Pak. 86/B4
Mandié, Moz. 105/F4
Mandiola (isl.), Indo. 81/G4
Mandira (res.), India 85/E4
Mandla, India 84/C4
Mandø (isl.), Den. 38/C4
Mándok, Hun. 41/M4
Mandoto, Madg. 107/H7
Mandoúdhion, Gre. 47/H3
Mándra, Gre. 47/N8
Mandrare (riv.), Madg. 107/H9
Mandritsara, Madg. 107/J6
Mandsaur, India 89/L4
Mandurah, Austl. 112/B5
Manduria, It. 47/E2
Māndvi, India 89/J4
Mandya, India 82/C5
Mane (pass), Nepal 84/D1
Manéngouba, Massif du (peak), Camr. 103/H5
Maner, India 85/E3
Manerbio, It. 58/D2
Manfalūt, Egypt 88/B3
Manfredonia, It. 46/D2
Manfredonia, Golfo di (gulf), It. 46/D2
Mang (riv.), China 72/B4
Manga, Braz. 154/B4
Manga, Burk. 103/E4
Mangabeiras, Chapada das (hills), Braz. 151/J6
Mangai, D.R. Congo 105/C1
Mangaia (isl.), Cookls. 117/K7
Mangaldai, India 83/F2
Mangaldan, Phil. 79/D4
Mangalia, Rom. 49/J4
Mangalisa (peak), Tanz. 104/C4
Mangalore, India 82/B5
Mangaratiba, Braz. 211/J7
Mangareva (isl.), FrPol. 117/M7
Manger, Nor. 38/A1
Mangghystaū (obl.), Kaz. 64/F5
Mangkalihat (cape), Indo. 81/E3
Mangla (dam), Pak. 86/B3
Mangla, Pak. 86/B3
Mangla (res.), Pak. 86/B3
Manglaralto, Ecu. 156/A1
Manglares (pt.), Col. 152/B4
Manglaur, India 84/A1
Mangles (bay), Austl. 112/K7
Mango, Togo 103/F4
Mangoche, Malw. 105/G3
Mangoky (riv.), Madg. 105/J11
Mangole (isl.), Indo. 81/G4
Mangoro (riv.), Madg. 107/J7
Mangotsfield, Eng, UK 32/D4
Māngrol, India 89/K4
Mangualde, Port. 44/B2
Mangueira (lake), Braz. 159/G2
Mangum, Ok, US 129/H4
Mangyshlak (plat.), Kaz. 63/K4
Mangyshlak (pen.), Kaz. 63/J3
Manhasset, NY, US 139/L8
Manhasset (bay), NY, US 139/L8
Manhattan, Mt, US 126/F4
Manhattan (isl.), NY, US 139/K9
Manhattan Beach, Ca, US 136/F8
Manhay, Belg. 53/E3
Manheim, Pa, US 138/B3
Manhiça, Moz. 105/F6
Manhuaçu, Braz. 155/D2
Manhumirim, Braz. 155/D2
Mania (riv.), Madg. 107/H7
Maniamba, Moz. 105/G3
Maniāri (riv.), India 84/C4
Manicoré (riv.), Braz. 150/F5
Manicoré, Braz. 150/F5
Manicouagan (riv.), Qu, Can. 123/K3
Manicouagan (res.), Can. 119/L4
Manifold (cape), Austl. 114/C3
Manigotagan, Mb, Can. 127/J3
Manihāri, India 85/F3
Manihi (isl.), FrPol. 117/L6
Manihiki (isl.), Cookls. 117/J6
Manikarchar, India 85/G3
Manila (cap.), Phil. 79/D5
Manilla, Austl. 115/D1
Maningory (riv.), Madg. 107/J7
Manipa (str.), Indo. 81/G4
Manipat (hills), India 84/D4
Manipur (state), India 70/F7
Manisa (prov.), Turk. 62/D5
Manistee (riv.), Mi, US 130/C2
Manistee, Mi, US 130/C2
Manistique, Mi, US 130/C2
Manitoba (prov.), Can. 122/G3
Manitoba (lake), Can. 119/G4
Manitou (riv.), Can. 131/H1
Manitou Springs, Co, US 129/F3
Manitoulin (isl.), Can. 130/D2
Manitowoc, Wi, US 127/M4
Maniwaki, Qu, Can. 130/F2
Manizales, Col. 150/C2
Manja, Madg. 107/H8
Manjakandriana, Madg. 107/J7
Manjimup, Austl. 112/C5
Mankono, C.d'Iv. 102/D4
Manley Hot Springs, Ak, US 134/H2
Manlleu, Sp. 44/D1
Manlyutka, Rus. 61/R4
Manmād, India 89/K4
Mannar, SrL. 82/C6
Mannar (gulf), SrL.,India 67/G9
Männedorf, Swi. 57/E3
Mannetjiesberg (peak), SAfr. 106/C4
Mannheim, Ger. 54/B4
Manning, SC, US 133/H3
Manning (cape), NW, Can. 123/Q7
Manning, Ab, Can. 122/E3
Mannington Meadow (lake), NJ, US 138/C4
Männlifluh (peak), Swi. 56/D4
Mannum, Austl. 113/H5
Mano (riv.), Libr. 96/C6
Manokotak, Ak, US 134/G4
Manolo Fortich, Phil. 79/D6
Manombo, Madg. 107/G8
Manono, D.R. Congo 105/E2
Manorville, NY, US 139/F2
Manosque, Fr. 42/F5
Manouane (riv.), Can. 131/G1
Manouane (lake), Can. 131/G1
Manp'o, NKor. 73/D2
Manra (Sydney) (isl.), Kiri. 117/H5
Manresa, Sp. 45/K6
Mansa, Zam. 104/A5
Mānsa, India 86/C5
Mansa Konko, Gam. 102/B3
Mansalay, Phil. 81/F1
Mānsehra, Pak. 86/B2
Mansel (isl.), NW, Can. 123/H2
Mansfield, Austl. 115/C3
Mansfield, Oh, US 130/D3
Mansfield, La, US 129/J4
Mansfield, Eng, UK 35/G5
Mansfield Woodhouse, Eng, UK 35/G5
Mansilla de las Mulas, Sp. 44/C1
Manta, Ecu. 152/A5
Mantalingajan (mt.), Phil. 81/E2
Mantaro (riv.), Peru 150/C6
Manteca, Ca, US 128/B3
Mantecal, Ven. 152/D3
Manteigas, Port. 44/B2
Mantena, Braz. 155/D1
Manthani, India 82/C4
Manti, Ut, US 128/E3
Mantiqueira, Serra da (mts.), Braz. 151/K8
Mantorp, Swe. 38/F2
Mantova (prov.), It. 58/D2
Mantova, It. 59/D2
Mäntsälä, Fin. 39/L1
Mantua, Ut, US 137/K11
Mantua, Cuba 145/E1
Mantua, NJ, US 138/C4
Manturovo, Rus. 61/K4
Mäntyharju, Fin. 39/M1
Manu (riv.), India 150/D6
Manú, Peru 156/D4
Manú, PN, Peru 150/D6
Manua (isls.), ASam. 117/J6
Manuae Atoll (atoll), Cookls. 117/K6
Manuel Alves da Natividade (riv.), Braz. 151/J6
Manuel Benavides, Mex. 132/C4
Manuel J. Cobo, Arg. 159/K11
Manui (isl.), Indo. 81/F4
Manuk (riv.), Indo. 80/C5
Manukau, NZ 117/S10
Manumuskin (riv.), NJ, US 138/D5
Manuripe (riv.), Bol. 150/E6
Manuripe Heath Amazonica, Reserva Nacional, Bol. 156/D4
Manus (isl.), PNG 116/D5
Manville, NJ, US 138/D2
Many, La, US 129/J5
Many Farms, Az, US 128/E3
Manyara (lake), Tanz. 104/B3
Manych (riv.), Rus. 64/E5
Manych-Gudilo (lake), Rus. 63/G3
Manzanares, Sp. 44/D3
Manzanares (riv.), Sp. 45/N8
Manzanares el Real, Sp. 45/N8
Manzanillo, Mex. 142/D5
Manzanillo (int'l arpt.), Mex. 142/D5
Manzanillo, Cuba 145/G1
Manzano (mts.), NM, US 132/B3
Manzano, It. 59/G1
Manzhouli, China 71/L2
Manzil Bū Zalafah, Tun. 46/B4
Manzil Tamīn, Tun. 46/B4
Manzilah, Buḩayrat al (lake), Egypt 91/B4
Manzini, Swaz. 107/E2
Mao, Chad 96/J5
Maoke (mts.), Indo. 116/C5
Maoming, China 83/K3
Mapastepec, Mex. 144/C3
Mapi (riv.), Indo. 81/J5
Mapimí, Bolsón de (depr.), Mex. 142/D3
Mapire, Ven. 153/E3
Maple (riv.), ND, US 127/J4
Maple Creek, Sk, Can. 126/F3
Maple Grove, Qu, Can. 131/N7
Maple Park, Il, US 135/N16
Maple Shade, NJ, US 138/D4
Maple Valley, Wa, US 135/C3
Mapleton, Ut, US 137/K13
Maplewood, Mo, US 137/G8
Maplewood, NJ, US 139/H9
Maporal, Ven. 152/D3
Mapuera (riv.), Braz. 150/G3
Maputo (int'l arpt.), Moz. 107/F2
Maputo (cap.), Moz. 107/F2
Maqdam (cape), Sudan 101/D5
Maqên Gangri (peak), China 70/G5
Maquan (Damqog) (riv.), China 84/E1
Maquinchao, Arg. 158/C4
Maquoketa (riv.), Ia, US 129/K2
Mar (mts.), Braz. 147/E5
Mar (reg.), Sc, UK 36/D2
Mar Chiquita (lake), Arg. 157/D3
Mar de Ajó, Arg. 159/F3
Mar del Plata, Arg. 158/F3
Mar del Tuyú, Arg. 159/F3
Mara (pol. reg.), Tanz. 104/B3
Mara (riv.), Tanz. 104/B3
Marabá, Braz. 151/J5
Maracá, Ilha de (isl.), Braz. 151/H3
Maracaibo, Ven. 152/D2
Maracaibo (lake), Ven. 147/B2
Maracaju, Serra de (mts.), Braz. 151/G8
Maracás, Braz. 154/B4
Maracás, Chapada de (hills), Braz. 154/B4
Maracay, Ven. 150/E1
Maracena, Sp. 44/D4
Marādah, Libya 96/J2
Maradi, Niger 103/G3
Maradi (dept.), Niger 103/G3
Marāgheh, Iran 88/E1
Mārahra, India 84/B2
Marahuaca (peak), Ven. 153/E4
Marais de St-Gond (swamp), Fr. 52/C6
Marais des Cygnes (riv.), US 129/J3
Marajó (bay), Braz. 147/E3
Marajó, Ilha de (isl.), Braz. 147/D3
Maralal, Kenya 104/C2
Maralinga-Tjarutja Abor. Land, Austl. 113/F4
Maramag, Phil. 79/E6
Marambaia, Ilha (isl.), Braz. 211/K8
Maramureş (co.), Rom. 41/M5
Marana, Az, US 128/E4
Marana (lag.), Cro. 59/G1
Marand, Iran 63/H5
Marang, Malay. 80/B2
Marangani, Peru 156/D4
Maranguape, Braz. 154/C1
Maranhão (riv.), Braz. 151/J6
Maranhão (state), Braz. 154/A2
Marano Lagunare, It. 59/G1
Marano sul Panaro, It. 59/D4
Marano Vicentino, It. 59/E1
Maranoa (riv.), Austl. 109/D3
Marañón (riv.), Peru 147/B3
Marans, Fr. 42/C3
Maraoue, PN de la, C.d'Iv. 102/D5
Marapi (peak), Indo. 80/B4
Maras (peak), Indo. 80/C4
Mărăşeşti, Rom. 49/H3
Marathon, On, Can. 127/M3
Marathon, Fl, US 133/H5
Marathon, Tx, US 132/C4
Marathón, Gre. 47/N8
Marau, Braz. 155/A4
Maraulīānwāla, Pak. 86/B3
Maravatío de Ocampo, Mex. 143/E5
Marawi, Phil. 81/F2
Marbach, Swi. 56/D4
Marbach am Neckar, Ger. 54/C5
Marbache, Fr. 53/F6
Marbella, Sp. 44/C4
Marble Bar, Austl. 112/C2
Marbleton, Wy, US 126/F5
Marburg, Ger. 43/H1
Marburg (lake), Pa, US 138/B4
Marca, Ponta da (pt.), Ang. 105/B4
Marcali, Hun. 48/C2
Marcallo, It. 58/B2
Marcapata, Peru 156/D4
March, Eng, UK 33/G1
Marche (prov.), It. 43/K5
Marche (mts.), Fr. 42/D3
Marche-en-Famenne, Belg. 53/E3
Marchémoret, Fr. 30/L4
Marchena, Sp. 44/C4
Marchena (isl.), Ecu. 156/E6
Marcheno, It. 58/D1
Marchiennes, Fr. 52/C3
Marchin, Belg. 53/E3
Marchtrenk, Aus. 55/H6
Marciana Marina, It. 46/B1
Marcilly, Fr. 30/L4
Marcilly-sur-Tille, Fr. 56/B2
Marck, Fr. 52/A2
Marckolsheim, Fr. 56/D1
Marco, Braz. 154/B1
Marco, Fl, US 133/H5
Marco Polo (int'l arpt.), It. 59/F2
Marcoing, Fr. 52/C3
Marcon, It. 59/F1
Marcona, Peru 156/C4
Marconi (mt.), BC, Can. 126/E3
Marcos Juárez, Arg. 158/E2
Marcoussis, Fr. 30/J6
Marcovia, Hon. 144/E3
Marcq-en-Barœul, Fr. 52/C2
Marcus Baker (mt.), Ak, US 134/J3
Marcy (mt.), NY, US 130/F2
Mardān, Pak. 86/B2
Marden, Eng, UK 30/E3
Mardeuil, Fr. 52/C5
Mardin (town), Turk. 90/E2
Marecchia (riv.), It. 59/F5
Maree (lake), Sc, UK 31/R8
Mareeba, Austl. 114/B2
Mareil-sur-Mauldre, Fr. 30/H5
Marengo, Il, US 135/N15
Marennes, Fr. 42/C4
Mareuil-sur-Ourcq, Fr. 30/M4
Marfa, Tx, US 129/F5
Margalla Hills NP, Pak. 86/B3
Marganets', Ukr. 62/E3
Margao (Madgaon), India 89/K5
Margaret (mt.), Austl. 112/C2
Margaret River, Austl. 112/B5
Margarita (peak), Ca, US 136/C4
Margarita, Isla de (isl.), Ven. 150/F1
Margarítion, Gre. 47/G3
Margate, SAfr. 107/E3
Margate, Eng, UK 33/H4
Margate City, NJ, US 138/D5
Margeride, Monts de la (mts.), Fr. 42/E4
Margherita (peak), Ugan. 104/A2
Marghilon, Uzb. 87/F4
Marghita, Rom. 48/F2
Margny-lès-Compiègne, Fr. 52/B5
Margos, Peru 156/B3
Margosatubig, Phil. 81/F2
Margraten, Neth. 53/E2
Mari, Braz. 154/D2
Mari El Aut. Rep., Rus. 64/Q6
Maria (mt.), Austl. 115/D4
María Cleófas (isl.), Mex. 142/D4
Maria da Fé, Braz. 211/H7
Maria Island NP, Austl. 115/D4
María Madre (isl.), Mex. 142/D4
María Magdalena (isl.), Mex. 142/D4
Maria van Diemen (cape), NZ 117/S9
Mariāhū, India 84/D3
Marian, Austl. 114/C3
Marianao, Cuba 145/F1
Marianna, Fl, US 133/G4
Marianna, Ar, US 129/K4
Mariano Comense, It. 58/C1
Mariano Marcos, Phil. 79/D6
Mariánské Lázně, Czh. 55/F3
Marias (riv.), Mt, US 126/F3
Mariato (pt.), Pan. 152/A3
Maribo, Den. 38/D4
Maribor, Slov. 43/L3
Maricá, Braz. 211/L7
Maricopa (co.), Az, US 137/R18
Marié (riv.), Braz. 150/E4
Marie Byrd Land (phys. reg.), Ant. 160/S
Marie-Galante (isl.), Dom. 141/J4
Mariehamn (int'l arpt.), Fin. 39/H1
Mariel, Cuba 145/F1
Marienhafe, Ger. 51/E1
Marienheide, Ger. 53/G1
Mariental, Namb. 105/C5
Mariestad, Swe. 38/E2
Marietta, Ok, US 129/H4
Marietta, Ga, US 133/G3
Marietta, Pa, US 138/B3
Marignane, Fr. 42/F5
Marigot, Dom. 141/N9
Marijampolė, Lith. 39/K4
Marília, Braz. 155/B2
Marín, Sp. 44/A1
Marin (co.), Ca, US 135/J10
Marin-Epagnier, Swi. 56/D3
Marina, It. 46/D3
Marina del Rey, Ca, US 136/F8
Marina del Rey (har.), Ca, US 136/F8
Marina di Andora, It. 58/B5
Marina di Montemarciano, It. 59/G5
Marina di Ravenna, It. 59/F4
Marine Nat'l Rsv., Kenya 104/D3
Marine World Africa USA, Ca, US 135/K10
Marineland, Austl. 113/M8
Marines, Fr. 30/H4
Marinette, Wi, US 127/M4
Maringá, Braz. 155/B2
Marinha Grande, Port. 44/A3
Marinhas, Port. 44/A2
Marion, Ky, US 130/B4
Marion, Mi, US 130/C2
Marion, In, US 130/C3
Marion, Oh, US 130/D3
Marion (reef), Austl. 109/E2
Marion, Al, US 133/G3
Marion (lake), SC, US 125/K5
Maripa, Ven. 153/E3
Mariposa, Ca, US 128/C3
Mariscal Estigarribia, Par. 150/F8
Mariscal Sucre (int'l arpt.), Ecu. 152/B5
Maritime Alps (mts.), Fr. 43/G4
Maritsa (riv.), Bul. 62/C4
Mariupol' (int'l arpt.), Ukr. 62/F3
Mariupol', Ukr. 62/F3
Marj 'Uyūn, Leb. 91/D3
Mark (riv.), Belg. 50/B6
Mark Twain (lake), Mo, US 129/J3
Mark Twain NWR, Mo, US 137/G8
Mark Twain NWR, Il, US 137/F7
Marka (riv.), Ger. 51/E3
Marka (Merca), Som. 97/P7
Markam, China 83/G2
Markaryd, Swe. 38/E3
Markdorf, Ger. 57/F2
Markelsdorfer (pt.), Ger. 38/D4
Marken (isl.), Neth. 50/C4
Markerwaard (polder), Neth. 50/C3
Market Harborough, Eng, UK 33/F2
Markgroningen, Ger. 54/C5
Markham, On, Can. 131/R8
Markham (bay), NW, Can. 123/J2
Marki, Pol. 41/L2
Markinch, Sc, UK 36/C4
Markit, China 87/G5
Markleeville, Ca, US 128/C3
Markneukirchen, Ger. 55/F2
Markópoulon, Gre. 47/N9
Markovac, Yugo. 48/E3
Marks, Rus. 63/H2
Marksville, La, US 129/J5
Markt Bibart, Ger. 54/D3

Markt Erlbach, Ger. 54/D4
Markt Indersdorf, Ger. 55/E6
Markt Rettenbach, Ger. 57/G2
Markt Sankt Florian, Aus. 55/H6
Markt Schwaben, Ger. 55/E6
Marktbreit, Ger. 54/D3
Marktheidenfeld, Ger. 54/C3
Marktl, Ger. 55/F6
Marktoberdorf, Ger. 57/G2
Marktredwitz, Ger. 55/F3
Marl, Ger. 51/E5
Marla, Austl. 113/G3
Marlboro, NJ, US 138/D3
Marlboro (Upper Marlboro), Md, US 138/B6
Marle, Fr. 52/C4
Marlengo (Marling), It. 57/H4
Marlenheim, Fr. 53/G6
Marles-en-Brie, Fr. 30/L5
Marles-les-Mines, Fr. 52/B3
Marlow, Eng, UK 33/F3
Marlow, Ger. 38/E4
Marlton, NJ, US 138/D4
Marly, Fr. 53/F5
Marly, Fr. 52/C3
Marly-la-Ville, Fr. 30/K4
Marly-le-Roi, Fr. 30/J5
Marmagão, India 89/K5
Marmande, Fr. 42/D4
Marmara, Turk. 49/H5
Marmara (isl.), Turk. 49/H5
Marmara (sea), Turk. 62/D4
Marmaraereğlisi, Turk. 49/H5
Marmaris, Turk. 90/B2
Marmelos (riv.), Braz. 150/F5
Marmion (lake), Austl. 109/A3
Marmirolo, It. 59/D2
Marmolada (peak), It. 43/J3
Marmolejo, Sp. 44/C3
Marmontana (peak), It. 57/F5
Marmora, NJ, US 138/D5
Marmoutier, Fr. 53/G6
Marnay, Fr. 56/B3
Marnaz, Fr. 56/C5
Marne (riv.), Fr. 42/F2
Marne, Ger. 38/C5
Marne (dept.), Fr. 52/C6
Marne au Rhin, Canal de la (canal), Fr. 53/D6
Maro Reef (reef), Hi, US 117/H2
Maroa, Ven. 153/E4
Maroantsetra, Madg. 107/J6
Marokau (isl.), FrPol. 117/L6
Marolambo, Madg. 107/J8
Maroldsweisach, Ger. 54/D2
Marolles-en-Brie, Fr. 30/M5
Marolles-en-Hurepoix, Fr. 30/J6
Maromokotro (peak), Madg. 107/J6
Marondera, Zim. 105/F4
Marone, It. 58/D1
Maroni (riv.), FrG.,Sur. 147/D2
Maroochydore-Mooloolaba, Austl. 114/D4
Maroon Town, Jam. 145/G2
Marostica, It. 59/E1
Marotandrano, Madg. 107/J7
Marotiri (Bass Is.) (isls.), FrPol. 117/L7
Marotta, It. 59/G5
Maroua, Camr. 96/H5
Marouini (riv.), FrG. 153/H4
Marovato, Madg. 107/J6
Marovoay, Madg. 107/H7
Marowijne (dist.), Sur. 153/H3
Marpingen, Ger. 53/G5
Marple, Eng, UK 35/F5
Marquan (riv.), China 82/E2
Marquard, SAfr. 106/D3
Marquarie (riv.), Austl. 116/D8
Marquesas (isls.), FrPol. 117/M5
Marquise, Fr. 52/A2
Marracuene, Moz. 107/F2
Marradi, It. 59/E4
Marrah (mts.), Sudan 97/K5
Marrah (peak), Sudan 97/K5
Marrakech, Mor. 98/D3
Marrero, La, US 137/P17
Marromeu, Moz. 105/G4
Marrupa, Moz. 105/G3
Mars (peak), It. 58/A1
Marsá al Burayqah, Libya 96/J1
Marsá Maṭrūḥ (cap.), Egypt 101/A2
Marsabit, Kenya 104/C2
Marsabit Nat'l Rsv., Kenya 104/C2
Marsala, It. 46/C4
Marsange (riv.), Fr. 30/L5
Marsannay, Fr. 56/A3
Marsberg, Ger. 51/F6
Marsciano, It. 43/K5
Marsdiep Texelstroom (chan.), Neth. 50/B3
Marseille, Fr. 42/F5
Marseille-en-Beauvaisis, Fr. 52/A4
Marsh (isl.), La, US 140/C2
Marshall, Sk, Can. 126/F2
Marshall, Mn, US 127/K4
Marshall, Tx, US 129/J4
Marshall, Mo, US 129/J3
Marshall, Co, US 137/B3
Marshall, Ut, US 137/J12
Marshall (riv.), Austl. 113/H2
Marshall Islands (ctry.) 116/G3
Marshallton, De, US 138/C4
Marshalltown, Ia, US 127/K5
Marshdale, Co, US 137/B3
Marshfield, Mo, US 129/J3
Märsta, Swe. 38/G2
Marston (lake), Co, US 137/B3
Marsyandi (riv.), Nepal 85/E1
Marta, It. 46/B1
Marta (mts.), Col. 145/H4
Martaban, Myan. 78/B2
Martaban (gulf), Myan. 78/B2
Martapura, Indo. 80/D4
Marte R. Gomez, Mex. 142/C3
Martelange, Belg. 53/E4
Martellago, It. 59/F1
Martensville, Sk, Can. 126/G2
Martfeld, Ger. 51/G3
Martha's Vineyard (isl.), Ma, US 131/G3
Martignacco, It. 59/G1
Martigny, Swi. 56/D5
Martigny-les-Bains, Fr. 56/B1
Martigues, Fr. 42/F5
Martil, Mor. 100/B2
Martin, Tn, US 130/B4
Martin (lake), Al, US 133/G3
Martin Vaz (isls.), Braz. 151/N8
Martina Franca, It. 47/E2
Martinengo, It. 58/C1
Martinez, Ga, US 133/H3
Martínez de la Torre, Mex. 143/M6
Martinho Campos, Braz. 155/C1
Martinique (isl.), Fr. 119/L8
Martinique Passage (chan.), Dom.,Mart. 141/J4
Martínon, Gre. 47/H3
Martinópole, Braz. 154/B1
Martinópolis, Braz. 155/B2
Martins, Braz. 154/C2
Martins Creek, Pa, US 138/C2
Martinsburg, WV, US 130/E4
Martinsville, Va, US 130/E4
Martorell, Sp. 45/K7
Martos, Sp. 44/D4
Martre (riv.), Can. 130/F1
Martres-Tolosane, Fr. 42/D5
Marty, SD, US 127/J5
Marugame, Japan 74/C3
Maruim, Braz. 154/C3
Maruko, Japan 75/F2
Marum, Neth. 50/D2
Maruoka, Japan 74/E2
Marutea (isl.), FrPol. 117/M7
Marv Dasht, Iran 88/F3
Marxheim, Ger. 54/D5
Mary, Trkm. 89/H1
Mary Anne Passage, Austl. 112/B2
Mary Esther, Fl, US 133/G4
Mary-sur-Marne, Fr. 30/M4
Maryborough, Austl. 115/B3
Maryborough, Austl. 114/D4
Marydale, SAfr. 106/C3
Marydel, Md, US 138/C5
Maryfield, Sk, Can. 127/H3
Maryland (co.), Lbr. 102/C5
Maryland (state), US 125/L4
Maryland City, Md, US 138/B5
Maryland Heights, Mo, US 137/G8
Maryland Line, Md, US 138/B4
Marystown, Nf, Can. 131/L2
Marysville, Ks, US 129/H3
Marysville, Pa, US 138/B3
Maryville, Tn, US 133/H3
Maryville, Il, US 137/H8
Marzabotto, It. 59/E4
Marzano (peak), It. 46/D2
Marzo (pt.), Col. 152/B3
Marzūq, Libya 96/H2
Masada (ruin), Isr. 91/D4
Masai Mara Nat'l Rsv., Kenya 105/F1
Masai Steppe (grsld.), Tanz. 104/C4
Masaka, Ugan. 104/A3
Masākin, Tun. 46/B5
Masamagrell, Sp. 45/E3
Masamba, Indo. 81/F4
Masan, SKor. 73/E5
Masangwe (hill), Tanz. 104/A4
Masaya, Nic. 144/E4
Masbate (isl.), Phil. 116/B3
Mascara, Alg. 100/F5
Mascarene (isls.), Mrts 107/T15
Mascota, Mex. 142/D4
Mascouche, Qu, Can. 131/N6
Maselheim, Ger. 57/F1
Maserà di Padova, It. 59/E2
Maseru (cap.), Les. 106/D3
Masevaux, Fr. 56/D2
Masfjorden, Nor. 38/A1
Mashan, China 79/A3
Mashhad (int'l arpt.), Iran 87/C5
Mashike, Japan 76/B2
Māshkīd (riv.), Iran 89/H3
Mashtūl as Sūq, Egypt 91/B4
Mashū (lake), Japan 76/D2
Masiaca, Mex. 142/C3
Maside, Sp. 44/A1
Masim (peak), Rus. 63/L1
Masindi, Ugan. 104/A2
Maṣīrah, Jazīrat (isl.), Oman 67/F5
Masisea, Peru 156/C3
Masjed-e Soleymān, Iran 88/E2
Mask (lake), Ire. 31/P10
Masker (peak), Mor. 98/D2
Masnou, Sp. 45/L7
Masoala (pen.), Madg. 105/L10
Masoala (cape), Madg. 107/J6
Masoarivo, Madg. 107/H7
Mason, Mi, US 130/C3
Mason, Tx, US 129/H5
Mason (lake), Wa, US 135/B3
Mason (co.), Wa, US 135/A3
Mason and Dixon Line, Pa, US 138/B4
Masone, It. 58/B4
Masonville, Co, US 137/B2
Masquefa, Sp. 45/K6
Massa, It. 58/D4
Massa-Carrara (prov.), It. 58/C4
Massa Finalese, It. 59/E3
Massa Fiscaglia, It. 59/F3
Massa Lombarda, It. 59/E4
Massa Marittima, It. 43/J5
Massa Martana, It. 43/K5
Massachusetts (bay), Ma, US 131/G3
Massachusetts (state), US 125/M3
Massaciuccoli, Lago di (lake), It. 58/D5
Massafra, It. 47/E2
Massangena, Moz. 105/F5
Massapê, Braz. 154/B1
Massapequa, NY, US 139/M9
Massapequa Park, NY, US 139/M9
Massarosa, It. 58/D5
Massbach, Ger. 54/D2
Massena, NY, US 130/F2
Masset, BC, Can. 134/M4
Massey (sound), NW, Can. 123/S7
Massey, Md, US 138/C5
Massillon, Oh, US 130/D3
Massy, Fr. 30/J5
Masterton, NZ 117/T11
Mastgat (chan.), Neth. 50/B5
Mastic, NY, US 139/F2
Mastic Beach, NY, US 139/F2
Mastník (riv.), Czh. 55/H3
Mastūj (riv.), Pak. 86/A2
Mastung, Pak. 89/J3
Masuda, Japan 74/B3
Masuho, Japan 77/A2
Masurai (peak), Indo. 80/B4
Masvingo, Zim. 105/F5
Maswa Game Rsv., Tanz. 104/B3
Maṣyāf, Syria 91/E2
Mat (riv.), Alb. 47/F2
Mata Grande, Braz. 154/C3
Mata Utu, Fr. 117/H6
Mātābhānga, India 85/G2
Matadi, D.R. Congo 105/B2
Matador, Tx, US 129/G4
Matagalpa, Nic. 144/E3
Matagami (lake), Can. 130/E1
Matagorda (bay), Tx, US 140/B2
Matagorda (isl.), Tx, US 140/B2
Matale, SrL. 82/D6
Matam, Sen. 102/B3
Matamoras, Pa, US 138/D1
Matamoros, Mex. 142/E3
Ma'ṭan as Sarra (well), Libya 97/K3
Matandu (riv.), Tanz. 104/C5
Matane (riv.), Can. 131/H1
Matane, Qu, Can. 131/H1
Matanga, Madg. 107/H8
Matanzas, Cuba 140/E3
Matão, Braz. 155/B2
Matape (riv.), Mex. 142/C2
Matapedia (riv.), Can. 131/H1
Mataquito (riv.), Chile 158/C2
Matara (ruin), Erit. 88/C6
Matara, SrL. 82/D6
Mataram, Indo. 81/E5
Matarânga, Gre. 47/G3
Mataró, Sp. 45/L6
Matatiele, SAfr. 106/E3
Mataura (riv.), NZ 117/R12
Matawan, NJ, US 139/J10
Matehuala, Mex. 143/E4
Matéri, Ben. 103/F4
Maternillos (pt.), Cuba 141/F3
Mátészalka, Hun. 41/M5
Mathay, Fr. 56/C3
Matheniko Game Rsv., Ugan. 104/B2
Mathew's (peak), Kenya 104/C2
Mathews (lake), Ca, US 136/C3
Mathis, Tx, US 132/D4
Mathoura, Austl. 115/C2
Mathurā, India 84/A2
Mati, Phil. 81/G2
Matias Barbosa, Braz. 211/K6
Matias Olímpio, Braz. 154/B1
Matías Romero, Mex. 144/C2
Matiguas, Nic. 144/E3
Matilija (dam), Ca, US 136/A2
Matinha, Braz. 154/A2
Matinhos, Braz. 155/B3
Matinicock (pt.), NY, US 139/L8
Mātir, Tun. 46/A4
Matiyuri (riv.), Ven. 152/D3
Mātla (riv.), India 85/G5
Matlock, Eng, UK 35/G5
Mato Grosso (plat.), Braz. 147/D4
Mato Grosso do Sul (state), Braz. 155/A1
Mato Grosso, Planalto do (plat.), Braz. 151/H6
Mato Verde, Braz. 154/B4
Matopos, Zim. 105/E5
Matosinhos, Port. 44/A2
Matoya (bay), Japan 77/L7
Maṭraḥ, Oman 89/G4
Matrei am Brenner, Aus. 57/H3
Matrei in Osttirol, Aus. 43/K3
Matriz de Camaragibe, Braz. 154/D3
Matroosberg (peak), SAfr. 106/L10
Matsalu (gulf), Est. 39/K2
Matsapa (Manzini) (int'l arpt.), Swaz. 107/E2
Matsiatra (riv.), Madg. 107/H8
Matsoandakana, Madg. 107/J6
Matsubara, Japan 77/J6
Matsubushi, Japan 77/D2
Matsuda, Japan 77/C3
Matsudo, Japan 77/D2
Matsue, Japan 74/C3
Matsuida, Japan 77/B1
Matsumae, Japan 76/B3
Matsumoto, Japan 75/E2
Matsuo, Japan 77/E2
Matsusaka, Japan 77/L6
Matsushima, Japan 76/B4
Matsutō, Japan 74/E2
Matsuyama, Japan 74/C4
Matt, Swi. 57/F4
Mattagami (riv.), Can. 130/D1
Mattarello, It. 57/H6
Mattawa, On, Can. 130/E2
Matterhorn (peak), It,Swi. 56/D6
Mattertal (valley), Swi. 56/D5
Mattese, Mo, US 137/G9
Matthews (mtn.), Ak, US 134/H2
Mattig (riv.), Aus. 55/G6
Mattighofen, Aus. 55/G6
Mattituck, NY, US 139/F2
Mattmarksee (lake), Swi. 56/D5
Mattō, Japan 74/E2
Mattock (riv.), Ire. 34/B4
Mattsee, Aus. 55/G7
Matucana, Peru 156/B3
Maturín, Ven. 153/F2
Matusadona NP, Zim. 105/E4
Matutum (mt.), Phil. 81/G2
Matzen, Aus. 49/P7
Maú (riv.), Guy. 150/G3
Mau (peak), Kenya 104/B3
Mau Aimma, India 84/C3
Mau Rānīpur, India 84/B3
Mauá, Braz. 155/C2
Maubert-Fontaine, Fr. 53/D4
Maubeuge, Fr. 52/C3
Maubourguet, Fr. 42/D5
Mauchline, Sc, UK 36/B5
Maud (pt.), Austl. 112/B2
Maud, Sc, UK 36/D1
Maudaha, India 84/C3
Mauerbach, Aus. 49/N7
Mauerkirchen, Aus. 55/G6
Maués, Braz. 150/G4
Maués Açu (riv.), Braz. 150/G4
Maug (isls.), NMar. 116/D2
Mauganj, India 84/C3
Maughold, IM, UK 34/D3
Maughold (pt.), IM, UK 34/D3
Mauguio, Fr. 42/F5
Maui (isl.), Hi, US 117/K2
Mauke (isl.), CookIs. 117/K7
Maulbronn, Ger. 54/B5
Mauldre (riv.), Fr. 52/A6
Maule (pol. reg.), Chile 158/B2
Maule (riv.), Chile 158/C2
Maule, Fr. 30/H5
Mauléon, Fr. 42/C3
Maullín, Chile 158/B4
Maumee (riv.), US 130/C3
Maun, Bots. 105/D4
Mauna Kea (peak), Hi, US 124/U11
Mauna Loa (peak), Hi, US 124/U11
Maunath Bhanjan, India 84/D3
Maungdaw, Myan. 83/F3
Mauperthuis, Fr. 30/M5
Maupertus (int'l arpt.), Fr. 42/C2
Maupiti (isl.), FrPol. 117/K6
Maur, Swi. 57/E3
Maurāwān, India 84/C2
Maurecourt, Fr. 30/J5
Maurepas (lake), La, US 137/P16
Maurepas, Fr. 52/A6
Mauriac, Fr. 42/E4
Maurice (lake), Austl. 109/C3
Maurice (riv.), NJ, US 138/C5
Mauricetown, NJ, US 138/D5
Maurienne (valley), Fr. 43/G4
Maurilândia, Braz. 155/B1
Mauritania (ctry.) 93/A3
Mauriti, Braz. 154/C2
Mauritius (ctry.) 107/T15
Mauston, Wi, US 127/L5
Mauthausen, Aus. 55/H6
Mauvoisin, Barrage de (dam), Swi. 56/D6
Mavrommátion, Gre. 47/H3
Mavrovo NP, Macd. 47/G2
Maw Daung (pass), Thai. 78/B4
Mawāna, India 84/A1
Mawlaik, Myan. 83/F3
Mawlamyine (Moulmein), Myan. 78/B2
Mawson, Austl., Ant. 160/E
Maxaranguape, Braz. 154/D2
Maxcanú, Mex. 144/D1
Maxdorf, Ger. 54/B4
Maxéville, Fr. 53/F6
Maxhütte-Haidhof, Ger. 55/F4
May (cape), NJ, US 138/D5
May-en-Multien, Fr. 30/M4
May, Isle of (isl.), Sc, UK 36/D4
May Pen, Jam. 145/G2
Maya (isl.), Indo. 80/C4
Maya (riv.), Rus. 67/N4
Maya (mts.), Guat. 144/D2
Maya-san (peak), Japan 77/H6
Mayaguana (isl.), Bahm. 119/K7
Mayaguana Passage (chan.), Bahm. 145/H1
Mayagüez, PR 141/M8
Mayakovskogo (peak), Taj. 89/K1
Mayang, China 83/J2
Mayarí, Cuba 145/H1
Maybee, Mi, US 135/E8
Maybole, Sc, UK 36/B6
Maydān, Iraq 88/E2
Mayen, Ger. 53/G3
Mayenne, Fr. 42/C2
Mayenne (riv.), Fr. 42/C3
Mayerthorpe, Ab, Can. 126/E2
Mayfield, Ky, US 130/B4
Mayfield, Sc, UK 36/C5
Maykop, Rus. 62/G3
Maymyo, Myan. 83/G3
Maynooth, Ire. 31/Q10
Mayo (riv.), Arg. 157/B6
Mayo, Yk, Can. 134/L3
Mayo, Md, US 138/B6
Mayotte (isl.), May. 107/H6
Mays Landing, NJ, US 138/D5
Maysville, Ky, US 130/D4
Maythalūn, WBnk. 91/G7
Mayville, ND, US 127/J4
Maywood, NJ, US 139/J8
Maywood, Il, US 135/Q16
Maywood, Ca, US 136/F8
Mazabuka, Zam. 105/E4
Mazagão, Braz. 151/H4
Mazamet, Fr. 42/E5
Mazán, Peru 156/C1
Mazār-e Sharīf, Afg. 89/J1
Mazara del Vallo, It. 46/C4
Mazara, Val di (valley), It. 46/C4
Mazarrón, Sp. 44/E4
Mazaruni (riv.), Guy. 150/G2
Mazatán, Mex. 142/C2
Mazatenango, Guat. 144/D3
Mazatlán, Mex. 142/D4
Mažeikiai, Lith. 39/K3
Mazeppa NP, Austl. 114/B3
Mazgirt, Turk. 90/D2
Mazıkıran (pass), Turk. 90/D2
Mazingarbe, Fr. 52/B3
Mazocruz, Peru 156/D5
Mazong (peak), China 70/G3
Mazury (reg.), Pol. 41/L2
Mazyr, Bela. 62/D1
Mbabala (isl.), Zam. 104/A5
Mbabane (cap.), Swaz. 107/E2
Mbabo (peak), Camr. 96/H6
Mbacké, Sen. 102/B3
Mbaïki, CAfr. 96/J7
Mbakaou, Lac de (lake), Camr. 96/H6
Mbala, Zam. 104/A5
Mbale, Ugan. 104/B2
Mbalmayo, Camr. 96/H7
Mbandaka, D.R. Congo 97/J7
Mbarangandu (riv.), Tanz. 104/C5
Mbarara, Ugan. 104/A3
Mbata, CAfr. 97/J7
Mbeya (peak), Tanz. 104/B5
Mbeya (range), Tanz. 105/F2
Mbeya, Tanz. 104/B5
Mbeya (pol. reg.), Tanz. 104/B5
Mbini, EqG. 96/G7
Mbini (riv.), EqG.,Gabo 96/H7
Mbirizi, Ugan. 104/A3
Mbomou (riv.), CAfr. 97/L6
M'Bour, Sen. 102/A3
Mbuji-Mayi, D.R. Congo 105/D2
Mbwemburu (riv.), Tanz. 104/C5
McAdoo, Pa, US 138/C2
McAfee, NJ, US 138/D1
McAlester, Ok, US 129/J4
McAlisterville, Pa, US 138/A2
Mcallen, Tx, US 132/D5
McBride, BC, Can. 126/C2
Mccall, Id, US 126/D4
Mccarran (int'l arpt.), Nv, US 128/D3
McCarthy, Ak, US 134/K3
Mcclain (co.), Ok, US 137/M15
McClure, Pa, US 138/A2
Mcclusky, ND, US 127/H4
Mcclusky, Il, US 137/G7
Mccomb, Ms, US 129/K5
McConaughy (lake), Ne, US 127/H5
Mccook, Ne, US 129/G2
Mccormick, SC, US 133/H3
Mccreary, Mb, Can. 127/J3
McCullom Lake, Il, US 135/P15
McDaniel, Md, US 138/B6
Mcdermitt, Nv, US 126/D5
McDonald (mt.), Ak, US 134/F3
McDonald (isls.), Austl. 23/N8
McDonnell (mt.), Austl. 113/H5
Mcdougall (pass), Can. 134/L2
Mcdowell (mts.), Az, US 137/S18
McElhattan, Pa, US 138/A1
Mcghee Tyson (int'l arpt.), Tn, US 133/H3
Mcgrath, Ak, US 134/G3
McGregor (riv.), Can. 126/C2
McGregor, On, Can. 135/G7
McHenry (co.), Il, US 135/N15
McKean (isl.), Kiri. 117/H5
McKeand (riv.), NW, Can. 123/K2
McKee City, NJ, US 138/D5
Mckeesport, Pa, US 130/E3
Mckenzie, Tn, US 130/B4
McKinlay, Austl. 114/A3
McKinley (mt.), Ak, US 134/H3
McKinleyville, Ca, US 126/B5
Mclaughlin, SD, US 127/H4
McLean, Va, US 138/A6
Mclennan, Ab, Can. 126/D2
Mcleod (riv.), Can. 126/D2
McLeod (lake), Austl. 109/A3
McLeod (bay), NW, Can. 122/E2
Mcleod Lake, BC, Can. 126/C2
M'Clintock (chan.), Can. 119/G2
Mcloud, Ok, US 137/N15
M'Clure (str.), NW, Can. 119/E2
Mcminnville, Or, US 126/C4
Mcminnville, Tn, US 130/C5
McMurdo, US, Ant. 160/M
McNeil (isl.), Wa, US 135/B3
Mcpherson, Ks, US 129/H3
Mcqueeney, Tx, US 137/U20
Mdantsane, SAfr. 106/D4
M'diq, Mor. 100/B2
Me-akan-dake (peak), Japan 76/C2
Mead, Co, US 137/C2
Mead (lake), Az,Nv, US 119/F6
Meade (riv.), Ak, US 134/G2
Meadow Lake, Sk, Can. 126/F2
Meadow Valley Wash (riv.), Nv, US 128/D3
Meadowbrook, Il, US 137/G8
Meadowlands Sports Complex, NJ, US 139/J8
Meadows, Md, US 138/B6
Meadville, Ms, US 133/F4
Meadville, Pa, US 130/D3
Mealhada, Port. 44/A2
Meall a' Bhuiridh (peak), Sc, UK 36/B3
Meall Buidhe (peak), Sc, UK 36/B3
Meall Dearg (peak), Sc, UK 36/C3
Meall Dubh (peak), Sc, UK 36/B2
Meall nam Fuaran (peak), Sc, UK 36/C4
Meall Tairneachan (peak), Sc, UK 36/C3
Mearim (riv.), Braz. 151/J5
Meat (mtn.), Ak, US 134/F2
Meath (co.), Ire. 34/B4
Meath Park, Sk, Can. 127/G2
Méaulte, Fr. 52/B4
Meaux, Fr. 30/L5
Mecapalapa, Mex. 143/M6
Mècatina,Rivière du Petit (riv.), Nf,Qu, Can. 123/K3
Mecca, Mo, US 137/H8
Mechanicsburg, Pa, US 138/A3
Mechanicsburg Naval Rsv., Pa, US 138/B3
Mechelen, Belg. 53/D1
Mecheria, Alg. 99/E2
Mechi (zone), Nepal 85/F2
Mechra-Bel-Ksiri, Mor. 100/B2
Mecidiye, Turk. 47/K2
Mecitözü, Turk. 62/E4
Meckenbeuren, Ger. 57/F2
Meckenheim, Ger. 53/G2
Mecklenburg-Vorpommern (state), Ger. 38/E5
Mecklenburger (bay), Ger. 40/F1
Mecuia (peak), Moz. 105/G3
Meda, It. 58/C1
Medak, India 82/C4
Medan, Indo. 80/A3
Médanos, Arg. 158/E3
Medanos de Coro, PN, Ven. 152/D2
Medanosa (pt.), Arg. 159/D6
Mede Lomellina, It. 58/B2
Médéa, Alg. 100/G4
Médéa (prov.), Alg. 100/G4
Medebach, Ger. 51/F6
Medeiros Neto, Braz. 154/B5
Medel (peak), Swi. 57/E4
Medellín, Col. 150/C2
Medemblik, Neth. 50/C3
Meden (riv.), Eng, UK 35/G5
Medesano, It. 58/D3
Medetsiz (peak), Turk. 90/C2
Medford, Or, US 126/C5
Medford, NY, US 139/E2
Medford Lakes, NJ, US 138/D4
Medgidia, Rom. 49/J3
Media, Pa, US 138/C4
Media Luna, La (isls.), Hon. 145/F3
Mediaş, Rom. 49/G2
Medical Lake, Wa, US 126/D4
Medicine Bow, Wy, US 127/G5
Medicine Bow (range), Wy, US 128/F2
Medicine Hat, Ab, Can. 126/F3
Medina, ND, US 127/J4
Medina (riv.), Tx, US 129/H5
Medina, Braz. 154/B5
Medina, Oh, US 130/D3
Medina, Col. 152/C3
Medina, Wa, US 135/C2
Medina de Pomar, Sp. 44/D1
Medina de Rioseco, Sp. 44/C2
Medina del Campo, Sp. 44/C2
Medina-Sidonia, Sp. 44/C4
Medinaceli, Sp. 44/D2
Medinipur, India 85/F4
Mediouna, Mor. 98/D2
Mediterranean (sea) 27/E5
Mednogorsk, Rus. 63/L2
Medole, It. 58/D2
Medolla, It. 59/E3
Međugorje, Bosn. 48/C4
Medveditsa (riv.), Rus. 64/E5
Medvezh'i (isls.), Rus. 65/S2
Medvezh'yegorsk, Rus. 60/G3
Medvode, Slov. 43/L3
Meekatharra, Austl. 112/C3
Meeker, Co, US 128/F2
Meeker Park, Co, US 137/A2
Meerbusch, Ger. 50/D6
Meerhout, Belg. 53/E1
Meersburg, Ger. 57/F2
Meerssen, Neth. 53/E2
Meerut, India 84/A1
Meeteetse, Wy, US 126/F4
Megála Kalívia, Gre. 47/G3
Megáli Panayía, Gre. 47/H2
Megálon Khorion, Gre. 90/A2
Megalópolis, Gre. 47/H4
Megantic (peak), Can. 131/G2
Mégara, Gre. 47/H3
Megève, Fr. 56/C6
Meghālaya (state), India 70/F6
Meghalaya (state), India 83/F2
Meghna (riv.), Bang. 85/H4
Megiddo, Isr. 91/G6
Mégiscane (lake), Can. 130/E1
Mégiscane (riv.), Can. 130/E1
Megista (isl.), Greece 91/A1
Mehaigne (riv.), Belg. 53/E2
Mehamn, Nor. 37/H1
Meharry (mt.), Austl. 112/C2
Mehdia, Alg. 100/F5
Mehdiya-Plage, Mor. 100/A2
Mehe (riv.), Ger. 51/G1
Mehedinţi (prov.), Rom. 48/F3
Mehlingen, Ger. 53/G4
Mehlville, Mo, US 137/G9
Mehndāwal, India 84/D2
Mehrān (riv.), Iran 89/F3
Mehring, Ger. 53/F4
Mehrnbach, Aus. 55/G6
Mehtar Lām, Afg. 86/A2
Mei (riv.), China 79/C3
Meia Ponte (riv.), Braz. 155/B1
Meiganga, Camr. 96/H6
Meighen (isl.), NW, Can. 123/R7
Meigu, China 83/H2
Meihekou, China 71/N3
Meikle Bin (peak), Sc, UK 36/B4
Meikle Black Law (hill), Sc, UK 36/D5
Meikle Says Law (peak), Sc, UK 36/D5
Meiktila, Myan. 83/G3
Meilen, Swi. 57/E3
Meine, Ger. 51/H4
Meiners Oaks, Ca, US 136/A2
Meinersen, Ger. 51/H4
Meinerzhagen, Ger. 53/G1
Meiningen, Ger. 54/D1
Meiringen, Swi. 56/E4
Meisenheim, Ger. 53/G4
Meishan (res.), China 72/C5
Meissen, Ger. 41/G3
Meissner (peak), Ger. 51/G6
Meitan, China 79/A2
Meitingen, Ger. 54/D5
Meiwa, Japan 77/L6
Meix-devant-Virton, Belg. 53/E4
Meizhou, China 79/C3
Mejaniga, It. 59/E2
Mejaouda (well), Mrta. 98/D5
Mejorada del Campo, Sp. 45/N9
Mek'elē, Eth. 97/N5
Meknès (prov.), Mor. 100/B3
Meknès, Mor. 100/B3
Mekong (riv.), Asia 70/G5
Mekong, Mouths of the (delta), Viet. 83/J6
Mekongga (peak), Indo. 81/F4
Mekoryuk, Ak, US 134/E3
Melaka, Malay. 80/B3
Melanesia (reg.) 116/E5
Melappālaiyam, India 82/C6
Melawi (riv.), Indo. 80/D4
Melbeck, Ger. 51/H2
Melbourne, Fl, US 133/H4
Melbourne (isl.), NW, Can. 122/F2
Melbourne, Austl. 115/G5
Melbu, Nor. 37/E1
Melchor (isl.), Chile 158/B5
Melchor Múzquiz, Mex. 132/C5
Melchor Ocampo, Mex. 143/Q9
Meldola, It. 59/F4
Meldorf, Ger. 38/C4
Mele (cape), It. 58/B5
Melegnano, It. 58/C2
Melenci, Yugo. 48/E3
Melenki, Rus. 60/J5
Melesse, Fr. 42/C2
Meleuz, Rus. 63/K1
Mélèzes (riv.), Qu, Can. 123/J3
Melezza (riv.), It. 57/E5
Melfi, It. 46/D2
Melfort, Sk, Can. 127/G2
Melgar de Fernamental, Sp. 44/C1
Melhus, Nor. 37/D3
Melibocus (peak), Ger. 54/B3
Melide, Swi. 57/E6
Meligalás, Gre. 47/G4
Meliki, Gre. 47/H2
Melilli (peak), Kenya 104/C3
Melilla, Sp. 100/C2
Melimoyu (peak), Chile 158/B5
Melipilla, Chile 158/N8
Mélisey, Fr. 56/C2
Melissano, It. 47/F3
Melita, Mb, Can. 127/H3
Melito di Porto Salvo, It. 46/D4
Melitopol', Ukr. 62/E3
Melitota, Md, US 138/B5
Melkbosstrand, SAfr. 106/L10
Melksham, Eng, UK 32/D4
Mella (riv.), It. 58/D2
Mellan Fryken (lake), Swe. 38/E2
Melle, Ger. 51/F4
Melle, Belg. 52/C2
Mellea (riv.), It. 58/A3
Mellègue, Oued (riv.), Alg. 100/K7
Mellerud, Swe. 38/E2
Mellid, Sp. 44/A1
Mellieħa, Malta 46/L7
Mellingen, Swi. 57/E3
Mellizo Sur (peak), Chile 159/B6
Mellrichstadt, Ger. 54/D2
Mellum (isl.), Ger. 51/F1
Melmoth, SAfr. 107/E3
Mělník, Bul. 47/H2
Mělník, Czh. 55/H2
Melo, Uru. 157/F3
Melocheville, Qu, Can. 131/N7
Melrose, Md, US 138/B4
Melrose, Sc, UK 36/D5
Melrose Abbey, Sc, UK 36/D5
Melrose Park, Il, US 135/Q16
Mels, Swi. 57/F3
Melsungen, Ger. 51/G6
Meltham, Eng, UK 35/G4
Melton, Austl. 115/C3
Melton Mowbray, Eng, UK 33/F1
Melun, Fr. 30/K6
Melville (cape), Phil. 81/E2
Melville, Sk, Can. 127/H3
Melville (isl.), Austl. 109/C2
Melville (bay), Austl. 109/C2
Melville, Il, US 137/G8
Melville (cape), Austl. 114/B1
Melville (lake), Nf, Can. 123/L3
Melville (pen.), Can. 119/J3
Melville, NY, US 139/M8
Melvindale, Mi, US 135/F7
Mélykút, Hun. 48/D2
Melzo, It. 58/C2
Memāri, India 85/G4
Memmert (isl.), Ger. 50/D1
Memmingen, Ger. 57/G2
Memphis, Mo, US 127/K5
Memphis (int'l arpt.), Tn, US 129/K4
Memphis, Tx, US 129/G4
Memphis, Tn, US 129/K4
Memphis (ruin), Egypt 91/B5
Memphis, Mi, US 135/G6
Mena, Ar, US 129/J4
Mena, Ukr. 62/D2
Menaggio, It. 57/F5
Menai (str.), Wal, UK 34/D5
Menai Bridge, Wal, UK 34/D5
Ménaka, Mali 103/F3
Menaldum, Neth. 50/C2
Menarandra (riv.), Madg. 107/H9
Menard, Tx, US 129/H5
Menasalbas, Sp. 44/C3
Menavava (riv.), Madg. 107/H7
Mendawai (riv.), Indo. 80/D4
Mende, Fr. 42/E4
Menden, Ger. 51/E6
Mendenhall (cape), Ak, US 134/E4
Mendes, Braz. 211/K7
Méndez, Mex. 143/F3
Mendham, NJ, US 138/D2
Mendig, Ger. 53/G3
Mendip (hills), Eng, UK 32/D4
Mendocino, Ca, US 128/B3
Mendocino (cape), Ca, US 124/A3
Mendooran, Austl. 115/D1
Mendoza, Peru 156/B2
Mendoza, Cuba 145/E1
Mendoza (prov.), Arg. 158/C2
Mendoza, Arg. 158/C2
Mendoza (El Plumerillo) (int'l arpt.), Arg. 158/C2
Mendrisio, Swi. 57/E6
Mene Grande, Ven. 152/D2
Menegosa (peak), It. 58/C3
Menemen, Turk. 62/C5
Menen, Belg. 52/C2
Menengai Crater, Kenya 104/C3
Menengiyn (plain), Mong. 65/M5
Menfi, It. 46/C4
Meng Xian, China 72/C4
Mengcheng, China 72/D4
Mengen, Ger. 57/F1
Mengersgereuth-Hämmern, Ger. 54/D2
Mengerskirchen, Ger. 54/B1
Mengeš, Slov. 43/L3
Menggala, Indo. 80/C4
Menghai, China 78/C1
Mengibar, Sp. 44/D4
Mengkofen, Ger. 55/F5
Mengla, China 78/C1
Menglian Daizu Lahuzu Vazu Zizhixian, China 83/G3
Mengjin, China 72/D4
Mengzi, China 83/H3
Menindee, Austl. 115/B2
Menindee (dam), Austl. 115/B2
Menindee (lake), Austl. 113/J5
Meningie, Austl. 115/A2
Menlo Park, Ca, US 135/K12
Menlo Park, NJ, US 139/H9
Menlolat (peak), Chile 158/B5
Mennecy, Fr. 30/K6
Menomonee Falls, Wi, US 130/B3
Menomonie, Wi, US 127/L4
Menongue, Ang. 105/C3
Menorca (int'l arpt.), Sp. 45/H3
Menorca (Minorca) (isl.), Sp. 45/H2
Mentasta Lake, Ak, US 134/K3
Mentawai (str.), Indo. 80/A4
Mentawai (isls.), Indo. 67/J10
Menteroda, Ger. 51/H6
Menthon-Saint-Bernard, Fr. 56/C6
Mentone, Tx, US 129/G5
Mentone, Ca, US 136/C2
Mentor, Oh, US 130/D3
Mentue (riv.), Swi. 56/C4
Menucourt, Fr. 30/H4
Menuma, Japan 77/C1
Menyapa (peak), Indo. 81/E3
Menzel Bourguiba, Tun. 46/A4
Menzie (mt.), Can. 134/M3
Menzies, Austl. 112/D4
Menziken, Swi. 56/E3
Menzingen, Swi. 57/E3
Menznau, Swi. 56/E3
Meolo, It. 59/F1
Meon (riv.), Eng, UK 33/E5
Meoqui, Mex. 132/B4
Mepistskaro (peak), Geo. 63/G4
Meppel, Neth. 50/D3
Meppen, Il, US 137/F8
Meppen, Ger. 51/E3
Mequinenzo, Embalse de (res.), Sp. 45/E2
Mer, Fr. 42/D3
Mera (riv.), It. 57/F5
Meramec (riv.), Mo, US 129/K3
Merano, It. 57/H4
Merate, It. 58/C1
Meratus (mts.), Indo. 80/D4
Meraux, La, US 137/Q17
Merbein, Austl. 115/B2
Mercaderes, Col. 152/B4
Mercantour, PN du, Fr. 43/G4
Mercatello sul Metauro, It. 59/F5
Mercato Saraceno, It. 59/F5
Merced (riv.), Ca, US 128/B3
Merced, Ca, US 128/B3
Mercedario (peak), Arg. 157/B3
Mercedes, Arg. 157/E2
Mercedes, Arg. 158/D2
Mercedes, Arg. 159/J11
Mercedes, Uru. 159/J10
Mercer (co.), NJ, US 138/D3
Mercer (isl.), Wa, US 135/C2
Mercer Island, Wa, US 135/C2
Mercerville-Hamilton Square, NJ, US 138/D3
Merchtem, Belg. 53/D2
Mercier, Qu, Can. 131/N7
Mercoal, Ab, Can. 126/D2
Mercy (cape), NW, Can. 123/K2

Mercy – Moksh

Mercy-le-Bas, Fr. 53/E5
Méré, Fr. 30/H5
Meredith (lake), Tx, US 129/G4
Meredith (cape), UK 19/F5
Merefa, Ukr. 62/F2
Merelbeke, Belg. 54/B1
Merenberg, Ger. 54/B1
Mergozzo, It. 57/E6
Mergui (arch.), Myan. 83/G5
Mergui (Myeik), Myan. 78/B3
Meriç, Turk. 49/H5
Méricourt, Fr. 30/G4
Méricourt, Fr. 52/B3
Mérida, Sp. 44/B3
Mérida, Ven. 152/D2
Mérida (state), Ven. 152/E2
Mérida, Mex. 144/D1
Mérida, Cordillera de (mts.), Ven. 150/D2
Meridian, Ms, US 133/F3
Meridian, Ok, US 137/N14
Mérignac, Fr. 42/C4
Merignac (int'l arpt.), Fr. 42/C4
Merimbula, Austl. 115/D3
Merinda, Austl. 114/C3
Mering, Ger. 54/D6
Merinos, Uru. 159/K10
Merja Zerga (lake), Mor. 100/A2
Mérk, Hun. 48/F2
Merkendorf, Ger. 54/D4
Merksem, Belg. 50/B6
Merksplas, Belg. 50/B6
Merlimont, Fr. 52/A3
Merlo, Arg. 159/J11
Meroe (ruin), Sudan 88/B5
Merone, It. 58/C1
Merredin, Austl. 112/C4
Merriam, Ks, US 137/D5
Merrick, NY, US 139/L9
Merrick (peak), Sc, UK 34/D1
Merrill, Wi, US 127/L4
Merrill Creek (res.), NJ, US 138/C2
Merrimack, NH, US 131/G3
Merritt, BC, Can. 126/C3
Merritt Island, Fl, US 133/H5
Merriwa, Austl. 115/D2
Mers-les-Bains, Fr. 52/A3
Mersch, Lux. 53/F4
Merse (reg.), Sc, UK 36/D5
Mersey (riv.), Eng, UK 35/F5
Merseyside (co.), Eng, UK 35/F5
Mersing, Malay. 80/B3
Mertert, Lux. 53/F4
Mertesdorf, Ger. 53/F4
Merthyr Tydfil, Wal, UK 32/C3
Mértola, Port. 44/B4
Merton (bor.), Eng, UK 30/C2
Mertzon, Tx, US 129/G5
Mertzwiller, Fr. 53/G6
Meru (mt.), Tanz. 104/C3
Meru, Kenya 104/C2
Méru, Fr. 52/B5
Meru NP, Kenya 104/C2
Merville, Fr. 52/B2
Merwedekanaal (riv.), Neth. 50/C5
Méry-sur-Oise, Fr. 30/J4
Merzen, Ger. 51/E4
Merzenich, Ger. 53/F2
Merzifon, Turk. 62/E4
Merzig, Ger. 53/F5
Mesa (mtn.), Ak, US 134/G3
Mesa, Az, US 129/D4
Mesa (peak), Arg. 159/C6
Mesa Verde NP, Co, US 128/E3
Mesabi (range), Mn, US 127/K4
Mesach Mellet (hills), Libya 99/H4
Mesagne, It. 47/E2
Mesaras (gulf), Gre. 47/J5
Mescalero (ridge), NM, US 132/C3
Meschede, Ger. 51/F6
Mesco, Punta di (pt.), It. 58/C4
Mescolino (riv.), It. 59/F5
Meseta de Montemayor (plat.), Arg. 158/D5
Mesgouez (lake), Can. 130/F1
Mesola, It. 59/F3
Mesolóngion, Gre. 47/G3
Mesomeloka, Madg. 107/J8
Mesopotamia (reg.), Arg. 157/E3
Mesoraca, It. 46/E3
Mespelbrunn, Ger. 54/C3
Mesquite, Tx, US 129/H4
Mesrouh (peak), Mor. 98/E2
Messaad, Alg. 96/F1
Messancy, Belg. 53/E4
Messel, Ger. 54/B3
Messina, SAfr. 105/F5
Messina, It. 46/D4
Messina, It. 46/D3
Messini (gulf), Gre. 47/H4
Messíni, Gre. 47/H4
Messkirch, Ger. 57/F2
Messstetten, Ger. 57/E2
Messy, Fr. 30/L5
Mesta (riv.), Bul. 59/F2
Mestre, It. 59/F2
Mestrino, It. 59/E2
Mesumba (riv.), Tanz. 104/C4
Mesurado (cape), Libr. 102/C5
Meta (dept.), Col. 152/C4

Meta (riv.), Col.,Ven. 147/C2
Meta Incognita (pen.), NW, Can. 123/K2
Metabetchouan, Qu, Can. 131/G1
Métabetchouane (riv.), Qu, Can. 131/F1
Metairie, La, US 137/P17
Metallifere, Colline (mts.), It. 59/D6
Metamora, Mi, US 135/F6
Metán, Arg. 157/D2
Metapontum (ruin), It. 46/E2
Metauro (riv.), It. 43/K5
Metelen, Ger. 51/E4
Meteóra, Gre. 47/G3
Metepec, Mex. 143/Q10
Methven, Sc, UK 36/C4
Metković, Cro. 47/E1
Metlakatla, Ak, US 134/M4
Metlatonoc, Mex. 144/B2
Metlili Chaamba, Alg. 99/F2
Metnitz, Aus. 43/L3
Metro Toronto Zoo, On, Can. 131/R8
Metropolis, Il, US 130/B4
Metropolitan Oakland (int'l arpt.), Ca, US 128/B3
Metropolitana de Santiago (pol. reg.), Chile 158/N8
Métsovon, Gre. 47/G3
Mettawa, Il, US 135/Q15
Mettenheim, Ger. 55/F6
Mettet, Belg. 53/D3
Mettingen, Ger. 51/E4
Mettlach, Ger. 53/F4
Mettmach, Aus. 55/G6
Mettmann, Ger. 50/D6
Metu, Eth. 97/N6
Metuchen, NJ, US 139/H9
Metulla, Isr. 91/D3
Metz, Fr. 53/F5
Metz-Nancy-Lorraine (int'l arpt.), Fr. 53/F6
Metzingen, Ger. 54/C5
Metztitlán, Mex. 143/L6
Meudon, Fr. 30/J5
Meulan, Fr. 30/H4
Meulebeke, Belg. 52/C2
Meurthe (riv.), Fr. 56/C1
Meurthe-et-Moselle (dept.), Fr. 53/E6
Meuse (riv.), Fr. 40/C4
Meuse (dept.), Fr. 53/E6
Meuzin (riv.), Fr. 56/A3
Mevasseret Ziyyon, Isr. 91/G8
Mexborough, Eng, UK 35/G5
Mexia, Tx, US 129/H5
Mexiana, Ilha (isl.), Braz. 151/J3
Mexicalcingo, Mex. 143/Q10
Mexicali, Mex. 128/C4
Mexico, Mo, US 129/K3
México (state), Mex. 140/A5
Mexico (ctry.) 119/G7
Mexico (gulf), NAm. 119/H7
Meximieux, Fr. 56/B6
Meybod, Iran 88/F2
Meyers Chuck, Ak, US 134/M4
Meyerton, SAfr. 106/Q13
Meymaneh, Afg. 89/H1
Meyrin, Swi. 56/C5
Meythet, Fr. 56/C6
Meyzieu, Fr. 56/A6
Mèze, Fr. 42/E5
Mezdra, Bul. 59/E1
Mezen' (riv.), Rus. 64/E3
Mezen' (bay), Rus. 61/J2
Mezha (riv.), Bela. 39/P4
Mezhdurechensk, Rus. 64/J4
Mezhdusharskiy (isl.), Rus. 64/E2
Mézières-sur-Seine, Fr. 30/H5
Mezőberény, Hun. 40/E3
Mezőkovácsháza, Hun. 48/E2
Mezőkövesd, Hun. 41/L5
Mezőtúr, Hun. 48/E2
Mezquital (riv.), Mex. 142/D4
Mezzana (peak), It. 57/G5
Mezzocorona, It. 57/H5
Mezzogoro, It. 59/F3
Mezzolombardo, It. 57/H5
Mfangano (isl.), Kenya 104/B3
Mga (riv.), Rus. 61/U7
M'goun (peak), Mor. 98/D3
Mhamdia Fūshānah, Tun. 46/N4
Mhòr (lake), Sc, UK 36/B2
Mhow, India 89/L4
Mi-shima (isl.), Japan 74/B3
Mi Xian, China 72/C4
Miahuatlán de Porfirio Díaz, Mex. 143/L8
Miajadas, Sp. 44/C3
Mianchi, China 72/B4
Miāndarreh, Iran 88/E1
Miandrivazo, Madg. 107/H7
Miāneh, Iran 88/E1
Miāni, Pak. 86/B3
Mianning, China 83/H2
Mianwāli, Pak. 86/A3
Mianyang, China 70/H5

Mianzhu, China 70/H5
Miao'er (peak), China 79/B2
Miarinarivo, Madg. 107/H7
Miary, Madg. 107/G8
Miass, Rus. 61/P5
Miass (riv.), Rus. 61/P5
Miastko, Pol. 38/G4
Mica Creek, BC, Can. 126/D2
Michalovce, Slvk. 41/L4
Michelfeld, Ger. 55/E3
Michelson (mt.), Ak, US 134/K2
Michelstadt, Ger. 54/C3
Michendorf, Ger. 40/Q7
Michigan (state), US 123/K3
Michigan (lake), US 119/J5
Michigan City, In, US 130/C3
Michipicoten (isl.), Can. 127/M4
Michoacán de Ocampo (state), Mex. 140/A4
Michurin, Bul. 49/H4
Michurinsk, Rus. 63/G1
Mickle Fell (peak), Eng, UK 35/F2
Mico (riv.), Nic. 140/E5
Micronesia (reg.) 116/E3
Micronesia, Federated States of (ctry.) 116/D4
Mid Glamorgan (co.), Wal, UK 32/C3
Mid Yell, Sc, UK 31/W13
Midal (well), Niger 103/G2
Midale, Sk, Can. 127/H3
Middelburg, SAfr. 106/D3
Middelburg, Neth. 50/A5
Middelfart, Den. 38/D4
Middelharnis, Neth. 50/B5
Middelkerke, Belg. 52/B1
Middle (bay), NY, US 139/L9
Middle Alkali (lake), Ca, US 128/C2
Middle Andaman (isl.), India 83/T8
Middle Caicos (isl.), UK 145/J1
Middle Concho (riv.), Tx, US 132/C4
Middle Raccoon (riv.), Ia, US 129/J2
Middle River, Md, US 138/B5
Middle Sister (peak), Or, US 126/C4
Middleberg, Ok, US 137/M15
Middleburg, Md, US 138/A4
Middleburg, Pa, US 138/A2
Middlebury, Vt, US 130/F2
Middlemount, Austl. 114/C3
Middleport, Pa, US 138/B2
Middlesboro, Ky, US 130/D4
Middlesbrough, Eng, UK 35/G2
Middlesex (reg.), Eng, UK 33/F4
Middleton, Sk, Can. 127/G3
Middleton, Eng, UK 35/F4
Middletown, Pa, US 138/B3
Middletown, De, US 138/C5
Middletown, NJ, US 139/J10
Middletown, NY, US 139/E1
Middletown, Mor. 98/D2
Midi (canal), Fr. 42/D5
Midi-Pyrénées (pol. reg.), Fr. 42/D4
Midland, Mi, US 130/D3
Midland, On, Can. 130/E2
Midland (int'l arpt.), Tx, US 142/E2
Midland, Wa, US 135/C3
Midland Park, NJ, US 139/J8
Midleton, Ire. 31/P11
Midlothian, Il, US 135/Q16
Midlum, Ger. 51/F1
Midongy Atsimo, Madg. 107/H8
Midou (riv.), Fr. 42/C5
Midsayap, Phil. 79/D6
Midu, China 83/H2
Midvale, Ut, US 137/K12
Midway, Il, US 137/H8
Midway, De, US 138/C6
Midway (isls.) 116/H2
Midway (reg.), Pac., US 116/H2
Midyan (reg.), SAr. 88/C3
Midyat, Turk. 90/E2
Midzŏr (peak), Yugo. 49/F4
Mie (pref.), Japan 74/E3
Mie, Japan 74/E3
Mi Xian, China 72/B4
Miechów, Pol. 62/B2
Międzychód, Pol. 41/H2
Międzylesie, Pol. 41/J3
Międzyrzec Podlaski, Pol. 62/B1
Międzyrzecz, Pol. 41/M3
Międzyzdroje, Pol. 38/F5
Miehlen, Ger. 53/G3
Miami (co.), In, US 137/D6
Miami Beach, Fl, US 133/H5
Mimiesbach...

Mianyang, China 70/H5

Miguel Alemán, Mex. 142/C2
Miguel Aleman, Presa (dam), Mex. 143/M8
Miguel Alves, Braz. 154/B2
Miguel Auza, Mex. 142/E3
Miguel Calmon, Braz. 154/B3
Miguel Hidalgo (int'l arpt.), Mex. 142/E4
Miguel Hidalgo (res.), Mex. 142/C2
Miguel Pereira, Braz. 211/K7
Miguel Riglos, Arg. 158/E3
Miguelete, Uru. 159/K11
Miguelópolis, Braz. 155/B2
Miguelturra, Sp. 44/D3
Mihama, Japan 74/D3
Mihara, Japan 74/C3
Mihara, Japan 77/J6
Miharu, Japan 75/G2
Mihla, Ger. 51/H6
Miho, Japan 77/E2
Mihrābpur, Pak. 89/J3
Mijares (riv.), Sp. 45/E2
Mijas, Sp. 44/C4
Mijdrecht, Neth. 50/B4
Mikasa, Japan 76/B2
Mikata, Japan 77/J4
Mikata (lake), Japan 77/J4
Mikawa (bay), Japan 77/M6
Mikhaylovka, Rus. 63/G2
Mikhmoret, Isr. 91/F7
Miki, Japan 77/G6
Mikinai, Japan 47/H4
Mikinai (Mycenae) (ruin), Gre. 47/H4
Mikkeli, Fin. 37/H3
Mikkeli (prov.), Fin. 37/H3
Mikonos (isl.), Gre. 47/J4
Mikonos, Gre. 47/J4
Mikri Prespa (lake), Alb.,Gre. 47/G2
Mikri Prespa NP, Gre. 47/G2
Mikuma, Japan 77/L6
Mikuni, Japan 74/E2
Mikuni-tōge (pass), Japan 75/F2
Mikura (isl.), Japan 75/F4
Mila (prov.), Alg. 100/H4
Milagro, Ecu. 152/B5
Milak, India 84/B1
Milan (Milano), It. 43/H4
Milang, Austl. 115/A2
Milano (prov.), It. 58/C2
Milano (Milan), It. 43/H4
Milas, Turk. 90/A2
Milazzo, It. 46/D3
Milbank, SD, US 127/J4
Mildura, Austl. 115/B2
Miles, Tx, US 132/C4
Miles, Austl. 114/C4
Miles City, Mt, US 127/G4
Milešovka (peak), Czh. 55/G1
Milestone, Sk, Can. 127/G3
Miletto (peak), It. 46/D2
Milevsko, Czh. 55/H4
Milford (lake), US 132/D2
Milford, Ut, US 128/D3
Milford, NJ, US 138/C2
Milford, Ct, US 139/E1
Milford, De, US 138/C5
Milford, Mi, US 135/E6
Milford Haven, Wal, UK 32/A3
Milford Haven (inlet), Wal, UK 32/A3
Milgis (riv.), Kenya 104/C2
Mili (isl.), Mrsh. 116/G4
Miliana, Alg. 100/G4
Milicz, Pol. 41/J3
Mililani Town, Hi, US 124/V13
Milk (hill), Eng, UK 33/E4
Milk River, Ab, Can. 126/E3
Mill (isl.), NW, Can. 123/J2
Mill (riv.), Ct, US 139/L8
Mill Neck, NY, US 139/L8
Millaa Millaa, Austl. 114/B2
Millau, Fr. 42/E4
Millbrae, Ca, US 135/K11
Millbrook (res.), Austl. 113/M8
Millburn, NJ, US 139/H9
Millcreek, Ut, US 137/K12
Mille Îles (riv.), Qu, Can. 129/J4
Mille Lacs (lake), Mn, US 125/H2
Milledgeville, Ga, US 133/H4
Millerovo, Rus. 63/G2
Millers Ferry (dam), Al, US 133/G3
Millersburg, Pa, US 138/B2
Millersville, Pa, US 138/B3
Millerton (lake), Ca, US 135/L10
Millerton, NY, US 139/E1
Millington, Md, US 138/C5

Millinocket, Me, US 131/G2
Millisle, NI, UK 34/C2
Millmerran, Austl. 114/C4
Millmont, Pa, US 138/A2
Millport, Sc, UK 36/B5
Mills Junction, Ut, US 137/J12
Millstadt, Il, US 137/G9
Millstone, NJ, US 138/D3
Millstream-Chichester NP, Austl. 112/D4
Millthorpe, Austl. 115/D2
Milltown, NJ, US 139/H10
Milltown Malbay, Ire. 31/P10
Millville, Pa, US 138/B1
Millville, NJ, US 138/C5
Millwood (lake), Ar, US 132/C3
Milmay, NJ, US 138/D5
Milnathort, Sc, UK 36/E5
Milne (bay), PNG 116/E5
Milne, It. 77/J6
Milnrow, Eng, UK 35/F4
Milo, Me, US 131/G2
Milo (riv.), Gui. 102/C4
Milolii, Hi, US 124/U11
Miltenberg, Ger. 54/C3
Milton, Austl. 115/D2
Milton, Fl, US 133/G4
Milton, NH, US 131/G3
Milton, On, Can. 131/R9
Milton, NZ 117/R12
Milton (res.), Co, US 137/F8
Milton, Ut, US 137/K11
Milton, Pa, US 138/B1
Milton, Wa, US 135/C3
Milton-Freewater, Or, US 126/D4
Milton Keynes, Eng, UK 33/F2
Milton Ness (pt.), Sc, UK 36/D3
Milton of Campsie, Sc, UK 36/B5
Milwaukee, Wi, US 127/M5
Milwaukee (co.), Wi, US 135/P14
Milwaukee, Wi, US 135/P14
Milz (riv.), Ger. 54/D2
Mimi (riv.), Japan 74/B4
Mimizan, Fr. 42/C4
Mimmaya, Japan 76/B3
Min (riv.), China 70/H5
Min Xian, China 70/H5
Minʿūf, Egypt 91/B4
Minab, Iran 89/G3
Minamata, Japan 77/K6
Minami Alps NP, Japan 75/F3
Minami-tori-shima, Japan 116/E2
Minamiaki, Japan 77/B1
Minamiashigara, Japan 77/C3
Minamichita, Japan 77/L6
Minamidaitō (isl.), Japan 75/L8
Minamiiō (isl.), Japan 116/D2
Minamikawara, Japan 77/C1
Minamimaki, Japan 77/A2
Minamiyamashiro, Japan 77/J6
Minano, Japan 77/C1
Minas (peak), Ecu. 152/B5
Minas, Cuba 145/G1
Minas, Uru. 159/G2
Minas de Matahambre, Cuba 145/F1
Minas de Ríotinto, Sp. 44/B4
Minas Gerais (state), Braz. 154/A5
Minas Novas, Braz. 154/B5
Minatitlán, Mex. 144/C2
Minbu, Myan. 83/F3
Minbya, Myan. 83/F3
Minch, The (North Minch) (str.), Sc, UK 31/Q8
Minchinābād, Pak. 86/B4
Minchinmávida (vol.), Chile 158/B4
Mincio (riv.), It. 59/D2
Mindanao (sea), Phil. 81/F2
Mindanao (isl.), Phil. 67/M9
Mindel (riv.), Ger. 40/F4
Mindelheim, Ger. 57/G1
Mindelo, CpV. 93/J10
Minden, La, US 129/J4
Minden, Ne, US 129/H2
Minden, Ger. 51/F4
Mindoro (str.), Phil. 79/C5
Mindoro (isl.), Phil. 79/C5
Mine, Ire. 31/O10
Mineiros, Braz. 151/H7
Mineola, Tx, US 129/J4
Mineola, NY, US 139/L8
Mineral del Monte, Mex. 143/L6
Mineral Wells, Tx, US 129/H4
Mineral'nye Vody, Rus. 63/G3
Mineral'nye Vody, Rus. 63/G3
Minerbe, It. 59/E2
Minerbio, It. 59/E2
Minersville, Pa, US 138/B2
Minfeld, Ger. 54/B4
Minfeng, China 70/D4
Mingäçevir, Azer. 63/H4
Mingäçevir Su Anbari (res.), Azer. 63/H4

Mingãora, Pak. 86/B2
Mingenew, Austl. 112/B4
Minganilla, Sp. 44/E3
Mingshui, China 71/N2
Mingxi, China 79/C2
Minhe, China 70/H4
Minhla, Myan. 83/G4
Minho (riv.), Sp. 44/A1
Minigwal (lake), Austl. 112/D4
Minisantla, Mex. 143/N7
Minitonas, Mb, Can. 127/H2
Minlaton, Austl. 113/H5
Minle, China 70/H4
Minna, Nga. 103/G4
Minneapolis, Mn, US 127/K4
Minneapolis-St. Paul (Wold-Chamberlain) (int'l arpt.), Mn, US 127/K4
Minnedosa, Mb, Can. 127/J3
Minnesota (riv.), Mn, US 127/K4
Minnesota (state), US 125/G2
Minnipa, Austl. 112/D5
Minnitaki (lake), On, Can. 127/L4
Miño (riv.), Port.,Sp. 44/A1
Mino, Japan 77/A4
Minobu, Japan 75/F3
Minokamo, Japan 77/M5
Mino'o, Japan 77/H6
Minori, Japan 77/E1
Minot, ND, US 127/H3
Minqin, China 70/H4
Minqing, China 79/C2
Minquan, China 72/C4
Minsener Oog (isl.), Ger. 51/F1
Minsk (cap.), Bela. 39/M5
Minsk (int'l arpt.), Bela. 39/M5
Mińsk Mazowiecki, Pol. 41/L2
Minskaya (prov.), Bela. 62/C1
Mintaka (pass), Pak. 87/F5
Mintaka (pass), China 89/K1
Mintlaw, Sc, UK 36/E1
Minto, Ak, US 134/J2
Minto, NB, Can. 131/H2
Minto (inlet), NW, Can. 122/D1
Minto, On, Can. 131/Q8
Minturn, Co, US 137/F3
Minturno, It. 58/C5
Minusinsk, Rus. 64/K4
Minusio, Swi. 57/E5
Minya al Qamḥ, Egypt 91/B4
Minyip, Austl. 115/B3
Minyu, China 70/E3
Miquan, China 70/E3
Miquelon (isl.), St.P.&M. 131/K2
Mira, Port. 44/A2
Mira (riv.), Col. 152/B4
Mira Loma, Ca, US 136/C2
Mira Monte, Ca, US 136/B2
Mira Taglio, It. 59/F2
Mirabel (int'l arpt.), Can. 131/M6
Mirabel, Qu, Can. 131/M6
Mirabela, Braz. 154/A5
Mirabello, It. 59/E3
Miracema, Braz. 155/D2
Miracema do Norte, Braz. 151/J5
Mirado Terme, It. 58/C2
Mirador, Braz. 154/A2
Mirador (pass), Chile 158/C4
Miraflores, Peru 156/B3
Miraflores, Mex. 142/C4
Miraflores, Col. 152/C4
Miraflores, Col. 152/C4
Miraflores, Haiti 145/H2
Miraj, India 89/K5
Miramar, Ca, US 136/C5
Miramar, Arg. 158/F3
Miramar Naval Air Station, Ca, US 136/C5
Mirambéllou (gulf), Gre. 47/J5
Miramont-de-Guyenne, Fr. 42/D4
Miranda (riv.), Braz. 151/G8
Miranda de Ebro, Sp. 44/D1
Miranda do Corvo, Port. 44/A2
Miranda do Douro, Port. 44/B2
Mirande, Fr. 42/D5
Mirandela, Port. 44/B2
Miranda (isl.), Braz. 43/J4
Mirandópolis, Braz. 155/B2
Mirano, It. 59/F2
Mīrānpur, India 84/B1
Mirante do Paranapanema, Braz. 155/B2
Mirassol, Braz. 155/B2
Mirassol d'Oeste...
Mitha Tiwāna, Pak. 86/B3
Mithankot, Pak. 86/A3
Mithi, Pak. 89/J4
Mithimna, Gre. 47/K3
Mitiaro, Cooks. 117/K6
Mitilini, Gre. 47/K3
Mitla (pass), Egypt 91/C4
Mitla (ruin), Mex. 144/B2
Mitlerovo, Braz. 211/G8
Mits'iwa, Erit. 97/N4
Mitsue, Japan 77/M6
Mitsukaidō, Japan 75/F2
Mitsuke, Japan 75/F2
Mittagong, Austl. 115/D2
Mittelspitze (peak), Aus. 57/F3
Modderrivier, SAfr. 106/D3
Modena (prov.), It. 59/D3

Mirzāpur, India 84/D3
Misa, It. 59/G5
Misäha (well), Egypt 101/A4
Misaki, Japan 77/B2
Misaki, Japan 74/D3
Misaki, Japan 77/F3
Misano Adriatico, It. 59/F5
Misantla, Mex. 143/N7
Misato, Japan 77/C1
Misato, Japan 77/D2
Misawa, Japan 76/B3
Mishan, China 71/P2
Mishawaka, In, US 130/C3
Misheguk (mtn.), Ak, US 134/F2
Mishima, Japan 75/F3
Mishmi, It. 46/C3
Misilmeri, It. 46/C3
Misiones, Sierra de (mts.), Arg. 157/E2
Miskito, Cayos (isls.), Nic. 140/E5
Miskolc, Hun. 41/L4
Misono, Japan 77/L6
Misool (isl.), Indo. 116/B5
Misquah (hills), Mn, US 127/L4
Misrātah (prov.), Libya 97/L1
Misrātah, Libya 96/J1
Missanaibi (lake), Can. 130/D1
Missinaibi (riv.), On, Can. 123/H3
Mission, Tx, US 132/D5
Mission (bay), Ca, US 136/C5
Mission Beach, Austl. 114/B2
Mission Hills, Ca, US 136/C2
Mission Ind. Res., Ca, US 136/C3
Mission San Buenaventura, Ca, US 136/B2
Mission San Jose, Ca, US 135/L12
Mission San Juan Capistrano, Ca, US 136/C3
Mission Viejo, Ca, US 136/C3
Missis (lake), Can. 127/M2
Mississauga, On, Can. 131/Q8
Mississippi (pt.), Can. 89/K1
Mississippi (riv.), US 119/H6
Mississippi (state), US 125/H4
Mississippi (delta), US 119/J7
Mississippi River Gulf Outlet (canal), La, US 137/Q17
Missoula, Mt, US 126/E4
Missouri (state), US 125/H4
Missouri (riv.), US 119/F5
Missouri City, Tx, US 129/J5
Missouri City, Mo, US 137/R9
Mistaken (pt.), Can. 131/K2
Mistassibi (riv.), Can. 131/F1
Mistassini Nord-Est (riv.), Can. 131/G1
Mistassini, Qu, Can. 131/F1
Mistassini (lake), Qu, Can. 123/J3
Mistelbach an der Zaya, Aus. 41/H4
Misti (vol.), Peru 156/D5
Mistissini, Qu, Can. 130/F1
Mistrás (ruin), Gre. 47/H4
Mistretta, It. 46/D4
Misty Fjords Nat'l Mon., US 134/M4
Misty Fjords Nat'l Mon., Ak, US 122/C3
Misugi, Japan 77/K6
Mita, Punta de (pt.), Mex. 142/D4
Mitaka, Japan 77/T2
Mitama, Japan 77/C3
Mitamia, It. 59/G5
Mitare, Ven. 152/D2
Mitchell, SD, US 127/H4
Mitchell (mt.), NC, US 133/H3
Mitchell, Il, US 137/G8
Mitchell, Austl. 114/C4
Mitchell River NP, Austl. 115/C2
Mithapur, India 86/A3
Mithimna, Gre. 47/K3
Mitiaro, Cooks. 117/K6
Mitilini, Gre. 47/K3
Mitla (pass), Egypt 91/C4
Mitla (ruin), Mex. 144/B2
Mito, Japan 77/F2
Mitomi, Japan 77/B2
Mitra (peak), EqG. 96/G7
Mitrovica...

Mittelberg, Aus. 57/G3
Mittelland (canal), Ger. 51/F4
Mittelradde (riv.), Ger. 51/E3
Mittelwald, Ger. 51/F6
Mittenwald, Ger. 57/H3
Mittersill, Aus. 43/K3
Mitterteich, Ger. 55/F3
Mittlere-Isar (canal), Ger. 55/E6
Mittweida, Ger. 40/Q3
Mitú, Col. 152/D4
Mitumba, Monts (mts.), D.R. Congo 105/E2
Mitwitz, Ger. 54/E2
Miura, Japan 77/D3
Miura (pen.), Japan 77/D3
Miwa, Japan 77/H5
Miwa, Japan 77/L5
Miwa, Japan 77/H4
Mixco Viejo (ruin), Guat. 144/D3
Mixquiahuala, Mex. 143/K6
Mixteco (riv.), Mex. 143/K8
Miya (riv.), Japan 77/K7
Miya, Japan 77/K7
Miyagawa, Japan 77/K7
Miyagi (pref.), Japan 76/B4
Miyajima (isl.), Japan 75/F3
Miyake (isl.), Japan 79/E3
Miyako, Japan 76/B4
Miyako (isls.), Japan 75/H8
Miyakonojō, Japan 74/B4
Miyama, Japan 77/J5
Miyama, Japan 76/B4
Miyanojō, Japan 74/B5
Miyashiro, Japan 77/D2
Miyazaki (pref.), Japan 74/B4
Miyazaki, Japan 74/B5
Miyazu (bay), Japan 77/H4
Miyazu, Japan 77/H4
Miyi, China 83/H2
Miyoshi, Japan 74/C3
Miyoshi, Japan 77/M5
Miyoshi, Japan 77/D3
Miyoshi, Japan 77/M5
Miyota, Japan 77/C1
Miyun (res.), China 72/H6
Miyun, China 72/H6
Mizen (pt.), Ire. 34/B6
Miziya, Bul. 49/F4
Mizoram (state), India 70/F7
Mizpah, NJ, US 138/D5
Mizpe Ramon, Isr. 91/D4
Mizuho, Japan 77/D1
Mizuho, Japan 77/H5
Mizunami, Japan 77/M5
Mizusawa, Japan 76/B4
Mjölby, Swe. 38/F2
Mjøndalen, Nor. 38/D3
Mjörn (lake), Swe. 38/E3
Mjøsa (lake), Nor. 37/D3
Mkata (plain), Tanz. 104/C4
Mkokotoni, Tanz. 104/C4
Mkomazi Game Rsv., Tanz. 104/C4
Mkombo (riv.), Tanz. 104/C4
Mkondoa (riv.), Tanz. 104/C4
Mkorn (reg.), Mor. 98/D3
Mkumbi (pt.), Tanz. 104/C4
Mkushi, Zam. 105/E3
Mkuze (riv.), SAfr. 107/F2
Mladá Boleslav, Czh. 55/H3
Mladá Vožice, Czh. 55/H4
Mladenovac, Yugo. 48/E3
Mława, Pol. 41/L2
Mljet (isl.), Cro. 47/E1
Mljet NP, Cro. 47/E1
Mmabatho, SAfr. 106/D2
Mnyera (riv.), Tanz. 104/B5
Mo Duc, Viet. 79/E5
Mo (riv.), SLeo. 102/C5
Moa, Cuba 145/H1
Moa (riv.), SLeo. 102/C5
Moa (isl.), Indo. 116/G6
Moab, Ut, US 128/E3
Moala Group (isl.), Fiji 116/G6
Moama, Austl. 115/C1
Moamba, Moz. 107/F2
Moaña, Sp. 44/A1
Moanda, Gabon 96/H8
Moate, Ire. 31/Q10
Mobara, Japan 77/E3
Mobaye, CAfr. 97/K7
Moberly, Mo, US 129/J3
Moberly Lake, BC, Can. 126/C2
Mobile, Al, US 137/G4
Mobile (riv.), Al, US 137/G4
Mobridge, SD, US 127/H4
Moca (pass), Turk. 90/C1
Mocache, Ecu. 152/B5
Mocajuba, Braz. 152/B5
Mojave (des.), Ca, US 124/C5
Mojave, Ca, US 128/C4
Mojiang Hanizu Zizhixian, China 83/H3
Mojikit (lake), Can. 127/L3
Mojkovac, Yugo. 47/F1
Mojos, Llanos de (plain), Bol. 150/E6
Moju (riv.), Braz. 151/J4
Moju, Braz. 75/F2
Mokameh, India 85/E3
Mokapu (pt.), Hi, US 124/W13
Mokau, NZ 117/S10
Mokelumne (riv.), Ca, US 128/C3
Mokelumne (aqueduct), Ca, US 135/M11
Mokena, Il, US 135/Q16
Mokil (isl.), Micr. 116/E4
Mokochu, Thai. 78/B3
Mokohinau (isls.), NZ 117/S9
Mokokchūng, India 83/F7
Mokolo, Camr. 96/H5
Mokp'o, SKor. 73/D5
Mokpō, Yugo. 49/H2
Moksha (riv.), Rus. 63/G1

Mokuleia, Hi, US	124/V12	Mondragone, It.	46/C2
Mol, Yugo.	48/E3	Mondsee (lake),	
Mol, Belg.	50/C6	Aus.	55/G7
Moláoi, Gre.	47/H4	Mondsee, Aus.	55/G7
Molare, It.	58/B3	Moneglia, It.	58/C4
Molas, Punta (pt.),		Monemvasia, Gre.	47/H4
Mex.	144/E1	Mones Cazón,	
Molat (isl.), Cro.	48/B3	Arg.	158/E3
Molatón (peak),		Monesterio, Sp.	44/B3
Sp.	44/E3	Money (pt.),	
Molbergen, Ger.	51/E3	Sc, UK	34/C2
Mold, UK	35/E5	Moneyreagh,	
Moldavia (reg.),		NI, UK	34/C2
Rom.	49/H2	Monfalcone, It.	43/H4
Moldavian Carpathians		Monferrato (reg.), It.	43/H4
(range), Rom.	49/G2	Monforte, Sp.	44/B1
Molde, Nor.	37/C3	Monforte, Port.	44/B3
Moldova (riv.),		Monagaguá, Braz.	211/G9
Rom.	49/G2	Mongers (isl.),	
Moldova (ctry.)	27/G4	Austl.	109/A3
Moldova Nouă,		Monghidoro, It.	59/E4
Rom.	48/E3	Mongo (riv.), Gui.	102/C4
Moldoveanu (peak),		Mongu, Zam.	105/D4
Rom.	49/G3	Monte Albán (ruin),	
Mole (riv.),		Mex.	144/B2
Eng, UK	32/C5	Monte Alegre,	
Mole NP, Gha.	103/E4	Braz.	151/H4
Môle Saint-Nicolas,		Monte Alegre de Goiás,	
Haiti	145/H2	Braz.	154/A4
Molepolole, Bots.	105/E5	Monte Alegre de Minas,	
Molina, Sp.	44/E2	Braz.	155/B1
Molina, Chile	158/C2	Monte Alegre do Piauí,	
Molina de Segura,		Braz.	154/A3
Sp.	44/E3	Monte Alto, Braz.	155/B2
Moline, Il, US	127/L5	Monte Azul, Braz.	154/B4
Molinella, It.	59/E2	Monte Carmelo,	
Molinicos, Sp.	44/D3	Braz.	155/C1
Molino de Flores, PN,		Monte Carmelo,	
Mex.	143/R9	Ven.	152/D2
Molins de Rei, Sp.	45/L7	Monte Caseros,	
Molise (reg.), It.	46/D2	Arg.	157/E3
Molkom, Swe.	38/E2	Monte Comán, Arg.	158/D2
Möll (riv.), Aus.	43/K3	Monte Escobedo,	
Mellebjerg (peak),		Mex.	142/E4
Den.	37/D5	Monte Maíz, Arg.	158/E2
Mollendo, Peru	156/C5	Monte Pascoal, PN de,	
Mollerußa, Col du (pass),		Braz.	151/L7
Swi.	56/B5	Monte Pascoal, PN de,	
Mollerußa, Sp.	45/F2	Braz.	154/C5
Molles (pt.), Chile	158/D3	Monte Rosa (mts.), It.	59/E6
Molles, Uru.	159/K10	Monte San Savino,	
Mollet del Vallès,		It.	59/D6
Sp.	45/L6	Montealegre, Sp.	44/E3
Mollis, Swi.	57/F3	Montebello (isls.),	
Mölndal, Swe.	38/E3	Austl.	109/A3
Mölnlycke, Swe.	38/E3	Montebello, Ca, US	136/F7
		Montebello	
Mono (riv.), Togo	96/F6	Vincentino, It.	59/E2
Molodezhnaya,		Montebelluna, It.	59/F1
Rus., Ant.	160/D	Mono (lake),	
Mologa (riv.), Rus.	60/G4	Ca, US	128/C3
Molokai (isl.),		Mono (prov.),	
HI, US	117/K2	Ben.	103/F5
Moloma (riv.), Rus.	61/L4	Monocacy (riv.),	
Molong, Austl.	115/D2	Md, US	138/A4
Molopo (riv.),		Monor, Hun.	48/D2
Bots.	93/E7	Monóvar, Sp.	45/E3
Mólos, Gre.	47/H3	Monreal del Campo,	
Molsheim, Fr.	56/D1	Sp.	44/E2
Molteno, SAfr.	106/D3	Monreale, It.	46/C3
Molu (isl.), Indo.	81/H5	Monroe, Wi, US	127/L5
Molucca (sea),		Monroe, Ut, US	128/D3
Indo.	67/M10	Monroe, Ga, US	133/H3
Molucca (sea),		Monroe (lake),	
Asia	67/M10	In, US	133/G2
Moluccas (arch.),		Monroe, La, US	129/J4
Indo.	81/G3	Monroe, NC, US	133/H3
Molveno (lake), It.	57/G5	Monroe, Mi, US	130/D3
Molveno, It.	57/G5	Monroe, Ct, US	139/E1
Mombaça, Braz.	154/C2	Monroe, NY, US	138/D1
Mombasa, Kenya	104/C4	Monroe, Wa, US	135/C2
Mombetsu, Japan	76/C1	Monroe City,	
Mombetsu, Japan	76/C2	Il, US	137/G9
Mömbris, Ger.	54/C2	Monroeville,	
Momchilgrad, Bul.	47/J2	Al, US	133/G4
Momfafa (cape),		Monroeville,	
Indo.	81/H4	NJ, US	138/C4
Momignies, Belg.	53/D3	Monrovia (cap.),	
Mömlingen, Ger.	54/C3	Libr.	102/C5
Momo, It.	58/B1	Monrovia, Ca, US	136/G7
Momoishi, Japan	76/B3	Mons, Belg.	52/C3
Mompós, Col.	152/C2	Monsanto, Port.	44/B2
Mon (state),		Monschau, Ger.	53/F2
Myan.	83/G4	Monsefú, Peru	156/B2
Mon (riv.), Myan.	83/F3	Monselice, It.	43/J4
Møn (isl.), Den.	37/E5	Monsenhor Tabosa,	
Mona (isl.), PR	141/M8	Braz.	154/C2
Mona (passg.),		Monsey, NY, US	139/J7
NAm.	119/L8	Monsheim, Ger.	54/B3
Monaco (ctry.)	27/E4	Monster, Neth.	52/B2
Monaco (cap.)		Mönsterås, Swe.	38/G3
Mona.	58/J8	Monsummano Terme, It.	59/D5
Monaco, Port of (har.),		Mont-de-Marsan, Fr.	42/C5
Mona.	58/J8	Mont-Joli, Qu, Can.	131/G1
Monadhliath (mts.),		Mont-Laurier,	
Sc, UK	36/B2	Qu, Can.	130/F2
Monagas (state),		Mont Peko, PN du,	
Ven.	153/F2	C.d'Iv.	102/D4
Monaghan (co.),		Mont-Royal,	
Ire.	34/A3	Qu, Can.	131/N6
Monagrillo, Pan.	152/A3	Mont-Saint-Martin, Fr.	53/E4
Monagrillo (ruin),		Mont-Saint-Michel,	
Pan.	152/A2	Fr., Can.	130/F2
Monar (lake),		Mont Sangbé, PN du,	
Sc, UK	36/A2	C.d'Iv.	102/D4
Monashee (mts.),		Mont-Sous-Vaudrey,	
Can.	126/D3	Fr.	56/B4
Moncada, Sp.	45/E3	Montà, It.	58/A3
Moncalieri, It.	43/G4	Monta Fon (mts.),	
Moncalvo, It.	58/B2	Aus.	57/F3
Monção, Braz.	154/A1	Montabaur, Ger.	53/G3
Moncayo, Sierra del (range),		Montagnana, It.	57/H5
Sp.	44/E2	Montagne d'Ambre NP,	
Mönch (peak), Swi.	56/D4	Madg.	107/J6
Monchegorsk, Rus.	60/G2	Montagny-Sainte-Félicité,	
Mönchengladbach,		Fr.	106/M10
Ger.	50/D6	Montagu, SAfr.	
Monchique, Serra de (mts.),		Montague (str.),	
Port.	44/A4	Ak, US	134/J2
Monchique, Port.	44/A4	Montague, Tx, US	137/H18
Moncks Corner,		Montague,	
SC, US	133/H3	Ca, US	135/J2
Monclova, Mex.	132/C5	Montague, NJ, US	138/D1
Moncton,		Montague (isl.),	
NB, Can.	131/H2	Uru.	159/K11
Mondego (cape),		Montaigu, Fr.	42/C3
Port.	44/A2	Montaione, It.	59/D5
Mondego (riv.),		Montalbán, Sp.	45/E2
Port.	44/A2	Montalbano Jonico, It.	46/E2
Mondéjar, Sp.	44/D2	Montale, It.	59/E5
Mondolfo, It.	59/G5	Montale, It.	59/D5
Mondoñedo, Sp.	44/B1	Montalieu-Vercieu, Fr.	56/B6
Mondorf-les- Bains,		Montalvo, Port.	44/B3
Lux.	53/F4	Montalvo, Sp.	44/A2
Mondovi, It.	58/A4	Montana (prov.),	
Mondragón, Sp.	44/D1	Bul.	47/H1

Montana, Bul.	49/F4	Montfort-L'Amaury,	
Montana, Swi.	56/D5	Fr.	52/A6
Montana (state), US	126/E1	Montgeron, Fr.	30/K5
Montanaro, It.	58/A2	Montgomery,	
Montánchez, Sp.	154/B5	WV, US	130/D4
Montargis, Fr.	42/E3	Montgomery (cap.),	
Montataire, Fr.	52/B5	Al, US	133/G3
Montauban, Fr.	42/D4	Montgomery,	
Montauk, NY, US	139/G1	Wal, UK	32/C1
Montauk (pt.),		Montgomery,	
NY, US	139/G1	Pa, US	138/B1
Montbard, Fr.	42/F3	Montgomery (co.),	
Montbéliard, Fr.	43/H4	Md, US	138/A5
Montblanc, Sp.	45/F2	Montgomery Village,	
Montcada i Reixac,		Md, US	138/A5
Sp.	45/L7	Montgomeryville,	
Montceau-les-Mines,		Pa, US	138/C3
Fr.	42/F3	Montgrand (peak), Fr.	42/E5
Montclair, Ca, US	136/C2	Monthermé, Fr.	53/D4
Montclair, NJ, US	139/J8	Monthey, Swi.	56/C5
Montcornet, Fr.	52/D4	Monthureux-sur-Saône,	
Montdidier, Fr.	52/B4	Fr.	56/B1
Monte Albán (ruin),		Monthyon, Fr.	30/L4
Mex.	144/B2	Monticelli d'Ongina,	
		It.	58/C2
		Monti Sabini (mts.), It.	46/C1
		Monticelli Terme, It.	58/D3
		Monticello,	
		Mo, US	127/L5
		Monticello, In, US	130/C4
		Monticello, La, US	129/K4
		Monticello, Fl, US	133/H4
		Monticello, Va, US	133/J2
		Monticello Conte Otto,	
		It.	59/E1
		Montichiari, It.	57/H5
		Montier-en-Der, Fr.	56/A1
		Montignies-le-Tilleul,	
		Belg.	53/D3
		Montigny-en-Gohelle,	
		Fr.	52/B3
		Montigny-le-Bretonneux,	
		Fr.	30/J5
		Montigny-le-Roi, Fr.	56/B2
		Montijo, Sp.	44/B3
		Montijo, Port.	45/Q10
		Montilla, Sp.	44/C4
		Montivilliers, Fr.	42/D2
		Montlebon, Fr.	56/C3
		Montluçon, Fr.	30/J6
		Montlhéry, Fr.	42/E3
		Montluel, Fr.	56/B6
		Montmagny,	
		Qu, Can.	131/G2
		Montmédy, Fr.	53/E4
		Montmelian, Fr.	57/E3
		Montmirail, Fr.	52/C6
		Montmorency, Fr.	30/J5
		Montmorillon, Fr.	42/D3
		Montmorot, Fr.	56/B4
		Montoire, Fr.	30/H5
		Montoir-de-Bretagne,	
		Fr.	42/B3
		Montois-la-Montagne,	
		Fr.	53/F5
		Montone (riv.), It.	59/E3
		Montopoli, It.	59/D5
		Montorio Veronese, It.	59/D5
		Montoro, Sp.	44/C3
		Montour (ridge),	
		Pa, US	138/B2
		Montour Falls,	
		NY, US	138/B1
		Montoursville,	
		Pa, US	138/B1
		Montpelier (cap.),	
		Vt, US	131/F2
		Montpellier, Fr.	42/E5
		Montreal (lake),	
		Can.	127/G2
		Montreal (riv.),	
		Can.	130/C2
		Montréal, Qu, Can.	131/N6
		Montréal-Est,	
		Qu, Can.	131/N6
		Montréal-la-Cluse,	
		Fr.	56/B5
		Montréal-Nord,	
		Qu, Can.	131/N6
		Montredon, Fr.	42/D5
		Montreuil, Fr.	30/K5
		Montreuil, Fr.	52/A3
		Montreuil-Bellay, Fr.	42/C3
		Montreuil-sur-Epte, Fr.	30/G4
		Montreux, Swi.	56/C5
		Montreux-Château, Fr.	56/C2
		Montrevel-en-Bresse,	
		Fr.	42/F2
		Montrichard, Swi.	56/C4
		Montricher, Swi.	56/C4
		Montrose, Co, US	128/F3
		Montrose (basin),	
		Sc, UK	36/D3
		Montrose, Sc, UK	36/D3
		Montrouge, Fr.	30/J5
		Montry, Fr.	30/L5
		Montsalvy, Fr.	42/E4
		Montsec, Pic de	
		(peak), Fr.	45/L6
		Montseny, PN, Sp.	45/L6
		Montserrado (co.),	
		Libr.	102/C5
		Montserrat (peak), Sp.	45/F2
		Montserrat (dpcy.), UK	119/L8
		Montsoult, Fr.	30/J4
		Montvale, NJ, US	139/J7
		Montville, NJ, US	139/H8
		Monywa, Myan.	83/G3
		Monza, It.	58/C1
		Monze, Zam.	105/E4
		Monzingen, Ger.	53/G4
		Monzón, Peru	156/B3
		Monzón, Sp.	45/F2
		Mooirivier, SAfr.	107/E3
		Mool (riv.),	
		NC, US	133/J3
		Moonta, Austl.	113/H5
		Moora, Austl.	112/C4
		Moorcroft,	
		Wy, US	127/G4
		Moordrecht, Neth.	50/B5
		Moore (lake),	
		Austl.	109/A3
		Moore, Ok, US	137/N15
		Moore Haven,	
		Fl, US	133/H5
		Moore River NP,	
		Austl.	112/B4
		Moorea (isl.),	
		FrPol.	117/K6
		Moorenweis, Ger.	57/H1
		Mooresboro,	
		NJ, US	138/D4

Mooresville,		Moreton Island NP,	
NC, US	133/H3	Austl.	114/D4
Mooretown,		Moreuil, Fr.	52/B4
On, Can.	135/H6	Moreyu (riv.), Rus.	61/P2
Moorfoot (hills),		Morez, Fr.	56/C4
Sc, UK	36/C5	Morgan (riv.), US	137/K11
Moorhead, Mn, US	127/J4	Morgan, Ut, US	137/K11
Moorook, Austl.	115/B2	Morgan, Austl.	113/H5
Moorpark, Ca, US	136/B2	Morgan City,	
Mooreesburg,		La, US	129/K5
SAfr.	106/L10	Morganfield,	
Mooreslede, Belg.	52/C2	Ky, US	130/C4
Moosburg, Ger.	55/E6	Morgantina (ruin), It.	46/D4
Moose (mtn.),		Morganton,	
Can.	127/H3	NC, US	133/H3
Moose (riv.),		Morgantown,	
Can.	130/D1	Ky, US	130/C4
Moose Creek,		Morgantown,	
Ak, US	134/J3	WV, US	130/D4
Moose Jaw,		Morgenzon, SAfr.	107/E2
Sk, Can.	127/G3	Morges, Swi.	56/C4
Moose Pass,		Morghāb (riv.),	
Ak, US	134/J3	Afg.	64/G6
Moosehead (lake),		Morgongāva, Swe.	38/G2
Me, US	125/N2	Mori, It.	57/H5
Mooseheart (mtn.),		Mori, Japan	76/B2
Ak, US	134/H3	Mori Kazak Zizhixian,	
Mooseheart,		China	70/F3
Il, US	135/P16	Morialta Conservation Park,	
Moosinning, Ger.	55/E6	Austl.	113/M8
Morganje, Fr.	56/C4	Moriarty, NM, US	129/F4
Moosomin,		Morice (lake),	
Sk, Can.	127/G3	BC, Can.	126/B2
Moosonee,		Morie (lake),	
On, Can.	130/D1	Sc, UK	36/B1
Moosseedorf, Swi.	56/D3	Moriguchi, Japan	77/J6
Mopti (pol. reg.),		Morin Dawa Daurzu Zizhiqi,	
Mali	102/E3	China	71/M2
Mopti, Mali	102/E3	Moringen, Ger.	51/G5
Moquegua (dept.),		Morinville	
Peru	156/D5	Ab, Can.	126/E2
Moquegua, Peru	156/D5	Morioka, Japan	76/B4
Moquehuá, Arg.	159/J11	Morlaix, Fr.	42/B2
Mór, Hun.	48/D2	Morlanwelz, Belg.	53/D3
Mora (riv.), India	85/E3	Mörlenbach, Ger.	54/B3
Mora, NM, US	129/F4	Morley, Eng, UK	35/G4
Mora, NM, US	129/F4	Mormant, Fr.	30/L6
Mora, Sp.	44/D3	Mormond (hill),	
Mora, Port.	44/A3	Sc, UK	36/D1
Mora de Rubielos,		Mornington (isl.),	
Sp.	45/E2	Austl.	109/C2
Moraga, Ca, US	135/K11	Mornington,	
Morada Nova,		Austl.	115/C3
Braz.	154/C2	Moro, Pak.	89/J3
Morada Nova de Minas,		Moro (gulf), Phil.	116/B4
Braz.	155/C1	Morocco (ctry.)	93/E1
Morafenobe,		Morocelli, Hon.	144/E3
Madg.	107/H7	Morococha, Peru	156/B3
Morag, Pol.	48/D1	Morogoro (pol. reg.),	
Mörnsheim, Ger.	54/D5	Tanz.	104/C4
Moro, Pak.	89/J3	Morombe, Madg.	107/G8
Morahalom, Hun.	48/D2	Morón (isl.),	
Morainvilliers,		Mong.	70/H2
Fr.	30/H5	Morón, Ven.	152/D2
Moral de Calatrava,		Morón, Ven.	152/D2
Sp.	44/D3	Mórón, Arg.	159/J11
Moraleja, Sp.	44/B2	Morón de la Frontera,	
Morales, Guat.	144/D3	Sp.	44/C4
Moramanga, Madg.	107/J7	Morona (riv.),	
Moranbah, Austl.	114/C3	Peru	150/C4
Morane (isl.),		Morona-Santiago (dept.),	
FrPol.	117/M7	Ecu.	152/B5
Morangis, Fr.	30/K5	Morondava (riv.),	
Morano Calabro, It.	46/E3	Madg.	107/H8
Morant Bay, Jam.	145/G2	Morondava, Madg.	107/H8
Morar (lake),		Moroni (cap.),	
Sc, UK	31/R8	Com.	107/G5
Morarano Chrome,		Morotai (str.),	
Madg.	107/J7	Indo.	81/G3
Morat (lake), Swi.	56/D4	Morotai (isl.),	
Morata de Tajuña,		Indo.	67/M9
Sp.	45/N9	Moroto (str.),	
Moratalla, Sp.	44/E3	Ugan.	104/B2
Moratuwa, SrL.	82/C6	Moroto, Ugan.	104/B2
Moravia (reg.),		Morowa, Austl.	112/C4
Czh.	41/J4	Moroyama, Japan	77/C2
Moravská Třebová,		Morpará, Braz.	154/B3
Czh.	41/J4	Morpeth, Eng, UK	35/G1
Moravské Budějovice,		Morphou, Cyp.	91/C2
Czh.	41/H4	Morphou (bay),	
Morawa, Austl.	112/C4	Cyp.	91/C2
Moray Firth (inlet),		Morra (lake),	
Sc, UK	36/B1	Neth.	50/C2
Morbach, Ger.	53/G4	Morrinhos, Braz.	155/B1
Morbier, Fr.	56/C4	Mórristown, Sp.	45/N9
Morbio Inferiore,		Morris, Mb, Can.	127/K4
Swi.	57/F6	Morris, NY, US	139/H8
Morbras (riv.), Fr.	30/K5	Morris (res.),	
Mørbylånga, Swe.	38/G3	Ca, US	136/D2
Morcenx, Fr.	42/C4	Morris (mt.), Austl.	113/F3
Morciano di Romagna,		Morris (isl.),	
It.	59/F5	Ca, US	136/D2
Mordaga, China	71/M2	Morrison, Co, US	137/N8
Morden, Mb, Can.	127/J3	Morristown,	
Mordovia Aut. Rep.,		NJ, US	139/H8
Rus.	64/Q6	Morristown NHP,	
Møre Og Romsdal (co.),		NJ, US	139/H8
Nor.	37/C3	Morrisville, Pa, US	138/D3
Moreau (riv.),		Morro Bay, Ca, US	128/B3
SD, US	127/H4	Morro de Môco (peak),	
Morecambe (bay),		Ang.	105/C2
Eng, UK	35/E3	Morro de Puercos (pt.),	
Moree, Austl.	115/D1	Pan.	145/F4
Morehead, Ky, US	130/D4	Morro do Chapéu,	
Morehead City,		Braz.	154/B3
NC, US	133/J3	Morrocoy, PN,	
Morelia, Mex.	143/E5	Ven.	152/D2
Morella, It.	45/E2	Motta Visconti, It.	58/B2
Morelos (state),		Motta di Livenza, It.	59/F1
Mex.	145/A5	Mottarone (peak), It.	58/B1
Morena, Sierra (range),		Motueka, NZ	117/S11
Sp.	44/C3	Motul de Carrillo Puerto,	
Moreni, Rom.	49/G3	Mex.	144/D1
Moreno Valley,		Morrosquillo (gulf),	
Ca, US	136/C3	Col.	145/G4
Moresby (isl.),		Mõrrum, Swe.	38/F3
BC, Can.	122/C3	Mers (isl.), Den.	38/C3
Moreton (isl.),		Morsang-sur-Orge, Fr.	30/K6
Austl.	114/D4	Morsbach, Fr.	53/F5

Morschwiller-le-Bas,		Moudon, Swi.	56/C4
Fr.	56/D2	Mougris (well),	
Morel, Fr.		Mrta.	102/B2
Morse, Ks, US	137/D6	Mouhoun (prov.),	
Morse Mill,		Burk.	102/E3
Mo, US	137/F9	Mouila, Gabon	96/H8
Morskoy (isl.),		Mouïna (well), Alg.	99/F3
Kaz.	63/J3	Moul (well), Niger	96/H4
Morsum, Ger.	51/G3	Moulamein (riv.),	
Mortagne (riv.), Fr.	56/C1	Austl.	115/C2
Mortagne-sur-Sèvre, Fr.	42/C3	Moulamein, Austl.	115/C2
Mortara, It.	58/B2	Moulay Idriss,	
Mortcerf, Fr.	30/L5	Mor.	100/B2
Morte (pt.),		Moulins, Fr.	42/E3
Eng, UK	32/B4	Moulouya (riv.),	
Morteau, Fr.	56/C3	Mor.	100/C2
Mortefontaine, Fr.	30/K4	Moultrie, Ga, US	133/H4
Mortegliano, It.	59/G1	Moultrie (lake),	
Mortes, Rio das (riv.),		SC, US	133/J3
Braz.	151/H6	Moundou, Chad	96/J6
Mortlake, Austl.	115/B3	Moundsville,	
Morton, Wa, US	126/C4	WV, US	130/D4
Morton, Il, US	137/P10	Mount Aberdeen NP,	
Morton, K2 (peak),		Austl.	114/C4
China	89/K2	Mount Abu, India	89/K4
Morton Grove,		Mount Airy, NC, US	130/D4
Il, US	135/Q15	Mount Airy, Md, US	138/A5
Morton NP,		Mount Allan Abor. Land,	
Austl.	115/D2	Austl.	113/G2
Morton NWR,		Mount Aspiring NP,	
NY, US	139/F2	NZ	117/R11
Mortsel, Belg.	50/B6	Mount Baker-Snoqualmie,	
Moruga (riv.),		Wa, US	135/D1
Chile	158/B3	Mount Baker-Snoqualmie	
Morhange, Fr.	53/F6	Nat'l For., Wa, US	135/D3
Morungaba, Braz.	211/G7	Mount Baldy,	
Moruya, Austl.	115/D2	Ca, US	136/C2
Morvan (plat.), Fr.	42/E3	Mount Barker,	
Morven, Wa, US	126/C4	India	89/K4
Morton, Il, US	129/K2	Mount Barker,	
Morven (peak),		Austl.	112/C5
Sc, UK	36/C2	Mount Barker,	
Morvi, India	89/K4	Austl.	113/M9
Morvillars, Fr.	56/C2	Mount Barkly Abor. Land,	
Morwell, Austl.	115/C3	Austl.	113/G2
Morzine, Fr.	56/C5	Mount Beauty,	
Mos, Sp.	44/A1	Austl.	115/C3
Mosbach, Ger.	54/C4	Mount Bold (res.),	
Mosby, Mo, US	137/E5	Austl.	113/M9
Moscavide, Port.	45/P10	Mount Buffalo NP,	
Moscow, Id, US	126/D4	Austl.	115/C3
Moscow (upland),		Mount Carmel,	
Rus.	60/F5	Il, US	130/C4
Moscow Oblast,		Mount Carmel,	
Rus.	60/H5	Pa, US	138/B2
Moscow University Ice Shelf,		Mount Darwin,	
Ant.	160/J	Zim.	105/F4
Moselle (riv.), Fr.	43/G2	Mount Diablo State Park,	
Moselle (dept.), Fr.	53/F5	Ca, US	135/L11
Moselotte (riv.), Fr.	56/C2	Mount Eccles NP,	
Moses Lake,		Austl.	115/B3
Wa, US	126/D4	Mount Elgon NP,	
Mosfellsbær, Ice.	37/N7	Ugan.	104/B2
Mosgiel, NZ	117/S12	Mount Elliot NP,	
Moshaweng (riv.),		Austl.	114/B2
SAfr.	106/C2	Mount Everard,	
Moshi, Tanz.	104/C3	Austl.	114/B2
Moshoeshoe (Maseru)		Mount Field NP,	
(int'l arpt.), Les.	106/D3	Austl.	115/C4
Mosina, Pol.	41/J2	Mount Gambier,	
Moskva (Moscow) (cap.),		Austl.	115/B3
Rus.	60/G5	Mount Garnet,	
Moskva (Moscow) (cap.),		Austl.	114/B2
Rus.	62/F1	Mount Holly,	
Mosonmagyaróvár,		NJ, US	138/D4
Hun.	48/C2	Mount Holly Springs,	
Mosquera, Col.	152/B4	Pa, US	138/A3
Mosquero,		Mount Imlay NP,	
NM, US	129/G4	Austl.	115/D3
Mosquitia (phys. reg.),		Mount Isa, Austl.	113/H2
Hon.	145/E3	Mount Joy,	
Mosquito (pt.),		Pa, US	138/B3
Pan.	145/G4	Mount Kaputar NP,	
Mosquitos, Golfo de los		Austl.	115/D1
(gulf), Pan.	150/B2	Mount Kenya NP,	
Mosrona (riv.),		Kenya	104/C2
Peru	150/C4	Mount Kisco,	
Moss Beach,		NY, US	139/E1
Ca, US	135/J11	Mount Larcom,	
Moss Bluff,		Austl.	114/C3
La, US	129/K5	Mount Laurel,	
Moss Point,		NJ, US	138/D4
Ms, US	133/F4	Mount Lofty (ranges),	
Moss-Side, NI, UK	34/B1	Austl.	109/C4
Moss Vale, Austl.	115/D2	Mount Lofty (range),	
Mosses, Col des (pass),		Austl.	113/M9
Swi.	56/D5	Mount Magnet,	
Mossel Bay, SAfr.	106/D4	Austl.	112/C4
Mossendjo, Congo	104/B4	Mount Mistake NP,	
Mossi Highlands (uplands),		Austl.	114/D4
Burk.	102/E4	Mount Morgan,	
Mossman, Austl.	114/B2	Austl.	114/C3
Mossoró, Braz.	154/C2	Mount Morris,	
Most, Czh.	55/G1	Mi, US	130/D3
Mostaganem (prov.),		Mount Nebo,	
Alg.	100/F4	Austl.	114/E6
Mostaganem, Alg.	100/F4	Mount Olive,	
Móstoles, Sp.	45/N9	NC, US	133/J3
Mostar, Bosn.	47/E1	Mount Pearl,	
Mostardas, Braz.	155/B4	Nf, Can.	131/L2
Mosul, Iraq	80/D6	Mount Penn,	
Motagua (riv.),		Pa, US	138/C3
Guat.	140/D4	Mount Pleasant,	
Motala, Swe.	38/F2	Ia, US	127/L5
Motherwell, Sc, UK	36/B5	Mount Pleasant,	
Motian (mtn.),		Ut, US	128/E3
China	72/E2	Mount Pleasant,	
Moṭihāri, India	85/E2	Mi, US	130/C3
Motilla del Palancar,		Mount Pleasant,	
Sp.	44/E3	Tx, US	129/K4
Motma, Japan	75/J7	Mount Pleasant,	
Motnik, Slov.	57/L3	De, US	138/C4
Motomiya, Japan	75/G2	Mount Pleasant	
Motono, Japan	77/L5	(int'l arpt.), UK	159/F6
Motosu (lake),		Mount Pocono,	
Japan	77/L5	Pa, US	138/C1
Motovski (gulf),		Mount Prospect,	
Rus.	37/K1	Il, US	135/P15
Motoyoshi, Japan	76/B4	Mount Rainier,	
Motozintla de Mendoza,		Md, US	138/B6
Mex.	144/C3	Mount Rainier NP,	
Motril, Sp.	44/D4	Wa, US	135/D3
Motsuta-misaki (cape),		Mount Remarkable NP,	
Japan	76/A2	Austl.	113/H5
Motul, ND, US	127/H4	Mount Revelstoke NP,	
Motueka, NZ	117/S11	Can.	126/D3
Mouaskar (prov.),		Mount Richmond NP,	
Alg.	100/F4	Austl.	115/B3
Mouchoir Passage (chan.),		Mount Rushmore Nat'l Mem.,	
UK	145/J1	SD, US	127/H4
		Mount Spec NP,	
		Austl.	114/B2
		Mount St. Helens Nat'l	
		Volcanic Mon.,	
		Wa, US	126/C4

Mount Sterling,		
Ky, US	130/D4
Mount Torrens,		
Austl.	113/M8
Mount Vernon,		
Wa, US	126/C3
Mount Vernon,		
Il, US	129/K3
Mount Vernon,		
Oh, US	130/D3
Mount Vernon,		
Va, US	138/A6
Mount Vernon,		
SC, US	133/J3
Mount Vernon,		
NY, US	139/K8
Mount Walsh NP,		
Austl.	114/C4
Mount Warning NP,		
Austl.	114/D5
Mount Welcome Abor. Land,		
Austl.	112/C2
Mount William NP,		
Austl.	115/D4
Mount Wolf,		
Pa, US	138/B3
Mountain (lake),		
Can.	127/G3
Mountain (riv.),		
NW, Can.	122/D2
Mountain Ash,		
Wal, UK	32/C3
Mountain Green,		
Ut, US	137/K11
Mountain Grove,		
Mo, US	129/J3
Mountain Home,		
Id, US	126/E5
Mountain Lakes,		
NJ, US	139/H8
Mountain Point,		
Ak, US	134/M4
Mountain Top,		
Austl.	138/C1
Mountain View,		
Ar, US	129/J4
Mountain View,		
Hi, US	124/U11
Mountain View,		
Ca, US	135/K12
Mountain Village,		
Ak, US	134/F3
Mountain Zebra NP,		
SAfr.	106/D4
Mountainhome,		
Pa, US	138/C1
Mountainside,		
NJ, US	139/H9
Mountlake Terrace,		
Wa, US	135/C2
Mountmellick, Ire.	31/Q10
Mountrath, Ire.	31/Q10
Mount's (bay),		
Eng, UK	32/A6
Mountville,		
Pa, US	138/B3
Moura, Braz.	150/E4
Moura, Port.	44/B3
Moura, Austl.	114/C4
Mourenx, Fr.	42/C5
Mourmelon-le-Grand,		
Fr.	53/D5
Mourmelon-le-Petit,		
Fr.	53/D5
Mourne (mts.),		
NI, UK	34/B3
Mourniai, Gre.	47/H5
Mourne, Fr.	30/M5
Mouscron, Belg.	52/C2
Mousseaux-sur-Seine,		
Fr.	30/G4
Moussoro, Chad	96/J5
Moussy-le-Neuf, Fr.	30/K4
Moussy-le-Vieux, Fr.	30/K4
Mouths of the Niger,		
Nga.	96/G6
Moutier, Swi.	56/D3
Mouvaux, Fr.	52/C2
Mouy, Fr.	52/B5
Mouydir (plat.),		
Alg.	99/G4
Mouzákion, Gre.	47/G3
Mouzon (riv.), Fr.	56/B1
Mouzon, Fr.	53/E4
Moville, Ire.	34/A1
Moxotó (riv.),		
Braz.	154/C3
Moy, NI, UK	34/B3
Moyamba, SLeo.	102/B4
Moye (isl.), China	73/B4
Moyen Atlas (mts.),		
Mor.	96/D1
Moyenmoutier, Fr.	56/C1
Moyeuvre-Grande, Fr.	53/F5
Moyle (dist.),		
NI, UK	34/B1
Moyo (isl.), Indo.	81/E5
Moyo, Ugan.	104/A2
Moyobamba, Peru	156/B2
Moyowosi (riv.),		
Tanz.	104/A3
Moyu, China	70/C4
Moyu (riv.), China	70/C4
Mozambique (ctry.)	93/F6
Mozambique (chan.),		
Afr.	93/F7
Mozhaysk, Rus.	60/H5
Mozhga, Rus.	61/M4
Mozzecane, It.	58/C2
Mozzecane, It.	59/D2
Mpanda, Tanz.	104/A4
Mpigi, Ugan.	104/B2
Mpika, Zam.	104/A5
Mporokoso, Zam.	104/A4
Mpraeso, Gha.	103/E5
Mpulungu, Zam.	104/A4
Mpumalanga (prov.),		
SAfr.	107/E2
Mpwapwa, Tanz.	104/B4
Mrągowo, Pol.	39/J5
Mrkonjić Grad,		
Bosn.	48/C3
M'Sila (prov.),		
Alg.	99/F2
M'sila, Alg.	100/H5
M'sila (riv.), Alg.	100/H5
Msoun (riv.),		
Mor.	100/C2
Msta (riv.), Rus.	60/G4
Mszana Dolna, Pol.	41/L4

Mtorwi (peak), Tanz. 104/B5
Mtsensk, Rus. 62/F1
Mtubatuba, SAfr. 107/F3
Mtunzini, SAfr. 107/E3
Mtwara, Tanz. 104/D5
Mtwara (pol. reg.), Tanz. 104/C5
Mu-kawa (riv.), Japan 76/C2
Mu Ko Similan NP, Thai. 78/B4
Mu Ko Surin NP, Thai. 78/B4
Mualama, Moz. 105/G4
Muan, SKor. 73/D5
Muang Hinboun, Laos 78/D2
Muang Khammouan, Laos 78/D2
Muang Khong, Laos 78/D3
Muang Khongxedon, Laos 78/D3
Muang Pak-lay, Laos 78/C2
Muang Pakxan, Laos 78/C2
Muang Sing, Laos 83/H3
Muang Vangviang, Laos 78/C2
Muang Xaignabouri, Laos 78/C2
Muang Xay, Laos 83/H3
Muar, Malay. 80/B3
Muarabungo, Indo. 80/B4
Muari (riv.), Pak. 89/J4
Mubārakpur, India 84/D2
Mubende, Ugan. 104/A2
Mucajaí (riv.), Braz. 150/F3
Much, Ger. 53/G2
Muchinga (mts.), Zam. 105/F3
Muck (isl.), Sc, UK 31/Q8
Muckleshoot Ind. Res., Wa, US 135/C3
Mucojo, Moz. 105/H3
Mucupina (mtn.), Hon. 144/E3
Mucur, Turk. 90/C2
Mucuri (riv.), Braz. 151/K7
Mud Mountain (dam), Wa, US 135/D3
Mud Mountain (lake), Wa, US 135/D3
Mudanjiang, China 71/N3
Mudanya, Turk. 49/J5
Mudau, Ger. 54/C3
Mudbach (riv.), Ger. 54/C3
Muddan (riv.), China 65/N5
Muddas NP, Swe. 37/G2
Muddy Run (res.), Pa, US 138/B4
Müden, Ger. 51/H3
Mudersbach, Ger. 53/G2
Mudgee, Austl. 115/D2
Mudjatik (riv.), Sk, Can. 122/F3
Mudon, Myan. 78/B2
Mudurnu, Turk. 49/K5
Muela (peak), Chile 159/B7
Muerte, Cerro de la (peak), CR 145/F4
Muff, Ire. 34/A1
Mufulira, Zam. 105/E3
Mugardos, Sp. 44/A1
Mugegawa, Japan 77/L4
Mughal Sarai, India 84/D3
Mugi, Japan 77/L4
Mugia, Sp. 44/A1
Muğla, Turk. 90/B2
Muğla (prov.), Turk. 90/B2
Muğla (prov.), Turk. 91/A1
Mugodzharskoye (mts.), Kaz. 87/C3
Muhamdi, India 84/C2
Muḥammad (pt.), Egypt 101/C3
Muhammadābad, India 84/D3
Muhavura (vol.), Rwa. 104/A3
Muhila, Monts (mts.), D.R. Congo 105/E3
Mühlacker, Ger. 54/B5
Mühlbach (riv.), Ger. 54/A2
Mühldorf, Ger. 55/F6
Mühleberg, Swi. 56/D4
Mühlenbeck, Ger. 40/Q6
Mühlhausen, Ger. 55/E4
Mühlheim am Main, Ger. 54/B2
Mühlheim an der Donau, Ger. 57/E1
Mühltroff, Ger. 55/E1
Mühlviertel (reg.), Aus. 41/G4
Muhos, Fin. 60/E2
Muhu (isl.), Est. 60/D4
Muiden, Neth. 50/C4
Muir of Ord, Sc, UK 36/B1
Muir Woods Nat'l Mon., Ca, US 128/B3
Muir Woods Nat'l Mon., Ca, US 135/J11
Muirkirk, Sc, UK 36/B5
Muizon, Fr. 52/C5
Muju, SKor. 73/D4
Mukacheve, Ukr. 41/M4
Mukawa, Japan 76/B2
Mukawwar (isl.), Sudan 101/C3
Mukden, Bol. 156/D3
Mukeriān, India 86/C4
Mukhayyam al Yarmūk, Syria 91/E3
Mukhmās, Isr. 91/G8
Mukinbudin, Austl. 112/C4
Mukō, Japan 77/J6
Mukono, Ugan. 104/B2
Mukoshima (isls.), Japan 116/D2
Muktsar, India 86/C4

Mukwonago, Wi, US 135/P14
Mula, Sp. 44/E3
Mulanje, Malw. 105/G4
Mulchatna (riv.), Ak, US 134/G4
Mulchén, Chile 158/B3
Mulde (riv.), Ger. 40/G3
Mulegé, Mex. 142/C3
Muleshoe, Tx, US 129/G4
Mulhacén, Cerro de (peak), Sp. 44/D4
Mülheim an der Ruhr, Ger. 50/D6
Mulhouse, Fr. 56/D2
Muli (riv.), Indo. 81/J5
Muli Zangzu Zizhixian, China 83/H2
Muling (pass), China 72/D3
Mulkhet (riv.), Turk. 62/D5
Mull (isl.), Sc, UK 31/R8
Mull of Galloway (pt.), Sc, UK 34/D2
Mull of Kintyre (pt.), Sc, UK 34/C1
Mull of Logan (pt.), Sc, UK 34/D2
Mullach Coire Mhic Fhearchair (peak), Sc, UK 36/A1
Mullaghcleevaun (peak), Ire. 34/B5
Mullaghmore (peak), Ire. 34/B2
Mullaittivu, SrL. 82/D6
Mullardoch (lake), Sc, UK 36/A2
Muller (mts.), Indo. 80/D4
Müllheim, Ger. 56/D2
Müllheim, Swi. 57/F2
Mullica (riv.), NJ, US 138/D4
Mullica Hill, NJ, US 138/C4
Mullingar, Ire. 31/Q10
Mullins, SC, US 133/J3
Mullumbimby, Austl. 115/E1
Mulobezi, Zam. 105/E4
Multai, India 84/B5
Multān, Pak. 86/A4
Multnomah (falls), Or, US 126/C4
Mulu (peak), Malay. 80/D3
Mulwala, Austl. 115/C2
Mum Nauk (pt.), Thai. 78/B5
Mumbai (Bombay), India 89/K5
Mumbwa, Zam. 105/E3
Mümling (riv.), Ger. 54/B3
Mumoni (peak), Kenya 104/C3
Mun (riv.), Thai. 83/H4
Muna (isl.), Indo. 116/B5
Muna, Mex. 144/D1
Munamägi (hill), Est. 39/M3
Muñani, Peru 156/D4
Muncar, Indo. 80/D5
Münchberg, Ger. 55/E2
München (Munich), Ger. 55/E6
Münchenstein, Swi. 56/D2
Munchique (peak), Col. 152/B4
Munchique, PN, Col. 152/B4
Münchmünster, Ger. 55/E5
Muncie, In, US 130/C3
Muncy, Pa, US 138/B1
Mundaring, Austl. 112/L6
Munday, Tx, US 129/H4
Mundelein, Il, US 135/Q15
Mundemba, Camr. 103/H5
Münden, Ger. 51/G6
Munderfing, Aus. 55/G6
Munderkingen, Ger. 57/F1
Mundo Novo, Braz. 157/F1
Mundo Novo, Braz. 154/B3
Mundubbera, Austl. 114/C4
Munera, Sp. 44/D3
Mungaoli, India 84/B3
Mungeli, India 84/C4
Munger, India 85/F3
Mungo NP, Austl. 115/B2
Mun'gyŏng, SKor. 73/D4
Munising, Mi, US 127/M4
Munkebo, Den. 38/D4
Munkedal, Swe. 38/D2
Munkfors, Swe. 38/E2
Munku-Sardyk (peak), Rus. 70/H1
Münnerstadt, Ger. 54/D2
Muñoz Gamero (pen.), Chile 157/B7
Munsan, SKor. 73/F6
Munsfield, Ger. 54/D6
Münsingen, Swi. 56/D4
Münsingen, Ger. 54/C4
Munster (reg.), Ire. 31/P10
Münster, Ger. 51/E5
Munster, Ger. 51/H3
Münster, Swi. 57/E5
Münster, Fr. 56/D1
Münster, In, US 135/R16
Münster, Ger. 54/B3
Münster/Osnabrück (int'l arpt.), Ger. 51/E4
Münstereifel, Ger. 53/F2
Münsterhausen, Ger. 54/D6
Münsterland (reg.), Ger. 40/D2
Münstermaifeld, Ger. 53/F2
Muntele Mare (peak), Rom. 41/F2
Muntendam, Neth. 50/D2
Muntok, Indo. 80/C4
Müntschemier, Swi. 56/D4
Münzenberg, Ger. 54/B2
Münzkirchen, Aus. 55/G6
Munzur Vadisi NP, Turk. 62/F5
Muonio, Fin. 37/G2
Muonioälven (riv.), Swe. 37/G1

Muotathal, Swi. 57/E4
Mupa, PN da, Ang. 105/C4
Muping, China 72/E3
Muqdisho (Mogadishu) (cap.), Som. 97/Q7
Muqeibila, Isr. 91/G6
Mur (riv.), Aus. 43/L3
Mura (riv.) Slov.,Hun 48/C2
Muradiye, Turk. 90/E2
Murādnagar, India 86/D5
Murakami, Japan 75/F1
Murallón (peak), Chile 159/B6
Murano, It. 59/F2
Murat (peak), Turk. 62/D5
Muratlı, Turk. 90/E2
Muratlı, Turk. 49/H5
Murayama, Japan 76/B4
Murchison, Austl. 115/C3
Murchison (riv.), Austl. 109/A3
Mustafābād, Pak. 86/B4
Murchison, NZ 117/S11
Murchison (mt.), Austl. 112/C3
Murcia, Sp. 45/E4
Murcia (aut. comm.) Sp. 44/E4
Murderkill (riv.), De, US 138/C6
Murdochville, Qu, Can. 131/H1
Murdock (pt.), Austl. 114/B1
Mürefte, Turk. 49/H5
Mureş (riv.), Rom. 41/F2
Mureş (prov.), Rom. 49/G2
Muret, Fr. 42/D5
Murfreesboro, Ar, US 129/J4
Murg (riv.), Ger. 53/H6
Murgab (riv.), Turk. 87/D5
Murgap (riv.), Trkm. 64/G6
Murgon, Austl. 114/C4
Muri, Swi. 57/E3
Muri bei Bern, Swi. 56/D2
Muria (peak), Indo. 80/D5
Muriaé, Braz. 155/D2
Murias de Paredes, Sp. 44/B1
Murici, Braz. 154/D3
Murīdke, Pak. 86/C4
Müritz (lake), Ger. 40/G2
Murliganj, India 85/F3
Múynoq, Uzb. 63/L4
Murmansk, (int'l arpt.), Rus. 60/G1
Murmansk Oblast, Rus. 37/J1
Murnau, Ger. 55/E6
Muro, Sp. 45/G3
Muro, It. 77/K6
Muro Lucano, It. 46/D2
Murom, Rus. 60/J5
Muroran, Japan 76/B2
Muros (isl.), Indo. 116/B5
Muroto, Japan 74/D4
Muroto-zaki (pt.), Japan 74/D4
Murowana Goślina, Pol. 41/J2
Murphy, NC, US 133/G3
Murphy, Mo, US 137/G9
Murr (riv.), Ger. 54/C5
Murrumarang NP, Austl. 115/D2
Murray (lake), SC, US 133/H3
Murray (riv.), Austl. 109/D4
Murray, Ky, US 130/B4
Murray, Ut, US 137/K12
Murray Bridge, Austl. 113/H5
Murraysburg, SAfr. 106/C3
Murrayville, Austl. 115/B2
Murree, Pak. 86/B3
Murrieta, Ca, US 136/C3
Murrieta Hot Springs, Ca, US 136/C3
Murrumbidgee (riv.), Austl. 109/D4
Murrumburrah, Austl. 115/D2
Murrurundi, Austl. 115/D2
Murshidābād, India 85/G3
Murtala Muhammed (int'l arpt.), Nga. 103/F5
Murtaröl (peak), Swi. 57/G4
Murten, Swi. 56/D4
Murten (lake), Swi. 56/D4
Murtoa, Austl. 115/B3
Murud (peak), Malay. 80/D3
Murupara, NZ 117/T10
Mururoa (isl.), FrPol. 117/M7
Murwāra, India 84/C4
Murwillumbah, Austl. 115/E1
Murzuq (dist.), Libya 97/H3
Mürzzuschlag, Aus. 41/H5
Muş (prov.), Turk. 90/E2
Muş, Turk. 90/E2
Musabeyli, Turk. 91/E1
Musafīrkhāna, India 84/C2
Musala (peak), Bul. 41/F4
Musan, NKor. 73/E1
Musashino (riv.), Japan 77/J2
Muscat, Oman 89/G4
Musconetcong (riv.), NJ, US 138/C2
Muscoot (res.), NY, US 138/C2
Muscoy, Ca, US 136/C2
Musekwapoort (pass), SAfr. 105/C5
Museum of Flight, Wa, US 135/C2
Musgrave (ranges), Austl. 109/D3
Musgrave (range), Austl. 116/D2
Musgrave Harbour, Nf, Can. 131/L1
Mushābani, India 85/F4

Mushie, D.R. Congo 96/J8
Mushin, Nga. 103/F5
Musi (riv.), Indo. 80/B4
Musile di Piave, It. 59/F1
Musinga (peak), Col. 152/B3
Muskego, Wi, US 135/P14
Muskegon, Mi, US 130/C3
Muskegon (riv.), Mi, US 130/C3
Muskingum (riv.), Oh, US 130/D4
Muskoka (lake), Can. 130/E2
Musoma, Tanz. 104/B3
Musquaro (riv.), Can. 131/J1
Mussau (isl.), PNG 116/D5
Musselburgh (riv.), Sc, UK 36/C5
Musselshell (riv.), Mt, US 124/F2
Mussomeli, It. 46/C4
Musson, Belg. 53/E4
Mustafakemalpaşa, Turk. 62/D4
Müstair, Swi. 57/G4
Mustang, Ok, US 137/M15
Musters (lake), Arg. 158/C5
Musu-dan (pt.), NKor. 73/F3
Musún (mtn.), Nic. 144/E3
Muşutişte, Yugo. 47/G1
Muswellbrook, Austl. 115/D2
Müt, Egypt 101/B3
Mut, Turk. 90/C2
Mutá, Ponta do (pt.), Braz. 154/C4
Mutare, Zim. 105/F4
Muthill, Sc, UK 36/C4
Mutis (peak), Indo. 81/F5
Mutsamudu, Com. 107/H6
Mutsu (bay), Japan 76/B3
Mutsu, Japan 76/B3
Mutsuzawa, Japan 77/E3
Muttenz, Swi. 56/D2
Mutters, Aus. 57/H3
Mutterstadt, Ger. 54/B4
Muttler (peak), Swi. 57/G4
Muttonville, Mi, US 135/F7
Mutum, Braz. 155/D1
Mutzig, Fr. 52/D2
Müynoq, Uzb. 63/L4
Muzaffargarh, Pak. 86/A4
Muzaffarnagar, India 86/D5
Muzaffarpur, India 85/F3
Muzamba, Braz. 211/G6
Muzon (cape), Ak, US 134/M4
Muztag (peak), China 70/D4
Muztagata (peak), China 87/G5
Muzzana del Turgnano, It. 59/G1
Mwadui, Tanz. 104/B3
Mwanza (cape), Kenya 104/D3
Mwanza (pol. reg.), Tanz. 104/B3
Mwanza, Tanz. 104/B3
Mweelrea (peak), Ire. 31/P10
Mweka, D.R. Congo 105/D1
Mwene-Ditu, D.R. Congo 105/D2
Mwense, Zam. 104/A5
Mweru (lake), D.R. Congo 93/E5
Mweru-Wantipa NP, Zam. 104/A5
Mwesi (riv.), Tanz. 104/A4
Mwinilunga, Zam. 105/D3
My Son Temples (ruin), Viet. 78/E3
My Tho, Viet. 78/D4
Myall Lakes NP, Austl. 115/E2
Myanaung, Myan. 83/G4
Myanmar (Burma) (ctry.) 67/J7
Myebon, Myan. 83/F3
Myerstown, Pa, US 138/B3
Myggenäs, Swe. 38/D2
Myingyan, Myan. 83/G3
Myitkyinā, Myan. 83/G2
Myjava, Slvk. 41/J4
Mykolayiv, Ukr. 49/L2
Mykolayiv (int'l arpt.), Ukr. 49/L2
Mykolayivs'ka (obl.), Ukr. 62/D3
Mylau, Ger. 55/F1
Mymensingh (pol. reg.), China 85/F1
Mynämäki, Fin. 39/J1
Mynydd Eppynt (mts.), Wal, UK 32/C2
Mynydd Pencarreg (peak), Wal, UK 32/B2
Mynydd Preseli (mtn.), Wal, UK 32/B3
Myōgi, Japan 77/J1
Myohaung, Myan. 83/F3
Myōkō-san (peak), Japan 75/F2
Myrhorod, Ukr. 62/E2
Myrtle Beach, SC, US 133/J3
Myrtle Creek, Or, US 126/C5
Myrtleford, Austl. 115/C3
Mysen, Nor. 38/D2
Myślenice, Pol. 41/K4
Myślibórz, Pol. 41/H2
Myslivna (peak), Czh. 55/H5
Mysore, India 85/K6
Mystery Bay Rec. Area, Wa, US 135/B1
Mystic Island, NJ, US 138/D4
Mystic Harbour, Nf, Can. 131/L1
Myszków, Pol. 41/K3
Mytishchi, Rus. 61/W9

Mže (riv.), Czh. 40/G4
Mzimba, Malw. 104/B5
Mzuzu, Malw. 104/B5

N

Na (riv.), Viet. 78/C1
Naab (riv.), Ger. 43/J2
Naaldwijk, Neth. 50/B5
Naalehu, Hi, US 124/U11
Naama, Alg. 99/F2
Naantali, Fin. 39/K1
Naarden, Neth. 50/C4
Naarn im Machlande, Aus. 55/H6
Nababeep, SAfr. 106/B3
Nabari, Japan 77/K6
Nabari (riv.), Japan 77/K6
Nabberu (lake), Austl. 115/D5
Nabburg, Ger. 55/F4
Naberezhnye Chelny, Rus. 61/M5
Nabha, India 86/D4
Nabiac, Austl. 115/E2
Nabisipi (riv.), Can. 131/J1
Nabón, Ecu. 156/B1
Nabq, Tun. 79/D5
Nābul, Tun. 46/B4
Nābul (gov.), Tun. 46/B4
Nacala, Moz. 105/H3
Nacaome, Hon. 144/E3
Nácori Chico, Mex. 142/C2
Nacozari de García, Mex. 142/C2
Nadbai, India 84/A2
Nadder (riv.), Eng, UK 32/D4
Nadiād, India 89/K4
Nādlac, Rom. 48/E2
Nador (prov.), Mor. 100/C2
Nador, Mor. 100/C2
Nadur, Malta 46/L6
Naejang-san NP, SKor. 73/D5
Näfels, Swi. 57/F3
Nafūsah, Jabal (mts.), Libya 99/H3
Naga, Phil. 79/D5
Nagagami (riv.), Can. 130/C1
Nagahama, Japan 74/C4
Nagahama, Japan 77/K5
Nagai, Japan 75/G1
Nagaizumi, Japan 77/B3
Nagano, Japan 75/F2
Nagano (pref.), Japan 75/E3
Naganuma, Japan 76/B2
Nagaokakyō, Japan 77/J6
Nagaon (Nowgong), India 83/F2
Nagar, India 84/A2
Nagara (riv.), Japan 75/E3
Nagārbāri, India 85/H2
Nāgārjuna Sāgar (res.), India 82/C4
Nagarote, Nic. 140/D5
Nagarzê, China 85/H1
Nagas (pt.), Can. 134/M5
Nagasaka, Japan 77/A2
Nagasaki (int'l arpt.), Japan 74/A4
Nagasaki (pref.), Japan 74/A4
Nagasaki Peace, Japan 74/A4
Nagashima, Japan 77/L5
Nagato, Japan 74/B3
Nagato, Japan 77/C1
Nagaur, India 89/K3
Nāgercoil, India 82/C6
Nagina, India 84/B1
Nago, Japan 75/J7
Nago-Torbole, It. 57/G6
Nagold (riv.), Ger. 54/B5
Nagold, Ger. 54/B5
Nagorno-Karabakh (prov.), Azer. 63/H5
Nagoya (int'l arpt.), Ukr. 49/L2
Nagoya Castle, Japan 77/L5
Nagpula (pass), China 85/F1
Nagqu, Japan 82/C3
Nagriamel, Japan 77/L5
Nags Head, NC, US 133/K3
Naguri, Japan 77/D1
Nagu-Milic (peak), Hun. 41/L4
Nagyatád, Hun. 40/D3
Nagyecsed, Hun. 41/M5
Nagyhalász, Hun. 41/L4
Nagykáta, Hun. 48/D2
Nagykörös, Hun. 48/E2
Nagyléta, Hun. 41/L4
Nahanni NP, NW, Can. 122/D2
Nahāvand, Iran 88/F2
Nagybarwon (peak), China 85/F1
NahJ Lel Shillo (riv.), Isr.,WBnk 91/G7
Nāhan, India 86/D4
Nahenaud (riv.), Micr. 116/F4
Nahendi, Iran 88/G2
Nahendi Soreq (riv.), Isr. 91/F8
Nahouri (prov.), Burk. 103/E3
Nahr 'Atbarah (riv.), Sudan 101/B4
Nahr Mufjir (riv.), Isr.,WBnk 91/G7

Nahr Ouassel (riv.), Alg. 100/F5
Nahuel Huapi (lake), Arg. 147/B7
Nahuel Huapi, PN, Arg. 157/B5
Nahuel Huapi, PN, Arg. 158/C4
Nahuelbuta, PN, Chile 158/B3
Naica, Mex. 142/D3
Naihāti, India 85/G4
Naila, Ger. 55/E2
Naiman Qi, China 72/E2
Nā'īn, Iran 88/F2
Nain, Nf, Can. 123/K3
Nainital, India 84/B1
Naintré, Fr. 42/D3
Nairn, Sc, UK 36/B2
Nairn, Austl. 113/M9
Nairobi (cap.), Kenya 104/C3
Nairobi NP, Kenya 104/C3
Naivasha, Kenya 104/C3
Najafābād, Iran 88/F2
Nájera, Sp. 44/D1
Najibabad, India 83/G3
Najin, NKor. 71/P3
Naju, SKor. 73/D5
Naka (riv.), Japan 74/D4
Naka, Japan 77/G5
Nakadōri (isl.), Japan 74/A4
Nakamichi, Japan 77/C3
Nakaminato, Japan 75/G2
Nakamura, Japan 74/C4
Nakano (lag.), Japan 74/C3
Nakasato, Japan 76/B3
Nakashibetsu, Japan 76/D2
Nakasongola, Ugan. 104/B2
Nakatane, Japan 75/L5
Nakatomi, Japan 77/A3
Nakatsu, Japan 74/B4
Nakatsugawa, Japan 75/E3
Nakhodka, Rus. 71/P4
Nakhon Nayok, Thai. 78/C3
Nakhon Pathom, Thai. 78/C3
Nakhon Phanom, Thai. 78/D2
Nakhon Ratchasima, Thai. 78/C3
Nakhon Sawan, Thai. 78/C3
Nakhon Si Thammarat, Thai. 78/B4
Nakina, Japan 77/J6
Nakkila, Fin. 39/J1
Naknek, Ak, US 134/G4
Nakodar, India 86/C4
Nakonde, Zam. 104/B5
Naksan-sa, SKor. 73/E3
Nakskov, Den. 38/D4
Naktong (riv.), SKor. 74/A3
Nakūr, India 86/D5
Nakuru, Kenya 104/C3
Nakusp, BC, Can. 126/D3
Nāl (riv.), Pak. 89/J3
Nalayh, Mong. 70/J2
Nalbach, Ger. 53/F4
Nālbāri, India 85/H2
Nalchik (int'l arpt.), Rus. 63/G4
Nālchik, Rus. 63/G4
Nalgonda, India 82/C4
Nālhāti, India 85/F3
Naliya, India 89/J4
Nalihan, Turk. 49/K5
Nallamala (riv.), India 82/C4
Nālūt, Libya 99/H3
Nam (riv.), NKor. 73/D3
Nam Dinh, Viet. 83/J3
Nam Ngum NP, Thai. 78/C2
Nam Un (res.), Thai. 78/D2
Namakzār-e Shadād (salt pan), Iran 89/G2
Namangan (pol. reg.), Uzb. 87/F4
Namangan, Uzb. 87/F4
Namanqualand (reg.), SAfr. 106/B3
Namaripi (cape), Indo. 81/J4
Namasagali, Ugan. 104/B2
Namatanai, PNG 116/F5
Namborn, Ger. 53/F4
Nambour, Austl. 114/D4
Nambu, Japan 77/A3
Nāmdo (isl.), SKor. 73/D5
Namhae, SKor. 73/D5
Namib (des.), Namb. 93/D6
Namibe, Ang. 105/B3
Namibia (ctry.) 93/D7
Namie, Japan 77/G2
Namioka, Japan 76/B3
Namja (pass), Nepal 82/D2
Namjagbarwa (peak), China 85/F1
Namling, China 82/E2
Namloser Wetterspitze (peak), Aus. 57/G3
Namoku, Japan 77/L4
Namoi (riv.), Austl. 109/D4
Namonuito (isl.), Micr. 116/F4
Namorik (isl.), Mrsh. 116/F4

Namp'o, NKor. 73/C3
Nampula, Moz. 105/G4
Namsē (pass), China 82/D2
Namsos, Nor. 37/D2
Namu (isl.), Mrsh. 116/F4
Namur, Belg. 53/D3
Namwŏn, SKor. 73/D5
Namysłów, Pol. 41/J3
Nan (riv.), Thai. 83/H4
Nan, Thai. 78/C2
Nanae, Japan 76/B3
Nanaimo, BC, Can. 126/C3
Nanakuli, Hi, US 124/V13
Nanam, NKor. 73/E2
Nanango, Austl. 114/D4
Nanao, Japan 75/E2
Nanatsu, India 86/D5
Nanbu, Japan 77/A3
Nancagua, Chile 158/C2
Nanchang, China 79/C2
Nancheng, China 79/C2
Nancheng, China 79/C2
Nanchong, China 70/J5
Nancy, Fr. 53/F6
Nanda Devi (peak), India 70/D5
Nanded, India 82/C4
Nariño (dept.), Col. 152/B4
Narita (int'l arpt.), Japan 75/G3
Narita, Japan 77/D2
Nariz (peak), Chile 159/C7
Narli, It. 46/C1
Narni, It. 46/C1
Narodnaya (peak), Rus. 61/P2
Narok, Kenya 104/B3
Narón, Sp. 44/A1
Narooma, Austl. 115/D3
Nārowāl, Pak. 86/C3
Nærøy, Nor. 37/D2
Naushahra, India 86/C3
Naushahra Virkhan, Pak. 86/B4
Nauta, Peru 156/C2
Nautla, Mex. 143/N6
Nauvo (Nagu), Fin. 39/J1
Nava, Mex. 132/C4
Nava, Colle di (pass), It. 58/A4
Nava del Rey, Sp. 44/C2
Navajo (res.), NM, US 128/F3
Navajo Nat'l Mon., Az, US 128/E3
Navalcarnero, Sp. 45/M9
Navalmoral de la Mata, Sp. 44/C3
Navan (bay), Sc, UK 44/C3
Narva, Est. 39/N2
Narva (riv.), Est.Rus. 60/E4
Narva (bay), Sc, UK 39/M2
Navapolatsk, Bela. 39/N4
Navarin (cape), Rus. 65/T3
Navarino (isl.), Chile 157/C8
Navarra (aut. comm.), Sp. 44/D1
Navarro, Arg. 159/J11
Navarro, Sp. 45/F2
Nâsâud, Rom. 49/G2
Navas de San Juan, Sp. 44/D3
Navasota (riv.), Tx, US 143/F7
Navassa (isl.), Myan. 145/H2
Navax (pt.), Eng, UK 32/A6
Navene, Fr. 58/D1
Naver, It. 56/C2
Navia, Sp. 44/B1
Navia (riv.), Sp. 44/B1
Navidad, Chile 158/N8
Navidad, Ok, US 137/M14
Navarra, Braz. 157/F1
Năvodari, Rom. 49/J3
Navojoa, Mex. 142/C3
Navolato, Mex. 142/D3
Navpaktos, Gre. 47/G3
Návplion, Gre. 47/H4
Navsāri, India 89/K4
Navy Board (inlet), Can. 123/H1
Navy Yard City, Wa, US 135/B2
Nawābganj, India 84/B1
Nawābganj, India 84/C2
Nawābganj, Bang. 85/G3
Nawābshāh, Pak. 89/J3
Nawāda, India 85/E3
Nawān Jandānwāla, Pak. 86/A3
Nawāshahr, India 86/D4
Nawāshahr, Pak. 86/B2
Nāwshar, It. 87/E4
Nawoiy (pol. reg.), Uzb. 87/D4
Nayoro, Japan 76/C1
Nayramdīn (peak), Mong. 70/E2
Nazyatash (pass), Taj. 87/F5
Nazaré, Braz. 154/C4
Nazaré do Piauí, Braz. 154/B2
Nazaré Paulista, Braz. 211/G8
Nazareth, Belg. 52/C2
Nazas (riv.), Mex. 142/D3
Nazas, Mex. 142/D3
Nazca, Peru 156/C4
Nazca Ridge, 75/K6
Naze, The (pt.), Eng, UK 33/H3
Nazerat (Nazareth), Isr. 91/G6
Nazilli, Turk. 90/B2
Nazret, Eth. 97/N6
Nazyvayevsk, Rus. 87/F1
Nchelenge, Zam. 104/A5

National Museum, Mona. 58/J8
National Security Agency, Md, US 138/B5
Natitingou, Ben. 103/F4
Natl, Jor. 91/D4
Natron (lake), Tanz. 104/B3
Natternbach, Aus. 55/G6
Natron, Ger. 54/D5
Narashino, Japan 77/E2
Nathiawat, Thai. 78/C5
Nättraby, Swe. 38/F3
Natuna (isls.), Indo. 67/K9
Natural Bridge Caverns, Tx, US 137/U20
Natural Bridges Nat'l Mon., Ut, US 128/E3
Naturaliste (cape), Austl. 115/C4
Naturaliste (chan.), Austl. 112/B3
Naturaliste (cape), Austl. 112/B5
Naturno (Naturns), It. 57/G4
Naturns (Naturno), It. 43/J3
Naucalpan, Mex. 143/Q10
Naucelle, Fr. 42/E4
Nauders, Aus. 57/G4
Naudesnek (pass), SAfr. 106/E3
Nauen, Ger. 40/F6
Naugachhia, India 85/F3
Naugaon Sādāt, India 84/B1
Nauhcampatépetl (vol.), Mex. 143/M7
Nauheim, Ger. 54/B3
Naumburg, Ger. 51/G6
Naumburg, Ger. 40/F3
Naumburg, Ger. 53/G3
Naʿūr, Jor. 91/D4
Nauru (ctry.) 116/F5
Nāushahra, India 86/C3
Naushahra Virkhan, Pak. 86/B4

Ncheu, Malw. 105/F3
Ndalatando, Ang. 105/B2
Ndali, Ben. 103/F4
Ndele, CAfr. 97/K6
Ndende (isl.), Sol. 116/F6
N'djamena (cap.), Chad 96/J5
Ndola, Zam. 105/E3
Ndrhamcha (lake), Mrta. 102/B2
Né (riv.), Fr. 42/C4
Néa Alikarnassós, Gre. 47/J5
Néa Ankhíalos, Gre. 47/H3
Néa Artáki, Gre. 47/H3
Néa Ionía, Gre. 47/H3
Néa Ionía, Gre. 47/N8
Néa Kallikrátia, Gre. 47/H4
Néa Kíos, Gre. 47/H4
Néa Mikhanióna, Gre. 47/H2
Néa Moudhaniá, Gre. 47/H2
Néa Potídhaia, Gre. 47/H2
Néa Tríglia, Gre. 47/H2
Néa Zíkhni, Gre. 47/H2
Neagh (lake), NI, UK 34/B2
Neale (lake), Austl. 109/C3
Neales (riv.), Austl. 113/G3
Neamt (prov.), Rom. 49/H2
Neaoophli-le-Château, Fr. 30/H5
Neápolis, Gre. 47/H4
Neápolis, Gre. 47/G2
Neápolis, Gre. 47/J5
Near (isls.), US 134/A5
Neath, Wal, UK 32/C3
Neath (riv.), Wal, UK 32/C3
Neavitt, Md, US 138/B6
Nebbi, Ugan. 104/A2
Nebel-Horn (peak), Ger. 57/G3
Nebikon, Swi. 56/D3
Nebitdag, Trkm. 63/K5
Neblina (peak), Braz. 153/E4
Nebo (mt.), Austl. 114/E6
Nebrodi (mts.), It. 46/C4
Nechako (riv.), BC, Can. 122/D3
Nechisar NP, Eth. 97/N6
Nechranice (res.), Czh. 55/G2
Neckar (riv.), Ger. 40/D4
Neckarbischofsheim, Ger. 54/B4
Neckargemünd, Ger. 54/B4
Neckarsteinach, Ger. 54/B4
Neckarsulm, Ger. 54/C4
Necker (isl.), Hi, US 117/J2
Necochea, Arg. 158/F3
Necocli, Col. 152/B2
Necrópoli (ruin), It. 46/C1
Neda, Sp. 44/A1
Nedelino, Bul. 47/J2
Nedelišce, Cro. 43/M3
Nederland, Tx, US 129/G5
Nederland, Co, US 137/A3
Nederweert, Neth. 50/C6
Neede, Neth. 50/D4
Needles, Ca, US 128/D4
Needles, The, Eng, UK 33/E5
Needmore, Ok, US 137/N15
Neepawa, Mb, Can. 127/J3
Neerabup NP, Austl. 112/K6
Neerpelt, Belg. 50/C6
Neetze (riv.), Ger. 51/H2
Neetze (riv.), Ger. 51/H2
Neffelbach (riv.), Ger. 53/F2
Neftekamsk, Rus. 61/M4
Nefud (des.), SAr. 67/B7
Nefyn, Wal, UK 34/D6
Negёlё, Eth. 97/N6
Negev (reg.), Isr. 90/C4
Negoiu (peak), Rom. 49/G3
Negombo, SrL. 82/C6
Negotin, Yugo. 48/F3
Negotino, Macd. 47/H2
Negra (pt.), Peru 156/A2
Negra (range), Braz. 154/A3
Negra (pt.), Belz. 144/D2
Negrais (cape), Myan. 83/F4
Negreira, Sp. 44/A1
Negreşti, Rom. 49/H2
Negritos, Peru 156/A2
Negro (riv.), Uru. 157/E3
Negro (riv.), Arg. 157/D5
Negro (peak), Arg. 158/C3
Negros (isl.), Phil. 67/M9
Nehbandān, Iran 89/H2
Nei Monggol (aut. reg.), China 71/K3
Nei Monggol (plat.), China 71/K3
Neiafu, Tonga 117/H6
Neiba, DRep. 141/G4
Neiba (mts.), DRep. 145/J2
Neiderösterreich (prov.), Aus. 43/L2
Neige, Crêt de la (peak), Fr. 56/B5
Neihuang, China 72/C4
Neijiang, China 70/J6
Neilston, Sc, UK 36/B5
Neiqiu, China 72/C3
Neisse (riv.), Ger. 41/H3
Neiva, Col. 152/C4
Neixiang, China 72/B4
Nejanilini (lake), Mb, Can. 122/G3
Nejdek, Czh. 55/F2
Nejrab (int'l arpt.), Syria 91/E1
Nek'emtё, Eth. 97/N6
Nekso, Den. 38/F4
Nelas, Port. 44/B2
Nelidovo, Rus. 60/G4
Nellingen, Ger. 54/C5
Nellore, India 82/C5
Nelson (cape), Austl. 115/B3

Nelson (isl.), Ak, US 134/E3
Nelson (str.), Nelson, BC, Can. 126/D3
Nelson, NZ 117/S11
Nelson (riv.), Mb, Can. 122/G3
Nelson, Eng, UK 35/F4
Nelson-Atkins Museum of Fine Art, Mo, US 135/H2
Nelson Bay, Austl. 115/E2
Nelson Lagoon, Ak, US 134/F4
Nelson Lakes NP, NZ 117/S11
Nelspruit, SAfr. 105/F6
Néma, Mrta. 102/D2
Neman (riv.), Rus. 41/M1
Nembro, It. 58/C1
Nemea, Gre. 47/H4
Nemingha, Austl. 115/D1
Nemira (peak), Rom. 49/H2
Nemours, Fr. 42/E2
Nemunas (riv.), Lith. 60/D5
Nemuro (pen.), Japan 76/D2
Nemuro, Japan 76/D2
Nenjiang, China 71/N2
Nen (riv.), China 67/M5
Nenagh, Ire. 31/P10
Nenana, Ak, US 134/J3
Nendaz, Swi. 57/E2
Nene (riv.), Eng, UK 35/G6
Nenetsia Aut. Okrug, Rus. 61/L2
Nenjiang, China 71/N2
Nenthead, Eng, UK 35/F3
Nentershausen, Ger. 51/G6
Nentershausen, Ger. 53/G3
Nenzing, Aus. 57/F3
Neo Volcanica, Cordillera (mts.), Mex. 143/Q10
Néon Petritsíon, Gre. 47/H2
Neoria Husainpur, India 84/B1
Néos Marmarás, Gre. 47/H2
Neosho (riv.), US 125/G4
Neosho, Mo, US 125/H5
Nepal (ctry.) 67/H7
Nepālganj, Nepal 84/C1
Nepean, On, Can. 130/F2
Nepean (riv.), Austl. 114/C4
Nepeña, Peru 156/B3
Nepessing (lake), Mi, US 138/E3
Nephi, Ut, US 128/E3
Nepisiguit (riv.), Can. 131/H2
Nepomuk, Czh. 55/G4
Neptune City, NJ, US 138/D3
Nera (riv.), It. 43/K5
Nérac, Fr. 42/D4
Neratovice, Czh. 55/H3
Nerekhta, Rus. 60/J4
Neresheim, Ger. 54/D5
Neretva (riv.), Bosn. 46/D4
Neris (riv.), Lith. 60/E5
Nerja, Sp. 44/D4
Nermete (pt.), Peru 156/A2
Nerokoúros, Gre. 47/J5
Nerone (peak), It. 59/F5
Nerpio, Sp. 44/D3
Nersingen, Ger. 54/D6
Nerva, Sp. 44/B4
Nervesa della Battaglia, It. 59/F1
Nerviano, It. 58/B1
Nes, Neth. 50/C2
Nes, Nor. 38/D1
Nes Ziyyona, Isr. 91/F8
Nesbyen, Nor. 38/C1
Nesebŭr, Bul. 47/K1
Nesher, Isr. 91/G7
Neskaupstadhur, Ice. 37/Q6
Nesle, Fr. 52/B5
Nesles-la-Vallée, Fr. 30/J4
Nesquehoning, Pa, US 138/C2
Ness (riv.), Sc, UK 36/B2
Ness (lake), Sc, UK 36/B2
Nesselrode (mt.), Ak, US 134/M4
Nesselwang, Ger. 57/G2
Nesslau, Swi. 57/F3
Neston, Eng, UK 35/E5
Nestórion, Gre. 47/G2
Néstos (riv.), Gre. 49/G5
Netanya, Isr. 91/F7
Netarhat, India 85/E4
Netcong, NJ, US 138/D2
Nethe (riv.), Ger. 51/G5
Netherlands (ctry.) 27/E2
Netherlands Antilles (dpcy.), Neth. 119/L8
Netolice, Czh. 55/H4
Netphen, Ger. 53/H2
Netstal, Swi. 57/F3
Nette (riv.), Ger. 50/D6
Nettersheim, Ger. 53/F3
Nettetal, Ger. 50/D5
Nettilling (lake), NW, Can. 123/J2
Nettuno, It. 46/C2
Netzschkau, Ger. 55/F1
Neu Darchau, Ger. 51/H2
Neu-Isenburg, Ger. 54/B2
Neu-Ulm, Ger. 54/D6
Neu Zittau, Ger. 40/Q7
Neubrandenburg, Ger. 41/H3
Neubulach, Ger. 54/B5
Neuburg an der Donau, Ger. 54/E5
Neuburg an der Kammel, Ger. 54/E5
Neuchâtel, Swi. 56/C4
Neuchâtel (canton), Swi. 56/C4
Neuchâtel, Lac de (lake), Swi. 43/G3
Neuenbürg, Ger. 54/B5
Neuenburg am Rhein, Ger. 56/D2

Neuendettelsau, Ger. 54/D4
Neuenhagen, Ger. 40/Q6
Neuenhaus, Ger. 50/D3
Neuenkirchen, Ger. 51/F3
Neuenkirchen, Ger. 51/F3
Neuenkirchen, Ger. 51/E6
Neuenrade, Ger. 51/E6
Neuenstadt am Kocher, Ger. 54/C4
Neuenstein, Ger. 54/C4
Neuerburg, Ger. 53/F3
Neuf-Brisach, Fr. 56/D1
Neufahrn bei Freising, Ger. 55/E6
Neufchâteau, Fr. 56/B1
Neufchâteau, Belg. 53/E4
Neufchâtel-en-Bray, Fr. 42/D2
Neufchâtel-Hardelot, Fr. 30/M4
Neufchelles, Fr. 30/M4
Neufmanil, Fr. 53/D4
Neufmoutiers-en-Brie, Fr. 30/L5
Neuhaus am Inn, Ger. 55/G6
Neuhaus am Rennweg, Ger. 54/E1
Neuhaus-Schiersnitz, Ger. 54/E2
Neuhäusel, Ger. 53/G3
Neuhausen am Rheinfall, Swi. 57/E2
Neuhof, Ger. 54/C2
Neuhof an der Zenn, Ger. 54/D4
Neuhofen, Ger. 54/B4
Neuhofen an der Krems, Aus. 55/H6
Neuilly-en-Thelle, Fr. 52/B5
Neuilly-L'Évêque, Fr. 56/B2
Neuilly-sur-Marne, Fr. 30/K5
Neuilly-sur-Seine, Fr. 30/J5
Neukirchen, Ger. 54/E2
Neukirchen, Ger. 51/H5
Neukirchen, Ger. 53/G5
Neukirchen, Ger. 53/G5
Neukirchen-Seelscheid, Ger. 53/G2
Neukirchen vorm Wald, Ger. 55/G5
Neumarkt (Enga), It. 57/H5
Neumarkt im Mühlkreis, Aus. 55/H6
Neumarkt in der Oberpfalz, Ger. 55/F4
Neumarkt-Sankt Veit, Ger. 55/F6
Neumünster, Ger. 38/C4
Neunkirch, Swi. 57/E2
Neunkirchen, Aus. 43/M3
Neunkirchen, Ger. 54/E2
Neunkirchen, Ger. 53/G5
Neunkirchen, Ger. 53/G5
Neunkirchen-Seelscheid, Ger. 55/G4
Neupotz, Ger. 54/B4
Neuquén (riv.), Arg. 157/C4
Neuquén (prov.), Arg. 158/C3
Neuquén, Arg. 158/C3
Neuruppin, Ger. 40/G2
Neusäss, Ger. 54/D6
Neuse (riv.), NC, US 133/J3
Neusiedl am See, Aus. 43/M3
Neusiedler (lake), Aus. 41/J5
Neusiedler See (lake), Aus. 43/M3
Neuss, Ger. 50/D6
Neustadt am Rübenberge, Ger. 51/F4
Neustadt an der Aisch, Ger. 54/D4
Neustadt an der Donau, Ger. 55/E5
Neustadt an der Waldnaab, Ger. 55/F4
Neustadt an der Weinstrasse, Ger. 54/B4
Neustadt bei Coburg, Ger. 54/E2
Neustadt in Holstein, Ger. 38/D4
Neustift im Stubaital, Aus. 57/H3
Neustrelitz, Ger. 40/G2
Neutraubling, Ger. 55/F5
Neuves-Maisons, Fr. 56/C1
Neuvic, Fr. 42/D4
Neuville-sur-Saône, Fr. 56/A6
Neuwied, Ger. 53/G3
Neuzelle, Ger. 41/H2
Nevada, Mo, US 129/J3
Nevada (mts.), Col. 145/H4
Nevada (state), US 124/C4
Nevada, Sierra (mts.), Sp. 44/D4
Nevado de Colima PN, Mex. 142/D5
Nevado de Toluca PN, Mex. 143/K7
Nevado del Huila PN, Col. 150/C3
Nevado, Sierra del (mts.), Arg. 158/C3
Nevel', Rus. 39/N3
Nevele, Belg. 52/C1
Nevel'sk, Rus. 61/R5
Nevers, Fr. 42/E3
Nevesinje, Bosn. 46/F1
Nevinnomyssk, Rus. 61/H6
Nevis (peak), StK. 141/N8
Nevis (isl.), UK 141/J4
Nevşehir, Turk. 59/G5
Nevşehir (prov.), Turk. 90/C2
New (riv.), Az, US 137/R18
New Albany, In, US 130/C4
New Albany, Ms, US 133/F3
New Amsterdam, Guy. 153/G3
New Ancholme (riv.), Eng, UK 35/H4
New Athens, Il, US 137/H9
New Baltimore, Mi, US 135/G6
New Bataan, Phil. 79/E6

New Bedford, Ma, US 131/G3
New Berlin, Tx, US 137/U21
New Berlin, Pa, US 138/B2
New Berlin, Wi, US 135/P14
New Berlinville, Pa, US 138/C3
New Bern, NC, US 133/J3
New Braunfels, Tx, US 137/U20
New Britain, Ct, US 131/F3
New Britain (isl.), PNG 116/D5
New Brunswick (prov.), Can. 123/K4
New Brunswick, NJ, US 131/G2
New Buffalo, Mi, US 138/B3
New Buildings, NI, UK 34/A2
New Caledonia (isl.), NCal. 116/F7
New Caledonia (terr.), Fr. 116/F6
New Canaan, Ct, US 139/M7
New Castle, In, US 130/C4
New Castle, Pa, US 130/D3
New Castle, De, US 138/C4
New Castle (co.), De, US 138/C5
New Chicago, Pa, US 138/B1
New City, NY, US 139/K7
New Columbia, Pa, US 138/B1
New Columbus, Pa, US 138/B1
New Cumberland, Pa, US 138/B3
New Cumnock, Sc, UK 36/B6
New Delhi (cap.), India 86/D5
New Denver, BC, Can. 126/D3
New Egypt, NJ, US 138/D3
New England NP, Austl. 115/E1
New Freedom, Pa, US 138/B4
New Galloway, Sc, UK 34/D1
New Georgia (isls.), Sol. 116/E5
New Georgia (sound), Sol. 116/E5
New Yam, Isr. 91/F6
Newell, Ger. 53/F4
Newell, Austl. 114/B2
Newellton, La, US 129/K4
Newenham (cape), Can.,US 131/N6
New Gretna, NJ, US 138/D4
New Guinea (isl.), PNG 67/N10
New Hampshire (state), US 125/M3
New Hanover, SAfr. 107/E3
New Hanover, Il, US 137/G9
New Hanover (isl.), PNG 116/D5
New Haven, Ct, US 131/F3
New Haven, Ak, US 134/H4
New Haven, Mi, US 135/G6
New Haven (bor.), Eng, UK 30/D2
New Hebrides (isls.), Van. 116/F6
New Holland, Pa, US 138/B3
New Hope, Pa, US 138/D3
New Hyde Park, NY, US 139/L9
New Iberia, La, US 129/K5
New Ireland (isl.), PNG 116/E5
New Jersey (state), US 125/M3
New Kensington, Pa, US 130/E3
New Kowloon, China 71/U10
New Lenox, Il, US 135/Q16
New Lisbon, NJ, US 138/D4
New Liskeard, On, Can. 130/E2
New London, Ct, US 131/F3
New Madrid, Mo, US 129/K3
New Market, Md, US 138/A5
New Meadows, Id, US 126/D4
New Mexico (state), US 124/E5
New Milford, NJ, US 139/J8
New Mills, Eng, UK 35/F5
New Norfolk, Austl. 115/C4
New Orleans, La, US 137/P17
New Orleans (Moisant Field), La, US 137/P17
New Oxford, Pa, US 138/A4
New Philadelphia, Oh, US 130/D3
New Philadelphia, Pa, US 138/B2
New Pitsligo, Sc, UK 36/D1
New Plymouth, NZ 117/S10
New Port Richey, Fl, US 133/H4
New Providence (isl.), Bahm. 141/F3
New Providence, NJ, US 139/H9
New Richmond, Qu, Can. 131/H1
New River (mts.), Az, US 137/R18
New River, Az, US 137/R18
New Rochelle, NY, US 139/K8
New Rockford, ND, US 127/J4
New Romney, Eng, UK 33/G5
New Ross, Ire. 31/Q10
New Rossington, Eng, UK 35/H5
New Sarpy, La, US 137/P17
New Schwabenland (phys. reg.), Ant. 160/Z

New Scone, Sc, UK 36/C4
New Siberian (isls.), Rus. 67/N2
New Smyrna Beach, Fl, US 133/H4
New South Wales, Austl. 115/D1
New South Wales (state), Austl. 109/D4
New Stuyahok, Ak, US 134/G4
New Town, ND, US 127/H4
New Tripoli, Pa, US 138/C2
New Ulm, Mn, US 127/K4
New Waterford, NS, Can. 131/K2
New Westminster, BC, Can. 126/C3
New Windsor, Md, US 138/A5
New York (state), US 125/L3
New York, NY, US 139/K9
New York, Eng, UK 61/W9
New Zealand (ctry.) 117/R10
Ngabang, Indo. 80/C3
Ngabordamlu (cape), Indo. 81/H5
Ngabu, Malw. 105/F4
Ngami (lake), Bots. 105/D5
Ngamring, China 85/F1
Nganda (peak), Malw. 104/D5
Ngangerabeli (plain), Kenya 104/D3
Ngaoundéré, Camr. 96/H6
Ngarkat Conservation Park, Austl. 113/J5
Ngatik (isl.), Micr. 116/E4
Ngoan Muc (pass), Viet. 78/D4
Ngoc Linh (peak), Viet. 78/E4
Ngomeni (cape), Kenya 104/D3
Ngong, Kenya 104/C3
Ngonye (falls), Zam. 105/D4
Ngorongoro Consv. Area, Tanz. 104/B3
Ngoudié (riv.), Gabon 96/H8
Nguigmi, Niger 96/H5
Ngulu (isl.), Micr. 116/C4
Ngumbe Sukani (peak), Tanz. 104/C5
Nguru (riv.), Tanz. 104/C5
Ngwenya (peak), Swaz. 107/F2
Nha Trang, Viet. 78/E4
Nhamunda (riv.), Braz. 147/D3
Nhill, Austl. 115/B3
Nhlangano, Swaz. 107/E2
Nieves, Mex. 142/E3
Niagara (co.), US 131/N9
Niagara (falls), Can.,US 134/F4
Niagara (riv.), Can.,US 131/N9
Niagara Falls, NY, US 131/N9
Niagara Falls, On, Can. 131/N9
Niagara-on-the-Lake, On, Can. 131/N9
Niamey (dept.), Niger 103/F3
Niamey (cap.), Niger 103/F3
Niamey (int'l arpt.), Niger 103/F3
Niamtougou, Togo 103/F4
Niandan (riv.), Gui. 102/C4
Niangara, D.R. Congo 97/L7
Niangay (lake), Mali 96/E4
Niangxi (pass), China 72/A3
Nias (isl.), Indo. 67/J9
Niassa (prov.), Moz. 104/B5
Nicaragua (lake), Nic. 119/J4
Nicaragua (ctry.) 119/J8
Nicastro-Sambiase, It. 46/E3
Nice, Fr. 43/G5
Niceville, Fl, US 133/G4
Nichinan, Japan 74/B5
Nichlaul, India 84/D2
Nichol (bay), Austl. 112/C2
Nichols, NY, US 138/B1
Nichols Hills, Ok, US 137/M14
Nicholson (range), Austl. 112/C3
Nickerie (dist.), Sur. 153/G3
Nickerie (riv.), Sur. 153/G3
Nikolai, Ak, US 134/H3
Nicobar (isls.), India 67/H9
Nicolás Bravo, Mex. 144/D2
Nicolás Romero, Mex. 143/Q9
Nicolet, Qu, Can. 131/F2
Nicolls (isl.), NY, US 139/T7
Nicoma Park, Ok, US 137/N15
Nicosia (isl.), Kiri. 117/H5
Nicosia, It. 46/D4
Nicosia (cap.), Cyp. 91/C2
Nicosia (int'l arpt.), Cyp. 91/C2
Nicotera, It. 46/D3
Nicoya (gulf), CR 140/D6
Nicoya, CR 144/E4
Nicoya, Peninsula de (pen.), CR 150/A1
Nidau, Swi. 56/D3
Nidd (riv.), Eng, UK 35/G3
Niddatal, Ger. 54/B2
Nidda (riv.), Ger. 54/B2
Nidda, Ger. 54/C2
Nidzica, Pol. 41/L2
Nideggen, Ger. 53/F2
Nidge (riv.), Turk. 90/C2
Nidwalden (canton), Swi. 57/E4
Niebüll, Ger. 38/C4
Nied (riv.), Fr. 53/F5
Niederanven, Lux. 53/F4
Nieder-Olm, Ger. 54/B3
Niederbipp, Swi. 56/D3
Niederbronn-les-Bains, Fr. 53/G6

Niedere Tauern (mts.), Aus. 43/K3
Niederfischbach, Ger. 53/G2
Niederlausitz (reg.), Ger. 41/G3
Niedernhausen, Ger. 54/B2
Niederösterreich (prov.), Aus. 48/B2
Niedersachsen (state), Ger. 38/C5
Niedersächsisches Wattenmeer NP, Ger. 51/E1
Niederstetten, Ger. 54/D4
Niederstotzingen, Ger. 54/D5
Niederurnen, Swi. 57/F3
Niederwerrn, Ger. 54/D3
Niederwinkling, Ger. 55/F5
Niederzier, Ger. 53/F2
Niederzissen, Ger. 53/G3
Niefern-Öschelbronn, Ger. 54/B5
Niegocin (lake), Pol. 39/J5
Nieheim, Ger. 51/G5
Nienburg, Ger. 51/G3
Nienhagen, Ger. 51/H3
Niénokoué (peak), C.d'Iv. 102/C5
Nieppe, Fr. 52/B2
Niéri (riv.), Sen. 102/B2
Niers (riv.), Ger. 53/F1
Nierstein, Ger. 54/B4
Niet Ban Tinh Xa, Viet. 78/D4
Nieuw-Amsterdam, Sur. 151/G2
Nieuw-Bergen, Neth. 50/D5
Nieuw-Loosdrecht, Neth. 50/C4
Nieuw-Nickerie, Sur. 153/G3
Nieuw-Schoonebeek, Neth. 50/D3
Nieuw-Vossemeer, Neth. 50/B5
Nieuwe Pekela, Neth. 50/D2
Nieuwegein, Neth. 50/C4
Nieuwerkerk aan de IJssel, Neth. 50/B5
Nieuwerschans, Neth. 51/E2
Nieuwkoop, Neth. 50/C4
Nieuwleusen, Neth. 50/D3
Nieuwolde, Neth. 50/D2
Nieuwpoort, Belg. 52/B1
Nieuwoudtville, SAfr. 106/B3
Nièvre (dept.), Fr. 42/E3
Niğde, Turk. 90/C2
Nigel, SAfr. 106/F2
Niger (riv.), Afr. 96/F5
Niger (delta), Nga. 103/G5
Niger (co.), Can. 131/B9
Niger (ctry.) 93/C3
Nigeria (ctry.) 93/C4
Nigg (bay), Sc, UK 36/C2
Nighthawk (lake), On, Can. 130/D1
Nightmute, Ak, US 134/F3
Nigrán, Sp. 44/A1
Nigrita, Gre. 47/H2
Nihoa (isl.), Hi, US 117/J2
Nihonmatsu, Japan 75/G2
Nihtaur, India 84/B1
Nii (isl.), Japan 75/F3
Niigata, Japan 75/F2
Niigata (pref.), Japan 76/A4
Niihama, Japan 74/C4
Niihari, Japan 77/E1
Niihau (isl.), Hi, US 117/J2
Niimi, Japan 74/C3
Niitsu, Japan 75/F2
Niiza, Japan 77/D2
Nijar, Sp. 44/D4
Nijkerk, Neth. 50/D1
Nijlen, Belg. 50/D1
Nijmegen, Neth. 50/D5
Nikaia, Gre. 47/H3
Nikel', Rus. 37/J1
Nikel (bay), Bang. 145/F1
Nikki, Ben. 103/F4
Nikkō, Japan 75/F2
Nikkō NP, Japan 75/F2
Niklasdorf, Aus. 43/L3
Nikol'sk, Rus. 61/H4
Nikolai, Ak, US 134/H3
Nikolayevsk-na-Amure, Rus. 65/Q4
Nikol'sk, Rus. 63/H1
Nikolski, Ak, US 134/E5
Nikonga (riv.), Tanz. 104/A3
Nikopol', Ukr. 62/E3
Nikopol, Bul. 49/G4
Niksar, Turk. 62/F4
Nīkshahr, Iran 89/H3
Nikšić, Yugo. 47/F1
Nikumaroro (Gardner) (isl.), Kiri. 117/H5
Nile (isl.), Kiri. 116/G5
Nile (prov.), Ugan. 104/A2
Nile (delta), Egypt 88/B2
Nile (riv.), Afr. 97/F2
Niles, Oh, US 130/D3
Niles, Il, US 135/Q15
Nidau, Swi. 150/A1
Nilgiri, India 85/F4
Nilópolis, Braz. 151/K7
Nilsiä, Fin. 60/F3
Nilüfer (riv.), Turk. 90/C2
Nimach, India 82/B2
Nīmāj, India 84/B2
Nimba (co.), Libr. 102/C4
Nimba (peak), C.d'Iv. 102/C5
Nîmes, Fr. 42/F5
Nimmitabel, Austl. 115/D3
Nimpkish (riv.), BC, Can. 126/B3
Nimrod (int'l arpt.), Libya 97/K2
Nimrud (ruin), Iraq 90/E2
Nimule NP, Sudan 104/A2
Nin, Cro. 43/K4
Nīnawá (gov.), Iraq 90/E2
Nīnawā (Nineveh) (ruin), Iraq 90/E2
Ninepin Group (isls.), China 71/V11
Ninfas (pt.), Arg. 158/D4

Ning'an, China 71/N3
Ningbo, China 72/E3
Ningde, China 79/C2
Ningdu, China 79/C2
Ningguang, China 83/K2
Ningguo, China 79/C2
Ninghua, China 79/C2
Ningjin, China 72/C3
Ningjin, China 72/D3
Ningxiang Yizu Zizhixian, China 83/H2
Ningling, China 72/C4
Ningming, China 83/J3
Ningxia (aut. reg.), China 71/J4
Ningxiang, China 79/B2
Ningyang, China 72/D4
Ningyuan, China 83/K2
Ninh Binh, Viet. 78/D2
Ninh Hoa, Viet. 78/D3
Ninh, Vinh (bay), Viet. 78/D1
Ninigo (isls.), PNG 116/C4
Ninohe, Japan 77/C3
Ninomiya, Japan 77/H4
Ninove, Belg. 52/D2
Niobara (riv.), US 124/F3
Niobe, Ger. 76/B3
Niobrara (riv.), US 117/H5
Niokolo-Koba, PN du, Sen. 96/C5
Niokolo-Koba, PN du, Sen. 102/B3
Niono, Mali 102/D3
Nioro-du-Rip, Sen. 102/B3
Nioro du Sahel, Mali 102/D3
Niort, Fr. 42/C3
Nipawin, Sk, Can. 127/H2
Nipe (bay), Cuba 145/H1
Nipigon, On, Can. 127/L3
Nipigon (lake), On, Can. 122/G3
Nipissing (lake), Can. 123/J4
Niquelândia, Braz. 149/K5
Niquero, Cuba 145/G1
Nirasaki, Japan 75/F3
Nirayama, Japan 77/H6
Nirmal, India 82/C4
Nirmali, India 85/F2
Niš, Yugo. 47/F1
Niša (riv.), Yugo. 47/H1
Niscemi, It. 46/D4
Nishiazai, Japan 77/K5
Nishibiwajima, Japan 77/L5
Nishiharu, Japan 77/L5
Nishikatsura, Japan 77/B2
Nishiki, Japan 74/B3
Nishino'omote, Japan 74/B5
Nishino, Japan 77/M6
Nishiwaki, Japan 74/C4
Nisko, Pol. 41/M3
Nisqually, Wa, US 135/B3
Nisqually (riv.), Wa, US 135/B3
Nisqually Ind. Res., Wa, US 135/B3
Nisqually Reach (str.), Wa, US 135/B3
Nissan (isl.), PNG 116/E5
Nisser (lake), Nor. 38/C2
Nisshin, Japan 77/M5
Nissum (bay), Den. 38/C3
Nisswa, Mn, US 127/K4
Nistru (riv.), Mol. 49/H1
Niterói, Braz. 211/K7
Nith (riv.), Sc, UK 36/C6
Nitra, Slvk. 48/D1
Nitra (riv.), Slvk. 41/K4
Nitra (riv.), Rus. 61/P4
Nitta, Japan 77/C1
Nittedal, Nor. 38/D1
Nittel, Ger. 53/F4
Niuafo'ou (isl.), Tonga 117/H6
Niuatoputapu Group (isls.), Kiri. 117/H6
Niue (terr.), NZ 117/H7
Niue (isl.), Niue 117/J6
Niulakita (isl.), Tuv. 116/G6
Niulan (riv.), China 83/H7
Niut (peak), Indo. 80/C3
Niutao (isl.), Tuv. 116/G5
Nivelles, Belg. 53/D2
Nivernais, Collines de (hills), Fr. 42/E3
Niverville, Mb, Can. 127/J3
Niwot, Co, US 137/B7
Niyazov (int'l arpt.), Trkm. 87/C5
Niyodo (riv.), Japan 74/C4
Nizāmābād, India 82/C4
Nizhnekama (res.), Rus. 61/M4
Nizhnekamsk, Rus. 61/L5
Nizhneudinsk, Rus. 65/K4
Nizhnevartovsk, Rus. 64/H3
Nizhniy Lomov, Rus. 63/G1
Nizhniy Novgorod, Rus. 61/K4
Nizhniy Novgorod Oblast, Rus. 63/G1
Nizhniy Tagil, Rus. 64/G4
Nizhyn, Ukr. 62/D2
Nizke Tatry NP, Slvk. 41/K4
Nizzanim, Isr. 91/F8
Njarðvík, Ice. 37/M7
Njombe, Tanz. 104/B4
Nkhata Bay, Malw. 104/B5
Nkongsamba, Camr. 103/H5
Nkulu, Tanz. 104/B4
Nkusi (riv.), Ugan. 104/A2

Noailles, Fr. 52/B5
Noäkhāli (pol. reg.), Bang. 85/H4
Noale, It. 59/F1
Noāmundi, India 85/E4
Noank, Ct, US 139/T11
Noatak, Ak, US 134/F2
Noatak (riv.), Ak, US 134/F2
Noatak Nat'l Prsv., Ak, US 134/F2
Nobeoka, Japan 74/B4
Noble, Ok, US 137/N15
Noboribetsu, Japan 76/B3
Noboa, Ecu. 152/A5
Noce (riv.), It. 57/G5
Noceto, It. 58/D3
Noci, It. 47/E2
Nockamixon State Park, Pa, US 138/C3
Noda, Japan 77/D2
Nogales, Japan 74/B4
Noé (cape), Alg. 100/D2
Nogales, Mex. 143/M8
Nogara, It. 59/E2
Nogaro, Fr. 42/C5
Nogat (riv.), Pol. 39/H4
Nogata, Japan 74/B4
Nogent, Fr. 56/B1
Nogent-l'Artaud, Fr. 52/C6
Nogent-le-Rotrou, Fr. 42/D2
Nogent-sur-Oise, Fr. 52/B5
Nogent-sur-Seine, Fr. 42/E2
Nogi, Japan 77/D1
Noginsk, Rus. 61/X9
Nogoa (riv.), Austl. 114/B4
Nogon-san (peak), SKor. 73/D5
Nogoonnuur, Mong. 70/F2
Nogoyá, Arg. 157/E3
Nógrád (co.), Hun. 41/K5
Nogwak-san (peak), SKor. 74/A2
Nohar, India 86/C5
Noheji, Japan 76/B3
Nohfelden, Ger. 53/G4
Noidans-lès-Vesoul, Fr. 56/C2
Noire (riv.), Can. 130/E2
Noires, Montagnes (mts.), Fr. 42/B2
Noirmoutier, Île de (isl.), Fr. 42/B3
Noisiel, Fr. 52/B6
Noisy-le-Grand, Fr. 30/K5
Noisy-le-Mec, Fr. 30/K5
Noisy-le-Roi, Fr. 30/J5
Nojima-zaki (pt.), Japan 75/F3
Nokia, Fin. 39/K1
Nokilalaki (peak), Indo. 81/F4
Nola, CAfr. 96/J7
Noli, It. 58/B4
Noli, Capo di (cape), It. 58/B4
Nomadgi NP, Austl. 115/D2
Nombre de Dios (mts.), Hon. 144/E3
Nombre de Dios, Mex. 142/D4
Nome (cape), Ak, US 134/F3
Nome, Ak, US 134/F3
Noménby, Fr. 53/F6
Nomexy, Fr. 56/C1
Nomo-misaki (pt.), Japan 74/B5
Nomo-zaki (pt.), Japan 74/A4
Nonacho (lake), NW, Can. 122/F2
Nonantola, It. 59/E3
Nondalton, Ak, US 134/H4
None, It. 43/G4
Nonette, It. 52/B5
Nong Han (res.), Thai. 78/D2
Nong Khai, Thai. 78/C2
Nong'an, China 71/N3
Nongoma, SAfr. 107/F2
Nongstoin, India 85/H3
Nonnweiler, Ger. 53/F4
Nonoava, Mex. 142/D3
Nonouti (isl.), Kiri. 116/G5
Nonri (isl.), China 72/E5
Nonsan, SKor. 73/D4
Nontron, Fr. 42/D4
Noord-Brabant (prov.), Neth. 50/C5
Noord Holland (prov.), Neth. 50/B3
Noordbeveland (isl.), Neth. 50/A5
Noorderhaaks (isl.), Neth. 50/B3
Noordhollandsch Kanaal (riv.), Neth. 50/B3
Noordoostpolder (polder), Neth. 50/C3
Noordwijk aan Zee, Neth. 50/B4
Noordwijkerhout, Neth. 50/B4
Noormarkku, Fin. 39/J1
Noorvik, Ak, US 134/F2
Nootka (isl.), Can. 126/B3
Nora, Swe. 38/F2
Norala, Phil. 81/F2
Norberg, Swe. 38/F2
Norberto de la Riestra, Arg. 159/J11
Norchia (ruin), It. 46/C3
Norco, It. 46/C3
Norco, La, US 137/P16
Nizze Tatry NP, Slvk. 62/A2
Nizza Monferrato, It. 58/B3
Qu, Can. 131/M6
Nord (prov.), Fr. 52/C3
Nørdjdtvík, Ice. 37/M7
Nord (dept.), Fr. 52/C3
Nord-Kivu (pol. reg.), D.R. Congo 104/A3
Nord-Ostsee (Kiel) (canal), Ger. 51/G1
Nord-Ouest (prov.), Camr. 103/H5
Nord-Ouest (pol. reg.), Mor. 100/D2

Nord – Okeec

Nord-Pas-de-Calais
(pol. reg.), Fr. 42/D1
Nord-Radde (riv.),
Ger. 51/E3
Nord-Sud Kanal (canal),
Ger. 51/E2
Nord-Trøndelag (co.),
Nor. 37/E2
Nordborg, Den. 38/C4
Nordby, Den. 38/D4
Norddeich, Ger. 51/E1
Nordela (int'l arpt.),
Azor., Port. 45/T13
Norden, Ger. 51/E1
Nordenham, Ger. 51/F1
Nordenskjöld (arch.),
Rus. 64/J2
Norderney, Ger. 51/E1
Norderney (isl.),
Neth. 51/E1
Norderstedt, Ger. 51/G1
Nordhausen, Ger. 40/F3
Nordholz, Ger. 51/F1
Nordhorn, Ger. 51/E4
Nordhouse, Fr. 56/D1
Nordjylland (co.),
Den. 38/C3
Nordkapp (cape),
Nor. 37/H1
Nordkapp, Nor. 37/H1
Nordkinn (pt.),
Nor. 37/H1
Nordkirchen, Ger. 51/E5
Nordland (co.),
Nor. 37/E2
Nordmaling, Swe. 37/H3
Nordreisa, Nor. 37/G1
Nordrhein-Westfalen
(state), Ger. 40/C3
Nords Wharf,
Austl. 115/D2
Nordwalde, Ger. 51/E4
Nore (riv.), Ire. 31/Q10
Noresund, Nor. 38/C1
Norfolk (mt.),
Austl. 115/C4
Norfolk (lake), US 129/J3
Norfolk, Ne, US 127/J5
Norfolk (isl.),
Austl. 116/F7
Norfolk Broads (swamp),
Eng, UK 33/H1
Norg, Neth. 50/D2
Norheimsund, Nor. 38/B1
Norikura-dake (peak),
Japan 75/E2
Noril'sk, Rus. 64/J3
Normal, Il, US 127/L5
Norman, Ok, US 137/N15
Norman Manley (int'l arpt.),
Jam. 145/G2
Norman Wells,
NW, Can. 122/D2
Normanby (isl.),
PNG 116/E6
Normandie, Collines de
(hills), Fr. 42/C2
Normandy (reg.), Fr. 42/C2
Normandy Beach,
NJ, US 138/D4
Normandy Park,
Wa, US 135/C3
Normanton, Austl. 114/A2
Normanton South,
Eng, UK 35/G4
Norotshama (peak),
Namb. 106/B3
Norquay, Sk, Can. 127/H3
Norquinco, Arg. 158/C4
Norrbotten (co.),
Swe. 37/G2
Nørre Alslev, Den. 38/D4
Nørre Nebel, Den. 38/C4
Nørre Vorupør,
Den. 38/C3
Norridge, Il, US 135/Q16
Norris (lake), Tn, US 130/E3
Norristown,
Pa, US 138/C3
Norrköping, Swe. 38/G2
Norrland (reg.), Swe. 37/F2
Norrsundet, Swe. 38/G1
Norrtälje, Swe. 39/H2
Nors, Den. 38/C3
Norseman, Austl. 112/D5
Norsjö, Swe. 37/H2
Norte (pt.), Arg. 159/F3
Norte (pt.), Arg. 158/E4
Norte, Cabo do (cape),
Braz. 151/H3
Norte de Santander (dept.),
Col. 145/H4
Norte Los Rodeos (int'l arpt.),
Sp. 98/A3
Norte, Serra do (mts.),
Braz. 150/G6
Nortelândia, Braz. 151/G6
Nörten-Hardenberg,
Ger. 51/G5
North (pt.), Austl. 115/C4
North (cape), Can. 131/J2
North (cape),
Ak, US 135/P14
North (cape), NZ 117/S9
North (isl.), NZ 116/G8
North (pt.),
Austl. 112/B4
North (pt.),
Md, US 138/B5
North (sound),
Sc, UK 31/V14
North (sea), Eur. 36/C4
North (chan.), UK 30/E4
North Albanian Alps (mts.),
Yugo. 47/F1
North America (cont.) 119
North Andaman (isl.),
India 83/F5
North Arlington,
NJ, US 139/J8
North Aulatsivik (isl.),
Nf, Can. 123/K3
North Aurora,
Il, US 135/P16
North Battleford,
Sk, Can. 126/F2
North Bay, On, Can. 130/E2
North Bay, Wi, US 135/Q14

North Beach,
Md, US 138/B6
North Beach Haven,
NJ, US 138/D4
North Bellmore,
NY, US 139/L9
North Bend,
Or, US 128/B2
North Bend,
Wa, US 135/D3
North Bergen,
NJ, US 139/J8
North Berwick,
Sc, UK 36/D4
North Branch,
NJ, US 138/D2
North Branch (riv.),
Md, US 138/B5
North Branford,
Ct, US 139/F1
North Brunswick,
NJ, US 138/D3
North Buganda (prov.),
Ugan. 104/B2
North Caicos (isl.), UK 145/J1
North Caldwell,
NJ, US 139/J8
North Canadian (riv.),
Ok, US 129/H3
North Cape May,
NJ, US 138/D6
North Cariboo (lake),
On, Can. 122/H3
North Carolina
(state), US 125/L4
North Cascades NP,
Wa, US 126/C3
North Central (plain),
Tx, US 143/F1
North Charleston,
SC, US 133/J3
North Cowichan,
BC, Can. 126/C3
North Dakota
(state), US 124/F2
North Dorset Downs
(uplands), Eng, UK 32/D5
North Down (dist.),
NI, UK 34/C2
North East, Pa, US 130/E3
North East (pt.),
Austl. 114/C3
North East, Md, US 138/C4
North Eastern (prov.),
Kenya 104/C2
North Esk (riv.),
Sc, UK 36/C5
North Foreland (pt.),
Eng, UK 33/H4
North Fork Crow (riv.),
Mn, US 127/K4
North Fort Myers,
Fl, US 133/H5
North French (riv.),
Can. 130/D1
North Frisian (isls.),
Ger. 40/D1
North Front
(int'l arpt.), UK 98/D1
North Gauhāti,
India 85/H2
North Haledon,
NJ, US 139/J8
North Hero,
Vt, US 130/F2
North Highlands,
Ca, US 135/L9
North Kansas City,
Mo, US 137/D5
North Kitui Nat'l Rsv.,
Kenya 104/C3
North Korea (ctry.) 71/N4
North Lakhimpur,
India 83/F2
North Las Vegas,
Nv, US 128/D3
North Lindenhurst,
NY, US 139/M9
North Little Rock,
Ar, US 137/J4
North Luangwa NP,
Zam. 105/F3
North Minch (The Minch) (str.),
Sc, UK 31/Q8
Northport, Al, US 133/G3
Northport
(Old Northport), NY, US 139/E2
Northumberland
(str.), Can. 131/J2
Northumberland,
Pa, US 138/B2
Northumberland NP,
Eng, UK 36/D6
Northvale, NJ, US 139/K7
Northville, Mi, US 135/E7
Northway, Ak, US 134/K3
Northwest Gander
(riv.), Can. 131/L2
Northwest Territories
(terr.), Can. 124/E2
Northwich, Eng, UK 35/F5
Northwood, ND, US 127/J4
Norton (bay),
Ak, US 134/F3
Norton (sound),
Ak, US 119/A3
Norton Shores,
Mi, US 130/C3
Nortorf, Ger. 38/C4
Norvegia (cape),
Ant. 160/Y
Nörvenich, Ger. 57/F4
Norwalk, Oh, US 130/D3
Norwalk, Ca, US 135/C3
Norwalk, Ct, US 139/M7
Norwegian (bay),
NW, Can. 123/S7
Norwegian (sea),
Eur. 27/D2
Norwich, NY, US 130/F3
Norwich, Eng, UK 33/H1
Norwood (int'l arpt.),
Eng, UK 33/H1
Norwood, NJ, US 139/K8
Nos Emine (cape),
Bul. 49/H4
Nos Kaliakra (pt.),
Bul. 49/J4
Nos Maslen Nos (pt.),
Bul. 49/H4
Nosappu-misaki (cape),
Japan 76/D2
Nose, Japan 77/H6

North Tyne (riv.),
Eng, UK 35/F1
North Uist (isl.),
Sc, UK 31/Q8
North Umpqua (riv.),
Or, US 128/B2
North Valley Stream,
NY, US 139/L9
North Vancouver,
BC, Can. 122/D4
North Wales,
Pa, US 138/C3
North Weald Bassett,
Eng, UK 30/D1
North West (cape),
Austl. 112/B2
North-West Frontier (co.),
India 86/A3
North West Highlands
(uplands), Sc, UK 31/R8
North Wildwood,
NJ, US 138/D6
North Wilton,
Ct, US 139/E1
North York, Can. 131/Q8
North York Moors NP,
Eng, UK 35/G3
North Yorkshire (co.),
Eng, UK 35/G3
Northallerton,
Eng, UK 35/G3
Northam, Austl. 112/C4
Northampton, Ma, US 131/F3
Northampton, Eng, UK 33/F2
Northampton, Austl. 112/B4
Northampton (co.),
Eng, UK 33/F2
Northampton,
Pa, US 138/C2
Northampton
(state), US 138/C2
Northampton Uplands
(uplands), Eng, UK 33/E2
Northamptonshire (co.),
Eng, UK 33/E2
Northbrook, Il, US 135/Q15
Northeast (cape),
Ak, US 134/E3
Nouâdhibou, Mrta. 98/A5
Nouadhibou (int'l arpt.),
Mrta. 98/A5
Nouakchott (cap.),
Mrta. 102/B2
Nouakchott (int'l arpt.),
Mrta. 102/B2
Nouna, Burk. 102/E3
Noupoort, SAfr. 106/C4
Nouvion-sur-Meuse, Fr. 53/D4
Nœux-les-Mines, Fr. 53/D3
Nouzonville, Fr. 53/D4
Nova
Braz. 151/H8
Nova Cruz, Braz. 151/L5
Nová Dubnica, Slvk. 41/K4
Nova Friburgo, Braz. 211/L7
Nova Gorica, Slov. 59/G1
Nová Gradiška, Cro. 48/C3
Nova Iguaçu, Braz. 211/K7
Nova Kakhovka, Ukr. 44/G2
Nova Olinda, Braz. 154/C2
Nova Olinda do Norte,
Braz. 150/G4
Nova Pazova, Yugo. 48/E3
Nova Prata, Braz. 155/B4
Nova Russas,
Braz. 154/B2
Nova Scotia (prov.),
Can. 123/K4
Nova Sintra, CpV. 93/J11
Nova Soure, Braz. 154/C3
Nova Varoš, Yugo. 48/D4
Nova Venécia,
Braz. 155/D1
Nova Xavantina,
Braz. 151/H6
Nova Zagora, Bul. 47/K1
Novaci, Rom. 49/F3
Novafeltria, It. 59/F5
Novara, It. 58/B2
Novate Mezzola, It. 57/F5
Novaya Sibir' (isl.),
Rus. 65/R2
Novaya Zemlya (isl.),
Rus. 160/C
Nove, It. 59/E1
Nové Hrady, Czh. 55/H5
Nové Město nad Váhom,
Slvk. 41/J4
Nové Strašeci, Czh. 55/G3
Nové Zámky, Slvk. 48/D2
Novelda, Sp. 45/E3
Novellara, It. 59/D3
Novena di Piave, It. 59/F1
Noventa Vicentina, It. 59/E1
Novgorod, Rus. 39/P2
Novgorod Oblast,
Rus. 60/D4
Novi, Mi, US 135/E7
Novi Bečej, Yugo. 48/E3
Novi di Modena, It. 59/D3
Novi Iskür, Bul. 47/H1
Novi Ligure, It. 43/H4
Novi Pazar, Yugo. 47/G1
Novi Pazar, Bul. 49/H4
Novi Sad, Yugo. 48/D3
Novi Vinodolski,
Cro. 48/B3
Novillars, Fr. 56/C3
Nóvita, Col. 152/B3
Novo
Braz. 211/K6
Novo Alexeyevka,
Ecu. 152/C5
Novo Aripuanã,
Braz. 150/F5
Novo Hamburgo,
Braz. 155/B4
Novo Horizonte,
Braz. 155/B1
Novo Miloševo,
Yugo. 48/E3
Novo Oriente,
Braz. 154/C2
Novoanninskiy, Rus. 63/G2
Novocheboksarsk,
Rus. 61/K4
Novocherkassk,
Rus. 63/G3
Novogrudok, Bela. 62/D3
Novohrad-Volyns'kyy,
Ukr. 62/D3
Novohradské Hory (mts.),
Czh. 55/H5
Novokuybyshevsk,
Rus. 63/J1
Novokuznetsk, Rus. 64/J4

Noshappu-misaki (cape),
Japan 76/B1
Noshaq (peak), Afg. 89/K1
Noshiro, Japan 76/B3
Nosivka, Ukr. 62/D2
Nosong (cape),
Malay. 81/E2
Noṣratābād, Iran 89/G3
Noss Head (pt.),
Sc, UK 31/S7
Nossa Senhora da Glória,
Braz. 154/C3
Nossa Senhora das Dores,
Braz. 154/C3
Nossebro, Swe. 38/E2
Nosy-varika, Madg. 107/J8
Notch (cape), Chile 159/B6
Notec (riv.), Pol. 41/J2
Noto (pen.), Japan 75/E2
Noto, It. 46/D4
Noto Antica (ruin), It. 46/D4
Noto, Golfo di (gulf), It. 46/D4
Noto, Val di (valley), It. 46/D4
Notodden, Nor. 38/C2
Notogawa, Japan 77/K5
Notoro (lake), Japan 76/C1
Notre Dame (mts.),
On, Can. 123/J4
Notre Dame (bay),
Nf, Can. 123/L4
Notre Dame, Fr. 30/K5
Notre-Dame-de-l'Île-Perrot,
Qu, Can. 131/N7
Notsé, Togo 103/F5
Nott (mt.), Austl. 113/G5
Nottaway (riv.),
Qu, Can. 123/J3
Nøtterøy, Nor. 38/D2
Nottingham (isl.),
NW, Can. 123/H2
Nottingham,
Eng, UK 35/G6
Nottingham-Shire (co.),
Eng, UK 35/G6
Nottuln, Ger. 51/E5
Nouakchott (cap.),
Mrta. 102/B2

Novolazarevskaya,
Rus., Ant. 160/A
Novomoskovsk, Rus. 62/F1
Novomoskovsk, Rus. 62/F3
Novorossiysk, Rus. 62/F3
Novoshakhtinsk,
Rus. 62/F3
Novosibirsk (res.),
Rus. 87/H2
Novosibirsk, Rus. 87/H1
Novosibirsk Oblast,
Rus. 87/G1
Novosibirsk (Tolmachevo)
(int'l arpt.), Rus. 87/H1
Novotroitsk, Rus. 63/L2
Novoukrayinka, Ukr. 62/D3
Novovolyns'k, Ukr. 62/D2
Novovyatsk, Rus. 61/L4
Novozybkov, Rus. 62/D1
Novska, Cro. 48/C3
Nový Jičín, Czh. 41/K4
Nowa Dęba, Pol. 41/M4
Nowa Ruda, Pol. 41/H3
Nowa Sarzyna, Pol. 41/M3
Nowa Sól, Pol. 41/H3
Nowata, Ok, US 129/J3
Nowe, Pol. 41/K2
Nowe Miasto Lubawskie,
Pol. 41/K2
Nowgong, India 84/B3
Nowitna (riv.),
Ak, US 119/A4
Nowitna NWR, US 134/G3
Nowogard, Pol. 38/F5
Nowood (riv.),
Wy, US 128/F1
Nowshāk (peak),
Afg. 87/F5
Nowshera, Pak. 86/A2
Nowy Dwór Gdański,
Pol. 39/M4
Nowy Sącz, Pol. 41/L4
Nowy Sącz (prov.),
Pol. 41/L4
Nowy Staw, Pol. 39/M4
Nowy Targ, Pol. 41/L4
Nowy Tomyśl, Pol. 41/H2
Noya (riv.),
Mrta. 44/A1
Noye (riv.), Fr. 52/B4
Noyon, Fr. 52/C4
Nsanje, Malw. 105/G4
Nsawam, Gha. 103/E5
Nsumbu NP, Zam. 104/A5
Nsuta, Gha. 103/E5
Ntoroko, Ugan. 104/A2
Ntungamo, Ugan. 104/A3
Ntusi, Ugan. 104/A3
Nu, Crêt du (peak), Fr. 56/B5
Nuanggla, Ugan. 138/C1
Nuuk (Godthåb),
Grld. 119/M3
Nubian (des.),
Sudan 93/F2
Nucet, Rom. 48/F2
Nucla, Co, US 132/A2
Nucourt, Fr. 30/H4
Nüdlingen, Ger. 54/D2
Nueces (riv.),
Tx, US 140/B2
Nueltin (lake),
NW, Can. 122/G2
Nuenen, Neth. 50/C6
Nueva Alejandría,
Peru 156/C2
Nueva Concepción,
Guat. 144/D3
Nueva Esparta (state),
Ven. 153/E2
Nueva Florida,
Ven. 152/D2
Nueva Gerona,
Cuba 145/D1
Nueva Helvecia,
Uru. 159/K11
Nueva Imperial,
Chile 158/B3
Nueva Italia de Ruiz,
Mex. 142/D4
Nueva Loja, Ecu. 152/B4
Nueva Ocotepeque,
Hon. 144/D3
Nueva Palmira,
Uru. 159/J10
Nueva Rosita,
Mex. 132/C5
Nueva Villa de Padilla,
Mex. 143/F3
Nueve de Julio,
Arg. 158/E2
Nuevas, Cuba 145/G1
Nueve, Ca, US 135/C3
Nuevitas, Cuba 145/G1
Nuevo Balsas,
Mex. 143/F5
Nuevo Berlín,
Uru. 159/J10
Nuevo Casas Grandes,
Mex. 142/D2
Nuevo Chagres,
Pan. 145/F4
Nuevo Gulfo (gulf),
Arg. 158/D5
Nuevo Ideal, Mex. 142/D3
Nuevo Ixcatlán,
Mex. 144/A2
Nuevo Laredo,
Mex. 132/D5
Nuevo Leon (state),
Mex. 140/A2
Nuevo Rocafuerte,
Ecu. 152/C5
Nufenen, Swi. 57/F4
Nufenenpass (pass),
Swi. 57/E5
Nuguria (isls.),
PNG 116/E5
Nuhne (riv.), Ger. 51/F6
Nui (isl.), Tuv. 116/H5
Nuiqsut, Ak, US 134/H1
Nuits-Saint-Georges,
Fr. 56/A3
Nukey Bluff (mt.),
Austl. 113/G5
Nukiki, Sol. 116/J6
Nuku'alofa (cap.),
Tonga 116/H7
Nukufetau (isl.),
Tuv. 116/H5
Nukulaelae (isl.),
Tuv. 116/H5
Nukumanu (atoll),
PNG 116/F5
Nukunonu (isl.), Tok. 116/H5
Nukuoro (isl.), Micr. 116/E4
Nukus (isl.), Uzb. 64/J4
Nukus (int'l arpt.),
Uzb. 87/C4

Nukus, Uzb. 87/C4
Nukutavake (isl.),
FrPol. 117/M6
Nulato, Ak, US 134/G3
Nules, Sp. 45/E3
Nullagine (riv.),
Austl. 109/B4
Nullarbor NP, Austl. 113/F4
Nullarbor (plain),
Austl. 109/B4
Numan, Nga. 103/G5
Numansdorp, Neth. 50/B5
Numata, Japan 75/F2
Numazu, Japan 75/F3
Numfoor (isl.), Indo. 81/H4
Numurkah, Austl. 115/C3
Nun (mts.), Turk. 91/E1
Nun (riv.), Kaz. 87/F2
Nunap Isua (cape),
Grld. 119/N3
Nunchia, Col. 152/C3
Nundle, Austl. 115/D1
Nuneaton, Eng, UK 33/E1
Nunivak (isl.),
Ak, US 119/A4
Nunnington, Austl. 112/C4
Nunspeet, Neth. 50/C4
Nuon (riv.), Libr. 102/D5
Nuoro, It. 46/A2
Nuqui, Col. 152/B3
Nura (riv.), Kaz. 87/G1
Nuremberg, Pa, US 138/B2
Nürnberg (int'l arpt.),
Ger. 54/E3
Nürnberg, Ger. 54/E4
Nürpur, Pak. 86/B3
Nurri (mt.), Austl. 115/C1
Nürtingen, Ger. 54/C5
Nushagak (riv.),
Ak, US 134/G4
Nushki, Pak. 89/J3
Nutbery (hill),
Sc, UK 36/C5
Nuth, Neth. 53/E2
Nuthe-Graben (riv.),
Ger. 40/Q7
Nutley, NJ, US 139/J8
Nutwood, Il, US 137/F7
Nyah, Austl. 115/B2
Nyah West, Austl. 115/B2
Nyainqêntanglha (peak),
China 70/F5
Nyaki NP, Malw. 104/B5
Nyalam, China 85/E1
Nyamlell, Sudan 97/K5
Nyala, Sudan 97/K5
Nyandoma, Rus. 60/J3
Nyanza (prov.),
Kenya 104/B3
Nyasa (lake), Malw. 93/F6
Nybro, Swe. 38/F3
Nyêmo, China 85/H1
Nyeri, Kenya 104/C3
Nyima, China 70/E5
Nyíradony, Hun. 41/L5
Nyírbátor, Hun. 41/M5
Nyíregyháza, Hun. 41/L5
Nyírmada, Hun. 41/M5
Nyíru (mt.), Kenya 104/C2
Nykøbing, Den. 38/C3
Nykøbing, Den. 38/D4
Nyköping, Swe. 38/G2
Nylstroom, SAfr. 105/E5
Nynäshamn, Swe. 38/G2
Nyngan, Austl. 115/C1
Nyoman (riv.), Bela. 62/D3
Nyon, Swi. 56/C5
Nyons, Fr. 42/F4
Nýrsko, Czh. 55/G3
Nyūzen, Japan 75/E2
Nzega, Tanz. 104/B4
Nzérékoré (pol. reg.),
Gui. 102/C4
Nzérékoré, Gui. 102/C5
Nzi (riv.), C.d'Iv. 96/E6

Oa, Mull of (pt.),
Sc, UK 31/Q9
Oahe (dam), SD, US 127/H4
Oahe (lake),
ND,SD, US 124/F2
Oʻahu (isl.), Hi, US 117/K2
Oak Forest, Il, US 135/Q16
Oak Grove,
Mo, US 137/E6
Oak Hill, WV, US 130/D4
Oak Park, Il, US 135/Q16
Oak Park, Mi, US 135/E7
Oak Ridge, Tn, US 130/E3
Oak View, Ca, US 136/A2
Oakbank, Mb, Can. 127/J3
Oakdale, La, US 129/J5
Oakes, ND, US 127/H4
Oakey, Austl. 114/C4
Oakham, Eng, UK 33/F1
Oakhurst, Ca, US 136/C3
Oakland, Md, US 138/B5
Oakland (lake),
Mi, US 135/F6
Oakland, NJ, US 139/J7
Oakland Falls, BC, Can. 126/B2

Oakland (bay),
Wa, US 135/A3
Ocean Grove, NJ, US 138/D3
Ocean View, NJ, US 138/D5
Oceanographic Museum,
Mona. 58/J8
Oceanside, Ca, US 136/C4
Oceanside, NY, US 139/L9
Oceanville, NJ, US 138/D5
Och'amch'ire, Geo. 63/G4
Ocheltree, Ks, US 137/P17
Ochiishi-misaki (cape),
Japan 76/D2
Ochil (hills), Sc, UK 36/C4
Ocho Rios, Jam. 145/G2
Ochsenfurt, Ger. 54/D3
Ochsenhausen, Ger. 57/F2
Ochsenkopf (peak),
Ger. 57/F3
Ochtendung, Ger. 53/G3
Ochtrup, Ger. 51/E4
Ochtum (riv.), Ger. 51/F2
Ockelbo, Swe. 38/G1
Ockenheim, Ger. 53/G4
Ocmulgee (riv.),
Ga, US 133/H3
Ocmulgee Nat'l Mon.,
Ga, US 133/H3
Ocna Mureş, Rom. 41/F4
Ocna Sibiului, Rom. 49/G3
Ocoña, Peru 156/C5
Ocoña (riv.), Peru 156/C5
Oconee (lake),
Ga, US 133/H3
Oconee (riv.), Can. 127/L3
Oconto, Wi, US 130/C2
Ocosingo, Mex. 144/C2
Ocotal, Nic. 144/E3
Ocotlán, Mex. 142/E4
Ocotlán de Morelos,
Mex. 144/B2
Ocoyoacac, Mex. 143/Q10
Ocozocoautla de Espinosa,
Mex. 144/C2
Ocracoke, NC, US 133/K3
Ocros, Peru 156/B3
Octeville, Fr. 42/C2
October Revolution (isl.),
Rus. 67/H2
Oda (peak), Sudan 101/G4
Oda, Japan 74/C3
Ōda, Japan 74/C3
Ōdaejan NP, SKor. 74/A2
Ōdaigahara-san (peak),
Japan 77/K7
Ōdate, Japan 76/B3
Odawara, Japan 75/F3
Odda, Nor. 38/B1
Odder, Den. 38/D4
Odeborn (riv.), Ger. 51/F6
Odelzhausen, Ger. 54/E6
Ōdemira, Port. 44/A4
Ōdemiş, Turk. 90/A2
Odendaalsrus,
SAfr. 106/D2
Odense, Den. 38/D4
Odense (int'l arpt.),
Den. 38/D4
Odenthal, Ger. 53/G1
Odenton, Md, US 138/B5
Odenwald (reg.),
Ger. 54/B3
Oder (Odra) (riv.),
Ger.,Pol. 41/H2
Oder-Spree Kanal (canal),
Ger. 40/Q7
Oderen, Fr. 56/C2
Oderhaff (lag.),
Ger. 41/H1
Oderzo, It. 59/F1
Odesa, Ukr. 62/D3
Odes'ka (obl.), Ukr. 62/D3
Odessa, Wa, US 126/D4
Odessa, Tx, US 129/G5
Odessa, De, US 138/C5
Odet (riv.), Fr. 52/B5
Odienné, C.d'Iv. 102/C4
Odintsovo, Rus. 61/W9
Odiongan, Phil. 79/D5
Odivelas, Port. 45/P10
Odobeşti, Rom. 49/H3
Odon (riv.), Fr. 30/C3
Odoorn, Neth. 50/D3
Odorheiu Secuiesc,
Rom. 49/G3
Odžaci, Yugo. 48/D3
Odzala, PN d',
Congo 103/J7
Oe, Japan 77/H5
Ōe-yama (peak),
Japan 77/H5
Oegstgeest, Neth. 50/B4
Oeiras, Braz. 154/B2
Oeiras, Port. 45/P10
Oelde, Ger. 51/F5
Ojo de Agua, Mex. 143/Q9
Oelsnitz, Ger. 55/F2
Oeno (isl.), Pitc. 117/N7
Oensingen, Swi. 56/D3
Oer-Erkenschwick,
Ger. 51/E5
Oesling (mts.), Lux. 53/E4
Oesterdam (dam),
Neth. 50/B6
Oestrich-Winkel,
Ger. 53/H3
Oeta Np, Gre. 47/H3
Oey'ŏn (isl.), SKor. 73/D3
Of, Turk. 63/H4
O'Fallon, Mo, US 137/F6
O'Fallon, Il, US 137/F6
Ofanto (riv.), It. 46/D2
Ofaqim, Isr. 91/D4
Ofenhorn (peak),
Swi. 57/E5
Offa, Nga. 103/G4
Offaly (co.), Ire. 31/P9
Offanengo, It. 58/C2
Offement, Fr. 54/B2
Offenbach, Ger. 54/B2
Offenbach an der Queich,
Ger. 54/B4
Offenburg, Ger. 54/D1
Offingen, Ger. 54/D5
Offstein, Ger. 54/B3
Oftersheim, Ger. 54/B3
Oftringen, Swi. 56/D3
Ofunato, Japan 76/B4
Oga, Japan 76/A4
Oga (pen.), Japan 76/A4
Ogachi, Japan 76/B4
Ogaden (reg.),
Eth. 97/P6

Ōgaki, Japan 77/L5
Ogano, Japan 77/C2
Ogasawara, Japan 116/D2
Ogatsu, Japan 76/B4
Ogawa, Japan 77/E1
Ogawara, Japan 77/E1
Ogawara (lake),
Japan 76/B3
Ogbomosho, Nga. 103/G4
Ogden, Ut, US 137/K11
Ogden Bay (bay),
Ut, US 137/J11
Ogden, South Fork (riv.),
Ut, US 137/K11
Ogdensburg, NY, US 130/F2
Ogdensburg, NJ, US 138/D1
Ogeechee
(riv.), Ga, US 133/H3
Oggiono, It. 58/C1
Ogi, Japan 75/F2
Ogidaki (mtn.),
On, Can. 130/D2
Ogies, SAfr. 106/E2
Ogilvie (mts.), Yk, Can. 122/C2
Ogilvie (riv.), Yk, Can. 122/C2
Ogles, Il, US 137/G8
Oglesby, Tx, US 143/F2
Oglio (riv.), It. 43/J4
Ognon (riv.), Fr. 40/C5
Ogoamas (peak),
Indo. 81/F3
Ogoki (lake), Can. 127/M3
Ogoki (res.), Can. 127/L3
Ogoki (riv.), Can. 127/L3
Ogooué (riv.), Gabon 93/C5
Ogose, Japan 77/C2
Ogosta (riv.), Bul. 49/F4
Ogre, Lat. 39/L3
Oguchi, Japan 77/L5
Ogulin, Cro. 48/B3
Ogun (riv.), Nga. 96/F6
Ogun (state), Nga. 103/F5
Ogurchinskiy (isl.),
Trkm. 63/K5
Oğuz, Turk. 62/F5
Oh Me Edge (hill),
Eng, UK 36/D6
Ōhara, It. 77/E3
Oharu, Japan 77/L5
Ōhata, Japan 76/B3
Ohey, Belg. 53/E3
O'Higgins (pol. reg.),
Chile 158/B1
O'Higgins (lake),
Chile 159/B6
Ohio (riv.), US 119/J6
Ohio (state), US 125/K3
Ōhira, Japan 77/D1
Ohlsdorf, Aus. 55/G7
Ohlstadt, Ger. 57/H2
Ohm (riv.), Ger. 54/C1
Ōho, Japan 77/E1
Ohoopee (riv.),
Ga, US 133/H3
Ohře (riv.), Czh. 40/H3
Ohře (riv.), Ger. 51/G7
Ohrid, Macd. 47/G2
Ohrid (lake),
Alb., Mac 47/G2
Oi (riv.), China 30/J5
Ōi, Japan 77/J6
Ōi, Japan 77/C3
Ōi, Japan 77/D2
Oiapoque (riv.),
Braz. 151/H3
Oiapoque, Braz. 151/H3
Oich (lake), Sc, UK 36/B2
Oieras, Port. 45/P10
Oignies, Fr. 52/B3
Oignin (riv.), Fr. 58/B5
Oil City, Pa, US 130/E3
Oinófita, Gre. 47/N8
Oinoi, Gre. 47/N8
Oirschot, Neth. 50/C5
Oise (dept.), Fr. 52/B5
Oise (riv.), Fr. 52/B3
Oise à l'Aisne, Canal de l'
(canal), Fr. 53/C5
Oiseaux du Djoudj, PN des,
Sen. 102/A2
Ōiso, Japan 77/C3
Oisterwijk, Neth. 50/C5
Ōita, Japan 74/B4
Ōita (pref.), Japan 74/B4
Ōita (riv.), Japan 74/B4
Ōizumi, Japan 77/C1
Ōizumi, Japan 77/D2
Ojai, Ca, US 136/A2
Ojcowski NP, Pol. 41/K3
Ojebyn, Swe. 37/G2
Ojima, Japan 77/C1
Ojinaga, Mex. 129/F5
Ojiya, Japan 75/F2
Ojo de Liebre (lag.),
Mex. 142/A2
Ojocaliente, Mex. 142/B3
Ojos del Salado (peak),
Chile 157/C2
Ojos Negros, Sp. 44/E2
Ojuelos de Jalisco,
Mex. 143/E4
Oka, Nga. 103/G5
Oka (riv.), Rus. 65/L4
Oka, Qu, Can. 131/M7
Okabe, Japan 77/C3
Okahandja, Namb. 105/C5
Okak (isl.), Nf, Can. 123/K3
Okanagan (lake),
BC, Can. 122/D4
Okanagan Falls,
BC, Can. 126/D3
Okanda, PN de l',
Gabon 105/B1
Okanogan, Wa, US 126/D3
Okanogan (riv.),
Wa, US 126/D3
Okawa, Japan 74/B4
Okaya, Japan 75/F2
Okayama, Japan 74/C3
Okayama (pref.),
Japan 74/C3
Okazaki, Japan 77/M6
Okch'ŏn, SKor. 77/D1
Okecie (int'l arpt.),
Pol. 41/L2
Okeechobee,
Fl, US 133/H5

Okeechobee (lake), Fl, US 125/K6
Okegawa, Japan 77/D2
Okement (riv.), Eng, UK 32/B5
Okha, Rus. 65/Q4
OkhiÒros (peak), Gre. 47/J3
Okhotsk (sea), Rus. 67/P4
Okhotsk, Sea of (sea), Japan,Rus 71/R2
Okhta (riv.), Rus. 61/T6
Okhtyrka, Ukr. 62/E2
Oki (isls.), Japan 65/P6
Okidaitō (isl.), Japan 75/L8
Okiep, SAfr. 106/B3
Okinawa (isl.), Japan 67/M7
Okinawa (pref.), Japan 75/J8
Okino-shima (isl.), Japan 74/C4
Okinoerabu (isl.), Japan 75/K7
Okitipupa, Nga. 103/G5
Okkan, Myan. 83/G4
Okku, SKor. 73/D5
Oklahoma (state), US 125/G4
Oklahoma City (cap.), Ok, US 137/M15
Okmulgee, Ok, US 129/J4
Oko, Nga. 103/G5
Okobaji (lakes), Ia, US 127/K5
Okok (riv.), Ugan. 104/B2
Okoppe, Japan 76/C1
Okotoks, Ab, Can. 126/E3
Okovango (riv.), Namb. 93/E6
Øksbøl, Den. 38/C4
Oksskolten (peak), Nor. 37/E2
Oktyabr'sk, Rus. 63/J1
Oktyabr'skiy, Rus. 61/M5
Ōkuchi, Japan 74/B4
Okulovka, Rus. 60/G4
Okushiri, Japan 76/A2
Okutama (lake), Japan 77/C2
Okutama, Japan 77/C2
Okwa (riv.), Bots. 105/D5
Ol Doinyo Sabuk NP, Kenya 104/C3
Ólafsfjördhur, Ice. 37/N6
Ólafsvík, Ice. 37/M7
Olalla, Wa, US 135/B3
Olan, Pic d' (peak), Fr. 43/G4
Olanchito, Hon. 144/E3
Öland (isl.), Swe. 37/F4
Ölands södra udde (pt.), Swe. 38/G3
Olathe, Ks, US 137/D6
Olavarria, Arg. 158/E3
Oł awa, Pol. 41/J3
Ölbach (riv.), Ger. 51/F5
Olberg, Az, US 137/S19
Olbia, It. 46/A2
Olching, Ger. 55/E6
Olcott, NY, US 131/S9
Old (riv.), Ca, US 135/L11
Old Bahama (chan.), Cuba 145/G1
Old Bar, Austl. 115/E1
Old Bedford (canal), Eng, UK 33/G2
Old Bethpage, NY, US 139/M9
Old Bridge, NJ, US 139/H10
Old City, Isr. 91/G8
Old Crow, Yk, Can. 134/L2
Old Faithful Geyser, Wy, US 126/F4
Old Field (pt.), NY, US 139/E2
Old Fort Niagara, NY, US 131/R9
Old Harbor, Ak, US 134/H4
Old Man of Hoy, Sc, UK 31/V14
Old Mill Creek, Il, US 135/Q15
Old Nene (riv.), Eng, UK 33/F2
Old Rhine (riv.), Neth. 50/B3
Old Saybrook, Ct, US 139/F1
Old Tappan, NJ, US 139/K8
Old Town, Me, US 131/G2
Old Windsor, Eng, UK 30/B2
Old Wives (lake), Can. 127/G3
Oldeani (peak), Tanz. 104/B3
Oldebroek, Neth. 50/C4
Oldemarkt, Neth. 50/C3
Oldenburg, Ger. 51/F2
Oldenburg, Ger. 38/D4
Oldenzaal, Neth. 50/D4
Oldham, Eng, UK 35/F4
Oldman (riv.), Can. 126/E3
Oldmeldrum, Sc, UK 36/D2
Oldoog (riv.), Est. 51/E1
Olds, Ab, Can. 126/E3
Olduvai Gorge, Tanz. 104/B3
Oldwick, NJ, US 138/D2
Olean, NY, US 130/E3
Olecko, Pol. 39/K4
Oleggio, It. 58/B1
Oleiros, Port. 44/B3
Oleiros, Sp. 44/A1
Olekma (riv.), Rus. 65/N4
Oleksandriya, Ukr. 62/E2
Olele, Wa, US 135/B2
Ølen, Nor. 38/A2
Olenegorsk, Rus. 60/G1
Oleněk (riv.), Rus. 65/L3
Oléron, Île (isl.), Fr. 42/C4
Olesa de Montserrat, Sp. 45/K6
Oleśnica, Pol. 41/J3
Olesno, Pol. 41/K3
Oley, Pa, US 138/C3
Olfen, Ger. 51/E5
Olga (mt.), Austl. 113/F3
Olginate, It. 58/C1
Ölgiy, Mong. 70/E2
Ølgod, Den. 38/C4

Olhão, Port. 44/B4
Oliena, It. 46/A2
Olifantshoek, SAfr. 106/P12
Olifantsrivier (riv.), SAfr. 105/C5
Ōmu, Japan 76/C1
Olimarao (isl.), Micr. 116/D4
Olímbia (Olympia) (ruin), Gre. 47/G4
Ólimbos, Gre. 90/A3
Ólimbos NP (Olympos NP), Gre. 47/H2
Olímpia, Braz. 155/B2
Olimpos Beydağları NP, Turk. 91/B1
Olinalá, Mex. 144/B2
Olinda, Braz. 154/D3
Olindina, Braz. 154/C3
Oliva, Sp. 45/E3
Oliva de la Frontera, Sp. 44/B3
Olivais, Port. 44/A3
Oliveira, Braz. 155/C2
Olivenza, Sp. 44/B3
Oliver, BC, Can. 126/D3
Olivet, Fr. 42/D3
Olivone, Swi. 57/E4
Olla, La, US 129/J5
Ollachea, Peru 156/C4
Ollagüe (vol.) 150/E8
Ollainville, Fr. 30/J6
Olleria, Sp. 45/E3
Olleros, Peru 156/B3
Ollon, Swi. 56/D5
Olūr, India 82/C5
Olmaliq, Uzb. 87/E4
Olmedo, Sp. 44/C2
Olmos, Peru 156/B2
Olmos Park, Tx, US 137/U21
Olney, Eng, UK 33/F2
Olney, Il, US 137/C1
Olney, Tx, US 129/H4
Olney, Md, US 138/A5
Olofström, Swe. 38/F3
Olomane (riv.), Can. 131/J1
Olomouc, Czh. 41/J4
Olongapo, Phil. 79/D5
Olonne-sur-Mer, Fr. 42/C3
Olorgasailie Nat'l Mon., Kenya 104/C3
Oloron-Sainte-Marie, Fr. 42/C5
Olot, Sp. 45/G1
Oloy (range), Rus. 65/S3
Olpe, Ger. 51/F6
Olpe, Ks, US 129/H2
Olsberg, Ger. 51/F6
Olst, Neth. 50/C4
Olsztyn, Pol. 39/J5
Olsztyn (prov.), Pol. 39/J5
Olsztynek, Pol. 41/L2
Olt (riv.), Rom. 62/C3
Olt (prov.), Rom. 49/G3
Olte, Sierra de (hills), Arg. 158/C4
Olten, Swi. 56/D3
Olteniţa, Rom. 49/H3
Olteţ (riv.), Rom. 49/F3
Oltre il Colle, It. 57/F6
Oltu (riv.), Turk. 63/G4
Oltu, Turk. 63/G4
Olur, Turk. 63/G4
Olvera, Sp. 44/C4
Olympia (cap.), Wa, US 126/C4
Olympic (isls.), Ok, US 132/D2
Olympic Dam, Austl. 113/H4
Olympic Game Farm, Wa, US 135/A1
Olympic National Forest, Wa, US 135/A2
Olympic NP, Wa, US 126/B3
Olympic Park, SKor. 73/G6
Olympos (Mount Olympus) (peak), Gre. 47/H2
Olympus (mt.), Cyp. 91/C2
Olyutorskiy (bay), Rus. 65/S3
Oma (riv.), Rus. 61/K2
Ōma-zaki (pt.), Japan 76/B3
Ōmachi, Japan 75/E2
Omae-zaki (pt.), Japan 75/E3
Ōmagari, Japan 76/B4
Omagh (dist.), NI, UK 34/A2
Omagh, NI, UK 34/A2
Omak, Wa, US 126/D3
Oman (gulf), Asia 67/E7
Oman (ctry.) 67/G5
Omar Torrijos Herrera (int'l arpt.), Pan. 152/B2
Omaruru, Namb. 105/C5
Omas, Peru 156/B4
Omatako (riv.), Namb. 105/C4
Omate, Peru 156/C4
Ombai (str.), Indo. 81/F5
Ombrone (riv.), It. 43/J5
Ombúes de Lavalle, Uru. 159/K10
Ōme, Japan 77/C2
Omeath, Ire. 34/B3
Omegna, It. 43/H4
Omei, Austl. 115/C2
Ōmerli, Turk. 90/E2
Ometepe (isl.), Nic. 144/E4
Ometepec, Mex. 144/B2
Ōmihachiman, Japan 77/K5
Omiš, Cro. 48/C4
Ōmitlan (riv.), Mex. 144/B2
Ōmiya, Japan 75/G2
Ōmiya, Japan 77/H4
Ōmmaney (cape), Ak, US 134/M4
Ommen, Neth. 50/D3
Ōmnōgovĭ (prov.), Mong. 70/H3
Omo NP, Eth. 97/N7
Omo Wenz (riv.), Eth. 93/F4
Omodeo (lake), It. 46/A2
Omolon (riv.), Rus. 67/Q3
Omono (riv.), Japan 76/B4

Omsk, Rus. 87/F1
Omsk (int'l arpt.), Rus. 87/F1
Omsk Oblast, Rus. 87/F1
Ōmu, Japan 76/C1
Omul (peak), Rom. 49/G3
Ōmura, Japan 74/A4
Omurtag, Bul. 49/H4
Ōmuta, Japan 74/B4
Omutninsk, Rus. 61/M4
Onagawa, Japan 76/B4
Onalaska, Tx, US 129/J5
Onaping (lake), Can. 130/D2
Oñate, Sp. 44/D1
Onaway, Mi, US 130/C2
Onchan, IM, UK 34/D3
Onda, Sp. 45/E3
Ondava (riv.), Slvk. 41/L4
Ondjiva, Ang. 105/C4
Ondo, Nga. 103/G5
Ondo (state), Nga. 103/G5
Öndörhaan, Mong. 71/K2
Onè, It. 59/E1
Onega (lake), Rus. 160/D
Onega (riv.), Rus. 64/D3
Onega (bay), Rus. 60/G2
Onega, Rus. 60/H3
Oneida, NY, US 130/F3
Oneida, Pa, US 138/B2
Oneonta, NY, US 130/F3
Onex, Swi. 56/C5
Ongjin, NKor. 73/C4
Ongole, India 82/D4
Ongtüstik Qazaqstan, Kaz. 64/G5
Onhaye, Belg. 53/D3
Onida, SD, US 127/H4
Onil, It. 45/E3
Onilahy (riv.), Madg. 107/G8
Onishi, Chile 158/N8
Onitsha, Nga. 103/G5
Onjuku, Japan 77/E3
Onkaparinga (riv.), Austl. 113/M8
Onny (riv.), Eng, UK 32/D2
Ōno, Japan 74/E3
Ōno, Japan 77/L5
Onoda, Japan 74/B4
Onomichi, Japan 74/C3
Onon, Mong. 71/K2
Onoto, Ven. 153/E2
Onotoa (isl.), Kiri. 116/G5
Onrusrivier, SAfr. 106/L11
Onslow, Austl. 112/B2
Ontake-san (peak), Japan 75/E3
Ontario, Or, US 126/D4
Ontario, Ca, US 136/C2
Ontario (prov.), Can. 122/H3
Ontario (lake) 36/B4
Oncano di Pesaro, It. 59/F5
Orco, It. 58/A4
Onteniente, Sp. 45/E3
Ontonagon, Mi, US 127/L4
Ontong Java (isls.), Sol. 116/E5
Onyang, SKor. 73/D4
Onzaga, Col. 152/C2
Oologah (lake), Ok, US 132/D2
Oona River, BC, Can. 134/M5
Oost-Vlaanderen (prov.), Belg. 52/C2
Oost-Vlieland, Neth. 50/C2
Oostburg, Neth. 52/C1
Oostelijk Flevoland (polder), Neth. 50/C3
Oostende (Ostend), Belg. 52/B1
Oosterhout, Neth. 50/B5
Oosterscheidedam (dam), Neth. 50/A5
Oosterschelde (riv.), Neth. 40/B3
Oosterwolde, Neth. 50/D3
Oosterzele, Belg. 52/C1
Oostkamp, Belg. 52/C1
Oostvaardersplassen (lake), Neth. 50/C4
Oostzaan, Neth. 50/C4
Ootmarsum, Neth. 50/D4
Opaka, Bul. 49/H4
Opalenica, Pol. 41/J2
Opasatika (riv.), Can. 130/D1
Opatija, Cro. 48/B3
Opatów, Pol. 41/L3
Opava, Czh. 41/J4
Opelika, Al, US 133/G3
Opelousas, La, US 129/J5
Opera, It. 58/C2
Öpfingen, Ger. 57/F1
Opglabbeek, Belg. 53/E1
Ophir (riv.), NZ 117/R12
Ophir, Ak, US 134/G3
Ophir, Ut, US 137/J13
Ophthalmia (range), Austl. 112/C2
Oploo, Neth. 50/C5
Opmeer, Neth. 50/B3
Opobo, Nga. 103/G5
Opochka, Rus. 60/F3
Opoczno, Pol. 41/L3
Opole, Pol. 41/J3
Opole Lubelskie, Pol. 41/L3
Opovo, Yugo. 48/E3
Opp, Al, US 133/G4
Oppdal, Nor. 37/D3
Oppeano, It. 46/A2
Oppenau, Ger. 56/E1
Oppenheim, Ger. 51/G3
Oppland (co.), Nor. 37/D3
Opportunity, Wa, US 126/D4
Opua (riv.), NY, US 139/F1
Oqu'Aqiva, Isr. 91/F6
Or, Mont d' (peak), Fr. 56/C4
Or Yehuda, Isr. 91/F7
Ora (riv.), Mex. 142/D3
Öra, Japan 77/C1
Oradell, NJ, US 139/J8
Oradell (res.), NJ, US 139/J8
Orahovac, Yugo. 47/G1
Orahovica, Cro. 48/D3
Orai, India 84/B3

Oral, Kaz. 63/J2
Oran, Alg. 100/E5
Orang (riv.), NKor. 73/E2
Orange (cape), Braz. 151/H3
Orange (mts.), Sur. 151/G3
Orange, Austl. 115/D2
Orange, Fr. 43/A3
Orange, Va, US 130/E4
Orange, Tx, US 129/J5
Orange, Fr. 42/F4
Orange (co.), NY, US 138/D1
Orange, Ct, US 139/E1
Orange (co.), NY, US 139/H7
Orange, Ca, US 136/C2
Orange, NJ, US 139/J8
Orange Park, Fl, US 133/H4
Orange Walk, Belz. 144/D2
Orangeburg, SC, US 133/H3
Orangeburg, Il, US 139/K7
Orange, On, Can. 130/D3
Orangeville, Pa, US 138/B2
Orangeville, On, Can. 130/D3
Orango (isl.), GBis. 102/A4
Oranienburg, Ger. 40/O6
Oranjekanaal (riv.), Neth. 50/D3
Oranjemund, Namb. 106/B3
Oranjestad, Aruba. 152/D1
Oranmore, Ire. 31/P10
Orapa, Bots. 105/E6
Oras, Phil. 79/E5
Orăştie, Rom. 49/F3
Oravita, Rom. 48/E3
Orb (riv.), Fr. 42/E5
Ørbaek, Den. 38/D4
Orbe (riv.), Swi. 56/C4
Orbe, Swi. 56/C4
Orbey, Fr. 56/D1
Orbigo (riv.), Sp. 44/C1
Orbost, Austl. 115/D3
Ørbyhus, Swe. 38/G1
Orcemont, Fr. 30/H6
Orcera, Sp. 44/D3
Orchamps, Fr. 56/B3
Orchamps-Vennes, Fr. 56/C3
Orchard (lake), Mi, US 135/F6
Orchard City, Co, US 128/F3
Orchard Farm, Mo, US 137/G8
Orchard Homes, Mt, US 126/E4
Orchard Lake Village, Mi, US 135/F6
Orchid (isl.), Tai. 79/D3
Orchies, Fr. 52/C3
Orchy (riv.), Sc, UK 36/B4
Orco (riv.), It. 58/A4
Orcopampa, Peru 156/C4
Orcotuna, Peru 156/C3
Ordaz (int'l arpt.), Ven. 153/E2
Orden, Sp. 44/A1
Ordes, Sp. 44/A1
Ordesa y Monte Perdido, PN de (park), Sp. 45/F1
Orosei, Golfo di (gulf), It. 46/A2
Ordos (des.), China 70/J4
Ordos (Mu Us Shamo) (des.), China 70/F4
Ordu, Turk. 62/E4
Ordu (prov.), Turk. 62/E4
Ore, Nga. 103/G5
Oreálla, Guy. 153/G3
Örebro, Swe. 38/F2
Örebro (int'l arpt.), Swe. 38/F2
Oregon (state), US 124/B3
Oregon Caves Nat'l Mon., Or, US 126/C3
Oregon City, Or, US 126/C4
Öregrund, Swe. 38/H1
Orekhovo-Zuyevo, Rus. 60/H5
Orël Oblast, Rus. 62/E1
Orel (riv.), Rus. 62/F1
Orellana, Peru 156/C2
Orellana la Vieja, Sp. 44/C3
Orenburg (int'l arpt.), Rus. 63/K1
Orenburg Oblast, Rus. 63/K2
Orense, Sp. 44/B1
Orestiás, Gre. 47/H5
Øresund (sound), 38/E4
Oreti (riv.), NZ 117/R12
Orford, Austl. 115/C4
Orford, Fr. 42/G4
Orford Ness (cape), Eng, UK 33/H2
Organ Pipe Cactus Nat'l Mon., Az, US 142/B1
Orgaz, Sp. 44/D3
Orgelet, Fr. 56/B4
Orgeval, Fr. 30/H5
Orgosolo, It. 46/A2
Orhangazi, Turk. 62/D5
Orhei, Mol. 49/J2
Orhon (riv.), Mong. 70/J2
Oria, Sp. 44/D4
Orient (pt.), NY, US 139/F1
Oriental, Cordillera (mts.), Ecu.,Col. 152/C3
Orientale (prov.), D.R. Congo 104/A2
Orihuela, Sp. 45/E3
Orihuela del Tremedal, Sp. 44/E2
Orillia, On, Can. 130/E2
Orimattila, Fin. 39/L1
Orinda, Ca, US 135/K11
Orinoco (riv.), Ven. 148/G8
Orinoco (delta), Ven. 153/F2
Oristán, Arg. 158/E3
Col.,Ven. 147/C2

Orio al Serio (int'l arpt.), It. 58/C1
Oriolo, It. 46/E2
Orion (lake), Mi, US 135/F6
Orissa (state), India 70/D7
Orissa Coast (canal), India 85/F5
Oristano, It. 46/A3
Oristano, Golfo di (gulf), It. 46/A3
Orivesi, Fin. 39/L1
Oriximiná, Braz. 211/G8
Orizaba, Mex. 143/M8
Orizona, Braz. 154/A5
Osborn (mt.),
Ørje, Swe. 38/E2
Orjen (peak), Yugo. 47/F1
Ørjiva, Sp. 44/D4
Orke (riv.), Ger. 51/F6
Örkelljunga, Swe. 38/E3
Orkhomenós, Gre. 47/H3
Orkney, SAfr. 106/D2
Orkney (isls.), UK 160/G
Orland, Tx, US 132/C4
Orland Park, Il, US 133/Q16
Orlândia, Braz. 155/C2
Orlando (int'l arpt.), Fl, US 133/H4
Orlando, Fl, US 133/H4
Orlando, Capo d' (cape), It. 46/D3
Orléanais (reg.), Fr. 42/D2
Orleans (co.), La, US 137/P16
Orléans, Fr. 42/D2
Orléans, Fr. 42/D2
Orleans, It. 58/A4
Orlik (res.), Czh. 55/H3
Orlová, Czh. 41/K4
Orly (int'l arpt.), Fr. 42/E2
Orly, Fr. 30/K5
Ormanli, Turk. 49/K5
Ormea, It. 58/A4
Ormília, Gre. 47/H2
Ormiston, Sc, UK 36/D5
Ormoc, Phil. 81/F1
Ormond Beach, Fl, US 133/H4
Ormskirk, Eng, UK 35/F4
Ornain (riv.), Fr. 42/F2
Ornans, Fr. 56/C3
Ornavasso, It. 57/E6
Ørnes, Nor. 37/E2
Ōrneta, Japan 39/J4
Örnsköldsvik, Swe. 37/F3
Oro (riv.), Mex. 154/C2
Oro Grande, Ca, US 136/C2
Oro, Monte d' (peak), Fr. 46/A1
Oro Valley, Az, US 128/E4
Orocó, Braz. 154/C3
Orocué, Col. 152/D3
Orodara, Burk. 102/D4
Orofino, Id, US 126/D4
Orolo (riv.), Micr. 116/E4
Oron-la-Ville, Swi. 56/C4
Orona (Hull) (isl.), Kiri. 117/H5
Orono, Me, US 131/G2
Orontes (riv.), Syria 90/D3
Oropesa, Sp. 44/C3
Orogen Zizhiqi, China 71/M1
Orós, Braz. 154/C2
Orosei, It. 46/A2
Orosei, Golfo di (gulf), It. 46/A2
Orosháza, Hun. 48/E2
Oroszlány, Hun. 48/D2
Orovada, Nv, US 126/D5
Oroville, Wa, US 126/D3
Oroville, Ca, US 128/B3
Orphin, Fr. 30/H6
Orpund, Swi. 56/D3
Orrefors, Swe. 38/F3
Orrell, Eng, UK 35/F4
Orrick, Mo, US 137/E5
Orrin (riv.), Sc, UK 36/B2
Orrin (res.), Sc, UK 36/B2
Orroroo, Austl. 113/H5
Orry-la-Ville, Fr. 30/K4
Orsa, Swe. 38/F1
Orsago, It. 59/F1
Orsay, Fr. 30/J5
Orsett, Eng, UK 30/E2
Orsha, Bela. 39/P4
Orsières, Swi. 56/D5
Orsk, Rus. 63/L2
Orsogna, It. 46/C2
Orsório, Braz. 155/B4
Orsova, Rom. 48/F3
Orta (lake), It. 43/H4
Orta Nova, It. 46/D2
Orta, Turk. 62/E4
Ortaca, Turk. 90/C2
Ortaköy, Turk. 62/E4
Ortaköy, Turk. 51/E2
Orth an der Donau, Aus. 49/P7
Orthez, Fr. 42/C5
Ortigueira, Sp. 44/B1
Ortiz, Mex. 142/C2
Ortiz, Ven. 152/E2
Ortles (peak), It. 57/J4
Ortón (riv.), Bol. 150/D6
Ortona, It. 46/C2
Ortonville, Mi, US 135/F6
Ortonville, Mn, US 127/J4
Orūmiyeh, Iran 90/F2
Oruro, Bol. 156/D4
Orust (isl.), Swe. 38/D2
Orvieto, It. 46/B2
Orvilliers, Fr. 30/G5
Orwell (riv.), Eng, UK 33/H2
Orwigsburg, Pa, US 138/B2
Oryahovo, Bul. 49/F4
Orzysz, Pol. 39/L5
Os, Nor. 38/A1
Osa, Rus. 61/M4

Osa, Peninsula de (pen.), CR 150/B2
Osage (riv.), Mo, US 129/J3
Osage Beach, Mo, US 129/J3
Ōsaka (pref.), Japan 74/D3
Ōsaka (int'l arpt.), Japan 74/D3
Ōsaka, Japan 77/H6
Ōsaka Castle, Japan 77/H6
Osan, SKor. 73/D4
Osasco, Braz. 211/G8
Ōsato, Japan 77/C1
Osborn (mt.),
Osburg, Ger. 53/F4
Osby, Swe. 38/E3
Osceola, Ar, US 130/B5
Osceola, Ia, US 129/J3
Oschersleben, Ger. 40/F2
Oschiri, It. 46/A2
Oscura (mts.), NM, US 132/B3
Osdorf, Ger. 51/G1
Osh (obl.), Kyr. 87/F4
Osh, Kyr. 87/F4
Oshamambe, Japan 76/B2
Oshawa, On, Can. 131/S8
Oshika, Japan 76/B4
Oshikango, Namb.
Oshima, Japan 77/B3
Oshkosh, Ne, US 127/H5
Oshnoviyeh, Iran 90/F2
Oshogbo, Nga. 103/G5
Osijek, Cro. 48/D3
Osio Sotto, It. 58/C1
Osipaovicha, Yugo. 48/E3
Oskarshamn, Swe. 38/G3
Oskarström, Swe. 38/E3
Oskol (riv.), Rus.,Ukr. 62/F2
Oslo (cap.), Nor. 38/D2
Osmānābād, India 89/L5
Osmancık, Turk. 62/E4
Osmaneli, Turk. 49/K5
Osmaniye, Turk. 91/E1
Osnabrück, Ger. 51/E4
Osny, Fr. 30/J4
Oso (riv.), D.R. Congo 104/A3
Oso (mt.), Ca, US 135/M12
Osogna, Swi. 57/E4
Osório, Braz. 155/B4
Osorno, Chile 158/B4
Osorno, BC, Can. 126/D3
Osoyoos, BC, Can. 126/D3
Ospedaletti, It. 58/A5
Ospedaletto, It. 58/B1
Ospitaletto, It. 58/D1
Osprey (reef), Austl. 109/D2
Oss, Neth. 50/C5
Ossa (mt.), Austl. 115/C4
Ossa, Sierra de (mts.), Port. 44/B3
Osse (riv.), Nga. 103/G5
Osséja, Fr. 42/D5
Ossett, Eng, UK 35/G4
Ossi, It. 46/A2
Ossining, NY, US 139/K7
Ostashkov, Rus. 60/G4
Ostbevern, Ger. 51/E4
Ostellato, It. 59/E3
Osten, Ger. 51/G1
Osterburg, Ger. 40/F2
Osterburken, Ger. 54/C4
Österbymo, Swe. 38/F3
Ostercappeln, Ger. 51/F4
Osterdalälven (riv.), Swe. 38/F1
Osterems (chan.), Ger. 50/D1
Osterholz-Scharmbeck, Ger. 51/F2
Osteria Grande, It. 59/D3
Ostermiething, Aus. 55/F6
Osterode am Harz, Ger. 51/H5
Östersund, Swe. 37/E3
Östervåla, Swe. 38/G1
Ostfildern, Ger. 54/C5
Ostfold (co.), Nor. 37/D4
Ostfriesland (reg.), Ger. 50/D2
Osthammar, Swe. 38/H1
Osthofen, Ger. 54/B3
Ostia Antica (ruin), It. 46/C2
Ostiano, It. 58/C2
Ostiglia, It. 58/D2
Ostional NWR, CR 144/E4
Ostra, It. 59/F5
Östra Silen (lake), Swe. 38/D2
Ostra Vetere, It. 59/F5
Ostrach (riv.), Ger. 54/C6
Ostrava, Czh. 41/K4
Ostróda, Pol. 41/K2
Ostrogozhsk, Rus. 62/F2
Ostroh, Ukr. 41/N3
Ostrołęka, Rus. 41/L2
Ostrov, It. 58/C2
Ostrov, Czh. 55/G3
Ostrov, Rus. 60/F3
Ostrów Mazowiecka, Pol. 41/L2
Ostrów Wielkopolski, Pol. 41/J3
Ostrowiec Świętokrzyski, Pol. 41/L3
Ostrzeszów, Pol. 41/J3
Ostseebad Binz, Ger. 38/F4
Ostseebad Göhren, Ger.
Ostseebad Prerow, Ger.
Osttirol (reg.), Aus.
Ostuni, It. 46/D2
Osūm (riv.), Alb. 47/F2
Osūm (riv.), Bul. 49/G4
Osumi (isls.), Japan 74/B5
Osun (state), Nga. 103/G5
Osuna, Sp. 44/C4
Osvaldo Cruz, Braz. 155/B2
Oswaldtwistle, Eng, UK 35/F4
Oswego, NY, US 130/E3
Oswego, Il, US 135/P16

Oswestry, Eng, UK 35/E6
Oświęcim (Auschwitz), Pol. 41/K3
Ōta (riv.), Japan 74/C3
Ōta, Japan 75/F2
Ōtaki, Japan 77/H6
Ōtaki, Japan 75/G3
Ōtaki, Japan 77/B2
Ōtakine-yama (peak), Japan 75/G2
Otava (riv.), Czh. 43/F2
Otavalo, Ecu. 152/B4
Otavi, Namb. 105/C4
Otawara, Japan 75/G2
Otay, Ca, US 136/C5
Oţelu Roşu, Rom. 48/F3
Otero de Rey, Sp. 44/B1
Oteros (riv.), Mex. 142/C3
Otgon Tenger (peak), Camr.
Othello, Wa, US 126/D4
Othis, Fr. 30/K4
Othonoi (isl.), Gre. 47/F3
Oti (riv.), Gha. 103/F4
Otijwarongo, Namb. 105/C5
Otočac, Cro. 48/B3
Otofuke, Japan 76/C2
Otog Qi, China 70/J4
Otok, Cro. 48/D3
Ōtone, Japan 77/D1
Otopeni (int'l arpt.), Rom. 49/H3
Otoskwin (riv.), Can. 130/C1
Otowa, Japan 77/M6
Otra (riv.), Nor. 64/A4
Otradnyy, Rus. 61/M5
Otranto, Strait of (str.), It. 47/F2
Otrokovice, Czh. 41/J4
Otse, Bots. 106/D2
Ōtsu, Japan 77/J5
Ōtsuchi, Japan 76/C3
Otta (riv.), Nor. 103/F5
On, Japan 130/F2
Ottawa (cap.), Can. 130/F2
Ottawa, Oh, US 130/C3
Ottawa, Ks, US 129/J3
Ottawa (int'l arpt.), Can. 130/F2
Ottawa (isls.), Can. 119/J4
Ottawa (riv.), Can. 119/K5
Ottensheim, Aus. 55/H6
Otter (riv.), Eng, UK 32/C5
Otterbach, Ger. 53/G5
Otterberg, Ger. 53/F5
Otterndorf, Ger. 51/F1
Ottersberg, Ger. 51/G2
Ottershaw, Eng, UK 30/B2
Otterville, Il, US 137/Q8
Ottignies-Louvain-la-Neuve, Belg. 53/D2
Öttingen im Bayern, Ger. 54/E4
Ottmarsheim, Fr. 56/D2
Ottnang an Hausruck, Aus. 55/G6
Otto, Mo, US 137/F9
Ottobeuren, Ger. 57/G2
Ottobrunn, Ger. 55/E6
Ottone, It. 58/C2
Ottosdal, SAfr. 106/D2
Ottsville, Pa, US 138/C2
Ottumwa, Ia, US 127/K5
Ottweiler, Ger. 53/G5
Otumba de Gómez Farías, Mex. 143/L7
Otuzco, Peru 156/B2
Otway (cape), Austl. 115/B3
Otway (bay), Chile 159/C7
Otway NP, Austl. 115/B3
Outeau, Fr. 42/A2
Otwock, Pol. 41/L2
Ötztal Alps (mts.), Aus. 43/J3
Ötztaler Ache (riv.), Aus.
Ou (mts.), Japan 76/B4
Ouachita (mts.), 125/G5
Ouachita (riv.), Ar,La, US
Ouadda, CAfr. 97/K6
Ouaddaï (reg.), Chad 97/J5
Ouadi Haddad (riv.), Chad
Ouadi Rimé (riv.), Chad 96/J5
Ouagadougou (int'l arpt.), Burk. 103/E3
Ouagadougou (cap.), Burk. 103/E3
Ouahigouya, Burk. 103/E3
Ouaka (riv.), CAfr. 97/K6
Oualâta, Dhar (cliff), Mrta. 102/D2
Ouallam, Niger 103/F3
Ouanda Djallé, CAfr. 97/K6
Ouanne (riv.), Fr. 42/E3
Ouarane (pol. reg.), Mrta.
Ouarane (reg.), Mrta. 98/C5
Ouargla (prov.), Alg.
Ouargla, Alg. 99/G3
Ouarkziz, Jebel (ridge), Mor. 98/D3
Ouarzazate (int'l arpt.), Mor. 98/D3
Ouarzazate, Mor. 98/D3
Ouassemscar (riv.), Can. 130/F1
Oubangui (riv.), CAfr. 97/J7
Oubritenga (prov.), Burk.
Ouche (riv.), Fr. 56/B3
Oud-Beijerland, Neth. 50/B5
Ŏuda (prov.), Japan 77/J7
Oudalan (prov.), Burk.
Oude IJssel (riv.), Neth. 50/D5
Oude Pekela, Neth. 50/E2
Oudega, Neth. 50/D1
Oudenaarde, Belg. 52/C2
Oudenbosch, Belg. 50/B5
Oudenburg, Belg. 52/C1
Oudewater, Neth. 50/B4
Oudon (riv.), Fr. 42/C3
Oudtshoorn, SAfr. 106/C4
Oued el Hadjar (well), Mali 102/E2
Oued Moulouyadeu (riv.), Mor. 96/E1
Oued Sous (riv.), Mor.
Oued Zem, Mor. 98/F6
Ouémé (riv.), Ben. 103/G5
Ouémé (prov.), Ben. 103/G5
Ouenza, Alg. 100/L7
Ouerrha (riv.),
Ouessant (isl.),
Ouessé, Ben. 103/F4
Ouessé, Congo 96/J7
Ouest (prov.),
Ouest, Camr. 103/H5
Ouest (pt.), Haiti 145/H1
Ouest (pt.), Haiti 145/H1
Ouezzane, Mor. 100/D2
Ougham (riv.), CAfr. 96/J6
Ouidah, Ben. 100/D2
Oujda (prov.), Mor.
Oujda, Mor. 100/D2
Oujda (Angads) (int'l arpt.), Mor. 98/C3
Oulad Teïma, Mor.
Oulangan NP, Fin. 60/F2
Ould Birni (well), Alg. 99/E4
Oulnina (peak), Austl. 113/H5
Oulu (prov.), Fin. 60/E2
Oulu, Fin. 60/F2
Oulujärvi (lake),
Oum El Bouaghi, Alg. 100/K7
Oum er Rbia, Oued (riv.),
Oum er Rhia (riv.),
Ōunasjoki (riv.), Fin.
Oupeye, Belg. 53/E2
Ource (riv.), Fr. 42/F3
Ourcq (riv.), Fr. 40/B4
Ourcq, Canal de l' (canal), Fr. 30/K5
Øure Anarjokka NP, Nor. 37/H1
Øure Dividal NP,
Ouricuri, Braz. 156/B2
Ourinhos, Braz. 155/B2
Ourique, Port. 44/A4
Ouro Fino, Braz. 211/G7
Ouro Preto, Braz. 155/D2
Ouro, Ponta de (pt.),
Ouroux-sur-Saône, Fr. 56/A4
Ourthe Occidentale (riv.),
Ourthe Orientale (riv.),
Ouse (riv.), Eng, UK 35/H4
Oust (riv.), Fr. 42/B3
Outardes (riv.),
Outardes Quatre (lake), Can. 131/G1
Outeïd Arkas (well), Mali 102/D2
Outer Hebrides (isls.), Sc, UK 31/P8
Outjo, Namb. 105/C5
Outlook, Sk, Can. 126/G3
Outreau, Fr. 52/A2
Outremont, Qu, Can. 131/N6
Ouvéze (riv.), Fr.
Ouyen, Austl. 115/B2
Ouzinkie, Ak, US 134/H4
Ovacık, Turk. 62/F5
Ovacık, Turk.
Ovada, It. 58/B3
Ovalle, Chile 157/B3
Ovana (peak), Ven. 158/D2
Ovar, Port. 44/A2
Overath, Ger. 53/G2
Ouddadà, CAfr. 97/K6
Overflakkee (isl.),
Overhalla, Nor. 37/D2
Overholser (lake), Ok, US 137/M14
Overijse, Belg. 53/D2
Overijssel (prov.), Neth. 50/D3
Overijssels (riv.),
Overkalix, Swe. 37/G2
Overland, Mo, US 137/G8
Overland Park, Ks, US 137/D6
Overlea, Md, US 138/B5
Overpelt, Belg. 50/C6
Overton, Nv, US 128/D2
Overtorneå, Swe. 60/D2
Overum, Swe. 38/G3
Oviedo, Sp. 44/C1
Övörhangay (prov.), Mong.
Ovruch, Ukr. 34/B6
Öwer (mt.), NZ 117/S11
Owen, Austl. 113/H5
Owen, Wi, US 127/L4
Owen Falls (dam), Ugan. 104/B2
Owen Roberts (int'l arpt.), UK 145/F2
Owen Sound, On, Can. 130/D2
Owensboro, Ky, US 130/C4
Owenskillew (riv.),
NI, UK 34/A2

Owerri, Nga. 103/G5
Owingen, Ger. 57/F2
Owings, Md, US 138/B6
Owings Mills, Md, US 138/B5
Owl Creek (mts.), Wy, US 126/F4
Owo, Nga. 103/G5
Owosso, Mi, US 130/C3
Owyhee, Nv, US 126/D5
Owyhee (lake), Or, US 128/C2
Owyhee (riv.), Id, US 128/C2
Owyhee, South Fork (riv.), Nv, US 126/D5
Oxapampa, Peru 156/C3
Oxbow, Sk, Can. 127/H3
Oxbow (lake), Mi, US 135/F6
Oxelösund, Swe. 38/G2
Oxford (canal), Eng, UK 33/E3
Oxford, Ms, US 133/F3
Oxford, Eng, UK 33/E3
Oxford, Pa, US 138/C4
Oxford, NY, US 135/F6
Oxfordshire (co.), Eng, UK 33/E3
Oxie, Swe. 38/E4
Oxkutzcab, Mex. 144/D1
Oxnard, Ca, US 136/A2
Oxnard Beach, Ca, US 136/A2
Oxon Hill (farm), Md, US 138/A6
Oxon Hill-Glassmanor, Md, US 138/B6
Oxted, Eng, UK 30/D3
Oyabe, Japan 75/E2
Oyama, Japan 75/F2
Oyama, Japan 77/B3
Oyama, Japan 77/K6
Ōyamazaki, Japan 77/J6
Oyapock (riv.), Fr. 151/H3
Oye-Plage, Fr. 52/B2
Oyem, Gabon 96/H7
Oyen, Ab, Can. 126/F3
Øyer, Nor. 38/D1
Øykell (riv.), Sc, UK 31/R8
Oyo (state), Nga. 103/F4
Oyo, Nga. 103/F5
Oyodo, Japan 74/B5
Ōyodo, Japan 77/J7
Oyón, Peru 156/B3
Oyonnax, Fr. 56/B5
Oyster Bay, NY, US 139/L8
Oyster Bay (har.), NY, US 139/L8
Oyster Bay Cove, NY, US 139/L8
Oyster Bay NWR, NY, US 139/L8
Oyten, Ger. 51/G2
Ozamiz, Phil. 79/D6
Ozark (plat.), Mo, US 129/K3
Ozark, Ar, US 129/J4
Ozark, Al, US 133/G4
Ozark (mts.), Ar,Mo, US
Ozarks (lake), Mo, US 125/H4
Ozd, Hun. 41/L4
Ozernoy (cape), Rus. 65/S4
Ozette (lake), Wa, US 126/B3
Ozhiski (lake), Can. 127/L3
Ozieri, It. 46/A2
Ozimek, Pol. 41/K3
Ozoir-la-Ferrière, Fr. 30/L5
Ozona, Tx, US 129/G5
Ozorków, Pol. 41/K3
Ozouer-le-Voulgis, Fr. 30/L6
Ozu, Japan 74/C4
Ozuluama de Mascareñas, Mex. 144/B1
Ozzano dell'Emilia, It. 59/E4

P

P. K. Le Rouxdam (res.), SAfr. 106/D3
Pa, Myan. 78/B2
Pa Sak (riv.), Thai. 83/H4
Paar (riv.), Ger. 40/F4
Paarden Eiland, SAfr. 106/L10
Paarl, SAfr. 106/L10
Paauilo, Hi, US 124/U10
Pabbi, Pak. 86/A2
Pabellón de Arteaga, Mex. 142/E4
Pabianice, Pol. 41/K3
Pabna, Bang. 85/G3
Pabna (pol. reg.), Bang. 85/G3
Pacaás Novos, PN dos, Braz. 150/F6
Pacaás Novos, Serra dos (mts.), Braz. 150/F6
Pacajus, Braz. 154/C2
Pacaltsdorp, SAfr. 106/C4
Pacaraimã, Serra (mts.), Braz. 150/F3
Pacaya Samiria, Reserva Nacional, Peru 156/C2
Pacasmayo, Peru 156/C2
Paceco, It. 46/C4
Pachacamac (ruin), Peru 156/B3
Pachaconas, Peru 156/C3
Pachamarca (riv.), Peru 156/C3
Pachino, It. 46/D4
Pachitea (riv.), Peru 156/C3
Pachiza, Peru 156/B2
Pachmarhī, India 84/B4
Pachuca, Mex. 143/L6
Pacific (ocean) 81/H3
Pacific (range), Can. 126/C2
Pacific, Wa, US 135/C3
Pacific Palisades, Hi, US 124/W13

Pacifico (mtn.), Ca, US 136/B2
Pacinan (cape), Indo. 80/D5
Pacitan, Indo. 80/D5
Paço de Arcos, Port. 45/P10
Pad Idan, Pak. 89/J3
Padampur, India 82/D3
Padang, Indo. 80/B4
Padangpanjang, Indo. 80/B4
Padangsidempuan, Indo. 80/A3
Paddock Lake, Wi, US 135/P14
Paddock Wood, Eng, UK 30/E3
Paderborn, Il, US 137/G9
Paderborn, Ger. 51/F5
Paderno, It. 59/F1
Padiham, Eng, UK 35/F4
Padilla, Bol. 150/F7
Padina, Yugo. 48/E3
Padjelanta NP, Swe. 37/F2
Padova (prov.), It. 59/E2
Padova, It. 59/E2
Padrão, Ponta do (pt.), Ang. 105/B2
Padrauna, India 84/D2
Padre (isl.), Tx, US 125/G6
Padre Island Nat'l Seashore, Tx, US 143/F3
Padrón, Sp. 44/A1
Paducah, Tx, US 129/G4
Paducah, Ky, US 130/B4
Padul, Sp. 44/D4
Padula, It. 46/D2
Paektŏk-san (peak), SKor. 73/E4
Paektu-san (peak), NKor. 73/E2
Paese, It. 59/F1
Páez, Col. 152/C3
Páez, Col. 152/C4
Pafúri, Moz. 105/F5
Pag, Cro. 48/B3
Pag (isl.), Cro. 48/B3
Pagadian, Phil. 81/F2
Pagai Selatan (isl.), Indo. 80/B4
Pagai Utara (isl.), Indo. 80/B4
Pagan, Myan. 83/F3
Pagan (isl.),NMar. 116/D3
Paganica, It. 46/C1
Page, Az, US 128/E3
Pager (riv.), Ugan. 104/B2
Pagny-sur-Moselle, Fr. 53/F6
Pagosa Springs, Co, US 128/F3
Pagwachuan (riv.), Can. 130/C1
Pahala, Hi, US 124/U11
Pahang (riv.), Malay. 80/B3
Pāhara (lag.), Nic. 145/F3
Pahārpur, Pak. 86/A3
Pahāsu, India 84/B1
Pahlgām, India 86/C2
Pahrump, Nv, US 128/D3
Pahuatlán, Mex. 143/L6
Pahute (mesa), Nv, US 128/C3
Pai (lake), China 72/C5
Paia, Hi, US 124/T10
Paignton, Eng, UK 32/C6
Paiján, Peru 156/B2
Päijänne (lake), Fin. 37/H3
Paikü (lake), China 85/E1
Pailolo (chan.), US 124/T10
Paimio, Fin. 39/K1
Paine (peak), Chile 159/B6
Paine, Chile 158/N8
Painesville, Oh, US 130/D3
Paint (lake), Can. 127/J2
Paint Rock, Tx, US 132/D4
Painted (des.), Az, US 124/D4
Paipa, Col. 152/C3
País Vasco (aut. comm.), Sp. 44/D1
Paisley, Sc, UK 36/B5
Paita, Peru 156/A2
Paithan, India 82/C4
Pajala, Swe. 37/G2
Paján, Ecu. 152/A5
Pajęczno, Pol. 41/K3
Pakanbaru, Indo. 80/B3
Pakch'ŏn, NKor. 73/C3
Pakenham, Austl. 115/G6
Pakenham (cape), Chile 159/B6
Pākhnes (peak), Gre. 47/J5
Pakhra (riv.), Rus. 61/W9
Pakistan (ctry.) 67/F7
Paklenica NP, Cro. 48/B3
Pakokku, Myan. 83/G3
Pakowki (lake), Can. 126/F3
Pākpattan, Pak. 86/B4
Pakrac, Cro. 48/C3
Paks, Hun. 48/D2
Pakwach, Ugan. 104/A2
Pakxe, Laos 78/D3
Pala, Chad 96/H6
Pala, Ca, US 136/C4
Pala Ind. Res., Ca, US 136/C4
Palace, Mona. 58/J8
Palafrugell, Sp. 45/G2
Palagonia, It. 46/D4
Palagruža (isls.), Cro. 46/E1
Palairos, Gre. 47/G3
Palaiseau, Fr. 30/J5
Pālakollu, India 82/D4
Palamás, Gre. 47/H3
Palamós, Sp. 45/G2
Palana, Rus. 65/R4
Palangkaraya, Indo. 80/D4
Pālanpur, India 89/K4
Palaoa (pt.), Hi, US 124/T10
Palapye, Bots. 105/E5
Palar (riv.), India 82/C5
Palas de Rey, Sp. 44/B1
Palāsbāri, India 85/H2
Palatine, Il, US 135/P15
Palatka, Fl, US 133/H4
Palau (ctry.) 116/C4
Palau We (isl.), Indo. 80/A2
Palaw, Myan. 78/B3
Palawan (isl.), Phil. 67/L9
Palawan Passage (chan.), Phil. 81/E2
Pālayankottai, India 82/C6
Palazzolo Acreide, It. 46/D4
Palazzolo dello Stella, It. 59/G1
Palazzolo sull'Oglio, It. 58/C1
Palé, EqG. 96/G8
Pale, Bosn. 48/D4
Paleleh, Indo. 81/F3
Palembang, Indo. 80/B4
Palena (riv.), Chile 158/B4
Palena, Chile 158/C4
Palencia, Sp. 44/C1
Palenque, Mex. 144/D2
Palenque, PN, Mex. 144/C2
Palermo, It. 46/C3
Palermo, NJ, US 138/D5
Palese (int'l arpt.), It. 46/E2
Palestine (lake), Tx, US 132/E3
Palestro, It. 58/B2
Pālghar, India 89/K5
P'algong-san (peak), SKor. 73/D5
P'algong-san (peak), SKor. 74/A2
Palgrave (mt.), Austl. 112/B2
Palhano, Braz. 154/C2
Palhoça, Braz. 155/B3
Pāli, India 89/K3
Pali-Aike, PN, Chile 159/C7
Paliā Kalān, India 84/C1
Palić, Yugo. 48/D2
Palikea (peak), Hi, US 124/V13
Palikir (cap.), Micr. 116/E4
Palioúrion (cape), Gre. 47/H3
Palisades (cliff), NJ,NY, US 139/K8
Palisades, NY, US 139/K8
Palisades Interstate Park, NJ, US 138/D1
Palisades Park, NJ, US 139/K8
Paliseul, Belg. 53/E4
Pālitāna, India 89/K4
Palizada, Mex. 140/C4
Paljenik (peak), Bosn. 48/C3
Palk (str.), India 82/C6
Pallamallawa, Austl. 115/D1
Pallarenda, Austl. 114/B2
Pallas-Ounastunturin NP, Fin. 37/H1
Pallasca, Peru 156/B3
Pallastunturi (peak), Fin. 37/H1
Palliser (cape), NZ 117/T11
Palm Bay, Fl, US 133/H4
Palm Beach (int'l arpt.), Fl, US 133/H5
Palm City, Ca, US 136/C5
Palm Harbor, Fl, US 133/H4
Palm Island Aboriginal Settlement, Austl. 114/B2
Palm Springs, Ca, US 128/C4
Palma (riv.), Braz. 151/J6
Palma, Moz. 104/D5
Palma, Sp. 45/G3
Palma del Río, Sp. 44/C4
Palma di Montechiaro, It. 46/C4
Palma Mallorca (int'l arpt.), Sp. 45/G3
Palma Soriano, Cuba 145/H1
Palmácia, Braz. 154/C2
Palmanova, It. 59/G1
Palmar (riv.), Ven. 145/H4
Palmares, Braz. 154/D3
Palmarito, Ven. 152/D3
Palmas, Braz. 155/A3
Palmas (cape), Libr. 102/D5
Palmdale, Ca, US 136/B1
Palmeira, Braz. 155/B3
Palmeira, CpV. 93/K10
Palmeira dos Índios, Braz. 154/C3
Palmeirais, Braz. 154/B2
Palmeiras (riv.), Braz. 154/A4
Palmeiras, Braz. 154/B4
Palmeirinhas, Ponta das (pt.), Ang. 105/B2
Palmela, Port. 45/Q10
Palmer, Ak, US 134/J3
Palmer, US, Ant. 160/V
Palmer, Wa, US 135/D3
Palmer Land (phys. reg.), Ant. 160/V
Palmerston, NZ 117/S12
Palmerston (cape), Austl. 114/C3
Palmerston Atoll (atoll), Cookls. 117/J6
Palmerston North, NZ 117/T11
Palmerston NP, Austl. 114/B2
Palmerton, Pa, US 138/C2
Palmetto, Fl, US 133/H5
Palmi, It. 46/D3
Palmilla, Chile 158/C2
Palmillas (pt.), Cuba 145/F1
Palmira, Col. 152/B4
Palmital, Braz. 155/B2
Palmitas, Uru. 159/K10
Palmyra, Ut, US 137/K13
Palmyra (isl.), PacUS 117/J4
Palmyra, Pa, US 138/B3
Palmyra (Tadmur) (ruin), Syria 90/D3
Palmyras (pt.), India 82/E3
Palni, India 82/C5
Palo, Phil. 79/D5
Palo Alto, Ca, US 128/B3
Palo Alto, Pa, US 138/B2
Palo Pinto, Tx, US 129/H4
Palo Verde, PN, CR 140/D5
Palomeu (riv.), Sur. 153/H4
Palon (peak), It. 59/E1
Palos (cape), Sp. 45/E4
Palos de la Frontera, Sp. 44/B4
Palos Hills, Il, US 135/Q16
Palos Verdes (hills), Ca, US 136/F8
Palos Verdes (pt.), Ca, US 136/F8
Palos Verdes Estates, Ca, US 136/F8
Palosco, It. 58/C1
Palpalá, Arg. 157/C1
Palpetu (cape), Indo. 81/G4
Paltamo, Fin. 60/E2
Palu, Indo. 81/E4
Palu, Turk. 62/F5
Paluan, Phil. 79/D5
Palwal, India 84/A1
Pamangkat, Indo. 80/C3
Pambula, Austl. 115/D3
Pamiers, Fr. 42/D5
Pamir (riv.), Afg.,Taj. 64/H6
Pamir (reg.), Taj.,China 64/H6
Pamlico (riv.), NC, US 133/J3
Pamlico (sound), NC, US 133/J3
Pampa, Tx, US 129/G4
Pampachiri, Peru 156/C4
Pampacolca, Peru 156/C4
Pampas (riv.), Peru 156/C4
Pampas, Peru 156/C4
Pampas, Peru 156/B3
Pampas (plain), Arg. 147/C6
Pampilhosa da Serra, Port. 44/B2
Pamplona, Sp. 44/E1
Pamplona, Col. 152/C3
Pampulha (int'l arpt.), Braz. 155/D1
Pāmpur, India 86/C2
Pamukova, Turk. 49/K5
Pan de Azúcar, PN, Chile 157/B2
Panaba, Mex. 144/D1
Panabo, Phil. 79/E6
Panāgar, India 84/B4
Panagyurishte, Bul. 47/J1
Panaitan (isl.), Indo. 80/B5
Panaji, India 89/K5
Panamá (bay), Pan. 145/G4
Panamá (cap.), Pan. 152/B2
Panama (ctry.) 119/J9
Panama (gulf), Pan. 119/K9
Panama (canal), Pan. 119/K9
Panama City, Fl, US 133/G4
Panama, Isthmus of (isth.), Pan. 150/C2
Panamá Viejo (ruin), Pan. 152/B2
Panamint (range), Ca, US 128/C3
Panao, Peru 156/B3
Panaro (riv.), It. 43/J4
Panay (isl.), Phil. 67/M8
Pancake (range), Nv, US 128/C3
Pančevo, Yugo. 48/E3
Pančićev vrh (peak), Yugo. 47/G1
Pancilet (res.), India 85/F4
Panciu, Rom. 49/H3
Pandamatenga, Bots. 105/E4
Pandharpur, India 89/L5
Pandino, It. 58/C2
Pando, Uru. 159/L11
Pāndoh, India 86/D4
Pandrup, Den. 38/C3
Pandua, India 85/G4
Panevėžys, Lith. 39/L4
Panfilov, Kaz. 70/D3
Pangai, Tonga 117/H6
Pangaion (peak), Gre. 47/J2
Pangani, Tanz. 104/C4
Pangani (riv.), Tanz. 104/C3
Pangkalanberandan, Indo. 80/A3
Pangkalaseang (cape), Indo. 81/F4
Pangkalpinang, Indo. 80/C4
Pangnirtung, NW, Can. 123/K2
Panguipulli, Chile 158/B3
Panguitch, Ut, US 128/D3
Pangutaran, Phil. 81/F2
Pangutaran (isl.), Phil. 79/C6
Panjai (lake), Indo. 81/J4
Paniau (peak), Hi, US 124/R10
Pānihāti, India 85/G4
Pānīpat, India 86/D5
Paniqui, Phil. 79/D4
Panj (riv.), Afg. 89/K1
Panjwīn, Iraq 88/E1
Panke (riv.), Ger. 40/Q6
P'anmunjŏm, NKor. 73/D4
Panna, India 84/C3
Pannawonica, Austl. 112/C2
Pannikin (isl.), Austl. 114/F7
Pano Lefkara, Cyp. 91/C2
Panorama, Braz. 155/B2
Pantanal (lowland), Braz. 150/G7
Pantanal Matogrossense, PN, Braz. 150/G7
Pantelleria, It. 46/B4
Pantelleria (isl.), It. 27/F5
Pantigliate, It. 58/C2
Panton, Fr. 30/K5
Pantoja, Peru 152/C5
Pantón, Sp. 44/B1
Pantukan, Phil. 79/E6
Pánuco (riv.), Mex. 140/B3
Pánuco, Mex. 144/B1
Panzhihua, China 83/H2
Panzós, Guat. 144/D3
Pão de Açúcar, Braz. 154/C3
Paola, It. 46/E3
Paola, Malta 46/M7
Paoli, Pa, US 138/C3
Paonia, Co, US 128/F3
Paonta Sahib, India 86/D4
Paoua, CAfr. 96/J6
Pápa, Hun. 48/C2
Papa Westray (isl.), Sc, UK 31/V14
Papagayo (gulf), CR 140/D5
Papaikou, Hi, US 124/U11
Papanduva, Braz. 155/B3
Papantla, Mex. 143/M6
Papaplaya, Peru 156/C2
Papenburg, Ger. 51/E2
Papendrecht, Neth. 50/B5
Paphos, Cyp. 91/C2
Paphos (dist.), Cyp. 91/C2
Papingut (peak), Alb. 47/G2
Papisoi (cape), Indo. 81/H4
Pappenheim, Ger. 54/D5
Papua (gulf), PNG 116/D5
Papua New Guinea (ctry.) 116/D5
Papudo, Chile 158/C2
Papunya, Austl. 113/F2
Pará (riv.), Braz. 151/H4
Pará (state), Braz. 154/A1
Para (dist.), Sur. 153/H3
Pará (falls), Ven. 153/E3
Pará de Minas, Braz. 155/C1
Para, South (riv.), Austl. 113/M8
Para Wirra NP, Austl. 113/M8
Paraburdoo, Austl. 112/C2
Paracambi, Braz. 211/K7
Paracas (pen.), Peru 156/B4
Paracas, Reserva Nacional, Peru 156/B4
Paracatu, Braz. 154/A5
Paracatu (riv.), Braz. 154/A5
Paracel (isls.), China 83/K4
Paracho de Verduzco, Mex. 142/E5
Paraćin, Yugo. 48/E4
Paracuru, Braz. 154/C1
Paradhísion (int'l arpt.), Gre. 90/B2
Paradip, India 82/E3
Paradis, La, US 137/P17
Paradise (valley), Az, US 137/R18
Paradise, Mo, US 137/D5
Paradise, Pa, US 138/B4
Paradise Valley, Az, US 137/S18
Paragominas, Braz. 154/A1
Paraguá (riv.), Bol. 150/F6
Paragua (riv.), Ven. 150/F2
Paraguaçu, Braz. 211/H6
Paraguaçu (riv.), Braz. 147/E4
Paraguaçu Paulista, Braz. 155/B2
Paraguai (riv.), SAm. 147/D5
Paraguaipoa, Ven. 152/D2
Paraguaná, Peninsula de (pen.), Ven. 150/D1
Paraguarí, Par. 157/E2
Paraguay (ctry.) 157/E1
Paraguay (riv.), Par. 157/E1
Paraíba (state), Braz. 154/C2
Paraíba do Sul, Braz. 211/K7
Paraíba do Sul (riv.), Braz. 147/E5
Paraibano, Braz. 154/B2
Paraibuna (riv.), Braz. 211/H8
Paraim (riv.), Braz. 154/A3
Parainen (Pargas), Fin. 39/K1
Paraíso, Mex. 144/C2
Paraíso, CR 145/F4
Paraíso do Norte de Goiás, Braz. 151/J6
Paraisópolis, Braz. 211/H7
Parakou, Ben. 103/F4
Paramaribo (cap.), Sur. 151/G2
Paramaribo (dist.), Sur. 153/H3
Parambu, Braz. 154/B2
Paramillo (peak), Col. 152/C3
Paramillo, PN, Col. 150/C2
Paramirim (riv.), Braz. 151/K6
Paramirim, Braz. 154/B4
Paramithía, Gre. 47/G3
Paramount, Ca, US 136/F8
Paramus, NJ, US 139/J8
Paramushir (isl.), Rus. 67/Q5
Paraná, Arg. 157/D3
Paraná (riv.), Braz. 151/J6
Paraná (state), Braz. 155/B3
Paraná (riv.), SAm. 147/D5
Paraná Ibicuy (riv.), Arg. 159/J10
Paraná Urariá (riv.), Braz. 153/G5
Paranaguá, Braz. 155/B3
Paranaguá, Baía de (bay), Braz. 155/B3
Paranaíba (riv.), Braz. 151/J7
Paranaíba, Braz. 155/B1
Paranapanema (riv.), Braz. 157/F1
Paranapiacaba, Serra do (mts.), Braz. 157/G2
Paranatinga (riv.), Braz. 147/D4
Paranavaí, Braz. 157/F1
Parang, Phil. 81/F2
Paraopeba, Braz. 155/C1
Parapetí (riv.), Bol. 150/F7
Parati, Braz. 211/J8
Paratico, It. 58/C1
Paratinga, Braz. 154/B4
Paratinga (riv.), Braz. 211/H8
Paray-Vieille-Poste, Fr. 30/K5
Paràzinho, Braz. 154/D2
Pārbati (riv.), India 89/L4
Parbhani, India 89/L5
Parchim, Ger. 40/F2
Parczew, Pol. 41/M3
Pardes HLanna-Karkur, Isr. 91/F7
Pārdi, India 89/K4
Pardo (riv.), Braz. 151/J8
Pardone (cape), SAfr. 106/D4
Pardubice, Czh. 41/H3
Pare, Indo. 80/D5
Pare (mts.), Tanz. 104/C3
Parece Vela (Okino-Tori-Shima) (isl.), Japan 67/N7
Parecis (mts.), Braz. 147/C4
Parede, Port. 45/P10
Paredes de Nava, Sp. 44/C1
Paredón, Mex. 144/C2
Paredones, Chile 158/C2
Parelhas, Braz. 154/C2
Parempuyre, Fr. 42/C4
Parenda, India 82/C4
Parent (lake), Can. 130/E1
Parentis-en-Born, Fr. 42/C4
Parepare, Indo. 81/E4
Parera, Arg. 158/D2
Parets del Valles, Sp. 45/L6
Pargny-sur-Saulx, Fr. 53/D6
Paria (riv.), Ut, US 128/E3
Paria (gulf), Trin.,Ven. 147/C1
Paria, Peninsula de (pen.), Ven. 150/F1
Pariacoto, Peru 156/B3
Pariaguán, Ven. 153/E2
Pariaman, Indo. 80/B4
Parikkala, Fin. 37/J3
Parima (riv.), Braz. 153/F4
Parima, Serra (mts.), Braz. 150/F3
Parinacota (peak), Bol. 156/D5
Parinari, Peru 156/C2
Pariñas (pt.), Peru 156/A2
Paringa, Austl. 115/B2
Parîngu Mare (peak), Rom. 49/F3
Parintins, Braz. 151/G4
Paris, Ar, US 129/J4
Paris, Tx, US 129/J4
Paris (cap.), Fr. 30/K5
Paris (dept.), Fr. 52/B6
Parita (bay), Pan. 145/F4
Park (range), US 128/F2
Park (pt.), Eng, UK 32/A5
Park City, Ut, US 137/L12
Park City, Il, US 135/Q15
Park Falls, Wi, US 127/L4
Park Rapids, Mn, US 127/K4
Park Ridge, Il, US 135/Q16
Park Ridge, NJ, US 139/J7
Park River, ND, US 127/J3
Parkano, Fin. 37/G3
Parker, Tx, US 129/H4
Parker, Az, US 128/D4
Parker, Co, US 137/C3
Parkersburg, WV, US 130/D4
Parkes, Austl. 115/D2
Parkesburg, Pa, US 138/C4
Parkgate, NI, UK 34/B2
Parksdale, Mo, US 137/F9
Parkside, Pa, US 138/C4
Parkstetten, Ger. 55/F5
Parkton, Md, US 138/B4
Parkville, Mo, US 137/D5
Parkville, Md, US 138/B5
Parkville, Pa, US 138/B4
Parkway-Sacramento, Ca, US 135/L9
Parla, Sp. 45/N9
Parlakhemundi, India 82/D4
Parli, India 89/L5
Parma, Oh, US 130/D3
Parma (prov.), It. 58/C3
Parma (riv.), It. 58/D3
Parma, It. 58/D3
Parmain, Fr. 30/J4
Parnaguá, Braz. 154/A3
Parnaíba, Braz. 154/B1
Parnaíba (riv.), Braz. 147/E3
Parnamirim, Braz. 154/C3
Parnamirim, Braz. 151/L5
Parnarama, Braz. 154/B2
Parnassós (peak), Gre. 47/H3
Parnassós NP, Gre. 47/H3
Párnis (peak), Gre. 47/N8
Párnis Óros NP, Gre. 47/N8
Párnon (mts.), Gre. 47/H4
Pärnu (bay), Est. 39/L2
Pärnu, Est. 39/L2
P'aro-ho (lake), SKor. 73/D3
Paron, Fr. 42/E2
Parona di Valpolicella, It. 59/D2
Paroo (riv.), Austl. 109/D3
Páros (isl.), Gre. 47/J4
Páros, Gre. 47/J4
Parow, SAfr. 106/L10
Parowan, Ut, US 128/D3
Parpan, Swi. 57/F4
Parral, Chile 158/C3
Parras de la Fuente, Mex. 142/E3
Parrett (riv.), Eng, UK 32/D4
Parrita, CR 145/E4
Parry (isls.), Can. 119/F2
Parry (bay), NW, Can. 123/H2
Parry (chan.), Can. 119/F2
Parry Sound, On, Can. 130/D2
Parsberg, Ger. 55/E4
Parseierspitze (peak), Aus. 57/G3
Parshall, ND, US 127/H4
Parsippany-Troy Hills, NJ, US 139/H8
Parsnip (riv.), Can. 126/C2
Pårtefjället (peak), Swe. 37/F2
Partenstein, Ger. 54/C2
Parthenay, Fr. 42/C3
Partille, Swe. 38/E3
Partinico, It. 46/C3
Partizansk, Rus. 71/P3
Partizánske, Slvk. 41/K4
Partridge (riv.), Can. 130/D1
Partūr, India 89/L5
Paru (riv.), Braz. 151/H4
Paru de Oeste (riv.), Braz. 147/D2
Paruro, Peru 156/D4
Pārvathīpuram, India 82/D4
Parys, SAfr. 106/D2
Pas-de-Calais (dept.), Fr. 52/A3
Pas de Morgins (pass), Fr. 56/C5
Pasadena, Tx, US 129/J5
Pasadena, Nf, Can. 131/K1
Pasadena, Md, US 138/B5
Pasadena, Ca, US 136/F7
Pasado (cape), Ecu. 152/A5
Pasaje, Ecu. 156/B1
Pasaman (peak), Indo. 80/B3
Pasān, India 84/D4
Pascagoula, Ms, US 133/F4
Paşcani, Rom. 49/H2
Pasching, Aus. 55/H6
Pasco, Wa, US 126/D4
Pasco (dept.), Peru 156/C3
Pascua (riv.), Chile 159/B6
Pascua, Isla de (Easter) (isl.), Chile 117/Q7
Pascuales, Ecu. 156/B1
Pasewalk, Ger. 38/E5
Pasian di Prato, It. 59/G1
Pasiano, It. 59/F1
Pasig, Phil. 79/D5
Pasinler, Turk. 63/G5
Pasión, Río de la (riv.), Guat. 144/D2
Pasłęk, Pol. 39/H4
Pasłęka (riv.), Pol. 41/L2
Pasley (cape), Austl. 112/D5
Pašman (isl.), Cro. 48/B4
Pasni, Pak. 89/H3
Paso de Indios, Arg. 158/C4
Paso de los Libres, Arg. 157/E2
Paso de los Toros, Uru. 159/K10
Paso de Ovejas, Mex. 143/N7
Paso del Macho, Mex. 143/N8
Paso del Planchón (peak), Chile 158/C2
Paso Robles (El Paso de Robles), Ca, US 128/B4
Pasrūr, Pak. 86/C3
Pass (peak), Can. 134/M3
Passa Quatro, Braz. 211/J7
Passagem Franca, Braz. 154/B2
Passaic (riv.), NJ, US 138/D2
Passaic, NJ, US 139/J8
Passau, Ger. 55/G5
Passero (pt.), It. 46/D4
Passo Fundo, Braz. 155/A4
Passo Fundo, Barragem do (res.), Braz. 155/A3
Passons, It. 59/G1
Passoré (prov.), Burk. 103/E3
Passos, Braz. 155/C2
Passwang (peak), Swi. 56/D3
Passy, Fr. 56/C6
Pastavy, Bela. 39/M4
Pastaza (riv.), Ecu.,Peru 147/B3
Pastaza (dept.), Ecu. 152/B5
Pastek (riv.), Pol. 39/J5
Pasto, Col. 152/B4
Pastol (bay), Ak, US 134/F3
Pastoriza, Sp. 44/B1
Pastos Bons, Braz. 154/A2
Pasuruan, Indo. 80/D5
Pásztó, Hun. 41/K5
Pata, Bol. 156/D4
Patagonia (phys. reg.), Arg. 147/B8
Patah (peak), Indo. 80/B4
Pātan, India 84/B4
Pātan, India 89/K4
Pataná (peak), Braz. 155/B3
Patapsco (riv.), Md, US 138/A5
Patapsco, Md, US 138/B4
Pataudi, India 86/D5
Pataz, Peru 156/B2
Patchogue, NY, US 139/E2
Paterna, Sp. 45/E3
Paternò, It. 46/D4
Paterson, NJ, US 139/J8
Pathalgaon, India 84/D4
Pathānkot, India 86/C3
Pathein (Bassein), Myan. 83/F4
Pathfinder (res.), Wy, US 126/G5
Pati, Indo. 80/D5
Patía (riv.), Col. 150/C3
Patía, Col. 152/B4
Patiāla, India 86/D4
Patikul, Phil. 81/F2
Patna, India 85/E3
Patna, Sc, UK 36/B6
Patnongon, Phil. 81/F1
Patnos, Turk. 90/E2
Pato Branco, Braz. 155/A3
Patoka (riv.), In, US 133/G2
Patos, Braz. 154/C2
Patos, Alb. 47/F2
Patos de Minas, Braz. 155/C1
Patos, Lagoa dos (lake), Braz. 157/F3
Patrai (gulf), Gre. 47/G3
Pátrai, Gre. 47/G3
Pātrasāer, India 85/F4
Patrātu, India 85/E4
Patricia (mt.), Austl. 113/F2
Patricio Lynch (isl.), Chile 159/A6
Patrocínio, Braz. 155/C1
Patscherkofel (peak), Aus. 57/H3
Pattani, Thai. 78/C5
Pattensen, Ger. 51/G4
Patti, India 86/C4
Patti, It. 46/D3
Pattoki, Pak. 86/B4
Pattukkottai, India 82/C5
Pattullo (mt.), Can. 134/N4
Patuākhāli (pol. reg.), Bang. 85/G4
Patuākhāli, Bang. 85/H4
Patuca (riv.), Hon. 140/D5
Patuca (mts.), Hon. 144/E3
Patuca (pt.), Hon. 145/E3
Patuxent (riv.), Md, US 138/B5
Patuxent NWR, Md, US 138/B5
Patuxent River State Park, Md, US 138/B5
Páty, Hun. 49/Q9
Pátzcuaro, Mex. 143/E5
Pau, Fr. 42/C5
Pau Brasil, Braz. 154/C4
Pau dos Ferros, Braz. 154/C2
Paucarbamba, Peru 156/C4
Paucartambo, Peru 156/C3
Paucartambo, Peru 156/D4
Pauillac, Fr. 42/C4
Pauini (riv.), Braz. 150/E5
Paulaya (riv.), Hon. 144/E3
Paulínia, Braz. 211/F7
Paulins Kill (riv.), NJ, US 138/D2
Paulistana, Braz. 154/B3
Paullo, It. 58/C2
Paulo Afonso, Braz. 154/C3
Paulo Afonso, PN de, Braz. 154/C3
Paulo Ramos, Braz. 154/A2
Paulpietersburg, SAfr. 107/E2
Pauls Valley, Ok, US 129/H4
Paulsboro, NJ, US 138/C4
Pauma Valley, Ca, US 136/D4
Paungde, Myan. 83/G4
Pavão, Braz. 154/B5
Pavel Banya, Bul. 47/J1
Pavia (prov.), It. 58/C2
Pavia, It. 58/C2
Pavie, Fr. 42/D5
Pavlikeni, Bul. 49/G4
Pavlodar (obl.), Kaz. 87/G2
Pavlodar, Kaz. 87/G2
Pavlof (vol.), Ak, US 134/F4
Pavlohrad, Ukr. 62/E2
Pavlovo, Rus. 60/J5
Pavone Canavese, It. 58/A2
Pavone del Mella, It. 58/D2
Pavullo nel Frignano, It. 59/D4
Paw Paw, Mi, US 130/C3
Pawan (riv.), Indo. 80/D4
Pawāyan, India 84/C1
Pawhuska, Ok, US 129/H3
Pawnee (riv.), US 129/G3
Pawtucket, RI, US 131/G3
Paxoí (isl.), Gre. 47/F3
Paxson, Ak, US 134/J3
Paxton, Austl. 115/D2
Pay-Khoy (mts.), Rus. 64/G3
Payakumbuh, Indo. 80/B4
Payerne, Swi. 56/C4
Payette (riv.), Id, US 126/D5
Payne (lake), Qu, Can. 123/J3
Paynesville, Austl. 115/C3
Pays de Caux (reg.), Fr. 42/D2
Pays de France (reg.), Fr. 30/K4
Pays de la Loire (reg.), Fr. 42/C3
Paysandú, Uru. 159/J10
Payson, Ut, US 128/E2
Payson, Az, US 128/E4
Payún (peak), Arg. 158/C3
Paz (riv.), Guat. 144/D3
Paz de Ariporo, Col. 152/D3
Paz de Río, Col. 152/C3
Pazar, Turk. 90/D1
Pazar, Turk. 63/G4
Pazarcık, Turk. 90/D2
Pazardzhik, Bul. 47/J1
Pazaryeri, Turk. 62/D5
Pazin, Cro. 48/A3
Peabiru, Braz. 155/A2
Peace (riv.), BC, Can. 122/D3
Peace Memorial Park, Japan 74/C3
Peaceful Valley, Co, US 137/B2
Peachland, BC, Can. 126/D3
Peachtree City, Ga, US 133/G3
Peak Charles NP, Austl. 112/D5
Peak District NP, Eng, UK 35/G5
Peak Hill, Austl. 112/C3
Peal de Becerro, Sp. 44/D4
Peapack-Gladstone, NJ, US 138/D2
Pearblossom, Ca, US 136/C1
Pearl, Ms, US 133/F3
Pearl (har.), US 124/W13
Pearl (riv.), La,Ms, US 125/J5
Pearl and Hermes (reef), Hi, US 117/H2
Pearl Beach, Mi, US 135/G6
Pearl City, Hi, US 124/W13
Pearl River (estu.), China 79/B3
Pearl River, La, US 137/Q16
Pearl River, NY, US 139/J7
Pearland, Ca, US 136/B1
Pearsall, Tx, US 129/H5
Pearson (int'l arpt.), Can. 131/Q8
Pearston, SAfr. 106/D4
Peary (chan.), NW, Can. 123/R7
Pease (riv.), Tx, US 129/G4
Pebane, Moz. 105/G4
Pebas, Peru 156/D1
Pebble (isl.), Mald. 159/E6
Peccia, Swi. 57/E5
Peccioli, It. 59/D5
Pécel, Hun. 49/R10
Pech de Guillaument (peak), Fr. 42/E5
Pechanga Ind. Res., Ca, US 136/C4
Pechora, Rus. 61/N2
Pechora (riv.), Rus. 67/C3
Pechora (bay), Rus. 61/M1
Peckham, Co, US 137/C2
Peconic (riv.), NY, US 139/F2
Pecos, Tx, US 132/C4
Pecos (riv.), US 119/G6
Pecq, Belg. 52/C2
Pecquencourt, Fr. 52/C3
Pécs, Hun. 48/D2
Peculiar, Mo, US 137/E6
Pecy, Fr. 30/M6
Pedasí, Pan. 152/A3
Pedder (lake), Austl. 109/D5
Pedemonte, It. 59/D2
Pedernales (riv.), Tx, US 143/F2
Pederneiras, Braz. 155/B2
Pedley, Ca, US 136/C3
Pedra Azul, Braz. 154/B5
Pedra Lume, CpV. 93/K10
Pedralva, Braz. 211/H7
Pedregal, Ven. 152/D2
Pedreguer, Sp. 45/F3
Pedreira, Braz. 211/G7
Pedreiras, Braz. 154/A2
Pedricktown, NJ, US 138/C4
Pedro (pt.), SrL. 82/D6
Pedro Avelino, Braz. 154/C2
Pedro Bay, Ak, US 134/H4
Pedro Betancourt, Cuba 145/F1
Pedro Carbo, Ecu. 152/A5
Pedro Cays (isl.), Jam. 141/F4
Pedro Ii, Braz. 154/B2
Pedro IV (isl.), Braz. 153/E4
Pedro Juan Caballero, Par. 157/E1
Pedro Leopoldo, Braz. 155/C1
Pedro Luro, Arg. 158/E3
Pedro Osório, Braz. 155/A4
Peebles, Sc, UK 36/C5
Peedamulla Abor. Land, Austl. 112/B2
Peekskill, NY, US 138/E1
Peel (co.), Can. 131/Q8
Peel (inlet), Austl. 112/B5
Peel (riv.), Yk, Can. 122/C2
Peel (sound), NW, Can. 122/G1
Peel (isl.), Austl. 114/F6
Peel, IM, UK 34/D3
Peel Fell (peak), Eng, UK 36/D6
Peene (riv.), Ger. 38/E5
Peer, Belg. 53/E1
Pegasus (bay), NZ 117/S11
Pegnitz, Ger. 55/E3
Pegnitz (riv.), Ger. 40/F4
Pego, Sp. 45/E3
Pego do Altar, Barragem de (res.), Port. 44/A3
Pegognaga, It. 59/D3
Pegwell (bay), Eng, UK 33/H4
Pehlivanköy, Turk. 49/H5
Pehowa, India 86/D5
Pehuajó, Arg. 158/E2
Pehuenche (pass), Chile 158/C2
Pei Xian, China 72/D4
Peine, Ger. 51/H4
Peipus (lake), Est.,Rus. 64/C4
Peiting, Ger. 57/G2
Peixe (riv.), Braz. 155/B2
Peixoto, Reprêsa de (res.), Braz. 155/C2
Pekalongan, Indo. 80/C5
Pekan, Malay. 80/B3
Pekan Nanas, Malay. 80/B3
Pekhora (riv.), Rus. 61/W9
Pekin, Il, US 127/L5
Pelada, Pampa (plain), Arg. 158/C5
Pelado (vol.), Mex. 143/Q10
Pelagie (isls.), It 46/C5
Peleaga (peak), Rom. 48/F3
Pelee (pt.), Can. 130/D3
Pelee (isl.), Can. 130/D3
Pelée (peak), Fr. 141/N9
Pelham, Al, US 133/G3
Pelham, On, Can. 131/R9
Pelham, NY, US 139/K8
Pelham Bay Park, NY, US 139/K8
Pelham Manor, NY, US 139/K8
Pelhřimov, Czh. 41/H4
Pelican (mts.), Can. 126/E2
Pelican (lake), US 127/H2
Pelican, Ak, US 134/L4
Pelican Narrows, Sk, Can. 127/H2
Pelindã, Ponta de (pt.), GBis. 102/A4
Pelister (peak), Macd. 47/G2
Pelister NP, Macd. 47/G2
Peljekaise NP, Swe. 37/F2
Pelješac (pen.), Cro. 47/E1
 Pelješec (pen.), Cro. 48/C4
Pell Lake, Wi, US 135/P14
Pélla (ruin), Gre. 47/H2
Pélla, Gre. 47/H2
Pellegrini, Arg. 158/E3
Pellestrina, It. 59/F2
Pello, Fin. 60/E2
Pelly (riv.), Yk, Can. 122/C2
Pelly (bay), NW, Can. 122/H2
Pelly Bay, NW, Can. 122/H2
Peloponnesus (reg.), Gre. 47/G3
Peloritani, Monti (mts.), It. 46/D4
Pelotas (riv.), Braz. 157/F2
Pelotas, Braz. 155/A4
Pelplin, Pol. 39/H5
Pemali (cape), Indo. 81/F5
Pemali (cape), Indo. 81/F4
Pematangsiantar, Indo. 80/A3
Pemba, Moz. 105/H3
Pemba (isl.), Tanz. 105/G2
Pemba (prov.) 104/C4
Pemberton, BC, Can. 126/C3
Pemberton, Austl. 112/C5
Pemberton, NJ, US 138/D4
Pembina (riv.), ND, US 126/E2
Pembina, ND, US 127/J3
Pembroke, On, Can. 130/E2
Pembroke, Wal, UK 32/B3
Pembrokeshire Coast NP, Wal, UK 32/A3
Pembury, Eng, UK 33/G4
Pemuco, Chile 158/B3
Pen Argyl, Pa, US 138/C2
Pen, The (lake), La, US 137/P17
Pen-y-Ghent (peak), Eng, UK 35/F3
Pen-y-Gogarth (pt.), Wal, UK 34/E5
Pen y Gurnos (peak), Wal, UK 32/C2
Peña Blanca (mtn.), Pan. 145/F4
Peña de Cerredo (mtn.), Sp. 44/C1
Peñafiel, Sp. 44/C2
Penafiel, Port. 44/A2
Peñaflor, Chile 158/N8
Penalva, Braz. 154/A1
Penamacor, Port. 44/B2
Penápolis, Braz. 155/B2
Peñaranda de Bracamonte, Sp. 44/C2
Peñarroya (peak), Sp. 45/E2
Peñarroya-Pueblonuevo, Sp. 44/C3
Penarth, Wal, UK 32/C4
Peñas (cape), Sp. 44/C1
Peñas (cape), Arg. 159/D7
Penas, Golfo de (gulf), Chile 157/A6
Peñasco (riv.), NM, US 129/F4
Pench (riv.), India 84/B5
Penchard, Fr. 30/L5
Penco, Chile 158/B3
Pend Oreille (lake), Id, US 126/D4
Pendelikón (peak), Gre. 47/N8
Pendembu, SLeo. 102/C4
Pendências, Braz. 154/C2
Pendjar (riv.), Burk. 103/F4
Pendjari, PN de la, Ben. 96/F5
Pendle (hill), Eng, UK 35/F4
Pendleton, Or, US 126/D4
Peneda-Gerês NP, Port. 44/A2
Penedo, Braz. 154/C3
Penetanguishene, On, Can. 130/E2
Penghu (Pescadores) (isls.), Tai. 79/C3
Penglai, China 72/E3
Penguin, Austl. 115/C4
Penha, Braz. 155/B3
Penhold, Ab, Can. 126/E2
Penibético, Sistema (range), Sp. 44/C4
Penice (peak), It. 58/C3
Peniche, Port. 44/A3
Penicuik, Sc, UK 36/C5
Península de Paria, PN, Ven. 153/F2
Peñíscola, Sp. 45/F2
Penitente, Serra do (mts.), Braz. 151/J5
Penmaenmawr, Wal, UK 34/E5
Penmarch, Fr. 42/A3
Penmarc'h, Pointe de (pt.), Fr. 42/A3
Penn Forest (res.), Pa, US 138/C2
Penn Hills, Pa, US 130/E3
Penn Yan, NY, US 130/E3
Penna, Punta della (cape), It. 46/D1
Penne (pt.), It. 47/E2
Penne, It. 46/C1
Penner (riv.), India 82/C5
Pennine Alps (mts.), Swi. 43/G4
Pennine Chain (mts.), Eng, UK 35/F2
Pennington, NJ, US 138/D3
Pennino (peak), It. 43/K5
Penns Creek (mtn.), Pa, US 138/A2
Penns Grove, NJ, US 138/C4
Penns Park, Pa, US 138/D3
Pennsauken, NJ, US 138/C4
Pennsburg, Pa, US 138/C3
Pennsville, NJ, US 138/C4
Pennsylvania (state), US 125/L3
Penny (str.), NW, Can. 123/S7

Penobscot (riv.), Me, US	131/G2
Penola, Austl.	115/B3
Peñon Blanco, Mex.	142/D3
Penon de Al Hoceima (isl.), Sp.	100/C2
Penonomé, Pan.	152/A2
Penrhyn Mawr (pt.), Wal, UK	34/D6
Penrhyn Mawr (pt.), IM, UK	34/D5
Penrith, Eng, UK	35/F2
Pensacola, Fl, US	133/G4
Pensacola (mts.), Ant.	160/X
Pense, Sk, Can.	127/G3
Penshurst, Austl.	115/B3
Pentagon Fed. Govt. Res., Va, US	138/A6
Pentecost (riv.), Van.	116/F6
Pentecoste, Braz.	154/C1
Penteleu (peak), Rom.	49/H3
Penthalaz, Swi.	56/C4
Penticton, BC, Can.	126/D3
Pentire (pt.), Eng, UK	32/B5
Pentland, Austl.	114/B3
Pentland (hills), Sc, UK	36/C5
Pentland Firth (inlet), Sc, UK	31/V14
Peñuelas, PN, Chile	158/N8
Penwith (pen.), Eng, UK	32/A6
Penza, Rus.	63/H1
Penza Oblast, Rus.	63/G1
Penzance, Eng, UK	32/A6
Penzberg, Ger.	57/H2
Penzhina (riv.), Rus.	65/S3
Penzhina (bay), Rus.	65/S3
Penzing, Ger.	57/G1
Penzlin, Ger.	40/G2
Peoria, Az, US	137/R18
Pepe (cape), Cuba	145/F1
Pepeekeo, Hi, US	124/U11
Pepeekeo, Hi, US	124/U11
Pepel, SLeo.	102/B4
Pepinster, Belg.	53/E2
Pequannock, NJ, US	139/H8
Pequeña Isla del Maíz (isl.), Nic.	145/F3
Pequest (riv.), NJ, US	138/D2
Perabumulih, Indo.	80/B4
Perales (riv.), Sp.	45/M9
Peralta, Sp.	44/E1
Pérama, Gre.	47/J5
Pérama, Gre.	47/N9
Percé, Qu, Can.	131/H1
Percée (peak), Fr.	56/C6
Perche, Collines du (hills), Fr.	42/D2
Perchtoldsdorf, Aus.	49/N7
Percival (lakes), Austl.	109/B3
Percy (isls.), Austl.	109/E3
Percy Isles (chan.), Austl.	114/C3
Perdekop, SAfr.	107/E2
Pérdhika, Gre.	47/G3
Perdida (riv.), Braz.	154/A3
Perdido (mtn.), Sp.	45/F1
Peregian Beach, Austl.	114/D4
Pereira, Col.	150/C3
Pereira Barreto, Braz.	155/B2
Pereiro, Braz.	154/C2
Perelló, Sp.	45/F2
Perenjori, Austl.	112/C4
Peretola (int'l arpt.), It.	59/E5
Perg, Aus.	158/E2
Pergamino, Arg.	158/E2
Pergamum (ruin), Turk.	62/C5
Pergine Valsugana, It.	57/H5
Pergola, It.	43/K5
Péribonca (riv.), Can.	131/G1
Perico, Cuba	145/G1
Pericos, Mex.	142/D3
Pericos, Mex.	142/D4
Périgueux, Fr.	42/D4
Perijá, Sierra de (mts.), Col.	150/D2
Peristéra (isl.), Gre.	47/H3
Peristéri, Gre.	47/N8
Perito Moreno, Arg.	158/C5
Perito Moreno, PN, Arg.	157/B6
Perkasie, Pa, US	138/C3
Perl, Ger.	53/F5
Perlas (lag.), Nic.	140/E5
Perlas (pt.), Nic.	145/F3
Perleberg, Ger.	40/F2
Perlis (state), Malay.	78/B5
Perm', Rus.	61/N4
Perm' Oblast, Rus.	87/C1
Perm' Oblast, Rus.	61/N4
Pérmet, Alb.	47/G2
Permyakia Aut. Okrug, Rus.	61/M3
Pernambuco (state), Braz.	154/C3
Pernate, It.	58/B2
Pernes-les-Fontaines, Fr.	42/F4
Pernik, Bul.	47/H1
Perniö, Fin.	39/K1
Peron (pt.), Austl.	112/B3
Péronne, Fr.	52/B4
Perote, Mex.	143/M7
Pérouges, Fr.	56/B6
Perpignan, Fr.	42/E5
Perray (riv.), Fr.	30/H6
Perrigny, Fr.	56/B4
Perris (res.), Ca, US	136/C3
Perris, Ca, US	136/C3
Perris State Rec. Area, Ca, US	136/C3
Perros-Guirec, Fr.	131/N7
Perrot, Île (isl.), Qu, Can.	131/N7
Perry, Ga, US	133/H4
Perry, Ok, US	129/H3

Perry, Fl, US	133/H4
Perry, Ut, US	137/J11
Perry (co.), Pa, US	138/B3
Perry (riv.), NW, Can.	122/F2
Perry Hall, Md, US	138/B5
Perryman, Md, US	138/B5
Perryton, Tx, US	129/G3
Perryville, Ak, US	134/G4
Perryville, Md, US	138/B4
Persan, Fr.	30/J4
Perstorp, Swe.	38/E3
Perth, Austl.	115/C4
Perth, On, Can.	130/E2
Perth (int'l arpt.), Austl.	112/K6
Perth, Austl.	112/K6
Perth, Sc, UK	36/C4
Perth Zoo, Austl.	112/K6
Pertuis, Fr.	42/F5
Pertuis Breton (inlet), Fr.	42/C3
Pertusato (cape), Fr.	46/A2
Peru, In, US	127/L5
Peru, In, US	130/C3
Peru (ctry.)	147/B3
Perúcáčko (lake), Bosn.	48/D4
Perugia, It.	43/K5
Peruíbe, Braz.	211/G9
Peruque, Mo, US	137/P8
Perushtitsa, Bul.	47/J1
Péruwelz, Belg.	52/C2
Pervari, It.	90/E2
Pervomaysk, Ukr.	49/K1
Pervomays'k, Rus.	63/G1
Pervomays'k, Rus.	61/N4
Perwez, Belg.	53/D2
Péry, Swi.	56/D3
Pesa (riv.), It.	59/E5
Pesagi (peak), Indo.	80/B4
Pesaro, It.	59/F5
Pesaro e Urbino (prov.), It.	59/F5
Pescadores (Penghu) (isls.), China	79/C3
Pescantina, It.	59/D2
Pescara, It.	46/D1
Peschanyy (cape), Kaz.	63/J4
Pescia, It.	59/D5
Peseux, Swi.	56/C4
Pesha (riv.), Rus.	61/J2
Peshāwar, Pak.	86/A2
Peshāwar (int'l arpt.), Pak.	86/A2
Peshtera, Bul.	47/J1
Peshtigo, Wi, US	127/M4
Peshtigo (riv.), Wi, US	130/B2
Peski, Rus.	56/B2
Peso da Régua, Port.	44/B2
Pesqueira, Braz.	154/C3
Pessac, Fr.	42/C4
Pest (prov.), Hun.	48/D2
Pestovo, Rus.	61/W9
Pestovo, Rus.	60/G4
Petal, Ms, US	133/F4
Petal.L Tiqwa, Isr.	91/F7
Petalión (gulf), Gre.	47/J4
Petaluma, Ca, US	135/J10
Pétange, Lux.	53/E4
Petare, Ven.	150/E2
Pétas, Gre.	47/G3
Petatlán, Mex.	142/D3
Petatlán, Mex.	143/E5
Petauke, Zam.	105/F3
Petawawa, On, Can.	130/E2
Petawawa (riv.), On, Can.	130/E2
Peten Itzá (lake), Guat.	144/D2
Petenwell (lake), Wi, US	127/L4
Peter (isl.), Nor.	160/U
Peterborough, On, Can.	130/E2
Peterborough, Eng, UK	33/F1
Peterborough, Austl.	113/H5
Peterhead, Sc, UK	127/H4
Peterlee, Eng, UK	35/G2
Petermann Abor. Land, Austl.	113/F2
Peteroa (vol.), Chile	158/C2
Petersaurach, Ger.	54/D4
Petersberg, Ger.	54/C1
Petersburg, Ak, US	134/M4
Petersfield, Eng, UK	33/F4
Petershagen, Ger.	51/F4
Petershagen, Ger.	40/G2
Petershausen, Ger.	55/G6
Peterson, Ut, US	137/K11
Pétervására, Hun.	41/L4
Petilia Policastro, It.	46/E3
Pétionville, Haiti	145/H1
Petit Goâve, Haiti	145/H2
Petit Lac Manicouagan (lake), Can.	131/H1
Petit Loango, PN du, Gabon	105/A2
Petit-Noir, Fr.	56/B4
Petit Rosne (riv.), Fr.	30/J2
Petitcodiac, NB, Can.	131/H2
Petite Miquelon (isl.), Can.	131/K2
Petite Rivière de l'Artibonite, Haiti	145/H2
Petite Rivière Noire (peak), Kiri.	117/H5
Petite-Rosselle, Fr.	53/F5
Petitt Morin (riv.), Fr.	42/E2
Petkeljärvi NP, Fin.	39/G2
Petlād, India	89/K4
Petlalcingo, Mex.	143/M7
Peto, Mex.	144/D1
Petorca, Chile	158/C2
Petoskey, Mi, US	130/C2
Petra (riv.), Rus.	65/M2
Petrel, Sp.	45/E3
Petrella (peak), It.	46/C2
Petrich, Bul.	47/H2
Petrified Forest NP, Az, US	128/E4
Petrila, Rom.	49/G3
Petrodvorets, Rus.	61/S7
Petrokhanski Prokhod (pass), Bul.	47/H1

Petrokrepost' (bay), Rus.	61/U7
Petrolándia, Braz.	154/C3
Petrolina, Braz.	154/B3
Petropavl, Kaz.	87/E2
Petropavlovsk-Kamchatskiy, Rus.	65/R4
Petrópolis, Braz.	211/K7
Petrovaradin, Yugo.	48/D3
Petrovsk, Rus.	30/J4
Petrovsk-Zabaykal'skiy, Rus.	70/J1
Petrozavodsk, Rus.	60/G3
Petrusburg, SAfr.	106/D3
Petrus Steyn, SAfr.	106/D2
Petrusville, SAfr.	106/D3
Pettenbach, Aus.	55/H1
Petteril (riv.), Eng, UK	35/F2
Petzeck (peak), Aus.	55/G6
Peuerbach, Aus.	55/H1
Peulik (mt.), Ak, US	134/G4
Peumo, Chile	158/N9
Pevely, Mo, US	137/G9
Pewaukee, Wi, US	135/X13
Pewaukee, Wi, US	135/P13
Peyrehorade, Fr.	42/C5
Peza (riv.), Rus.	61/K2
Pézenas, Fr.	42/E5
Pfaffenhausen, Ger.	57/G1
Pfaffenhofen an der Ilm, Ger.	57/G1
Pfaffenhofen an der Ilm, Ger.	54/D6
Pfaffenhoffen, Fr.	55/E5
Pfäffikon, Swi.	57/E3
Pfaffing, Ger.	55/G6
Pfaffnau, Swi.	56/D3
Pfahl (riv.), Ger.	55/F4
Pfälzer Wald (mts.), Ger.	54/A4
Pfälzerwald (mts.), Ger.	54/A4
Pfalzgrafenweiler, Ger.	54/B5
Pfarrhof Esternberg, Ger.	55/G5
Pfarrkirchen, Ger.	55/F6
Pfatter, Ger.	55/F5
Pfeffenhausen, Ger.	55/E5
Pfettrach (riv.), Ger.	55/F5
Pfieffe (riv.), Ger.	51/G6
Pfinztal, Ger.	54/B5
Pforzheim, Ger.	54/B5
Pfreimd, Ger.	55/F3
Pfreimd (riv.), Ger.	55/F3
Pfronstetten, Ger.	57/F1
Pfronten, Ger.	57/G2
Pfroslkopf (peak), Aus.	57/G4
Pfullendorf, Ger.	57/F2
Pfunds, Aus.	57/G4
Pfungstadt, Ger.	54/B3
Phagwāra, India	86/D5
Phalauda, India	86/D5
Phalempin, Fr.	52/C2
Phālia, Pak.	86/C2
Phalodi, India	89/K3
Phalsbourg, Fr.	53/G6
Phan Rang, Viet.	78/E4
Phan Thiet, Viet.	78/E4
Phanat Nikhom, Thai.	78/C3
Phang Hoei (range), Thai.	78/C2
Phangnga, Thai.	78/B4
Phanom Dongrak (mts.), Thai.	78/C3
Pharr, Tx, US	132/D5
Phatthalung, Thai.	78/C2
Phaya Fo (peak), Thai.	78/B2
Phayao, Thai.	78/B2
Phelan, Ca, US	136/C2
Phenix City, Al, US	133/G4
Phet Buri, Thai.	78/B3
Phetchabun, Thai.	78/C2
Phichit, Thai.	78/C2
Philadelphia, Ms, US	133/F4
Philadelphia, Pa, US	138/C4
Philadelphia (int'l arpt.), Pa, US	138/C4
Philip, SD, US	127/H4
Philip S.W. Goldson (int'l arpt.), Belz.	144/D2
Philippeville, Belg.	53/D3
Philippi, WV, US	130/D4
Philippine Asia	79/D4
Philippine (sea), Asia	67/M8
Philippines (ctry.), Asia	67/M8
Philippines (ctry.)	67/M8
Philippsburg, Ger.	54/B4
Philipsburg, Ven.	152/D2
Philipstown, SAfr.	106/D3
Phillaur, India	86/C4
Phillipsburg, NJ, US	138/C3
Phimai (ruin), Thai.	78/C3
Phitsanulok, Thai.	78/C2
Phnom Penh (Phnum Pénh) (cap.), Camb.	78/D4
Phnum Pénh (int'l arpt.), Camb.	78/D4
Pho (pt.), Thai.	78/C5
Phoenix (cap.), Az, US	137/R19
Phoenix, Az, US	137/R19
Phoenix (isls.), Kiri.	117/H5
Phoenix Park, Ire.	34/B5
Phoenix Sky Harbor (int'l arpt.), Az, US	137/S19
Phoenixville, Pa, US	138/C3
Phongsali, Laos	78/D3
Phongsali, Laos	78/D3
Phou Huatt (peak), Viet.	83/H4
Phou Loi (peak), Laos	78/D3
Phou Xai Lai Leng (peak), Laos	78/D3
Phra Nakhon Si Ayutthaya, Thai.	78/C3
Phra Thong (isl.), Thai.	78/B4
Phrae, Thai.	78/C2
Phu Hin Rong Kla NP, Thai.	78/C2

Phu Kradung NP, Thai.	78/C2
Phu Luong (peak), Viet.	83/H3
Phu Phan NP, Thai.	78/D2
Phu Quoc (isl.), Viet.	78/D4
Phu Rua NP, Thai.	78/C2
Phu Tho, Viet.	83/J3
Phuket (isl.), Thai.	83/G6
Phuket, Thai.	78/B5
Phulwaran, Pak.	86/B3
Phūlpur, India	84/D3
Piaçabuçu, Braz.	154/C3
Piacenza, It.	58/C2
Piacenza (prov.), It.	58/C2
Piadena, It.	58/D2
Pian di Serra, It.	59/F6
Pian-Upe Game Rsv., Ugan.	104/B2
Piancastagnaio, It.	46/B1
Piancó, Braz.	154/C2
Pianello val Tidone, It.	58/C2
Pianezza, It.	58/A2
Piangipane, It.	59/E4
Pianoro, It.	59/E4
Pianosa (isl.), It.	46/A1
Piaro, It.	58/C4
Pianosa (isl.), It.	46/A1
Piatra Neamţ, Rom.	49/H2
Piauí (riv.), Braz.	154/B3
Piauí (state), Braz.	154/B3
Piave (riv.), It.	43/K3
Piazza, It.	58/D1
Piazza, It.	58/D1
Piazza al Serchio, It.	58/D4
Piazza Armerina, It.	46/D4
Piazza Brembana, It.	58/C1
Piazzola sul Brenta, It.	59/E1
Pic (riv.), Can.	130/C1
Pic de Nore (peak), Fr.	42/E5
Pic d'Orhy (peak), Fr.	42/C5
Pic du Canigou (peak), Fr.	42/E5
Pica, Chile	150/E8
Picacho del Centinela (peak), Mex.	129/G5
Picahos, Cerro Dos (peak), Mex.	142/B2
Picardie (pol. reg.), Fr.	42/E2
Picardy (reg.), Fr.	52/B4
Picatinny Arsenal, NJ, US	138/D2
Picayune, Ms, US	133/F4
Piccolo (lag.), It.	43/K4
Pichanal, Arg.	159/J12
Pichidegua, Chile	158/N9
Pichilemu, Chile	158/B2
Pichincha (dept.), Ecu.	152/B4
Pichincha (vol.), Ecu.	152/B4
Pichl bei Wels, Aus.	55/G6
Pichor, India	86/D4
Pichucalco, Mex.	144/C2
Pickens, Ms, US	129/K4
Pickering, On, Can.	131/R8
Pickering, Eng, UK	35/H3
Pickering, Vale of (valley), Eng, UK	35/H3
Pickle Lake, On, Can.	127/L3
Picnic Bay, Austl.	114/B2
Pico da Neblina, PN do, Braz.	150/F3
Pico de Orizaba, PN, Mex.	143/M7
Pico Rivera, Ca, US	136/F8
Pico Truncado, Arg.	158/D5
Picos, Braz.	154/B3
Picota, Peru	152/B2
Picsi, Peru	152/B2
Picton, On, Can.	130/E2
Pictou, NS, Can.	131/J2
Picture Rocks, Pa, US	138/B1
Pictured Rocks Nat'l Lakeshore, Mi, US	127/M4
Pictured Rocks Nat'l Lakeshore, Mi, US	130/C2
Picui, Braz.	154/C2
Picun Leufú (riv.), Arg.	158/C3
Piddle (riv.), Eng, UK	32/D5
Pidurutagala (peak), SrL.	82/D6
Piedade, Port.	45/P10
Piedade do Rio Grande, Braz.	211/J6
Piedimulera, It.	57/E6
Piedmont, Al, US	133/G3
Piedmont (upland), US	133/H3
Piedmont, Ok, US	137/M14
Piedra Grande, Ven.	152/D2
Piedrabuena, Sp.	44/C3
Piedras, Arg.	159/J5
Piedras Coloradas, Uru.	159/K10
Piedras Negras, Mex.	132/C4
Piedras Negras, Mex.	143/N8
Piedras, Rio de las (riv.), Peru	150/D6
Piedritas, Arg.	158/E2
Piekary Śląskie, Pol.	41/K3
Piekenierskloof (pass), SAfr.	106/L10
Pieksämäki, Fin.	60/E3
Pielinen (lake), Fin.	37/J3
Piemonte (reg.), It.	43/G4
Pienza, It.	59/E6
Pieński NP, Pol.	41/L4
Pieńsk, Pol.	41/H3
Piera, SAfr.	45/K6
Pierce, Ne, US	127/J5
Pierce, Co, US	137/C1
Pierceland, Sk, Can.	126/F2
Pieris, It.	59/G1
Piermont, NY, US	139/J7
Pierowall, Sc, UK	31/V14
Pierre (cap.), SD, US	127/H4
Pierre-de-Bresse, Fr.	56/B4
Pierre-Lévée, Fr.	30/M5
Pierrefitte-sur-Seine, Fr.	30/K5
Pierrefonds, Qu, Can.	131/N7

Pierrefontaine-les-Varans, Fr.	56/C3
Pierrelatte, Fr.	42/F4
Pierrelaye, Fr.	30/J4
Pierrevert, Fr.	42/F5
Pierry, Fr.	52/C5
Piešťany, Slvk.	41/J4
Pieski, Ak, US	160/S
Piest'any (int'l arpt.), Slvk.	49/P7
Pieterlen, Swi.	56/D3
Pietermaritzburg, SAfr.	107/E3
Pietersburg, SAfr.	105/E5
Pietra Ligure, It.	58/B4
Pietralunga, It.	59/F6
Pietramelara, It.	46/D2
Pietrasanta, It.	59/D5
Pietravairano, It.	58/A1
Pieve del Cairo, It.	58/B2
Pieve di Cento, It.	59/E3
Pieve di Soligo, It.	59/F1
Pieve di Teco, It.	58/A4
Pieve Emanuele, It.	58/C2
Pieve Porto Morone, It.	58/C4
Pieve Santo Stefano, It.	59/F5
Pieve Vergonte, It.	58/D4
Pievepelago, It.	58/D4
Pigeon (lake), Can.	126/E2
Pigeon (lake), Can.	126/E2
Pigeon Chau (isl.), China	71/V9
Piggott, Ar, US	129/K3
Pigs (bay), Cuba	140/E3
Pigüé, Arg.	158/E3
Pigüé, Arg.	158/E3
Piława, India	84/C2
Piława, India	84/C2
Pijijiapan, Mex.	144/C3
Pijnacker, Neth.	50/B4
Pijol (peak), Hon.	144/E3
Pike (co.), Pa, US	138/C1
Pikelot (isl.), Micr.	116/D4
Pikes Creek (res.), Pa, US	138/B1
Pikesville, Md, US	138/B5
Piketberg, SAfr.	106/L10
Pikeville, Ky, US	130/D4
Pikit, Phil.	79/D5
Pikou, China	72/C3
Pila, Arg.	159/J12
Pila (riv.), Pol.	41/J2
Pilanesberg (range), SAfr.	106/P12
Pilani, India	86/C5
Pilão Arcado, Braz.	154/B3
Pilar, Arg.	157/E2
Pilar, Arg.	154/D3
Pilar, Phil.	158/E1
Pilatus (peak), Swi.	57/E4
Pilaya (riv.), Bol.	150/F8
Pilchuck (riv.), Wa, US	135/D1
Pilcomayo (riv.), SAm.	147/C5
Pili, Phil.	79/D5
Pilibhit, India	84/B1
Pilica (riv.), Pol.	62/B2
Pilica (peak), Gre.	47/H1
Pilis, Hun.	48/D2
Pilinel, Port.	44/B2
Piniós (riv.), Gre.	47/G4
Pilis (peak), Hun.	41/K4
Piliscsaba, Hun.	49/Q9
Pilisvörösvár, Hun.	49/Q9
Pilkhua, India	86/D5
Pillar (cape), SAm.	147/C5
Pillar, Ca, US	115/C4
Pillar (pt.), Ca, US	135/J12
Pillar (peak), Austl.	113/G5
Pilliga, Austl.	115/D1
Pillon, Col du (pass), Swi.	56/D5
Pilões (riv.), Braz.	154/A5
Pilões, Serra dos (mtn.), Braz.	154/A5
Pilos, Gre.	47/G4
Pilot (mtn.), Tn, US	130/C4
Pilot Point, Ak, US	134/G4
Pilot Station, Ak, US	134/F3
Pilsting, Ger.	55/F5
Pima, Az, US	128/E4
Pima, Az, US	128/E4
Pimpri-Chinchwad, India	89/K5
Piña (pt.), Pan.	145/G5
Pináculo (peak), Arg.	159/B6
Pinamar, Arg.	159/F3
Pinang (cape), Malay.	80/A2
Pinang (isl.), Malay.	80/A2
Pinar del Río, Cuba	145/F1
Pınarbaşı, Turk.	90/D2
Pınarhisar, Turk.	49/H5
Piñas, Ecu.	156/B1
Pinatubo (mt.), Phil.	79/D5
Pinawa, Mb, Can.	127/K3
Pincher Creek, Ab, Can.	126/E3
Pinconning, Mi, US	130/D3
Pincourt, Qu, Can.	131/N7
Pindamonhangaba, Braz.	211/H7
Pindaré (riv.), Braz.	154/B2
Pindaré-Mirim, Braz.	154/A2
Pindhos NP, Gre.	47/G3
Pindi Bhattiān, Pak.	86/B2
Pindi Gheb, Pak.	86/B3
Pindobaçu, Braz.	154/B3
Pindus (mts.), Gre.	47/G3
Pindwara, India	86/B3
Pine Barrens (phys. reg.), NJ, US	138/D3
Pine Bluff, Ar, US	129/J4
Pine Bluffs, Wy, US	127/G5
Pine Creek (pt.), Ct, US	139/E1
Pine Falls, Mb, Can.	127/J3

Pine Grove, Pa, US	138/B2
Pine Hill, NJ, US	138/D4
Pine Island, Mn, US	130/A2
Pine Island Bay (flat), Ant.	160/S
Pine Lawn, Mo, US	137/Q7
Pine Point, NW, Can.	122/E2
Pine Ridge, SD, US	127/H5
Pine, South Branch (riv.), Mi, US	130/D3
Pine, The (hills), US	135/G6
Pinecliff (lake), NJ, US	139/H7
Pinecliffe, Co, US	137/D4
Pinedale, Wy, US	126/F5
Pinega (riv.), Rus.	64/C3
Pineimuta (riv.), Can.	127/L2
Pinelands, SAfr.	106/L10
Piñeira (riv.), Braz.	151/L5
Pinerolo, It.	43/G4
Pinetown, SAfr.	107/E3
Pineui, Fr.	42/D4
Pineview (res.), Ut, US	137/K11
Pineville, La, US	129/J5
Pinewood Springs, Co, US	137/D3
Pinga (riv.), Thai.	83/G4
Pingbian Miaozu Zizhixian, China	83/H3
Pingding, China	72/C3
Pingdingshan, China	72/D3
Pingdu, China	72/D3
Pingelap (isl.), Micr.	116/F4
Pingguo, China	83/J3
Pinghe, China	77/H1
Pinghu, China	77/L9
Pingjiang, China	79/B3
Pingjing (pass), China	72/C5
Pingnan, China	79/B3
Pingquan, China	72/D2
Pingshan, China	72/C3
Pingtan, China	79/C2
Pingtang, China	83/J2
P'ingtung, Tai.	79/D3
Pingxiang, China	83/J3
Pingxiang, China	83/J3
Pingxing Guan (pass), China	72/C3
Pingyao, China	72/C3
Pingyi, China	72/D3
Pingyin, China	72/D3
Pingyu, China	72/C4
Pingyuan, China	72/D3
Pinhal, Braz.	211/G7
Pinhal Novo, Port.	45/U10
Pinhão, Braz.	155/B3
Pinheiro, Braz.	154/A1
Pinheiros, Braz.	155/D2
Pinhel, Port.	44/B2
Pinjar (lake), Austl.	112/K6
Pinjarra, Austl.	112/B5
Pink, Ok, US	137/N15
Pink Mountain, BC, Can.	124/AA13
Pinkafeld, Aus.	48/C2
Pinkawillinie Conservation Park, Austl.	113/G5
Pinkegat (chan.), Neth.	50/C2
Pinnacles Nat'l Mon., Ca, US	136/B3
Pinnaroo, Austl.	113/J5
Pinneberg, Ger.	51/G1
Pinole, Ca, US	135/K10
Pinon Hills, Ca, US	136/C2
Pinos, Mex.	143/E4
Pinos (pt.), Ca, US	128/B3
Pinos, Mex.	143/E4
Pinos, Isla de (Isla de la Juventud) (isl.), Cuba	140/E3
Pinos-Puente, Sp.	44/D4
Pinoso, Sp.	45/E3
Pins, Île des (isl.), NCal.	116/F7
Pinsdorf, Aus.	55/H3
Pinsk, Bela.	62/C1
Pinta, Isla (isl.), Ecu.	156/E6
Pinto, Arg.	159/K7
Pinto, Chile	158/C3
Pinto, It.	59/D3
Pinzolo, It.	57/G5
Pio IX, Braz.	154/B2
Pio Xii, Braz.	154/A2
Piobbico, It.	59/E5
Pioche, Nv, US	128/D3
Piombino, It.	59/D5
Piombino Dese, It.	59/F1
Pioneer World, Austl.	112/L7
Pioner (isl.), Rus.	64/J2
Pionki, Pol.	41/L3
Piorini (riv.), Braz.	150/F4
Piota (riv.), It.	58/B3
Piotrków Trybunalski, Pol.	41/K3
Piove di Sacco, It.	59/F2
Pipa (riv.), It.	151/J4
Pipar, India	86/B3
Pipe Spring Nat'l Mon., Az, US	128/D3
Piper, Ks, US	137/Q15
Pipersville, Pa, US	138/D3
Pipestone (riv.), On, Can.	127/L2
Pipestone, Mn, US	127/J5
Piplān, Pak.	86/B3
Pipmuacan (res.), Qu, Can.	131/J2
Pippingarra Abor. Land, Austl.	112/C2
Pipra (riv.), India	84/D2
Pipraich, India	84/D2
Piqua, Oh, US	130/C4

Piquet Carneiro, Braz.	154/C2
Piquete, Braz.	211/H7
Piquiri (riv.), Braz.	151/H7
Pir Mahal, Pak.	86/B4
Pir Panjal (range), India	86/C3
Piracanjuba, Braz.	155/B5
Piracicaba, Braz.	155/B3
Piracuruca, Braz.	154/B1
Plai Mat (riv.), Thai.	78/C3
Piraeus, Gre.	47/N9
Pirae-bong (peak), NKor.	73/C2
Pirai, Braz.	211/K7
Piraí do Sul, Braz.	155/B3
Piraiévs, Gre.	47/N9
Piraju, Braz.	155/B2
Pirajuí, Braz.	155/B2
Pirámide (peak), Chile	159/B6
Piran, Slov.	59/G1
Piranga, Arg.	157/E2
Piranhas (riv.), Braz.	151/L5
Piranji (riv.), Braz.	154/C2
Pirapemas, Braz.	154/A1
Pirapora, Braz.	154/A3
Pirapòzinho, Braz.	155/A2
Pirarajá, Uru.	159/G2
Pirassununga, Braz.	155/C2
Pires do Rio, Braz.	155/B2
Pirgos, Gre.	47/G4
Pirgos, Gre.	47/H2
Pírgos, Gre.	47/J5
Piripolis, Uru.	159/G2
Pirin (peak), Bul.	47/H2
Pirin NP, Bul.	47/H2
Piripiri, Braz.	154/B2
Piritiba, Braz.	154/B3
Piritu, Ven.	152/D2
Pirmasens, Ger.	53/F3
Pirna, Ger.	41/G3
Piro, India	85/E3
Pirot, Yugo.	47/H1
Pirovano, Arg.	152/B2
Pirthipur, India	84/B3
Piru, Ca, US	136/B2
Piru, Ca, US	136/B2
Piryion, Gre.	59/D6
Pisa (prov.), It.	58/D5
Pisa, It.	58/D5
Pisac, Peru	150/D6
Pisanino (peak), It.	58/D4
Pisco (riv.), Peru	150/C6
Pisco, Peru	156/B4
Piscobamba, Peru	156/B3
Pisek (peak), Rus.	55/H3
Pisek, Czh.	55/H4
Pishan, China	70/C4
Pishin, Pak.	89/J2
Pishīn, Iran	89/H3
Piskavica, Bosn.	48/C3
Pisogne, It.	58/D1
Pissis (peak), Arg.	157/C2
Pistakee (lake), Il, US	135/P15
Pisticci, It.	46/E2
Pistoia (prov.), It.	59/D5
Pistoia, It.	59/D5
Pisuerga (riv.), Sp.	44/C1
Pisz, Pol.	41/L2
Pit (riv.), Ca, US	128/B2
Pitalito, Col.	152/B4
Pitanga, Braz.	155/A3
Pitcairn, Pa, US	138/L6
Pitcairn Islands (dpcy.), UK	117/N7
Piteå, Swe.	37/F2
Piteålven (riv.), Swe.	37/F2
Piteşti, Rom.	49/G3
Pithiviers, Fr.	42/E2
Pithorāgarh, India	84/C1
Pitigliano, It.	46/B1
Pitiquito, Mex.	142/B2
Pitjantjatjara Abor. Lands, Austl.	113/F3
Pitkas Point, Ak, US	134/F3
Pitlochry, Sc, UK	36/C4
Pitman, NJ, US	138/C4
Pitmedden, Sc, UK	36/D2
Pitomača, Cro.	48/C3
Piton de la Fournaise (peak), Reun.	107/S15
Piton des Neiges (peak), Reun.	107/S15
Pitrufquén, Chile	158/B3
Pitt Water (bay), Austl.	114/H8
Pittenweem, Sc, UK	36/D4
Pittsburg, Ks, US	129/J3
Pittsburgh, Pa, US	130/E3
Pittsfield, Ma, US	139/F2
Pittsfield, Ma, US	139/F2
Pittston, Pa, US	138/C2
Pittstown, NJ, US	138/C2
Pittsworth, Austl.	114/C4
Piui, Braz.	155/G6
Piumazzo, It.	59/E3
Piura (dept.), Peru	156/A2
Piura, Peru	156/A2
Pividnny Buh (riv.), Ukr.	64/C5
Pixley, Ca, US	136/C3
Pixoyal, Mex.	140/C4
Piz d'Err (peak), Swi.	57/F4
Piz di Sacco, It.	57/F4
Pizarra, Sp.	44/C4
Pizhma (riv.), Rus.	61/K2
Pizol (peak), Swi.	57/F4
Pizzighettone, It.	58/C2
Pizzo, It.	46/E3
Pizzo dei Tre Signori (peak), It.	57/E5
Pizzo della Presolana (peak), It.	57/F6
Pizzo di Coca (peak), It.	57/G6
Pizzo di Vogorno (peak), It.	57/E5
Pizzuto (peak), It.	46/C1

Placentia (bay), Can.	131/L2
Placentia, Ca, US	136/G8
Placer, Phil.	79/E6
Placer (co.), Ca, US	135/M9
Placetas, Cuba	145/G1
Plachkovtsi, Bul.	47/J1
Plaffeien, Swi.	56/D4
Plai Mat (riv.), Thai.	78/C3
Plaidt, Ger.	53/G2
Plain City, Ut, US	137/J11
Plain Dealing, Mt, US	127/G4
Plaine (riv.), Fr.	56/C1
Plainfield, Il, US	135/P16
Plains, Tx, US	129/G4
Plains, Pa, US	138/C1
Plainsboro, NJ, US	138/D3
Plainview, Tx, US	129/G4
Plainview, Mn, US	130/A2
Plainview, NY, US	139/M8
Plan-les-Ouates, Swi.	56/C5
Planá, Czh.	55/F3
Plana Cays (isls.), Bahm.	145/H1
Planaltina, Braz.	154/A4
Plancher-Bas, Fr.	56/C2
Plancher-les-Mines, Fr.	56/C2
Plandište, Yugo.	48/E3
Planeta Rica, Col.	152/C2
Planken, Lcht.	57/F3
Plankstadt, Ger.	54/B4
Plano, Tx, US	129/H4
Plant City, Fl, US	133/H4
Plantation, Fl, US	133/H5
Plaquemines, La, US	137/Q17
Plasencia, Sp.	44/B2
Plaski, Cro.	55/L4
Plaston, SAfr.	106/L10
Plata (estu.),	147/D5
Plata, Col.	150/C3
Platani (riv.), It.	46/C4
Plate Taille, Barrage de la (dam), Belg.	53/D3
Plateau (state), Nga.	103/H4
Platí, It.	47/H2
Platinum, Ak, US	134/F4
Plato, Col.	152/C2
Platón Sánchez, Mex.	144/B1
Platte (riv.), US	119/G5
Platte City, Mo, US	137/D5
Platte, North (riv.), US	129/K3
Platte, South (riv.), US	124/E3
Platteville, Co, US	137/C2
Plattling, Ger.	55/F5
Plattsburgh, NY, US	130/F2
Plauen, Ger.	55/F1
Plav, Yugo.	47/F1
Plavna Dadaint (peak), Swi.	57/G4
Playa de los Muertos (ruin), Hon.	144/E3
Playa del Carmen, Mex.	144/E1
Playa Noriega (lake), Mex.	142/C2
Playa Vicente, Mex.	144/C2
Playas (lake), NM, US	128/E5
Playgreen (lake), Mb, Can.	127/J2
Pleasant (lake), Az, US	137/R18
Pleasant Grove, Ut, US	137/K13
Pleasant Hill, Mo, US	137/E6
Pleasant Hill, Ca, US	135/K11
Pleasant Hills, Md, US	138/B5
Pleasant Valley, Mo, US	137/E6
Pleasant View, Ut, US	137/K11
Pleasant View, Co, US	137/B3
Pleasanton, Tx, US	129/H5
Pleasanton, Ca, US	135/L11
Pleasantville, NJ, US	138/D4
Pleasantville, NY, US	139/K7
Pleaux, Fr.	42/E4
Pleiku, Viet.	78/D3
Pleinfeld, Ger.	54/D4
Plein, Fr.	37/D3
Plesná (riv.), Czh.	55/F2
Pleso (int'l arpt.), Cro.	48/C3
Plessisville, Qu, Can.	131/G2
Plettenberg, Ger.	51/E6
Pleumeur, Fr.	42/B2
Pleven, Bul.	49/G4
Pljevlja, Yugo.	47/F1
Plitvice Lakes NP, Cro.	48/B3
Ploče, Cro.	40/C2
Plochingen, Ger.	54/C5
Płock, Pol.	41/K2
Pločno (peak), Bosn.	48/C4
Ploemeur, Fr.	42/B3
Ploieşti, Rom.	49/H3
Plomárion, Gre.	47/K3
Plombières, Belg.	53/E2
Plombières-lès-Dijon, Fr.	56/A3
Plön, Ger.	38/D4
Płońsk, Pol.	41/L2
Plottier, Arg.	158/C3
Ploučnice (riv.), Czh.	41/H3

Ploufragan, Fr.	42/B2
Plougastel-Daoulas, Fr.	42/A2
Plouguernével, Fr.	42/B2
Plouzané, Fr.	42/A2
Plovdiv (pol. reg.), Bul.	
Plover Cove (res.), China	71/U10
Plozévet, Fr.	42/A3
Pluffgan (int'l arpt.), Fr.	42/A3
Plum (isl.), NY, US	139/F1
Plumridge Lakes Nature Rsv., Austl.	112/E4
Plumstead, Pa, US	138/C3
Plungė, Lith.	39/J4
Plymouth, NC, US	133/J3
Plymouth, NH, US	131/G3
Plymouth, In, US	130/C3
Plymouth, Wi, US	130/C3
Plymouth (cap.), Monts.	141/N8
Plymouth, Eng, UK	32/B6
Plymouth (sound), Eng, UK	32/B6
Plymouth, Pa, US	138/C1
Plynlimon (peak), Wal, UK	32/C2
Plzeň, Czh.	55/G3
Pniel, SAfr.	106/L10
Pniewy, Pol.	41/J2
Pô, Burk.	103/E4
Po (riv.), It.	27/F4
Po di Venezia (riv.), It.	59/F2
Po di Volano (riv.), It.	59/E3
Po Klong Garai Cham Towers, Viet.	78/E4
Po, Mouths of the (delta), It.	43/K4
Pô, PN de, Burk.	103/E4
Po Toi Group (isls.), China	71/V11
Poá, Braz.	211/G8
Poa (riv.), Ven.	153/E2
Poag, Il, US	137/G8
Pobé, Ben.	103/F5
Pobedy (peak), Kyr.	70/D3
Pobiedziska, Pol.	41/J2
Pobla de Segur, Sp.	45/F1
Pocahontas, Ar, US	129/K3
Poção de Pedra, Braz.	154/A2
Pochep, Rus.	62/E1
Poch'ŏn, SKor.	73/G6
Pocinhos, Braz.	154/C2
Pöcking, Ger.	57/H2
Pöcking, Ger.	55/G6
Pocklington Reef (reef), PNG	116/E6
Poço Fundo, Braz.	211/H6
Poções, Braz.	154/B4
Pocola, Ok, US	129/J4
Poconé, Braz.	151/G7
Pocono (mts.), Pa, US	138/C2
Pocono (lake), Pa, US	138/C1
Pocono Lake, Pa, US	138/C1
Pocono Pines, Pa, US	138/C1
Poços de Caldas, Braz.	211/G6
Pocrí, Pan.	152/A2
Podbořany, Czh.	55/G2
Poddębice, Pol.	41/K3
Podenzano, It.	58/C3
Podgorica, Yugo.	47/F1
Podlasie (reg.),	
Podol'sk, Rus.	61/W9
Podor, Sen.	102/B2
Podporozh'ye, Rus.	60/G3
Podravska Slatina, Cro.	48/C3
Podujevo, Yugo.	47/G1
Pofadder, SAfr.	106/B3
Poggibonsi, It.	59/E5
Poggio Renatico, It.	59/E3
Poggio Rusco, It.	59/E2
Poggiola, It.	59/E6
Pogromni (vol.), Ak, US	134/F5
P'ohang, SKor.	74/A2
Pohénégamook, Qu, Can.	131/G2
Pohja (Pojo), Fin.	39/K1
Pohjanmaa (reg.), Fin.	37/D3
Pohjois-Karjala (prov.), Fin.	60/F3
Pohnpei (isl.), Micr.	116/E4
Pohoiki, Hi, US	124/U11
Pohopoco Mtn. (mtn.), Pa, US	138/C2
Poigny-la-Forêt, Fr.	30/H5
Poinsett (cape), Ant.	160/H
Point (lake), NW, Can.	122/E2
Point au Fer (isl.), La, US	129/K6
Point Baker, Ak, US	134/M4
Point Fortin, Trin.	153/F2
Point Hope, Ak, US	134/E2
Point Lay, Ak, US	134/F2
Point Lookout (peak), Austl.	114/D4
Point Mugu Naval Air Sta., Ca, US	136/B2
Point Mugu State Park, Ca, US	136/A2
Point of Aire (pt.), Wal, UK	35/E5
Point of Ayre (pt.), IM, UK	34/D3
Point Pelee NP, Can.	130/D3
Point Pleasant, WV, US	130/D4
Point Pleasant, Pa, US	138/C3
Point Pleasant, NJ, US	138/D3

Point Pleasant Beach, NJ, US 138/D3
Point Salines (int'l arpt.), Gren. 153/F1
Point Salvation Abor. Rsv., Austl. 112/D4
Pointe-à-Pitre, Fr. 141/N8
Pointe à Raquette, Haiti 145/H2
Pointe-aux-Trembles, Qu, Can. 131/P6
Pointe-Calumet, Qu, Can. 131/N6
Pointe-Claire, Qu, Can. 131/N7
Pointe de Chassiron (pt.), Fr. 42/C3
Pointe de l'Arcouest (pt.), Fr. 42/B2
Pointe des Verres (peak), Fr. 56/C6
Pointe-du-Lac, Qu, Can. 131/F2
Pointe du Sablon (pt.), Fr. 42/F5
Pointe-Noire, Congo 105/B1
Poirino, It. 58/A3
Poissonier (pt.), Austl. 112/C1
Poissy, Fr. 30/J5
Poitiers, Fr. 42/D3
Poitou (reg.), Fr. 42/C3
Poitou-Charentes (reg.), Fr. 42/C3
Poix-de-Picardie, Fr. 52/A4
Poix-Terron, Fr. 53/D4
Pojuca, Braz. 154/C4
Pok Liu Chau (isl.), China 71/U11
Pokaran, India 89/K3
Pokharā, Nepal 84/D1
Pokhvistnevo, Rus. 63/K1
Pol-e Khomrī, Afg. 89/J1
Pola de Laviana, Sp. 44/C1
Pola de Lena, Sp. 44/C1
Pola de Siero, Sp. 44/C1
Polabská Nížina (phys. reg.), Czh. 43/L1
Pol'ana (peak), Slvk. 62/A2
Poland (ctry.) 27/F3
Połaniec, Pol. 41/L3
Polatlı, Turk. 62/E5
Polatsk, Bela. 39/N4
Polch, Ger. 53/G3
Połczyn-Zdrój, Pol. 38/G5
Pole of Inaccessibility, Ant. 160/E
Polesella, It. 59/E3
Polesine (reg.), It. 59/E3
Poleski NP, Pol. 41/M3
Polgár, Hun. 48/E2
Pŏlgyo, SKor. 73/D5
Poliaigos (isl.), Gre. 47/J4
Policastro, Golfo di (gulf), It. 46/D3
Police, Pol. 38/F5
Policoro, It. 46/E2
Poligny, Fr. 56/B4
Polikastron, Gre. 47/H2
Polikhni, Gre. 47/H2
Polikhnítos, Gre. 47/K3
Polillo (isl.), Phil. 79/D4
Polis, Cyp. 91/C2
Polistena, It. 46/E3
Políyiros, Gre. 47/H2
Polje, Slov. 43/L3
Polkowice, Pol. 41/J3
Polla, It. 46/D2
Pollença, Sp. 45/G3
Polochic (riv.), Guat. 144/D3
Polomolok, Phil. 81/G2
Polonia (cape), Uru. 159/G2
Polonnaruwa, SrL. 82/D6
Polonne, Ukr. 62/C2
Polski Trŭmbesh, Bul. 49/G4
Polson, Mt, US 126/E4
Poltava, Ukr. 62/E2
Poltavs'ka (obl.), Ukr. 62/E2
Poluška (peak), Czh. 55/H5
Polvijärvi, Fin. 60/F3
Polyarnyy, Rus. 60/G1
Polynesia (reg.) 116/G6
Pomabamba, Peru 156/B3
Pomarance, It. 43/J5
Pomarico, It. 46/E2
Pomáz, Hun. 49/R9
Pomba (riv.), Som. 155/D2
Pombal, Braz. 154/C2
Pombal, Port. 44/A3
Pombas, CpV. 93/J9
Pomerania (reg.), Pol. 38/F4
Pomeranian (bay), Ger.,Pol. 38/F4
Pomerode, Braz. 155/B3
Pomeroon-Supenaam (pol. reg.), Guy. 153/G3
Pomeroy, Wa, US 126/D4
Pomeroy, NI, UK 34/B2
Pommersfelden, Ger. 54/D3
Pomona, Ca, US 136/C2
Pomona, NJ, US 138/D5
Pomona, Md, US 138/B5
Pomorie, Bul. 49/H4
Pomos (pt.), Cyp. 91/C2
Pompano Beach, Fl, US 133/H5
Pompei (ruin), It. 46/D2
Pompeu, Braz. 155/C1
Pompey, Fr. 53/F6
Pompiano, It. 58/C2
Pompton (riv.), NJ, US 139/H8
Pompton Lakes, NJ, US 139/H8
Poncarale, It. 58/D2
Ponce, PR 141/M8
Ponchatoula, La, US 137/P16
Poncheville (lake), Can. 130/E1
Pond, Mo, US 137/F8
Pond (inlet), NW, Can. 123/J1
Pond (pt.), Ct, US 139/E1
Pond Inlet, NW, Can. 123/J1
Pondicherry (terr.), India 70/D8
Pondicherry, India 82/C5
Ponente, Riviera di (coast), Fr. 58/B5
Ponferrada, Sp. 44/B1
Pongdong, SKor. 73/D5
Ponghwa, SKor. 74/A2
Pongolo (riv.), SAfr. 107/E2
Poni (prov.), Burk. 102/E4
Poniatowa, Pol. 41/M3
Ponnaiyar (riv.), India 82/C5
Ponoka, Ab, Can. 126/E2
Ponoy (riv.), Rus. 64/D3
Pons, Fr. 42/C4
Ponsacco, It. 58/D5
Pont-à-Celles, Belg. 53/D3
Pont-à-Marcq, Fr. 52/C2
Pont-D'Ain, Fr. 56/B5
Pont-de-Chéruy, Fr. 56/B6
Pont-de-Roide, Fr. 56/C3
Pont-de-Vaux, Fr. 56/A5
Pont-de-Veyle, Fr. 56/A5
Pont-du-Château, Fr. 42/E4
Pont-Remy, Fr. 52/A3
Pont-Saint-Esprit, Fr. 42/F4
Pont-Saint-Martin, It. 58/A1
Pont-Sainte-Maxence, Fr. 52/B5
Ponta Delgada, Azor., Port. 45/T13
Ponta do Pico (peak), Azor., Port. 45/S12
Ponta Grossa, Braz. 155/B3
Ponta Porã, Braz. 157/E1
Pontalina, Braz. 155/B1
Pontarlier, Fr. 56/C4
Pontarmé, Fr. 30/K4
Pontassieve, It. 59/E5
Pontault-Combault, Fr. 30/K5
Pontax (riv.), Can. 130/E1
Pontcarré, Fr. 30/L5
Pontchartrain (lake), La, US 125/H5
Pontchâteau, Fr. 42/B3
Ponte Alta do Bom Jesus, Braz. 154/A4
Ponte Alta do Tocantins, Braz. 154/A3
Ponte Buggianese, It. 59/D5
Ponte de Sor, Port. 44/A3
Ponte dell'Olio, It. 58/C3
Ponte di Legno, It. 57/G5
Ponte di Piave, It. 59/F1
Ponte do Lima, Port. 44/A2
Ponte Lambro, It. 58/C1
Ponte Nova, Braz. 155/D2
Ponte San Nicolò, It. 59/E2
Pontecagnano, It. 46/D2
Pontecorvo, It. 46/C2
Pontecurone, It. 58/B3
Pontedera, It. 58/D5
Pontefract, Eng, UK 35/G4
Ponteland, Eng, UK 35/G1
Pontelongo, It. 59/F2
Pontenure, It. 58/C3
Pontes e Lacerda, Braz. 150/G7
Pontestura, It. 58/B2
Pontevedra, Sp. 44/A1
Pontevico, It. 58/D2
Ponthévrard, Fr. 30/H6
Ponthieu (reg.), Fr. 52/A3
Pontiac, Il, US 127/L5
Pontiac, Mi, US 130/D3
Pontiac (lake), Mi, US 135/E6
Pontianak, Indo. 80/C4
Pontivy, Fr. 42/B2
Pontoise, Fr. 30/J4
Pontoon Beach, Il, US 137/G8
Pontotoc, Ms, US 133/F3
Pontpoint, Fr. 52/B5
Pontremoli, It. 58/C4
Pontresina, Swi. 57/F5
Pontypool, Wal, UK 32/C3
Ponza, It. 46/C2
Ponziane, Isole (isls.), It. 46/C2
Poole (bay), Eng, UK 33/E5
Poole, Eng, UK 32/E5
Poolewe, Sc, UK 31/R8
Poona (Pune), India 89/K5
Poondarrie (peak), Austl. 112/C3
Poondinna (mt.), Austl. 113/F3
Poopó (lake), Bol. 147/C4
Poortugaal, Neth. 50/B5
Pöösapää (pt.), Est. 39/K2
Poosepatuck Ind. Res., NY, US 139/F2
Popayán, Col. 152/B4
Poperinge, Belg. 52/B2
Popigochic (riv.), Mex. 142/C2
Popilta (lake), Austl. 113/J5
Popio (lake), Austl. 115/B2
Poplar, Mt, US 127/G3
Poplar (riv.), Mb,On, Can. 122/G3
Poplar (isl.), Md, US 138/B6
Poplar Bluff, Mo, US 129/K3
Poplarville, Ms, US 133/F4
Popocatépetl (vol.), Mex. 143/L7
Popovo, Bul. 49/H4
Poppberg (peak), Ger. 55/E4
Poppenhausen, Ger. 54/D2
Poppenhausen, Ger. 54/C2
Poppi, It. 59/E5
Poprad, Slvk. 41/L4
Poprad (riv.), Slvk. 41/L4
Poranga, Braz. 154/B2
Porangatu, Braz. 151/J6
Porbandar, India 89/J4
Porcari, It. 58/D5
Porce (riv.), Col. 152/C3
Porcheville, Fr. 30/H5
Porcia, It. 59/F1
Porcuna, Sp. 44/C4
Porcupine (riv.), Can.,US 119/C3
Porcupine Gorge NP, Austl. 114/B3
Porcupine Plain, Sk, Can. 127/H2
Pordenone (prov.), It. 59/F2
Pordenone, It. 59/F1
Pordim, Bul. 49/G4
Pore, Col. 152/D3
Poreč, Cro. 59/G2
Poretta (int'l arpt.), Fr. 46/A1
Pori (int'l arpt.), Fin. 39/J1
Pori, Fin. 39/J1
Porirua, NZ 117/S11
Porlezza, It. 57/F5
Pornic, Fr. 42/B3
Porongurup NP, Austl. 112/C5
Póros, Gre. 47/H4
Porpoise (bay), Ant. 160/J
Porrentruy, Swi. 56/D3
Porretta Terme, It. 59/D4
Porriño, Sp. 44/A1
Porsangen (inlet), Nor. 37/H1
Porsgrunn, Nor. 38/C2
Porsuk (riv.), Turk. 62/D5
Port (isl.), Japan 77/H6
Port Alberni, BC, Can. 126/B3
Port Albert, Austl. 115/C3
Port Alexander, Ak, US 134/M4
Port Alfred, SAfr. 106/D4
Port Alice, BC, Can. 126/B3
Port Angeles, Wa, US 126/C3
Port Antonio, Jam. 145/G2
Port Appin, Sc, UK 36/A3
Port Arthur, Tx, US 129/J5
Port au Choix, Nf, Can. 131/K1
Port-au-Prince (cap.), Haiti 145/H2
Port Augusta, Austl. 113/H5
Port Bannatyne, Sc, UK 36/A5
Port Blair, India 83/F5
Port Blakely, Wa, US 135/C2
Port Bolivar, Tx, US 132/E4
Port-Bouët, C.d'Iv. 102/E5
Port Bouet (Abidgan) (int'l arpt.),= C.d'Iv. 102/E5
Port Broughton, Austl. 113/H5
Port Canning, India 85/G4
Port Carbon, Pa, US 138/B2
Port Charlotte, Fl, US 133/H5
Port Chester, NY, US 139/L8
Port Clements, BC, Can. 134/M5
Port Clinton, Oh, US 130/D3
Port Clinton, Pa, US 138/B2
Port Colborne, On, Can. 131/R10
Port Columbus (int'l arpt.), Oh, US 130/D4
Port Davey (har.), Austl. 115/C4
Port-de-Paix, Haiti 145/H2
Port Deposit, Md, US 138/B4
Port Dickson, Malay. 80/B3
Port Discovery (bay), Wa, US 135/B1
Port Douglas, Austl. 114/B2
Port Edward, BC, Can. 134/M4
Port Elgin, On, Can. 130/D2
Port Elizabeth, SAfr. 106/D4
Port Elizabeth, NJ, US 138/D5
Port Ellen, Sc, UK 31/Q9
Port Elliot, Austl. 113/H5
Port Erin, IM, UK 34/D3
Port-Eynon (pt.), Wal, UK 32/B3
Port Fairy, Austl. 115/B3
Port Gamble, Wa, US 135/B2
Port Gamble Ind. Res., Wa, US 135/B2
Port-Gentil, Gabon 96/G8
Port Gibson, Ms, US 129/K5
Port Glasgow, Sc, UK 36/B5
Port Graham, Ak, US 134/H4
Port Harcourt (int'l arpt.), Nga. 103/G5
Port Harcourt, Nga. 103/G5
Port Hardy, BC, Can. 126/B3
Port Hawkesbury, NS, Can. 131/J2
Port Hedland, Austl. 112/C2
Port Hedland (int'l arpt.), Austl. 112/C2
Port Heiden, Ak, US 134/G4
Port Hueneme, Ca, US 136/A2
Port Huron, Mi, US 130/D3
Port Isaac (bay), Eng, UK 32/B5
Port Jefferson, NY, US 139/E2
Port-la-Nouvelle, Fr. 42/E5
Port Lambton, On, Can. 135/H6
Port Lavaca, Tx, US 129/H5
Port Lincoln, Austl. 113/G5
Port Lions, Ak, US 134/H4
Port Loko, SLeo. 102/B4
Port-Louis, Fr. 141/N8
Port Louis (cap.), Mrts. 107/T15
Port Macdonnell, Austl. 115/B3
Port Macquarie, Austl. 115/E1
Port Madison Ind. Res., Wa, US 135/B2
Port Maria, Jam. 145/G2
Port McNeill, BC, Can. 126/B3
Port-Menier, Qu, Can. 131/H1
Port Monmouth, NJ, US 139/J10
Port Nolloth, SAfr. 106/B3
Port Norris, NJ, US 138/C5
Port of Ness, Sc, UK 31/Q7
Port-of-Spain (cap.), Trin. 153/F2
Port Orange, Fl, US 133/H4
Port Penn, De, US 138/C4
Port Phillip (bay), Austl. 115/C3
Port Pirie, Austl. 113/H5
Port Reading, NJ, US 139/J9
Port Republic, NJ, US 138/D4
Port Royal, Pa, US 138/A2
Port Saint Joe, Fl, US 133/G4
Port-Saint-Louis-du-Rhône, Fr. 42/F5
Port Saint Lucie, Fl, US 133/H5
Port Saint Mary, IM, UK 34/D3
Port Shepstone, SAfr. 107/E3
Port Stevens (bay), Austl. 109/E4
Port-sur-Saône, Fr. 56/C2
Port Townsend, Wa, US 126/C3
Port-Vendres, Fr. 42/E5
Port Victoria, Austl. 113/H5
Port-Vila (cap.), Van. 116/F6
Port Wakefield, Austl. 113/H5
Port Washington, NY, US 139/L8
Port Weld, Malay. 80/B3
Porta Westfalica (pass), Ger. 51/F4
Porta Westfalica, Ger. 51/F4
Portachuelo, Bol. 150/F7
Portadown, NI, UK 34/B3
Portaferry, NI, UK 34/C3
Portage, Mi, US 130/C3
Portage Des Sioux, Mo, US 137/G8
Portage la Prairie, Mb, Can. 127/J3
Portalegre (dist.), Port. 44/B3
Portalegre, Port. 44/B3
Portales, NM, US 129/G4
Portarlington, Ire. 31/Q10
Portbou, Sp. 42/E5
Porteirinha, Braz. 154/B4
Portel, Braz. 151/H4
Porters (lake), Pa, US 138/C1
Porterville, Ca, US 127/C3
Porterville, Ut, US 137/K12
Porterville, SAfr. 106/L10
Portes-lès-Valence, Fr. 42/F4
Portet-sur-Garonne, Fr. 42/D5
Portete (bay), Col. 145/J3
Portglenone, NI, UK 34/B2
Portimão, Port. 44/A4
Portishead, Eng, UK 32/D4
Portknockie, Sc, UK 36/D1
Portland, Austl. 115/D2
Portland (cape), Austl. 115/C4
Portland, Austl. 115/B3
Portland (int'l arpt.), Or, US 126/C4
Portland, Or, US 126/C4
Portland, Tn, US 130/C4
Portland, In, US 130/C3
Portland, Me, US 131/G3
Portland (pt.), Jam. 145/G2
Portland Canal (inlet), Can. 134/M4
Portland Jetport (int'l arpt.), Me, US 131/G3
Portlaoise, Ire. 31/Q10
Portlaw, Ire. 31/Q10
Portlethen, Sc, UK 36/D2
Portmarnock, Ire. 35/B3
Portmore, Jam. 145/G2
Portneuf (riv.), Can. 131/G1
Porto (dist.), Port. 44/A2
Porto (int'l arpt.), Port. 44/A2
Porto (gulf), Fr. 46/A1
Porto, Port. 44/A2
Porto Azzurro, It. 43/J5
Porto Belo, Braz. 155/B3
Porto Calvo, Braz. 154/D3
Porto Ceresio, It. 57/E6
Pôrto da Fôlha, Braz. 154/C3
Porto de Mós, Port. 44/A3
Porto Empedocle, It. 46/C4
Porto Ercole, It. 46/B1
Porto Ferreira, Braz. 155/C2
Porto Franco, Braz. 154/A2
Porto Garibaldi, It. 59/F3
Porto Inglês, CpV. 93/K10
Porto Nacional, Braz. 151/J6
Porto-Novo (cap.), Ben. 103/F5
Porto Potenza Picena, It. 59/G6
Porto Recanati, It. 59/G6
Porto Sant'Elpidio, It. 43/K5
Porto Santo (isl.), Port. 98/A2
Porto Santo Stefano, It. 46/B1
Porto Seguro, Braz. 154/C5
Porto Tolle, It. 59/F3
Porto Torres, It. 46/A2
Porto União, Braz. 155/B3
Porto Valtravaglia, It. 57/E6
Porto-Vecchio, Fr. 46/A2
Porto Velho, Braz. 150/F5
Portobelo, PN, Pan. 145/G4
Portocannone, It. 46/D2
Portocivitanova, It. 43/K5
Portoferraio, It. 43/J5
Portofino, It. 58/C4
Portogruaro, It. 59/F1
Portomaggiore, It. 59/E3
Portovenere, It. 58/C4
Portoviejo, Ecu. 152/A5
Portpatrick, Sc, UK 34/C2
Portree, Sc, UK 31/Q8
Portrush, NI, UK 34/B1
Portsea (isl.), Eng, UK 33/E5
Portslade-by-Sea, Eng, UK 33/F5
Portsmouth, NH, US 131/G3
Portsmouth, Dom. 141/N9
Portsmouth, Eng, UK 33/E5
Portsoy, Sc, UK 36/D1
Portstewart, NI, UK 34/B1
Portugal (ctry.) 27/D5
Portugalete, Sp. 44/D1
Portuguesa (riv.), Ven. 141/H6
Portuguesa (state), Ven. 152/D2
Portumna, Ire. 31/P10
Porvenir, Uru. 159/K10
Porvenir, Chile 159/C7
Porzuna, Sp. 44/C3
Posada, It. 46/A2
Posadas, Arg. 157/E2
Posadas, Sp. 44/C4
Posavina (valley), Bosn. 48/C3
Poschiavo, Swi. 57/G5
Posio, Fin. 60/F2
Poso (lake), Indo. 81/F4
Posof, Turk. 63/G4
Posŏng (riv.), SKor. 73/D5
Posŏng, SKor. 73/D5
Posorja, Ecu. 152/A5
Posse, Braz. 154/A4
Possession (pt.), Wa, US 135/C2
Possession (sound), Wa, US 135/C2
Post, Tx, US 129/G4
Post Falls, Id, US 126/D4
Poste Maurice Cortier (ruin), Alg. 99/F5
Postmasburg, SAfr. 106/C3
Postojna, Slov. 43/L4
Postoloprty, Czh. 55/G2
Potam, Mex. 142/C3
Potamós, Gre. 47/H5
Potaro-Siparuni (pol. reg.), Guy. 153/G3
Potchefstroom, SAfr. 106/D2
Poteau, Ok, US 129/J4
Potenza (riv.), It. 46/C1
Potenza, It. 46/D2
Potenza Picena, It. 59/G6
Potes, Sp. 44/C1
Potholes (res.), Wa, US 126/D4
Poti (riv.), Braz. 151/K5
P'ot'i, Geo. 63/G4
Potiraguá, Braz. 154/C4
Potomac (riv.), US 130/E4
Potomac, Md, US 138/A5
Potosí, Bol. 150/E7
Potosi, Mo, US 129/K3
Potrerillos, Chile 157/C2
Potsdam, NY, US 130/F2
Potsdam, Ger. 40/G7
Potta-Watomie (co.), Ok, US 137/N15
Pottendorf, Aus. 43/M3
Pottenstein, Ger. 55/E3
Potters Bar, Eng, UK 30/C1
Pöttmes, Ger. 54/E5
Pottstown, Pa, US 138/C3
Pottsville, Pa, US 138/B2
Pottuvil, SrL. 82/D6
Poudre d'Or, Mrts. 107/T15
Poughkeepsie, NY, US 130/F3
Pouilley-les-Vignes, Fr. 56/B3
Poulaphouca (res.), Ire. 34/B5
Poulter (riv.), Eng, UK 35/G5
Poulton-le-Fylde, Eng, UK 35/F4
Poŭn, SKor. 73/D4
Pourri (peak), Fr. 43/G4
Pouru-Saint-Remy, Fr. 53/E4
Pouso Alegre, Braz. 211/H7
Pouthisat (riv.), Camb. 83/H5
Pouzauges, Fr. 42/C3
Považská Bystrica, Slvk. 41/K4
Povegliano Veronese, It. 59/D2
Poverty Point Nat'l Mon., La, US 129/K4
Poviglio, It. 58/D3
Póvoa de Varzim, Port. 44/A2
Povoação, Azor., Port. 45/T13
Povorino, Rus. 63/G2
Povungnituk (riv.), Qu, Can. 123/J2
Povungnituk, Qu, Can. 123/J2
Poway, Ca, US 136/C5
Powder (riv.), Mt,Wy, US 124/E2
Powell, Wy, US 126/F4
Powell (lake), Az,Ut, US 119/F6
Powell River, BC, Can. 126/B3
Power (res.), US 131/R9
Powers (lake), Wi, US 135/P14
Powys (co.), Wal, UK 35/E6
Powys, Vale of (valley), Wal, UK 32/C1
Poxoreo, Braz. 151/H7
Poyang (lake), China 79/C2
Poynton, Eng, UK 35/F5
Poyo, Sp. 44/A1
Poysdorf, Aus. 41/J4
Poza Rica, Mex. 143/M6
Požarevac, Yugo. 48/E3
Požega, Yugo. 48/E4
Poznań, Pol. 41/J2
Pozo Alcón, Sp. 44/D4
Pozoblanco, Sp. 44/C3
Pozohondo, Sp. 44/E3
Pozuelo de Alarcón, Sp. 45/N9
Pozuelos, Ven. 153/E2
Pozuzo, Peru 156/C3
Pozza, It. 59/D3
Pozzallo, It. 46/D4
Pozzolo Formigaro, It. 58/B3
Pozzonovo, It. 59/E2
Ppa. de Salamanca (plain), Arg. 158/F1
Prabuty, Pol. 39/H5
Pracham Hiang (pt.), Thai. 78/B4
Prachatice, Czh. 55/H4
Prachin Buri (riv.), Thai. 78/C3
Prachin Buri, Thai. 78/C3
Prachuap Khiri Khan, Thai. 78/B4
Praděd (peak), Czh. 41/J3
Pradera, Col. 152/B4
Prades, Fr. 42/E5
Prado, Braz. 154/C5
Prado del Rey, Sp. 44/C4
Prado Flood Control (basin), Ca, US 136/C3
Pragelpass (pass), Swi. 57/E4
Praha (pol. reg.), Czh. 41/H3
Praha (peak), Czh. 55/G3
Praha (Prague) (cap.), Czh. 55/H2
Prahova (prov.), Rom. 49/G3
Praia (cap.), CpV. 93/K11
Praia (int'l arpt.), CpV. 93/K11
Praia da Vitória, Azor., Port. 45/S12
Praia Grande, Braz. 211/G9
Prairie Dog Town Fk. (riv.), Tx, US 124/F4
Prairie du Chien, Wi, US 127/L5
Prairie Grove, Il, US 135/P15
Prairie View, Tx, US 129/J5
Prairie Village, Ks, US 137/D6
Prairies (riv.), Qu, Can. 131/N6
Prairietown, Il, US 137/H8
Pralboino, It. 58/D2
Pralungo, It. 58/B1
Pram (riv.), Aus. 55/G6
Prambachkirchen, Aus. 55/G6
Pran Buri (res.), Thai. 83/G5
Prangins, Swi. 56/C5
Prānhita (riv.), India 82/C4
Prapat, Indo. 80/A3
Præstø, Den. 38/E4
Praszka, Pol. 41/K3
Prat, Chile, Ant. 160/W
Prata (riv.), Braz. 154/A5
Prata, Braz. 155/B1
Prata di Pordenone, It. 59/F1
Prathersville, Mo, US 137/E5
Prätigau (valley), Swi. 57/F4
Prato, It. 59/E5
Prato allo Stelvio (Prad am Stilfserjoch), It. 57/G4
Prato (Leventina), Swi. 57/E5
Pratola Peligna, It. 46/C1
Pratomagno (mts.), It. 59/E5
Pratovecchio, It. 59/E5
Pratt, Ks, US 129/H3
Pratt (isl.), Chile 159/B6
Pratteln, Swi. 56/D2
Prattville, Al, US 133/G3
Prauthoy, Fr. 56/B2
Pravets, Bul. 47/H1
Pravia, Sp. 44/B1
Prawle (pt.), Eng, UK 32/C6
Praxedis G. Guerrero, Mex. 129/F5
Praya, Indo. 81/E5
Pré-Saint-Didier, It. 56/C6
Preah Vihear (ruin), Camb. 78/D3
Précy-sur-Oise, Fr. 52/B5
Predappio, It. 59/E4
Predazzo, It. 43/J3
Predeal, Rom. 49/G3
Predosa, It. 58/B3
Preeceville, Sk, Can. 127/H3
Preetz, Ger. 38/D4
Preganziol, It. 59/F1
Pregarten, Aus. 55/H6
Pregolya (riv.), Pol. 39/J4
Pregolya (riv.), Rus. 41/L1
Pregonero, Ven. 152/D2
Preissac (lake), Can. 130/E1
Premana, It. 57/F5
Prémery, Fr. 42/E3
Premià de Mar, Sp. 45/L7
Prenzlau, Ger. 41/G2
Přerov, Czh. 41/J4
Presanella (peak), It. 57/G5
Prescot, Eng, UK 35/F5
Prescott, Az, US 128/D4
Prescott, On, Can. 130/F2
Preševo, Yugo. 47/G1
Presidencia Roque Sáenz Peña, Arg. 157/D2
Presidente Dutra, Braz. 154/A2
Presidente Epitácio, Braz. 155/A2
Presidente Olegário, Braz. 155/C1
Presidente Venceslau, Braz. 155/B2
Presidential Lake Estates, NJ, US 138/D4
Presidio, Tx, US 129/F5
Presidio (riv.), Mex. 142/D4
Preslav, Bul. 49/H4
Presles, Fr. 30/J4
Presles-en-Brie, Fr. 30/L5
Prešov, Slvk. 41/L4
Prespa (lake), Eur. 47/G2
Presque Isle, Me, US 131/G2
Pressath, Ger. 55/E3
Pressbaum, Aus. 49/N7
Prestatyn, Wal, UK 35/E5
Prestea, Gha. 103/E5
Prestfoss, Nor. 38/C1
Přeštice, Czh. 55/G3
Preston (cape), Austl. 112/C2
Preston, Md, US 138/C6
Preston, Wa, US 135/D2
Preston, Eng, UK 35/F4
Prestonpans, Sc, UK 36/D5
Prestonsburg, Ky, US 130/D4
Prestwich, Eng, UK 35/F4
Prestwick (int'l arpt.), Sc, UK 36/B5
Prestwick, Sc, UK 36/B6
Prêto (riv.), Braz. 151/J6
Pretoria (cap.), SAfr. 106/E2
Pretty Boy (res.), Md, US 138/B4
Preussisch Olendorf, Ger. 51/F4
Prevalje, Slov. 43/L3
Préveza, Gre. 47/G3
Prévost, Qu, Can. 131/M6
Prey Veng, Camb. 78/D4
Pribilof (isls.), Ak, US 134/D4
Priboj, Yugo. 48/D4
Příbram, Czh. 55/H3
Price (riv.), Ut, US 128/E3
Price, Ut, US 128/E3
Price, Md, US 138/C5
Prichard, Al, US 133/F4
Prichsenstadt, Ger. 54/D3
Priego, Sp. 44/D2
Priego de Córdoba, Sp. 44/C4
Prien am Chiemsee, Ger. 55/F7
Prieska, SAfr. 106/C3
Priest (lake), Id, US 126/D3
Priest River, Id, US 126/D3
Prieta (mtn.), Sp. 44/C1
Prievidza, Slvk. 41/K4
Prignitz (reg.), Ger. 40/F2
Prijedor, Bosn. 48/C3
Prijepolje, Yugo. 47/F1
Prikaspian (plain), Kaz.,Rus. 64/E5
Prikumsk, Rus. 63/H3
Prilep, Macd. 47/G2
Prilly, Swi. 56/C4
Prima Porta, It. 46/C1
Prima Tapia, Mex. 128/C4
Prime Hook NWR, De, US 138/C6
Primeira Cruz, Braz. 154/B1
Primero (cape), Chile 159/B6
Primorskiy Kray, Rus. 65/P5
Primorsko, Bul. 49/H4
Primorsko-Akhtarsk, Rus. 62/F3
Prims (riv.), Ger. 53/F4
Prince Albert, Sk, Can. 127/G2
Prince Albert, SAfr. 106/C4
Prince Albert (pen.), NW, Can. 122/E1
Prince Albert (sound), NW, Can. 122/E1
Prince Albert NP, Sk, Can. 122/F3
Prince Alfred (cape), NW, Can. 123/Q7
Prince Charles (isl.), NW, Can. 123/J2
Prince Edward (prov.), Can. 131/J2
Prince Edward (isl.), Can. 119/L5
Prince Edward (isls.), SAfr. 23/L7
Prince Edward Island (prov.), Can. 123/K4
Prince Edward Island NP, Can. 131/J2
Prince George, BC, Can. 126/C2
Prince Georges (co.), Md, US 138/B6
Prince Gustav Adolf (sea), NW, Can. 123/R7
Prince Leopold (isl.), NW, Can. 122/G1
Prince of Wales (str.), NW, Can. 122/E1
Prince of Wales (isl.), Ak, US 122/C3
Prince Olav (coast), Ant. 160/D
Prince Patrick (isl.), Can. 119/E2
Prince Regent (inlet), NW, Can. 122/G1
Prince Rupert, BC, Can. 134/M4
Prince William (sound), Ak, US 122/B2
Princenhof (lake), Neth. 50/C2
Princes Risborough, Eng, UK 33/F3
Princes Town, Trin. 141/J5
Princesa Isabel, Braz. 154/C2
Princess Charlotte (bay), Austl. 109/D2
Princess Margaret (range), NW, Can. 123/S6
Princess Royal (isl.), BC, Can. 122/C3
Princeton, Mn, US 127/K4
Princeton, BC, Can. 126/C3
Princeton, In, US 130/C4
Princeton, Ky, US 130/C4
Princeton, NJ, US 138/D3
Princeton Junction, NJ, US 138/D3
Princeville, Hi, US 124/S9
Principe (isl.), SaoT. 96/G7
Prindle (vol.), Ak, US 134/K3
Prineville, Or, US 126/C4
Pringsewu, Indo. 80/B5
Pringy, Fr. 56/C6
Prinsenbeek, Neth. 50/B5
Prinses Margriet (canal), Neth. 50/C3
Prinzapolka, Nic. 145/F3
Prinzapolka (riv.), Nic. 145/E3
Priolo di Gargallo, It. 46/D4
Prior (cape), Sp. 44/A1
Priore (peak), It. 43/K5
Priozersk, Rus. 39/P1
Pripet Marshes (swamp), Bela.,Ukr 62/C1
Prīpyat' (riv.), Ukr. 62/C2
Prisdorf, Ger. 51/G1
Priština, Yugo. 47/G1
Prittriching, Ger. 57/G1
Pritzwalk, Ger. 40/G2
Privas, Fr. 42/F4
Privolzhskiy, Rus. 63/H2
Priyutovo, Rus. 63/K1
Prizren, Yugo. 47/G1
Prnjavor, Yugo. 48/D3
Prnjavor, Bosn. 48/C3
Probištip, Macd. 47/H1
Probolinggo, Indo. 80/D5
Probstzella, Ger. 55/E1
Proctor (lake), Tx, US 132/D3
Proctor (pt.), La, US 137/Q17
Proddatūr, India 82/C5
Proença-a-Nova, Port. 44/B3
Profondeville, Belg. 53/D3
Progreso, Pan. 145/F4
Progreso, Mex. 144/D1
Progreso, Uru. 159/K11
Progreso, Mex. 143/K6
Progress, Rus. 71/N2
Progresso, It. 59/E3
Prokhladnyy, Rus. 63/G4
Prokuplje, Yugo. 47/G1
Promised Land (lake), Pa, US 138/C1
Promissão, Braz. 155/B2
Promissão, Reprêsa (res.), Braz. 155/B2
Propriá, Braz. 154/C3
Propriano, Fr. 46/A2
Proserpine, Austl. 114/C3
Prosna (riv.), Pol. 41/J2
Prospect Park, NJ, US 139/J8
Prospector (mtn.), Can. 134/L3
Prosperidad, Phil. 79/E6
Prosperous, Ire. 31/Q10
Prostějov, Czh. 41/J4
Proston, Austl. 114/C4
Proszowice, Pol. 41/L3
Protivín, Czh. 55/H4
Provadiya, Bul. 49/H4
Provence (reg.), Fr. 42/F5
Provence (int'l arpt.), Fr. 42/F5
Provence-Alpes-Côte-d'Azur, Fr. 43/G4
Providence (cap.), RI, US 131/G3
Providencia, Isla de (isl.), Col. 140/E5
Providência, Serra de (mts.), Braz. 150/F6
Providenciales (isl.), Bahm. 145/H1
Provins, Fr. 42/E2
Provo (riv.), Ut, US 137/K13
Provo (peak), Ut, US 137/K13
Provo, Ut, US 137/K13
Provost, Ab, Can. 126/F2
Prozor, Bosn. 48/C4
Prudentópolis, Braz. 155/B3
Prudhoe (bay), Ak, US 119/C2
Prudhoe, Eng, UK 35/G2
Prudhoe Bay, Ak, US 134/J1
Prudnik, Pol. 41/J3
Prüm (riv.), Ger. 40/D4
Prüm, Ger. 53/F3
Prunay-en-Yvelines, Fr. 30/H6
Prunelli-di-Fiumorbo, Fr. 46/A1
Pruszcz Gdański, Pol. 38/H4
Pruszków, Pol. 41/L2
Prut (riv.), Eur. 64/C5
Prutz, Aus. 57/G3
Pryluky, Ukr. 62/E2
Pryor, Ok, US 129/J3
Prypyats' (riv.), Bela. 64/C4
Przasnysz, Pol. 41/L2
Przemków, Pol. 41/H3
Przemyś (prov.), Pol. 41/M4
Przemyśl, Pol. 41/M4
Przeworsk, Pol. 41/M3
Przylądek Rozewie (cape), Pol. 38/H4
Przysucha, Pol. 41/L3
Psakhná, Gre. 47/H3
Psará (isl.), Gre. 47/J3
Psárion, Gre. 47/G4
Psël (riv.), Rus.,Ukr. 62/E2
Pskov (lake), Rus. 60/E5
Pskov, Rus. 39/N3
Pskov Oblast, Rus. 60/F4
Pšovka (riv.), Czh. 55/H2
Pszczyna, Pol. 41/K4
Ptolemaïs, Gre. 47/G2
Ptuj, Slov. 43/L3
Pu Xian, China 72/B3
Puan, SKor. 73/D5
Pubei, China 79/A3
Pucacaca, Peru 156/B2
Pucallpa, Peru 156/C3
Pucará, Ecu. 156/B1
Pucará, Peru 156/B2
Pucará, Peru 156/D4
Pucarani, Bol. 156/D5
Pucaurco, Peru 152/D5
Puchenau, Aus. 55/H6
Pucheng, China 79/C2
Pucheng, China 72/B4
Puchheim, Ger. 55/E6
Puch'on, SKor. 73/F7
Puchuncaví, Chile 158/N8
Pucioasa, Rom. 49/G3
Puck, Pol. 38/H4
Pucking, Aus. 55/H6
Pucón, Chile 158/C3
Pucusana, Peru 156/B4
Pudasjärvi, Fin. 60/E2
Puderbach, Ger. 53/G2
Pudsey, Eng, UK 35/G4
Pudu (riv.), China 83/H2
Puebla (state), Mex. 140/B4
Puebla, Mex. 143/L7
Puebla de Alcocer, Sp. 44/C3
Puebla de Don Fadrique, Sp. 44/D4
Puebla de la Calzada, Sp. 44/B3
Puebla de Sanabria, Sp. 44/B1
Puebla de Trives, Sp. 44/B1
Puebla del Caramiñal, Sp. 44/A1
Pueblillo, Mex. 143/M6
Pueblito, Col. 152/C2
Pueblo, Co, US 129/F3
Pueblo Nuevo, Nic. 144/E3
Pueblo Nuevo, Ven. 152/D2
Pueblo Yaqui, Mex. 142/C3
Puente (hills), Ca, US 136/G8
Puente Alto, Chile 158/N8
Puente Caldelas, Sp. 44/A1
Puente-Ceso, Sp. 44/A1
Puente de Ixtla, Mex. 143/K8
Puente del Inca, Arg. 158/C2
Puente-Genil, Sp. 44/C4
Puente Nacional, Col. 152/C3
Puente Piedra, Peru 156/B3
Puenteareas, Sp. 44/A1
Puentedeume, Sp. 44/A1
Puentes de García Rodríguez, Sp. 44/B1
Pueo (pt.), Hi, US 124/R10
Puerco (riv.), NM, US 128/E4
Puerto Acosta, Bol. 156/D4
Puerto Aisén, Chile 158/B5
Puerto América, Peru 156/B2
Puerto Á ngel, Mex. 144/B3
Puerto Armuelles, Pan. 145/F4
Puerto Asís, Col. 152/B4
Puerto Ayacucho, Ven. 153/E3
Puerto Ayora, Ecu. 156/E7
Puerto Baquerizo Moreno, Ecu. 156/F7
Puerto Barrios, Guat. 144/D3
Puerto Bermúdez, Peru 156/C3
Puerto Berrío, Col. 152/C3
Puerto Cabello, Ven. 152/D2
Puerto Cabezas, Nic. 145/F3
Puerto Carreño, Col. 153/E3
Puerto Cisnes, Chile 158/B5
Puerto Cortés, Mex. 142/C3
Puerto Cortés, Hon. 144/E3
Puerto Cumarebo, Ven. 152/D2
Puerto de la Cruz, Sp. 98/A3
Puerto de la Libertad, Mex. 142/B2
Puerto de Navacerrada (pass), Sp. 45/M8
Puerto del Rosario, Sp. 98/B3
Puerto del Son, Sp. 44/A1
Puerto Deseado, Arg. 159/D5
Puerto El Carmen, Ecu. 152/C4
Puerto Escondido, Col. 152/B2
Puerto Escondido, Mex. 144/B3
Puerto Heath, Bol. 156/D4
Puerto Iguazú, Arg. 157/F2
Puerto Inca, Peru 156/C3
Puerto Ingeniero Ibáñez, Chile 158/C5
Puerto Inírida, Col. 152/E4
Puerto La Cruz, Ven. 153/E2
Puerto Leguízamo, Col. 152/C5
Puerto Lempira, Hon. 145/F3
Puerto López, Col. 152/C3
Puerto Lumbreras, Sp. 44/E4
Puerto Madero, Mex. 144/C3
Puerto Madryn, Arg. 158/D4
Puerto Magdalena, Mex. 142/B3
Puerto Maldonado, Peru 156/D4
Puerto Montt, Chile 158/B4
Puerto Morazán, Nic. 144/E3
Puerto Morelos, Mex. 140/D3
Puerto Napo, Ecu. 152/B5
Puerto Natales, Chile 159/B6
Puerto Obaldía, Pan. 152/B2
Puerto Ocopa, Peru 156/C3
Puerto Padre, Cuba 145/G1
Puerto Páez, Ven. 153/E3
Puerto Peñasco, Mex. 128/D5
Puerto Píritu, Ven. 153/E2
Puerto Portillo, Peru 156/C3
Puerto Prado, Peru 156/C3
Puerto Princesa, Phil. 81/E2
Puerto Quellón, Chile 158/B4
Puerto Real, Sp. 44/B4
Puerto Rico, Col. 152/C4
Puerto Rico, Col. 152/C4
Puerto Rico (dpcy.), US 119/L8
Puerto Rondón, Col. 152/D3
Puerto San Carlos, Mex. 142/B3
Puerto San Julián, Arg. 159/D6
Puerto Santa Cruz, Arg. 159/C6
Puerto Serrano, Sp. 44/C4
Puerto Suárez, Bol. 150/G7
Puerto Supe, Peru 156/B3
Puerto Tejada, Col. 152/B4
Puerto Vallarta, Mex. 142/D4
Puerto Varas, Chile 158/B4
Puerto Viejo, CR 145/E4
Puerto Villamil, Ecu. 156/E7
Puerto Wilches, Col. 152/C3
Puerto Williams, Chile 159/D7
Puertollano, Sp. 44/C3
Pueyrredón (lake), Arg. 158/C5
Puffin (isl.), Wal, UK 34/D5
Pugachev, Rus. 63/J1

Puget (sound), Wa, US 124/B2
Puglia (pol. reg.), It. 46/E2
Puglia (prov.), It. 48/C5
Puigcerdà, Sp. 45/F1
Puiseux-en-France, Fr. 30/K4
Pujehun, SLeo. 102/C5
Pujiang, China 79/C2
Pujilí, Ecu. 152/B5
Pujŏn (lake), NKor. 73/D2
Pujut (cape), Indo. 80/C5
Pukalani, Hi, US 124/T10
Puk'an-san (peak), SKor. 73/F6
Puk'an-san NP, SKor. 73/D4
Pukapuka (isl.), Cookls. 117/J6
Pukarua (isl.), FrPol. 117/M6
Pukaskwa NP, Can. 130/C1
Pukch'ŏng, NKor. 73/E2
Pukdae (riv.), NKor. 73/E2
Pukhan (riv.), NKor.,SKor 73/D3
Pukhrāyān, India 84/B2
Pukovac, Yugo. 47/G1
Pukp'ot'ae-san (peak), NKor. 73/E2
Pula, Cro. 48/A3
Pulacayo, Bol. 150/E8
Pulandian (bay), China 73/A3
Pulanduta (pt.), Phil. 81/F1
Pulap (isl.), Micr. 116/D4
Pulaski, Va, US 130/D4
Pulaski, Tn, US 133/G3
Pulau (riv.), Indo. 81/J5
Puľawy, Pol. 41/L3
Pulguk-sa, SKor. 74/A3
Pulheim, Ger. 53/F2
Pulisan (cape), Indo. 81/G3
Pulkovo (int'l arpt.), Rus. 61/T7
Pullach im Isartal, Ger. 57/H1
Pullman, Wa, US 126/D4
Pully, Swi. 56/C5
Pulsnitz (riv.), Ger. 41/G3
Puľtusk, Pol. 41/L2
Pülümür, Turk. 62/F5
Puluwat (isl.), Micr. 116/D4
Pulversheim, Fr. 56/D2
Pum (riv.), China 85/F1
Puma (lake), China 85/H1
Pumu (pass), China 83/F2
Puna de Atacama (plat.), Arg. 157/C2
Puná, Isla (isl.), Ecu. 150/B4
Punākha, Bhu. 85/G2
Punata, Bol. 150/E7
Pūnch, India 86/C3
Pūnch (riv.), India 86/C3
Pūndri, India 86/D5
Pune (Poona), India 89/K5
Punggai (cape), Malay. 80/B3
P'unggi, SKor. 73/E4
P'ungsan, NKor. 73/E2
Pungwe (falls), Zim. 105/F4
Punjab (plain), Pak. 89/K2
Punjab (state), Pak. 82/B2
Puno, Peru 156/D4
Puno (dept.), Peru 156/D4
Pūnpūn (riv.), India 85/E3
Punta, Ca, US 136/A2
Punta Alta, Arg. 158/E3
Punta Arena (pt.), Mex. 142/C4
Punta Arenas, Chile 159/C7
Punta Banda (cape), Mex. 142/A2
Punta Cardón, Ven. 152/D2
Punta Celarain (pt.), Mex. 144/E1
Punta Colnett (pt.), Mex. 142/A2
Punta Colonet, Mex. 142/A2
Punta de Bombón, Peru 156/D5
Punta de Mata, Ven. 153/F2
Punta del Este, Uru. 159/G2
Punta del Este (Capitán Curbelo) (int'l arpt.), Uru. 159/G2
Punta Gorda, Fl, US 133/H5
Punta Gorda (bay), Nic. 140/E5
Punta Gorda, Belz. 144/D2
Punta Marina, It. 59/F4
Punta Raisi (int'l arpt.), It. 46/C3
Punta Umbría, Sp. 44/B4
Puntarenas, CR 145/E4
Puolo (pt.), Hi, US 124/S10
Pupiales, Col. 152/B4
Pupuya (peak), Bol. 156/D4
Puquio, Peru 156/C4
Pur (riv.), Rus. 64/H3
Puracé (vol.), Col. 152/B4
Puracé, PN, Col. 150/C3
Pūranpur, India 84/C1
Purbeck (isl.), Eng, UK 32/D5
Purcell (mts.), Can. 126/D3
Purcell, Ok, US 129/H4
Puré (riv.), Col. 152/D5
Purén, Chile 158/B3
Purgatoire (riv.), Co, US 129/G3
Pürgen, Ger. 57/G1
Purgstall an der Erlauf, Aus. 43/L2
Purī, India 82/D3
Purificación, Col. 152/C4
Purikari (pt.), Est. 39/L2
Purkersdorf, Aus. 49/N7
Purmerend, Neth. 50/B3
Pūrna, India 82/C4
Purnia, India 85/F3
Purranque, Chile 157/B5
Puruê (riv.), Braz. 152/D5
Purūlia, India 85/F4
Puruni (riv.), Guy. 153/G3
Purús (riv.), Braz. 147/C3
Purushottampur, India 82/D4
Pŭrvomay, Bul. 47/J1
Purwa, India 84/C2
Purwokerto, Indo. 80/C5
Pusad, India 82/C4
Pusan, SKor. 71/N4
Pusan-jikhalsi (prov.), SKor. 74/A3
Pusat Gayo (mts.), Indo. 80/A3
Puschendorf, Ger. 54/D3
Pushkin, Rus. 61/T7
Püspökladány, Hun. 48/E2
Pusur (riv.), Bang. 85/G4
Putaendo, Chile 158/C2
Putian, China 79/C2
Putina, Peru 156/D4
Puting (cape), Indo. 80/D4
Putla de Guerrero, Mex. 144/B2
Putomayo (dept.), Col. 152/C4
Putorana (mts.), Rus. 64/K3
Putrachoique (peak), Arg. 158/C4
Putre, Chile 156/D5
Puttalam, SrL. 82/C6
Putte, Belg. 53/D1
Puttelange-aux-Lacs, Fr. 53/F5
Putten, Neth. 50/C4
Putten (isl.), Neth. 50/B5
Püttlach (riv.), Ger. 55/E3
Püttlingen, Ger. 53/F5
Putu (range), Libr. 102/C5
Putumayo (riv.), SAm. 152/C5
Putumayo (riv.), SAm. 147/B3
Putussibau, Indo. 80/D3
Puu Kukui (peak), Hi, US 124/T10
Puu Moaulanui (peak), Hi, US 124/T10
Puu o Mahuka Heiau State Mon., Hi, US 124/V12
Puuanahulu, Hi, US 124/U11
Puuiki, Hi, US 124/T10
Puula (lake), Fin. 39/M1
Puurs, Belg. 53/D1
Puuwai, Hi, US 124/R10
Puy de Sancy (peak), Fr. 42/E4
Puyallup, Wa, US 126/C4
Puyallup (riv.), Wa, US 135/C3
Puyallup Ind. Res., Wa, US 135/C3
Puyang, China 72/C4
Puyehué (lake), Chile 158/B4
Puyehue (vol.), Chile 158/B4
Puylaurens, Fr. 42/E5
Puymorens, Col de (pass), Fr. 42/D5
Puyŏ, SKor. 73/D4
Puyo, Ecu. 152/B5
Puzal, Sp. 45/E3
Pwani (pol. reg.), Tanz. 104/C4
Pwllheli, Wal, UK 34/D6
Pyandzh (riv.), Taj. 87/F5
Pyaozero (lake), Rus. 37/J2
Pyapon, Myan. 83/G4
Pyasina (riv.), Rus. 64/J2
Pyatigorsk, Rus. 63/G3
Pyfara (peak), Fr. 42/F4
Pyhä-Häkin NP, Fin. 60/E3
Pyhäjärvi, Fin. 60/E3
Pyhäjärvi (lake), Fin. 39/K1
Pyhäntä, Fin. 60/E2
Pyhätunturi (peak), Fin. 60/E2
Pyinmana, Myan. 83/G4
P'yŏngan-bukto (prov.), NKor. 73/C2
P'yŏngan-namdo (prov.), NKor. 73/C3
P'yŏngch'ang, SKor. 73/E4
P'yŏnggang, NKor. 73/D3
P'yŏnghae, SKor. 73/E4
P'yŏngsan, NKor. 73/D3
P'yŏngsong, NKor. 73/C3
Pyŏngt'aek, SKor. 73/D4
P'yŏngyang (int'l arpt.), NKor. 73/C3
P'yŏngyang (cap.), NKor. 73/C3
P'yŏngyang-si (prov.), NKor. 73/C3
Pyŏnsanbando NP, SKor. 73/D5
Pyramid (lake), Nv, US 128/B3
Pyramid (mtn.), Can. 134/M4
Pyramid (lake), Ca, US 124/C3
Pyramids Of Jīzah, Egypt 91/B5
Pyrenees (mts.), Fr.,Sp. 27/D4
Pyrénées Occidental, PN des, Fr. 42/C5
Pyryatyn, Ukr. 62/E2
Pyrzyce, Pol. 41/H2
Pyshma (riv.), Rus. 61/Q4
Pyu, Myan. 83/G4
Pyuthān, Nepal 84/D1

Q

Qā 'al Jafr (salt pan), Jor. 90/D4
Qā'al Jafr (salt pan), Jor. 91/E4
Qabalān, WBnk. 91/G7
Qabāṭiyah, WBnk. 91/G7
Qābis, Tun. 96/H1
Qābis (gov.), Tun. 99/H2
Qadima, Isr. 91/F7
Qādirpur Rān, Pak. 86/A4
Qā'en, Iran 89/G2
Qafa e Malit (pass), Alb. 47/G1
Qaffīn, WBnk. 91/G7
Qafṣah, Tun. 96/G1
Qafṣah (gov.), Tun. 99/H2
Qahar Youyi Qianqi, China 72/C2
Qahar Youyi Zhongqi, China 72/C2
Qaidam (basin), China 70/F4
Qalansuwa, Isr. 91/F7
Qal'at Al Andalus, Tun. 46/B4
Qal'at Dizah, Iraq 90/F2
Qal'eh-ye Now, Afg. 87/D6
Qalqīlyah, WBnk. 91/F7
Qalyūb, Egypt 91/B4
Qamdo, China 70/G5
Qamīnis, Libya 96/K1
Qandahār, Afg. 89/J2
Qapshagay Bögeni (res.), Kaz. 87/G4
Qapshaghay, Kaz. 87/G4
Qaraghandy, Kaz. 87/F3
Qaraghandy (obl.), Kaz. 87/F3
Qarataū, Kaz. 87/F4
Qarataū (mts.), Kaz. 87/E4
Qareh Chāy (riv.), Iran 88/E2
Qareh Sū (riv.), Iran 63/H5
Qarqan (riv.), China 70/E4
Qarrit (pass), Alb. 47/G2
Qarshi, Uzb. 87/E5
Qārūn (lake), Egypt 101/B2
Qashqadaryo (pol. reg.), Uzb. 87/D5
Qaṣr-e Qand, Iran 89/H3
Qaṣr-e-shīrīn, Iran 88/E2
Qaṣr Hallāl, Tun. 46/B5
Qa'ṭabah, Yem. 88/D6
Qatar (ctry.) 67/E7
Qattara (depr.), Egypt 90/A4
Qaṭṭīnah, Buḩayrat (lake), Syria 91/E2
Qayyārah, Iraq 90/E3
Qāzi Ahmad, Pak. 82/A2
Qazvīn, Iran 88/F1
Qedma, Isr. 91/F8
Qendrevica (peak), Alb. 47/F2
Qezel Owzan (riv.), Iran 88/E1
Qi Xian, China 72/C4
Qian (mts.), China 73/B2
Qian (riv.), China 72/D5
Qian'an, China 71/M3
Qianxi, China 72/J6
Qianyang, China 79/B2
Qiaojia, China 83/H2
Qibyā, Isr. 91/G8
Qidong, China 83/K2
Qidong, China 72/L8
Qiemo, China 70/E4
Qihe, China 72/D3
Qijiang, China 79/A2
Qila Dīdār Singh, Pak. 86/C3
Qila Sobha Singh, Pak. 86/C3
Qilian (peak), China 70/G4
Qilian (mts.), China 67/J6
Qimantag (mts.), China 70/F4
Qimen, China 79/C2
Qin (mts.), China 72/B4
Qinā (gov.), Egypt 101/C3
Qing (riv.), China 79/B1
Qing'an, China 71/N2
Qingdao, China 72/E3
Qingfeng, China 72/C4
Qinghai (mts.), China 70/G4
Qinghai (prov.), China 70/G4
Qinghe, China 72/C3
Qinglong, China 72/D2
Qingpu, China 72/L8
Qingshui (riv.), China 79/A2
Qingshuihe, China 72/B3
Qingyuan, China 83/K3
Qingyun, China 72/D3
Qingzhou, China 72/D3
Qinhuangdao, China 72/D3
Qinshui, China 72/C4
Qinyang, China 72/C4
Qinyuan, China 72/C3
Qinzhou, China 83/J3
Qionghai, China 83/K4
Qionglai (mts.), China 70/H5
Qiongshan, China 83/K4
Qiongzhong, China 78/E2
Qiqihar, China 71/M2
Qira, China 70/D4
Qiryat Ata, Isr. 91/G6
Qiryat Bialik, Isr. 91/G6
Qiryat Gat, Isr. 91/D4
Qiryat Mal'akhi, Isr. 91/F8
Qiryat Motzkin, Isr. 91/G6
Qiryat Shemona, Isr. 91/D3
Qiryat Tiv'on, Isr. 91/G6
Qiryat Yam, Isr. 91/G6
Qitai, China 70/E3
Qitaihe, China 71/P2
Qixia, China 72/E3
Qixing (riv.), China 65/P5
Qizilqum (des.), Kaz. 64/G5
Qogir (peak), China 89/L1
Qom (riv.), Iran 88/F2
Qom, Iran 88/F2
Qomsheh, Iran 88/F2
Qondūz (riv.), Afg. 89/J1
Qonggyai, China 85/H1
Qoraqalpoghiston Aut. Rep., Uzb. 63/L3
Qormi, Malta 46/L7
Qorveh, Iran 88/E1
Qostanay (obl.), Kaz. 87/D2
Qostanay (int'l arpt.), Kaz. 61/P5
Qostanay, Kaz. 61/P5
Qoṭūr, Iran 90/F2
Qu (riv.), China 71/L6
Quabbin (res.), Ma, US 131/F3
Quairading, Austl. 112/C5
Quakenbrück, Ger. 51/E3
Quakertown, Pa, US 138/C3
Quambatook, Austl. 115/B2
Quanah, Tx, US 129/H4
Quanbao (mtn.), China 72/B4
Quang Ngai, Viet. 78/E3
Quang Tri, Viet. 78/D2
Quanjiao, China 72/D4
Quannan, China 79/B3
Quantocks, The (hills), Eng, UK 32/C4
Quanzhou, China 79/C3
Qu'appelle (dam), Sk, Can. 127/G3
Qu'appelle (riv.), Can. 127/G3
Qu'appelle, Sk, Can. 127/H3
Quaqtaq, Qu, Can. 123/K2
Quaregnon, Belg. 52/C3
Quarles (mts.), Indo. 81/E4
Quarona, It. 58/B1
Quarrata, It. 59/D5
Quarryville, Pa, US 138/B4
Quarto d'Altino, It. 59/F1
Quartu Sant'Elena, It. 46/A3
Quartz Hill, Ca, US 136/B1
Quatre Bornes, Mrts. 107/T15
Quattervals (peak), Swi. 57/G4
Quba, Azer. 63/J4
Qūchān, Iran 89/G1
Queanbeyan, Austl. 115/D2
Québec (int'l arpt.), Can. 131/G2
Québec (cap.), Qu, Can. 131/G2
Québec (prov.), Can. 123/J3
Quebra-Cangalha, Serra (mts.), Braz. 211/H8
Quecholac, Mex. 143/M8
Quechutenango, Mex. 143/F5
Quedal (pt.), Chile 158/B4
Queen Alia (int'l arpt.), Jor. 91/E4
Queen Anne, Md, US 138/C6
Queen Annes (co.), Md, US 138/C5
Queen Charlotte (str.), BC, Can. 126/B3
Queen Charlotte, BC, Can. 134/M5
Queen Charlotte (isls.), BC, Can. 122/C3
Queen Charlotte (sound), BC, Can. 122/C3
Queen City, Tx, US 129/J4
Queen Creek, Az, US 137/S19
Queen Elizabeth (isls.), Can. 119/E2
Queen Mary (coast), Ant. 160/G
Queen Mary (res.), Eng, UK 30/B2
Queen Mary, Ca, US 136/F8
Queen Maud (gulf), NW, Can. 122/F2
Queen Maud (mts.), Ant. 160/P
Queen Maud Land (phys. reg.), Ant. 160/Z
Queen Victoria Spring Nature Reserve, Austl. 112/D4
Queens (chan.), NW, Can. 123/S7
Queens (co.), NY, US 139/E2
Queensberry (peak), Sc, UK 36/C6
Queensferry, Sc, UK 36/C5
Queensland, Austl. 115/B1
Queensland (state), Austl. 109/C3
Queenstown, Austl. 115/C4
Queenstown, SAfr. 106/D3
Queenstown, NZ 117/R12
Queenstown, Md, US 138/B6
Queich (riv.), Ger. 53/H5
Queidersbach, Ger. 53/G5
Queilén, Chile 158/B4
Queimada, Ilha (isl.), Braz. 151/H4
Queimadas, Braz. 154/D2
Queimadas, Braz. 154/C3
Quelimane, Moz. 105/G4
Queluz, Port. 45/P10
Quemado, Punta del (pt.), Cuba 145/H1
Quemú Quemú, Arg. 158/E3
Quepos, CR 145/E4
Quequén, Arg. 158/F3
Quequén Grande (riv.), Arg. 158/F3
Querecotillo, Peru 156/A2
Querétaro, Mex. 143/E4
Querétaro de Arteaga (state), Mex. 140/A5
Quero, It. 59/E1
Querobabi, Mex. 142/C2
Quesada, Sp. 44/D4
Quesada, CR 145/E4
Queshan, China 72/C4
Quesnel, BC, Can. 126/C2
Quesnel (lake), BC, Can. 122/D3
Quesnoy-sur-Deûle, Fr. 52/C2
Questa, NM, US 129/F3
Questembert, Fr. 42/B3
Quetigny, Fr. 56/B3
Quetta, Pak. 89/J2
Queulat, PN, Chile 158/B5
Quevedo, Ecu. 150/C4
Quevedo (riv.), Ecu. 152/B5
Quezaltenango, Guat. 144/D3
Quezon, Phil. 81/E2
Quezon City, Phil. 79/D5
Qufu, China 72/D4
Qui Nhon, Viet. 78/E3
Quibdó, Col. 152/B3
Quiberon, Fr. 42/B3
Quiberon (bay), Fr. 42/B3
Quíbor, Ven. 152/D2
Quicacha, Peru 156/C4
Quiçama, PN da, Ang. 105/B2
Quickborn, Ger. 51/G1
Quiers, Fr. 30/L6
Quierschied, Ger. 53/G5
Quila, Mex. 142/D3
Quilán (cape), Chile 158/B4
Quilca, Peru 156/C5
Quilcene, Wa, US 135/B2
Quiliano, It. 58/B4
Quilicura, Chile 158/N8
Quill (lakes), Can. 127/G2
Quill Lakes, Sk, Can. 122/F3
Quillabamba, Peru 156/C4
Quillacollo, Bol. 150/E7
Quillagua (pt.), Chile 158/B4
Quillan, Fr. 42/E5
Quilleco, Chile 158/C3
Quillota, Chile 158/N8
Quilmaná, Peru 156/B4
Quilon, India 82/C6
Quilpie, Austl. 114/B4
Quilpué, Chile 158/N8
Quimilí, Arg. 157/D2
Quimper, Fr. 42/A2
Quimperlé, Fr. 42/B3
Quincey, Fr. 56/C2
Quincy, Wa, US 126/D4
Quincy, Fl, US 133/G4
Quincy, Ma, US 131/G3
Quincy-sous-Sénart, Fr. 30/K5
Quincy-Voisins, Fr. 30/L5
Quindío (dept.), Col. 152/A4
Quinhagak, Ak, US 134/F4
Quinn (riv.), Nv, US 128/C2
Quinns Rocks, Austl. 112/K6
Quintana de la Serena, Sp. 44/C3
Quintana Roo (state), Mex. 140/D4
Quintanar de la Orden, Sp. 44/D3
Quintanar del Rey, Sp. 44/E3
Quintero, Chile 158/N8
Quinto, Sp. 45/E2
Quinto, Swi. 57/E4
Quinto (riv.), Arg. 158/D2
Quinto di Treviso, It. 59/F1
Quinto di Valpantena, It. 59/E2
Quinton, NJ, US 138/C4
Quinzano d'Oglio, It. 58/C2
Quionga, Moz. 104/D5
Quipapá, Braz. 154/C3
Quirihue, Chile 158/B3
Quirimba, Arquipélago de (arch.), Moz. 105/H3
Quirindi, Austl. 115/D1
Quirinópolis, Braz. 155/B1
Quiriquire, Ven. 153/F2
Quiroga, Mex. 143/E5
Quiroga, Sp. 44/B1
Quiruvilca, Peru 156/B3
Quisiro, Ven. 152/D2
Quispamsis, NB, Can. 131/H2
Quissico, Moz. 105/F5
Quistello, It. 59/D3
Quitilipi, Arg. 157/D2
Quitman, Ga, US 133/H4
Quitman, Ms, US 133/F3
Quito (cap.), Ecu. 152/B5
Quixeramobim, Braz. 154/C2
Qujiang, China 83/K3
Qujing, China 83/H2
Qulaybīyah, Tun. 46/B4
Quogue, NY, US 139/F2
Quoich (riv.), NW, Can. 122/G2
Quoich (lake), Sc, UK 36/A2
Quoile (riv.), NI, UK 34/C3
Quoin (pt.), SAfr. 106/L11
Quorn, Austl. 113/H5
Qŭqon, Uzb. 87/F4
Quranbāliyah, Tun. 46/B4
Qurbah, Tun. 46/B4
Qŭrghonteppa, Taj. 89/J1
Qurnat as Sawdā' (peak), Leb. 91/E2
Qūṣ, Egypt 101/C3
Qusum, China 70/F6
Quṣūr As Sāf, Tun. 46/B5
Quwo, China 72/B4
Quwu (mts.), China 70/H4
Quyang, China 72/C3
Quzhou, China 79/C2
Quzhou, China 72/C3
Qyzylorda, Kaz. 87/E4
Qyzylorda (obl.), Kaz. 87/D4

R

Raab (riv.), Aus. 43/L3
Raab, Aus. 55/G6
Raabs an der Thaya, Aus. 41/H4
Raahe, Fin. 60/E2
Raalte, Neth. 50/D4
Raamsdonk, Neth. 50/B5
Ra'ananna, Isr. 91/F7
Raanes (pen.), NW, Can. 123/S7
Rab (isl.), Cro. 48/B3
Rab, Cro. 48/B3
Rába (riv.), Hun. 48/C2
Rábahidvég, Hun. 43/M3
Rabat (cap.), Mor. 100/A2
Rabat, Malta 46/L7
Rabat (Sale) (int'l arpt.), Mor. 100/A2
Rabat (Victoria), Malta 46/L6
Rabbi (riv.), It. 43/K4
Rabgala (pass), China 85/F2
Rabil, CpV. 93/K10
Rabinal, Guat. 144/D3
Rabiusa (riv.), Swi. 57/F4
Rabka, Pol. 41/K4
Rabkavi-Banhatti, India 89/L5
Raby (pt.), Can. 131/S8
Racconigi, It. 43/G4
Raccoon (pt.), La, US 129/K5
Rach Gia (bay), Viet. 78/D4
Rach Gia, Viet. 78/D4
Racibórz, Pol. 41/K3
Racine, Wi, US 127/M5
Racine (peak), Swi. 56/C3
Racine (co.), Wi, US 135/P14
Rada Tilly, Arg. 158/D5
Radaur, India 86/D4
Rădăuṭi, Rom. 49/G2
Radbuza (riv.), Czh. 40/G4
Radcliffe, Eng, UK 35/F4
Raddestorf, Ger. 51/F4
Rade de Caen (bay), Fr. 42/C2
Radeč (peak), Czh. 55/G3
Radevormwald, Ger. 51/E6
Radisson, Sk, Can. 126/G2
Radlett, Eng, UK 30/C2
Radnice, Czh. 55/G3
Radolfzell, Ger. 57/E2
Radom (prov.), Pol. 41/L3
Radom, Pol. 41/L3
Radomir, Bul. 47/H1
Radomsko, Pol. 41/K3
Radoviš, Macd. 47/H2
Radovljica, Slov. 43/L3
Radøy (isl.), Nor. 38/A1
Radstadt, Aus. 43/K3
Radviliškis, Lith. 39/K4
Raḍwá, Jabal (peak), SAr. 88/C4
Radziejów, Pol. 41/K2
Radzymin, Pol. 41/L2
Radzyń Podlaski, Pol. 41/M3
Rae (isth.), NW, Can. 123/H2
Rae (riv.), NW, Can. 122/E2
Rāe Bareli, India 84/C2
Rae-Edzo, NW, Can. 122/E2
Raeford, NC, US 133/J3
Raeren, Belg. 53/F2
Raesfeld, Ger. 50/D5
Raeside (lake), Austl. 112/D4
Rafael J. Garcia, Mex. 143/M7
Rafael Núñez (int'l arpt.), Col. 152/C2
Rafaela, Arg. 157/D3
Rafaḥ, Gaza 91/D4
Rafai, CAfr. 97/K7
Rafīdīyah, WBnk. 91/G7
Rafiganj, India 85/E3
Rafína, Gre. 47/P8
Rafsanjān, Iran 89/G2
Raft (riv.), Id, US 126/E5
Rafz, Swi. 57/E2
Ragang (mt.), Phil. 81/F2
Ragged (mt.), Austl. 112/D5
Ragged (pt.), Chile 159/B7
Rāghugarh, India 84/A3
Raghunāthpur, India 85/F4
Rago NP, Nor. 37/E2
Ragstone (range), Eng, UK 30/D3
Ragusa, It. 46/D4
Rāhatgarh, India 84/B4
Rahden, Ger. 51/F4
Rahīmyār Khān, Pak. 86/A5
Rahole Nat'l Rsv., Kenya 104/C2
Råholt, Nor. 38/D1
Rāhuri, India 82/B4
Rahway, NJ, US 139/H9
Raiatea (isl.), FrPol. 117/K6
Raichūr, India 82/C4
Raiganj, India 85/G3
Raigarh, India 84/D5
Raikot, India 86/C4
Railroad, Pa, US 138/B4
Railroad Canyon (res.), Ca, US 136/C3
Rainbach im Mühlkreis, Aus. 55/H5
Rainbow, Austl. 115/B2
Rainbow (valley), Az, US 137/R19
Rainbow, Ca, US 136/C4
Rainbow Beach, Austl. 114/D4
Rainbow Bridge Nat'l Mon., Ut, US 128/E3
Rainier (mt.), Wa, US 126/C4
Rainsville, Al, US 133/G3
Rainy (lake), On, Can. 122/G4
Rainy Lake (riv.), US,Can. 127/K3
Rainy River, On, Can. 127/K3
Raipur, India 82/D3
Rairoa (atoll), FrPol. 117/L6
Raisdorf, Ger. 38/D4
Raisen, India 84/A4
Rāisinghnagar, India 86/B5
Raisio, Fin. 39/K1
Raismes, Fr. 52/C3
Raivavae (isl.), FrPol. 117/L7
Rāiwind, Pak. 86/C4
Raizeux, Fr. 30/H6
Rāj Gāngpur, India 85/E4
Raja (pt.), Indo. 80/A3
Rāja Jang, Pak. 86/C4
Rājahmundry, India 82/D4
Rājampet, India 82/C5
Rajang (riv.), Malay. 80/D3
Rājanpur, Pak. 86/A5
Rājaori, India 86/C3
Rājapālaiyam, India 82/C6
Rājāpur, India 84/C3
Rājāpur, India 89/K5
Rājasthān (state), India 82/B2
Rājbirāj, Nepal 85/F2
Rājgarh, India 84/A2
Rājgarh, India 86/C5
Rājgarh, India 89/L4
Rājgir, India 85/E3
Rajka, Hun. 48/C1
Rājkot, India 89/K4
Rājmahal (hills), India 85/F3
Rājmahāl, India 85/F3
Rājpur, India 85/G4
Rājpura, India 86/D4
Rājshāhi (pol. reg.), Bang. 85/G3
Rājshāhi (pol. div.), Bang. 85/G3
Rājshāhi, Bang. 85/G3
Rājula, India 89/K4
Raka (riv.), China 85/F1
Rakahanga (isl.), Cookls. 117/J5
Rakamaz, Hun. 48/E1
Rakaposhi (peak), Pak. 86/C1
Rakhine (div.), Myan. 70/F8
Rakhine (state), Myan. 83/F4
Rakhshān (riv.), Pak. 89/H3
Rakkestad, Nor. 38/D2
Rakos-patak (riv.), Hun. 49/R9
Rakovnicky Potok (riv.), Czh. 55/G2
Rakovník, Czh. 55/G2
Rakovski, Bul. 47/J1
Rakushechnyy (cape), Kaz. 87/B4
Rakvere, Est. 39/M2
Raldon, It. 59/E2
Raleigh (cap.), NC, US 133/J3
Raleigh-Durham (int'l arpt.), NC, US 133/J3
Ralik Chain (isls.), Mrsh. 116/F4
Ralingen, Ger. 53/F4
Ralston, Ab, Can. 126/F3
Rām Allāh, Isr. 91/G8
Ramalho, Serra do (mts.), Braz. 151/K6
Ramapo (riv.), NJ, US 138/J7
Ramapo (mts.), NJ, US 139/H7
Ramat Gan, Isr. 91/F7
Ramat Hasharon, Isr. 91/F7
Rambervillers, Fr. 56/C1
Rame (pt.), Eng, UK 32/B6
Ramenskoye, Rus. 61/X9
Rāmeswaram, India 82/C6
Rāmgangā (riv.), India 84/B1
Rāmgarh, India 85/E4
Rāmhormoz, Iran 88/E2
Ramírez, Mex. 143/M7
Rāmjībanpur, India 85/F4
Ramla, Isr. 91/F8
Ramlu (peak), Erit. 88/D6
Ramme, Den. 38/C3
Rammūn, Isr. 91/G8
Rāmnagar, India 84/B1
Rāmnagar, India 84/D3
Rāmnagar, India 86/C3
Ramnäs, Swe. 38/G2
Ramonchamp, Fr. 56/C2
Ramor (lake), Ire. 34/A4
Ramos (riv.), Mex. 132/B5
Ramosch, Swi. 57/G4
Rampart, Ak, US 134/H2
Rampillon, Fr. 30/M6
Rāmpur, India 84/B1
Rāmpur, India 86/D4
Rāmpur Hāt, India 85/F3
Rāmpura Phūl, India 86/C4
Ramree (isl.), Myan. 83/F4
Rāmsanehīghāt, India 84/C2
Ramsbottom, Eng, UK 35/F4
Ramsden Heath, Eng, UK 30/E2
Ramsen, Swi. 57/E2
Ramsey (lake), Can. 130/D2
Ramsey (isl.), Wal, UK 32/A3
Ramsey, NJ, US 139/J7
Ramsey, IM, UK 34/D3
Ramsey (bay), IM, UK 34/D3
Ramsgate, Eng, UK 33/H4
Ramstein-Miesenbach, Ger. 53/G5
Ramu (riv.), PNG 116/D5
Rana, Nor. 37/E2
Rānāghāt, India 85/G4
Rancagua, Chile 158/N9
Rance (riv.), Fr. 42/E5
Rancharia, Braz. 155/B2
Rancheria (riv.), Col. 152/C2
Rānchī, India 85/E4
Rancho Palos Verdes, Ca, US 136/F8
Rancho Santa Fe, Ca, US 136/C4
Ranchos, Arg. 158/F2
Ranco (lake), Chile 158/B4
Rancocas, NJ, US 138/D4
Rancul, Arg. 158/D2
Randaberg, Nor. 38/A2
Randallstown, Md, US 138/B5
Randalstown, NI, UK 34/B2
Randazzo, It. 46/D4
Randburg, SAfr. 106/P13
Randers, Den. 38/D3
Randolph, NJ, US 138/D2
Randow (riv.), Ger. 41/H2
Randsfjorden (lake), Nor. 38/D1
Råneå, Swe. 60/D2
Rang (peak), Thai. 78/C2
Rang-du-Fliers, Fr. 52/A3
Rāngāmāti (pol. reg.), Bang. 85/H4
Rāngāmāti, Bang. 83/F3
Rangasa (cape), Indo. 81/E4
Rangely, Co, US 128/E2
Ranger, Tx, US 129/H4
Rangia, India 85/H2
Rangiora, NZ 117/S11
Rangiroa (isl.), FrPol. 117/L6
Rangoon (Yangon) (cap.), Myan. 83/G4
Rangpur, Bang. 85/G3
Rangpur (pol. reg.), Bang. 85/G3
Rangsdorf, Ger. 40/Q7
Rānībennur, India 89/L6
Rānīganj, India 85/F4
Rānīkhet, India 84/B1
Rānīpur, India 84/B3
Rankin, Tx, US 129/G5
Rankweil, Aus. 57/F3
Rannoch (lake), Sc, UK 36/B3
Ranohira, Madg. 107/H8
Ranomafana, Madg. 107/H8
Ranong, Thai. 78/B4
Ranotsara, Madg. 107/H8
Ransbach-Baumbach, Ger. 53/G3
Ransomville, NY, US 131/S9
Ranst, Belg. 50/B6
Ranstadt, Ger. 54/B2
Rantabe, Madg. 107/J6
Rantekombola (peak), Indo. 81/F4
Rantigny, Fr. 52/B5
Rantīs, WBnk. 91/G7
Rantoul, Il, US 127/L5
Rantsila, Fin. 60/E2
Ranzan, Japan 77/C1
Rao Co (peak), Laos 78/D2
Raon-l'Étape, Fr. 56/C1
Raoping, China 79/C3
Raoui, 'Erg er (des.), Alg. 98/E3
Raoul (isl.), NZ 116/H7
Raoyang (riv.), China 73/A2
Raoyang, China 72/C3
Rapa (isl.), FrPol. 117/L7
Rapallo, It. 58/C4
Rapel (lake), Chile 158/N9
Rapid City, SD, US 127/H4
Rappahannock (riv.), Va, US 130/E4
Rapper (cape), Chile 158/B5
Rāpti (zone), Nepal 84/D1
Rapti (riv.), India 82/D2
Rara NP, Nepal 84/D1
Raritan (bay), NJ, US 138/D3
Raritan (riv.), NJ, US 138/D2
Raritan, South Branch (riv.), NJ, US 138/D2
Raron, Swi. 56/D5
Rarotonga (isl.), Cookls. 117/J7
Ra's al 'Ayn, Syria 90/E2
Ra's al Basīt (pt.), Syria 91/D2
Ra's Al Jabal, Tun. 46/B4
Ra's al Khaymah, UAE 89/G3
Ra's al Unūf, Libya 97/J7
Ra's An Naqb, Jor. 91/D5
Ra's aṭ Ṭīb (Cape Bon) (cape), Tun. 46/B4
Ras Dashen (peak), Eth. 97/N5
Râs el Ma, Alg. 100/D2
Râs el Oued, Alg. 100/H5
Ras il-Qammieħ (pt.), Malta 46/L7
Ras San Dimitri (pt.), Malta 46/L6
Ra's Şawqirah (pt.), Oman 89/G5
Rasa (pt.), Arg. 158/E4
Raschau, Ger. 55/F1
Rashaant, Mong. 70/F2
Rasharkin, NI, UK 34/B2
Rāshayyā, Leb. 91/D3
Rashīd, Egypt 91/B4
Rasht, Iran 88/E1
Raška, Yugo. 47/G1
Rasmussen (basin), NW, Can. 122/G2
Raso (cape), Port. 45/P10
Rason (lake), Austl. 109/B3
Rasrā, India 84/D3
Rassina, It. 59/E5
Rasskazovo, Rus. 63/G1
Rastatt, Ger. 54/B5
Rastede, Ger. 51/F2
Rasūlnagar, Pak. 86/B3
Rat (isls.), Ak, US 134/B6
Rat Buri, Thai. 78/B3
Rata (cape), Indo. 80/B5
Ratak Chain (isls.), Mrsh. 116/F3
Ratangarh, India 89/K3
Ratanpur, India 84/D4
Rāth, India 84/B3
Rathbun (lake), Ia, US 127/K5
Rathcoole, Ire. 34/B5
Rathdowney, Ire. 31/Q10
Rathdrum, Ire. 34/B6
Rathedaung, Myan. 83/F3
Rathenow, Ger. 40/G2
Rathfriland, NI, UK 34/B3
Rathkeale, Ire. 31/P10
Rathlin (isl.), NI, UK 34/B1
Rathlin (sound), NI, UK 34/B1
Rathluirc, Ire. 31/P10
Rathmore, Ire. 31/P10
Rathnew, Ire. 34/B6
Ratia, India 86/C5
Ratingen, Ger. 50/D6
Ratlām, India 89/L4
Ratnāgiri, India 89/K5
Ratnapura, SrL. 82/D6
Ratoath, Ire. 34/B4
Raton, NM, US 129/F3
Rattray (pt.), Sc, UK 36/E1
Rättvik, Swe. 38/F1
Raub, Malay. 80/B3
Rauch, Arg. 158/F3
Raudales Malpaso, Mex. 144/C2
Raudhinúpur (pt.), Ice. 37/P6
Raufarhöfn, Ice. 37/P6
Raufoss, Nor. 38/D1
Rauhe Ebrach (riv.), Ger. 54/D3
Raul Soares, Braz. 155/D2
Rauma, Fin. 39/J1
Raunheim, Ger. 54/B2
Raurkela, India 85/E4
Rausu, Japan 76/D1
Rautjärvi, Fin. 39/N1
Ravanusa, It. 46/C4
Rāvar, Iran 89/G2
Ravarino, It. 59/E3
Ravels, Belg. 50/B6
Ravenna, It. 59/F4
Ravenna (prov.), It. 59/E4
Ravenna, Ca, US 136/B2
Ravensburg, Ger. 57/F2
Ravensdale, Wa, US 135/D3
Ravenshoe, Austl. 114/B2
Ravensthorpe, Austl. 112/D5
Ravenswood, WV, US 130/D4
Rāvi (riv.), Ind.,Pak. 89/K2
Ravne na Koroškem, Slov. 43/L3
Rawa Mazowiecka, Pol. 41/L3
Rāwah, Iraq 90/E3
Rawaki (Phoenix) (isl.), Kiri. 117/H5
Rāwalpindi, Pak. 86/B3
Rāwatsār, India 86/C5
Rawicz, Pol. 41/J3
Rawlins, Wy, US 126/G5
Rawlinson (mt.), Austl. 113/E3
Rawmarsh, Eng, UK 35/G5
Rawson, Arg. 158/D4
Rawtenstall, Eng, UK 35/F4
Raxaul Bazar, India 85/E2
Ray (cape), Can. 131/K2
Raya (peak), Indo. 80/D4
Rāyadrug, India 82/C5
Raychikhinsk, Rus. 71/N2
Rayleigh, Eng, UK 33/G3
Raymond, Ab, Can. 126/E3
Raymond, Wa, US 126/C4
Raymond, Co, US 137/B2
Raymond, Wi, US 135/P14
Raymondville, Tx, US 132/D5
Raymore, Sk, Can. 127/G3
Raymore, Mo, US 137/E6
Rayón, Mex. 143/F4
Rayón, Mex. 142/C2
Rayón, Mex. 143/Q10
Rayón, PN, Mex. 143/E5
Rayong, Thai. 78/C3
Raytown, Mo, US 137/E5
Rayville, La, US 129/K4
Raz, Pointe de (pt.),Fr. 42/A2
Razelm (lake), Rom. 49/J3
Razgrad, Bul. 49/H4
Razlog, Bul. 47/H2
Re di Castello (peak), It. 57/G5
Ré, Île de (isl.), Fr. 42/C3
Rea (riv.), Eng, UK 32/D1
Reading, Eng, UK 33/F4
Reading, Pa, US 138/C3
Real, Cordillera (mts.), Peru 150/E7
Realicó, Arg. 158/D2
Realp, Swi. 57/E4
Reamstown, Pa, US 138/B3
Reao (isl.), FrPol. 117/M6
Réau, Fr. 30/K6
Rebais, Fr. 52/C6
Rebecca (lake), Austl. 109/B4
Rębiechowo (int'l arpt.), Pol. 38/H4
Rebouças, Braz. 155/B3
Rebstein, Swi. 57/F3
Rebun, Japan 76/B1
Recanati, It. 59/G6
Recco, It. 58/C4
Recherche (arch.), Austl. 109/B4
Rechnitz, Aus. 43/M3
Rechthalten, Swi. 56/D4
Rechytsa, Bela. 62/D1
Recife (cape), SAfr. 106/D4
Recke, Ger. 51/E4
Reckingen, Swi. 57/E5
Recklinghausen, Ger. 51/E5
Recknitz (riv.), Ger. 40/G2
Réclère, Swi. 56/C3
Recoaro Terme, It. 59/E1
Reconquista, Arg. 157/E2
Reconvilier, Swi. 56/D3
Recuay, Peru 156/B3
Red (riv.), US 129/J5
Red (riv.), Can. 127/J3
Red (riv.), Ok, US 129/H4
Red (hills), US 133/D2
Red (riv.), China,Vie 70/H7
Red (riv.), La, US 140/C1
Red (riv.), Viet. 83/H3
Red (sea), Afr.,Asia 67/C7
Red (riv.), Mn, US 125/G2
Red (lakes), Mn, US 122/G4
Red (bay), NI, UK 34/B1
Red Bank, NJ, US 138/D3
Red Bluff (lake), Tx, US 129/G5
Red Bluff, Ca, US 128/B2
Red Cliffs, Austl. 115/B2
Red Cloud, Ne, US 129/H2
Red Deer, Ab, Can. 126/E2
Red Deer (riv.), Sk, Can. 122/E3
Red Devil, Ak, US 134/G3
Red Hill (peak), Hi, US 124/T10
Red Hill, Pa, US 138/C3
Red Indian (lake), Can. 131/K1
Red Lake (riv.), Mn, US 127/K3
Red Lake, On, Can. 127/K3
Red Lion, De, US 138/C4
Red Lion, Pa, US 138/B4
Red Lodge, Mt, US 126/F4
Red, North Fork (riv.), US 129/G4
Red River of the North (riv.), US,Can. 127/J3
Red Rock (lake), Ia, US 127/K5
Red Rocks (pt.), Austl. 113/E5
Red Sea (hills), Sudan 93/F2
Red Volta (riv.), Burk. 103/E4
Red Wing, Mn, US 127/K4
Reda, Pol. 38/H4
Redange-sur-Attert, Lux. 53/E4
Redbridge (bor.), Eng, UK 30/D2
Redcar, Eng, UK 35/G2
Redcliff, Ab, Can. 126/F3
Redcliffe (mt.), Austl. 112/D4
Redden, De, US 138/C6
Reddersburg, SAfr. 106/D3
Redding, Ca, US 128/B2
Redding, Ct, US 139/E1
Redditch, Eng, UK 33/E2
Rede (riv.), Eng, UK 35/F1
Redenção do Gurguéia, Braz. 154/A3
Redfield, SD, US 127/J4
Redford, Mi, US 135/F7
Redhill, Eng, UK 30/C3
Rédics, Hun. 48/C2
Redland, Md, US 138/A5
Redlands, Ca, US 136/C2
Redmond, Or, US 126/C4
Rednitz (riv.), Ger. 54/D4
Redon, Fr. 42/B3
Redondela, Sp. 44/A1
Redondo, Port. 44/B3
Redondo, Wa, US 135/C3
Redondo Beach, Ca, US 136/F8
Redoubt (vol.), Ak, US 134/H3
Redstone (riv.), NW, Can. 122/D2
Redvers, Sk, Can. 127/H3
Redwater, Ab, Can. 126/E2
Redway, Ca, US 126/C5
Redwood Falls, Mn, US 127/K4
Redwood NP, Ca, US 128/A2
Ree, Lough (lake), Ire. 31/P10
Reed City, Mi, US 130/C3
Reeding, Ok, US 137/M14
Reedley, Ca, US 128/C3
Reeds (bay), NJ, US 138/D5
Reedsburg, Wi, US 127/L5
Reef (pt.), Belz. 143/J5
Reef (isls.), Sol. 116/F6
Reefton, NZ 117/S11
Rees, Ger. 50/D5
Reese (riv.), Nv, US 124/C4
Reessum, Ger. 51/G2
Reest (riv.), Neth. 50/D3
Reeuwijk, Neth. 50/B4
Refahiye, Turk. 90/D2
Reforma, Mex. 144/C2

Refugio, Tx, US 132/D4
Rega (riv.), Pol. 38/F5
Regen, Ger. 55/G5
Regen (riv.), Ger. 55/F4
Regência, Pontal da (pt.), Braz. 155/E1
Regeneração, Braz. 154/B2
Regensburg, Ger. 55/E2
Regensdorf, Swi. 57/E3
Regenstauf, Ger. 55/E2
Reggane, Alg. 99/F4
Regge (riv.), Neth. 50/D4
Reggello, It. 59/E5
Reggio, La, US 137/Q17
Reggio di Calabria (prov.), It. 46/D3
Reggio di Calabria, It. 46/D3
Reggio nell' Emilia (prov.), It. 58/D3
Reggio nell'Emilia, It. 58/D3
Reggiolo, It. 59/D3
Reghin, Rom. 49/G2
Regina (cap.), Sk, Can. 127/G3
Régina, FrG. 151/H3
Regina, NM, US 132/B2
Regina Beach, Sk, Can. 127/G3
Región Metropolitana Santiago (pol. reg.), Chile 158/B1
Registro, Braz. 155/C3
Regnitz (riv.), Ger. 43/J2
Regoledo, It. 57/F5
Reguengos de Monsaraz, Port. 44/B3
Rehau, Ger. 55/F2
Rehburg-Loccum, Ger. 51/G4
Rehfelde, Ger. 40/Q6
Rehli, India 84/B4
Rehling, Ger. 54/D6
Rehlingen-Siersburg, Ger. 53/F5
Rehoboth, Namb. 105/C5
Rehon, Fr. 53/E4
RehLovot, Isr. 91/F8
Rehrersburg, Pa, US 138/B3
Reichelsheim, Ger. 54/B2
Reichelsheim, Ger. 54/B3
Reichenbach, Ger. 55/F1
Reichenbach im Kandertal, Swi. 56/D4
Reichenbach-Steegen, Ger. 53/G4
Reichenberg, Ger. 54/C3
Reichertshausen, Ger. 55/E6
Reichhof, Ger. 53/G2
Reichshoffen, Fr. 53/G6
Reichstett, Fr. 53/G6
Reid (lake), Austl. 126/F3
Reiden, Swi. 56/D3
Reigate, Eng, UK 30/C3
Reignier, Fr. 56/C5
Reims, Fr. 52/D5
Reina Adelaida (arch.), Chile 157/A7
Reina Beatrix (int'l arpt.), NAnt. 152/D1
Reinach, Swi. 56/D3
Reinach, Swi. 56/E3
Reinbek, Ger. 51/H1
Reindeer (riv.), Can. 127/H1
Reindeer (isl.), Can. 127/J2
Reindeer (lake), Sk, Can. 119/G4
Reinerton-Orwin-Muir, Pa, US 138/B2
Reinheim, Ger. 54/B3
Reinosa, Sp. 44/C1
Reinsfeld, Ger. 53/F4
Reischach, Ger. 55/F6
Reisdorf, Lux. 53/F4
Reisduoddarhal'di (peak), Nor. 37/G1
Reiskirchen, Ger. 54/B1
Reisterstown, Md, US 138/B5
Reitdiep (riv.), Neth. 50/D2
Reitz, SAfr. 106/E2
Rejón (int'l arpt.), Mex. 144/D1
Rekkam (plat.), Mor. 100/C2
Reliance, NW, Can. 122/F2
Relizane (prov.), Alg. 100/F5
Relizane, Alg. 100/F5
Rellingen, Ger. 51/G1
Remagen, Ger. 53/G2
Remanso, Braz. 154/B3
Remanzacco, It. 59/G1
Remarde (riv.), Fr. 30/H6
Remarkable (mt.), Austl. 113/H5
Rembang, Indo. 80/D5
Remchi, Alg. 100/D2
Remedios, Pan. 145/F4
Remich, Lux. 53/F4
Remicourt, Belg. 53/E4
Rémire, FrG. 151/H3
Remiremont, Fr. 56/C1
Remlingen, Ger. 51/H4
Rems (riv.), Ger. 43/H2
Remscheid, Ger. 51/E6
Remy, Fr. 52/B5
Rena, Nor. 38/D1
Renala Khurd, Pak. 86/B4
Renan, Swi. 56/C3
Renarde (riv.), Fr. 30/J6
Renazzo, It. 59/E3
Renca, Chile 158/N8
Rench (riv.), Ger. 54/A5
Renchen, Ger. 54/B5
Rend (lake), Il, US 133/F2
Rendeux, Belg. 52/D5
Rendsburg, Ger. 38/C4
Renens, Swi. 56/C4
Renfrew, On, Can. 130/E2
Renfrew, Sc, UK 36/B5
Rengam, Malay. 80/B3
Rengat, Indo. 80/B4
Rengo, Chile 158/N9
Rengsdorf, Ger. 53/G3
Renhua, China 83/K2
Reni, Ukr. 49/J3
Renish (pt.), Sc, UK 31/Q8
Renkum, Neth. 50/C5

Renmark, Austl. 113/J5
Rennell (isl.), Sol. 116/F6
Rennerod, Ger. 53/H2
Rennertshofen, Ger. 54/E5
Rennes, Fr. 42/C2
Renningen, Ger. 54/B5
Reno, Nv, US 128/C3
Reno (riv.), It. 59/E1
Renoster (riv.), SAfr. 106/C3
Renqiu, China 72/D3
Rensselaer, In, US 130/C3
Rentchler, Il, US 137/H9
Renteria, Sp. 44/E1
Renton, Wa, US 126/C4
Renton, Sc, UK 36/B5
Renwez, Fr. 52/C3
Réo, Burk. 103/E3
Reoti, India 85/E3
Répcelak, Hun. 43/M3
Repelón, Col. 145/H4
Repentigny, Qu, Can. 131/P6
Replonges, Fr. 56/A5
Republican (riv.), Ks,Ne, US 125/G3
Republic, Wa, US 126/D3
Repulse (bay), Austl. 109/D3
Repulse Bay (isl.), Austl. 114/C3
Repulse Bay, NW, Can. 123/H2
Requena, Peru 156/C2
Requena, Sp. 45/E3
Requínoa, Chile 158/N9
Reriutaba, Braz. 154/B2
Reşadiye, Turk. 62/F4
Reschensee (Resia) (lake), It. 57/G4
Rescue (pt.), Chile 158/B5
Resegone (peak), It. 58/C1
Resen, Macd. 47/G2
Resende, Port. 44/B2
Resende, Braz. 155/D1
Reserve, NM, US 128/E4
Resia, Passo di (pass), It. 57/G4
Resia (Reschensee) (lake), It. 57/G4
Resistencia, Arg. 157/E2
Reşiţa, Rom. 48/E3
Resolution (isl.), NW, Can. 123/K2
Respenda de la Peña, Sp. 44/C1
Resplendor, Braz. 155/D1
Restigouche (riv.), Can. 131/H2
Reston, Mb, Can. 127/H3
Reston, Va, US 138/A6
Reszel, Pol. 39/J4
Retalhuleu, Guat. 144/D3
Rethel, Fr. 53/D4
Réthimnon, Gre. 47/J5
Retie, Belg. 55/E6
Retrezap NP, Rom. 62/B3
Rétság, Hun. 48/D2
Rettenberg, Ger. 57/G2
Retz, Aus. 41/H4
Réunion (dpcy.), Fr. 107/S15
Reus, Sp. 45/F2
Reusel, Neth. 50/C6
Reuterstadt Stavenhagen, Ger. 38/E5
Reutlingen, Ger. 54/C6
Reutov, Rus. 61/W9
Reutte, Aus. 57/G3
Revadim, Isr. 91/F8
Réveillon (riv.), Fr. 30/K5
Revel, Fr. 42/D5
Revelstoke, BC, Can. 126/D3
Revin, Fr. 53/D4
Revillagigedo (isls.), Mex. 119/F8
Revin, Fr. 53/D4
Revolyutsii (peak), Taj. 87/F5
Revsbotn (inlet), Nor. 37/G1
Rewa, India 84/C3
Rewa (riv.), Guy. 153/G4
Richard's Bay, SAfr. 107/F3
Rewari, India 84/C2
Rex (mtn.), Ak, US 134/J3
Rey (isl.), Pan. 141/F6
Rey, Isla del (isl.), Pan. 150/C2
Reyes, Bol. 150/E4
Reyes (pt.), Ca, US 128/B3
Reyhanlı, Turk. 91/E1
Reykjanestá (cape), Ice. 37/M7
Reykjavik (int'l arpt.), Ice. 37/N7
Reykjavik (cap.), Ice. 37/N7
Reynosa, Mex. 132/D5
Reyssouze (riv.), Fr. 56/B5
Rezé, Fr. 42/C3
Rēzekne, Lat. 39/M3
Rezzato, It. 58/D1
Rhaetian Alps (mts.), Swi.,Aus. 43/H3
Rhallamane (reg.), Mrta. 98/C5
Rhallamane (lake), Mrta. 98/C4
Rhar (peak), Mor. 98/D3
Rhat (peak), Mor. 98/D3
Rhätikon (mts.), Swi.,Aus. 57/F3
Rheda-Wiedenbrück, Ger. 51/F5
Rhede, Ger. 51/E2
Rheden, Neth. 50/D4
Rheidol (riv.), Wal, UK 32/C2
Rheinau, Swi. 57/E3
Rheinberg, Ger. 50/D5
Rheinbreitbach, Ger. 53/G2
Rheinböllen, Ger. 53/G3
Rheine, Ger. 51/E4
Rheinfall, Swi. 57/E2
Rheinfelden, Ger. 56/D2
Rheinland-Pfalz (state), Ger. 54/A3
Rheinwaldhorn (peak), Swi. 57/E3
Rheinzabern, Ger. 54/B4
Rhemiles (well), Alg. 100/D3
Rhenen, Neth. 50/C5
Rheris, Oued (riv.), Mor. 98/D3
Rhinau, Fr. 56/D1

Rhine (riv.), Eur. 27/E4
Rhine-Herne (canal), Ger. 51/E5
Rhinns (pt.), Sc, UK 31/Q9
Rhinns, The (pt.), Sc, UK 34/C2
Rhino Camp, Ugan. 104/A2
Rhiou (riv.), Alg. 100/F5
Rhiou (riv.), Alg. 100/F5
Rhir (cape), Mor. 98/C3
Rhisnes, Belg. 53/D3
Rhiw (riv.), Wal, UK 32/C1
Rho, It. 58/C1
Rhode Island (state), US 125/M3
Rhodes (isl.), Gre. 27/G5
Rhön (mts.), Ger. 54/D1
Rhondda, Wal, UK 32/C3
Rhône (dept.), Fr. 56/A6
Rhône (glacier), Swi. 57/E3
Rhône (riv.), Fr. 27/E4
Rhône-Alpes (pol. reg.), Fr. 56/B5
Rhône au Rhin (canal), Fr. 56/B3
Rhonelle (riv.), Fr. 52/C2
Rhoslianerchrugog, Wal, UK 35/E6
Rhum (isl.), Sc, UK 31/Q8
Rhume (riv.), Ger. 51/H5
Rhumel, Oued el (riv.), Alg. 100/J4
Rhyddhywel (peak), Wal, UK 32/C2
Rhyl, Wal, UK 34/E5
Riachão, Braz. 154/A2
Riachão das Neves, Braz. 154/C3
Riachão do Jacuípe, Braz. 154/C3
Riacho de Santana, Braz. 154/B2
Riachuelo, Arg. 154/C2
Rialto, Ca, US 136/C2
Rialto (pt.), Chile 157/B7
Rianjo, Sp. 44/A1
Riaño, Sp. 44/C1
Riāsi, India 86/C3
Riau (isls.), Indo. 80/B3
Riaza, Sp. 44/D2
Ribadeo, Sp. 44/B1
Ribadesella, Sp. 44/C1
Riban'i Manamby (mts.), Madg. 107/H9
Ribble (riv.), Eng, UK 35/F4
Ribblesdale (valley), Eng, UK 35/F3
Ribe (co.), Den. 38/C4
Ribe, Den. 38/C4
Ribeauvillé, Fr. 56/D1
Ribécourt-Dreslincourt, Fr. 52/B4
Ribeira (riv.), Braz. 155/C3
Ribeira Brava, CpV. 93/J10
Ribeira de Pena, Port. 44/B2
Ribeira do Pombal, Braz. 154/C3
Ribeira Grande, Azor., Port. 45/T13
Ribeira Grande, CpV. 93/J9
Ribeirão, Braz. 154/D3
Ribeirão do Pinha, Braz. 155/B2
Ribeiro Gonçalves, Braz. 154/A2
Ribera, It. 46/C4
Riberalta, Bol. 150/E6
Ribniţa, Mol. 49/J2
Ribnitz-Damgarten, Ger. 38/E4
Říčany u Prahy, Czh. 55/H3
Ricaurte, Col. 152/B4
Riccia, It. 46/D2
Riccione, It. 59/F5
Ricco'del Golfo, It. 58/C4
Rice (lake), Can. 130/E2
Richard Toll, Sen. 102/B2
Richards (isl.), NW, Can. 122/C2
Richardson (lakes), Me, US 131/G2
Richboro, Pa, US 138/C3
Riche (cape), Austl. 112/C5
Richebourg, Fr. 53/D4
Richel (isl.), Neth. 50/C2
Richelieu, Qu, Can. 131/P7
Richfield, Ut, US 128/D3
Richfield, Pa, US 138/A2
Richhill, NI, UK 34/B3
Richland, Wa, US 126/D4
Richland, Ok, US 137/M14
Richland, NJ, US 138/D5
Richland, Mo, US 137/E9
Richland Balsam (peak), NC, US 133/H3
Richland Center, Wi, US 127/L6
Richland Creek (res.), US 129/H5
Richlandtown, Pa, US 138/C3
Richmond, BC, Can. 126/C3
Richmond, Ky, US 130/C4
Richmond, Qu, Can. 131/F2
Richmond, Va, US 130/E4
Richmond, SAfr. 106/C3
Richmond, SAfr. 106/D3
Richmond, NJ, US 138/D3
Richmond, Austl. 114/A3
Richmond (co.), NY, US 138/D2
Richmond, Il, US 135/P15
Richmond Beach-Innis Arden, Wa, US 135/A1
Richmond Heights, Mo, US 137/G8
Richmond Hill, On, Can. 131/N6
Richmond Park (bor.), Eng, UK 30/C2
Richmond Upon Thames (bor.), Eng, UK 30/B2
Richmond-Windsor, Austl. 114/C4
Richtersveld NP, SAfr. 106/B3
Richtersweil, Swi. 57/E3
Richwiller, Fr. 56/D2
Rickenbach, Ger. 56/D2
Ricketts Glen State Park, Pa, US 138/B1
Rickmansworth, Eng, UK 30/C2

Ricla, Sp. 44/E2
Ricse, Hun. 41/L4
Ridá', Yem. 88/D6
Ridderkerk, Neth. 50/B5
Rideau (lake), Can. 130/E2
Ridgecrest, Ca, US 128/C4
Ridgefield, Ct, US 139/E1
Ridgefield, NJ, US 139/K8
Ridgefield Park, NJ, US 139/J8
Ridgeland, Ms, US 129/K4
Ridgely, Md, US 138/C6
Ridgely, Mo, US 137/D5
Ridgewood, NJ, US 139/J8
Ridgewood State Park, NJ, US 138/D2
Riding Mountain NP, Can. 127/H3
Ridlees Cairn (hill), Eng, UK 36/D6
Riecito (riv.), Col. 152/D3
Ried im Innkreis, Aus. 55/G6
Ried im Traunkreis, Aus. 55/H6
Riede, Ger. 51/F3
Riedenburg, Ger. 55/E5
Riedisheim, Fr. 56/D2
Riedlingen, Ger. 57/F1
Riegelsberg, Ger. 53/F5
Riegelsville, Pa, US 138/C2
Riegsee (lake), Ger. 57/H2
Riehen, Swi. 56/D2
Riemst, Belg. 53/E2
Rieneck, Ger. 54/C2
Riesa, Ger. 41/G3
Rieschweiler-Mühlbach, Ger. 53/G5
Riesco (isl.), Chile 157/B7
Riese Pio X, It. 59/E1
Riet (riv.), SAfr. 106/D3
Rietberg, Ger. 51/F5
Rietbron, SAfr. 106/C4
Rieti, It. 46/C1
Riffe (lake), Wa, US 126/C4
Rifle, Co, US 128/F3
Rifsnes (pt.), Ice. 37/N6
Rift Valley (prov.), Kenya 104/B2
Riga (gulf), Eur. 64/C4
Riga (cap.), Lat. 39/L3
Rigby, Id, US 126/F5
Rigestan (pol. reg.), Afg. 89/H2
Riggins, Id, US 126/D4
Rigi (peak), Swi. 57/E3
Rignano sull'Arno, It. 59/E5
Rigolet, Nf, Can. 123/L3
Rihand (dam), India 84/D3
Rihand (riv.), India 84/D3
Rihand Sägar (res.), India 82/D3
Riihimäki, Fin. 39/L1
Riiser-Larsen (pen.), Ant. 160/C
Riiser-Larsen Ice Shelf, Ant. 160/Y
Riisitunturin NP, Fin. 37/N3
Rijeka, Cro. 48/B3
Rijksmuseum Kröller Müller, Neth. 50/C4
Rijnsburg, Neth. 50/B4
Rijsbergen, Neth. 50/B5
Rijssen, Neth. 50/D4
Rijswijk, Neth. 50/B4
Rikers (isl.), NY, US 139/K8
Rikitea, FrPol. 117/M7
Rikubetsu, Japan 76/C4
Rikuchū-Kaigan NP, Japan 76/C4
Rikuzentakata, Japan 76/B4
Rila (mts.), Bul. 47/H1
Rila, Bul. 47/H1
Rillieux-la-Pape, Fr. 56/A6
Rilski Manastir, Bul. 47/H1
Rimatara (isl.), FrPol. 117/K7
Rimavská Sobota, Slvk. 41/L4
Rimbach, Ger. 54/B3
Rimbey, Ab, Can. 126/D2
Rimforsa, Swe. 38/F2
Rimini, It. 59/F5
Rîmnicu Sărat, Rom. 49/H3
Rîmnicu Vîlcea, Rom. 49/G3
Rimogne, Fr. 53/D4
Rimouski, Qu, Can. 131/G1
Rimpar, Ger. 54/C3
Rimpfischhorn (peak), Swi. 56/D5
Rinas (int'l arpt.), Alb. 56/D5
Rinbung, China 85/G1
Rinchnach, Ger. 55/G5
Rincón de la Vieja, PN, CR 140/D5
Rincón de Romos, Mex. 144/D5
Ringarooma, Austl. 115/C4
Ringboy (pt.), NI, UK 34/C3
Ringebu, Nor. 38/D1
Ringelspitz (peak), Swi. 57/F4
Ringgold, La, US 129/J4
Ringkøbing (fjord), Den. 38/B3
Ringkøbing (co.), Den. 38/B3
Ringkøbing, Den. 38/B3
Ringoes, NJ, US 138/D3
Ringsend, NI, UK 34/B1
Ringsted, Den. 38/D3
Ringvaart (riv.), Neth. 50/B4
Ringvassøy (isl.),Nor. 37/F1
Ringwood, Eng, UK 33/E5
Ringwood, NJ, US 139/H7
Ringwood State Park, NJ, US 139/H7
Rinia (isl.), Gre. 47/J4
Rinteln, Ger. 51/F4
Rinxent, Fr. 52/A2
Rio Abiseo, PN, Peru 150/C5
Rio Azul, Braz. 155/B3
Rio Blanco, Mex. 143/M8
Rio Bonito, Braz. 211/L7
Rio Branco, Braz. 150/D6
Rio Branco do Sul, Braz. 155/B3
Rio Bravo, Mex. 143/F2
Rio Bueno, Chile 158/B4
Rio Casca, Braz. 155/D1
Rio Cauto, Cuba 145/G1

Río Clarillo, PN, Chile 158/N8
Rio Claro, Braz. 211/J7
Rio Claro, Trin. 153/F2
Rio Colorado, Arg. 158/D2
Rio de Janeiro (state), Braz. 155/D2
Rio de Janeiro (int'l arpt.), Braz. 211/K7
Rio Dell, Ca, US 126/B5
Rio Gallegos, Arg. 159/C6
Rio Grande (riv.), US,Mex. 125/F5
Rio Grande, Braz. 155/A5
Rio Grande (plain), Tx, US 140/B2
Rio Grande, NJ, US 138/D5
Rio Grande, Arg. 159/D7
Rio Grande City, Tx, US 132/D5
Rio Grande da Serra, Braz. 211/G8
Rio Grande Do Norte (state), Braz. 154/C2
Rio Grande do Piaui, Braz. 154/B2
Rio Grande Valley (int'l arpt.), Tx, US 140/B2
Rio Jaú, PN do, Braz. 153/G5
Rio Lagartos, Mex. 144/D1
Rio Maior, Port. 44/A3
Rio Mayo, Arg. 159/C5
Rio Negrinho, Braz. 155/B3
Rio Negro, Braz. 155/B3
Rio Negro (prov.), Arg. 158/B3
Rio Negro, Embalse de (res.), Uru. 157/E3
Rio Paranaíba, Braz. 155/C1
Rio Pardo, Braz. 155/A4
Rio Pilcomayo, PN, Arg. 157/E2
Rio Prêto (range), Braz. 154/A3
Rio Rancho, NM, US 128/F4
Rio Real, Braz. 154/C3
Rio Salceto, It. 59/D3
Rio Simpson, PN, Chile 158/B5
Rio Tala, Arg. 159/J10
Rio Tercero, Arg. 158/D3
Rio Tigre, Ecu. 152/B5
Rio Tinto, Braz. 154/D2
Rio Verde, Chile 157/B7
Rio Verde, Mex. 143/F4
Rio Verde de Mato Grosso, Braz. 151/H7
Rio Vista, Ca, US 135/L10
Riobamba, Ecu. 152/B5
Riohacha, Col. 152/C2
Rioja, Peru 156/B2
Riolândia, Braz. 155/B1
Riolo Terme, It. 59/E4
Riom, Fr. 42/E4
Riom-ès-Montagne, Fr. 42/E4
Riomaggiore, It. 58/C4
Rion-des-Landes, Fr. 42/C5
Rionero in Vulture, It. 46/D2
Rios (lake), Chile 158/B5
Riosucio, Col. 152/B3
Rioz, Fr. 56/C3
Ripalti, Punta dei (pt.), It. 58/D5
Ripanj, Yugo. 48/E3
Riparbella, It. 58/D6
Ripley, Ms, US 133/F3
Ripley, Eng, UK 35/G5
Ripoll, Sp. 45/G1
Ripoll (riv.), Sp. 45/L6
Ripollet, Sp. 45/L6
Ripon, Wi, US 127/L5
Ripon, Eng, UK 35/G3
Riposto, It. 46/D4
Rippowam (riv.), Ct, US 139/E2
Risan, Yugo. 47/E1
Risaralda (dept.), Col. 152/A4
Rishikesh, India 84/C1
Rishiri, Japan 76/B1
Rishiri-Rebun-Sarobetsu NP, Japan 76/B1
Rishon Leziyyon, Isr. 91/F8
Rising Sun, Md, US 138/B4
Rising Sun-Lebanon, Md, US 138/B4
Risle (riv.), Fr. 42/C2
Ris-Orangis, Fr. 30/K6
Risnjak (peak), Cro. 48/B3
Risnjak NP, Cro. 48/B3
Rîsnov, Rom. 49/G3
Rison, Ar, US 129/J4
Risør, Nor. 38/C2
Riss (riv.), Ger. 57/F1
Ristiina, Fin. 39/M1
Ritacuba (peak), Col. 152/C3
Ritaiō (isl.), Japan 116/D2
Ritchie, SAfr. 106/D3
Ritterhude, Ger. 51/F2
Rittō, Japan 77/J5
Ritzville, Wa, US 126/D4
Riva, It. 57/G6
Riva Ligure, It. 58/B5
Riva Presso Chieri, It. 58/A3
Riva San Vitale, Swi. 57/E6
Rivadavia, Arg. 157/C3
Rivadavia, Arg. 158/D2
Rivalta di Torino, It. 58/A3
Rivalta, It. 58/A3
Rivanazzano, It. 58/B3
Rivarolo Canavese, It. 58/A2
Rivarolo Mantovano, It. 58/D2
Rivas, Nic. 144/E4
Rive-de-Gier, Fr. 42/E4
River Cess, Libr. 102/C5
River Edge, NJ, US 139/J8
River Hall, SC, US 133/H4
River Kwai Bridge, Thai. 78/B3
River Rouge, Mi, US 135/F7
River Vale, NJ, US 139/J8

Rivera, Uru. 157/E3
Rivera, Swi. 57/E5
Rivera (isl.), Chile 158/B5
Rivera (isl.), Chile 158/B5
Riverdale, Ut, US 137/K11
Riverdale, Md, US 138/B6
Rivergaro, It. 58/C2
Riverhead, NY, US 139/F1
Riverside (inlet), NY, US 139/K9
Rivers (inlet), Can. 126/B3
Rivers, Mb, Can. 127/H3
Rivers (state), Nga. 103/G5
Riverside (co.), US,Mex. 136/C3
Riverside, Ca, US 136/C3
Riverside, Mo, US 137/D5
Riverton, NC, US 133/J3
Riverton, Austl. 114/C4
Riverton, Mb, Can. 131/G2
Riverton, Me, US 131/G2
Riverton, On, Can. 130/F2
Riverton, NZ 117/R12
Riverton, Ut, US 137/K12
Riverview, NB, Can. 131/H2
Riverwoods, Il, US 135/Q15
Riviera Beach, Fl, US 133/H5
Riviera Beach, Md, US 138/B6
Rivière-du-Loup, Qu, Can. 131/G2
Rivne, Ukr. 62/C2
Rivne (prov.), Ukr. 62/C2
Rivne's'ka (obl.), Ukr. 62/C2
Rivoli, It. 43/G4
Rivoli d'Adda, It. 58/C2
Rixensart, Belg. 53/D2
Rixheim, Fr. 56/D2
Riyāq, Leb. 91/D3
Rize (prov.), Turk. 63/G4
Rize, Turk. 63/G4
Rizhao, China 72/D4
Rizokarpasso, Cyp. 91/D2
Rjukan, Nor. 38/C2
Rkîz (lake), Mrta. 102/B2
Roa, Sp. 44/D2
Roa, Nor. 38/D1
Road Town (cap.), BVI 141/M8
Roan (plat.), US 128/E3
Roan Fell (hill), Sc, UK 35/F1
Roanne, Fr. 42/F3
Roanoke, Al, US 133/G3
Roanoke, Va, US 130/D4
Roanoke (riv.), US 129/P7
Roatán (isl.), Hon. 140/D4
Roatán, Hon. 144/E2
Robāt Karīm, Iran 88/F1
Robbiate, It. 58/C1
Robbins (isl.), Austl. 115/C4
Robbio, It. 58/B2
Robe, Austl. 115/A3
Robe (mt.), Austl. 115/B1
Robe (riv.), Ire. 31/P10
Robert (peak), Fr. 56/B5
Robert Lee, Tx, US 129/G5
Roberts (mtn.), Ak, US 134/E4
Roberts (Monrovia) (int'l arpt.), Libr. 102/C5
Robertsfors, Swe. 37/G2
Robertsganj, India 84/D3
Robertson, SAfr. 106/L10
Robertson, Libr. 102/C5
Robertstown, Qu, Can. 131/Q10
Roberval, Qu, Can. 131/F1
Robesonia, Pa, US 138/B3
Robinson (range), Austl. 109/A3
Robinson Crusoe (isl.), Chile 147/B6
Robinson Gorge NP, Austl. 114/C4
Robinvale, Austl. 115/B2
Roblin, Mb, Can. 127/H3
Robore, Bol. 150/G7
Robson (mt.), BC, Can. 126/D2
Robstown, Tx, US 132/D5
Roby, Tx, US 129/G4
Roc du Haut du Faite (peak), Fr. 56/D1
Roca, Cabo da (cape), Port. 45/P10
Roca Partida (isl.), Mex. 142/B5
Roca Partida, Punta (pt.), Mex. 144/C2
Rocafuerte, Ecu. 152/A5
Rocas (isl.), Braz. 151/M4
Rocca San Casciano, It. 59/E4
Roccabianca, It. 58/D2
Roccastrada, It. 43/G5
Rocciamelone (peak), It. 58/A3
Rocha (dept.), Uru. 159/G2
Rocha, Uru. 159/G2
Rochdale, Eng, UK 35/F4
Roche, Swi. 56/D5
Roche du Sapin Sec (peak), Fr. 56/C1
Roche-lez-Beaupré, Fr. 56/C3
Rochefort, Fr. 42/C4
Rochefort, Belg. 52/D3
Rochelle Park, NJ, US 139/J8
Rochers du Bourbet (peak), Fr. 56/C3
Rochester, Austl. 115/C3
Rochester, Mn, US 127/K4
Rochester, NY, US 130/E2
Rochester, NH, US 131/G3
Rochester, Eng, UK 33/G4
Rochester, Mi, US 135/F5
Rochford, Eng, UK 30/D2
Rock (riv.), Il, US 125/L3
Rock Creek, Yk, Can. 134/L3
Rock Forest, Qu, Can. 131/F2
Rock Glen, Pa, US 138/B2
Rock Hall, Md, US 138/B5
Rock Hill, SC, US 133/H4
Rock Island, Il, US 130/B3
Rock Springs, Wy, US 126/F5

Rockall (isl.), UK 27/C3
Rockaway (riv.), NJ, US 138/D1
Rockaway (pt.), NY, US 139/K9
Rockaway, NJ, US 138/D1
Rockaway (inlet), NY, US 139/K9
Rockdale, Il, US 135/P17
Rockefeller (plat.), Ant. 160/R
Rockenhausen, Ger. 53/G4
Rockford, Il, US 127/L5
Rockglen, Sk, Can. 127/J3
Rockhampton, Austl. 114/C4
Rockingham, Austl. 112/K7
Rockingham, NC, US 133/J3
Rockingham, Me, US 131/G2
Rockland, On, Can. 130/F2
Rockland (co.), NY, US 138/D1
Rockland Lake, NY, US 139/K7
Rocklands (res.), Austl. 109/D4
Rockledge, Fl, US 133/H4
Rockledge, Pa, US 138/C3
Rockport, Tx, US 132/D4
Rocks, Md, US 138/B4
Rocksprings, Tx, US 129/G5
Rockstone, Guy. 153/G3
Rockville, In, US 130/C4
Rockville Centre, NY, US 139/L9
Rockwall, Tx, US 129/H4
Rockwood, Tn, US 133/G3
Rocky (mtn.), Ky, US 130/D4
Rocky (mts.), Can.,US 119/E4
Rocky (riv.), SAfr. 106/C4
Rocky, NY, US 139/F1
Rocky Cape NP, Austl. 115/C4
Rocky Harbour, Nf, Can. 131/K1
Rocky Island (lake), Can. 130/D2
Rocky Mount, NC, US 133/J3
Rocky Mountain House, Ab, Can. 126/D2
Rocky Mountain NP, Co, US 128/F2
Rocky Mountain NP, Co, US 137/A1
Rodach (riv.), Ger. 55/E2
Rodach bei Coburg, Ger. 54/D2
Rodalben, Ger. 53/G5
Rødberg, Nor. 38/C1
Rødbyhavn, Den. 38/D4
Roddickton, Nf, Can. 131/K1
Rödental, Ger. 54/D2
Roden (riv.), Eng, UK 35/F6
Rodenbach, Ger. 54/C2
Rodeo, Mex. 142/D3
Rodeo, Ca, US 135/K10
Rödermark, Ger. 54/B3
Rodewisch, Ger. 55/F1
Rodez, Fr. 42/E4
Rodholívos, Gre. 47/H2
Ródhos (ruin), Gre. 90/B2
Ródhos (Rhodes), Gre. 90/B2
Rodigo, It. 58/D1
Roding (riv.), Eng, UK 30/D2
Roding, Ger. 55/E2
Rodinga (mt.), Austl. 113/G3
Rödinghausen, Ger. 51/F4
Rodnei (mts.), Rom. 49/G2
Rodney (cape), Ak, US 134/E3
Rodoč, Bosn. 47/E1
Rodolfo Sánchez Toboada, Mex. 142/A2
Rodríguez, Uru. 159/K11
Roe (riv.), NI, UK 34/B2
Roebourne, Austl. 109/A3
Roebuck (bay), Austl. 109/B2
Roeland Park, Ks, US 137/D5
Roermond, Neth. 50/D6
Roes Welcome Sound (str.), NW, Can. 123/H2
Roeselare, Belg. 52/C2
Roesiger (lake), Wa, US 135/D2
Rogagua (lake), Bol. 150/E6
Rogaška Slatina, Slov. 43/B3
Rogatec, Slov. 40/B2
Rogers (mt.), Va, US 130/D4
Rogers City, Mi, US 130/D2
Rogersville, Tn, US 133/H3
Roggwil, Swi. 56/D3
Rogliano, It. 46/E3
Rognon, Fr. 56/B2
Rogozno, Pol. 41/J2
Rogue (riv.), Or, US 128/B2
Rohl (riv.), Sudan 104/B3
Rohr, Ger. 55/E5
Rohrbach bei Mattersburg, Aus. 43/M3
Rohrbach in Oberösterreich, Aus. 55/G5
Rohrbach-lès-Bitche, Fr. 53/G5
Rohri, Pak. 89/J3
Röhrmoos, Ger. 55/E6
Rohtak, India 84/C2
Roi Et, Thai. 78/C2
Roine (lake), Fin. 39/L1
Roissy, Fr. 30/K5
Roissy-en-France, Fr. 30/K4
Rojas, Arg. 158/E3
Rojo (cape), PR 141/M8
Rojo, Cabo (cape), Mex. 144/A3
Rokan (riv.), Indo. 80/B3
Rokel (riv.), SLeo. 102/C4
Rokkasho, Japan 76/B3
Rokkō-san (peak), Japan 77/A3
Rokugō, Japan 77/J5
Rokycany, Czh. 55/H2
Rokytka (riv.), Czh. 55/H2
Rolampont, Fr. 56/B2

Rolândia, Braz. 155/B2
Rolava (riv.), Czh. 55/F2
Rolde, Neth. 50/D3
Rolla, ND, US 127/J3
Rolla, BC, Can. 126/C2
Rolla, Mo, US 129/K3
Rolle, Swi. 56/C4
Rolling Fork, Ms, US 129/K4
Rolling Hills Estates, Ca, US 136/F8
Rolling Meadows, Il, US 135/P15
Rollingbay, Wa, US 135/A2
Rollinsville, Co, US 137/A3
Rolo, It. 59/D3
Rom (peak), Ugan. 104/B2
Roma (Rome) (cap.), It. 46/C2
Roma, Swe. 38/H3
Roma, Austl. 114/C4
Romagnano Sesia, It. 58/B1
Romagnat, Fr. 42/E4
Romain (cape), SC, US 133/J3
Romaine (riv.), Qu, Can. 123/K3
Roman, Bul. 47/H1
Roman, Rom. 49/H2
Romang (str.), Indo. 81/G5
Romang (isl.), Indo. 81/G5
Romania (ctry.) 27/G4
Romano Canavese, It. 58/A2
Romano, Cayo (isl.), Cuba 145/G3
Romano di Lombardia, It. 58/C1
Romans d'Isonzo, It. 59/G1
Romans-sur-Isère, Fr. 42/F4
Romanzof (cape), Ak, US 134/E3
Rombas, Fr. 53/F5
Romblon, Phil. 81/F1
Rome, NY, US 130/F3
Rome, Ga, US 133/G3
Rome, Wi, US 135/N14
Romeny, Fr. 56/B4
Romeoville, Il, US 135/P16
Römhild, Ger. 54/D2
Romilly-sur-Seine, Fr. 42/E2
Rommani, Mor. 98/D2
Rommerskirchen, Ger. 53/D1
Romney Marsh (phys. reg.), Eng, UK 33/G4
Romny, Ukr. 62/E2
Romodan, Ukr. 62/E2
Romoland, Ca, US 136/C3
Romont, Fr. 56/C4
Romorantin-Lanthenay, Fr. 42/D3
Romsey, Eng, UK 33/E5
Rømskog, Nor. 38/D2
Ronald Reagan Washington National (int'l arpt.), DC, US 138/A6
Ronan, Mt, US 126/E3
Roncade, It. 59/F1
Roncador Cay (isl.), Col. 141/F5
Roncador, Serra do (mts.), Braz. 151/H6
Ronchamp, Fr. 56/C2
Ronchi dei Legionari (int'l arpt.), It. 59/G1
Ronchi dei Legionari, It. 59/G1
Ronciglione, It. 46/C1
Ronco (riv.), It. 59/F5
Ronco All'Adige, It. 59/E1
Ronco Scrivia, It. 58/B3
Roncoferraro, It. 58/D2
Roncq, Fr. 52/C2
Ronda, Sp. 44/C4
Rondane NP, Nor. 37/D3
Ronde, Tête (peak), Fr. 56/D5
Ronde (riv.), Fr. 30/K5
Rondônia (state), Braz. 150/F6
Rondonópolis, Braz. 151/H7
Rong (riv.), China 83/J2
Rong Xian, China 83/K3
Rongcheng, China 73/B4
Rongcheng, China 72/G7
Rongelap (isl.), Mrsh. 116/F3
Rongerik (isl.), Mrsh. 116/F3
Ronge (lake), Sk, Can. 122/F3
Ronkonkoma, NY, US 139/F2
Rønne, Den. 38/E4
Ronne Ice Shelf, Ant. 160/W
Ronneby, Swe. 38/F3
Ronnenberg, Ger. 51/G4
Ronse, Belg. 52/C2
Roodepoort, SAfr. 106/P13
Roosendaal, Neth. 50/B5
Roosevelt (canal), Az, US 137/S19
Roosevelt (riv.), Braz. 147/D3
Roosevelt (isl.), Ant. 160/N
Roosevelt, NY, US 139/F2
Root (mt.), Ak, US 134/L4
Root, West Branch (riv.), Wi, US 135/P14

Rosa Punta (pt.), Mex. 142/D3
Rosa Zárate, Ecu. 152/B3
Rosablanche (peak), Swi. 56/D5
Rosal, Sp. 44/A2
Rosales, Mex. 132/B4
Rosamorada, Mex. 142/D4
Rosanna (riv.), Aus. 57/G3
Rosário, Braz. 154/A1
Rosario, Mex. 142/D4
Rosario, Mex. 142/D4
Rosario, Arg. 158/E3
Rosario, Uru. 159/K11
Rosario de la Frontera, Arg. 157/D2
Rosario del Tala, Arg. 159/J10
Rosarito, Mex. 132/C4
Rosarno, It. 46/D3
Rosas, Col. 152/B4
Rosas, Golfo di (gulf), Sp. 45/G1
Rosate, It. 58/C2
Rosay, Fr. 30/G5
Rosbach vor der Höhe, Ger. 54/B2
Rosche, Ger. 51/H3
Roscommon, Ire. 31/P10
Roscoff, Fr. 42/B2
Roscrea, Ire. 31/Q10
Rosdorf, Ger. 51/G5
Rose (pt.), Can. 134/M4
Rose (isl.), ASam. 107/T15
Rose Belle, Mrts. 107/T15
Roseau, Mn, US 127/K3
Roseau (riv.), Mn, US 127/J3
Roseaux, Haiti 145/H2
Rosebery, Austl. 115/C4
Rosebud, Or, US 126/C5
Rosedale, It. 59/G1
Rosedale, Il, US 137/F7
Rosedale, Md, US 138/B5
Rosehearty, Sc, UK 36/D1
Roseland, NJ, US 139/H8
Roselette, Aiguille de (peak), Fr. 56/C6
Roselle, Il, US 135/P16
Roselle Park, NJ, US 139/H9
Rosemead, Ca, US 136/F7
Rosemère, Qu, Can. 131/N6
Rosenberg, Tx, US 129/J5
Rosenberg, Ger. 57/E1
Rosenhayn, NJ, US 138/C5
Rosenheim, Ger. 43/K3
Roses, Sp. 45/G1
Roseto, Pa, US 138/C2
Roseto degli Abruzzi, It. 43/L5
Rosetown, Sk, Can. 126/G3
Rosetta (riv.), Egypt 91/B4
Roseville, Mi, US 135/G6
Roseville, Il, US 137/G8
Rosh Ha'ayin, Isr. 91/F7
Rosh Hakarmel (pt.), Isr. 91/F6
Rosh Haniqra (pt.), Isr. 91/D3
Rosheim, Fr. 56/D1
Rosières-en-Santerre, Fr. 52/B4
Rosignano Marittimo, It. 58/D6
Roșiori de Vede, Rom. 49/G3
Roskilde, Den. 38/E4
Roskilde (co.), Den. 38/D4
Roslavl', Rus. 62/E1
Roslev, Den. 38/C3
Rosmalen, Neth. 50/C5
Rosmaninhal, Port. 44/B3
Rosneath, Sc, UK 36/B4
Rosny-sous-Bois, Fr. 30/K5
Rosolina, It. 59/F2
Rosolini, It. 46/D4
Rosporden, Fr. 42/B3
Ross, Austl. 115/C4
Ross (pt.), Can. 127/J2
Ross (isl.), Ant. 160/N
Ross (sea), Ant. 160/P
Ross (isl.), Sc, UK 36/C1
Ross Ice Shelf, Ant. 160/N
Rossa, It. 43/K3
Rossa, Swi. 57/E4
Rossall (pt.), Eng, UK 35/E4
Rossano Stazione, It. 46/E3
Rossano Veneto, It. 59/E1
Rossbach, Ger. 55/F5
Rossberg (peak), Ger. 56/D2
Rossdorf, Ger. 54/B3
Rossel (isl.), PNG 116/E6
Rosselange, Fr. 53/F5
Rosshaupten, Ger. 57/G2
Rossignol (lake), Can. 131/H2
Rosslare, Ire. 31/P9
Rossland, BC, Can. 126/D3
Rosso, Mrta. 102/B2
Rossosh', Rus. 62/F2
Rosstock (mt.), Swi. 57/E4
Rosstal, Ger. 54/D3
Rossville, Ok, US 137/N14
Rost, Nor. 37/E2
Rosthern, Sk, Can. 127/J3
Rostock, Ger. 38/E4
Rostock (reg.), Ger. 38/E4
Rostov, Rus. 62/G1
Rostov (int'l arpt.), Rus. 62/F2
Rostov Oblast, Rus. 60/H4
Rostov-na-Donu, Rus. 62/F2
Rostrenen, Fr. 42/B2
Rostrevor, NI, UK 34/B3
Roswell, NM, US 129/F4
Roswell, Ga, US 133/G3
Rota, Sp. 44/B4
Rota (isl.), NMar. 116/D3
Rote Wand (peak), Aus. 57/G3
Rotenburg an der Fulda, Ger. 51/G7

Roter Main (riv.), Ger. 40/F3
Rötgen, Ger. 53/F2
Roth (riv.), Ger. 57/G1
Roth bei Nürnberg, Ger. 54/E4
Rothaargebirge (mts.), Ger. 51/F6
Rothau, Fr. 56/D1
Röthenbach an der Pegnitz, Ger. 54/E4
Rothenberg, Ger. 54/B3
Rothenburg, Swi. 57/E3
Rothenburg ob der Tauber, Ger. 54/D4
Rothera, UK, Ant. 160/V
Rotherham, Eng, UK 35/G5
Rothes, Sc, UK 36/C1
Rothesay, Sc, UK 36/A5
Rotheux-Rimière, Belg. 53/E2
Rothschild, Wi, US 127/L4
Rothwell, Eng, UK 33/F2
Rothwell, Eng, UK 35/G4
Roti (isl.), Indo. 81/F6
Rotorua, NZ 117/T10
Rotselaar, Belg. 53/D2
Rott (riv.), Ger. 40/G4
Rott am Inn, Ger. 55/F7
Rottach-Egern, Ger. 40/F5
Rotte (riv.), Fr. 53/F6
Rotten (riv.), Swi. 56/E5
Rottenacker, Ger. 57/F1
Röttenbach, Ger. 54/E4
Rottenberg, Ger. 54/C2
Rottenburg am Neckar, Ger. 54/B6
Rottenburg an der Laaber, Ger. 55/F5
Rotterdam (int'l arpt.), Neth. 50/B5
Rotterdam, Neth. 50/B5
Rotthalmünster, Ger. 55/G6
Röttingen, Ger. 54/C3
Rottne, Swe. 38/F3
Rottnest (isl.), Austl. 112/B5
Rottofreno, It. 58/C2
Rottum (riv.), Ger. 57/F1
Rottumeroog (isl.), Neth. 50/D1
Rottumerplaat (isl.), Neth. 50/D1
Rottweil, Ger. 57/E1
Rotuma (isl.), Fiji 116/G6
Rötz, Ger. 55/F4
Roubaix, Fr. 52/C2
Roubion (riv.), Fr. 42/F4
Roudnice nad Labem, Czh. 55/H2
Rouen, Fr. 42/D2
Rouffach, Fr. 56/D2
Rouge (riv.), Qu, Can. 123/J4
Rouge, Middle (riv.), Mi, US 135/F7
Rougemont, Fr. 56/C3
Rougemont-le-Château, Fr. 56/C2
Rough (riv.), Ky, US 133/G2
Roullet-Saint-Estèphe, Fr. 42/D4
Round (hill), Pa, US 138/B3
Round Hill (pt.), Austl. 114/C4
Round Lake, Il, US 135/P15
Round Lake Beach, Il, US 135/P15
Round Lake Park, Il, US 135/P15
Round Rock, Tx, US 129/H5
Round Valley (res.), NJ, US 138/D2
Roundup, Mt, US 126/F4
Roundway (hill), Eng, UK 32/E4
Rousay (isl.), Sc, UK 31/V14
Rousies, Fr. 52/D3
Rousínov, Czh. 41/J4
Roussillon, Fr. 42/F4
Rouvres, Fr. 30/M4
Rouvroy, Belg. 53/E4
Rouxville, SAfr. 106/D3
Rouyn-Noranda, Qu, Can. 130/E1
Rovaniemi, Fin. 60/E2
Rovaniemi (int'l arpt.), Fin. 60/E2
Rovasenda, It. 58/B1
Rovato, It. 58/C1
Roverbella, It. 59/D2
Rovereto, It. 59/D3
Rovereto, It. 57/H6
Rovigo (prov.), It. 59/E2
Rovigo, It. 59/E2
Rovinj, Cro. 59/G2
Rovuma (riv.), Moz. 104/B5
Rowley (isl.), NW, Can. 123/J2
Rowley Shoals (isl.), Austl. 109/A2
Roxa (isl.), GBis. 102/B4
Roxana, Il, US 137/G8
Roxas, Phil. 81/E1
Roxas, Phil. 81/F1
Roxas, Phil. 79/D4
Roxboro, NC, US 130/E4
Roxen (lake), Swe. 38/F2
Roxo (cape), Sen. 102/A3
Roy, NM, US 132/B3
Roy, Ut, US 137/J11
Roy, Wa, US 135/B3
Roya (riv.), Fr. 43/G5
Royal (canal), Ire. 35/B3
Royal Botanical Garden, On, Can. 131/Q9
Royal Chitwan NP, Nepal 85/E2
Royal Lakes, Il, US 137/H7
Royal Natal NP, SAfr. 106/E3
Royal NP, Austl. 115/D2
Royal NP, The, Austl. 114/H9
Royal Oak, Mi, US 135/F7
Royal Paekje Tombs, SKor. 73/D4
Royal Tombs, Viet. 78/D2
Royal Tunbridge Wells, Eng, UK 33/G4
Royale, Isle (isl.), Mi, US 127/L4
Royalton, Pa, US 138/B3
Royan, Fr. 42/C4
Roye, Fr. 56/C2
Roye, Fr. 52/B4
Royersford, Pa, US 138/C3
Røyken, Nor. 38/D2
Royston, Eng, UK 33/F2
Royston, Eng, UK 35/G4
Royton, Eng, UK 35/F4
Rožaj, Yugo. 47/G1
Rozay-en-Brie, Fr. 52/B6
Rozenburg, Neth. 50/B5
Rozhaya (riv.), Rus. 61/W9
Rožmberk (lake), Czh. 55/H4
Rožmital pod Třemšínem, Czh. 55/G3
Rožňava, Slvk. 41/L4
Roztoczański NP, Pol. 62/B2
Roztoczański PN, Pol. 41/M3
Roztoky, Czh. 55/H2
Rozzano, It. 58/C2
Rrëshen, Alb. 47/F2
Rt Kamenjak (cape), Cro. 48/A3
Rt Ploča (pt.), Cro. 48/B4
Rtishchevo, Rus. 63/G1
Ruacana (falls), Ang. 105/B4
Ruaha NP, Tanz. 104/B4
Ruaha NP, Tanz. 105/F2
Ruapehu (vol.), NZ 117/T10
Rub' al Khali (des.), SAr. 67/D7
Rubelles, Fr. 30/L6
Rubeshibe, Japan 76/C2
Rubí, Sp. 45/L7
Rubidoux, Ca, US 136/C3
Rubiera, It. 59/D3
Rubigen, Swi. 56/D4
Rubim, Braz. 154/B5
Rubizhne, Ukr. 62/F2
Rubondo NP, Tanz. 104/A3
Řubřina (riv.), Czh. 55/G4
Ruby, Ak, US 134/G3
Ruby (lake), Nv, US 128/D2
Ruby (mts.), Nv, US 128/D2
Rubyvale, Austl. 114/B3
Rucheng, China 79/B2
Rucphen, Neth. 50/B5
Ruda Woda (lake), Pol. 41/K2
Rudall River NP, Austl. 112/D2
Rūdarpur, India 84/D2
Rudauli, India 84/C2
Rüdersdorf, Ger. 40/Q7
Rüdesheim, Ger. 53/G4
Rudiano, It. 58/C2
Rudkøbing, Den. 38/D4
Rudnik, Pol. 41/M3
Rūdnyy, Kaz. 61/P5
Rudolf (isl.), Rus. 64/F1
Rudolstadt, Ger. 43/J1
Rudong, China 72/E4
Rūdsar, Iran 88/F1
Rue, Swi. 56/C4
Rue (pt.), NI, UK 34/B1
Rue, Fr. 52/A3
Rueda, Sp. 44/C2
Rueil-Malmaison, Fr. 30/J5
Ruell (riv.), Sc, UK 36/A4
Ruelle-sur-Touvre, Fr. 42/D4
Ruen (peak), Bul. 48/F4
Ruetzbach (riv.), Aus. 57/H3
Ruffano, It. 47/F3
Ruffec, Fr. 42/D3
Rufiji (riv.), Tanz. 93/F5
Rufina, It. 59/E5
Rufino, Arg. 158/E2
Rufisque, Sen. 102/A3
Rugao, China 72/E4
Rugby, ND, US 127/J3
Rugby, Eng, UK 33/E2
Rugeley, Eng, UK 33/E1
Rügen (isl.), Ger. 38/E4
Ruggell, Lcht. 57/F3
Ruhmannsfelden, Ger. 55/F5
Ruhnu saar (isl.), Lat. 39/K3
Ruhr (riv.), Ger. 40/D3
Ruhr (reg.), Ger. 40/E3
Ruhrgebiet (phys. reg.), Ger. 50/D6
Ruhstorf an der Rott, Ger. 55/F5
Rui'an, China 79/D2
Ruicheng, China 72/B4
Ruidoso, NM, US 129/F4
Ruinen, Neth. 50/D3
Ruiselede, Belg. 52/C1
Ruiz, Mex. 142/D4
Rujen (peak), Macd. 47/H1
Ruki (riv.), D.R. Congo 93/D5
Rukwa (pol. reg.), Tanz. 104/B4
Rukwa (lake), Tanz. 93/F5
Rulles (riv.), Belg. 53/E4
Rülzheim, Ger. 54/B4
Rum, Aus. 57/H3
Rum Cay (isl.), Bahm. 141/G3
Ruma, Yugo. 48/D3
Ruma NP, Kenya 104/B3
Rumbek, Sudan 97/L6
Rumes, Belg. 52/C2
Rumford, Me, US 131/G2
Rumia, Pol. 38/H4
Rumilly, Fr. 56/B6
Rümlang, Swi. 57/E3
Rumoi, Japan 76/B2
Rumphi, Malw. 104/B5
Rumson, NJ, US 138/E3
Rumst, Belg. 53/D1
Rumuruti, Kenya 104/C2
Runabay (pt.), NI, UK 34/B1
Runan, China 72/C4
Runcorn, Eng, UK 35/F5
Runding, Ger. 55/F4
Rundu, Namb. 105/C4
Rungwa (riv.), Tanz. 104/B4
Rungwa Game Rsv., Tanz. 104/B4
Rungwe (peak), Tanz. 104/B5
Runkel, Ger. 54/B2
Runn (lake), Swe. 38/F1
Runnemede, NJ, US 138/C4
Running Springs, Ca, US 136/C2
Ruo (riv.), China 65/K5
Ruokolahti, Fin. 39/N1
Ruoqiang, China 70/E4
Rupat (isl.), Indo. 80/B3
Rupea, Rom. 49/G2
Rupel (riv.), Belg. 53/D1
Rupert (riv.), Qu, Can. 123/J3
Rūpnagar, India 86/D4
Ruppichteroth, Ger. 53/G2
Rupt-sur-Moselle, Fr. 56/C2
Rupununi (riv.), Guy. 153/G4
Rur (riv.), Ger. 40/D3
Rur-Strasse (lake), Ger. 53/F2
Rurrenabaque, Bol. 150/E6
Rurutu (isl.), FrPol. 117/K7
Rusape, Zim. 105/F4
Rüschegg, Swi. 56/D4
Rüschlikon, Swi. 57/E3
Ruscom (riv.), On, Can. 135/G7
Ruse (pol. reg.), Bul. 47/K1
Ruse, Bul. 49/G4
Rusera, India 85/F3
Rush (lake), Ut, US 137/J13
Rush, Ire. 34/B4
Rushan, China 72/E3
Rushden, Eng, UK 33/F2
Rushville, In, US 130/C4
Rusk, Tx, US 129/J5
Russ, Fr. 56/D1
Russ Lake Nat'l Rec. Area, Wa, US 126/C3
Russbach (riv.), Aus. 49/N7
Russel (lake), Can. 127/H1
Russell, Mb, Can. 127/H3
Russell (lake), US 133/H3
Russell (isl.), NW, Can. 123/S7
Russell (isls.), Austl. 114/F7
Russell Gulch, Co, US 137/A3
Russellville, Al, US 133/G3
Russellville, Ar, US 129/J4
Russellville, Ky, US 130/C4
Rüsselsheim, Ger. 54/B3
Russi, It. 59/F4
Russia (ctry.) 70/F1
Russian (riv.), Ca, US 128/B3
Russian Mission, Ak, US 134/F3
Russkaya, Rus., Ant. 160/Q
Rust'avi, Geo. 63/H4
Rustenburg, SAfr. 105/E6
Ruston, La, US 129/J4
Ruston, Wa, US 135/C3
Rute, Sp. 44/C4
Ruteng, Indo. 81/F5
Rüthen, Ger. 51/F6
Rutherford, NJ, US 139/J8
Rutherglen, Sc, UK 36/B5
Rüthi, Swi. 57/F3
Ruthin, Wal, UK 35/E5
Ruthven, On, Can. 135/G7
Rüti, Swi. 57/E3
Rüti, Swi. 57/F4
Rutland, Vt, US 130/F3
Rutland Water (res.), Eng, UK 33/F1
Rutog, China 70/C5
Rutshuru (riv.), D.R. Congo 104/A3
Ruukki, Fin. 60/E2
Ruurlo, Neth. 50/D4
Ruvo di Puglia, It. 46/E2
Ruvu (riv.), Tanz. 104/C4
Ruvubu (riv.), Buru. 104/A3
Ruvuma (pol. reg.), Tanz. 104/C5
Ruvuma (riv.), Moz.,Tanz 104/B5
Ruwāndūz, Iraq 90/F2
Ruwenzori (range), Ugan. 104/A2
Ruwenzori NP, Ugan. 104/A3
Ruy Barbosa, Braz. 154/B4
Ruyang, China 72/C4
Ruzayevka, Rus. 63/H1
Ruzizi (riv.), D.R. Congo 104/A3
Ružomberok, Slvk. 41/K4
Ruzyně (int'l arpt.), Czh. 55/H2
Rwanda (ctry.) 93/F5
Ryan (mt.), Austl. 115/D2
Ryan (mt.), Austl. 114/A1
Ryan (inlet), Sc, UK 34/C2
Ryazan', Rus. 63/G1
Ryazan', Rus. 60/H5
Ryazhsk, Rus. 62/G1
Rybachiy (pen.), Rus. 37/K1
Rybinsk, Rus. 60/H4
Rybinsk (res.), Rus. 27/J2
Rybnik, Pol. 41/K3
Rycroft, Ab, Can. 126/D2
Ryd, Swe. 38/F3
Rydaholm, Swe. 38/F3
Ryde, Eng, UK 33/E5
Ryde, Ca, US 135/L10
Rydet, Swe. 38/D3
Rye (bay), Eng, UK 33/G5
Rye, Eng, UK 33/G5
Rye, NY, US 139/L8
Rye (riv.), Eng, UK 35/H3
Rye Brook, NY, US 139/L7
Rye Patch (res.), Nv, US 128/C2
Rygge, Nor. 38/D2
Ryki, Pol. 41/L3
Rylstone, Austl. 115/D2
Ryn-Peski (plain), Kaz. 63/J2
Ryōkami, Japan 77/B2
Ryōtsu, Japan 75/F1
Ryōzen-yama (peak), Japan 77/K5
Rypin, Pol. 41/K2
Rysy (peak), Pol. 41/L4
Ryton, Eng, UK 35/G2
Rytterknægten (peak), Den. 38/F4
Ryūgasaki, Japan 75/G3
Ryukyu (isls.), Japan 67/M7
Ryūō, Japan 77/B2
Ryūō, Japan 77/K5
Rzeszów (prov.), Pol. 41/M3
Rzeszów, Pol. 41/M3
Rzhev, Rus. 60/G4

S

S. Aust., Austl. 115/B2
's-Graveland, Neth. 50/C4
's Gravendeel, Neth. 50/B5
's Heerenberg, Neth. 50/D5
's Hertogenbosch, Neth. 50/C5
Sa Dec, Viet. 78/D4
Saab (int'l arpt.), Swe. 38/F2
Sääksjärvi (lake), Fin. 39/K1
Saal an der Donau, Ger. 55/E5
Saalbach (riv.), Ger. 54/B4
Saaldorf, Ger. 55/E2
Saale (riv.), Ger. 40/F3
Saales, Col de (pass), Fr. 56/D1
Saalfeld, Ger. 43/J1
Saalfelden am Steinernen Meer, Aus. 43/K3
Saane (riv.), Swi. 56/D5
Saanen, Swi. 56/D5
Saanta (peak), Kenya 104/C2
Saar (riv.), Ger. 53/F5
Saarbrücken, Ger. 53/F5
Saarburg, Ger. 53/F4
Saaremaa (isl.), Est. 60/D4
Saarland (state), Ger. 43/G2
Saarlouis, Ger. 53/F5
Saas, Swi. 57/F4
Saas Fee, Swi. 56/D5
Saastal (valley), Swi. 56/D5
Sab (riv.), Camb. 78/D3
Saba (isl.), NAnt. 141/N8
Šabac, Yugo. 48/D3
Sabadell, Sp. 45/L6
Sabae, Japan 74/E3
Sabah (reg.), Malay. 67/L9
Sabalgarh, India 84/A2
Sabana (arch.), Bang. 145/F1
Sabana de Uchire, Ven. 153/E2
Sabanalarga, Col. 152/C3
Sabanalarga, Col. 152/C2
Sabancuy, Mex. 144/D2
Sabaneta, Ven. 152/D2
Sabang, Indo. 80/A2
Sabanita, Pan. 145/G4
Sabasţīyah, WBnk. 91/G7
Sabat (riv.), Sudan 93/F4
Sabbio Chiese, It. 58/D1
Sabbioneta, It. 58/D3
Sabhā, Libya 96/H2
Sabie (riv.), Moz. 107/F2
Sabinal, Cayo (isl.), Cuba 145/G1
Sabiñánigo, Sp. 45/E1
Sabinas, Mex. 132/C5
Sabinas (riv.), Mex. 140/A2
Sabinas Hidalgo, Mex. 132/C5
Sabine (lake), US 129/J5
Sabine (riv.), La, US 140/C1
Sabinópolis, Braz. 155/D1
Sabkhat al Bardawīl (lag.), Egypt 91/C4
Sabkhat al Jabbūl (lake), Syria 90/D3
Sabkhat al Mūḩ (lake), Syria 90/D3
Sablayan, Phil. 81/F1
Sable (isl.), Can. 131/K3
Sable (cape), Can. 131/H3
Sablé-sur-Sarthe, Fr. 42/C3
Saboeiro, Braz. 154/C2
Sabor (riv.), Port. 44/B2
Sabra (cape), Indo. 81/H4
Sabrina (coast), Ant. 160/J
Sabugal, Port. 44/B2
Sabzevār, Iran 89/G1
Sacajawea (peak), Or, US 126/D4
Sácama, Col. 152/C3
Sacaton, Az, US 137/S19
Sacavém, Port. 45/P10
Saccarello (peak), It. 58/A4
Sacco (riv.), It. 46/C2
Sacedón, Sp. 44/D2
Săcele, Rom. 49/G3
Sachigo (lake), Can. 127/K2
Sachigo (riv.), On, Can. 122/G3
Sachs Harbour, NW, Can. 122/D1
Sachseln, Swi. 57/E4
Sachsen (state), Ger. 40/G3
Sachsen-Anhalt (state), Ger. 40/F3
Sachsenbrunn, Ger. 54/D2
Sachsenhagen, Ger. 51/G4
Sacile, It. 59/F1
Säckingen, Ger. 56/D2
Sackville, NB, Can. 131/H2
Saclay, Fr. 30/J5
Saco, Me, US 131/G3
Sacramento (cap.), Ca, US 128/B3
Sacramento, Braz. 155/C1
Sacramento (valley), Ca, US 128/B3
Sacramento (riv.), Ca, US 124/B4
Sacramento (mts.), NM, US 124/E5
Sacramento (co.), Ca, US 135/M10
Sacramento, Pampa del (plain), Peru 156/C2
Sacramento River Deep Water Ship Canal, Ca, US 135/L10
Sacratif (cape), Sp. 44/D4
Sacred (falls), Hi, US 124/W12
Sacro (peak), It. 46/E2
Sacro Monte, It. 58/B1
Sada, SAfr. 106/D4
Sádaba, Sp. 44/E1
Sadābād, India 84/B2
Sa'dah, Yem. 88/D5
Saddam (int'l arpt.), Iraq 90/F3
Saddle (hills), Can. 126/C2
Saddle (riv.), NJ, US 139/J8
Saddle Brook, NJ, US 139/J8
Saddle River, NJ, US 139/J7
Saddle Rock, NY, US 139/K8
Saddle, The (peak), Sc, UK 36/A2
Saddleworth, Austl. 113/H5
Sādhaura, India 86/D4
Sādiqābād, Pak. 89/K3
Sado (isl.), Japan 71/Q4
Sado (riv.), Port. 44/A3
Sadovo, Bul. 47/J1
Sadowara, Japan 74/B4
Sādri, India 89/K3
Sadripante (mt.), Phil. 81/F1
Sadulshahar, India 86/C5
Saerbeck, Ger. 51/E4
Saeul, Lux. 53/E4
Safājah (well), Egypt 101/C3
Safāqis, Tun. 96/H1
Safāqis (gov.), Tun. 99/H2
Safed Koh (range), Pak. 86/A3
Saffānīyah, Ra's as (pt.), SAr. 88/E3
Saffig, Ger. 53/G3
Säffle, Swe. 38/E2
Safford, Az, US 128/E4
Saffron Walden, Eng, UK 33/G2
Safi (cape), Mor. 98/C2
Safi, Mor. 98/C2
Safīd (riv.), Afg. 89/J1
Safid Khers (mts.), Afg. 89/K1
Safid Kūh (mts.), Afg. 89/H2
Safidon, India 86/D5
Safien, Swi. 57/F4
Safīpur, India 84/C2
Şāfītā, Syria 91/E2
Safonovo, Rus. 60/G5
Safranbolu, Turk. 62/E4
Sag Harbor, NY, US 139/F2
Saga (pref.), Japan 74/A4
Saga, China 85/E1
Saga, Japan 74/B4
Sagae, Japan 76/B4
Sagaing (div.), Myan. 70/F7
Sagaing, Myan. 83/G3
Sagaing (state), Myan. 83/F3
Sagami (sea), Japan 75/F3
Sagami (riv.), Japan 77/C2
Sagami (lake), Japan 77/C2
Sagami (bay), Japan 77/C3
Sagamihara, Japan 75/F3
Sagamiko, Japan 77/C2
Sagamore Hill Nat'l Hist. Site, NY, US 139/M8
Sāgar, India 84/B4
Sagard, Ger. 38/E4
Sagarmatha (zone), Nepal 85/F2
Sagarmatha (Everest) (mtn.), China,Nepa 85/F2
Sagarmatha NP, Nepal 85/F2
Sagauli, India 85/E2
Sagavanirktok (riv.), Ak, US 134/J2
Sagay, Phil. 81/F1
Saggart, Ire. 34/B5
Saginaw, Mi, US 130/D3
Saginaw (bay), Mi, US 130/D3
Saglek (bay), Nf, Can. 123/K3
Sagone, Golfe de (gulf), Fr. 46/A1
Sagter Ems (riv.), Ger. 51/E2
Sagua de Tánamo, Cuba 145/H1
Sagua la Grande, Cuba 145/F1
Saguaro NP, Az, US 128/E4
Saguenay (riv.), Can. 131/G1
Saguia el Hamra (riv.), WSah. 96/C2
Sagunto, Sp. 45/E3
Sagy, Fr. 30/H4
Sa'gya, China 85/G1
Sagyz (riv.), Kaz. 63/K2
Saḩāb, Jor. 91/D4
Sahagún, Sp. 44/C1
Sahagún, Col. 152/C2
Sahagún, Mex. 143/L7
Saḩam, Jor. 91/D3
Sahand (mtn.), Iran 88/E1
Sahara (des.), Afr. 93/B2
Sahāranpur, India 86/D5
Saharsa, India 85/F3
Sahaspur, India 84/B1
Sahaswān, India 84/B1
Sahavato, Madg. 107/J8
Sahāwar, India 84/B2
Sahel (riv.), Alg. 100/H4
Sāhibganj, India 85/F3
Şahinli, Turk. 49/H5
Sāhīwāl, Pak. 86/B4
Sahiwal, Pak. 86/B4
Şaḩrā Marzūq (des.), Libya 96/H3
Şaḩrā' Rabyānah (des.), Libya 97/K3
Sahrho, Jebel (mts.), Mor. 98/D3
Sahuaripa, Mex. 142/C2
Sahuayo de Morelos, Mex. 142/E4
Šahy, Slvk. 41/K4
Sai (canal), India 82/D2
Sai Yok NP, Thai. 78/B3
Saïda, Alg. 100/F5
Saidpur, Bang. 85/G3
Saidpur, India 84/D3
Saignelégier, Swi. 56/D3
Saigō, Japan 74/C2
Saigon, Viet. 78/D4
Saijō, Japan 74/C4
Saikai NP, Japan 74/A4
Saiki, Japan 74/B4
Sailly, Fr. 30/H4
Sailly-sur-la-Lys, Fr. 52/B2
Sailu, India 89/L5
Saimaa (lake), Fin. 37/J3
Sain Alto, Mex. 142/E4
Sainghin-en-Weppes, Fr. 52/B2
Sains-du-Nord, Fr. 52/D3
Saint Abb's (pt.), Sc, UK 36/D5
Saint-Affrique, Fr. 42/E5
Saint Agnes (pt.), Eng, UK 32/A6
Saint Albans, WV, US 130/D4
Saint Alban's, Nf, Can. 131/L2
Saint Albans, Vt, US 130/F2
Saint Albans, Eng, UK 30/C1
Saint Albert, Ab, Can. 126/E2
Saint-Amable, Qu, Can. 131/P6
Saint-Amand-les-Eaux, Fr. 52/C3
Saint-Amand-Montrond, Fr. 42/E3
Saint-Amarin, Fr. 56/D2
Saint-Ambroise, Qu, Can. 131/G1
Saint-Amé, Fr. 56/C1
Saint-André, Reun. 107/S15
Saint-André, Fr. 52/C2
Saint-André-de-Cubzac, Fr. 42/C4
Saint-André-les-Vergers, Fr. 42/F2
Saint Andrew's (bay), Sc, UK 36/D4
Saint Andrews, Sc, UK 36/D4
Saint Ann (cape), SLeo. 102/B5
Saint Anns, On, Can. 131/Q9
Saint Ann's (pt.), Wal, UK 32/A3
Saint Ann's Bay, Jam. 141/F4
Saint Anthony, Nf, Can. 131/L1
Saint-Antoine, Qu, Can. 131/N6
Saint Arnaud, Austl. 115/B3
Saint-Arnoult-en-Yvelines, Fr. 30/H6
Saint Aubin, Chl, UK 42/B2
Saint-Aubin, Swi. 56/C4
Saint-Aubin, Fr. 56/B3
Saint-Augustin, Fr. 30/M5
Saint Augustine, Fl, US 133/H4
Saint Augustine Beach, Fl, US 133/H4
Saint Austell (bay), Eng, UK 32/B6
Saint Austell, Eng, UK 32/B6
Saint-Avé, Fr. 42/B3
Saint-Avold, Fr. 53/F5
Saint-Barthélemy (isl.), Fr. 141/N8
Saint-Barthélemy-d'Anjou, Fr. 42/C3
Saint-Barthélemy, Pic de (peak), Fr. 42/D5
Saint Bees (pt.), Eng, UK 34/E2
Saint-Benoît, Fr. 42/D3
Saint-Benoît, Reun. 107/S15
Saint-Benoît, Qu, Can. 131/M6
Saint Bernard (co.), La, US 137/Q17
Saint Bernard, La, US 137/Q17
Saint-Berthevin, Fr. 42/C2
Saint-Blaise, Swi. 56/C3
Saint-Blaise, Qu, Can. 131/P7
Saint Blaize (cape), SAfr. 106/C4
Saint Boswells, Sc, UK 36/D5
Saint-Brice-Courcelles, Fr. 52/C5
Saint-Brice-sous-Forêt, Fr. 30/K5
Saint Bride's (bay), Wal, UK 32/A3
Saint-Brieuc, Fr. 42/B2
Saint-Brieuc (bay), Fr. 42/B2
Saint-Bruno-de-Montarville, Qu, Can. 131/P6
Saint-Calais, Fr. 42/D3
Saint-Canut, Qu, Can. 131/M6
Saint Catharines, On, Can. 131/R9
Saint Catherine (mt.), Gren. 153/F1
Saint Catherine's (pt.), Eng, UK 33/E5
Saint Catherine's (hill), Eng, UK 33/E5
Saint-Céré, Fr. 42/D4
Saint-Cergue, Swi. 56/C5
Saint-Cergues, Fr. 56/C5
Saint-Chamond, Fr. 42/F4
Saint Charles, Md, US 130/E4
Saint Charles, Mo, US 137/G8
Saint Charles (co.), La, US 137/P17
Saint Charles (co.), Mo, US 137/F8
Saint Charles, Il, US 135/P16
Saint-Chély-d'Apcher, Fr. 42/E4
Saint-Chéron, Fr. 30/J6
Saint Christoffel (peak), NAnt. 152/D1
Saint Clair, Mi, US 130/D3
Saint Clair (peak), Az, US 137/S18
Saint Clair, Pa, US 138/B2
Saint Clair (lake), Can.,US 135/G7
Saint Clair (co.), Mi, US 135/G6
Saint Clair Beach, On, Can. 135/G7
Saint Clair Shores, Mi, US 135/G6
Saint-Claude, Fr. 56/B5
Saint Cloud, Mn, US 127/K4
Saint-Cloud, Fr. 30/J5
Saint-Constant, Qu, Can. 131/N7
Saint Croix (riv.), US 130/A2
Saint Croix (isl.), USVI 141/M8
Saint Cyr (mt.), Can. 134/M3
Saint-Cyr-l'école, Fr. 30/J5
Saint-Cyr-sous-Dourdan, Fr. 30/J6
Saint-Cyr-sur-Morin, Fr. 30/M5
Saint David's (pt.), Wal, UK 32/A3
Saint David's, Wal, UK 32/A3
Saint-Denis, Fr. 30/K5
Saint-Denis, Reun. 107/S15
Saint-Denis-en-Bugey, Fr. 56/B6
Saint-Dié, Fr. 56/C1
Saint-Dizier, Fr. 53/D6
Saint-Doulchard, Fr. 42/E3
Saint-édouard, Qu, Can. 131/N7
Saint Eleanors, PE, Can. 131/J2
Saint Elias (mt.), Ak, US 134/K3
Saint Elias (cape), Ak, US 134/K4
Saint Elias (mts.), Ak, US 122/B2
Saint-Éloy-les-Mines, Fr. 42/E3
Saint-Esprit, Qu, Can. 131/N6
Saint-Estève, Fr. 42/E5
Saint-Étienne, Fr. 42/F4
Saint-Étienne-au-Mont, Fr. 52/A2
Saint-Étienne-de-Baïgorry, Fr. 42/C5
Saint-Étienne-de-Tinée, Fr. 43/G4
Saint-Étienne-du-Rouvray, Fr. 42/D2
Saint-Étienne-lès-Remiremont, Fr. 56/C1
Saint-Eustache, Qu, Can. 131/N6
Saint Eustatius (isl.), NAnt. 141/N8
Saint-Fargeau-Ponthierry, Fr. 30/K6
Saint-Félicien, Qu, Can. 131/F1
Saint-Félix, Fr. 56/B6
Saint-Florent-sur-Cher, Fr. 42/E3
Saint-Florentin Fr. 42/E2
Saint-Floris, PN de, CAfr. 97/K6
Saint-Four, Fr. 42/E4
Saint Francis (riv.), Ar, US 129/K4
Saint Francis (riv.), Mo, US 133/F2
Saint Francis, Ks, US 129/G3
Saint Francis (cape), SAfr. 106/D4
Saint Francis, Wi, US 135/Q14
Saint Francisville, La, US 129/K5
Saint Francois (mts.), US 133/F2
Saint Gallen (canton), Swi. 57/F3
Saint-Gaudens, Fr. 42/D5
Saint-Genis-Pouilly, Fr. 56/C5
Saint George (isl.), Ak, US 134/E4
Saint George, Ak, US 134/E4
Saint George (pt.), Ca, US 126/B5
Saint George, SC, US 133/H3
Saint George, Ut, US 128/D3
Saint George, NB, Can. 131/H2
Saint George (cape), Can. 131/K1
Saint George, Austl. 114/C5
Saint George's (bay), Can. 131/J2
Saint George's, Nf, Can. 131/K1
Saint-Georges, Qu, Can. 131/G2
Saint George's (cap.), Gren. 153/F1
Saint Georges, De, US 138/C4
Saint George's (chan.), Ire.,UK 31/Q11
Saint-Germain, Fr. 56/C2
Saint-Germain-de-la-Grange, Fr. 30/H5
Saint-Germain-du-Bois, Fr. 56/B4
Saint-Germain-du-Corbéis, Fr. 42/D2
Saint-Germain-du-Plain, Fr. 56/A4
Saint-Germain-en-Laye, Fr. 30/J5
Saint-Germain-lès-Corbeil, Fr. 30/K6
Saint-Germain-sous Doue, Fr. 30/M5
Saint-Germain-sur-Morin, Fr. 30/L5
Saint-Germer-de-Fly, Fr. 52/A5
Saint-Gervais, Fr. 30/H4
Saint-Gervais-les-Bains, Fr. 56/C6
Saint-Ghislain, Belg. 52/C3
Saint-Gilles, Fr. 42/F5
Saint-Gilles-Croix-de-Vie, Fr. 42/C3
Saint-Gingolph, Swi. 56/C5
Saint-Girons, Fr. 42/D5
Saint-Gobain, Fr. 52/C4
Saint Govan's (pt.), Wal, UK 32/B3
Saint-Gratien, Fr. 30/J5
Saint Hedwig, Tx, US 137/U21
Saint Helena (bay), SAfr. 105/C7
Saint Helena (isl.), Austl. 114/F6
Saint Helens, Austl. 115/D4
Saint Helens (pt.), Austl. 115/D4
Saint Helens (mt.), Wa, US 126/C4
Saint Helens, Or, US 126/C4
Saint Helens, Eng, UK 35/F5
Saint Helier (cap.), Chl, UK 42/B2
Saint-Herblain, Fr. 42/C3
Saint-Hilarion, Fr. 30/H6
Saint-Hippolyte, Fr. 56/C3
Saint-Honoré, Qu, Can. 131/G1
Saint-Hubert, Qu, Can. 131/P6
Saint-Hubert, Belg. 53/E3
Saint-Hyacinthe, Qu, Can. 130/F2
Saint Ignace (isl.), Can. 127/L3
Saint Ignace, Mi, US 130/C2
Saint-Imier, Swi. 56/D3
Saint-Isidore-de-Laprairie, Qu, Can. 131/N7
Saint Ives (bay), Eng, UK 32/A6
Saint Ives, Eng, UK 33/F2
Saint Ives, Eng, UK 32/A6
Saint Jacques (int'l arpt.), Fr. 42/C2
Saint-Jacques-le-Mineur, Qu, Can. 131/P7
Saint James, NY, US 139/E2
Saint James (cape), BC, Can. 122/C3
Saint-Jean (riv.), Can. 131/H1
Saint-Jean (lake), Qu, Can. 123/J4
Saint-Jean-d'Angély, Fr. 42/C4
Saint-Jean-de-la-Ruelle, Fr. 42/D3
Saint-Jean-de-Losne, Fr. 56/B3
Saint-Jean-Port-Joli, Qu, Can. 131/G2
Saint-Jean-sur-Richelieu, Qu, Can. 130/F2
Saint-Jeoire, Fr. 56/C5
Saint-Jêrôme, Qu, Can. 131/N6
Saint Joe, La, US 137/Q16
Saint Joe (riv.), Id,Wa, US 124/C2
Saint John, NB, Can. 131/H2
Saint John (isl.), USVI 141/M8
Saint John (riv.), Me, US 123/K4
Saint John The Baptist (co.), La, US 137/P16
Saint Johns (riv.), US 133/H4
Saint Johns, Az, US 128/E4
Saint John's (cap.), Anti. 141/N8
Saint John's (pt.), NI, UK 34/C3
Saint Johnsbury, Vt, US 131/F2
Saint Jones (riv.), De, US 138/C5
Saint Joseph (riv.), US 130/C3
Saint Joseph (isl.), Can. 130/C2
Saint Joseph, La, US 129/K5
Saint Joseph, Mo, US 129/J3
Saint Joseph (lake), On, Can. 122/G3
Saint-Joseph, Reun. 107/S15
Saint-Juéry, Fr. 42/E5
Saint-Julien, Fr. 56/B3
Saint-Julien-en-Genevois, Fr. 56/C5
Saint-Julien-les-Villas, Fr. 42/F2
Saint-Junien, Fr. 42/D4
Saint-Just-en-Chaussée, Fr. 52/B4
Saint Kilda (isl.), UK 31/P8
Saint Kitts (isl.), StK. 141/J4
Saint Kitts and Nevis (ctry.) 119/L8
Saint-Lambert, Qu, Can. 131/P6
Saint Laurent, Mb, Can. 127/J3
Saint-Laurent (riv.), Can. 131/G1
Saint-Laurent, Qu, Can. 131/N6
Saint-Laurent-Blangy, Fr. 52/B3
Saint-Laurent-de-Cerdans, Fr. 42/E5
Saint-Laurent du Maroni, FrG. 151/H2
Saint-Laurent-en-Grandvaux, Fr. 56/B4
Saint-Laurent-sur-Saône, Fr. 56/A5
Saint Lawrence, Nf, Can. 131/L2
Saint Lawrence (riv.), US,Can. 130/F2
Saint Lawrence, Pa, US 138/C3
Saint Lawrence (isl.), Ak, US 119/A3
Saint Lawrence (gulf), Can. 119/L5
Saint Lawrence Islands NP, Can. 130/E2
Saint-Lazare, Qu, Can. 131/M7
Saint-Léger, Belg. 53/E4
Saint-Léger-en-Yvelines, Fr. 30/H5
Saint-Léger-lès-Domart, Fr. 52/B3
Saint Leonard (mt.), Austl. 115/G5
Saint-Léonard, Qu, Can. 131/N6
Saint-Léonard, Fr. 52/A2
Saint-Leu, Reun. 107/S15
Saint-Leu-d'Esserent, Fr. 52/B5
Saint-Leu-la-Forêt, Fr. 30/J4
Saint Llorenc del Munt, PN, Sp. 45/K6
Saint-Lô, Fr. 42/C2
Saint Louis, Sk, Can. 127/G2
Saint Louis (riv.), Mn, US 130/A2
Saint-Louis, Sen. 102/A2
Saint-Louis (pol. reg.), Sen. 102/B3
Saint Louis, Mo, US 137/G8
Saint Louis (co.), Mo, US 137/F8
Saint-Louis, Fr. 56/D2
Saint Louis (lake), Qu, Can. 131/N7
Saint-Louis, Reun. 107/S15
Saint-Louis-de-Gonzague, Qu, Can. 131/N7
Saint-Louis-de-Kent, NB, Can. 131/H2
Saint-Louis du Nord, Haiti 145/H2
Saint-Loup-sur-Semouse, Fr. 56/C2
Saint-Lubin-des-Joncherets, Fr. 42/D2
Saint-Luc, Qu, Can. 131/P7
Saint Lucia (lake), SAfr. 107/F3
Saint Lucia (cape), SAfr. 107/F3
Saint Lucia (chan.), Mart.,StL. 141/N9
Saint Lucia (ctry.) 119/L8
Saint Lucia Estuary, SAfr. 107/F3
Saint-Lucien, Fr. 30/G6
Saint Maarten (isl.), NAnt. 141/N8
Saint Magnus (bay), Sc, UK 31/W13
Saint-Maixent l'Écale, Fr. 42/C3
Saint Malo, Mb, Can. 127/J3
Saint-Malo, Fr. 42/B2
Saint-Malo, Golfe de (gulf), Fr. 42/B2
Saint-Mandrier-sur-Mer, Fr. 42/F5
Saint-Marc, Haiti 145/H2
Saint-Marc-sur-Richelieu, Qu, Can. 131/P6
Saint-Marcel, Fr. 56/A4
Saint-Mard, Fr. 30/L4
Saint Maries, Id, US 126/D4
Saint Martin (lake), Can. 127/J3
Saint-Martin (isl.), Fr. 141/J4
Saint-Martin, Swi. 56/D5
Saint-Martin-Boulogne, Fr. 52/A2
Saint-Martin-d'Ablois, Fr. 52/C6
Saint-Martin-d'Hères, Fr. 42/F4
Saint-Martin-du-Tertre, Fr. 30/K4
Saint-Martin-la-Garenne, Fr. 30/H4
Saint Martinville, La, US 129/K5
Saint Mary (cape), Gam. 102/A3
Saint Mary (peak), Austl. 113/H4
Saint Mary's, Ak, US 134/F3
Saint Marys, Austl. 115/D4
Saint Marys, Ga, US 133/H4
Saint Marys, Pa, US 130/E3
Saint Mary's, On, Can. 130/D3
Saint Mary's (riv.), Can. 131/J2
Saint-Mathieu-de-Beloeil, Qu, Can. 131/N7
Saint Matthew (isl.), Ak, US 119/A4
Saint Matthews, SC, US 133/H3
Saint Matthias Group (isls.), PNG 116/E5
Saint-Maur-des-Fossés, Fr. 30/K5
Saint-Maurice, Swi. 56/D5
Saint-Maurice (riv.), Qu, Can. 123/J4
Saint-Max, Fr. 53/F6
Saint-Maximin-la-Sainte-Baume, Fr. 42/F5
Saint-Memmie, Fr. 53/D6
Saint-Méry, Fr. 30/L6
Saint Michael, Ak, US 134/F3
Saint Michaels, Md, US 138/B6
Saint-Michel (bay), Fr. 42/C2
Saint-Michel, Fr. 53/D4
Saint-Michel-sur-Meurthe, Fr. 56/C1
Saint-Michel-sur-Orge, Fr. 30/J6
Saint-Mihiel, Fr. 53/E6
Saint Monance, Sc, UK 36/D4
Saint-Nabord, Fr. 56/C1
Saint-Nazaire, Fr. 42/B3
Saint Neots, Eng, UK 33/F2
Saint-Nicolas, Belg. 53/E2
Saint-Nicolas-d'Aliermont, Fr. 42/D2
Saint Niklaus, Swi. 56/D5
Saint-Nom-la-Bretèche, Fr. 30/J5
Saint-Omer, Fr. 52/B2
Saint-Omer-en-Chaussée, Fr. 52/A4
Saint-Ouen, Fr. 52/B3
Saint-Ouen-en-Brie, Fr. 30/L6
Saint-Ouen-L'Aumône, Fr. 30/J4
Saint-Pamphile, Qu, Can. 131/G2
Saint-Pascal, Qu, Can. 131/G2
Saint-Pathus, Fr. 30/L4
Saint Paul, Ak, US 134/D4
Saint Paul (riv.), Libr. 96/C6
Saint Paul (isl.), Ak, US 134/W23
Saint Paul (cap.), Mn, US 127/K4
Saint Paul, Ab, Can. 126/F2
Saint Paul, Ks, US 132/E2
Saint Paul (cape), Gha. 103/F5
Saint Paul, Reun. 107/S15
Saint-Paul-lès-Dax, Fr. 42/C5
Saint Paul Rocks (isl.), Braz. 22/H5

Saint Paul's Church Nat'l Hist. Site, NY, US 139/K8
Saint-Pé-de-Bigorre, Fr. 42/C5
Saint Peter, Mn, US 127/K4
Saint Peter (isl.), Austl. 113/G5
Saint Peter Port (cap.), Chl, UK 42/B2
Saint Peters, Mo, US 137/F8
Saint Petersburg, Fl, US 133/H5
Saint Petersburg, Rus. 61/T7
Saint-Philippe-de-Laprairie, Qu, Can. 131/P7
Saint-Pierre (isl.), Can. 131/K2
Saint-Pierre, Fr. 131/K2
Saint-Pierre, Fr. 141/N9
Saint-Pierre, Reun. 107/S15
Saint Pierre and Miquelon (dpcy.), Can. 131/K2
Saint-Pierre-du-Mont, Fr. 42/C5
Saint-Pierre-du-Perray, Fr. 30/K6
Saint-Pierre-en-Faucigny, Fr. 56/C5
Saint Pierre-Jolys, Mb, Can. 127/J3
Saint-Pierre-sur-Dives, Fr. 42/C2
Saint-Point (lake), Fr. 56/C4
Saint-Pol-de-Léon, Fr. 42/B2
Saint-Pol-sur-Mer, Fr. 52/B1
Saint-Pol-sur-Ternoise, Fr. 52/B3
Saint-Pourçain-sur-Sioule, Fr. 42/E3
Saint-Prex, Swi. 56/C5
Saint-Prix, Fr. 30/J4
Saint-Quentin, Fr. 52/C4
Saint-Quentin, Canal de (canal), Fr. 52/C4
Saint-Rambert-en-Bugey, Fr. 56/B6
Saint-Raphaël, Fr. 43/G5
Saint-Rémi, Qu, Can. 131/N7
Saint-Rémy-de-Provence, Fr. 42/F5
Saint-Rémy-lès-Chevreuse, Fr. 30/J5
Saint-Rémy-l'Honoré, Fr. 30/H5
Saint-Roch-de-l'Achigan, Qu, Can. 131/N6
Saint Rose, La, US 137/P17
Saint Sampson's, Chl, UK 42/B2
Saint-Saulve, Fr. 52/C3
Saint-Sauveur, Fr. 56/C2
Saint-Sauveur-des-Monts, Qu, Can. 131/M6
Saint-Sever, Fr. 42/C5
Saint Simons (isl.), Ga, US 133/H4
Saint Simons Island, Ga, US 133/H4
Saint-Soupplets, Fr. 30/L4
Saint Stephen, NB, Can. 131/H2
Saint-Sulpice, Fr. 42/D5
Saint Tammany, La, US 137/Q16
Saint Tammany (co.), La, US 137/P16
Saint Thomas, On, Can. 130/D3
Saint Thomas (isl.), USVI 141/H4
Saint-Timothée, Qu, Can. 131/M7
Saint-Trivier-de-Courtes, Fr. 56/B5
Saint-Tropez, Fr. 43/G5
Saint-Urbain-Premier, Qu, Can. 131/N7
Saint-Ursanne, Swi. 56/D3
Saint-Valery-en-Caux, Fr. 42/D2
Saint-Valery-sur-Somme, Fr. 52/A3
Saint-Vallier, Fr. 42/F3
Saint-Vaury, Fr. 42/D3
Saint Vincent (pt.), Austl. 115/C4
Saint Vincent (isl.), StV. 141/N9
Saint Vincent, It. 58/A1
Saint Vincent and the Grenadines (ctry.) 119/L8
Saint-Vincent-de-Tyrosse, Fr. 42/C5
Saint Vincent Passage (chan.), StL.,StV. 141/N9
Saint-Vit, Fr. 56/B3
Saint-Vith, Belg. 53/F3
Saint-Vrain, Fr. 30/K6
Saint Walburg, Sk, Can. 126/F2
Saint-Witz, Fr. 30/K4
Saint-Yrieix-la-Perche, Fr. 42/D4
Sainte-Agathe-des-Monts, Qu, Can. 130/F2
Sainte-Anne-des-Monts, Qu, Can. 131/H1
Sainte-Anne-des-Plaines, Qu, Can. 131/N6
Sainte-Aulde, Fr. 30/M5
Sainte-Croix, Swi. 56/C4
Sainte-Croix-aux-Mines, Fr. 56/D1
Sainte-Foy, Qu, Can. 131/G2
Sainte-Geneviève-des-Bois, Fr. 30/K6
Sainte-Julie, Qu, Can. 131/P6
Sainte-Marie, Qu, Can. 131/G2
Sainte-Marie, Fr. 141/N9
Sainte-Marie-aux-Chênes, Fr. 53/F5
Sainte Marie, Nosy (isl.), Madg. 105/L10
Sainte-Martine, Qu, Can. 131/N7
Sainte-Maxime, Fr. 43/G5
Sainte-Mesme, Fr. 30/H6
Sainte Rose du Lac, Mb, Can. 127/J3
Sainte-Sigolène, Fr. 42/F4
Sainte-Thérèse, Qu, Can. 131/N6
Sainte-Tulle, Fr. 42/F5
Saintes, Fr. 42/C4
Sainthia, India 85/F4
SaintPierre-des-Corps, Fr. 42/D3
Sainy Clair (co.), Il, US 137/G9
Sāipal (peak), Nepal 82/D2
Saipan (isl.), NMar. 116/D3
Saitama (pref.), Japan 75/F2
Saito, Japan 74/B4
Saiwa Swamp NP, Kenya 104/B2
Sajama, Bol. 156/D5
Sajama, PN, Bol. 156/D5
Sajószentpéter, Hun. 41/L4
Sak (riv.), SAfr. 106/C3
Sakado, Japan 77/C2
Sakae, Japan 77/E2
Sakahogi, Japan 77/L5
Sakai, Japan 74/E2
Sakai, Japan 75/F2
Sakai (riv.), Japan 77/C3
Sakai, Japan 77/C1
Sakaide, Japan 74/C3
Sakaigawa, Japan 77/B2
Sakaiminato, Japan 74/C3
Sakakawea (lake), ND, US 127/H3
Sakami (lake), Qu, Can. 123/J3
Sakaraha, Madg. 107/H8
Sakarya (riv.), Turk. 62/D4
Sakarya (prov.), Turk. 62/D4
Sakauchi, Japan 77/K4
Sakawa, Japan 74/C4
Sakay (riv.), Madg. 107/H7
Sakçagöze, Turk. 90/D2
Sakeny (riv.), Madg. 107/H7
Sakété, Ben. 103/F5
Sakhalin (gulf), Rus. 65/Q4
Sakhalin (isl.), Rus. 67/P4
Sakhalin Oblast, Rus. 65/Q4
Sakhnīn, Isr. 91/G6
Sakht Sar, Iran 88/F1
Şäki, Azer. 63/H4
Sakishima (isl.), Japan 67/M7
Sakmara (riv.), Rus. 87/C2
Sakon Nakhon, Thai. 78/D2
Sakrand, Pak. 89/J3
Sakti, India 84/D4
Saku, Japan 75/F2
Saku, Japan 77/A1
Sakura, Japan 77/E1
Sakura, Japan 77/E2
Sakuragawa, Japan 77/E2
Sakurai, Japan 77/J6
Saky, Ukr. 62/E3
Sakya Monastery, China 85/G1
Säkylä, Fin. 39/K1
Sal (riv.), Rus. 63/G3
Sal (pt.), Hon. 144/E3
Sal (isl.), CpV. 93/K10
Sal Rei, CpV. 93/K10
Šal'a, Slvk. 48/C1
Sala, Swe. 38/G2
Sala Baganza, It. 58/D3
Sala Consilina, It. 46/D2
Salada (lake), Mex. 142/B1
Saladas, Arg. 157/E2
Saladilio (riv.), Arg. 159/J11
Saladillo, Arg. 158/F2
Salado (riv.), Mex. 132/D5
Salado (riv.), Arg. 147/C6
Salado del Norte (riv.), Arg. 147/C5
Salaga, Gha. 103/E4
Şalaḩ Ad Din (gov.), Iraq 90/E3
Sălaj (co.), Rom. 41/M5
Sălaj (prov.), Rom. 49/F2
Salālah, Oman 88/F5
Salamá, Guat. 144/D3
Salamajärven NP, Fin. 60/E3
Salamanca, NY, US 130/E3
Salamanca, Mex. 143/E4
Salamanca, Sp. 44/C2
Salamat (riv.), Chad 96/J6
Salamatof, Ak, US 134/H3
Salamina, Col. 152/C2
Salamís, Gre. 47/H3
Salamís (isl.), Gre. 47/N9
Salamīyah, Syria 91/E2
Salangen, Nor. 37/F1
Salas, Peru 156/B2
Salas, Sp. 44/B1
Salas de los Infantes, Sp. 44/D1
Salavat, Rus. 63/K1
Salaverry, Peru 156/B3
Salayar (isl.), Indo. 116/B5
Salbris, Fr. 42/E3
Salcantay (peak), Peru 156/C4
Saldaña, Sp. 44/C1
Saldanhabaai (bay), Safr. 106/K10
Saldus, Lat. 39/K3
Sale, Austl. 115/C3
Sale, It. 58/B3
Salé, Mor. 100/A2
Salé (prov.), Mor. 100/A3
Sale, Eng, UK 35/F5
Sale Marasino, It. 58/D1
Salebabu (isl.), Indo. 81/G3
Salekhard, Rus. 64/G3
Salem (cap.), Or, US 126/C4
Salem, NH, US 131/G3
Salem, In, US 130/C4
Salem, India 82/C5
Salem, Ger. 57/F2
Salem (co.), NJ, US 138/C4
Salem, NJ, US 138/C4
Salem, Mi, US 135/E7
Salemi, It. 46/C4
Salentina (pen.), It. 47/F2
Salerno, It. 46/D2
Salerno, Golfo di (gulf), It. 46/D2
Sales (pt.), Eng, UK 33/G3
Saleux, Fr. 52/B4
Salfīt, WBnk. 91/G7
Salford, Eng, UK 35/F5
Salgado Filho (int'l arpt.), Braz. 155/B4
Salgar, Col. 152/C3
Salgesch, Swi. 56/D5
Salgótarján, Hun. 41/K4
Salgueiro, Braz. 154/C3
Salhus, Nor. 38/A1
Salies-de-Béarn, Fr. 42/C5
Salies-du-Salat, Fr. 42/D5
Şalīf, Yem. 88/D5
Salihli, Turk. 62/D5
Salihorsk, Bela. 62/C1
Salima, Malw. 105/F3
Salīmah (oasis), Sudan 101/B4
Salina, Ut, US 128/E3
Salina (isl.), It. 46/D3
Salina (pt.), Bahm. 145/H1
Salina Cruz, Mex. 144/C2
Salinas (riv.), Ca, US 128/B3
Salinas, Braz. 154/B5
Salinas, Ca, US 128/B3
Salinas (cape), Sp. 45/G3
Salinas, Ecu. 152/A5
Salinas de Hidalgo, Mex. 143/E4
Salinas Pueblo Missions Nat'l Mon., NM, US 129/F4
Salinas Y Aguada Blanca, Reserva Nacional, Peru 156/D4
Saline (riv.), US 132/D2
Saline, It. 59/D6
Saline, Sc, UK 36/C4
Salinópolis, Braz. 151/J4
Salins-les-Bains, Fr. 56/B4
Salisbury, NC, US 133/H3
Salisbury (plain), Eng, UK 32/D4
Salisbury, Eng, UK 33/E4
Salisbury (isl.), NW, Can. 123/J2
Salisbury, NY, US 139/L9
Salitre (riv.), Braz. 154/B3
Salitre, Ecu. 152/B5
Salla, Fin. 60/F2
Salladasburg, Pa, US 138/A1
Sallanches, Fr. 56/C6
Salland (phys. reg.), Neth. 50/D4
Sallatouk (pt.), Gui. 102/B4
Sallaumines, Fr. 52/B3
Sallent, Sp. 45/F2
Salliqueló, Arg. 158/E3
Sallisaw, Ok, US 129/J4
Sally (pass), Ire. 34/B5
Salm (riv.), Ger. 53/F3
Salmān Pāk, Iraq 90/F3
Salmās, Iran 90/F2
Salmon, Id, US 126/E4
Salmon (riv.), Can. 126/C2
Salmon (riv.), Id, US 124/C2
Salmon Arm, BC, Can. 126/D3
Salmon Falls (riv.), US 128/D2
Salmon River (mts.), Id, US 124/C2
Salmon, South Fork (riv.), US 128/C2
Salmtal, Ger. 53/F4
Salò, It. 58/D1
Salo, Fin. 39/K1
Salon, India 84/C2
Salon (riv.), Fr. 40/C5
Salon-de-Provence, Fr. 42/F5
Salonga, PN de la, D.R. Congo 97/K8
Salonta, Rom. 48/E2
Salouël, Fr. 52/B4
Salpausselkä (mts.), Fin. 39/M1
Salpo, Peru 156/B3
Salses-le-Château, Fr. 42/E5
Sal'sk, Rus. 63/G3
Salso (riv.), It. 46/C4
Salsomaggiore Terme, It. 58/C3
Salt (riv.), SAfr. 106/C4
Salt (riv.), Az, US 137/R19
Salt (range), Pak. 86/B3
Salt Cay (isl.), UK 145/J1
Salt Draw (riv.), Tx, US 142/D2
Salt Fork Arkansas (riv.), US 129/H3
Salt Fork Red (riv.), US 129/G4
Salt Lake (co.), Ut, US 137/J12
Salt Lake City (cap.), Ut, US 126/F5
Salt Lake City, Ut, US 137/K12
Salt Meadow NWR, Ct, US 139/F1
Salt, North Fork (riv.), Mo, US 129/J2
Salt River Ind. Res., Az, US 137/S18
Salta, Arg. 157/C1
Saltaire, NY, US 139/E2
Saltash, Eng, UK 32/B6
Saltcoats, Sc, UK 36/B5
Saltdal, Nor. 37/E2
Saltee (isls.), Ire. 31/Q10
Saltfjorden (inlet), Nor. 37/E2
Saltillo, Mex. 143/E3
Salto, Uru. 157/E3
Salto, Braz. 155/C2
Salto, Arg. 158/E2
Salto da Divisa, Braz. 154/C5
Salto del Guairá, Par. 157/F1
Salto Grande (res.), Arg. 157/E3
Salto Santiago, Représa de (res.), Braz. 155/A3
Salton Sea (lake), Ca, US 124/C5
Saltvik, Fin. 39/J1
Saluda (riv.), SC, US 133/H3
Salug, Phil. 79/D6
Saluggia, It. 58/B2
Salunga-Landisville, Pa, US 138/B3
Sālūr, India 82/D4
Salurn (Salorno), It. 57/H5
Salut, Îles du (isls.), FrG. 151/H2
Saluzzo, It. 43/G4
Salvación (bay), Chile 159/B6
Salvador (lake), La, US 137/P17
Salvaleón de Higüey, DRep. 141/H4
Salvaterra de Magos, Port. 44/A3
Salvatierra, Mex. 143/E4
Salvatierra de Miño, Sp. 44/A1
Salween (riv.), Asia 67/J8
Salyan, Azer. 63/J5
Salyersville, Ky, US 130/D4
Salza (riv.), Aus. 41/H5
Salzach (riv.), Ger. 40/G5
Salzano, It. 59/F1
Salzbergen, Ger. 51/E4
Salzburg, Aus. 43/K3
Salzburg (int'l arpt.), Aus. 43/K3
Salzburg (prov.), Aus. 41/G5
Salzgitter, Ger. 51/H4
Salzhausen, Ger. 51/H2
Salzhemmendorf, Ger. 51/G4
Salzkotten, Ger. 51/F5
Salzwedel, Ger. 40/F2
Sam Rayburn (res.), Tx, US 140/C1
Sam Sao (mts.), Laos,Viet. 78/C1
Sam Son, Viet. 78/D2
Sama, Sp. 44/C1
Samak (cape), Indo. 80/C4
Samales Group (isls.), Phil. 81/F2
Samālkha, India 86/D5
Sāmalkot, India 82/D4
Samāna, India 86/D4
Samaná (cape), DRep. 141/H4
Samana (isl.), Bahm. 145/H1
Samandağı, Turk. 91/D1
Samani, Japan 76/C2
Samaniego, Col. 152/B4
Samannūd, Egypt 91/B4
Samaqua (riv.), Can. 131/F1
Samar, Jor. 91/D3
Samar (isl.), Phil. 67/M8
Samara (riv.), Rus. 87/B2
Samara (int'l arpt.), Rus. 63/J1
Samara, Rus. 63/J1
Samara Oblast, Rus. 87/A2
Samarai, PNG 116/E6
Samarate, It. 58/B1
Samaria (reg.), WBnk. 91/G7
Samarinda, Indo. 81/E4
Samarqand, Uzb. 87/E5
Samarqand (pol. reg.), Uzb. 87/E5
Sāmarrā', Iraq 90/E3
Samasata, Pak. 86/A5
Samāstipur, India 85/E3
Şamaxi, Azer. 63/J4
Sāmba, India 86/C3
Sambalpur, India 82/D3
Sambao (riv.), Madg. 107/H7
Sambar (cape), Indo. 80/D4
Sambas, Indo. 80/C3
Sambava, Madg. 107/J6
Sambhal, India 84/B1
Sambir, Ukr. 41/M4
Sambor Prei Kuk (ruin), Camb. 78/D3
Samborobón (riv.), Arg. 159/K11
Samborombón (bay), Arg. 159/F2
Sambre (riv.), Fr. 40/C3
Sambre à l'Oise, Canal de (canal), Fr. 52/C4
Sambriāl, Pak. 86/C3
Sambu, Japan 77/E2
Samburu Nat'l Rsv., Kenya 104/C2
Samch'ŏk, SKor. 74/A2
Samch'ŏnp'o, SKor. 73/E5
Samedan, Swi. 57/F4
Samer, Fr. 52/A2
Samfya Mission, Zam. 104/A5
Sámi, Gre. 47/G3
Samiria (riv.), Peru 156/C2
Samit (cape), Camb. 78/C4
Samkos (peak), Camb. 78/C3
Sammamish (lake), Wa, US 135/C2
Sammeron, Fr. 30/M5
Samnangjin, SKor. 74/A3
Samnaun, Swi. 57/G4
Samoa (ctry.) 117/H6
Samobor, Cro. 48/B3
Samoëns, Fr. 56/C5
Samoggia (riv.), It. 59/E4
Samokov, Bul. 47/H1
Samora (riv.), Port. 45/Q10
Samora Correia, Port. 45/Q10
Sámos (isl.), Gre. 90/A2
Sámos, Gre. 90/A2
Samothráki, Gre. 47/J2
Sampacho, Arg. 158/D2
Samper de Calanda, Sp. 45/E2
Sampit (riv.), Indo. 80/D4
Sampit, Indo. 80/D4
Samsø (isl.), Den. 38/D4
Samsø Bælt (chan.), Den. 38/D4
Samson (mt.), Austl. 114/E6
Samsonvale (lake), Austl. 114/E6
Samsun, Turk. 62/F4
Samsun (prov.), Turk. 62/E4
Samthar, India 84/B3
Samugheo, It. 46/A3
Samui (isl.), Thai. 83/H6
Samukawa, Japan 77/C3
Samundri, Pak. 86/B4
Samur (riv.), Azer.,Rus. 64/E5
Samut Prakan, Thai. 78/C3
Samut Sakhon, Thai. 78/C3
Samut Songkhram, Thai. 78/B3
Samye Monastery, China 85/H1
San, Mali 102/D3
San (riv.), Pol. 62/B2
San (riv.), Camb. 78/D3
San Adrián, Cabo de (cape), Sp. 44/A1
San Agustin (cape), Phil. 81/G2
San Agustín, Col. 152/B4
San Agustin de Guadalix, Sp. 45/N8
San Agustín, Parque Arqeológico, Col. 152/B4
San Ambrosio (isl.), Chile 147/B5
San Andreas (lake), Ca, US 135/J11
San Andres (mts.), NM, US 128/F4
San Andrés (lake), Mex. 144/B1
San Andrés, Col. 152/C3
San Andrés, Col. 145/F3
San Andrés Cuexcontitlán, Mex. 143/Q10
San Andrés de Giles, Arg. 159/J11
San Andrés de Machaca, Bol. 156/D5
San Andrés del Rabanedo, Sp. 44/C1
San Andrés, Isla de (isl.), Col. 140/E5
San Andrés Tuxtla, Mex. 144/C2
San Angelo, Tx, US 132/C4
San Anselmo, Ca, US 135/J11
San Antonio, Peru 156/B4
San Antonio (int'l arpt.), Tx, US 129/H5
San Antonio, Mex. 142/C4
San Antonio (riv.), Tx, US 140/B2
San Antonio (mt.), Ca, US 136/C2
San Antonio, Ecu. 152/B4
San Antonio, Ven. 153/F2
San Antonio (cape), Arg. 159/F3
San Antonio, Uru. 159/K11
San Antonio, Chile 158/N8
San Antonio Abad, Sp. 45/F3
San Antonio de Areco, Arg. 159/J11
San Antonio de Caparo, Ven. 152/D3
San Antonio del Golfo, Ven. 153/F2
San Antonio del Táchira, Ven. 152/C3
San Antonio Oeste, Arg. 158/D4
San Antonio, Punta (pt.), Mex. 142/B2
San Augustine, Tx, US 132/E4
San Bartolo, Peru 156/B4
San Bartolomé de Tirajana, Canl. 45/X17
San Bartolome Tlaltelulco, Mex. 143/Q10
San Bartolomeo in Bosco, It. 59/E3
San Bartolomeo in Galdo, It. 46/D2
San Bautista, Uru. 159/L11
San Benedetto (range), It. 59/E5
San Benedetto del Tronto, It. 43/K5
San Benedetto in Alpe, It. 59/E5
San Benedetto Po, It. 59/D2
San Benedicto (isl.), Mex. 142/C5
San Bernardino (co.), Ca, US 136/C2
San Bernardino (mts.), Ca, US 136/C2
San Bernardino, Ca, US 136/C2
San Bernardino Nat'l Forest, Ca, US 136/C2
San Bernardo (pt.), Col. 152/C2
San Bernardo, Chile 158/N8
San Blas (cape), Fl, US 133/G4
San Blas, Mex. 142/D4
San Blas, Mex. 142/C3
San Bonifacio, It. 59/E2
San Borja, Bol. 150/E6
San Bruno, Mex. 142/B3
San Bruno, Ca, US 135/K11
San Buenaventura, Mex. 132/C5
San Buenaventura (Ventura), Ca, US 136/A2
San Candido (Innichen), It. 43/K3
San Carlos (lake), Az, US 128/E4
San Carlos, Mex. 129/G5
San Carlos, Phil. 79/D4
San Carlos, Mex. 143/F3
San Carlos, Pan. 152/B2
San Carlos, Ven. 152/D2
San Carlos, Nic. 145/E4
San Carlos, Chile 158/C3
San Carlos, Uru. 159/G2
San Carlos, Ca, US 135/K11
San Carlos de Bariloche, Arg. 158/C4
San Carlos de Bariloche (int'l arpt.), Arg. 158/C4
San Carlos de Río Negro, Ven. 153/E4
San Carlos del Zulia, Ven. 152/D2
San Casciano in Val di Pesa, It. 59/E5
San Cataldo, It. 47/F2
San Cayetano, Arg. 158/F3
San Cesario sul Panaro, It. 59/E3
San Ciro de Acosta, Mex. 143/F4
San Clemente (isl.), Ca, US 128/C4
San Clemente, Ca, US 136/C4
San Clemente, Sp. 44/D3
San Clemente, Chile 158/C2
San Clemente del Tuyú, Arg. 159/F3
San Colombano al Lambro, It. 58/C2
San Cristóbal, Arg. 157/D3
San Cristobal (isl.), Sol. 116/F6
San Cristóbal (vol.), Nic. 144/E3
San Cristóbal, Ven. 152/C3
San Cristóbal, Cuba 145/F1
San Cristóbal (isl.), Ecu. 156/F7
San Cristóbal de las Casas, Mex. 144/C2
San Cristobal Wash (riv.), Az, US 142/B1
San Damiano d'Asti, It. 58/B3
San Diego, Tx, US 132/D5
San Diego (aqueduct), Ca, US 136/C4
San Diego (bay), Ca, US 136/C5
San Diego, Ca, US 136/C5
San Diego (co.), Ca, US 136/C4
San Diego (cape), Arg. 159/D7
San Diego International-Lindbergh Field (int'l arpt.), Ca, US 136/C5
San Diego Naval Station Naval Sta., Ca, US 136/C5
San Diego Wild Animal Park, Ca, US 136/C4
San Diego Zoo, Ca, US 136/C5
San Diequito (riv.), Ca, US 136/C5
San Dimas, Ca, US 136/C2
San Donà di Piave, It. 59/F1
San Donnino, It. 59/E5
San Dorligo della Valle, It. 59/G1
San Esteban de Gormaz, Sp. 44/D2
San Felice Circeo, It. 46/C2
San Felice del Benaco, It. 58/D1
San Felice sul Panaro, It. 59/E3
San Felipe, Mex. 142/B2
San Felipe, Ven. 152/D2
San Felipe, Chile 158/N8
San Felipe de Puerto Plata, DRep. 141/G4
San Felipe de Vichayal, Peru 156/A2
San Felipe Jalapa de Díaz, Mex. 143/F5
San Felipe Torres Mochas, Mex. 143/E4
San Felix (isl.), Chile 147/A5
San Fernando (riv.), Mex. 132/D5
San Fernando, Phil. 79/D4
San Fernando, Phil. 79/D4
San Fernando (valley), Ca, US 136/B2
San Fernando, Sp. 44/B4
San Fernando, Trin. 153/F2
San Fernando, Chile 158/C2
San Fernando, Arg. 159/J11
San Fernando, Ca, US 136/F7
San Fernando de Apure, Ven. 153/E3
San Fernando de Atabapo, Ven. 152/E3
San Fernando de Henares, Sp. 45/N9
San Fernando de Presas, Mex. 143/F3
San Fior di Sopra, It. 59/F1
San Francesco al Campo, It. 58/A2
San Francisco, Arg. 157/D3
San Francisco (int'l arpt.), Ca, US 128/B3
San Francisco (riv.), US 128/E4
San Francisco, Ca, US 128/B3
San Francisco, Phil. 79/E6
San Francisco, Col. 152/B4
San Francisco, ESal. 144/D3
San Francisco, Ven. 152/D2
San Francisco (co.), Ca, US 135/K11
San Francisco Acuautla, Mex. 143/R10
San Francisco Bay NWR, Ca, US 135/K11
San Francisco, Cabo de (cape), Ecu. 152/A4
San Francisco Chimalpa, Mex. 143/Q10
San Francisco de la Paz, Hon. 144/E3
San Francisco de Macorís, DRep. 141/G4
San Francisco de Mostazal, Chile 158/N8
San Francisco del Mezquital, Mex. 142/D4
San Francisco del Monte de Oro, Arg. 158/D2
San Francisco del Oro, Mex. 142/D3
San Francisco del Rincón, Mex. 143/E4
San Francisco Telixtlahuaca, Mex. 140/B4
San Fratello, It. 46/D3
San Gabriel (riv.), Ca, US 136/C2
San Gabriel (pt.), Mex. 142/B2
San Gabriel (res.), Ca, US 136/C2
San Gabriel, Ecu. 152/B4
San Gabriel, Ca, US 136/F7
San Gavino Monreale, It. 46/A3
San Germán, Cuba 145/G1
San Germano Vercellese, It. 58/B2
San Gil, Col. 152/C3
San Gimignano, It. 59/E6
San Giorgio delle Pertiche, It. 59/E1
San Giorgio di Piano, It. 59/E3
San Giorgio Ionico, It. 47/E2
San Giorgio Piacentino, It. 58/C3
San Giovanni al Natisone, It. 59/G1
San Giovanni Bianco, It. 58/C1
San Giovanni Gemini, It. 46/C4
San Giovanni in Croce, It. 58/D2
San Giovanni in Fiore, It. 46/E3
San Giovanni in Marignano, It. 59/F5
San Giovanni in Persiceto, It. 59/E3
San Giovanni Lupatoto, It. 59/E2
San Giovanni Valdarno, It. 59/E5
San Giuliano, It. 58/B3
San Giuliano Terme, It. 58/D5
San Giustino, It. 59/F5
San Giusto Canavese, It. 58/A2
San Gorgonio (mtn.), Ca, US 128/C4
San Gottardo, Passo del (pass), Swi. 57/E4
San Gregorio, Arg. 158/E2
San Gregorio, Uru. 159/L10
San Gregorio, Ca, US 135/K12
San Guiliano Milanese, It. 58/C2
San Hipólito Punta (pt.), Mex. 142/B3
San Ignacio, Bol. 150/E6
San Ignacio, Peru 156/B2
San Ignacio, Bol. 150/F7
San Ignacio, Mex. 142/B3
San Ignacio, Mex. 142/D4
San Ignacio, Belz. 144/D2
San Ignacio, Chile 158/B3
San Ildefonso, Sp. 44/D2
San Isidro, Nic. 144/E3
San Isidro, CR 145/F4
San Jacinto, Col. 152/C2
San Jacinto, Uru. 159/L11
San Javier, Sp. 45/E4
San Javier, Chile 158/C2
San Javier, Uru. 159/J10
San Jerónimo, Mex. 142/E3
San Joaquín, Bol. 150/F6
San Joaquin (riv.), Ca, US 128/C3
San Joaquín, Col. 152/C3
San Joaquin (hills), Ca, US 136/G8
San Joaquin (co.), Ca, US 135/L11
San Joaquín (peak), Ecu. 156/F7
San Jorge (bay), Mex. 142/B2
San Jorge (riv.), Col. 145/H5
San Jorge (gulf), Arg. 147/C7
San Jorge (cape), Arg. 158/D5
San Jorge, Golfo di (gulf), Sp. 45/F2
San Jose, Phil. 81/F1
San José, Peru 156/D4
San José, Peru 156/B2
San Jose (int'l arpt.), Ca, US 128/B3
San Jose, Phil. 79/D4
San Jose, Phil. 79/D5
San Jose, Ca, US 128/B3
San José (isl.), Mex. 142/C3
San José, Sp. 45/F3
San José, Col. 152/B4
San José (cap.), CR 145/E4
San José (gulf), Arg. 158/D4
San Jose (hills), Ca, US 136/G7
San José (dept.), Uru. 159/K11
San Jose (riv.), Uru. 159/K10
San José de Chiquitos, Bol. 150/F7
San José de Guanipa, Ven. 153/E2
San José de Guaribe, Ven. 153/E2
San José de Jáchal, Arg. 157/C3
San José de la Esquina, Arg. 158/E2
San Jose de Los Molinos, Peru 156/C4
San José de los Remates, Nic. 144/E3
San José de Maipo, Chile 158/N8
San José de Mayo, Uru. 159/K11
San José de Raíces, Mex. 143/E3
San José de Seque, Ven. 152/D2
San José del Cabo, Mex. 142/C4
San José del Guaviare, Col. 152/C4
San José Iturbide, Mex. 143/E4
San José Viejo, Mex. 142/C4
San Juan, Arg. 157/C3
San Juan (riv.), Arg. 157/C3
San Juan, Peru 156/C4
San Juan (basin), NM, US 132/A2
San Juan (riv.), NM, US 132/B2
San Juan, Phil. 79/D5
San Juan, PR 141/M8
San Juan (riv.), Nic. 140/E5
San Juan (pt.), ESal. 144/D3
San Juan (mts.), Co, US 124/E4
San Juan (cape), Arg. 159/E7
San Juan Abajo, Mex. 142/D4
San Juan Bautista, Par. 157/E2
San Juan Bautista Coixtlahuaca, Mex. 144/B2
San Juan Bautista Tuxtepec, Mex. 144/B2
San Juan Bautista Valle Nacional, Mex. 144/B2
San Juan Capistrano, Ca, US 136/C3
San Juan de Alicante, Sp. 45/E3
San Juan de Aznalfarache, Sp. 44/B4
San Juan de la Costa, Mex. 142/C3
San Juan de Lima (pt.), Mex. 142/E5
San Juan de los Cayos, Ven. 152/D2
San Juan de los Lagos, Mex. 142/E4
San Juan de los Morros, Ven. 150/E2
San Juan del Norte, Nic. 145/F4
San Juan del Río, Mex. 143/F4
San Juan Guichicovi, Mex. 140/B4
San Juan Hot Springs, Ca, US 136/C3
San Juan Ixcaquixtla, Mex. 143/M8
San Juan Juquila Mixes, Mex. 144/C2
San Juan Nepomuceno, Col. 152/C2
San Juanico, Mex. 142/B3
San Juanico Punta (pt.), Mex. 142/B3
San Juanito, Mex. 142/D2
San Justo, Arg. 157/D3
San Lázaro (cape), Mex. 142/B3
San Lazzaro, It. 59/E4
San Leandro, Ca, US 135/K11
San Leandro (res.), Ca, US 135/K11
San Lorenzo (cape), Ecu. 150/B4
San Lorenzo, Bol. 150/E6
San Lorenzo, Peru 156/D3
San Lorenzo (riv.), Mex. 142/D3
San Lorenzo (cape), It. 46/A3
San Lorenzo, Nic. 144/E3
San Lorenzo, Hon. 144/E3
San Lorenzo, Ecu. 152/B4
San Lorenzo, Ca, US 135/K11
San Lorenzo (peak), Chile 159/B5
San Lorenzo al Mare, It. 58/A5
San Lorenzo de El Escorial, Sp. 45/M8
San Lorenzo in Campo, It. 59/F5
San Lucas, Nic. 144/E3
San Lucas, Cabo (cape), Mex. 142/C4
San Luis, Peru 156/B4
San Luis (valley), Co, US 132/B2
San Luis, Ven. 152/D2
San Luis, Guat. 144/D2
San Luis, Cuba 145/H1
San Luis, Arg. 158/D2
San Luis Acatlán, Mex. 144/B2
San Luis al Medio, Uru. 159/G2
San Luis de la Paz, Mex. 143/E4
San Luis Obispo, Ca, US 128/B4
San Luis Potosí (state), Mex. 140/A3
San Luis Potosí, Mex. 143/E4
San Luis Rey (riv.), Ca, US 136/C4
San Luis Rey, Ca, US 136/C4
San Luis Río Colorado, Mex. 128/D4
San Luis, Sierra de (mts.), Arg. 158/D2
San Manuel, Az, US 128/E4
San Marcello Pistoiese, It. 59/D4
San Marcos, Peru 156/B3
San Marcos, Peru 156/B2
San Marcos, Tx, US 129/H5
San Marcos, Ca, US 136/C4
San Marcos, Mex. 140/B4
San Marcos, Guat. 144/D3
San Marcos, CR 145/E4
San Marcos, Col. 152/C2
San Maria di Porto Novo, It. 59/G5
San Mariano, Phil. 79/D4
San Marino (cap.), SMar. 59/F5
San Marino (ctry.) 27/F4
San Marino, Ca, US 136/F7
San Martín (riv.), Bol. 150/F6
San Martín (dept.), Peru 156/B2
San Martín, Mex. 143/R9
San Martín, Col. 152/C4
San Martín (lake), Arg. 147/B7
San Martín, Arg. 158/C2
San Martin Cuautlalpan, Mex. 143/R10
San Martín de los Andes, Arg. 158/C4
San Martín de Valdeiglesias, Sp. 44/C2
San Martino Buon Albergo, It. 59/E2
San Martino-di-Lota, Fr. 46/A1
San Martino di Lupari, It. 59/E1
San Martino di Venezze, It. 59/E2
San Martino in Passiria (Sankt Martin in Passieir), It. 57/H4
San Martino in Rio, It. 59/D3
San Martino in Strada, It. 58/C2
San Martino Siccomario, It. 58/C2
San Mateo, Peru 156/B3
San Mateo (mts.), NM, US 132/B3
San Mateo, Ca, US 128/B3
San Mateo, Sp. 45/F2
San Mateo, Ven. 153/E2
San Mateo (co.), Ca, US 135/K12
San Mateo Atarasquillo, Mex. 143/Q10
San Mateo Xoloc, Mex. 143/Q9
San Matías, Bol. 150/G7
San Matías, Golfo de (gulf), Arg. 147/C7
San Maurizio d'Opaglio, It. 58/B1
San Mauro Pascoli, It. 59/F4
San Mauro Torinese, It. 58/A2
San Michele al Tagliamento, It. 59/F1
San Miguel (riv.), Bol. 150/F6
San Miguel, Peru 156/B2
San Miguel, Peru 156/C4
San Miguel, Mex. 132/C4
San Miguel, ESal. 144/D3
San Miguel (gulf), Pan. 145/G4
San Miguel (riv.), Col. 152/B4
San Miguel Coatlincham, Mex. 143/R10
San Miguel de Allende, Mex. 143/E4
San Miguel de los Bancos, Ecu. 152/B4
San Miguel de Tucumán, Arg. 157/C2
San Miguel del Monte, Arg. 159/J11
San Miguel Tlaixpan, Mex. 143/R9
San Miguel Totolapan, Mex. 140/A4
San Miniato, It. 59/D5
San Nicolas (isl.), Ca, US 128/B4
San Nicolás de los Arroyos, Arg. 158/E2
San Nicolò, It. 58/C2
San Onofre (mtn.), Ca, US 136/C4
San Onofre, Ca, US 136/C4
San Onofre, Col. 152/C2
San Pablo, Peru 156/B2
San Pablo, Phil. 79/D5
San Pablo (int'l arpt.), Sp. 44/C4
San Pablo, Ven. 153/E2
San Pablo, Col. 152/B4
San Pablo, Chile 158/B4
San Pablo, Ca, US 135/K11
San Pablo (res.), Ca, US 135/K11
San Pablo Bay NWR, Ca, US 135/K10
San Pablo de las Salinas, Mex. 143/Q9
San Pablo Huixtepec, Mex. 144/B2
San Paolo, It. 58/D2
San Pawl il-Baħar, Malta 46/L7
San Pedro, Arg. 157/D1
San Pedro, Par. 157/E1
San Pedro (vol.), Chile 157/C1
San Pedro (riv.), Mex. 132/B5
San Pédro, C.d'Iv. 102/D5
San Pedro, Belz. 144/E2
San Pedro (riv.), Guat. 144/D2
San Pedro, Chile 158/N8
San Pedro, Arg. 159/J10
San Pedro Arriba, Mex. 143/Q10
San Pedro Carchá, Guat. 144/D3
San Pedro de Cajas, Peru 156/C3
San Pedro de la Cueva, Mex. 142/C2
San Pedro de las Colonias, Mex. 132/C5
San Pedro de Lloc, Peru 156/B2
San Pedro de Lóvago, Nic. 145/E3
San Pedro de Macorís, DRep. 141/H4
San Pedro del Pinatar, Sp. 45/E4
San Pedro Huamelula, Mex. 144/C2
San Pedro Pochutla, Mex. 144/B3
San Pedro, Sierra de (mts.), Sp. 44/B3
San Pedro Sula, Hon. 144/D3
San Pedro Tapanatepec, Mex. 144/C2
San Pedro Totoltepec, Mex. 143/Q10
San Pellegrino Terme, It. 58/C1
San Piero a Sieve, It. 59/E5
San Piero in Bagno, It. 59/E5
San Pietro (isl.), It. 46/A3
San Pietro in Casale, It. 59/E3
San Pietro in Gù, It. 59/E1
San Pietro in Vincoli, It. 59/F4
San Pietro in Volta, It. 59/F2
San Polo d'Enza, It. 58/D3
San Polo di Piave, It. 59/F1
San Possidonio, It. 59/D3
San Quentin, Ca, US 135/K11
San Quintín (cape), Mex. 142/B2
San Quintín, Mex. 142/B2
San Rafael (riv.), Ut, US 128/E3
San Rafael, Peru 156/B3
San Rafael, Peru 156/B2
San Rafael, Mex. 143/N6
San Rafael, Arg. 158/C2
San Rafael (hills), Ca, US 136/F7
San Rafael del Moján, Ven. 152/D2
San Ramón, Peru 156/C3
San Ramón, CR 145/E4
San Ramon, Ca, US 135/L11
San Ramón, Uru. 159/L11
San Ramón de la Nueva Orán, Arg. 157/D1
San Remo, It. 58/A5
San Rocco al Porto, It. 58/C2
San Romano, It. 59/D5

San Roque, Sp. 44/C4
San Rosendo, Chile 158/B3
San Saba (riv.), Tx, US 143/F2
San Salvador (cap.), ESal. 144/D3
San Salvador (riv.), Uru. 159/J10
San Salvador de Jujuy, Arg. 157/C1
San Salvador el Seco, Mex. 143/M7
San Salvador, Isla (isl.), Bahm. 141/G3
San Salvador (Watling) (isl.), Bahm. 141/G3
San Salvatore Monferrato, It. 58/B3
San Salvo, It. 46/D1
San Sebastián, Sp. 44/E1
San Sebastián de los Reyes, Sp. 45/N8
San Sebastián de Yalí, Nic. 144/E3
San Sebastiano, It. 58/D1
San Secondo Parmense, It. 58/D3
San Severo, It. 46/D2
San Telmo (pt.), Mex. 142/E5
San Timoteo, Ven. 152/D2
San Valentín (peak), Chile 158/B5
San Valentino, It. 59/G1
San Vicente (res.), Ca, US 136/D5
San Vicente, Mex. 142/A2
San Vicente, ESal. 144/D3
San Vicente, Chile 158/C2
San Vicente de Alcántara, Sp. 44/B3
San Vicente de Cañete, Peru 156/B4
San Vicente del Caguán, Col. 152/C4
San Vicente del Raspeig, Sp. 45/E3
San Vicino (peak), It. 43/K5
San Vincenzo, It. 43/J5
San Vito (cape), It. 46/C3
San Vito, CR 145/F4
San Vito al Tagliamento, It. 59/F1
San Ysidro, Ca, US 136/C5
Saña, Peru 156/B2
Sana (riv.), Bosn. 48/C3
Şan'ā (Sanaa) (cap.), Yem. 88/D5
Sanae III, SAfr., Ant. 160/Z
Sanaga (riv.), Camr. 93/C4
Sanak (isl.) 134/F5
Sanana (isl.), Indo. 81/G4
Sanandaj, Iran 88/E1
Sananduva, Braz. 155/B3
Sanaur, India 86/D4
Sānāwad, India 89/L4
Sanborn, NY, US 131/S9
Sanch'ŏng, SKor. 73/D5
Sancti Spíritu, Arg. 158/E2
Sancti Spíritus, Cuba 145/G1
Sand (hills), Can. 126/F2
Sand (riv.), SAfr. 106/D3
Sand (pt.), Eng, UK 32/D4
Sand (hills), Ne, US 124/F3
Sand, Nor. 38/B2
Sand am Main, Ger. 54/D3
Sand Point, Ak, US 134/F4
Sanda, Japan 77/H6
Sanda (isl.), Sc, UK 34/C1
Sandakan, Malay. 81/E2
Sandane, Nor. 37/C3
Sandanski, Bul. 47/H2
Sandarne, Swe. 38/G1
Sanday (isl.), Sc, UK 31/V14
Sandbach, Eng, UK 35/F5
Sandberg, Ger. 54/C2
Sande, Ger. 51/F1
Sandefjord, Nor. 38/D2
Sandersville, Ga, US 133/H3
Sandhurst, Eng, UK 33/F4
Sandia, Peru 156/D4
Sandıklı, Turk. 90/B2
Sandīla, India 84/C2
Sandino, Cuba 140/E3
Sandnes, Nor. 38/A2
Sandomierz, Pol. 41/L3
Sandoná, Col. 152/B4
Sándorfalva, Hun. 48/E2
Sandougou (riv.), Sen. 102/B3
Sandover (riv.), Austl. 113/G2
Sandoway, Myan. 83/F4
Sandpoint, Id, US 126/D3
Sandrakatsy, Madg. 107/J7
Sandrigo, It. 59/E1
Sands (pt.), NY, US 139/L8
Sands Point, NY, US 139/L8
Sandspit, BC, Can. 134/M5
Sandstedt, Ger. 51/F2
Sandstone, Austl. 112/C3
Sandu Shuizu Zizhixian, China 83/J2
Sandusky, Mi, US 130/D3
Sandusky, Oh, US 130/D3
Sandvika, Nor. 38/D2
Sandviken, Swe. 38/G1
Sandweiler, Lux. 53/F4
Sandwich, Eng, UK 33/H4
Sandwich (cape), Austl. 114/B2
Sandwīp (isl.), Bang. 85/H4
Sandy, Ut, US 137/K12
Sandy (cape), Austl. 114/D4
Sandy (lake), On, Can. 122/G3
Sandy (pt.), RI, US 139/G1
Sandy Bay, Sk, Can. 127/H2
Sandy Hook (bay), NJ, US 138/D3
Sandy Hook (bar), NJ, US 139/J10
Sandy Hook Lighthouse, NJ, US 139/J10
Sandy Springs, Ga, US 133/G3
Sanem, Lux. 53/E4
Sånfjällets NP, Swe. 37/E3
Sanford (mt.), Ak, US 134/K3
Sanford, Me, US 131/G3
Sanford, NC, US 133/J3
Sanford, Fl, US 133/H4
Sangamner, India 89/K5
Sangamon (riv.), Il, US 129/K3
Sangān (mtn.), Afg. 89/H2
Sangaria, India 86/C5
Sangatte, Fr. 52/A2
Sangay (vol.), Ecu. 152/B5
Sangay, PN, Ecu. 150/C4
Sangenjo, Sp. 44/A1
Sanggan (riv.), China 72/C2
Sanggau, Indo. 80/D3
Sanggou (bay), China 73/B4
Sangha (riv.), CAfr. 96/J7
Sangihe (isl.), Indo. 81/G3
Sangihe (isl.), Phil. 67/M9
Sangju, SKor. 73/E4
Sangkulirang, Indo. 81/E3
Sāngla, Pak. 86/B4
Sāngli, India 89/K5
Sangmélima, Camr. 96/H7
Sangō, Japan 77/J6
Sangre de Cristo (mts.), US 129/F3
Sangre Grande, Trin. 153/F2
Sangri, China 85/J1
Sangro (riv.), It. 46/D2
Sangrūr, India 86/C4
Sangster (int'l arpt.), Jam. 145/G2
Sangue, Rio do (riv.), Braz. 150/G6
Sangüesa, Sp. 44/E1
Sanguie (prov.), Burk. 103/E4
Sanguinetto, It. 59/E2
Sangzhi, China 79/B2
Sanhe, China 72/H7
Sani (pass), Les. 106/E3
Sāni Bheri (riv.), Nepal 84/D1
San'in Kaigin NP, Japan 74/D3
Saniquellie, Libr. 102/C5
Sanjō, Japan 75/F2
Sankanbiriwa (peak), SLeo. 102/C4
Sankh (riv.), India 85/E4
Sankoroni (riv.), Gui. 102/C4
Sankosh (riv.), India 85/G2
Sankt Aegyd am Neuwalde, Aus. 43/L3
Sankt Agatha, Aus. 55/G6
Sankt Andrä, Aus. 43/L3
Sankt Andrä-Wördern, Aus. 49/N7
Sankt Andreasberg, Ger. 51/H5
Sankt Anton am Arlberg, Aus. 57/G3
Sankt Augustin, Ger. 53/G2
Sankt Blasien, Ger. 56/E2
Sankt Florian am Inn, Aus. 55/G6
Sankt Gallen, Swi. 57/F3
Sankt Gallenkirch, Aus. 57/F3
Sankt Georgen bei Salzburg, Aus. 55/F7
Sankt Georgen im Attergau, Aus. 55/G7
Sankt Georgen im Schwarzwald, Ger. 57/E1
Sankt Goar, Ger. 53/G3
Sankt Goarshausen, Ger. 53/G3
Sankt Ingbert, Ger. 53/G5
Sankt Johann im Pongau, Aus. 43/K3
Sankt Johann in Tirol, Aus. 43/K3
Sankt Leonhard im Pitztal, Aus. 57/G3
Sankt Leonhard in Passeier (San Leonardo in Passiria), It. 57/H4
Sankt Marien, Aus. 55/H6
Sankt Martin im Mühlkreis, Aus. 55/H6
Sankt Michael in Obersteiermark, Aus. 43/L3
Sankt Moritz, Swi. 57/F5
Sankt Oswald bei Freistadt, Aus. 55/H5
Sankt Pantaleon, Aus. 55/F6
Sankt Peter am Hart, Aus. 55/G6
Sankt Peter in der Au, Aus. 55/H6
Sankt Peter-Ording, Ger. 38/C4
Sankt Pölten, Aus. 41/H4
Sankt Stephan, Swi. 56/D4
Sankt Ulrich bei Steyr, Aus. 55/H6
Sankt Valentin, Aus. 55/H6
Sankt Veit, Aus. 48/B1
Sankt Veit an der Glan, Aus. 43/L3
Sankt Wendel, Ger. 53/G5
Sankt Wolfgang, Ger. 55/F6
Sanlúcar de Barrameda, Sp. 44/B4
Sanmatenga (prov.), Burk. 103/E3
Sanmen, China 79/D2
Sanmenxia, China 72/B4
Sanming, China 79/C2
Sannan, Japan 77/H5
Sannazzaro de'Burgondi, It. 58/B2
Sannicandro Garganico, It. 46/D2
Sannikova (str.), Rus. 65/P2
San'nohe, Japan 76/B3
Sannois, Fr. 30/J5
Sano, Japan 75/F2
Sanok, Pol. 41/M4
Sanquhar, Sc, UK 36/C6
Sanquianga, PN, Col. 150/C3
Sans Bois (mts.), Ok, US 132/E3
Sansepolcro, It. 59/F5
Sanshui, China 79/B3
Sant Adrià de Besòs, Sp. 45/L7
Sant Boi de Llobregat, Sp. 45/L7
Sant Carles de la Ràpita, Sp. 45/F2
Sant Celoni, Sp. 45/L6
Sant Cugat del Vallès, Sp. 45/L7
Sant Feliu de Guíxols, Sp. 45/G2
Sant Feliu de Llobregat, Sp. 45/L7
Sant Julià, And. 42/D5
Sant Pere de Ribes, Sp. 45/K7
Sant Sadurní d'Anoia, Sp. 45/K7
Sant Vicenç de Castellet, Sp. 45/K6
Sant Vicenç dels Horts, Sp. 45/L7
Santa (riv.), Peru 156/B3
Santa, Peru 156/B3
Santa Ana, Bol. 150/E6
Santa Ana (mts.), Ca, US 136/C3
Santa Ana (riv.), Ca, US 136/C3
Santa Ana, Mex. 142/C2
Santa Ana (vol.), ESal. 144/D3
Santa Ana, ESal. 144/D3
Santa Ana, Ecu. 152/A5
Santa Ana, Ven. 152/C3
Santa Ana, Ven. 152/D2
Santa Ana, Hon. 144/E3
Santa Ana, Ca, US 136/G8
Santa Ana del Alto Beni, Bol. 150/E7
Santa Anna, Tx, US 129/H5
Santa Bárbara, Braz. 155/D1
Santa Bárbara, Mex. 142/D3
Santa Barbara, Ca, US 136/A2
Santa Barbara (co.), Ca, US 136/A1
Santa Bárbara, Ven. 152/D3
Santa Bárbara, Chile 158/B3
Santa Bárbara, Ven. 152/D2
Santa Bárbara, Hon. 144/D3
Santa Bárbara d'Oeste, Braz. 155/C2
Santa Barbara Mountains NRA, Ca, US 136/E7
Santa Catalina, Phil. 79/D6
Santa Catalina, Ven. 152/D3
Santa Catalina, Pan. 145/F4
Santa Catalina (isl.), CA, US 124/B5
Santa Catalina, Gulf of (gulf), Ca, US 128/C4
Santa Catarina (state), Braz. 155/B3
Santa Catarina, Mex. 143/E3
Santa Catarina, Ilha de (isl.), Braz. 157/G2
Santa Cecília, Braz. 155/B3
Santa Clara, Mex. 142/E3
Santa Clara, Ven. 153/E2
Santa Clara, Cuba 145/G1
Santa Clara (co.), Ca, US 135/L12
Santa Clara, Ca, US 135/L12
Santa Clara, Barragem de (res.), Port. 44/A4
Santa Clara de Olimar, Uru. 159/G2
Santa Clarita, Ca, US 136/B2
Santa Clotilde, Peru 152/C5
Santa Coloma de Farners, Sp. 45/G2
Santa Coloma de Gramanet, Sp. 45/L7
Santa Comba, Sp. 44/A1
Santa Croce di Magliano, It. 46/D2
Santa Croce sull'Arno, It. 59/D5
Santa Cruz (riv.), Az, US 129/E5
Santa Cruz, Braz. 154/C2
Santa Cruz, Peru 156/C2
Santa Cruz, Mex. 128/E5
Santa Cruz, Phil. 79/E6
Santa Cruz, Phil. 79/D5
Santa Cruz, Ca, US 128/B3
Santa Cruz, Phil. 79/D5
Santa Cruz (isls.), Sol. 116/F6
Santa Cruz (riv.), Arg. 147/B8
Santa Cruz (mts.), Guat. 144/D3
Santa Cruz, CR 144/E4
Santa Cruz, Chile 158/C2
Santa Cruz (prov.), Arg. 158/C5
Santa Cruz (isl.), Ecu. 156/E7
Santa Cruz da Graciosa, Azor., Port. 45/S12
Santa Cruz da Vitória, Braz. 154/C4
Santa Cruz das Flores, Azor., Port. 45/R12
Santa Cruz de Bucaral, Ven. 152/D2
Santa Cruz de El Seibo, DRep. 141/H4
Santa Cruz de la Palma, Sp. 98/A3
Santa Cruz de la Sierra, Bol. 150/F7
Santa Cruz de la Zarza, Sp. 44/D3
Santa Cruz de Mudela, Sp. 44/D3
Santa Cruz de Orinoco, Ven. 153/E2
Santa Cruz de Tenerife, Sp. 98/A3
Santa Cruz del Quiché, Guat. 144/D3
Santa Cruz del Sur, Cuba 145/G1
Santa Cruz do Capibaribe, Braz. 154/C2
Santa Cruz do Piauí, Braz. 154/B2
Santa Cruz do Rio Pardo, Braz. 155/B2
Santa Cruz do Sul, Braz. 155/A4
Santa Cruz Island (isl.), Ca, US 128/C4
Santa Elena, Peru 156/C2
Santa Elena (bay), CR 144/E4
Santa Elena, Hon. 144/E3
Santa Elena (cape), CR 144/E4
Santa Elena, Ecu. 152/A5
Santa Elena (peak), Arg. 158/D5
Santa Elena de Uairén, Ven. 153/F3
Santa Eugenia de Ribeira, Sp. 44/A1
Santa Eulalia del Río, Sp. 45/F3
Santa Fe, Arg. 157/D3
Santa Fe, Cuba 145/F1
Santa Fe (cap.), NM, US 129/F4
Santa Fe (riv.), Fl, US 133/H4
Santa Fé, Sp. 44/D4
Santa Fé do Sul, Braz. 155/B2
Santa Fe Springs, Ca, US 136/F8
Santa Felicia (dam), Ca, US 136/B2
Santa Filomena, Braz. 154/A3
Santa Giustina (lake), It. 57/H5
Santa Helena, Braz. 154/A1
Santa Helena de Goiás, Braz. 155/B1
Santa Inés (isl.), Chile 157/B7
Santa Inês, Braz. 154/C4
Santa Inês, Braz. 154/A1
Santa Isabel, Ecu. 156/B1
Santa Isabel, Braz. 211/G8
Santa Isabel (isl.), Sol. 116/E5
Santa Isabel (riv.), Guat. 144/D2
Santa Isabel, Arg. 158/D3
Santa Isabel, Arg. 158/E2
Santa Isabel de Sihuas, Peru 156/C5
Santa Isabel, Pico de (peak), EqG. 96/G7
Santa Juliana, Braz. 155/C1
Santa Lucía, Peru 156/D4
Santa Lucía, Canl. 45/X17
Santa Lucía, Ven. 152/D2
Santa Lucía, Ecu. 152/B5
Santa Lucía, Uru. 159/K11
Santa Lucia di Piave, It. 59/F1
Santa Luz, Braz. 154/C3
Santa Luzia, Braz. 154/A1
Santa Luzia, Braz. 155/D1
Santa Luzia, Braz. 154/C2
Santa Luzia (isl.), CpV. 93/J10
Santa Magdalena (isl.), Mex. 142/B3
Santa Magdalena, Arg. 158/E2
Santa Margarita (isl.), Mex. 142/B3
Santa Margarita (riv.), Ca, US 136/C4
Santa Margherita Ligure, It. 58/C4
Santa Maria, Braz. 157/F2
Santa Maria, Ca, US 128/B4
Santa Maria (riv.), Mex. 132/B4
Santa Maria (riv.), Mex. 142/D2
Santa Maria (bay), Mex. 142/C3
Santa Maria (cape), Port. 44/B4
Santa Maria (isl.), Azor., Port. 45/T13
Santa Maria (isl.), Chile 158/B3
Santa Maria, CpV. 93/K10
Santa María, Chile 158/N8
Santa María, Ecu. 156/E7
Santa María (isl.), Ecu. 156/E7
Santa Maria a Monte, It. 59/D5
Santa Maria, Cabo de (cape), Moz. 107/F2
Santa Maria Capua Vetere, It. 46/D2
Santa Maria, Chapadão de (hills), Braz. 154/A4
Santa Maria da Boa Vista, Braz. 154/C3
Santa Maria da Vitória, Braz. 154/A4
Santa Maria de Cayón, Sp. 44/D1
Santa Maria de Ipire, Ven. 153/E2
Santa Maria de Nanay, Peru 156/C1
Santa Maria del Oro, Mex. 142/D3
Santa Maria della Versa, It. 58/C3
Santa Maria di Leuca, Capo (cape), It. 47/F3
Santa Maria do Suaçuí, Braz. 154/B5
Santa Maria Maddalena, It. 59/E3
Santa Maria Maggiore, It. 57/E5
Santa Maria Nuova, It. 59/G6
Santa María Xadani, Mex. 140/B4
Santa Marta, Col. 152/C2
Santa Marta Grande (cape), Braz. 155/B4
Santa Marta, Sierra Nevada de (mts.), Col. 152/C2
Santa Monica (bay), Ca, US 136/B3
Santa Monica (mts.), Ca, US 136/B2
Santa Monica, Ca, US 136/F7
Santa Monica Mountains Nat'l Rec. Area, Ca, US 128/C4
Santa Monica Mountains NRA, Ca, US 136/B2
Santa Olalla del Cala, Sp. 44/B4
Santa Paula (peak), Ca, US 136/A2
Santa Paula, Ca, US 136/A2
Santa Pola, Sp. 45/E3
Santa Pola, Cabo de (cape), Sp. 45/E3
Santa Quitéria, Braz. 154/B2
Santa Quitéria do Maranhão, Braz. 154/B1
Santa Rita, Braz. 154/A1
Santa Rita, Braz. 154/D2
Santa Rita, Ven. 152/D2
Santa Rita de Cássia, Braz. 154/A3
Santa Rita do Sapucaí, Braz. 211/H7
Santa Rosa, Arg. 157/C3
Santa Rosa, Braz. 157/F2
Santa Rosa, Peru 156/D4
Santa Rosa, Ecu. 156/B1
Santa Rosa, Arg. 150/F8
Santa Rosa (range), Nv, US 128/C2
Santa Rosa, NM, US 129/F4
Santa Rosa, Ca, US 128/B3
Santa Rosa, CR 144/E4
Santa Rosa, Ven. 152/D2
Santa Rosa, Arg. 158/D3
Santa Rosa (mts.), Nv, US 124/C3
Santa Rosa, Uru. 159/K11
Santa Rosa, Bajo de (plain), Arg. 158/D4
Santa Rosa de Aguán, Hon. 144/E3
Santa Rosa de Copán, Hon. 144/D3
Santa Rosa de Osos, Col. 152/C3
Santa Rosa de Viterbo, Braz. 155/C2
Santa Rosa Island (isl.), Ca, US 128/B4
Santa Rosalia (pt.), Mex. 142/B2
Santa Rosalía, Mex. 142/B3
Santa Rosalía, Ven. 152/D2
Santa Rosalía, Ven. 153/E3
Santa Sofia, It. 59/E5
Santa Susana (mts.), Ca, US 136/B2
Santa Teresa (riv.), Braz. 151/J6
Santa Teresa, Austl. 113/G3
Santa Teresa Abor. Land, Austl. 113/G2
Santa Teresa, PN, Uru. 159/G2
Santa Teresinha, Braz. 151/H6
Santa Teresita, Arg. 159/F3
Santa Vitória, Braz. 155/B1
Santa Vitória do Palmar, Braz. 159/G2
Santa Ynez (mts.), Ca, US 136/A2
Sant'Antioco (isl.), It. 46/A3
Santaella, Sp. 44/C4
Sant'Agata Bolognese, It. 59/E3
Sant'Agata di Militello, It. 46/D3
Sant'Agata Feltria, It. 59/F5
Sant'Agostino, It. 59/E3
Sant'Alberto, It. 59/F3
Santan (canal), Az, US 137/S19
Santana, Braz. 154/A4
Santana (isl.), Braz. 154/B1
Santana do Acaraú, Braz. 154/B1
Santana do Ipanema, Braz. 154/C3
Santana do Livramento, Braz. 157/E3
Santander, Sp. 44/D1
Santander (dept.), Col. 145/H5
Santander de Quilichao, Col. 152/B4
Santander Jiménez, Mex. 143/F3
Sant'Angelo in Vado, It. 59/F5
Sant'Angelo Lodigiano, It. 58/C2
Sant'antioco, It. 46/A3
Sant'Antonio, It. 59/D2
Santañy, Sp. 45/G3
Sant'Apollinare in Classe, It. 59/F4
Santarcángelo, It. 59/F4
Santarém, Braz. 151/H4
Santarém (dist.), Port. 44/A3
Santarém, Port. 44/A3
Sant'arsenio, It. 46/D2
Santee (riv.), SC, US 133/J3
Santee, Ca, US 136/D5
Sant'Eufemia (gulf), It. 46/D3
Santena, It. 58/A3
Santerno (riv.), It. 43/J4
Santeuil, Fr. 30/H4
Santhià, It. 58/B2
Santiago, Braz. 157/F2
Santiago, Peru 156/C4
Santiago, Phil. 79/D4
Santiago (res.), Ca, US 136/C3
Santiago (peak), Ca, US 136/C3
Santiago (int'l arpt.), Sp. 44/A1
Santiago (riv.), Peru 152/B5
Santiago, Pan. 152/A2
Santiago (mtn.), Pan. 145/F4
Santiago (mts.), Tx, US 124/F5
Santiago (cap.), Chile 158/N8
Santiago (cape), Chile 159/B6
Santiago Cuautlalpan, Mex. 143/R10
Santiago Cuautlalpan, Mex. 143/Q9
Santiago de Cao, Peru 156/B2
Santiago de Chocorvos, Peru 156/C4
Santiago de Chuco, Peru 156/B3
Santiago de Compostela, Sp. 44/A1
Santiago de Cuba, Cuba 145/H1
Santiago de los Caballeros, DRep. 141/G4
Santiago de Machaca, Bol. 156/D5
Santiago del Estero, Arg. 157/D2
Santiago do Cacém, Port. 44/A3
Santiago Ixcuintla, Mex. 142/D4
Santiago Jamiltepec, Mex. 144/B2
Santiago Juxtlahuaca, Mex. 144/B2
Santiago Miahuatlán, Mex. 143/M8
Santiago Papasquiaro, Mex. 142/D3
Santiago Pinotepa Nacional, Mex. 144/B2
Santiago Tilapa, Mex. 143/Q10
Santiago Tolman, Mex. 143/R9
Santiago Vázquez, Uru. 159/K11
Santiago Zacatepec, Mex. 144/C2
Sant'Ilario d'Enza, It. 58/D3
Sāntipur, India 85/G4
Säntis (peak), Swi. 57/F3
Santisteban del Puerto, Sp. 44/D3
Santō, Japan 77/G5
Santō, Japan 77/K5
Santo Amaro, Braz. 154/C4
Santo Amaro, Ilha de (isl.), Braz. 211/G8
Santo Anastácio, Braz. 155/B2
Santo André, Braz. 211/G8
Santo Ângelo, Braz. 157/F2
Santo Antão (isl.), CpV. 93/J9
Santo António, SaoT. 96/G7
Santo Antônio de Jesus, Braz. 154/C4
Santo Antônio de Pádua, Braz. 155/D2
Santo Antônio do Içá, Braz. 152/E5
Santo Antônio do Jacinto, Braz. 154/B5
Santo Antônio dos Lopes, Braz. 154/A2
Santo Domingo (cap.), DRep. 141/H4
Santo Domingo, Mex. 143/E4
Santo Domingo (pt.), Mex. 142/B3
Santo Domingo, Cuba 145/F1
Santo Domingo, Chile 158/N8
Santo Domingo de la Calzada, Sp. 44/D1
Santo Domingo de los Colorados, Ecu. 152/B5
Santo Domingo Petapa, Mex. 144/C2
Santo Domingo Tehuantepec, Mex. 144/C2
Santo Domingo Zanatepec, Mex. 144/C2
Santo Estêvão, Braz. 154/C4
Santo Onofre (riv.), Braz. 154/B4
Santo Stefano Belbo, It. 58/B3
Santo Stefano d'Aveto, It. 58/C3
Santo Stefano di Magra, It. 58/C4
Santo Stino di Livenza, It. 59/F1
Santo Tomás, Peru 156/C4
Santo Tomás, Peru 156/B2
Santo Tomás, Mex. 142/A2
Santo Tomás (pt.), Mex. 142/A2
Santo Tomás (vol.), Ecu. 156/E7
Santo Tomé, Arg. 157/E2
Santo Tomé, Arg. 157/D3
Santoña, Sp. 44/D1
Santorso, It. 59/E1
Santos, Braz. 211/G8
Santos Dumont (int'l arpt.), Braz. 211/K7
Santos Dumont, Braz. 211/K6
Santos Reyes Nopala, Mex. 144/B2
Santuario di Crea, It. 58/B2
Santuario di Oropa, It. 58/A1
Şānūr, WBnk. 91/G7
Sanwa, Japan 77/D1
São Benedito, Braz. 154/B2
São Benedito do Rio Prêto, Braz. 154/B1
São Bento, Braz. 154/C2
São Bento, Braz. 154/A1
São Bento do Sapucaí, Braz. 211/H7
São Bento do Sul, Braz. 155/B3
São Bento do Una, Braz. 154/C3
São Bernardo do Campo, Braz. 211/G8
São Borja, Braz. 157/E2
São Carlos, Braz. 155/C2
São Cristóvão, Braz. 154/C3
São Desidério, Braz. 154/A4
São Domingos (riv.), Braz. 154/A4
São Domingos, Braz. 154/A4
São Domingos do Maranhão, Braz. 154/B2
São Félix do Xingu, Braz. 151/H5
São Fidélis, Braz. 155/D2
São Filipe, CpV. 93/J11
São Francisco, Braz. 154/A4
São Francisco (riv.), Braz. 147/F3
São Francisco do Sul, Braz. 155/B3
São Francisco, Ilha de (isl.), Braz. 157/G2
São Fransisco de Paula, Braz. 155/B4
São Gabriel, Braz. 157/F3
São Gabriel da Palha, Braz. 155/D1
São Gonçalo, Braz. 211/K7
São Gonçalo do Abaeté, Braz. 154/A5
São Gonçalo do Sapucaí, Braz. 211/H6
São Gotardo, Braz. 155/C1
São Joachim da Barra, Braz. 155/C2
São João Batista, Braz. 154/A1
São João Batista, Braz. 155/B3
São João da Aliança, Braz. 154/A4
São João da Barra, Braz. 155/D2
São João da Boa Vista, Braz. 211/G6
São João da Madeira, Port. 44/A2
São João da Pesqueira, Port. 44/B2
São João da Ponte, Braz. 154/A4
São João das Lampas, Port. 45/P10
São João de Meriti, Braz. 211/K7
São João del Rei, Braz. 155/C2
São João do Paraíso, Braz. 154/B4
São João do Piauí, Braz. 154/B3
São João dos Patos, Braz. 154/B2
São João Evangelista, Braz. 155/D1
São João, Ilhas de (isl.), Braz. 151/K4
São João Nepomuceno, Braz. 211/K6
São João, Serra de (mts.), Braz. 150/F5
São Joaquim, Braz. 155/B4
São Joaquim, PN de, Braz. 155/B4
São Jorge (isl.), Azor., Port. 45/S12
São José, Braz. 155/B3
São José da Laje, Braz. 154/C3
São José de Mipibu, Braz. 154/D2
São José de Piranhas, Braz. 154/C2
São José de Ribamar, Braz. 154/A1
São José do Belmonte, Braz. 154/C2
São José do Egito, Braz. 154/C2
São José do Norte, Braz. 155/A5
São José do Peixe, Braz. 154/B2
São José do Rio Pardo, Braz. 211/G6
São José do Rio Prêto, Braz. 155/B2
São José dos Campos, Braz. 211/H8
São José dos Pinhais, Braz. 155/B3
São Julião, Braz. 154/B2
São Leopoldo, Braz. 155/B4
São Lourenço (riv.), Braz. 151/G7
São Lourenço, Braz. 211/H7
São Lourenço, Port. 45/P11
São Lourenço do Sul, Braz. 155/A5
São Luís, Braz. 154/A1
São Luís do Curu, Braz. 154/C1
São Luís do Quitunde, Braz. 154/D3
São Manoel, Braz. 155/B2
São Marcos (riv.), Braz. 155/C1
São Marcos (bay), Braz. 147/E3
São Martinho do Porto, Port. 44/A3
São Mateus, Braz. 155/E1
São Mateus (riv.), Braz. 155/D1
São Mateus do Maranhão, Braz. 154/A2
São Mateus do Sul, Braz. 155/B3
São Miguel, Braz. 154/C2
São Miguel (isl.), Azor., Port. 45/T13
São Miguel Arcanjo, Braz. 155/C2
São Miguel do Tapuio, Braz. 154/B2
São Miguel dos Campos, Braz. 154/C3
São Nicolau (isl.), CpV. 93/J10
São Paulo (state), Braz. 155/B2
São Paulo, Braz. 211/G8
São Paulo de Olivença, Braz. 150/E4
São Paulo do Potengi, Braz. 154/D2
São Pedro da Aldeia, Braz. 155/D2
São Pedro do Piauí, Braz. 154/B2
São Pedro do Sul, Port. 44/A2
São Raimundo das Mangabeiras, Braz. 154/A2
São Raimundo Nonato, Braz. 154/B3
São Romão, Braz. 154/A5
São Roque, Cabo de (cape), Braz. 154/D2
São Roque do Pico, Azor., Port. 45/S12
São Sebastião (pt.), Moz. 105/G5
São Sebastião, Braz. 211/H8
São Sebastião do Paraíso, Braz. 155/C2
São Sebastião, Ilha de (isl.), Braz. 155/C2
São Simão, Barragem de (res.), Braz. 155/B1
São Teotónio, Port. 44/A4
São Tiago, Braz. 155/C2
São Tiago (isl.), CpV. 93/K10
São Tomé (cap.), SaoT. 96/G7
São Tomé (isl.), SaoT. 96/G7
São Tomé and Príncipe (ctry.) 93/C4
São Tomé, Cabo de (cape), Braz. 155/D2
São Vicente, Braz. 211/G8
São Vicente (cape), Port. 44/A4
São Vicente (isl.), CpV. 93/J10
Saône (riv.), Fr. 42/F3
Saône-et-Loire (dept.), Fr. 56/B4
Saori, Japan 77/L5
Saouru (riv.), Alg. 96/E1
Sápai, Gre. 47/J2
Sapallanga, Peru 156/C4
Sapanca, Turk. 49/K5
Sapatgrām, India 85/H2
Sapé, Braz. 154/D2
Sapele, Nga. 103/G5
Sapelo (isl.), Ga, US 133/H4
Şaphane, Turk. 62/D5
Sapiéndza (isl.), Gre. 47/G4
Sapkyo, SKor. 73/D4
Sapo (mts.), Pan. 145/G5
Sapo NP, Libr. 102/C5
Saposoa, Peru 156/B2
Sapemeer, Neth. 50/D2
Sapphire, Austl. 114/B3
Sappington, Mo, US 137/G8
Sapporo, Japan 76/B2
Sapri, It. 46/D2
Sapsi (isl.), SKor. 73/D3
Sapt Kosi (riv.), Nepal 85/F2
Sapucaí (riv.), Braz. 211/H7
Sapucaia, Braz. 211/L6
Saqqez, Iran 88/E1
Saquena, Peru 156/C2
Saquisilí, Ecu. 152/B5
Šar (mts.), Yugo 47/G1
Sar Dasht, Iran 90/F2
Sar-e Pol, Afg. 87/E5
Sara Buri, Thai. 78/C3
Sarāb, Iran 88/E1
Saraguro, Ecu. 156/B1
Sarāi Alamgīr, Pak. 86/B3
Sarāi Sidhu, Pak. 86/A4
Sarajevo (cap.), Bosn. 48/D4
Saraland, Al, US 133/F4
Saramacca (dist.), Sur. 153/H3
Saran (peak), Indo. 80/D4
Saran', Kaz. 87/F3
Saranac Lake, NY, US 130/F2
Sarandapótamos (riv.), Gre. 47/N8
Sarandë, Alb. 47/G3
Sarandí de Navarro, Uru. 159/K10
Sarandí del Yi, Uru. 159/G2
Sarandí Grande, Uru. 159/K10
Sarangani (isls.), Phil. 81/G2
Sārangpur, India 89/L4
Saransk, Rus. 63/H1
Sarapul, Rus. 61/M4
Sarare (riv.), Ven. 152/D3
Sarasota, Fl, US 133/H5
Saratoga, Wy, US 126/G5
Saratoga, Ca, US 135/K12
Saratoga Springs, NY, US 130/F3
Saratov (res.), Rus. 63/J1
Saratov, Rus. 63/H2
Saratov Oblast, Rus. 87/A2
Saravan, Laos 78/D3
Sarawak (reg.), Malay. 67/L9
Saray, Turk. 49/H5
Sarayacu, Ecu. 152/B5
Sarāyan (riv.), India 84/C2
Saraykōy, Turk. 90/B2
Sarayönü, Turk. 90/C2
Sárbogárd, Hun. 48/D2
Sarcelles, Fr. 30/K5
Sārda (riv.), India 84/C1
Sārda (canal), India 84/C2
Sārda (riv.), India 82/D2
Sardara, It. 46/A3
Sardārshahar, India 86/C5
Sardegna (prov.), It. 46/A2
Sardhana, India 86/D5
Sardinata, Col. 152/C2
Sardinaux, Cap des (cape), Fr. 43/G5
Sardinia (isl.) 46/A2
Sardis (lake), Ms, US 129/K4
Sardis (lake), Ok, US 129/J4
Sareks NP, Swe. 37/F2
Sarektjåkko (peak), Swe. 37/F2
Sarempaka (peak), Indo. 81/E4
Sarentino, It. 57/H4
Serezzo, It. 58/D1
Sargans, Swi. 57/F3
Sargodha, Pak. 86/B3
Sarh, Chad 96/J6
Sārī, Iran 88/F1
Sari-Solenzara, Fr. 46/A2
Sariaya, Phil. 79/D5
Saribi (cape), Indo. 81/J4
Sarigan (isl.), NMar. 116/D3
Sarıgöl, Turk. 90/B2
Sarıkamış, Turk. 63/G4
Sarikaya (prov.), Turk. 62/E5
Sarıkaya, Turk. 62/E5
Sarikei, Malay. 80/D3
Sarina, Austl. 114/C3
Sarine (riv.), Swi. 43/G4
Sariñena, Sp. 45/E2
Sarīr Kalanshiyū (des.), Libya 96/K2
Sarīr Tibastī (des.), Libya 96/J3
Sarita, Tx, US 132/D5
Sariwŏn, NKor. 73/C3
Sarju (riv.), India 84/C1
Sark (isl.), Chl, UK 42/B2
Sarkad, Hun. 48/E2
Sarkant, Kaz. 70/C2
Şarkikaraağaç, Turk. 90/B2
Şarkışla, Turk. 62/F5
Şarköy, Turk. 49/H5
Sarlat-la-Canéda, Fr. 42/D4
Sarleinsbach, Aus. 55/G5
Sarmato, It. 58/C2
Sarmeola, It. 59/E2
Sarmiento, Arg. 158/C5
Sarmiento (peak), Chile 159/C7
Särna, Swe. 38/E1
Sarnano, It. 43/K5
Sarnen, Swi. 57/E4
Sarnia, On, Can. 130/D3
Sarnico, It. 58/C1
Sarny, Ukr. 62/C2
Saroma (lake), Japan 76/C1
Saronic (gulf), Gre. 47/H4
Saronno, It. 58/C1
Saros (gulf), Turk. 62/C4
Sárospatak, Hun. 41/L4
Sarpsborg, Nor. 38/D2
Sarralbe, Fr. 53/G6
Sarre (riv.), Fr. 52/F6
Sarre-Union, Fr. 53/G6
Sarrebourg, Fr. 53/G6
Sarria, Sp. 44/B1
Sarroch, It. 46/A3
Sarry, Fr. 53/D6
Sarsāwa, India 86/D4
Sarsina, It. 59/F5
Sarstedt, Ger. 51/G4
Sarstún (riv.), Guat. 144/D3
Sartang (riv.), Rus. 65/P3
Sarteano, It. 46/B1
Sartène, Fr. 46/A2
Sarthe (riv.), Fr. 42/C3
Sartrouville, Fr. 30/J5
Sarufutsu, Japan 76/C1
Saruhanlı, Turk. 62/C5
Sárvár, Hun. 43/M3
Sárvíz (riv.), Hun. 48/D2
Sary Ishikotrau (des.), Kaz. 70/C2
Saryshaghan, Kaz. 87/F3
Sarysu (riv.), Kaz. 64/G5
Sarzana, It. 58/C4
Sas Van Gent, Neth. 52/C1
Sasaginnigack (lake), Can. 127/K3
Sasarām, India 85/E3
Sasayama, Japan 77/H5
Sasayama (riv.), Japan 77/H5
Sásd, Hun. 48/D2
Sasebo, Japan 74/A4
Sashima, Japan 77/D1
Saskatchewan (prov.), Can. 126/F2
Saskatchewan (riv.), Can. 119/G4
Saskatoon, Sk, Can. 126/G2
Saslaya (mtn.), Nic. 144/E3
Saslaya, PN, Nic. 144/E3
Sāsni, India 84/B2
Sasolburg, SAfr. 106/D2
Sasovo, Rus. 63/G1
Saspamco, Tx, US 137/U21
Sassafras, Md, US 138/C5
Sassafras (riv.), Md, US 138/B5
Sassandra (riv.), C.d'Iv. 96/D6
Sassandra, C.d'Iv. 102/D5
Sassari, It. 46/A2
Sassello, It. 58/B4
Sassenberg, Ger. 51/F4
Sassenheim, Neth. 50/B4
Sassnitz, Ger. 38/E4
Sasso Marconi, It. 59/E4
Sassocorvaro, It. 59/F5
Sassoferrato, It. 59/F6
Sassuolo, It. 59/D3
Sástago, Sp. 45/E2
Sasyk (lake), Ukr. 49/J3
Sata-misaki (cape), Japan 74/B5
Sātāra, India 89/K5
Satawan (isl.), Micr. 116/E4
Säter, Swe. 38/F1
Saticoy, Ca, US 136/A2
Satilla (riv.), Ga, US 133/H4
Satipo, Peru 156/C3
Sātkhira, Bang. 85/G4
Sátoraljaújhely, Hun. 41/L4
Satpayev, Kaz. 87/E3
Satpura (range), India 89/K4
Satte, Japan 77/D1
Satteins, Aus. 57/F3
Satteldorf, Ger. 54/D4
Sattler, Tx, US 137/U20
Satu Mare (co.), Rom. 41/M5
Satu Mare, Rom. 41/M5
Satun, Thai. 78/C5
Sauce, Peru 156/B2
Sauce Grande (riv.), Arg. 158/E3
Saucillo, Mex. 132/B4
Sauda, Nor. 38/B2
Saúde, Braz. 154/B3
Saudhárkrókur, Ice. 37/N6
Saudi Arabia (ctry.) 67/B7
Sauer (riv.), Ger. 51/F5
Sauerlach, Ger. 57/H2
Sauerland (reg.), Ger. 40/D3
Sauêruiná (riv.), Braz. 150/G6
Saugatuck (riv.), Ct, US 139/E1
Saujon, Fr. 42/C4
Sauk (riv.), Mn, US 127/K4
Sauk Centre, Mn, US 127/K4
Sauk Rapids, Mn, US 127/K4
Saül, FrG. 151/H3
Sauland, Nor. 38/C2
Sauldre (riv.), Fr. 42/D3
Saulgau, Ger. 57/F1
Saulheim, Ger. 54/B3
Saulieu, Fr. 42/F3
Sault-lès-Rethel, Fr. 53/D5
Sault Sainte Marie, On, Can. 130/C2
Sault Ste. Marie, Mi, US 130/C2
Saulx, Fr. 56/C2
Saulx (riv.), Fr. 40/C4
Saulxures-sur-Moselotte, Fr. 56/C2
Saumur, Fr. 42/C3
Saunders (peak), Austl. 112/E3
Saura (riv.), India 85/F3
Saurimo, Ang. 105/D2
Sausalito, Ca, US 135/J11

Sausseron (riv.), Fr. 30/J4
Sauteurs, Gren. 153/F1
Sava, It. 47/E2
Sava (riv.), Slov. 43/L3
Savá, Hon. 144/E3
Savage (dam), Ca, US 136/D5
Savage River, Austl. 115/C4
Savai'i (isl.), Sam. 117/H6
Savalou, Ben. 103/F5
Savane (riv.), Can. 131/G1
Savanna-la-Mar, Jam. 145/G2
Savannah, Ga, US 133/H3
Savannah, Tn, US 133/F3
Savannah (riv.), US 119/J6
Savannakhet, Laos 78/D2
Savant (lake), Can. 127/L3
Sāvantvādi, India 82/B4
Sävar, Swe. 37/G3
Savaştepe, Turk. 62/C5
Save (riv.), Moz. 93/F7
Sāveh, Iran 88/F1
Savena (riv.), It. 59/E4
Sāveni, Rom. 49/H2
Saverdun, Fr. 42/D5
Saverne, Fr. 53/G6
Savièse, Swi. 56/D5
Savigliano, It. 43/G4
Savignano sul Panaro, It. 59/E4
Savignano sul Rubicone, It. 59/F4
Savigny-le-Temple, Fr. 30/K6
Savigny-sur-Orge, Fr. 30/K5
Savio (riv.), It. 43/K5
Sāvja, Swe. 38/G2
Savognin, Swi. 57/F4
Savoie (dept.), Fr. 56/C6
Savona, BC, Can. 126/C3
Savona (prov.), It. 58/B4
Savona, It. 58/B4
Savoonga, Ak, US 134/D3
Savoy (reg.), Fr. 42/F4
Savoy Alps (mts.), Fr. 56/C6
Şavşat, Turk. 63/G4
Sävsjö, Swe. 38/F3
Savu (sea), Phil. 67/M10
Sawahlunto, Indo. 80/B4
Sawankhalok, Thai. 78/B2
Sawara, Japan 75/G3
Sawaski-bana (pt.), Japan 75/F2
Sawatch (range), Co, US 128/F3
Sawdā', Jabal (peak), SAr. 88/D5
Saweba (cape), Indo. 81/H4
Sawel (mtn.), NI, UK 34/A2
Sawtell, Austl. 115/E1
Sawtooth (range), Id, US 126/E4
Sawtooth Nat'l Rec. Area, Id, US 126/E5
Sawu (isls.), Indo. 81/F6
Sax, Sp. 45/E3
Saxman, Ak, US 134/M4
Saxon, Swi. 56/D5
Say, Niger 103/F3
Saya, Japan 77/L5
Sayama, Japan 75/F3
Sayama, Japan 77/J6
Sayán, Peru 156/B3
Şaydā, Leb. 91/D3
Sayil (ruin), Mex. 144/D1
Saynbach (riv.), Ger. 53/G2
Sayreville, NJ, US 139/H10
Sayville, NY, US 139/E2
Saywūn, Yem. 88/E5
Sazan (isl.), Alb. 47/F2
Sázava (riv.), Czh. 43/L2
Sbaa, Alg. 99/E3
Scafell Pikes (peak), Eng, UK 35/E3
Scalasaig, Sc, UK 31/Q8
Scald Law (peak), Sc, UK 36/C5
Scalea, It. 46/D3
Scalino (peak), It. 57/F5
Scalloway, Sc, UK 31/W13
Scammon Bay, Ak, US 134/E3
Scandia, Wa, US 135/B12
Scandiano, It. 59/D3
Scandicci, It. 59/E5
Scapa Flow (chan.), Sc, UK 31/V14
Scar Water (riv.), Sc, UK 34/E1
Scarborough, Can. 131/R8
Scarborough, Eng, UK 35/H3
Scarborough Shoal (isl.), Phil. 79/C4
Scardovari, It. 59/F3
Scarpe (riv.), Fr. 40/B3
Scarperia, It. 59/E5
Scarsdale, La, US 137/Q17
Scarsdale, NY, US 139/K7
Sceaux, Fr. 30/J5
Scenic Oaks, Tx, US 137/T20
Scey-sur-Saône-et-St-Albin, Fr. 56/B2
Schaefferstown, Pa, US 138/B3
Schaerbeek, Belg. 50/C5
Schaffhausen (canton), Swi. 57/E2
Schaffhausen, Swi. 57/E2
Schäftlarn, Ger. 57/H2
Schagen, Neth. 50/B3
Schaijk, Neth. 50/C5
Schalchen, Aus. 55/G6
Schalkau, Ger. 54/E2
Schalksmühle, Ger. 51/E6
Schanck (cape), Austl. 115/C3
Schangnau, Swi. 56/D4
Schardenberg, Aus. 55/G5
Schärding, Aus. 55/G5
Scharfreiter (peak), Aus. 57/H3
Scharhorn (isl.), Ger. 51/F1

Scharnebeck, Ger. 51/H2
Scharnitz (pass), Ger. 57/H3
Scharnstein, Aus. 55/G7
Schashagen, Ger. 40/F1
Schattdorf, Swi. 57/E4
Schauenstein, Ger. 55/E2
Schaumburg, Il, US 135/P15
Scheemda, Neth. 50/D2
Scheer, Ger. 57/F1
Scheessel, Ger. 51/G2
Schefferville, Qu, Can. 123/K3
Scheibbs, Aus. 41/H4
Scheidegg, Ger. 57/F2
Scheinfeld, Ger. 54/D3
Schelde (riv.), Belg. 42/E1
Schelklingen, Ger. 54/C6
Schell Creek (range), Nv, US 128/D3
Schellerten, Ger. 51/H4
Schellville, Ca, US 135/K10
Schenectady, NY, US 130/F3
Schenefeld, Ger. 51/G1
Schermbeck, Ger. 50/D5
Scherpenzeel, Neth. 50/C3
Schertz, Tx, US 137/U20
Schesaplana (peak), Aus. 57/F3
Schesslitz, Ger. 54/E3
Scheyern, Ger. 55/E5
Schiedam, Neth. 50/B5
Schieder-Schwalenberg, Ger. 51/G5
Sgurr na Lapaich (peak), Sc, UK 32/C2
Schier Monnikoog (isl.), Neth. 40/D2
Schierling, Ger. 55/F5
Schiermonnikoog (isl.), Neth. 50/D1
Schiermonnikoog, Neth. 50/D2
Schiers, Swi. 57/F4
Schifferstadt, Ger. 54/B4
Schiffweiler, Ger. 53/G5
Schijndel, Neth. 50/C5
Schilde, Belg. 50/B6
Schildmeer (lake), Neth. 50/D2
Schillighörn (cape), Ger. 51/F1
Schillingfürst, Ger. 54/D4
Schiltach, Ger. 57/E1
Schiltigheim, Fr. 56/D1
Schinnen, Neth. 53/E2
Schinznach-Dorf, Swi. 56/E3
Schio, It. 59/D2
Schipbeek (riv.), Neth. 50/D4
Schirmeck, Fr. 56/D1
Schkumbin (riv.), Alb. 47/G2
Schladen, Ger. 51/H4
Schladming, Aus. 43/K3
Schlanders (Silandro), It. 43/J3
Schlangen, Ger. 51/F5
Schlangenbad, Ger. 54/B2
Schleiden, Ger. 53/F2
Schleitheim, Swi. 57/E2
Schleiz, Ger. 55/E1
Schlema, Ger. 55/F1
Schleswig, Ger. 38/C4
Schleswig-Holstein (state), Ger.
Schleswig-Holsteinisches Wattenmeer NP, Ger. 38/C4
Schleuse (riv.), Ger. 54/D2
Schleusingen, Ger. 54/D1
Schliengen, Ger. 56/D2
Schlierbach, Aus. 55/H7
Schlieren, Swi. 57/E3
Schloss Herrenchiemsee, Ger. 55/F7
Schloss Holte-Stukenbrock, Ger. 51/F5
Schloss Sansoucci, Ger.
Schloss Wilhelmstein, Austl. 113/M8
Schlotheim, Ger. 51/H6
Schluchsee, Ger. 56/E2
Schlüchtern, Ger. 54/C2
Schlüsselfeld, Ger. 54/D3
Schlüsslberg, Aus. 55/G6
Schmalkalden, Ger. 43/J1
Schmallenberg, Ger. 51/F6
Schmelz, Ger. 53/G5
Schmiech (riv.), Ger. 54/C6
Schmitten, Ger. 54/B2
Schmitten, Swi. 56/D4
Schmutter (riv.), Ger. 54/D5
Schnaitsee, Ger. 55/F6
Schnaittach, Ger. 55/E4
Schnaittenbach, Ger. 55/F4
Schnarrtanne, Ger. 55/F1
Schnecksville, Pa, US 138/C2
Schneeberg (peak), Ger.
Schneeberg, Ger. 55/E2
Schneeberg, Ger. 55/F1
Schneeberg (peak), Ger. 54/C3
Schneifel (upland), Ger. 40/D2
Schneverdingen, Ger. 51/G2
Schofield Barracks, Hi, US 124/V12
Schollene, Ger. 40/G2
Schöllkrippen, Ger. 54/C2
Schömberg, Ger. 57/E1
Schömberg, Ger. 54/B5
Schönaich, Ger. 54/C5
Schönau im Schwarzwald, Ger. 56/D2
Schönberg, Ger. 56/D2
Schönberg, Ger. 38/D4
Schönberg, Ger. 54/B5
Schönebeck, Ger. 40/F2
Schönecken, Ger. 53/F3
Schönefeld (int'l arpt.), Ger. 40/Q7
Schongau, Ger. 57/H2
Schöningen, Ger. 51/H4
Schönsee, Ger. 55/F3
Schönungen, Ger. 54/D2
Schönwald, Ger. 55/E2

Schoonebeek, Neth. 50/D3
Schoonhoven, Neth. 50/D3
Schoorl, Neth. 50/B3
Schopfheim, Ger. 53/G4
Schopfloch, Ger. 54/D4
Schöppenstedt, Ger. 51/H4
Schörfling, Aus. 55/G7
Schorndorf, Ger. 54/C5
Schortens, Ger. 51/E1
Schoten, Belg. 50/B6
Schotten, Ger. 54/C1
Schouten (isl.), Austl. 115/D4
Schouten (isl.), Indo. 116/C5
Schouwen (isl.), Neth. 50/A5
Schramberg, Ger. 57/E1
Schrankogel (peak), Aus. 57/H3
Schreckhorn (peak), Swi. 56/E4
Schriesheim, Ger. 54/B4
Schrobenhausen, Ger. 55/E5
Schroffenstein (peak), Gabon 96/G1
Shattuck, Ok, US 132/B1
Shaunavon, Sk, Can. 126/F3
Shavano Park, Tx, US 137/T20
Shaw, Eng, UK 35/G4
Shawano, Wi, US 127/L4
Shawinigan, Qu, Can. 131/F2
Shawnee (res.), Ok, US 137/N15
Shawnee, Ks, US 137/D5
Shay Gap, Austl. 112/D2
Shaykhān, Iraq 90/E2
Shchara (riv.), Bela. 62/D1
Shchekino, Rus. 62/F1
Shchelkovo, Rus. 61/W9
Shchigry, Rus. 62/F2
Shchūchīnsk, Kaz. 87/G1
She Xian, China 79/C2
Shea Stadium, NY, US 139/K9
Shebelē Wenz (riv.), Eth. 97/P6
Sheberghān, Afg. 89/J1
Sheboygan, Wi, US 127/M5
Shediac, NB, Can. 131/H2
Sheelin (lake), Ire. 34/A4
Sheep (mtn.), Ak, US 134/F2
Shefar'am, Isr. 91/G6
Shefayim, Isr. 91/F7
Sheffield, Austl. 115/C4
Sheffield, Al, US 133/G3
Sheffield, Ct, US 139/M7
Sheffield, Eng, UK 35/G5
Shehuén (riv.), Arg. 157/B6
Shek Uk (peak), China 71/V10
Shekak (riv.), Can. 130/C1
Shekhūpura, Pak. 86/B4
Shelagskiy (cape), Rus. 65/S2
Shelburne, NS, Can. 131/H3
Shelby, Mt, US 126/F3
Shelby, Ms, US 129/K4
Shelby, Mi, US 130/C3
Shelby, NC, US 133/H3
Shelbyville, Il, US 133/F2
Shelbyville, Tn, US 133/G3
Shelbyville, In, US 130/C4
Sheldon Point, Ak, US 134/E3
Shelekhov (gulf), Rus. 67/Q3
Shelikof (str.), Ak, US 134/H4
Shell (pt.), Eng, UK 33/G4
Shell Lake, Wi, US 127/L4
Shell Rock, Ia, US 127/K5
Shellbrook, Sk, Can. 127/G2
Shelley (isl.), Pa, US 138/B3
Shelter (isl.), NY, US 139/F1
Shelter Island (sound), NY, US 139/F1
Shelton, Wa, US 126/C4
Shelton, Ct, US 139/E1
Shen Xian, China 72/C3
Shenandoah, Pa, US 138/B2
Shenandoah NP, Va, US 130/E4
Shenchi, China 72/C3
Sheng Xian, China 79/D2
Shenge (pt.), SLeo. 102/B5
Shennongjia, China 72/B5
Shenqiu, China 72/C4
Shenyang, China 73/B2
Shenzhen, China 78/K3
Shepetivka, Ukr. 62/C2
Shepherd (isl.), Van. 116/F6
Shepparton, Austl. 115/C3
Sheppey, Isle of (isl.), Eng, UK 33/G4
Shepshed, Eng, UK 33/E1
Sherbro (isl.), SLeo. 102/C5
Sherbrooke, Qu, Can. 131/G2
Shere (hill), Nga. 103/H4
Sheremetyevo (int'l arpt.), Rus. 61/W9
Sherghāti, India 85/E3
Sheridan, Wy, US 126/G4
Sheridan, Co, US 137/F2
Sherman, Tx, US 129/N4
Sherpur, Bang. 85/H3
Sherwood, Ct, US
Shetland (isls.), UK 160/G
Sheung Shui-Fanling, China 71/U10
Shevchenko (int'l arpt.), Kaz. 63/J4
Shexian, China 79/C2
Sheyang, China 72/E4
Sheyenne (riv.), ND, US 127/J4
Shi (riv.), China 72/C4
Shi San Ling, China 71/H8
Shibakawa, Japan 77/K3
Shibata, Japan 79/A2
Shibayama, Japan 75/F2
Shibecha, Japan 76/D2
Shibetsu, Japan 76/C1
Shibetsu, Japan 76/D1
Shibīn al Kaum, Egypt 91/B4
Shibīn al Qanāṭir, Egypt 91/B4
Shibogama (lake), Can. 127/L2

Shibotsu (isl.), Rus. 76/E2
Shibushi (bay), Japan 74/B5
Shicheng, China 79/D3
Shicheng (isl.), China 73/B1
Shickshinny, Pa, US 138/B1
Shiderty (riv.), Kaz. 87/F2
Shido, Japan 74/D3
Shigaraki, Japan 77/K6
Shihezi, China 70/D3
Shijak, Alb. 47/F2
Shijiazhuang, China 72/C3
Shijōnawate, Japan 77/J6
Shikabe, Japan 76/C2
Shikarpur, India 89/L5
Shikārpur, India 84/B1
Shikārpur, India 89/J5
Shikatsu, Japan 77/L5
Shikine (isl.), Japan 77/G6
Shikishima, Japan 77/K5
Shikohābād, India 84/B2
Shikoku (mts.), Japan 74/C4
Shikoku (isl.), Japan 67/N6
Shikotsu (lake), Japan 76/C2
Shikotsu-Tōya NP, Japan 76/B2
Shilka (riv.), Rus. 67/L4
Shilka, China 89/L2
Shilla (peak), India 84/C1
Shillington, Pa, US 138/C3
Shillong, India 85/H3
Shiloh, Il, US 137/H8
Shiloh, NJ, US 138/C5
Shilou, China 72/B3
Shimabara, Japan 77/B2
Shimada, Japan 77/D2
Shimagahara, Japan 77/K6
Shimane (pref.), Japan 77/J6
Shimanovsk, Rus. 77/K5
Shimasahi, Japan 77/K5
Shimizu, Japan 76/C2
Shimizu, Japan 77/B3
Shimo-koshiki (isl.), Japan 77/M5
Shimobe, Japan 77/A3
Shimoda, Japan 75/F3
Shimodate, Japan 75/F2
Shimofusa, Japan 77/M5
Shimoichi, Japan 77/J7
Shimokita (pen.), Japan 76/B3
Shimonita, Japan 77/B1
Shimonoseki, Japan 74/B4
Shimotsuma, Japan 77/M5
Shimoyama, Japan 77/M5
Shimukappu, Japan 76/C2
Shin, Japan 77/C1
Shin (lake), Sc, UK 31/R7
Shindo, SKor. 73/F6
Shindō, Japan 77/M4
Shingū, Japan 74/C4
Shinhyōn, SKor. 74/A3
Shinji (lake), Japan 74/C3
Shinjō, Japan 76/B4
Shinjō, Japan 77/J7
Shinkawa, Japan 77/M4
Shinminato, Japan 75/E2
Shinnecock (bay), NY, US 139/F2
Shinnecock Ind. Res., NY, US 139/F2
Shinsei, Japan 77/L5
Shintoku, Japan 76/C2
Shintone, Japan 77/M5
Shinyanga, Tanz. 104/B3
Shinyanga (pol. reg.), Tanz. 104/B3
Shio-no-misaki (cape), Japan 74/D4
Shiogama, Japan 75/G1
Shioya-saki (pt.), Japan 75/G2
Shioya-saki (pt.), Japan 75/G2
Shipley, Eng, UK 35/G4
Shippagan, NB, Can. 131/H2
Shippensburg, Pa, US 138/A3
Shiprock, NM, US 128/E3
Shīr (mtn.), Iran 88/F2
Shirakami-misaki (cape), Japan 76/B3
Shirakawa, Japan 75/G2
Shirakawa-tōge (pass), Japan 74/E3
Shirako, Japan 77/M4
Shiranuka, Japan 76/D2
Shiraoka, Japan 77/D1
Shirāz, Iran 88/F3
Shirbīn, Egypt 91/B4
Shiretoko-misaki (cape), Japan 76/D1
Shiriya-zaki (pt.), Japan 76/B3
Shirley, NY, US 139/F2
Shirone, Japan 75/F2
Shiroishi, Japan 75/G2
Shiroyama, Japan 77/A2
Shīrvān, Iran 89/G1
Shishaldin (vol.), Ak, US 134/F5
Shīshgarh, India 84/B1
Shishi, China 79/C3
Shishmaref, Ak, US 134/E2
Shishou, China 79/B2
Shithātha, Iraq 90/E3
Shivpuri NP, India 84/A3
Shixing, China 83/K3
Shiyan, China 79/A1
Shizawa, China 79/A2
Shizugawa, Japan 75/G1
Shizuishan, China 72/A3
Shizukuishi, Japan 75/G1
Shizuoka (pref.), Japan 75/F3
Shō (riv.), Japan 75/E2
Shkodër, Alb. 47/F1
Shmidta (cape), Rus. 134/C2
Shoal Lake, Mb, Can. 127/H3

Shoalhaven (riv.), Austl. 115/D2
Shōbara, Japan 74/C3
Shōbu, Japan 77/D1
Shōdo (isl.), Japan 74/D3
Shokanbetsu-dake (peak), Japan 76/B2
Sholāpur, India 89/L5
Sholl (peak), Arg. 159/D6
Shomron (ruin), WBnk. 91/G8
Shoranur, India 89/H6
Shoreham-by-Sea, Eng, UK 33/F5
Shorewood, Wi, US 135/Q13
Shorewood, Il, US 135/P16
Shorkot, Pak. 86/B4
Short (mtn.), Tn, US 133/G3
Shortland (isls.), Sol. 116/E5
Shoshone (riv.), Wy, US 126/F4
Shoshone (mts.), Nv, US 128/C3
Shoshoni, Wy, US 126/F5
Shostka, Ukr. 62/E2
Shotts, Sc, UK 36/C5
Shou Xian, China 72/D4
Shouguang, China 72/D3
Shouyang, China 72/C3
Show Low, Az, US 128/E4
Shōwa, Japan 77/B2
Shōwa, Japan 77/D2
Shpanberga (chan.), Rus. 76/E2
Shpola, Ukr. 62/D2
Shreveport, La, US 129/J4
Shrewsbury, Mo, US 137/G8
Shrewsbury, Eng, UK 32/D1
Shrewsbury, Pa, US 138/B4
Shriner (mtn.), Ca, US 138/A2
Shropshire (co.), Eng, UK 35/E6
Shropshire Union (canal), Eng, UK 35/E6
Shū (riv.), Kaz. 65/H5
Shu (riv.), China 72/D5
Shuangbai, China 83/H3
Shuangcheng, China 71/N2
Shuangliao, China 72/E2
Shuangyang, China 83/K2
Shuangyashan, China 71/P2
Shu'ayb, Jabal an (peak), Yem. 88/D5
Shubrā al Khaymah, Egypt 91/B4
Shubrā Khīt, Egypt 91/B4
Shucheng, China 72/D5
Shu'fāṯ, Isr. 91/G8
Shufu, China 87/G5
Shuiyang (riv.), China 72/D5
Shujāābād, Pak. 86/A5
Shulan, China 71/N3
Shule, China 87/G5
Shule (riv.), China 64/K6
Shumagin (isls.), Ak, US 134/G4
Shumen, Bul. 49/H4
Shumerlya, Rus. 61/K5
Shuna (isl.), Sc, UK 36/A3
Shunak (peak), Kaz. 87/F3
Shungnak, Ak, US 134/G2
Shunyi, China 72/H6
Shuo Xian, China 72/C3
Shūr (riv.), Iran 89/G2
Shurugwi, Zim. 105/E4
Shūshtar, Iran 88/F2
Shuswap (lake), Can. 126/D3
Shuya, Rus. 60/J4
Shuyang, China 72/D4
Shwegyin, Myan. 83/G3
Shyghys Qazaqstan (obl.), Kaz. 64/J5
Shymkent, Kaz. 87/F4
Shyok (riv.), India 89/L2
Si Satchanalai (ruin), Thai. 78/B2
Si Xian, China 72/D4
Siah Kūh (mts.), Afg. 89/H2
Siak (riv.), Indo. 80/B3
Sialkot, Pak. 86/C3
Siánow, Pol. 38/G4
Siapa (riv.), Ven. 153/E4
Siargao (isl.), Phil. 79/E6
Siasi, Phil. 81/F2
Siaton, Phil. 79/D6
Siaton, Phil. 81/F2
Šiauliai, Lith. 39/K4
Šibalom, Phil. 79/D5
Sibay, Rus. 63/L1
Sibay, Phil. 79/D5
Sibenik, Cro. 48/B4
Siberia, Rus. 67/J3
Siberut (isl.), Indo. 67/J10
Sibi, Pak. 89/J3
Sibiloi NP, Kenya 97/N7
Sibiti, Congo 105/B1
Sibiu (prov.), Rom. 49/G2
Sibiu, Rom. 49/G2
Sibley, Mo, US 137/S5
Sibolga, Indo. 80/A3
Sibsāgar, India 70/D3
Sibu, Malay. 80/D3
Sibuco, Phil. 81/F2
Sibut, CAfr. 97/J6
Sibuyan (sea), Phil. 81/F1
Sibuyan (isl.), Phil. 81/F1
Sicamous, BC, Can. 126/D3
Sichuan (prov.), China 70/H5
Sicilia (pol. reg.), It. 46/C4
Sicily (isl.), It. 27/F5
Sicily, Strait of (str.), It. 46/B3
Sico (riv.), Hon. 140/D4
Sicuani, Peru 156/D4
Siddhapur, India 82/C4
Siddipet, India 82/C4
Sidero, Marina, It. 47/E3
Sidewinder (mtn.), Ca, US 136/C1
Sīdhi, India 84/C3
Sidhaulī, India 84/C2
Sīdi, India 85/E3
Sidlao, Mex. 143/E4
Sīlat az Zahr, WBnk. 91/G8

Sīdī Bū Zayd (gov.), Tun. 46/A5
Sidi Ifni, Mor. 98/C3
Sidi Kacem, Mor. 100/B2
Sidi Kacem (prov.), Mor. 100/B2
Sidi Slimane, Mor. 100/B2
Sidi Yahya du Rharb, Mor. 100/A2
Sidlaw (hills), Sc, UK 36/C3
Sidmouth, Eng, UK 32/C5
Sidney, BC, Can. 126/C3
Sidney, Mt, US 126/G3
Sidney, Oh, US 130/C3
Sidney Lanier (lake), Ga, US 133/H3
Sidra (gulf), Libya 93/D1
Sieci, It. 59/E5
Siedlce, Pol. 41/M2
Siedlce (prov.), Pol. 41/L2
Sieg (riv.), Ger. 43/G1
Siegburg, Ger. 53/F2
Siegen, Ger. 53/F2
Siegenburg, Ger. 55/E5
Siegendorf im Burgenland, Aus. 43/M3
Siemianówka (lake), Pol. 41/M2
Siemiatycze, Pol. 41/M2
Siemreab, Camb. 78/C3
Siena (prov.), It. 59/E6
Siena, It. 43/J5
Sienne (riv.), Fr. 42/C2
Sieradz, Pol. 41/K3
Sieradz (prov.), Pol. 41/K3
Sierck, Pol.
Sierning, Aus. 55/H6
Sierpc, Pol. 41/K2
Sierra (peak), Ca, US 136/C3
Sierra Blanca, Tx, US 129/F5
Sierra de la Macarena, PN, Col.
Sierra de San Pedro Mártir, Mex. 142/B2
Sierra Estrella (mts.), Az, US 137/J10
Sierra Grande, Arg. 158/D4
Sierra Leone (cape), SLeo. 102/C4
Sierra Leone (ctry.), 102/B4
Sierra Madre, Ca, US 136/F7
Sierra Nevada (mts.), Mex. 132/C5
Sierra Nevada de Santa Marta, PN, Col. 152/C4
Sierra Nevada de Santa Marta, PN, Col. 152/C4
Sierra Nevada, PN, Ven. 150/D2
Sierra Nevada, PN, Ven. 141/G6
Sierra Vieja (mts.), US, Mex. 132/B4
Sierras Bayas, Arg. 158/E3
Siete Picos (peak), Sp. 45/M8
Siete Tazas, PN, Chile 158/C2
Sieve (riv.), It. 59/E5
Sif Fatima, Alg. 99/H3
Sifnos (isl.), Gre. 47/J4
Sifton, Pa, US 138/B4
Sig, Alg. 100/D2
Sigatoka, Fiji 117/H6
Sigean, Fr. 42/E5
Siġġiewi, Malta 46/L7
Sighetu Marmaţiei, Rom. 49/G2
Sighişoara, Rom. 49/G2
Sighty Crag (hill), Eng, UK 35/F2
Sigli, Indo. 80/A3
Sigli (cape), Alg. 100/H4
Siglufjördhur, Ice. 37/N6
Sigmaringen, Ger. 57/F2
Sigmarszell, Ger. 57/F2
Signa, It. 59/E5
Signal de la Mère Boitier (peak), Fr. 42/F2
Signal de Toussaines (peak), Fr. 42/D2
Signal Hill, Ca, US 136/F8
Signau, Swi. 56/D4
Signy-L'Abbaye, Fr. 53/D4
Signy-le-Petit, Fr. 53/D4
Signy-Signets, Fr. 30/M6
Sigriswil, Swi. 56/D4
Siguatepeque, Hon. 144/E3
Sigüenza, Sp. 45/E2
Sihl (riv.), Swi. 57/E3
Sihlsee (lake), Swi. 57/E3
Siilinjärvi, Fin. 60/E3
Siirt, Turk. 90/E2
Siirt (prov.), Turk. 90/E2
Sikandarābād, India 84/A1
Sikandarpur, India 85/E3
Sikandra Rao, India 84/B2
Sikanni Chief (riv.), BC, Can. 122/G2
Sīkar, India 89/L3
Sikasso, Mali 102/D3
Sikasso (pol. reg.), Mali 102/D3
Sikeston, Mo, US 129/K3
Sikhote-Alin' (mts.), Rus. 65/P5
Sikinos (isl.), Gre. 47/J4
Sikkim (state), India 84/F2
Siklós, Hun. 40/E5
Sikonge, Tanz. 104/B4
Sil (riv.), Sp. 44/B1
Silai (riv.), India 85/E3
Silandro (Schlanders), It. 43/J3
Silao, India 85/E3
Silao, Mex. 143/E4
Sīlat az Zahr, WBnk. 91/G8
Silay, Phil. 81/F1
Silchar, India 83/F2
Şile, Turk. 62/B4
Šilea, It.
Silenen, Swi. 57/E4

Silesia (reg.), Pol. 41/H3
Silgadhī, Nepal 84/C1
Silifke, Turk. 91/C1
Siliguri, India 85/G3
Silistra, Bul. 49/H3
Siljan (lake), Swe. 38/F1
Siljansnäs, Swe. 38/F1
Silkeborg, Den. 38/C3
Sill (riv.), Aus. 57/H3
Silla, Sp. 45/E3
Silla Tombs, SKor. 74/A3
Sillamäe, Est. 39/M2
Sillaro (riv.), It. 59/E4
Silleda, Sp. 44/A1
Silloth, Eng, UK 35/E2
Sillustani (ruin), Peru 156/D4
Silopi, Turk. 90/E2
Silsbee, Tx, US 129/J5
Silsden, Eng, UK 35/G4
Silsersee (lake), Swi. 57/F5
Silute, Lith. 39/J4
Silvan (dam), Turk. 90/E2
Silvaplana, Swi. 57/F5
Silvassa, India 82/B3
Silver (lake), Or, US 128/C2
Silver (riv.), Or, US 128/C2
Silver Bay, Mn, US 127/L4
Silver City, NM, US 128/E4
Silver Lake, Wi, US 135/P14
Silver Lake-Fircrest, Wa, US 135/C12
Silver Meadow (lake), NJ, US 138/C4
Silver Run, Md, US 138/A4
Silver Spring, Md, US 138/A6
Silverado, Ca, US 136/D3
Silverton, Or, US 126/C4
Silverton, Co, US 128/F3
Silverton, NJ, US 138/D3
Silverwood (lake), Ca, US 136/C2
Silves, Port. 44/A4
Silvi, It. 46/D1
Silvia, Col. 152/B4
Silvies (riv.), Or, US 128/C2
Silvretta (mts.), Aus. 57/G3
Silyānah (gov.), Tun. 46/A4
Silyānah, Tun. 100/L6
Silz, Aus. 57/G3
Sim (cape), Mor. 98/C3
Simão Dias, Braz. 154/C3
Simard (lake), Can. 130/E2
Simbach am Inn, Ger. 55/G6
Simcoe, On, Can. 130/D3
Simcoe (lake), Qu, Can. 123/J4
Simdega, India 85/E4
Simen (mts.), Eth. 97/N5
Simeria, Rom. 48/F3
Simeonof (isl.), Ak, US 134/G4
Simferopol', Ukr. 62/E3
Simi Valley, Ca, US 136/B2
Similaun (peak), It. 43/J3
Simití, Col. 152/C3
Simiyu (riv.), Tanz. 104/B3
Simla, India 84/B1
Simla, Co, US 136/B4
Simleu Silvaniei, Rom. 49/F2
Simme (riv.), Swi. 56/D5
Simmelsdorf, Ger. 55/E3
Simmerath, Ger. 53/F2
Simmerbach (riv.), Ger. 53/G4
Simmern, Ger. 53/G3
Simmozheim, Ger. 54/C5
Simón Bolívar (int'l arpt.), Ven. 152/D2
Simoncello (peak), It. 59/F5
Simonstown, SAfr. 106/L11
Simplício Mendes, Braz. 154/B2
Simplon, Swi. 56/E5
Simplonpass (pass), Swi. 56/E5
Simpson (des.), Austl. 113/G4
Simpson (pen.), NW, Can.
Simpson Desert Conservation Park, Austl. 113/H3
Simpson Desert NP, Austl. 113/H3
Simpsons Gap NP, Austl. 113/G3
Simrishamn, Swe. 38/F4
Simunul, Phil. 81/F3
Sin-le-Noble, Fr. 52/C3
Sinai (peak), Egypt 91/M1
Sinaia, Rom. 49/G3
Sinaloa (state), Mex. 142/C3
Sinaloa de Leyva, Mex. 142/C3
Sinalunga, It. 43/J5
Sinan, China 79/A2
Sīnāwin, Libya 99/H3
Sincé, Col. 152/C2
Sincelejo, Col. 152/C2
Sinch'ang, NKor. 73/D2
Sinch'ŏn, NKor. 73/C3
Sinclair (lake), Ga, US 133/H3
Sinclair (pt.), Austl. 113/G5

Sincorá, Serra do (range), Braz. 154/B4
Sind (riv.), India 84/C1
Sind (prov.), Pak. 82/A2
Sindangan, Phil. 79/D6
Sindangbarang, Indo. 80/D5
Sindelfingen, Ger. 54/C5
Sindirgi, Turk. 62/C5
Sindri (prov.), Pak. 82/A2
Sindhulimādi, Nepal 85/E2
Sindri, India 85/F4
Singapore (cap.), Singapore 80/B3
Singapore (ctry.), 67/K9
Singen, Ger. 57/E2
Sîngeorz-Bāi, Rom. 49/G2
Singida (pol. reg.), Tanz. 104/B3
Singida, Tanz. 104/B4
Singitic (gulf), Gre. 47/H2
Singkang, Indo. 80/C3
Singkawang, Indo. 80/C3
Singkep (isl.), Indo. 80/B4
Singleton, Austl. 115/D2
Singleton (mt.), Austl. 112/C4
Singleton (mt.), Austl. 113/F2
Singou, Réserve Totale de Faune du, Burk. 103/F4
Sinincay, Ecu. 152/B5
Siniscola, It. 46/A2
Sinjār, Iraq 90/E2
Sinjil, WBnk. 91/G7
Sinn (riv.), Ger. 40/E3
Sinnamary, FrG. 153/H2
Sinnamary, Co, US 137/C1
Sinnicolau Mare, Rom. 48/E2
Sinoe (co.), Libr. 102/C5
Sinnyŏng, SKor. 74/E4
Sinoe (lake), Rom. 49/J3
Sinop, Braz. 151/G6
Sinop (prov.), Turk. 62/E4
Sinop, Turk. 62/E4
Sint-Genesius-Rode, Belg. 53/D2
Sint-Gillis-Waas, Belg. 50/B6
Sint-Kateljne-Waver, Belg. 50/D1
Sint-Laureins, Belg. 52/C1
Sint-Martens-Voeren, Belg. 53/E2
Sint-Michielsgestel, Neth. 50/C5
Sint-Niklaas, Belg. 50/C6
Sint-Oedenrode, Neth. 50/C5
Sint-Pieters-Leeuw, Belg. 53/D2
Sint-Truiden, Belg. 53/E2
Sintang, Indo. 80/D3
Sintra (range), Port. 45/P10
Sintra, Port. 45/P10
Sinú (riv.), Col. 150/C2
Sinŭiju, NKor. 73/C2
Sinzheim, Ger. 54/B5
Sinzig, Ger. 53/G2
Sió (riv.), Hun. 48/D2
Siocon, Phil. 81/F2
Siófok, Hun. 40/E5
Sioma Ngwezi NP, Zam. 105/D4
Sion, Swi. 56/D5
Sion Mills, NI, UK 31/Q9
Sioule (riv.), Fr. 42/E4
Sioux City, Ia, US 127/J5
Sioux Lookout, Can. 127/L3
Sipalay, Phil. 79/D6
Sipaliwini (dist.), Sur. 153/H4
Sipanok (chan.), Can. 127/H2
Siparia, Trin. 153/F2
Siping, China 72/F2
Sipiwesk (lake), Can. 122/G3
Siponto (ruin), It. 59/F5
Sipsey (riv.), Al, US 133/G3
Simpelveld, Neth. 53/E2
Siqueira Campos, Braz. 155/B2
Siquia (riv.), Nic. 140/E5
Sira (riv.), Nor. 38/B2
Sīrajganj, Bang. 85/G3
Sirha, Nepal 85/F3
Sirhind, India 86/D4
Sirik (cape), Malay. 80/D3
Sīrik, Iran 89/G3
Sirinhaém, Braz. 154/D2
Sirius, Rus. 62/C...
Sīrjān, Iran 89/G3
Sirmione, It. 58/D2

Sirnach, Swi. 57/F3
Şırnak, Turk. 90/E2
Sirolo, It. 59/G5
Sironj, India 84/A3
Síros (isl.), Gre. 47/J4
Siroua (peak), Mor. 98/D3
Sirsa, India 86/C5
Sirsāganj, India 84/B2
Sirsi, India 84/B1
Sirsi, India 89/K6
Sisak, Cro. 48/C3
Sisaket, Thai. 78/D3
Sishui, China 72/D4
Sisikon, Swi. 57/E4
Sisipuk (lake), Can. 127/H2
Sissach, Swi. 56/D3
Sisseton, SD, US 127/J4
Sissili (prov.), Burk. 103/E4
Sissonne, Fr. 52/C4
Sissonville, WV, US 130/D4
Sisterdale, Tx, US 137/T20
Sisteron, Fr. 42/F4
Siswā Bāzār, India 84/D2
Sitacocha, Peru 156/B2
Sītākunda, Bang. 83/F3
Sītāmarhi, India 85/E2
Sītāpur, India 84/C2
Sitārganj, India 84/B1
Siteki, Swaz. 107/E2
Sitges, Sp. 45/K7
Sithoniá (pen.), Gre. 62/C5
Sitía, Gre. 47/K5
Sitidgi (lake), Can. 134/M2
Sítio Novo do Grajaú, Braz. 154/A2
Sitka, Ak, US 134/L4
Sitno (peak), Slvk. 48/D1
Sittard, Neth. 53/E2
Sittensen, Ger. 51/G2
Sitter (riv.), Swi. 57/F3
Sittingbourne, Eng, UK 33/G4
Sitton (peak), Ca, US 136/C3
Sittwe (Akyab), Myan. 83/F3
Sivac, Yugo. 48/D3
Sivakāsi, India 82/C6
Sīvand, Iran 88/F2
Sivas (prov.), Turk. 62/F5
Sivas, Turk. 62/F5
Siverek, Turk. 90/D2
Siviriez, Swi. 56/C4
Sivrihisar, Turk. 62/D5
Sivry-Courtry, Fr. 30/L6
Siwa Oasis (oasis), Egypt 101/A2
Sīwah, Egypt 97/L2
Siwalik (range), Nepal 70/C5
Siwān, India 85/E2
Siwāni, India 86/C5
Six Flags Great Adventure, NJ, US 138/D3
Six Flags Great America, Il, US 135/Q15
Six Flags Magic Mountain, Ca, US 136/B2
Sixmilecross, NI, UK 34/A2
Sixth (falls), Sudan 97/M4
Siyabuswa, SAfr. 105/E6
Siyāna, India 84/B1
Siyang, China 72/D4
Siziano, It. 58/C2
Siziwang, China 71/K3
Sjælland (isl.), Den. 37/D5
Sjenica, Yugo. 47/G1
Sjöbo, Swe. 38/E4
Sjónfridh (peak), Ice. 37/M6
Sjuntorp, Swe. 38/E2
Skaftafell NP, Ice. 37/P7
Skagen, Den. 38/D3
Skagens (The Skaw) (cape), Den. 38/D3
Skagern (lake), Swe. 38/F2
Skagerrak (str.), Nor.,Den. 27/E3
Skaget (peak), Nor. 38/C1
Skagway, Ak, US 134/L3
Skála, Gre. 47/H4
Skälderviken (bay), Swe. 38/E3
Skálfandafljót (riv.), Ice. 37/P7
Skalica, Slvk. 41/J4
Skalice (riv.), Czh. 43/K2
Skalka (res.), Czh. 55/F2
Skælskør, Den. 38/D4
Skanderborg, Den. 38/C3
Skåne (reg.), Swe. 38/E4
Skanes (int'l arpt.), Tun. 46/B5
Skånland, Nor. 37/F1
Skänninge, Swe. 38/F2
Skanör, Swe. 38/E4
Skantzoura (isl.), Gre. 47/J3
Skara, Swe. 38/E2
Skaraborg (co.), Swe. 37/E4
Skärblacka, Swe. 38/F2
Skåre, Swe. 38/E2
Skarszewy, Pol. 38/H4
Skarżysko-Kamienna, Pol. 41/L3
Skateraw, Sc, UK 36/D5
Skattkärr, Swe. 38/E2
Skawina, Pol. 41/K4
Skeena (riv.), BC, Can. 124/AA13
Skeena (mts.), BC, Can. 122/D3
Skegness, Eng, UK 35/J5
Skellefteå, Swe. 37/G2
Skellefteälven (riv.), Swe. 37/F2
Skelleftehamn, Swe. 37/G2
Skelmersdale, Eng, UK 35/F4
Skelmorlie, Sc, UK 36/B5
Skerne (riv.), Eng, UK 35/G2
Skerries, Ire. 34/B4
Skhimatárion, Gre. 47/H3
Skhirat, Mor. 100/A3
Skhirat Temara (prov.), Mor. 100/A3
Skhiza (isl.), Gre. 47/G4
Skhodnya (riv.), Rus. 61/W9
Ski, Nor. 38/D2
Skíathos, Gre. 47/H3
Skiatook, Ok, US 129/H3
Skibbereen, Ire. 31/P11
Skidegate, BC, Can. 134/M5
Skídhra, Gre. 47/H2
Skien, Nor. 38/C2
Skierniewice (prov.), Pol. 41/K3
Skierniewice, Pol. 41/L3
Skikda, Alg. 100/K6
Skinári (cape), Gre. 47/G4
Skinnskatteberg, Swe. 38/F2
Skipton, Eng, UK 35/F4
Skirfare (riv.), Eng, UK 35/F3
Skíros, Gre. 47/J3
Skive, Den. 38/C3
Skjærhollen, Nor. 38/D2
Skjeberg, Nor. 38/D2
Skjelåtinden (peak), Nor. 37/E2
Skjern, Den. 38/C4
Skjern (riv.), Den. 38/C4
Škofja Loka, Slov. 43/L3
Skoghall, Swe. 38/E2
Skogstorp, Swe. 38/G2
Skokholm (isl.), Wal, UK 32/A3
Skokie (riv.), Il, US 135/Q15
Skokloster, Swe. 38/G2
Sköllersta, Swe. 38/F2
Skolniki Park, Rus. 61/W9
Skomer (isl.), Wal, UK 32/A3
Skópelos (isl.), Gre. 47/H3
Skópelos, Gre. 47/H3
Skopin, Rus. 62/F1
Skopje (cap.), Macd. 47/G1
Skopje (int'l arpt.), Macd. 48/E5
Skotterud, Nor. 38/E2
Skoútari, Gre. 47/H2
Skövde, Swe. 38/E2
Skowhegan, Me, US 131/G2
Skukum (mt.), Can. 134/L3
Skull, Ire. 31/P11
Skultorp, Swe. 38/E2
Skultuna, Swe. 38/G2
Skunk (riv.), Ia, US 130/A3
Skurup, Swe. 41/G1
Skutskär, Swe. 38/G1
Skwentna, Ak, US 134/H3
Skwierzyna, Pol. 41/H2
Skye (isl.), Sc, UK 31/Q8
Skyring (sound), Chile 159/B7
Skytop, Pa, US 138/C1
Slagelse, Den. 38/D4
Slakovský Les (for.), Czh. 55/F2
Slamannan, Sc, UK 36/C5
Slana, Ak, US 134/K3
Slaná (riv.), Slvk. 41/L4
Slane, Ire. 34/B4
Slaney (riv.), Ire. 31/Q10
Slănic, Rom. 49/G3
Slănic-Moldova, Rom. 49/H2
Slantsy, Rus. 39/N2
Slaný, Czh. 55/H2
Slapy (res.), Czh. 55/H3
Slatedale, Pa, US 138/C2
Slatina, Rom. 49/G3
Slatington, Pa, US 138/C2
Slaton, Tx, US 129/G4
Slattum, Nor. 38/D1
Slaughter Beach, De, US 138/C6
Slaughterville, Ok, US 137/N15
Slave (coast), Afr. 103/F5
Slave (riv.), NW, Can. 122/E2
Slave Lake, Ab, Can. 126/E2
Slavgorod, Rus. 87/G2
Slavkov u Brna, Czh. 43/M2
Slavonia (reg.), Cro. 48/C3
Slavonska Požega, Cro. 48/C3
Slavonski Brod, Cro. 48/D3
Slavuta, Ukr. 62/C2
Slavyanovo, Bul. 49/G4
Slavyansk-na-Kubani, Rus. 62/F3
Sławno, Pol. 38/G4
Sleen, Neth. 50/D3
Sleeper (isls.), On, Can. 123/H3
Sleeping Bear Dunes Nat'l Lakeshore, US 130/C2
Sleepy Hollow, NY, US 139/K7
Sleepy Hollow, Il, US 135/P15
Sleetmute, Ak, US 134/G3
Slidell, La, US 137/Q16
Sliedrecht, Neth. 50/B5
Sliema, Malta 46/M7
Slieve Binnian (peak), NI, UK 34/C3
Slieve Croob (peak), NI, UK 34/C3
Slieve Donard (peak), NI, UK 34/C3
Slieve Gullion (peak), NI, UK 34/B3
Slieve Snaght (peak), Ire. 34/A1
Slioch (peak), Sc, UK 36/A1
Slite, Swe. 39/H3
Sliven, Bul. 47/K1
Slivnitsa, Bul. 47/H1
Sloan, NY, US 131/S10
Sloatsburg, NY, US 139/J7
Slobodskoy, Rus. 61/L4
Slobozia, Rom. 49/H3
Slochteren, Neth. 50/D2
Sloten, Neth. 50/C3
Slotermeer (lake), Neth. 50/C3
Slough, Eng, UK 30/B2
Slovakia (ctry.) 27/F4
Slovenia (ctry.) 27/F4
Slovenj Gradec, Slov. 43/L3
Slovenska Bistrica, Slov. 43/L3
Slovenska Ľupča, Slvk. 41/K4
Slovenske Konjice, Slov. 43/L3
Slovenské Rudohorie (mts.), Slvk. 41/L4
Slov'yans'k, Ukr. 62/F2
Słowiński PN, Pol. 38/G4
Słubice, Pol. 41/H2
Sluch' (riv.), Ukr. 62/C2
Sluderno (Schluderns), It. 57/G4
Sluis, Neth. 52/C1
Słupca, Pol. 41/J2
Słupia (riv.), Pol. 38/G4
Słupsk, Pol. 38/G4
Słupsk (prov.), Pol. 38/G4
Slutsk, Bela. 62/C1
Slyne Head (pt.), Ire. 30/F10
Smålandsstenar, Swe. 38/E3
Smallwood (res.), Can. 119/L4
Smeaton, Sk, Can. 127/G2
Smederevo, Yugo. 48/E3
Smederevska Palanka, Yugo. 48/E3
Smedjebacken, Swe. 38/F1
Smendou (riv.), Alg. 100/J4
Śmigiel, Pol. 41/J2
Smila, Ukr. 62/D2
Smilde, Neth. 50/D3
Smith (riv.), Mt, US 126/F4
Smith (inlet), Can. 126/B3
Smith (isl.), Qu, Can. 123/J2
Smith Mountain (lake), Va, US 130/E4
Smith Village, Ok, US 137/N15
Smithburg, NJ, US 138/D3
Smithers, BC, Can. 126/B2
Smithfield, Ut, US 126/F5
Smithfield, NC, US 133/J3
Smiths Creek, Mi, US 135/G6
Smiths Falls, On, Can. 130/E2
Smithton, Austl. 115/C4
Smithton, Il, US 137/H9
Smithtown (bay), NY, US 139/E2
Smithtown, NY, US 139/E2
Smithville, Ok, US 132/E3
Smithville (lake), Mo, US 137/D5
Smithville, Mo, US 137/D5
Smoky (cape), Austl. 115/E1
Smoky (hills), US 129/H3
Smoky (riv.), Ab, Can. 122/E3
Smoky Hill (riv.), Ks, US 124/F4
Smoky Lake, Ab, Can. 126/E2
Smøla (isl.), Nor. 37/C3
Smolensk, Rus. 60/G5
Smolensk Oblast, Rus. 60/F5
Smólikas (peak), Gre. 47/G2
Smolyan, Bul. 47/J2
Smooth Rock Falls, On, Can. 130/D1
Smrčina (peak), Czh. 55/G5
Smutná (riv.), Czh. 55/H4
Smyadovo, Bul. 49/H4
Smyrna, Ga, US 133/G3
Smyrna (riv.), De, US 138/C5
Smyrna, De, US 138/C5
Snaefell (peak), IM, UK 34/D3
Snake (riv.), US 119/F5
Snake River (plain), Id, US 126/E5
Snares (isls.), NZ 117/R12
Snåsa, Nor. 37/E2
Snedsted, Den. 38/C3
Sneek, Neth. 50/C2
Sneekermeer (lake), Neth. 50/C2
Sneeuberg (peak), SAfr. 106/B4
Sneeuberg (mts.), SAfr. 106/D3
Sneeuwkop (peak), SAfr. 106/L11
Snejbjerg, Den. 38/C3
Sněžka (peak), Czh. 41/H3
Snežnik (peak), Slov. 43/L4
Sni Mills, Mo, US 137/E6
śniardwy (lake), Pol. 41/L2
Snodland, Eng, UK 33/G4
Snøhetta (peak), Nor. 37/D3
Snohomish, Wa, US 135/C2
Snohomish (co.), Wa, US 135/C2
Snohomish (riv.), Wa, US 135/C2
Snoqualmie (riv.), Wa, US 135/D2
Snoqualmie (falls), Wa, US 135/D2
Snoqualmie, Wa, US 135/D2
Snoqualmie Falls, Wa, US 135/D2
Snoqualmie, Middle Fk. (riv.), Wa, US 135/D2
Snoqualmie, North Fork (riv.), Wa, US 135/D2
Snoqualmie, South Fork (riv.), Wa, US 135/D3
Snøtind (peak), Nor. 37/E2
Snowdon (peak), Wal, UK 34/D5
Snowdonia NP, Wal, UK 34/D6
Snowdrift, NW, Can. 122/E2
Snowflake, Az, US 128/E4
Snowtown, Austl. 113/H5
Snowy (peak), Ak, US 134/K2
Snowy (riv.), Austl. 115/D3
Snowy River NP, Austl. 115/D3
Snyder (co.), Pa, US 138/A2
Snydertown, Pa, US 138/B2
Snyderville, Ut, US 137/K12
Soalala, Madg. 107/H7
Soanierana-Ivongo, Madg. 107/J7
Soanindrariny, Madg. 107/H7
Soar (riv.), Eng, UK 35/G6
Soavina, Madg. 107/H8
Soavina, Madg. 107/J8
Soavinandriana, Madg. 107/H7
Sobaek (mts.), SKor. 73/D5
Soběslav, Czh. 55/H4
Sobger (riv.), Indo. 81/K4
Sobhādero, Pak. 89/J3
Sobradinho, Represa (res.), Braz. 147/E3
Sobral, Braz. 154/B1
Sobretta (peak), It. 57/G5
Sobue, Japan 77/L5
Soc Trang, Viet. 78/D4
Soča (riv.), Slov. 43/K3
Socabaya, Peru 156/D5
Sochaczew, Pol. 41/L2
Sochi, Rus. 62/F4
Sŏch'ŏn, SKor. 73/D4
Söchtenau, Ger. 55/F7
Soci, It. 59/E5
Society (isls.), FrPol. 117/K6
Socorro, Tx, US 129/F5
Socorro, NM, US 128/F4
Socorro, Braz. 211/G7
Socorro (isl.), NM, Mex. 142/C5
Socorro, Col. 152/C3
Socota, Peru 156/B2
Socotá, Col. 152/C3
Socotra (isl.), Yem. 67/E8
Socuéllamos, Sp. 44/D3
Soda Springs, Id, US 126/F5
Sodankylä, Fin. 60/E2
Sodegaura, Japan 77/D3
Söderbärke, Swe. 38/F1
Söderfors, Swe. 38/G1
Söderhamn, Swe. 38/G1
Söderköping, Swe. 38/G2
Södermanland (co.), Swe. 37/E4
Södertälje, Swe. 38/G2
Sodo, Eth. 97/N6
Sŏdu (riv.), NKor. 73/E2
Sodwana Bay NP, SAfr. 107/F2
Soest, Ger. 51/F5
Soest, Neth. 50/C4
Soeste (riv.), Ger. 40/D2
Sofádhes, Gre. 47/H3
Sofia (int'l arpt.), Bul. 47/H1
Sofia (riv.), Madg. 107/J6
Sofia (Sofiya) (cap.), Bul. 47/H1
Sofiya (prov.), Bul. 47/H1
Sogamoso (riv.), Col. 152/C3
Sogamoso, Col. 152/C3
Sögel, Ger. 51/E3
Sogn Og Fjordane (co.), Nor. 37/C3
Sognafjorden (inlet), Nor. 37/C3
Sogndal, Nor. 38/B1
Søgne, Nor. 38/B2
Sogollé (well), Chad 96/J4
Soğuksu NP, Turk. 62/E4
Söğüt, Turk. 62/D5
Söğütlü, Turk. 49/K5
Sogwass (peak), Ugan. 104/B2
Sohāgpur, India 84/B4
Sohren, Ger. 53/G4
Sŏhŭng, NKor. 73/D3
Soignies, Belg. 53/D2
Soignolles-en-Brie, Fr. 30/L6
Soissons, Fr. 52/C5
Sōja, Japan 74/C3
Sojat, India 89/K3
Sŏjosŏn (bay), NKor. 73/C3
Sok (riv.), Rus. 63/J1
Sok (riv.), Thai. 78/C3
Sōka, Japan 77/D2
Sokch'o, SKor. 73/E3
Söke, Turk. 90/A2
Sokhós, Gre. 47/H2
Sokhumi, Geo. 63/G4
Sokna, Nor. 38/C1
Soko (isls.), China 71/T11
Soko Banja, Yugo. 48/E4
Sokodé, Togo 103/F4
Sokol, Rus. 60/J4
Sokol (peak), Czh. 55/G4
Sokółka, Pol. 41/M2
Sokolov, Czh. 55/F2
Sokołów Podlaski, Pol. 41/M2
Sokoto (plain), Nga. 96/F5
Sokoto (riv.), Nga. 96/F5
Sokoto, Nga. 103/G3
Sokoto (state), Nga. 103/G3
Sol, Costa del (coast), Sp. 44/C4
Sol'-Iletsk, Rus. 63/K2
Sola, Nor. 38/A2
Sola (int'l arpt.), Nor. 38/A2
Solana, Phil. 79/D4
Solana Beach, Ca, US 136/C5
Solânea, Braz. 154/D2
Solano, Phil. 79/D4
Solano (pt.), Col. 152/B3
Solano (co.), Ca, US 135/L10
Solarolo, It. 59/E4
Solca, Rom. 49/G2
Sölden, Aus. 57/H4
Soldier (riv.), Ia, US 129/J2
Soldotna, Ak, US 134/H3
Soledad, Col. 152/C2
Soledad, Ven. 153/F2
Soledad Canyon (canyon), Ca, US 136/B2
Soledad de Doblado, Mex. 143/N7
Soledad de Graciano, Mex. 143/E4
Soledade, Braz. 155/A4
Solent, The (chan.), Eng, UK 33/E5
Solesino, It. 59/E2
Solesmes, Fr. 52/C3
Soleuvre (peak), Lux. 53/E4
Solferino, It. 58/D2
Solhan, Turk. 90/E2
Soliera, It. 59/D3
Soligo, It. 59/F1
Solihull, Eng, UK 33/E2
Solimões (riv.), Braz. 153/E5
Solingen, Ger. 50/E6
Sollefteå, Swe. 37/F3
Sollentuna, Swe. 38/G2
Sóller, Sp. 45/G3
Sollerön, Swe. 38/F1
Solling (mts.), Ger. 40/E3
Solmsbach (riv.), Ger. 54/B2
Søln (peak), Nor. 37/D3
Solnan (riv.), Fr. 42/F3
Solntsevo, Rus. 61/W9
Solo (riv.), Indo. 80/D5
Solok, Indo. 80/B4
Sololá, Guat. 144/D3
Solomon, Ak, US 134/F3
Solomon (riv.), US 129/H3
Solomon (sea), PNG,Sol. 116/D5
Solomon Islands (ctry.) 116/E6
Solomon, North Fork (riv.), US 129/G3
Solonchak Goklenkui (swamp), Trkm. 87/C4
Solonópole, Braz. 154/C2
Solothurn, Swi. 56/D3
Solothurn (canton), Swi. 56/D3
Solovetskiy (isls.), Rus. 60/G2
Solre-le-Château, Fr. 53/D3
Solsona, Sp. 45/F2
Solt, Hun. 48/D2
Šolta (isl.), Cro. 46/E1
Soltau, Ger. 51/G3
Soltustik Qazaqstan (obl.), Kaz. 64/G4
Soltvadkert, Hun. 48/D2
Solunska (peak), Macd. 47/G2
Solva (riv.), Wal, UK 32/A3
Solvang, Ca, US 128/B4
Sölvesborg, Swe. 38/F3
Solway Firth (inlet), Eng.,Sc, UK 34/E2
Solwezi, Zam. 105/E3
Solymár, Hun. 49/Q9
Sōma, Japan 75/G2
Soma, Turk. 62/C5
Somain, Fr. 52/C3
Somalia (ctry.) 93/G4
Sombor, Yugo. 48/D3
Sombra, On, Can. 135/H6
Sombreffe, Belg. 53/D2
Sombrerete, Mex. 142/E4
Sombrio, Braz. 155/B4
Someren, Neth. 50/C6
Somero, Fin. 39/K1
Somers, Mt, US 126/E3
Somers, Wi, US 135/Q14
Somers Point, NJ, US 138/D5
Somerset, Ky, US 130/C4
Somerset, NY, US 131/S9
Somerset, Tx, US 137/T21
Somerset (co.), Eng, UK 32/D4
Somerset, NJ, US 138/D3
Somerset (isl.), NW, Can. 122/G1
Somerset East, SAfr. 106/D4
Somerset West, SAfr. 106/L11
Somersworth, NH, US 131/G3
Somerton, Az, US 128/D4
Somerville (lake), Tx, US 129/H5
Somerville, NJ, US 138/D2
Someş (riv.), Rom. 62/B3
Someşul Mare (riv.), Rom. 49/G2
Someswar (range), India 85/E2
Somis, Ca, US 136/B2
Sŏmjin (riv.), SKor. 73/D5
Somma Lombardo, It. 58/B1
Sommacampagna, It. 59/D2
Sommam (riv.), Alg. 100/H4
Sommariva del Bosco, It. 58/A3
Somme (bay), Fr. 42/D1
Somme (dept.), Fr. 52/B4
Somme (riv.), Fr. 40/B3
Somme, Canal de la (canal), Fr. 52/B4
Somme-Leuze, Belg. 53/E3
Somme-Soude (riv.), Fr. 53/D6
Sommedieue, Fr. 53/E5
Sommen (lake), Swe. 38/F2
Sommet de Finiels (peak), Fr. 42/E4
Sommevoire, Fr. 56/A1
Somogy (prov.), Hun. 48/C2
Somoto, Nic. 144/E3
Son (riv.), India 70/D7
Son Servera, Sp. 45/G3
Sona, It. 59/D2
Sonāmukhi, India 85/F4
Sonāmura, India 85/H4
Sonār (riv.), India 84/B4
Sonchamp, Fr. 30/H6
Sŏnch'ŏn, NKor. 73/C3
Soncino, It. 58/C2
Sondalo, It. 57/G5
Sønder Nissum, Den. 38/C3
Sonderborg (int'l arpt.), Den. 38/C4
Sønderborg, Den. 38/C4
Sonderend (riv.), SAfr. 106/L11
Sønderjylland (co.), Den. 38/C4
Sondica (int'l arpt.), Sp. 44/D1
Sondrio, It. 57/F5
Sondrio (dept.), It. 57/F5
Sonepur, India 82/D3
Song (peak), China 72/C4
Song Xian, China 72/C4
Songea, Tanz. 104/B5
Songeons, Fr. 52/A4
Songhua (riv.), China 67/M5
Sŏnghwan, SKor. 73/D4
Songi (isl.), SKor. 73/C5
Songino, Mong. 70/G2
Songjiang, China 72/L8
Sŏngju, SKor. 73/E5
Songkhla, Thai. 78/C5
Songkhram (riv.), Thai. 83/H4
Songling, China 71/M2
Songming, China 83/H2
Sŏngnam, SKor. 73/G7
Songnim, NKor. 73/C3
Songololo, D.R. Congo 105/B2
Songt'an, SKor. 73/D4
Songtao Miaozu Zizhixian, China 79/A2
Songxi, China 79/C2
Songzi, China 79/B1
Songzi (pass), China 72/C5
Soni, Japan 77/K6
Sonid Youqi, China 71/K3
Sonid Zuoqi, China 71/K3
Sonīpat, India 86/D5
Sonneberg, Ger. 54/E2
Sonnefeld, Ger. 54/E2
Sonnjoch (peak), Aus. 57/H3
Sonntagshorn (peak), Ger. 43/K3
Sonobe, Japan 77/H5
Sonoma (mts.), Ca, US 135/J10
Sonoma (co.), Ca, US 135/J10
Sonora, Ca, US 128/B3
Sonora, Tx, US 129/G5
Sonora (state), Mex. 142/C2
Sonoyta, Mex. 128/D5
Sonoyta (riv.), Mex. 142/B2
Sonpur, India 85/E3
Sonqor, Iran 88/E2
Sŏnsan, SKor. 73/E4
Sonsbeck, Ger. 50/D5
Sonseca, Sp. 44/D3
Sonsonate, ESal. 144/D3
Sonsorol (isls.), Palau 116/C4
Sonta, Yugo. 48/D3
Sontheim, Ger. 57/G2
Sontheim an der Brenz, Ger. 54/D5
Sonthofen, Ger. 57/G2
Sontra, Ger. 51/G6
Sonvico, Swi. 57/E5
Sopetrán, Col. 152/C3
Sopi (cape), Indo. 81/G3
Sopor, India 86/C2
Sopot, Bul. 47/J1
Sopot, Pol. 38/H4
Sopron, Hun. 43/M3
Sŏr (riv.), Wal, UK 32/D3
Sor Karatuley (salt pan), Kaz. 87/C4
Sor Kaydak (swamp), Kaz. 63/K3
Sor Mertvyy Kultuk (swamp), Kaz. 87/B3
S'ør-Trøndelag (co.), Nor. 37/D3
Sør-Varanger, Nor. 37/J1
Sora, It. 46/C2
Soragna, It. 58/D3
Sŏrak-san (peak), SKor. 73/E3
Sŏraksan NP, SKor. 73/E3
Sorata, Bol. 150/E7
Sorbas, Sp. 44/D4
Sorbolo, It. 58/D3
Sorcy-Saint-Martin, Fr. 53/E6
Sorel, Qu, Can. 130/F2
Sorell-Midway Point, Austl. 115/C4
Soresina, It. 58/C2
Sörforsa, Swe. 38/G1
Sorgues, Fr. 42/F5
Sorgun, Turk. 62/E5
Sori, It. 58/C4
Soria, Sp. 44/D2
Soriano (dept.), Uru. 158/G3
Soriano, Uru. 159/J10
Sorikmerapi (peak), Indo. 80/A3
Soritor, Peru 156/B2
Sormonne (riv.), Fr. 53/D4
Sorø, Den. 38/D4
Soro, Rio do (riv.), Braz. 151/J5
Soroca, Mol. 49/J1
Sorocaba, Braz. 155/C2
Sorochinsk, Rus. 63/K1
Sorol (isl.), Micr. 116/D4
Soron, India 84/B2
Sorong, Indo. 81/H4
Soroti, Ugan. 104/B2
Sørøya (isl.), Nor. 37/G1
Sørøysundet (chan.), Nor. 37/G1
Sorpestausee (lake), Ger. 51/E6
Sorraia (riv.), Port. 44/A3
Sorrento, It. 46/D2
Sorsele, Swe. 37/F2
Sorso, It. 46/A2
Sorsogon, Phil. 79/D5
Sort, Sp. 45/F1
Sõrve (pt.), Est. 39/K3
Sos del Rey Católico, Sp. 44/E1
Sŏsan, SKor. 73/D4
Sŏsan Haean NP, SKor. 73/C4
Sösdala, Swe. 38/E3
Söse (riv.), Ger. 51/H5
Soshanguve, SAfr. 105/E6
Sosna (riv.), Rus. 62/F1
Sosneado (peak), Arg. 158/C2
Sosnogorsk, Rus. 61/M3
Sosnovka, Rus. 62/G1
Sosnowiec, Pol. 41/K3
Sospiro, It. 58/D2
Sosúa, DRep. 141/G4
Sos'va (riv.), Rus. 64/G3
Sot (riv.), India 84/B1
Soto del Real, Sp. 44/D2
Soto la Marina, Mex. 143/F4
Sotouboua, Togo 103/F4
Sottrum, Ger. 51/G2
Sotuta, Mex. 144/D1
Soude (riv.), Fr. 53/D6
Souderton, Pa, US 138/C3
Soúdha, Gre. 47/J5
Souffelweyersheim, Fr. 53/G6
Soufflenheim, Fr. 53/G6
Souflíon, Gre. 47/K2
Soufrière (peak), StV. 141/N9
Soufrière (peak), Guad. 141/N8
Souillac, Fr. 42/D4
Souillac, Mrts. 107/T15
Souk Ahras, Alg. 100/K6
Souk Ahras (prov.), Alg. 100/K6
Souk el Arba du Rharb, Mor. 100/A2
Sŏul (Seoul) (cap.), SKor. 71/N4
Soultz-Haut-Rhin, Fr. 56/D2
Soultz-sous-Forêts, Fr. 54/A5
Soum (prov.), Burk. 103/E3
Soumagne, Belg. 53/E2
Sound, The (chan.), Den. 37/E5
Souppes-sur-Loing, Fr. 42/E2
Sour El Ghozlane, Alg. 100/G4
Sources, Mont aux (peak), Les. 106/E3
Soure, Braz. 151/J4
Soure, Port. 44/A2
Souris, Mb, Can. 127/H3
Souris, PE, Can. 131/J2
Souris (riv.), Can.,US 122/F4
Sourou (prov.), Burk. 102/E3
Sous le Vent, Îles (isls.), FrPol. 117/K6
Sousa, Braz. 154/C2
Sout (riv.), SAfr. 106/C3
South (mts.), Can. 131/H2
South (cape), NZ 117/R12
South (mtn.), Pa, US 138/A3
South (bay), NW, Can. 123/H2
South (isl.), NZ 109/H7
South Africa (ctry.) 105/D6
South Amboy, NJ, US 139/H10
South America (cont.) 147
South Andaman (isl.), India 83/F5
South Anna (riv.), Va, US 133/J2
South Augusta, Ga, US 133/H3
South Aulatsivik (isl.), Nf, Can. 123/K3
South Australia, Austl. 115/B1
South Australia (state), Austl. 109/C3
South Bend, Wa, US 126/C4
South Bend, In, US 130/C3
South Benfleet, Eng, UK 33/G3
South Buganda (prov.), Ugan. 104/A3
South Burlington, Vt, US 130/F2
South Caicos (isl.), UK 145/J1
South Carolina (state), US 125/K5
South China (sea), Asia 67/L8
South Colby, Wa, US 135/B2
South Dakota (state), US 124/F3
South Dorset Downs (uplands), Eng, UK 32/D5
South Downs (hills), Eng, UK 33/F5
South Dum Dum, India 85/G4
South East (pt.), Austl. 115/C3
South East (cape), Austl. 109/D5
South Elgin, Il, US 135/P16
South Esk (riv.), Austl. 115/C4
South Esk (riv.), Sc, UK 36/C3
South Farmingdale, NY, US 139/M9
South Fork, Co, US 132/B2
South Fulton, Tn, US 130/B4
South Gate, Md, US 138/B5
South Gate, Ca, US 136/F8
South Georgia (isl.), UK 22/H8
South Glamorgan (co.), Wal, UK 32/C4
South Hams (plain), Eng, UK 32/C6
South Holland, Il, US 135/Q16
South Island NP, Kenya 104/C2
South Jordan, Ut, US 137/K12
South Koel (riv.), India 85/E4
South Korea (ctry.) 67/M6
South Lake Tahoe, Ca, US 128/C3
South Loup (riv.), Ne, US 127/J5
South Luangwa NP, Zam. 105/F3
South Lyon, Mi, US 135/E7
South Magnetic Pole, Ant. 160/K
South Moose (lake), Can. 127/J2
South Moresby NP and Prsv., Can. 134/M5
South Naknek, Ak, US 134/G4
South Normanton, Eng, UK 35/G5
South Nyack, NY, US 139/K7
South Ockenden, Eng, UK 30/D2
South Ogden, Ut, US 137/K11
South Orange, NJ, US 139/H9
South Orkney (isls.), UK 160/X
South Ossetia (reg.), Geo. 63/G4
South Oxhey, Eng, UK 30/B2
South Oyster (bay), NY, US 139/M9
South Pacific (ocean) 22/B7
South Para (res.), Austl. 113/M8
South Pasadena, Ca, US 136/F7
South Pine (riv.), Austl. 114/E6
South Plainfield, NJ, US 139/H9
South Platte (riv.), Co, US 137/C2
South Polar (plat.), Ant. 160/Y
South Pole, Ant. 160/A
South Prairie, Wa, US 135/C3
South River, NJ, US 139/H10
South Rockwood, Mi, US 135/F7
South Ronaldsay (isl.), Sc, UK 31/V14
South Roxana, Il, US 137/G8
South Salt Lake, Ut, US 137/K12
South San Francisco, Ca, US 135/K11
South Sandwich (isls.), UK 22/H8
South Saskatchewan (riv.), Sk, Can. 122/E3
South Seaville, NJ, US 138/D5
South Shetland (isls.), UK 160/W
South Shields, Eng, UK 35/G2
South Sioux City, Ne, US 127/J5
South Skunk (riv.), Ia, US 129/J2
South Taranaki Bight (bay), NZ 117/S10
South Turkana Nat'l Rsv., Kenya 104/B2
South Tyne (riv.), Eng, UK 35/F2
South Ubian, Phil. 81/F2
South Uist (isl.), Sc, UK 31/Q8
South Umpqua (riv.), Or, US 128/B2
South Valley Stream, NY, US 139/L9
South Weber, Ut, US 137/K11
South West (cape), Austl. 115/C4
South West NP, Austl. 115/C4
South West Rocks, Austl. 115/E1
South Whittier, Ca, US 136/F8
South Williamsport, Pa, US 138/B1
South Woodham Ferrers, Eng, UK 30/E2
South Yorkshire (co.), Eng, UK 35/G5
Southampton, On, Can. 130/D2
Southampton, Eng, UK 33/E5
Southampton (cape), NW, Can. 123/H2
Southampton, NY, US 139/F2
Southampton (isl.), NW, Can. 123/H2
Southampton Water (inlet), Eng, UK 33/E5
Southaven, Ms, US 129/K4
Southeast (cape), Ak, US 134/E3
Southeast (pt.), Bahm. 145/H1
Southeast (pt.), Jam. 145/G2
Southend (int'l arpt.), Eng, UK 33/G3
Southend-on-Sea, Eng, UK 33/G3
Southern (prov.), Ugan. 104/A3
Southern (dist.), Isr. 91/D4
Southern (mts.), NZ 109/G7
Southern (riv.), Austl. 112/K7
Southern Cook (isls.), Cookls. 117/J6
Southern Cross, Austl. 112/C4
Southern Indian (lake), Mb, Can. 122/G3
Southern NP, Sudan 97/L6
Southern Pines, NC, US 133/J3
Southern Uplands (hills), Sc, UK 35/D1
Southern Ural (mts.), Rus. 61/N5
Southesk Tablelands (plat.), Austl. 109/B2
Southold, NY, US 139/F1
Southport, NC, US 133/J3
Southport, Eng, UK 35/E4
Southton, Tx, US 137/U21
Southwark (bor.), Eng, UK 30/A1
Southwood NP, Austl. 114/C4
Southworth, Wa, US 135/C3
Sovata, Rom. 49/G2
Soverato Marina, It. 46/E3
Sovere, It. 58/D1
Sovetsk, Rus. 39/J4
Sŏwa, Japan 77/D1
Sowerby Bridge, Eng, UK 35/G4
Soweto, SAfr. 106/D2
Sōya-misaki (cape), Japan 76/B1
Soyana (riv.), Rus. 60/J2
Soyang (lake), SKor. 74/A2
Soyaux, Fr. 42/D4
Soyen, Ger. 55/F6
Soyhières, Swi. 56/D3
Sozh (riv.), Bela. 62/D1
Sozopol, Bul. 49/H4
Spa, Belg. 53/E3
Spada (lake), Wa, US 135/D2
Spain (ctry.) 27/D4
Spalding, Austl. 113/H5
Spalding, Eng, UK 35/H6
Spalt, Ger. 54/D4
Spanish Lake, Mo, US 137/G8
Spanish Town, Jam. 145/G2
Spannort (peak), Swi. 57/E4
Sparanise, It. 46/D2
Sparks, Nv, US 128/C3
Sparlingville, Mi, US 135/G6
Sparreholm, Swe. 38/G2
Sparta, Wi, US 127/L5
Sparta, Tn, US 130/C5
Sparta, NC, US 130/D4
Sparta, NJ, US 138/D1
Spartanburg, SC, US 133/H3
Spartel (cape), Mor. 100/B2
Spárti (Sparta), Gre. 47/H4
Spartivento (cape), It. 46/E4
Sparwood, BC, Can. 126/E3
Spassk-Dal'niy, Rus. 71/P3
Spáta, Gre. 47/N9
Spátha (cape), Gre. 47/H5
Spean (riv.), Sc, UK 36/B3
Speer (peak), Swi. 57/F3
Speer Canal (canal), Co, US 137/C2
Speicher, Swi. 57/F3
Speicher, Ger. 53/F4
Speichersdorf, Ger. 55/E3
Speke (gulf), Tanz. 104/B3
Speke (int'l arpt.), Eng, UK 35/F5
Spelle, Ger. 51/E4
Spence Bay, NW, Can. 122/G2
Spencer (pt.), Ak, US 134/E2
Spencer, Ia, US 127/K5
Spencer (gulf), Austl. 109/C4
Spencer, Ok, US 137/N14
Spencer (cape), Austl. 113/H5
Spenge, Ger. 51/F4
Spennymoor, Eng, UK 35/G2
Spentrup, Den. 38/D3
Sperkhiás, Gre. 47/H3
Sperkhios (riv.), Gre. 47/H3
Sperrin (mts.), NI, UK 34/A2
Spessart (range), Ger. 54/C3
Spétsai, Gre. 47/H4
Spey (riv.), Sc, UK 36/B2
Spey (bay), Sc, UK 36/C1
Speyer, Ger. 54/B4
Speyerbach (riv.), Ger. 54/B4
Spezzano Albanese, It. 46/E3
Špičák (peak), Czh. 55/F2
Spicer (isls.), NW, Can. 123/H2
Spiekeroog (isl.), Ger. 51/E1
Spiez, Swi. 56/D4
Spigno Monferrato, It. 58/B3
Spijkenisse, Neth. 50/B5
Spike (mtn.), Ak, US 134/K2
Spilamberto, It. 59/E3
Spílion, Gre. 47/J5
Spilve (int'l arpt.), Lat. 39/L3
Spina (peak), It. 46/A2
Spinetta Marengo, It. 58/B3
Spino d'Adda, It. 58/C2
Spirano, It. 58/C1
Spirit River, Ab, Can. 126/D2
Spiritwood, Sk, Can. 126/G2
Spišská Nová Ves, Slvk. 41/L4
Spiti (riv.), India 86/D3
Spitsbergen (isl.), Sval. 160/E
Split, Cro. 48/C4
Split (int'l arpt.), Cro. 48/C4
Split (lake), Mb, Can. 122/G3
Splitrock (res.), NJ, US 139/H8
Spluga, Passo dello (pass), Swi. 57/F5
Splügen, Swi. 57/F4
Spokane, Wa, US 126/D4
Spokane (riv.), Wa, US 126/D4
Spöl (riv.), It. 57/G5
Spoleto, It. 43/K5
Spoon (riv.), Il, US 130/B3
Spooner, Wi, US 127/L4
Spotorno, It. 58/B4
Spotswood, NJ, US 139/H10
Sprague, Mb, Can. 127/K3
Sprang, Neth. 50/C5
Spratly (isls.) 80/D2
Spree (riv.), Ger. 41/H2
Sprendlingen, Ger. 53/G4
Spresiano, It. 59/F1
Sprimont, Belg. 53/E3
Spring, Tx, US 129/J5
Spring City, Pa, US 138/C3
Spring Grove, Pa, US 138/B4
Spring Grove, Il, US 135/P15
Spring Hill, Ks, US 137/D6
Spring Lake, NJ, US 138/D3
Spring Valley, Ca, US 136/D5

Spring – Swarz

Spring Valley, NY, US 139/J7
Springbok, SAfr. 106/B3
Springdale, Nf, US 131/K1
Springdale, Ar, US 129/J3
Springe, Ger. 51/G4
Springer, NM, US 129/F3
Springerville, Az, US 128/E4
Springfield, Or, US 126/C4
Springfield, Tn, US 130/C4
Springfield, Vt, US 131/H3
Springfield, Ma, US 131/F3
Springfield, Mo, US 129/J3
Springfield, Va, US 138/A6
Springfield, NJ, US 139/H9
Springfontein, SAfr. 106/D3
Springhill, La, US 129/J4
Springhill, NS, Can. 131/H2
Springs, SAfr. 106/E2
Springs, NY, US 139/F1
Springside, Sk, Can. 123/J2
Springsure, Austl. 114/C4
Springville, Ut, US 137/K13
Sprockhövel, Ger. 51/E6
Spruce (peak), WV, US 130/E4
Spruce Run (res.), NJ, US 138/C2
Spui (riv.), Neth. 50/B5
Spurn (pt.), Eng, UK 35/J4
Squamish, BC, Can. 126/C3
Squaw Harbor, Ak, US 134/F4
Squaxin Island Ind. Res., Wa, US 135/A3
Squillace, Golfo di (gulf), It. 46/E3
Squinzano, It. 47/F2
Squires (mt.), Austl. 113/E3
Srbobran, Yugo. 48/D3
Srebrenica, Bosn. 48/D3
Sredna (mts.), Bul. 47/J1
Srednogorie, Bul. 47/J1
Šrem, Pol. 41/J2
Sremčica, Yugo. 48/E3
Sremska Mitrovica, Yugo. 48/D3
Sreng (riv.), Camb. 78/C3
Srepok (riv.), Camb. 78/D3
Sri Dungargarh, India 89/K3
Sri Gangānagar, India 86/B5
Sri Jayawardanapura (Kotte), Sri Lanka (ctry.) 67/H9
Srīkākulam, India 86/C2
Srīnagar, India 86/C2
Srīvardhan, India 89/K5
Šroda Śląska, Pol. 41/J3
Šroda Wielkopolska, Pol. 41/J2
St. Albans, Vale of (valley), Eng, UK 30/B1
St. John's (cap.), Nf, Can. 131/L2
Stabbursdalen NP, Nor. 37/H1
Staberhuk (pt.), Ger. 38/D4
Stabroek, Belg. 50/B6
Stade, Ger. 51/G4
Staden, Belg. 52/C2
Stadl-Paura, Aus. 55/G6
Stadtbergen, Ger. 54/D6
Stadthagen, Ger. 51/G4
Stadtlauringen, Ger. 54/D2
Stadtlohn, Ger. 50/D5
Stadtoldendorf, Ger. 51/G5
Stadtsteinach, Ger. 55/E2
Stäfa, Swi. 57/E3
Staffanstorp, Swe. 38/E4
Staffelberg (peak), Ger. 54/E2
Staffelegg (pass), Swi. 56/E3
Staffelsee (lake), Ger. 57/H2
Staffhorst, Ger. 51/F2
Staffora (riv.), It. 58/C3
Stafford, Eng, UK 35/F6
Stagno, It. 58/D5
Stagnone Isole Della (isl.), It. 46/B4
Stahnsdorf, Ger. 40/Q7
Staines, Eng, UK 30/K5
Stains, Fr. 30/K5
Stakes (mt.), Ca, US 135/M12
Stakhanov, Ukr. 62/F2
Stalden, Swi. 56/D5
Stalingrad (Volgograd), Rus. 63/H2
Stallings, Il, US 137/G8
Stallworthy (cape), NW, Can. 123/S6
Stalowa Wola, Pol. 41/M3
Stalybridge, Eng, UK 35/M4
Stamboliyski, Bul. 47/J1
Stamford, Ct, US 139/H12
Stamford, Eng, UK 33/F1
Stamford, Ct, US 139/L7
Stampa, Swi. 57/F5
Stampriet, Namb. 105/C5
Stamullen, Ire. 34/B4
Standerton, SAfr. 106/E2
Standish-with-Langtree, Eng, UK 35/F4
Standley (lake), Co, US 137/B3
Stanford-le-Hope, Eng, UK 30/K4
Stange, Nor. 38/D1
Stanger, SAfr. 107/E3

Stanghella, It. 59/E2
Stanhope, NJ, US 138/D2
Staniśić, Yugo. 48/D3
Stanislaus (riv.), Ca, US 128/B3
Stanislaus (co.), Ca, US 135/M12
Stanley, Austl. 115/C4
Stanley (falls), D.R. Congo 97/L8
Stanley, ND, US 127/H3
Stanley, NB, Can. 131/H2
Stanley, Ks, US 137/D6
Stanley (res.), India 82/C5
Stanley (mt.), Austl. 113/F2
Stanley (cap.), Falk. 159/F6
Stanley, Sc, UK 36/C4
Stanley, Eng, UK 35/G2
Stanley Draper (lake), Ok, US 137/N15
Stanovo, Yugo. 48/E4
Stanovoy (range), Rus. 67/M4
Stans, Swi. 57/E4
Stansted (int'l arpt.), Eng, UK 33/G3
Stanthorpe, Austl. 114/C5
Stanton, Ky, US 130/D4
Stanton, Tx, US 129/G4
Stanton, De, US 138/C4
Stanton, NJ, US 138/D2
Stanton, Ca, US 136/G8
Staphorst, Neth. 50/D3
Staplehurst, Eng, UK 33/G4
Staples, On, Can. 135/G7
Stąporków, Pol. 41/L3
Stara Pazova, Yugo. 48/E3
Stara Planina (mts.), Yugo. 48/F3
Stara Zagora, Bul. 47/J1
Starachowice, Pol. 41/L3
Staranzano, It. 59/G1
Staraya Russa, Rus. 39/P2
Starbuck (isl.), Kiri. 117/K5
Starcke NP, Austl. 114/B1
Stargard Szczeciński, Pol. 38/F5
Starke, Fl, US 133/H4
Starkville, Ms, US 133/F3
Starnbergersee (lake), Ger. 57/H2
Starodub, Rus. 62/E1
Starogard Gdański, Pol. 38/H5
Start (bay), Eng, UK 32/C6
Start (pt.), Eng, UK 32/C6
Start (pt.), Sc, UK 31/V14
Startup, Wa, US 135/D2
Staryy Oskol', Rus. 62/F2
Staszów, Pol. 41/L3
State College, Pa, US 130/E3
State Fairgrounds, De, US 138/C6
State Park Place, Il, US 137/G8
Staten (isl.), NY, US 138/D2
States (int'l arpt.), Chl, UK 42/B2
Statesboro, Ga, US 133/H3
Statesville, NC, US 133/H3
Statue of Liberty Nat'l Mon., NY, US 139/J9
Staufen im Breisgau, Ger. 56/D2
Staufenberg, Ger. 40/E3
Stavanger, Nor. 38/A2
Staveley, Eng, UK 35/G5
Stavelot, Belg. 53/E3
Staveren, Neth. 50/C3
Stavern, Nor. 38/D2
Stavropol', Rus. 63/G3
Stavropol' Kray, Rus. 64/E5
Stavrós, Gre. 47/H2
Stawell, Austl. 115/B3
Stayton, Or, US 126/C4
Ste-Marguerite (riv.), Can. 131/H1
Steamboat Slough (riv.), Ca, US 135/L10
Steamboat Springs, Co, US 128/F2
Steckborn, Swi. 57/E2
Stederau (riv.), Ger. 51/H2
Steeg, Aus. 57/G3
Steele, ND, US 127/J4
Steele's Knowe (hill), Sc, UK 36/C4
Steelpoortrivier (riv.), SAfr. 107/E2
Steelton, Pa, US 138/B3
Steenbergen, Neth. 50/B5
Steens (mtn.), Or, US 128/C2
Steensby (inlet), NW, Can. 123/J1
Steenvoorde, Fr. 52/B2
Steenwijk, Neth. 50/D3
Steep (pt.), Austl. 112/B3
Steep Holm (isl.), Eng, UK 32/C4
Steep Pond, Md, US 138/B5
Steephill (lake), Sk, Can. 127/G1
Steeping (riv.), Eng, UK 35/J5
Steese Nat'l Conservation Area, Ak, US 134/J2
Stefansson (isl.), NW, Can. 122/F1
Steffen (peak), Chile 158/C5
Steffisburg, Swi. 56/D5
Steg, Swi. 56/D5
Stege, Den. 38/E4
Steiermark (prov.), Aus. 41/H5
Steigerwald (for.), Ger. 43/J2
Steilacoom, Wa, US 135/B3
Steimbke, Ger. 51/G3
Stein, Neth. 53/E2
Stein am Rhein, Swi. 57/E2
Stein bei Nürnberg, Ger. 54/E4
Steina (riv.), Ger. 57/E2
Steinach, Ger. 55/F5
Steinach (riv.), Ger. 54/E4

Steinach am Brenner, Aus. 57/H3
Steinbach, Mb, Can. 127/J3
Steinbach an der Steyr, Aus. 55/H7
Steinbourg, Fr. 53/G6
Steinen, Ger. 56/D2
Steinerkirchen an der Traun, Aus. 55/G6
Steinfeld, Ger. 51/F3
Steinfeld, Ger. 54/B4
Steinfeld, Ger. 54/C3
Steinfort, Lux. 53/E4
Steingaden, Ger. 57/G2
Steinhausen, Swi. 57/E3
Steinhausen an der Rottum, Ger. 57/F1
Steinheim, Ger. 51/G5
Steinheim am Albuch, Ger. 54/D5
Steinheim an der Murr, Ger. 54/C5
Steinhorst, Ger. 51/H3
Steinhuder (lake), Ger. 51/G4
Steinkjer, Nor. 37/D2
Steinsland, Nor. 38/A1
Steinweiler, Ger. 54/B4
Stekene, Belg. 50/B6
Stella, SAfr. 106/D2
Stella (peak), It. 57/F5
Stellarton, NS, Can. 131/J2
Stelle, Ger. 51/H2
Stellenbosch, SAfr. 106/L10
Stello (peak), Fr. 43/H5
Stelvio, Passo di (pass), It. 57/G4
Stelvio, PN Dello (pass), It. 43/J3
Stenay, Fr. 53/E5
Stendal, Ger. 40/F2
Steneto NP, Bul. 47/J1
Stenhousemuir, Sc, UK 36/C4
Stenløse, Den. 38/E1
Stenungsund, Swe. 38/D2
Stephansposching, Ger. 55/F5
Stephenville, Nf, Can. 131/K1
Stephenville, Tx, US 129/H4
Sterkstroom, SAfr. 106/D3
Sterling, Ak, US 134/H3
Sterling, Co, US 129/G2
Sterlitamak, Rus. 63/K1
Sternstein (peak), Aus. 55/H5
Sterzing (Vipiteno), It. 57/H3
Steszew, Pol. 41/J2
Šteti, Czh. 55/H2
Stettler, Ab, Can. 126/F2
Steubenville, Oh, US 130/D3
Stevenage, Eng, UK 33/F3
Stevens Village, Ak, US 134/J2
Stevenson (lake), Can. 127/J2
Stevenson Entrance (str.), Ak, US 134/H4
Stevenston, Sc, UK 36/B5
Stevensville, Mt, US 126/E4
Stevensville, Md, US 138/B6
Stevinsluizen (dam), Neth. 50/C3
Stevzing (Vipiteno), It. 43/J3
Stewart (riv.), Yk, Can. 122/C2
Stewart (isl.), NZ 109/G7
Stewart Crossing, Yk, Can. 134/L3
Stewarton, Sc, UK 36/B5
Stewartstown, Pa, US 138/B4
Stewartstown, NI, UK 34/B2
Stewartville, Mn, US 127/K5
Steynrus, SAfr. 106/D2
Steynsburg, SAfr. 106/D3
Steyr, Aus. 55/H6
Steyr (riv.), Aus. 41/H5
Steyregg, Aus. 55/H6
Steytlerville, SAfr. 106/C4
Stia, It. 59/E5
Stiava, It. 58/D5
Stickney (pt.), Wa, US 135/D2
Stiens, Neth. 50/C2
Stigler, Ok, US 129/J4
Stigtomta, Swe. 38/G2
Stikine (riv.), NW, Can. 134/M4
Stilbaai, SAfr. 106/C4
Stilfontein, SAfr. 106/D2
Stilis, Gre. 47/H3
Still Creek (riv.), Pa, US 138/C2
Still Pond, Md, US 138/B5
Stilling, Den. 38/D3
Stillings, Mo, US 137/T4
Stillwater (range), Nv, US 128/C3
Stillwater, Ok, US 129/H3
Stillwater, Pa, US 138/B1
Stillwater (lake), Pa, US 138/C1
Stilo (cape), It. 46/E3
Stilwell, Ok, US 129/J4
Stilwell, Ks, US 137/D6
Štimlje, Yugo. 47/G1
Stimpfach, Ger. 54/D4
Stinchar (riv.), Sc, UK 34/D1
Stinnett, Tx, US 129/G4
Štip, Macd. 47/H2
Stiring-Wendel, Fr. 53/F5
Stirka (peak), SAfr. 55/G4
Stirling (int'l.), Austl. 112/C4
Stirling, Sc, UK 36/C4
Stirling Range NP, Austl. 112/C5
Stirone (riv.), It. 58/D2
Stjørdal (riv.), Nor. 37/D3
Stob a' Choin (peak), Sc, UK 36/B4

Stob Choire Claurigh (peak), Sc, UK 36/B3
Stochov, Czh. 55/G2
Stock, Eng, UK 30/E2
Stock (lake), Fr. 53/F6
Stockach, Ger. 57/F2
Stockerau, Aus. 49/N7
Stockertown, Pa, US 138/C2
Stockholm (co.), Swe. 38/G2
Stockholm (cap.), Swe. 37/F4
Stockhorn (peak), Swi. 56/D4
Stockport, Eng, UK 35/F5
Stocks (res.), Eng, UK 35/F4
Stocksbridge, Eng, UK 35/G5
Stockstadt am Rhein, Ger. 54/B3
Stockton (lake), Mo, US 129/J3
Stockton, Ca, US 128/B3
Stockton (plat.), Tx, US 142/E2
Stockton, NJ, US 137/J13
Stockton, NJ, US 138/D3
Stockton-on-Tees, Eng, UK 35/G2
Stod, Czh. 55/G3
Stoddard, Ut, US 137/K11
Stoke (pt.), Eng, UK 32/B6
Stoke-on-Trent, Eng, UK 35/F6
Stoke Poges, Eng, UK 30/D2
Stokenchurch, Eng, UK 30/A2
Stokes (pt.), Austl. 115/B4
Stokes NP, Austl. 112/D5
Stokes (bay), Eng, UK 30/A6
Stolac, Bosn. 47/E1
Stolberg, Ger. 53/E2
Stolbovoy (isl.), Rus. 65/P2
Stöllet, Swe. 38/E1
Stolzenau, Ger. 51/G3
Stompneuspunt (pt.), SAfr. 106/K10
Stone, Eng, UK 35/F6
Stone Harbor, NJ, US 138/D4
Stonehaven, Sc, UK 36/D3
Stonehenge, Eng, UK 32/E4
Stonehouse, Sc, UK 36/C5
Stonewall, Mb, Can. 127/J3
Stoney Creek, On, Can. 131/Q9
Stoney Point, On, Can. 135/G7
Stoneyburn, Sc, UK 36/C5
Stonington, Ct, US 139/G1
Stony (pt.), Mb, Can. 127/J2
Stony Brook, NY, US 139/E2
Stony Creek (lake), Mi, US 135/E7
Stony Mountain, Mb, Can. 127/J3
Stony Point, NY, US 138/E1
Stony River, Ak, US 134/G3
Stony Tunguska (riv.), Rus. 67/J3
Stonybrook-Wilshire, Pa, US 138/B4
Stooping (riv.), Co, US 130/D1
Stor (isl.), NW, Can. 123/S7
Stör (riv.), Ger. 51/G1
Stör-Elvdal, Nor. 38/D1
Storå, It. 38/F2
Stora Le (lake), Swe. 38/D2
Stora Sjöfallets NP, Swe. 37/F2
Stora Strand, Arg. 159/C6
Storavan (lake), Swe. 37/F2
Stord (isl.), Nor. 38/A2
Store Bælt (chan.), Den. 38/D4
Storebø, Nor. 38/A1
Støren, Nor. 37/D3
Storfors, Swe. 38/F1
Storm (bay), Austl. 109/D5
Stormberg (mtn.), SAfr. 106/D3
Stormont, NI, UK 34/C2
Stornoway, Sc, UK 31/Q7
Storo, It. 58/D1
Stronie Śląskie, Pol. 41/J3
Storr, The (peak), Sc, UK 31/V14
Storsjön (lake), Swe. 37/E3
Storsteinsfjellet (peak), Nor. 37/F1
Storstrøm (co.), Den. 38/D1
Storvik, Swe. 38/G1
Storvreta, Swe. 38/G2
Story, Wy, US 126/G4
Stoughton, Sk, Can. 127/H3
Stoumont, Belg. 53/E3
Stour (riv.), Eng, UK 32/D5
Stourbridge, Eng, UK 32/D2
Stourport-on-Severn, Eng, UK 32/D2
Støvring, Den. 38/C3
Stowe, Pa, US 138/C2
Stowmarket, Eng, UK 33/G2
Stra, It. 59/E2
Strabane (dist.), NI 34/A2
Strabane, NI, UK 36/B3
Stradella, It. 58/C2
Straelen, Ger. 50/D6
Strahan, Austl. 115/C4
Strakonice, Czh. 55/G4
Straldzha, Bul. 47/K1
Stralsund, Ger. 38/G4
Strambino, It. 58/A2
Strand, SAfr. 106/L11
Strand, NI, UK 34/C3
Strangford (lake), NI, UK 34/C3

Strangford (lake), Sc, UK 34/C3
Strängnäs, Swe. 38/G2
Strangways (mt.), Austl. 113/G2
Stranocum, NI, UK 34/B1
Stranraer, Sc, UK 34/B1
Strasbourg, Fr. 56/D1
Strasbourg (Entzheim) (int'l arpt.), Fr. 56/D1
Strasburg, Mo, US 137/E6
Strasburg, Pa, US 138/B4
Strassen, Lux. 53/E4
Strasshof an der Nordbahn, Aus. 49/P7
Strasswalchen, Aus. 55/G6
Stratford, Tx, US 129/G3
Stratford, On, Can. 130/D3
Stratford, NZ 117/S10
Stratford, Ct, US 139/E1
Stratford, NJ, US 138/C4
Stratford (pt.), Ct, US 139/L8
Stratford and Worcester (canal), Eng, UK 32/D2
Stratford-upon-Avon, Eng, UK 32/D2
Strathalbyn, Austl. 113/H5
Strathbeg (bay), Sc, UK 36/E1
Strathblane, Sc, UK 36/B5
Strathclyde (pol. reg.), Sc, UK 36/B5
Strathearn (valley), Sc, UK 36/C4
Strathmore, Ab, Can. 126/E3
Strathmore (valley), India 85/E4
Strathpeffer, Sc, UK 36/B1
Strathspey (valley), Sc, UK 36/C2
Straubing, Ger. 55/F5
Strausberg, Ger. 40/Q6
Strausberg, Alpe di (peak), It. 58/D4
Strausstown, Pa, US 138/B3
Suceava, Rom. 49/H2
Suceava (prov.), Rom. 49/H2
Strawberry (peak), Ca, US 135/L11
Strawberry Bay, Austl. 113/G5
Středočeská Žulová Vrchovina (mts.), Czh. 41/H4
Středočeský (pol. reg.), Czh. 43/L2
Středoslovenský (pol. reg.), Czh. 41/H3
Streich (peak), Austl. 112/D4
Strekov, Czh. 41/G3
Strelley Abor. Land, Austl. 112/C2
Strel'na (riv.), Rus. 60/H2
Strengelbach, Swi. 56/D3
Strengen, Aus. 57/G3
Stresa, It. 58/B1
Stretford, Eng, UK 35/F5
Strettoia, It. 58/D5
Streu (riv.), Ger. 54/D2
Streymoy (isl.), Den. 38/A4
Strichen, Sc, UK 36/D1
Strigno, It. 57/H5
Strijen, Neth. 50/B5
Strimón (gulf), Gre. 62/C4
Strimónas (riv.), Gre. 47/H2
Striven (lake), Sc, UK 36/A5
Strobel (lake), Arg. 159/C6
Stroeder, Arg. 158/E4
Strofádhes (isl.), Gre. 47/G4
Strom Thurmond (lake), US 133/H3
Stromberg, Ger. 54/B2
Stromboli (isl.), It. 46/D3
Stromness, Sc, UK 31/V14
Strömstad, Swe. 38/D2
Strömsund, Swe. 37/E3
Strona (riv.), It. 57/E6
Strongoli, It. 46/E3
Stronsay (isl.), Sc, UK 31/V14
Stronsay Firth (inlet), Sc, UK 31/V14
Strood, Eng, UK 30/E2
Stropnice (riv.), Czh. 55/H5
Stroppiana, It. 58/B2
Stroud, Eng, UK 32/D3
Stroudsburg, Pa, US 138/C2
Struan, Sc, UK 31/Q8
Struer, Den. 38/C3
Struga, Macd. 47/G2
Strullendorf, Ger. 51/H6
Struma (riv.), Bul. 62/B4
Strumble (pt.), Wal, UK 32/A2
Strumica, Macd. 47/H2
Struthers, Oh, US 130/D3
Stryn, Nor. 37/C3
Strzelce, Pol. 41/K3
Strzelce Krajeńskie, Pol. 41/H2
Strzelce Opolskie, Pol. 62/D2
Strzelecki (mt.), Austl. 115/D4
Strzelecki (riv.), Austl. 113/H3
Strzelin, Pol. 41/J3
Strzelno, Pol. 41/K2
Strzyżów, Pol. 41/L4
Stuart (lake), BC, Can. 126/B2

Stuart (riv.), BC, Can. 126/B2
Stuart, Fl, US 133/H5
Stuart (mt.), Va, US 130/E4
Stuarts Draft, Va, US 130/E4
Stubbekøbing, Den. 38/E4
Stubbenkammer (pt.), Ger. 38/E4
Stühlingen, Ger. 57/E2
Stukaba, Slvk. 43/M2
Stupava, Slvk. 43/M2
Stupino, Rus. 60/H5
Stura di Lanzo (riv.), It. 58/A2
Sturgeon (lake), Can. 127/L3
Sturgeon (bay), Can. 127/L3
Sturgeon (riv.), Can. 130/D2
Sturgis, Mi, US 130/C3
Sturgis (des.), Austl. 109/D3
Sturt (mt.), Austl. 113/J4
Sturt (riv.), Austl. 113/M8
Sturt NP, Austl. 115/B1
Sturup (str.), Swe. 38/E4
Stutterheim, SAfr. 106/D4
Stuttgart, Ger. 54/C5
Stykkishólmur, Ice. 37/M6
Styr (riv.), Ukr. 62/C2
Su açuı Grande (riv.), Braz. 155/D1
Suakin (arch.), Sudan 97/N4
Suam (riv.), Kenya 104/B2
Suaqui Grande, Mex. 142/C2
Suār, India 84/B1
Suárez (riv.), Col. 152/C3
Subang, Indo. 80/C5
Subanarekhā (riv.), India 85/E4
Sübät (riv.), Sudan 97/M6
Subay'tilah, Tun. 100/L7
Subei Monggolzu Zizhixian, China 70/F4
Subi (isl.), Indo. 80/C3
Subic (bay), Phil. 80/C3
Subotica, Yugo. 48/D2
Succasunna-Kenvil, NJ, US 138/D2
Succiso, Alpe di (peak), It. 58/D4
Suceava, Rom. 49/H2
Suceava (prov.), Rom. 49/H2
Suchedniów, Pol. 41/L3
Suches, Bol. 156/D4
Suck (riv.), Ire. 31/P10
Sucre (cap.), Bol. 150/E7
Sucre (state), Ven. 153/F2
Sucre (dept.), Col. 145/H4
Sucre (prov.), Ecu. 152/B5
Sucumbíos (prov.), Ecu. 152/B4
Sucunduri (riv.), Braz. 150/G5
Sucúpira do Norte, Braz. 154/A2
Sucy-en-Brie, Fr. 30/K5
Sud (pol. reg.), Mor. 98/C3
Sud-Ouest (prov.), Camr. 103/H5
Suda (riv.), Rus. 60/H4
Sudama, Japan 77/A2
Sudan (cty.) 93/E3
Sudbury, On, Can. 130/D2
Sudbury, Eng, UK 33/G2
Suddie, Guy. 153/G3
Süderbrarup, Ger. 38/C4
Sudetes (mts.), Czh.,Pol. 41/H3
Sudlersville, Md, US 138/C5
Sudogda, Rus. 60/J5
Sue (riv.), Sudan 93/K4
Sue Creek, Md, US 137/E5
Sugar Grove, Il, US 135/P16
Sugar Land, Tx, US 142/E4
Sugar Loaf (peak), Wal, UK 32/C3
Sugar Notch, Pa, US 138/C1
Sugenheim, Ger. 54/D3
Sugito, Japan 77/D1
Suhāj (gov.), Egypt 101/B3
Suhāj, Egypt 101/B3
Sühbaatar (prov.), Mong. 71/K2
Suhl, Ger. 54/D1
Suhl (dir.), Ger. 54/D1
Suhlendorf, Ger. 51/H3
Suhr, Swi. 56/D3
Sui (riv.), China 79/B3
Sui Xian, China 72/C4
Sui-Missu (riv.), Braz. 151/H6
Suibin, China 75/D2
Suica, Bosn. 47/E1
Suita, Japan 77/J6
Suitland-Silver Hill, Md, US 138/B6

Suixi, China 83/K3
Suixi, China 72/D4
Suiyang, China 79/A2
Suize (riv.), Fr. 56/B2
Suizhong, China 72/E2
Suizhou, China 71/K5
Sukabumi, Indo. 80/C5
Sukadana (bay), India 85/G5
Sukadana, Indo. 80/C4
Sukagawa, Japan 75/G2
Sukheke, Pak. 86/B4
Sukhindol, Bul. 47/J1
Sukhinichi, Rus. 62/E1
Sukhodol'skoye (lake), Rus. 39/N1
Sukhothai (ruin), Thai. 78/B2
Sukhothai, Thai. 78/B2
Sukkur, Pak. 89/J3
Sükösd, Hun. 48/D2
Sukumo, Japan 74/C4
Sula (isls.), Phil. 67/M10
Sula (isls.), Indo. 80/B4
Sula (riv.), Rus. 61/L2
Sulaimān (range), Pak. 89/J3
Sulakyurt, Turk. 62/E4
Sulawesi (Celebes) (isl.), Indo. 81/E4
Sulb Temple (ruin), Sudan 101/B4
Sulby (riv.), IM, UK 34/D3
Sulechów, Pol. 41/H2
Sulęcin, Pol. 41/H2
Sulejów, Pol. 41/K3
Sulejówek, Pol. 41/L2
Sulina, Rom. 49/J3
Sulina Branch (riv.), Rom. 49/J3
Sulingen, Ger. 51/F3
Sulitjelma (peak), Nor. 37/E2
Sullana, Peru 156/A2
Sullivan (lake), Can. 126/F3
Sullivan, Qu, Can. 130/E1
Sullivan, Wi, US 135/N13
Sully-sur-Loire, Fr. 42/E3
Sulmona, It. 46/C1
Sulphur (riv.), Tx, US 129/J4
Sulphur, Ok, US 129/H4
Sulphur Springs, Tx, US 129/J4
Sulphur Springs, Ca, US 136/A2
Sultan (riv.), Wa, US 135/D2
Sultan (cap.), Bol. 156/D4
Sultan Kudarat, Phil. 79/D6
Sultānpur, India 84/D2
Sulu (arch.), Phil. 67/L9
Sulu (sea), Asia 67/M9
Sülüklü, Turk. 90/C2
Suluova, Turk. 62/E4
Sulūq, Libya 97/K1
Sülüsap, Hun. 49/R10
Sulz, Swi. 56/E2
Sulz (riv.), Ger. 55/E4
Sülz (riv.), Ger. 53/G2
Sulz am Neckar, Ger. 54/B6
Sulzbach, Ger. 53/G5
Sulzbach, Ger. 54/C4
Sulzbach am Main, Ger. 54/C3
Sulzbach-Rosenberg, Ger. 54/E3
Sulzberger (bay), Ant. 160/Q
Sulzburg, Ger. 56/D2
Sulzemoos, Ger. 57/H1
Sulzfeld (peak), Aus. 57/F1
Sulzheim, Ger. 54/D3
Sumadija (mts.), Yugo. 48/E3
Sumampa, PN, Col. 152/C4
Sumatra (isl.), Indo. 67/J9
Sumba (str.), Indo. 81/E5
Sumba (isl.), Indo. 67/L11
Sumbar (riv.), Trkm. 87/C5
Sumbawa (isl.), Indo. 67/L10
Sumbawa Besar, Indo. 81/E5
Sumbawanga, Tanz. 104/A4
Sumbe, Ang. 103/D3
Sumburgh Head (pt.), Sc, UK 31/W14
Sumdum (mt.), Ak, US 134/M4
Sümeg, Hun. 48/C2
Sumedang, Indo. 80/C5
Sumisho (isl.), Japan 76/D2
Sumiswald, Swi. 56/D3
Summer Land, BC, Can. 126/D3
Summerland, Ca, US 136/A2
Summerside, PE, Can. 131/J2
Summerville, Ga, US 133/G3
Summerville, SC, US 133/H3
Summit (co.), Ut, US 137/K11
Summit, NJ, US 139/H9
Summit Bridge, De, US 138/C5
Summit Hill, Pa, US 138/C2
Sumner, Wa, US 135/C3
Sumoto, Japan 74/D3
Šumperk, Czh. 41/J4
Sumqayyt, Azer. 63/J4
Sums'ka (obl.), Ukr. 62/E1
Sumter, SC, US 133/H3
Sumy, Ukr. 62/E1
Sun (riv.), Mt, US 128/E1
Sun City, SAfr. 106/E2
Sun City, Az, US 137/R18
Sun City, Ca, US 136/C3
Sun City West, Az, US 137/R18
Sun Kosi (riv.), Nepal 85/F2
Sun Lakes, Az, US 137/S19
Sunagawa, Japan 75/F1
Sunām, India 86/C4
Sunami, Japan 77/L5
Sunbury, Pa, US 138/B2
Sunbury-on-Thames, Eng, UK 30/B2

Sunch'ang, SKor. 73/D5
Sunch'ŏn, NKor. 73/C3
Sunch'ŏn, SKor. 73/D5
Suncook, NH, US 131/G3
Sunda (isls.), Indo. 67/J10
Sunda (str.), Indo. 67/K10
Sundance, Wy, US 127/G4
Sundarbans (phys. reg.), India 85/G5
Sundargarh, India 85/E4
Sundarnagar, India 86/D4
Sundays (riv.), SAfr. 106/D4
Sunderland, Eng, UK 35/G2
Sundern, Ger. 51/F6
Sundhouse, Fr. 56/D1
Sundown, Tx, US 129/G4
Sundown NP, Austl. 115/D1
Sundre, Ab, Can. 126/E3
Sunderland, Or, US 126/C5
Sundsvall, Swe. 37/F3
Sunds, Den. 38/C3
Sungai Petani, Malay. 83/H6
Sungaipenuh, Indo. 80/B4
Sungurlu, Turk. 62/E4
Suning, China 72/C3
Sunndal, Nor. 37/D3
Sunne, Swe. 38/E2
Sunningdale, Eng, UK 30/A2
Sunnyside, Ca, US 136/C5
Sunnyside, Il, US 135/P15
Sunnyvale, Ca, US 128/B3
Sunol, Ca, US 135/L11
Sunomata, Japan 77/L5
Sunrise (mtn.), NJ, US 138/D1
Sunset, Ut, US 137/J11
Sunset Beach, Hi, US 124/V12
Sunset Beach, Ca, US 136/F8
Sunset Country (reg.), Austl. 115/B2
Sunset Crater Volcano Nat'l Mon., Az, US 128/E4
Suntar-Khayata (mts.), Rus. 65/P3
Süntel (mts.), Ger. 51/G4
Sunwi (isl.), NKor. 73/C4
Sunwu, China 71/N2
Sunyani, Gha. 103/E5
Sunzu (peak), Zam. 104/A5
Suo (sea), Japan 74/B4
Suomenlinna, Fin. 39/L1
Suomenselkä (reg.), Fin. 37/H3
Supawna Meadows NWR, NJ, US 138/C4
Supe, Peru 156/B3
Superior, Mt, US 126/E4
Superior, Az, US 128/E4
Superior (upland), US 137/B3
Superior, Co, US 137/B3
Superior (lake), Can.,US 119/J5
Suphan Buri, Thai. 78/C3
Supiori (isl.), Indo. 81/J4
Sup'ung (res.), China 73/C2
Sup'ung (dam), NKor. 73/C2
Süq ash Shuyükh, Iraq 88/E2
Suqian, China 72/D4
Sūr, Leb. 91/D3
Sur (riv.), Ca, US 159/F3
Sur Reina Sofia (int'l arpt.), Sp. 90/A3
Sura (riv.), Rus. 61/K5
Surabaya, Indo. 82/D4
Surada, India 82/D4
Surahammar, Swe. 38/G2
Sürajgarh, India 86/C5
Surak-san (peak), SKor. 73/D3
Surakarta, Indo. 82/D5
Surallah, Phil. 81/F2
Suran (riv.), Fr. 31/P7
Šurany, Slvk. 48/D1
Surat, India 89/K4
Surat, Austl. 114/C4
Surat Thani, Thai. 78/C3
Suratgarh, India 86/B5
Surčin, Yugo. 48/E3
Surduc, Ab, Can. 126/E2
Surdulica, Yugo. 47/H1
Sûre (riv.), Lux. 53/E4
Surendranagar, India 89/K4
Surf City, NJ, US 138/D4
Surgères, Fr. 42/C3
Surgut, Rus. 64/H3
Süri, India 85/F4
Súria, Sp. 45/F2
Surigao, Phil. 81/G2
Surin, Thai. 78/C3
Suriname (ctry.) 147/D2
Surma (riv.), Bang. 85/G4
Surprise, Az, US 137/R18
Surrey, BC, Can. 126/C3
Surrey (co.), Eng, UK 33/F4
Sursee, Swi. 56/D3
Surt, Libya 96/J1
Surt (gulf), Libya 96/J1
Surtsey (isl.), Ice. 37/N7
Suruga (bay), Japan 75/F3
Surumu (riv.), Braz. 153/F4
Surveyor General's Corner, Austl. 113/F3
Surwakwima (falls), Guy. 153/F3
Susa, It. 58/A2
Susah, Tun. 46/B5
Süsah (gov.), Tun. 46/B5
Susaki, Japan 74/C4
Susanville, Ca, US 126/C5
Suşehri, Turk. 62/E4
Susian (well), Libya 99/H4
Sušice, Czh. 55/G4
Susitna (riv.), Ak, US 134/H3
Suso, Japan 75/F3

Susquehanna (riv.), US 130/E3
Susquehanna NWR, Md, US 138/B5
Sussex, NB, Can. 131/H2
Sussex (co.), De, US 138/D1
Sussex, NJ, US 138/D1
Sussex Inlet, Austl. 115/D2
Sussex, Vale of (valley), Eng, UK 33/F4
Sustenhorn (peak), Swi. 57/E4
Sustenpass (pass), Swi. 57/E4
Susteren, Neth. 53/E1
Susuman, Rus. 65/Q3
Susurluk, Turk. 62/D5
Sütçüler, Turk. 90/B2
Sutherland, SAfr. 106/C4
Sutherland Springs, Tx, US 137/U21
Sutherlin, Or, US 126/C5
Sutjeska NP, Bosn. 47/F1
Sutlej (riv.), India 70/C5
Sutter (co.), Ca, US 135/L9
Sutton, Ak, US 134/J3
Sutton (bor.), Eng, UK 30/C2
Sutton Coldfield, Eng, UK 33/E1
Sutton in Ashfield, Eng, UK 35/G5
Suttsu, Japan 76/B2
Suurberge (mts.), SAfr. 106/D4
Suurbraak, SAfr. 106/C4
Suvorovo, Bul. 49/H4
Suwa, Japan 75/F2
Suwałki, Pol. 39/K5
Suwałki, Pol. 39/K4
Suwannee (riv.), Fl, US 140/E1
Suwanose (isl.), Japan 75/K6
Suwarrow (isl.), Cooks. 117/K10
Suwayliḥ, Jor. 91/D3
Suwon, SKor. 73/G7
Suyo, Peru 156/B2
Suzaka, Japan 75/F2
Suzhou, China 72/D4
Suzhou, China 72/E4
Suzi (riv.), China 73/C2
Suzu, Japan 75/F2
Suzu-misaki (cape), Japan 75/E2
Suzuka, Japan 75/E3
Suzuka (range), Japan 77/K6
Suzzara, It. 59/D2
Švaneke, Den. 38/F4
Svängsta, Swe. 38/F3
Svanstein, Swe. 60/D2
Svatava (riv.), Czh. 55/F2
Svealand (reg.), Swe. 37/E4
Svedala, Swe. 38/E4
Sveio, Nor. 38/A2
Svelvik, Nor. 38/D2
Svendborg, Den. 38/D4
Svendsen (pen.), NW, Can. 123/S7
Svenstrup, Den. 38/C3
Sverdlovsk Oblast, Rus. 87/D1
Sverdlovsk Oblast, Rus. 64/G4
Sverdrup (chan.), NW, Can. 123/S7
Sverdrup (isl.), Rus. 64/H2
Sverdrup (isls.), Can. 119/G2
Svetlogorsk, Bela. 62/D1
Svetlograd, Rus. 63/G2
Svetlyy, Rus. 63/M2
Svetozarevo, Yugo. 48/E4
Sviahnúkar (peak), Ice. 37/P7
Svilajnac, Yugo. 48/E3
Svilengrad, Bul. 47/K2
Svishtov, Bul. 49/G4
Svislach, Bela. 41/N2
Svobodnyy, Rus. 71/N1
Svoge, Bul. 47/H1
Svolvær, Nor. 37/E1
Svratka (riv.), Czh. 43/M2
Svyatyy Nos (cape), Rus. 65/Q2
Swābi, Pak. 86/B2
Swadlincote, Eng, UK 33/E1
Swain (reefs.), Austl. 109/E3
Swainsboro, Ga, US 133/H3
Swakopmund, Namb. 105/B5
Swale, The (riv.), Eng, UK 33/G4
Swalmen, Neth. 50/D6
Swan (riv.), Austl. 109/E3
Swan (isls.), Hon. 140/E4
Swan (riv.), Austl. 113/G2
Swan (hills), Ab, Can. 126/E2
Swan Hill, Austl. 115/B3
Swan Hills, Ab, Can. 126/E2
Swan Reach, Austl. 126/E2
Swan River, Mb, Can. 127/H2
Swanscombe, Eng, UK 30/D2
Swansea, Austl. 115/C4
Swansea, Il, US 137/H8
Swansea (bay), Wal, UK 32/B3
Swansea, Wal, UK 32/B3
Swart Kei (riv.), SAfr. 106/D3
Swarthmore, Pa, US 138/C4
Swartswood (lake), NJ, US 138/D1
Swarzędz, Pol. 41/J2

Swarzenbach an der Sächsischen Saale, Ger. 55/E2
Swarzrand (mts.), Namb. 106/B2
Swāt (riv.), Pak. 86/B2
Swatragh, NI, UK 34/B2
Swayambhunath, Nepal 85/E2
Swaziland (ctry.) 93/F7
Swedesboro, NJ, US 138/C4
Sweet Home, Or, US 126/C4
Sweetwater (riv.), Wy, US 126/F5
Sweetwater, Tx, US 129/G4
Sweetwater (res.), Ca, US 136/D5
Swellendam, SAfr. 106/C4
Świdnica, Pol. 41/J3
Świdnik, Pol. 41/M3
Świdwin, Pol. 38/F5
Świebodzice, Pol. 41/J3
Świebozin, Pol. 41/H2
Świecie, Pol. 41/K2
Świętokrzysky NP, Pol. 41/L3
Swift Current, Sk, Can. 126/G3
Swifts Creek, Austl. 115/C3
Swilly, Lough (inlet), Ire. 31/Q9
Swimming River (res.), NJ, US 138/D3
Swindon, Eng, UK 33/E3
Świnoujście, Pol. 38/F5
Swinton, Eng, UK 35/G5
Swist Bach (riv.), Ger. 53/F2
Switzerland (ctry.) 27/E4
Swords, Ire. 34/B5
Swoyersville, Pa, US 138/C1
Syamozero (lake), Rus. 60/G3
Sych, Moel (peak), Wal, UK 35/E6
Syców, Pol. 41/J3
Sydney, NS, Can. 131/J2
Sydney, Austl. 114/H8
Sydney-Kingsford Smith (int'l arpt.), Austl. 114/H8
Syeverodonets'k, Ukr. 62/F2
Syke, Ger. 51/F3
Sykesville, Md, US 138/B5
Sykkylven, Nor. 37/C3
Syktyvkar, Rus. 61/L3
Sylacauga, Al, US 133/G3
Sylarna (peak), Swe. 37/E3
Sylhet (pol. reg.), Bang. 85/H3
Sylva (riv.), Rus. 61/N4
Sylvan Lake, Mi, US 135/F6
Sylvania, Oh, US 130/D3
Sylvenstein-Stausee (lake), Ger. 57/H2
Sými, Gre. 90/A2
Syntagma, Gre. 47/N8
Syosset, NY, US 139/L8
Syowa, Japan, Ant. 160/C
Syracuse, NY, US 130/E3
Syracuse, Ut, US 137/J11
Syracuse Hancock (int'l arpt.), NY, US 130/E3
Syrdarīya (riv.), Kaz. 67/F5
Syria (ctry.) 67/B6
Syriam, Myan. 83/G4
Syrian (des.), Jor. 88/C2
Sysmä, Fin. 39/L1
Sysola (riv.), Rus. 61/L3
Syzran', Rus. 63/J1
Szabolcs-Szatmár-Bereg (co.), Hun. 41/L4
Szamotuły, Pol. 41/J2
Szarvas, Hun. 48/E2
Százhalombatta, Hun. 49/Q10
Szczebrzeszyn, Pol. 41/M3
Szczecin, Pol. 38/F5
Szczecin (prov.), Pol. 38/F5
Szczecinek, Pol. 38/G5
Szczytna, Pol. 41/J3
Szczytno, Pol. 41/L2
Szeged, Hun. 48/E2
Szeghalom, Hun. 48/E2
Székesfehérvár, Hun. 48/D2
Szekszárd, Hun. 48/D2
Szendro, Hun. 48/E1
Szent László-Vize (riv.), Hun. 49/Q10
Szentendre, Hun. 49/R9
Szentes, Hun. 48/E2
Szentlorinc, Hun. 48/C2
Szerencs, Hun. 41/L4
Szeskie (peak), Pol. 39/K4
Sziget-Szentmiklós, Hun. 49/R10
Szigetvár, Hun. 48/C2
Szirák, Hun. 41/K5
Szolnok, Hun. 48/E2
Szombathely, Hun. 43/M3
Szprotawa, Pol. 41/H3
Sztum, Pol. 39/H5
Szubin, Pol. 41/J2
Szydłowiec, Pol. 41/L3

T

Ta Khmau, Camb. 78/D4
Taabo, Barrage de (dam), C.d'Iv. 102/D5
Tabaco, Phil. 79/D5
Tabaquite, Trin. 153/F2
Ţabarqah, Tun. 100/L6
Ţabas, Iran 89/G2
Tabasará (mts.), Pan. 145/F4
Tabasco (state), Mex. 140/C4
Tabatinga, Serra da (mts.), Braz. 151/K6
Tabayama, Japan 77/B2
Tabelbala, Alg. 98/E3
Tabelbalet (well), Alg. 99/G4
Ta'benghisa, Ponta (pt.), Malta 46/L7
Taber, Ab, Can. 126/E3
Tabernes de Valldigna, Sp. 45/E3
Tabiang, Kiri. 116/F5
Tabira, Braz. 154/C2
Tabiteuea (isl.), Kiri. 116/G5
Tablas (isl.), Phil. 81/F1
Tablas de Daimiel NP, Sp. 44/D3
Table (bay), SAfr. 106/B4
Table (mtn.), SAfr. 106/L10
Table Rock (lake), Mo, US 129/J3
Tabligbo, Togo 103/F5
Tábor, Czh. 55/H4
Tabora (pol. reg.), Tanz. 104/B4
Tabora, Tanz. 104/B4
Tabou, C.d'Iv. 102/D5
Tabuk, Phil. 79/D4
Tabūk, SAr. 88/C3
Tabuleiro do Norte, Braz. 154/C2
Ţaburbah, Tun. 46/A4
Tabwemasana (peak), Van. 116/F6
Tacabamba, Peru 156/B2
Tacámbaro de Codallos, Mex. 143/E5
Tacaná (vol.), Mex. 144/C3
Tacarcuna (mtn.), Pan. 152/B2
Tacheng, China 70/D2
Tachibana (bay), Japan 74/A4
Tachikawa, Japan 75/F3
Tachinger (lake), Ger. 55/F7
Tachira (state), Ven. 145/H5
Tachov, Czh. 55/F3
Tacloban, Phil. 79/E5
Tacna, Peru 156/D5
Tacna (dept.), Peru 156/D5
Tacoma, Wa, US 126/C4
Tacora (vol.), Chile 156/D5
Tacotalpa, Mex. 144/C2
Tacuarembó, Uru. 157/E3
Tacuarembó (dept.), Uru. 159/G2
Tacutu (riv.), Braz. 153/F4
Tadaoka, Japan 77/H7
Ta'Delimara (pt.), Malta 46/M7
Tademaït, Plateau du (plat.), Alg. 96/F2
Tādepallegūdem, India 82/D4
Tadley, Eng, UK 33/E4
Tadmur, Syria 90/D3
Tadó, Col. 152/B3
Tado, Japan 77/L5
Tadohae Hasang NP, SKor. 73/C5
Tadotsu, Japan 74/C3
Tādpatri, India 82/C5
Tadrart (mts.), Alg.,Liby 96/H2
Tadworth, Eng, UK 30/C3
T'aean, SKor. 73/D4
T'aebaek, SKor. 73/E4
Taebudo (isl.), SKor. 73/F7
Taech'ŏn, SKor. 73/D4
Taech'ŏng (isl.), SKor. 73/C4
Taedŏk, SKor. 73/D5
Taedong (riv.), NKor. 73/D3
Taegang-got (pt.), NKor. 73/D3
Taegu, SKor. 73/E5
Taegu-jikhalsi (prov.), SKor. 74/A3
Taehŭksan (isl.), SKor. 73/C5
Taehwa (isl.), NKor. 73/C3
T'aein, SKor. 73/D5
Taejŏn, SKor. 73/D4
Taejŏn-jikhalsi (prov.), SKor. 73/D4
Taeryŏng (riv.), NKor. 73/C2
Tafalla, Sp. 44/E1
Tafassasset, Oued (riv.), Alg. 99/H4
Taff (riv.), Wal, UK 32/C3
Tafí Viejo, Arg. 157/C2
Tafraout, Mor. 98/C3
Taft, La, US 137/P17
Taft, Iran 88/F2
Taftān (mtn.), Iran 89/H3
Taga, Japan 77/K5
Taganrog, Rus. 62/F3
Tagant (pol. reg.), Mrta. 102/C2
Tagarav (peak), Trkm. 63/L5
Tagawa, Japan 74/B4
Taggia, It. 58/A5
Taghit, Alg. 99/E3
Tagish, Yk, Can. 134/M3
Tagliamento (riv.), It. 43/K3
Taglio di Po, It. 59/F3
Tagolo (pt.), Phil. 81/F2
Taguasco, Cuba 145/G1
Taguatinga, Braz. 151/J7
Tagula (isl.), PNG 116/E6
Tagum, Phil. 81/G2
Tagun (riv.), Rus. 61/P4
Tagus (riv.), Sp. 27/D5
Tagus Rio Tejo (lake), Port. 45/P10
Tagus (Tajo) (riv.), Sp. 44/C3
Tahan (peak), Malay. 80/B3
Tahanea (isl.), FrPol. 117/L6
Tahanroz'ka Zatoka (gulf), Rus.,Ukr. 62/F3
Tahara, Japan 77/M6
Tahat (peak), Alg. 99/G5
Tahat, Oued et (riv.), Alg. 100/F5
Tahe, China 71/M1
Tahilt, Mong. 70/G2
Tahir (pass), Turk. 63/G5
Tahiti (isl.), FrPol. 117/L6
Tahkuna (pt.), Est. 39/K2
Tahlequah, Ok, US 129/J4
Tahmoor, Austl. 115/D2
Tahneta (pass), Ak, US 134/J3
Tahoe (lake), Ca,Nv, US 122/D5
Tahoka, Tx, US 129/G4
Tahoua (dept.), Niger 103/G3
Tahoua, Niger 103/G3
Tahsis, BC, Can. 126/B3
Tahuamanu (riv.), Peru 156/D3
Tahuamanú, Peru 156/D3
Tahuata (isl.), FrPol. 117/L6
Tahulandang (isl.), Indo. 81/G3
Tahuya, Wa, US 135/A3
Tahuya (riv.), Wa, US 135/B3
Tai Long Wan (bay), China 71/V10
Tai Mo Shan (peak), China 71/U10
Taï, PN de, C.d'Iv. 96/D6
Tai Po, China 71/U10
Tai Xian, China 72/E4
Tai'an, China 73/B2
Tai'an, China 72/D3
Taiaret (well), Mor. 98/B5
Taibus, China 71/L3
Taicang, China 72/L8
T'aichung, Tai. 79/D3
Taiei, Japan 77/E2
Taieri (riv.), NZ 117/S12
Taigu, China 72/C3
Taihang (mts.), China 72/C3
Taihe, China 79/B2
Taihe, China 72/C4
Taikang, China 72/C4
Taiki, Japan 76/C2
Tailem Bend, Austl. 113/H5
Taima, Japan 77/J6
Tain, Sc, UK 36/B1
T'ainan, Tai. 79/D3
Taínaron (cape), Gre. 47/H4
Taingainony, Madg. 107/H8
Taino, It. 58/B1
Taiobeiras, Braz. 154/B4
T'aipei (cap.), Tai. 79/D2
Taiping, Malay. 80/B3
Taiping, China 79/C1
Taisha, Japan 74/C3
Taishan, China 79/B3
Taishi, Japan 77/J6
Taishun, China 79/C2
Taiskirchen im Innkreis, Aus. 55/G6
Taissy, Fr. 53/D5
Taitao (pen.), Chile 147/B7
Taiti (peak), Kenya 104/B2
T'aitung, Tai. 79/D3
Taiwan (ctry.) 67/M7
Taiwan (str.), China,Tai 116/A2
Taixing, China 72/E4
Taíyetos (mts.), Gre. 47/H4
Taiyuan, China 72/C3
Taizhou, China 72/D4
Taizi (riv.), China 72/F2
Ta'izz, Yem. 88/D6
Tāj Mahal, India 84/B2
Tajikistan (ctry.) 67/G6
Tajima, Japan 75/F2
Tajimi, Japan 77/M5
Tajiri, Japan 77/H7
Tājpur, India 84/B1
Tajrīsh, Iran 88/F1
Tajumulco (vol.), Guat. 144/D3
Tajuña (riv.), Sp. 44/D2
Tak, Thai. 78/B2
Takahagi, Japan 75/G2
Takahama, Japan 77/J5
Takahama, Japan 77/L6
Takahashi (riv.), Japan 74/C3
Takahashi, Japan 74/C3
Takahata, Japan 75/G1
Takaishi, Japan 77/H6
Takamatsu, Japan 74/D3
Takami-yama (peak), Japan 77/K7
Takanabe, Japan 74/B4
Takane, Japan 77/A2
Takanosu, Japan 76/B3
Takanosu-yama (peak), Japan 77/C2
Takaoka, Japan 75/E2
Takapuna, NZ 117/S10
Takarazuka, Japan 77/H6
Takaroa (isl.), FrPol. 117/L6
Takasaki, Japan 75/F2
Takashima, Japan 77/K5
Takatomi, Japan 77/L5
Takatori, Japan 77/J7
Takatsuki, Japan 77/K5
Takatsuki, Japan 77/J6
Takayama, Japan 75/E2
Takefu, Japan 74/E3
Takehara, Japan 74/C3
Tākestān, Iran 88/E1
Taketa, Japan 74/B4
Taketoyo, Japan 77/L6
Takhatgarh, India 82/B2
Takhatpur, India 84/C4
Takht-e Jamshīd (ruin), Iran 88/F3
Takht-i-Bhāi, Pak. 86/A2
Taki, Japan 77/L7
Takijuq (lake), NW, Can. 122/E2
Takikawa, Japan 76/B2
Takino, Japan 77/G6
Takla (lake), Can. 126/B2
Takla Makan (des.), China 67/H6
Tako, Japan 77/E2
Takoradi, Gha. 103/E5
Takouch (cape), Alg. 100/K6
Taksony, Hun. 49/R10
Tala, Mex. 142/E4
Talā, Egypt 91/B4
Tala, Uru. 159/L11
Talagang, Pak. 86/B3
Talagante, Chile 158/N8
Talāja, India 89/K4
Talak (phys. reg.), Niger 96/G4
Talamanca (mts.), CR 145/F4
Talamba, Pak. 86/B4
Talamona, It. 57/F5
Talang (peak), Indo. 80/B4
Talanga, Hon. 144/E3
Talange, Fr. 53/F5
Talant, Fr. 56/A3
Talara, Peru 156/A2
Talas (obl.), Kyr. 87/F4
Talas, Turk. 90/C2
Talas, Kyr. 87/F4
Talas (riv.), Kaz. 87/F4
Talaud (isl.), Phil. 67/M9
Talavera de la Reina, Sp. 44/C3
Talawakele, SrL. 82/D6
Talayuela, Sp. 44/C3
Talbingo, Austl. 115/D2
Talbot (mt.), Austl. 112/E3
Talbot (co.), Md, US 138/B6
Talca, Chile 158/C2
Talcahuano, Chile 158/B3
Tālcher, India 82/E3
Taldyqorghan (obl.), Kaz. 87/G3
Taldyqorghan, Kaz. 87/G3
Talence, Fr. 42/C4
Talent (riv.), Swi. 56/C4
Talfer (Talvera) (riv.), It. 57/H4
Talgar, Kaz. 87/G4
Taliabu (isl.), Indo. 81/F4
Taliouine, Mor. 98/D3
Talkeetna, Ak, US 134/H3
Ţalkhā, Egypt 91/B4
Tall 'Afar, Iraq 90/E2
Tall al Muqayyar (ruin), Iraq 88/E2
Tall 'āsūr (peak), Isr. 91/G8
Tall Kayf, Iraq 90/E2
Talladega, Al, US 133/G3
Tallahassee (cap.), Fl, US 133/G4
Tallahatchie (riv.), Ms, US 129/K4
Tallangatta, Austl. 115/C3
Tallanstown, Ire. 34/B4
Tallering (peak), Austl. 112/B4
Talleyville, De, US 138/C4
Tallinn (cap.), Est. 39/L2
Tallman Mountain State Park, NY, US 139/K7
Talloires, Fr. 56/C6
Tallow, Ire. 31/Q10
Tallulah, La, US 129/K4
Tallulah (falls), Ga, US 133/H3
Talmassons, It. 59/G1
Talo (peak), Eth. 97/N5
Taloda, India 89/K4
Tāloqān, Afg. 89/J1
Talpa de Allende, Mex. 142/D4
Talsperre Pöhl (res.), Ger. 55/F1
Taltal, Chile 157/B2
Taltson (riv.), NW, Can. 122/E2
Talumphuk (pt.), Thai. 78/C4
Talvera (Talfer) (riv.), It. 57/H4
Talwāra, India 86/C4
Tam Ky, Viet. 78/E3
Tama, Japan 77/C2
Tama (riv.), Japan 77/D2
Tamagawa, Japan 77/C2
Tamaho, Japan 77/B2
Tamaki, Japan 77/L7
Tamalameque, Col. 152/C2
Tamale, Gha. 103/E4
Tamamura, Japan 77/C1
Taman, Indo. 80/D5
Taman-Rasset, Oued (riv.), Alg. 99/F5
Tamaná (peak), Col. 152/B3
Tamana (isl.), Kiri. 116/G5
Tamanar, Mor. 98/C3
Tamanghasset (prov.), Alg. 103/F1
Tamanghasset, Oued (riv.), Alg. 99/F5
Tamanrasset, Alg. 99/G5
Tamanrasset (prov.), Alg. 99/F4
Tamaqua, Pa, US 138/C2
Tamar (riv.), Eng, UK 32/B5
Tamara (isl.), Japan 75/H8
Tamari, Japan 77/E1
Tamarindo NWR, CR 144/E4
Tamarite de Litera, Sp. 45/F2
Tamaro (peak), Swi. 57/E5
Tamási, Hun. 48/D2
Tamatsukuri, Japan 77/E1
Tamaulipas (state), Mex. 140/B3
Tamazula de Gordiano, Mex. 142/E5
Tamazunchale, Mex. 144/B1
Tamba, Japan 77/H5
Tamba (uplands), Japan 77/H5
Tambacounda (pol. reg.), Sen. 102/B3
Tambacounda, Sen. 102/B3
Tambaoura, Falaise de (cliff), Mali 102/C3
Tambelan (isls.), Indo. 80/C3
Tambellup, Austl. 112/C5
Tambo (riv.), Peru 156/C3
Tambo (peak), Swi. 57/F5
Tambo, Austl. 114/B4
Tambo Colorado (ruin), Peru 156/C4
Tambo de Mora, Peru 156/B4
Tambo Grande, Peru 156/A2
Tambobamba, Peru 156/C4
Tambohorano, Madg. 107/G7
Tambopata (riv.), Peru 156/D4
Tambora (peak), Indo. 81/E5
Tamboril, Braz. 154/B2
Tamboritha (mt.), Austl. 115/C3
Tambov, Rus. 63/G1
Tambov Oblast, Rus. 63/G1
Tambre (riv.), Sp. 44/A1
Tame (riv.), Eng, UK 33/E1
Tame, Col. 152/D3
Tâmega (riv.), Port. 44/B2
Tamentit, Alg. 99/E4
Tamgak (peak), Niger 103/H2
Tamgue (mass.), Gui. 102/B3
Tamiahua, Mex. 144/B1
Tamiahua (lag.), Mex. 144/B1
Tamil Nādu (state), India 82/C5
Taminango, Col. 152/B4
Ţāmiyah, Egypt 91/B5
Tamlūk, India 85/F4
Tammany (mt.), NJ, US 138/C2
Tammela, Fin. 39/K1
Ţammūn, WBnk. 91/D3
Tampa, Fl, US 133/H5
Tampa (int'l arpt.), Fl, US 133/H5
Tampere, Fin. 39/K1
Tampere-Pirkkala (int'l arpt.), Fin. 39/K1
Tampico, Mex. 144/B1
Tampoc (riv.), FrG. 153/H4
Tampon Ambohitra (peak), Madg. 107/J6
Tampulonanjing (peak), Indo. 80/A3
Tamra, Isr. 91/G6
Tamshiyacu, Peru 156/C2
Tamuín (riv.), Mex. 144/B1
Tamuín, Mex. 144/B1
Tamur (riv.), Nepal 85/F2
Tamworth, Austl. 115/D1
Tamworth, Eng, UK 33/E1
Tamyang, SKor. 73/D5
Tan (riv.), China 83/K3
Tan An, Viet. 78/D4
Tan-Tan, Mor. 98/C3
Tana (riv.), Kenya 93/G5
Tana (lake), Eth. 93/F3
Tana River Primate Nat'l Rsv., Kenya 104/D3
Tanabe, Japan 74/D4
Tanabe, Japan 77/J6
Tanabi, Braz. 155/B2
Tanacross, Ak, US 134/K3
Tanafjorden (estu.), Nor. 37/J1
Tanaga (vol.), Ak, US 134/C6
Tanaga (isl.), Ak, US 65/U4
Tanagura, Japan 75/G2
Tanah Merah, Malay. 83/H6
Tanahbala (isl.), Indo. 80/A4
Tanakpur, India 84/C1
Tanambe, Madg. 107/J7
Tanami (des.), Austl. 109/C2
Tanana, Ak, US 134/H2
Tanana (riv.), Ak, US 119/C3
Tanandava, Madg. 107/G8
Tanaro (riv.), It. 43/G4
Tancheng, China 72/D4
Tanch'ŏn, NKor. 73/E2
Tancítaro, Pico de (peak), Mex. 142/E5
Tancitaro, PN de, Mex. 140/A4
Tanda (lake), Mali 102/D3
Tandā, India 84/D2
Tānda, India 84/B1
Tandag, Phil. 81/G2
Ţăndărei, Rom. 49/H3
Tandil, Arg. 158/F3
Tāndliānwāla, Pak. 86/B4
Tando Ādam, Pak. 89/J3
Tando Allāhyār, Pak. 89/J3
Tando Muhammad Khān, Pak. 89/J3
Tandou (lake), Austl. 109/D4
Tandragee, NI, UK 34/B3
Tanem (range), Thai. 83/G4
Tanezrouft (des.), Alg. 93/B2
Tanezrouft-n-Ahenet (des), Alg. 99/F5
Tang (riv.), China 72/C4
Tanga (pol. reg.), Tanz. 104/C4
Tanga, Tanz. 104/C4
Tangail, Bang. 85/G3
Tangail (pol. reg.), Bang. 85/G3
Tanganyika (lake), D.R. Congo 93/F5
Tangará da Serra, Braz. 150/G6
Tangent (pt.), Ak, US 134/G1
Tanger, Mor. 100/B2
Tanger (prov.), Mor. 100/A2
Tangerhütte, Ger. 40/F2
Tangermünde, Ger. 40/F2
Tanggula (mts.), China 70/E5
Tanghe, China 72/C4
Tangi, Pak. 86/A2
Tangipahoa (riv.), La, US 137/P16
Tangipahoa (co.), La, US 137/P16
Tangjin, SKor. 73/D4
Tanglewilde-Thompson Place, Wa, US 135/B3
Tangshan, China 72/J7
Tangub, Phil. 79/D6
Tangyin, China 72/C4
Tangyuan, China 71/N2
Tanhaçu, Braz. 154/B4
Tanigumi, Japan 77/L4
Tanimbar (isl.), Indo. 67/N10
Taninges, Fr. 56/C5
Tanintharyi (state), Myan. 83/G5
Tanjay, Phil. 79/D6
Tanjungbalai, Indo. 80/A3
Tanjungkarang-Telukbetung, Indo. 80/C5
Tanjungpandan, Indo. 80/C4
Tanjungpinang, Indo. 80/B3
Tanjungpura, Indo. 80/A3
Tānk, Pak. 86/A3
Tankwa Karoo NP, SAfr. 106/B4
Tann, Ger. 55/F6
Tanna (isl.), Van. 116/F6
Tannan, Japan 77/H5
Tannersville, Pa, US 138/C1
Tannheim, Aus. 57/G3
Tannu-Ola (mts.) 70/F1
Tano (riv.), Gha. 96/E6
Tânout, Niger 103/H3
Tanquián de Escobedo, Mex. 144/B1
Tansen, Nepal 84/D2
Ţanţā, Egypt 91/B4
Tantallon, Md, US 138/A6
Tantō, Japan 77/G5
Tantoyuca, Mex. 144/B1
Tanuku, India 82/D4
Tanumshede, Swe. 38/D2
Tanunda, Austl. 115/A2
Tanyang, SKor. 73/E4
Tanzania (ctry.) 93/F5
Tanzawa-yama (peak), Japan 77/C3
Tao (isl.), Myan. 78/B4
Taolañaro, Madg. 107/H9
Taormina, It. 46/D4
Tāoru, India 86/D5
Taos, NM, US 129/F3
Taounate (town), Mor. 100/B2
Taounate, Mor. 100/B2
Taourirt, Alg. 99/F4
Taourirt, Mor. 100/C2
T'aoyüan, Tai. 79/D2
Taoyuan, China 83/K2
Tap Mun Chau (isl.), China 71/V10
Tap O'Noth (hill), Sc, UK 36/D2
Tapa, Est. 39/L2
Tapachula, Mex. 144/C3
Tapajós (riv.), Braz. 147/D3
Tapanahoni (riv.), Sur. 151/G3
Tapanti Nat'l Wild. Ref., CR 145/F4
Tapauá (riv.), Braz. 150/E5
Tapauá, Braz. 150/F5
Tapaz, Phil. 79/D5
Tapejara, Braz. 155/A4
Tapes, Braz. 155/B4
Tapeta, Libr. 102/C5
Tapia de Casariego, Sp. 44/B1
Tapiche (riv.), Peru 156/C2
Tapilula, Mex. 144/C2
Tapis (peak), Malay. 80/B3
Tapo, Peru 156/C3
Tapoa (prov.), Burk. 103/F3
Tapolca, Hun. 48/C2
Tappahannock, Va, US 130/E4
Tappan, NY, US 139/K7
Tappan Zee (lake), NY, US 139/E1
Tappan Zee (riv.), NY, US 139/K7
Tappi-zaki (pt.), Japan 76/B3
Tapps (lake), Wa, US 135/C3
Tāpti (riv.), India 89/J4
Ţāq Kisrá (Ctesiphon) (ruin), Iraq 90/F3
Taquara, Braz. 155/B4
Taquari (riv.), Braz. 151/G7
Taquari, Braz. 155/B4
Taquaritinga, Braz. 155/B2
Taquarituba, Braz. 155/B2
Taquil, Ecu. 156/B1
Tar (riv.), Kyr. 87/F4
Tara, Rus. 87/F1
Tara (riv.), Yugo. 48/D4
Tara, Austl. 114/C4
Taraba (state), Nga. 103/H5
Taraba (riv.), Nga. 103/H4
Tarābulus, Leb. 91/D2
Ţarābulus (Tripoli) (cap.), Libya 96/H1
Tarakan, Indo. 81/E3
Taraklı, Turk. 49/K5
Taraku (isl.), Rus. 76/E2
Taralga, Austl. 115/D2
Taranagar, India 86/C5
Tarancón, Sp. 44/D2
Tarangire NP, Tanz. 105/G1
Taranto, It. 47/E2
Taranto, Golfo di (gulf), It. 46/E2
Tarapoto, Peru 156/B2
Tarare, Fr. 42/F4
Tarariras, Uru. 159/K11
Tarascon, Fr. 42/F5
Tarascon-sur-Ariège, Fr. 42/D5
Tarata, Peru 156/D5
Tarauacá, Braz. 156/D3
Tarauacá (riv.), Braz. 156/D2
Taravai (isl.), FrPol. 117/M7
Tarawa (cap.), Kiri. 116/G4
Tarawa (isl.), Kiri. 116/G4
Tarazona, Sp. 44/E3
Tarazona, Sp. 44/E2
Tarbagatay (mts.), Kaz. 70/D2
Tarbat Ness (pt.), Sc, UK 36/C1
Tarbela (dam), Pak. 86/B2
Tarbela (res.), Pak. 86/B2
Tarbes, Fr. 42/D5
Tarbolton, Sc, UK 36/B5
Tarboro, NC, US 133/J3
Tarcento, It. 43/K3
Tarcutta, Austl. 115/C2
Tardes (riv.), Fr. 42/E3
Tardienta, Sp. 45/E2
Tardoire (riv.), Fr. 42/D4
Taree, Austl. 115/E1
Tarf Water (riv.), Sc, UK 34/D2
Tarfâwi (well), Egypt 101/B4
Tarfaya, Mor. 98/B4
Target Rock NWR, NY, US 139/M8
Targuist, Mor. 100/B2
Tarhūnah, Libya 96/H1
Tarifa, Ecu. 156/B1
Tarifa, Sp. 44/C4
Tarija, Bol. 150/F8
Tariku (riv.), Indo. 81/J4
Tariku-Taritatu (plain), Indo. 81/J4
Tarim (basin), China 64/J6
Tarim (riv.), China 64/J5
Tarin (riv.), Afg. 89/J2
Tarin (Torino), It. 43/G4
Taritatu (riv.), Indo. 81/J4
Tarkastad, SAfr. 106/D4
Tarkhankut (cape), Ukr. 49/L3
Tarkwa, Gha. 103/E5
Tarlac, Phil. 79/D4
Tarma, Peru 156/C3
Tarmstedt, Ger. 51/G2
Tarn (riv.), Fr. 42/D5
Tarn Tāran, India 86/C4
Tarnak (riv.), Afg. 89/J2
Tarnobrzeg, Pol. 41/L3
Tarnobrzeg (prov.), Pol. 41/M3
Tarnów, Pol. 41/L3
Tärnsjö, Swe. 38/G1
Taro (riv.), It. 43/J4
Tarō, Japan 76/B4
Ţārom, Iran 89/G3
Taroom, Austl. 114/C4
Tarouca, Port. 44/B2
Taroudannt, Mor. 98/C3
Tarp, Ger. 38/C4
Tarpa, Hun. 48/F1
Tarpon Springs, Fl, US 133/H4
Tarquinia, It. 46/B1
Tarqūmiyah, WBnk. 91/D4
Tarrafal, CpV. 93/K10
Tarragona, Sp. 45/F2
Tarraleah, Austl. 115/C4
Tàrrega, Sp. 45/F2
Tarrenz, Aus. 57/G3
Tarrytown, NY, US 139/K7
Tarsney Lakes, Mo, US 137/E6
Tarsus, Turk. 91/D1
Tarsus (riv.), Turk. 91/D1
Tartagal, Arg. 157/D1
Tartaro (riv.), It. 59/E2
Tartarstan Aut. Rep., Rus. 64/Q6
Tartas, Fr. 42/C5
Tartu, Est. 39/M2
Ţarţūs (prov.), Syria 90/C3
Ţarţūs, Syria 91/D2
Tarui, Japan 77/L5
Tarumizu, Japan 74/B5
Tarutao NP, Thai. 78/B5
Tarvagatay (mts.), Mong. 70/G2
Taşağıl, Turk. 91/B1
Täsch, Swi. 56/D5
Taşçı, Turk. 90/C2
Tashkent (cap.), Uzb. 87/E4
Tashkent (int'l arpt.), Uzb. 87/E4
Tasikmalaya, Indo. 80/C5
Taşkent, Turk. 91/C1
Taşköprü, Turk. 62/E4
Taşlıçay, Turk. 63/G5
Tasman (pen.), Austl. 109/D5
Tasman (sea), Austl.,NZ 116/E8
Tasman (bay), NZ 109/H7
Tasman Head (cape), Austl. 115/C4
Tasmania, Austl. 115/C3
Tasmania (state), Austl. 109/D5
Tăşnad, Rom. 48/F2
Taşova, Turk. 62/F4
Tasquillo, Mex. 143/K6
Tassili-n-Ajjer (mts.), Alg. 99/G4
Tassili Oua-n Ahaggar (mts.), Alg. 99/G5
Tasu, BC, Can. 134/M5
Taşucu, Turk. 91/C1
Tata, Mor. 98/D3
Tata, Hun. 48/D2
Tatabánya, Hun. 48/D2
Tatachikapika (riv.), Can. 130/D2
Tatakoto (isl.), FrPol. 117/L6
Tatamy, Pa, US 138/C2
Tatar (str.), Rus. 67/P5
Tatarlar, Turk. 47/K2
Tatarsk, Rus. 87/G1
Tatāwīn, Tun. 96/H1
Tatāwīn (gov.), Tun. 99/H2
Tate-yama (peak), Japan 75/E2
Tatebayashi, Japan 77/D1
Tateshina, Japan 77/A1
Tateyama, Japan 75/F3
Tathlina (lake), NW, Can. 122/E2
Tathra, Austl. 115/D3
Tatilt (well), Mrta. 102/B2
Tatitlek, Ak, US 134/J3
Tatnam (cape), Mb, Can. 122/G3
Tatomi, Japan 77/B2
Tatranský NP, Slvk. 41/K4
Tatsuno, Japan 75/E3
Tatsuta, Japan 77/L5
Tatura, Austl. 115/C3
Tatvan, Turk. 90/E2
Tauá, Braz. 154/B2
Taubaté, Braz. 211/H8
Tauber (riv.), Ger. 40/E4
Tauberbischofsheim, Ger. 54/C3
Tauca, Peru 156/B3
Taufkirchen, Ger. 55/F6
Taufkirchen an der Pram, Aus. 55/G6
Taufstein (peak), Ger. 54/C1
Taulihawa, Nepal 84/D2
Taung, SAfr. 106/D2
Taungdwingyi, Myan. 83/G3
Taunggyi, Myan. 83/G3
Taungup, Myan. 83/F4
Taunsa, Pak. 86/A4
Taunton, Ma, US 131/G3
Taunton, Eng, UK 32/C4
Taunus (range), Ger. 54/A2
Taunusstein, Ger. 54/B2
Taupo, NZ 117/T10
Taupo (lake), NZ 109/H6
Tauragė, Lith. 39/K4
Tauranga, NZ 117/T10
Taurion (riv.), Fr. 42/D3
Taurisano, It. 47/F3
Taurus (mts.), Turk. 90/C2
Tauste, Sp. 44/E2
Taute (riv.), Fr. 42/C2
Tauu (isls.), PNG 116/E5
Tavanbulag, Mong. 70/H2
Tavannes, Swi. 56/D3
Tavaputs (plat.), Ut, US 128/E3
Tavarnelle, It. 59/E5
Tavarnuzze, It. 59/E5
Tavas, Turk. 90/B2
Tavaux, Fr. 56/B3
Tavazzano, It. 58/C2
Tavda (riv.), Rus. 64/G4
Tavernerio, It. 58/C1
Taverny, Fr. 30/J4
Taviano, It. 47/F3
Tavira, Port. 44/B4
Tavoy (pt.), Myan. 78/B3
Tavoy (Dawei), Myan. 78/B3
Tavşanlı, Turk. 62/D5
Tavy (riv.), Eng, UK 32/B6
Taw (riv.), Eng, UK 32/C5
Tawaramoto, Japan 77/J6
Tawas City, Mi, US 130/D2
Tawau, Malay. 81/E3
Tawe (riv.), Wal, UK 32/C3
Tawern, Ger. 53/F4
Tāwi (riv.), India 86/C3
Tawi-tawi (isl.), Phil. 79/C6
Ţāwūq, Iraq 90/F3
Tawzar, Tun. 96/G1
Tawzar (gov.), Tun. 99/G2
Taxco, Mex. 143/K8
Taxila (ruin), Pak. 86/B3
Taxila, Pak. 86/B3
Taxkorgan Tajik Zizhixian, China 89/L1
Tay (lake), Sc, UK 36/B3
Tay (riv.), Sc, UK 36/C3
Tay, Firth of (inlet), Sc, UK 36/C4
Tay Ninh, Viet. 78/D4
Tayabamba, Peru 156/B3
Taylor, Mi, US 135/F7
Taylorsville-Bennion, Ut, US 137/K12
Taymyr (riv.), Rus. 64/K2
Taymyr (isl.), Rus. 65/L2
Taymyr (pen.), Rus. 67/H2
Tayoltita, Mex. 142/D3
Tayport, Sc, UK 36/D4
Tayrona, PN, Col. 152/C2
Tayshet, Rus. 65/K4
Tayside (pol. reg.), Sc, UK 36/C3
Taytay, Phil. 81/E1
Taz (riv.), Rus. 67/H3
Taza (prov.), Mor. 100/C2
Taza, Mor. 100/B2
Tazawako, Japan 76/B4
Tazekka (peak), Mor. 100/B2
Tazenakht, Mor. 98/D3
Tazewell, Tn, US 130/D4
Tāzirbū (oasis), Libya 97/K2
Tazumal (ruin), ESal. 144/D3
T'bilisi (cap.), Geo. 63/H4
T'boli, Phil. 79/D6
Tchamba, Togo 103/F4
Tchaourou, Ben. 103/F4
Tchefuncta (riv.), La, US 137/P16
Tchibanga, Gabon 96/H8
Tcholliré, Camr. 96/H6
Tczew, Pol. 39/H4
Te Anau, NZ 117/R12
Te Araroa, NZ 117/T10
Te Aroha, NZ 117/T10
Te Awamutu, NZ 117/T10
Te Kao, NZ 117/S9
Te Kuiti, NZ 117/T10
Tea (riv.), Braz. 150/E4
Teacapán, Mex. 142/D4
Teague, Tx, US 129/H5
Teaneck, NJ, US 139/J8
Teano, It. 46/D2
Teapa, Mex. 144/C2
Tearce, Macd. 47/G1
Tebak (peak), Indo. 80/B4
Tébessa (prov.), Alg. 99/G2
Tebessa (mts.), Alg. 100/L7
Tébessa, Alg. 100/L7
Tebesselamane (well), Mali 103/F2
Tebicuary (riv.), Par. 157/E2
Tebingtinggi, Indo. 80/A3
Tebulos-mta (peak), Rus. 63/H4
Tecalitlán, Mex. 142/E5
Tecamac, Mex. 143/R9
Tecamachalco, Mex. 143/M8
Tecate, Mex. 128/C4
Tech (riv.), Ger. 42/E5
Techirghiol, Rom. 49/J3
Tecirli, Turk. 90/D2
Tecka, Arg. 158/C4
Tecka (riv.), Arg. 158/C4
Tecklenberg, Ger. 51/E4
Tecolutla, Mex. 143/M6
Tecomán, Mex. 142/E5
Tecozautla, Mex. 143/K6
Tecpan de Galeana, Mex. 143/E5
Tecuala, Mex. 142/D4
Tecuci, Rom. 49/H3
Tecumseh, Mi, US 130/D3
Tecumseh, Ne, US 129/H2
Tecumseh, On, Can. 135/G7
Tedjert (well), Alg. 99/H1
Tedzhen (riv.), Trkm. 64/G6
Tees (bay), Eng, Uk 35/G2
Tees (riv.), Eng, UK 35/G3
Teesside (int'l arpt.), Eng, UK 35/G3
Tefé (riv.), Braz. 150/E4
Tefé, Braz. 150/F4
Teferič, Yugo. 48/E4
Tega (lake), Japan 77/E2
Tegal, Indo. 80/C5
Tegel (int'l arpt.), Ger. 40/Q6
Tegelen, Neth. 50/D6
Tegeler (lake), Ger. 40/Q6
Tegheri (well), Libya 99/H4
Teghra, India 85/E3
Tegid, Llyn (lake), Wal, UK 34/E6
Teglio, It. 57/G5
Tégouma (riv.), Niger 103/H3
Tegsh, Mong. 70/G2
Tegucigalpa (cap.), Hon. 144/E3
Tehek (lake), NW, Can. 122/G2
Tehrān (cap.), Iran 88/F1
Tehuacán, Mex. 143/M8
Tehuantepec (isth.), Mex. 143/G5
Tehuantepec (riv.), Mex. 144/C2
Tehuantepec (gulf), Mex. 119/H8
Teide, Pico de (peak), Sp. 98/A3
Teifi (riv.), Wal, UK 32/B2
Teifiside (valley), Wal, UK 32/B2
Teiga (plat.), Sudan 97/L4
Teign (riv.), Eng, UK 32/C5
Teignmouth, Eng, UK 32/C5
Teisendorf, Ger. 55/F7
Teith (riv.), Sc, UK 36/B4
Tejen, Trkm. 89/H1
Tejn, Den. 38/F4
Tejupilco de Hidalgo, Mex. 143/E5
Tekamah, Ne, US 127/J5
Tekāri, India 85/E3
Tekax de Álvaro Obregón, Mex. 144/D1
Teke, Turk. 49/J5
Tekeli, Kaz. 87/G4
Tekes (riv.), China 64/J5
Tekezē Wenz (riv.), Eth. 97/N5
Tekiliktag (peak), China 70/D4
Tekirdağ, Turk. 49/H5
Tekirdag (prov.), Turk. 62/C4
Tekirdağ (prov.), Turk. 49/H5
Tekit, Mex. 144/D1
Tekkali, India 82/D4
Tekke, Turk. 90/D1
Tekkeköy, Turk. 62/F4
Tekman, Turk. 63/G5
Tel Aviv (dist.), Isr. 91/D3
Tel Aviv-Yafo, Isr. 91/F7
Tel Megiddo (ruin), Isr. 91/G6
Tela, Hon. 144/E3
Télagh, Alg. 100/D2
T'elavi, Geo. 63/H4
Telde, Sp. 98/B3
Télé (lake), Mali 102/D2
Telêmaco Borba, Braz. 155/B3
Telemark (co.), Nor. 37/D4
Telen (riv.), Indo. 81/E3
Teleorman (prov.), Rom. 49/G4
Telertheba (peak), Alg. 99/G4
Teles Pires (riv.), Braz. 147/D3
Telford, Pa, US 138/C3
Telford Dawley, Eng, UK 32/D1
Telfs, Aus. 57/H3
Telgate, It. 58/C1
Telgte, Ger. 51/E5
Telica, Nic. 144/E3
Télig (well), Mali 98/E5
Télimélé, Gui. 102/B4
Telkwa, BC, Can. 126/B2
Tell City, In, US 130/C4
Teller, Ak, US 134/E2
Telli (lake), Mrta. 98/C4
Tellicherry, India 82/C5
Tellin, Belg. 53/E3
Telluride, Co, US 128/F3
Telok Anson, Malay. 80/B3
Teloloapan, Mex. 143/F5
Telšiai, Lith. 39/K4
Teltow, Ger. 40/Q7
Teltow (reg.), Ger. 41/G2
Tema, Gha. 103/E5
Temagami (lake), Can. 130/D2
Temax, Mex. 144/D1
Tembilahan, Indo. 80/B4
Tembisa, SAfr. 106/E2
Temblador, Ven. 153/F2
Teme (riv.), Eng, UK 32/C2
Temecula, Ca, US 136/C4
Temelkovo, Bul. 47/H1
Temerin, Yugo. 48/D3
Temerloh, Malay. 80/B3
Temirtaū, Kaz. 87/F2
Témiscamie (riv.), Can. 131/F1
Témiscaming, Qu, Can. 130/E2
Temoaya, Mex. 143/Q10
Temoe (isl.), FrPol. 117/M7
Temora, Austl. 115/C2
Tempe, Az, US 137/S19
Tempio Pausania, It. 46/A2
Temple, Pa, US 138/C3
Temple City, Ca, US 136/F7
Temple of Lady Chua Xu, Viet. 78/D4
Templemore, Ire. 31/Q10
Templepatrick, NI, UK 34/B2
Templeuve, Fr. 52/C2
Templeville, Md, US 138/C5
Templin, Ger. 41/G2
Templiner (lake), Ger. 40/Q7
Tempoal de Sánchez, Mex. 144/B1
Temryuk, Rus. 62/F3
Temse, Belg. 53/D1
Temuco, Chile 158/B3
Temuka, NZ 117/S11
Ten Boer, Neth. 50/D2
Tena, Ecu. 152/B5
Tena Kourou (peak), Mali 96/D5
Tenabo, Mex. 144/D1
Tenafly, NJ, US 139/K8
Tenakee Springs, Ak, US 134/L4
Tenancingo, Mex. 143/K8
Tenango, Mex. 143/R10
Tenango de Arista, Mex. 143/Q10

Tenasserim (range), Myan. 78/B3
Tenasserim, Myan. 78/B3
Tenay, Fr. 56/B6
Tenby, Wal, UK 32/B3
Tende, Fr. 43/G4
Tende, Col de (pass), Fr. 58/A4
Tenderovsk (bay), Ukr. 49/K2
Tenderovsk Spit (isl.), Ukr. 49/K2
Tendō, Japan 76/B4
Tendre (lake), Swi. 56/C4
Ténenkou, Mali 102/D3
Ténéré (des.), Niger 96/G4
Ténéré du Tafassasset (des.), Niger 96/G3
Tenerife (isl.), Sp. 152/C2
Tenerife (isl.), Sp. 93/A2
Ténès, Alg. 100/F4
Tenes (riv.), Sp. 45/L6
Teng (riv.), Myan. 83/G3
Teng Xian, China 72/D4
Tenggarong, Indo. 81/E4
Tengger (des.), China 70/H4
Tengiz (lake), Kaz. 64/G4
Tenguel, Ecu. 152/B5
Tenibres (peak), It. 43/G6
Teniente Enciso, PN, Par. 157/D1
Teningen, Ger. 56/D1
Tenja, Cro. 48/D3
Tenkodogo, Burk. 103/E4
Tenmile (riv.), Az, US 128/D4
Tennessee (state), US 129/K4
Tennessee (riv.), US 125/J5
Tennessee (state), US 125/J4
Tenneville, Belg. 53/E3
Tennuaca (well), Mor. 98/B5
Teno, Chile 158/C2/A6
Tenojoki (riv.), Fin. 37/H1
Tenosique de Pino Suárez, Mex. 144/D2
Tenri, Japan 77/J6
Tenryū, Japan 75/E3
Tenryū (riv.), Japan 75/E3
Tensift (pol. reg.), Mor. 98/C3
Tensift, Oued (riv.), Mor. 98/C3
Tenterfield, Austl. 115/E1
Tentolomatinan (peak), Indo. 81/F3
Tenus (peak), Kenya 104/B2
Teo, Sp. 44/A1
Teocaltiche, Mex. 140/A3
Teocelo, Mex. 143/N7
Teodelina, Arg. 158/E2
Teodoro Sampaio, Braz. 155/A2
Teófilo Otoni, Braz. 154/B5
Teopisca, Mex. 144/C2
Teotihuacán (ruin), Mex. 143/P9
Teotihuacán, Mex. 143/P9
Teotitlán del Camino, Mex. 144/B2
Tepache, Mex. 142/C2
Tepalcatepec, Mex. 142/E5
Tepalcingo, Mex. 143/L8
Tepatitlán de Morelos, Mex. 140/A3
Tepatlaxco, Mex. 143/M7
Tepeapulco, Mex. 143/L7
Tepebaşı, Turk. 91/C1
Tepehuaje, Mex. 143/F4
Tepehuanes, Mex. 142/D3
Tepeji del Río de Ocampo, Mex. 143/K7
Tepelenë, Alb. 47/G2
Tepelská Plošina (mts.), Czh. 55/F2
Tepetlaoxtoc, Mex. 143/P9
Tepexi, Mex. 143/M8
Tepexpan, Mex. 143/P9
Tepic, Mex. 142/D4
Teplá (Tiber) (riv.), Czh. 40/G3
Teplá Vltava (riv.), Czh. 55/G5
Teplice, Czh. 41/G3
Tepoca (cape), Mex. 142/B2
Tepoca, Cabo (cape), Mex. 142/B2
Tepoto (isl.), FrPol. 117/L6
Tepotzotlán, Mex. 143/O9
Tepoztlán, Mex. 143/K8
Tequila, Mex. 142/E4
Tequisquiapan, Mex. 143/F4
Tequixquiac, Mex. 143/K7
Ter (riv.), Sp. 45/G1
Ter Aar, Neth. 50/B4
Téra, Niger 103/F3
Tera (riv.), Sp. 44/C2
Teraina (Washington) (isl.), Kiri. 117/J4
Teramo, It. 43/K5
Terang, Austl. 115/B3
Tercan, Turk. 62/G5
Terceira (isl.), Azor., Port. 45/S12
Terek (riv.), Rus. 63/N5
Terepaima, PN, Ven. 152/D2
Teresina, Braz. 154/B2
Teresópolis, Braz. 211/J4
Terespol, Pol. 41/M2
Tergnier, Fr. 52/C4
Tergun Daba (mts.), China 70/F4
Terheijden, Neth. 50/C5
Teriberskiy (pt.), Rus. 60/G1
Terkaplesterpoelen (lake), Neth. 50/C2
Terlan (Tirol), It. 57/H4
Temas de Rio Hondo, Arg. 157/D2
Términi Imerese, It. 46/C4
Términos (lag.), Mex. 144/D2
Termiz, Uzb. 89/J1
Termo, Ca, US 126/C5
Termoli, It. 46/D1
Termunten, Neth. 50/E2
Ternate, Indo. 81/G3
Ternberg, Aus. 55/H7

Terneuzen, Neth. 50/A6
Terni, It. 46/C1
Ternin (riv.), Fr. 42/F3
Ternoise (riv.), Fr. 52/B3
Ternopil', Ukr. 62/C2
Ternopil's'ka (obl.), Ukr. 62/C2
Terpeniya (bay), Rus. 65/O5
Terpni, Gre. 47/H2
Terra Nova, Braz. 154/B4
Terra Nova, Braz. 154/C3
Terra Nova NP, Can. 131/L1
Terrace, BC, Can. 126/A2
Terrace Bay, On, Can. 127/M3
Terracina, It. 46/C2
Terråk, Nor. 37/E2
Terralba, It. 46/A3
Terranuova Bracciolini, It. 59/E5
Terrassa, Sp. 45/L6
Terrasson-la-Villedieu, Fr. 56/B1
Terre Hill, Pa, US 138/B3
Terrebonne, Fr. 56/D2
Terrell Hills, Tx, US 137/U21
Terri (peak), Swi. 57/F4
Terry, Mt, US 127/G4
Terry (lake), Co, US 137/B2
Terrytown, La, US 137/P17
Terschelling (isl.), Neth. 50/C2
Tertenia, It. 46/A3
Teruel, Sp. 45/E2
Terutao (isl.), Thai. 83/G6
Tervel, Bul. 49/H4
Terza Grande (peak), It. 43/K3
Terzo d'Aquileia, It. 59/J3
Tešanj, Bosn. 48/C3
Tescou (riv.), Fr. 42/D5
Tešedíkovo, Slvk. 40/D5
Tesero, It. 57/H5
Teshekpuk (lake), Ak, US 134/G1
Teshikaga, Japan 76/D2
Teshio (riv.), Japan 76/C1
Teshio, Japan 76/B1
Teshio-dake (peak), Japan 76/C2
Teslić, Bosn. 48/C3
Teslin (riv.), Yk, Can. 122/C2
Teslin (lake), BC, Can. 122/C3
Tessaoua, Niger 103/G3
Tessenderlo, Belg. 53/E1
Tessenei (Teseney), Erit. 88/C3
Test (riv.), Eng, UK 33/E4
Testa del Gargano (pt.), It. 46/E2
Tét, Hun. 48/C2
Tete, Moz. 105/F4
Tête de l'Estrop (peak), Fr. 43/G4
Tetela, Mex. 143/M7
Teterow, Ger. 38/E5
Teteven, Bul. 47/J1
Tetiaroa (isl.), FrPol. 117/L6
Tetlin, Ak, US 134/K3
Tetlin NWR, US 134/K3
Teton (riv.), Mt, US 127/G4
Tétouan (prov.), Mor. 100/B2
Tétouan, Mor. 100/B2
Tetovo, Macd. 47/G1
Tettnang, Ger. 57/F2
Tetulia (riv.), Bang. 85/H4
Teublitz, Ger. 55/F4
Teuco (riv.), Arg. 157/D1
Teufen, Swi. 57/F3
Teúl de González Ortega, Mex. 142/E4
Teulada (cape), It. 46/A3
Teulon, Mb, Can. 127/J3
Teupasenti, Hon. 144/E3
Teuri (isl.), Japan 76/B1
Teuschnitz, Ger. 55/E2
Teutoburger Wald (for.), Ger. 51/F4
Tevere (Tiber) (riv.), It. 46/C1
Teverya, Isr. 91/D3
Teviot (riv.), Sc, UK 36/D2
Teviotdale (valley), Sc, UK 36/D2
Tewantin-Noosa, Austl. 114/D4
Tewkesbury, Eng, UK 32/D3
Texarkana, Tx, US 129/J4
Texas (state), US 124/F5
Texas City, Tx, US 129/J5
Texcoco, Mex. 143/P9
Texel (isl.), Neth. 50/B2
Texhoma, Ok, US 132/C2
Texmelucan, Mex. 143/L7
Texoma (lake), US 125/G5
Teyateyaneng, Les. 106/D3
Teykovo, Rus. 60/J4
Tezio (peak), It. 43/K5
Teziutlán, Mex. 143/M7
Tezonapa, Mex. 143/N8
Tezontepec, Mex. 143/L7
Tezontepec de Aldama, Mex. 143/K6
Tezpur, India 70/F6
Tezu, India 83/G2
Tezze, It. 59/E1

Thaleischweiler-Fröschen, Ger. 53/G5
Thalerhof (int'l arpt.), Aus. 43/L3
Thalgau, Aus. 55/G7
Thalheim bei Wels, Aus. 55/H6
Thalmässing, Ger. 54/E4
Thalwil, Swi. 57/E3
Thamar, Jabal (peak), Yem. 88/E6
Thame (riv.), Eng, UK 33/F3
Thames (riv.), Can. 130/D3
Thames (riv.), NZ 117/T10
Thames, Eng, UK 33/G4
Thames Barrier, Eng, UK 30/D2
Thāna, India 89/K5
Thāna Bhawan, India 86/D5
Thānesar, India 86/D5
Thangool, Austl. 114/C4
Thanh Hoa, Viet. 83/J4
Thanjavur, India 82/C5
Thann, Fr. 56/D2
Thannhausen, Ger. 57/G1
Thaon-les-Vosges, Fr. 56/C1
Thar (des.), Pak. 86/A5
Tharad, India 89/K4
Thargomindah, Austl. 114/A5
Tharrawaddy, Myan. 78/B3
Thásos, Gre. 47/J2
Thásos (isl.), Gre. 47/J2
Thatcham, Eng, UK 33/E4
Thatcher, Az, US 128/E4
Thaton, Myan. 78/B2
Thaur, Aus. 57/H3
Thaya (riv.), Aus. 41/H4
Thayetmyo, Myan. 83/G4
Thaynges, Swi. 57/E2
Thārū, Myan. 83/G3
The Alamo, Tx, US 137/U21
The Dalles, Or, US 126/C4
The Hague ('s-Gravenhage) (cap.), Neth. 50/B4
The Oaks, Ca, US 136/B1
The Pas, Mb, Can. 127/H2
The Rock, Austl. 115/C2
The Valley (cap.), Angu. 141/N8
The Village, Ok, US 137/M14
The Woodlands, Tx, US 129/J5
Thebes (ruin), Egypt 101/C3
Theilheim, Ger. 54/C3
Thelma, Tx, US 137/T21
Thelon (riv.), Can. 119/G3
Thémericourt, Fr. 30/H4
Theo (mt.), Austl. 113/F2
Theodore, Sk, Can. 127/G3
Theodore, Austl. 114/C4
Theodore Roosevelt (lake), Az, US 128/E4
Theodore Roosevelt NP, US 127/G4
Thérain (riv.), Fr. 42/D2
Thermaic (gulf), Gre. 62/B4
Thérmi, Gre. 47/H2
Thermopílai (Thermopylae) (pass), Gre. 47/H3
Thermopolis, Wy, US 126/F5
Thérouanne (riv.), Fr. 30/L4
Thesprotikón, Gre. 47/G3
Thessalon, On, Can. 130/D2
Thessaloníki, Gre. 47/H2
Thessaly (reg.), Gre. 47/H3
Thet (riv.), Eng, UK 33/G2
Thetford, Eng, UK 33/G2
Thetford Mines, Qu, Can. 131/G2
Theunissen, SAfr. 106/D3
Theux, Belg. 53/E2
Thève (riv.), Fr. 30/K4
Theydon Bois, Eng, UK 30/D2
Thiais, Fr. 30/K5
Thiámis (riv.), Gre. 47/G3
Thiant, Fr. 52/C3
Thiaucourt-Regniéville, Fr. 53/E6
Thief River Falls, Mn, US 127/J3
Thielle (riv.), Swi. 56/C4
Thielsen (mt.), Or, US 126/C5
Thiene, It. 59/E1
Thiérache (reg.), Fr. 52/C4
Thierhaupten, Ger. 54/D5
Thiers, Fr. 42/E4
Thiers-sur-Thève, Fr. 30/K4
Thierville-sur-Meuse, Fr. 53/E5
Thiès (pol. reg.), Sen. 102/A3
Thiès, Sen. 102/A3
Thika, Kenya 104/C3
Thimphu (cap.), Bhu. 85/F2
Thingvellir NP, Ice. 37/N7
Thionville, Fr. 53/F5
Thira (peak), It. 43/K5
Thíra, Gre. 47/J4
Thíra (isl.), Gre. 47/J4
Third Cataract (falls), Sudan 101/B4
Third Lake, Il, US 135/Q15
Thirlmere (lake), Eng, UK 35/E2
Thirsty (mt.), Austl. 112/D5
Thirtymile (pt.), NY, US 131/V9
Thise, Fr. 56/C3
Thisted, Den. 38/C3
Thistilfjördhur (estu.), Ice. 37/P6
Thistle (mtn.), Can. 134/L3
Thistle (isl.), Austl. 113/H5
Thitu (isl.) 79/B5
Thívai, Gre. 47/H3
Thiverval-Grignon, Fr. 30/H5
Thjósa (riv.), Ice. 37/N7
Thlewiaza (riv.), NW, Can. 122/G2
Thoiry, Fr. 30/H5
Tholen (isl.), Neth. 50/B5
Tholen, Neth. 50/B5
Tholey, Ger. 53/G5

Thomaston, Ga, US 133/G3
Thomasville, Ire. 31/Q10
Thomasville, Al, US 133/G3
Thomasville, NC, US 133/H3
Thomasville, Ga, US 133/H4
Thomasville, Pa, US 138/B4
Thompson, Mb, Can. 127/J2
Thompson (riv.), Can. 126/C2
Thompson (lake), Austl. 112/K7
Thompson Falls, Mt, US 126/E4
Thomsen (riv.), NW, Can. 122/E1
Thomson, Ga, US 133/H3
Thongwa, Myan. 78/B2
Thonnance-lès-Joinville, Fr. 56/B1
Thoreau, NM, US 128/E3
Thorens-Glières, Fr. 56/C6
Thorhild, Ab, Can. 126/E2
Thorigny-sur-Marne, Fr. 30/L5
Thorlákshöfn, Ice. 37/N7
Thornaby-on-Tees, Eng, UK 35/G2
Thornbury, Eng, UK 32/D3
Thorndale, Pa, US 138/C4
Thorne, Eng, UK 35/H4
Thorne Bay, Ak, US 134/M4
Thornhill, Sc, UK 34/E1
Thornhurst, Pa, US 138/C2
Thornton, Co, US 137/C3
Thornton, Ca, US 135/M10
Thornton Cleveleys, Eng, UK 35/E4
Thorold, On, Can. 131/R9
Thouars, Fr. 42/C3
Thouet (riv.), Fr. 42/C3
Thourotte, Fr. 30/B5
Thousand Oaks, Ca, US 136/B2
Thowa (riv.), Kenya 104/C3
Thrace (reg.), Gre.,Turk 62/C4
Thracian (sea), Gre. 62/C4
Thredbo Village, Austl. 115/D3
Three Bridges, NJ, US 138/D2
Three Forks, Mt, US 126/F4
Three Guardsmen (mtn.), Can. 134/L3
Three Hills, Ab, Can. 126/E3
Three Hummock (isl.), Austl. 114/C4
Three Kings (isls.), NZ 116/G8
Three Mile (isl.), Pa, US 138/B3
Three Pagodas (pass), Myan. 78/B3
Three Points (cape), Gha. 103/E5
Three Rivers, Mi, US 130/C3
Three Rivers, Austl. 112/B4
Three Springs, Austl. 112/B4
Throssell (lake), Austl. 109/B3
Thrushel (riv.), Eng, UK 32/B5
Thu Dau Mot, Viet. 78/D4
Thuin, Belg. 53/D3
Thuir, Fr. 42/E5
Thulba (riv.), Ger. 54/C2
Thule Air Base, Den. 123/T7
Thun, Swi. 56/D4
Thunderbird (lake), Ok, US 137/N15
Thunder Bay, Braz. 155/B3
Thuner See (lake), Swi. 56/D4
Thung Salaeng Luang NP, Thai. 78/C2
Thüngersheim, Ger. 54/C3
Thur (riv.), Swi. 57/F3
Thurgau (canton), Swi. 57/F2
Thüringen (state), Ger. 43/J1
Thüringen, Aus. 57/F3
Thüringer Schiefergebirge (mts.), Ger. 54/D2
Thüringer Wald (for.), Ger. 43/J1
Thurles, Ire. 31/Q10
Thurman, Md, US 138/B6
Thurn, By, Den. 38/D6
Thurso, Sc, UK 31/V14
Thurso (riv.), Ant. 160/T
Thurston (co.), Fr.
Thusis, Swi. 57/F4
Thyez, Fr. 56/C5
Thyolo, Malw. 105/G4
Ti-m-Merhsoï (riv.), Niger 103/G2
Ti-n-Jedane, Oued (riv.), Mali 99/G4
Ti-n-Zaouâten, Alg. 96/F3
T-Tree Abor. Land, Austl. 113/G2

Tianzhu, China 83/J2
Tiaret, Alg. 100/F5
Tibagi, Braz. 155/B3
Tibaji (riv.), Braz. 155/B3
Tibaná, Col. 152/C3
Tibati, Camr. 96/H6
Tibba, Pak. 86/A5
Tibé, Pic de (peak), Gui. 102/C4
Tiber (Tevere) (riv.), It. 43/J5
Tiberias (lake), Isr. 91/D3
Tibesti (mts.), Chad 93/D3
Tibet (reg.), China 67/H6
Tibet (Xizang) (aut. reg.), China 70/D5
Tibro, Swe. 38/F2
Tiburon (cape), Haiti 141/G4
Tiburon, Ca, US 135/K11
Tiburón, Isla (isl.), Mex. 142/B2
Ticaco, Peru 156/D5
Tichigan (lake), Wi, US 135/P14
Tichît, Dhar (cliff), Mrta. 102/C2
Ticino (canton), Swi. 57/E5
Ticleni, Rom. 49/F3
Ticlios, Peru 156/B3
Ticonderoga, NY, US 130/F3
Ticul, Mex. 144/D1
Tidaholm, Swe. 38/E2
Tidikelt (plain), Alg. 96/F2
Tidjikdja, Mrta. 102/C2
Tidone (riv.), It. 58/C3
Tidore, Eng, UK 35/H4
Tidore (isl.), Indo. 81/G3
Tidra, Île (isl.), Mrta. 102/A2
Tiede, PN del, Sp. 98/A3
Tiefencastel, Swi. 57/F4
Tiel, Neth. 50/C5
Tieling, China 72/E2
Tielt, Belg. 52/C1
Tielt-Winge, Belg. 53/D2
Tiemba (riv.), C.d'Iv. 102/D4
Tiengen, Ger. 57/E2
Tienen, Belg. 53/D2
Tierney (riv.), Austl. 114/C3
Tieroko (peak), Chad 96/J3
Tierp, Swe. 38/G1
Tierra Amarilla, NM, US 128/F3
Tierra Blanca, Mex. 143/N8
Tierra Colorada, Mex. 143/F4
Tierra del Fuego (isl.), Arg. 147/C8
Tierra del Fuego, Antártida e Islas del Atlántico Sur, Arg. 159/C7
Tierradentro, Col. 152/B4
Tierranueva, Mex. 143/E4
Tietê (riv.), Braz. 147/D5
Tiffin, Oh, US 130/D3
Tiflet, Mor. 100/A3
Tifton, Ga, US 133/H4
Tigeaux, Fr. 30/L5
Tighina (Bendery), Mol. 49/J2
Tighvein (hill), Sc, UK 34/C1
Tignère, Camr. 96/H6
Tignieu-Jameyzieu, Fr. 56/B6
Tigre (riv.), Ven. 150/C4
Tigre (riv.), Peru 153/F2
Tigre, Arg. 159/J11
Tigris (riv.), Iraq 67/C6
Tigui (well), Chad 96/J4
Tiguidit, Falaise de (cliff), Niger 103/G2
Tigzirt, India 82/C5
Tihosuco, Mex. 144/D1
Tihuatlán, Mex. 144/B1
Tiilikkajärven NP, Fin. 60/F3
Tijâra, India 84/A2
Tijuana, Mex. 136/C5
Tijucas, Braz. 155/B3
Tijuco (riv.), Braz. 155/B1
Tikal (ruin), Guat. 144/D2
Tikamgarh, India 84/B3
Tikchik (lakes), Ak, US 134/G3
Tikhoretsk, Rus. 62/G3
Tikhvin, Rus. 60/G4
Tikrit, Iraq 90/E3
Tiksi, Rus. 66/L2
Tila, Mex. 144/C2
Tilburg, Neth. 50/C5
Tilbury, Eng, UK 30/E2
Tilden, Tx, US 132/D4
Tilghman, Md, US 138/B6
Tilghman (isl.), Md, US 138/B6
Tilhar, India 84/B2
Tillabéry, Niger 103/F3
Tillamook, Or, US 126/C4
Tille (riv.), Fr. 40/C5
Tillicoultry, Sc, UK 34/C4
Tilst, Den. 38/D3
Tiltil, Chile 158/N8
Tim, Den. 38/C3
Timan (ridge), Rus. 64/F2
Timanfaya, PN de, Sp. 98/B3
Timaru, NZ 117/S11
Timashevsk, Rus. 62/G3
Timbákion, Gre. 47/J5
Timbaúba, Braz. 154/D2
Timbédra, Mrta. 102/C2
Timber Lake, SD, US 127/H4
Timberlane, Pa, US
Timberwood Park, Tx, US 137/U20
Timbiras, Braz. 154/B2
Timbó, Braz. 155/B3
Timboon, Austl. 115/B3

Timehri (int'l arpt.), Guy. 153/G3
Timelkam, Aus. 55/G6
Timfristós (peak), Gre. 47/G3
Timimoun, Alg. 99/F3
Timiris (peak), Mrta. 102/A2
Timiş (prov.), Rom. 48/E3
Timiş (riv.), Rom. 62/B3
Timişoara (int'l arpt.), Rom. 48/E3
Timişoara, Rom. 48/E3
Timmath, Co, US 137/C1
Timmins, On, Can. 130/D1
Timms (hill), Wi, US 127/L4
Timon, Braz. 154/B2
Timonium, Md, US 138/B5
Timor (sea), Asia,Austl. 67/M11
Timor (isl.), Indo. 67/M12
Timóteo, Braz. 155/D1
Timpanogos Cave Nat'l Mon., Ut, US 137/K13
Timpanogos Nat'l Mon., Ut, US 137/K13
Timpson, Tx, US 129/J5
Timpton (riv.), Rus. 65/N4
Tims Ford (lake), 133/G3
Tin Can Bay, Austl. 114/D4
Tin Shui Wai, China 71/T10
Tina (riv.), SAfr. 106/B1
Tinaca (pt.), Phil. 81/G2
Tinaco, Ven. 152/D2
Tindivanam, India 82/C5
Tindouf, Alg. 98/C4
Tindouf (prov.), Alg. 98/D3
Tineo, Sp. 44/B1
Tingalpa (res.), Austl. 114/F7
Tingha (mts.), SLeo. 102/C4
Tingi, India 115/D1
Tingley, China 70/G5
Tingmerkpuk (mtn.), Ak, US 134/F2
Tingo María, Peru 156/C3
Tingsryd, Swe. 38/F3
Tiní, Austl. 114/C3
Tinharé, Ilha de (isl.), Braz. 151/L6
Tinian (isl.), NMar. 116/D3
Tinicum Nat'l Conserv. Area, Pa, US 138/C4
Tinley Park, Il, US 135/Q16
Tinogasta, Arg. 157/C2
Tinos, Gre. 47/J4
Tinos (isl.), Gre. 47/J4
Tinqueux, Fr. 52/C5
Tinrhir, Mor. 98/D3
Tinta, Peru 156/D4
Tintagel (pt.), Eng, UK 32/B5
Tintern Abbey, Wal, UK 32/D3
Tintigny, Belg. 53/E4
Tintina, Austl. 115/B2
Tinto (riv.), Sp. 44/B4
Tinto (peak), Sc, UK 36/C5
Tinton Falls (New Shrewsbury), NJ, US 138/D3
Tinyahuarco, Peru 156/B3
Tioga, ND, US 127/H3
Tioman (isl.), Malay. 80/B3
Tione di Trento, It. 57/G5
Tipasa (prov.), Alg. 100/F4
Tipasa, Alg. 100/G4
Tipperary, Ire. 31/P10
Tiptür, India 82/C5
Tir Rhiwiog (peak), Wal, UK 32/C1
Tiracambu, Serra do (mts.), Braz. 151/J4
Tiran (isl.), Egypt, SA 101/C3
Tiran (isl.), Egypt,SAr. 101/C3
Tirán (isl.), Egypt 97/M2
Tirano, It. 57/G5
Tirari (des.), Austl. 113/H4
Tiraspol, Mol. 49/J2
Tirat Karmel, Isr. 91/F6
Tire, Turk. 90/A2
Tirebolu, Turk. 62/F4
Tiree (isl.), Sc, UK 31/Q8
Tirest (well), Mali 99/F3
Tirgovişte, Rom. 49/G3
Tirgu Bujor, Rom. 49/H3
Tirgu Cărbuneşti, Rom. 49/F3
Tirgu Frumos, Rom. 49/H2
Tirgu Jiu, Rom. 49/F3
Tirgu Lăpuş, Rom. 49/F2
Tirgu Mureş, Rom. 49/G2
Tirgu Neamţ, Rom. 49/G2
Tirgu Ocna, Rom. 49/H2
Tirgu Secuiesc, Rom. 49/H2
Tirich Mīr (peak), Pak. 89/K1
Tiris Zemmour (pol. reg.), Mrta. 98/C4
Tiris (isl.), WSah. 98/B5
Tirna Mare (riv.), Rom. 49/F2
Tirna Mică (riv.), Rom. 49/F2
Tirnăveni, Rom. 49/G2
Tirnavos, Gre. 47/H3
Tiros, Braz. 155/C1
Tirschenreuth, Ger. 55/F3
Tiruchchirāppalli, India 82/C5
Tiruchendūr, India 82/C6
Tirunelveli, India 82/C6
Tiruntán, Peru 156/C2
Tirupati, India 82/C5
Tiruppattūr, India 82/C5
Tiruppūr, India 82/C5
Tiruvannāmalai, India 82/C5
Tisa (riv.), Ukr. 49/G1
Tisa (riv.), India 84/B2
Tisdale, Sk, Can. 127/G2
Tishomingo, Ok, US 129/H4

Tissa, Mor. 100/B2
Tissemsilt (prov.), Alg. 100/F5
Tissemsilt, Alg. 100/F5
Tista (riv.), Bang. 85/G2
Tisza (riv.), Hun. 62/B3
Tiszaföldvár, Hun. 48/E2
Tiszafüred, Hun. 48/E2
Tiszakécske, Hun. 48/E2
Tiszalök, Hun. 48/E1
Tiszavasvári, Hun. 41/L5
Titano (peak), SMar. 59/F5
Titel, Yugo. 48/E3
Titicaca (lake), Bol.,Peru 147/B4
Titisee-Neustadt, Ger. 56/E2
Titlagarh, India 84/B5
Titlis (peak), Swi. 57/E4
Tito, It. 46/D2
Titov Veles, Macd. 47/G2
Titov vrh (peak), Macd. 47/G2
Titting, Ger. 54/E5
Tittmoning, Ger. 55/F6
Titu, Rom. 49/G3
Titusville, Fl, US 133/H4
Titusville, NJ, US 138/D3
Tiva (riv.), Kenya 104/C3
Tivaouane, Sen. 102/A3
Tivat, Yugo. 47/F1
Tiverton, Eng, UK 32/C5
Tiverton, RI, US 138/E3
Tivoli, It. 46/C2
Tixán, Ecu. 156/B1
Tixtla de Guerrero, Mex. 143/F5
Tizayuca, Mex. 143/L7
Tizi Ouzou (prov.), Alg. 100/H4
Tizi Ouzou, Alg. 100/H4
Tizimín, Mex. 144/D1
Tiznap (riv.), China 89/L3
Tiznit, Mor. 98/C3
Tjæreborg, Den. 38/C4
Tjeldstø, Nor. 38/A1
Tjeukemeer (lake), Neth. 50/C3
Tjøme, Nor. 38/D2
Tjorn (isl.), Den. 38/D3
Tjörn (isl.), Swe. 38/D2
Tlachichuca, Mex. 143/N7
Tlacolula de Matamoros, Mex. 144/B2
Tlacotepec, Mex. 143/F5
Tlahualilo de Zaragoza, Mex. 132/C5
Tlalixcoyan, Mex. 143/N8
Tlalmanalco, Mex. 143/Q10
Tlalnepantla, Mex. 143/Q9
Tláloc (vol.), Mex. 143/Q10
Tlaltenango de Sánchez Román, Mex. 142/E4
Tlaltizapan, Mex. 143/K8
Tlapa de Comonfort, Mex. 144/B2
Tlapacoya (ruin), Mex. 143/M7
Tlapacoyan, Mex. 143/M7
Tlapehuala, Mex. 143/E5
Tlaquepaque, Mex. 142/E4
Tlaquiltenango, Mex. 143/K8
Tlatlauquitepec, Mex. 143/M7
Tlaxcala (state), Mex. 143/M7
Tlaxcala, Mex. 143/L7
Tlaxco, Mex. 143/L7
Tlaxcoapan, Mex. 143/K6
Tlell, BC, Can. 134/K5
Tlemcen, Alg. 100/E5
Toabré, Pan. 152/A2
Toaca (peak), Rom. 49/H2
Toachi (riv.), Ecu. 152/B4
Toamasina (prov.), Madg. 107/J7
Toamasina, Madg. 107/J7
Toano, It. 59/D4
Toao (isl.), FrPol. 117/L6
Toay, Arg. 158/D3
Toba (lake), Indo. 80/A3
Toba (inlet), Can. 126/B3
Toba, Japan 70/G5
Toba Kākar (range), Pak. 89/J2
Toba Tek Singh, Pak. 86/B4
Tobago (isl.), Trin. 150/F2
Tobarra, Sp. 44/E3
Tobbio (peak), It. 58/B3
Tobias Barreto, Braz. 154/C3
Tobin (lake), Austl. 109/C3
Tobique (riv.), Can. 131/H2
Tobishima, Japan 75/F3
Tobol (riv.), Rus. 61/Q5
Tobol, Kaz. 64/H4
Tobruk, Libya 77/A1
Tobyhanna (lake), 138/C1
Tobyhanna, Pa, US 138/C1
Tobyhanna St. Park, Pa, US 138/C1
Tocache, Peru 156/B3
Tocantinópolis, Braz. 154/A2
Tocantins (state), Braz. 154/A2
Tocantins (riv.), Braz. 147/E4
Toccoa, Ga, US 133/H3
Toce (riv.), It. 43/H3
Tochigi (pref.), Japan 75/F2
Tochigi, Japan 75/F2
Tochimilco, Mex. 143/L8
Tochio, Japan 75/F2
Tocina, Sp. 44/C4
Töcksfors, Swe. 38/D2
Toco, Trin. 153/F2
Tocopilla, Chile 157/B1
Tocumen, Pan. 152/B2
Tocumwal, Austl. 115/C2
Tocuyito, Ven. 152/D2
Tocuyo (riv.), Ven. 152/D1
Toda, Japan 77/D2
Toda Bhīm, India 84/A2
Todi, It. 46/C1
Tödi (peak), Swi. 57/F4

Todmorden, Eng, UK 35/F4
Todos os Santos, Baíaa de (bay), Braz. 154/C4
Todos Santos, Mex. 142/C4
Todtmoos, Ger. 56/E2
Todtnau, Ger. 56/D2
Toekomstig (res.), Sur. 150/G3
Toffia (hill), Mrta. 98/C5
Toffo, Ben. 103/F5
Tofield, Ab, Can. 126/E2
Tofua (isl.), Tonga 117/H6
Tōgane, Japan 77/F2
Togba (well), Mrta. 102/C2
Toggenburg (valley), Swi. 57/F3
Togher, Ire. 34/B5
Togiak, Ak, US 134/F3
Togiak NWR, US 134/F4
Togo (ctry.) 93/C4
Tōgō, Japan 77/M5
Togō, Mong. 70/F2
Togtoh, China 72/B2
Tōgyu-san NP, SKor. 73/G4
Tohāna, India 86/C5
Tohatchi, NM, US 132/A3
Tōhoku (prov.), Japan 75/F1
Toi, Japan 75/F3
Tōin, Japan 77/L5
Toiyabe (range), Nv, US 130/C4
Tōjō, Japan 74/C3
Tōjō, Japan 77/H6
Tok, Ak, US 134/K3
Tokachi (riv.), Japan 76/C2
Tōkai, Japan 77/M6
Tokaj, Hun. 41/L4
Tōkamachi, Japan 75/F2
Tokar Nat'l Rsv., Sudan 101/B4
Tokara (isls.), Japan 116/B1
Tokat (prov.), Turk. 62/F4
Tokat, Turk. 62/F4
Tokelau (terr.), NZ 117/H5
Tokelau, Japan 77/M5
Toki, Japan 77/M6
Tokigawa, Japan 77/C2
Tokke, Japan 77/L6
Tokoname, Japan 77/L6
Tokoro (riv.), Japan 76/D1
Tokoro, Japan 76/D1
Tokoroa, NZ 117/T10
Tokorozawa, Japan 77/D2
Toksook Bay, Ak, US 134/E3
Toksun, China 70/E3
Tokuno (isl.), Japan 75/K7
Tokunoshima, Japan 75/K7
Tokushima (pref.), Japan 73/G3
Tokushima, Japan 74/C4
Tokuyama, Japan 74/B3
Tōkyō (cap.), Japan 75/F3
Tōkyō (pref.), Japan 75/F3
Tōkyō (bay), Japan 77/D2
Tōkyō Disneyland, Japan 77/D2
Tola, Nic. 144/E4
Tola, Mong. 70/F2
Tolaga Bay, NZ 117/F1
Toledo, Braz. 157/F1
Toledo, Phil. 79/D5
Toledo, Oh, US 130/D3
Toledo, Sp. 44/D3
Toledo, Col. 152/C3
Toledo, Uru. 159/K11
Toledo Bend (dam), US 129/J5
Toledo Bend (res.), US 129/J5
Toledo, Montes de (mts.), Sp. 44/C3
Tolentino, It. 43/K5
Tolima (dept.), Col. 152/C3
Tolitoli, Indo. 81/F3
Tolleson, Az, US 137/R19
Tolmezzo, It. 43/K3
Tolna (prov.), Hun. 48/D2
Tolna, Hun. 48/D2
Tolo (chan.), China 71/U10
Tolo, Gulf of (gulf), Indo. 81/F4
Tolosa, Sp. 44/D1
Tolosa, Madg. 107/G8
Tolsan (isl.), SKor. 73/D5
Tolt (riv.), Wa, US 135/C2
Tolt (res.), Wa, US 135/C2
Tolt, North Fork (riv.), Wa, US 135/D2
Tolt, South Fork (riv.), Wa, US 135/D2
Toltén, Chile 158/B3
Tolú Viejo, Col. 152/C2
Tol'yatti, Rus. 63/J1
Tom Price, Austl. 112/C2
Tom White (mt.), Ak, US 134/K3
Tomakomai, Japan 76/B2
Tomamae, Japan 76/C2
Tomar, Port. 44/A3
Tomaszów Lubelski, Pol. 41/M3

Tomaszów Mazowiecki, Pol. 41/L3
Tomatlán, Mex. 142/D5
Tomb of Qinshihuang, China 72/B4
Tombador, Serra do (mts.), Braz. 150/G6
Tombigbee (riv.), Al,Ms, US 125/J5
Tombolo, It. 59/E1
Tombouctou, Mali 102/E2
Tombouctou (pol. reg.), Mali 98/D5
Tombstone, Az, US 128/E5
Tombua, Ang. 105/B4
Tomé, Chile 158/B3
Tomé, Île (isl.), Fr. 42/B2
Tomelilla, Swe. 38/E4
Tomelloso, Sp. 44/D3
Tomika, Japan 77/L5
Tomini (gulf), Indo. 67/M10
Tomiño, Sp. 44/A2
Tomioka, Japan 77/B1
Tomisato, Japan 77/D3
Tomiura, Japan 77/D3
Tomizawa, Japan 77/A3
Tomiya, Japan 75/F3
Tommot, Rus. 65/N4
Tompa, Hun. 48/D2
Tompkinsville, Ky, US 130/C4
Toms (riv.), NJ, US 138/D3
Toms River, NJ, US 138/D4
Tomsk, Rus. 64/J4
Tōmū, Turk. 91/D1
Tonalá, Mex. 144/C2
Tonale, Passo del (pass), It. 57/G5
Tonasket, Wa, US 126/C3
Tonawanda, NY, US 131/S9
Tonawanda Ind. Res., NY, US 131/S9
Tonbridge, Eng, UK 30/D3
Toncontín (int'l arpt.), Hon. 144/E3
Tondabayashi, Japan 77/J7
Tondano, Indo. 81/F3
Tondou, Massif du (plat.), CAfr.,Sud 97/K6
Tondu (peak), Fr. 56/C6
Tone (riv.), Japan 75/G3
Tone, Japan 77/E2
Tonekābon, Iran 88/F1
Tonelagee (peak), Ire. 34/B5
Tonga (cty.) 117/H7
Tongaat, SAfr. 107/E3
Tongareva (Penrhyn) (isl.), Cookls.
Tongariro NP, NZ 117/T10
Tongatapu (isl.), Tonga 117/H7
Tongbu, China 72/C4
Tongcheng, China 79/B2
Tongcheng, China 72/C4
Tongchuan, China 72/B4
Tongchuan, China 72/B4
Tongduch'ŏn, SKor. 73/G6
Tongeren, Belg. 53/E2
Tonggu (peak), China 71/J2
Tonggu, China 83/K2
Tonghae, SKor. 73/E4
Tonghua, China 73/C2
Tonghua, China 73/C2
Tongliao, China 72/E2
Tongling, China 71/L5
Tongren, China 83/J2
Tongo (lake), Austl. 81/E5
Tongobory, Madg. 107/H8
Tongren, China 83/J2
Tongsa (riv.), Bhu. 85/F2
Tongsa Dzong, Bhu. 85/F2
Tongshan, China 79/B2
Tongue (riv.), 44/C2
Tongue, Sc, UK 31/F7
Tongxu, China 72/C4
Tongyu, China 71/M3
Tongzi, China 79/A2
Tonino-Anivskiy (pen.), Rus. 76/C1
Tönisvorst, Ger. 50/D6
Tonk, India 89/J3
Tonkawa, Ok, US 129/H3
Tonkin (gulf), China,Viet. 67/K7
Tonkin, Gulf of (gulf), Asia 70/J7
Tonle Sap (lake), Camb. 83/H5
Tonnerre, Fr. 42/E3
Tönning, Ger. 38/B5
Töno, Japan 76/B4
Tonopah, Nv, US 128/D3
Tonoshō, Japan 74/D3
Tonosí, Pan. 152/A3
Tonota, Bots. 105/E5
Tons (riv.), India 84/C3
Tønsberg, Nor. 38/D2
Tønsberg, Ak, US 134/M4
Tonto Nat'l For., Az, US 137/S18
Tonto Nat'l Mon., Az, US 128/E4
Tonya, Turk. 62/F4
Toobeah, Austl. 114/C4
Tooele (co.), Ut, US 137/J13
Tooele, Ut, US 137/J12
Toowoomba, Austl. 114/C4
Topanga State Park, Ca, US 136/B2
Topanga, Ca, US 136/B2
Topanga Beach, Ca, US 136/E7
Tope de Coroa (mtn.), CpV. 93/J3
Topia, Mex. 142/D3

Topley, BC, Can.	126/B2	Torroella de Montgrí,	
Toplița, Rom.	49/G2	Sp.	45/G1
Topol'čany, Slvk.	41/K4	Torrone Alto (peak),	
Topolobampo, Mex.	142/C3	Swi.	57/F5
Topoloveni, Rom.	49/G3	Torrox, Sp.	44/D4
Topolovgrad, Bul.	47/K1	Torsa (riv.), Bhu.	85/G2
Topozero,		Torsås, Swe.	38/F3
Rus.	37/J2	Torsby, Swe.	38/E1
Toppenish, Wa, US	126/C4	Tortola (isl.), UK	141/J4
Toprakkale, Turk.	91/E1	Tortoli, It.	46/A3
Topton, Pa, US	138/C3	Tortona, It.	58/B3
Tor (bay), Eng, UK	32/C6	Tortosa, It.	58/D1
Torahime, Japan	77/K5	Tortosa (cape), Sp.	45/F2
Torata, Peru	156/D5	Tortosa, Sp.	45/F2
Torawitan (cape),		Tortuga (isl.),	
Indo.	81/G3	Haiti	141/H5
Torbalı, Turk.	90/A2	Tortuguero, PN, CR	145/F4
Torbat-e Ḩeydarīyeh,		Tortum, Turk.	63/G4
Iran	89/G1	Torüd, Iran	89/F1
Torbat-e Jām, Iran	87/D5	Torugart (pass), Kyr.	87/G4
Torbay, Nf, Can.	131/K2	Torul, Turk.	62/F4
Torbeck, Haiti	145/H2	Toruń, Pol.	41/K2
Torbert (mt.),		Torup, Swe.	38/E3
Ak, US	134/H3	Tory (isl.), Ire.	31/P9
Torcy, Fr.	30/K5	Torysa (riv.), Slvk.	41/L4
Tordera (riv.), Sp.	45/L6	Torzhok, Rus.	60/G4
Tordesillas, Sp.	44/C2	Tosa, Japan	74/C4
Töreboda, Swe.	38/F2	Tosagua, Ecu.	152/A5
Torelló, Sp.	45/G1	Tosashimizu, Japan	74/C4
Torgelow, Ger.	38/E5	Toscana (reg.), It.	58/D3
Torghay (riv.),		Toscana (prov.), It.	43/J5
Kaz.	87/D3	Toscanella, It.	59/E4
Torghay, Kaz.	64/G4	Toscolano-Maderno,	
Torhamnsudde (pt.),		It.	58/D1
Swe.	38/F3	Toshi (isl.), Japan	77/L6
Torhout, Belg.	52/C1	Toshibetsu (riv.),	
Tori-shima (isl.),		Japan	76/A2
Japan	116/K1	Toshkent (pol. reg.),	
Toride, Japan	77/M6	Uzb.	87/E4
Torigni-sur-Vire, Fr.	42/C2	Tosna (riv.), Rus.	61/T7
Torii-tōge (pass),		Tosno, Rus.	39/P2
Japan	75/E3	Tosontsengel,	
Toriñana (cape), Sp.	44/A1	Mong.	70/G2
Torino (prov.), It.	58/A2	Töss (riv.), Swi.	37/H3
Torino (Turin), It.	43/G4	Tosson (hill),	
Torkestān (mts.),		Eng, UK	36/E6
Afg.	89/H1	Tostado, Arg.	157/D2
Tormes (riv.), Sp.	44/C2	Tostedt, Ger.	36/D5
Torndirrup NP,		Tosu, Japan	74/B4
Austl.	112/C5	Tosya, Turk.	90/C1
Torne (riv.),		Totana, Sp.	44/E4
Eng, UK	35/H4	Totness, Sur.	153/G3
Torneälven (riv.),		Totowa, NJ, US	139/J8
Swe.	60/D2	Totten (inlet),	
Tornesch, Ger.	51/G1	Wa, US	135/A3
Tornik (peak),		Tottenham, Austl.	115/C2
Yugo.	48/D4	Tottington,	
Tornio, Fin.	37/H2	Eng, UK	35/F4
Tornionjoki (riv.),		Tottori, Japan	74/D3
Fin.	37/G2	Tottori (pref.),	
Toro, Sp.	44/C2	Japan	74/C3
Toro, Cerro del (peak),		Totutla, Mex.	143/N7
Arg.,Chil	157/C2	Touat (reg.), Alg.	99/E4
Toro Nat'l Rsv.,		Touba, C.d'Iv.	102/D4
Ugan.	104/A2	Toubkal (peak),	
Toro, PN, Ven.	152/D2	Mor.	98/D3
Törökbálint, Hun.	49/Q10	Toubkal, PN du,	
Törökszentmiklós,		Mor.	98/D3
Hun.	48/E2	Touchwood (hills),	
Toronaic (gulf),		Can.	127/G3
Gre.	47/H1	Toucy, Fr.	42/E3
Torondoy, Ven.	152/D2	Toudao (riv.), China	73/D1
Toronto, Can.	131/R8	Tougan, Burk.	102/E3
Toronto (cap.),		Touggourt, Alg.	99/G2
On, Can.	131/R8	Toughkenamon,	
Toronto (isl.),		Pa, US	138/C4
Can.	131/R8	Touil (riv.), Alg.	100/G5
Toropets, Rus.	39/P3	Toul, Fr.	53/E6
Tororo, Ugan.	104/B2	Toulnustouc (riv.),	
Torote (riv.), Sp.	45/N8	Can.	131/H1
Torp (int'l arpt.),		Toulon, Fr.	42/F5
Nor.	38/D2	Toulouse, Fr.	42/D5
Torpa, Swe.	38/E3	Toumodi, C.d'Iv.	102/D4
Torquay, Austl.	115/C3	Toungoo, Myan.	83/G4
Torquay, Eng, UK	32/C6	Touquin, Fr.	30/M5
Torquemada, Sp.	44/C1	Toura, Monts du (mts.),	
Torr (pt.), NI, UK	34/B1	C.d'Iv.	102/D4
Torrance, Ca, US	136/F8	Tourcoing, Fr.	52/C2
Torraz, Tête du		Tourfourine (well),	
(peak), Fr.	56/C6	Mali	98/D4
Torrazza Piemonte, It.	58/A2	Tourlaville, Fr.	42/C2
Torre de Moncorvo,		Tournai, Belg.	52/C2
Port.	44/B2	Tournan-en-Brie, Fr.	30/M5
Torre dè Passeri, It.	46/C1	Tournus, Fr.	56/A4
Torre del Campo,		Touros, Braz.	154/D2
Sp.	44/D4	Tours, Fr.	42/D3
Torre del Greco, It.	46/D2	Tous, Embalse de (res.),	
Torre del Lago Puccini,		Sp.	45/E3
It.	46/D2	Toussidé (peak),	
Torre-Pacheco, Sp.	45/E4	Chad	96/J3
Torrebelvicino, It.	59/E1	Touws (riv.),	
Torreblanca, Sp.	45/F2	CAfr.	97/K6
Torredonjimeno, Sp.	44/D4	Touws (riv.),	
Torreglia, It.	59/E2	SAfr.	106/C4
Torrejón de Ardoz,		Touwsrivier,	
Sp.	45/N9	SAfr.	106/M10
Torrejoncillo, Sp.	44/B3	Toužim, Czh.	55/G2
Torrelaguna, Sp.	44/D2	Töv (prov.), Mong.	70/J2
Torrelavega, Sp.	44/C1	Tovar, Ven.	152/D2
Torrelodones, Sp.	45/N9	Tove (riv.),	
Torremaggiore, It.	46/D2	Eng, UK	33/E2
Torremolinos, Sp.	44/C4	Towaco, NJ, US	139/H8
Torrens (lake),		Towada, Japan	75/G2
Austl.	109/C4	Towada (lake), Japan	76/B3
Torrens (riv.),		Towada-Hachimantai NP,	
Austl.	113/M8	Japan	76/B3
Torrens (isl.),		Tower City,	
Austl.	113/M8	Pa, US	138/B2
Torrente, Sp.	45/E3	Tower Hamlets (bor.),	
Torreón, Mex.	142/E4	Eng, UK	30/A1
Torreperogil, Sp.	44/D3	Tower of London,	
Tôrres, Braz.	155/B4	Eng, UK	30/C2
Torres (isl.),		Treinta de Agosto,	
Austl.,PNG	116/D6	Arg.	159/D4
Torres (isls.),		Towner, ND, US	126/H4
Van.	116/F6	Townend (mt.),	
Torres del Paine, PN,		Wa, US	135/A2
Chile	157/B7	Townsends (inlet),	
Torres del Paine, PN,		NJ, US	138/D4
Chile	159/B6	Townshend (cape),	
Torres Novas,		Austl.	110/B5
Port.	44/A3	Townsville, Austl.	114/B2
Torres Vedras,		Towson, Md, US	138/B5
Port.	44/A3	Towuti (lake), Indo.	81/G4
Torrevieja, Sp.	45/E4	Toya (lake), Japan	76/B2
Torridge (riv.),		Toyah, Tx, US	137/E3
Eng, UK	32/B5	Toyahvale, Tx, US	132/C4
Torrijos, Sp.	44/C3	Toyama, Japan	75/E2
Torrington,		Toyama (pref.),	
Wy, US	127/G5	Japan	75/E2
Torrita di Siena, It.	43/J5	Toyoake, Japan	77/M5
		Toyohashi, Japan	75/E3

Toyokawa, Japan	75/E3	Tremšín (peak),	
Toyonaka, Japan	77/H6	Czh.	55/G3
Toyono, Japan	77/H6	Trenche (riv.),	
Toyo'oka, Japan	74/D3	Can.	130/F1
Toyosato, Japan	77/E1	Trenčín, Slvk.	41/K4
Toyoshina, Japan	77/K5	Trenel, Arg.	158/D2
Toyota, Japan	75/E2	Trenque Lauquen,	
Toyoyama, Japan	77/M5	Arg.	158/D2
Toyotomi, Japan	77/B2	Trent (riv.),	
Tozeur, Tun.	96/G1	Eng, UK	35/F6
Tozi (mt.), Ak, US	134/H2	Trent and Mersey (canal),	
Tra Vinh, Viet.	78/D4	Eng, UK	35/F6
Traben-Trarbach,		Trentino-Alto Adige	
Ger.	53/G4	(pol. reg.), It.	43/J3
Trabuco Canyon,		Trento (prov.), It.	57/H5
Ca, US	136/C3	Trenton, On, Can.	130/E2
Trabzon, Turk.	62/F4	Trenton, Ga, US	133/G3
Trabzon (prov.),		Trenton, Fl, US	133/H4
Turk.	62/F4	Trenton, Tn, US	130/B5
Tracadie,		Trenton, Mo, US	129/J2
NB, Can.	131/H2	Trenton (cap.),	
Trachselwald, Swi.	56/D3	NJ, US	138/D3
Tracy, Qu, Can.	130/D3	Trepassey,	
Tracy, Mo, US	137/D5	Nf, Can.	131/K2
Tracyton, Wa, US	135/B2	Trepuzzi, It.	47/F2
Tradate, It.	58/B1	Tres Algarrobos,	
Trafalgar (cape),		Arg.	158/D2
Sp.	44/B4	Tres Arroyos,	
Tragwein, Aus.	55/H6	Arg.	158/E3
Traiguén, Chile	158/B3	Três Corações,	
Trail, BC, Can.	126/D3	Braz.	211/H6
Traini, Braz.	154/C1	Três Irmãos, Reprêsa (res.),	
Traisen (riv.), Aus.	41/H5	Braz.	155/C2
Traiskirchen, Aus.	49/N7	Três Lagoas, Braz.	155/B2
Traismauer, Aus.	41/H4	Tres Lomas, Arg.	158/D3
Trakai NP, Lith.	39/L4	Três Marias,	
Traki, Lith.	39/L4	Braz.	154/A5
Tralee (riv.), Ire.	31/P10	Tres Marías (isls.),	
Tralee, Ire.	31/P10	Mex.	142/D4
Tramandaí, Braz.	155/B4	Tres Marías,	
Tramelan, Swi.	56/D3	Mex.	143/Q10
Tramin (Termeno), It.	57/H5	Tres Marías, Reprêsa (res.),	
Tranås, Swe.	38/F2	Braz.	43/L3
Tranbjerg, Den.	38/D3	Trofaiach, Aus.	58/A3
Trancoso, Port.	44/B2	Trofarello, It.	
Tranebjerg, Den.	38/D4	Tshikapa,	
Tranemo, Swe.	38/E3	D.R. Congo	105/D2
Tranent, Sc, UK	36/D5	Troia, It.	46/D2
Tranet (peak), Fr.	53/D4	Tshuapa (riv.),	
Trang, Thai.	78/B5	D.R. Congo	93/E5
Trangan (isl.)		Tsiafajavona (peak),	
Indo.	81/H5	Madg.	107/H7
Trangie, Austl.	115/C2	Tulle, Fr.	42/D4
Trängsletsjön (lake),		Tsimlyansk (res.),	
Swe.	38/E1	Rus.	64/F5
Trani, It.	46/E2	Tsing Yi (isl.),	
Tranoroa, Madg.	107/H9	China	71/U10
Transantarctic (mts.),		Tsiribihina (riv.),	
Ant.	160/W	Madg.	107/G7
Transylvania (reg.),		Tsiroanomandidy,	
Rom.	48/F2	Madg.	107/H7
Transylvanian Alps (mts.),		Tsitsikamma Forest and	
Rom.	62/B3	Coastal NP, SAfr.	106/D4
Trapani, It.	46/C3	Tsivory, Madg.	107/H9
Trapper (peak),		Ts'khinvali, Geo.	63/G4
Mt, US	126/E4	Tsna (riv.), Rus.	60/G4
Trappes, Fr.	30/J5	Tsomo (riv.), SAfr.	106/D3
Trasacco, It.	46/C2	Tsomog, Mong.	71/J2
Trasimeno (lake), It.	43/K5	Tsu, Japan	75/E3
Träslövsläge, Swe.	38/D3	Tsu (isl.), Japan	74/B3
Traun (riv.), Aus.	49/H4	Tsubame, Japan	75/F2
Traun, Aus.	55/H6	Tsubata, Japan	75/E2
Traunreut, Ger.	55/F7	Tsuchiura, Japan	75/G2
Traunsee (lake),		Tsuchiyama, Japan	77/K6
Aus.	41/H4	Tsuen Wan, China	71/U10
Traunstein, Ger.	55/F7	Tsugaru (pen.),	
Traveller's (isl.),		Japan	76/B3
Austl.	109/D4	Tsuge, Japan	77/J6
Travemunde, Ger.	40/F2	Tsukigase, Japan	77/K6
Traverse (peak),		Tsukuba, Japan	77/E1
Ak, US	134/G2	Tsukude, Japan	77/M6
Traverse (lake), US	127/J4	Tsukui, Japan	77/C2
Traverse City,		Tsukumi, Japan	74/B4
Mi, US	130/C2	Tsumagoi, Japan	77/F1
Traversetolo, It.	57/E2	Tsumeb, Namb.	105/C4
Travis (lake),		Tsuna, Japan	77/G7
Tx, US	132/D4	Tsuru, Japan	75/F3
Travis AFB,		Tsuruga, Japan	74/E3
Ca, US	135/L10	Tsurugashima, Japan	77/E2
Travnik, Bosn.	48/C3	Tsurugi, Japan	74/E2
Trawsalt (peak),		Tsurugi-san (peak),	
Wal, UK	32/C2	Japan	74/D4
Trawsfynydd, Llyn (lake),		Tsurumi (isl.),	
Wal, UK	34/D6	Indo.	80/A3
Trbovlje, Slov.	43/L3	Tsushima, Japan	77/L5
Tré-la-Tête (peak), Fr.	56/C6	Tsushima (co.), Nor.	37/F1
Treachery (mt.),		Tsvelerheim, Geo.	63/G4
Austl.	113/G2	Tsuyama, Japan	74/D3
Trebaseleghe, It.	59/F1	Tua (cape), Indo.	80/C5
Trebbia (riv.), It.	43/H4	Tua (riv.), Port., Sp.	44/B2
Trébeurden, Fr.	42/B2	Tuam, Ire.	31/P10
Trebinje, Bosn.	47/F1	Tuamapu (chan.),	
Trebisacce, It.	46/E3	Chile	158/B4
Trebišov, Slvk.	41/L4	Tuamotu (arch.),	
Trebnje, Slov.	40/B3	FrPol.	117/L6
Treboń, Czh.	41/H4	Tuan (pt.), Indo.	80/A3
Tregaron, Wal, UK	32/C2	Tuan (riv.), China	72/B4

Trinidad and Tobago		Tryavna, Bul.	47/J1
(ctry.)	119/L8	Trysil, Nor.	38/E1
Trinity (isls.),		Trysilelva (riv.),	
Ak, US	134/H4	Nor.	38/D1
Trinity (range),		Tryssa, Pol.	41/J2
Nv, US	128/C2	Trzcianka, Pol.	41/H2
Trinity (mts.),		Trzebiatów, Pol.	38/F4
Ca, US	126/C5	Trzebnica, Pol.	41/J3
Trinity (bay), Can.	131/L2	Trzemeszno, Pol.	41/J2
Trinity, West Fork (riv.),		Tsabong, Bots.	106/C2
Tx, US	140/B1	Tsagaan Bogd (peak),	
Trino, It.	58/B2	Mong.	70/G4
Triolet, Mrts.	107/T15	Tsakane, SAfr.	106/O13
Tripolis, Gre.	47/H4	Tsalgar, Mong.	70/F2
Tripoli (reg.),		Tsant, Mong.	70/J2
Libya	96/H1	Tūkh, Egypt	91/B4
Trippstadt, Ger.	53/G5	Tsao, Bots.	105/D3
Tripunittura, India	82/C6	Tsaratanana,	
Tripura (cap.),		Madg.	107/H6
India	70/F7	Tsaratanana (mass.),	
Trisanna (riv.),		Madg.	107/H7
Aus.	57/G4	Tsast (bay),	
Trissino, It.	59/E1	Mong.	70/F2
Tristan da Cunha (isl.),		Tsatsana (peak),	
StH.	22/J7	Les.	106/E3
Triste (peak),		Tsavo East NP,	
Arg.	158/E3	Kenya	105/G1
Trisuli (riv.), Nepal	85/E2	Tsavo West NP,	
Trittau, Ger.	51/H1	Kenya	105/G1
Trivandrum, India	82/C6	Tschagguns, Aus.	57/F3
Trivero, It.	58/B1	Tschierv, Swi.	57/G4
Trnava, Slvk.	48/C1	Tschlin, Swi.	57/G4
Trobriand (isls.),		Tselfat (reg.), Mor.	100/B2
PNG	116/E5	Tselinograd (Astana),	
Trochtelfingen,		Kaz.	64/H4
Ger.	57/F1	Tsévié, Togo	103/F5
Troesnes (riv.), Fr.	52/A5	Tshane, Bots.	105/D5
Trofaiach, Aus.	43/L3	Tshela,	
Trofarello, It.	58/A3	D.R. Congo	105/B2
Tulla (lake), Sc, UK	36/B3	Tulla, Ire.	129/K2
Tullahoma, Tn, US	133/G3	Turkey (ctry.)	67/B5
Tullamarine (int'l arpt.),		Türkeli, Turk.	57/G1
Austl.	115/F5	Türkistan, Kaz.	87/E4
Tullamore, Austl.	115/C2	Turkmenistan (ctry.)	67/E6
Tullamore, Ire.	31/Q10	Türkoğlu, Turk.	90/D2
Tulle, Fr.	42/D4	Turks (isls.), Haiti	141/G3
Tullibody, Sc, UK	36/C4	Turks and Caicos	
Tsimlyansk (res.),		(isls.), UK	119/K7
Rus.	64/F5	Turks Island Passage	
Tullow, Ire.	31/Q10	(chan.), UK	145/J1
Tully, Austl.	114/B2	Turku (int'l arpt.),	
Tullytown, Pa, US	138/D3	Fin.	37/D3
Tulsa, Ok, US	129/J3	Turku Ja Pori (prov.),	
Tulsipur, Nepal	84/D1	Fin.	37/D3
Tulsipur, India	143/Q9	Turkwel (riv.),	
Tultitlán, Mex.	143/Q9	Kenya	104/B2
Tuluá, Col.	152/B3	Turlock, Ca, US	128/B3
Tulukak, Sc, UK	134/F3	Turmalina, Braz.	154/B5
Tulum, Mex.	144/E1	Turneffe (isls.), Belz.	144/D1
Tulum, PN, Mex.	144/E1	Turner (mt.),	
Tulun, Rus.	65/L4	Austl.	112/C2
Tumacacori Nat'l Hist. Park,		Turnersville,	
Az, US	128/E5	NJ, US	138/C4
Tumaco, Col.	152/B4	Turnhouse (int'l arpt.),	
Tsu, Japan	75/E3	Sc, UK	36/C4
Tumatumari, Guy.	153/G3	Turnhout, Belg.	50/B6
Tumauini, Phil.	79/D4	Turnor (lake),	
Tumba, Japan	75/F2	Sk, Can.	126/F1
Tumba (lake),		Turnu Măgurele,	
D.R. Congo	96/J8	Rom.	49/G4
Tumbarumba, Austl.	115/D2	Turnu-Severin, Rom.	64/E3
Tumbes (dept.),		Turón (pt.),	
Peru	156/A1	Cuba	145/G2
Tumbes, Peru	156/A1	Turriaco, It.	59/G1
Tumen (riv.),		Turriff, Sc, UK	36/D1
China	73/D2	Turt, Mong.	70/H1
Tumen, China	73/D1	Turtle (isl.),	
Tumen (depr.),		SLeo.	83/H6
China	70/E3	Turtleford,	
Tumeremo, Ven.	152/F3	Sk, Can.	126/F2
Tumkūr, India	82/C5	Turugart (pass),	
Tummel (riv.),		China	87/G4
Sc, UK	36/C3	Turukhansk, Rus.	64/J3
Tumpat, Malay.	83/H6	Tuscaloosa, Al, US	133/G3
Tumpu (peak), Indo.	81/F4	Tuscania, It.	46/B1
Tumu, Gha.	102/E3	Tuscano (arch.), It.	
Tumuc-Humac (mts.),		Tuscarora, Nv, US	128/C2
Braz.	151/G3	Tuscarora Ind. Res.,	
Tumut, Austl.	115/D2	Pa, US	138/A3
Tunadal, Swe.	60/C3	Tuskegee, Al, US	133/G3
Tunceli (prov.),		Tustin, Ca, US	136/D8
Turk.	90/D2	Tuszyn, Pol.	
Tunceli, Turk.	90/D2	Tutak, Turk.	63/G5
Tunchang, China	83/K4	Tutayev, Rus.	60/H4
Tundla, India	84/B2	Tuticorin, India	82/C6
Tundzha (riv.), Bul.	47/K1	Tuttlingen, Ger.	37/E2
Tungabhadra (res.),		Tuttungurahua (prov.),	
India	82/C4	Ecu.	152/B5
Tungabhadra (riv.),		Tutupaca (vol.),	
India	82/C4	Peru	156/D5

Tuenno, It.	57/H5	Tuparro (riv.), Col.	152/E2
Tufanbeyli, Turk.	90/D2	Tupelo, Ms, US	133/F3
Tug Fork (riv.), US	133/H2	Tupi Paulista,	
Tugela (riv.),		Braz.	155/B2
SAfr.	107/E3	Tupiza, Bol.	150/E8
Tugela, SAfr.	107/E3	Tupper Lake,	
Tugela (falls),		NY, US	130/F2
SAfr.	107/E3	Tupungato, Arg.	158/C2
Tughlakabad (ruin),		Tupungato (peak),	
India	86/D5	Arg.	158/P8
Tuguegarao, Phil.	79/D4	Tura, India	85/H3
Tuguegarao (isls.),		Tura (riv.), Rus.	64/G4
Mong.	70/D4	Tura, Rus.	65/L3
Indo.	81/F5	Turaiçu (riv.),	
Tūkh, Egypt	91/B4	Braz.	154/A1
Tuktoyaktuk,		Turan Lowland (plain),	
NW, Can.	134/M2	Uzb.	64/G5
Tukums, Lat.	39/K3	Tweed Heads,	
Tukung,		Austl.	114/D5
Indo.	80/D4	Twello, Neth.	50/D4
Tukuyu, Tanz.	104/B5	Twente, Neth.	
Tukwila, Wa, US	135/C3	Twente (int'l arpt.),	
Tula (riv.), Kenya	104/C3	Neth.	50/D4
Tula, Mex.	143/F4	Twentynine Palms,	
Tula, Rus.	62/F1	Ca, US	
Tula (riv.), Mex.	143/K6	Twin Buttes (res.),	
Tula, Rus.	143/K6	Tx, US	129/G5
Tula Oblast, Rus.	62/F1	Turčiansky Svätý Martin,	
Tula, PN, Mex.	143/K6	Slvk.	62/A2
Tulancingo, Mex.	143/L6	Twin Hills, Ak, US	134/F4
Tulare, Ca, US	128/C3	Tureia (isl.),	
Tularosa (valley),		FrPol.	117/M7
NM, US	129/F4	Turek, Pol.	41/K2
Tularosa, NM, US	129/F4	Turgeon (riv.),	
Tulcán, Ecu.	152/B4	Can.	130/E1
Tulcea, Rom.	49/J3	Turhal, Turk.	62/E2
Tulcea (prov.), Rom.	49/J3	Türgovishte, Bul.	49/H4
Tule (canal),		Turia (riv.), Sp.	45/E3
Ca, US	135/L9	Turiaçu, Braz.	151/A4
Tulebras (peak),		Turkana (Rudolf) (lake),	
Sp.	45/E5	Kenya	93/G4
Tulia, Tx, US	129/G4	Türkeli, Turk.	62/E4
Tulik (vol.),		Türkeve, Hun.	48/E2
Ak, US	134/E5		
Tulin (isls.), PNG	116/E5		

Tuparro (riv.), Col.	152/E2	Tuzla, Turk.	91/D1
Tupelo, Ms, US	133/F3	Tuzluca, Turk.	63/G4
Tupi Paulista,		Tuzluca, Turk.	90/B2
Braz.	155/B2	Tvååker, Swe.	38/E3
Tupiza, Bol.	150/E8	Tvedestrand, Nor.	38/C2
Tupper Lake,		Tver', Rus.	60/G4
NY, US	130/F2	Tver' Oblast, Rus.	39/P3
Tupungato, Arg.	158/C2	Tvertsa (riv.),	
Tupungato (peak),		Rus.	60/G4
Arg.	158/P8	Tvůrditsa, Bul.	47/J1
Tura, India	85/H3	Twardogóra, Pol.	41/J3
Tura (riv.), Rus.	64/G4	Tweed (riv.),	
Tura, Rus.	65/L3	Sc, UK	36/C5
Turaiçu (riv.),		Tweed Heads,	
Braz.	154/A1	Austl.	114/D5
Turan Lowland (plain),		Twello, Neth.	50/D4
Uzb.	64/G5	Twente, Neth.	50/D4
Turango, NZ	117/T10	Twente (int'l arpt.),	
Turbaco, Col.	152/C2	Neth.	50/D4
Turbe, Pak.	89/H3	Twin Buttes (res.),	
Turbenthal, Swi.	57/E3	Tx, US	129/G5
Turbo, Col.	152/B2	Twin Hills, Ak, US	134/F4
Turbotville,		Twin Lakes,	
Neth.	50/D4	Wi, US	135/P14
Twin Buttes (res.),		Twin Rivers,	
Tx, US	129/G5	NJ, US	138/D3
Turčiansky Svätý Martin,		Twiste (riv.), Ger.	51/G6
Slvk.	62/A2	Twistringen, Ger.	
Twin Hills, Ak, US	134/F4	Twizel, NZ	117/S11
Two Hills, Ab, Can.	126/F2	Two Rivers,	
Two Rivers,		Wi, US	127/M4
Wi, US	127/M4	Twofold (bay),	
Twofold (bay),		Austl.	115/D3
Austl.	115/D3	Twyford, Eng, UK	33/F4
Twyford, Eng, UK	33/F4	Twymyn (riv.),	
Twymyn (riv.),		Wal, UK	32/C1
Wal, UK	32/C1	Tyatya (vol.), Rus.	76/F1
Tyatya (vol.), Rus.	76/F1	Tychy, Pol.	41/K3
Tychy, Pol.	41/K3	Tyendinaga,	
Tyendinaga,		On, Can.	130/E2
On, Can.	130/E2	Tyger (riv.),	
Tyger (riv.),		SC, US	133/H3
SC, US	133/H3	Tyldesley, Eng, UK	35/F4
Tyldesley, Eng, UK	35/F4	Tylersville, Pa, US	138/A2
Tylersville, Pa, US	138/A2	Tyne (riv.), Sc, UK	41/H4
Tyne (riv.), Sc, UK	36/D5	Tyne and Wear (co.),	
Tyne and Wear (co.),		Eng, UK	35/G2
Eng, UK	35/G2	Tynemouth, Eng, UK	35/G1
Tynemouth, Eng, UK	35/G1	Tynset, Nor.	37/D3
Tynset, Nor.	37/D3	Tyonek, Ak, US	134/H3
Tyonek, Ak, US	134/H3	Tyrifjorden (lake),	
Tyrifjorden (lake),		Nor.	38/C1
Nor.	38/C1	Tyringe, Swe.	38/E3
Tyringe, Swe.	38/E3	Tyrnyauz, Rus.	63/G4
Tyrnyauz, Rus.	63/G4	Tyrrell (lake),	
Tyrrell (lake),		Austl.	115/B2
Austl.	115/B2	Tyrrhenian (sea), It.	27/F4
Tyrrhenian (sea), It.	27/F4	Tysnes (isl.),	
Tysnes (isl.),		Nor.	38/A1
Nor.	38/A1	Tysnesøy (isl.),	
Tysnesøy (isl.),		Nor.	38/A2
Nor.	38/A2	Tysons Corner,	
Tysons Corner,		Va, US	138/A6
Va, US	138/A6	Tysse, Nor.	38/A1
Tysse, Nor.	38/A1	Tystberga, Swe.	38/G2
Tystberga, Swe.	38/G2	Tyub-Karagan (pt.),	
Tyub-Karagan (pt.),		Kaz.	63/J3
Kaz.	63/J3	Tyuleni (isls.), Rus.	87/B3
Tyuleni (isls.), Rus.	87/B3	Tyuleniy (isls.), Rus.	63/H3
Tyuleniy (isls.), Rus.	63/H3	Tyumen (int'l arpt.),	
Tyumen (int'l arpt.),		Rus.	61/Q4
Rus.	61/Q4	Tyumen', Rus.	61/Q4
Tyumen', Rus.	61/Q4	Tyumen' Oblast,	
Tyumen' Oblast,		Rus.	87/E1
Rus.	87/E1	Tywi (riv.),	
Tywi (riv.),		Wal, UK	32/B3
Wal, UK	32/B3	Tzaneen, SAfr.	105/F5
Tzaneen, SAfr.	105/F5	Tzucacab, Mex.	144/D1
Tzucacab, Mex.	144/D1		

Ubundu, D.R. Congo 97/L8
Ucayali (dept.), Peru 156/C3
Ucayali (riv.), Peru 147/B3
Uccle, Belg. 53/D2
Ucha (riv.), Rus. 61/W9
Uchaly, Rus. 61/N5
Uchāna, India 86/D5
Uchinskoye (res.), Rus. 61/W9
Uchiza, Peru 156/B3
Uchte, Ger. 51/F3
Uchte (riv.), Ger. 40/F2
Uchumarca, Peru 156/B2
Uchumayo, Peru 156/D5
Uchur (riv.), Rus. 65/P4
Ücker (riv.), Ger. 38/E5
Uckermark (reg.), Ger. 41/G2
Uckfield, Eng, UK 33/G5
Ucluelet, BC, Can. 126/B3
Uda (riv.), Rus. 65/M4
Udagamandalam, India 82/C5
Udaipur, India 89/K4
Udaipura, India 84/B4
Uddevalla, Swe. 38/D2
Uddingston, Sc, UK 36/B5
Uddjaure (lake), Swe. 37/F2
Üdem, Ger. 50/D5
Uden, Neth. 50/C5
Udenhout, Neth. 50/C5
Udgīr, India 82/C4
Udhampur, India 86/C3
Udine (prov.), It. 59/G1
Udine, It. 43/K3
Udipi, India 82/B5
Udmurtia Aut. Rep., Rus. 64/G6
Udmurtiya Aut. Rep., Rus. 87/B1
Udon Thani, Thai. 78/C2
Ueckermünde, Ger. 38/F5
Ueda, Japan 75/F2
Uele (riv.), D.R. Congo 93/E4
Uelsen, Ger. 50/D3
Uelzen, Ger. 51/H3
Ueno, Japan 77/B1
Ueno, Japan 77/K6
Uenohara, Japan 75/F3
Uetendorf, Swi. 56/D4
Uetersen, Ger. 51/G1
Uetze, Ger. 51/H4
Ufa (riv.), Rus. 87/D1
Ufa, Rus. 61/M5
Uffenheim, Ger. 54/D3
Uffing, Ger. 57/H2
Ugalla (riv.), Tanz. 104/A4
Ugalla River Game Rsv., Tanz. 104/A4
Uganda (ctry.) 93/F4
Ugento, It. 47/F3
Ugie (riv.), Sc, UK 36/E1
Ugine, Fr. 56/C6
Uglich, Rus. 60/H4
Ugod, Hun. 48/C2
Ugra (riv.), Rus. 60/G5
Ugŭrchin, Bul. 47/J1
Uherské Hradiště, Czh. 41/J4
Uhingen, Ger. 54/C5
Úhlava (riv.), Czh. 41/G4
Úhlavka (riv.), Czh. 55/F3
Uibaí, Braz. 154/B3
Uíge, Ang. 105/C2
Ŭihŭng, SKor. 73/E4
Ŭijŏngbu, SKor. 73/G6
Ŭiju, NKor. 73/C2
Uil (riv.), Kaz. 87/B3
Uilkraal (riv.), SAfr. 106/L11
Uilpata (peak), Rus. 63/G4
Uinta (mts.), Ut, US 128/E2
Uintah, Ut, US 137/K11
Uiraúna, Braz. 154/C2
Ŭiryŏng, SKor. 73/E5
Ŭisŏng, SKor. 74/A2
Uitenhage, SAfr. 106/D4
Uitgeest, Neth. 50/B3
Uithoorn, Neth. 50/B4
Uithuizen, Neth. 50/D2
Ujae (isl.), Mrsh. 116/F4
Ujelang (isl.), Mrsh. 116/F4
Újfehértó, Hun. 41/L5
Ujhāni, India 84/B1
Uji (riv.), Japan 74/D3
Uji, Japan 77/J6
Ujitawara, Japan 77/J6
Ujjain, India 89/L4
Ujung Pandang, Indo. 81/E5
Ukara (isl.), Tanz. 104/B3
Ukerewe (isl.), Tanz. 104/B3
Ukhta, Rus. 61/M3
Ukiah, Ca, US 128/B3
Uklāna, India 86/C5
Ukmergė, Lith. 39/L4
Ukraine (ctry.) 27/G4
Ulaanbaatar (cap.), Mong. 70/J2
Ulaangom, Mong. 70/F2
Ulaanjirem, Mong. 70/J2
Ulanhot, China 71/M2
Ulchin, SKor. 74/A2
Ulcumayo, Peru 156/C3
Ulefoss, Nor. 38/C2
Ulemiste (int'l arpt.), Est. 39/L2
Ulhāsnagar, India 89/K5
Uliastay, Mong. 70/G2
Ulindi (riv.), D.R. Congo 97/L8
Ulithi (isl.), Micr. 116/C3
Uljma, Yugo. 48/E3
Ulla (riv.), Sp. 44/A1
Ulla Ulla, Bol. 156/D4
Ulla Ulla, Reserva Nacional, Bol. 156/D4
Ulladulla, Austl. 115/D2
Ullapool, Sc, UK 31/R8
Ullared, Swe. 38/E3
Ulldecona, Sp. 45/F2
Ullensvang, Nor. 38/B1
Üllő, Hun. 49/R10
Ullsfjorden (estu.), Nor. 37/F1
Ullswater (lake), Eng, UK 35/F2
Ulm, Ger. 54/C6
Ulmarra, Austl. 115/E1
Ulmen, Ger. 53/F3
Ulricehamn, Swe. 38/E3
Ulrichen, Swi. 57/E5
Ulrichsberg, Aus. 55/G5
Ulrichstein, Ger. 54/C1
Ulrum, Neth. 50/D2
Ulsan, SKor. 74/A3
Ulstein, Nor. 37/C3
Ulster (reg.), Ire. 34/A3
Ulster (riv.), Ger. 54/C1
Ulster American Folk Park, NI, UK 34/A2
Ulúa (riv.), Hon. 140/D4
Ulua (riv.), Hon. 144/E3
Uluçınar, Turk. 91/D1
Uludağ (peak), Turk. 62/D4
Uludoruk (peak), Turk. 88/D1
Uluguru (mts.), Tanz. 104/C4
Ulukışla, Turk. 90/C2
Ulundi, SAfr. 107/E3
Uluru NP, Austl. 113/F3
Ulverston, Eng, UK 35/E3
Ulverstone, Austl. 115/C4
Ulvik, Nor. 38/B1
Ulvila, Fin. 39/J1
Ul'yanovka, Rus. 39/P2
Ul'yanovsk, Rus. 61/L5
Ul'yanovsk Oblast, Rus. 63/H1
Ulytaū (mts.),Kaz. 87/E3
Ulytau (peak), Kaz. 87/E3
Umag, Cro. 48/A3
Uman', Ukr. 62/D2
Umán, Mex. 144/D1
Umarizal, Braz. 154/C2
Umarkot, India 82/D4
Umāsi La (pass), India 86/D3
Umbertide, It. 43/K5
Umbogintwini, SAfr. 107/E3
Umboi (isl.), PNG 116/D5
Umbrail (peak), Swi. 57/G4
Umbrailpass (pass), Swi. 57/G4
Umbria (prov.), It. 43/K5
Ume (riv.), Swe. 64/B3
Umeå, Swe. 37/G3
Umeälven (riv.), Swe. 37/F2
Umfolozi (riv.), SAfr. 107/E3
Umgeni (riv.), SAfr. 107/E3
Umhausen, Aus. 57/G3
Umiat, Ak, US 134/H2
Umkirch, Ger. 56/D1
Umkomaas, SAfr. 107/E3
Umm Durmān, Sudan 88/B5
Umm el Fahm, Isr. 91/G6
Umm Hibal (well), Egypt 101/C4
Ummendorf, Ger. 57/F1
Umnak (isl.), Ak, US 65/V4
Umnak Pass (chan.) 134/E5
Umpqua (riv.), Or, US 124/B3
Ümraniye, Turk. 62/D5
Ŭmsŏng, SKor. 73/D4
Umtata, SAfr. 106/E3
Umuahia, Nga. 103/G5
Umuarama, Braz. 157/F1
Umurbey, Turk. 47/K2
Umzimvubu (riv.), SAfr. 106/E3
Umzinto, SAfr. 107/E3
Una, Braz. 154/C4
Una, India 86/D4
Una (mt.), NZ 117/S11
Una (riv.), Bosn.,Cro 43/L4
Unaí, Braz. 154/A5
Unalakleet, Ak, US 134/F3
Unalaska, Ak, US 134/E5
Unalaska (isl.), Ak, US 65/V4
Uncastillo, Sp. 45/E1
Unchahra, India 84/C3
Uncompahgre (plat.), Co, US 128/E3
Unden (lake), Swe. 38/F2
Undenheim, Ger. 54/B3
Underberg, SAfr. 106/E3
Underbool, Austl. 115/B2
Underwood, ND, US 127/H4
Unecha, Rus. 62/E1
Unga (isl.), Ak, US 134/F4
Ungama (bay), Kenya 105/H1
Ungarie, Austl. 115/C2
Ungava (pen.), Can. 119/K3
Ungava (bay), Can. 119/L4
Ungheni, Mol. 49/H2
Unhošt, Czh. 55/H2
União, Braz. 154/B2
União da Vitória, Braz. 155/B3
União dos Palmares, Braz. 154/C3
Unimak (isl.), Ak, US 65/V4
Unimak Pass (str.), Ak, US 134/E5
Unini (riv.), Braz. 150/F4
Union, Or, US 126/D4
Union, Mo, US 129/K3
Union, SC, US 133/H3
Union (lake), NJ, US 138/C5
Unión, Arg. 158/D2
Union, NJ, US 139/H9
Union (canal), Sc, UK 36/C5
Union Beach, NJ, US 139/J10
Union Bridge, Md, US 138/A4
Union City, Tn, US 130/B4
Union City, Ca, US 135/K11
Union City, NJ, US 139/J8
Unión de Reyes, Cuba 145/F1
Unión de Tula, Mex. 142/D5
Unión Hidalgo, Mex. 144/C2
Union Mills, Md, US 138/A4
Union Springs, Al, US 133/G3
Uniondale, SAfr. 106/C4
Uniondale, NY, US 139/L9
Uniontown, Pa, US 130/E4
Uniontown, Md, US 138/A4
Unionville, Mo, US 127/K5
United Arab Emirates (ctry.) 67/C7
United Kingdom (ctry.) 27/D3
United Nations, NY, US 139/K9
United Nations Mem. Cemetery, SKor. 74/A3
United States (range), NW, Can. 123/T6
United States (ctry.) 119/G5
United States Coast Guard Receiving Center, NJ, US 138/D6
United States Department of Energy, Md, US 138/A5
United States Naval Academy, Md, US 138/B6
United States Naval Reservation Mil. Res., PR 141/M8
Unity, Sk, Can. 126/F2
University City, Mo, US 137/G8
University Place, Wa, US 135/B3
Unjha, India 89/K4
Unkel, Ger. 53/G2
Unna, Ger. 51/E5
Unnāo, India 84/C2
Ŭnsan-ŭp, NKor. 73/D3
Unst (isl.), Sc, UK 31/W13
Unter Pleichfeld, Ger. 54/D3
Unterägeri, Swi. 57/E3
Unterargen (riv.), Ger. 57/F2
Untergriesbach, Ger. 55/G5
Unterhaching, Ger. 55/E6
Unteriberg, Swi. 57/E3
Unterkulm, Swi. 56/E3
Unterlüss, Ger. 51/H3
Unterschleissheim, Ger. 55/E6
Untersee (lake), Swi. 57/E2
Unterseen, Swi. 56/D4
Untersiggenthal, Swi. 57/E3
Unterthingau, Ger. 57/G2
Untervaz, Swi. 57/F4
Unterweissenbach, Aus. 55/H6
Ünye, Turk. 62/F4
Unzen-Amakusa NP, Japan 74/A4
Unzen-Dake (peak), Japan 74/B4
Unzha (riv.), Rus. 64/E4
Uozu, Japan 75/E2
Upala, CR 145/E4
Upanema, Braz. 154/C2
Upata, Ven. 153/F2
Upemba, Lac (lake), D.R. Congo 105/E2
Upemba, PN de l', D.R. Congo 105/E2
Uphall, Sc, UK 36/C5
Upington, SAfr. 106/C3
Upland, Pa, US 138/C4
Upleta, India 89/K4
Upolu (pt.), Hi, US 124/U10
Upolu (isl.), Sam. 117/H6
Upper (lake), Ca, US 128/B2
Upper (bay), NY, US 138/D2
Upper (pen.), Mi, US 125/J2
Upper Arrow (lake), Can. 126/D3
Upper Darby, Pa, US 138/C4
Upper Demerara-Berbice (pol. reg.), Guy. 153/G3
Upper East (pol. reg.), Gha. 103/E4
Upper Engadine (valley), Swi. 57/F5
Upper Falls, Md, US 138/B5
Upper Ganges (canal), India 84/A1
Upper Hutt, NZ 117/T11
Upper Iowa (riv.), Ia, US 129/J2
Upper Klamath (lake), Or, US 126/C5
Upper Lough Erne (lake), NI, UK 31/Q9
Upper Peoria (lake), Il, US 127/L5
Upper Red (lake), Mn, US 127/K3
Upper Rouge (riv.), Mi, US 135/F7
Upper Saddle River, NJ, US 139/J7
Upper Takutu-Upper Essequibo (pol. reg.), Guy. 153/G4
Upper Thames (valley), Eng, UK 33/E3
Upper Trajan's Wall, Mol. 62/D3
Upper West (pol. reg.), Gha. 103/E4
Upperlands, NI, UK 34/B2
Upplands-Väsby, Swe. 38/G2
Uppsala, Swe. 38/G2
Uppsala (co.), Swe. 37/F3
Upright (cape), Ak, US 134/D3
Upstart (cape), Austl. 114/B2
Upton, Wy, US 127/G4
Urabá (gulf), Col. 145/G4
Uracoa, Ven. 153/F2
Urad Qianqi, China 72/B2
Uraga (chan.), Japan 77/D3
Urahoro, Japan 76/C2
Uraim (riv.), Braz. 154/A1
Urakawa, Japan 76/C2
Ural (mts.), Rus. 27/L2
Uralla, Austl. 115/D1
Urana, Austl. 115/C2
Urandi, Braz. 154/B4
Uraricoera (riv.), Braz. 150/F3
Urasoe, Japan 75/J7
Urawa, Japan 75/F3
Uray, Rus. 64/G3
Urayasu, Japan 77/D2
Urbach, Ger. 54/C5
Urbana, Md, US 138/A5
Urbania, It. 59/F5
Urbano Santos, Braz. 154/B1
Urbenville, Austl. 114/D5
Urbino, It. 59/F5
Urcos, Peru 156/D4
Urda, Sp. 44/D3
Urdinarrain, Arg. 159/J10
Urdorf, Swi. 57/E3
Ure (riv.), Eng, UK 35/G3
Ures, Mex. 142/C2
Ureshino, Japan 77/K6
Urewera NP, NZ 117/T10
Urfa (prov.), Turk. 90/D2
Urfa, Turk. 90/D2
Urft (riv.), Ger. 51/G6
Urft (lake), Ger. 53/F2
Urganch, Uzb. 87/D4
Urgnano, It. 58/C1
Urho Kekkosen NP, Fin. 37/H1
Uri, India 86/C2
Uri-Rotstock (peak), Swi. 57/E4
Uriangato, Mex. 143/E4
Uribante (riv.), Ven. 152/D3
Uribia, Col. 152/C2
Urie (riv.), Sc, UK 36/D2
Uriménil, Fr. 56/C1
Urique (riv.), Mex. 142/D3
Urjala, Fin. 39/K1
Urk, Neth. 50/C3
Urla, Turk. 62/C5
Urlați, Rom. 49/H3
Urmar, India 86/C4
Urmia (lake), Iran 90/F2
Urmitz, Ger. 53/G3
Urmston, Eng, UK 35/F5
Urnäsch, Swi. 57/F3
Urnersee (lake), Swi. 57/E4
Uroševac, Yugo. 47/G1
Urr Water (riv.), Sc, UK 34/E1
Ursensollen, Ger. 55/E4
Ursulo Galván, Mex. 143/N7
Uruaçu, Braz. 151/J6
Uruapan, Mex. 142/E5
Urubamba (riv.), Peru 150/D6
Urubamba, Peru 156/C4
Urubu (riv.), Braz. 150/G4
Uruburetama, Braz. 154/C1
Uruçuca, Braz. 154/C4
Uruçuí, Braz. 154/A2
Uruçuí Preto (riv.), Braz. 154/A3
Uruçuí, Serra do (mts.), Braz. 151/K5
Urucuia (riv.), Braz. 151/J7
Uruguaiana, Braz. 157/E2
Uruguay (ctry.) 147/D6
Uruguay (riv.), SAm. 147/D5
Urumaco, Ven. 152/D2
Ürümqi, China 70/E3
Urunga, Austl. 115/E1
Uruoca, Braz. 154/B1
Urup (isl.), Rus. 67/Q5
Ururi, It. 46/D2
Urussanga, Braz. 155/B4
Uryupinsk, Rus. 63/G2
Urziceni, Rom. 49/H3
Us, Fr. 30/H4
Usa, Japan 74/B4
Usa (riv.), Rus. 64/G3
Uşak (prov.), Turk. 90/B2
Uşak, Turk. 62/D5
Usakos, Namb. 105/C5
Usborne (mt.), UK 159/F6
Uscio, It. 58/C4
Usedom (isl.), Ger. 38/F4
Useldange, Lux. 53/E4
Useless Loop, Austl. 112/B3
Ushibori, Japan 77/F2
Ushibuka, Japan 74/B4
Ushiku, Japan 77/E2
Ushtobe, Kaz. 87/G3
Ushuaia, Arg. 159/C7
Usibelli, Ak, US 134/J3
Usicayos, Peru 156/D4
Usilampatti, India 82/C6
Usingen, Ger. 54/B2
Üsküp, Turk. 49/H5
Uslar, Ger. 51/G5
Usman', Rus. 62/F1
Uspallata, Arg. 158/C2
Uspallata, Paso de (pass), Chile 158/N8
Usquil, Peru 156/B2
Ussel, Fr. 42/E4
Ussel (riv.), Ger. 54/D5
Usses (riv.), Fr. 56/C5
Ussuri (riv.), China,Rus. 65/P5
Ussuriysk, Rus. 71/P3
Ussy-sur-Marne, Fr. 30/M5
Ust'-Ilimsk, Rus. 65/L4
Ust'-Kamchatsk, Rus. 65/S4
Ust'-Kut, Rus. 65/L4
Úštěk, Czh. 55/H1
Uster, Swi. 57/E3
Ústí nad Labem, Czh. 43/L1
Ustica (isl.), It. 46/C3
Ustica, It. 46/C3
Ustka, Pol. 38/G4
Ustrzyki Dolne, Pol. 41/M4
Ust'ya (riv.), Rus. 61/K3
Ustyurt (plat.), Kaz. 67/D5
Usu, China 70/D3
Usuda, Japan 75/F2
Usuki, Japan 74/B4
Usulután, ESal. 144/D3
Usumacinta (riv.), Mex. 140/C4
Utah (lake), Ut, US 128/D2
Utah (co.), Ut, US 137/K13
Utah (state), US 124/D4
Utangan (riv.), India 84/A2
Utano, Japan 77/J7
Utashinai, Japan 76/C2
Utena, Lith. 39/L4
Uterský (riv.), Czh. 55/G3
Uthai Thani, Thai. 78/C3
Utica, NY, US 130/F3
Utica, Mi, US 135/F6
Utiel, Sp. 44/E3
Utik (lake), Can. 127/J2
Utila (isl.), Hon. 144/E2
Utinga, Braz. 154/B4
Utirik (isl.), Mrsh. 116/G3
Utiroa, Kiri. 116/G5
Utmānzai, Pak. 86/A2
Utopia Abor. Land, Austl. 113/G2
Utraulā, India 84/D2
Utrecht, SAfr. 107/E2
Utrecht, Neth. 50/C4
Utrecht (prov.), Neth. 50/C4
Utrera, Sp. 44/C4
Utsunomiya, Japan 75/F2
Uttar Pradesh (state), India 70/C6
Uttaradit, Thai. 78/C2
Uttenweiler, Ger. 57/F1
Uttoxeter, Eng, UK 35/G6
Utuado, PR 141/M8
Utupua (isl.), Sol. 116/F6
Uturoa, FrPol. 117/K6
Utzenstorf, Swi. 56/D3
Uusikaupunki, Fin. 39/J1
Uusimaa (prov.), Fin. 37/H3
Uva (riv.), Col. 150/E3
Uvalde, Tx, US 129/H5
Uvarovo, Rus. 63/G2
Uverito, Ven. 153/E2
Uvira, D.R. Congo 104/A3
Uvongo, SAfr. 107/E3
Uvs (prov.), Mong. 70/F2
Uwajima, Japan 74/C4
Uwimmerah (riv.), Indo. 81/K5
Uxin Qi, China 72/B3
Uxmal (ruin), Mex. 144/D1
Üydzin, Mong. 70/J3
Uyo, Nga. 103/G5
Üyönch, Mong. 70/F2
Uyuni, Bol. 150/E8
Uzbekistan (ctry.) 67/E5
Uzbekistan Nat'l. Park, Uzb. 87/E5
Uzein (int'l arpt.), Fr. 42/C5
Uzerche, Fr. 42/D4
Uzès, Fr. 42/F4
Uzhhorod, Ukr. 41/M4
Uzhok (pass), Ukr. 41/M4
Užice, Yugo. 48/D4
Uzlovaya, Rus. 62/F1
Uznach, Swi. 57/E3
Üzümlü, Turk. 62/F5
Uzunköprü, Turk. 47/K2
Uzwil, Swi. 57/F3

V

V.P. Rosales, PN, Chile 158/B4
Vaal (riv.), SAfr. 93/E7
Vaala, Fin. 37/H2
Vaalbos NP, SAfr. 106/D3
Vaaldam (res.), SAfr. 106/D2
Vaals, Neth. 53/F2
Vaalserberg (hill), Neth. 53/E2
Vaasa (prov.), Fin. 37/G3
Vaasa (int'l arpt.), Fin. 37/G3
Vaasa (Vasa), Fin. 37/G3
Vaassen, Neth. 50/C4
Vác, Hun. 48/D2
Vaca (mts.), Ca, US 135/K10
Vaca (mt.), Ca, US 135/K10
Vacaria, Braz. 155/B4
Vacaville, Ca, US 128/B3
Vachon (riv.), Qu, Can. 123/J2
Vada, It. 58/D6
Vado Ligure, It. 58/B4
Vadret (peak), Swi. 57/F4
Vadsø, Nor. 37/J1
Vadstena, Swe. 38/F2
Vaduz (cap.), Lcht. 57/F3
Vaernes (int'l arpt.), Nor. 37/D3
Vaga (riv.), Rus. 60/J3
Vågå, Nor. 37/D3
Vågan, Nor. 37/E1
Vaganski vrh (peak), Cro. 48/B3
Vagay (riv.), Rus. 61/R4
Vaggeryd, Swe. 38/F3
Vagney, Fr. 56/C1
Vagos, Port. 44/A2
Vågsøy, Nor. 37/C3
Váh (riv.), Slvk. 41/J4
Vahitahi (isl.), FrPol. 117/M6
Vaiano, It. 59/E5
Vaiano Cremasco, It. 58/C2
Vaich (lake), Sc, UK 36/B1
Vaihingen an der Enz, Ger. 54/B5
Vaijāpur, India 89/K5
Vail, Co, US 129/F3
Vailate, It. 58/C2
Vair (riv.), Fr. 56/B1
Vaisali (riv.), India 84/B2
Vaitupu (isl.), Tuv. 116/G5
Vaivre-et-Montoille, Fr. 56/C2
Vakfıkebir, Turk. 62/F4
Vakh (riv.), Rus. 64/J3
Vakhān (mts.), Afg. 89/K1
Vakhsh (riv.), Taj. 89/J1
Vál, Hun. 48/D2
Val-de-Marne (dept.), Fr. 52/B6
Val-d'or, Qu, Can. 130/E1
Val Lagarina (valley), It. 59/D1
Val Marie, Sk, Can. 126/G3
Val Venosta (valley), It. 57/G4
Val Verda, Ut, US 137/K12
Val Verde, Ca, US 136/B2
Valais (canton), Swi. 56/D5
Valbo, Swe. 38/G1
Valburg, Neth. 50/C5
Valcheta, Arg. 158/D4
Valdagno, It. 59/E1
Valdahon, Fr. 56/C3
Valdai (hills), Rus. 60/G4
Valdarno (valley), It. 59/E5
Valdecañas, Embalse de (res.), Sp. 44/C3
Valdemarsvik, Swe. 38/G2
Valdemorillo, Sp. 45/M8
Valdense, Uru. 159/K11
Valdepeñas, Sp. 44/D3
Valderas, Sp. 44/C1
Valderrobres, Sp. 45/F2
Valdés, Península de (pen.), Arg. 147/C7
Valdeverdeja, Sp. 44/C3
Valdez, Ak, US 134/J3
Valdez, Ecu. 152/B4
Valdivia, Col. 152/C3
Valdivia, Chile 158/B3
Valdobbiadene, It. 59/F1
Valdoie, Fr. 56/C2
Valdosta, Ga, US 133/H4
Valdoviño, Sp. 44/A1
Vale, Or, US 126/D5
Valeggio sul Mincio, It. 59/D2
Valemount, BC, Can. 126/D2
Valença, Braz. 154/C4
Valença, Braz. 211/K7
Valença, Port. 44/A1
Valença do Piauí, Braz. 154/B2
Valence, Fr. 42/D4
Valence, Fr. 42/F4
Valence-sur-Baïse, Fr. 42/D5
Valencia, Ven. 150/E1
Valencia (int'l arpt.), Sp. 45/E3
Valencia, Sp. 45/E3
Valencia (aut. comm.), Sp. 44/E2
Valencia, Ecu. 152/B5
Valencia (isl.), Ire. 30/P11
Valencia de Alcántara, Sp. 44/B3
Valencia de Don Juan, Sp. 44/C1
Valencia, Golfo de (gulf), Sp. 45/F3
Valenciennes, Fr. 52/C3
Valendas, Swi. 57/F4
Vălenii de Munte, Rom. 49/H3
Valente, Braz. 154/C3
Valentigney, Fr. 56/C3
Valentim (range), Braz. 154/B2
Valentine, Tx, US 132/B4
Valentines, Uru. 159/G2
Valenton, Fr. 30/K5
Valenza, It. 58/B2
Våler, Nor. 38/D1
Våler, Nor. 38/D2
Valera, Ven. 152/D2
Valff, Fr. 56/D1
Valga, Est. 39/M3
Valhalla, NY, US 139/K7
Valinco, Golfe de (gulf), Fr. 46/A2
Valinhos, Braz. 211/F7
Valjevo, Yugo. 48/D3
Valkeakoski, Fin. 39/K1
Valkeala, Fin. 39/M1
Valkenburg, Neth. 53/E2
Valkenswaard, Neth. 50/C6
Vall de Uxó, Sp. 45/E3
Valladolid, Sp. 44/C2
Valladolid (int'l arpt.), Sp. 44/C2
Valladolid, Mex. 144/D1
Vallangoujard, Fr. 30/J4
Valle, Ecu. 152/B5
Valle, Nor. 38/B2
Valle d'Aosta (pol. reg.), It. 43/G4
Valle de Bravo, Mex. 143/E5
Valle de Cauca (dept.), Col. 152/B4
Valle de Guanape, Ven. 153/E2
Valle de La Pascua, Ven. 150/E2
Valle de Santiago, Mex. 143/E4
Valle de Zaragoza, Mex. 132/B5
Valle Hermoso, Mex. 143/F3
Valle Lomellina, It. 58/B2
Valle Mosso, It. 58/B1
Vallecitos de Zaragoza, Mex. 143/E5
Vallecrosia, It. 43/G5
Valledupar, Col. 152/C2
Vallée de l'Azaouak (riv.), Mali 103/G2
Vallée du Ferlo (riv.), Sen. 102/B3
Vallée du Mboune (riv.), Sen. 102/B3
Vallée du Saloum (riv.), Sen. 102/B3
Vallée du Serpent (riv.), Mali 102/C3
Vallegrande, Bol. 150/F7
Vallehermoso, Sp. 98/A3
Vallejo, Ca, US 128/B3
Vallenar, Chile 157/B2
Vallendar, Ger. 53/G3
Valleroy, Fr. 53/E5
Valletta (cap.), Malta 46/M7
Valley Brook, Ok, US 137/N15
Valley Center, Ca, US 136/C4
Valley City, ND, US 127/J4
Valley Cottage, NY, US 139/K7
Valley East, On, Can. 130/D2
Valley Forge Nat'l Hist. Park, Pa, US 138/C3
Valley of Desolation, SAfr. 106/D4
Valley of the Kings, Egypt 101/C3
Valley Park, Mo, US 137/G8
Valley Spring, Tx, US 129/H5
Valley Stream, NY, US 139/L9
Vallière (riv.), Fr. 56/B4
Vallorbe, Swi. 56/C4
Valls, Sp. 45/F2
Valluga (peak), Aus. 57/G3
Valmayor (res.), Sp. 45/M8
Valme (riv.), Ger. 51/F6
Valmeyer, Il, US 137/G9
Valmiera, Lat. 39/L3
Valmondois, Fr. 30/J4
Valognes, Fr. 42/C2
Valois (reg.), Fr. 52/B5
Valona, Bay of (bay), Alb. 47/F2
Valpaços, Port. 44/B2
Vālpārai, India 82/C5
Valparaiso, Fl, US 133/G4
Valparaiso, In, US 130/C3
Valparaíso, Mex. 142/E4
Valparaíso (pol. reg.), Chile 158/C2
Valparaíso, Chile 158/N8
Valpovo, Cro. 48/D3
Valréas, Fr. 42/F4
Vals (riv.), SAfr. 106/D2
Vals, Swi. 57/F4
Vals-les-Bains, Fr. 42/F4
Valsād, India 89/K4
Valsaquillo (res.), Mex. 143/L8
Valsbaai (bay), SAfr. 105/C7
Valserine (riv.), Fr. 56/B5
Valserrhein (riv.), Swi. 57/F4
Valsura (riv.), It. 57/G4
Valtellina (valley), It. 57/F5
Valtice, Czh. 43/M2
Valuyki, Rus. 62/F2
Valverde, Sp. 98/A4
Valverde del Camino, Sp. 44/B4
Valyermo, Ca, US 136/C2
Våmhus, Swe. 38/F1
Vammala, Fin. 39/K1
Vámos, Gre. 47/J5
Vámosmikola, Hun. 48/D2
Vámospércs, Hun. 48/E2
Van, Turk. 90/E2
Van (lake), Turk. 64/E6
Van Buren, Me, US 131/H2
Van Buren, Ar, US 129/J4
Van Cortlandt Park, NY, US 139/K8
Van Diemen (cape), Austl. 109/C2
Van Diemen (gulf), Austl. 109/C2
Van Harinxmakanaal (riv.), Neth. 50/C2
Van Horn, Tx, US 129/F5
Van Norman Lakes, Ca, US 136/B2
Van Rees (mts.), Indo. 81/J4
Van Wert, Oh, US 130/C3
Vana-Javesi (lake), Fin. 39/K1
Vanadzor, Arm. 63/H4
Vanavara (isl.), FrPol. 117/L7
Vancouver (mt.), Can. 134/L3
Vancouver, Wa, US 126/C4
Vancouver, BC, Can. 126/C3
Vancouver (int'l arpt.), BC, Can. 126/C3
Vancouver (cape), Austl. 112/C5
Vancouver (isl.), BC, Can. 122/D4
Vandalia, Mo, US 129/K3
Vandans, Aus. 57/F3
Vanderbijlpark, SAfr. 106/D2
Vanderbilt Museum, NY, US 139/E2
Vanderhoof, BC, Can. 126/B2
Vandœuvre-Lès-Nancy, Fr. 53/F6
Vanegas, Mex. 143/E4
Vänern (lake), Swe. 64/B4
Vänersborg, Swe. 38/E2
Vangaindrano, Madg. 107/H8
Vanier (isl.), NW, Can. 123/R7
Vanikolo (isl.), Sol. 116/F6
Vanil Noir (peak), Swi. 56/D4
Vanimo, PNG 116/D5
Vännäs, Swe. 37/F3
Vanne (riv.), Fr. 42/E2
Vannes, Fr. 42/B3
Vanoise, PN de la, Fr. 43/G4
Vanreenenpas (pass), SAfr. 106/E3
Vanrhynsdorp, SAfr. 106/B3
Vansbro, Swe. 38/F1
Vanse, Nor. 38/B2
Vansittart (isl.), NW, Can. 123/H2
Vantaa, Fin. 39/L1
Vanua Levu (isl.), Fiji 116/G6
Vanuatu (ctry.) 116/F6
Vanwyksvlei, SAfr. 106/C3
Var (riv.), Fr. 43/G5
Vara (riv.), It. 58/C4
Vara, Swe. 38/E2
Varadero, Cuba 145/F1
Varaita (riv.), It. 58/A3
Varallo, It. 58/B1
Varāmīn, Iran 88/F1
Vārānasi, India 84/D3
Varanger-Halvøya (pen.), Nor. 37/J1
Varangerfjorden (estu.), Nor. 37/J1
Varangéville, Fr. 53/F6
Varano (lake), It. 46/D2
Varano Borghi, It. 58/B1
Varaždin, Cro. 43/M3
Varazze, It. 58/B4
Varberg, Swe. 38/E3
Vardar (riv.), Macd. 47/G2
Varde, Den. 38/C4
Várdha, Gre. 47/G3
Vardø, Nor. 37/J1
Varel, Ger. 51/F2
Varenne (riv.), Fr. 42/C2
Varennes, Qu, Can. 131/P6
Varennes-Jarcy, Fr. 30/K5
Varennes-Vauzelles, Fr. 42/E3
Vareš, Bosn. 48/D3
Varese, It. 58/B1
Varese (prov.), It. 57/E6
Varese Ligure, It. 58/C4
Vårgårda, Swe. 38/E2
Vargem Grande, Braz. 154/B1
Vargem Grande do Sul, Braz. 211/G6
Varginha, Braz. 211/H6
Vári, Gre. 47/H4
Varilhes, Fr. 42/D5
Värmeln (lake), Swe. 38/E2
Värmland (co.), Swe. 37/E3
Varna (pol. reg.), Bul. 47/K1
Varna, Bul. 49/H4
Värnamo, Swe. 38/F3
Varois-et-Chaignot, Fr. 56/B3
Varoška Rijeka, Bosn. 48/C3
Várpalota, Hun. 48/D2
Varraddes, Fr. 30/L5
Varsi, It. 58/C3
Vårsta, Swe. 38/G2
Vartholomiôn, Gre. 47/G4
Varto, Turk. 90/E2
Vartry (res.), Ire. 34/B5
Vartry (riv.), Ire. 34/B5
Várzea Alegre, Braz. 154/C2
Várzea da Palma, Braz. 154/A5
Várzea Grande, Braz. 154/B2
Várzea Grande, Braz. 151/G7
Varzelândia, Braz. 154/A4
Varzi, It. 58/C3
Varzo, It. 57/E5
Varzuga (riv.), Rus. 60/H2
Vas (prov.), Hun. 48/C2
Vasa Barris (riv.), Braz. 151/L5
Vásárosnamény, Hun. 41/M4
Vașcău, Rom. 48/F2
Vashka (riv.), Rus. 61/K2
Vashon, Wa, US 135/C3
Vashon (isl.), Wa, US 135/C3
Vasiliká, Gre. 47/H2
Vasil'yevskiy (isl.), Rus. 61/S7
Vaslui (prov.), Rom. 49/H2
Vaslui, Rom. 49/H2
Vassar, Mi, US 130/D3
Vassdalsegga (peak), Nor. 38/B2
Vassouras, Braz. 211/K7
Västerås, Swe. 38/G2
Västerbotten (co.), Swe. 37/F2
Västerdalälven (riv.), Swe. 38/E1
Västernorrland (co.), Swe. 37/F3
Västervik, Swe. 38/G3
Västmanland (co.), Swe. 37/E3
Vasto, It. 46/D1
Västra Silen (lake), Swe. 38/E2
Vasvár, Hun. 48/C2
Vasyl'kiv, Ukr. 62/D2
Vaterstetten, Ger. 55/E6
Vatican City (ctry.) 27/F4
Vatnajökull (glacier), Ice. 37/P7
Vatomandry, Madg. 107/J7
Vatra Dornei, Rom. 49/G2
Vättern (lake), Swe. 37/E4
Vaucouleurs (riv.), Fr. 30/H5
Vaud (canton), Swi. 56/C4
Vaudoy-en-Brie, Fr. 30/M5
Vaudreuil-Dorion, Qu, Can. 131/M7
Vaughan, On, Can. 131/Q8
Vaughn, NM, US 129/F4
Vaughn, Wa, US 135/B3
Vaulruz, Swi. 56/C4
Vaulx-en-Velin, Fr. 56/A6
Vaupés (dept.), Col. 152/D4
Vaupés (riv.), Col. 147/B2
Vauréal, Fr. 30/J4
Vauvert, Fr. 42/F5
Vauvillers, Fr. 56/C2
Vaux (riv.), Fr. 40/C4
Vaux-sur-Seine, Fr. 30/H4
Vaux-sur-Sûre, Belg. 53/E4
Vauxhall, Ab, Can. 126/E3
Vavatenina, Madg. 107/J7
Vava'u Group (isls.), Tonga 117/H6
Vavuniya, SrL. 82/D6
Vawkavysk, Bela. 41/N2
Vaxjo (int'l arpt.), Swe. 38/F3
Växjö, Swe. 38/F3
Vaygach (isl.), Rus. 160/B
Vazante, Braz. 154/A5
Vázea Paulista, Braz. 211/G8
Vazuza (res.), Rus. 60/G5
Vazzola, It. 59/F1
Vecchiano, It. 58/D5
Vechigen, Swi. 56/D4
Vecht (riv.), Neth. 50/D3
Vechta, Ger. 51/F3
Vechte (riv.), Ger. 50/D3
Vecsés, Hun. 48/D2
Vedano Olona, It. 58/B1
Veddige, Swe. 38/E3
Vedea (riv.), Rom. 49/G3
Vedelago, It. 59/F1
Vedia, Arg. 158/E2
Vedra, Sp. 44/A1
Veendam, Neth. 50/D2
Veenendaal, Neth. 50/C4
Veere, Neth. 50/A5
Veerse Meer (res.), Neth. 50/A5
Vefsn, Nor. 37/E2
Vega, Tx, US 128/G4
Vega (pt.), Ak, US 134/B6
Vega (isl.), Nor. 37/D2
Vega de Alatorre, Mex. 143/N6
Vegafjorden (estu.), Nor. 37/D2
Veghel, Neth. 50/C5
Végreville, Ab, Can. 126/E2
Végueta, Peru 156/B3
Vehkalahti, Fin. 39/M1
Vehne (riv.), Ger. 51/F2
Veigné, Fr. 42/D3
Veinticinco de Mayo, Arg. 158/E2
Veinticinco de Mayo, Arg. 158/D3
Veinticinco de Mayo, Uru. 159/K11
Veintiocho de Mayo, Ecu. 156/B1
Veintiocho de Noviembre, Arg. 159/B6
Veitsch, Aus. 48/B2
Veitshöchheim, Ger. 54/C3
Vejen, Den. 38/C4
Vejer de la Frontera, Sp. 44/C4
Vejle, Den. 38/C4
Vejle (co.), Den. 38/C4
Vejprty, Czh. 55/G2
Vela, Cabo de la (pt.), Col. 152/C1
Vela Luka, Cro. 46/E1
Velaines, Fr. 53/E6
Vélan (peak), Swi. 56/D6
Velardeña, Mex. 142/E3
Velas, Azor., Port. 45/S12
Velasco Ibarra, Ecu. 152/B5
Velázquez, Uru. 159/G2
Velbert, Ger. 50/E6
Velburg, Ger. 55/E4
Velddrif, SAfr. 106/L10
Velden, Ger. 55/F6
Velden am Wörthersee, Aus. 43/L3
Veldhoven, Neth. 50/C6
Velen, Ger. 50/D5
Velešta, Macd. 47/G2
Velestínon, Gre. 47/H3
Vélez, Col. 152/C3
Vélez-Blanco, Sp. 44/D4
Vélez-Málaga, Sp. 44/C4
Vélez-Rubio, Sp. 44/D4
Velhas, Rio das (riv.), Braz. 151/K7
Velika Gorica, Cro. 48/C3
Velika Kladuša, Bosn. 43/L4
Velika Plana, Yugo. 48/E3
Velikaya (riv.), Rus. 60/F4
Velikiy Ustyug, Rus. 61/K3
Velikiye Luki, Rus. 39/P3
Veliko Tŭrnovo, Bul. 47/J1
Velille, Peru 156/D4
Vélingara, Sen. 102/B3
Vélizy-Villacoublay, Fr. 30/J5
Vel'ké Kapušany, Slvk. 48/F1
Vel'ký Krtíš, Slvk. 41/K4
Velký Zvon (peak), Czh. 55/F3
Vellberg, Ger. 54/C4
Velletri, It. 46/C2
Vellinge, Swe. 38/E4
Vellmar, Ger. 51/G6
Vellón (res.), Sp. 45/N8
Vellore, India 82/C5
Vélon, Gre. 47/H4
Vel'sk, Rus. 60/J3
Veluwe (phys. reg.), Neth. 50/C4
Veluwemeer (lake), Neth. 50/C4
Veluwezoom, NP, Neth. 50/C4
Velva, ND, US 127/H3
Velvary, Czh. 55/H2
Velvendós, Gre. 47/H2
Vémars, Fr. 30/K4
Vemb, Den. 38/C3
Véménd, Hun. 48/D2
Venachar (lake), Sc, UK 36/B4
Venado Tuerto, Arg. 158/E2
Venafro, It. 46/D2
Venamo (peak), Ven. 153/F3
Venâncio Aires, Braz. 155/A4
Venaria, It. 43/G4
Vence, Fr. 43/G5
Venceslau Brás, Braz. 155/B2
Vendas Novas, Port. 44/A3
Vendôme, Fr. 42/D3
Vendrell, Sp. 45/F2
Vendrest, Fr. 30/M4
Veneta, Laguna (lake), It. 59/F2
Venetie, Ak, US 134/J2
Veneto (pol. reg.), It. 43/J4
Venezia (prov.), It. 59/F1
Venezia, Golfo di (gulf), Eur. 43/K4
Venezia (Venice), It. 59/F2
Venezuela (gulf), Col.,Ven. 147/B1
Venezuela (ctry.) 147/C2
Vengurla, India 89/K5
Veniaminof (vol.), Ak, US 134/G4
Venice, Fl, US 133/H5
Venice, Il, US 137/G8
Venice (Venezia), It. 43/K4
Vénissieux, Fr. 42/F4
Venjan, Swe. 38/E1
Venjansjön (lake), Swe. 38/E1
Venkatagiri, India 82/C5
Venlo, Neth. 50/D6
Vennesla, Nor. 38/C2
Veno (bay), Den. 38/C3
Venoge (riv.), Swi. 56/C4
Venosa, It. 46/D2
Venray, Neth. 50/C5
Vent, Îles du (isls.), FrPol. 117/L6
Venta (riv.), Lat. 60/D4
Venta de Baños, Sp. 44/C2

Ventauri (riv.), Ven. 150/E3
Ventersburg, SAfr. 106/D3
Ventersdorp, SAfr. 106/D2
Venterstad, SAfr. 106/D3
Ventiseri, Fr. 46/A2
Ventnor, Eng, UK 33/E5
Ventnor City, NJ, US 138/D5
Ventspils, Lat. 39/J3
Ventuari (riv.), Ven. 153/E3
Ventura (riv.), Ca, US 136/A2
Ventura (co.), Ca, US 136/A2
Venturina, It. 43/J5
Venturosa, Braz. 154/C3
Venustiano Carranza, Mex. 140/C4
Venustiano Carranza (res.), Mex. 143/E3
Vép, Hun. 43/M3
Ver-sur-Launette, Fr. 30/L4
Vera, Arg. 157/D2
Vera, Sp. 44/E4
Vera Cruz, Pan. 152/B2
Veracruz, Mex. 143/N7
Veracruz-Llave (state), Mex. 140/B3
Veranópolis, Braz. 155/B4
Verāval, India 89/K4
Verbania, It. 57/E6
Verberie, Fr. 52/B5
Verbicaro, It. 46/D3
Vercelli, It. 58/B2
Vercelli (prov.), It. 56/E6
Verdal, Nor. 37/D3
Verde (riv.), Par. 157/D1
Verde (cape), Sen. 96/B5
Verde (riv.), Braz. 151/G6
Verde (riv.), Mex. 143/F4
Verde (coast), Sp. 44/B1
Verde (cape), It. 58/A5
Verde (bay), Arg. 158/E3
Verde Grande (riv.), Braz. 151/K7
Verden, Ger. 51/G3
Verdhikoússa, Gre. 47/G3
Verdigris (riv.), US 129/J3
Verdinho (riv.), Braz. 155/B1
Verdon (riv.), Fr. 42/F5
Verdugo (mts.), Ca, US 136/F7
Verdun, Qu, Can. 131/N7
Vereeniging, SAfr. 106/D2
Verena (peak), It. 57/H6
Vereshchagino, Rus. 61/M4
Veretskiy (pass), Ukr. 41/M4
Verga (cape), Gui. 102/B4
Vergara, Uru. 159/G2
Vergato, It. 59/E4
Vergennes, Vt, US 130/F2
Vergiate, It. 58/B1
Vergína (ruin), Gre. 47/H2
Verigenstadt, Ger. 57/F1
Verín, Sp. 44/B2
Veríssimo, Braz. 155/B1
Verkhnetulomskiy (res.), Rus. 60/F1
Verkhoyansk (range), Rus. 67/M2
Verkhoyansk, Rus. 65/P3
Verl, Ger. 51/F5
Vermenagna (riv.), It. 58/A4
Vermilion (range), Mn, US 127/K4
Vermilion, Ab, Can. 126/F2
Vermilion (riv.), Can. 126/F2
Vermillion, SD, US 127/J5
Vermont (state), US 125/M3
Vernal, Ut, US 128/E2
Vernayaz, Swi. 56/D5
Vernazza, It. 58/C4
Verneuil-sur-Avre, Fr. 42/D2
Verneuil-sur-Seine, Fr. 30/H5
Verneukpan (salt pan), SAfr. 106/C3
Vernier, Swi. 56/C5
Vernon, BC, Can. 126/D3
Vernon, Fr. 42/D2
Vernon Hills, Il, US 135/Q15
Vernon Valley, NJ, US 138/D1
Vernouillet, Fr. 30/H5
Vero Beach, Fl, US 133/H5
Véroia, Gre. 47/H2
Verolanuova, It. 58/D2
Verolavecchia, It. 58/D2
Verolengo, It. 58/A2
Verona (prov.), It. 59/D1
Verona (int'l arpt.), It. 59/D2
Verona, It. 59/D2
Verona, NJ, US 139/J8
Verónica, Arg. 159/K11
Verrès, It. 58/A1
Verret, La, US 137/Q17
Verrières-le-Buisson, Fr . 30/J5
Versa (riv.), It. 58/B3
Versailles, Ky, US 130/C4
Versailles, Fr. 30/J5
Versigny, Fr. 30/L4
Verskla (riv.), Ukr.,Rus. 64/D4
Versmold, Ger. 51/F4
Versoix, Swi. 56/C5
Vert-le-Grand, Fr. 30/K6
Vert-le-Petit, Fr. 30/K6
Vert-Saint-Denis, Fr. 30/K6
Vertana (peak), It. 57/G4
Verte (peak), Fr. 56/C6
Vertemate, It. 58/C1
Vertientes, Cuba 145/G1
Vertou, Fr. 42/C3
Vertova, It. 58/C1
Vertus, Fr. 52/D6
Verviers, Belg. 53/E2
Vervins, Fr. 52/C4
Verwoerdburg, SAfr. 106/Q12
Veryan (bay), Eng, UK 32/B6
Verzasca (riv.), Swi. 57/E5
Verzasca (Gerra), Swi. 57/E5
Verzenay, Fr. 53/D5
Verzuolo, It. 43/G4
Verzy, Fr. 53/D5
Vescovato, Fr. 46/A1
Vescovato, It. 58/D2
Vesdre (riv.), Belg. 42/F1
Veselí nad Lužnicí, Czh. 55/H4
Veselyy (res.), Rus. 63/G3
Vesgre (riv.), Fr. 52/A6
Vesijärvi (lake), Fin. 39/L1
Vesle (riv.), Fr. 40/C4
Vesoul, Fr. 56/C2
Vespolate, It. 58/B2
Vest-Agder (co.), Nor. 37/C4
Vest-Sjælland (prov.), Den. 38/D4
Vest-Vlaanderen (prov.), Belg. 52/B2
Vestbjerg, Den. 38/C3
Vestby, Nor. 38/D2
Vesterålen (isls.), Nor. 37/E1
Vestfjorden (inlet), Nor. 37/E2
Vestfold (co.), Nor. 37/D4
Vestmannaeyjar, Ice. 37/N7
Vestone, It. 58/D1
Vestvågøy, Nor. 37/E1
Vestvågøya (isl.), Nor. 37/E1
Vesuvio (Vesuvius) (vol.), It. 46/D2
Veszprém (prov.), Hun. 48/C2
Veszprém, Hun. 48/C2
Vészto, Hun. 48/E2
Vet (riv.), SAfr. 106/D3
Vétheuil, Fr. 30/H4
Vetlanda, Swe. 38/F3
Vetluga (riv.), Rus. 64/E4
Vetralla, It. 46/C1
Vétraz, Fr. 56/C5
Větřni, Czh. 55/H5
Vettore (peak), It. 43/K5
Veude (riv.), Fr. 42/D3
Veurne, Belg. 52/B1
Vevey, Swi. 56/C5
Vex, Swi. 56/D5
Veybach (riv.), Ger. 53/F2
Veyle (riv.), Fr. 56/B5
Veyrier-du-Lac, Fr. 56/C6
Vézelise, Fr. 56/C1
Vézère (riv.), Fr. 42/D4
Vezirköprü, Turk. 62/E4
Vezza d'Oglio, It. 57/G5
Vezzano Ligure, It. 58/C4
Viacha, Bol. 150/E7
Viadana, It. 58/D3
Viana, Braz. 154/A1
Viana del Bollo, Sp. 44/B1
Viana do Alentejo, Port. 44/A3
Viana do Castelo, Port. 44/A2
Viana do Castelo (dist.), Port. 44/A2
Vianden, Lux. 53/F4
Vianen, Neth. 50/C4
Viangchan (Vientiane) (cap.), Laos 78/C2
Viar (riv.), Sp. 44/C4
Viareggio, It. 58/D5
Viarmes, Fr. 30/K4
Viaur (riv.), Fr. 42/E4
Vibbard, Mo, US 137/E5
Vibo Valentia, It. 46/E3
Viborg, Den. 38/C3
Viborg (co.), Den. 38/C3
Vic, Sp. 45/G2
Vic-en-Bigorre, Fr. 42/D5
Vic-Fezensac, Fr. 42/D5
Vicam, Mex. 142/C3
Vícar, Sp. 44/D4
Vicarello, It. 58/D5
Vicchio, It. 59/E6
Vice, Peru 156/A2
Vicente (pt.), Ca, US 136/F8
Vicente Guerrero, Mex. 142/E4
Vicente Guerrero, Mex. 142/A2
Vicente López, Arg. 159/J11
Vicenza, It. 59/E1
Vicenza (prov.), It. 57/H6
Vichada (riv.), Col. 150/E3
Vichada (dept.), Col. 152/D3
Vichaya, Bol. 156/D5
Vichuga, Rus. 60/J4
Vichy, Fr. 42/E3
Vickham (cape), Austl. 115/B3
Vicksburg, Ms, US 129/K4
Vicksburg Nat'l Mil. Park, Ms, US 129/K4
Vico, Fr. 46/A1
Vico (lake), It. 46/C1
Vico del Gargano, It. 48/B5
Vicopisano, It. 58/D5
Viçosa, Braz. 154/C3
Viçosa, Braz. 155/D2
Viçosa do Ceará, Braz. 154/B1
Vicosoprano, Swi. 57/F5
Vicou Gorge NP, Gre. 47/G3
Vicq, Fr. 30/H5
Victor Harbor, Austl. 113/H5
Víctor Rosales, Mex. 142/E4
Victoria, Malay. 80/E2
Victoria (peak), Phil. 81/E2
Victoria, Austl. 115/B2
Victoria (falls), Zim. 105/E4
Victoria, Arg. 157/D3
Victoria (cap.), BC, Can. 126/C3
Victoria (riv.), Austl. 109/C2
Victoria (state), Austl. 109/D4
Victoria, China 83/K3
Victoria (mt.), Myan. 83/F3
Victoria, Rom. 49/G3
Victoria, Hon. 144/E3
Victoria, Chile 158/B3
Victoria (peak), Belz. 144/D2
Victoria, Gren. 153/F1
Victoria (isl.), NW, Can. 122/E1
Victoria (str.), NW, Can. 122/F2
Victoria (lake), Ugan. 93/F5
Victoria de las Tunas, Cuba 145/G1
Victoria Land (pol. reg.), Ant. 160/M
Victoria Nile (riv.), Ugan. 97/M7
Victoria West, SAfr. 106/C3
Victorias, Phil. 79/D5
Victoriaville, Qu, Can. 131/G2
Victorica, Arg. 158/D3
Victorville, Ca, US 136/C1
Victory Junction, Ks, US 137/D5
Vicuña Mackenna, Arg. 158/D2
Vidal (cape), SAfr. 107/F3
Vidalia, La, US 129/K5
Vidalia, Ga, US 133/H3
Videira, Braz. 155/B3
Videle, Rom. 49/G3
Vidhošt (peak), Czh. 55/G4
Vidigueira, Port. 44/B3
Vidigulfo, It. 58/C2
Vidin, Bul. 49/F4
Vidisha, India 84/A4
Vidnoye, Rus. 61/W9
Vidor, Tx, US 129/J5
Vidor, It. 59/F1
Vidöstern (lake), Swe. 38/F3
Vidourle (riv.), Fr. 42/E5
Vie (riv.), Fr. 42/D2
Viechtach, Ger. 55/F4
Viedma, Arg. 158/E4
Viedma (lake), Arg. 159/B6
Viehberg (peak), Aus. 55/H5
Vieille-Eglise-en-Yvelines, Fr. 30/H6
Viejo (peak), Peru 156/B2
Viella, Sp. 45/F1
Vielsalm, Belg. 53/E3
Vienenburg, Ger. 51/H5
Vienna, WV, US 130/D4
Vienna, Va, US 138/A6
Vienne, Fr. 42/F4
Vienne (riv.), Fr. 42/D3
Vientiane (int'l arpt.), Laos 78/C2
Vientiane (Viangchan) (cap.), Laos 78/C2
Vieques (isl.), PR 141/M8
Viére (riv.), Fr. 53/D6
Vierlingsbeek, Neth. 50/D5
Viernheim, Ger. 54/B3
Vierre (riv.), Belg. 53/E4
Viersen, Ger. 50/D6
Vierzon, Fr. 42/E3
Viesca, Mex. 142/E3
Vieste, It. 46/E2
Viet., Viet. 79/A5
Viet Tri, Viet. 83/J3
Vietnam (ctry.) 67/K8
Vieux-Boucau-les-Bains, Fr . 42/C5
Vieux Carré, La, US 137/P17
Vieux-Charmont, Fr. 56/C2
Vieux-Condé, Fr. 52/C3
Vieux Fort, StL. 141/N9
Vieux-Thann, Fr. 56/D2
Vieze (riv.), Swi. 56/C5
Viga, Phil. 79/D5
Vigan, Phil. 79/D4
Vigarano Mainarda, It. 59/E3
Vigasio, It. 59/D2
Vigevano, It. 58/B2
Viggiù, It. 57/E6
Vigia, Braz. 151/J4
Vigliano Biellese, It. 58/B1
Viglio (peak), It. 46/C2
Vignacourt, Fr. 52/B3
Vignanello, It. 46/C1
Vignemale (peak), Fr. 42/C5
Vigneulles-lès-Hattonchâtel, Fr. 53/E6
Vigneux-sur-Seine, Fr. 30/K5
Vignola, It. 59/D4
Vignot, Fr. 53/E6
Vigo, Sp. 44/A1
Vigodarzere, It. 59/E2
Vigonovo, It. 59/F2
Vigonza, It. 59/E2
Vigrestad, Nor. 38/A2
Viguzzolo, It. 58/B3
Vihanti, Fin. 60/E2
Vihāri, Pak. 86/B4
Vihti, Fin. 39/L1
Viitasaari, Fin. 60/E3
Vijayawada, India 82/D4
Vík, Ice. 37/N7
Vik, Nor. 38/B1
Vikersund, Nor. 38/C2
Vikesâ, Nor. 38/B2
Vikhren (peak), Bul. 47/H2
Viking, Ab, Can. 126/F2
Vikmanshyttan, Swe. 38/F1
Vila Bittencourt, Braz. 152/D5
Vila de Sena, Moz. 105/G4
Vila do Bispo, Port. 44/A4
Vila do Conde, Port. 44/A2
Vila do Porto, Azor., Port. 45/T13
Vila Franca de Xira, Port. 45/P10
Vila Franca do Campo, Azor., Port. 45/T13
Vila Nova de Fozcoa, Port. 44/B2
Vila Nova de Gaia, Port. 44/A2
Vila Nova de Milfontes, Port. 44/A4
Vila Pouca de Aguiar, Port. 44/B2
Vila Real, Port. 44/B2
Vila Real (dist.), Port. 44/B2
Vila Velha Argolas, Braz. 155/D2
Vila Velha de Ródão, Port. 44/B3
Vila Verde, Port. 44/A2
Vila Viçosa, Port. 44/B3
Viladecans, Sp. 45/K7
Vilafranca del Penedès, Sp. 45/K7
Vilaine (riv.), Fr. 42/B3
Vilanandro (cape), Madg. 107/H7
Vilanculos, Moz. 105/G5
Vilanova i la Geltrù, Sp. 45/K7
Vilar Formoso, Port. 44/B2
Vilcabamba, Peru 156/B3
Vîlcea (prov.), Rom. 49/F3
Vilches, Sp. 44/D3
Vilhelmina, Swe. 37/F2
Vilhena, Braz. 150/F6
Viliya (riv.), Bela. 60/E5
Viljandi, Est. 39/L2
Viljoenskroon, SAfr. 106/D2
Vil'kitsogo (str.), Rus. 65/K2
Villa Alemana, Chile 158/N8
Villa Alhué, Chile 158/N9
Villa Ángela, Arg. 157/D2
Villa Atuel, Arg. 158/D2
Villa Bartolomea, It. 59/E2
Villa Bruzual, Ven. 152/D2
Villa Cañás, Arg. 158/E2
Villa Carcina, It. 58/D1
Villa Carlos Paz, Arg. 157/D3
Villa Chañar Ladeado, Arg. 158/E2
Villa Constitución, Arg. 158/E2
Villa Corzo, Mex. 144/C2
Villa Cuauhtemoc, Mex. 143/Q10
Villa d'Almè, It. 58/C1
Villa de Arista, Mex. 143/E4
Villa de Cos, Mex. 142/E4
Villa de Costa Rica, Mex. 142/D3
Villa de La Paz, Mex. 143/E4
Villa de Reyes, Mex. 143/E4
Villa del Carbón, Mex. 143/Q9
Villa del Carmen, Uru. 159/K10
Villa del Río, Sp. 44/C4
Villa di Serio, It. 58/C1
Villa Dolores, Arg. 157/C3
Villa Dolores, Arg. 158/D1
Villa Flores, Mex. 144/C2
Villa Gesell, Arg. 159/F3
Villa Guardia, It. 58/C1
Villa Hidalgo, Mex. 142/D4
Villa Hidalgo, Mex. 142/C2
Villa Huidobro, Arg. 158/D2
Villa Iris, Arg. 158/E3
Villa Isabela, DRep. 145/J2
Villa Jaragua, DRep. 145/J2
Villa Juárez, Mex. 142/C3
Villa Juárez, Mex. 142/D3
Villa La Angostura, Arg. 158/C4
Villa Lázaro Cárdenas, Mex. 143/M6
Villa López, Mex. 142/D3
Villa Mantero, Arg. 159/J10
Villa María, Arg. 157/D3
Villa Minozzo, It. 58/D4
Villa Montes, Bol. 150/F8
Villa Nueva, Guat. 144/D3
Villa Nueva, Nic. 144/E3
Villa Nueva, Arg. 158/C2
Villa Opicina, It. 59/G1
Villa Park, Il, US 135/Q16
Villa Park, Ca, US 136/G8
Villa Regina, Arg. 158/D3
Villa Rica, Peru 156/C3
Villa Rosario, Col. 152/C3
Villa Sandino, Nic. 145/E3
Villa Sarmiento, Arg. 158/D2
Villa Serrano, Bol. 150/F7
Villa Unión, Arg. 157/C2
Villa Unión, Mex. 142/D4
Villa Valeria, Arg. 158/D2
Villa Verucchio, It. 59/F5
Villaba, Sp. 44/E1
Villablino, Sp. 44/B1
Villacañas, Sp. 44/D3
Villacarrillo, Sp. 44/D3
Villada, Sp. 44/C1
Villadiego, Sp. 44/C1
Villadose, It. 59/E2
Villadossola, It. 57/E5
Villafamés, Sp. 45/E2
Villafranca, Sp. 44/E1
Villafranca d'Asti, It. 58/B3
Villafranca de los Barros, Sp. 44/B3
Villafranca del Bierzo, Sp. 44/B1
Villafranca del Cid, Sp. 45/E2
Villafranca di Verona, It. 59/D2
Villafranca in Lunigiana, It. 58/C4
Villagarcía, Sp. 44/A1
Villagrán, Mex. 143/F3
Villaguay, Arg. 157/E3
Villahermosa, Sp. 44/D3
Villahermosa, Mex. 144/C2
Villajoyosa, Sp. 45/E3
Villalba, Sp. 44/B1
Villalcampo, Embalse de (res.), Sp. 44/B2
Villaldama, Mex. 132/C5
Villalón de Campos, Sp. 44/C1
Villalonga, Arg. 158/E3
Villalpando, Sp. 44/C2
Villamartín, Sp. 44/C4
Villandro (peak), It. 57/H4
Villanova, It. 59/F4
Villanova, It. 59/E4
Villanova d'Asti, It. 58/A3
Villanova Mondovì, It. 58/A4
Villanterio, It. 58/C2
Villanueva, Mex. 142/E4
Villanueva, Col. 152/C2
Villanueva, Hon. 144/E3
Villanueva de Arosa, Sp. 44/A1
Villanueva de Córdoba, Sp. 44/C3
Villanueva de la Serena, Sp. 44/C3
Villanueva de los Infantes, Sp. 44/D3
Villanueva de Oscos, Sp. 44/B1
Villanueva del Arzobispo, Sp. 44/D3
Villanuova sul Clisi, It. 58/D1
Villány, Hun. 48/D3
Villar del Arzobispo, Sp. 45/E3
Villarcayo, Sp. 44/D1
Villardevós, Sp. 44/B2
Villarreal de los Infantes, Sp. 45/E3
Villarrica, Par. 157/E2
Villarrica, Chile 158/B3
Villarrica (vol.), Chile 158/C3
Villarrica (lake), Chile 158/B3
Villarrica, PN, Chile 158/C3
Villarrobledo, Sp. 44/D3
Villarrubia de los Ojos, Sp. 44/D3
Villars-les-Dombes, Fr. 56/B6
Villars-sur-Glâne, Swi. 56/D4
Villas, NJ, US 138/D5
Villasana de Mena, Sp. 44/D1
Villasanta, It. 58/C1
Villastellone, It. 58/A3
Villaverde del Río, Sp. 44/C4
Villaverla, It. 59/E1
Villavicencio, Col. 152/C3
Villaviciosa, Sp. 44/C1
Villaviciosa de Odón, Sp. 45/N9
Villazón, Bol. 157/C1
Villecresnes, Fr. 30/K5
Villefranche-de-Rouergue, Fr. 42/E4
Villefranche-sur-Saône, Fr. 42/F4
Villejuif, Fr. 30/K5
Villemur-sur-Tarn, Fr. 42/D5
Villena, Sp. 45/E3
Villeneuve, Swi. 56/C5
Villeneuve-d'Ascq, Fr. 52/C2
Villeneuve-le-Comte, Fr. 30/L5
Villeneuve-le-Roi, Fr. 30/K5
Villeneuve-lès-Avignon, Fr. 42/F5
Villeneuve-Saint-Denis, Fr . 30/L5
Villeneuve-Saint-Georges, Fr. 30/K5
Villeneuve-Saint-Germain, Fr. 52/C5
Villeneuve-sur-Lot, Fr. 42/D4
Villeneuve-sur-Yonne, Fr. 42/E2
Villeneuve-Tolosane, Fr. 42/D5
Villennes-sur-Seine, Fr. 30/H5
Villeparisis, Fr. 30/K5
Villepinte, Fr. 30/K5
Villepreux, Fr. 30/J5
Villeroy, Fr. 30/L4
Villers-Bretonneux, Fr. 52/B4
Villers-Cotterêts, Fr. 52/C5
Villers-en-Arthies, Fr. 30/H4
Villers-le-Bouillet, Belg. 53/E2
Villers-le-Lac, Fr. 56/C3
Villers-lès-Nancy, Fr. 53/F6
Villers-Saint-Genest, Fr . 30/L4
Villers-Saint-Paul, Fr. 52/B5
Villers-Semeuse, Fr. 53/D4
Villersexel, Fr. 56/C2
Villerupt, Fr. 53/E5
Villette, Fr. 30/H5
Villeurbanne, Fr. 56/A6
Villevaudé, Fr. 30/K5
Villiers, SAfr. 106/E2
Villiers-en-Lieu, Fr. 53/D6
Villiers-le-Bel, Fr. 30/K4
Villiers-Saint-Georges, Fr. 52/C6
Villiers-sur-Marne, Fr. 30/K5
Villiers-sur-Morin, Fr. 30/L5
Villiersdorp, SAfr. 106/L10
Villieu-Loyes-Mollon, Fr. 56/B6
Villingen-Schwenningen, Ger. 57/E1
Villmar, Ger. 54/B2
Villongo, It. 58/C1
Villorba, It. 59/F1
Vilnius (int'l arpt.), Lith. 39/L4
Vilnius (cap.), Lith. 39/L4
Vils, Aus. 57/G2
Vils (riv.), Ger. 40/F4
Vilsbiburg, Ger. 55/F6
Vilseck, Ger. 55/E3
Vilshofen, Ger. 55/G5
Vilters, Swi. 57/F3
Vilvoorde, Belg. 53/D2
Vilyuy (riv.), Rus. 67/L3
Vilyuy (range), Rus. 65/M3
Vimercate, It. 58/C1
Vimeu (reg.), Fr. 52/A3
Vimmerby, Swe. 38/F3
Vimodrone, It. 58/C2
Vimperk, Czh. 55/G4
Vina (riv.), Camr. 96/H6
Viña del Mar, Chile 158/N8
Vinanivao, Madg. 107/J6
Vinaroz, Sp. 45/F2
Vincennes, In, US 130/C4
Vincennes (lake), Fr. 30/L5
Vincennes (bay), Ant. 160/H
Vincennes, Fr. 30/K5
Vincent, Ca, US 136/B1
Vincentown, NJ, US 138/D4
Vinces, Ecu. 152/B5
Vincey, Fr. 56/C1
Vinchos, Peru 156/C4
Vinci, It. 59/D5
Vindeby, Den. 38/D4
Vindeln, Swe. 37/F2
Vindhya (range), India 84/A4
Vineland, NJ, US 138/C5
Vineland Station, On, Can. 131/R9
Vineuil, Fr. 42/D3
Vingåker, Swe. 38/F2
Vinh, Viet. 78/D2
Vinh An, Viet. 79/A4
Vinh Long, Viet. 78/D4
Vinh Yen, Viet. 78/D1
Vinhais, Port. 44/B2
Vinhedo, Braz. 211/G8
Vinica, Macd. 47/H2
Vinita, Ok, US 129/J3
Vînju Mare, Rom. 48/F3
Vinkovci, Cro. 48/D3
Vinningen, Ger. 53/G5
Vinnyts'ka (prov.), Ukr. 49/J1
Vinnyts'ka (obl.), Ukr. 62/D2
Vinnytsya, Ukr. 62/D2
Vinon-sur-Verdon, Fr. 42/F5
Vinson Massif (peak), Ant. 160/U
Viola, De, US 138/C5
Viola, NY, US 139/J7
Violet, La, US 137/Q17
Violet Town, Austl. 115/C3
Viosne (riv.), Fr. 52/A5
Virac, Phil. 79/D5
Viracopos (int'l arpt.), Braz. 211/F7
Viranşehir, Turk. 90/D2
Virār, India 89/K5
Virden, Mb, Can. 127/H3
Vire, Fr. 42/C2
Vire (riv.), Fr. 42/C2
Viren (lake), Swe. 38/F2
Vireux-Wallerand, Fr. 53/D3
Virgem da Lapa, Braz. 154/B5
Virgin (riv.), US 128/D3
Virgin (isls.), UK,US 119/L8
Virgin Gorda (isl.), UK 141/M8
Virgin Islands NP, USVI 141/M8
Virginia, SAfr. 106/D3
Virginia (state), US 125/L4
Virginia City, Nv, US 128/C3
Virginia Water, Eng, UK 30/B2
Viriat, Fr. 56/B5
Virieu-le-Grand, Fr. 56/B6
Viroflay, Fr. 30/J5
Viroin (riv.), Belg. 53/D3
Viroqua, Wi, US 129/K2
Virovitica, Cro. 48/C3
Virserum, Swe. 38/F3
Virton, Belg. 53/E4
Virú, Peru 156/B3
Virudunagar, India 82/C6
Virunga, D.R. Congo 104/A3
Virunga NP, D.R. Congo 104/A3
Viry-Châtillon, Fr. 30/K6
Vis (isl.), Cro. 48/C4
Visaginas, Lith. 39/M4
Visalia, Ca, US 128/C3
Visandre (riv.), Fr. 30/M5
Visayan (sea), Phil. 81/F1
Visbek, Ger. 51/F3
Visby, Swe. 38/H3
Visconde do Rio Branco, Braz. 155/D2
Viscount Melville (sound), NW, Can. 123/R7
Visé, Belg. 53/E2
Višegrad, Bosn. 48/D4
Viseu, Port. 44/B2
Viseu (dist.), Port. 44/B2
Vişeu de Sus, Rom. 49/G2
Vishākhapatnam, India 82/D4
Vishera (riv.), Rus. 61/L3
Vishoek, SAfr. 106/L11
Viskafors, Swe. 38/E3
Vislanda, Swe. 38/F3
Visnagar, India 89/K4
Višnjevac, Cro. 48/D3
Visoko, Bosn. 48/D4
Visp, Swi. 56/D5
Visperterminen, Swi. 56/D5
Visselhövede, Ger. 51/G3
Vissenbjerg, Den. 38/D4
Vissoie, Swi. 56/D5
Vista, Ca, US 136/C4
Vistonís (lake), Gre. 47/J2
Vistula (riv.), Pol. 27/H3
Vit (riv.), Bul. 47/J1
Vita, Mb, Can. 127/J3
Viterbo, It. 46/C1
Vitez, Bosn. 48/C3
Viti Levu (isl.), Fiji 116/G6
Vitigudino, Sp. 44/B2
Vitim (plat.), Rus. 65/M4
Vitim (riv.), Rus. 67/L4
Vítkuv Kamen (peak), Czh. 55/H5
Vitomirica, Yugo. 47/G1
Vitor, Peru 156/D5
Vitória, Braz. 155/D2
Vitoria, Sp. 44/D1
Vitória da Conquista, Braz. 154/B4
Vitória de Santo Antão, Braz. 154/D3
Vitória do Mearim, Braz. 154/A1
Vitorino Freire, Braz. 154/A2
Vitosha NP, Bul. 47/H1
Vitré, Fr. 42/C2
Vitrey-sur-Mance, Fr. 56/B2
Vitrolles, Fr. 42/F5
Vitry-en-Artois, Fr. 52/B3
Vitry-le-François, Fr. 53/D6
Vitry-sur-Seine, Fr. 30/K5
Vitsyebsk, Bela. 39/P4
Vitsyebskaya (prov.), Bela. 60/E5
Vittangi, Swe. 37/G2
Vittel, Fr. 56/B1
Vittoria, It. 46/D4
Vittorio Veneto, It. 43/K4
Vivarais, Monts du (mts.), Fr. 42/F4
Viveiro, Sp. 44/B1
Viverone (lake), It. 58/B2
Viverone, It. 58/B2
Vivian, La, US 129/J4
Vivonne, Fr. 42/D3
Vizcaíno, Sierra (mts.), Mex. 142/B3
Vize, Turk. 49/H5
Vizhas (riv.), Rus. 61/K2
Vizianagaram, India 82/D4
Vlaardingen, Neth. 50/B5
Vlădeasa (peak), Rom. 49/F2
Vladikavkaz, Rus. 63/H4
Vladimir, Rus. 60/J4
Vladimir Oblast, Rus. 60/J5
Vladivostok, Rus. 71/P3
Vlagtwedde, Neth. 51/E2
Vlăhiţa, Rom. 49/G2
Vlajna (peak), Yugo. 47/G1
Vlasenica, Bosn. 48/D3
Vlašim, Czh. 43/L2
Vlasotince, Yugo. 47/H1
Vlieland (isl.), Neth. 40/C2
Vliestroom (chan.), Neth. 50/C2
Vlijmen, Neth. 50/C5
Vlissingen, Neth. 50/A6
Vlotho, Ger. 51/F4
Vltava (riv.), Czh. 41/H4
Vnukovo (int'l arpt.), Rus. 61/W9
Vobarno, It. 58/D1
Vöcklabruck, Aus. 55/G6
Vöcklamarkt, Aus. 55/G6
Vodice, Cro. 48/B3
Vodlozero (lake), Rus. 60/H3
Vodňany, Czh. 55/H4
Vodskov, Den. 38/D3
Voerde, Ger. 50/D5
Vogan, Togo 103/F5
Vogelsberg (mts.), Ger. 43/H1
Voghera, It. 58/C3
Vogogna, It. 57/E6
Vogorno (lake), Swi. 57/E5
Vogtareuth, Ger. 55/F7
Vogtland (reg.), Ger. 40/F3
Vohenstrauss, Ger. 55/F3
Vohilava, Madg. 107/H8
Vohimena (cape), Madg. 107/H9
Vohipeno, Madg. 107/H8
Vohiposa, Madg. 107/H8
Voi, Kenya 104/C3
Void-Vacon, Fr. 53/E6
Voil (lake), Sc, UK 36/B4
Voinjama, Libr. 102/C4
Voinsles, Fr. 30/M5
Voiron, Fr. 42/F4
Voise (riv.), Fr. 42/D2
Voisey (bay), Nf, Can. 123/K3
Voiteur, Fr. 56/B4
Vojosë (riv.), Alb. 48/D5
Vojvodina (prov.), Yugo. 48/D3
Völklingen, Ger. 53/F5
Volano, It. 57/H6
Volary, Czh. 55/G5
Volcán Barú, PN, Pan. 145/F4
Volcán Poás, PN, CR 145/E4
Volcano, Hi, US 124/U11
Volcano (isls.), Japan 116/C2
Volcans NP, Rwa. 104/A3
Volchiy Nos (cape), Rus. 39/Q1
Volda, Nor. 37/C3
Volendam, Neth. 50/C3
Volga (riv.), Rus. 27/J3
Volga-Baltic Waterway (canal), Rus. 60/H3
Volgelsheim, Fr. 56/D1
Volgodonsk, Rus. 63/G3
Volgograd (int'l arpt.), Rus. 63/H2
Volgograd (res.), Rus. 63/H2
Volgograd Oblast, Rus. 63/G2
Volkach (riv.), Ger. 54/D3
Volkach, Ger. 54/D3
Volkeradam (dam), Neth. 50/B5
Völkermarkt, Aus. 43/L3
Volketswil, Swi. 57/E3
Volkhov (riv.), Rus. 60/F4
Volkhov, Rus. 39/Q2
Volkmarsen, Ger. 51/G6
Volksrust, SAfr. 107/E2
Volodymyr-Volyns'kyy, Ukr. 62/C2
Vologda, Rus. 60/H4
Vologda Oblast, Rus. 60/J3
Vologne (riv.), Fr. 40/D4
Volos (gulf), Gre. 47/H3
Vólos, Gre. 47/H3
Volpago del Montello, It. 59/F1
Volpiano, It. 58/A2
Völs, Aus. 57/H3
Vol'sk, Rus. 63/H1
Volta (riv.), Gha. 96/F6
Volta (pol. reg.), Gha. 103/F5
Volta (lake), Gha. 93/B4
Volta Mantovana, It. 58/D2
Volta Redonda, Braz. 211/J7
Voltana, It. 59/E3
Volterra, It. 59/D6
Voltlage, Ger. 51/E4
Volturino (peak), It. 46/D2
Volturno (riv.), It. 46/D2
Volubilis (ruin), Mor. 100/B2
Vólvi (lake), Gre. 47/H2
Volyně, Czh. 55/G4
Volyňka (riv.), Czh. 55/G4
Volyns'ka (obl.), Ukr. 62/C2
Volzhsk, Rus. 61/L5
Volzhskiy, Rus. 63/H2
Von Frank (mtn.), Ak, US 134/H3
Von Ormy, Tx, US 137/T21
Vondrozo, Madg. 107/H8
Vónitsa, Gre. 47/G3
Vonne (riv.), Fr. 42/D3
Voorburg, Neth. 50/B4
Voorne (isl.), Neth. 50/B5
Voorschoten, Neth. 50/B4
Voorst, Neth. 50/D4
Vopnafjördhur, Ice. 37/P6
Vorab (peak), Swi. 57/F4
Vorarlberg (prov.), Aus. 40/E5
Vorbach (riv.), Ger. 54/C4
Vorchdorf, Aus. 55/G6
Vorden, Neth. 50/D4
Vorderrhein (riv.), Swi. 43/H3
Vorderweissenbach, Aus. 55/H5
Vordingborg, Den. 38/D4
Voreppe, Fr. 42/F4
Vorkuta, Rus. 61/P2
Vorkuta (int'l arpt.), Rus. 61/Q2
Vormsi (isl.), Est. 39/K2
Vóroi, Gre. 47/J5
Vorona (riv.), Rus. 63/G1
Voronezh (int'l arpt.), Rus. 62/F2
Voronezh (riv.), Rus. 62/F1
Voronezh, Rus. 62/F2
Voronezh Oblast, Rus. 63/G2
Voron'ya (riv.), Rus. 60/G1
Vorskla (riv.), Ukr. 62/E2
Vorst, Belg. 53/E1
Võrts (lake), Est. 60/E4
Võru, Est. 39/M3
Vorya (riv.), Rus. 61/X8
Vosburg, SAfr. 106/C3
Vösendorf, Aus. 49/N7
Vosges (dept.), Fr. 56/C1
Vosges (mts.), Fr. 40/D5
Voskresensk, Rus. 60/H5
Voss, Nor. 38/B1
Vostok (isl.), Kiri. 117/K6
Vostok (cape), Ant. 160/V
Vostok, Rus., Ant. 160/H
Votice, Czh. 55/H3
Votkinsk, Rus. 61/M4
Votkinsk (res.), Rus. 61/M4
Votorantim, Braz. 155/C2
Votuporanga, Braz. 155/B2
Vouga (riv.), Port. 44/A2
Vouglans (lake), Fr. 56/B5
Vouglans, Barrage de (dam), Fr. 56/B5
Voujeaucourt, Fr. 56/C3
Voúla, Gre. 47/N9
Voulangis, Fr. 30/L5
Vouvry, Swi. 56/C5
Voúxa (cape), Gre. 47/H5
Vouziers, Fr. 53/D5
Voy-Vozh, Rus. 61/M3
Voyageurs NP, Mn, US 130/A1
Voyeykov Ice Shelf, Ant. 160/J
Voytolovka (riv.), Rus. 61/T7
Vozhe (lake), Rus. 60/H3
Voznesens'k, Ukr. 49/K2
Vozrozhdeniya (isl.), Uzb. 87/C4
Vrå, Den. 38/C3
Vraine (riv.), Fr. 56/B1
Vrancea (prov.), Rom. 49/H3
Vrangelya (isl.), Rus. 67/T2
Vranjska Banja, Yugo. 47/G1
Vranov nad Teplou, Slvk. 41/L4
Vrapčište, Macd. 47/G2
Vratsa, Bul. 47/H1
Vrbas, Yugo. 48/D3
Vrbas (riv.), Bosn. 48/C3
Vrchy (peak), Czh. 55/H4
Vrede, SAfr. 106/E2
Vredefort, SAfr. 106/D2
Vreden, Ger. 50/D4
Vredenburg-Saldanha, SAfr. 106/K10
Vredendal, SAfr. 106/B3
Vresse-sur-Semois, Belg. 53/D4
Vrhnika, Slov. 43/L4
Vries, Neth. 50/D2
Vriezenveen, Neth. 50/D4
Vrigstad, Swe. 38/F3
Vrin (riv.), Fr. 40/B5
Vrindāban, India 84/A2
Vrnjačka Banja, Yugo. 48/E4
Vrondádhos, Gre. 47/K3
Vršac, Yugo. 48/E3
Vryburg, SAfr. 106/D2
Vryheid, SAfr. 107/E2
Vsetín, Czh. 41/K4
Vsevidof (mt.), Ak, US 134/E5
Vsevolozhsk, Rus. 61/T6
Vtáčnik (peak), Slvk. 41/K4
Vught, Neth. 50/C5
Vukovar, Cro. 48/D3
Vulcan, Ab, Can. 126/E3
Vulcan, Rom. 49/F3
Vulcano (isl.), It. 46/D3
Vŭlchedrŭm, Bul. 49/F4
Vŭlchi Dol, Bul. 49/H4
Vulci (ruin), It. 46/B1
Vung Tau, Viet. 78/D4
Vuohijärvi (lake), Fin. 39/M1
Vuollerim, Swe. 37/G2
Vuoska (lake), Rus. 39/N1
Vuotso, Fin. 60/E1
Vŭrbitsa, Bul. 47/K1
Vuria (peak), Kenya 104/C3
Vŭrshets, Bul. 49/F4
Vyāra, India 89/K4
Vyatka (riv.), Rus. 64/E4
Vyatskiye Polyany, Rus. 61/L4
Vyazemskiy, Rus. 71/P2
Vyaz'ma, Rus. 60/G5
Vyborg, Rus. 39/N1
Vyborg (bay), Rus. 39/N1
Vychegda (riv.), Rus. 64/F3
Východočeský (pol. reg.), Czh. 41/H3
Vychodoslovensky (pol. reg.), Slvk. 41/L4
Vygozero (lake), Rus. 60/G3
Vyhorlat (peak), Slvk. 41/M4
Vyksa, Rus. 60/J5
Vym' (riv.), Rus. 61/L3
Vynohradiv, Ukr. 41/M4
Vyrnwy (riv.), Wal, UK 32/C1
Vyshniy Volochek, Rus. 60/G4
Vyškov, Czh. 41/J4

W

W du Benin, PN du, Ben. 103/F4
W du Burkino Faso, PN du, Burk. 103/F4
W du Niger, PN du, Ben. 96/F5
W du Niger, PN du, Niger 103/F3
W. J. van Blommestein (lake), Sur. 151/G2
Wa, Gha. 103/E4
Waal, Ger. 57/G2
Waal (riv.), Neth. 50/C5
Waalre, Neth. 50/C6
Waalwijk, Neth. 50/C5
Waarschoot, Belg. 52/C1
Wabasca, Ab, Can. 126/E2
Wabasca (riv.), Ab, Can. 122/E3
Wabash, In, US 130/C3
Wabash (riv.), Il,In, US 125/J4
Wabē Shebelē Wenz (riv.), Eth. 93/G4
Wabern, Ger. 51/G6
Wabigoon (lake), Can. 127/K3
Wabowden, Mb, Can. 127/J2
Wąbrzeźno, Pol. 41/K2
Wabu (lake), China 72/D4
Wabu, SKor. 73/G6
Wachenheim an der Weinstrasse, Ger. 54/B4
Wachi, Japan 77/H5
Wachtebeke, Belg. 52/C1
Wachtendonk, Ger. 50/D6
Wächtersbach, Ger. 54/C2
Wackernheim, Ger. 54/B3
Wackersdorf, Ger. 55/F4
Waco, Tx, US 129/H5
Waconda (lake), US 129/H3
Waconia, Mn, US 127/K4
Wad Medanī, Sudan 88/B6
Wada, Japan 77/E3
Wadayama, Japan 77/G5
Wadbilliga NP, Austl. 115/D3
Waddān, Libya 96/J2
Waddell, Az, US 137/R18
Waddell (dam), Az, US 137/R18
Waddenzee (sound), Neth. 40/C2
Waddington (mt.), BC, Can. 126/B3
Waddinxveen, Neth. 50/B4
Waddy (pt.), Austl. 114/D4
Wadena, Sk, Can. 127/H3
Wadena, Mn, US 127/K4
Wädenswil, Swi. 57/E3
Wadern, Ger. 53/F4
Wadersloh, Ger. 51/F5
Wadgassen, Ger. 53/F5
Wādī al Layl, Tun. 100/M6
Wādī As Sīr, Jor. 91/D4
Wādī Majardah (riv.), Tun. 46/A4
Wādī Mūsá, Jor. 91/D4
Wading (riv.), NJ, US 138/D4
Wading River, NY, US 139/F2
Wadowice, Pol. 41/K4
Wadsworth, Il, US 135/Q15
Waegwan, SKor. 73/E5
Wafangdian, China 73/A3
Wagenfeld-Hasslingen, Ger. 51/F3
Wageningen, Neth. 50/C5
Wager (bay), NW, Can. 119/H3
Wagga Wagga, Austl. 115/C2
Waggaman, La, US 137/P17
Waghäusel, Ger. 54/B4
Wagin, Austl. 112/C5
Waging am See, Ger. 55/F7
Waginger (lake), Ger. 55/F7
Wägitaler-see (lake), Swi. 57/E3
Wagna, Aus. 43/L3
Wagner, Braz. 154/B4
Wągrowiec, Pol. 41/J2
Wagstaff, Ks, US 137/D6
Wāh, Pak. 86/B3
Wah Wah (range), Ut, US 128/D3
Wahiawa, Hi, US 124/V12
Wahlern, Swi. 56/D4
Wahpeton, ND, US 127/J4
Wahrenholz, Ger. 51/H3
Wai, India 82/B4
Waialee, Hi, US 124/V12
Waialua, Hi, US 124/V12
Waianae, Hi, US 124/V13
Waiau (riv.), NZ 117/S11
Waibamiao, China 72/D2
Waiblingen, Ger. 54/C5
Waidhaus, Ger. 55/F3
Waidhofen an der Thaya, Aus. 43/L2
Waidhofen an der Ybbs, Aus. 55/H7
Waigeo (isl.), Indo. 116/C4
Waigolshausen, Ger. 54/D3
Waihou (riv.), NZ 117/T10
Waikane, Hi, US 124/W12
Waikari, NZ 117/S11
Waikato (riv.), NZ 109/H6
Waikerie, Austl. 113/H5

Waikiki, Hi, US 124/W13
Waikoloa Village, Hi, US 124/U11
Wailuku, Hi, US 124/T10
Waimanalo, Hi, US 124/W13
Waimanalo Beach, Hi, US 124/W13
Waimate, NZ 117/S11
Waimea, Hi, US 124/S10
Waimea (falls), Hi, US 124/V12
Waimes, Belg. 53/F3
Wainfleet, On, Can. 131/R10
Waingangā (riv.), India 82/C3
Waini (riv.), Guy. 153/G2
WaiNWRight, Ak, US 134/F1
Wainwright, Ab, Can. 126/F2
Waipahu, Hi, US 124/V13
Waipio, Hi, US 124/U10
Waipio Acres, Hi, US 124/V13
Waipukurau, NZ 117/T10
Wairau (riv.), NZ 117/S11
Wairoa, NZ 117/T10
Waischenfeld, Ger. 55/E3
Waitaki (riv.), NZ 117/S11
Waitara, NZ 117/S10
Waizenkirchen, Aus. 55/G6
Wajima, Japan 75/E2
Waka (cape), Indo. 81/G4
Wakakusa, Japan 77/A2
Wakasa, Japan 74/D3
Wakasa (bay), Japan 77/H4
Wakaw, Sk, Can. 127/G2
Wakayama, Japan 74/D3
Wakayama (pref.), Japan 74/D4
Wake (isl.), Pac., US 116/F3
Wakefield, Mi, US 130/B2
Wakefield, Eng, UK 35/G4
Wakema, Myan. 83/G4
Waki, Japan 74/D3
Wakkanai, Japan 76/B1
Wakool, Austl. 115/C2
Wakuya, Japan 76/B4
Wakwayowkastic (riv.), Can. 130/D1
Wala (riv.), Tanz. 104/B4
Walachia (reg.), Rom. 49/G3
Walagunya Abor. Land, Austl. 112/D2
Wałbrzych, Pol. 41/J3
Wałbrzych (prov.), Pol. 41/J3
Walbury (hill), Eng, UK 33/E4
Walcha, Austl. 115/D1
Walcheren (isl.), Neth. 50/A5
Walcourt, Belg. 53/D3
Wałcz, Pol. 41/J2
Wald, Swi. 57/E3
Wald, Ger. 55/F4
Waldbillig, Lux. 53/F4
Waldbreitbach, Ger. 53/G2
Waldbröl, Ger. 53/G2
Waldbronn, Ger. 54/B5
Waldbrunn, Ger. 54/C3
Waldburg, Ger. 57/F2
Walden, Co, US 129/F2
Waldenbuch, Ger. 54/C5
Waldenburg, Swi. 56/D3
Waldenburg, Ger. 54/C4
Waldershof, Ger. 55/F3
Waldesch, Ger. 53/G3
Waldheim, Sk, Can. 126/G2
Waldighofen, Fr. 56/D2
Walding, Aus. 55/H6
Waldkirch, Ger. 56/D1
Waldmünchen, Ger. 55/F4
Waldnaab (riv.), Ger. 55/F3
Waldrach, Ger. 53/F4
Waldron, Mo, US 137/D5
Waldsassen, Ger. 55/F3
Waldshut-Tiengen, Ger. 57/E2
Waldstetten, Ger. 54/C5
Waldviertel (reg.), Aus. 41/H4
Waldwick, NJ, US 139/J8
Walea (str.), Indo. 81/F4
Waleabahi (isl.), Indo. 81/F4
Walensee (lake), Swi. 57/F3
Walenstadt, Swi. 57/F3
Wales, Ak, US 134/E2
Wales, UK 32/B3
Wales (isl.), NW, Can. 123/H2
Wales, Wi, US 135/P14
Walferdange, Lux. 53/F4
Walgett, Austl. 115/D1
Walhalla, ND, US 127/J3
Walhalla, SC, US 133/H3
Walhalla, Ger. 55/F4
Walker (riv.), Nv, US 128/C3
Walker (lake), US 128/C3
Walker (bay), SAfr. 106/L11
Walkerston, Austl. 114/C3
Walkerton, On, Can. 130/D2
Walkill (riv.), NY, US 138/D1
Walla Walla, Austl. 115/C2
Walla Walla, Wa, US 126/D4
Wallace, Id, US 126/E4
Wallaceburg, On, Can. 130/D3
Wallaroo, Austl. 113/H5
Wallasey, Eng, UK 35/E5
Walldorf, Ger. 54/B4
Walldürn, Ger. 54/C3
Walled (lake), Mi, US 135/F6
Walled City Hist. Site, SKor. 73/G7
Walled Lake, Mi, US 135/F6
Wallenhorst, Ger. 51/F4
Wallern im Burgenland, Aus. 43/M3
Wallers, Fr. 52/C3
Wallersee (lake), Aus. 55/G7
Wallerstein, Ger. 54/D5
Wallington, NJ, US 139/J8
Wallis (isls.), Wall. 117/H6
Wallis and Futuna (dpcy.), Fr. 116/G6
Wallisellen, Swi. 57/E3
Walloon Brabant (prov.), Belg. 53/D2
Wallowa (mts.), Or, US 126/D4
Wallsend, Eng, UK 35/G2
Wallumbilla, Austl. 114/C4
Walney, Isle of (isl.), Eng, UK 35/E3
Walnut, Ca, US 136/G7
Walnut Canyon Nat'l Mon., Az, US 128/E4
Walnut Creek, Ca, US 135/K11
Walnut Grove, Ca, US 135/L10
Walnut Park, Ca, US 136/F8
Walnut Ridge, Ar, US 129/K3
Walnutport, Pa, US 138/C2
Walpole, Austl. 112/C5
Walpole-Nornalup NP, Austl. 112/C5
Walrus (isls.), Ak, US 134/F4
Walsall, Eng, UK 32/E1
Walsenburg, Co, US 129/F3
Walsingham (cape), NW, Can. 123/K2
Walsrode, Ger. 51/G3
Waltenhofen, Ger. 57/G2
Walter F. George (res.), US 133/G4
Walterboro, SC, US 133/H3
Walter's Ash, Eng, UK 30/A2
Waltham Abbey, Eng, UK 30/D1
Waltham Forest (bor.), Eng, UK 30/A1
Walton-on-Thames, Eng, UK 30/B2
Waltrop, Ger. 51/E5
Walvis Bay, Namb. 105/B5
Walworth, Wi, US 135/N14
Walworth (co.), Wi, US 135/N14
Walyahmoning (peak), Austl. 112/C4
Walyunga NP, Austl. 112/L6
Walzenhausen, Swi. 57/F3
Wamba, Kenya 104/C2
Wamba, D.R. Congo 97/L7
Wamel, Neth. 50/C5
Wami (riv.), Tanz. 104/C4
Wampool (riv.), Eng, UK 35/E2
Wamsutter, Wy, US 126/G5
Wanaka, NZ 117/R11
Wanamassa, NJ, US 138/D3
Wanaque (res.), NJ, US 138/D1
Wanaque, NJ, US 139/H7
Wanda (mts.), China 71/P2
Wanda, Il, US 137/G8
Wandering, Austl. 112/C5
Wanding, China 83/G3
Wando, SKor. 73/D5
Wandoan, Austl. 114/C4
Wandsworth (bor.), Eng, UK 30/C2
Wanfried, Ger. 51/H6
Wang (riv.), Thai. 83/G4
Wang Hip (peak), Thai. 78/B4
Wanganui, NZ 117/T10
Wangaratta, Austl. 115/C3
Wangdu, China 72/C3
Wangen, Ger. 57/F2
Wangen an der Aare, Swi. 56/D3
Wangen bei Olten, Swi. 56/D3
Wangerooge (isl.), Ger. 51/E1
Wanggamet (peak), Indo. 81/F6
Wanghai Shan (peak), China 73/A2
Wängi, Swi. 57/E3
Wangjiang, China 79/C1
Wangpan (bay), China 72/E5
Wani (peak), Indo. 81/F4
Wanica (dist.), Sur. 153/H3
Wank (peak), Ger. 57/H2
Wanning, China 83/K4
Wanouchi, Japan 77/L5
Wanquan, China 72/C2
Wanrong, China 72/B4
Wansbeck (riv.), Eng, UK 35/G1
Wantagh, NY, US 139/M9
Wanxian, China 70/J5
Wanze, Belg. 53/E2
Wapakoneta, Oh, US 130/C3
Wapawekka (lake), Can. 127/G2
Wapiti (riv.), Can. 126/D2
Wapoga (riv.), Indo. 81/J4
Wappapello (lake), Mo, US 129/K3
Wapsipinicon (riv.), Ia, US 127/K5
Wapwallopen, Pa, US 138/B1
Warabi, Japan 77/D2
Warangal, India 82/C4
Waratah, Austl. 115/C4
Warburg, Ger. 51/G6
Warburton, Pak. 86/B4
Warburton, Austl. 112/E3
Warburton Range Abor. Rsv., Austl. 112/E3
Warche (riv.), Belg. 53/F3
Ward, Co, US 137/A2
Ward, NZ 117/S11
Ward Cove, Ak, US 134/M4
Warden, SAfr. 106/E2
Warden (pt.), Eng, UK 33/G4
Wardenburg, Ger. 51/F2
Wardha, India 82/C3
Ward's Stone (peak), Eng, UK 35/F3
Ware, Eng, UK 33/F3
Waregem, Belg. 52/C2
Waremme, Belg. 53/E2
Waren, Ger. 38/E5
Warendorf, Ger. 51/E5
Waretown, NJ, US 138/D4
Warffum, Neth. 50/D2
Wargrave, Eng, UK 33/F4
Warialda, Austl. 115/D1
Warin Chamrap, Thai. 78/D3
Waringstown, NI, UK 34/B3
Warka, Pol. 41/L3
Warkworth, NZ 117/S10
Warlingham, Eng, UK 30/C3
Warmbad, Namb. 106/B3
Warme Bode (riv.), Ger. 51/H5
Warmebach (riv.), Ger. 51/G6
Warmenhuizen, Neth. 50/B3
Warmeriville, Fr. 53/D5
Warmia (reg.), Pol. 41/K1
Warminster, Eng, UK 32/D4
Warminster, Pa, US 138/C3
Warner (mts.), Ca, US 126/C5
Warner Robins, Ga, US 133/H3
Warnow (riv.), Ger. 38/D5
Warnsveld, Neth. 50/D4
Waroona, Austl. 112/B5
Warr Acres, Ok, US 137/M14
Warrabri, Austl. 113/G2
Warrandirinna (lake), Austl. 113/H3
Warrego (range), Austl. 109/D3
Warrego (riv.), Austl. 109/D3
Warren (pt.), Can. 134/M2
Warren, Austl. 115/C1
Warren, Mn, US 127/J3
Warren, Oh, US 130/D3
Warren, Pa, US 130/E3
Warren, Ar, US 129/J4
Warren, Mi, US 130/D3
Warren, Ut, US 137/J11
Warren (riv.), Austl. 112/C5
Warren, NJ, US 138/D2
Warren (co.), NJ, US 138/C2
Warrenpoint, NI, UK 34/B3
Warrensburg, Mo, US 129/J3
Warrenton, SAfr. 106/D3
Warrenville, Il, US 135/P16
Warri, Nga. 103/G5
Warrington, Fl, US 133/G4
Warrington, Eng, UK 35/F5
Warrnambool, Austl. 115/B3
Warroad, Mn, US 127/K3
Warrumbungle NP, Austl. 115/D1
Warsaw, In, US 130/C3
Warsaw (Warszawa) (cap.), Pol. 41/L2
Warscheneck (peak), Aus. 48/B2
Warsop, Eng, UK 35/G5
Warstein, Ger. 51/F6
Warszawa (prov.), Pol. 41/L2
Warta (riv.), Pol. 62/A1
Wartberg an der Krems, Aus. 55/H7
Wartberg ob der Aist, Aus. 55/H6
Wartburg, Il, US 137/G9
Warwick, RI, US 131/G3
Warwick, Ok, US 137/N14
Warwick, Eng, UK 33/E2
Warwick, Austl. 114/D5
Warwick, NY, US 138/D1
Warwick, Md, US 138/C5
Warwickshire (co.), Eng, UK 33/E2
Wasatch (co.), Ut, US 137/K12
Wasatch (range), Ut, US 124/D4
Wasbank, SAfr. 107/E3
Wasburn (riv.), Eng, UK 35/G4
Wasco, Ca, US 128/C4
Waseca, Mn, US 127/K4
Wash, The (bay), Eng, UK 35/J6
Washburn (lake), NW, Can. 122/F1
Washimiya, Japan 77/D1
Washington, Il, US 127/L5
Washington (isl.), Wi, US 127/M4
Washington, NC, US 133/J3
Washington, Pa, US 130/D3
Washington (mt.), NH, US 131/G2
Washington, NJ, US 138/D2
Washington (state), US 124/B2
Washington (cap.), US 138/A6
Washington (lake), Wa, US 135/C2
Washington, Eng, UK 35/G2
Washington Dulles (int'l arpt.), Va, US 130/E4
Washington Park, Il, US 137/G8
Washington Terrace, Ut, US 137/K11
Washingtonville, Pa, US 138/B1
Washita (riv.), US 129/H4
Washtenaw (co.), Mi, US 135/E7
Wasilków, Pol. 41/M2
Wasilla, Ak, US 134/J3
Waskaganish (Rupert House), Qu, Can. 130/E1
Waskasa (bay), Japan 74/D3
Waskey (mt.), Ak, US 134/G4
Waspán, Nic. 145/F3
Wasselonne, Fr. 53/G6
Wassen, Swi. 57/E4
Wassenaar, Neth. 50/B4
Wassenberg, Ger. 53/F1
Wasserbillig, Lux. 53/F4
Wasserburg, Ger. 54/D6
Wasserburg am Inn, Ger. 55/F6
Wasserkuppe (peak), Ger. 54/C2
Wassuk (range), Nv, US 124/C4
Wassy, Fr. 56/A1
Wast Water (lake), Eng, UK 35/E3
Wasur-Rawa Biru NP, Indo. 81/K5
Waswanipi (lake), Can. 130/E1
Wat Phu, Laos 78/D3
Watampone, Indo. 81/F4
Watarai, Japan 77/L7
Watarase (riv.), Japan 75/F2
Watari, Japan 75/G1
Watch Hill (pt.), RI, US 139/G1
Watchung, NJ, US 139/H9
Watchung (mts.), NJ, US 139/H9
Water of Ae (riv.), Sc, UK 34/E1
Water of Girvan (riv.), Sc, UK 36/B6
Water of Ken (riv.), Sc, UK 34/D1
Waterbury, Ct, US 130/F3
Wateree (lake), SC, US 133/H3
Wateree (riv.), SC, US 133/H3
Waterford, Mi, US 130/D3
Waterford, Ire. 31/Q10
Waterford, Ct, US 139/F1
Waterford Works, NJ, US 138/D4
Watergate (bay), Eng, UK 32/A6
Waterhen (riv.), Can. 126/F2
Waterhen (lake), Can. 127/J2
Waterloo, On, Can. 130/D3
Waterloo, Il, US 137/G9
Waterloo, Ok, US 137/M14
Waterloo, Belg. 53/D2
Waterloo Battlesite, Belg. 53/D2
Waterloo Village, NJ, US 138/D2
Watermael-Boitsfort, Belg. 52/D2
Waterton Lakes NP, Can. 126/E3
Waterton Lks. Nat'l Pk., Ab, Can. 122/E4
Watertown, SD, US 127/J4
Watertown, NY, US 130/F3
Waterville, Wa, US 126/C4
Waterville, Me, US 131/G2
Waterville, Ire. 30/N11
Waterway, La, US 137/P17
Watford, Eng, UK 30/B1
Watford City, ND, US 127/H4
Wath-upon-Dearne, Eng, UK 35/G4
Watheroo NP, Austl. 112/B4
Watkins, Co, US 137/C3
Watonwan (riv.), Mn, US 129/J1
Watowato (peak), Indo. 81/G3
Watrous, Sk, Can. 127/G3
Watsa, D.R. Congo 104/A2
Watseka, Il, US 130/C3
Watson Lake, Yk, Can. 124/AA13
Watsontown, Pa, US 138/B1
Watsonville, Ca, US 128/B3
Watten, Fr. 52/B2
Wattenberg, Co, US 137/C2
Wattenheim, Ger. 54/B3
Wattens, Aus. 57/H3
Wattignies, Fr. 52/C2
Wattrelos, Fr. 52/C2
Wattwil, Swi. 57/F3
Wauchope, Austl. 115/E1
Wauchula, Fl, US 133/H5
Wauconda, Il, US 135/P15
Waukarlycarly (lake), Austl. 109/B3
Waukesha, Wi, US 129/K2
Waukesha (co.), Wi, US 135/P14
Waun Fâch (peak), Wal, UK 32/C3
Waun-Oer (peak), Wal, UK 32/C1
Wauna, Wa, US 135/B3
Waupun, Wi, US 127/L5
Waurika, Ok, US 129/H4
Wauseon, Oh, US 130/C3
Waveney (riv.), Eng, UK 33/H2
Waver (riv.), Eng, UK 35/E2
Wavre, Belg. 53/D2
Wavrin, Fr. 52/B2
Wāw, Sudan 97/L6
Wawa (riv.), Nic. 145/E3
Wawagosic (riv.), Can. 130/E1
Wawasang (peak), Nic. 145/E3
Wawayanda State Park, NJ, US 138/D1
Waxahachie, Tx, US 129/H4
Waycross, Ga, US 133/H4
Wayne, Ne, US 127/J5
Wayne (co.), Pa, US 138/C3
Wayne, Pa, US 138/C3
Wayne, NJ, US 139/J8
Wayne, Mi, US 135/F7
Wayne, Il, US 135/P16
Waynesboro, Pa, US 130/E4
Waynesboro, Ms, US 133/F4
Waynesboro, Ga, US 133/H3
Waynesville, NC, US 133/H3
Waynesville, Mo, US 129/J3
Waziers, Fr. 52/C3
Wazīrābād, Pak. 86/C3
Wazuka, Japan 77/J6
Wda (riv.), Pol. 41/K2
Weald, The (grsld.), Eng, UK 33/F4
Wear (riv.), Eng, UK 35/F2
Weatherby Lake, Mo, US 137/D5
Weatherford, Tx, US 132/D3
Weatherly, Pa, US 138/C2
Weaver (riv.), Eng, UK 35/F5
Weaverville, Ca, US 128/B2
Weber (co.), Ut, US 137/J11
Weber (riv.), Ut, US 137/J11
Weber Hill, Mo, US 137/F9
Webi Jubba (riv.), Som. 93/G4
Webster, SD, US 127/J4
Webster City, Ia, US 127/K5
Webster Groves, Mo, US 137/G8
Weddell (isl.), Mald. 159/E6
Weddell (sea) 160/X
Wedderburn, Austl. 115/B3
Weddin Mountains NP, Austl. 115/C2
Wedel, Ger. 51/G1
Wedemark, Ger. 51/G3
Wee Waa, Austl. 115/D1
Weed, Ca, US 128/B2
Weehawken, NJ, US 139/J8
Weekapaug, RI, US 139/G1
Weenen, SAfr. 107/E3
Weerselo, Neth. 50/D4
Weert, Neth. 50/C6
Weesen, Swi. 57/F3
Weesp, Neth. 50/C4
Wegberg, Ger. 53/F1
Weggis, Swi. 57/E3
Węgorzewo, Pol. 39/J4
Węgrów, Pol. 41/M2
Wegscheid, Ger. 55/G5
Wehingen, Ger. 57/E1
Wehr, Ger. 56/D2
Wehra (riv.), Ger. 56/D2
Wehre (riv.), Ger. 51/G6
Wehrheim, Ger. 54/B2
Wei Xian, China 72/C3
Wei Xian, China 72/C3
Weibersbrunn, Ger. 54/C3
Weichang, China 71/L3
Weida, Ger. 43/K1
Weiden, Ger. 55/F3
Weidenthal, Ger. 54/A4
Weifang, China 72/D3
Weihai, China 73/B4
Weihenzell, Ger. 54/D4
Weikersheim, Ger. 54/C4
Weil (riv.), Ger. 54/B2
Weil der Stadt, Ger. 54/B5
Weilburg, Ger. 54/B2
Weiler-Simmerberg, Ger. 57/F2
Weilerswist, Ger. 53/F2
Weilheim, Ger. 57/H2
Weilheim an der Teck, Ger. 54/C5
Weilmünster, Ger. 54/B2
Weimar, Ger. 40/F3
Weinan, China 72/B4
Weinfelden, Swi. 57/F2
Weingarten, Ger. 57/F2
Weingarten, Ger. 54/B4
Weinheim, Ger. 54/B3
Weinsberg, Ger. 54/C4
Weinstadt, Ger. 54/C5
Weinviertel (reg.), Aus. 43/M2
Weirton, WV, US 130/D3
Weisendorf, Ger. 54/D3
Weisenheim am Berg, Ger. 54/B3
Weiser (riv.), Id, US 126/D4
Weishan, China 72/D4
Weishi, China 72/C4
Weiskirchen, Ger. 53/F4
Weismain, Ger. 54/E2
Weiss (lake), US 133/G3
Weissach, Ger. 54/B5
Weisse Elster (riv.), Ger. 40/G3
Weisse Laber (riv.), Ger. 55/E4
Weissenbach am Lech, Aus. 57/G3
Weissenburg im Bayern, Ger. 54/D4
Weissenfels, Ger. 40/F3
Weissenhorn, Ger. 57/G1
Weissenstadt, Ger. 55/E2
Weissenthurm, Ger. 53/G3
Weisser (peak), Ger. 53/F3
Weisser Main (riv.), Ger. 55/E2
Weisshorn (peak), Swi. 56/D5
Weissmies (peak), Swi. 56/D5
Weisswasser, Ger. 41/H3
Weistrach, Aus. 55/H6
Weitefeld, Ger. 53/G2
Weiterstadt, Ger. 54/B3
Weitra, Aus. 41/H4
Weixi, China 83/G2
Weiyuan, China 70/H4
Weiz, Aus. 43/L3
Weizhou (isl.), China 83/J3
Wejherowo, Pol. 38/H4
Welby, Co, US 137/C3
Welch, WV, US 130/D4
Welch (hill), Pa, US 138/A3
Weld (co.), Co, US 137/C2
Welden, Ger. 54/D6
Weldiya, Eth. 97/N5
Weldon Spring, Mo, US 137/F8
Welel (peak), Eth. 97/M6
Weligama, SrL. 82/D6
Welkenraedt, Belg. 53/E2
Welkom, SAfr. 106/D3
Welland (canal), Can. 131/R10
Welland, On, Can. 131/R10
Welland (riv.), Eng, UK 35/H6
Wellandport, On, Can. 131/R9
Wellen, Belg. 53/E2
Wellesley (isls.), Austl. 109/C2
Wellin, Belg. 53/E3
Wellingborough, Eng, UK 33/F2
Wellington (lake), Austl. 115/C3
Wellington, Austl. 115/D2
Wellington, Tx, US 129/G4
Wellington (int'l arpt.), NZ 117/S11
Wellington (cap.), NZ 117/S11
Wellington, Eng, UK 32/C5
Wellington (chan.), NW, Can. 123/S7
Wellington (isl.), Chile 147/B7
Wellington, SAfr. 106/L10
Wells, BC, Can. 126/C2
Wells, Nv, US 126/E5
Wells (lake), Austl. 109/B3
Wells, Eng, UK 32/D4
Wellston, Oh, US 130/D4
Wellston, Ok, US 137/N14
Wellsville, Pa, US 138/B3
Wellton, Az, US 128/D4
Wels, Aus. 55/H6
Welschbillig, Ger. 53/F4
Welshnofen (Nova Levante), It. 57/H5
Welshpool, Wal, UK 32/C1
Welty, Co, US 137/B2
Welver, Ger. 51/E5
Welzheim, Ger. 54/C5
Wembere (riv.), Tanz. 105/F1
Wembley, Ab, Can. 126/D2
Wembley Stadium, Eng, UK 30/C2
Wemding, Ger. 54/D5
Wemmel, Belg. 53/D2
Wemyss Bay, Sc, UK 36/B5
Wen Xian, China 72/C4
Wenatchee, Wa, US 126/C4
Wenchang, China 83/K4
Wencheng, China 79/D2
Wenchi, Gha. 103/E5
Wendeburg, Ger. 51/H4
Wenden, Ger. 53/G2
Wendeng, China 73/B4
Wendover, Nv, US 126/E5
Wendover, Eng, UK 33/F3
Wengyuan, China 83/K3
Wenling, China 79/D2
Wenlock Edge (ridge), Eng, UK 32/D2
Wenne (riv.), Ger. 51/F6
Wennigsen, Ger. 51/G4
Wenonah, NJ, US 138/C4
Wenshan, China 83/H3
Wenshang, China 72/D4
Wenshui, China 72/C3
Wensleydale (valley), Eng, UK 35/F3
Went (riv.), Eng, UK 35/G4
Wentworth, Austl. 115/B2
Wenxi, China 72/B4
Wenzhou, China 79/D2
Wepener, SAfr. 106/D3
Wer, India 84/A2
Werdau, Ger. 43/K1
Werdohl, Ger. 51/E6
Werkendam, Neth. 50/B5
Werl, Ger. 51/E5
Werlte, Ger. 51/E3
Wermelskirchen, Ger. 53/G1
Wern (riv.), Ger. 54/C3
Wernberg-Köblitz, Ger. 55/F3
Werne an der Lippe, Ger. 51/E5
Werneck, Ger. 54/D3
Wernigerode, Ger. 51/H5
Werong (mt.), Austl. 115/D2
Werra (riv.), Ger. 40/E3
Werre (riv.), Ger. 40/E2
Werrikimbe NP, Austl. 115/E1
Werris Creek, Austl. 115/D1
Werse (riv.), Ger. 51/E5
Wertach (riv.), Ger. 54/D6
Wertheim, Ger. 54/C3
Wertheim NWR, NY, US 139/F2
Werther, Ger. 51/F4
Wertingen, Ger. 54/D5
Wervershoof, Neth. 50/C3
Wervik, Belg. 52/C2
Weschnitz (riv.), Ger. 54/B3
Wesefgebirge (mts.), Ger. 51/F4
Wesel, Ger. 50/D5
Wesel-Datteln (canal), Ger. 51/E5
Weser (riv.), Ger. 40/E2
Weslaco, Tx, US 132/D5
Wesley Hills, NY, US 139/J7
Wessel (isls.), Austl. 109/C2
Wesselburen, Ger. 38/C4
Wesselsbron, SAfr. 106/D2
Wessex (reg.), Eng, UK 32/D4
Wessington Springs, SD, US 127/J4
West (pt.), Austl. 115/C4
West, Tx, US 129/H5
West (cape), NZ 117/R12
West (pt.), Wa, US 135/C2
West Allis, Wi, US 129/K2
West Alton, Mo, US 137/G8
West Babylon, NY, US 139/E2
West Bank 101/C2
West Bank (occ. zone), Isr. 90/C3
West Bank 91/G7
West Bank (ctry.) 91/D3
West Bend, Wi, US 127/L5
West Bengal (state), India 70/E7
West Bountiful, Ut, US 137/K12
West Branch, Mi, US 130/C2
West Bridgford, Eng, UK 35/G6
West Bromwich, Eng, UK 32/E1
West Caicos (isl.), UK 145/H1
West Calder, Sc, UK 36/C5
West Caldwell, NJ, US 139/H8
West Cap Howe NP, Austl. 112/C5
West Chester, Pa, US 138/C4
West Chicago, Il, US 135/P16
West Chyulu Game Consv. Area, Kenya 104/C3
West Coast NP, SAfr. 106/L10
West Columbia, SC, US 133/H3
West Covina, Ca, US 136/G7
West Creek, NJ, US 138/D4
West Elk (mts.), Co, US 132/B2
West End, Eng, UK 30/B3
West Falkland (isl.), Falk. 157/D7
West Fargo, ND, US 127/J4
West Fayu (isl.), Micr. 116/D4
West Frisian (isls.), Neth. 40/C2
West Glamorgan (co.), Wal, UK 32/C3
West Glen (riv.), Eng, UK 35/H6
West Grove, Pa, US 138/C4
West Haven, Ct, US 139/F1
West Haverstraw, NY, US 138/E1
West Helena, Ar, US 129/K4
West Hempstead, NY, US 139/L9
West Hills, NY, US 139/M8
West Hollywood, Ca, US 136/F7
West Humber (riv.), Can. 131/Q8
West Ice Shelf, Ant. 160/F
West Indies (isls.), NAm. 119/L7
West Islet (isl.), Austl. 109/E3
West Islip, NY, US 139/E2
West Jordan, Ut, US 137/K12
West Kilbride, Sc, UK 36/B5
West Kingsdown, Eng, UK 30/D3
West Knock (peak), Sc, UK 36/D3
West Lamma (chan.), China 71/U11
West Lincoln, Ne, US 129/H2
West Lunga NP, Zam. 105/D3
West Memphis, Ar, US 129/K4
West Midlands (co.), Eng, UK 33/E1
West Milford, NJ, US 139/H7
West Milton, Pa, US 138/B1
West Monroe, La, US 129/J4
West New York, NJ, US 139/J8
West Nyack, NY, US 139/K7
West Orange, NJ, US 139/J8
West Palm Beach, Fl, US 133/H5
West Paterson, NJ, US 139/J8
West Pensacola, Fl, US 133/G4
West Plains, Mo, US 129/K3
West Point, Ne, US 127/J5
West Point (lake), US 133/G3
West Point, Ms, US 133/F3
West Point, Ut, US 137/J11
West Reading, Pa, US 138/C3
West Redding, Ct, US 139/E1
West Road (riv.), Can. 126/B2
West Sacramento, Ca, US 135/L9
West Sayville, NY, US 139/E2
West Seneca, NY, US 131/S10
West Siberian (plain), Rus. 64/H3
West Sussex (co.), Eng, UK 33/F4
West-Terschelling, Neth. 50/C2
West Valley City, Ut, US 137/K12
West Vancouver, BC, Can. 126/C3
West Virginia (state), US 125/K4
West Warren, Ut, US 137/J11
West Water (riv.), Sc, UK 36/D3
West Weber, Ut, US 137/J11
West Wyalong, Austl. 115/C2
West York, Pa, US 138/B4
West Yorkshire (co.), Eng, UK 35/G4
Westall (pt.), Austl. 113/G5
Westbrook, Ct, US 139/F1
Westbury, NY, US 139/L9
Westchester (co.), NY, US 139/E1
Westcott, Eng, UK 30/B3
Westerbork, Neth. 50/D3
Westerburg, Ger. 53/G2
Westerham, Eng, UK 30/D3
Westerheim, Ger. 57/G1
Westerholt, Ger. 51/E1
Westerkappeln, Ger. 51/E4
Westerland, Ger. 38/C4
Westerlo, Belg. 53/D1
Western (prov.), Kenya 104/B2
Western (des.), Egypt 97/L2
Western (prov.), Ugan. 104/A2
Western (pol. reg.), Gha. 103/E5
Western (chan.), SKor. 74/A3
Western Area (prov.), SLeo. 102/B4
Western Australia (state), Austl. 109/B3
Western Cape (prov.), SAfr. 106/C4
Western Ghats (mts.), India 89/K5
Western Run (riv.), Md, US 138/B4
Western Sahara 93/A2
Western Sayans (mts.), Rus. 64/J4
Westerschelde (chan.), Belg. 50/A6
Westerstede, Ger. 51/E2
Westerville, Oh, US 130/D3
Westervoort, Neth. 50/C5
Westerwald (mts.), Ger. 40/D3
Westfield, NJ, US 139/H9
Westgat (chan.), Neth. 50/D2
Westhampton, NY, US 139/F2
Westhampton Beach, NY, US 139/F2
Westhausen, Ger. 54/D5
Westheim, Ger. 54/B4
Westhill, Sc, UK 36/D2
Westhofen, Ger. 54/B3
Westhoughton, Eng, UK 35/F4
Westkapelle, Neth. 50/A5
Westlake Village, Ca, US 136/B2
Westland, Mi, US 135/F7
Westland NP, NZ 117/R11
Westminster, Co, US 137/B3
Westminster, Md, US 138/B4
Westminster, Ca, US 136/F8
Westminster, City of (bor.), Eng, UK 30/A1
Westmont (Haddon), NJ, US 138/C4
Westmorland (reg.), Eng, UK 35/F3
Westmount, Qu, Can. 131/N7
Weston, Mo, US 137/D5
Weston, Ct, US 139/E1
Weston-super-Mare, Eng, UK 32/D4
Westonaria, SAfr. 106/P13
Westport, Ire. 31/P10
Westport, NZ 117/S11
Westport, Ct, US 139/E1
Westray (isl.), Sc, UK 31/V14
Westview, Il, US 137/G8
Westwego, La, US 137/P17
Westwood, Ks, US 137/D5
Westwood, NJ, US 139/J8
Wet (mts.), Co, US 132/B2
Wetar (str.), Indo. 81/G5
Wetar (isl.), Indo. 67/M10
Wetaskiwin, Ab, Can. 126/E2
Wete, Tanz. 104/C4
Wétetnagami (riv.), Can. 130/E1
Wetherell (lake), Austl. 115/B2
Wetter, Ger. 51/E6
Wetter (riv.), Ger. 54/B2
Wetterau (reg.), Ger. 54/C2
Wetteren, Belg. 52/C2
Wetterhorn (peak), Swi. 56/E4
Wettingen, Swi. 57/E3
Wettringen, Ger. 51/E4
Wetzikon, Swi. 57/E3
Wetzlar, Ger. 54/B1
Wetzstein (peak), Ger. 55/E2
Wevelgem, Belg. 52/C2
Wewak, PNG 116/D5
Wewoka, Ok, US 129/H4
Wexford, Ire. 31/Q10
Wey (riv.), Eng, UK 30/A3
Weybridge, Eng, UK 30/B2
Weyburn, Sk, Can. 127/H3
Weygand (ruin), Alg. 99/F4
Weyhausen, Ger. 51/H4
Weyland (pt.), Austl. 113/G5
Weymouth, Eng, UK 32/D5
Weymouth (bay), Eng, UK 32/D5
Whakatane, NZ 117/T10
Whale Cove, NW, Can. 122/G2
Whalsey (isl.), Sc, UK 31/W13
Whangarei, NZ 117/S10
Wharfe (riv.), Eng, UK 35/G3
Wheat Ridge, Co, US 137/B3
Wheatland, Wy, US 127/G5
Wheaton, Il, US 130/B3
Wheaton-Glenmont, Md, US 138/A5
Wheaton Village, NJ, US 138/C5
Wheeler (peak), Nv, US 128/D3
Wheeler (peak), NM, US 129/F3
Wheeler (lake), Al, US 133/G3
Wheeler Springs, Ca, US 136/A1
Wheeling, WV, US 130/D3
Wheeling, Il, US 135/Q15
Wheelwright, Arg. 158/E2
Whernside (peak), Eng, UK 35/F3
Whickham, Eng, UK 35/G2
Whidbey (pt.), Austl. 113/G5
Whinham (mt.), Austl. 113/F3
Whitburn, Sc, UK 36/C5
Whitby, On, Can. 131/S8
Whitby, Eng, UK 35/H3
White (lake), La, US 129/J5
White (riv.), US 129/J4
White (riv.), Tx, US 129/K2
White (riv.), SD, US 127/H5
White (lake), Austl. 109/B3
White (lake), Can. 130/C1
White (riv.), Can. 131/K1
White (riv.), In, US 130/C4
White (pass), Ak, US 134/L3
White (sea), Rus. 60/H2
White (bay), Nf, Can. 123/L3
White City, Sk, Can. 127/G3
White Cliffs, Austl. 115/B1
White Coomb (peak), Sc, UK 36/C6
White Esk (riv.), Sc, UK 36/C6
White Fox, Sk, Can. 127/G2
White Hall, Md, US 138/B4
White Haven, Pa, US 138/C1
White Marsh, Md, US 138/B5
White Mountain, Ak, US 134/F3
White Mountains Nat'l Rec. Area, Ak, US 134/J2
White Nile (riv.), Sudan 93/F4
White Oak, Md, US 138/B5
White Otter (lake), Can. 127/K3
White Plains, NY, US 139/K7
White River, On, Can. 130/C1
White Rock, NM, US 132/B3
White Sands, NM, US 128/F4
White Sands Nat'l Mon., NM, US 128/F4
White Sulphur Springs, Mt, US 126/F4
White Volta (riv.), Gha. 93/B4

White, West Fork (riv.), In, US 130/C4
Whiteadder Water (riv.), Sc, UK 36/D5
Whitecourt, Ab, Can. 126/E2
Whiteface (riv.), Mn, US 127/K4
Whitefield, Eng, UK 35/F4
Whitefish, Mt, US 126/E3
Whitefish (bay), US,Can. 130/C2
Whiteford (pt.), Wal, UK 32/B3
Whiteford, Md, US 138/B4
Whitehall, Mt, US 126/E4
Whitehall, Mi, US 130/C3
Whitehaven, Eng, UK 34/E2
Whitehead, NI, UK 34/C2
Whitehills, Sc, UK 36/D1
Whitehorse (cap.), Yk, Can. 134/L3
Whitehorse (hill), Eng, UK 33/E3
Whitehouse, Tx, US 129/J4
Whitemouth (riv.), Can. 127/K3
Whiteriver, Az, US 128/E4
Whiteside (chan.), Chile 159/C7
Whitesville, NJ, US 138/D3
Whiteville, NC, US 133/J3
Whitewater (lake), Can. 127/L3
Whitewood, Sk, Can. 127/H3
Whithorn, Sc, UK 34/D2
Whiting, In, US 135/R16
Whitley Bay, Eng, UK 35/G1
Whitmore Village, Hi, US 124/V12
Whitney (lake), Tx, US 129/H4
Whitney, Tx, US 129/H5
Whitsand (bay), Eng, UK 32/B6
Whitstable, Eng, UK 33/H4
Whitsunday (isl.), Austl. 109/D3
Whittaker, Mi, US 135/E7
Whittier, Ak, US 134/J3
Whittier, Ca, US 136/F8
Whittlesea, Austl. 115/G5
Whitton, Austl. 115/C2
Whitworth, Eng, UK 35/F4
Wholdaia (lake), NW, Can. 122/F2
Whyalla, Austl. 113/H5
Wi (isl.), SKor. 73/D5
Wiang Kosai NP, Thai. 78/B2
Wiarton, On, Can. 130/D2
Wiawso, Gha. 103/E5
Wichabai, Guy. 153/G4
Wichelen, Belg. 52/C2
Wichita (riv.), Tx, US 129/H4
Wichita (mts.), Ok, US 129/H4
Wichita Falls, Tx, US 129/H4
Wick, Sc, UK 31/S7
Wickenburg, Az, US 128/D4
Wickepin, Austl. 112/C5
Wickford, Eng, UK 30/E2
Wickham, Austl. 112/C2
Wicklow (mts.), Ire. 31/Q10
Wicklow (pass), Ire. 34/B5
Wicklow, Ire. 34/B6
Wicklow (pt.), Ire. 34/B6
Wickriede (riv.), Ger. 51/F4
Wid (riv.), Eng, UK 30/E2
Widnau, Swi. 57/F3
Widnes, Eng, UK 35/F5
Więcbork, Pol. 41/J2
Wied (riv.), Ger. 43/G1
Wiedau (riv.), Ger. 51/G2
Wiefelstede, Ger. 51/F2
Wiehengebirge (ridge), Ger. 51/F4
Wiehl, Ger. 53/G2
Wielenbach, Ger. 57/H2
Wieliczka, Pol. 41/L4
Wielkopolski NP, Pol. 62/A1
Wielkopolski NP, Pol. 41/J2
Wielsbeke, Belg. 52/C2
Wieluń, Pol. 41/K3
Wien (riv.), Aus. 49/N7
Wien (prov.), Aus. 41/J4
Wien (Vienna) (cap.), Aus. 49/N7
Wiener Neudorf, Aus. 49/N7
Wiener Neustadt, Aus. 43/M3
Wienerwald (reg.), Aus. 49/N7
Wienwald (reg.), Aus. 43/L2
Wieprz (riv.), Pol. 62/B2
Wierden, Neth. 50/D4
Wieringermeerpolder (polder), Neth. 50/B3
Wieringerwerf, Neth. 50/C3
Wieruszów, Pol. 41/K3
Wiesbaden, Ger. 54/B2
Wiese (riv.), Ger. 43/G3
Wiese (isl.), Rus. 160/A
Wieseck (riv.), Ger. 54/B1
Wiesendangen, Swi. 57/E2
Wiesensteig, Ger. 54/C5
Wiesent (riv.), Ger. 54/E4
Wiesentheid, Ger. 54/D3
Wiesloch, Ger. 54/B4
Wiesmoor, Ger. 51/E2
Wietmarschen, Ger. 51/D4
Wietze, Ger. 51/G3
Wietze (riv.), Ger. 51/G3
Wietzendorf, Ger. 51/G3
Wiezyca (peak), Pol. 38/H4
Wigan, Eng, UK 35/F4
Wiggins, Ms, US 133/F4
Wight (isl.), UK 42/C1
Wigierski NP, Pol. 41/M1
Wignehies, Fr. 52/D3
Wigry (lake), Pol. 39/K5
Wigston, Eng, UK 33/E1
Wigtown, Sc, UK 34/D2
Wigtown (bay), Sc, UK 34/D2
Wijchen, Neth. 50/C5
Wijhe, Neth. 50/D4
Wijk bij Duurstede, Neth. 50/C5
Wil, Swi. 57/F3
Wilber, Ne, US 129/H2
Wilberforce, Austl. 114/G8
Wilbur, Wa, US 126/D4
Wilburton, Ok, US 129/J4
Wilcannia, Austl. 115/B1
Wilchingen, Swi. 57/E2
Wilczek (isl.), Rus. 64/G1
Wild (coast), SAfr. 106/E4
Wild Creek (res.), Pa, US 138/C2
Wild Rice (riv.), Mn, US 127/J4
Wild World, Md, US 138/B6
Wildau, Ger. 40/Q7
Wildbad im Schwarzwald, Ger. 54/B5
Wildberg, Ger. 54/B5
Wilder, Ks, US 137/D5
Wilderswil, Swi. 56/D4
Wildeshausen, Ger. 51/F3
Wildflecken, Ger. 54/C2
Wildgrat (peak), Aus. 57/G3
Wildhaus, Swi. 57/F3
Wildhorn (peak), Swi. 56/D5
Wildomar, Ca, US 136/C3
Wildspitze (peak), Aus. 57/G4
Wildstrubel (peak), Swi. 56/D5
Wildwood, NJ, US 138/D6
Wildwood Crest, NJ, US 138/D6
Wilge (riv.), SAfr. 106/E2
Wilhelm II (coast), Ant. 160/F
Wilhelmina (mts.), Sur. 150/G3
Wilhelminakanaal (canal), Neth. 50/C5
Wilhelmshaven, Ger. 51/F1
Wilhering, Aus. 55/H6
Wilkes-Barre, Pa, US 138/C1
Wilkes Land (phys. reg.), Ant. 160/J
Wilkesboro, NC, US 130/D4
Wilkeson, Wa, US 135/C3
Wilkie, Sk, Can. 126/F2
Wilkins (sound), Ant. 160/U
Will (mt.), Can. 134/N4
Will (co.), Il, US 135/P16
Willamette (riv.), Or, US 126/C4
Willandra NP, Austl. 115/C2
Willapa (bay), Wa, US 126/B4
Willard (bay), Ut, US 137/J11
Willard (res.), Ut, US 137/J11
Willard, Ut, US 137/J11
Willaura, Austl. 115/B3
Willcox, Az, US 128/E4
Willebadessen, Ger. 51/G5
Willebroek, Belg. 53/D1
Willemstad, Neth. 50/B5
Willemstad (cap.), NAnt. 152/D1
William (mt.), Austl. 115/B3
William B. Hartsfield Atlanta (int'l arpt.), Ga, US 133/G3
William Bay NP, Austl. 112/C5
Williams, Az, US 128/D4
Williams, Austl. 112/C5
Williams Lake, BC, Can. 126/C2
Williamsburg, Ky, US 130/C4
Williamsport, Pa, US 138/A1
Williamston, NC, US 133/J3
Williamstown, Pa, US 138/B2
Williamstown, NJ, US 138/D4
Williamsville, NY, US 131/S10
Willich, Ger. 50/D6
Willingboro, NJ, US 138/D3
Willingen, Ger. 51/F6
Willis, Tx, US 129/J5
Willis Islets (isls.), Austl. 109/E2
Willisau, Swi. 56/D3
Williston, ND, US 127/H3
Williston, Fl, US 133/H4
Williston, SAfr. 106/C3
Williston (lake), BC, Can. 122/D3
Williston Park, NY, US 139/L9
Willits, Ca, US 128/B3
Willmar, Mn, US 127/K4
Willow, Ak, US 134/H3
Willow (riv.), Can. 126/C2
Willow Bunch, Sk, Can. 127/G3
Willow Grove, Pa, US 138/C3
Willow Grove, De, US 138/C5
Willow Grove Naval Air Sta., Pa, US 138/C3
Willow River, BC, Can. 126/C2
Willow Street, Pa, US 138/B4
Willow Tree, Austl. 115/D1
Willowbrook, Ca, US 136/F8
Willowbrook, Il, US 135/P16
Willowmore, SAfr. 106/C4
Willows, Ca, US 128/B3
Wills (lake), Austl. 109/B3
Wills Point, La, US 137/Q17
Willstätt, Ger. 56/D1
Willunga, Austl. 113/H5
Wilmette, Il, US 135/Q15
Wilmington, NC, US 133/J3
Wilmington, Austl. 113/H5
Wilmington, De, US 138/C4
Wilmington Island, Ga, US 133/H4
Wilmslow, Eng, UK 35/F5
Wilnsdorf, Ger. 53/H2
Wilrijk, Belg. 50/B6
Wilseder (peak), Ger. 51/G2
Wilson, NC, US 133/J3
Wilson (co.), Tx, US 137/U21
Wilson, NY, US 131/S9
Wilson (mt.), Ca, US 136/B2
Wilson, Pa, US 138/C2
Wilson (cape), NW, Can. 123/H2
Wilsons Promontory (pen.), Austl. 109/D4
Wilsons Promontory NP, Austl. 115/C3
Wilsonville, Il, US 137/H7
Wilstedt, Ger. 51/G2
Wilster, Ger. 51/G1
Wilsum, Ger. 50/D3
Wilton, Eng, UK 33/E4
Wilton, Ct, US 139/E1
Wiltshire (co.), Eng, UK 33/E4
Wiltz, Lux. 53/E4
Wiltz (riv.), Lux. 53/E4
Wiluna, Austl. 112/D3
Wimborne Minster, Eng, UK 32/E5
Wimereux, Fr. 52/A2
Wimmis, Swi. 56/D4
Winam (gulf), Kenya 104/B3
Winburg, SAfr. 106/D3
Winchester, Ky, US 130/C4
Winchester, Tn, US 133/G3
Winchester, Ca, US 136/C3
Winchester, Eng, UK 33/E4
Winchester Mystery House, Ca, US 135/L12
Wind (riv.), Wy, US 126/F5
Wind (lake), Wi, US 135/P14
Wind Cave NP, SD, US 129/G2
Wind Gap, Pa, US 138/C2
Wind Lake, Wi, US 135/P14
Wind Point, Wi, US 135/Q14
Wind River (range), Wy, US 128/E2
Windach (riv.), Ger. 57/G2
Windach, Ger. 54/E6
Winder, Ga, US 133/H3
Windermere (lake), Eng, UK 35/F3
Windermere, Eng, UK 35/F3
Windesheim, Ger. 53/G4
Windhoek (cap.), Namb. 105/C5
Windlesham, Eng, UK 30/B2
Window Rock, Az, US 128/E4
Windrush (riv.), Eng, UK 33/E3
Windsbach, Ger. 54/D4
Windsor, Nf, Can. 131/L1
Windsor, NS, Can. 131/H2
Windsor, Qu, Can. 131/G2
Windsor, On, Can. 130/D3
Windsor, Co, US 137/C2
Windsor (res.), Co, US 137/C1
Windsor, Eng, UK 33/F4
Windsor, Pa, US 138/B4
Windward (isls.), StV. 141/J5
Windward Passage (passg.), Cuba,Haiti 119/K8
Winfield, BC, Can. 126/D3
Winfield, Ks, US 129/H3
Winfield, Pa, US 138/B2
Winfield, Md, US 138/A5
Wingene, Belg. 52/C1
Winger, On, Can. 131/R10
Wingham, Austl. 115/E1
Winifred (lake), Austl. 112/D2
Winifreda, Arg. 158/D3
Winisk (riv.), On, Can. 123/H3
Winkler, Mb, Can. 127/J3
Winneba, Gha. 103/E5
Winnebago (lake), Wi, US 127/L5
Winnenden, Ger. 54/C5
Winner, SD, US 127/J5
Winnetka, Il, US 135/Q15
Winnett, Mt, US 126/F4
Winnfield, La, US 129/J5
Winningen, Ger. 53/G3
Winnipeg (cap.), Mb, Can. 127/J3
Winnipeg (int'l arpt.), Can. 127/J3
Winnipeg (riv.), Can. 127/K3
Winnipeg (lake), Mb, Can. 119/H4
Winnipeg Beach, Mb, Can. 127/J3
Winnipegosis, Mb, Can. 127/J3
Winnipegosis (lake), Mb, Can. 119/G4
Winnsboro, La, US 129/K4
Winnsboro, SC, US 133/H3
Winnweiler, Ger. 53/G4
Winschoten, Neth. 50/E2
Winsford, Eng, UK 35/F5
Winslow, Az, US 128/E4
Winslow, NJ, US 138/D4
Winslow, Wa, US 135/B2
Winston-Salem, NC, US 133/H2
Winsum, Neth. 50/D2
Winter Haven, Fl, US 133/H4
Winter Park, Fl, US 133/H4
Winterberg, Ger. 51/F6
Winterberge (mts.), SAfr. 106/D4
Winterlingen, Ger. 57/F1
Winters, Tx, US 129/H5
Winters, Ca, US 135/K9
Winters Run (riv.), Md, US 138/B4
Winterstaude (peak), Aus. 57/F3
Winterswijk, Neth. 50/D5
Winterthur, Swi. 57/E3
Winterthur Museum and Gardens, De, US 138/C4
Winthrop, Me, US 131/G2
Winton, Austl. 114/A3
Wintzenheim, Fr. 56/D1
Wipper (riv.), Ger. 40/F3
Wipperau (riv.), Ger. 51/H2
Wipperfürth, Ger. 53/G1
Wirges, Ger. 53/G3
Wirrabara, Austl. 113/H5
Wirral (pen.), Eng, UK 35/E5
Wisbech, Eng, UK 33/G1
Wisch, Neth. 50/D5
Wischhafen, Ger. 51/G1
Wisconsin (riv.), Wi, US 127/L5
Wisconsin (state), US 125/H3
Wiseman, Ak, US 134/H2
Wisenta (riv.), Ger. 55/E1
Wishaw, Sc, UK 36/C5
Wishek, ND, US 127/J4
Wisła, Pol. 41/K4
Wiślany (lag.), Pol. 39/H4
Wisłoka (riv.), Pol. 41/L4
Wismar, Ger. 38/D5
Wisner, La, US 129/K5
Wissant, Fr. 52/A2
Wissembourg, Fr. 53/G5
Wissen, Ger. 53/G2
Wissey (riv.), Eng, UK 33/G1
Wit Kei (riv.), SAfr. 106/D3
Witbank, SAfr. 106/E2
Witham, Eng, UK 33/G3
Witham (riv.), Eng, UK 35/H5
Witherspoon (mt.), Ak, US 134/J3
Withlacoochee (riv.), US 133/H4
Withnell, Eng, UK 35/F4
Witjira NP, Austl. 113/G3
Witkowo, Pol. 41/J2
Witney, Eng, UK 33/E3
Witnica, Pol. 41/H2
Witry-lès-Reims, Fr. 53/D5
Wittelsheim, Fr. 56/D2
Wittem, Neth. 53/E2
Witten, Ger. 51/E6
Wittenbach, Swi. 57/F3
Wittenberg, Ger. 40/G3
Wittenberge, Ger. 40/F2
Wittenburg, Ger. 38/D5
Wittenheim, Fr. 56/D2
Wittenoom, Austl. 112/C2
Wittingen, Ger. 51/H3
Wittislingen, Ger. 54/D5
Wittlich, Ger. 53/F4
Wittman, Md, US 138/B6
Wittmund, Ger. 51/E1
Wittmunder (riv.), Ger. 51/E1
Witton (pen.), Ger. 41/G1
Wittstock, Ger. 40/G2
Witu, Kenya 104/D3
Witwatersrand (reg.), SAfr. 106/P12
Witzenhausen, Ger. 51/G6
Wivenhoe (lake), Austl. 109/E3
Wixom, Mi, US 135/E6
Wkra (riv.), Pol. 60/D5
Władysławowo, Pol. 38/H4
Włocławek, Pol. 41/K2
Włocławek (prov.), Pol. 41/K2
Włocławskie (lake), Pol. 41/K2
Włodawa, Pol. 41/M3
Włoszczowa, Pol. 41/K3
Wobulenzi, Ugan. 104/B2
Wodonga, Austl. 115/C3
Wodzisław Śląski, Pol. 41/K4
Woensdrecht, Neth. 50/B6
Woerden, Neth. 50/B4
Wognum, Neth. 50/C3
Wohlen, Swi. 57/E3
Wohlen bei Bern, Swi. 56/D4
Wohlford (lake), Ca, US 136/C4
Woippy, Fr. 53/F5
Wokam (isl.), Indo. 81/H5
Woking, Eng, UK 30/B3
Wokingham, Eng, UK 33/F4
Wŏlch'ul-san NP, SKor. 73/D5
Wolcott, Ks, US 137/D5
Wolcottsville, NY, US 131/S9
Wołczyn, Pol. 41/K3
Woleai (isl.), Micr. 116/D4
Wolf (mtn.), Ak, US 134/H2
Wolf (riv.), Wi, US 130/B2
Wolf (vol.), Ecu. 156/E7
Wolf (isl.), Ecu. 156/E6
Wolf (lake), In, US 135/Q16
Wolf Creek (mtn.), Ak, US 134/F3
Wolf Creek, Mt, US 126/E4
Wolf Point, Mt, US 127/G3
Wolfach, Ger. 57/E1
Wolfach (riv.), Ger. 54/B6
Wolfegg, Ger. 57/F2
Wolfen, Ger. 40/G3
Wolfenbüttel, Ger. 51/H4
Wolfern, Aus. 55/H6
Wölfersheim, Ger. 54/B2
Wolfhagen, Ger. 51/G6
Wolframs-Eschenbach, Ger. 54/D4
Wolfsburg, Ger. 51/H4
Wolfsegg am Hausruck, Aus. 55/G6
Wolfurt, Aus. 57/F3
Wolgast, Ger. 38/E4
Wolhusen, Swi. 56/E3
Wolin, Pol. 38/F5
Woliński PN, Pol. 41/H2
Wolkersdorf, Aus. 49/P7
Wollaston (isl.), Chile 157/C8
Wollaston (lake), Sk, Can. 122/F3
Wollaston (pen.), NW, Can. 122/E2
Wollemi NP, Austl. 115/D2
Wollerau, Swi. 57/E3
Wollongong, Austl. 115/D2
Wöllstadt, Ger. 54/B2
Wöllstein, Ger. 53/G4
Wolmaransstad, SAfr. 106/D2
Wolnzach, Ger. 55/E5
Wologizi (range), Libr. 96/C6
Wołomin, Pol. 41/L2
Wołów, Pol. 41/J3
Wolseley, SAfr. 106/L10
Wolsztyn, Pol. 41/J2
Woluwé-saint-Lambert, Belg. 53/D2
Wolvega, Neth. 50/D3
Wolverhampton, Eng, UK 32/D1
Wolverine Lake, Mi, US 135/F6
Wolziger (lake), Ger. 40/Q7
Woman (riv.), Can. 130/D2
Wombourne, Eng, UK 32/D1
Wombwell, Eng, UK 35/G4
Womelsdorf, Pa, US 138/B3
Wondai, Austl. 114/C4
Wonder (lake), Il, US 135/P16
Wondervu, Co, US 137/B3
Wondreb (riv.), Ger. 55/F3
Wong Chu (riv.), Bhu. 85/G2
Wongan Hills, Austl. 112/C4
Wŏnju, SKor. 73/D4
Wonnangatta-Moroka NP, Austl. 115/C3
Wŏnsan, NKor. 73/D3
Wonthaggi, Austl. 115/C3
Wonyulgunna (peak), Austl. 112/C3
Wood (mt.), Can. 134/K3
Wood (riv.), Can. 127/H2
Wood (mtn.), Sk, Can. 126/G3
Wood (riv.), Il, US 137/G8
Wood Buffalo NP, NW,Ab, Can. 122/E2
Wood Dale, Il, US 135/P16
Wood-Ridge, NJ, US 139/J8
Wood River, Il, US 137/G8
Woodbine, NJ, US 138/D5
Woodbine, Md, US 138/A5
Woodbridge, Ct, US 139/E1
Woodbridge, Ca, US 135/M10
Woodbridge, NJ, US 139/H9
Woodburn, Austl. 115/E1
Woodburn, Or, US 126/C4
Woodburn, Il, US 137/G7
Woodburn, On, Can. 131/Q9
Woodbury, NJ, US 138/C4
Woodcliff Lake, NJ, US 139/J7
Woodenbong, Austl. 115/E1
Woodenbridge, Ire. 34/B6
Woodend, Austl. 115/C3
Woodgate, Austl. 114/D4
Woodgate NP, Austl. 114/D4
Woodinville, Wa, US 135/C2
Woodland, Ca, US 128/B3
Woodlark (isl.), Sol. 116/E5
Woodlawn, Md, US 138/B5
Woodlawn Park, Ok, US 137/M14
Woodmere, NY, US 139/L9
Woodmont, Ct, US 139/F1
Woodridge, Il, US 135/P16
Woodroffe (mt.), Austl. 113/F3
Woods, Ok, US 137/N15
Woods (lake), On, Can. 122/G4
Woods Cross, Ut, US 137/K12
Woods Heights, Mo, US 137/E5
Woodsboro, Md, US 138/A4
Woodside, De, US 138/C5
Woodside, Austl. 113/M8
Woodside, Ca, US 135/K12
Woodside-Drifton, Pa, US 138/C2
Woodstock, Austl. 115/D2
Woodstock, NB, Can. 131/H2
Woodstock, Il, US 129/K2
Woodstock, Eng, UK 33/E3
Woodstock, Md, US 138/B5
Woodstown, NJ, US 138/C4
Woodville, Ms, US 129/K5
Woodway, Wa, US 135/C2
Woolgoolga, Austl. 115/E1
Wooli, Austl. 115/E1
Woolrich, Pa, US 138/A1
Woomera, Austl. 113/H4
Woomera Prohibited Area, Austl. 113/G4
Woonsocket, SD, US 129/H1
Woorabinda Aboriginal Community, Austl. 114/C4
Wooramel (riv.), Austl. 112/B3
Wooster, Oh, US 130/D3
Worb, Swi. 56/D4
Worcester, Ma, US 131/G3
Worcester, Eng, UK 32/D2
Worcester, SAfr. 106/L10
Worcester and Birmingham (canal), Eng, UK 32/D2
Worden, Il, US 137/H8
Wörgl, Aus. 43/K3
Workington, Eng, UK 34/E2
Worksop, Eng, UK 35/G5
Workum, Neth. 50/C3
Worland, Wy, US 126/G4
World 22
World Trade Center, NY, US 139/J9
Wormer, Neth. 50/B3
Wormhoudt, Fr. 52/B2
Worms (pt.), Wal, UK 32/B3
Worms, Ger. 54/B3
Wörnitz (riv.), Ger. 43/J2
Worpswede, Ger. 51/F2
Wörrstadt, Ger. 54/B3
Wórsbach (riv.), Ger. 54/B2
Worsbrough, Eng, UK 35/G4
Worth, Il, US 135/Q16
Wörth am Rhein, Ger. 54/B4
Wörth an der Donau, Ger. 55/F4
Wörth an der Isar, Ger. 55/F5
Wortham, Tx, US 129/H5
Worthing, Eng, UK 33/F5
Wörthsee (lake), Ger. 54/E6
Worton, Md, US 138/B5
Wotho (isl.), Mrsh. 116/F3
Wotje (isl.), Mrsh. 116/G4
Woudenberg, Neth. 50/C4
Woudrichem, Neth. 50/B5
Wounta (lake), Nic. 145/F3
Wouw, Neth. 50/B5
Wowoni (isl.), Indo. 81/F4
Wrangel (isl.), Rus. 160/U
Wrangell, Ak, US 134/M4
Wrangell (mts.), Ak, US 122/B2
Wrangell-St. Elias NP and Prsv., Ak, US 134/K3
Wrath (cape), Sc, UK 31/R7
Wray, Co, US 129/G2
Wraysbury, Eng, UK 30/B2
Wraysbury (res.), Eng, UK 30/B2
Wreck (reef), Austl. 109/E3
Wreck (pt.), SAfr. 106/B3
Wrekin, The (hill), Eng, UK 32/D1
Wremen, Ger. 51/E2
Wrexham, Wal, UK 35/F5
Wright, Wy, US 127/G5
Wrightstown, NJ, US 138/D3
Wrightwood, Ca, US 136/C2
Wrigley, NW, Can. 122/D2
Writtle, Eng, UK 33/G3
Wrocław, Pol. 41/J3
Wrocław (prov.), Pol. 41/J3
Września, Pol. 41/J2
Wschowa, Pol. 41/J3
Wu (riv.), China 79/A2
Wu'an, China 72/C3
Wuchang, China 71/N3
Wuchang (lake), China 72/D5
Wucheng, China 72/D3
Wuchuan, China 79/A2
Wuchuan, China 79/B3
Wuchuan, China 72/B2
Wudang (mtn.), China 72/B4
Wudi, China 72/D3
Wuding (riv.), China 72/B3
Wudinna, Austl. 113/G5
Wufeng, China 79/B1
Wugang, China 79/B2
Wuhai, China 70/J4
Wuhan, China 79/B1
Wuhe, China 72/D4
Wuhle (riv.), Ger. 40/Q6
Wuhu, China 72/D5
Wuhu, China 72/D5
Wuhua, China 79/C3
Wujal Wujal Aboriginal Community, Austl. 114/B1
Wujiang, China 72/L8
Wular (lake), India 86/C2
Wülfrath, Ger. 50/E6
Wulften, Ger. 51/H5
Wulian, China 72/D4
Wuling (mts.), China 79/B2
Wulong, China 83/J2
Wum, Camr. 103/H5
Wumang (isl.), China 73/B3
Wümme (riv.), Ger. 51/F2
Wūn, India 82/C3
Wungong (res.), Austl. 112/L7
Wuning, China 79/C2
Wünnenberg, Ger. 51/F5
Wünnewil, Swi. 56/D4
Wunsiedel, Ger. 55/F2
Wunstorf, Ger. 51/G4
Wupatki Nat'l Mon., Az, US 128/E4
Wuppertal, Ger. 51/E6
Wuqi, China 72/B3
Wuqia, China 87/G5
Wuqiang, China 72/C3
Wuqiao, China 72/D3
Würm (riv.), Ger. 53/H6
Würm K. (canal), Ger. 57/H1
Würselen, Ger. 53/F2
Würzburg, Ger. 54/C3
Wusheng (pass), China 72/C5
Wushi, China 70/C3
Wüstegarten (peak), Ger. 51/G6
Wüstenrot, Ger. 54/C4
Wusuli (riv.), China 71/P2
Wutach (riv.), Ger. 57/E2
Wutai (peak), China 72/C3
Wutai, China 72/C3
Wuteve (mt.), Libr. 102/C4
Wutha-Farnroda, Ger. 54/D1
Wutöschingen, Ger. 57/E2
Wuustwezel, Belg. 50/B6
Wuwei, China 70/H4
Wuwei, China 72/D5
Wuxi, China 72/L8
Wuxiang, China 72/C3
Wuyang, China 72/C4
Wuyi (mts.), China 79/C2
Wuyi, China 72/C3
Wuyuan, China 70/J3
Wuyuan, China 79/C2
Wuzhai, China 72/B3
Wuzhi (peak), China 83/J4
Wuzhi, China 72/C4
Wuzhi (peak), China 72/J6
Wuzhou, China 83/K3
Wyalkatchem, Austl. 112/C4
Wyandanch, NY, US 139/M8
Wyandotte (co.), Ks, US 137/D5
Wyandotte County (lake), Ks, US 137/D5
Wyandotte NWR, Mi, US 135/F7
Wyangala (dam), Austl. 115/D2
Wycheproof, Austl. 115/B3
Wyckoff, NJ, US 139/J8
Wye (riv.), Eng, UK 32/C2
Wye Mills, Md, US 138/B6
Wyee, Austl. 115/D2
Wyk, Ger. 38/C4
Wynigen, Swi. 56/D3
Wynne, Ar, US 129/K4
Wynyard, Austl. 115/C4
Wynyard, Sk, Can. 127/G3
Wyoming (range), Wy, US 128/E2
Wyoming, Mi, US 130/C3
Wyoming (state), US 124/E3
Wyoming, De, US 138/C5
Wyoming, Pa, US 138/C1
Wyomissing, Pa, US 138/C3
Wyperfeld NP, Austl. 115/B2
Wyralinu (peak), Austl. 112/D5
Wyre (riv.), Eng, UK 35/F4
Wyrzysk, Pol. 41/J2
Wysokie Mazowieckie, Pol. 41/M2
Wyszków, Pol. 41/L2

X

X-Can, Mex. 144/E1
Xa Binh Long, Viet. 78/D4
Xaçmaz, Azer. 63/J4
Xagħra, Malta 46/L6
Xai-Xai, Moz. 105/F6
Xainza, China 70/E5
Xaitongmoin, China 85/G1
Xaltianguis, Mex. 143/F5
Xan (riv.), Viet. 79/A5
Xankändı, Azer. 63/H5
Xanten, Ger. 50/D5
Xánthi, Gre. 47/J2
Xanxerê, Braz. 155/A3
Xar Moron (riv.), China 65/M5
Xarba (pass), China 85/E1
Xavantes, Represa de (res.), Braz. 155/B2
Xavantes, Serra dos (mts.), Braz. 151/J6
Xayar, China 70/D3
Xel-há (ruin), Mex. 144/E1
Xenia, Oh, US 130/D4
Xerta, Sp. 45/F2
Xertigny, Fr. 56/C1
Xi (riv.), China 67/L7
Xi (lake), China 72/E2
Xiaguan, China 83/H2
Xiajin, China 72/C3
Xiamen, China 79/C3
Xiamen (int'l arpt.), China 79/C3
Xi'an, China 72/B4
Xiang (riv.), China 71/K6
Xiangcheng, China 83/G2
Xiangcheng, China 72/C4
Xiangcheng, China 72/C4
Xiangfan, China 72/C4
Xiangfen, China 72/B4
Xianghe, China 72/H7
Xiangkhoang, Laos 78/C2
Xiangning, China 72/B4
Xiangshan, China 79/D2
Xiangshui, China 72/D4
Xiangtan, China 83/K2
Xiangxiang, China 79/B2
Xiangyuan, China 72/C3
Xiangyun, China 83/H2
Xianju, China 79/D2
Xianning, China 79/B2
Xiantao, China 79/B1
Xianyang, China 70/J5
Xiao Hinggang (mts.), China 71/N2
Xiao Xian, China 72/D4
Xiaogan, China 71/K5
Xiaoqing (riv.), China 72/D3
Xiaoshan, China 72/L9
Xiaowutai (peak), China 72/C3
Xiaoyi, China 72/B3
Xiapu, China 79/C2
Xiayi, China 72/D4
Xichang, China 83/H2
Xichou, China 83/H3
Xico, Mex. 143/N7
Xicohténcatl, Mex. 143/F4
Xicotepec, Mex. 143/M6
Xifei (riv.), China 72/C4
Xifeng, China 70/J4
Xifeng, China 83/J2
Xifeng, China 72/F2
Xigazê, China 85/G1
Xihua, China 72/C4
Xilin, China 83/J3
Xilitla, Mex. 144/B1
Xilókastron, Gre. 47/H3
Ximeng Vazu Zizhixian, China 83/G3
Xin (riv.), China 79/C2
Xin Barag Zuoqi, China 71/L2
Xin'an, China 72/C4
Xin'an (riv.), China 72/D5
Xin'anjiang (res.), China 79/C2
Xin'anjiang (res.), China 72/D5
Xinbin, China 73/C2
Xincai, China 72/C4
Xinchang, China 79/D2
Xincheng, China 79/A3
Xincheng, China 72/G7
Xinfeng, China 79/B2
Xinfeng, China 83/K3
Xinfengjiang (res.), China 79/B3
Xing'an, China 79/B2
Xingcheng, China 72/E2
Xinghua, China 72/D4
Xinglong, China 72/H6
Xingshan, China 72/B5
Xingtai, China 72/C3
Xingu (riv.), Braz. 147/D3
Xingu, PN do, Braz. 151/H6
Xingyang, China 72/C4
Xingzi, China 79/C2
Xinhe, China 70/D3
Xinhe, China 72/C3
Xinhua, China 79/B2
Xinhuang Dongzu Zizhixian, China 79/A2
Xining, China 70/H4
Xinji, China 72/C3
Xinjiang, China 72/B4
Xinjiang (reg.), China 67/H5
Xinjin, China 73/A3
Xinle, China 72/C3
Xinmin, China 73/B1
Xintai, China 72/D4
Xinxiang, China 72/C4
Xinyang, China 71/K5
Xinyang, China 72/C4
Xinye, China 72/C4
Xinyi, China 83/K3
Xinyi, China 72/D4
Xinyu, China 79/B2
Xinyuan, China 70/D3
Xinzheng, China 72/C4
Xinzo de Limia, Sp. 44/B1
Xiong Xian, China 72/H7
Xiping, China 72/C4
Xiqing (mts.), China 70/H5
Xique-Xique, Braz. 154/B3
Xitang, China 72/L9
Xitiao (riv.), China 72/K9
Xiu (riv.), China 79/B2
Xiuning, China 79/C2
Xiuwen, China 83/J2
Xiuwu, China 72/C4
Xiuyan, China 73/B2
Xixabangma (peak), China 85/E1
Xixia, China 72/B4
Xiyang (riv.), China 83/J3
Xizang (Tibet) (aut. reg.), China 70/D5
Xochicalco (ruin), Mex. 143/K8
Xonacatlán, Mex. 143/Q10
Xpujil, Mex. 144/D2
Xu (riv.), China 79/C2
Xuan'en, China 79/A2
Xuanhua, China 72/G6
Xuchang, China 72/C4
Xun (riv.), China 79/B3
Xun Xian, China 72/C4
Xunke, China 71/N2
Xunwu, China 79/C3
Xunyang, China 72/B4
Xupu, China 79/B2
Xuwen, China 83/K3
Xuyi, China 72/D4
Xuzhou, China 72/D4

Y

Y Llethr (peak), Wal, UK 34/E6
Ya'an, China 70/H6
Ya'bad, Isr. 91/G7
Yabassi, Camr. 96/G7
Yablanitsa, Bul. 47/J1
Yablonovyy (range), Rus. 67/L4
Yabrūd, Isr. 91/G8
Yabucoa, PR 141/M8
Yabuki, Japan 75/G2
Yabuzukahon, Japan 77/C1
Yachi (riv.), China 70/J6
Yachiho, Japan 77/A1
Yachimata, Japan 77/E2
Yachiyo, Japan 77/D1
Yachiyo, Japan 77/G5
Yachiyo, Japan 77/E2
Yacimiento Río Turbio, Arg. 159/B6
Yacuiba, Bol. 150/F8
Yacuma (riv.), Bol. 150/E6
Yacumbu, PN, Ven. 152/D2
Yādgīr, India 82/C4
Yadkin (riv.), NC, US 133/H2
Yaeyama (isls.), Japan 75/G8
Yāfā, Isr. 91/G6
Yağcılar, Turk. 62/D5
Yagi, Japan 77/J5
Yagorlytsk (gulf), Ukr. 49/K2
Yagoua, Camr. 96/J5
Yagradagzê (peak), China 70/G4
Yaguale (riv.), Hon. 144/E3
Yaguarón (riv.), Uru. 159/G2
Yaguas (riv.), Peru 152/D5
Yague del Sur (riv.), DRep. 145/J2
Yagur, Isr. 91/G6
Yahagi (riv.), Japan 77/M6
Yahualica de Gonzalez Gallo, Mex. 142/E4
Yahyalı, Turk. 90/C2
Yáios (Paxoí), Gre. 47/G3
Yaita, Japan 75/F2
Yaizu, Japan 75/F3
Yajalón, Mex. 144/C2
Yakacık, Turk. 91/E1
Yakapınar, Turk. 91/D1
Yakima (riv.), Wa, US 126/C4
Yakima, Wa, US 126/C4
Yakishiri (isl.), Japan 76/B1
Yako, Burk. 103/E3
Yakoruda, Bul. 47/H1
Yakumo, Japan 76/B2
Yakuno, Japan 77/G5
Yakutat (bay), Ak, US 122/B3
Yakutsk, Rus. 65/N3
Yala, Thai. 78/C5
Yalahua (lag.), Mex. 144/E1
Yalangoz, Turk. 91/E1
Yalata Abor. Land, Austl. 113/F4
Yalbac (hills), Belz. 144/D2
Yalgoo, Austl. 112/C4
Yalgorup NP, Austl. 112/B5
Yalnızçam, Turk. 63/G4
Yaloké, CAfr. 96/J6
Yalong (riv.), China 67/K6
Yalova, Turk. 49/J5
Yalova, Turk. 49/H5
Yalpuh (lake), Ukr. 49/J3
Yalta, Ukr. 62/E3
Yalu (riv.), China,NKor 65/N5
Yalutorovsk, Rus. 87/E1
Yalvaç, Turk. 90/B2
Yamada, Japan 76/B4
Yamaga, Japan 74/B4
Yamagata, Japan 71/Q4
Yamagata, Japan 75/G1
Yamagata (pref.), Japan 76/A4
Yamaguchi (pref.), Japan 74/B3
Yamaguchi, Japan 74/B3
Yamakita, Japan 77/C3
Yamal (pen.), Rus. 67/F2
Yamanaka (lake), Japan 77/B3
Yamanashi, Japan 77/B2
Yamanie (falls), Austl. 114/B2
Yamanie Falls NP, Austl. 114/B2
Yamantau (peak), Rus. 61/N5
Yamaoka, Japan 77/M5
Yamarna Abor. Rsv., Austl. 112/D4
Yamashiro, Japan 77/J6
Yamato, Japan 77/B2
Yamato, Japan 77/E1
Yamato, Japan 77/C3
Yamato (riv.), Japan 77/J6
Yamato-kōriyama, Japan 77/J6
Yamatotakada, Japan 77/J6
Yamazoe, Japan 77/K6
Yamba, Austl. 115/E1
Yambio, Sudan 97/L7
Yambol, Bul. 47/K1
Yambrasbamba, Peru 156/B2
Yamdena (isl.), Indo. 81/H5
Yamethin, Myan. 83/G3
Yamin (peak), Indo. 81/K4
Yamma Yamma (lake), Austl. 109/D3
Yamoto, Japan 76/B4
Yamoussoukro (cap.), C.d'Iv. 102/D5
Yampa (riv.), Co, US 128/F2
Yamuna (riv.), India 70/C6
Yamunānagar, India 86/D4
Yamzho Yumco (lake), China 83/F2
Yan (riv.), SrL. 82/D6
Yan Yean (res.), Austl. 115/G5
Yana (riv.), Rus. 67/N3
Yanagawa, Japan 74/B4
Yanahuanca, Peru 156/B3
Yanai, Japan 74/C4
Yanaizu, Japan 77/L5
Yan'an, China 72/B3
Yanaoca, Peru 156/D4
Yanaul, Rus. 61/M4
Yanbian, China 83/H2
Yancheng, China 72/C4
Yancheng, China 72/E4
Yanchep NP, Austl. 112/B4
Yanco, Austl. 115/C2
Yandeearra Abor. Rsv., Austl. 112/C2
Yandoon, Myan. 83/G4
Yanfolila, Mali 102/C4
Yangambi, D.R. Congo 97/K7
Yangbi (riv.), China 83/G2
Yangcheng, China 72/C4
Yangcheng (lake), China 72/L8
Yangchun, China 79/B3
Yangdang (mts.), China 79/C2
Yangdŏk, NKor. 73/D3
Yanggang-do (prov.), NKor. 73/D2
Yanggao, China 72/C2
Yanggu, SKor. 73/D3
Yanggu, China 72/C3
Yangiyul', Uzb. 87/E4
Yangjiang, China 83/K3
Yangma (isl.), China 73/A4

Yango – Zywie

Yangon (state), Myan. 83/G4
Yangp'yŏng, SKor. 73/D4
Yangqu, China 72/C3
Yangquan, China 72/C3
Yangsan, SKor. 73/E5
Yangshan, China 83/K3
Yangtze (Chang) (riv.), China 79/C1
Yangudi Rassa NP, Eth. 97/P5
Yangxin, China 79/C2
Yangxin, China 72/D3
Yangyang, SKor. 73/E3
Yangzhong, China 87/G5
Yangzhou, China 72/D4
Yanhe, China 79/A2
Yanji, China 71/N3
Yanjin, China 83/H2
Yanjin, China 72/C4
Yankari NP, Nga. 97/H6
Yankee Stadium, NY, US 139/K8
Yanling, China 72/C2
Yanmen (pass), China 72/C3
Yanshan, China 79/C2
Yanshan, China 83/H3
Yanshan, China 72/C4
Yanshi, China 72/C4
Yanshou, China 71/N2
Yantai, China 72/E3
Yanyuan, China 83/H2
Yanzhou, China 72/D4
Yao, China 79/H2
Yao'an, China 83/H2
Yaotsu, Japan 77/M5
Yaoundé (cap.), Camr. 96/H7
Yap (isls.), Micr. 68/C3
Yapacana, PN, Ven. 150/E3
Yapei, Gha. 103/E4
Yapen (isl.), Indo. 116/C5
Yapen (str.), Indo. 81/J4
Yapraklı, Turk. 62/E4
Yaqui (riv.), Mex. 119/G7
Yara, Cuba 145/G1
Yaracuy (state), Ven. 152/D2
Yaralıgöz (peak), Turk. 62/E4
Yaransk, Rus. 61/K4
Yardımcı (pt.), Turk. 62/E4
Yardley, Pa, US 138/D3
Yardville-Groveville, NJ, US 138/D3
Yare (riv.), Eng, UK 33/H1
Yarí (riv.), Col. 150/D3
Yari-ga-take (peak), Japan 75/E2
Yarımca, Turk. 49/J5
Yaritagua, Ven. 152/D2
Yarkant (riv.), China 64/H6
Yarloop, Austl. 115/C5
Yarlung Zangbo (Brahmaputra) (riv.), China 85/G1
Yarmouth, NS, Can. 131/H3
Yaroslavl', Rus. 60/H4
Yaroslavl' Oblast, Rus. 60/H4
Yarpuz, Turk. 91/E1
Yarra (riv.), Austl. 115/G5
Yarra Glen, Austl. 115/G5
Yarram, Austl. 115/C3
Yarraman, Austl. 114/D4
Yarrawonga, Austl. 115/C3
Yarrow Point, Wa, US 135/C2
Yartsevo, Rus. 64/K3
Yarumal, Col. 152/C2
Yasato, Japan 77/E1
Yasawa Group (isls.), Fiji 116/G6
Yasel'da (riv.), Bela. 62/C1
Yashima, Japan 76/B4
Yashio, Japan 77/D2
Yashiro, Japan 63/L2
Yasothon, Thai. 115/D2
Yass, Austl. 115/D2
Yasu (riv.), Japan 77/K6
Yasu, Japan 77/K5
Yasugi, Japan 88/F2
Yāsūj, Iran 88/F2
Yasun Burnu (pt.), Turk. 62/F4
Yasuni, PN, Ecu. 150/C4
Yatabe, Japan 75/G2
Yatağan, Turk. 90/B2
Yateley, Eng, UK 33/F4
Yatenga (prov.), Burk. 103/E3
Yathkyed (lake), NW, Can. 122/G2
Yatomi, Japan 77/L5
Yatsuga-take (peak), Japan 77/A2
Yatsuo, Japan 75/F2
Yatsushiro, Japan 77/B2
Yattah, WBnk. 91/D3
Yauca, Peru 156/C4
Yauca, Peru 156/C4
Yauco, PR 141/M8
Yauli, Peru 156/B5
Yaután, Peru 156/C4
Yauyos, Peru 156/C4
Yauza (riv.), Braz.,Peru 147/B3
Yavarí Mirim (riv.), Peru 156/C2
Yavaros, Mex. 142/C3
Yavay (pen.), Rus. 64/H2
Yavne, Isr. 91/F8
Yavuzeli, Turk.
Yawahara, Japan 77/E2
Yawata, Japan 77/J6
Yawatahama, Japan 74/C4
Yaxchilán (ruin), Guat. 144/D2

Yaygın, Turk. 90/E2
Yayladağı, Turk. 91/E2
Yayladere, Turk. 90/E2
Yazd, Iran 89/F2
Yazmān, Pak. 86/A5
Yazoo (riv.),
Yazoo City, Ms, US 129/K4
Yazoo, Ms, US 129/K4
Ybbs (riv.), Aus. 41/H4
Ybbsitz, Aus. 43/L3
Yding Skovhøj (peak), Den. 38/C3
Ye Xian, China 72/D3
Yeay Sen (cape), Camb. 78/C4
Yecheng, China 87/G5
Yech'ŏn, SKor. 73/E4
Yecla, Sp. 45/E3
Yécora, Mex. 142/C2
Yecuatla, Mex. 143/N7
Yedigöller Nat'l Park, Turk. 49/K5
Yeditepe, Turk. 91/E2
Yéfira, Gre. 47/H2
Yefremov, Rus. 62/F1
Yegizkara (peak), Kaz. 87/D3
Yegorlak (riv.), Rus. 63/G3
Yehialtepec, Mex. 143/M8
Yehud, Isr. 91/F7
Yejmiadzin, Arm. 63/H4
Yekaterinburg (Sverdlovsk), Rus. 61/P4
Yekateriny (chan.), Rus. 76/E1
Yelabuga, Rus. 61/M5
Yelan', Rus. 63/G2
Yelarbon, Austl. 114/C5
Yelets, Rus. 62/F1
Yélimané, Mali 102/C3
Yelizovo, Rus. 65/H4
Yell (isl.), Sc, UK 31/W13
Yellow, Alg. 100/F5
Yellow (riv.), US 133/G4
Yellow (sea), Asia 67/M6
Yellow Grass, Sk, Can. 127/G3
Yellowknife (riv.), NW, Can. 122/E2
Yellowknife (cap.), NW, Can. 122/E2
Yellowstone (lake), Wy, US 126/F4
Yellowstone (riv.), US 119/G5
Yellowstone NP, US 128/E1
Yellville, Ar, US 129/J3
Yemen (ctry.) 67/D8
Yenakiyeve, Ukr. 62/F2
Yenangyaung, Myan. 83/F3
Yenda, Austl. 115/C2
Yendi, Gha. 103/E4
Yengisar, China 87/G5
Yeniçağa, Turk. 49/L5
Yenice, Turk. 91/D1
Yenice, Turk. 49/L5
Yenice, Turk. 62/E4
Yenice, Turk. 49/H6
Yeniceoba, Turk. 90/C2
Yenişehir, Turk. 49/J5
Yenişehir, Turk. 85/G1
Yeniseysk, Rus. 64/K4
Yeo (lake), Austl. 109/B3
Yeo Lake Nature Rsv., Austl. 112/E3
Yeoval, Austl. 115/D2
Yeovil, Eng, UK 32/D5
Yeppoon, Austl. 114/C3
Yeraifia (well), WSah. 98/B4
Yerakovoúni (peak), Gre. 47/H3
Yères (riv.), Fr. 52/A4
Yerevan (int'l arpt.), Arm. 63/H4
Yerington, Nv, US 128/C3
Yerköy, Turk. 62/E5
Yerlisu, Turk. 47/K2
Yermak, Kaz. 87/G2
Yeroham, Isr. 91/D4
Yerolimín, Gre. 47/H4
Yerres (riv.), Fr. 42/D2
Yerres, Fr. 30/K5
Yerupaja (peak), Peru 156/B3
Yesagyo, Myan. 83/G3
Yesan, SKor. 73/D5
Yeşilhisar, Turk. 90/C2
Yeşilırmak (riv.), Turk. 62/E4
Yeşilkent, Turk. 91/E1
Yeşilova, Turk. 90/B2
Yesodot, Isr. 91/F8
Yessentuki, Rus. 63/G3
Yeste, Sp. 44/D3
Yetti (reg.), Mrta. 98/D4
Yettem, Ca, US 135/C3
Yevlax, Azer. 63/H4
Yevpatoriya, Ukr. 62/E3
Yèvre (riv.), Fr. 53/D5
Yeya (riv.), Rus. 62/G3
Yeysk, Rus. 62/F3
Ygos-Saint-Saturnin, Fr. 42/C5
Yi (riv.), Uru. 159/F2
Yialousa, Cyp. 91/D2
Yiánnitsá, Gre. 47/H2
Yiánnouli, Gre. 47/H3
Yibin, China 70/H6
Yichang, China 71/K5
Yicheng, China 72/C5
Yicheng, China 72/B4
Yichun, China 72/C4
Yichun, China 83/K2
Yiğilca, Turk. 49/K5
Yıldız (peak), Turk. 90/D1
Yıldızeli, Turk. 62/F5
Yilehuli (mts.), China 71/M1
Yiliang, China 72/B4
Yimen, China 83/H3
Yin (mts.), China 65/L5

Yinan, China 72/D4
Yinchuan, China 70/J4
Yindarlgooda (lake), Austl. 109/B4
Yingcheng, China 71/K5
Yingcheng, China 79/B3
Yingkou, China 73/B2
Yingshang, China 72/C5
Yingshang, China 79/C2
Yinshui, China 72/D4
Yishui, China 72/D4
Yitong (riv.), SKor. 73/B2
Yiwu, China 70/F3
Yixing, China 72/K8
Yiyang, China 83/K2
Yiyang, China 72/C4
Yiyuan, China 72/D3
Yizhang, China 83/K2
Yizheng, China 72/D4
Ylöjärvi, Fin. 39/K1
Yngaren (lake), Swe. 38/G2
Yobe (state), Nga. 103/H3
Yóch'ŏn, SKor. 73/D5
Yodo (riv.), Japan 77/J6
Yoduma (riv.), Rus. 65/P4
Yoff (Dakar) (int'l arpt.), Sen. 102/A3
Yogo, Japan 77/K4
Yogoum (well), Chad 97/J4
Yŏgyang, Turk. 49/H5
Yogyakarta, Indo. 80/D5
Yoho NP, Can. 126/D3
Yoichi, Japan 76/B2
Yojoa (lake), Hon. 144/D3
Yōju, SKor. 73/D4
Yokadouma, Camr. 96/J7
Yōkaichi, Japan 77/K5
Yokawa, Japan 77/H6
Yokkaichi, Japan 77/L6
Yokohama, Japan 75/F3
Yokoshiba, Japan 77/E2
Yokosuka, Japan 75/F3
Yokote, Japan 76/B4
Yokoze, Japan 77/C2
Yola, Nga.
Yolaina (mts.), Nic. 145/E4
Yolboyu, Turk. 90/D2
Yolo, Ca, US 135/L10
Yolo (co.), Ca, US 135/L9
Yom (riv.), Thai. 83/H4
Yovi (peak), Ven. 153/E3
Yozgat, Turk. 62/E5
Ypsilanti, Mi, US 135/E7
Yr Eifl (peak), Wal, UK 34/D6
Yreka, Ca, US 119/G7
Yser (riv.), Fr. 40/B3
Ysieux (riv.), Fr. 30/K4
Ystad, Swe. 38/E4
Ysyk-Köl (lake), Kyr. 70/C3
Ysyk-Köl (obl.), Kyr. 87/G4
Ythan (riv.), Sc, UK 36/D2
Ytterby, Swe. 38/D3
Ytterbyn, Swe. 37/G2
Yü (peak), Tai. 79/D3
Yu Xian, China 72/C3
Yu Xian, China 72/C4
Yuan (riv.), China 71/K6
Yuan (riv.), China 72/B5
Yuan'an, China 72/B5
Yuanlin, Tai. 79/D3
Yuanping, China 72/B4
Yuanqu, China 72/B4
Yuanshi, China 72/C3
Yuanyang, China 72/C4
Yuba City, Ca, US 128/B3
Yūbari, Japan 76/B1
Yūbetsu, Japan 76/C1
Yūbetsu (riv.), Japan 76/C2
Yucaipa, Ca, US 136/C2
Yucatán (state), Mex. 144/D3
Yucatán (pen.), Mex. 119/J7
Yuci, China 72/C3
Yuen Long, China 71/U10
Yuendumu, Austl. 113/F2
Yuendumu Abor. Land, Austl. 113/F2
Yueqing, China 71/M4
Yueyang, China 79/B2
Yug (riv.), Rus. 64/E4
Yugawara, Japan 77/C3
Yugorskiy (riv.), Rus. 61/P1
Yugoslavia (ctry.) 40/C2
Yuhang, China 79/D2
Yuhuan, China 79/D2
Yui, Japan 77/B3
Yujiang, China 79/B3
Yūki, Japan 77/D2
Yukon, Ok, US 137/M14
Yukon (riv.), Can.,US 119/B3
Yukon-Charley Rivers Nat'l Prsv., Ak, US 134/K2
Yukon Delta NWR, US 134/D3
Yukon Flats NWR, US 134/J2
Yukon Territory (terr.), Can. 134/L2
Yukuhashi, Japan 74/B4
Yulara, Austl. 114/C4
Yuleba, Austl. 114/C4
Yulin, China 83/J4
Yulin, China 72/B3
Yuma, Az, US 128/D4
Yuma, Az, US 124/D5
Yumbarra Consv. Park, Austl. 113/H5
Yumbel, Chile 158/B3

Yumbo, Col. 152/B4
Yumen, China 70/G4
Yumin, China 70/D2
Yumurtalık, Turk. 91/D1
Yun (riv.), China 72/C5
Yun Xian, China 83/H3
Yun Xian, China 72/B5
Yunak, Turk. 90/B2
Yuncheng, China 72/C3
Yuncheng, China 72/C4
Yundum (Banjul) (int'l arpt.), Gam. 102/A3
Yungang Caves, China 72/C3
Yungas (phys. reg.), Bol. 150/E7
Yungay, Chile 158/B3
Yungay, Peru 156/B3
Yunguyo, Peru 156/D5
Yunkanjini Abor. Land, Austl. 113/F2
Yunlong, China 83/G2
Yunnan (prov.), China 70/H7
Yuntai (peak), China 72/C3
Yunxi, China 72/B4
Yunxiao, China 72/C3
Yunyi (riv.), China 72/C4
Yunzhong (mtn.), China 72/C3
Yuping, China 83/J2
Yupukarri, Guy. 153/G4
Yuqiao (res.), China 72/H7
Yuracyacu, Peru 156/B2
Yurimaguas, Peru 156/B2
Yuruari (riv.), Ven. 153/F3
Yürük, Turk. 49/H5
Yur'yevets, Rus. 60/J4
Yuryuzan' (riv.), Rus. 61/N5
Yuscarán, Hon. 144/E3
Yushan, China 79/C2
Yushe, China 72/C3
Yushu, China 71/N3
Yushu, SKor. 73/G4
Yusufeli, Turk. 63/G4
Yutai, China 72/D4
Yutian, China 72/D4
Yutian, China 72/H7
Yutz, Fr. 73/F5
Yuxi, Japan 76/A4
Yuzawa, Japan 76/B4
Yuzhno-Sakhalinsk, Rus. 71/R2
Yverdon, Swi. 56/C4
Yvette (riv.), Fr. 52/B6
Yvetot, Fr. 32/D2
Yvonand, Swi. 56/C4
Yvoir, Belg. 53/D3
Yvonne, Swi. 55/C4
Yzeure, Fr. 42/E5

Z

Za (riv.), Mor. 100/C2
Zaachila, Mex. 144/B2
Zaandam, Neth. 50/B4
Zaanstad, Neth. 50/B4
Zaber (riv.), Ger. 51/H5
Żabia, Malta 46/M7
Zábki, Pol. 41/L2
Ząbkowice Śląskie, Pol. 41/J3
Żabljak, Yugo. 47/F1
Zabło, Pol. 41/M2
Żabreh, Cro. 48/B3
Zabrze, Pol. 41/K3
Zacapa, Guat. 144/D3
Zacapoaxtla, Mex. 143/M7
Zacapu, Mex. 143/E5
Zacatecas (state), Mex. 140/A3
Zacatecas, Mex. 142/E4
Zacatecoluca, ESal. 144/D3
Zacatelco, Mex. 143/L7
Zacatepec, Mex. 143/K8
Zacatlán, Mex. 143/M7
Zachary, La, US 132/F4
Zacoalco de Torres, Mex. 142/E4
Zacualtipán, Mex. 144/B1
Zadar, Cro. 43/L4
Zadetkyi (isl.), Myan. 80/A2
Zafarwāl, Pak. 86/C3
Zafra, Sp. 44/B3
Zagań, Pol. 41/H3
Zaghouan (gov.), Tun. 46/A4
Zaghwān, Tun. 100/M6
Zagora, Mor. 98/D2
Zagorá, Gre. 47/H3
Zagorje ob Savi, Slov. 43/L3
Zagreb (cap.), Cro. 48/B3
Zagros (mts.), Iran 66/F6
Zāhedān, Iran 89/H3
Zahirābād, India 82/C4
Zahlah, Leb. 91/D3
Zahrez Chergui (dry lake), Alg. 100/G5
Zaidín, Sp. 45/F2
Zaïo, Mor. 100/C2
Zaire (see Congo, Democratic Republic of the)
Zakamensk, Rus. 70/H1
Zakarpats'ka (obl.), Ukr. 41/K4
Zakháro, Gre. 47/G4
Zakhodnyaya Dzvina (riv.), Bela. 60/E5
Zakho, Iraq 90/E2
Zákinthos (isl.), Gre. 47/G4
Zakopane, Pol. 41/K4
Zakouma, PN de, Chad 97/J5
Zala (prov.), Hun. 48/C2
Zalaegerszeg, Hun. 48/C2
Zalamea de la Serena, Sp. 44/C3
Zalamea la Real, Sp. 44/C4
Zalaszentgrót, Hun. 48/C2
Zalău, Rom. 41/K5
Zaltan (well), Libya 96/J2
Zaltbommel, Neth. 50/C5
Zalun, Myan. 83/G4

Zama, Japan 77/C3
Zamania, India 84/D3
Zambezi, Zam. 105/D3
Zambezi (riv.), Moz. 93/E6
Zamboanga, Phil. 81/F2
Zambrów, Pol. 41/M2
Zamora, Turk. 90/B2
Zamora, Ecu. 156/B2
Zamora, Sp. 44/C2
Zamora-Chinchipe (prov.), Ecu. 156/B2
Zamora de Hidalgo, Mex. 142/E5
Zamość (prov.), Pol. 41/M3
Zamość, Pol. 41/M3
Zams, Aus. 37/G3
Záncara (riv.), Sp. 44/D3
Zanda, China 70/C5
Zandkreekdam (dam), Neth. 50/A5
Zandvoort, Neth. 50/B4
Zanè, It. 59/E1
Zanhuang, China 72/C3
Zanjan, Iran 88/E1
Zanjón (riv.), Mex. 128/E5
Zánka, Hun. 48/C2
Zanzibar, Tanz. 104/C4
Zanzibar (isl.), Tanz. 93/F5
Zanzibar (Kisauni) (int'l arpt.), Tanz. 104/C4
Zanzibar North (prov.), Tanz. 104/C4
Zanzibar South (pol. reg.), Tanz. 104/C4
Zanzibar West (pol. reg.), Tanz. 104/C4
Zanzuzí (hill), Tanz. 104/B3
Zaō-san (peak), Japan 75/G1
Zaoqing, China 72/C3
Zaouiet Kounta, Alg. 99/E4
Zaozhuang, China 72/D4
Zaoyang, China 72/C4
Západočeský (pol. reg.), Czh. 43/K2
Zapadocesky (pol. reg.), Czh. 40/G4
Zapadoslovensky (pol. reg.), Slvk. 41/J4
Zapaleri (peak), SA 157/C1
Zapallar, Chile 158/C2
Zapata (pen.), Cuba 145/F1
Zapata, Tx, US 132/D5
Zapatoca, Col. 152/C3
Zapatosa (lake), Col. 152/C2
Zapolyarnyy, Rus. 60/F1
Zapopan, Mex. 142/E4
Zaporizhzhya, Ukr. 62/E3
Zaporizhzhya (int'l arpt.), Ukr. 62/E3
Zaporiz'ka (prov.), Ukr. 62/E3
Zapotal, Ecu. 152/B5
Zapotillo, Ecu. 156/A2
Zapotiltic, It. 46/D2
Zapreśić, Cro. 48/B3
Zara, It. 62/F5
Zaragoza, Mex. 132/C4
Zaragoza (int'l arpt.), Sp. 45/E2
Zaragoza, Mex. 143/M7
Zaragoza, Col. 152/C3
Zaragoza (Saragossa), Sp. 45/E2
Zarah, Ks, US 137/D6
Zarand, Iran 89/G2
Zaranda (hill), Nga. 103/H4
Zárate, Arg. 159/J11
Zarauz, Sp. 44/D1
Zaraza, Ven. 153/E2
Zareh (mtn.), Iran 88/F2
Zareh Sharan, Afg. 89/J2
Zārgän, Iran 88/F3
Zaria, Nga. 103/G4
Zarmast (pass), Afg. 89/H2
Zarnovica, Slvk. 48/D1
Zarnesti, Rom. 41/H5
Zarqā', Jor. 91/E3
Zaruma, Ecu. 156/B2
Zarumilla, Peru 156/A1
Zary, Pol. 41/H3
Zarza la Mayor, Sp. 44/B2
Zarzal, Col. 152/B3
Zaskár (range), India 66/G5
Zäskär (riv.), India 86/D2
Zastron, SAfr. 104/D3
Zatah, Leb. 55/G2
Žatec, Czh. 41/J3
Zavala, Arg. 158/E2
Zavalla, Arg. 158/E2
Zavdi'el, Isr. 91/F8
Zaventem, Belg. 53/D2
Zavet, Bul. 49/H4
Zavidovići, Bosn. 48/D3
Zawiercie, Pol. 41/K3
Zawadzkie, Pol. 41/K3
Zawiye, Pol. 41/K3
Zaysan, Kaz. 70/D2
Zaysan (lake), Kaz. 65/L4
Zayü (riv.), China 83/G2
Zazáu, Cuba 145/G1
Zazárida, Ven. 152/D2
Zbąszyń, Pol. 41/H2
Zázhū, Iraq 90/E2
Žďár nad Sázavou, Czh. 41/H4
Zdice, Czh. 55/G3
Zduńska Wola, Pol. 41/K3
Zeballos, BC, Can. 126/C3

Zegrzyńskie (res.), Pol. 41/L2
Zehdenick, Ger. 41/G2
Zeil (int'l arpt.), Austl. 113/G2
Zeil, Ger. 54/D2
Zeiselmauer, Aus. 49/N7
Zeist, Neth. 50/C4
Zeitz, Ger. 40/G3
Zejtun, Malta 46/M7
Zekharya, Isr. 91/F8
Zele, Belg. 52/D1
Zelenodol'sk, Rus. 61/L5
Zelenogorsk, Rus. 61/S6
Zelenogradsk, Rus. 63/G3
Zelhem, Neth. 50/D4
Zell, Swi. 57/E3
Zell, Ger. 51/G3
Zell, Swi. 56/D3
Zell am Harmersbach, Ger. 56/E1
Zell am Main, Ger. 54/C3
Zell am Moos, Aus. 55/G7
Zell am See, Aus. 43/K3
Zell an der Pram, Aus. 55/G6
Zell in Wiesental, Ger. 56/D2
Zellersee (lake), Aus. 54/G7
Zellingen, Ger. 54/C3
Zelów, Pol. 41/K3
Zeltingen-Rachtig, Ger. 51/G4
Zeltweg, Aus. 43/L3
Zelzate, Belg. 52/C1
Zemaitija NP, Lith. 39/J3
Zembra (isls.), Tun. 46/B4
Zemen, Bul. 47/H1
Zemio, CAfr. 97/L6
Zemmer, Ger. 53/F4
Zemmora, Alg. 100/F5
Zempoala, Mex. 143/N7
Zempoala (peak), Mex. 143/Q10
Zempoaltepec, Cerro (peak), Mex. 144/C2
Zemst, Belg. 53/D2
Zenica, Bosn. 48/C3
Zenith, Wa, US 135/C3
Zenn (riv.), Ger. 43/J2
Zenne (riv.), Belg. 53/D1
Zenon Park, Sk, Can. 127/H2
Zentsūji, Japan 74/C3
Zepče, Bosn. 48/D3
Zepu, China 87/G5
Zeralda, Alg. 100/G4
Zeravshan (riv.), Taj.,Uzb. 87/J5
Zermatt, Swi. 56/D5
Zernez, Swi. 56/D5
Zernograd, Rus. 62/G3
Zero Branco, It. 59/F1
Zeta (lake), NW, Can. 122/F1
Zetel, Ger. 51/E2
Zeuthen, Ger. 40/Q7
Zeven, Ger. 51/G2
Zevenaar, Neth. 50/D5
Zevenbergen, Neth. 50/B5
Zevgolation, Gre. 47/H4
Zevio, It. 57/J5
Zeya (res.), Rus. 67/M4
Zeya (riv.), Rus. 65/N4
Zeya-Bureya (plain), Rus. 71/N2
Zézere (riv.), Port. 44/A3
Zgharta, Leb. 91/D2
Zgierz, Pol. 41/K2
Zgorzelec, Pol. 41/H3
Zhambyl (obl.), Kaz. 87/H4
Zhambyl, Kaz. 87/H4
Zhangaözen, Kaz. 87/H4
Zhangaqazaly, Kaz. 87/D3
Zhanghua, Tai. 79/D3
Zhangjiakou, China 72/C3
Zhangping, China 79/C2
Zhangqiu, China 72/D3
Zhangshu, China 79/B3
Zhangwei (riv.), China 72/D3
Zhangye, China 70/H4
Zhangye, China 79/C3
Zhangzi (isl.), China 73/B3
Zhanhe, China 71/K5
Zhanjiang, China 70/J7
Zhanyi, China 70/H6
Zhao Xian, China 72/C3
Zhao'an, China 79/C3
Zhaojue, China 83/H2
Zhaoqing, China 71/K7
Zhaotong, China 83/H2
Zhaozhou, China 71/N2
Zháyuq (Ural) (riv.), Kaz.,Rus. 64/F2
Zhayyq (riv.), Kaz. 64/K5
Zhecheng, China 72/C4
Zhejiang (prov.), China 71/M5
Zhelaniya (cape), Rus. 64/G2
Zheleznodorozhnyy, Rus. 61/L3
Zheleznogorsk, Rus. 62/F1
Zheleznogorsk-Ilimskiy, Rus. 70/D2
Zhen'an, China 72/B4
Zhengzhou, China 72/C4
Zhenjiang, China 72/D4
Zhenning Bouyeizu Miaozu, China 83/J2
Zhenping, China 72/C4
Zhenwu (mtn.), China 79/C3
Zhenxiong, China 83/H2
Zhenyuan, China 83/J2
Zhetigara, Kaz. 63/N1

Zhezqazghan (obl.), Kaz. 87/E3
Zhicheng, China 79/B2
Zhigulevsk, Rus. 63/J1
Zhijiang, China 79/B1
Zhijin, China 83/J2
Zhiloy (isl.), Azer. 63/J4
Zhlobin, Bela. 62/D1
Zhmerynka, Ukr. 62/D2
Zhob, Pak. 89/J2
Zhob (riv.), Pak. 89/J2
Zhodino, Bela. 39/N4
Zhokhov (riv.), Rus. 65/P2
Zhongba, China 79/K3
Zhongshan, China 83/K3
Zhongxiang, China 72/C5
Zhongxiang, China 72/B3
Zhoushan (isls.), China 57/E5
Zhouzhou, China 72/D3
Zhovtneve, Ukr. 49/L2
Zhuanghe, China 73/B3
Zhuzhou, China 72/D4
Zhuhai, China 83/K3
Zhuji, China 79/D2
Zhujiang Kou (bay), China 71/T10
Zhukovka, Rus. 62/E1
Zhukovskiy, Rus. 61/X9
Zhumadian, China 72/C4
Zhuolu, China 72/G6
Zhuozi, China 72/C2
Zhushan, China 72/B4
Zhuxi, China 72/B4
Zhuzhou, China 83/K2
Zhuzhou, China 83/K2
Zhuzhou, China 50/D3
Zhytomyr, Ukr. 62/D2
Zhytomyr's'ka (obl.), Ukr. 62/C2
Zi (riv.), China 79/B2
Zia (int'l arpt.), Bang. 85/H4
Zibo, China 72/D3
Zielona Góra, Pol. 41/H3
Zierenberg, Ger. 51/G6
Zierikzee, Neth. 50/A5
Zifta, Egypt 103/M6
Zigong, China 83/H2
Zigui, China 72/B5
Ziguinchor (int'l arpt.), Sen. 102/A3
Ziguinchor, Sen. 102/A3
Ziguinchor (pol. reg.), Sen. 102/A3
Zihuatanejo, Mex. 143/E5
Zijing (mtn.), China 72/H6
Zikhron Ya'aqov, Isr. 91/F6
Zile, Turk. 62/E4
Žilina, Slvk. 41/K4
Zillah, Libya 96/J2
Ziller (riv.), Aus. 43/K3
Zillisheim, Fr. 56/D2
Zimapán, Mex. 143/F4
Zimatlán de Álvarez, Mex. 144/B2
Zimba, Zam. 105/E4
Zimbabwe (ctry.) 105/E4
Zimla (well), Alg. 98/E4
Zimnicea, Rom. 49/G4
Zinapécuaro de Figueroa, Mex. 143/E5
Zinave, PN de, Moz. 105/F5
Zinder, Niger 103/H3
Zinder (dept.), Niger 103/H3
Ziniaré, Burk. 103/E3
Zinjin, China 79/C3
Zion, Md, US 138/C4
Zion NP, Ut, US 128/D3
Zippori, Isr. 91/G6
Zirc, Hun. 48/C2
Zirje (isl.), Cro. 48/B4
Zirl, Aus. 57/H3
Ziro, India 63/J2
Zitácuaro, Mex. 143/E5
Žitava (riv.), Slvk. 41/K5
Zittau, Ger. 41/H3
Živinice, Bosn. 48/D3
Ziwa Magharibi (pol. reg.), Tanz. 104/A3
Zixi, China 79/C3
Zixing, China 83/K2
Ziya (riv.), China 72/D3
Ziyyon, Isr. 91/G8
Ziz, Oued (riv.), Mor. 98/D2
Zlatna, Rom. 48/F2
Zlatograd, Bul. 47/J2
Zlatoust, Rus. 61/N5
Zlín, Czh. 41/J4
Zliv, Czh. 55/H4
Złocieniec, Pol. 41/J2
Złot, Yugo. 48/E3
Zlotoryja, Pol. 41/H3
Złotów, Pol. 41/J2
Żlutice, Czh. 41/J3
Żmigród, Pol. 41/J3
Znam'yanka, Ukr. 62/E2
Znin, Pol. 41/J2
Znojmo, Czh. 41/J4
Zocca, It. 59/D4
Zoersel, Belg. 52/D5
Zoetermeer, Neth. 50/B4
Zoeterwoude, Neth. 50/B4
Zofingen, Swi. 56/D3
Zogno, It. 58/C1
Zográfos, Gre. 47/N9
Zohreh (riv.), Iran 88/F2
Zola, It. 59/E4
Zollikon, Swi. 57/E3
Zolotonosha, Ukr. 62/E2
Zomba, Malw. 105/G4
Zongo, Zaire 97/J6
Zongolica, Mex. 143/N8
Zonguldak (prov.), Turk. 62/E4
Zonguldak, Turk. 49/K5
Zonhoven, Belg. 53/E2
Zonnebeke, Belg. 52/C2
Zonza, Fr. 46/A4
Zorge (riv.), Ger. 51/H5
Zorgo, Burk. 103/E3
Zorn (riv.), Fr. 50/E6
Zorneding, Ger. 37/J6
Zörnig, Ger. 55/C4
Zorritos, Peru 156/A1
Zössen, Ger. 40/C2
Zottegem, Belg. 52/C2
Zou (prov.), Ben. 103/F5

Zou Xian, China 72/D4
Zouérat, Mrta. 98/B5
Zound-Wéego (prov.), Burk. 103/E4
Zouping, China 72/D3
Zoustana, Oued (riv.), Alg. 99/E3
Zrenjanin, Yugo. 48/E3
Zschopau (riv.), Ger. 55/F1
Zuata, Ven. 153/E2
Zubia, Sp. 44/D4
Zubȗbā, Isr. 91/G6
Zuchero (canal), Belg.,Neth. 50/C6
Zuckerhütl (peak), Swi. 57/E5
Zuehl, Tx, US 137/U21
Zug, Swi. 57/E3
Zug, Swi. 57/E3
Zugdidi, Geo. 63/H4
Zugersee (lake), Swi. 43/H3
Zugspitze (peak), Ger. 37/G3
Zuhai, China 83/K3
Zuid Holland (prov.), Neth. 50/A5
Zuid-Willemsvaart (canal), Belg.,Neth. 50/C6
Zuidbeveland (isl.), Neth. 50/A6
Zuidelijk Flevoland (polder), Neth. 50/C4
Zuidhorn, Neth. 50/D2
Zuidlaardermeer (lake), Neth. 50/D2
Zuidland, Neth. 50/D2
Zuidwolde, Neth. 50/D3
Zújar, Sp. 44/D3
Zújar (riv.), Sp. 44/C3
Zújar, Embalse del (res.), Sp. 44/C3
Zulia (state), Ven. 150/D2
Zulia (riv.), Ven. 145/H4
Zülpich, Ger. 53/F2
Zululand (reg.), SAfr. 107/E2
Zumárraga, Sp. 44/D1
Zumba, Ecu. 156/B2
Zumbo, Moz. 105/F4
Zumpango de Ocampo, Mex. 143/K7
Zumpango del Río, Mex. 143/F5
Zundert, Neth. 50/B6
Zunheboto, India 72/H6
Zunhua, China 72/H6
Zuni, NM, US 128/E4
Zuni (riv.), NM, US 128/E4
Zuni (mts.), NM, US 132/A3
Zunyi, China 83/J2
Zuo (riv.), China 79/A3
Zuo Jiang (riv.), China 78/D1
Zuoquan, China 72/C3
Zuoyun, China 72/C3
Żupanja, Cro. 48/D3
Zurbātīyah, Iraq 88/E2
Zürich (canton), Swi. 57/E2
Zürich, Swi. 57/E3
Zürich (int'l arpt.), Swi. 57/E3
Zürichsee (lake), Swi. 43/H3
Zurrieq, Malta 46/L7
Zurzach, Swi. 57/E2
Zusam (riv.), Ger. 37/J2
Zusmarshausen, Ger. 54/D6
Zutphen, Neth. 50/D4
Zuurberg NP, SAfr. 106/D4
Zuwārah, Libya 96/H1
Zuyevka, Rus. 61/L4
Zvishavane, Zim. 105/F5
Zvolen, Slvk. 62/A2
Zvornik, Bosn. 48/D3
Zvornićko (lake), Bosn. 48/D3
Zwarte Meer (lake), Neth. 50/D3
Zwartsluis, Neth. 50/D3
Zweibrücken, Ger. 53/G5
Zweisimmen, Swi. 51/G6
Zwesten, Ger. 51/G6
Zwevelgem, Belg. 52/C2
Zwickau, Ger. 43/K1
Zwickauer Mulde (riv.), Ger. 40/G3
Zwijndrecht, Belg. 53/D1
Zwischenahner Meer (lake), Ger. 51/F2
Zwischenwasser, Swi. 57/F3
Zwoleń, Pol. 41/L3
Zwolle, Neth. 50/D3
Zyrardów, Pol. 41/L2
Żywiec, Pol. 41/K4

Acknowledgements

COMPUTERIZED CARTOGRAPHIC ADVISORY BOARD

Mitchell J. Feigenbaum, Ph.D
Chief Technical Consultant
Toyota Professor, The Rockefeller University
Wolf Prize in Physics, 1986
Member, The National Academy of Sciences

Judson G. Rosebush, Ph.D
Computer Graphics Animation
Producer, Director and Author

Gary Martin Andrew, Ph.D
Consultant in Operations Research,
Planning and Management

Warren E. Schmidt, B.A.
Former U.S. Geological Survey,
Chief of the Branch of Geographic
and Cartographic Research

HAMMOND PUBLICATIONS ADVISORY BOARD

John P. Augelli
Professor and Chairman,
Department of Geography-Meteorology,
University of Kansas

Roger S. Boraas
Former Professor of Religion,
Upsala College

Alice C. Hudson
Chief, Map Division,
The New York Public Library

P. P. Karan
Professor, Department of Geography,
University of Kentucky

Vincent H. Malmstrom
Professor, Department of Geography,
Dartmouth College

Tom L. McKnight
Professor, Department of Geography,
University of California, Los Angeles

Christopher L. Salter
Professor and Chairman,
Department of Geography,
University of Missouri

Whitney Smith
Executive Director,
The Flag Research Center,
Winchester, Massachusetts

Norman J. W. Thrower
Professor, Department of Geography,
University of California, Los Angeles

HAMMOND INCORPORATED

C. Dean Hammond III
Chairman & CEO

Kathleen D. Hammond, President
Publisher

Caleb D. Hammond
Chairman Emeritus

Brian O'Leary, Sr. V.P.
Associate Publisher

Charles L. Koch, V.P.
Sales Administration

DATABASE RESOURCES

Theophrastos E. Giouvanos, V.P.

Joseph F. Kalina, Jr.
Information Resources Manager

Walter H. Jones, Jr.
Database Assistant Manager

Database Specialists
William Webster Adams
Barry A. Moraller
Nadejda Naiman

DIGITAL CARTOGRAPHY/ EDITORIAL

Luis A. Lugo, Jr.
Director

Terri J. Michos
Assistant Manager

James Padykula
Digital Technical Support

Senior Cartographers
Andrew J. Murphy
Thomas J. Scheffer

Cartographers
Carlee J. Britsch
James C. Labate

Associate Cartographer
Robert A. Carruthers

Cartographic Support Specialists
Sharon Lightner
Harry E. Morin
Lincoln Penn

Senior Art Designer
Regina Golan

Associate Art Designer
John A. DiGiorgio

TECHNOLOGY

Andrey Rogalsky
Manager

System Specialist / Webmaster
James F. Bayne

SPECIAL ADVISORS

Martin A. Bacheller
Editor in Chief, Emeritus

Ernst G. Hofmann
Manager Emeritus, Topographic Arts

DESIGN CONSULTANT
Pentagram

TECHNOLOGY
Michael E. Agishtein, Ph.D
Shou-Wen Chen

CONTRIBUTING WRITER
Frederick A. Shamlian

Population Research Center
University of Texas
Austin, Texas

Office of Population Research
Princeton University
Princeton, New Jersey

ARCTIC REGION
160

GREENLAND

ALASKA
134

CANADA
122

NORTH AMERICA
119

UNITED STATES
124

139
Metropolitan
New York

136
Metropolitan Los Angeles

Oahu
124

HAWAII
124

142
MEXICO

Mexico-Veracruz
143

Mexico
143

CUBA
140

BAHAMAS

HAITI

DOM.
REP.
141

JAMAICA

HON.

GUAT.

NICAR.

COSTA RICA

PANAMA

VENEZUELA
132

COLOMBIA

ECU.

SUR.

GUIANA

FR. GUIANA

NORTHERN
SOUTH AMERICA
150

156
Galápagos Is.

156
PERU

BOLIVIA

BRAZIL
154

CENTRAL
PACIFIC OCEAN
116

SOUTH AMERICA
147

PAR.

155
Rio de Janiero-
São Paulo
155

CHILE

ARGENTINA

158
Santiago-
Valparaíso
158

UR.
159
Rio de la
Plata

SOUTHERN
SOUTH AMERICA
157

159

Iceland

EUROPE
27

London
30

Paris
30

Monaco
58

45
Azores

Madeira
45

MOROCCO

Canary
45

NORTHERN
AFRICA
96

ALGERIA
98

93
Cape Verde

MAURITANIA

SEN.

GUINEA

LIBR.

CÔTE
D'IV.

MALI

B.F.

GHANA

TOGO

BENIN

NIGER

NIGER

AFRICA
93

SOUTHERN
AFRICA
105

UNITED STATES / CANADA

BC

AB

SK

MB

ON

QU

NF

CANADA

Seattle-Tacoma
135

WA

OR

Sacramento-San
Francisco-San Jose
135

ID

Salt Lake City
137

MT
126

ND

MN

WI

SD

WY

Montreal
131

Toronto-Buffalo
131

NB

ME

NS

Detroit
135

MI

NY

130

CA

NV

UT

Co

NE

IA

Chicago-Milwaukee
135

IL

IN

OH

PA

136

AZ

NM

Denver
137

Ks

Kansas City
137

Mo

St. Louis
137

KY

WV

VA

128

Phoenix
137

TX

Oklahoma City
137

OK

AR

TN

NC

SC

San Antonio
137

MS
132

AL

GA

LA

New Orleans
137

FL

MEXICO

KEY TO ATLAS MAPS

1:12,000,000   ASIA 67
AND SMALLER SCALES

1:9,000,000   134

1:6,000,000   156

1:3,000,000   106

1:1,000,000   143

1:500,000   ● London 30
AND LARGER SCALES